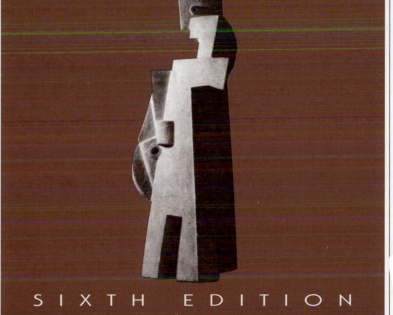

The Mainstream of CIVILIZATION

SINCE 1500

SIXTH EDITION

STANLEY CHODOROW
University of California, San Diego

MACGREGOR KNOX
University of Rochester

CONRAD SCHIROKAUER
The City College of The City University of New York

JOSEPH R. STRAYER
Late of Princeton University

HANS W. GATZKE
Late of Yale University

THE HARCOURT PRESS

Harcourt Brace College Publishers

Fort Worth Philadelphia San Diego New York Orlando Austin San Antonio
Toronto Montreal London Sydney Tokyo

Publisher	Ted Buchholz
Acquisitions Editor	Drake Bush
Senior Project Editor	Kay Kaylor
Associate Project Editor	Sandy Walton
Senior Production Manager	Kathleen Ferguson
Art Director	Burl Sloan
Picture Editor	Lili Weiner

Cover: Yale University Art Gallery. Background © 1990 Tatsuhiko Shimada / Photonica

Address for Editorial Correspondence: Harcourt Brace College Publishers, 301 Commerce Street, Suite 3700, Fort Worth, TX 76102

Address for Orders: Harcourt Brace & Company, 6277 Sea Harbor Drive, Orlando, FL 32887; 1-800-782-4479 or 1-800-433-0001 (in Florida)

ISBN: 0-15-501199-5
Library of Congress Catalog Card Number: 93-78964
Printed in the United States of America
3 4 5 6 7 8 9 0 1 2   048   9 8 7 6 5 4 3 2 1

PREFACE

Writing a history of civilization is an almost foolhardy enterprise. But it is easier to do if you have done it before, as the authors of the first four editions of this history, Joseph R. Strayer and Hans W. Gatzke, noted dryly in their preface to the Fourth Edition. We, their successors, had not done it before the mid-1980s. But we did have the robust framework the original authors left to us. In this Sixth Edition of *The Mainstream of Civilization,* we have built on that framework and on the major recasting of the work carried out in the Fifth Edition.

That edition integrated into the text new themes—such as social history and the history of women—that had figured less in earlier editions. Especially in the modern period, it emphasized the great driving forces—technology, demography, economics, and nationalism—that have made the twentieth century immensely different from any earlier age. It sought to explain the origins of key events, such as the Industrial Revolution, the Great Depression, and the World Wars. And unlike its predecessors, it used charts and graphs to present chronological and other quantitative data vividly, new picture captions to integrate the illustrations into the text, new boxed quotations from primary sources (some of them translated for the purpose), and frequent primary-source quotations in the text to convey the flavor of the past.

Yet the Fifth Edition also drew on the greatest strength of earlier editions—their global perspective. Like its predecessors, it sought to follow the "mainstream of civilization" by gradually shifting its geographic focus from the Mediterranean to Europe, and ultimately to the wider world. It offered detailed treatment of the major civilizations east and south of Europe, from Byzantium and Islam to India, China, and Japan. And as that "mainstream" flowed toward the present, the text provided increasingly detailed analysis and narrative in order to make that present understandable. That narrative attempted to convey to readers the texture and flavor of past civilizations and the astonishing variety of human possibilities and accomplishments. It sought to emphasize the interrelationships of all spheres of life, from politics and warfare to economics, art, scholarship, and religion. It sought to suggest at least some of the differing ways in which contemporaries and historians have understood the past. But above all, the text attempted to explain that past, to explain historical change and the recurring patterns visible in the past. Why and how have states, institutions, and ideas risen, flourished, and crumbled into dust? Why did events happen as they did and not otherwise?

This new Sixth Edition, we are confident, has kept the strengths of its predecessors. But it also contains much that is new both in presentation and substance. We have reviewed and rewritten the entire text sentence by sentence for clarity and readability; the result is slightly shorter than the Fifth Edition. We have reorganized Chapters 9, 10, and 11 to group related topics more effectively and to strengthen the narrative line. We have sometimes written new chapter introductions to make clearer how the material presented in topical chapters, such as 24, 25, and 27, fits into our overall chronological and thematic framework. We have rewritten or added subheadings where necessary to group the text into more easily understood segments. And we have revised and updated the bibliographical suggestions at the end of each chapter.

The Sixth Edition also incorporates recent research and new material on topics that range from humanity's origins to the end of the Cold War. We have added material on Hebrew culture to provide a better understanding of the background of European religion. We have reorganized and strengthened the sections on Hellenistic civilization to better explain the transition from Greece to Rome. We have radically rewritten and shortened our chapter on the post-1945 non-Western world to simplify the presentation and bring it up to 1992. Finally, we have rewritten the final chapter almost completely to offer both narrative and interpretation of recent momentous events. We are confident that Chapters 34–36 of the new *The Mainstream of Civilization* offer the best short analysis of the world since the Second World War available in any similar textbook.

The Sixth Edition also comes with a totally recast package of ancillary materials: a testbook (also available in software form) and film guide with learning objectives, 50 map transparencies, and 25 color transparencies of major works of art and architecture. Above all, the Sixth Edition study guide is completely new; it contains new chapter summaries, chapter objectives, time-lines, maps and map questions, identifications, and numerous probing essay questions also designed to serve as topics for class discussion.

This edition, like its predecessors, inevitably draws heavily upon the publications, contributions, and advice of other scholars. We have sought wherever possible to hint at our major debts in the Suggestions for Further Reading that follow each chapter. We owe special thanks to Conrad Schirokauer, City College of the City University of New York, for his contribution of Chapters 6 and 15. We thank Carl Abrams, Bob Jones University; Ron Brown, Charles County Community College; Ann Sumner Holmes, Louisiana State University; Gilberto Ramirez, Auburn University; Randall Rogers, Louisiana State University; Alan Schaffer, Clemson University; and Marian E. Strobel, Furman University, for their perceptive comments and criticisms. And we are profoundly grateful to Everett M. Sims, who edited the final manuscript with tact, decisiveness, and a brilliant choice of synonyms. All have helped to make this book better, but they bear no responsibility for sins of omission or commission and errors of fact or judgment, which belong to the authors alone.

Finally, we remain deeply indebted to the late Hans W. Gatzke. Despite the debilitating effects of a tragic illness, he oversaw with tact and consideration the transition from one "team" of authors to the next. He set ambitious goals for the new team: a major revision and recasting of the book. He shaped the plan for that revision and suggested a number of the new themes that we have attempted to emphasize. To his memory, and to that of the late Joseph R. Strayer, we thankfully dedicate this Sixth Edition.

Stanley Chodorow   MacGregor Knox

A Note on the Paperbound Editions

This volume is one of a number of variant paintings of the Sixth Edition of *The Mainstream of Civilization*. It is not a revised or condensed text. Many users of the Fourth Edition found the various paperbound versions of that edition useful because the variant printings made it possible for them to fit the text into their own patterns of teaching and scheduling. In the Sixth Edition, the publishers have continued the practice of preparing separate paperbound volumes. Users may choose the volume that best corresponds to the chronological period covered by their courses. The variants are:

In all the variant printings, the pagination, index (except for *To 1500*, which has its own index), illustrations, maps, and other related materials from the one-volume version are retained. The difference between the one-volume and the other versions of this book is a difference only in form.

1. A two-volume edition

The first volume, To 1715 *(Chapters 1 through 21), starts with the beginnings of Western civilization in the ancient Middle East and continues to the end of the Middle Ages. The second volume,* Since 1660 *(Chapters 20 through 36), begins with the seventeenth century and carries the account forward to the present day.*

2. A two-volume edition

The first volume, To 1500 *(Chapters 1 through 15), starts with the beginnings of Western civilization in the ancient Middle East and continues to the end of the Middle Ages. The second volume,* Since 1500 *(Chapters 16 through 36), after a Prologue that summarizes events to the year 1500, begins with the Renaissance and carries the account forward to the present day.*

CONTENTS

29

EUROPEAN FROM BALANCE TO BREAKDOWN, 1871–1914 / 739

30

WAR AND REVOLUTION, 1914–1929 / 769

31

THE WORLD BETWEEN THE WARS, 1919–1939 / 799

32

THE TOTALITARIAN STATES / 827

LIST OF MAPS

INTRODUCTION

History as Foresight and Memory

History is the story of the human past. It is also the only available introduction to the human future. That was how the first critically thinking historian, Thucydides the Athenian, justified his history of the great war between the rival Greek city-states of Athens and Sparta in the fifth century B.C. Thucydides addressed his work to those "who want to understand clearly the events which happened in the past and which (human nature being what it is) will, at some time or other and in much the same ways, be repeated in the future." He added that his book was "not a piece of writing designed to meet the taste of an immediate public, but was done to last for ever."

No modern historian would dare make that claim. Forever is a length of time beyond human grasp, and the tastes of the immediate public now have a weight that Thucydides the aristocrat would have roundly condemned. But Thucydides' book, the most penetrating historical work of the ancient world, has nevertheless survived for 2400 years, and has probably enjoyed more readers in the last three centuries than in its entire previous existence. Thucydides' claim that human affairs follow patterns meaningful to the trained eye has remained the fundamental argument for studying history.

The future is by definition unknowable and unpredictable; events are unique, and never repeat themselves precisely. But they often follow patterns. Individuals are unique, and are free to make their own history. That freedom gives the unfolding of history its element of suspense. But individuals also band together to create societies. Those societies have structures—languages, religions, intellectual traditions, artistic styles, and political, social, economic, and military institutions—that limit how individuals can make history, and that restrict the range of thoughts and actions open to them. Those historical structures operate in consistent and often predictable ways. Historical situations separated by centuries and continents have similarities, and sometimes develop according to a similar logic. Historical analogies—comparisons between one set of historical structures or events and another—are powerful if treacherous tools for probing future possibilities.

Historical analysis inevitably has limits. Evidence about the past is always incomplete. Politics, warfare, religion, philosophy, and art have left more traces than everyday life. The few with power and leisure loom far larger in the surviving sources than the peasants and workers on whose drudgery that power and leisure rested. Men appear in the sources more frequently than women. Societies with writing have left far more behind them than those without. Twentieth-century technology—aerial photography, radiocarbon dating, precise chemical analysis, meticulous archaeological technique—has told us much about voiceless societies and groups, and has broadened our knowledge even of societies that left extensive literatures. Source criticism—close scrutiny of the style, content, context, purposes, and reliability of surviving texts—has deepened our understanding of the written sources and of the societies that created them. The fragmentary nature of the evidence transmitted from the past nevertheless limits the historian's ability to see clearly and to draw valid conclusions. And in the nineteenth and twentieth centuries, the written record has swollen geometrically with the coming of mass literacy and the creation of immense bureaucracies. Too much evidence rather than too little is the burden of the historian of the recent past.

The historian's own values also color and sometimes drastically distort both the selection of evidence and the analysis of ideas and events. The past is the key to the present, but the present can also crush the past. Crusading religions and combative secular ideologies such as nationalism or Marxism-Leninism alter history to fit dogma. Traumatic experiences such as wars, revolutions, or economic catastrophes sometimes lead the historian to seek escape in a largely imaginary and far more pleasant distant past, or to rewrite recent events as a one-way street leading inevitably to the unhappy present. And historians, although their craft should lead them to take the long view, sometimes fall victim to passing fads. The historian's only defenses against ideological distortion and trendiness are the search for detachment and the passionate commitment to the verifiable evidence that has distinguished the best historical writing from Thucydides onward. For history, if painstakingly and honestly written, gives to those who pursue it a sense of the probabilities, of the range of outcomes inherent in a given historical situation. Historical knowledge can teach us how the world works.

That knowledge is also indispensable in a second way. History is memory. Historical knowledge is self-knowledge. It tells us how our world, our own society, and we as individuals got to where we are. Memory can give pleasure, but is also decisive in our lives. For the individual, memory is identity. For society, the "collective memory" or knowledge of the society's past and shared values is equally central. It is part of the glue that binds society together. When a society suffers collective amnesia, when it loses its historical consciousness, the values formed through that society's history erode. That decay undermines the society's political, social, and intellectual cohesion, and may threaten its survival.

In the empires, city-states, monarchies, and tribal polities of the past and in the single-party dictatorships of the present, religion, custom, political indoctrination, and force have usually maintained cohesion. But our own civilization has over the last three centuries evolved a historically unique concept: laws that guarantee the rights of the ruled against the rulers, the rights of individuals against the state. Those laws have given individuals a measure of freedom unprecedented in history: freedom to worship as they please, to follow their economic interests, to pursue private happiness. The victories of rights against the state in the seventeenth and eighteenth centuries and of representative democratic government in the nineteenth and twentieth centuries marked an immense leap forward in human freedom and economic dynamism. But that freedom also carried with it the possibility that its heirs might one day lose it, through forgetfulness of the sacrifices and struggles that has secured it and through ignorance of its historical uniqueness and potential fragility. Historical knowledge can guard against that danger as no other knowledge can.

History as the History of Civilization

Our present comes from our past, but what is the shape of that past? All readers of this book, by the fact that they read the English language, are heirs to a tradition that stretches back to the first millennium B.C., to the Greeks on the one hand and to the Hebrew authors of the Old Testament on the other. That *civilization*—a term coined in the eighteenth century and derived from the Roman word for city, *civitas*—is the civilization of the West, the civilization of Europe.

Civilization above all means cities, a human institution less than 10,000 years old. Cities demand a highly developed peasant agriculture to feed them, architects and laborers to erect them, artisans to people them, bureaucrats to organize and tax them, soldiers to defend them, rulers to rule them, and religious or communal myths and customs to foster loyalty to the existing order. Cities mean a degree of social stratification, of differences between the high and the low, unknown in the hunter-gatherer or cattle-herding nomad societies that preceded them. Cities mean *literacy, organization,* and *specialization* of work. And the degree of literacy, organization, and specialization affects the density of population that a given civilization can support and the character and attainments of that civilization. The Greek city-states were capable of efforts and achievements far surpassing those of the Scythian nomads to their north and of the ramshackle Persian empire to their east.

Cities have meant the intensified development of religion, philosophy, technology, art, and literature. The great religions, from those of ancient Egypt and Mesopotamia through Hinduism and Buddhism to Christianity and Islam, were or became urban civilizations. Philosophy, the quest for the principles and realities underlying human knowledge and existence, was an offshoot of religion that first arose in the Greek cities and in the urban civilizations of China and India. Technological advance—from improvements in tools and weapons to the building of fortifications, roads, and aqueducts—made cities possible, and cities in turn accelerated technological advance. Highly developed art, from architecture and sculpture to ceramics and painting, has been the mark of urban civilizations. And writing, invented for the tax accounting of the bureaucrats and the records of the city priesthoods, eventually made possible the flowering of poetry, drama, history, and science.

Cities have meant common values that bind the inhabitants together, that inspire them to accept the sacrifices—often without immediate or apparent compensating benefits—that specialization and organization impose. Those values can derive from a variety of sources. The great religions, the cult of the nation-state, the modern ideologies that claim to grasp the meaning and destination of history, and the sense of duty toward the community that is the "civic religion" of democracies have all provided the myths and values needed to sustain urban civilization. Those myths and values have been closely related to the type of civilization they spring from and support.

Finally, cities have meant conflict as well as achievement. Hunter-gatherers and nomads raid their neighbors for booty, women, slaves, and cattle. All adult males are by definition warriors. But in urban civilizations, specialization of work extends to warfare: hereditary warrior castes or standing armies and navies that may command the entire resources of the state. Urban civilizations, by virtue of literacy, organization, and specialization, can wield violence far longer and more systematically than their predecessors. That violence led to the formation of *state systems,* of highly competitive groups of rival states. In such systems, as the greatest of Greek philosophers, Plato, bitingly remarked, "What most people call peace . . . is just a name; in fact there is by nature an everlasting undeclared war of all against all." And even within the city walls, fierce conflicts between rival groups among the ruling few or between the few and the downtrodden many have frequently broken the peace.

A history of civilization must therefore try to explain the gradual increase of literacy, organization, and specialization over the last three millennia. Such a history must be a political history, for politics is the key to understanding the nature, growth, and collapse of *states*—the large-scale political units whose character, success, or failure has been a matter of life or death for the inhabitants of all known civilizations. A history of civilization must be an economic and social history, for economic and social relationships shape politics and are in turn shaped by politics. A history of civilization must be a history of art, literature, and ideas—for art, literature, and ideas define and reflect the systems of shared beliefs without which no civilization is possible. Above all, a history of civilization has to explore the interconnections of politics, economics, and ideas that determine the character, development, and fate of civilizations.

And as seen from the late twentieth century, the history of human civilization as a whole centers around the history of the West, the history of Europe. For Europe's civilization, although at first merely one of the world's major traditions, spread outward after 1492 to dominate the entire globe. That outcome was not foreordained, for Europe started late. The earliest civilizations arose as early as 3000 B.C. in the great river valleys of Egypt, Mesopotamia, India, and China. The first recognizably Western civilization only appeared after 1000 B.C. in the Greek city-states of Greece, Asia Minor, southern Italy, and Sicily. The Greeks borrowed much from their predecessors to the east and south, including the alphabet they took from their Phoenician rivals. But the Greeks were unique. In the space of little more than three centuries—the sixth through fourth centuries B.C.—they invented the Western traditions of philosophical, historical, and scientific inquiry. They created the concept of individual freedom. They laid the foundations of Western literature. They made Western civilization self-conscious, inquiring, and *historical*. And in the fourth century B.C., the immense conquests of Alexander of Macedon, heir to a half-barbarian kingdom on Greece's northern border, spread Greek civilization—and Greek-ruled cities named Alexandria—from Egypt to the borders of India.

The successors of Alexander, the Romans, dominated the entire Mediterranean basin for five centuries. In art and literature they borrowed much from the Greeks. In law, statecraft, and military organization they were bold and ruthless innovators who solved brilliantly the problem that had perplexed the Greeks: how to create large-scale and long-lasting political units ruling over citizens and non-citizens alike. The only contemporary civilization that rivaled the brillance of Rome and the extent of Rome's power was China, which experienced a merciless unification in the same centuries as the Roman conquest of the Mediterranean.

Roman legions, Roman roads, Roman cities, and Roman laws civilized Europe as far east as the great river barriers of the Rhine and the Danube and as far north as the wild borders of Scotland. Rome provided the political order within which a new religion, which blended the Hebrew traditions of the Old Testament with the philosophical conceptions of the Greeks, could spread and prosper. In the fourth century A.D., that new religion, Christianity, became the official religion of the empire. By that point Rome was near collapse. Interrelated and mutually reinforcing pressures from within and without brought the empire down: bloody civil wars, brigandage and piracy, economic decay, plague epidemics, loss of intellectual self-confidence and social cohesion, and vastly increased barbarian pressure on the Rhine-Danube frontier.

In the fifth century A.D., Rome fell to waves of invaders, as the pitiless Huns on their shaggy steppe ponies drove the warlike Germanic tribes across Rome's crumbling frontiers. The western half of the empire collapsed. The unity of the Mediterranean basin was gone. A Greek-speaking remnant of the Empire centered on Byzantium survived in the East for another thousand years, but had small influence on developments in the West. In the seventh and eighth centuries A.D., the Arabian tribes, under the green banner of their new religion, Islam, conquered the eastern Mediterranean and swept across northern Africa to Spain. Those conquests further divided Rome's inland sea—between the heirs of Greece, Rome, and Jerusalem and the heirs of the prophet Mohammed. The *ancient world,* the Greco-Roman civilization of the Mediterranean basin, had ceased to exist.

The new *medieval* civilization that eventually arose in western Europe after the eighth century was thus thrown back on its own resources. It saved only a fragment of its Roman inheritance, as Rome itself had been only a part of the ancient world. And the new rulers of western Europe, the Germanic peoples, had never been part of that world. They only gradually absorbed the fragments of Latin literature and Roman law that Rome had left behind. They were slow to blend with the Latin peoples they had conquered. They and their subjects were equally slow to absorb Christianity. But the fusion over some six centuries of those diverse ethnic and cultural elements ultimately produced a distinctive European civilization.

Once its character was set, medieval Europe developed rapidly. It eagerly received lost Greek texts, decimal numbers, and algebra from its neighbors, the more highly developed Byzantines and Arabs. Many of its basic institutions and ideas, such as universities and representative assemblies, originated in the twelfth and thirteenth centuries. Its centers were in the north, in the triangle bounded by the formerly Roman cities of Paris (*Lutetia Parisiorum*), Cologne (*Colonia*), and London (*Londinium*) and in north Italian cities such as Florence, Bologna, and Padua. Its periphery, from Sicily, Spain, and Ireland to Scandinavia, Poland, and Bohemia, developed more slowly. And beyond that periphery Western influence almost ceased. Byzantium remained apart: Greek in language, despotic in politics, and Orthodox rather than Catholic in religion. Byzantium's influence dominated the southern and eastern Slavic peoples who had moved into eastern Europe as the Germanic tribes had moved west. Byzantium likewise inspired the early Russian state, until Mongol conquerors subjugated Moscow and Kiev in the thirteenth century and forced them to face eastward for more than 200 years.

South and east of Byzantium lay the civilizations of Islam, which began to close themselves off from new ideas just as Europe was beginning its ascent. Still further east lay the great civilizations of India, China, and Japan. Each had characteristic values—religious in India, scholarly and bureaucratic in China, military and bureaucratic in Japan. All three had on occasion borrowed from their neighbors, but they nevertheless tended toward self-absorption and the perfection of existing modes of thought rather than the acquisition of new knowledge. India suffered Moslem conquest, constant wars, and crushing taxation. China after the fifteenth century showed little interest in exploration or seaborne trade. Japan, which had borrowed much from China, fiercely walled itself off after 1600. And after pioneering efforts—gunpowder, rockets, firearms, crucible steel, iron smelting with coke—none of the Eastern civilizations developed a tradition of scientific inquiry and technological innovation rivaling that of the West.

By the fifteenth century, medieval Europe had begun to break out of its original social and religious mold and out of its narrow and rain-sodden peninsula off the Eurasian landmass. Since the twelfth century, Europeans had shown an insatiable scholarly curiosity about distant lands and a thirst for trade and booty. They had shown a fascination with machinery—from clocks and windmills to ships and cannon—rarely seen to the south and east. European scholars had begun to lay the groundwork for the seventeenth-century scientific revolution that immeasurably increased humanity's mastery over nature and transformed its view of its place in the universe.

In the last decade of the fifteenth century, Europeans leapt across the globe—the Spaniards to the Americas in 1492 and the Portuguese around Africa to India in 1498. Europe's new seaborne empires—the empires of the *early modern* age of Western expansion—soon dominated the fringes of Africa and Asia and conquered three newly discovered continents: North America, South America, and Australia.

Then came two further revolutions within Europe itself. The collapse of the French monarchy in 1788–89 opened 25 years of revolution and war that spread the democratic ideas of the French revolutionaries and the notion of nationalism—the political religion of the nation-state—eastward across Europe. Simultaneously, an industrial revolution that transformed humanity's power over nature and over its own existence began in Britain. Those twin revolutions—of mass politics and nationalism, and of engine-powered machines and economic freedoms—have been the driving forces of the *modern* era in which we still live. They transformed Europe and the world. For the first time in history, one civilization brought all others into increasingly direct contact with it, and forced its rivals to adopt its techniques and ideas or go under.

Those rivals ultimately maintained or reasserted their independence—within the framework of the worldwide international system that Europe established—by adopting Western ideas and techniques. The world has not become one; mortal rivalries between states, religions, ideologies, and cultures continue to rend it. But for good or ill a recognizably Western global civilization has taken shape, bound together by an accelerating revolution of science and technology, an ever-expanding world market, and a thickening web of mass communications. That is the present that any history of civilization must seek to explain.

Prologue: From the Beginnings to 1500

Three words that appear repeatedly in this book look simple but are difficult to define: *civilization, western,* and *modern.* What is civilization? When and how did a distinct type of civilization—Western civilization—develop in Europe? And when did Western civilization begin to manifest traits that we call modern?

Every group of scholars interested in humankind and society gives a different meaning to the word *civilization.* Even historians are by no means in full agreement, though during the last century a good many of them have reached a consensus. When they speak of a civilization, they mean a society in which there is some degree of economic and political organization, some measure of occupational specialization, and a set of beliefs or values that is accepted by most members of the society. Organization, specialization, and common beliefs in turn combine to generate a distinct pattern of living that is recognizable over long periods of time.

Organization in its simplest form provides security against external and internal enemies, some control of the environment (for example, irrigation, community building, or collective agricultural operations), and some reasonably stable means of exchanging products. Without some measure of organization, each family or small group of families has to strive for self-sufficiency and so is doomed to live at a bare subsistence level. No one will stop procuring food to spend time making cloth unless there is some assurance that the cloth can be exchanged—safely and regularly—for food. And if everyone has to give over every day to hunting animals or collecting grain, no one is likely to become a very good clothmaker. As soon as a group of people has attained an acceptable level of security, however, and has set up regular procedures for exchanging

| ca. 3100 B.C. | ca. 2700 | ca. 2150 | ca. 2050 | ca. 1650 | ca. 1550 | ca. 1100 | ca. 650 |
| Early Dynastic | Old Kingdom | | Middle Kingdom | | New Kingdom | 3rd Intermediate Period |

1st Intermediate Period

2nd Intermediate Period

Homo Habilis made tools by striking flint off of a core.

goods, individual members of the group can develop specialized skills. Effective organization, even in a small community, can stimulate a high degree of specialization. A few thousand Greeks working together in a city-state managed to produce or acquire almost every object they wanted from almost anywhere in the Mediterranean world, in spite of the poverty of their soil and the lack of other natural resources. By contrast, a few thousand North American Indians who were divided into small, wandering bands barely managed to survive, though they lived in a much richer country.

Organization requires a certain amount of cooperation from the people who make up the community. Cooperation is not achieved by coldly rational appeals to self-interest, nor can it be maintained simply through threats and punishments. People who share common beliefs, however, are likely to cooperate in carrying out the tasks of their society. So long as a group believes that it is working toward generally accepted goals through forms of organization that seem right and proper, it will attain at least some of its objectives and will survive as a group. Once a group, or some part of a group, loses that assurance, either an altered set of beliefs or a restructured society will emerge. One of the problems faced by every civilization is how to maintain common beliefs and common values in the face of technical, economic, and social change. Once those common beliefs and values are lost, the civilization dies.

THE ANCIENT MIDDLE EAST

The earliest examples of organization, specialization, and cooperation based on common beliefs are found in the city-states of the great river valleys of Eurasia—first in the Tigris-Euphrates valley of Mesopotamia, next in the Nile valley of Egypt and the Indus River valley of India, and last in the Yellow River valley of China. *City-state* is too grand a term for the earliest settlements, which were hardly more than big villages. But the emergence of the village itself marks an important stage in organization and specialization; it was the product of a social and economic revolution that took place at the end of the Old Stone Age, about 10,000 B.C.

When people began to grow their food in cleared fields instead of relying on hunting and food gathering, when they settled in one place rather than roaming over a wide area, and when they built permanent homes instead of hastily erecting temporary shelters, the need for organization grew more pressing and the opportunities for specialization grew more frequent. A settled population is more vulnerable to attack and to internal strife than is a migratory population. It cannot solve its problems simply by moving on or by splitting up into smaller groups. The members of a village using primitive farming methods have to cooperate in clearing and planting fields, herding animals, and controlling the water supply. At the same time, the existence of a settled community means that there is a permanent market in which specialized craftsmen can produce and exchange goods. Even in the very earliest settlements there was a differentiation of social, economic, and political roles. There was a governing group, a priestly group, a merchant group, an artisan group, and an agricultural group. One person may have played several roles—ruler and priest, or priest and merchant.

Over time, the villages grew into cities, and the cities into states. The influence of an urban center spread farther and farther across the countryside until it touched the area dominated by another urban center. The frictions that developed when two spheres of influence met often led to war, and a series of wars in turn sometimes gave rise to the development of a fairly large kingdom. War itself was likely to strengthen political institutions, and a kingdom required more elaborate forms of organization. The creation of a kingdom also required a conscious attempt to establish common beliefs and loyalties. The victors might, for example, substitute their gods for the gods of the defeated, they might simply subordinate the gods of the defeated to their own greater gods (who had proved their greatness by bringing victory), or the victors and the defeated might decide that they had been worshiping the same gods all along, though under different names. A good deal of local variation in worship was tolerated so long as special respect was paid to the ruler's god or to the ruler himself as an embodiment of that god.

This bone shows the cut marks of the butchering process.

Origins of Agriculture   6000 B.C.

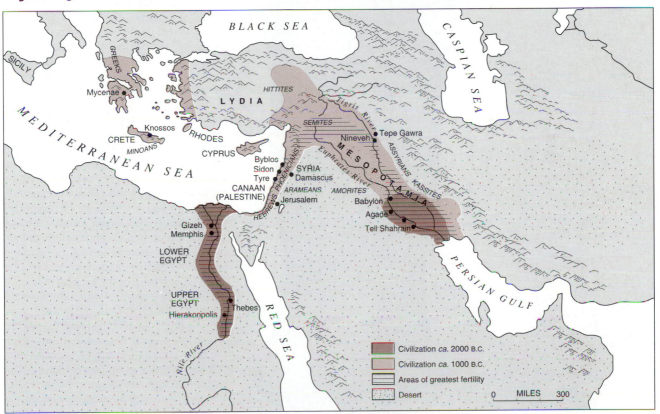

The gold-plated inner coffin of the pharaoh Tutankhamen (ca. 1340 B.C.)

In this brief introduction we cannot trace the long history of the kingdoms that arose in India and in China. China, for some time, had few contacts with the rest of the world. And, though India was in fairly close touch with Mesopotamia, ideas that reached the West from India were absorbed into existing cultures and did not survive as a separate tradition. On the other hand, the kingdom of Egypt and the various kingdoms and empires that succeeded one another in the Mesopotamian area laid the foundation for the ancient Mediterranean civilization from which Western civilization arose. Equally important were the border states—especially those of the Phoenicians and the Hebrews—that grew up in Asia Minor and in the contested lands that lay between Egypt and the successive kingdoms of the Tigris-Euphrates area. The Phoenicians invented (or at least perfected) the alphabet, and the Hebrew tradition lies at the root of two great world religions.

There were some striking differences among the peoples of the ancient Middle East. For example, the king of Egypt was a god, owner of the whole country, master of all its inhabitants; the Mesopotamian kings were only servants of the gods, and their subjects had full rights over their own property and considerable freedom of action. Egypt was built in stone, Mesopotamia in brick. In the Nile valley the chief agricultural problem was irrigation; in Mesopotamia it was drainage. But beneath the diversity was a certain degree of uniformity. With very few exceptions, all the societies of the Middle East were agricultural societies. A vast number of agricultural workers supported a much smaller population of artisans and traders, and an even smaller population of priests, bureaucrats, nobles, and members of the royal family. Most of the surplus produced by many thousands of agricultural workers was consumed by a tiny elite.

Some of the surplus was used to finance wars, and every kingdom—even the little kingdom of the Hebrews—went through a phase of empire-building. War, migration, and trade brought a mixing of peoples from various regions and an exchange of ideas and techniques. Curiously, however, some of those ideas and techniques did not spread very far. For example, every Middle Eastern society either invented or borrowed the technique of writing; yet only a few of the border peoples capitalized on the immense improvement made possible by the invention of the alphabet. The Egyptians and other peoples were intensely interested in religion, yet none of them adopted the rigid monotheism of the Jews. But such cases were rare.

All the peoples of the ancient Middle East drew on a common fund of experience and knowledge. That fund was rich and varied. By the end of the second millennium B.C., political organization had reached a stage at which vast areas and hundreds of thousands of people could be governed from a single center, power could be safely delegated to provincial administrators, and large armies could be raised and kept in the field year after year. Economic organization made possible not only a host of local traders and specialized artisans but a class of merchants who traveled thousands of miles every year. Masterpieces of architecture, sculpture, and

An alabaster relief showing an Assyrian king on a hunt.

The great pyramid of Khufu with the Sphinx in the foreground.

ca. 2000 B.C.	ca. 1700	ca. 1400	ca. 1100	ca. 800	ca. 600	404	323	Conquest by Rome 146 B.C.
Minoan Civilization on Crete			"Dark Ages"	Archaic Period	Classical Period		Hellenistic Era	
Arrival of Greeks	Mycenaean Civilization in Aegean Area							

Decline of City-State System and Conquest by Macedon

painting were being produced, and religious writers were expressing ideas that would have a profound influence on future generations. Knowledge of astronomy, arithmetic, and geometry was already considerable and was advancing steadily. In short, by 1000 B.C. the ancient Middle East had achieved a level of civilization that was equaled only by China and India.

THE GREEKS

To the west of this Middle Eastern civilization lived the Greeks. They were almost certainly invaders from the north who had settled on the Greek peninsula, in the Aegean Islands, and on the coast of Asia Minor around 2000 B.C. This is an area in which small patches of fertile land are cut

The reconstructed throne room of the palace at Knossos, Crete.

off from one another by rocky hills and barren mountains—a topography that encouraged the founding of many small kingdoms. Each king had a fortified palace or town from which he could protect the farmers in his district. The invasions from the north continued for many centuries, and the early settlers resented the intrusion of the later arrivals. Persistent warfare strengthened the tendency toward political fragmentation. The Greeks clung to their separate states until the fourth century B.C., when Alexander the Great incorporated them into his Mediterranean empire.

Given the geography of the peninsula, the Greeks inevitably became a seafaring people. Every path led toward the coast, and young Greeks grew up with the smell of the sea in their nostrils. Inland, one could make only a bare living farming the thin soil, but overseas there were rich communities with cheap food and seductive luxuries. Soon after the first invasions, certainly by 1700 B.C., Greek sailors were sailing the Aegean in search of unoccupied land, trading with wealthy neighbors, and sacking enemy towns. Though these early traders had many competitors and few commodities to offer in trade, they managed in time to dominate the commerce of the eastern Mediterranean. Greek colonies along the coasts of Thrace, the Black Sea, and southern Italy produced grain for the homeland population, enabling the richer farmers there to concentrate on raising grapes and olive trees that flourished on the hillsides where grain would not grow. Exports of wine, olive oil, pottery, and metal work, together with shipping and middlemen's profits, produced a favorable balance of trade. As early as the second millennium B.C., the Greeks were engaged in commerce, and by the seventh century B.C. they had become the most successful merchants of the Mediterranean.

Finally, geography put the early Greeks into contact with a remarkable civilization that was flourishing on the nearby island of Crete. This Minoan civilization, named after the legendary King Minos, showed the influence of many Middle Eastern cultures, especially that of Egypt.

But the Minoans had achieved a quality of grace and elegance that was all their own. Instead of the massive buildings and statues of Egypt that dwarfed the observer, the Minoan style was restrained, sensitive, proportioned to the human body—a style that the Minoans may have passed on to the Greeks, along with other influences. The Minoans too were a seafaring people. Their ships plied the Aegean, trading with the Greeks and the Phoenicians. And the Minoans may even have established a sort of overlordship over some of the little Greek kingdoms. Later (about 1630 B.C.)

Greek vase of the late sixth century B.C. depicting a foot race. The vase was awarded to the winner of the race at the Panathenaic festival in Athens.

The Aegean World   *ca.* 1500–146 B.C.

a great disaster struck Crete, a terrific volcanic explosion. The ruined palaces and cities of the island were rebuilt by a people who wrote a primitive form of Greek, suggesting that the Greeks were now the lords of Crete. In any case, the earliest Greek civilization—the Mycenaeans who destroyed Troy shortly after 1200 B.C.—had many affinities with the Minoan civilization.

Around 1150 B.C. the Mycenaean civilization fell into eclipse, probably as a result of new invasions from the north. In the dark ages that followed, the Greeks almost vanish from view. When the Greeks reappear (about 800 B.C.), they are still divided into small kingdoms built around fortified towns; they are still bothered by the limited agriculture production resulting from the peninsula's poor soil; and they are still engaged in overseas

trade. Now, however, they seem more curious about the world and more willing to try out new ideas and new forms of organization.

Those who settled along the western coast of Asia Minor also learned from their immediate neighbors. Asia Minor was fully integrated into the ancient Middle Eastern civilization, and it was here that the Greeks acquired some of their earliest ideas about astronomy, mathematics, and philosophy. They also learned the use of coined money, a notable invention made about 700 B.C. in a kingdom of Asia Minor. Using coins instead of weighing out chunks of gold or silver made trade easier, an advantage that the Greeks were quick to recognize.

The Greeks also saw that the only way small states could survive in a world of large states was to make the fullest use of their human resources. Under a monarchical or an aristocratic government most of the people were barred from the political process and hence were unable to contribute fully to the common welfare. Under a democratic government, by contrast, citizens could hold responsible positions in the army and in government. In Athens by the fifth century B.C., every citizen—that is, the free male natives of the city—could vote and hold office. Perhaps half the population was still excluded, but in Athens and other Greek city-states citizens enjoyed greater political freedom than was permitted in any other society at the time.

That freedom, together with a generous measure of curiosity, fostered speculation about all sorts of social and natural phenomena. The Greeks argued and wrote about politics and ethics, about philosophy and poetry, about mathematics and science. They sought first principles and general laws that could be applied universally. They borrowed many of their facts from other societies and subjected them to daring generalizations. In fact, they tended to rely more heavily on logical reasoning—formal logic was a Greek invention—than on observation. Euclid's geometry (*ca*. 300 B.C.), for example, contains many propositions that were already known (including the hypothesis that the square of the legs of a right triangle could reveal the square of the hypotenuse) but had never been proved or fitted into a coherent, logical system. Euclid's system rests on axioms that he thought were self-evident and needed no proof. In philosophy, Plato's emphasis on abstract ideas and Aristotle's theory that form shapes matter were based on logical argument rather than on observation, but they were profound intuitions that shaped Western thinking and led to centuries of discussion.

In Greek art and literature, the human being was always the measure, but it was

The Parthenon at Athens.

the human being at the height of his or her powers. Temples were built to a human scale; the gods were glorified human beings and the heroes were demigods. Drama dealt with the fate of men and women in an unfriendly world, especially of those who lacked moderation and a sense of the fitness of things. History—an area in which the Greeks improved greatly on earlier work—dealt with the triumphs and failures of individuals.

A darker side of the Greek character expressed itself in the frenzies of secret religious rites and in the violence of political life. One reason why the Greeks stressed rationality, moderation, and a sense of proportion was their awareness that they were often emotional, overly ambitious, and unduly partisan. The Greek city-states were never able to work together, even when their very existence was threatened. The Persian Empire, the last of the great Middle Eastern monar-

chies, nearly overran the Greek world in the fifth century B.C. when the Greek cities insisted on fighting individually instead of under a common command. The elation that followed the eventual defeat of Persia led politicians into incredible excesses. Athens and Sparta, the two states that had done most to defeat Persia, entered into a crude game of power politics in an attempt to gain the leadership of Greece. Athens concentrated on fashioning a maritime empire; Sparta countered by building an alliance with city-states on the mainland. In the Peloponnesian War that followed (431–404 B.C.), Sparta emerged as the victor, but the long, bitter war left the Greeks too exhausted to deal with the next threat to their independence.

That threat came from Macedon, a half-Greek kingdom north of the Aegean. Philip of Macedon defeated a badly organized Greek alliance in 338 B.C. His son, Alexander the Great (356–323 B.C.), succeeded his father and permitted the Greeks a large measure of local autonomy but made it clear that he expected them to cooperate in his scheme to create an eastern empire. He conquered the entire ancient Middle East (Asia Minor, Syria, Egypt, Mesopotamia, Persia), along with western India. Though Alexander had no respect for Greek politicians, he had great respect for Greek culture. Throughout his vast empire he built new cities on the Greek model (including Alexandria in Egypt) and installed Greeks or Hellenized natives as the rulers of old cities. Greek became the language of the upper classes; Greek art and literature furnished the models for artists and writers. Greek culture never spread beyond the large cities, however, and even there the Greek veneer was sometimes thin. Yet the Greeks left an indelible mark on the ancient world. After Alexander's death in Babylon at the age of thirty-two, the generals who divided up his empire continued his policy of Hellenization. For almost a thousand years—the so-called Hellenistic period—the ruling group and the literate classes of the Middle East adhered to a tradition that was largely Greek. Although Jesus spoke Aramaic, his followers wrote the New Testament in Greek.

Pericles on Athens and Sparta

This oration, inserted by the Greek historian Thucydides in his History of the Peloponnesian War, *does not give Pericles' exact words. It does, however, express the pride of the Athenians in their city and its form of government.*

We are called a democracy, for the administration is in the hands of the many and not of the few. But . . . the claim of excellence is also recognized, and when a citizen is in any way distinguished, he is preferred to the public service, not as a matter of privilege, but as the reward of merit. . . . Our city is thrown open to the world, and we never expel a foreigner or prevent him from seeing or learning anything of which the secret, if revealed to an enemy, might profit him. . . . In the matter of education, whereas the Spartans from early youth are always undergoing laborious exercises which are to make them brave, we live at ease, and yet are equally ready to face the perils which they face. . . . For we are lovers of the beautiful, yet simple in our tastes, and we cultivate the mind without loss of manliness. . . . Such is the city for whose sake these men fought and died; . . . and every one of us who survive should gladly toil on her behalf.

From Pericles' Funeral Oration, in Thucydides, The History of the Peloponnesian War, *trans. by B. Jowett in Francis R. B. Godolphin, ed.,* The Greek Historians *(New York: Random House, 1942), Vol. I, pp. 648–50.*

The political collapse of Greece after the war between Athens and Sparta was not altogether disastrous. Plato (426–347 B.C.) wrote after the defeat of Athens, and Aristotle (384–322 B.C.) was the tutor of Alexander. Euclid devised his system of geometry about 300 B.C. The greatest achievements of Greek science—for example, the measurement of the circumference of the earth and the hypothesis that the earth moved around the sun—occurred in Alexandria during the Hellenistic period.

By this time, though the Greeks had lost none of their ingenuity, they had lost the self-confidence that came with being free citizens of free cities. The philosophies that arose during the Hellenistic period emphasized withdrawal from the world, the simple life, the search for internal harmony. The most successful of those philosophies—Stoicism—taught that men should act as public servants when duty called them, but it also taught that the wise man would not seek public office and that the life of a private citizen was better than the life of a statesman. At the same time,

the Greeks grew less arrogant and more tolerant of other peoples. Hellenistic philosophies emphasized the brotherhood of men and the existence of a universal law. These ideas—withdrawal from the world, self-control, a sense of duty, the equality of all men under a single law—passed from the Greeks to the new lords of the Mediterranean world, the Romans.

THE ROMANS

The Romans were one of various Italic peoples who had settled in the Italian peninsula during the second millennium B.C. Their land was more productive than that of the Greeks, and there were fewer harbors and no chain of islands to lure them out to sea. Rome and its neighboring communities were still agricultural while the Greeks were building their commercial empire. But Rome was surrounded by enemies, and the Romans learned almost as early as the Greeks that a small community could survive in a hostile world only by commanding the support of all its inhabit-

Idealized statue of Alexander, probably the work of an artist of Pergamum in Asia Minor.

Alexander's Empire   336–323 B.C.

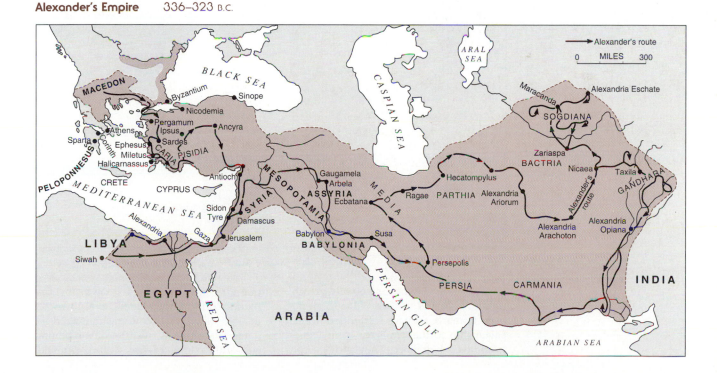

Early Italy　*ca.* 275 B.C.

ants. Not only did they eventually give the right to vote and to hold office to all free male Romans; they also extended Roman citizenship to their military colonies and to some of their allies. They allowed con-quered cities to keep their own governments so long as they agreed to help Rome in time of war. Thus Rome managed to extend its authority over the Italian peninsula and to draw a large, well-disciplined

Founding of City of Rome *ca.* 750 B.C.		*ca.* 600		*ca.* 500		264	146	27 B.C.
Independent Roman Kingdom		Etruscan Dominance		Rome Conquers Italian Peninsula		Punic Wars	Rome Conquers Entire Mediterranean Area	

army from the growing population of free citizens.

The test of this system came when the expanding Roman state ventured into the sphere of influence of an expanding North African state—Carthage. Carthage was a Phoenician settlement that had become far more powerful than the mother country itself; it controlled what is now Tunisia, much of Sicily, and the eastern part of Spain. Rome defeated Carthage in two long Punic Wars (264–241 B.C. and 218–202 B.C.), largely because Rome could always raise one more army, while Carthage, though it won many victories, eventually exhausted its resources. With the collapse of Carthage, Rome became master of the western Mediterranean. But it was hard for the dominant power in the West to avoid friction with the states of the East. One by one, Rome defeated the kingdoms that had grown out of Alexander's empire. Macedon, Greece, Asia Minor, Syria, and, last of all, Egypt came under Roman rule. Meanwhile Julius Caesar completed the process of subduing all the regions bordering on the Mediterranean by conquering Gaul (France) in a series of campaigns that lasted from 59 B.C. to 52 B.C. Although Britain and a small part of western Germany were added later, Rome had assembled its Mediterranean empire before the birth of Christ.

The Roman state was severely strained by the annexations that followed the defeat of Carthage and the eastern kingdoms. Rome continued to be generous with grants of Roman citizenship, but most citizens lived far from Rome. Since the Roman constitution was still that of a city-state, power theoretically resided in assemblies of all Roman citizens. But since Rome never developed the idea of representation, power actually lay in the hands of the citizens who happened to live in the city of Rome. A citizen who could not

get to Rome could not vote. The inhabitants of Rome were not well-informed and were easily swayed by cheap oratory, bribes, and threats of force. For several generations they followed the lead of the Senate, an assembly made up of rich landholders, heads of patrician families, and ex-officials. Most officeholders and generals were selected from senatorial families and took their seats in the Senate when their terms expired. The leaders of the Senate were ruthless, selfish men who had amassed fortunes while serving as provincial governors and army commanders. So long as they remained more or less united, they were able to preserve a fair degree of stability. After 100 B.C., however, they began to quarrel more and more openly over the spoils of office. Each faction sought the support of the Roman voters. Elections became so corrupt and tumultuous that eventually they could not be held at all. Riots in the city grew into civil wars that spread throughout the state. Just as Rome was about to unite the Mediterranean world, rival military commanders threatened to tear it apart.

In the end, however, one general emerged supreme. The Gallic wars had given Julius Caesar great personal prestige and control over an army of veterans. He used those assets to eliminate his rivals and to begin the rebuilding of the Roman government. But his assassination (44 B.C.) triggered a new round of civil wars. His grandnephew and heir, Octavian, succeeded, after years of intrigue and battle, in destroying all his opponents, and by 27 B.C. he was in full control of the Roman world. As the restorer of peace and prosperity, he was hailed by the Senate as Augustus (the revered, the majestic one). And it was as Augustus that he became the first Roman emperor.

Augustus's power rested on his command of the army ("emperor" is merely

Bust of Julius Caesar showing him at the time of his assassination.

the English form of the Latin *imperator,* commander-in-chief) and on his position as First Citizen (less politely, "boss") in the Roman political structure. But the early Empire was far from being a monolithic despotism. Although popular assemblies were soon a thing of the past, the Senate retained a good deal of its political influence and continued to administer some of the more peaceful provinces. Neither Augustus nor his immediate successors had a bureaucracy large enough to rule all parts of the Empire directly. The emperor was there to keep the peace and to intervene when trouble threatened, but not to oversee local administration.

As in the days when Rome was still a Republic, most of the work of government was done by allied or subject city-states under the general supervision of imperial authorities. Where city-states did not exist, as in parts of Gaul and Spain, the Roman governors created them. The founding of city-states throughout the West was one of the most important legacies of the Roman empire. It was through the city-states that the culture of Rome and of Greece flowed into the less-developed areas of the Empire. Because business had to be conducted in Latin according to Roman procedures, knowledge of Latin and of Roman laws and institutions spread throughout the provinces. It was to everyone's advantage to learn Roman ways.

In the East, however, with its older civilization, people felt culturally superior to Rome. And yet for several centuries there was a fruitful interchange of ideas between the Greek-speaking and Latin-speaking halves of the Empire. Roman law and administrative techniques were widely adopted in the East, and the West in turn acquired literary and artistic standards and an assortment of philosophies and religions from the East. By the end of the first century after Christ, ways in which people lived and thought were much the same throughout the Mediterranean world. A Roman citizen felt as much at home in Beirut or Alexandria as in Marseilles or Naples.

Augustus, who was determined to restore the ancient Roman religion, tried to prohibit the spread of the eastern mystery cults that were becoming popular in Roman society. In the East, the Jews were divided into several sects, and it was into this unsettled situation that Jesus, a Gali-

The ruins of public structures at Djemila, Algeria.

This fresco, found in a villa on the outskirts of Pompeii, depicts initiation rites of a Dionysian mystery cult, but they are rendered in such a way as to make precise interpretation difficult for the outsider.

lean Jew, was born. During his lifetime, his message found its way only to the community of Aramaic-speaking Jews. Shortly after the Romans crucified him as a rebel, however, Hellenized converts, principally Paul and his associates, spread his teachings throughout the Hellenized communities of the East. As the new religion absorbed Hellenistic religious ideas it lost its Jewishness and attracted converts who welcomed its promise of forgiveness and everlasting life.

Among the privileged classes of the Empire, Stoicism was almost an official creed, but Stoicism was too cold and rational for common people. Many of those searching for assurance that the individual was significant and that life was meaningful were drawn to the mystery cults, in which a god died and was resurrected, thereby assuring the salvation of his followers. Though the mystery cults brought consolation to many, they had little appeal for educated men and women. Some of the cults called for magical incantations and animal sacrifices and the worship of several gods. Fearful people might belong to two or three cults at the same time, perhaps worshiping Isis and Osiris, a cult from Egypt, and the Great Mother, a cult from Asia Minor.

By contrast, Christianity preserved the monotheism of the Jews and was intolerant of all other religions. For poor and humble people, it was enough to know that God was a loving Father who had sent his only Son to redeem mankind through his death on the cross. For better-educated people, Christianity was free of the crude and inconsistent claims of competing religions. One could talk about Christianity in the language of Greek philosophy or of Roman law—as Paul did, and as the author of the Gospel According to John did. Christianity spread steadily throughout the Empire, unchecked by occasional persecutions.

During the first century after Christ, the Roman Empire flourished despite palace intrigues and some detestable emperors. It grew even stronger in the second century under the rule of the "five good emperors." It was during these years that the Roman administrative system was perfected. A decline set in around A.D. 180 with the death of Marcus Aurelius, a Stoic and the last of the "good emperors." But the Empire remained stable for another fifty years, a time in which Roman law achieved its highest levels.

The Romans had long realized that the laws designed for the ancient city-state of Rome were archaic and inappropriate for a world empire. They allowed subject peoples to use their own laws in their own communities, but confusion set in when citizens of different communities sued each other or sued a Roman. For generations Roman lawyers had tried to formulate general rules with wide applicability.

The Roman Empire at Its Height   A.D. 117

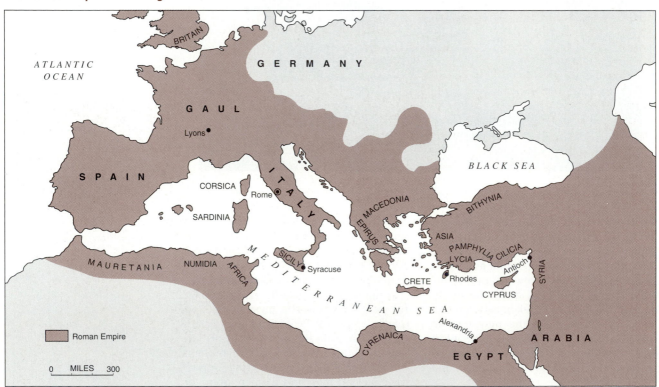

In their search for justice and equity they were encouraged by the emperors and by the Stoic belief in universal law. At last they devised the "law of nations," which became the common law of the Empire. Old distinctions between Roman citizens, allies, and subjects now became meaningless, and in A.D. 212 the emperor decreed that almost every person in the Empire was a Roman citizen.

The basic principles of Roman law had been worked out by A.D. 235, but the law continued to grow until it was summarized and codified in the sixth century by the emperor Justinian. Justinian's Code became the basic text for medieval and early modern lawyers and exercised a powerful influence on the law of many European states.

Just as the Empire was reaching a peak of efficiency in administration and law, it was struck by a series of disasters. Civil wars devastated many of the provinces and opened the way to barbarians pressing on the frontiers. The cities were so weakened by disorder and economic decline that they could no longer perform their old functions. From A.D. 235 to 285 the Empire verged on anarchy. Partial recovery came only when the emperor assumed the role of military dictator.

The Romans had never devised an orderly procedure for choosing a new emperor when the old one died or was overthrown. A competent emperor could nominate his successor, but the successor named by a weak emperor was ignored. Powerful generals fought for the throne, and the frontiers went undefended as their armies struggled with one another. During the third century even the few able emperors who emerged were toppled before they could restore order.

Economic decline brought further difficulties. During the centuries of expansion, Rome had lived off the plunder of conquered lands. When expansion came to an end, Rome was obliged to live off the vanishing resources of its empire. The mines, forests, and soil around the rim of the Mediterranean were nearly exhausted, and the Romans had not established stable settlements in the richer lands to the north. There was relatively little manufacturing,

A funerary relief showing a man and his wife, a portrait of an ancestor, and an attribute of the man's profession (first century B.C.).

and most of what was produced went to local markets. Because of the Romans' desire for luxury goods from the Orient, money was drained from the western parts of the Empire. Since most people were very poor, the cities had trouble collecting taxes. In fact, many citizens came to feel that it mattered little whether the Empire survived or collapsed—and that they might be better off if it did collapse. The soldiers (who were recruited from the poorest classes and received little pay) felt that their only chance for wealth was to

Third-century tomb relief showing an affluent banker and two struggling Roman laborers. The Roman economy was weakened by the gap between the wealthy few and the poor masses.

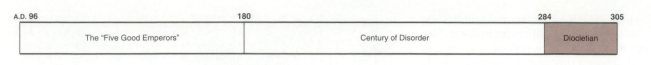

A.D. 96	180	284	305
The "Five Good Emperors"	Century of Disorder	Diocletian	

support a general who was fighting for the throne. There would be loot during the campaign and rewards for victory. Several generals were forced to make a bid for the throne by soldiers who simply wanted a chance to raid the imperial treasury.

Finally, there was a widespread attitude that the individual counted for nothing, that things would never get better, and that there was no use in trying to keep the machinery going. The mystery cults, and Christianity as well, counseled withdrawal from the world of warfare and strife. Only a few soldiers, government officials, and aristocrats loyal to the old Roman traditions were truly determined to keep the Empire going. They succeeded, but only at a price. That price was to transform the Empire into a despotism. The cities lost

their autonomy, and peasants, artisans, and even minor officials were bound to their jobs for life. The emperor's will was now law.

The transformation began with Diocletian (r. 284–305). Despite the growing rigidity of society and government, the fourth century was not a stagnant time. Diocletian's successor, Constantine (r. 307–37), first tolerated and then actively encouraged the Christian church. He certainly believed in the Christian God, and he may have sensed that Christianity brought a vital force to the Empire. The leading writers and thinkers were Christian, and Christian artists introduced eastern traditions into the classical style. Constantine built a new capital where the Black Sea empties into the Aegean, and Constantinople served as a bulwark of the eastern Empire for over a thousand years.

Constantine's successors completed the process of making Christianity the official religion of the Empire. They also transformed the Roman army from an army of peasants from the provinces into an army of barbarians from across the frontiers. By A.D. 400 almost every "Roman" general and almost all the soldiers were members of Germanic tribes. These men were loyal enough so long as they were paid on time, but they had little attachment to the Empire and little understanding of Roman ways.

As a result, when the next crisis came, a large part of the Empire simply disintegrated. An invasion of central Europe by the Huns (an Asian people) set the Germanic tribes milling about and pushed some of them into the western Empire. In A.D. 476, Roman authority in the West collapsed and German tribal kingdoms began to fill the gap.

By the time of the Empire's collapse in the late fifth century, the pope—bishop of Rome and successor of St. Peter—had emerged as head of the Roman church. Although the authority of the pope was challenged by the patriarch of Constanti-

Cicero and Ulpian on Justice

Cicero was an able lawyer and one of the leading Roman politicians of the first century B.C.

Since reason is given to all men by nature, so right reason is given to them, therefore they are also given law, which is right reason in commanding and forbidding; . . . thus a sense of what is right is common to all men.

From Cicero, *De legibus,* 1, 33.

Ulpian was one of the great Roman jurists of the early third century after Christ. These passages from Ulpian were quoted by Justinian's lawyers in the *Digest,* an authoritative treatise on Roman law.

Justice is a constant and perpetual will to give every man his due. The principles of law are these: to live virtuously, not to harm others, to give his due to everyone. Jurisprudence is the knowledge of divine and human things, the science of the just and the unjust.

Law is the art of goodness and justice. By virtue of this we [lawyers] may be called priests, for we cherish justice and we profess knowledge of goodness and equity, separating right from wrong and legal from the illegal. . . .

nople—the head of the eastern church—it was generally accepted in the West. Successive popes had difficulty exercising administrative authority over the early church, however. A bishopric was a profitable position, and barbarian kings named as bishops friends and relatives who were often ignorant and vicious men. And when good bishops were appointed, the kings tried to dominate them. The kings ignored repeated requests from the pope to respect the privileges and property of local churches.

The popes found loyal allies among the monks, men who had renounced the world and lived in tightly organized religious communities under the rule of an abbot. The monks formed a disciplined force in an undisciplined age, and the secular rulers treated them with greater respect than they did the clergy. During the seventh and eighth centuries the popes sent monks as missionaries to the heathen Anglo-Saxons in England, and the Anglo-Saxons, with the zeal of converts, were soon sending missionaries to the Low Countries and to Germany. The churches founded by these missionary monks proved more obedient to the pope than churches in areas like Gaul that had long been nominally Christian. Eventually a reform movement spread from the missionary churches to the rest of western Europe that brought about an improvement in the quality and character of the bishops and a strengthening of the authority of the pope. The reform succeeded largely because it was supported by the kings, however. It was not until the eleventh century that the pope began to gain effective administrative control over the church.

Meanwhile, the emperor Justinian (r. 527–65), determined to restore the splendor and unity of the Roman Empire, launched an ambitious building program (including the building of Hagia Sophia in Constantinople) and commissioned the codification of Roman law. But he failed in his effort to gain control over the West. He succeeded only in destroying the Gothic kingdom of Italy, the most advanced Germanic state, and in exhausting the resources of his eastern provinces. Italy soon fell into the hands of another

A sixth-century ivory panel depicting St. Michael. The panel may have decorated a portable altar or reliquary.

Germanic people, the Lombards, who were far less capable rulers than the Goths had been. Moreover, Justinian subjected Syria, Egypt, and North Africa to oppressive taxation and made it clear that he was willing to sacrifice their interests to his

The Germanic Migrations   Fourth to Sixth Centuries

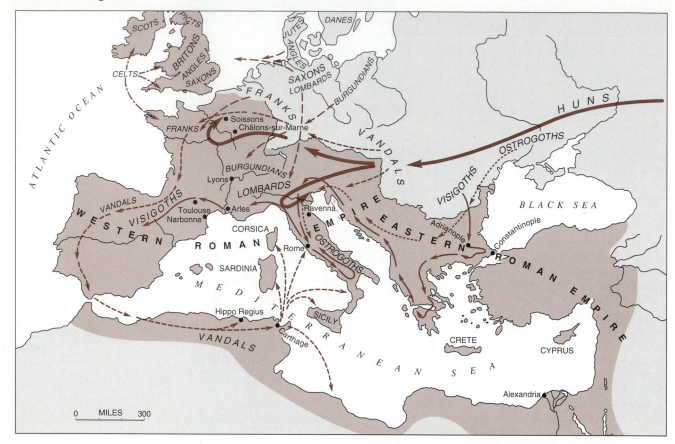

Hagia Sophia, built *ca.* 535. The minarets were added after the Ottoman Turks captured Constantinople in 1453.

efforts to strengthen himself in the West. In matters of theology, Justinian supported the doctrines of the Latin church rather than those of Egyptian and Syrian theologians. Since religion was almost the equivalent of patriotism for the easterners, their loyalty to the emperor was shaken. Justinian forced his bishops, most of whom were Greeks, to follow his policies, but in doing so he released long-suppressed feelings of resentment on the part of Egyptians and Syrians against domination by a Greek-speaking minority. In the crisis that was soon to come, the Egyptians and Syrians made little effort to preserve their ties to the Empire.

That crisis was caused by the rise of a new religion—Islam. The prophet Mohammed (*ca.* 570–632) had convinced his fellow Arabs that he had received a revelation from God that superseded all earlier revelations. Though he accepted many elements of the Jewish and Christian traditions, he emphasized strict monotheism (in opposition to the Christian doctrine of the Trinity) and the joys of Paradise and

Mohammed choosing Ali as his heir.

the pains of hell (in opposition to Jewish uncertainties concerning the afterlife). His religion was simple and easily taught. No

The Growth of the Islamic Empire   632–750

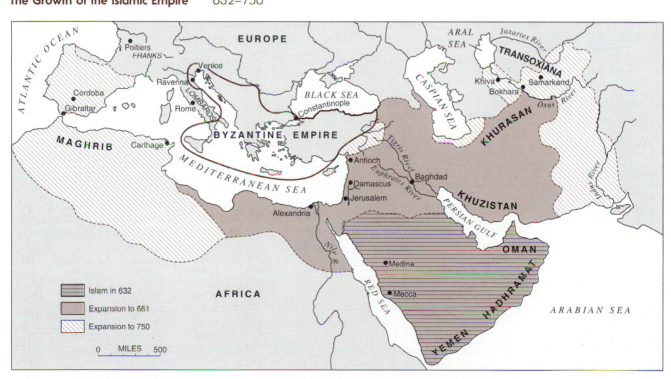

A Northumbrian cross (ca. 700).

priest or theologian was necessary. To become a Moslem—that is, a convert to Islam—one had only to believe in Allah and in his prophet Mohammed, to accept Mohammed's sayings (embodied in the Koran) as the word of God, to pray several times each day, and to fast from sunrise to sunset during the month of Ramadan.

Mohammed, who was a political and military leader as well as a prophet, succeeded in uniting most of the scattered tribes of the Arabian Peninsula. His successors, the caliphs, led the united tribes in their conquest of the Middle East. Syria, Egypt, and North Africa fell after brief struggles. And Persia, weakened by wars with the Roman Empire, also came under Moslem domination. Though not all the conquered peoples accepted Islam, the caliphs were able to raise new armies for new wars. In the West, the Moslems took Morocco, overran most of Spain, and raided Gaul. In the East, they pushed as far as the Indus Valley. In about a century the Moslems had created an empire larger than that of Rome at its greatest extent.

The Mediterranean world was now split into three fragments. Largest and richest were the lands of the Moslem caliphate. What was left of the Roman Empire included only Greece, the Balkans, and Asia Minor, though it was still a wealthy, well-organized state. Because the old name of Constantinople was Byzantium, this surviving portion of the old Roman state is usually called the Byzantine Empire. Finally, there was western Europe— a poor, backward, barbarous region.

Justinian's wars and the Moslem wars of conquest had isolated the West from its old neighbors even more effectively than had the earlier Germanic invasions. Not all contacts were broken, however. Trade between East and West continued; the Byzantine Empire maintained enclaves in Italy and sent embassies to western courts; pope and patriarch remained in communion with each other until the eleventh century. Westerners were profoundly suspicious of the Byzantines, who seemed arrogant, oversophisticated, and unreliable, and they were profoundly hostile to the Moslems, who were raiding Italy and southern Gaul. Neither the Byzantines nor the Moslems, in turn, saw much advantage in maintaining close relations with the undeveloped, poverty-stricken West. For several centuries contacts between the East and West remained at a low level.

Another result of Justinian's wars and the Moslem conquests was the demise of the Germanic kingdoms that had been established in southern France, northeastern Spain, and northern Italy. The Franks, whose strength lay along the lower Rhine and in northeastern Gaul, gradually picked up fragments of those kingdoms, and by the end of the eighth century they had become the dominant power in western Europe. The little Anglo-Saxon kingdoms in Britain had not yet united; there was only a beginning of political organization in Scandinavia, and the Slavs of central Europe lacked any organization at all. But the Frankish kings ruled the area that stretched from the Ebro to the Elbe and from the North Sea to Rome. Given the strength of local loyalties and the weakness of Frankish administration, such a vast area could not long remain united. For about a century, however, the Franks held their empire together, and during that time a distinctively Western civilization began to emerge.

REVIVAL OF THE WEST

That period is called the Carolingian Age, after the most famous of Frankish kings, Charles the Great, or Charlemagne (r. 768–814. The name of the dynasty comes from the Latin form of his name, *Carolus*). In many ways Charles the Great merely continued the work of his father and grandfather, and many of his plans (especially in cultural matters) were carried out by his son and grandsons. Throughout the Carolingian period the kings protected the pope from his enemies and supported the work of his missionaries in Germany. They encouraged church reform in Gaul, helped to strengthen relations between the pope and the bishops, and fostered an increase in the number of rural parishes. As a result, the church improved the quality of the clergy, strengthened its administrative system, and engaged in more frequent contacts with its communicants. In fact, it was during this time that people north of the Alps began to practice the Christian religion regularly.

In return, the church gave spiritual support to the Carolingians and encouraged its bishops and abbots to take an active role in the administration of the kingdom. The clergy was the only educated class of this time, and their participation in government was essential. Moreover, most of them were more loyal to the king than they were to the counts (district governors), and they often helped to counteract the influence of local strong men. Finally, since the prelates were drawn from all parts of Europe, they helped to spread a common culture across the Continent.

Charles the Great and his successors, eager to improve the education of the clergy, encouraged the use of a basic curriculum in all church schools. That curriculum included study of the Latin classics to improve skill in the use of that language; consequently many books that were on the verge of disappearing were copied and preserved. It also included study of the Bible, requiring copies of the Bible to be produced and errors in earlier texts to be corrected. Authoritative commentaries and explanations of the Scriptures led to additional copying and emendation. To expedite this vast enterprise, the script used by the copyists was simplified and refined. With the proliferation of materials, familiarity with the Latin and Christian intellectual heritage became widespread.

In 800, the pope crowned Charles the Great emperor of the Holy Roman Empire in St. Peter's Church in Rome. This act symbolized Charles's supremacy in the West and his role as protector of the church. Though it added somewhat to his moral authority over his subjects, it did nothing to augment his political power. It did, however, irritate the Byzantine emperor and helped widen the rift between eastern and western Europe. It also created problems that were to plague the West for centuries. What authority did the emperor have over Italy, especially Rome? If the pope could make an emperor, could

Ninth-century statue of Charlemagne or his grandson Charles the Bald on horseback. He wears a crown and carries an orb, symbol of royal power.

The Coronation of Charles the Great   800

Now when the king upon the most holy day of the Lord's birth was rising to the mass after praying before the tomb of the blessed Peter the Apostle, Leo the Pope, with the consent of all the bishops and priests and of the senate of the Franks and likewise of the Romans, set a golden crown upon his head, the Roman people also shouting aloud. And when the people had made an end of chanting praises, he was adored by the pope after the manner of the emperors of old. For this was also done by the will of God. For while the said Emperor abode at Rome certain men were brought to him who said that the name of Emperor had ceased among the Greeks, and that there the Empire was held by a woman called Irene, who had by guile laid hold on her son the Emperor and put out his eyes and taken the Empire to herself. . . . Which when Leo the Pope and all the assembly of the bishops and priests and abbots heard, and the senate of the Franks and all the elders of the Romans, they took counsel with the rest of the Christian people, that they should name Charles king of the Franks to be Emperor, seeing that he held Rome the mother of empire where the Caesars and Emperors always used to sit.

From Chronicle of Moissac, *trans. by J. Bryce*, The Holy Roman Empire *(New York: Macmillan and St. Martin's Press, 1911), p. 54.*

he also depose him? And if a pope could depose an emperor, could he not depose a king as well?

After Charles the Great's death in 814, internal strife among the Franks and a new wave of invasions from the north, east, and south threatened the survival of the Empire. Charles's grandsons entered into a bloody civil war and split the Frankish lands into three holdings. One grandson took France; another took the nucleus of what became Germany; the eldest took the so-called middle kingdom, which included the Netherlands, Belgium, Lorraine, part of Switzerland, Provence, and northern Italy. The middle kingdom was a long, narrow strip that lacked cohesion, and soon the kings of France and Germany began to fight over parts of it. That struggle has persisted into the twentieth century. Meanwhile the Scandinavian Vikings began to raid and conquer parts of Ireland, England, France, and Germany; the Magyars (a group of Asian nomads) occupied the Hungarian plain and plundered Germany and northern Italy; and the Moslems terrorized the coasts of Italy and southern France. Under the impact of war and invasion the Carolingian Empire disintegrated into kingdoms, the kingdoms into principalities, the principalities into counties, and the counties into castellanies (small areas ruled by the lord of a castle).

The disintegration was greatest in France and in western Germany. By 900 a new type of political organization was beginning to appear in those regions—a type of organization that came to be known as feudalism. Under feudalism, government was conducted by a lord assisted by a group of armed retainers called knights. Some lords ruled only the district around their castle; others managed to unite several castellanies; a very few (for example, the Duke of Normandy) extended their rule over several counties. Large or small, the territory ruled by a lord was an autonomous political unit. The lord owed allegiance and obedience to the king, or to some superior (a duke or a count) who stood between him and the king.

The knights, who had no independent political power, gradually emerged as a landlord class. Most lords had a great deal of land worked by peasant farmers, but their castles were small and crowded. Therefore, it was easier for a lord to give a knight some of the land and the services of peasants to work the land than it was to support him in the lord's household. By 1100 most knights possessed estates with attached villages, and they gradually acquired a sort of jurisdiction over their peasants. However, they remained politically dependent on barons, counts, or kings.

Feudalism was a rudimentary form of political organization in which the rulers treated their rights of government as if they were private property. It did, however, meet the needs of the time. The political unit—a county or a castellany—corresponded fairly closely to the economic unit—a district centered around a few local markets. A local lord was in a better position to provide local defense than a distant king. Since the lord thought of his rights of government as his private property, it was in his interest to improve that government and to make it more profitable. In time, feudal government became more effective and more popular than either the Germanic kingdoms or the Carolingian monarchy had been. Most modern European states grew out of feudal states.

A feudal knight accompanying a traveling king (eleventh century).

Feudalism brought heightened security to many parts of the West. Inside the larger counties relative peace prevailed; the quarrels of petty lords were less disruptive than the civil wars among Frankish kings. Feudal lords helped to beat back the invasions of Northmen and Moslems, though the major defensive campaigns were conducted by kings and popes. (The Magyar threat was repelled mainly by the efforts of the king of Germany.) In the eleventh century, there were very few major wars and almost no large-scale invasions of Europe.

Increased security meant increased population. The food needed to support that population could be provided only through improvements in agricultural techniques. As the population grew, the urban and professional classes experienced rapid growth, while industry and commerce expanded, as well. For example, fine woolen cloth made in Flanders was exchanged with Byzantines and Moslems for luxuries from the East. Together, political stability and economic expansion lifted the population of the West above the subsistence level for the first time in centuries.

Meanwhile, the church was extending its influence, though only slowly. This slow rate was the result of the difficulty of expanding the parish system, the setbacks caused by the barbarian invasions, the ignorance of many members of the clergy, and the weak administrative system of the church. Even so, the Northmen and the Magyars were converted during the eleventh century and a new reform movement improved the quality of the clergy and strengthened the authority of the pope. The laity became more devout (if not more virtuous), more eager to demonstrate their faith, and more willing to accept the leadership of the church.

THE MIDDLE AGES

These improvements in the condition of western Europe during the eleventh century produced a burst of energy that lasted for over two centuries. One of the first problems was to find land for the burgeoning population. The towns were growing, but they could accommodate only about 10 percent of the population. Everyone else had to live by farming. All

Norman troops on horseback engaging Anglo-Saxon foot soldiers in battle (detail from the Bayeux tapestry, late eleventh century).

Infants were swaddled in the Middle Ages to protect their "loose" limbs and bodies. Here two thirteenth-century nurses hold swaddled infants.

over Europe forests were cleared and swamps and marshes were drained. The Germans began to push into the half-empty Slavic lands between the Elbe and Oder rivers. Some peasant families traveled hundreds of miles in order to obtain small farms on this eastern frontier. The Norman conquest of England in 1066 was not just a military adventure: northern France was overpopulated, England was underpopulated, and most of William's army consisted of poor knights in search of land. The Norman conquest of southern Italy and Sicily also was manned by poor knights who could not make a living at home. And one of the motivations behind the long, slow reconquest of Spain from the Moslems was the existence of vacant land in the disputed area between the little Christian kingdoms of the north and the Moorish states of the south.

Another problem was to make governments strong enough to prevent internal disorder. In pursuit of this goal, however, rulers were frustrated by one of the strongest movements of the eleventh and twelfth centuries: the drive to reform the Church. No government could operate without the participation of the clergy; members of the clergy were better educated, more competent as administrators, and usually more reliable than laymen. Understandably, the kings and the greater feudal lords wanted to control the appointment of bishops and abbots in order to create a corps of capable and loyal public servants. But the reformers wanted a church that was completely independent of secular power, a church that would instruct and admonish lay rulers rather than serve them. The resulting struggle lasted half a century, from 1075 to the 1122.

The leading figures in the struggle were the pope and the king of Germany. Germany had suffered less severely from civil war and invasion than had France and consequently was in a more stable condition. The king wielded at least some power in most parts of the country, largely through the support of his appointed bishops and abbots. In 962 a German king managed to take control of northern Italy and to revive the title of emperor, which had lapsed after the collapse of the Carol-

ingian Empire in the late ninth century. From that time on, almost all the German kings served as emperors, as titular rulers of northern Italy, and as protectors of Rome and of the pope. In fact, they frequently installed men of their own choice in the papal office and on at least one occasion deposed a pope.

Such a situation was intolerable to the church reformers. Pope Nicholas II (r. 1059–61) forbade the emperor to interfere in papal elections; henceforth, the pope was to be chosen only by the cardinals. Pope Gregory VII (r. 1073–85) tried to keep Emperor Henry IV (r. 1056–1106) from naming bishops and abbots. Henry in turn tried to depose the pope. Gregory responded by releasing Henry's subjects from allegiance to their ruler, causing a rebellion to break out in Germany. Henry was so weakened that he had to seek the pope's forgiveness at Canossa (1077). This was not a complete victory for Gregory (Henry later succeeded in driving him from Rome), but it proved that secular rulers would have to make some concessions. Eventually, the successors of Gregory and Henry reached a compromise by which papal independence and papal authority over church affairs were clearly recognized. Secular influence over the appointment of bishops was permitted, and many bishops continued to act as advisers and officials of kings. The pope, however, could give orders to and discipline the bishops.

The net result of the struggle was to make the church completely independent of secular rulers. The church had demonstrated that it had enough support among people of all classes to enable it to shake any government that opposed it. In short, the church had assumed the leadership of western Europe.

An early demonstration of that fact was the First Crusade (1096–99). Pope Urban II had many reasons for wanting to send knights and nobles to fight the Moslems in the Holy Land. It would distract the crusaders from their petty wars in Europe. Moreover, if the crusaders could help regain some of the lost Byzantine provinces, they might heal the quarrels between the Greek and the Roman churches, which had culminated in the mutual excommunications of pope and patriarch in 1054. Finally, Urban earnestly desired to bring the Holy Land under Christian rule. His appeal for volunteers had enormous and unexpected success. Men from all parts of the West responded and under the leadership of a papal legate marched through Europe, Asia Minor, and Syria to capture the city of Jerusalem. No secular ruler could have raised such an army or persuaded men from so many countries to participate. Only the pope could draw on the religious fervor of the people. For two centuries crusaders protected the Holy Land from reconquest by the Moslems. The role of successive popes in initiating crusades gave them an opportunity to intervene in every aspect of life in the West.

The renewed energy of the West from the eleventh century on led to remarkable achievements in the arts and in scholarship. Europe was clothed in new churches, built first in the Romanesque style, an attempt to recapture the architecture of the Romans, and then in the new Gothic style. The new style was marked by height and light, with emphasis on vertical rather than horizontal lines and on greatly enlarged windows. Stained glass filled the windows, and statues adorned the exterior, especially the portals. Several arts were brought together to make the Gothic one of the most impressive architectural styles ever conceived.

By the twelfth century, there was a sharp rise in the number of students eager to gain an education. To teach them, a new institution was invented—the university. Texts that had long been neglected were studied once again. The university at Bologna concentrated on the study of Roman and canon law. Thousands of students from all parts of Europe studied at Bologna and carried home new ideas about the nature of government and the meaning of justice. The university at Paris emphasized the arts and theology. Since only a few basic texts on logic were known, a search was made for new material in Greek or Arabic translations from the Greek. Generations of devoted scholars spent their lives translating these ancient texts into Latin. In the process, all of

Aristotle's works on logic were recovered. Greek works on science and mathematics, amplified by the Arabs, entered the intellectual heritage of the West for the first time.

The scholars at Paris, for whom theology was the "queen of sciences," set about weaving all knowledge into a pattern of Christian theology and philosophy. The final synthesis was achieved by St. Thomas Aquinas (1225–74), who believed that all learning, even that of pagans, was inspired by Divine Reason, and that a truth

Principles of Gregory VII ca. 1075

This document, which was certainly drawn up in Gregory's circle, if not by the pope himself, expresses the views of those who were trying to strengthen papal power.

1. That the Roman church was founded by the Lord alone.

2. That only the Roman pontiff is rightly called universal.

3. That he alone can depose or reestablish bishops.

4. That his legate, even if of inferior rank, is above all bishops in council; and he can give sentence of deposition against them. . . .

12. That it is permitted to him to depose emperors. . . .

18. That his decision ought to be reviewed by no one, and that he alone can review the decisions of everyone.

19. That he ought to be judged by no one.

20. That no one may dare condemn a man who is appealing to the apostolic see.

21. That the greater cases of every church ought to be referred to him.

22. That the Roman church has never erred nor will ever err, as the Scripture bears witness.

23. That the Roman pontiff, if he has been canonically ordained, is indubitably made holy by the merits of the blessed Peter. . . .

24. That by his precept and license subjects are permitted to accuse their lords. . . .

27. That he can absolve the subjects of the unjust from their fealty.

From Dictatus Papae Gregorii VII, trans. by E. Lewis, Medieval Political Ideas (New York: Knopf, 1954), Vol. II, pp. 380–81.

The emergence of Gothic from Romanesque. *(Left)* Romanesque barrel vault (church of St. Savin, eleventh century). Although no light could be admitted in the upper part of the nave, the vault could be covered with fine Romanesque painting. *(Center)* Groin vault, formed by the intersection of two barrel vaults (Mont-Saint-Michel, twelfth century). The walls could now be pierced with windows. *(Right)* Early Gothic rib vault (Mont-Saint-Michel). Ribs reinforce the groin vault. Greater height and light are now being exploited.

A university lecture, as portrayed in a fourteenth-century Italian miniature. Attention to the lecturer is not undivided; several students are talking, and one is certainly asleep.

known by natural reason could not contradict a truth known by revelation. Thomas's interpretation allowed Europeans to consider concepts advanced by non-Christians, and thus a great deal of Greek and Moslem scholarship could be absorbed into western thought.

During this time, the church admitted that secular governments were necessary to keep the peace and to repress crime and taught that the chief duty of a ruler was to do justice. That view was reinforced by the revival of legal studies. It was also reinforced by the self-interest of kings and princes, who recognized that the best way to strengthen government was to improve the administration of justice and persuade their subjects to turn to the law courts when disputes arose. The states that emerged during the twelfth century were firmly based on law.

The process of state-building proceeded most swiftly in England and France. England had avoided fragmentation, partly because it was a small country, and partly because following the Norman conquest the invaders had destroyed the old Anglo-Saxon aristocracy that might have set up autonomous provincial governments in opposition to the king. The new Norman aristocracy was created by kings, was dependent on them, and enjoyed very limited powers. The kings had land, officers, and courts in every part of England. Therefore, it was easy for them to institute a reasonably efficient financial administration. Moreover, they made it easy for people to use the royal courts by sending judges around on regular circuits. The judges protected the property of all free men and used a jury to determine facts instead of depending on such practices as trial by battle. By 1300 uniform taxes had been imposed throughout England, and all important cases were being tried by royal courts.

In France the king at first had direct rule over only a small district running north and south of Paris. Even in this limited area, there were unruly and disobedient lords. Beyond this area were the feudal principalities, including Normandy, Flanders, and Burgundy, where the king had no power at all. After bringing the Paris

region under control in the early twelfth century, he turned to the delicate task of annexing the principalities. Some were acquired by way of marriages between royal princes and heiresses, and a few of the smaller ones were bought outright. However, the most effective means was by confiscating the lands of a lord who defied the jurisdiction of the king's court or disobeyed its orders. King John of England lost the duchy of Normandy in this way— a lesson that made a deep impression on other lords. By 1285 most of France was ruled directly by the king, and the feudal lords who ruled the rest were reasonably obedient to him.

The Expansion of the Royal Domain in France   1180–1314

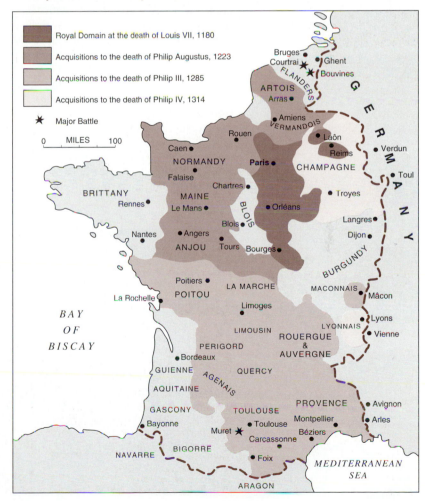

In France, however, government practice was less uniform than it was in England. England had one set of laws and one system of courts. In France each province was allowed to keep its old laws and courts even after it was annexed to the crown. The royal courts in England dealt directly with the people. The royal court in Paris dealt mainly with appeals from provincial officials and feudal lords. The lack of unity in France reduced royal income. France started to levy general taxes a century later than England, and even then local privileges limited the yield. Though France had four or five times the population of England, the royal revenues of the countries were often about the same.

Other countries were even less advanced than France. The Spanish kingdoms were still occupied with their struggle against the Moors; the Scandinavian kingdoms were still unstable; the Slavic kingdoms were just beginning to set up fully organized governments. Germany and Italy had been shattered by the struggle between the pope and emperor. In Germany the typical political unit was the principality, and in Italy, it was the city-state. Even these countries, however, had made progress since the invasions and civil wars that followed the collapse of the Carolingian Empire. Almost everywhere secular rulers—kings, princes, city magistrates—were repressing internal violence and providing greater security for all classes.

In eastern Europe, however, the thirteenth century was a time of troubles. In 1204, crusaders who had intended to attack the Moslems in the Holy Land were misled by Venetian politicians and Byzantine exiles and instead captured the city of Constantinople. The Byzantines eventually drove the westerners out (1261), but the restored Byzantine Empire never regained its strength and failed to halt the advance of the Turks in the fourteenth century.

At about the same time, Russia was struck by a series of Mongol invasions. After taking China, Persia, and Mesopotamia, the invaders drove across Russia to Hungary. Russia, which had been Christianized by the Byzantines, was in the intellectual and artistic orbit of Constantinople. Now the Russian princes were forced to retreat to the northern forests, and even there they had to pay tribute to the Mongols. Contacts with Constantinople declined, and contacts with the West almost ceased. Russia turned in on itself and became suspicious of all outsiders.

Thus the division between East and West that had opened centuries before grew even deeper. The Byzantines never forgot their humiliation in 1204, and the heirs of the Byzantine emperors were to be Turkish sultans rather than Christian kings from the West. For many generations, Russia was to look south and east to the camps of the Mongol khans rather than west to Latin Christendom, and the Moslems, under the influence of mystic theologians, turned inward. Moslem civilization in the twelfth century had been more akin to western civilization than was Moslem civilization in the fourteenth century.

The Grand Prince of Kiev, Vladimir I.

THE CRISIS OF THE LATER MIDDLE AGES

The West once more stood alone, though it was far stronger than it had been after the collapse of the Roman Empire. By the thirteenth century the main outlines of medieval civilization had been well established. It was clearly a Western civilization. Though largely Christian, its intellectual tradition was a unique combination of Greek, Roman, and Moslem thought, with some Jewish and even Hindu influence. Its arts were its own, as were its thought patterns. It had built new institutions—the church, the law-based monarchy, and the university. It had improved its technology and had reached an economic level at least as high as that of earlier civilizations. In fact, per capita income in western Europe in the thirteenth century was probably higher than it had been at the height of the Roman Empire. And yet the West was no richer, no stronger, and no more impressive in its intellectual and artistic accomplishments than China, India, or the Moslem world. Its economy was still based largely on peasant agriculture; industrial production was still low. Even the rich lived under conditions that would appall a slum-dweller today, and the peasants and textile workers lived short, miserable lives. By modern standards, western Europe in the thirteenth century was an underdeveloped society.

As the century advanced, Western civilization began to show signs of strain. The symptoms appeared first in the church, which found itself more deeply involved in worldly affairs but less capable of understanding those affairs. For example, it drew most of its income from the land and failed to appreciate the problems of the cities. It encouraged secular rulers to promote peace and justice but failed to realize that by doing so it was strengthening people's loyalty to those rulers. It insisted on independence from secular rulers but became embroiled in political matters. In resisting the emergence of a strong Italian state, the thirteenth-century popes drifted into a series of wars with the German emperors, who held Sicily and Naples and were trying to unite these southern territories with Lombardy and Tuscany. During the wars (1229–68) the popes taxed the clergy to support their armies, granted indulgences to supporters, and called on the kings of France and England for assistance. By playing politics,

the papacy became politicized; by appealing to secular rulers for help, the papacy sacrificed its independence; by opposing the creation of an Italian state, the papacy created such anarchy that the popes of the fourteenth century were obliged to abandon Rome and take refuge in France. Respect for the church as an institution declined sharply during the thirteenth century.

Western Europe remained firmly attached to the Christian faith, however. Two new religious orders, the Dominicans and the Franciscans, founded early in the thirteenth century, tried to reach people who had become alienated from or neglected by the rest of the clergy. Although these orders won considerable support from townspeople, intellectuals, and government officials, they had little influence on the behavior of the general population. People became more worldly, selfish, and critical of the church as time passed. The conflict between their Christian faith and their daily behavior, and between their professed piety and their cynical resistance to papal directives, created a dangerous instability in society.

Meanwhile, secular governments were gaining power and prestige. The thirteenth century was, on the whole, a peaceful age; even the papal wars in Italy were fought mostly on a local level and

In 1241 Frederick's fleet captured (or drowned) two cardinals and a hundred bishops who were on their way to a council summoned by Pope Gregory IX to depose the emperor. This manuscript illustration shows Frederick in the ship on the left, though actually he was not present. On the right, his soldiers attack the prelates in a ship bearing the papal ensign of the keys of St. Peter.

only occasionally led to large-scale battles. People tended to settle their quarrels by turning to the courts rather than by fighting, and the more cases that came to the courts, the stronger government became. Once again, loyalty was shifting. The showdown between church and state came at the end of the century.

When war broke out between France and England, the kings of England and France ordered the clergy to pay taxes to support the wars. At first the pope forbade the clergy to pay, but public protest forced him to admit that the clergy could be taxed for defense of the state. A few years later the king of France had a bishop arrested on charges of treason. When the pope ordered the bishop's release and criticized the king's behavior, an agent of the king tried to arrest the pope on trumped-up charges of heresy. The attempt very nearly succeeded. The ensuing propaganda attack on the pope grew so nasty that in the end he fully absolved the king and his ministers. The people, including many members of the clergy, had supported their king rather than the pope.

Such events put an end to the control of secular affairs that the church had exerted for two centuries. The secular states might have seized control for themselves, but they were not quite ready. No state had either a foreign office or a war department, and local power centers limited the effectiveness of central governments. No state was able to cope with the host of new problems that arose in the fourteenth century. Not until the end of the fifteenth century did secular states emerge as effective agents of government. For a century and a half, western Europe suffered a lack of leadership.

The fourteenth century was a time of grave problems. The economy had reached its limit; until new technology, industries, and markets were developed, Europe could neither produce more by itself nor import more from other areas. Population was rising rapidly. Peasants were living at barely subsistence levels,

This is a table of contents, in Gothic script, for a secular law book or treatise.

and the overcrowded cities offered them no escape. Landlords were finding it hard to live on their rents and had to borrow money at high rates of interest. Most kings and princes also were chronically short of funds and had to borrow heavily. The bankers from whom they borrowed were no better off, and most of them went bankrupt during the century. In short, western Europe had entered a severe economic depression.

Population pressure was relieved by the Black Death, an outbreak of bubonic plague that struck Europe in 1347, then swept through Italy, France, England, and Germany, returning several times during the century. In some areas a third or more of the population died. The psychological and economic shocks of the plague were enormous. Peasants were better off, because they could now concentrate on their richest lands; artisans were worse off, because they had lost many customers and had to pay more for food. Society as a whole was dangerously unstable.

Given the precarious state of affairs, pressures for armed conflict were great. Noblemen and members of the landed gentry raised companies of soldiers and roamed about in search of a windfall— plundering a town, for example, or taking a prominent man for ransom. Merchants tried to eliminate competitors. Kings did battle in order to expand their territory. Feudal lords fought over uncertain boundaries and in defiance of higher authorities. The fourteenth and early fifteenth centuries were periods of almost constant conflict.

The longest and most costly war was the Hundred Years' War between England and France, which sputtered along from 1337 to 1453. Since neither country could afford continuous fighting, the war was interrupted by long truces. Yet it consumed most of their revenues and devastated large areas of France. Wars in Scandinavia, Germany, Italy, and Spain were less spectacular but also caused widespread suffering.

Despite the warfare, however, territorial patterns remained much as they had been in the thirteenth century. Germany remained a divided land ruled by several

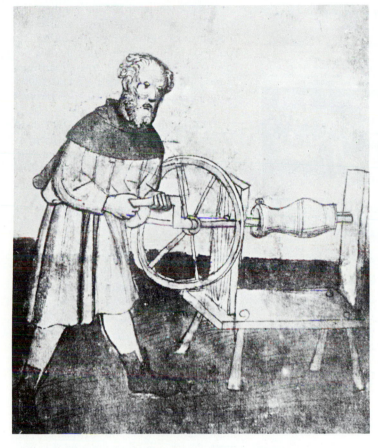

Miniature painting of a fourteenth-century pewterer turning a jug on a lathe, from the *Guild Book* of the Twelve Brothers' Foundation in Nuremburg.

independent princes, of whom the Habsburgs of Austria were the strongest. Northern Italy remained a region of city-states, which had grown wealthy from their virtual monopoly over the eastern trade. Despite their wealth they lacked political power, and by 1500 France and Spain were intervening in Italy. The district around Rome claimed by the pope was almost in a state of anarchy, and southern Italy was saddled with a decaying monarchy. In Spain, the kingdoms of Portugal, Castile, and Aragon had driven the Moors to the southernmost tip of the peninsula. Royal marriages were being arranged, which ultimately led to the merger of Castile and Aragon into the kingdom of Spain.

The outcome of the Hundred Years' War confirmed the unity of France and obliged the English to give up any hope of holding territory on the Continent. That war had ended when a peasant girl, Joan

The Battle of Sluys in 1340 established English control of the Channel. This illustration from a copy of Froissart's *Chronicles,* which recount the first half of the Hundred Years' War, shows an English ship engaging a French vessel.

of Arc, convinced that religious duty and loyalty to the French crown demanded that she drive the English out of France, led a victorious French army against the invaders. The English burned Joan as a heretic in 1431, but, to no avail, within twenty years they had lost all their French lands except Calais.

During the long years of war, England moved steadily toward establishing its unique institutions of government. England was a unitary state, not an assemblage of provinces. It had a single representative assembly, the Parliament, instead of an assembly for each province or region. Representative assemblies had been introduced into most European states during the thirteenth century by rulers who found them useful instruments for influencing public opinion. Occasionally the assemblies were asked to give advice on matters of policy, legislation, or taxation. Usually, however, especially in wartime, the king collected taxes without bothering to get the consent of the assemblies.

The English Parliament spoke for the whole country. Since the representatives of the propertied classes who sat in Parliament—landowners and townsmen—almost always agreed on important issues, class disputes did not arise. Moreover,

many of the members of Parliament were the same men who collected local taxes back home and who, as justices of the peace, maintained order in the counties. The support of these men was essential to the government, which was weakened by factional struggles among the nobility and civil wars that led to the death of five of the nine kings who ruled between 1307 and 1485. Each monarch turned to Parliament for support and the stamp of legitimacy. As time passed, Parliament became an essential part of the machinery of government; no statute could be enacted and no tax imposed without its consent. It survived the disorders of the fifteenth century and the strong monarchs of the sixteenth century, and by the seventeenth century it was a unique institution in Europe.

Futile wars, heavy taxes, inept administrations, and factional quarrels eroded respect for secular governments over the centuries. As we have seen, the church was experiencing similar troubles. Early in the fourteenth century, French pressure, coupled with disorder in Italy, prompted the popes to abandon Rome for Avignon, a city in southern France. There they stayed for over seventy years (1305–78) in the so-called "Babylonian Captivity." The Avignon popes were good administrators but poor spiritual leaders; they were sus-

An early gun, lighter and more portable than the first cannon. The gun was placed on a forked stand and was braced against the ground by its long tail (illustration from a German manuscript, *ca.* 1405).

pected (wrongly) of being puppets of the king of France, and a pope away from Rome hardly seemed a pope at all. Pope Gregory XI moved back to Rome and died there in 1378. His successor, Urban VI, who was chosen under pressure from a Roman mob, soon angered the cardinals, who fled back to Avignon, repudiated their election of Urban, and elected a rival pope, Clement VII. All attempts to settle the dispute failed, and for forty years there were two popes, one at Rome and one at Avignon. This Great Schism left Europe confused and divided. No one was sure who the rightful pope was, and everyone was disgusted by the bickering between the two camps. The Great Schism helped prepare the way for the Protestant Reformation of the sixteenth century.

In the darkest days of the fourteenth century, Western civilization seemed on the verge of collapse. And yet, though almost everything seemed to be working badly, nothing stopped working altogether. The church continued to function, and the vast majority of the people remained loyally Christian. Kings and ministers were overthrown, but the monarchies endured. The nobility gained power through its command of the armed forces, but it remained dependent on the central governments that paid the troops. Neither war nor plague halted the production of goods or the exchange of commodities. In some areas per capita production rose as peasants concentrated on farming their best land, and artisans moved into country districts to escape urban regulations on hours of labor and techniques of production. Pessimism did not stunt the intellectual life of the universities, where theologians engaged in subtle reasoning, and scholars made the first original European contributions to scientific theory. Scholars at Oxford came close to formulating the law of accelerated motion, for example. As other societies, notably the Moslem, lost interest in science, the western Europeans exercised a near-monopoly on the study of science from 1300 to 1500.

During that same time, significant advances in technology were being made. Ships were built that could sail the open ocean and voyage out to the distant Azores. Improved blast furnaces increased the production and quality of iron. The discovery of gunpowder changed warfare and advanced the art of metallurgy. New

The Black Death in England

Then that most grievous pestilence penetrated the coastal regions by way of Southampton and came to Bristol, and people died as if the whole strength of the city were seized by sudden death. For there were few who lay in their beds more than three days or two and a half days; then that savage death snatched them about the second day. In Leicester, in the little parish of St. Leonard, more than three hundred and eighty died; in the parish of the Holy Cross, more than four hundred, and in the parish of St. Margaret, more than seven hundred. . . .

And the price of everything was cheap, because of the fear of death, there were very few who took any care for their wealth, or for anything else. For a man could buy a horse for half a mark [about 7 shillings] which before was worth forty shillings, a large fat ox for four shillings, a cow for twelve pence, a heifer for sixpence, a large fat sheep for four pence. . . . And the sheep and cattle wandered about through the fields and among the crops, and there was no one to go after them or collect them. They perished in countless numbers everywhere, for lack of watching . . . since there was such a lack of serfs and servants, that no one knew what he should do. For there is no memory of a mortality so severe and so savage. . . . In the following autumn, one could not hire a reaper for less than eight pence [per day] with food, or a mower at less than twelve pence with food.

From Henry Knighton, Chronicle, in The Portable Medieval Reader, *ed. by J. B. Ross and M. M. McLaughlin (New York: Viking, 1949), 218–19.*

A fifteenth-century representation of Geoffrey Chaucer from the Ellesmere manuscript of the *Canterbury Tales.*

The Great Schism   1378–1417

0   MILES   300

SCOTLAND

NORTH SEA

NORWAY

SWEDEN

IRELAND

ENGLAND

DENMARK

BALTIC SEA

ATLANTIC OCEAN

POLAND-LITHUANIA

HOLY ROMAN EMPIRE

FRANCE

Avignon

HUNGARY

CASTILE & LEON

NAVARRE

PORTUGAL

ARAGON

CORSICA

Rome

ADRIATIC SEA

SARDINIA

KINGDOM OF NAPLES

SICILY

MEDITERRANEAN SEA

■ Land giving allegiance to Rome
■ Land giving allegiance to Avignon
□ Shifting and divided

Early mechanical clockworks (*ca.* 1500). The first clocks had only one moveable hand.

textiles were developed, and the first mechanical clocks appeared. Blast-furnace bellows driven by waterpower came into use, along with pumps to draw water out of deep mines.

The potential for growth was still great, as many people realized. They felt that if they could just get society back on track all the problems would vanish. They had already built the sovereign state, had expanded industry and long-distance commerce, and had reached new levels of competence in science and technology. Now the trick was to eliminate the disruptive forces that kept western Europe from moving forward. The word of the day was *reform.* And it was through efforts to reform society that western Europe entered the modern age.

Suggestions for Further Reading

W. H. McNeill, *The Rise of the West* (1963), is an excellent account that deals largely with the ancient world. V. G. Childe, *What Happened in History?* (1964), is a good summary of ancient history before the Greeks. M. I. Rostovtzeff, *A History of the Ancient World,* 2 vols. (1926), is somewhat out-of-date, but its superb illustrations and its treatment of social and economic history make it well worth consulting. The book covers Greece and Rome as well as the ancient Middle East.

M. I. Finley, *The Ancient Greeks* (1963), is a good introduction to Greek history. The standard textbook is G. W. Botsford and C. A. Robinson, *Hellenic History,* 5th ed., rev. by D. Kagan (1969). M. Grant, *The World of Rome* (1964); M. P. Charlesworth, *The Roman Empire* (1951); and H. Mattingly, *Roman Imperial Civilization* (1959), are all useful.

F. Lot, *The End of the Ancient World* (1931), is a classic study of the collapse of the Roman Empire. A stimulating book is P. Brown, *The World of Late Antiquity* (1971). L. M. Duchesne, *Early History of the Christian Church,* 3 vols. (1912–24), is still one of the best surveys of the subject.

C. Dawson, *The Making of Europe* (1934), is an excellent account of the early Middle Ages. It should be supplemented by F. L. Ganshof, *Feudalism,* 3rd Eng. ed. (1964), and R. Latouche, *The Birth of the Western Economy* (1961). R. W. Southern, *The Making of the Middle Ages* (1953), is a first-rate account of the culture of the High Middle Ages. See also C. Brooke, *The Twelfth Century Renaissance* (1969). On institutions, see R. S. Lopez, *The Birth of Europe* (1967), and R. S. Hoyt and S. Chodorow, *Europe in the Middle Ages,* 3rd ed. (1976).

W. K. Ferguson, *Europe in Transition* (1962), and D. Hay, *Europe in the Fourteenth and Fifteenth Centuries* (1967), are good introductions to Europe in the late Middle Ages.

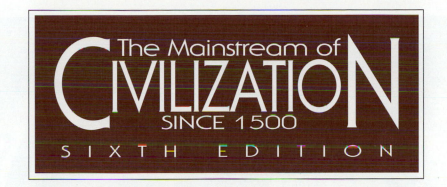

16

THE REVIVAL OF EUROPE

One of the most striking aspects of the late Middle Ages is that political leaders and scholars created so much that was new and exciting while society as a whole was suffering war, famine, and plague. Institutions that had stood for centuries gradually lost prestige and authority, but at the same time the seeds of a new era were being sown. In England, Parliament moved toward its modern status, and the idea that the judiciary should be independent of royal power won acceptance. Capitalism began to emerge as an economic system suitable for commerce and agriculture.

The writers and scholars of the fourteenth century were the first to recognize the vast distance between the culture of the classical world and the culture of their own time. Earlier scholars had thought of themselves as the continuers of ancient civilization; scholars of the new era thought of themselves as recoverers of that civilization. For them, ancient civilization had ended in the fifth century, when the Visigoths, Ostrogoths, and Franks overran western Europe. Scholars of the fifteenth and sixteenth centuries first referred to the thousand years dating from the end of the Roman Empire as the "middle ages."

With this new awareness came a new historical consciousness. Earlier historians, following the lead of Augustine (see p. 118), had divided history into epochs marked by crucial events in the relationship between man and God: History began with the Fall of Adam; the flood and Noah's rescue marked the beginning of a new epoch; Moses and the making of the covenant between God and the Jews marked a third epoch; the incarnation of God in Jesus inaugurated the current epoch; the Second Coming would bring all history to an end. Now, however, people

(OPPOSITE) SANDRO BOTTICELLI'S ALLEGORY OF SPRING SHOWS THE CLASSICAL INFLUENCE IN RENAISSANCE ART. BOTTICELLI WAS A MEMBER OF THE CIRCLE OF PLATONISTS GATHERED AT THE ACADEMY BY LORENZO DE MEDICI. THE IDEALIZATION OF THE HUMAN FIGURE IN ART IS "PAINTED PLATONISM."

were tracing the course of history according to intellectual and artistic milestones, not according to phases in the spiritual condition of humanity. At the moment, they were conscious of a revival of ancient civilization. Jakob Burckhardt, a Swiss historian of the nineteenth century, called that revival a renaissance.

Recently, however, historians have suggested that Burckhardt's term is somewhat inappropriate. True, there was a sharp break with medieval philosophy and a revival of classical learning, but in many other respects life in the fifteenth and sixteenth centuries was pretty much an extension of what life had been in the late Middle Ages. The economic and political changes that set in had little to do with the new ideas in scholarship and the arts. They were the consequences of a natural evolution from late-medieval society. The same is true of religious institutions, which went through profound changes in the sixteenth century. The next chapter is about those changes.

THE BACKGROUND OF THE RENAISSANCE

The new era opened against a background of economic depression, social unrest, and religious malaise. As we saw in Chapter 14, the droughts and famines that struck Europe toward the end of the thirteenth century had set off a decline in population that continued into the first half of the next century, and at midcentury the already weakened population was ravaged by the bubonic plague. During the next half-century the labor force continued its decline, a decline hastened by the breakdown of the manor and the guild. The structure of government and of society itself weakened, and the upper classes, led by the kings, tried desperately to preserve their privileges and fortunes by instituting drastic measures to keep prices and wages from rising. Europe was in woeful condition.

During the fifteenth century, institutions recovered their stability. The papacy regained much of its power with the defeat of the conciliar movement, even though it no longer exercised the universal authority it had once wielded. The monarchies of England and Spain began to bring their kingdoms under central control, and by the end of the century the French monarchy was following their lead. The population began to grow again, and technological advances gave the economy new impetus. Europeans turned more adventurous and by the end of the century had rounded Africa to reach the East Indies and had found their way to the Americas.

The seeds of this recovery had taken root in Italy toward the end of the fourteenth century. During the two centuries between the death of Dante (1321) and the sack of Rome by mutinous imperial troops (1527), Italy's influence over the rest of Europe had grown enormously. Italians set the style in architecture, sculpture, and painting; they dictated the literary taste and the educational practices that Europeans would follow for centuries. Northern Europeans flocked to Italy to study engineering, art, politics, and business, and Italians frequented the courts of princes and kings throughout Europe—even in remote Moscow. Italian navigators ventured out on bold explorations of uncharted waters.

Several reasons explain why it was Italy that pioneered the way into the new era. In close contact with the advanced civilizations of the Byzantine Empire and Islam, the Italian cities had begun to flourish as early as the tenth century, when northern Europe was just completing its move into feudalism. Because its focus was essentially rural, feudalism provided little impetus for the growth of cities. In Italy, feudalism never became very strong, and by the early fourteenth century it existed there in name only.

Moreover, because of the conflict between the papacy and the German empire a unified monarchy never emerged in Italy. Consequently, many of the medieval institutions that dominated the northern kingdoms never gained a foothold there. In intellectual matters, Italy was never dominated by scholasticism, as were the universities of the north, and Gothic architecture and sculpture had little influence in Italy. Thus, because the Italians' intellectual and artistic proclivities were outside the paradigms of medieval civilization, Italians were more receptive than northerners were to new ideas and to new ways of viewing the world. Also, though they experienced the famines and plagues of the fourteenth century, the cities of Italy were large enough, rich enough, and strong enough to recover more quickly than the cities of northern Europe.

THE CITY-STATES OF NORTHERN ITALY

The main business of the northern Italian cities was international trade. A third of the population of Florence, for example, was engaged in importing wool, making finished cloth, and selling it in foreign markets. Nearly all the people in Venice and Genoa depended for their livelihood either directly or indirectly on trade with the Levant and with northern Europe. Not surprisingly, affairs in the northern Italian cities were largely in the hands of bankers, export merchants, and textile manufacturers.

The political power of the cities reached deep into the adjacent region, which meant that they could act in the manner of urban principalities—that is, as city-states. Feudal lords in the neighborhood soon joined the city elite. And as the small market towns and villages of the countryside (called the *contado*) were annexed, some city-states came to control domains of several hundred square miles.

By the late twelfth century, the population of the city-states was divided into classes defined partly by social and partly by economic criteria. The merchant bankers—called the *popolo grasso,* or "fat people"—constituted the ruling class. The craftsmen, shopkeepers, and other members of the lesser bourgeoisie—the *popolo minuto,* or "little people"—made up the largest class. The lowest class consisted of poor day laborers, who had little say in the political life of the cities. Well-to-do families and craft guilds supported hospitals and other service agencies to take care of this indigent class. To be associated

with these institutions brought a certain social cachet.

Unlike the class groups in the northern cities, the classes in the Italian cities rarely organized themselves into cohesive political entities. This was because in virtually every Italian city political parties supported either the emperor or the pope in their endless struggle for power, and the membership of those parties cut across class lines. These parties were descendants of the eleventh-century *patarini,* groups of townspeople who had fought the bishops for political control. Because most of the bishops were appointed by the emperor, the *patarini* had usually allied themselves with the papacy.

In the twelfth century, supporters of the Hohenstaufen emperors came to be known as Ghibellines, while supporters of the papacy were called Guelfs. Ghibelline was the Italian version of Waiblingen, the name of one of the Hohenstaufen castles; the Guelfs took their name from the Welfs, the family of the Bavarian dukes who were traditional rivals of the Hohenstaufens. Every city had its Ghibellines and Guelfs. By the thirteenth century, however, the parties, which continued to be known by their old names, no longer concerned themselves with the conflict between the pope and the emperor. They were only competitors for control of the cities, which had governments elected by all citizens who owned a certain amount of property.

Each party was led by one of the leading families of the city. The party that was out of power at the moment tried to win the support of the *popolo minuto* by blasting the incumbents and by promising to undertake a program of reform if elected. Occasionally, as in Florence in 1378, some reforms really were carried out after a transfer of power. Such reforms lasted only a short time, however, before they were scrapped in a new election or *coup d'état.*

The never-ending turmoil caused by the struggle between the Ghibellines and Guelfs drove many leading citizens from their cities. Whenever an able man won power and succeeded in restoring order by dictatorial means, he was hailed by the populace and accorded widespread

Equestrian statue of the condottieri Captain Bartolommeo Colleoni, who tried to create a state between Milan and Florence in the fifteenth century.

support. Such despots, as they were called, gained control of many Italian cities in the last fourteenth and fifteenth centuries and continued to command support even though they exiled, imprisoned, and executed their opponents. They managed to stay in the public's good graces by improving the city's public services, strengthening its defenses, imposing equitable tax systems, and seeing that the streets were safe. Many of them engaged architects and sculptors to build and adorn magnificent public buildings. They also wooed the public by waging wars with rival cities.

The despots had a hard time raising forces to fight a war, however, because the merchants and shopkeepers of the city, though eager to expand their markets, had no stomach for battle. Moreover, the despots suspected that they might be making trouble for themselves if they armed the townspeople. They hired mercenary troops called *condottieri,* who were well trained and fairly reliable so long as they were paid on time. In a showdown, however, the *condottieri* tended to be more loyal to their captain than to the man who was paying them, and some of the captains managed to seize power for themselves.

War and Diplomacy

In time, the city-states of northern Italy became so independent and so powerful that they were engaging almost constantly in wars and alliances with one another. By the early fifteenth century, they had begun to send ambassadors to the courts of Europe to report on potential allies and potential enemies. This was the beginning of modern diplomacy.

In the second half of the century, the five leading states—Venice, Milan, Florence, the Papal States, and the Kingdom of Naples—entered into a kind of "balance of power" with an unwritten understanding that no one of them would be allowed to become strong enough to threaten the others. Later, when France and Spain intervened in Italian affairs, they too began to engage in the practice of diplomacy and soon were working out a balance of power of their own. By the mid-sixteenth

century, resident ambassadors were common throughout western and central Europe, and France and Spain were maintaining a rough balance of power.

Milan, Venice, and Florence

Milan, the largest city in the Po Valley was the exemplar of the classic Italian city-state. At the end of the fourteenth century, Milan was ruled by Gian Galeazzo Visconti, a despot who made Milan into a leading manufacturing and trading city and who almost succeeded in uniting all of northern Italy under his power.

Venice, Italy's greatest commercial center, had risen to prominence in the ninth century as a Byzantine protectorate. Along with other interests in the eastern Mediterranean, it controlled the trade with Constantinople and Fatimid Egypt (see pp. 186–88). Built on a meager cluster of islands in the Adriatic Sea, Venice had never been touched by feudalism and was the first Italian city to hazard life under a republican constitution. Its government, the most stable in Italy, was conducted by a small council of merchants—the Council of Ten—led by a head of state called the doge. Every ounce of energy of the Venetian state and of the Venetian people was devoted to commerce. Venetian history included no revolutions but more than a few conspiracies. Venetians proclaimed their city, "the most serene republic." Until Venice began to acquire territory on the mainland during the fifteenth century, the city was relatively isolated from Italian politics.

Florence had outstripped its rivals Pisa and Siena as the leading city of Tuscany during the eleventh century. Florence, like Venice, was a republic. Its citizens took pride in their constitutional government and scorned their rivals for tolerating the rule of despots. They were particularly proud of having resisted Gian Galeazzo Visconti's attempt to take over their city.

Florentine society and politics were dominated by wealthy merchant bankers and textile manufacturers. Florentine bankers were regarded as the most astute on the Continent, and Florentine textiles

The Italian City-States   1454

The rise of the Medici: Cosimo de' Medici has the look of the wily businessman.

as the finest to be had. Unlike Venice, however, Florence was the scene of endless political intrigues and conspiracies, with the losers usually being forced into exile. (Dante suffered that fate.) The victors repeatedly tampered with the constitution in an effort to hold onto their position. Finally, in 1434, a party led by the banker Cosimo de' Medici (1389–1464) took control of the city. Cosimo was a political boss who preferred to work through others and used bribes and threats to ensure that his supporters won election to city offices. His son Piero (1416–69) and his grandson Lorenzo the Magnificent (1449–92) followed his ex-

ample, and Florence enjoyed sixty years of stability.

Although the Medici were not themselves despots, they behaved in the manner of despots by strengthening the defenses of the city and by patronizing the best artists and architects of the age. The first three Medici made Florence the center of the Italian Renaissance, and their descendants, who remained prominent in the city until the eighteenth century, were faithful patrons of the arts. They allied their family with the leading families of Europe, and two of the Medici became queens of France.

The palace of the Medici in Florence. Cosimo began construction of it in 1444.

A Man of Virtù

Benvenuto Cellini, a Florentine goldsmith and sculptor, had struck medals and coins for Pope Clement VII (1523–34). He claimed that he had been insulted by a jeweler named Pompeo (who also worked for the pope), and after several quarrels, Cellini stabbed Pompeo to death in a street brawl. Clement VII had just died; Cardinal Farnese was elected pope on October 13, 1534, and took the name of Paul III.

After he had put affairs of greater consequence in order, the new Pope sent for me, saying that he did not wish any one else to strike his coins. To these words of his Holiness one of his gentlemen named Latino Juvinale [a Humanist] answered that I [Cellini] was in hiding for the murder of Pompeo of Milan, and set forth what could be argued for my justification in the most favorable terms. The Pope replied: "I know nothing of Pompeo's death but plenty of Benvenuto's provocation, so let a safe-conduct be at once made out for him." A great friend of Pompeo's was there; he was a Milanese called Ambrogio [Ambrogio Recalcati, a papal secretary]. This man said: "In the first days of your papacy it is not well to grant pardons of this kind." The Pope answered: "You know less about such matters than I do. Know then that men like Benvenuto, unique in their profession, stand above the law."

From Benvenuto Cellini, The Life of Benvenuto Cellini, *trans. by John Addington Symonds (New York: Scribner's, 1926), p. 144.*

ITALIAN URBAN CIVILIZATION

Baldassare Castiglione (1478–1529) in *The Courtier* defined the Renaissance man. The courtier combines the chivalric virtues—physical dexterity and strength, courage, skill in combat, courtesy—with the new virtues—knowledge of the classics, appreciation of art and literature, eloquence, and good taste. Above all, the courtier has grace; he excels effortlessly in everything he undertakes.

During the Middle Ages, courtliness had been associated with high birth. But the Renaissance courtier could be a self-made man, for talented and ambitious men were accorded considerable mobility. The *condottieri* captain Francesco Sforza (1401–66), for example, who overthrew the Visconti family to become Duke of Milan, founded a dynasty that ruled for a century. Leonardo da Vinci and the scholars Lorenzo Valla and Aeneas Silvius Piccolomini (who became Pope Pius II) were not highborn but were said to have *virtù,* a term that meant more than "virtue" in the modern sense; it also meant "virtuosity," that combination of genius and determination that made for greatness in statesmanship, art, and literature. Eventually, *virtù* came to mean the quality that makes for success.

Individualism

Above all else, the Italian Renaissance valued individualism. The Italians had never felt the full weight of feudal obligations, and their wealth came from commerce rather than from landed estates. That meant that their assets were readily available, making it possible for them to move from place to place whenever they found their situation oppressive or boring.

Mobility provided individuals with the opportunity to act independently and favored the man with the talent and courage to strike out on his own. Many merchants, craftsmen, scholars, and artists moved away from their hometowns, where they could find support from family and friends, to places where the market was good or patrons were ready to hire them, but where they would be on their own. Benvenuto Cellini (1500–71), a sculptor and goldsmith who described his violent and colorful career in his *Autobiography,* was an excellent case of the individualistic ethos occasioned by the mobility in Renaissance society. Cellini assumed that autobiography, which had been a rare literary genre in the Middle Ages, was a natural form of expression: "All men of whatsoever quality they be, who have done anything of excellence, . . . ought to describe their life with their own hand." He declared that ordinary laws of morality were meant for ordinary people, not for geniuses such as himself, and he claimed that the pope had once absolved him of murdering a man because the pope understood that he was above the law.

Secularism

The second characteristic of Renaissance society in Italy was its secular tone. People were endlessly interested in the things of this world—commerce, the design of houses, styles of dress, food and drink, and the enjoyment of leisure. In his *Decameron* (*ca.* 1350), Giovanni Boccaccio told one hundred stories featuring characters taken from contemporary society. The work provided a model for Italian prose writing but also presented personality types that reveal the interests and ideals of behavior of the period. Boccaccio's characters are not irreligious or anti-Christian, but they scorn the hypocrisy of priests and monks; they rejoice in the triumph of clever people over clerical busybodies; and they seem to say that paying attention to the affairs of this world is quite appropriate for the people who live in it. The secularism of the *Decameron* consisted of two components—a preoccupation with worldly affairs and a contempt for false spirituality and asceticism.

Humanism

Humanism derived from the study of classical literature; the humanist was a classical scholar. It was not the mere act of studying the classics that made the humanist but the implication that one who

---

Petrarch on the Classics and Christianity

You are well aware that from early boyhood of all the writers of all ages and races the one whom I most admire and love is Cicero. You agree with me in this respect as well as in so many others. I am not afraid of being considered a poor Christian by declaring myself so much a Ciceronian. [This is an allusion to a famous vision of St. Jerome in which God told him: "You are a Ciceronian and therefore not a Christian."] To my knowledge, Cicero never wrote one word that would conflict with the principles proclaimed by Christ. If, perchance, his works contained anything contrary to Christ's doctrine, that one fact would be sufficient to destroy my belief in Cicero and in Aristotle and in Plato. . . .

Christ is my God; Cicero is the prince of the language I use. I grant you that these ideas are widely separated, but I deny that they are in conflict with each other. Christ is the Word, and the Virtue and the Wisdom of God the Father. Cicero has written much on the speech of men, on the virtues of men, and on the wisdom of men—statements that are true and therefore surely acceptable to the God of Truth.

From a letter to Neri Morando, 1358, in Petrarch's Letters to Classical Authors, *trans. by M. E. Cosenza (Chicago: University of Chicago Press, 1910), pp. 18–19.*

---

did so was interested in the highest ideals of human behavior. Humanism was the study of man though the examples provided by classical literature and ancient history. As far back as the fourteenth century, the poet/scholar Petrarch (1304–74) had revived classical literary forms and had imitated the styles of the ancient writers. Later humanists followed his example, spurred on by Boccaccio's biography of Petrarch.

Led by Petrarch and Boccaccio, Renaissance Italians conceived a passion for everything relating to classical antiquity. Knowledge of classical literature was an indication of true gentility, and the humanists were held in high honor. Many humanists held positions as secretaries in the royal courts of Europe and as teachers of the children of noble families. Generally, they were self-made men who earned a living through their learning. Enthusiasm

Benvenuto Cellini did this bust of Bindo Altroviti about 1550.

Young student reading Cicero
(detail from a painting by
Vincenzo Foppa).

One humanist educator wrote, "We call those studies liberal which are worthy of a free man . . . that education which calls forth, trains, and develops those highest gifts of body and of mind which ennoble men." That is still the goal of liberal education.

Historical Consciousness

Petrarch and his fellow humanists were well aware that the Roman civilization they admired was quite different from their own and were careful to distinguish between the past and present. They could talk of the "fall of Rome" and of the "dark age" that separated the glorious time of Augustus, Vergil, and Cicero from their own. This was a new consciousness that enabled the humanists to see themselves and their society in historical context, which is a characteristic of the modern view of individuals and society.

FAMILY LIFE

The ideals of Renaissance family life were those of upper-class urban families—the families of bankers and merchants. The *populo minuto* imitated these ideals to the extent that their finances permitted.

Men got married rather late, usually to much younger women, and the husband was unchallenged head of the household. Because of the disparity of age, widows were almost as common as widowers. (Until modern times, men generally outlived their wife because of the frequency with which women died in childbirth.) A man was expected to have established himself as an upstanding member of the community before marrying, and his purpose in marrying was to have children who would carry on his family line and his profession. The role of the wife was to advance her husband's career by exhibiting her beauty, culture, and social grace. Consequently, it was important that women be faithful and virtuous, and a woman's virtue was a common theme in Renaissance literature. The need for a woman to remain faithful to her husband was so urgent that it even survived his

for the classics intensified after 1395, as scholars fled westward from Constantinople to escape the Ottoman Turks, who were advancing across Asia Minor. In Italy the Greeks found students eager to study the Greek language and Greek literature, and Lorenzo the Magnificent founded a Platonic Academy in Florence for the study and teaching of Greek philosophy. By the end of the fifteenth century a few Italians were studying Hebrew and Arabic in addition to Greek.

The humanists turned their attention to education as well. The secular schools of the Middle Ages had concentrated on preparing young men for a career in commerce. They taught reading, writing, and arithmetic, and little else. And the main purpose of the ecclesiastical schools had been to train clerics and monks; their intellectual standards were high, but of course all study focused on theology.

The humanists of the fifteenth century rediscovered the "liberal arts" that liberate the mind and the imagination through the study of great literature and philosophy. To that study they added training in behavior and athletic skill, thereby realizing the ancient goal of *mens sana in corpore sano* ("a sound mind in a sound body").

death. A man was advised to discourage his wife from remarrying after his death by arranging that his property would go to her only "if she remains a widow and lives with her children." Of course many widows did remarry, and families were often quite large.

A young woman married to an older man often had to cope with difficult circumstances. There might be little or no difference between her own age and the age of her husband's older children, and she might become embroiled in controversies between the various sibling groups. She might also be obliged to accept her husband's illegitimate children into the household and sometimes the children of his brothers or sisters as well. During prolonged absences of her husband, she was expected to manage the servants and their children, raise her children, run the household, and keep the family, the relatives, and the staff at peace.

Infants were normally put out for two years to a wet nurse—usually peasant women in the *contado*. When returned to the family household, they had to get to know their siblings and their parents and find a place for themselves in the family group. Many diaries from the period evidence the feelings of alienation and fear that often accompanied this entry into the home.

Between the ages of two and seven, children were almost exclusively under their mother's care. The father remained rather distant except in times of crisis, as when the child or the mother became seriously ill. The father entered the child's world when the child was ready to begin formal education, usually at the age of seven.

Boys were sent to a boarding school, where they spent three or four years learning to read and write both in Latin and the vernacular. They then spent another year or so studying accounting and business procedures and finally were placed as apprentices with a merchant or banker. Girls were educated at home in the household arts and in reading and writing.

Women were expected to come to their marriage with a dowry, and in Florence and many other cities parents could

How Children Should Be Raised

The Dominican Friar Giovanni Dominici (ca. 1356–ca. 1420) wrote a treatise on childrearing.

Children should be accustomed to eat coarse food, to wear cheap and common clothes. . . . They should also learn to wait on themselves, and to use as little as possible the services of maid and servant, setting and clearing the table, dressing and undressing themselves, putting on their own shoes and clothes and so forth.

After a boy reaches three years of age, he should know no distinction between male and female other than dress and hair. From then on let him be a stranger to being petted, embraced and kissed by you [the mother] until after the twenty-fifth year. Granted that there will not take place any thought or natural movement before the age of five . . . do not be less solicitous that he be chaste and modest always and, in every place, covered as modestly as if he were a girl.

Quoted by James Bruce Ross, "The Middle-Class Child in Urban Italy, Fourteenth to Early Sixteenth Century", The History of Childhood, *ed. by L. deMause (New York: Psychoanalytic Press, 1974).*

invest in dowry banks. They deposited a specified sum when their daughter was very young and let the fund grow through the accrual of interest until it was redeemed.

Women of the middle classes participated more directly in their husbands' affairs. From the little evidence we have, it appears that middle-class families emulated their betters by putting their children out to a wet nurse and providing them with a formal education. The men married late, and widowhood was common in this class. Some women found work in manufacturing—perhaps as weavers—and many women seem to have owned their own shops.

THE RENAISSANCE

Literature, Philosophy, and Scholarship

The early humanists tended to imitate the genres and styles of classical literature—letters, orations, moral essays, and poetry,

A seventeenth-century engraving showing a peasant father feeding his infant child.

Renaissance scholars created the discipline of critical scholarship, which calls for a careful linguistic and historical analysis of the literature of the past. Lorenzo Valla (*ca.* 1405–57) used linguistic analysis to prove that the Donation of Constantine (see p. 182), on which papal claims to temporal authority rested, was a crude forgery of the early Middle Ages. He also compared several Greek manuscripts of the New Testament with Jerome's vulgate translation (late fourth century) and uncovered many errors and distortions in the translation. His scholarly approach to literary texts influenced later scholars, including Erasmus (see p. 432), who produced the first critical edition of the Greek New Testament.

Social and Political Thought

Though most of the social and political thinkers of the Renaissance simply paraphrased the Greek and Roman classics, a few of them did original work. Leon Battista Alberti (1404–72), for example, in his *On the Family* analyzed the structure and interests of Florentine families. He reports that they prized prudence, thrift, foresight, and comfort; had strong family feeling and little interest in the affairs of society as a whole; and aspired to a house in the city and an estate in the country to produce the family's food. Alberti's account is one of the earliest treatments of what later came to be called the bourgeois virtues.

Baldassare Castiglione's *The Courtier* (written 1513–18, published 1528), as we have seen, dealt with the ideals of the noble class. Drawing on his experiences at the court of the duke of Urbino, Castiglione reformulated the ideal of "the gentleman." Though his work owed much to the chivalric tradition of the Middle Ages, it spoke of the goals of a liberal education and the idea that "nobility" derives from character rather than from the accident of birth.

Perhaps the greatest political theorist of the Renaissance was Niccolò Machiavelli (1469–1527), who combined wide reading in the classics, particularly history, with wide experience in politics. He served Florence as an ambassador to

for example. They also created new forms, however, such as the sonnet and the essay.

Renaissance philosophers drew heavily on the work of Plato, which had been introduced to the West by refugee Byzantine scholars in the 1390s. The leading members of the Platonic academy founded by the Medici were Marsilio Ficino (1433–99) and Pico della Mirandola (1463–94), who tried to reconcile Plato and Christianity much as Thomas Aquinas had tried to reconcile Aristotle and Christianity (see pp. 293–95).

France and as secretary of the state during a period when the Medici were out of power. When they returned to power in 1512, Machiavelli retired to his country estate. There he studied political history and reflected on what causes political breakdown, how political leaders obtain and hold power, and what can be learned from history.

In his long, rambling *Discourses on Livy* (Livy was a famous Roman historian) and in his brief essay, *The Prince,* Machiavelli sought to describe political life as he saw it, rather than as it should be. His analysis of the strengths and weaknesses of various types of constitutions shows that he favored the republican form of government, like that of Florence. In *The Prince,* however, he concentrated on the behavior of heads of state and their use of power. The book ends with a plea that Italians unify their country, throw out the foreign invaders, and recreate the glory of ancient Rome. *The Prince* became a grammar of political and diplomatic practice and was translated into many languages. Its realistic account of the world of politics and international relations earned Machiavelli a reputation as a proponent of dictatorship. Actually, although he believed that a strong, centralized state was desirable, he insisted that it must operate under a constitution suited to the character of the people. And the most educated populace would be best served by a republican constitution.

The Arts

Soon after the humanists rediscovered Roman literature, Renaissance architects turned their attention to Roman architecture. There were Roman buildings or their ruins everywhere, and architects set about analyzing the principles of design the Romans had followed. The greatest of the early Renaissance architects was Brunelleschi (*ca*. 1377–1446), who designed numerous churches with symmetrical design and stately facades. The most impressive example of Renaissance architecture was the church of St. Peter in Rome, which replaced a fourth-century basilica built by Emperor Constantine I. The largest church

A late sixteenth-century portrait of Niccolò Machiavelli by Santi di Tito. The artist has tried to suggest both the intellectual brilliance and the shrewdness of the man.

in Europe, St. Peter's was the work of several architects—including Bramante, Michelangelo, and Bernini—from 1506 to 1615.

Renaissance painting was strongly influenced by the techniques of Giotto (1276–1337), Dante's favorite painter, who introduced a sense of volume in his representations of figures and their surroundings, especially in a series of frescoes (paintings done on fresh plaster) in the church of St. Francis in Assisi. During the fourteenth century Italian painters had also become familiar with the realistic style favored by the Flemish painters of the Burgundian court. That style was raised to a new height by Masaccio (1401–*ca*. 1428), who suppressed irrelevant details and concentrated on the emotional aspects of the scenes he painted.

In the Middle Ages, painting and sculpture had usually been regarded as adjuncts to architecture. But during the Renaissance they emerged as independent forms of expression. Italian painters still painted frescoes on the walls of

Machiavelli on Cruelty and Clemency

Is it better to be loved than feared or feared than loved? It may be answered that one should wish to be both, but it is much safer to be feared than loved when one of the two must be chosen. Men on the whole are ungrateful, fickle, false, cowards, covetous. As long as you succeed, they are yours entirely. They will offer you their blood, property, life, and children when the need is distant, but when it approaches they turn against you. And a prince who, relying entirely on their promises, has neglected other precautions, is ruined. . . . Men have fewer scruples in offending one who is beloved than one who is feared, for love is preserved by the link of obligation which, owing to the baseness of men, is broken at every opportunity for their advantage, but fear preserves you by a dread of punishment which never fails.

Nevertheless, a prince should inspire fear in such a way that if he does not win love, he avoids hatred; because he can endure very well being feared while he is not hated, and this will be true as long as he abstains from taking the property of his subjects or their women. But when it is necessary for him to take the life of someone, he must do it with proper justification and for manifest cause, and above everything he must keep his hands off the property of others, because men more quickly forget the death of their father than the loss of their heritage.

From Niccolò Machiavelli, The Prince, *trans. by W. K. Marriott (London: Dent, n.d.), pp. 134–35.*

churches and monasteries, but they turned more and more to easel painting, creating pictures to be hung on the wall and enjoyed for their own sake. Though they still favored religious themes, they often drew on classical sources for their subjects, reflecting the influence of humanism.

Sculptors, too, turned to classical models for inspiration. Donatello (1368–1466), for example, was the first sculptor since Roman times to model a freestanding nude figure. His *David* opened the way to the creation of a succession of great sculptures that culminated in the masterpieces of Michelangelo (1475–1564). These works revived the Greco-Roman fascination with the beauty of the human body.

Many Renaissance artists achieved substantial public recognition and social prestige through their work. Although some patrons treated artists as common servants, many artists earned handsome commissions and lived as independent and honored members of society.

In their efforts to achieve realism, Renaissance painters studied the laws of perspective and human anatomy, and their notebooks and sketches contain countless studies of proportion and space and treatments of the human torso and limbs. They observed facial expressions and body posture so that they could reveal the exact emotional state of figures they portrayed. Leonardo da Vinci (1452–1519), for example, in his painting *The Last Supper,* departed from tradition by depicting, not the moment when Christ says to the apostles, "This is my body . . .," but instead the dramatic moment when Christ announces, "One of you will betray me." By conveying the psychological state of each apostle, he achieves tremendous dramatic power.

Da Vinci's wide-ranging curiosity extended to the workings of mechanical devices as well as to the workings of the human body. He created designs for a helicopter and a self-propelled vehicle and made studies of perspective, light, and optics.

Michelangelo followed Da Vinci in searching for the psychologically charged moment. His painting of the Creation on the ceiling of the Sistine Chapel in the Vatican is focused on God's animation of Adam. And in his statue of Moses, Michelangelo portrays him at the moment when he catches sight of the Golden Calf, sitting tense, with a fierce expression, trying to control his rage over his people's idolatry.

Throughout these examples we find the Renaissance emphasis on human beings as they live here and now, in this world—troubled, striving, with unknown potential. Pico della Mirandola remarked in a famous *Oration* on man's dignity (1486) that God had given man something he had given to no other creature—freedom. All other creatures have their set patterns of behavior, but man's nature and destiny, Pico declared, are in his own hands. The people of the Renaissance had not lost their belief in God, but they gave new meaning to the Judeo-Christian idea that man was made in God's image: Like

God, man is a creator, a creator of his own character and his own destiny.

Along with artists and writers, the urban courts of Italy employed hundreds of musicians, craftsmen, mechanics, and engineers. Working together in a relatively small space, these specialists often cooperated and advanced one another's endeavors. Artists and physicians shared their knowledge of human anatomy. Painters worked out the principles of perspective and contributed to the study of mathematics. Physicians studied astronomy, because in medieval medicine the stars were thought to affect health. In fact, many of the instruments used to observe the stars were designed by physicians.

During the sixteenth century Italy was the center of European cultural life. Northern Europe had begun to recover from the famines and plagues of the late Middle Ages, but northerners with an interest in the arts and humanism traveled to Italy to study. No northern city approached Florence, Venice, or Rome as a center of artistic and intellectual life.

ECONOMIC GROWTH IN NORTHERN EUROPE

The wealth of Italy was based primarily on trade and industry, and from the thirteenth century to the sixteenth century, Italy was the banking center of Europe. The wealth of the nations of northern Europe was based primarily on agriculture and mineral deposits. To be sure, northerners engaged in commerce and industry, and many cities had substantial communities of merchants and manufacturers; Flanders, for example, produced excellent cloth for which there was a lively demand. But agriculture was the main source of wealth, for northern Europe is one of the richest agricultural regions on earth, and the extensive network of rivers made it possible to move the produce to the markets at low cost.

During the fifteenth century, a series of technological advances fueled a new burst of economic activity in the North. And the new industries such as cannon founding and printing required large ini-

The Pitti Palace in Florence, now an art museum, was built by the early Renaissance architect Filippo Brunelleschi for the merchant Luca Pitti.

tial investments in plant and machinery. From the start, these industries were organized as capitalistic enterprises—that is, enterprises in which wealth was used to create new wealth. This was a departure from medieval practice, when most wealth was used to buy "consumer" goods and was rarely accumulated to invest in improvements and increased production.

The managers of these capitalistic enterprises drew their workers from both town and countryside and created a large, mobile labor force that was subject to the vagaries of an economy that neither they nor their workers could control. Consequently, the workers were wealthier and at the same time less secure than medieval peasants and craftsmen had been.

Progressive landlords tried to introduce capitalism into agriculture by producing only the most profitable crops and animal products. Particularly in England—where wool production was well established—many landlords fenced in, or "enclosed," open fields that had formerly been reserved for the use of villagers, and some of them even enclosed cultivated land to accommodate huge flocks of sheep. At the beginning of the sixteenth

Donatello's *David* (ca. 1430–32). Compare this statue with the *David* by Michelangelo on the opposite page.

century, Thomas More, chancellor of England, complained that the enclosure movement was ruining the small farmers and was creating a class of "sturdy beggars" or "vagabonds" who posed a problem for town governments. Actually, the reason for the vagabonds was the growth in population. After two centuries of decline, population growth had resumed, and it outpaced the creation of jobs. Town governments built prisons and workhouses to house the tramps.

The wealth produced by the new industries tended to find its way to a few hands in a few places. For a brief time, the most powerful banking house in northern Europe was that of the Fuggers of Augsburg in southern Germany. Jakob Fugger (1459–1525), banker to the Habsburgs of Austria (see p. 370) and to the popes, could invest in Austrian mines and Spanish colonies and carry on dealings with every part of the continent. From about 1476 to 1576, however, the real center of banking was Antwerp (now in Belgium), with Lyons in second place. In the following century, Amsterdam took over the lead. By the later sixteenth century, financial power was shifting from Italy to the north.

Leonardo da Vinci's design for a helicopter. The man uses a crank to flap the wings.

POLITICAL CONSOLIDATION AND CENTRALIZATION

Toward the end of the fifteenth century, the nations of northern Europe began to recover from the disastrous effects of war and plague. The War of the Roses (1455–85) produced a strong new dynasty in England (see p. 362), and after the end of the Hundred Years' War in 1453 the French kings were able to recover their power. In Germany, though the emperor remained weak, the marriage alliances contrived by the imperial family spread their influence across the Continent. And Spain too established a power base with the wealth extracted from its new colonies. In short, the kings of northern Europe were drawing close to achieving the absolute power that had eluded their medieval predecessors.

France

Although Charles VII (r. 1422–61) managed to drive the English from nearly all of their French territories, he was not a particularly effective ruler. He was, however, good at choosing able men to work for him (he was known as Charles "the Well-served") and getting them to strengthen the monarchy for him. In 1438, he asserted his authority over the French church by means of the Pragmatic Sanction of Bourges (see p. 428). In the 1440s, he solved his need for money by getting the Estates General to agree to a broad-based tax on land, which he continued to collect on his own authority thereafter. He organized a small but strong standing army (not more than 25,000 men). And he won the support of the merchant class, from which he recruited some of his best royal officials.

Charles's son Louis XI (r. 1461–83) was an able ruler who left the monarchy stronger than it had been since the early fourteenth century. He was a master of diplomacy—he was called "the Spider" because of his ability to trap his enemies in a web of intrigue—and won the admiration of Machiavelli. Louis's greatest enemy was Charles the Bold, duke of Burgundy (r. 1467–77), who outmaneuvered him while at the same time helping him to rid France of the last English troops. But Louis finally succeeded in stirring up Charles's eastern neighbors, and Charles died fighting a battle with Swiss pikemen.

The richest part of Charles the Bold's inheritance, the Netherlands, went to the Habsburg emperor Maximilian (r. 1493–1519) by way of his wife Mary, Charles's daughter. But the strategically located duchy of Burgundy went to Louis. Louis also married his son Charles VIII (r. 1483–98) to the heiress of Brittany, thus bringing the last feudal duchy under French control. Louis continued his father's policy of encouraging trade, maintaining the loyalty of the merchant class, and keeping firm control of the aristocracy and the church.

During the first years of his reign, however, Charles VIII spent most of his

Michelangelo's *David* (ca. 1501–04). Instead of representing David after his victory over Goliath, as Donatello had done, Michelangelo chose to represent him watching the approaching foe, with muscles tensed in gathering strength.

Michelangelo's statue of the horned Moses. The horns represent the rays of light that symbolize the divine inspiration of Moses as receiver of the Ten Commandments.

An early printing press, as shown in an early sixteenth-century French print.

gon (r. 1479–1516) and Isabella of Castile (r. 1474–1504) enabled them to carry out a common foreign policy and helped them to transform their joint kingdoms into a European power. Another marriage at about that time further enhanced the position of Spain. The emperor Maximilian and his wife Mary of Burgundy had a son, Philip, who was heir to Austria through his Habsburg father and heir to the Netherlands through his mother. Philip married Joanna, the daughter of Ferdinand and Isabella, and their son, Charles, eventually became king of Spain (r. 1516–56) and ruler of the Netherlands, Austria, Milan, Naples, and the Spanish colonies in the New World. In 1519, the German princes elected him emperor as Charles V (see pp. 437, 457).

At the end of the fifteenth century, Spain was not yet wealthy or fully unified. The kingdoms of Aragon and Castile clung to their old institutions and to their own languages. The Spanish armies, however, were among the best in Europe. Then, with Columbus's discoveries in the New World, gold and silver streamed into the kingdom and transformed Spain into the leading power of sixteenth-century Europe (see pp. 453–58).

England

Henry Tudor (Henry VII, r. 1485–1509), who brought the War of the Roses to an end, succeeded in reestablishing peace and proved himself one of the ablest kings in English history. The ranks of the aristocracy had been thinned during the wars, and Henry filled them out with men loyal to his monarchy. He kept England out of foreign wars, encouraged trade, restored royal revenues, and eliminated all pretenders to the throne.

Henry's son, Henry VIII (r. 1509–47), inherited a full treasury, a united nation, and a relatively efficient administration. He introduced humanist learning to England and helped foster the English Renaissance. With the help and advice of his ruthless chief minister, Cardinal Wolsey, he issued numerous statutes to reform the Common Law and to correct abuses. His reign was one of the most innovative periods in the history of the English law.

time consolidating his control of the country. Once that was done, he was ready to renew some of the ancient claims of the French monarchy. In 1494 he invaded Italy and asserted his claim to the kingdom of Naples as the heir of Charles of Anjou (see p. 322). The Spanish monarchy, which also had a claim to Italy, reacted quickly to the French invasion. For the next half-century, foreign armies ranging across Italy destroyed the prosperity and independence of the city-states. Eventually, Spain won out and made the kingdom of Naples a dependency of the Spanish crown. Though the French monarchy had suffered severe financial losses in the wars, it remained one of the most influential powers in Europe.

Spain

As we have seen, the momentous marriage (1469) between Ferdinand of Ara-

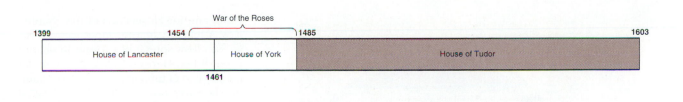

| 1399 | | 1454 | | 1485 | | 1603 |

War of the Roses

| House of Lancaster | House of York | House of Tudor |

1461

Henry married Catherine of Aragon, thereby joining England to the grand alliance of families associated with the royal house of Spain. But he and Catherine had only one daughter. Foreseeing a dynastic crisis, Henry sought to rid himself of his wife. When the pope refused to grant him a divorce, he proclaimed the Act of Supremacy in 1534, declaring himself the head of an English church free from the authority of the pope. Chancellor Thomas More, a humanist scholar and brilliant lawyer who succeeded Cardinal Wolsey in 1529, refused to accede to the king's assertion of authority and retired from his office in 1532. When he continued in his opposition to the king's remarriage and the Act of Supremacy, he was convicted of treason and was beheaded in 1535.

The Consolidation of Royal Power

During the sixteenth century, the European monarchs overcame the nobility, the representative assemblies, and the church in their determination to strengthen their power. They overcame the nobility either because it had been weakened by war, as in England, or because it could not afford the cost of the new military technology. Most of the kings compensated for the loss of the nobility by creating bureaucracies made up of educated, loyal men who strengthened royal finances by means of innovative taxes and sound financial management.

The representative assemblies—the Estates General in France, the Cortes in Spain, and Parliament in England—had achieved great power and influence during the fourteenth century, when the kings needed their help in dealing with the endless wars and the dire effects of the plague. In the fifteenth century, however, the power of the assemblies declined everywhere except in England. In most cases,

they themselves were to blame for their decline. Once the kings were no longer dependent on them for financial aid, the parochial interests of the delegates came

Jakob Fugger with his bookkeeper. The cabinet in the rear lists the names of cities where Fugger had branch offices—Innsbruck, Nuremburg, and Lisbon, among others (detail from a painting by Matthaus Schwartz, 1516).

Los Reyes don fernando y doña ysabel y la Reyna... alinfāta su hija doña   Juana.

Illumination of Ferdinand and Isabella of Spain—known as the "Catholic Kings"—with their daughter Joanna.

realm and for all sections of the country, it was hard to ignore. Moreover, it was an excellent source of support in time of need. When Henry VIII was trying to get the pope to grant him a divorce, for example, he summoned Parliament and asked for its support. By 1600, as a result of the frequent use Henry VIII and his successors made of it, Parliament had risen to a position of great influence in English government. By that time the representative assemblies on the Continent were hollow bodies under the control of absolute monarchs.

Finally, the monarchs overcame the church by preempting the appointment of prelates, by taxing the clergy without the permission of the pope, and by monitoring the appeal of cases to Rome. The kings of England and France had established the right to tax the clergy by 1300 (see p. 325), and the French king asserted the right to appoint prelates in 1438 in the Pragmatic Sanction of Bourges. In the Concordat of Bologna (1516) the pope granted Francis I (r. 1515–47) the right to nominate members of the higher clergy and to settle most ecclesiastical disputes that arose in France. The power to nominate amounted to the power to appoint. Even Ferdinand and Isabella, the Catholic Kings, asserted their right to appoint, to tax, and to reform the clergy within their kingdoms. In England, Henry VIII's Act of Supremacy (1534) gave him complete power over the church in one stroke.

The consolidation and centralization of power also proceeded in Norway and Sweden during the fifteenth and sixteenth centuries, and in Russia Ivan the Terrible (r. 1533–84) ruthlessly destroyed the power of the Russian nobility (see p. 346). But the process did not take place everywhere. Italy made no movement toward formation of a central government—to the dismay of Machiavelli—and in Germany the emperor was no more than a figurehead. When Charles V became emperor in 1519, his real strength lay in his position as duke of Austria, lord of the Netherlands, and king of Spain. In becoming emperor he gained some prestige, many responsibilities, but little power. Consequently, no one in Germany could resist the exactions

into play and destroyed the effectiveness of the assemblies. As the power of the kings rose during the fifteenth century, they manipulated the assemblies by playing the various factions off against one another, and the delegates began to avoid attending the meetings. The Estates General and Cortes met less and less frequently after the end of the fifteenth century.

In England, Henry VII used the Parliament to help establish his power. Once he was in control, however, he rarely called it into session. Nonetheless, because it spoke for all the privileged classes of the

Sir Thomas More, after Hans Holbein (1527).

of the papacy, which escalated steadily as the popes found themselves challenged elsewhere.

This lack of central authority in Germany was to be crucial in the sixteenth century. It contributed to the success of the Protestant Reformation, which became mixed up in the competition among the German princes. And it obliged the emperor to rely entirely on his hereditary domains in meeting the threat of the Ottoman Turks (see p. 189), who under Suleiman the Magnificent (r. 1520–66) captured Belgrade, took most of Hungary in the battle of Mohacs (1526), and almost seized Vienna in 1529.

Suggestions for Further Reading

General

The classic work on the Renaissance is J. Burckhardt, *The Civilization of the Renaissance in Italy* (1860). For a recent survey, see D. Hay, *The Italian Renaissance* (1977). W. K. Ferguson, *Europe in Transition: 1300–1520* (1963), emphasizes social and economic history. For a revolutionary view of the economic background of the Renaissance, see R. S. Lopez and H. A. Miskimin, "The Economic Depression of the Renaissance," *Economic History Review* 14 (1962), and the response by C. Cipolla, "Economic Depression of the Renaissance?" *Economic History Review* 16 (1963–64). For an overview, see A. Molho, *Social and Economic Foundations of the Italian Renaissance* (1969), and G. Huppert, *After the Black Death: A Social History of Early Modern Europe* (1986).

Italian Politics and Society

Recently, historians have written a series of works on individual Italian cities. See G. Brucker, *Renaissance Florence* (1969); D. Herlihy, *Pisa in the Early Renaissance* (1958); W. M. Bowsky, *The Finances of the Commune of Siena* (1970); D. S. Chambers, *The Imperial Age of Venice: 1380–1580* (1970); and C. M. Ady, *Milan under the Sforza* (1907). See also R. de Roover, *The Rise and Fall of the Medici Bank* (1963). For a general view, see D. Waley, *The Italian City Republics* (1969).

The classic work on the origins of modern diplomacy is G. Mattingly, *Renaissance Diplomacy* (1955). For background, see D. E. Queller, *The Office of Ambassador in the Middle Ages* (1967). On Renaissance warfare, see C. Oman, *History of the Art of War in the Sixteenth Century* (1937), and M. Mallett, *Mercenaries and their Masters* (1974).

On the Renaissance family, see L. deMause, ed., *The History of Childhood* (1974); J. Gage, *Life in Italy at the Time of the Medici* (1968); C. L. Lee, Jr., *Daily Life in Renaissance Italy* (1975); G. Brucker, *Giovanni and Lusanna: Love and Marriage in Renaissance Florence* (1986); and P. Aries, *Centuries of Childhood* (1962), a revolutionary work that uses art to show how views of children changed over time. *The Portable Renaissance Reader,* ed. by J. B. Ross and M. McLaughlin (1953), contains a selection from Alberti's *On the Family,* as well as other works. See J. Gadol, *Leon Battista Alberti: Universal Man of the Early Renaissance* (1969).

Humanism

On the origins of Renaissance humanism, see C. Trinkhaus, *The Poet as Philosopher: Petrarch and the Formation of the Renaissance Consciousness* (1979). On the humanist movement, see P. Kristeller, *Renaissance Thought,* 2 vols. (1961, 1965), and C. Trinkhaus, *The Scope of Renaissance Humanism* (1983). H. Baron, *The Crisis of the Early Italian Renaissance,* 2 vols. (1966), is an important treatment of the relationship between humanist thought and Florentine history in the early fifteenth century. On Renaissance political thought, see J. W. Allen, *Political Thought in the Sixteenth Century* (1928), and F. Chabod, *Machiavelli and the Renaissance* (1958). For an excellent biography of Machiavelli, see S. de Grazia, *Machiavelli in Hell* (1989).

Art and Architecture

There are many histories of Renaissance art and architecture. See P. and L. Murray, *The Art of the Renaissance* (1963); P. Murray, *Architecture of the Italian Renaissance* (1963); and E. H. Gombrich, *The Story of Art* (1953). See also Gombrich's article on the Medici as patrons of art in E. F. Jacob, ed., *Italian Renaissance Studies* (1960). For the early period, see R. Fremantle, *Florentine Gothic Painters from Giotto to Masaccio* (1975), and M. Meiss, *Painting in Florence and Siena after the Black Death* (1973). See also M. Baxendall, *Painting and Experience in Fifteenth Century Italy* (1972); J. R. Hale, *Italian Renaissance Painting from Masaccio to Titian* (1977); J. Pope-Hennessy, *An Introduction to Italian Sculpture,* 3rd ed., 3 vols. (1986); and R. Wittkower, *Architectural Principles in the Age of Humanism,* 4th ed. (1988).

Economic Growth

For a general history of the European economy, see the *Cambridge Economic History of Europe,* 3 vols. (1952–66). Volume 1 deals with agriculture; volume 2 with commerce and industry; and volume 3 with economic organization and policy. H. A. Miskimin, *The Economy of Early Renaissance Europe* (1969), is a good short survey. R. Ehrenberg, *Capital and Finance in the Age of the Renaissance* (1928), is the standard study of the Fuggers. See also E. Power and M. M. Postan, eds., *Studies in English Trade in the Fifteenth Century* (1953), and A. R. Bridbury, *Economic Growth: England in the Later Middle Ages* (1962). On the low countries; see H. Van Der Wee, *The Growth of the Antwerp Market and the European Economy* (1963). E. Eisenstein, *The Printing Press as an Agent of Change* (1979), is a good account of the invention and its effect.

France, England, and Spain

On late medieval France, see the works cited in Chapter 14. See also P. M. Kendall, *Louis the Eleventh* (1971); F. Pegues, *Lawyers of the Last Capetians* (1962); and J. H. Shennan, *The Parlement of Paris* (1968). On Spain, see the works cited in Chapter 14. On England, see the works cited in Chapter 14, and S. B. Chrimes, *Lancastrians, Yorkists, and Henry VII* (1964).

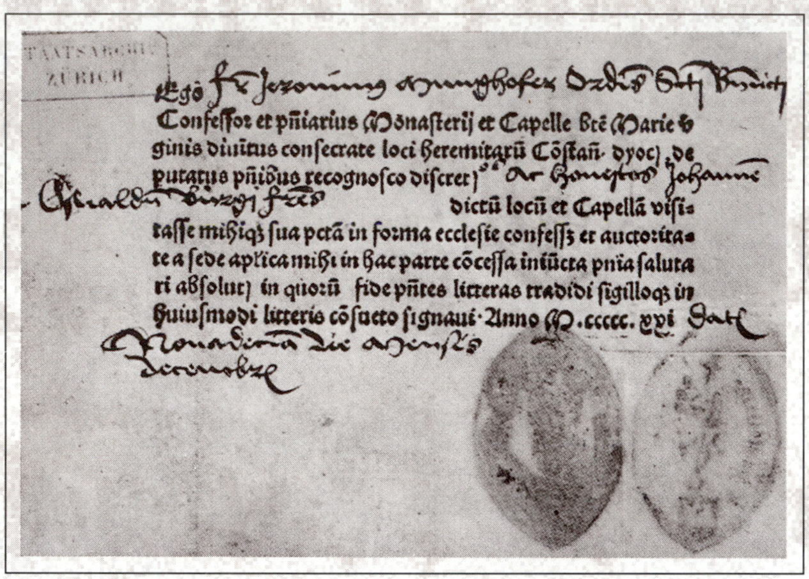

STAATSARCHIV ZÜRICH

Egō Fr Jeronimus Mungkofer Ordinis Sancti Benedicti
Confessor et pñiarius Monasterij et Capelle btē Marie v
ginis diuinitus consecrate loci heremitarū Cōstañ dyoc) de
putatus pñidus recognosco discret) ac honestum Johannem
Gheralden ... dictū locū et Capellā visi
tasse mihiq3 sua petā in forma ecclesie confess3 et auctorita
te a sede ap'lica mihi in hac parte cōcessa iniūcta pnīa saluta
ri absolut) in quorū fide pñtes litteras tradidi sigilloq3 in
huiusmodi litteris cōsueto signaui Anno M.ccccc.xxi Sab
... die mensis
decembris

17

RELIGIOUS REFORM AND REVOLUTION IN WESTERN CHRISTENDOM

As we have seen, religious institutions were changing in the late Middle Ages. By the sixteenth century, the national churches of Europe were essentially under the control of the kings and the status of the pope had dwindled to that of an Italian despot. Many people had grown suspicious of the church and contemptuous of its leaders. So outraged had they become by the church's incessant demands for money that many had stopped attending church services altogether. This did not mean that their interest in religion had waned; it meant simply that they were looking elsewhere for religious guidance. Evangelical preachers abounded and attracted enthusiastic followings who applauded their charge that the church had grown worldly and corrupt. It did not help that the church was a demanding landlord to peasants and townspeople throughout Europe.

The new class of capitalistic merchants and industrialists also was at odds with the church, which had never managed to incorporate business ethics into its system of values. The church still shared the view of the ancient Romans that business was inevitably corrupting and morally suspect, and it still imposed the Judaic injunction against usury (charging interest on loans). Throughout the Middle Ages, merchants had often borrowed money to finance their business and had resorted to ruses to escape the charge of usury. With the rise of capitalism, the tension between the commercial classes and the church intensified, because capitalism was based on the idea that money invested in an enterprise ought to produce a return. Moreover, businessmen were angered by the church's failure to practice what it preached, pointing out that many church officials were themselves greedy and unscrupulous.

One of the questions put to students in debating practice was, "Can an archdeacon be saved?" (The archdeacon was the principal administrative officer of a bishopric.)

EFFORTS TO REFORM THE CHURCH

Late Medieval Reform Movements

The state of the church during the papal stay in Avignon and the Great Schism (see pp. 354–58) seemed so dismal that many laymen began to seek salvation on their own. They did not break openly with the church; they simply ceased to rely on it. They came together in groups, small at first, such as the Brethren of the Common Life in the Low Countries and the Rhineland, to encourage one another to lead a devout Christian life and to seek direct contact with God through mystical experiences. The Brethren produced some impressive works of devotion, like the *Theologica Germanica* (the "German Theology"), that influenced later reformers. They also founded schools that contributed to the educational revival of the fifteenth and sixteenth centuries; Erasmus (see p. 432), for example, was educated in a Brethren school. Conservative churchmen looked on these reformers with suspicion, but most of the groups managed to remain within the bounds of orthodoxy.

A more radical element wanted to mount a thoroughgoing reform of the church, preferably directed by laymen. As early as 1324 Marsilius of Padua, in his *Defensor pacis,* had argued that the state should control the church just as it controlled other organizations, like guilds. If the state could regulate physicians, he reasoned, it could also regulate priests. The church condemned Marsilius's book, but reformers continued to be inspired by his ideas.

Another critic of the church was the Oxford professor John Wycliffe (*ca.* 1320–84). At first concerned with questions having to do with the ownership of private property, Wycliffe became convinced that the church was being corrupted by wealth and that the state should take over its property holdings. The secular rulers applauded this suggestion, of course, and protected Wycliffe from the wrath of the clergy. Wycliffe went on to question the orthodox doctrine that the bread and wine in the communion service are transformed into the body and blood of Christ. He ended up by attacking the whole administrative structure of the church as corrupt and unauthorized by the Bible. He also encouraged his followers to translate the Bible so ordinary people could understand its message without the mediation of the clergy.

Though Wycliffe had no intention of launching a popular movement, his ideas spread rapidly beyond the scholarly circles for which he wrote. Preachers carrying the Wycliffite English Bible traveled about the country telling people about his radical proposals. Many of those preachers became social reformers as well and gained an impressive following among the lower and middle classes in England. Their preaching contributed to the radicalism that triggered the great Peasants' Rebellion of 1381 (see p. 354). When the king and nobles put down the rebellion, they took care to suppress the radicals as well. But the suppression was not wholly successful. The radicals—called Lollards (from the Dutch word *lollaert,* meaning mumbler, which was used to describe religious radicals on the Continent)—went underground and continued to foment unrest until the English Reformation of the sixteenth century.

Such reform movements drew much of their strength from the decline of the church after the Great Schism. In 1395 the French became so exasperated with their pope, Benedict XIII of Avignon, that the French clergy, under pressure from the government, withdrew their obedience from him for five years. This was the first instance of a strategy that was to have a fateful future: the rejection of papal authority by the clergy of a large nation under pressure from the secular government.

John Huss

Even after Wycliffe's death, his ideas continued to exercise great influence on the

Continent as well as in England. The English king Richard II (r. 1377–99) married Anne of Bohemia, and Czech students began to come to England to study. When they returned home, they carried Wycliffe's teachings with them. In time, those teachings found a home at the University of Prague (founded 1348).

In 1402, John Huss (*ca.* 1369–1415), a brilliant young professor at the university, emerged as a leader of the Czech reformers. In his preaching he drew on the teachings of Wycliffe: Faith must be based on the Bible, which is the only source of authority; Christ, not the pope, is the true head of the church; salvation comes from God through Christ, not through ritual ceremonies and a corrupt priesthood. In 1414 Huss was excommunicated by the pope. But he remained at liberty, and his ideas were accepted by a majority of the Czech people.

In that same year, Huss was invited to defend his ideas at the Council of Constance (called to resolve the Great Schism; see p. 357). He eagerly accepted and traveled to Constance under the emperor Sigismund's guarantee of safe conduct. On his arrival he was charged with heresy and was imprisoned, the emperor's guarantee notwithstanding. In fact, Sigismund withdrew his protection as soon as the charge of heresy was leveled. The leaders of the council ordered Huss to recant his views in public, but he stood firm. In the dramatic trial that followed, the issue was whether the Bible and the individual's conscience were the source of religious authority, as Huss argued, or the Catholic church was, as the council insisted. Not surprisingly, the council fathers condemned Huss to death and ordered that he be burned at the stake. He was executed outside the walls of Constance in May 1415.

The following year, the council condemned a follower of Huss, Jerome, to be burnt at the stake, and before the council disbanded in 1418 civil war had broken out in Bohemia. Not until 1436 were some of the more conservative Hussites and the church able to reach an agreement. The agreement recognized a Bohemian church with control over its own ecclesiastical appointments and with its own liturgical practices, notably the right to offer the cup as well as the bread to communicants. For the first time, the Roman church had entered into an agreement with condemned heretics after excommunicating them and preaching a crusade against them.

A pair of woodcuts by Lucas Cranach the Elder contrasting Jesus and the pope. On the left, Jesus is driving the moneychangers from the temple; on the right, the pope is taking money for indulgences.

THE PAPACY'S TRIUMPH OVER THE CONCILIAR MOVEMENT

Though the Council of Constance succeeded in ending the Great Schism, it was unable to institute any meaningful reform, which had been one of its principal goals. The English and German delegates tried in vain to get the council to consider reform before turning to the election of a new pope; the other delegates were more interested in healing the schism first. Once Martin V (r. 1417–31) had been elected, the council leaders waved aside the mild report of a committee they had set up to study church abuses and declared the council ended without ever taking up the question of reform. So the fifteenth-century church continued to countenance corruption under the leadership of a pope who set a standard of worldliness.

The leaders of the council at Constance had decreed that the church must summon a general council every five years. But Martin V saw to it that the decree

1305	1378	1409	1417	1447	1527

Babylonian Captivity

Great Schism

Conciliar Movement

Renaissance Papacy

was ignored. At a time when most European kings were humbling their parliaments and their nobles, the popes chose to abolish regular councils and to humble the princes of the church, the cardinals. By the time Nicholas V (r. 1447–55) became pope, the possibility that the church might evolve into a limited monarchy had vanished. Since that time, every general council has been under the control of the pope.

That victory left the papacy stronger in some respects, weaker in others. No one within the church could any longer challenge the power of the pope, but the pope was now isolated from leaders of opinion—both clerical and lay—particularly in northern Europe. The period of the concordats followed (see p. 420). In France, Charles VII in effect created a national, or "Gallican," church, restricting the pope's power to appoint and tax the clergy. In England and Spain, the kings followed suit, but in Germany, which lacked a central government strong enough to stand up to the pope, the papacy retained its rights of appointment, taxation, and jurisdiction.

The period between the accession of Nicholas V to the papacy (1447) and the sack of Rome by imperial Spanish troops (1527) is often called the age of the Renaissance papacy. During that period, many of the popes were well-educated patrons of humanists and artists, while others were despots; some were both. Nicholas V founded the Vatican library, one of the world's great repositories of books and manuscripts. Pius II (r. 1458–64), before his election as pope, had been a celebrated Sienese humanist, Aeneas Sylvius Piccolomini. Julius II (r. 1503–13) initiated the rebuilding of St. Peter's. Sixtus IV (r. 1471–84) was said to have died in a fit of rage at the conclusion of a peace settlement; and Julius II was known as "the Warrior Pope." Alexander VI (r. 1492–1503) tried to carve a principality out of the Papal States for his illegitimate son, Cesare Borgia.

The papacy had often been embroiled in politics during the Middle Ages, but in those days politics meant international politics, with grand principles of political authority at stake. The Renaissance popes, by contrast, were embroiled mainly in Italian politics, with only dynastic interests at stake. In time, the papacy became thoroughly Italianized. (In fact, since the end of the Great Schism in 1417, only two non-Italians have ever been elected pope, in 1522 and 1979).

Julius Ii (r. 1503–13), the warrior pope, painted by Raphael.

THE PROBLEMS OF THE RENAISSANCE CHURCH

The Renaissance church had problems elsewhere besides in the papal curia where venality and nepotism reigned. Most of the bishops and archbishops of the church were of noble birth, and many of them had been appointed to their office by a king or a pope as a reward for their loyal service rather than for their piety or administrative ability. Typically, the newly appointed bishop paid a substantial part of his first year's income to whoever it was who had appointed him. Not only was this contrary to canon law, it gave the bishop a strong incentive to siphon off as much money as he could from his diocese. Moreover, many bishops and archbishops held more than one office—which also was contrary to canon law. In a diocese with an absentee bishop, the bishop's income was drained from the local economy, and the diocese was left to the mercy of the greedy priests and secular lords. One bishop is said to have visited his bishopric only once, to be buried.

Even conscientious bishops found that they had little power to appoint competent clergy or to reform abuses within their dioceses. Much of the power that had formerly belonged to the bishops had either fallen into the hands of local laymen or the pope. Consequently the parish priests tended to be ignorant and immoral. Moreover, because the priests had to raise money to pay taxes to their bishop and to local laymen, they became almost as rapacious as their superiors. Normally the income of a church consisted of tithes (that is, a tenth of the income of parishioners), first fruits (a small share of the early harvest), and oblations (gifts from parishioners). By the sixteenth century priests were augmenting that income by charging a fee for baptisms, marriages, and burials.

Monastic orders had also lost prestige. Many monasteries in the cities performed as parish churches because the population had grown too large for the parish priests to handle. This activity involved the monasteries in the affairs of the world, and they followed the example of the priests in squeezing their congregations for money.

By the late fifteenth century, the monastic orders were no longer attracting pious novices but men who wanted to serve parishes and to rise to positions of power and wealth in society. The monks acquired a reputation for living rich and secular lives.

The most common complaint leveled against the church was that it sold spiritual benefits for money. The church was land rich, but cash poor, and it had to find ways to support itself. But the methods it used to raise money and the purposes to which the money was allegedly put—wars, rich living, and the like—outraged many of the faithful. Clergy at all levels were criticized, but the papacy was considered the worst offender.

The sale of indulgences was the practice that aroused the most heated criticism, although it was far from the most important source of papal income. An indulgence was a remission of the temporal penalty for sin imposed by a priest in the sacrament of penance. Christians were required to confess their sins and receive penance (a penalty) at least once a year. Penances ranged from saying prayers to going on a crusade or a pilgrimage; the severity of the penance depended on the seriousness of the sin and the condition of the sinner.

During the Middle Ages, the practice of commuting a penance with a money payment had become common, and in the fourteenth century the popes devised a doctrine that held Christ and the saints had accumulated a "treasury of merits" from which Christ's vicars—the popes—could dispense benefits to the faithful through indulgences. In the fifteenth century, Sixtus IV (r. 1471–84) expanded this doctrine by claiming that the pope had the power to release the souls of the dead from the penances they were undergoing in purgatory—the state in which the soul purged its sins before being admitted to paradise. Sixtus's pronouncement transformed the traffic in indulgences into a booming business and a real moneymaker. It was hard for people to resist an opportunity to ease the suffering of the soul of a dead parent or spouse. Yet when it became clear that the money from the sale of indulgences was going not to pious purposes but to war and ostentatious living, many laymen concluded that the church was selling salvation for profit.

RESPONSES TO CORRUPTION

Criticism and Reform of the Church in the Fifteenth Century

Many church leaders of the late fifteenth century were of course conscientious, pious men who found it difficult to answer the criticism leveled at the church. Not only were the abuses undeniable; the status of churchmen in general had declined. The Europe of 1500 was more secular in its outlook than the Europe of 1400. Imbued with the ideas of the Renaissance, many people now considered a career in business, politics, or the arts to be as attractive as a career in the church and no less likely to lead to salvation.

Moreover, during the fifteenth century the lower and middle classes had come to embrace a popular piety accompanied by religious practices that verged on superstition and idolatry—the cults of the saints, for example, and the veneration of relics. In what one historian has called the "supersaturated" religious atmosphere of the fifteenth century, perceptive church leaders came to realize that the church was vulnerable to troublesome questions: What is the essence of Christianity? Is it the ritual and the elaborate hierarchy? Is it the veneration of relics or participation in a pilgrimage? Or is it loving one's neighbor and living simply, as Christ lived?

Church leaders were well aware of the new power of secular rulers to appoint bishops, tax the clergy, and limit papal control over the churches in their realms. And they knew that the kings could initiate religious reform of their own, often for political purposes. In fact, reform by royal command was sometimes well motivated and effective: In Spain, Cardinal Jiménez de Cisneros (1436–1517), backed by Ferdinand and Isabella, carried out many church reforms early in the sixteenth century. But always the danger remained that reform by a secular ruler, no matter how well motivated, might result in state control of the church and its property.

Several reform movements were launched within the church, none of them effective. The Brethren of the Common Life, as we have seen, pursued its quiet way of life and founded schools to educate a new Christian elite, but it had little effect on the church. In Florence between 1494 and 1498, one of the most remarkable preachers of the age, the Dominican Savonarola, tried to reform the inhabitants of one of the richest and most secular cities in Europe. He preached repentance and piety and attacked both secular and church leaders. Savonarola held to the medieval view that the church itself was divinely constituted and could never be in need of reform, but that when the individuals who served it grew corrupt they should and must be reformed.

That idea of reform had already begun to disappear. The intention of the leaders of the councils of Constance (1414–18) and Basel (1431–37) had been to reform the church by assigning substantial power to councils and by making the pope a limited monarch. Even more radical, John Huss preached the reform both of individual Christians and of the church as an institution. But the church demonstrated its unreadiness for such reform: it ignored the conciliar movement and had both Huss and Savonarola burned as heretics.

Christian Humanism

Humanism, which, as we have seen, extolled the eloquence and power of the ancient authors, spread from Italy to northern Europe during the fifteenth century and was well established there by the early sixteenth century. Northern Europeans came to Italy to study with humanists, books and translations were shipped north from Italy (some of the most important printing presses were in northern Italy), and Italian humanists kept up a lively correspondence with their northern counterparts.

The humanism that took root in northern Europe is often called Christian humanism to distinguish it from the

Italian variety, but the name is somewhat misleading. Even though the Italian humanists were primarily interested in pre-Christian authors, they were themselves Christians and never denied their Christian faith. The fact that the northern humanists were more interested in the early Christian authors and writings suggests that in some sense they were more "Christian" than the Italians, though at base their interests were the same.

In their studies of the New Testament, the Christian humanists sought to explore the faith of the apostles as revealed in the language of the biblical account. They concentrated especially on the letters of St. Paul, which constitute a substantial body of material. They also studied the works of the church fathers—Greek writers such as Origen and Gregory of Nazianzus and Latin writers such as Augustine and Jerome. There they found straightforward, detailed explanations of the Christian faith free of the abstruse theological accretions of medieval commentators and scholastic theologians. They held St. Jerome in the highest esteem, because his Latin was closest to that of Cicero and because he was the most accomplished literary scholar of the western church fathers.

The main goal of the Christian humanists was to retrieve the original texts of Christianity. During the Middle Ages, intellectuals read the Bible only with the aid of learned commentaries, just as they used a technical gloss when they read legal, medical, or philosophical texts. All the major works were accompanied by a standard commentary, called a *glossa ordinaria,* that became in effect part of the works themselves. The humanists scorned those commentaries, which were often ungrammatical, dense, and rich in jargon. They sought instead the eloquence of the early church writers, who spoke in the original voice of Christianity.

The Christian humanists first set out to produce accurate texts of the Bible and the early Christian writings. In Spain, Cardinal Jiménez set scholars to producing a monumental edition of the Bible in which the original Hebrew and Greek texts appeared in parallel columns with the Latin. In Germany, Johann Reuchlin (1455–1522) promoted the study of Hebrew as a means of understanding the Old Testament, while a group of German Dominicans—who saw such study as a threat to the authority of the church—sought to destroy all books written in Hebrew.

The Christian humanists were in a sense conservative in their attempt to get back to the original texts, but they were radical in their conviction that the individual human being had a unique spiritual capacity. They called for translations of the Bible into the vernacular so that ordinary people could participate in the Christian experience and understand the need for reform. In France, Jacques Lefèvre d'Etaples (1455–1536) translated the New Testament into French (1523). In England, Thomas More (1477–1535)—the royal chancellor who was executed in 1535 for his loyalty to the Roman church

A Catholic, Sir Thomas More, on the Church

The true Church of Christ is the common known church of all Christian people not gone out nor cast out. This whole body both of good and bad is the Catholic Church of Christ, which is in this world very sickly, and hath many sore members, as hath sometime the natural body of a man. . . . The Church was gathered, and the faith believed, before any part of the New Testament was put in writing. And which was or is the true scripture, neither Luther nor Tyndale [translator of the New Testament into English] knoweth but by the credence that they give to the Church. . . . The Church was before the gospel was written; and the faith was taught, and men were baptized and masses said, and the other sacraments ministered among Christian people, before any part of the New Testament was put in writing. . . . As the sea shall never surround and overwhelm the land, and yet it hath eaten many places in, and swallowed whole countries up, and made places now sea that sometime were well-inhabited lands, and hath lost part of his own possession in other parts again; so though the faith of Christ shall never be overflown with heresies, nor the gates of hell prevail against Christ's Church, yet in some places it winneth in a new people, so may there in some places by negligence be lost the old.

From The Workes of Sir Thomas More *(London: Scholar Press, 1978), pp. 527, 852, 853, 921.*

(see p. 419)—detailed in his book *Utopia* the ironies and hypocrisies of society and called for the spread of true Christianity through education.

Erasmus

The acknowledged leader of the Christian humanists was Erasmus of Rotterdam (*ca.* 1469–1536), who in his youth had attended a school run by the Brethren of the Common Life. He was committed to the study of early Christian writers and had absorbed the ideals—though not the secular interests—of the Italian humanists. Erasmus devoted his life to scholarship, in the conviction that knowledge would help save the church.

Erasmus, by Holbein.

After making an exhaustive comparison of ancient manuscripts, Erasmus produced the first critical edition of the Greek text of the New Testament (1516). In his preface, he urged that his work be used as the basis for new translations of the Scriptures into the vernacular languages. He summarized the goal of Christian humanism with this statement: "I utterly dissent from those who are unwilling that the sacred Scriptures should be read by the unlearned translated into their vulgar tongue, as though Christ had taught such subtleties that they can scarcely be understood even by a few theologians, or, as though the strength of the Christian religion consisted in men's ignorance of it." In countless letters and books Erasmus proclaimed a "philosophy of Christ"—the love of God and neighbor that to him was the essence of Christianity.

Erasmus, through his intellect, learning, literary skills, and lively sense of humor, had an enormous influence on his contemporaries. He acknowledged the Renaissance commitment to life in this world by insisting that the love of God and neighbor be expressed through a life of good works. He ridiculed monks and priests who insisted that withdrawal from the world was the ideal form of the Christian life. He also rejected ceremonies and fasts as routes to heaven by imagining what Christ might have said: "I promised [to Christians] the inheritance of my Father, not to cowls, prayers, or fasts, but to works of charity."

Although Christian humanism demonstrated the power of education to bring about reform, it was far too intellectual to arouse the interest of the general population.

LUTHER'S REVOLT

On October 31, 1517, an Augustinian friar named Martin Luther (1483–1546), who was professor of Bible in the little University of Wittenberg in Saxony, submitted 95 theses—or propositions—to his colleagues to serve as the material for a debate on the subject of indulgences. Luther had become outraged by the efforts of a Dominican friar named Tetzel to hawk indulgences to the residents of Magdeburg with the following sales pitch: "So soon as coin in coffer rings, the soul from Purgatory springs." Though the proceeds were supposed to go toward the building of the new church of St. Peter in Rome, half actually ended up with the archbishop of Mainz and the Fugger banking firm of Augsburg (see p. 416).

Luther's theses, which were immediately printed and debated throughout Germany, caused a sensation. They touched on a note of resentment that was ready to be sounded:

> *There is no divine authority for preaching that the soul flies out of purgatory immediately the money clinks in the bottom of the chest.... It is certainly possible that when the money clinks in the bottom of the chest, avarice and greed increase.... All those who believe themselves certain of their own salvation by means of letters of indulgence will be eternally damned, together with their teachers.... Any*

Erasmus's Preface to His Edition of the New Testament

I utterly dissent from those who are unwilling that the sacred Scriptures should be read by the unlearned translated into their vulgar tongue, as though Christ had taught such subtleties that they can scarcely be understood even by a few theologians, or, as though the strength of the Christian religion consisted in men's ignorance of it. The mysteries of kings it may be safer to conceal, but Christ wished his mysteries to be published as openly as possible. I wish that even the weakest woman should read the Gospel—should read the epistles of Paul. And I wish these were translated into all languages, so that they might be read and understood, not only by Scots and Irishmen, but also by Turks and Saracens. To make them understood is surely the first step. It may be that they might be ridiculed by many, but some would take them to heart. I long that the husbandman should sing portions of them to himself as he follows the plough, that the weaver should hum them to the tune of his shuttle, that the traveller should beguile with their stories the tedium of his journey.

From Erasmus, "Paraclesis," Novum Instrumentum, *trans. by Frederic Seebohm, in* The Oxford Reformers *(New York: Dutton, 1914), p. 203.*

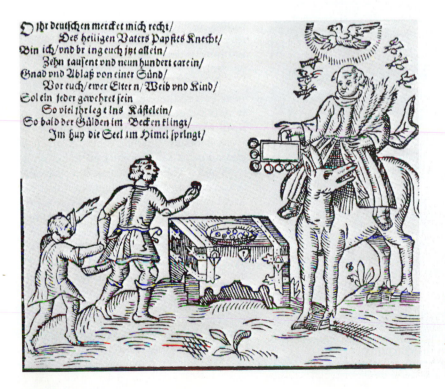

Contemporary caricature of Johann Tetzel hawking indulgences. The last line of the jingle is: "So soon as coin in coffer rings, the soul into heaven springs."

Christian whatsoever, who is truly repentant, enjoys plenary remission from penalty and guilt, and this is given him without letters of indulgence.

At this time, Luther was 34 years old, the brilliant son of a prosperous peasant turned miner who had been able to afford a university education for his son. As a young man, Luther had experienced several emotional crises and had eventually decided on the life of a friar. Though it was the age of humanism and the new learning, he chose to live a religious life and to pursue scholastic learning, which still dominated the university curriculum.

Luther found no spiritual solace in the prayers, confessions, and penances of the monastic community, however. He sought forgiveness of his sins but found no assurance of God's forgiveness in the ceremonial acts of worship. Instead, he became increasingly guilt-ridden and doubtful about his ability to save himself.

Suddenly he came to an understanding of what St. Paul had meant when he said that a man is saved not by obeying the Jewish law but by his faith in Christ alone. He realized that he had been trying to satisfy God by scrupulously observing church ritual, which was no less demanding and no more effective than the Jewish law against which Paul had preached. He found it unthinkable that human beings, corrupted by sin, could win God's favor by performing some good deed or sacramental act. He came to believe that God alone can save people's souls and that all the sinner can do is to have faith in the possibility of God's forgiveness.

In working out the revolutionary implications of his new understanding, Luther slowly came to the view that ceremonies and sacraments, pilgrimages and indulgences—everything the medieval church called "good works"—were irrelevant at best and dangerous at worst. His first act was to deny the efficacy of indulgences, causing sales of indulgences in Germany to drop off sharply. When the Dominicans, the chief dealers in indulgences, persuaded Pope Leo X (r. 1513–21) to condemn Luther's theses, he was gradually driven into denying the authority of the pope. He also came to believe that John Huss had been right on certain points, despite his being condemned by the Council of Constance, and this belief led him to deny the authority of councils as well.

At last Luther was summoned to appear before the emperor Charles V at an imperial diet (council) held at Worms in April 1521 to defend his theses. Like John Huss a century earlier, he was given a guarantee of safe conduct on his journey to Worms. There he declared to the emperor and assembled dignitaries that he was bound by the authority of the Scriptures and by his own conscience rather than by the authority of the pope or council. He could not recant his theses, he said, because his conscience was "captive of the Word of God" and because it was "neither safe nor right to go against conscience."

The emperor permitted Luther to return to the protection of Frederick, the Elector of Saxony, and until his death in 1546, Luther remained in Wittenberg

Luther on Justification by Faith

For the word of God cannot be received and honored by any works, but by faith alone. Hence it is clear that, as the soul needs the word alone for life and justification, so it is justified by faith alone and not by any works. For if it could be justified by any other means, it would have no need of the word, nor consequently of faith. . . .

It is evident that by no outward work or labor can the inward man be at all justified, made free and saved, and that no works whatever have any relation to him. And so, on the other hand, it is solely by impiety and incredulity of heart that he becomes guilty and a slave of sin, deserving condemnation; not by any outward sin or work.

Therefore the first care of every Christian ought to be to lay aside all reliance on works, and strengthen his faith alone more and more, and by it grow in the knowledge, not of works, but of Christ Jesus, who has suffered and risen again for him.

From Martin Luther, On Christian Liberty, *trans. by H. Wace and C. A. Buchheim, in* First Principles of the Reformation *(London: Murray, 1883), pp. 107–08.*

teaching, preaching, and writing. In his new view of Christianity, the active life of a merchant or a housewife was as spiritually rewarding as the life of a monk or a nun, and he himself married a former nun, with whom he had six children. Meanwhile, the revolt against the papacy that he had initiated gathered momentum and spread across northern Europe. By the late sixteenth century, the unity of western Christendom had been shattered.

Luther's Work

Luther's religious thought contained three main, closely related principles: salvation through faith rather than through good works, the ultimate authority of the Bible, and the priesthood of all believers. Luther wrote hundreds of letters and tracts defending his ideas, but his greatest literary accomplishment was his German translation of the Bible (completed in 1534). He wanted to put the Bible into the hands of every German, for he was convinced that there was no essential difference between a priest and a layman. A dedicated layman reverently reading the Scripture was closer to the divine truth than a worldly pope proclaiming the dogma of the church. Thus a pious layman could serve God as well as a priest or a monk. The literary quality of Luther's translation was so impressive that the work is considered to have been the foundation for the modern language known as High German.

Luther's original protest had been purely religious in nature, but by 1520 he was appealing to German nationalism. "What has brought us Germans to such a pass that we have to suffer this robbery and this destruction of our property by the Pope?" he asked. That question drew a quick response from princes eager to confiscate church property, from businessmen unhappy over papal taxation and over ecclesiastical rules governing business practices, and from devout laymen and priests shocked by the corruption of the church. Though the purpose of his revolt was to enable people to reconcile an honest life with the highest spiritual aspirations, some people seized on it for their own selfish purposes.

IV. D. Pl. I.

J. Buys, inv. et dolin.   Reinr. Vinkeles sculp. 178...

Luther burns papal bulls, symbolizing his rejection of papal authority.

Luther had no intention of setting up an independent church to compete with the church of Rome. But at last he became convinced that the church founded by Christ had strayed from its true path after the conversion of Constantine, when the church became entangled in worldly affairs, and that the bishop of Rome was not

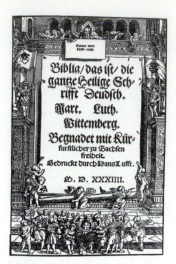

Title page of the first German translation of the Bible, by Martin Luther, printed in 1534 with the approval of the Elector of Saxony.

the true vicar of Christ but the Antichrist. He wanted the church to return to the pure faith and the simple religion of the apostles. In the purified church there would be only two sacraments—baptism and communion—rather than the seven sacraments of the Catholic church. There would be a simplified ritual in German rather than in Latin, and there would be more emphasis on the congregation's participation in the service. Luther wrote many hymns in which he incorporated these ideas, and those hymns are still sung today.

The split between the "Lutheran" and "Catholic" churches occurred gradually and without Luther's explicit approval. The conflict over the nature of the true church continued unresolved until at last each church embraced its own beliefs and rejected the beliefs of the other.

THE SPREAD OF LUTHERANISM

Unlike the failed reforms of the fifteenth century, Lutheranism—one of the most radical movements in Christian history—spread quickly across northern Europe. One reason for its rapid acceptance was the availability of the printing press, which Gutenberg had invented in the middle of the fifteenth century (see p. 373). Luther and his followers wrote hundreds of tracts and had them printed for widespread distribution. The nineteenth-century historian Leopold von Ranke calculated that in 1523 Luther and his supporters published nearly 400 books and pamphlets.

Another reason for the rapid acceptance of Lutheranism was the early support of the humanists. The humanists were themselves reformers, and they saw in Luther's program many of the principles they were espousing. Like them, Luther rejected the commentaries of the medieval theologians and sought to return to the unadorned text of the Bible. And like them, Luther respected the church fathers and attacked the financial abuses of the church. But while the humanists criticized the medieval commentators for obscuring the text of the Bible with their graceless prose, Luther criticized them for their

faulty theological opinions. And while the humanists valued the church fathers for what they said about the faith of the early Christians, Luther valued them for their simple, direct explications of the meaning of the biblical text. For Luther, the sole source of authority was the Bible, particularly the New Testament.

Further, the humanists wanted to reform only the practices of the church, while Luther and his followers came to view the church itself as illegitimate. Erasmus and Cardinal Jiménez, for example, concentrated on freeing the biblical text from the clutter of the medieval commentaries, whereas the Protestants (as Lutherans were called after 1529, when they presented a "protest" at an imperial diet) claimed that the Scripture was the sole basis for faith and for an understanding of Christ.

The difference is further illustrated by a comparison between a reform document that the cardinals, inspired by the humanists, presented to Pope Paul III (r. 1534–49) in 1538 and Luther's *Address to the Nobility of the German Nation* (1520). After affirming the authority of the church, the cardinals urged the reform of the parish churches, the elimination of nonresident bishops, a restriction on the sale of indulgences to one sale a year, and a reform of the judicial system. Luther complained about the same abuses, and in much harsher language, but he sought to eliminate their root causes. For example, the cardinals urged strict enforcement of the rule of celibacy to ensure the chastity of clerics; Luther argued that clerics should be permitted to marry.

Despite the differences between the humanist cardinals and Luther, many leading humanists, including Erasmus and Thomas More, supported him at first. More broke with him in 1523, in his *Letter against Luther,* and Erasmus broke with him in 1524.

Luther also received early support from many priests and monks, especially in the German cities. The cities had many grievances against the church: it controlled their prime real estate, and it insisted that the clergy be exempted from local taxes. Moreover, the church's tax levies fell most heavily on the urban populations. In city after city, conservative members of the clergy were quietly replaced by followers of Luther. Because so many of the cities held imperial charters, the reformed churches were in effect state churches, and in another decade or so Lutheranism would be established as the state religion by some of the German princes.

The peasants too responded to Luther's message at first, but they lost interest after the Peasants' Rebellion of 1524–25. Although the aims of the rebellion had to do with social reform—the abolition of serfdom and the burdens of the manorial system—the rebels interpreted Luther's pronouncements as support for their program: "Therefore do we find in the Scripture that we are free," they argued, "and we will be free." In a bitter condemnation of the rebels, Luther replied that the freedom he was speaking about was spiritual not social, and the rebels felt he had betrayed them. As time passed, Luther and his supporters found themselves caught between the reactionary Roman Catholic church and the radical lower classes.

Finally, Germany's lack of centralized government prevented its resistance to the spread of Lutheranism. Although the emperor Charles V (r. 1519–56) never wavered in his orthodoxy, he was preoccupied with trying to hold his vast dominions together and with repelling military threats on every side. From 1522 to 1559, Charles and his son Philip were fighting a series of wars with France, while Charles and his brother Ferdinand, Duke of Austria, were trying to stem the advance of the Turks up the Danube Valley.

Not until 1547—the year after Luther's death—did Charles turn his attention to Lutheranism, which by then had been accepted by about half the German principalities. He launched a confused religious war against the princes who supported Luther that dragged on until 1555, when he permitted his brother Ferdinand to conclude the Religious Peace of Augsburg. That peace allowed the free cities and principalities of the empire to choose between Lutheranism and Catholicism and bound them to respect each other's

Contemporary engraving depicting a noble lady and her son kneeling before peasant rebels to plead for their lives during the Peasants' Rebellion (1524–25).

choice. Essentially, the agreement made religion the prerogative of the ruler of each principality; anyone who disagreed with his ruler could migrate to another principality.

The Peace of Augsburg constituted the first official recognition that western Christendom was in a state of disunity and would remain so. In the end, northern Germany became mostly Protestant; southern Germany remained Catholic. Outside Germany, Lutheranism took root only in Scandinavia, where Denmark, Norway, and Sweden became Lutheran by midcentury. The German provenance of Lutheranism limited its appeal abroad, where another form of Protestantism, that of John Calvin, won acceptance.

OTHER PROTESTANT MOVEMENTS

In addition to Wittenberg, other important centers of reform were Zürich, Basel, Strasbourg, and especially Geneva. In each of these cities a form of Protestantism emerged that was significantly different from Lutheranism. The so-called "reformed" churches that resulted had a more highly developed system of theology and church organization and put greater stress on the moral conduct and political action of their members than did the Lutheran churches.

Bucer and Zwingli

Among the early leaders of these Protestant movements were the humanists Martin Bucer of Strasbourg (1491–1551) and the Swiss scholar Ulrich Zwingli (1484–1531). As a Dominican friar, Bucer had been influenced by the humanism of Erasmus. Once he became familiar with Luther's views, however, he left the Dominican order and married a nun. He was excommunicated in 1523, and from 1524 to 1548 he led the reform movement in Strasbourg, where he introduced various liturgical changes. Throughout the years he participated in colloquies held in Worms, Regensburg, and Hagenau aimed at reconciling Catholicism and Protestantism and also was active in trying to reconcile Lutheranism with other Protestant movements, particularly the one led by Zwingli.

Zwingli, who was born in a rural village in the Swiss Alps, studied classics in Basel. He too fell under Erasmus's influence and was especially attracted to the idea of a renascent Christianity based on the Scriptures. Zwingli became a priest, beginning as a village parson in 1506, and rose to become the "people's priest" in Zürich (1518). In this prestigious position, which enabled him to stay abreast of the ideas of the day, he became familiar with the activity of Martin Luther. Historians still debate the extent of the influence of Luther's ideas on Zwingli. Zwingli himself claimed that he had arrived at Luther's basic ideas on his own before reading Luther's works.

As in many other cities, the reform movement in Zürich proceeded by stages. In 1522, some of the citizens violated the church's dietary laws during the Lenten season, and the city council appointed a commission to investigate. The bishop of Constance, who had jurisdiction over Zürich, protested that he had the exclusive right to judge matters of religious discipline, but the commission, of which Zwingli was a member, proceeded anyway. The commission's report was equivocal, but Zwingli soon published a sermon in which he argued that, because Christians were free from the law, as St. Paul said,

they did not have to obey dietary rules imposed by the church. A person's faith, he argued, had to do with his or her beliefs and motivations, not with the observance of actions prescribed by the church. Luther, of course, had reached the same conclusion.

In 1523, the city council of Zürich, in an effort to dispel public confusion and unrest, announced a debate on questions of religion. Zwingli prepared for the debate by drawing up a list of 67 conclusions on matters of doctrine, morals, and church discipline. His main ideas reflected that the Scriptures alone were the basis of true Christianity, and they carried the day. After this, Protestantism was widely accepted in Zürich. The question now became whether the paintings, stained-glass windows, and sculptures should be removed from the city's churches. Zwingli's position was that once the church members had become true Christians they would no longer need such outward signs of faith, and he suggested that the images be removed gradually. The people were less patient, however, and in 1524 they stripped the interiors of the churches—whitewashing the walls, pulling down the crucifixes, and destroying the windows and sculptures. Finally, in 1525, the reformers, with Zwingli in the lead this time, replaced the Mass with a simple service in commemoration of the Last Supper. The city council supported their action by issuing a law that did away with the Mass altogether.

Calvinism

John Calvin (1509–64) was born in Noyon, France, and as a young man was sent to the University of Paris to study law. He was more interested in humanism than in law, however, and soon dropped his legal studies to concentrate on Greek and Latin. In 1532, he published a commentary on Seneca's treatise *Concerning Clemency.* Around this time he had what he later called a conversion to Protestantism, and in 1534 he moved to Basel, where there were many Protestants. In Basel, he wrote a theological treatise, called the *Institutes of the Christian Religion,* which he intended to be a comprehensive treatment of the Protestant religion. The first edition of this work, only six chapters long, was published in 1536. Calvin then revised and enlarged the work until the fourth edition, with eighty chapters, was published in 1559. The *Institutes* was the first systematic presentation of Protestant theology.

Calvin visited Geneva in 1536. He had no intention of staying until Guillaume Farel (1489–1565), a leading Protestant who had introduced Protestantism to the city two months before, persuaded him to become his assistant. Together, Farel and Calvin undertook a vigorous program of reform that aroused opposition because of their impatience and the strictness of their approach. In 1538, a majority of Catholics were elected to the city council, and Farel and Calvin were driven from the city. Farel went to Neuchâtel, where he remained the rest of his life. Calvin went to Strasbourg, where he came under the influence of the moderate reformer Martin Bucer.

Apparently, Protestantism had taken root in Geneva, however, because in 1541 the city council invited Calvin to return. Although he seems to have done so reluctantly, he remained there until his death in 1564. During those years, he worked diligently for reform in the church of Geneva and gradually asserted his power over the city council itself. By the late 1550s, Geneva had become a virtual theocracy—a city-state governed by the clergy.

Building on Luther's doctrine of salvation by faith alone, Calvin constructed a system that emphasized the sovereignty of God and the depravity of man. At the center of that system was the doctrine of predestination: God, through his inscrutable will, destined some men to be saved and others to be damned. Consequently, the idea that one can win salvation by performing "good works" is absurd. Calvin also held that a true and fervent faith in Christ and the Scriptures was a sign that one was among the elect of God and that the performance of good works was evidence of that faith.

In 1559, Calvin established an academy in Geneva comprising schools of arts, law, medicine, and theology. Perhaps because of his own fame, he was able to attract an excellent faculty, and within a few years the academy was flourishing, with more than 1,500 students from all over Europe. Geneva itself became a model for Presbyterian or Reformed churches in France, England, Scotland, the Netherlands, the Rhineland, Bohemia, and Hungary, and later for churches in North America and Dutch South Africa.

Calvin advocated that each local church should have a ruling body composed of ministers and elders (or presbyters) who were to meet regularly in councils (called synods) with the officials of the other churches in the district. Because Calvinism was particularly resistant to secular control, it never became "nationalized," as Lutheranism had. Moreover, because it possessed a systematic theology, it could be adopted by reformers everywhere.

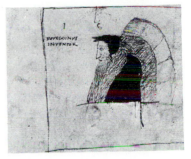

Sketch of John Calvin drawn by a student, perhaps during a lecture.

Calvin on Predestination

Predestination we call the eternal decree of God, by which he has determined in himself, what he would have to become of every individual of mankind. For they are not all created with a similar destiny; but eternal life is foreordained for some, and eternal damnation for others. . . .

In conformity, therefore, to the clear doctrine of the Scripture, we assert, that by an eternal and immutable counsel, God has once for all determined, both whom he would admit to salvation, and whom he would condemn to destruction. We affirm that this counsel, as far as concerns the elect, is founded on his gratuitous mercy, totally irrespective of human merit; but that to those whom he devotes to condemnation, the gate of life is closed by a just and irreprehensible, but incomprehensible, judgment. . . .

How exceedingly presumptuous it is only to inquire into the causes of the Divine will; which is in fact, and is justly entitled to be, the cause of everything that exists. . . . For the will of God is the highest rule of justice; so that what he wills must be considered just, for this very reason, because he wills it.

From John Calvin, Institutes of the Christian Religion, *trans. by John Allen (Philadelphia: Westminster Press, 1930), Book III, Ch. 21, pars. 5, 7; Ch. 23, par. 2.*

By the 1550s Calvinists were in many parts of Europe, but they constituted a majority only in Geneva and Scotland. Elsewhere, they formed a well-organized minority that left its mark on society. Calvinism gave rise to Puritanism in England, to the Huguenots in France, and to the Dutch Reformed church. It served as the militant wing of Protestantism.

THE RADICALS

Other reformers had more radical agendas linked to the social unrest of the period. In Germany particularly—where capitalism was making rapid progress—workers and peasants hard hit by economic change turned to old ideas of social and religious reform. During the 1520s in Switzerland and in the upper Rhine Valley, little groups of people came together and proclaimed that the only true church was a voluntary association of believers, not an official institution like the churches of the Lutherans or the Catholics. Holding that baptism was a sign of belief, many of these groups in-sisted that only adults could be baptized—an idea that dated back to certain heretical groups of the twelfth century. Their opponents called them Anabaptists, or re-baptizers. The Anabaptists had a simple liturgy and generally interpreted the Bible literally. Most of them refused to take an oath—in court or elsewhere—or to accept public office or serve in the army. Some of the groups practiced the sort of communism described in the second chapter of Acts (2:44–47).

The Anabaptists were persecuted by Catholics and Protestants alike. After being driven from southern Germany, many of them found their way to the Netherlands, Bohemia, Poland, and England. It was during the seventeenth century in England and in the English colonies in America that the ideas of the Anabaptists were fully realized. Modern Baptists (who practice only adult baptism), Congregationalists (who recognize the autonomy of local congregations), and Quakers (who rely on an "inner light") all trace their origins to the sixteenth-century Anabaptists.

The more rigid Protestants objected to all religious paintings and sculpture as leading to idolatry. In this engraving of 1579, Calvinists are pulling down statues of saints and destroying stained-glass windows.

ANGLICANISM

Although several kings took over their national churches during the late Middle Ages, they were not motivated by a desire for reform. In England, though the breach with Rome signaled by the Act of Supremacy in 1534 was followed by change, Henry VIII did not intend to depart from orthodox Catholic belief and practice. He made it clear that he would continue to suppress heresy, whether Lutheran or Anabaptist. Still, he found that he could not seal England off from Protestantism or maintain his break from Rome without the support of Protestant sympathizers. To evidence his willingness to compromise he approved the distribution of an English translation of the Bible.

By the time of Henry's death in 1547, a Protestant clergy had emerged within the English church under the leadership of Thomas Cranmer, archbishop of Canterbury (r. 1533–53). Under Henry's son, Edward IV (r. 1547–53), Cranmer set about transforming the English church into a Protestant church. He assembled the best parts of the Catholic liturgy and translated them into English to form the majestic Book of Common Prayer (1549). In his first version of his collection he tried to accommodate both Catholics and Protestants, but he satisfied neither. So he issued a fully Protestant version in 1552. This prayer book eventually became a literary symbol of Anglicanism, as Luther's Bible and Calvin's *Institutes* had come to symbolize Lutheranism and Calvinism.

The advance of Protestantism in England was further accelerated by Henry VIII's dissolution of the monasteries. Because the monasteries belonged to international orders, they were incompatible with the new national church headed by the king. Furthermore, monasticism had lost much of its appeal, and many of the houses were no longer abiding by the rules of their orders. Beginning in 1536, Henry confiscated the properties of the monastic communities and incorporated them into the crown lands. By 1539, the dissolution of the monasteries was complete. Although the confiscations virtually doubled the royal income, it was still not

enough to support the monarchy's costly wars. Consequently, Henry and his successors gradually sold the old monastic properties to aristocratic families, who thereby acquired an economic interest in preserving the breach with Rome.

The Protestant reformation in England came to a halt in 1553, when Henry's oldest child, Mary, daughter of Catherine of Aragon, came to the throne. To vindicate her mother, Mary tried to reunite

Radical Protestantism: The Teaching of Menno Simons

Menno Simons (1496–1561) was one of the ablest leaders of the radical wing of the Reformation. Simons's followers formed the Mennonite church, which still exists. His ideas also contributed to the development of the Baptist church. He never summed up his doctrine in a single document; it has to be put together from scattered pamphlets.

We do not find in Scripture a single word by which Christ has ordained the baptism of infants, or that his apostles taught and practiced it. We say that infant baptism is but a human invention. . . . To baptize before that which is required for baptism, namely faith, is to place the cart before the horse.

Never should any commandment be observed which is not contained in God's holy Word, either in letter or in spirit.

The regenerated do not go to war nor fight. . . . How can a Christian, according to Scripture, consistently retaliate, rebel, make war, murder, slay, torture, steal, rob, and burn cities and conquer countries?

Where have you read in the Scriptures, that Christ or the Apostles called upon the power of the magistracy against those who would not hear their doctrine or obey their words? . . . Faith is a gift of God, therefore it cannot be forced on anyone by worldly authorities or by the sword.

We must be born from above, must be changed and renewed in our hearts and thus be transplanted from the unrighteous and evil nature of Adam into the righteous and good nature of Christ, or we cannot be helped in eternity by any means, divine or human.

From "Selections from the Writings of Menno Simons," in The Medieval World and Its Transformations, *ed. by G. M. Straka (New York: McGraw-Hill, 1967), Vol. II, pp. 463, 466, 467, 468, 470.*

Title page of Daniel Featley's *Description* of 1645, known also as "The Dippers Dipt," a satirical view of the Anabaptists.

she was an educated, intelligent woman, and she knew that she would have to be patient. She had the Book of Common Prayer revised once again, to make it acceptable to Catholics and Protestants alike. She refused "to make windows into men's souls," as she put it—that is, she would persecute only those who openly and persistently opposed her. Even after the pope excommunicated her in 1570, she tolerated Catholics so long as they refrained from political activity. But she treated as a traitor anyone who challenged her right to the throne.

Elizabeth's moderate policies did not please all her subjects. Radical Protestants continued to demand that the English church be purified of all traces of Catholicism. These "Puritans" were strong in Parliament, and the queen occasionally had to deal harshly with them, but they helped to establish the idea that patriotism required independence from Rome.

The Anglican church viewed Presbyterianism—which was dominant in Scotland and had made some headway in England—with suspicion and was contemptuous of the Baptists. During the seventeenth century, the Anglican church became progressively more conservative, and today many Anglicans insist that their church is not "Protestant" at all. Rather, they argue, it was the Catholic church that strayed from the true path and Henry VIII and Cranmer who preserved the church of Christ.

THE CATHOLIC REFORMATION AND THE COUNTER REFORMATION

The leaders of Protestantism thought of themselves as reformers, and the movement they set in motion is still known as the Protestant Reformation. Catholics, of course, viewed them as rebels and their reformation as a revolt. For them, true reformation could take place only within the church. Churchmen and pious laymen had been calling for reform ever since the fourteenth century, but the Protestant challenge heightened the pressure and helped to precipitate a great new reform movement in the middle of the sixteenth

the English church with Rome. She canceled all antipapal legislation, deposed Cranmer, purged the church of his supporters, and had Cranmer and about 300 other Protestants burned as heretics. Mary's reign of terror (she was known as Bloody Mary) and her marriage to Philip II of Spain offended her English subjects as inhumane and as an affront to their patriotism. As a result, Protestantism came to be identified with patriotism in the public mind.

Mary died in 1558, and Elizabeth, the daughter of Henry VIII and his second wife, Anne Boleyn, succeeded to the throne as Elizabeth I (r. 1558–1603). Elizabeth understood that her legitimacy as queen depended on the validity of Henry's divorce and on his Act of Supremacy. But

century. Historians call that movement the Catholic Reformation, or the Counter-Reformation. Actually, these were two different movements. The Catholic Reformation was a reform of the church, while the Counter-Reformation was a Catholic response to the Protestants. That response was vigorous; the church used torture and imprisonment as well as gentler means of persuasion to bring wayward Catholics back to orthodoxy.

The pressure for the reform of the Catholic church had produced some action even before Luther sounded his pro-test. In the late fifteenth century, the Oratory of Divine Love was founded in Genoa as a lay brotherhood similar to the Brethren of the Common Life in the north. The Oratory sought to encourage a simple Christian life among laymen and to reform the clergy, who were gradually admitted to it as members. The movement spread to other Italian cities, and by the second quarter of the sixteenth century it had be-come the main source of ideas for reform within the church.

The impetus toward internal reform coincided with a decline in the political

Europe after the Reformations

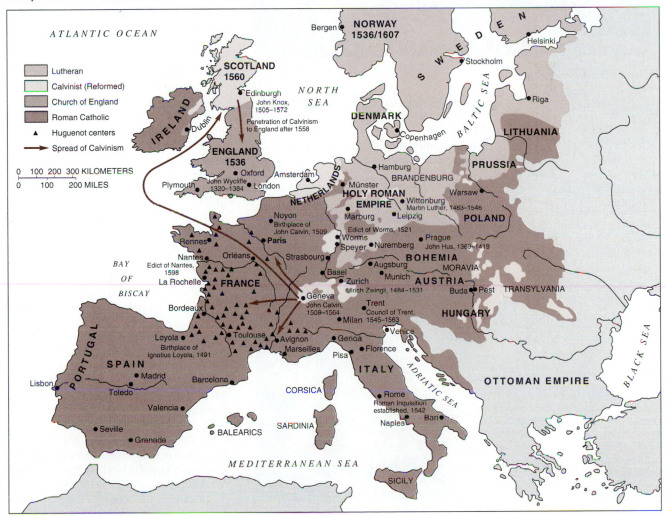

Engraving showing the third session of the Council of Trent (1562–63). An amphitheater was set up in the church of St. Maria Maggiore.

power of the papacy. The last of the politician popes of the Renaissance was Clement VII (r. 1523–34), who rejected calls for reform and acted like a traditional Italian despot. To counter the power of the em-

Ignatius of Loyola, founder of the Jesuit Order, holds a book with the text "to the greater glory of God."

peror Charles V, Clement entered into an alliance with Francis I of France. But with the sack of Rome in 1527 by undisciplined imperial troops, Italy came under imperial control and the political aspirations of the papacy vanished. Clement's successor, Paul III (r. 1534–49) turned his attention to reform and named cardinals who themselves were eager for reform. Eventually he summoned a great council to the city of Trent—which was under German control—to work out a reform program.

The Council of Trent met in three sessions—1545–48, 1551–52, and 1562–63. Toward the end of the first session, Emperor Charles V urged the council to open direct negotiations with the Protestants. To thwart that proposal, the pope moved the meeting to Bologna, knowing that no Protestant would appear in a city under papal control. For its second and third sessions, the council returned to Trent. In the third session, it issued a series of reform decrees.

Among those decrees was a declaration that salvation was indeed granted by God alone and that salvation resulted from faith, but that good works were a demonstration of faith and a confirmation of the working of God's mercy in the doer. The council also asserted that ultimate religious authority resided *both* in the Bible *and* in tradition, as interpreted by the Roman Catholic church. It urged that seminaries be established to train priests, and those seminaries did in fact foster a gradual reform of the priesthood. Finally, it ruled that clerics could not hold multiple offices and reaffirmed the absolute supremacy of the pope over the clerical hierarchy.

The second and third sessions of the council were dominated by Philip II of Spain (r. 1556–98), who was determined that Spain would resist the Protestant threat. He emerged as the leader of the Counter-Reformation, promoting the revival of a militant church throughout Europe. The spearhead of the Counter-Reformation was a new order founded by Ignatius of Loyola (1491–1556), a Spaniard of Basque descent. While serving as a soldier in the wars between the Habsburgs and the French, Ignatius had suffered a severe wound and had spent months recuperating. During his convalescence, he had read several books on the lives of the saints, the only reading material at hand, and had decided to become a Christian knight in the service of the Virgin Mary. As he found his way into his new life, he worked through a series of "spiritual exercises," which he later recommended to his followers. The exercises called for intense concentration on the most vivid details of hell and of the life and death of Christ as a means of strengthening one's will toward salvation. While Ignatius was studying at the University of Paris (John Calvin was a fellow student), he enlisted nine of his friends to become the nucleus of a new order called the Society of Jesus. Pope Paul III approved the order in 1540, and its members became known as Jesuits.

The Jesuits wore no distinctive habit; they dressed as their work required. They swore an oath of allegiance to the pope and underwent rigorous training for hazardous assignments. They carried out secret missions in Protestant regions, where they would be executed if caught. Through their clandestine operations, they strengthened the pope's control over the church; they ran the best schools in Europe; and they reclaimed most of Bohemia, Poland, Hungary, and southern Germany from Protestantism.

The inquisition was revived as an instrument of church reform when Ferdinand and Isabella instituted a royal inquisition in Spain in 1480. Their lead was followed by the Habsburgs in the Netherlands in 1523 and by Spanish powers in Italy in 1542. In 1559, the papacy instituted a system of censorship known as the Index. This was a list of printed books that Catholics were forbidden to read. The Index was approved, with some modifications, by the Council of Trent in 1563.

The Catholic Reformation brought new vitality to the church and enabled it to close ranks against the Protestants. By the second half of the sixteenth century a strong church, reorganized and backed by Spanish power, faced an array of Protes-

CALVIN   LE PAPE   LUTHER

Luther tweaks the beard of Calvin as both of them pull the hair of the pope. This satirical engraving presents a Catholic view of the Reformation controversy.

tant organizations that had already begun to compete with one another for followers.

The Results of the Reformation

Some of the results of the Protestant Reformation are clear: It split Christendom into several competing churches. It halted the trend toward secularism that had been evident in the late Middle Ages. After Luther, all issues were religious issues and for the next century the most serious conflicts in Europe were religious conflicts.

Modern historians have debated the political, economic, and cultural effects of the Protestant Reformation. Did it foster capitalism by recognizing the possibility of serving God in one's secular calling and by extolling the bourgeois virtues of thrift and self-discipline? Did it help kings create absolute monarchies by supporting the idea that royal power came directly from God? Did it deflect the course of art history by cleansing the medieval churches and refusing to decorate the new churches? The historical record does not furnish answers to these questions, but the effort to answer them has produced some influential historical works.

Suggestions for Further Reading

Background of the Reformation

Several works put the Reformation in a historical context. See S. Ozmont, *The Reformation in Medieval Perspective* (1971); G. Strauss, *Pre-Reformation Germany* (1972); and J. Bossy, *Christianity in the West, 1400–1750* (1985). On the background of Protestantism, see H. Oberman, *The Harvest of Medieval Theology* (1963), and A. McGrath, *The Intellectual Origins of the European Reformation* (1987). J. Huizinga's *The Waning of the Middle Ages* (1924) is the classic work on the cultural changes during the fourteenth and fifteenth centuries.

The Religious Upheaval

On the Hussite movement, see M. Spinka, *John Huss and the Czech Revolution* (1941); F. G. Heymann, *John Zizka and the Hussite Revolution* (1955); and H. Kaminsky, *A History of the Hussite Revolution* (1967). On the spread of humanism, see P. O. Kristeller, "The European Diffusion of Italian Humanism," *Renaissance Thought II* (1965), and L. Spitz, *The Religious Renaissance of the German Humanists* (1963). On Erasmus, see J. Huizinga, *Erasmus* (1952), and R. H. Bainton, *Erasmus of Christendom* (1969). For a specialized study of Erasmus's reform views, see J. B. Payne, *Erasmus: His Theology of the Sacraments* (1970). Erasmus's writings are widely available; see, for example, J. P. Dolan, ed., *The Essential Erasmus* (1964).

There are many histories of the Protestant Reformation. H. Holborn, *A History of Modern Germany: The Reformation* (1959), is excellent on Germany. See also B. Moeller, *Imperial Cities and the Reformation* (1972), and G. Strauss, *Luther's House of Learning* (1978). L. W. Spitz, *The Renaissance and Reformation Movements,* Vol. 2 (1971), is an excellent brief history. J. Lortz, *The Reformation in Germany,* 2 vols. (1969), gives a fair statement of the Catholic view. A. G. Dickens, *The German Nation and Martin Luther* (1972), emphasizes the urban nature of the Reformation. H. J. Hillerbrand, *The Protestant Reformation: A Narrative History* (1964), contains a good anthology of contemporary writings.

On the spread of Protestantism, see S. Ozment, *The Reformation of the Cities* (1975). On Zwingli, see W. P. Stephens, *The Theology of Huldrych Zwingli* (1986). On the iconoclasm of the Protestant movement, see C. M. N. Eire, *War Against the Idols* (1986), and C. Christensen, *Art and the Reformation in Germany* (1980). W. Bouwsma, *John Calvin* (1988), is a fine biography and introduction. F. Wendel, *Calvin, The Origin and Development of his Religious Thought* (1963), is an excellent introduction. On the radicals, see G. H. Williams, *The Radical Reformation* (1962); F. H. Littell, *The Free Church* (1958); R. H. Bainton, *The Travail of Religious Liberty* (1951); and C. L. Clausen, *Anabaptism: A Social History* (1972). The best work on England is A. G. Dickens, *The English Reformation* (1964). J. J. Scarisbrick, *Henry VIII* (1968), is a brilliant work. For the Puritans, see P. Collinson, *The Elizabethan Puritan Movement* (1967).

An excellent discussion of the Catholic Reformation is H. Daniel-Rops, *The Catholic Reformation,* 2 vols. (1961). See also A. G. Dickens, *The Counter Reformation* (1969). For the Council of Trent, the definitive work is H. Jedin, *History of the Council of Trent,* of which the first two volumes appeared in English translation in 1957.

Results of the Reformation

On the economic, political, and cultural consequences of the Reformation there are wide differences of opinion. The starting point of modern debate was an "essay" by M. Weber, *The Protestant Ethic and the Spirit of Capitalism* (1905). *Protestantism and Capitalism: The Weber Thesis and Its Critics,* ed. by R. W. Green (1973), is a convenient collection of selections from the literature. See also L. W. Spitz, *The Reformation: Basic Interpretations* (1972), and R. Kingdon and R. Linder, *Calvin and Calvinism: Sources of Democracy* (1972). For a readable and perceptive survey of the period, see A. G. Dickens, *Reformation and Society in Sixteenth-Century Europe* (1966).

THE AGE OF DISCOVERY

In the early Middle Ages, Europeans knew of the world beyond the horizon only from the works of the ancient geographers. Then they learned something more through their contacts with the Arabs, Moors, Vikings, Magyars, and Mongols. But they had only the vaguest notions of East Asia, except that it was the source of the spices and curiosities that the Arabs brought to market. And they knew nothing at all of the southern hemisphere or the vast American continents.

Consequently, the explorations of the late fifteenth century had a revolutionary effect on their consciousness of the world and their place in it. For the first time in history they had direct experience of all the inhabited continents of the world and of the people who lived on them. By the middle of the sixteenth century, European intellectuals were pondering the question of how to deal with people who had built impressive civilizations without the benefit of divine revelation or Christian sanction.

THE EMERGENCE OF OCEANIC TRADE

The Early Voyages

In 1400, Europeans knew scarcely more about the world than the Romans had, for only a few of them had ever ventured beyond the Mediterranean Basin. The crusades had enlarged the vision of western Europeans somewhat, but not beyond the limits of the ancient world.

Only the Scandinavians had caught a glimpse of far horizons. Their sagas tell of voyages of Leif Ericson and other bold Viking seamen to North America. During the eleventh century, the Icelanders established settlements on Greenland and around Hudson Bay and apparently coasted down the eastern shores of North America. The Hudson Bay settlements seem to have been abandoned after a short time, but the Greenland settlements survived until the middle of the thirteenth century, when a cooling trend in the earth's climate made them uninhabitable. The last official contact between Iceland and the Greenland settlements took place

(Top) Mediterranean war galley with lateen sail (*ca.* twelfth century); *(middle)* lateen-rigged vessel, much like Columbus's *Niña* (early fifteenth-century); *(bottom)* Spanish galleon of sixteenth century, the typical long-distance ship for Spanish commerce.

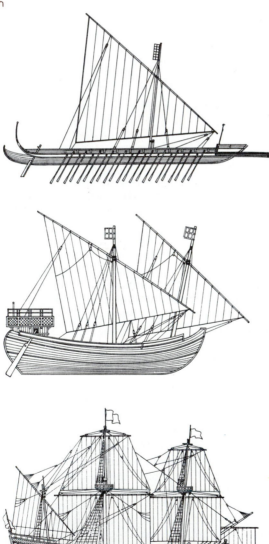

in 1258, though there is archaeological evidence that English sailors were still visiting them at the end of the century.

Meanwhile the Italians were opening up an overland trade route to China. The Polo family of Venice, and Franciscan friars as well, demonstrated that China could be reached by land across the vast steppes of central Asia. Marco Polo (*ca.* 1254–1324) traveled to China with his father and uncle in 1271 and remained at the court of the Mongol emperor for more than fifteen years. On his return in 1295, he wrote an account of the journey that was widely read in Europe and contributed greatly to the Europeans' knowledge of the East and stimulated their interest in Chinese civilization. But after the collapse of the Mongol empire in the fourteenth century, the overland route to China was no longer safe, and the demand for eastern wares was satisfied by Arab sailors operating in the Indian Ocean who brought spices and textiles to Alexandria and Beirut to be distributed by the Venetians to European markets.

By the end of the sixteenth century, these uncertain contacts with the East had been replaced by a regular trade of worldwide proportions. The ocean had become a busy highway on which Europeans controlled all the traffic, and it was becoming clear that the empires of the future would be built on mastery of the seas. When the first ship to circumnavigate the globe sailed into its home port in 1522, Europeans had already begun to build a network of trade around the earth that would bring all the civilizations of the world under their influence in the centuries ahead.

The Preconditions for Exploration

The age of exploration could not have occurred before revolutionary advances had been made in the design of ships and in the tools of navigation. The Vikings had made short voyages across the North Atlantic—Greenland was only a twelve-day sail from Norway—but in their small, open boats, even those trips were daring. What made the western explorations possible was a rare climatic condition that occasionally gave Scandinavian sailors a hazy glimpse of land beyond the horizon. From the western coast of Iceland they could "see" Greenland: In the winter, when the water is colder than the air, land far beyond the horizon—over the curvature of the earth—is sometimes reflected in the sky, giving would-be explorers confidence that they will reach land just beyond the range of sight.

But the Scandinavians' boats were too small and too unseaworthy to permit regular contact with the settlements in Greenland and North America. Before Europeans could push out across the Atlantic and plant colonies linked to the mother country, they needed more seaworthy ships and more reliable navigational aids.

It was a long time before oceangoing ships became available, however. The oar-propelled galleys of the Mediterranean served well enough in coastal waters, but sailors rarely struck out into the open sea—and then only to cross such narrow stretches as the passage between Sicily and North Africa. By the thirteenth century, Genoese and Venetian galleys were venturing out into the Atlantic to Morocco and Flanders, but they still hugged the coastline going and coming. To sail the open sea, mariners needed ships with sails rather than oars, and with broad, round hulls rather than the long, narrow hulls of the oar-propelled galleys. The fifty or more rowers who manned a galley burned up an enormous number of calories each day and consequently required vast amounts of food—far more than a galley could carry. Only sailing ships with small crews could make voyages across the Atlantic that lasted for months.

By the fifteenth century the Portuguese had designed such a vessel. The squat, three-masted caravel had two masts with the square sails favored by the Europeans and one mast with the triangular lateen sail favored by the Moslems. The square rigs were best for running before the wind, while the lateen rig was better suited to sailing close to the wind. The caravel was slower and less maneuverable than the galley, but it had more space for cargo and provisions for long voyages.

Mariners had had means of determining their direction of sail and their po-

sition for centuries. The astrolabe (already in use in the eleventh century and perhaps as early as the third century B.C.) enabled them to determine latitude by measuring the elevation of the sun and stars. The compass (used in Europe by the thirteenth century) gave them their direction in cloudy weather when the sun and stars were obscured. (No way to determine longitude precisely developed until the eighteenth century, when Edmund Halley—for whom the comet is named—devised a reasonably accurate method.)

The exploration of the oceans required substantial financial resources to construct and man the oceangoing vessels. City-states—from the Phoenicians to the Italians—were the original providers of shipping, but transoceanic voyages required resources far beyond the capacities of city-states. Only after the European monarchs had consolidated their power and unified their countries did there exist powers with enough wealth to man and equip fleets of oceangoing vessels. Thus, after 1400 the kingdoms gradually replaced the cities as the major supporters of shipping.

The Motivations for Exploration

The motivations of individual European ship captains varied, but it is clear that they had both religious and worldly motives. Christians believed that the longed-for end of the world would not take place until all were converted to Christianity. The desire to convert all the peoples of the world was always part of the motivation of explorers and their patrons.

One motivation for exploration was the desire to find new trade routes to East Asia. The spices used to preserve meats and make them palatable—pepper from India, cinnamon from Sri Lanka (Ceylon), ginger from China, nutmeg and cloves from the East Indies—were absolute necessities in an age without refrigeration. The Arabs controlled the trade between Alexandria and East Asia. The Venetians controlled it between Alexandria and Europe. And these monopolies made those necessities extremely expensive. The monarchs of western Europe were

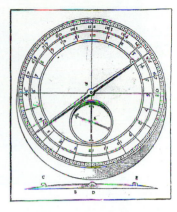

Drawing of an early compass, designed by Agricola (Georg Bauer, 1494–1555), the father of mineralogy.

Toynbee on the Age of Discovery

Since A.D. 1500 the map of the civilized world has indeed been transformed out of all recognition. Down to that date it was composed of a belt of civilizations girdling the Old World from the Japanese Isles on the north-east to the British Isles on the north-west. . . . The main line of communication was provided by the chain of steppes and deserts that cut across the belt of civilizations from the Sahara to Mongolia. For human purposes, the Steppe was an inland sea. . . . This waterless sea had its dry-shod ships and its quayless ports. The steppe-galleons were camels, the steppe-galleys horses, and the steppe-ports "caravan cities." . . . The great revolution was a technological revolution by which the West made its fortune, got the better of all the other living civilizations, and forcibly united them into a single society of literally world-wide range. The revolutionary Western invention was the substitution of the Ocean for the Steppe as the principal medium of world-communication. This use of the Ocean, first by sailing ships and then by steamships, enabled the West to unify the whole inhabited and habitable world.

From Arnold J. Toynbee, Civilization on Trial *(New York: Oxford University Press, 1948), pp. 67–70.*

most of it wrong—to make success seem likely. They took as fact Ptolemy's estimate that the circumference of the earth was about 8,000 miles. That meant that Japan and China lay only a few thousand miles west of Europe. And because they believed that Africa was much smaller than it is, they thought they could sail around it and soon arrive in Asia. In short, they reckoned that they could sail either east or west and reach their destination in a reasonable amount of time.

Portuguese Exploration

Prince Henry the Navigator (1394–1460), the young son of King John I of Portugal (r. 1385–1433) contributed a great deal to the scientific and seafaring knowledge of the day through his work at a remarkable observatory at Sagres on Cape St. Vincent, at the tip of Portugal. He devoted his life to organizing, equipping, and sending out fleets to explore the coast of Africa, and he had a notion that he could outflank the Moslems and discover lands they knew nothing about. But his main goal was to find gold—a goal he realized when his fleets reached the Gold Coast of Africa in the 1450s.

After Henry's death, the Portuguese lost interest in exploration for a time. They did discover and settle clusters of small islands in the Atlantic—the Madeiras and the Azores. Although the islands did not prove very profitable, the discovery showed that there was land to be found eight hundred miles out in the Atlantic and encouraged further exploration.

Henry's interest in voyages of discovery was taken up again by his grand-nephew, King John II (r. 1481–95), who encouraged Portuguese explorers to find an all-water route to India. By 1488 Bartholomeu Dias had discovered the Cape of Good Hope, and in 1497 Vasco da Gama rounded the Cape with four ships. He reached Calicut on the Malabar Coast of India in 1498 and was back in Lisbon with two of his ships in 1499. In 1500 Pedro Álvares Cabral led a large fleet to Brazil and then sailed on to India, where he established the first Portuguese trading stations. At first the Portuguese met with a

eager to find a way to lower the cost of importing them.

Another motivation was the need to find new sources of precious metals. The only way Europeans could pay for imports from Asia was with gold or silver bullion. Asians had no interest in accepting lumber or foodstuff in payment, and in any case such products were too bulky or perishable to be used in long-distance trade. By 1400 the gold and silver mines of Europe, which had never been especially productive, were nearly exhausted. To support the steady flow of gold and silver to Asia, European monarchs were eager to locate new sources of supply.

THE FIRST EXPLORATIONS

By the late fifteenth century many bold mariners along Europe's Atlantic coast were eager to set sail. They had the motivation, the ships, and the instruments they needed to venture out onto the unknown sea. They also had enough information—

hostile reception from the Hindus and the Moslems of India. Da Gama was not impressed by Indian civilization and apparently said as much. Several of Cabral's men were killed by Moslems. But within a few years the Portuguese had built a commercial empire in India under the bold leadership of Afonso de Albuquerque (1453–1515), who served as governor of Portuguese India from 1509 to 1515.

Albuquerque had already been active in the area before he became governor. He had conquered Goa, a coastal region in western India, which he later made his capital, and had established strategic fortresses in East Africa to disrupt the Arabs' trade with India. (The Arabs had established themselves along the East African coast in the Middle Ages and used the ports as staging posts for their trade in the Indian Ocean.) As governor, he seized Malacca to control the trade between the Spice Islands and the Indian Ocean, and took over Ormuz, an island in the Persian Gulf from which he could disrupt Arab shipping. He tried but failed to take Aden, which would have given him control of the Red Sea, through which the Arab-Venetian trade passed. By the time Albuquerque died, Portugal had taken control of much of the spice trade and had established strategic bases all the way from Africa to the East Indies.

That success was short-lived, however. Although Portugal drew large profits from these early ventures, it lacked the resources to maintain permanent colonies in India and to support the navy required to protect its trade. Italian, German, and Flemish bankers soon took over the Portuguese trade, and even the spices that still arrived at Lisbon were sent on to Antwerp for distribution. The burden of empire had grown heavy by the time Portugal fell under Spanish control in 1580.

Columbus and Spanish Exploration

In 1484, before the Portuguese had reached the Cape of Good Hope, a Genoese sailor named Christopher Columbus (1451–1506) had tried in vain to persuade the Portuguese king, John II, to back him

Vasco da Gama.

The Portuguese as others saw them: African bronze sculpture of a Portuguese man.

in a voyage of exploration to the west. Relying on the accounts of Portuguese sailors and on Ptolemy's estimate of the size of the earth, Columbus was convinced that he could reach Japan (then called Cipangu) by sailing due west. But he could find no one to back him with ships and money. The Portuguese were content to follow up the explorations of Henry the Navigator along the coast of Africa, and Ferdinand and Isabella were busy with the conquest of the kingdom of Granada, the last Moorish stronghold on the Iberian peninsula.

In January 1492, Granada fell to Spain, and Ferdinand and Isabella turned to other matters. After much hesitation, and against the advice of her counselors, Isabella agreed to back Columbus. With one brilliant voyage the Spanish reached the New World.

Columbus landed in the Bahamas on October 12, 1492, thinking he had come

The World of the Voyager

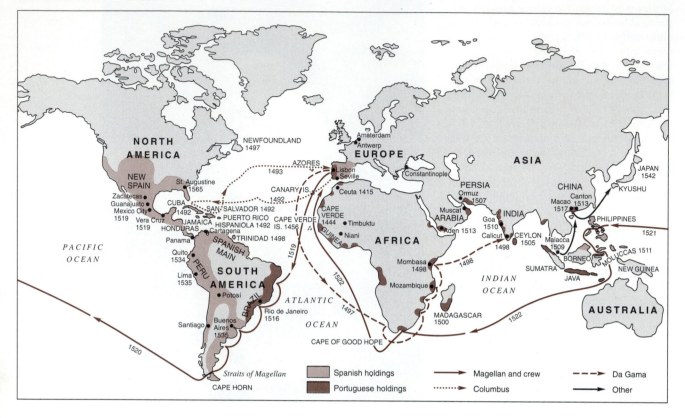

NORTH AMERICA

NEWFOUNDLAND 1497

EUROPE

ASIA

JAPAN 1542

NEW SPAIN

St. Augustine 1565

AZORES 1493

Amsterdam
Antwerp

KYUSHU

Zacatecas
Guanajuato
Mexico City 1519
Vera Cruz 1519

CUBA 1492

CANARY IS. 1492

Lisbon
Seville

Ceuta 1415

Constantinople

PERSIA
Ormuz 1507

CHINA
Macao 1517
Canton 1513

SAN SALVADOR 1492
PUERTO RICO
HISPANIOLA 1492

CAPE VERDE

Muscat
ARABIA

INDIA
Goa 1510
Calicut 1498

PHILIPPINES

1521

JAMAICA
HONDURAS
Cartagena

CAPE VERDE IS. 1456

VERDE 1444

Timbuktu
Niani

Aden 1513

CEYLON 1505

Malacca 1509

MOLUCCAS 1511

Panama

TRINIDAD 1498

GUINEA

BORNEO

NEW GUINEA

PACIFIC OCEAN

SPANISH MAIN

AFRICA

SUMATRA
JAVA

Quito 1534

1519

INDIAN OCEAN

AUSTRALIA

PERU

SOUTH AMERICA

Lima 1535

Potosí

Mombasa 1498

1498

BRAZIL

1522

ATLANTIC OCEAN

Mozambique

1522

Santiago

Buenos Aires 1535

Rio de Janeiro 1516

1497

MADAGASCAR 1500

1520

Straits of Magellan

CAPE OF GOOD HOPE

CAPE HORN

| | Spanish holdings | → Magellan and crew | ----→ Da Gama |
| | Portuguese holdings | ········→ Columbus | ——→ Other |

Christopher Columbus, the Genoese sailor who sailed west in search of Japan and found the New World. This portrait of Columbus is thought to be the closest existing likeness of him. It is a copy, made in about 1525, of an earlier painting that has been lost.

upon some islands in the Japanese archipelago. Throughout four voyages, until his death in 1506, he remained convinced, even after reaching the mainland, that he had reached Japan and China and gave the name "Indians"—at that time a general term for East Asians—to the people he found.

It was a fellow Italian, Amerigo Vespucci (1454–1512), head of a branch of the Medici bank in Seville, who recognized what Columbus had discovered. After voyages in 1499 and 1501, Vespucci described what he saw in letters that were published and read throughout Europe. In one he referred to the great southern continent in the west as *Mundus novus*, a New World. Later mapmakers labeled both the northern continent and the southern continent "America," after Amerigo.

Incidently, it was Vespucci's letters that inspired Thomas More to write his *Utopia* (see pp. 431–32).

The Treaty of Tordesillas, 1494

Spain and Portugal competed for possession of the western continents from the very beginning. (Portugal's claim rested on the voyage of Cabral in 1500.) To avoid going to war, they turned to the pope, Alexander VI, to settle their claims. Alexander, who was himself a Spaniard, drew a line of demarcation 100 leagues (about 300 miles) west of the Cape Verde Islands (off the coast of West Africa), which clearly favored Spain. Dissatisfied, the Portuguese persuaded the Spanish to negotiate the Treaty of Tordesillas (1494), which drew a line of demarcation from pole to pole 370 leagues west of the Cape Verde Islands.

The Portuguese assumed that the line applied only to the western hemisphere (it gave them Brazil, though they did not know it at the time), while the Spanish assumed that it went clear around the earth. According to their interpretation, the Spanish could claim the Moluccas, the heart of the Spice Islands, and part of what is now Indonesia. Given the progress the Portuguese were making in the East Indies, the conflicting interpretations of the treaty might have led to war after all. But Spain became so occupied with its new possessions in the Americas that in 1527 it sold its claims in the eastern hemisphere to Portugal.

The Spanish remained determined to find a westward route to the Orient, however. When the Spanish explorer Vasco Núñez de Balboa sighted the Pacific Ocean from the Isthmus of Darien in Central America, the Spanish thought that somewhere they might find a passage across the New World. In 1519, the Portuguese navigator Ferdinand Magellan—with Spanish backing—negotiated the treacherous straits off the southern tip of South America and sailed across the Pacific only to be killed by natives in the Philippines. His navigator, Sebastian del Cano, brought one of Magellan's five ships back to Lisbon in 1522 by way of the Cape of Good Hope. This was the first ship to circumnavigate the world.

THE SPANISH EMPIRE IN THE AMERICAS

While Magellan was on his historic voyage, Spanish conquistadors discovered and overcame wealthy civilizations in Mexico and Peru. The most notable of the conquistadors were Hernando Cortés and Francisco Pizarro. In 1519–21 Cortés conquered the formidable Aztec Empire in Mexico with 600 men, sixteen horses, and a few cannon, and in 1533–34 Pizarro, with an even smaller force, conquered the Incan Empire in the Andes Mountains of Peru.

The Aztecs and the Incans were wealthy, sophisticated peoples, but they were no match for the Spaniards. The Spanish troops were small, but well disciplined and daring, and their leaders took advantage of every opportunity. Moreover, both the Aztec and the Incan empires were highly centralized, and once

Cortés accepting the surrender of Quauhtemoc, last king of the Aztecs. The artist was a Spanish-trained native from Tlaxcala, who chronicled Cortés's conquest for Mexico. Notice the mixture of European and Indian styles.

the rulers had been disposed of there were no local leaders to take over. Even more destructive than the military superiority of the Spaniards were the diseases (especially smallpox) they brought with them. The native populations had no natural defenses against those diseases, and soon they were so reduced in numbers that resistance was impossible.

Though it is difficult to estimate the size of the population of Mexico before the conquest, it appears to have been at least 25 million. It had dropped to about 6 million by 1540, to 4 million by 1563, and to 2.5 million by 1600. By about 1650, it had reached 1.5 million. Thereafter, it climbed gradually and reached a little more than 3.5 million in 1793. By contrast, the population of goats, sheep, and cattle that the Spanish introduced into Mexico rose dramatically in the second half of the sixteenth century. From 1550 to 1620, the number of goats and sheep rose from about half a million to 8 million, while the number of cattle rose from about 10,000 to 100,000. The small plots once tended by the native farmers had been taken over by great herds of range animals that destroyed the vegetation and reduced the land to a desert.

Spain's new empire overseas created conflict between groups with different interests and different goals. The settlers who went out to the New World wanted to build a manorial system based on the old European model, using the forced labor of the native population. They were unwilling to take orders from the Spanish government or to serve its interests. The government in turn wanted to exercise absolute power over the colonies and to exploit the rich sources of precious metals it knew to be there. The friars wanted to convert the native population to Christianity.

The fact that the native population was civilized but non-Christian raised serious theological and moral questions. Spanish scholars turned for answers to the works of medieval thinkers who had speculated about whether the biblical texts that specify that rulers receive their authority from God (such as 1 Samuel 9–31 and Romans 13) applied to rulers who did not

accept or did not know the Bible. Questions also arose regarding marriages of the natives. The church considered marriage to be a sacrament in which God joins husband and wife. Were the marriages of heathens valid? Medieval theologians and lawyers had declared that marriages of non-Christians were valid but not licit. In other words, the union was created by God but the marriages were not recognized by the church. The distinction they were making was between acts performed in accordance with natural law (which stems directly from God) and acts performed in accordance with human law (which stems only indirectly from God, through the medium of human institutions). The sixteenth-century Spaniards made much of this distinction. They concluded that the Indians lived by natural law alone but that they were God's people even without the benefit of the church. The leading proponent of this theory was a Spanish Dominican, Bartolomé de Las Casas (1474–1566).

Las Casas had gone to the New World in 1502 to convert the heathens and had soon become engaged in a struggle to win them better treatment. He and his fellow missionaries wanted the converts to be treated as fellow Christians, and he made several trips to Spain to win support for that goal. In the early 1520s, he took part in a program to found free cities for Christianized Indians. But when the project failed, he returned to Spain and retired to a Dominican house. In retirement, he wrote many learned works promoting his scheme as well as a long *History of the Indians.*

In the end, a compromise was worked out among the conflicting interests of the settlers, the government, and the friars. The settlers were permitted to use the forced labor of the Indians, but under the regulation of the government. The friars were given freedom to evangelize and Europeanize the native population. By contemporary standards, these policies were quite humane, and the Spanish came close to achieving what the Portuguese had failed to accomplish in the East and what the English never attempted in North America: the Christianization and

Europeanization of a whole native population.

Nonetheless, the main goal of the Spanish Empire was economic exploitation. With the discovery of rich silver mines in Mexico in 1545, the Empire gave itself over to the extraction and shipment of silver. After 1564, a silver fleet of twenty to sixty ships would gather every spring in Havana harbor to be convoyed by warships to Seville. And every spring the government officials would wait anxiously until the bullion was safely landed; silver was the key to Spain's power.

Despite their obsession with silver production, the Spanish were also aware of the agricultural potential of their holdings. The wet lowlands of the Caribbean were well suited to sugar cane cultivation, and sugar became an important commodity. When it turned out that the Indian workers were highly vulnerable to disease, however, the Spaniards began to import black slaves from Africa. Eventually, many Spaniards and Indians intermarried, and the mestizos—offspring of mixed marriages—outnumbered the purebred of either race. The Africans, however, remained enslaved outside society.

IMPERIAL SPAIN: THE REIGN OF PHILIP II

With the wealth from its colonies in the New World, Spain became the most powerful nation in Europe. And with the succession of the Habsburg emperor Charles V (r. 1516–56) to the Spanish throne through his mother Joanna, the daughter of Ferdinand and Isabella, Spain acquired a new role in European affairs. Charles, who had inherited Austria through his father, Maximilian, and the Netherlands through his mother, Mary of Burgundy, was elected emperor in 1519. He used Spanish money and Spanish troops to counter the Protestant heretics, to protect Austria from the Turks, and to extend the Spanish conquest of the New World. Although these ambitious enterprises taxed Spain's resources, under Charles and his son King Philip II (r. 1556–98), the nation proved almost equal to the

Las Casas on the American Indians in the Sixteenth Century

It has been written that these peoples of the Indies, lacking human governance and ordered nations, did not have the power of reason to govern themselves—which was inferred only from their having been found to be gentle, patient and humble. It has been implied that God became careless in creating so immense a number of rational souls and let human nature, which He so largely determined and provided for, go astray in the almost infinitesimal part of the human lineage which they comprise. From this it follows that they have all proven themselves unsocial and therefore monstrous, contrary to the natural bent of all peoples of the world.

. . . Not only have [the Indians] shown themselves to be very wise peoples and possessed of lively and marked understanding, prudently governing and providing for their nations (as much as they can be nations, without faith in or knowledge of the true God) and making them prosper in justice; but they have equalled many diverse nations of the world, past and present, that have been praised for their governance, politics and customs, and exceed by no small measure the wisest of all these, such as the Greeks and Romans, in adherence to the rules of natural reason.

From Bartolomé de las Casas, Apologética historia de las Indias, *in* Introduction to Contemporary Civilization in the West, *3rd ed. (New York: Columbia University Press, 1960), Vol. 1, p. 539.*

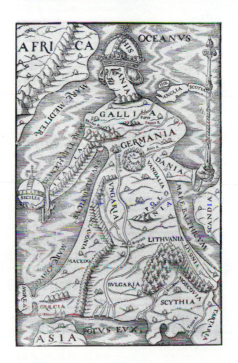

Contemporary map showing Spain as the head and crown of sixteenth-century Europe.

task. The sixteenth and early seventeenth centuries were the golden age of Spain.

In 1555–56 Charles V divided the Habsburg holdings between his brother Ferdinand and his son Philip. To Ferdinand went the Habsburg possessions in Austria, Bohemia, and Hungary, along with the imperial crown (still elective in theory, but by now always bestowed on a Habsburg). To Philip went the crowns of Castile and Aragon—still technically separate, but united since the death of Isabella (1504) and Ferdinand (1516). With Spain went its possessions in the New World, the kingdom of Naples, and the duchy of Milan (in effect control of all Italy), and the Netherlands. For a century and a half the "Austrian Habsburgs" and

the "Spanish Habsburgs," were separate ruling houses that cooperated closely in matters of dynastic policy. Even though Philip's realm included the Netherlands, it was more tightly knit and centralized than that of his uncle.

Although Philip was the scion of a central European family, he was thoroughly Spanish in speech, thought, and character. After 1559, when the Habsburgs concluded peace with France, he spent all his remaining years in Spain. Though conscientious, he was distrustful of his advisers, unable to delegate authority even in minor matters, and rigorously Catholic in religion. His goal was to restore the unity of Christendom with the Spanish king as its temporal head.

Europe about 1560

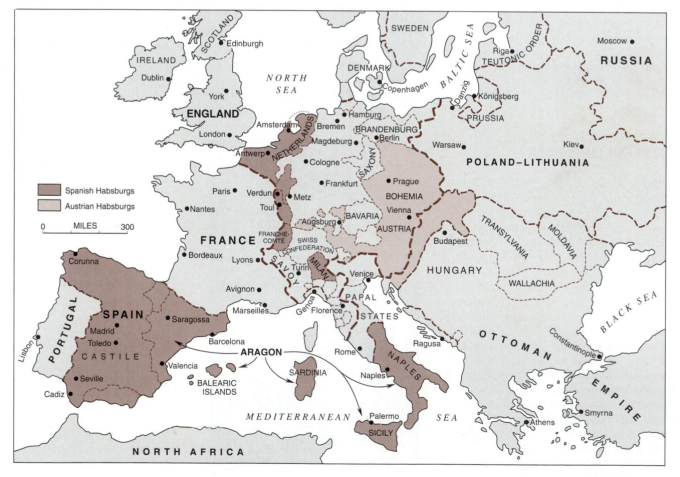

Economic Policy

After the discovery of the Mexican mines, the value of the annual shipments of silver rose dramatically. In the early years it amounted to something less than $300,000; by about 1550 it had risen to more than $4,000,000; and by 1600 it was about $12,000,000. Then a steady decline set in, and by about 1660 the average value was down to $1,200,000. The crown's share was about one-quarter of the total.

As a result of the influx of bullion into Spain, prices rose steeply after centuries of relative stability. By the middle of the sixteenth century, inflation was rampant and had spread to the rest of Europe. It has been estimated that prices in Spain quadrupled in the course of the century.

The rise in prices outstripped the rise in tax revenues, and Philip II was forced to repudiate his government's debts three times—in 1557, 1575, and 1596. These repudiations, which were tantamount to declarations of bankruptcy because Philip was announcing that he could not and would not repay his debts, sent shockwaves through the financial institutions of Europe. Besides damaging Spain's credit, the inflation ruined its infant industries, which had appeared robust early in the century. Because inflation developed first and rose fastest in Spain, its industrialists were at a disadvantage in the international market, and Spain suffered a regular trade imbalance. Spanish industry languished, and bullion flowed out of the country. When the silver mines in America began to peter out in the mid-seventeenth century, the Spanish economy had already been ruined, and the nation quickly declined into a second-rate power.

Religious Policy

Philip II's religious views were the most intolerant of his time. He once said that he would rather be king of a desert than of a land of heretics. His grandparents, Ferdinand and Isabella, had already forced the Moors to convert to Christianity, had expelled the Jews from their kingdoms (1492), and had delegated to the Spanish Inquisition responsibility for see-

On Philip II of Spain

The pallor of his complexion was remarked on by all observers, and most of them drew the proper conclusion, namely, that it indicated a weak stomach and lack of exercise. Reddened eyes were a penalty of his excessive devotion to the written word both day and night. . . . Reading and writing occupied the major portion of Philip's day. . . . He had taken deeply to heart his father's injunction to direct everything himself, and never to give his full confidence even to the most faithful of his ministers, and the natural result was that his time was completely occupied with receiving and answering reports and letters. . . . Reports, reports, and even more reports; Philip was literally submerged with them in his later years, and moreover he did not stop at reading them; he annotated them, as he went along, with comments on matters as absurdly trifling as the spelling and style of the men who had written them—all in that strange, sprawling hand of his, one of the most illegible hands of an age more than usually replete with chirographical difficulties.

From R. B. Merriman, The Rise of the Spanish Empire in the Old World and in the New *(New York: Macmillan, 1934), Vol. IV, pp. 21–24.*

ing that the converts remained Christian. Nonetheless, it was widely believed that the Moriscos (Moslems who had converted to Christianity) continued to practice Islam in private. In 1566, Philip ordered them to stop using the Arabic language, to give up their traditional dress, and to stop taking hot baths, as was their custom. Three years later, when the Moriscos rebelled in protest against this suppression of their cultural heritage, Philip savagely put down the rebellion and drove them out of Andalusia, where most of them lived. Many of them left Spain for North Africa, depriving Spain of their contributions as leaders of Spanish agriculture and industry.

Philip's actions were part of a comprehensive anti-Moslem policy. Philip led the struggle to control the Turks in the eastern Mediterranean, though with only limited success. In 1570 the Turks took Cyprus from the Venetians, and in 1571 a combined Spanish and Venetian fleet defeated the Turks at Lepanto in the Gulf of Corinth. Though the victory was hailed

The baptism of Moslem women, from a Spanish relief (1520).

throughout Europe, the Christian forces failed to follow it up.

For a short time after Lepanto, Philip was at the height of his power and prestige. But the moment was brief. During the last quarter of the sixteenth century, his dream of a revived Catholic Europe under his authority was shattered by the revolt of the Netherlands, the rise of English seapower, and the accession of a former Protestant to the throne of France.

THE REVOLT OF THE NETHERLANDS

In the sixteenth century, the 3 million people in the seventeen provinces of the Netherlands constituted one of the most prosperous populations in Europe. The comfortable houses of Bruges, Ghent, Antwerp, and Amsterdam had been built with the profits of a flourishing textile industry and a far-flung commercial net-

ca. 1400		1519	1581		1648
Low Countries United under Dukes of Burgundy		Spanish Rule	Dutch Wars of Independence		

work. Though the provinces had been united under the personal authority of the dukes of Burgundy during the preceding century, there was little sense of nationalism until Charles V became duke. Charles was the closest thing to a native ruler the united Netherlands had ever had, but once he became emperor he sacrificed the interests of the Dutch and Flemish cities to his imperial aims and prompted the first stirrings of nationalism in the provinces.

Under Philip II, religious tension added to the Netherlanders' alienation from Habsburg rule. The Netherlands were a crossroads of ideas as well as of commerce, and the teachings of Luther and Calvin had early taken root there. By the 1550s, well-organized Calvinist minorities existed in most of the cities.

Philip's intransigent religious policies were bound to alienate many of his Dutch and Flemish subjects. Their urban-commercial culture had for centuries been out of tune with the church's restrictive attitude toward business practices, and they had adopted an attitude of moderation in religious matters. That attitude had enabled them to countenance the rise and survival of such groups as the Brethren of the Common Life (see p. 426) and it was totally at odds with the king's religious fanaticism. To make matters worse, Philip violated the traditional limits of his authority as duke of the provinces by interfering in the internal affairs of the cities. In 1566 Calvinist mobs went on a rampage, breaking images of the saints and smashing stained-glass windows in Catholic churches throughout the Netherlands.

Philip sent the duke of Alva with about 10,000 Spanish regulars to suppress the iconoclasts, and Alva set up a regime that came to be known as the "Council of Blood." He boasted (with some exaggeration) that during his six years in the Netherlands (1567–73), he executed 18,000 people. His government also confiscated enormous tracts of land and imposed a 10

percent sales tax that seriously injured commerce.

Alva's measures served only to solidify resistance, and by 1572 the Dutch had found a leader in William the Silent, prince of Orange, the wealthiest landowner in the provinces. Although William lost almost every battle he fought against the Spanish, he had political wisdom, integrity, and patience. He also had a deep hatred of religious fanaticism. Dutch nationalism grew stronger under his leadership, helped by the actions of the Spanish themselves. In 1576, the Spanish responded to Calvinist excesses by staging a frightful sack of Antwerp, known as the "Spanish Fury." Frightened, the seventeen provinces rushed into an agreement to form a united front against Philip—the so-called Pacification of Ghent (1576).

The united front was led by moderate Calvinists and Catholics, but soon religious fanatics on both sides seized control. In the savage civil war that ensued, the Calvinists—who were better organized than the Catholics—gained the upper hand. The Catholics fled south to the ten Walloon provinces that were under the protection of the Spanish troops, while the Calvinists moved north to the Dutch provinces. In 1579 those provinces formed the Union of Utrecht, which ultimately evolved into the United Provinces, or the Dutch Netherlands, and declared their independence from Philip II in 1581. The

Example of propaganda badge worn by Dutch "Sea Beggars." The insurgents' hatred of Catholicism is expressed in the inscription: "Better the Turks than the pope."

The Division of the Netherlands   1581

southern provinces remained under Habsburg rule until 1830, when they became the kingdom of Belgium.

The Rise of the Dutch Netherlands

After declaring their independence, the Dutch Provinces struggled for two generations before achieving real independence. William the Silent was assassinated in 1584, and his successors carried on his able, disinterested leadership. Although the "United Provinces" was never more than a loose confederation, the Dutch fought with a fierce stubbornness whenever the need arose.

In 1578, Philip II, angered by the Pacification of Ghent, sent the duke of Parma—one of the age's best military leaders—to remedy the situation. But the Dutch privateers—"Sea Beggars"—joined with the English to control the English Channel and prevent Parma from resupplying the Spanish troops. This meant that Parma and Philip were in conflict with England—where Philip had once been Queen Mary's royal consort. This struggle led to the Spanish decision to send a great flotilla to clear the English Channel (see p. 464). The defeat of that armada ended any chance Spain might have had to reconquer the Dutch provinces. Not until 1648, however, did Spain formally recognize Dutch independence.

Dutch Prosperity

The Dutch emerged from the conflict with Spain as the most powerful commercial nation in Europe. By the early seventeenth century they were building more ships—and better ships—than all other nations combined. It was said that they built 2,000 per year, and they were taking over more and more of the carrying trade of Europe and of the world. During the war with Spain, the Dutch had closed off Antwerp—which was under Spanish control—by damming its harbor, and Amsterdam had become the commercial and financial capital of Europe.

The Dutch handled much of the grain trade of the Baltic and a large part of the carrying trade of England, France, Italy, and Portugal. When Philip II closed Lisbon to the Dutch—after seizing the Portuguese crown in 1580—the Dutch went directly to the source of spices in the Moluccas. In 1602 the Dutch East India Company was formed and was soon operating out of headquarters at Batavia on the island of Java. By the middle of the seventeenth century the Dutch had taken over Portugal's richest holdings in the East, and in 1652 they set up a colony at the Cape of Good Hope to serve as a way station on the route to Asia. A few decades earlier, they had almost ousted the Portuguese from Brazil and had founded the colony of New Amsterdam on Manhattan Island in the Hudson River (1624), which became the center for a large Dutch carrying trade in the New World. When the French and English began to develop their own overseas empires in the seventeenth century, they found the Dutch ahead of them wherever they went.

ELIZABETHAN ENGLAND

Elizabeth I (r. 1558–1603) was the last of the direct descendants of Henry VII Tudor

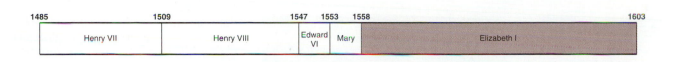

1485	1509	1547	1553	1558	1603
Henry VII	Henry VIII	Edward VI	Mary	Elizabeth I	

(r. 1485–1509; see p. 418). She was a cautious, reflective ruler whose instinct was to temporize and compromise. Although she could never submit to papal authority—the pope had declared the marriage of her mother, Anne Boleyn, to Henry VIII invalid—she followed a moderate religious policy and was conservative in matters of theology and liturgy.

Elizabeth temporized and compromised in foreign policy too. She tried to avoid committing herself, kept a dozen intrigues afoot to give herself an avenue of escape, and seems to have aimed at avoiding war at any cost. The chief foreign danger to the realm was the French influence over Scotland. Elizabeth's cousin, Mary Stuart, Queen of Scots, had married the heir to the French crown in 1558, and the alliance between the French and Scots promised to be troublesome.

But when the Scotsman John Knox returned from Geneva and began preaching Calvinism in 1559, he undermined the influence of Catholicism and the French. This time Elizabeth made a quick decision and allied herself with the Calvinist party in Scotland. By 1560, the Kirk (the Scottish church), the pro-English party, and Knox were in control, and the French had lost their foothold in Scotland.

In 1561, Mary Stuart returned to Scotland after the death of her husband, hoping to reestablish Catholicism along with her own authority. But she faced unbending opposition from Knox and the Kirk, and after a second marriage that turned out badly she was forced to abdicate in 1567. A year later Mary fled to England, where Elizabeth received her coolly but permitted her to stay. Mary soon became the center of French and Spanish plots against Elizabeth who kept a watch on her but refused to imprison or execute her. Then in 1587, when Elizabeth's ministers presented her with incontrovertible evidence of Mary's complicity in an assassination plot, Elizabeth reluctantly consented to Mary's execution.

The Conflict with Spain

Although there were many reasons for conflict between Spain and England—particularly English support of the Dutch—Philip II and Elizabeth I remained on good terms for more than twenty years. That stretch of tranquillity gave English industry and commerce a chance to expand and grow strong. When the inflationary spiral ruined Spanish industry, the English were ready to supply the Spanish colonies with manufactured goods. In 1562, an aggressive merchant named Sir John Hawkins was the first Englishman to carry goods from England and slaves from Africa directly to the Spanish settlements in the New World. The Spanish sought to prevent such direct traffic, which drew profit from their colonies and brought nothing to the mother country, and in 1569 Sir John and his cousin Sir Francis Drake were almost sunk by a Spanish fleet. In revenge, Drake seized that year's silver shipment from Peru to Spain. Then, from 1577 to 1580, he duplicated Magellan's voyage around the world, demonstrating the vulnerability of the Spanish Empire. Meanwhile, other English mariners probed the coasts of North America in search of a Northwest Passage that would outflank the Portuguese route to the East Indies.

It was the revolt of the Netherlands that finally broke the peace between Spain and England. For centuries, the English had had close commercial ties with the Low Countries; Flanders, for example, had long been the best customer for English wool and other goods. Moreover, Englishmen sympathized with their fellow Protestants in the United Provinces, and English privateers—the Sea Dogs—cooperated with the Sea Beggars, their Dutch counterparts, in disrupting Spanish shipping and communications. For their part, Philip II's ambassadors in England were deeply involved in plots against Elizabeth's life, one of which, as we have seen, led to the execution of Mary Stuart.

Elizabeth I of England, and her signature. The silver medal commemorates the defeat of the Spanish Armada.

The Armada

When the Spanish Armada challenged the ancient lords of the English on their own grounds, the impending conflict took on the aspect of a judicial duel in which as was expected in such duels, God would defend the right. . . . So when the two fleets approached their appointed battleground, all Europe watched. For the spectators of both parties, the outcome, reinforced, as everyone believed, by an extraordinary tempest, was indeed decisive. The Protestants of France and the Netherlands, Germany and Scandinavia saw with relief that God was, in truth, as they had always supposed, on their side. The Catholics of France and Italy and Germany saw with almost equal relief that Spain was not, after all, God's chosen champion. From that time forward, though Spain's preponderance was to last for more than another generation, the peak of her prestige had passed. . . . So, in spite of the long, indecisive war which followed, the defeat of the Spanish Armada really was decisive. It decided that religious unity was not to be reimposed by force on the heirs of medieval Christendom, and if, in doing so, it only validated what was already by far the most probable outcome, why, perhaps that is all that any of the battles we call decisive has ever done.

From Garrett Mattingly, The Spanish Armada *(Boston: Houghton Mifflin, 1959), pp. 400–01.*

Then in 1588 Philip decided to make a bold attempt on England itself. He assembled an enormous fleet, the so-called Invincible Armada, and sent it north to clear the English Channel and prepare the way for an invasion of England by the duke of Parma, who was engaged in operations against the Dutch. The English met the Armada with smaller, faster ships that could fire at longer range than the Spanish ships, and when the Armada anchored off Calais to await Parma, English fire ships caused panic among the Spaniards. The Armada fled north, and the English attacked again off Gravelines, scattering the Spanish ships. North Sea storms completed what the English had started, and fewer than half of the Armada's ships struggled home by sailing north and west around the British Isles.

The victory lifted the morale of Englishmen and Protestants everywhere. It ended the threat of a Spanish conquest of England and made it impossible for the Spanish to reconquer the United Provinces. When a peace was finally signed in 1604, the English and the Dutch met the Spaniards as near equals.

THE FRENCH WARS OF RELIGION

The rise of Spain and the relatively peaceful reign of Elizabeth I in England relied in part on the weakness of France, the largest and most populous nation in Europe. From 1562 to 1593 the French were embroiled in civil and religious strife that the monarchy was powerless to control.

Although France was the largest nation in Europe under a single monarch, it

The British fleet attack the Spanish Armada.

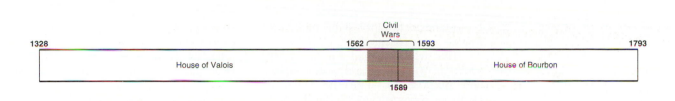

1328		1562	Civil Wars	1593		1793

House of Valois

House of Bourbon

1589

was less unified than either England or Spain. The aristocracy was still powerful, and the provinces still held on to their local customs and privileges. The divisiveness grew even more severe with the spread of Calvinism into France.

The French Calvinists—nicknamed the Huguenots (the origin of the name is unknown)—had about 2,500 churches. Huguenot congregations formed a small but well-organized and aggressive minority supported by people at the highest levels of French society. Arrayed against the Huguenots were the Catholic aristocracy, the University of Paris, and the Parlement (high court) of Paris. The monarchy itself was opposed to the spread of Calvinism, because it could not control the Protestant churches as it did the Catholic church under the Concordat of Bologna (1516).

After the death of King Henry II, husband of Mary Stuart of Scotland, in 1559, royal authority fell into the hands of the Queen Mother, Catherine de' Medici, who controlled the French government during the reigns of Henry's two weak brothers—Francis II (r. 1559–60) and Charles IX (r. 1560–74)—and during the reign of Henry's son Henry III (r. 1574–89). Catherine was an astute ruler, but she lacked formal authority and was powerless to prevent the religious fanatics—both Calvinist and Catholic—from making war on one another. Discontented nobles and the provinces sided with the Calvinists. The monarchy and most of the nobility sided with the Catholics. Both sides appealed for foreign support—the Huguenots to the English and Dutch, the Catholics to Spain. England and Spain actually sent troops, mostly at the beginning and the end of the wars.

The fighting was savage, and large areas of France were devastated. Though the Catholics won most of the battles, they could not destroy the Huguenots. In 1572 Catholic fanatics convinced Catherine that

they could put an end to the strife with one decisive blow. At two o'clock in the morning of St. Bartholomew's Day (August 23), armed bands of Catholics attacked and killed several Huguenot leaders who were in Paris for the wedding of the Huguenot Prince Henry of Navarre and the king's sister. The St. Bartholomew's Day Massacre touched off an explosion of violence that soon spread to other cities. Between late August and October, more than 10,000 Huguenots—3,000 in Paris alone—were murdered. The events intensified religious hatred in France and across Europe. Pope Gregory XIII and Philip II of Spain hailed the massacre as a milestone in the fight against

Religion and Patriotism

A Spanish ambassador reporting the words of a French Catholic in 1565:

Nowadays Catholic princes must not proceed as they once did. At one time friends and enemies were distinguished by the frontiers of provinces and kingdoms, and were called Italians, Germans, Frenchmen, Spaniards, Englishmen, and the like. Now we must say Catholics and heretics, and a Catholic prince must consider all Catholics of all countries as his friends, just as the heretics consider all heretics as friends and subjects whether they are their own vassals or not.

An English Protestant writing in 1589:

All dutiful subjects in this land desire with all their hearts the continuance of God's religion; the preservation of Queen Elizabeth; and the good success of the English navy. These particulars, I grant, are not expressed in flat in the Lord's Prayer; but they are contained within the compass of, and may be deduced from the petitions of that excellent prayer. Whosoever doubteth of this is void of learning.

As quoted in Erich Marks, Die Zusammenkunft von Bayonne (Strassburg: K. J. Trübner, 1889), p. 14; as quoted in Benjamin Hanbury, Historical Memorials Relating to the Independents (London: Congregational Union of England and Wales, 1839–44), Vol. I, p. 71.

Protestantism, but Protestants throughout Europe were horrified.

The wars dragged on for twenty years, growing more and more confused and purposeless, until the Huguenot Henry of Navarre came to the throne as Henry IV (r. 1589–1610). Although Henry was the nearest male heir to the crown, his relationship to Henry III was quite distant, and he had trouble making his claim stick. The Catholics took over Paris, and Spanish troops from the Netherlands moved into France led by the duke of Parma. After four years of fighting and maneuvering, Henry decided to renounce his Protestantism and become a Catholic, which he did in 1593. He did not, however, turn against his former co-religionists. Five years later he issued the Edict of Nantes, which granted the Huguenots freedom of conscience, freedom of worship, equal civil rights, and control of approximately 200 fortified towns. The Edict constituted the first official recognition that two religions could coexist within one nation.

The Effects of the Wars of Religion

In the world of Philip II and Elizabeth I, religion had a strong influence on political and social conflicts. The conflicts themselves grew out of economic changes that predated the Protestant Reformation, but religious convictions embittered every issue and made moderation impossible. Some monarchies that had been moving toward the consolidation of power—for example France and Germany—were weakened by the religious strife. Others— such as Spain and England—were strengthened. In Spain, Charles V and Philip II championed the cause of embattled Catholicism. In England, after Mary tried to reverse the reformation that grew out of the Act of Supremacy, Protestantism became associated with patriotism.

Just as the Great Schism in the Roman church (1378–1417) had motivated thinkers to devise a new constitutional theory of the church—conciliarism—so the wars of religion inspired new political theories. French theorists, for example, created a doctrine of political obligation that justified rebellion against constituted authority under certain conditions. And Protestants in Germany, the Netherlands, and France cited that doctrine to justify their rebellion against monarchs whom they accused of seeking to subject them to a false religion. After a generation of religious war, the French writer Jean Bodin (1530–96) developed a new, secular theory of political sovereignty that justified obedience to properly constituted authority without appeal to religious doctrine. That theory had a powerful influence on later political thought.

A less benign result of the religious paroxysm was a terrifying witch-craze in Europe that began in the mid-sixteenth century and lasted nearly a century. During the craze, thousands of people—mostly women—were burned at the stake or hanged as witches. The horror seems to have begun when the religious passions set off by the Protestant and Catholic Reformations got mixed up with ancient, pre-Christian superstitious beliefs and practices. Almost every community had its wizard and cunning woman to whom neighbors turned when the ministrations of priest or physician did not avail. From time to time during the Middle Ages, such women had been convicted of malevolent

Massacre of St. Bartholomew's Day, 1572 (detail from a painting by an eyewitness, François Dubois).

witchcraft—that is, of attempting to use occult means to inflict death or disease on others.

During the sixteenth century, the number of people accused of witchcraft increased dramatically. The accused were tortured into confessing the most fantastic acts—participating in obscene "witches' sabbaths" and creating diabolical schemes to harm their neighbors. Because they were also forced to name their accomplices in their pacts with the Devil, one arrest led to others. Often dozens, even hundreds, in a single community were burned at the stake.

By 1660 the craze was subsiding, and by 1700 it had all but disappeared as religious passions cooled and as toleration became the norm. Moreover, the rise of modern science led educated people to suspend belief in miracles, invisible spirits, and occult forces. The century-long witch-craze was one of the most tragic episodes in the history of Europe.

THE EUROPEAN WORLD IN THE LATE SIXTEENTH CENTURY

The Condition of the Peasants

Although we have been concentrating on urban life in the last two chapters, the vast majority of Europeans lived in the country during these years. By the end of the sixteenth century, significant changes had occurred in the economic and social condition of the peasants. In France and western Germany, the peasants' lot had improved. In Spain, eastern Germany, and other eastern European countries, it had deteriorated.

In most of western Europe, the disastrous plagues of the fourteenth century had undermined the old feudal system whereby peasants were obliged to perform services for their lords. As a result, life in the villages and regular cultivation of the fields broke down. When conditions began to improve in the fifteenth century, landholders granted favorable terms to the peasants to induce them to return to the fields. Some of the landholders had been ruined by the plagues and

Illumination from a Book of Hours (Flemish, *ca.* 1500) shows peasants harvesting grain.

had sold their land to their own peasants. By the late sixteenth century about 5 percent of the peasants in France and western Germany owned their own land, and another 5 percent remained bound in serfdom. The rest of them leased the land they worked. Increasingly, however, the law permitted them to sell or grant their rights in the properties they leased.

In 1480, the king of Castile released all peasants from serfdom and gave them proprietary rights in their land. But within a couple of generations the royal government was encouraging the importation of cheap grain, and the Castilian peasants derived little benefit from their emancipation. The peasants of Aragon, who had not been released from serfdom, also suffered under the government's policy. By the late sixteenth century, peasants throughout Spain were caught up in a serious economic depression.

When the condition of the peasants in Europe finally began to improve, the condition of the eastern peasants continued to sink lower and lower. In northeastern Germany, for example, a region of large estates with access to rivers to carry crops to market, the landholders imposed full-fledged serfdom on their peasants in the late sixteenth century. In Russia, Tsar Ivan the Terrible (r. 1533–84) rewarded his noblemen for service to the state by granting them large estates with the right to force the peasants into serfdom (see p. 345).

Urban Life in the Sixteenth Century

As far back as the twelfth century, the towns and cities of Europe had begun to achieve virtual independence through charters granted by kings and emperors. The charters freed them from the control of the feudal lords and gave them the right to govern themselves. By the sixteenth century, the cities had become independent in both political and economic matters, and their influence was felt throughout Europe.

One historian has compared citizenship in the early modern city to membership in a club. Every aspect of life was regulated by special associations under the control of the city council. Craft guilds and religious fraternities governed the lives of their members and provided social security.

Pieter Bruegel's *Children's Games.*

A young man could expect to be elected to a lower office in his guild about six years after becoming a master and to a higher office after another eight years. The principal officers of the major guilds were almost assured of an important position in the city government.

Most cities had religious confraternities or brotherhoods that cut across membership in the various guilds. These organizations were responsible for staging city-wide festivals in cooperation with the guilds, and the fact that men from all walks of life participated in these events helped reduce the potential for conflict among the guilds. Officeholders in a brotherhood often moved to positions in the city government.

Cities were usually divided into wards to facilitate the conduct of government. Each ward was responsible for ensuring security within its boundaries and for providing a certain number of men for the city militia. The wards also furnished men to stand night watch on the city walls and at the gates. Although some wards were dominated by one of the guilds (for example, butchers and tanners usually settled along a river), in most neighborhoods the population was quite mixed, with the rich living alongside the poor. About a fifth of the urban population, more in large cities, consisted of day laborers and other poor people who were not members of any guild. They did, however, have acknowledged status in their ward.

Usually the city gates were opened at 4 A.M. and closed at 8 P.M., about an hour after the workday ended. During the night a curfew was imposed on the city to discourage crime and keep the peace. Saturday was payday, when workers got off early, and Sunday was a day of rest. *Children's Games*, painted by the Flemish artist Pieter Bruegel the Elder (*ca.* 1525–69), suggests what a typical Sunday may have been like in a sixteenth-century city.

Because men did not marry until they had set themselves up as substantial citizens, there were usually many young men about town. Rape, including group rape, was common, and the authorities were always on the watch for such offenses. The larger cities usually had a public brothel in which the women were licensed. Even prostitutes who worked the streets were licensed and wore badges to prove it. The public bathhouse was another place where young upper-class men could find prostitutes.

In many cities young men's associations patterned themselves on the religious brotherhoods, though their purpose was anything but religious. The members amused themselves at the expense of the "establishment," and their officers bore such titles as Prince of Youth and Abbot of Fools.

Women played an important role in the sixteenth-century city not only as wives but as craftspeople and merchants. Their principal role was as wife and mother, but a craftsman could not function—indeed, some guilds would not permit him to function—without a wife. She raised the apprentices and often ran the shop where the master's products were sold. Although the guilds guarded their craft secrets jealously, members were permitted to share them with their wives.

Many women also participated in the commercial life of the cities. They engaged in silk weaving, retailing, and brewing and often functioned as agents for foreign merchants. They were accorded no role in city government, however, or in other public business.

ART, LITERATURE, AND SCIENCE

Art

Renaissance art reached its zenith in the first two decades of the century with the memorable accomplishments of Leonardo da Vinci (1452–1519), Raphael (1483–1520), Albrecht Dürer (1471–1528), and Michelangelo (1475–1564). In the last years of his life, Dürer, influenced by Luther's view that the style and subject matter of the Renaissance were too pagan, simplified his work and concentrated on biblical scenes. In the next generation, the German painter Hans Holbein the Younger (1497–1543) was a talented portraitist who traveled to Switzerland and England to execute commissions. He settled in England as a court painter and created portraits of Henry VIII, Thomas More, and other prominent figures.

Michelangelo also abandoned the high Renaissance style after 1520 and developed a new style that departed from the serenity of his early work. For example, his ceiling frescos in the Sistine Chapel, painted around 1510, are organized in carefully planned panels with figures reminiscent of the classical sculpture that inspired the Renaissance, and the Genesis story is represented in a series of static images. By contrast, his wall fresco of the Last Judgment in the same chapel, painted during the 1530s, is a crowded scene of twisted bodies in which the action of condemnation and salvation of souls is captured in dynamic fashion. In sculpture, too, Michelangelo proceeded from observance of the classical ideals of the Renaissance, through a rebellion against proportion and graceful lines, to the creation of tortured shapes of great emotional power.

Some artists, like the Venetian painter Titian (*ca.* 1477–1576), continued to work in the Renaissance style. Others favored a new style known as Mannerism, because they painted in the manner of (the late) Michelangelo. Two of the most notable Mannerists were Tintoretto (1518–94) and El Greco (*ca.* 1548–1614). Tintoretto was a Venetian who tried to combine the style of Titian with the late style of Michelangelo. He painted scenes of saints and miracles and executed some large wall paintings. His works convey a sense of movement and action, similar to that of Michelangelo's Last Judgment. El Greco (Domenicos Theotocopoulos, born on the island of Crete) studied in Venice and Rome and eventually settled in Spain, where he hoped to become a court painter. But Philip II favored the work of second-rate Spanish Mannerists, and El Greco (as the Spaniards nicknamed him) never found favor in Madrid, Philip's new capital. El Greco was a highly original artist who paintings exude a strong mystical aura and whole sparse, elongated figures project great tension and strength.

The Flemish artist Hieronymus Bosch (*ca.* 1450–1516) painted dark, foreboding

Virgin with Sts. Ines and Tecla, by El Greco.

showing agricultural labors appropriate to each month of the year. In his few religious paintings, such as the "Slaughter of the Innocents," he depicts the moment before the crucial scene occurs, so that the viewer is caught up in suspense. His son Pieter also painted scenes of peasant life, along with works depicting hell, and Jan favored landscapes and still lifes. Members of the Bruegel family were still painting well into the eighteenth century.

Literature

In literature, the sixteenth century was the great age of drama. Medieval drama evolved from the religious festivals at which the guilds staged plays dealing with the lives and miracles of the saints. University students too had been putting on plays since the thirteenth century. At first their plays were based on the stories of biblical figures, such as Daniel and Herod. But during the fifteenth and early sixteenth centuries the students turned to secular dramas fashioned on Roman models and intended for educated audiences. The great age of theater began in the 1570s when actors and playwrights in England and Spain formed professional companies that played to the general public.

In London, several companies were founded in the 1570s, and two playwrights attracted an enthusiastic following Thomas Kyd (1558–94) and Christopher Marlowe (1564–93). Kyd's *Spanish Tragedy* and Marlowe's *Tamburlaine* were the first popular successes of the English stage. Kyd's play, about a father who exacts revenge for his son's death, established revenge as a favorite theme of English tragedy. Marlowe's plays are dominated by powerful, romantic figures who control the action. He was the first playwright to use blank verse in dramatic writing.

It was Marlowe's contemporary, William Shakespeare (1564–1616), who emerged as the greatest English poet and dramatist. Shakespeare wrote his plays for a company of twenty or so actors, the Lord Chamberlain's Company (later called the King's Company), that continued to perform for more than two decades. Theater

works on religious themes that exaggerate the physicality of human life. Modern scholars have discovered in them a complex, visual language that reflects Bosch's mystical view of the world. The Bruegels—Pieter the Elder (*ca.* 1525–69), Pieter the Younger (1564–1637), and Jan (1568–1625)—preferred to paint scenes from everyday life. Pieter the Elder favored rural scenes, including a series

companies were expected to present a play six afternoons a week throughout the year and consequently had to keep about fifty plays in their repertory. Shakespeare must have written many plays that were never published, because he considered them the property of his company. Eighteen of them, however, were published in illegal editions during his lifetime. After his death, his friends published his surviving manuscripts in a folio volume in 1623. The first edition of Shakespeare's work contained 36 plays; since then scholars have added another, *Pericles*, on the likelihood that some of the scenes in it were written by Shakespeare. The plays consist of tragedies (*Hamlet* and *King Lear*), comedies (*Taming of the Shrew* and *As You Like It*), and histories (*Richard III* and *Henry V*). Shakespeare took his themes from classical and English history and from Italian works, which had become popular in England early in the sixteenth century.

The typical theater of Shakespeare's London was a large, round building without a roof that could hold as many as 3,000 people. In Shakespeare's Globe Theatre, the audience stood in the pit below the stage or in the boxes along the walls. Admission to the pit cost only a penny or two, which meant that watching a play was one of the most inexpensive pastimes in the city. Admission to the boxes cost much more.

There were smaller theaters as well, such as Blackfriars, where Shakespeare's company also performed. These were rectangular buildings that could hold only a few hundred people. Admission to these theaters was more expensive than admission to open theaters, and the plays written for them appealed to a more sophisticated audience. It is estimated that English playwrights wrote more than 6,000 plays between 1580 and 1640, about 2,000 of which have survived.

In Spain, the theater became popular soon after the middle of the century and, as in England, experienced a great increase in popularity during the 1570s. Spanish plays combined dramatic scenes with interludes of dance and musical entertainment. Unlike the English companies, the Spanish companies employed women as entertainers and actresses. The Spanish playwright Lope de Vega (1562–1632) wrote about 1,500 *comedias*, of which 500 have survived. In writing this stupendous number of plays he used only a few plot lines, but he achieved spectacular fame and great success.

By contrast, the greatest literary figure of sixteenth-century Spain, Miguel de Cervantes (1547–1616), led a life of hardship and penury. He began writing plays in the early 1560s, but after getting into trouble with the law he ran off to Rome. There he enlisted in the navy that Philip II was forming to fight the Turks, and he distinguished himself at the Battle of Lepanto (1571; see p. 459). In 1575, while on his way back to Spain to seek an officer's commission, he was captured and enslaved by the Turks of Algiers, and for the next five years he repeatedly tried to escape while his family tried to raise a ransom. Finally freed, he returned to Spain and took a job in the royal bureaucracy in Seville. Accounting was not his strong suit, however, and he was constantly in trouble with his superiors. He left the royal service in 1600.

While still working at his job in Seville, Cervantes began to write again and won first prize for poetry in a contest held in Zaragoza in 1595. After leaving government service, he spent three years writing a great satire on the chivalric romances that had become phenomenally popular in Spain. This work, *Don Quixote*, which recounts adventures of a knight and his squire, became immediately popular. Philip III (r. 1598–1621), observing a young man convulsed with laughter over a book, is said to have remarked that the young man was either crazy or was reading *Don Quixote*. The work was first translated into English in 1612 and has been translated into more languages than any other book except the Bible. Toward the end of his life, Cervantes published the first short stories to be written in Spanish, in a work titled *Twelve Exemplary Novelas* (1613).

Although theater did not become popular in France until the seventeenth century, French writers of the sixteenth century contributed to the foundations

A contemporary drawing (1596) of the Swan Theatre in London.

of modern literature. Michel Montaigne (1533–92), a French nobleman educated as a humanist, created the genre of the essay after retiring from the royal court in disgust over the fanaticism engendered by the wars between the Huguenots and the Catholics. In his *Essays,* Montaigne explored human nature in a manner both witty and wise.

Science

During the sixteenth century Nicholas Copernicus (1473–1543), Tycho Brahe (1546–1601), Johannes Kepler (1571–1630), and Galileo Galilei (1564–1642) combined theory with experimentation and observation to transform the medieval world view. Copernicus, who was educated at the universities of Padua and Cracow, spent most of his adult life in a monastery in Prussia trying to resolve the discrepancy between the observed movement of the planets and the Ptolemaic view that the planets and the sun orbit the earth. Eventually, in a work published the year of his death, he proposed that the earth and the other planets circle the sun.

Copernicus's heliocentric theory did not gain wide acceptance until late in the century. In fact, the Danish astronomer Tycho Brahe made careful observations of the movement of the planets in an effort to demonstrate the validity of the Ptolemaic view. Instead, they led him to the conclusion that Copernicus was right and that the discrepancy between the observed movements and the Ptolemaic theory was even greater than Copernicus had thought.

Copernicus had still subscribed to the ancient view that the planets move in circular orbits. Brahe's observations were not entirely consistent with that view, however, and his assistant, Johannes Kepler, eventually demonstrated that the planets follow elliptical orbits and provided a mathematical explanation for their movement.

Galileo, a professor at the University of Padua, confirmed Copernicus's theory by using a telescope he built after hearing about a spyglass that had been invented in Holland. The telescope, which magnified objects thirty times, enabled him to make many revolutionary discoveries. He was the first to observe the mountains on the moon, the rings of Saturn, and the components of the Milky Way. He also provided mathematical explanations of the movement of physical objects and described the behavior of the pendulum in clocks. In his most famous experiment he dropped objects of different weights from the leaning tower of Pisa to show that all objects fall with the same rate of acceleration and then devised a mathematical formula for the universal rate of acceleration of falling objects. Galileo once remarked, "The book of nature . . . is written in mathematical characters."

In Chapter 21, we will deal with the scientific revolution of the sixteenth century in greater detail.

Suggestions for Further Reading

Geographical Discovery

For a detailed account of the geographical discoveries of the fifteenth and sixteenth centuries, see J. H. Parry, *The Age of Reconnaisance* (1963). For the technological basis of the explorations, see C. Cipolla, *Guns and Sails in the Early Phase of the European Expansion* (1966). For the Mediterranean background of oceanic navigation, see M. E. Mallet, *Florentine Galleys of the Fifteenth Century* (1967), and F. C. Lane, *Venetian Ships and Shipbuilders of the Renaissance* (1934).

Effects on Europe

On the effect of the discoveries on Europe, see J. H. Elliott, *The Old World and the New* (1970). H. H. Hart, *The Road to the Indies* (1950), describes the Portuguese expeditions; J. B. Brebner, *The Explorers of North America, 1492–1806* (1933), and A. P. Newton, *The European Nations in the West Indies, 1493–1688* (1933), treat exploration in particular areas. The best account of Columbus is S. E. Morrison, *Admiral of the Ocean Sea*, 2 vols. (1942). For an overall view, see Morrison's

The European Discovery of America (1971). For good histories of the early Spanish colonies, see C. H. Haring, *The Spanish Empire in America* (1947); L. Hanke, *The Spanish Struggle for Justice in the Conquest of America* (1949); and R. Cameron, *Viceroyalties of the West* (1968).

Spain

On Spain in the sixteenth century, J. H. Elliott, *Imperial Spain, 1469–1716* (1964), is excellent. R. T. Davies, *The Golden Century of Spain, 1501–1621* (1937) and *Spain in Decline, 1621–1700* (1956), are sometimes controversial but good accounts. For the effect of imperialism on Spanish government, see J. H. Parry, *The Spanish Theory of Empire in the Sixteenth Century* (1940). E. J. Hamilton, *American Treasure and the Price Revolution, 1501–1650* (1934), is the starting point for studies of the economic effects of empire. See also C. Cipolla, *Money, Prices and Civilization in the Mediterranean World* (1967). The classic work on the Armada is G. Mattingly, *The Spanish Armada* (1959). F. Braudel, *The Mediterranean and the Mediterranean World in the Age of Philip II*, 2 vols. (1972–73), is a masterpiece.

The Netherlands

The best history of the Dutch rebellion is P. Geyl, *The Revolt of the Netherlands, 1555–1609* (1932) and *The Netherlands Divided, 1609–1648* (1936). For a well-written biography of William the Silent, see C. V. Wedgewood, *William the Silent* (1944), and on the English involvement in the rebellion, see C. Wilson, *Queen Elizabeth and the Revolt of the Netherlands* (1970).

Elizabethan England

There is a wealth of good scholarly books on Elizabethan England. See J. Neale, *Queen Elizabeth I* (1952). C. Read's thorough biographies, *Mr. Secretary Walsingham,* 3 vols. (1925), and *Mr. Secretary Cecil* (Lord Burghley), 2 vols. (1955, 1960), provide detailed information about the politics of the period. For a social history, see A. L. Rowse, *The England of Elizabeth* (1950) and *The Expansion of Elizabethan England* (1955). On the English explorations, see J. A. Williamson, *The Age of Drake,* 3rd ed. (1952).

France

There is not much work in English on sixteenth-century France. J. W. Salmon, *Society in Crisis: France in the Sixteenth Century* (1975), is the best general treatment. J. E. Neale, *The Age of Catherine de' Medici* (1943), and H. Pearson, *Henry of Navarre* (1963), are useful. On the government, see N. M. Sutherland, *The French Secretaries of State in the Age of Catherine de Medici* (1962). J. W. Thompson, *The Wars of Religion in France, 1559–1576* (1909), is still useful. For brief scholarly accounts, see F. C. Palm, *Calvinism and the Religious Wars* (1932), and A. J. Grant, *The Huguenots* (1934). On the development of French political thought during the civil wars, see W. F. Church, *Constitutional Thought in Sixteenth Century France* (1941).

Social History

On rural life in the sixteenth century, see E. Le Roy Ladurie, *The Peasants of Languedoc* (1974), and M. R. Weisser, *The Peasants of the Montes* (1976). N. Z. Davis covers various aspects of French social history in a series of essays in *Society and Culture in Early Modern France* (1975). See also L. Febvre, *Life in Renaissance France* (1979). G. Huppert, *After the Black Death: A Social History of Early Modern Europe* (1986), concentrates on urban society. There are several excellent studies of individual cities. See G. Strauss, *Nuremburg in the Sixteenth Century* (1976); C. R. Friedrichs, *Urban Society in an Age of War: Nördlingen, 1580–1720* (1979); and C. Pythian-Adams, *Desolation of a City* (1979), concerning Coventry, England. On urban women, see M. C. Howell, *Women, Production, and Patriarchy in Late Medieval Cities* (1986).

Art and Literature

On the art of the sixteenth century, see W. Friedländer, *Mannerism and Anti-Mannerism in Italian Painting* (1957). The works of Marlowe, Shakespeare, Lope de Vega, Cervantes, and Montaigne are available in numerous modern editions.

19

POLITICAL AND ECONOMIC CRISES: THE SEVENTEENTH CENTURY

The seventeenth century was the century in which modern European civilization took on recognizable form. Political, social, and economic upheavals almost as dangerous as those that had shaken medieval civilization in the fourteenth century convulsed Europe. In the 1640s, great rebellions weakened England, France, and Spain, the three most powerful European monarchies. The last wars of religion merged with wars to expand commerce or to overthrow or preserve the balance of power. Weather, famine, and plague compounded the ravages of war. In Germany and Spain, the Thirty Years' War (1618–48) and plague epidemics actually forced the population downward. Prolonged economic depression marked the middle decades of the century. Harvests repeatedly failed. Starvation and disease followed. The flow of silver from the New World that had stimulated the European economy dropped off sharply. After 1670, growth turned upward again, but only gradually. Poverty sharpened social unrest and inadequate revenues limited state power.

That unpromising environment nevertheless gave birth to a new Europe that was richer, controlled more of the world's commerce, and had more effective government in 1700 than in 1600. The troubles of the fourteenth century and the religious conflicts of the sixteenth century had slowed the process of building the sovereign territorial state begun in the thirteenth century. But it now proceeded rapidly. In the realm of theory, state-building required defining the concept of sovereignty. In the realm of practice, it meant concentrating supreme power in some organ of the state. And Europe simultaneously underwent an intellectual revolution, a sharp change in conceptions about humanity and the universe far deeper and broader in its consequences than the Italian Renaissance (see pp. 408–11).

FRANCE'S SEARCH FOR ORDER AND AUTHORITY, 1598–1661

The anarchy and religious violence that lasted from 1562 to the Edict of Nantes in 1598 deeply marked seventeenth-century France. Three feeble kings had allowed the unruly great nobles to challenge the monarchy. Civil wars had torn the fabric of trade that linked the merchants and manufacturers of the towns. The wanderings of ragged, undisciplined armies had savaged the peasantry. The population longed for security despite a continuing suspicion of any authority that might attack local privileges or increase taxes.

The lawyer Jean Bodin (*ca.* 1530–96), the most penetrating political thinker of the tragic years of the Wars of Religion, offered a theory that spoke to the universal yearning for order. Bodin's *The Republic*

(1576) argued that a well-ordered state must give supreme power—sovereignty—to some organ of the state, preferably the monarchy. Bodin defined sovereignty as the essential characteristic of the state: the power of "giving laws to the people as a whole without their consent."

The laws of God and nature still bound Bodin's sovereign. But Bodin insisted that no human agency must limit the sovereign. Power must be "absolute," not divided, to be effective. Neither *parlements* (the highest French law courts) nor the Estates General should veto or modify decisions of the sovereign.

Bodin defined sovereignty far more clearly than previous theorists. He persuasively presented it as the only alternative to insecurity and civil war. The French absolute monarchy of the seventeenth century appeared to fulfill Bodin's prescription and became the model and envy of many of Europe's rulers.

Henry IV and Sully: Order Restored

Henry IV (r. 1589–1610), ex-Huguenot and victorious founder of the Bourbon dynasty, began the process of restoring royal power and French prosperity. He was a popular king—courageous, vigorous, humorous, tolerant, and sound in his judgment of subordinates. But he spent much time in pursuit of game and women and happily left the routine business of government to his chief minister, Maximilien de Sully, an austere ex-Huguenot artillery officer. Sully restored the monarchy's solvency by canceling some debts, avoiding expensive foreign wars, and patching up the inefficient, corrupt, and inequitable tax system.

The monarchy, like most early modern governments, "farmed" its taxes—that is, it granted the right to collect taxes to private contractors who paid the government a fixed sum and then extracted all they could from the population. The tax burden fell most heavily on the peasants, because nobles and the upper classes in the towns were exempt from major taxes. The nobility opposed attempts to redistribute the tax burden and helped to bring

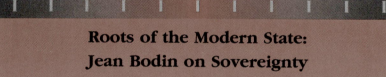

Roots of the Modern State: Jean Bodin on Sovereignty

Political thinkers had recognized the fact *of sovereignty for some time, but Bodin was the first to express the* idea *in clear and uncompromising terms.*

Sovereignty is supreme power over citizens and subjects unrestrained by laws. . . . A prince is bound by no law of his predecessor, and much less by his own laws. . . . He may repeal, modify, or replace a law made by himself and without the consent of his subjects. . . . The opinion of those who have written that the king is bound by the popular will must be disregarded; such doctrine furnishes seditious men with material for revolutionary plots. No reasonable ground can be found to claim that subjects should control princes or that power should be attributed to popular assemblies. . . . The highest privilege of sovereignty consists in giving laws to the people as a whole without their consent. . . . Under this supreme power of making and repealing laws it is clear that all other functions of sovereignty are included.

From Jean Bodin, Six Books Concerning the Republic, *from the Latin version of 1586, trans. by F. W. Coker, in* Readings in Political Philosophy *(New York: Macmillan, 1938), pp. 374–77, 380.*

Triumphal Entry of Henry IV into Paris, a large sketch by the great Peter Paul Rubens (*ca.* 1630).

The great cardinal: Richelieu, founder of the modern French state, painted by Philippe de Champaigne.

down the French monarchy in 1788–89 over that very issue (see pp. 584–85). Sully nevertheless did improve the system he inherited by attacking the crooked and inefficient tax farmers who as a rule pocketed as much as half the taxes collected before they reached the treasury. The reestablishment of internal order allowed agriculture and commerce to recover and increased the government's revenues, especially from customs duties. By the time a Catholic fanatic assassinated Henry IV in 1610, France's treasury contained a sizable surplus.

Richelieu and the Consolidation of the Monarchy, 1610–42

A few years of weakness at the center reduced the work of Henry IV and Sully to ruins. The regency of Henry's widow, Marie de' Medici, allowed rapacious courtiers the run of the treasury and permitted Spain to intervene once more in French affairs, sometimes in bizarre alliance with the Huguenots. Incompetence soon dissipated the financial surplus Sully had left and led in 1614 to a summoning of the Estates General of France to one of its rare meetings. But the deliberations of the Estates General soon produced deadlock over taxation and religious issues between the First and Second Estates (the clergy and the nobility) and the Third Estate (the middle classes of the towns, represented largely by provincial royal officers). The Estates General dissolved inconclusively, and did not meet again until 1789, on the eve of the French Revolution.

Fortunately for the monarchy, a minister far more powerful than Sully soon emerged. Henry IV's son, Louis XIII (r. 1614–43), assumed the throne and in 1624 appointed a brilliant young cardinal, Armand Jean du Plessis de Richelieu (1585–1642), as chief of the king's council. From then until his death Richelieu was the real ruler of France. The great Cardinal, rather than any member of the Bourbon dynasty, founded the French absolute monarchy.

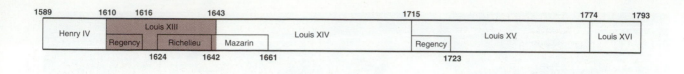

Richelieu had the clearest and most penetrating mind of any statesman of his generation as well as a largely deserved reputation for diabolical cleverness. He sought to establish beyond challenge the power and prestige of the French monarchy. He came to his task with a startling grasp of political and diplomatic possibilities, an infallible memory, and an inflexible will unconstrained by moral scruple. Richelieu admired Machiavelli (see pp. 412–14), and the heart of the Cardinal's political creed was *raison d'état,* "reason of state": the good of the state was the supreme good. That good justified the use of any means whatsoever—a stern creed that Richelieu nearly reconciled with his own religious conscience. He deemed it "essential to banish pity" when judging "crimes against the state," for mercy in the present only led to greater bloodshed in the future. He coolly sent innocent men to their death to terrify troublemakers. When Louis XIII expressed moral qualms, Richelieu beat the king's objections down with brutal frankness: "Man is immortal; his salvation is hereafter; the state has no immortality, its salvation is now or never."

Richelieu pursued four objectives: he sought to destroy the power of the Huguenots, crush the great nobles, exclude the Habsburgs from French internal politics, and decide in France's favor the Bourbon–Habsburg rivalry abroad that dated from the sixteenth century. The Edict of Nantes, the compromise of 1598 that ended the religious civil wars, had allowed the Huguenots to garrison about 200 towns. Richelieu persuaded Louis XIII that he would never be master in his own house until he had wiped out this "state within a state." A monopoly of force within its borders, then as now, was the essential characteristic of statehood.

Rumors that the government had decided to attack them provoked the Huguenots to rebel. Richelieu besieged and captured their chief stronghold at La Rochelle on the Atlantic coast. Despite his contempt for what he described as the "pretended Reformed religion," he nevertheless allowed the Huguenots to worship as they pleased once he had destroyed their political and military autonomy. He sought to conciliate Protestants abroad who might help him in war with Spain and Austria, and he hoped to make dependable citizens of the Huguenots. In that he was successful. The Huguenots served the crown in the war of 1635–59 against the Habsburgs and remained loyal in the great domestic crisis of the Fronde (see next section) that followed Richelieu's death.

Richelieu's attack on the nobility was less successful. Noble plotting threatened him until the end of his career. In response, he developed networks of spies, created a special tribunal to try noble lawbreakers, and sternly forbade duelling, a privilege that symbolized the nobility's freedom from ordinary restraints. The great nobles who had governed provinces almost by hereditary right gradually lost their powers to appointees of the crown called *intendants.* These temporary appointees came not from the old "nobility of the sword" but from the commons or the *noblesse de robe,* who were ennobled judicial officeholders of middle-class ancestry who had bought their offices from the crown. The economic and social privileges of the nobility survived Richelieu, but he curtailed its political power.

Richelieu was no financier and was no more interested in bettering the condition of the common people than were the rulers of other early modern states. He spent large sums to rebuild the armed forces and even more in wars against the Spanish and Austrian Habsburgs, Bourbon France's chief rivals for the leadership of Europe. He left the state's finances and the peasantry that supported those finances in worse condition than he had found them. But his subtle diplomacy and well-timed intervention in the Thirty Years' War (see pp. 489–91) made France instead of Spain the leading European power.

At his death in 1642, Richelieu left behind him the most powerful state in Europe. His success in establishing relative peace within France's own borders made economic growth possible, and France's steadily increasing power made Richelieu's creation the model for royal absolutism throughout the continent.

Mazarin, the Fronde, and the Coming of Louis XIV

Richelieu's death and that of Louis XIII in 1643 put the great Cardinal's work to a severe test. Louis XIV was a child of five when his father died, and his mother, Anne of Austria, became regent. She left the business of government to the man whom Richelieu had trained as his successor, the Italian Cardinal Giulio Mazzarini (1602–61), known in France as Mazarin.

Mazarin lacked his former master's relentless will and self-confidence. He sought to continue the war against Spain until the defeat of the Habsburgs, and to maintain the prestige of the monarchy that Richelieu had restored. But the nobility despised Mazarin as a foreign upstart, and the urban middle classes hated him for the high taxes that war demanded. The result was a movement known as the Fronde, the most serious rebellion against the monarchy before the Revolution of 1789.

The word *fronde* referred to a game of the unruly children of Paris, who threw dirt at passing coaches. The rebellion coincided with a period of severe harvest failures and lasted from 1648 to 1652. Like the children's game, it was annoying, but it ultimately failed to deflect the monarchy from its path. The Fronde's leaders were the judges of the *parlements,* or high courts; the chief financial officers who owned their offices and were thus heredi-

tary bureaucrats; and the nobility under the guidance of princes of the royal family. Each group hoped merely to increase its own influence, not destroy the French monarchy or upset the established social order.

They also failed to agree on a joint program beyond the purely negative policy of exiling Mazarin. The *parlements,* which began the struggle, stood for the privileges of the bureaucrats who controlled the courts and the ramshackle tax machinery. They wanted the king to rule with their advice rather than through councilors whom he could make or break at his pleasure. They insisted especially that he impose no tax without their consent. The nobles, who joined the rebellion later, had no intention of letting the *parlements* become dominant. They instead sought to abolish the upstart *intendants* and regain their old powers as provincial governors.

The result might have been different had any group dared to mobilize fully the deep-seated resentment of the lower classes—a resentment expressed throughout the century in urban riots and peasant rebellions against taxes and government. A few theorists, especially Huguenots, had argued that subjects possessed a "right of resistance" to unjust authority. But unlike the contemporary English rebellion, which asserted that right by defeating the king, the groups that led the Fronde were unwilling to unleash forces from below that might prove uncontrollable. Their conservatism, combined with the disunity of the rebels, eventually led to the Fronde's collapse.

Mazarin fled the country in 1651 and again in 1652–53 but returned to the saddle without difficulty, thanks to the support of Anne of Austria. By 1659, he had achieved victory over Spain. France gained two counties in the Pyrenees and the daughter of Philip IV of Spain as a bride for the young Louis XIV. That outcome symbolized the humiliation of Spain and the triumph of France as the leading power in Europe. The young king profited both from widespread revulsion against the disorders of the Fronde and from the prestige of foreign victories.

Cardinal Mazarin.

Fighting in Paris during the Fronde, 1648.

The morning after Mazarin's death in March 1661, Louis XIV announced to his ministers that he would henceforth be his own first minister. Richelieu had triumphed at last. The French monarchy had outlasted Huguenots and Fronde at home and Habsburgs abroad. Louis XIV henceforth ruled as an absolute monarch, endowed with a fuller sovereignty than any yet seen in the western Europe.

ENGLAND: IN SEARCH OF CIVIL AND RELIGIOUS LIBERTY, 1603–60

While Richelieu and Mazarin laid the foundations of absolute monarchy by divine right in France, England was slowly developing a constitutional, parliamentary system. The English groped toward a conception of sovereignty rooted in law and lodged in the hands of an assembly that represented the community—or at least its more wealthy and influential members. England was not alone in its resistance to absolute monarchy, but the result elsewhere tended to be anarchy and confusion as in Poland, or the victory of the crown as in France. In the end, the English example prevailed over absolutism. The "mother of parliaments" in London ultimately inspired parliamentary government in England's colonies and across modern Europe. But the road to constitutional monarchy in England was hard. It led through civil war and the execution of a king.

The Tudors: Crown and Parliament

England had always been peculiar. The strong monarchy of the Tudors (1485–1603) was part of a general European trend, but the survival and strengthening of Parliament under such a monarchy had no parallel elsewhere. While rulers on the Continent sought to abolish representative assemblies, the Tudors grudgingly used Parliament to legitimate laws and taxes. In the delicate area of religion, the Tudors found Parliament indispensable. Henry VIII had aspired to rule as an autocrat but had needed Parliament to break with Rome. Mary had asked Parliament to restore England to the Roman Church by statute. Elizabeth I had by statute once more broken with the Pope.

Elizabeth quarreled with her Parliaments, but the threat from Spain and the political good sense of both the queen and the parliamentary leaders had prevented a break. Both parties tacitly recognized that only Parliament could make a law or impose a tax. Parliament in turn recognized that making policy, especially foreign policy, lay within the sphere of "royal prerogative." Elizabeth's Parliaments tried more than once to reform the Anglican Church in a Puritan direction and to nudge the queen on foreign policy—presumptuous acts for which Elizabeth scolded them sharply. But she was too popular for Parliament to challenge her directly and too astute to demand a clear definition of her prerogative.

Under the Tudors, Parliament acquired a corporate feeling and a sense of being an integral part of government. The absence of provincial estates or privileges like those in France further increased its power. By the sixteenth century the lower house, called the House of Commons (see p. 363), represented both the landed gentry of the countryside and the richer merchants of the towns. The gentry also governed England at the local level as justices of the peace, for the English monarchy had failed to develop paid bureaucrats like the French *intendants*.

England was peculiar socially as well as politically. It lacked the Continent's rigid legal boundaries between social "orders." The gentry—baronets, knights, esquires, and simple "gentlemen"—were all commoners in the eyes of the law. Unlike its French counterpart, England's titled nobility was minuscule in numbers, a mere 121 English peers in 1641. The gentry included the younger sons of the nobility, who received neither land nor title thanks to the system of primogeniture that preserved noble estates by passing them in their entirety to the eldest son. Noble younger sons thus linked nobility and gentry; many pursued middle-class careers in the law or even commerce. At the same time, English merchants continually moved upward into the gentry by buying land. English society was hierarchical, but less so than continental societies. The comparative unity of England's gentry and nobility made the Parliament that represented them uniquely self-confident. That self-confidence was one source of the fateful clash between Crown and Parliament.

James I: Crown against Parliament

The Tudors had long ago put a stop to private wars waged by the high nobility. Under Elizabeth I, foreign and domestic

A formal meeting of Parliament in 1625. The Lords are seated; the Commons stand outside the bar.

1485		1603	1642	1660		1714
	House of Tudor		House of Stuart	Civil War and Republican Experiments	House of Stuart	

peril had rallied the Commons to the monarchy. But peace with Spain in 1604 and Europe's growing absorption in the Thirty Years' War after 1618 (see below) eliminated the danger of foreign invasion. The absence of threats inevitably lessened the authority of the Stuart family that succeeded Elizabeth, who was childless, in 1603.

James I (King of Scotland and of England, r. 1603–25) was the son of Mary, Queen of Scots. Well-meaning but pedantic, he failed to understand the political realities of the kingdom he had inherited from Elizabeth. The regents who ran Scotland after his mother's exile had raised him as a Protestant, but he had not relished that grim Presbyterian upbringing. His aims were entirely reasonable; he sought peace with Spain, toleration of England's Catholic minority, the union of England and Scotland, and a strong but benevolent monarchy.

But James, afflicted with a tendency to drool, preferred hunting, banqueting, and dalliance with male favorites to the sustained effort needed to govern. He failed to inspire confidence. And unlike Elizabeth, who often concealed her imperious will in ambiguous language, James made things dangerously clear. In a famous speech to the House of Commons in 1610, he proclaimed that "The state of monarchy is the supremist thing on earth; for kings are not only God's lieutenants upon earth, and sit upon God's throne, but even by God himself they are called gods." That lack of tact, his disorderly style of life, and the conspicuous financial corruption and bumbling foreign policy of the chief royal favorite, the Duke of Buckingham, offended many of the groups represented in Parliament.

The House of Commons began to attack the royal prerogative with arguments based on innovative readings of England's common law. The king in return denounced the parliamentary opposition.

The indolent James I.

The "country"—the nobility and gentry who ruled England at the local level and represented it in Parliament—attacked the "court party" of the increasingly friendless king. "Country" spokesmen denounced the court as secretly Catholic, influenced culturally by Spain and France, and financially and morally corrupt. The delicate Tudor balance collapsed.

Crown and Parliament clashed over three related issues: religion, money, and foreign policy. The Puritans and their sympathizers in the House of Commons wished to "purify" the Anglican Church of everything that still savored of Catholicism, from "Popish" ritual to the authority of bishops. James for his part knew from his youth in Scotland the Presbyterian system of church government that the Puritans sought. He was convinced that it would remove the church from royal control and threaten the monarchy itself. "No bishop, no king," he shouted in a moment of frustration.

Parliament continued to denounce the extravagance of the court and soon denied James the money needed to meet Elizabeth I's war debts and the rising cost of government in an age of inflation. James then raised money without parliamentary approval by increasing customs duties. Parliament contested his right to do so, but the courts ruled in the king's favor. The seeming subservience of the courts to the royal will further annoyed Parliament.

James I's foreign policy likewise exasperated his critics. He was too friendly with Catholic Spain for Puritan tastes, he did little to defend Protestants abroad against militant Catholicism, and he tried in vain to marry his son Charles to the daughter of the king of Spain. When James chided the House of Commons in 1621 for even discussing his foreign policy, the House bristled. It passed a unanimous Protestation defending its right to discuss "the arduous and urgent affairs concerning the King, State, and defence of the realm, and of the Church of England." That was revolutionary talk. James tore the resolution from the Commons' *Journal* with his own hand, but he could not undo what the Commons had done. An aggressive and influential element among his subjects demanded rights and powers that he was unwilling to grant.

Charles I and the English Revolution, 1642–49

This crisis rapidly worsened after Charles I (r. 1625–49), second of the Stuarts, came to the throne. Charles tried to placate Parliament by attacking Catholic states. But Buckingham, the foppish favorite inherited from his father, failed to capture Cadiz in Spain or to save the French Huguenots besieged at La Rochelle. Parliament had urged war but had failed to grant sufficient taxes. Charles therefore levied a forced loan and imprisoned those who objected. In 1628 Parliament drew up a formal protest, the "Petition of Right," and compelled Charles to approve it. The Petition established that the king should henceforth levy neither taxes nor loans "without common consent by Act of Parliament" and that the government should imprison no one without showing cause. The king's subjects had begun to claim ever-broader rights against the state.

In 1629 Charles again roused the House of Commons to fury by asserting his full control of church and state. The Commons in reply declared that whoever introduced practices savoring of Catholicism into the Anglican Church was "a capital enemy to this kingdom and commonwealth," and that anyone who advised or submitted to taxation without parliamentary consent was "a betrayer of the liberties of England." The Commons thus raised the issue of the power to make law. Where did that power lie—in the king or in Parliament? The old answer, that it lay in the "king-in-Parliament," was no longer convincing. James I and Charles I between them had brought into the open the conflict between royal prerogative and the traditional "liberties of England" that descended ultimately from the *Magna Carta* of the barons (see pp. 311–12).

Charles, more stubborn than his father, ruled without Parliament from 1629 to 1640. In an attempt to duplicate Richelieu's absolutism, he chose advisers whose slogan was "thorough," such as Thomas Wentworth, Earl of Strafford, for political matters, and William Laud, Archbishop of Canterbury, for church affairs. Charles and his advisers devised new methods of taxation that did not require Parliament's approval and provided money enough to run the government so long as it stayed out of war. Laud challenged the Calvinist doctrine of predestination and sought to reestablish the authority of the bishops and reintroduce ritual into the Anglican service. The Puritans denounced him as a disguised Catholic. Up to 20,000 religious dissenters emigrated to the Netherlands or to bleak and distant Massachusetts. And Charles was unable to raise enough money to create the twin pillars of French-style absolutism—a royal administrative machine and a royal standing army.

Charles nevertheless prevailed until 1637–38. Then Laud tried to force the Anglican Book of Common Prayer on fiercely Presbyterian Scotland while Charles, with amazingly poor timing, alienated the Scottish nobility by seeking to reclaim from them the church lands they had acquired under Henry VIII. A fierce Scottish army was soon encamped in northern England. Charles and Strafford, unable to raise an army willing to fight, had to summon Parliament to vote money to buy the Scots off. The "Long Parliament" met in November 1640 and remained in session until 1653. It became a workshop of revolution. It sent Strafford and eventually Laud to the execution block. It dictated that the king must summon Parliament at least every three years. It outlawed all nonparliamentary taxation. It abolished the special royal law courts that had been the chief instruments of Charles's "Eleven Years' Tyranny." In less than a year (1640–41) Parliament destroyed absolute monarchy in England.

Charles secretly vowed revenge but acquiesced. He had no choice, for his government had alienated virtually all of the traditionally loyal groups whose cooperation he needed to rule England. Then the Catholics of Ireland decisively altered the

The autocratic Charles I.

situation by imitating the Scottish revolt and slaughtering Protestant settlers whom Elizabeth I and James I had planted in Ireland. Suppressing the Irish required raising an army once more—and Parliament distrusted the vengeful king too much to allow him to control that army. Simultaneously, the radical Puritans in Parliament abolished bishops in the Anglican Church. The inescapable issue of whether king or Parliament was to control army and church thereupon split England's upper classes. The growing political and religious radicalism of the House of Commons gave Charles what he had until then lacked—a royalist party that would fight to reassert his prerogatives. He attempted to arrest his parliamentary opponents in January 1642. By summer England was at war.

What was at first a confused struggle between factions of nobility and gentry soon turned into the English Revolution. Both Parliamentarians and Royalists claimed to support traditional English political and religious freedoms. London,

The English Revolution   1642–49

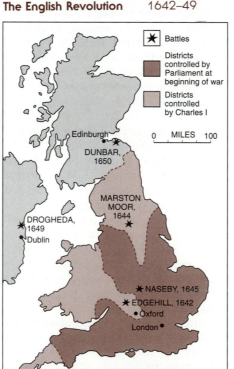

most towns, the middle classes, and the economically advanced southeast of England generally supported Parliament, although much of the population sought to remain neutral. Many rural areas and the backward northwest supported Charles. But the divisions between the parties did not correspond closely to England's economic, social, or regional divisions. Nobility, gentry, and artisans from all over England fought on both sides. The fierce religious and ideological issues at stake split many families, both noble and gentry.

Unlike the Fronde, in which narrow interest groups failed to proclaim programs with broad appeal, the English Civil War and Revolution offered dramatic alternatives to the established order—parliamentary monarchy instead of royal absolutism, and a Presbyterian Church with elected "presbyters," or elders, instead of an Anglican Church under crown-appointed bishops. Unlike the Fronde, the English Revolution produced radical movements that sought to abolish the monarchy, the established Church, and the landlords. "Levellers," "Diggers," and millenarian sects such as the "Fifth Monarchy Men" sought to inaugurate a new age of radical equality, or rule by "saints."

Parliament based itself in London, Europe's largest city, and proved more successful than the king at raising money and armies. Oliver Cromwell, a brilliant and ruthless cavalry officer, helped create a "New Model Army" drawn largely from his fellow Independents, strict Bible-reading Puritans who believed in democratically organized independent congregations with little or no church structure.

Cromwell and Parliament's numerically superior and ideologically motivated army ("Truly, I think he that prays best will fight best") defeated the king's forces decisively in June–July 1645. The king surrendered a year later. Then the army broke with the Presbyterians, who had dominated Parliament since the Anglicans had withdrawn in 1642 to join Charles I. Groups in Parliament and army with views ranging from social and religious moderation to extreme radicalism quarreled over the constitutional and religious settlement. The king sought to exploit the divisions among his opponents by devious negotiations. In November 1647 he escaped from custody to launch a brief second round of civil war.

The Independents in the army were now determined to root out all opposition. They purged Parliament of their Presbyterian rivals, defeated the king, and called the untrustworthy "Charles Stuart, that man of blood, to an account for the blood that he had shed." Cromwell, after initial hesitation, had Charles I executed in 1649, abolished the monarchy and the House of Lords, and set up a republic or "Commonwealth" with the "rump" of the Long Parliament as its government and with himself as its unchallenged leader. Parliament had tried a king ordained by divine right for treason against his own subjects, had cut off his head, and had abolished the very institution of kingship. England had set an example that was long remembered.

Cromwell's Dictatorship

Unlike later continental figures who seized command of a state through revolution, England's new dictator was a deeply religious man who did not initially seek supreme power. Yet power, and inevitable opposition to his will, brought out Cromwell's ruthlessness. He suppressed with fire and massacre the Irish rebellion that in 1641–42 had helped trigger the Civil War. He drubbed the Scots in two great battles when they intervened in favor of the son of Charles I. He presided over a naval war with the Dutch from 1652 to 1654. He wrathfully dissolved the rump of the Long Parliament in 1653, saying "You are no Parliament, I say you are no Parliament; I will put an end to your sitting." But he failed in his efforts to guarantee religious toleration to all Protestants except determined Anglicans and to find a satisfactory constitutional basis for government.

Cromwell attempted to rule with the consent of Parliament and through a written constitution, the "Instrument of Government"—the first such document in the history of a major state. He took the title of Lord Protector instead of king, but quar-

reled with Parliament as bitterly as had the Stuarts. In 1655 he installed an open military dictatorship to keep Parliament from disbanding his army and persecuting his coreligionists. Most Englishmen still rejected religious toleration, especially toleration of the religious and political radicals who made up a large part of Cromwell's army. And it became increasingly evident that England—like other states in the following centuries—could not break with history and set up a new regime simply by drafting a constitution. An unwritten "constitution" already existed, deeply ingrained in English political traditions.

Democratic Radicalism in the English Revolution

With victory assured, Cromwell's army turned to politics. In 1647 a Council of the Army debated constitutional issues at Putney, outside London. Radicals and representatives of the common soldiers, influenced by the Levellers, pressed for political rights for all men. Gentry figures such as General Ireton, Cromwell's forceful son-in-law, countered with the claim that only ownership of land conferred the right to representation.

MAJOR RAINBOROUGH: I think that the poorest he that is in England hath a life to live, as the greatest he, and therefore truly, sir, I think it's clear, that every man that is to live under a government ought first by his own consent to put himself under that government, and I do think that the poorest man in England is not at all bound in a strict sense to that government that he hath not had a voice to put himself under.

GENERAL IRETON: Government is to preserve property. . . . The objection does not lie in the making of the representation more equal but in the introducing of men . . . in this government who have no property in this kingdom. . . .

SEXBY [a representative of the troops]: I see that though liberty were our end, there is a degeneration from it. We have ventured our lives to recover our birthrights and privileges as Englishmen, and by the arguments urged there is none. There are many thousands of us soldiers that have ventured our lives; we have had little property . . . yet we have had a birthright. But it seems now, except a man hath a fixed estate in this kingdom, he hath no right in this kingdom. I wonder we were so much deceived.

From Puritanism and Liberty, *ed. by A. S. P. Woodhouse (Chicago: University of Chicago Press, 1951), pp. 53, 62, 69.*

Oliver Cromwell, by Samuel Cooper.

Cromwell's death in 1658 made General George Monck, his most important military subordinate, the most powerful figure in England. Monck recognized that Parliament was the only alternative to military dictatorship and that restoring Parliament also required recreating the monarchy. In 1660, a "Convention Parliament" under his protection invited the son of Charles I to return from France and take up the crown.

The Legacy of the English Revolution

The Civil War had made clear that England would not tolerate an absolute monarchy. Strafford and Laud had tried to do for Charles I what Richelieu and Mazarin had done for Louis XIV. But whereas the Frenchmen had died in their beds, the Englishmen had lost their heads to the executioner. The new Parliament confirmed many of the severe limits to royal power that the Long Parliament had set before the outbreak of the Civil War. The turmoil of the first half of the century left most Englishmen with half-expressed convictions that had lasting effects—a fear of too great a concentration of power, a deepened respect for government by law rather than by royal command, a reverence for Parliament as the defender of individual rights against royal despotism, and a fervent distaste for standing armies.

The restoration of King Charles II: the coronation in Westminster Abbey (from a contemporary print).

The early seventeenth century was a brilliant age in the history of English literature and thought. It included Shakespeare's mature work and the early years of the great poet John Milton. In 1611 the Authorized, or King James, Version of the Bible first emerged from the presses. Its sonorous cadences have influenced the writing of English to the present day. Statesmen and pamphleteers arguing for royalist, parliamentary, or radical principles likewise made this a formative period of modern political thought.

Thomas Hobbes's *Leviathan* (1651) distilled the political insights of the years of civil war. Under the influence of Thucydides' great history of the Peloponnesian War (see pp. 52–53), of which Hobbes wrote the first English translation, Hobbes saw in humanity "a perpetual and restless desire of power after power." Without some authority to enforce law, society would disintegrate into "a war of every man against every man." Life without government was "solitary, poor, nasty, brutish, and short." Hobbes, following Huguenot thinkers seeking to justify revolt against France's Catholic monarchy, postulated that humans set up sovereign powers through agreements or contracts.

But Hobbes drew from this "contract theory" of government conclusions opposite to those of the Huguenots, and of Cromwell and his army, who had declared "the king is king by contract" and had severed Charles I's head for violating that contract. For Hobbes, society agreed to obey the sovereign because the sovereign alone could maintain order. To ensure the maintenance of order, the sovereign's powers had to be absolute and unquestioned. Hobbes's contract therefore bound only the subjects, not the ruler. "There can happen no breach of the Covenant on the part of the Sovereign; and consequently none of his Subjects . . . can be freed from his subjection."

Hobbes thus took contract theory and transformed it into a justification of unfettered and arbitrary power. English political theorists during the remainder of the seventeenth century devoted much effort to finding some way to refute Hobbes— to subject political power to the restraint

of law and to the consent of the governed. But they, too, remained fearful of the ever-present threat of violence and chaos against which Hobbes had created his absolute sovereign.

GERMANY: DISINTEGRATION AND DISASTER, 1618–48

The consequences of the absence of sovereign power and the "war of every man against every man" were nowhere so visible as across the North Sea in Germany. While France built the mightiest monarchy

The title page of Thomas Hobbes's *Leviathan*, one of the fundamental works of Western political theory. Hobbes described the sovereign power of the state as "that great Leviathan, or rather (to speak more reverently) that mortal God, to which we owe under the Immortal God, our peace and defence."

in Europe and England underwent a crisis from which it emerged with new strength, the German-speaking peoples suffered the Thirty Years' War. It was in reality four successive wars that began in 1618 in Bohemia, spread to the rest of the Holy Roman Empire, and before its end in 1648 involved most major continental powers. It was a savage and demoralizing conflict that left central Europe poorer and weaker than the states to its west for the next 150 years.

The Causes of the Thirty Years' War

The war sprang from a complicated mixture of religious and political quarrels. The Peace of Augsburg (1555) had ended the previous round of religious war in central Europe (see p. 437) by dividing the German states between Catholic and Lutheran rulers. Each prince had received the right to determine the religion of his subjects. But in the following decades most Catholic bishoprics in north Germany had fallen into Lutheran or secular hands. The spread of Calvinism introduced a further source of friction, for the Peace of Augsburg had not recognized Calvinism nor assigned it any territories. Protestant successes caused increasing discontent in the Catholic camp.

In 1608, the foremost leader of the Catholics, Duke Maximilian of Bavaria, roughly disciplined the Protestant town of Donauwörth. That action led Frederick V, the Calvinist ruler of the Palatinate, a small state on the middle Rhine, to form a Protestant Union of German princes and cities. In reply, Maximilian organized a Catholic League with the support of German Catholic princes and the Jesuits. By 1609 the Holy Roman Empire had fractured once again into two hostile religious and military alliances. Protestant Union and Catholic League faced each other with hatred and suspicion, each determined to bar the other from further gains.

1. Revolt in Bohemia, 1618–20

These signs of anarchy and religious division within the Holy Roman Empire prompted the Habsburgs, who held the imperial title, to try to rebuild their authority. They began by seeking to consolidate their hold over their long-time family domains of Austria, Bohemia, and Hungary. The aging emperor Matthias secured the election of his heir-apparent, Ferdinand of Styria, as king of Bohemia in 1617.

Bohemia was a flourishing territory in which two chief nationalities (Germans and Czechs) and a variety of religions (Catholicism, Lutheranism, Calvinism, and remnants of the Hussite movement of the fifteenth century) lived in relative peace under Habsburg promises of toleration. But Ferdinand was a zealous Counter-Reformation Catholic. He had ruthlessly recatholicized Styria, and the Protestant majority in the Bohemian Estates rightly feared that he planned the same for Bohemia. In May 1618 the Bohemians therefore threw their imperial governors from the windows of Prague castle (an incident thereafter known as the "defenestration of Prague"). The Estates raised an army, declared Ferdinand deposed, and offered the crown of Bohemia to Frederick V of the Palatinate. Frederick's unwise acceptance extended the war from Bohemia to the Empire as a whole. His Protestant Union took the side of the Bohemian Estates, while Maximilian of Bavaria swung the Catholic League behind Ferdinand, who had been elected emperor.

The Bohemian phase of the war ended swiftly. In November 1620 the Imperial forces crushed the Bohemian rebels at the battle of the White Mountain near Prague. Frederick V fled, and Emperor Ferdinand proceeded to make Bohemia over at the cost of wrecking its economy and society. War and plague cut the population almost in half. The Czech nobility lost everything. Half the land in Bohemia changed hands through confiscation, and Ferdinand created a new nobility of adventurers from as far away as Ireland. The Jesuits, with Ferdinand's full backing, set out to reconvert the country to Catholicism by force. Within ten years they had stamped Protestantism out or driven it underground. The Czechs became a people without a ruling class and without a claim to an independent existence for two centuries. The Habsburgs and their Catholic allies had decisively won the first round of the great war.

2. Danish Intervention and Catholic Triumph, 1625–29

The fall of Bohemia terrified the German Protestants and elated the Catholics. The Spanish Habsburgs had also intervened against the Protestant states of north Germany, and the armies of the Catholic League were everywhere triumphant. But common danger failed to unite the Protestants. The Lutherans feared a Calvinist victory in Bohemia more than an Imperial triumph. The Lutheran kingdom of Saxony had actually helped Ferdinand put the Czechs down. And although Frederick V was the son-in-law of James I, Protestant England gave no help; James I and his successor Charles I were locked in their struggle with Parliament.

The king of Denmark joined his fellow Protestants in 1625, but his principal motive was greed for territory in north Germany. Within a year, the Catholics had beaten him back. Albrecht von Wallenstein, a brilliant military entrepreneur who had offered the emperor his services, crushed the Danes with an expert mercenary army that at its height numbered 125,000 men. Wallenstein's long-term aim was probably to secure central Europe for himself. His immediate goal was to build an Imperial Habsburg military machine that could eliminate the Protestants without the help of the Catholic League. By 1628 Wallenstein and the League were as much at odds on the Catholic side as Calvinists and Lutherans were on the Protestant. Religion slowly receded in significance as the war became a struggle between armies and states alone, a struggle for mastery in Europe.

The Habsburg and Catholic cause reached its high-water mark in 1629. Denmark withdrew, leaving Wallenstein's army supreme. The Catholic League and Jesuit advisers persuaded Ferdinand to issue an Edict of Restitution that restored to Catholic hands all church lands lost to Protestantism since 1552. Carrying out the edict meant yet more bloodshed to restore the dispossessed Catholic bishops of Protestant north Germany. That would also destroy both the rough religious balance between Catholicism and Protestantism in Germany and the power balance between the north German states on the one hand and Austria and Bavaria on the other. That threat finally roused Lutherans inside and outside Germany to action.

3. The "Lion of the North": Gustavus Adolphus, 1630–32

In 1630 Sweden, a country until now on the periphery of the European state system, intervened to check the Habsburgs. Its masterful king, Gustavus Adolphus, was the ablest ruler of his generation. Sweden had a population of roughly 1.25 million people, perhaps a fifteenth of the population of France. But Gustavus had cultivated rich copper and timber exports, a sophisticated iron and armament industry, and the most advanced army of the day. That army was not large, but it was the first in Europe recruited by universal conscription, and it possessed a high morale born of fierce patriotism. It also had the first uniforms, the first artillery light enough for battlefield maneuver, improved muskets, regular pay, and discipline, a rarity indeed in the Thirty Years' War. Its victories over Russia, Denmark, and Poland between 1611 and 1629 made the Baltic almost a Swedish lake.

Gustavus stepped into the great war in Germany to defend Sweden's Baltic interests, which Wallenstein appeared to threaten. But as the war continued, Gustavus began to toy with a broader aim— the creation of a federation of German Protestant states under Swedish leadership. He arrived too late to save the great city of Magdeburg from sack, massacre, and destruction by the Imperial forces in May 1631, an event that for generations symbolized the all-devouring brutality of this war. But in the fall of 1631 Gustavus shattered the Imperial armies at Breitenfeld in Saxony, and marched triumphantly to the Rhine.

That emergency compelled the Emperor to recall Wallenstein, whom he had dismissed at the insistence of the Catholic

League. Gustavus defeated Wallenstein decisively at Lützen in 1632, but paid for victory with his own life. Without Gustavus's leadership the outnumbered Swedes could not maintain their dominance in Germany. Swedish weakness in turn freed the Emperor from dependence on his over-mighty subject, Wallenstein, who perished by assassination at Ferdinand's orders. In the fall of 1634 the Imperial armies checked the Swedes at the battle of Nördlingen. Gustavus Adolphus had saved German Protestantism but had failed to decide the war.

4. France Intervenes, 1635–48

The most powerful state of all now acted, opening the fourth and final phase of the war. Since his appointment as chief minister in 1624, Richelieu had followed the war closely through his ever-present ambassadors and agents. His aim was to crush both Austrian and Spanish Habs-

burgs and to end Habsburg encirclement of France. Under his leadership, Catholic France accepted as allies all opponents of the Habsburgs regardless of religion. His first allies were the Protestant Dutch, who in 1621 had again gone to war with their ancestral enemy, Spain. Then Richelieu subsidized Sweden. But the Imperial defeat of the Swedes in 1634 forced him to choose between direct French intervention and Habsburg domination of Europe. In May 1635 he chose intervention; France declared war on Spain and allied itself with Sweden and Germany.

The Thirty Years' War had by then lasted for seventeen years. It continued drearily for a further thirteen years, for neither side had the strength to force a decision. French, Swedish, and Dutch armies slogged across central Europe pursuing or pursued by the Habsburg forces. The rebellions of Portugal and of the rich province of Catalonia in 1640 weakened Spain. In 1643, on the battlefield of Rocroi

MAGDEBURG.

The siege of Magdeburg in 1631 by Habsburg and Catholic forces, which ended with one of the bloodiest massacres of the war.

in the Netherlands, the French finally crushed the Spanish army and its legend of invincibility. Habsburg allies soon deserted the Empire, and the Swedes besieged Prague and menaced Vienna. The Habsburg attempt to roll back the Reformation in Germany and establish mastery over central Europe had failed.

Peace of Exhaustion: Westphalia, 1648

Habsburg defeat opened the way to the peace negotiated between 1644 and 1648 at the Congress of Westphalia. The gathering was Europe's first great peace conference and the first interstate meeting of importance since the Council of Constance of 1414–18 (see p. 427). But unlike Constance, the atmosphere and the business of the Congress that met at Münster in western Germany were entirely secular. The Congress was a meeting of sovereign states that recognized no earthly superior and only the most shadowy common interests. The unity of medieval "Christendom" had dissolved.

The Congress confirmed the importance of the sovereign state and set a framework for central European politics that lasted until 1801–06. In recognizing the right of the German principalities to make alliances and to declare war, the Congress accepted the disintegration of the Empire into more than 300 separate sovereignties. Switzerland and the Dutch Netherlands finally achieved recognition as independent states. France acquired ambiguous rights to Alsace, and Sweden gained strips of German territory along the Baltic and the North seas. The two German states of Brandenburg and Bavaria increased their territory and prestige.

As for religion, the Congress reaffirmed the principle of partition according to the religion of the ruler established in the Peace of Augsburg of 1555, and at last added Calvinism to Catholicism and Lutheranism as one of the recognized faiths. To prevent further dispute, the Congress froze the ownership of church lands as of 1624. North Germany remained Protestant and south Germany Catholic. Only France and Spain failed to reach

The Sack of Magdeburg   1631

For a generation after the destruction of this German city, the phrase "Magdeburg quarter" meant "no quarter."

Then was there naught but beating and burning, plundering, torture, and murder. Most especially was every one of the enemy bent on securing much booty. When a marauding party entered a house, if its master had anything to give he might thereby purchase respite and protection for himself and his family till the next man, who also wanted something, should come along. It was only when everything had been brought forth and there was nothing left to give that the real trouble commenced. Then, what with blows and threats of shooting, stabbing, and hanging, the poor people were so terrified that if they had had anything left they would have brought it forth if it had been buried in the earth or hidden away in a thousand castles. In this frenzied rage, the great and splendid city that had stood like a fair princess in the land was now, in its hour of direst need and unutterable distress and woe, given over to the flames, and thousands of innocent men, women, and children, in the midst of a horrible din of heartrending shrieks and cries, were tortured and put to death in so cruel and shameful a manner that no words would suffice to describe, nor no tears to bewail it.

From Otto von Guericke, in Readings in European History, *ed. by James Harvey Robinson (Boston: Ginn, 1906), Vol. II, pp. 211–12.*

agreement. Their war continued until Mazarin secured, in the Peace of the Pyrenees of 1659, the victory that Richelieu had sought.

The Consequences of the Thirty Years' War

The Thirty Years' War had been a terrifying demonstration of the anarchy that Europe's state-builders sought to avoid. It was one of the most destructive wars in recorded history. In Europe no later conflict matched it in ruthless devastation until the new "thirty years' war" of 1914–45. Armies pillaged, raped, and murdered their way across central Europe. The soldiery wiped towns off the map and reduced cities to a small fraction of their original populations. Cultivated land reverted to waste. Destruction of livestock even more than of crops crippled a primitive and mostly agrarian economy, for

Europe in 1648

plough and dairy animals were difficult to replace. Starvation and the massive plague epidemics that marched with the lice-ridden armies killed more than the sword.

The Holy Roman Empire (including Bohemia) lost an estimated 4 million out of roughly 21 million inhabitants. A few areas lost up to 80 percent of their population. The war also had deep psychological, social, political, and economic effects. The peoples of central Europe were soon happy to acknowledge any authority, however brutal, that promised peace. The fragmentation of the Holy Roman Empire

into small states quirkily divided by customs barriers hampered economic recovery. The war helped delay until the nineteenth century the emergence of a state called "Germany," and helped make its emergence an event that shook Europe and the world.

DUTCH UNREST AND SPANISH DECLINE

The political upheavals of the early seventeenth century touched many areas of

Europe other than France, England, and central Europe. Even distant Russia underwent an anarchic "Time of Troubles" before settling down uneasily under the rule of the first Romanov tsar in 1613. In the west, violent convulsions shook the Netherlands and Spain.

By 1609 the northern areas of the Netherlands had achieved effective independence from Spain and enormous economic success. An aggressively Calvinist party nevertheless pressed for renewed war against Spain in the southern Netherlands. Its leader was Maurice of Nassau, son of William the Silent, chief of the House of Orange and commander of the highly competent Dutch army. A second party, that of the merchant class, enjoyed the support of the religiously tolerant Arminians (those unwilling to accept Calvin's stern doctrine of predestination). It hoped to reestablish trade with Spain.

In 1619 Maurice of Nassau overthrew this "peace party" and had its leader executed after a political trial. The war with Spain resumed in 1621 and continued inconclusively until the Peace of Westphalia. Tensions between the House of Orange and the mercantile "regent class" continued throughout the century. For two decades after 1650 the "regents" dominated Dutch affairs. But when invasion—from France rather than Spain—came again in 1672, the old conflicts reopened. A mob in The Hague tore the leading regent, Johan de Witt, limb from limb and publicly sold his remains. The Dutch summoned the head of the House of Orange, the young Prince William, to lead them victoriously against overwhelming odds.

In Spain, religious-ethnic persecution marked the beginning of irreversible decline. In 1609 the monarchy and the Inquisition launched a campaign similar to the expulsion of Spain's 150,000 Jews after 1492 (see p. 459). In fanatical pursuit of religious uniformity and "purity of blood" *(limpieza de sangre),* the authorities deported to north Africa in 1609–14 as many as 275,000 Moriscos, the insufficiently converted descendants of the Moors who had given the Iberian peninsula much of its civilization. That savage persecution

deprived Spain of a creative minority that it sorely needed. Plague and economic collapse reduced the population dramatically, from perhaps 8.5 million in 1600 to 7.5 million in 1650.

War, both foreign and domestic, also contributed to Spain's decline. The leading minister from 1621 to 1643, the proud Count-Duke of Olivares, committed Spain to war in Germany in 1620 and against the Netherlands in 1621. War with France as well in 1635 placed unbearable tax burdens on the Spanish monarchy's patchwork of provinces jealous of their traditional rights and liberties. Olivares struggled gloomily to establish a centralized administration with an effective system of tax collection. But as so often happened in early modern Europe, centralization—the creation of a modern state machine—provoked bitter revolt. In 1640 Portugal, forcibly united with Spain since 1580, made good its independence by force. The rich province of Catalonia attracted French support and defied the monarchy until 1652. Spain's Italian possessions also revolted.

Spain thus had to yield to France the position of leading power in Europe in 1659. Spain's political and military decline was in part a consequence of the overambitious policies of Olivares. But its deeper causes were economic and internal. Of all the powers, Spain suffered most from the crises of the European and world economy of the seventeenth century.

EUROPE'S POPULATION AND ECONOMY IN CRISIS

A suddenly hostile climate and a drastic fall in prices intensified the ravages that never-ending war inflicted on the societies of seventeenth-century Europe. Despite the slowly gathering force of commerce and industry, agriculture still dominated Europe's economy. The tyranny of the seasons in turn dominated agriculture. And during what historians have termed the "little ice age," the cold century and a half between the 1590s and the 1740s, that tyranny was harsh indeed. Usually ice-free rivers repeatedly froze over in winter. Springs and summers turned rainy and cold.

Even in the relatively warm fifteenth and sixteenth centuries, England had suffered one poor harvest in four, and one disastrous harvest in six. Between 1594 and 1597 rain and cold wrecked four harvests in succession from Ireland to east central Europe; the result was widespread famine. The harvests from 1647 to 1652–53 were similarly catastrophic, especially in France and Spain. The 1690s were the coldest decade in 700 years; in 1696–97 about a quarter of the population of Finland perished by famine. The "great cold" of 1709–10 produced a general crop failure in France. Beggars froze to death in the streets of Paris.

Human and animal epidemics inevitably accompanied famine, for malnutrition reduces resistance to disease. Spain lost perhaps a half-million dead from bubonic plague in 1647–52, and outbreaks were widespread until the early eighteenth century. The population of Europe dipped slightly (see Figure 19-1). Only after 1750 did a mellower climate, crop-rotation techniques pioneered in the Low Countries, New World crops such as the potato and maize, and dramatic improve-

ments in transport allow a new and sustained increase in Europe's population.

A second force intensified the effects of the seventeenth-century climate on Europe's fragile economy and population—the movement of prices. In the sixteenth century two trends had united to produce a "price revolution": the sudden and massive influx of New World silver and gold, and the rapidly increasing sophistication of Europe's merchants and bankers, who had multiplied the effective volume of money by speeding its circulation and by using credit far more extensively than in the past. In consequence, by 1600 prices had reached levels four to five times above those of 1500. That inflation, although modest by twentieth-century standards, had deeply unsettling effects on societies that still adhered to the medieval myth of a "just" price. The penetration of money ever deeper into the countryside brought with it price fluctuations that intensified the distress of the peasantry and ruined aristocrats who failed to adapt to the hard new age of profit and loss.

After about 1620 the influx of New World silver slowed as production in the mines of Mexico and Peru peaked. Loss of revenue helped cripple the policies of Olivares. Throughout Europe price inflation gave way to deflation, and hectic growth to stagnation. The wars and troubles after 1620, from the Thirty Years' War to the English Revolution and the Fronde, further intensified the economic depression. Only after 1670 did some northern areas of Europe, most notably England and the Dutch United Provinces, once more begin to enjoy a steady prosperity. In Spain, the pressure of taxes to finance Olivares' wars and the dead hand of his bureaucracy crushed what little independence and enterprise the middle classes of Castile had possessed. In the countryside, as in the Spanish New World, sheep replaced peasants. In France, the pressure of the monarchy's taxation, further intensified in the wars of Louis XIV after 1667 (see pp. 510–12), caused repeated revolts.

Yet Europe survived and grew—despite the "little ice age," deflation, and war—thanks above all to economic innovation. In industry—the production of

FIGURE 19-1   **The Population of Europe, 1000–1700 (including Russia west of the Ural Mountains)**

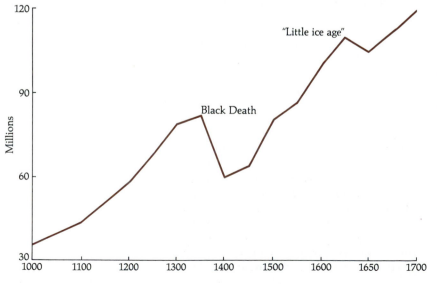

goods for market using specialized labor and machines—new techniques rapidly gained ground. In the 1580s, the Dutch introduced power saws worked by windmills. Water-driven power hammers for forging became common. Coal, at least in England, became the cheapest source of energy. Coal fueled London's growth from 200,000 inhabitants in 1600 to more than 550,000—Europe's largest city—by 1700. Coal made the English glass industry the most modern in Europe, and supplied London's shops with glass windowpanes at which visitors marveled.

All over Europe, commerce and industry began to break out from the medieval framework of town and guild monopolies. A new form of craft organization that bypassed the guilds, the "putting-out system," spread from the Low Countries. Traveling merchants supplied rural home workers with raw materials, then returned to collect the finished product. "Putting-out" was particularly effective in the greatest industry of early modern Europe, textiles. It was also well suited to an age in which techniques were simple and hand or animal power drove most industrial equipment. To the peasant family, it provided income that in years of crop failure might mean the difference between life and death. Putting-out slowly eroded guild restrictions, channeled money into the countryside, and dissolved the old peasant barter economy. It was a major source of Europe's economic growth.

In trade and finance, the century was one of continued rapid change. An ever-widening banking network spread across Europe, from Seville facing the New World to the grain and timber ports of the Baltic. A new institution apparently invented in Italy, the joint-stock company, made possible a far more widespread mobilization of capital than traditional family firms or partnerships. Individuals who were not necessarily traders could buy "shares" in great commercial enterprises such as the Muscovy Company (1553), the English East India Company (1600), and the Dutch East India Company (1602). The company directors then used the shareholders' money for their operations. Soon a vast market developed in the "shares" themselves, the ancestor of the modern stock exchange.

A further source of change was geographic. By the middle of the seventeenth century the westward and northward shift in Europe's economic center of gravity that had begun even before 1492 was complete. The Mediterranean and central Europe became backwaters. Venice, although victorious over the Turks at sea, suffered disastrous shrinkage both in its industries and in its trade with the eastern Mediterranean. The westward shift of trade to the New World and around the Cape of Good Hope helped destroy German banking dynasties such as the Fuggers of Augsburg. Then the Thirty Years' War completed Germany's economic ruin.

But even economies open to the ocean failed. Spain, thanks to religious persecution, rigid government controls, and high taxes, soon yielded much of its New World trade to Genoese and Dutch merchants. Antwerp, the great trading and banking center of northern Europe until the mid-sixteenth century, failed to assert its political independence from Spain. It lost its economic position as well to its Dutch neighbors to the north. The founding of the Bank of Amsterdam in 1609—the same year as the truce by which Spain recognized Dutch independence—symbolized the supremacy of the Dutch Republic as the center of Europe's economy, a supremacy that lasted throughout the seventeenth century. But the republic, with a tiny territory and a population that reached 2 million in 1650 but then remained essentially unchanged until 1800, was little more than a glorified city-state.

The future belonged to those powerful engines of growth, the modern "national markets" within the large territorial states, France and England. France seemed by far the richest, for it possessed the largest territory of any state west of Russia and a population greater than any other. But its agriculture suffered badly in the "little ice age." France's sheer size, the absence of good roads or navigable waterways, and the numerous customs barriers between provinces, and between towns and countryside likewise stunted growth. France's centralized war-making state crushed the peasants under a taxation that, along with dues to landlords and Church, deprived them of roughly half their income.

Nor did the efforts of France's government to promote economic growth help. The great finance minister of Louis XIV, Jean-Baptiste Colbert (see p. 506) made an almost despairing attempt to promote the development of industry and commerce in the face of the economic depression that lasted through the 1680s. In the 1670s he founded many enterprises, including cannon foundries and textile mills staffed with Dutch experts. He strengthened the guilds as a means of ensuring the quality and uniformity needed to promote exports. He attempted to crush the Dutch with tariffs and with Louis's wars. Colbert was the most consistent adherent of a series of loosely linked notions, characteristic of a world of warring states, usually known as "mercantilism"—state intervention to promote industry and maximize

Ships bearing precious merchandise from the far side of the world: the front of the earliest headquarters of the English East India Company. Photo courtesy of the Granger Collection.

FRONT OF THE OLD EAST INDIA HOUSE.

The world's first stock exchange, at Amsterdam, in the mid-seventeenth century.

exports, protective tariffs to prevent imports, and strenuous attempts to create a trade surplus that would suck in gold and silver from competitors. Such methods long outlived the seventeenth century, but they did not help France. Most of Colbert's industries proved ruinously unprofitable, and his reinforcement of the guilds was a disaster for French industry. His tariffs damaged France more than the Dutch. France's commercial economy developed, but largely despite Colbert.

England was different. It too employed "mercantilist" practices, such as the Navigation Acts that after 1651 restricted all trade with England and its colonies to English ships, and channeled colonial products through English ports. England, too, fought wars with the Dutch over commerce in 1652–54, 1665–67, and 1672–74. But internally, England was already a large unified market; its guilds were decayed relics; its textile, coal, and iron industries were gradually expanding. By 1700 its economy, the least "mercantilist" and

state-controlled in Europe, owed a third of its national product to commerce and industry, while the proportion in France was a fifth or less. In the long term, England's economy could not fail to have an impact on the wider world opened up in the age of discovery.

THE EUROPEAN EMPIRES

Europe's overseas expansion slowed briefly in the seventeenth century. Spain needed time to digest the conquered Aztec and Inca empires. In India, China, and Japan the Europeans faced ancient civilizations that still had the power to hold them at arm's length. Developing the North American wilderness required settlers in numbers unavailable until Europe's population growth resumed. And the extension to the outside world of the warlike competition between European states slowed Europe's economic penetration of the non-European world.

Trade and plunder had lured the Europeans overseas. Portugal persisted in that pattern, and its "colonies," with the exception of its early settlements on Madeira and its great land empire in Brazil, remained fortified trading posts that dealt in spices or slaves through native middlemen. The Dutch sought to follow the Portuguese example after 1600, when they seized control from Portugal of the Indian Ocean and China Sea. But in their Spice Islands south of the Philippines the Dutch soon found that maintaining exports required more than trading posts. As the Spaniards discovered during their feverish search for gold and silver in the Americas, trade and plunder led to rule and settlement.

The new model colonies of the seventeenth century were thus settlement colonies. The pattern dated from Portugal's settlement in the 1420s of the uninhabited Atlantic island of Madeira, and Spain had followed it in the Americas after the 1520s. The function of the settlement colonies was to produce raw materials essential to the mother country. That purpose required the export of European institutions, technology, plants, and animals to set up overseas societies on the European model. In Africa, malaria and yellow fever killed the vast majority of Europeans who attempted to penetrate inland, and Europe's military technology did not yet provide superiority over the natives on their own ground. Native middlemen and rulers continued to provide apparently inexhaustible supplies of slaves; the trading-post system persisted.

But in the New World, settlement was possible. And settlement meant production of the commodity most prized after gold and silver—sugar. Cultivating that addictive substance, first brought to Europe by the Crusaders, required backbreaking labor. As the Portuguese had demonstrated on Madeira, enslaved natives from the Canary Islands or from Africa most conveniently supplied that labor. Tobacco, coffee, and in East Asia tea and spices created similar patterns of cultivation and settlement. The riches that these products generated proved an irresistible source of conflict.

The Struggle for Mastery in the East

East of Africa and south of China the Portuguese soon lost the trading empire they had established after the voyages of Vasco de Gama. Dutch, English, and French interlopers appeared. Portugal was too economically and demographically weak and too technologically backward to hold empires both in the New World and in the East simultaneously, and its subordination to Spain from 1580 to 1640 exposed it to attack by Spain's enemy, the Dutch. Portugal's rivals founded powerful East India Companies: the English in 1600, the Dutch in 1602, the French in 1664. The Dutch proved the most ruthless, well-organized, and successful. Their seizure of the Cape of Good Hope in 1652 created the largest white community in Africa as a way-station for their shipping. Their massacre of English merchants on Amboina in 1623 and their control of Batavia on Java from 1619 and of the strategic Malacca strait after 1641 persuaded the English to concentrate on India. There England and France set up trading posts on the Portuguese model at Bombay, Madras, and Calcutta for England, and at Pondicherry for France. The Mughal empire that dominated South Asia barred the way inland. Only its collapse after 1707 opened the road by which Britain ultimately established its hegemony in the Mughals' place (see Chapters 22 and 27).

Sugar and Slavery in the Caribbean

In the Caribbean, the Dutch, English, and French competed for crumbs from Spain's overfilled table. After war between the Dutch and Spain resumed in 1621, the Dutch sought to damage Spain by seizing sugar-rich Brazil from Spain's dependency, Portugal. The Dutch failed, but they did take the Caribbean island of Curaçao as a base for raids on Spanish commerce. England settled Barbados in 1624 and gained Jamaica in 1655, while the French took Guadeloupe and Martinique. They had come for plunder like the Dutch, but they stayed to grow sugar. And sugar plantations required a ready supply of labor—

A tropical Amsterdam, complete with canals: the great Dutch port of Batavia, on Java (1682).

unfree labor. The Caribbean Indians were becoming extinct, thanks to smallpox, massacres, and slave labor exacted by Spain. The interloping powers therefore brought their own labor with them. On Barbados, white small farmers who cultivated tobacco gave way in the 1640s and 1650s to large, efficient plantations grouped around great sugar mills. At first white contract labor worked the plantations. These "indentured servants" worked off the price of their passage to the New World by years of servitude. But white labor could not compete with black slaves from Africa. Slaves were virtually unlimited in supply and cost less than whites—slavery was for life, not three, five, or seven years.

African rulers, Arabs, and Portuguese had pioneered the slave trade long before the discovery of the New World. The Portuguese had experimented with slave cultivation of sugar on Madeira. Extending that savage system to the New World required the transportation across the Atlantic of almost a million Africans in the course of the seventeenth century. Death rates ran as high as 20 percent during transport inside Africa and another 20 percent on the Atlantic crossing. Disease and ill-treatment prevented the slave populations in the New World from reproducing enough to increase their numbers. Expanding the sugar economy thus required the import of ever-greater numbers of slaves. A triangular trade pattern developed—Europeans took goods such as weapons, rum, or tobacco to Africa, bartered them for slaves whom the kings of west Africa had seized from neighboring tribes and kingdoms, and exchanged the slaves in the West Indies for tropical goods that included molasses from which to make more rum. As the Portuguese slowly lost control of the west coast of Africa, the Dutch, English, and French stepped in to supply slaves to their own sugar islands and—through smuggling—to the plantations of Spain. Slavery, whether in the European colonies, the Islamic world, or Africa itself, had as yet attracted little attention as an institution of peculiar cruelty.

North America: The Dutch, the French, and the English

North of the sugar islands lay an immense waste of swamp and woodland: North America. Its only known resources were the codfish off Newfoundland and the furs and timber of its great forests. But three powers nevertheless attempted settlements there in the hope of breaking Spain's near-monopoly of the New World. The failure of Sir Walter Raleigh to found a colony in Virginia during the 1580s revealed some of the difficulties. Cold winters and poor soil made the creation of a tropical plantation economy difficult. Hostile natives were still relatively strong. Planting a permanent colony in North America required the transport of a large labor force and its support over many years until the settlement achieved self-sufficiency. That demanded capital, numerous emigrants, and unshakable determination.

The Dutch and French failed both demographically and economically. The Dutch explored the Hudson River in 1609 and had settled New Amsterdam on Manhattan Island by 1624. But their colony of "New Netherland" never became more than a center for trade and fur exports. The English seized it in 1664, immediately before the second of their wars with the Dutch (see p. 514).

The French excelled in the backwoods. Jacques Cartier discovered the St. Lawrence River in 1535 and Robert de La Salle coursed the Mississippi in 1682. France's explorers and fur-trading *coureurs de bois* ("wood runners") were more adventurous and France's Jesuit missionaries more determined than the New World representatives of any other European state except perhaps the Portuguese of Brazil. By 1605 French settlers had planted villages in Acadia, and in 1608 Samuel de Champlain founded Québec. By 1640 perhaps 3,000 French inhabited Canada, but the population had reached only 10,000 by 1700.

Growth was slow because the French government succeeded too well in imposing French absolutism and social patterns on its colonies. It regulated and stultified economic life while granting land in large blocks to a few proprietors under semifeudal conditions. Except under Colbert in the 1660s and 1670s, it gave French peasants little inducement to emigrate. For religious reasons it strictly barred from Canada all Huguenots, who took their economic talents to the English colonies instead. A cluster of French settlements spread across the St. Lawrence Valley, but the English settlers to the south far outnumbered the "New France" of lords and peasants.

England's constitutional and religious struggles spurred emigration. English governments, whether Stuart or Cromwell, encouraged colonizing projects but left great latitude to individuals or joint-stock companies in founding colonies. Above all, English governments allowed religious

The inhabitants of the New World, as seen in the 1580s by John White, one of the leaders of Raleigh's failed attempt to establish a colony on Roanoke Island, Virginia.

minorities to settle in English colonies. That speeded mightily the growth of an enterprising, independent, and rapidly multiplying population.

The Virginia Company planted England's first successful colony at Jamestown in 1607. It almost failed, but then the settlers discovered the rage in Europe for a native weed, tobacco. That cash crop paid for the manufactured goods they needed from England—and ultimately for African slaves to cultivate the tobacco. The small band of religious dissenters who landed at Plymouth in 1620 lost half their number during the first winter. But the Massachusetts Bay Company, which founded Boston, was able to profit by the Pilgrims' experience. In 1630 it transported 900 settlers across the ocean in a large and well-planned operation. Thanks in part to Laud's persecution of dissenters, the population of Massachusetts had swelled within ten years to about 14,000. By 1650 the population of "New England" was about 20,000. The settlers were soon shipping fur, fish, and timber to England.

By 1700 the English colonies held almost 200,000 settlers and dominated the continent. Twelve colonies existed, offshoots of the original settlements or created by royal grants. Georgia, the thirteenth, was founded in 1732. And unlike New France, which suffered under a royal central administration of Québec, the English colonies were in effect self-governing. Each colony acquired an elected representative assembly that passed its laws and controlled taxation. A royal governor appointed by London was in theory not responsible to the assembly. But because the governor generally depended on the assembly for his salary, his executive power and London's reach were in practice limited. In the 1660s Parliament did its best to impose mercantilist practices by requiring the export of some colonial goods exclusively to England in English or colonial ships. Those restrictions caused much complaint and smuggling. After the Glorious Revolution of 1688 (see p. 515) London gradually became less insistent on asserting its authority. The colonists accepted regulation of their trade so long as enforcement was lenient.

Unlike the colonial subjects of all other powers, the inhabitants of British North America thus became increasingly accustomed to self-government. Without conscious design, England had fashioned a new kind of empire. Armed trade had been the foundation of the Portuguese and Dutch empires. The empire of Spain placed a ruling class of soldiers, planters, and missionaries in command of large native populations. But the Protestant English felt none of the responsibility for the Indians that weighed upon the missionaries of Spain, nor could the English exploit the labor of the thinly settled Indian populations of North America. Instead, the English settlers and the Dutch of New Holland simply displaced the natives. England transferred an entire European population to a new environment and allowed it to blend institutions brought from home with innovations that new surroundings demanded. The result was a unique, unplanned experiment in economic, political, and religious freedom.

Russia Reaches the Pacific

While France and Britain were pushing westward across North America, the Muscovite state was pressing eastward from the Ural Mountains across Siberia toward the Pacific. Muscovy reached the Pacific first; no ocean separated its new dominions from the center of its power around Moscow. In 1581 groups of Cossacks—the "pioneers" or "frontiersmen" who had earlier pushed back Tartars and Turks and had settled the lower valleys of the Dnieper, Don, and Volga rivers—struck eastward from the Urals. Their fierce leader, Yermak, enjoyed the patronage of Tsar Ivan IV, the Terrible. Like the French in Canada, the Cossacks sought furs, particularly the incomparable sable. They therefore followed the pine forests and the northern tundra rather than the open plains to the south. The innumerable rivers and lakes of Siberia allowed the Cossacks, like the French *coureurs de bois,* to flow swiftly eastward, occasionally halting to found fortified outposts.

The Cossacks reached the Pacific in the early 1640s, three generations and

3,000 miles after their eastward movement began. Unlike America, no great mountain chains barred the way. Resistance from the small Tartar states and the numerically weak tribal peoples of Siberia was slight. The advanced civilization of China ultimately checked Muscovite expansion in the Amur River valley. In 1689, Russia and China concluded their first treaty at Nerchinsk, and Russia withdrew from the Amur basin for almost 200 years.

Like the English, the Cossacks sought freedom as well as furs. Their early communities in Siberia were as wild and lawless as the later towns of the American West. But like the French administration in North America, the despotism of the tsars soon reached out across vast distances to clamp its administration and taxes on the lucrative fur trade. By 1700 several hundred thousand Russians had settled Siberia. By the end of the century, Russian traders had ventured across the Bering Strait to Alaska and down the North American coastline in search of seals. Long before the English in America reached the Pacific, the Russians had through individuals daring and government backing staked a claim to the northern half of Asia and had reached out toward the Western Hemisphere.

The first half of the seventeenth century was thus a period of fierce turmoil both within Europe and in Europe's relations with the wider world. The French monarchy consolidated itself but remained vulnerable to its turbulent nobles. The English monarchy for a time collapsed. From 1618 to 1648 the states of central Europe—and outside powers from France to Sweden—fought the last and bloodiest of the wars of religion. European economic and population growth faltered under the battering of wars, epidemics, and the "little ice age." Yet Europe's expansion into the outer world continued ceaselessly, if less swiftly than in the sixteenth century. The rise of Europe's new territorial states continued; new theories and methods of statecraft and new economic techniques made them bastions of order and relative prosperity in a violent and anarchic world. Yet after 1600, one state rose so high that it threatened to overthrow the balance of power on which Europe's state system rested.

Suggestions for Further Reading

General

D. Ogg, *Europe in the Seventeenth Century* (1925, 1960), and G. N. Clark, *The Seventeenth Century* (1931), offer useful surveys. G. Parker, *Europe in Crisis* (1979), reflects recent work in the field. For a model comparative analysis of the upheavals that convulsed most early modern states, see P. Zagorin, *Rebels and Rulers, 1500–1660* (1982). M. S. Anderson, *War and Society in Europe of the Old Regime, 1619–1789* (1988), surveys one powerful force for change.

The Great Powers

For events in France, see the detailed survey of R. R. Treasure, *Seventeenth Century France* (1966). C. V. Wedgwood, *Richelieu and the French Monarchy* (1962), and C. J. Burckhardt, *Richelieu: His Rise to Power* (1964), are informative. P. Goubert, *The Ancien Regime: French Society, 1600–1750* (1973), is excellent on French social structure. On England, see especially C. Hill, *The Century of Revolution, 1603–1714* (1961); L. Stone, *The Causes of the English Revolution, 1529–1642* (1972); and C. V. Wedgwood, *The King's Peace, 1637–1641* (1955), and *The King's War 1641–1647* (1958). M. Ashley, *The Greatness of Oliver Cromwell* (1966), and C. Hill, *God's Englishman* (1970), deal in lively fashion with a central figure. P. Laslett, *The World We Have Lost,* 2nd ed. (1971), gives an enthusiastic introduction to England's seventeenth-century social history. S. Schama, *The Embarrassment of Riches* (1988), is entertaining on the culture and politics of the Dutch Republic. On events in central Europe, see especially R. W. J. Evans, *The Making of the Habsburg Monarchy* (1979); C. V. Wedgwood, *The Thirty Years' War* (1938); and G. Parker et al., *The Thirty Years' War* (1974).

The European and World Economies

On Europe's economic crisis, see especially C. M. Cipolla, *Before the Industrial Revolution* (1976); F. Braudel, *Civilization and Capitalism, 15th–18th Centuries* (1982); and *The Cambridge Economic History of Europe,* Vol. 4 (1967). C. McEvedy and F. Jones, *Atlas of World Population History* (1978), provides the best set of—admittedly speculative—population figures.

For relations between Europe and the world, see particularly J. H. Parry, *The Age of Reconnaissance* (1964), and J. H. Elliott, *The Old World and the New* (1970). A. W. Crosby, *The Columbian Exchange* (1972), and *Biological Imperialism: The Biological Expansion of Europe, 900–1900* (1986), provide elegant treatments of neglected but decisively important events.

ABSOLUTISM AND CONSTITUTIONALISM
1660–1715

The last half of the seventeenth century was the age of France. Its population of roughly 18 million in 1650 dwarfed the 7.5 million of Spain and the roughly 5 million of England. Its economy and its bureaucratic-military machine were the largest in Europe. Much of Europe imitated its culture, a subject treated more fully in the following chapter.

But French power had limits. Internally, high taxation, government regulation of the economy, religious persecution, and oppressive censorship stunted economic growth. Externally, Louis XIV's attempts to dominate Europe created a series of coalitions against France. In the two great worldwide conflicts of 1689–97 and 1701–15, England, the Dutch Republic, and Habsburg Austria compelled even the "Sun King" of France to recognize the law of relations between states: the law of the balance of power.

Other powers declined with giddying speed, or stagnated. Sweden, outclassed militarily thanks to its small population, ceased to be a great power. The Ottoman Turks mounted their last great threat to western Europe, and then began the decline that soon made their empire the "sick man" of the state system. The internal anarchy and external decline of Poland that led to its disappearance from the map between 1772 and 1795 became visible. Spain sank further. The Dutch settled down to enjoy their riches.

Winners emerged as well. Austria defeated the Turks and consolidated the Habsburg hereditary possessions into a state more centralized than anything before it in south-central Europe. England took command of the outer seas from the Dutch, as the Dutch had taken it from Portugal. Russia, until now a backward power outside the European system, suffered the first of the barbaric "revolutions

(OPPOSITE) ABSOLUTISM: THE YOUNG LOUIS XIV, READY FOR THE PURSUIT OF GLORY, BY GIOVANNI LORENZO BERNINI, 1665.

The Sun King's emblem.

from above" that transformed it into a military giant. And the uncouth electorate of Brandenburg, an obscure state on the eastern fringes of Germany, began its fateful rise to great power status.

THE FRANCE OF LOUIS XIV

Louis XIV, the "Sun King" (r. 1643–1715), was the living symbol of French military,

political, and cultural domination. He was born in 1638 and took power decisively into his own hands the day after Mazarin's death in 1661. He died at the age of 77 and left the throne to his great-grandson. By temperament and training he incarnated divine-right monarchy—the notion that hereditary kingship was the only divinely approved form of government, that kings answered to God alone for their conduct, and that subjects owed absolute obedience to their king as the direct representative of God on earth. His education was sketchy, and he had little imagination and no sense of humor. But he had the qualities needed to rule—a willingness to work relentlessly, a commanding presence, and an imperious will.

Louis may not have spoken the famous words ascribed to him—"I am the state." But he practiced them. He sought to personify the concept of sovereignty. He took a deep interest in the elaborate etiquette and ceremonies of his court, for they dramatized his supremacy over the nobility. He also conducted the business of the state in person, as his own "first minister," from Mazarin's death in 1661 to his own in 1715, a dedication uncommon in monarchs. He set his preferred pastimes of hunting and womanizing aside when the state demanded it. "If you let yourself be carried away by your passions," he once remarked, "don't do it in business hours."

The administrative machine that served Louis XIV culminated in a three to five member "High Council" of great ministers that met with him almost daily. Professional "secretaries" at the head of bureaucracies then executed the decisions taken in council. In the provinces, the *intendants,* the royal administrative officers that Richelieu had created, received ever more power to enforce the king's will.

Three great ministers of middle-class origin—Jean-Baptiste Colbert, Michel Le Tellier, and his son, the Marquis de Louvois—directed the administration under the king's close supervision. Colbert, cold, gloomy, and fanatically precise, served as Controller General of Finance. He cut waste, streamlined the tax system, and gave France its first serious attempt at

Bishop Bossuet on Absolutism

Jacques Bénigne Bossuet was tutor to Louis XIV's son in the 1670s, and the most zealous and prominent theorist of the king's absolutism.

The royal power is absolute. With the aim of making this truth hateful and insufferable, many writers have tried to confound absolute government and arbitrary government. But no two things could be more unlike. . . . The Prince need render an account of his acts to no one. . . . Without this absolute authority the king could neither do good nor repress evil. . . . God is infinite, God is all. The prince, as prince, is not regarded as a private person: he is a public personage, all the state is in him; the will of all the people is included in his. As all perfection and all strength are united in God, so all the power of individuals is united in the person of the prince. What grandeur that a single man should embody so much! . . .

From Jacques Bénigne Bossuet, "Politics Drawn from the Very Words of Scripture," in Readings in European History, *ed. by James Harvey Robinson (Boston: Ginn, 1906), Vol. II, pp. 275–76.*

an annual budget. He sought to force France's economic growth by punitive tariffs against the Dutch, state-supported industrial projects, and colonial enterprises. He doubled the king's net income between 1661 and 1671. Le Tellier and Louvois, the ministers of war, then spent the proceeds.

The old French monarchy had imposed its authority through its law courts, the *parlements*. It had also frequently consulted provincial assemblies or the Estates General of France. The new monarchy that Richelieu had founded and Louis XIV perfected imposed its authority and its taxes by decree. Louis XIV checked the pretensions of the *parlements* and deliberately neglected to summon the Estates General. The new army paid for by Louis XIV's taxes mobilized French manpower and militarized French society to an unprecedented extent. It also provided the force to crush—often with mass hangings—the many attempts at tax rebellion in the provinces. Above all, the king completed Richelieu's work of destroying the political power of the French nobility.

The Domestication of the Nobility

The Fronde had forced Louis XIV to flee Paris three times, and had left him fiercely determined to break the turbulent nobility. His principal weapons were three: First, he denied the nobility its traditional share in the power of the state and sharply curtailed its independent power in the provinces. He chose his ministers almost exclusively from commoners, rotated *intendants* to prevent collusion with the local nobility, and treated *parlements* and provincial assemblies with contempt. Second, he cheapened the status of the nobility by increasing its numbers; the title of marquis soon became almost a joke. Finally, he required the high nobility to serve him at court.

That service was bound up with Louis XIV's deliberate display of himself as the symbol of the state. In 1683 he moved court and government from the Louvre palace in central Paris to Versailles, fifteen miles away. There he made his home in the formal gardens and ornate chateau that he had built on marshland, at great cost in lives and treasure.

Louis XIV on the Duties of a King

In the 1660s and 1670s, Louis XIV and his staff prepared notes to instruct his son in the art of ruling.

I have often wondered how it could be that love for work being a quality so necessary to sovereigns should yet be one that is so rarely found in them. Most princes, because they have a great many servants and subjects, do not feel obligated to go to any trouble and do not consider that if they have an infinite number of people working under their orders, there are infinitely more who rely on their conduct and that it takes a great deal of watching and a great deal of work merely to insure that those who act do only what they should and that those who rely tolerate only what they must. The deference and the respect that we receive from our subjects are not a free gift from them but payment for the justice and the protection that they expect to receive from us. Just as they must honor us, we must protect and defend them, and our debts toward them are even more binding than theirs to us, for indeed, if one of them lacks the skill or the willingness to execute our orders, a thousand others come in a crowd to fill his post, whereas the position of a sovereign can be properly filled only by the sovereign himself.

. . . of all the functions of sovereignty, the one that a prince must guard most jealously is the handling of finances. It is the most delicate of all because it is the one that is most capable of seducing the one who performs it, and which makes it easiest for him to spread corruption. The prince alone should have sovereign direction over it because he alone has no fortune to establish but that of the state.

From Louis XIV, Memoirs for the Instruction of the Dauphin, *ed. by Paul Sonnino (New York: Free Press, 1970), pp. 63–64.*

The medal on the left (1661) celebrates the young Louis's purported accessibility to his subjects. The one on the right (1685) extols the new discipline and professionalism of his armies.

The palace of Versailles (1686), with the king arriving by carriage.

Louis moved with impassive dignity through the innumerable court gatherings in the mirrored halls of Versailles. Years of self-conscious practice in kingship had given him a public façade—cool, courteous, impersonal, imperturbable—that fitted perfectly the artificiality of the small world of the court, as far removed from reality as Versailles itself was physically removed from the bustle of Paris. In that atmosphere, a ball seemed as important as a battle, and holding the basin for the king's morning ablutions became a task as coveted as the command of armies. Instead of competing in the provinces for political power against the monarchy, nobles squandered their fortunes in jockeying for prestige under the king's vigilant eye.

He left the nobility one other outlet—war. Military service harnessed the nobility's inborn aggressiveness to the purposes of the state. But that outlet also had a political cost. It created a noble "war party" at court that encouraged the king's own megalomania.

The Destruction of the Huguenots

The only potential challenges to Louis's absolutism besides the nobility were religious forces and groups. The king clashed with several popes who disputed his "Gallican" claim to control the Church in France. But those quarrels never led to a break with Rome, for in doctrine Louis XIV was strictly orthodox. And after 1680 he became increasingly concerned about the fate of his own soul. When his queen, Maria Theresa, died in 1683, he gave up all mistresses except the pious Madame de Maintenon, whom he secretly married. The king's growing piety naturally expressed itself politically. The wars of religion were over, but in the late seventeenth century religion and affairs of state remained tightly intertwined.

Louis XIV enthusiastically persecuted the Jansenists, an austere group of Catholic "puritans" who emphasized the teachings of St. Augustine on original sin, human depravity, and the need for divine grace. Louis, whose confessors were Jesuits, thought the Jansenists impertinent in their disapproval of his numerous mistresses, and subversive as well, for the pope had condemned them. In 1710–12 Louis razed their principal monastic center to the ground.

But it was the Huguenots, one of the most loyal and industrious groups in France, who felt the full force of Louis XIV's religious enthusiasm. Two religions under one prince was indeed, by seventeenth-century standards, an anomaly. And the French clergy had long insisted that the continued existence of Protestantism in France was an insult to the king's dignity and authority. After 1679 Louis apparently embraced the idea of atoning for his own numerous sins of the flesh—and his negotiations with the Ottoman Turks, enemies of Catholic Habsburg Austria—by crushing heresy in France.

He began by gradually tightening his interpretation of the Edict of Nantes, by which Henry IV had granted toleration to the Huguenots and ended France's religious civil wars in 1598. He forced Protestants to convert, destroyed their chapels, and quartered royal troops on their families. In 1685 he took the final step. At the urging of his Jesuit advisers, he announced that since all heretics had reconverted to Catholicism, the Edict of Nantes no longer served any purpose and was therefore revoked. The state closed all remaining Protestant churches and schools, and the Church baptized all Protestant children as Catholics. Louis enforced the revocation with imprisonment, torture, and condemnation to the galleys. Many Huguenots continued to practice their faith in secret. Perhaps 200,000, more than a fifth of the Protestant population of France, fled to England, the Dutch Netherlands, Brandenburg, and the New World. Their industry and skill contributed mightily to the rapid economic growth of their new homes.

The revocation of the Edict of Nantes was an act of religious intolerance that rivaled the Spanish expulsion of the Moriscos in 1609–14, the Habsburg ravaging of Bohemia after the battle of the White Mountain in 1620, or the systematic impoverishment and degradation of the Catholics of Ireland by English conquerors from Elizabeth I to Cromwell and his successors. But in those cases, unlike that of France, ethnic hatred had compounded religious savagery. The revocation of the Edict of Nantes was unique in the seventeenth century—a major act of barbarism that was *purely* religious in intention. It was the last such act in western Europe until Germany's attempt to exterminate the European Jews between 1941 and 1944.

Literature and Fashion: The Primacy of France

To dramatize his conception of kingship, Louis chose as his emblem the sun god,

Apollo. The symbol of the sun, on whose rays all earthly life depends, became the theme of the architecture and sculpture of the new palace at Versailles. The "Sun King" patronized and presided over an "Augustan Age" of French culture. As befitted such a patron, the prevailing taste was classical. It emphasized form, order, balance, and proportion—the presumed ideals of reasonable individuals throughout history.

In 1636, Pierre Corneille (1606–84), the father of French classical tragedy, wrote *Le Cid,* the first of a series of powerful dramas that glorified willpower and the quest for perfection. Corneille was still active when Louis began his personal rule, but the dramatist's brilliant younger contemporary, Jean Racine (1639–99), soon eclipsed him. Racine wrote more realistically than Corneille about human beings in the grip of violent and sometimes coarse passions. He brought French tragedy to its highest perfection between 1667 and 1677. Then he underwent a religious conversion that caused him to renounce drama as immoral.

Some of the admirers of the tragedies of Corneille and Racine had little respect for the comic playwright Molière (1622–73), but his biting satirical drama became a model for future dramatists. From 1659 to his death he was the idol of aristocratic audiences at Versailles. All three playwrights concentrated on portraying types, not individuals—the hero, the man of honor violently in love, the miser, the hypocrite—embodiments of human passions and foibles that belonged to all times and places. Partly as a result, French classical drama of the age of Louis XIV was easily exportable. French literary standards influenced cultivated Europeans everywhere, although French literary creativity flagged in the later years of Louis XIV's reign, as religious persecution, political censorship, and economic exhaustion intensified.

In the other arts, and in social conventions, France likewise swayed the rest of Europe, although Louis XIV's growing religious intolerance and military aggressiveness prompted resistance to French culture, especially in Protestant republics

Engraving of a performance of Molière's last play, *Le Malade imaginaire* (1673). Molière died on stage on the fourth night of the performance.

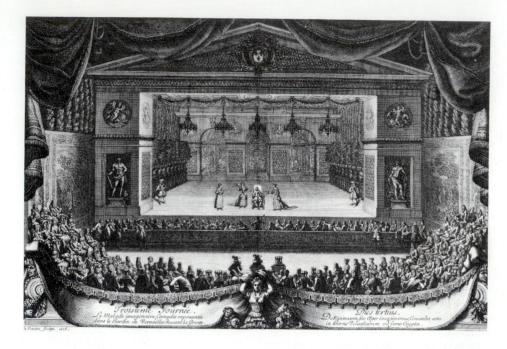

such as the Dutch United Provinces, where middle-class art and manners flourished. French fashions in dress nevertheless spread across Spain, Italy, and much of Germany. The heavy French Baroque style, exemplified by Louis's palace at Versailles, broke the supremacy in architecture that Italy had enjoyed since the Renaissance. French became the language of diplomacy and polite conversation, and the court of the "Sun King" set the tone for countless smaller courts throughout Catholic Europe. As Florence had been the center of the Italian Renaissance, and Spain of the Counter-Reformation, so France in the late seventeenth century was the center of European politics, diplomacy, and culture.

France's Bid for the Domination of Europe

Richelieu and Mazarin had begun the process of creating a large, dependable standing army to replace the disorderly semi-mercenary, semi-feudal military system of the preceding century. Louis and his formidable ministers of war, Le Tellier and Louvois, completed the task. The ministers subordinated the aristocratic officer corps and the provincial private armies to royal authority, developed an efficient supply system, standardized the organization of infantry and artillery, and followed the example of Gustavus Adolphus by having the troops wear uniforms. The Seigneur de Vauban, the father of modern military engineering, invented the first effective bayonet and perfected the science of building—and smashing—fortifications in the age of gunpowder. Above all, Le Tellier and Louvois provided Louis with numbers. By the 1660s he possessed by far the largest and best-equipped army in Europe: 100,000 men in peace and up to 400,000 in war, numbers not seen in the West since the fall of Rome.

This unprecedented power inevitably brought the temptation to use it. War aroused the enthusiasm of the nobility and kept it occupied in ways that did not threaten the state. War exercised and justified the enormous and costly standing army. Above all, successful war enhanced the glory of the monarch, a glory that was Louis XIV's constant concern. Perhaps war would make him the arbiter not only of France but of Europe as well.

Louis XIV's first two wars (1667–68, 1672–79) were relatively limited in aim.

The decline of Spain and the collapse of the Holy Roman Empire left a power vacuum on France's eastern borders; Louis therefore sought to annex the Spanish Netherlands (later Belgium), Franche-Comté, and parts of western Germany and to reduce the Dutch to vassalage. In each of the two wars, alliances that at different times included the United Provinces, Sweden, and the Habsburg monarchy checked him after initial French victories. The Dutch held off his first onslaught in 1672 by opening their dikes and flooding the countryside. England simultaneously attacked the Dutch by sea but withdrew from the war in 1674. By 1678 Louis had gained only Franche-Comté and a few border fortresses in Flanders.

Thereafter, Louis briefly chose legal chicanery over musketry. He established French courts called Chambers of Reunion to "reunite" to France all lands on France's borders that had in the past been dependencies of French territories. That gave him control of the independent Protestant republic of Strasbourg in 1681, much to the indignation of the inhabitants and of Protestants throughout Europe. The revocation of the Edict of Nantes in 1685 provided further evidence of his arrogance.

In 1686 the Habsburg emperor, along with Spain, Sweden, and several German states, formed the defensive League of Augsburg. Habsburg victories in Hungary over the Turks, who were allied with Louis, shifted the balance in the West against Bourbon France. Louis replied with the most senseless atrocity since the Thirty Years' War—his armies systematically devastated the Palatinate, a rich region of western Germany, in 1688 simply to cow his enemies. That act instead helped weld them together. And French distraction in Germany allowed William of Orange, ruler of the Dutch Netherlands and Louis XIV's most implacable enemy, to claim the English throne in 1688–89. England and the Dutch, the two greatest economic and sea powers of the age, then joined the League of Augsburg and closed the circle around over-mighty France.

The participants' worldwide interests made this war the first *world* war, waged in India, the Caribbean, and North Amer-

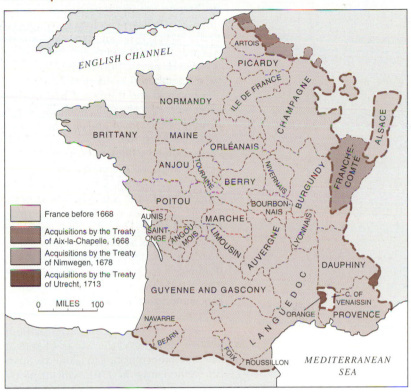

The Conquest of Louis XIV   1661–1715

ENGLISH CHANNEL

ARTOIS
PICARDY
ILE DE FRANCE
CHAMPAGNE
ALSACE
NORMANDY
BRITTANY
MAINE
ORLÉANAIS
ANJOU
TOURAINE
NIVERNAIS
BERRY
BURGUNDY
FRANCHE-COMTÉ
POITOU
AUNIS
SAINT-ONGE
ANGOUMOIS
MARCHE
BOURBONNAIS
LIMOUSIN
AUVERGNE
LYONNAIS
DAUPHINY
GUYENNE AND GASCONY
LANGUEDOC
C. OF VENAISSIN
ORANGE
PROVENCE
NAVARRE
BÉARN
FOIX
ROUSSILLON
MEDITERRANEAN SEA

France before 1668
Acquisitions by the Treaty of Aix-la-Chapelle, 1668
Acquisitions by the Treaty of Nimwegen, 1678
Acquisitions by the Treaty of Utrecht, 1713

0   MILES   100

ica as well as in Europe. After ten years of fighting, France agreed to the Peace of Ryswick in 1697. Louis retained the gains made before 1678 but had to renounce nearly all conquests after that date except Strasbourg. England emerged from the war stronger than it had been in 1689, and France weaker.

The War of the Spanish Succession, 1701–14

The Peace of Ryswick lasted only four years. Louis had made peace in the hope of gaining a greater prize than any for which he had yet contended—the Spanish Empire. Charles II of Spain, bizarre end-product of generations of syphilitic degeneration and Habsburg inbreeding, and last of the Spanish Habsburg line that had ruled since 1516, was losing a 30-year struggle against numerous diseases. By 1697 he was close to death and had no direct heir. That raised an issue of vital

Officer and musketeer of the French Guard (late seventeenth century).

importance to all Europe: would the Spanish Empire fall to Emperor Leopold I of the Austrian Habsburg line, would it pass to the French Bourbon dynasty (for Louis XIV was both the son and the widower of Spanish Habsburg princesses), or would it be dismembered by its rivals?

England and the Dutch had obvious economic and strategic interests in preventing France from grasping Spain's colonial trade or the Spanish Netherlands. Louis seemed willing to compromise and twice concluded secret treaties that partitioned the Spanish dominions with the English and Dutch. But when news of the second treaty reached Madrid, the dying Charles II refused to see parts of his Catholic empire pass to Protestant powers. Instead, he made a will that left all his dominions to a grandson of Louis XIV. After the death of Charles II in 1699, Spain proclaimed that grandson King Philip V of Spain.

Louis XIV tore up the secret partition treaties, recognized the will of Charles II, and sent French troops to claim the Spanish Netherlands. In 1701 William of Orange formed yet another coalition against France. England, Holland, and Emperor Leopold I of Austria bound themselves to fight until they had ended the threat of Bourbon control of Spain and of the Spanish colonies. Louis had made his last and most far-reaching bid for the domination of Europe. But this time his enemies were as unyielding and powerful as he was.

Warfare had by now become thoroughly professional. In the long wars since 1618, innovators such as Gustavus Adolphus, Maurice of Orange, Le Tellier, and Louvois had replaced noble amateurs and independent military contractors with professional officers corps that bore the "king's commission." Ragged bands of freebooters yielded to disciplined ranks rigidly drilled in the new fire tactics. The combination of musket and bayonet united fire and shock in one weapon and drove out the clumsy combinations of pikemen and musketeers that had ruled the battlefield since the Spanish victory at Pavia in 1525. Commanders learned to coordinate infantry, the new mobile artillery, and cavalry. Sieges, thanks to Vauban, became scientific exercises.

In the new world war of 1701–14, the French soon found themselves outdone. Two commanders of genius led the Allied armies—England's John Churchill, first Duke of Marlborough, and the great Habsburg general and scourge of the Turks, Prince Eugene of Savoy. Marlborough's diplomacy held the ramshackle coalition together. His generalship smashed the great armies of Louis XIV in four battles of unprecedented slaughter that cost France up to 80,000 casualties—Blenheim (1704), Ramillies (1706), Oudenarde (1708), and Malplaquet (1709). England trounced the French at sea and seized Gibraltar, from which it thereafter dominated the western Mediterranean. An allied army even invaded Spain and several times took Madrid.

Louis XIV, with France exhausted militarily and in the grip of famine, sued for peace in 1709–10 on almost any terms. The Allies thereupon demanded that he send French troops to help expel his own grandson from Madrid. That was too great a humiliation. Louis XIV refused, and appealed with success to his subjects. Famine and economic crisis filled the French armies with new recruits, who preferred the risks of the battlefield to the certainty of starvation. An anti-foreign reaction in Spain helped drive the English and Austrian invaders out. In 1710 the English war party, the Whigs, gave way to the Tories, and a war-weary England recalled Marlborough. In 1712 the French severed Prince Eugene of Savoy's communications and forced him to retreat. It was the Allies' turn to seek peace.

The Peace of Utrecht, 1713–14

In theory, the Peace of Utrecht of 1713 and other treaties of 1714 that ended the war of the Spanish Succession gave France the prize that Louis had sought since 1701. Louis's grandson remained on the throne of Spain—but only on condition that no subsequent Bourbon should unite the crowns of Spain and France. And Louis gave up all conquests east of the Rhine and his bid for the Spanish Netherlands and Spain's colonial trade. France survived as the greatest single power. But the war had drained it of money and blood, and had made Louis XIV's government bankrupt and hated. When the great king died at last in 1715, France's common people reputedly "openly returned thanks to God."

England was the chief victor. It emerged from the war with the dominance of the seas that it held until the twentieth century. From France it took Newfoundland, Acadia (modern New Brunswick and Nova Scotia), and the Hudson's Bay Territory. It kept Gibraltar and Minorca, seized from Spain, and received the *Asiento*—the profitable privilege of supplying African slaves to the Spanish colonies.

The Austrian Habsburgs gained the Spanish Netherlands (which now became the Austrian Netherlands) and replaced Spain as the dominant power in Italy through the acquisition of Milan, Naples, and Sicily. Two new smaller powers, Brandenburg-Prussia and the Duchy of Savoy, increased their territories and prestige; they had chosen the winning side. The Dutch achieved their minimum war aim—they kept the Scheldt River closed, thus blocking the trade of Antwerp, the chief port of the Austrian Netherlands. But the long strain of fighting France for almost half a century had demoralized them. They could no longer compete at sea with England and soon slipped from the ranks of the great powers.

The Peace of Utrecht ended the first bid for European hegemony since the days of Philip II of Spain. Louis XIV's attempt to gain for France the domination of western Europe and the wider world had summoned up, through the workings of the balance of power, the coalition that had checked France. War had prevented the universal domination of one power. The European state system had survived a challenge to its very existence.

ENGLAND: THE EMERGENCE OF PARLIAMENTARY MONARCHY

While Louis XIV consolidated absolute monarchy in France, the English created a constitutional monarchy controlled by Parliament. The restoration of king, Parliament, and Anglican Church in 1660 had established a balance between Crown and Parliament. But that balance had remained unstable. Who was to exercise sovereignty—the king, or the gentry and merchants of Parliament? What would the religious settlement be, and who would make it? Who would control foreign policy? These questions had dominated the preceding forty years of turmoil and civil war. They still awaited answers.

Charles II and the "Cavalier Parliament"

Charles II (r. 1660–85), unlike his too stubborn father, was witty, attractive, worldly, a king of hearty sexual appetites and shrewd political sense. He had lived long in exile in France and took his cousin Louis XIV as his model. Charles was resolved not to risk exile or execution in the manner of his father. He instead hoped to restore England to Catholicism and to establish a French-style absolute monarchy through stealth, manipulation, and compromise. That ambition Charles II pursued through 25 years of court intrigue, party politics, and secret diplomacy that kept both Parliament and ministers guessing about his intentions.

The "Cavalier Parliament" of 1661–79 held a commanding position at the beginning of the reign. It was the preserve of the gentry, and of the aristocracy, now partly restored to its ancient influence in both local and national government. Both groups were for the moment strongly royalist and determined to stamp out all remaining political and religious radicalism. But they also had no intention of allowing the Crown to be financially independent of Parliament.

In place of the old idea that "the king should live of his own," Parliament now granted Charles a regular income from customs and excise duties. But it was not enough to meet even the ordinary expenses of government, let alone the expenses of Charles's wild doings at court or of his numerous mistresses and illegitimate children. And foreign war was unthinkable unless Parliament voted money. Charles therefore allowed Parliament, under the leadership of his father's adviser, Edward Hyde, Earl of Clarendon, to have its way for a time.

The House of Commons, on the Great Seal of England (1651).

Charles II, the "Merry Monarch."

Parliament thus dictated the religious settlement. The Cavalier Parliament was as strongly pro-Anglican as it was pro-royalist. Between 1661 and 1665 it passed statutes known inaccurately as the "Clarendon Code"—Clarendon himself favored toleration—that excluded from local government Puritans who "dissented" from the established Church and purged Puritan ministers from the Anglican clergy. Later legislation barred dissenters from Parliament, from service in the army or navy, and from the universities at Oxford or Cambridge.

Puritanism and social radicalism appeared to be intertwined. The Cavalier Parliament was therefore determined to stamp out the first and discourage the second. But while the Clarendon Code lowered the social status of dissenters and narrowed their opportunities, it did not greatly decrease their number. Presbyterians, Congregationalists, Baptists, and Quakers formed persistent religious minorities that bitterly opposed both Anglicanism and Catholicism. Charles himself sought toleration as a first step to restoring Catholicism. In 1672 he issued a "Declaration of Indulgence" that suspended the operation of the Code against both Puritans and Catholics and appeared to assert—in the manner of Charles I—that royal prerogative could thwart acts of Parliament. Parliament forced him to withdraw the Declaration and imposed on him a Test Act that excluded non-Anglicans from civil and military office. To the Anglican gentry of Parliament, Puritans remained radicals and Catholics traitors.

Foreign Policy: The French Alliance

Two natural calamities, a fierce outbreak of bubonic plague that killed 60,000 of the 450,000 inhabitants of London in 1665 and a fire that destroyed much of the city in 1666, contributed to widespread unrest. Public opinion blamed the fire on an imaginary Catholic plot. Uneasiness increased as king and Parliament drifted apart over foreign policy. In 1665 Parliament forced Charles into a war with the Dutch over trade, but denied him the money needed to win. When swift victories did not follow, Parliament unfairly held Clarendon responsible and exiled him.

After Louis XIV began his attack on the Spanish Netherlands in 1667, English opinion began to see the military power of Catholic France as more threatening than the commercial rivalry of the Protestant Dutch. But Charles held to his connection with Louis, and in 1670 Charles allied England with France against the Dutch through the notorious secret Treaty of Dover. In the Treaty, Louis XIV offered money and French troops if Charles were to declare himself a Catholic and reconvert England to Catholicism.

Charles was probably unsure of how far down that road he meant to travel. He did acquire both a pro-French foreign policy and a French mistress who reported secretly to Louis XIV's ambassador. English forces also attacked the Dutch along with the French in 1672. Between 1675 and 1681 Charles concluded with Louis four additional secret agreements in which he undertook to thwart Parliament's anti-French moves in return for more French money. The existence of this close understanding with Louis inevitably leaked out and created fear of French domination and a return to Catholicism. The landed classes represented in Parliament were increasingly suspicious of Charles II and prone to panic.

London's catastrophic great fire of 1666.

Whigs and Tories: The Origins of Modern Party Politics

In 1678 these accumulated fears exploded in the lurid "Popish Plot." A disreputable former Anglican clergyman named Titus Oates concocted a story about a Jesuit plot to kill the king, to place his Catholic brother James, Duke of York, on the throne with French help, and to massacre England's Protestants. Parliament described it as "a damnable and hellish plot, for assassinating and murdering the king and rooting out and destroying the Protestant religion." A new civil war seemed about to break out.

The Earl of Shaftesbury, a great land-owner who had fought for Parliament in the Civil War, rallied a "Country Party" that campaigned fiercely to exclude James from the succession to the throne. In response, an Anglican and royalist "Court Party" assembled, although at first without much enthusiasm, to support Charles II and his brother. The Court Party denigrated the Shaftesbury group as "Whigs," a name hitherto applied to Scottish Presbyterian rebels. The Whigs in turn baptized their antagonists "Tories," a kind of Irish Catholic brigand.

The Whigs controlled the three brief Parliaments that followed the dissolution of the Cavalier Parliament in 1679. Shaftesbury and his associates merrily pressed the execution of some 35 Catholics for alleged complicity in the imaginary Popish Plot. But the Whig leaders overplayed their hand. Opinion swung back toward the king, and it was soon the turn of the Whigs to suffer. By 1681 Shaftesbury had fled abroad, the inventors of the Popish Plot were disgraced or executed, and Charles II was stronger than any monarch since the early days of James I. Until his death in 1685 Charles ruled without Parliament, with his brother James by his side and with the subsidies of Louis XIV filling his coffers.

These difficult years were nevertheless momentous for the West's tradition of political liberty. This struggle between the king and factions of the gentry in Parliament created the ancestors of modern political parties—groups organized for the purpose of electioneering and of controlling government through a representative assembly. Whigs and Tories were in part the descendants of the Parliamentarians and Royalists of the 1640s. But the great crisis of the 1680s produced, instead of civil war, the system of Parliamentary rule that England later passed on to its colonies and indirectly to the West as a whole.

The "Glorious Revolution" of 1688

James, Duke of York, succeeded his brother Charles II in 1685 as James II (r. 1685–88). He was a bigoted convert to Catholicism who lacked Charles's shrewdness and flexibility. Within three years he had infuriated almost every political and religious group of importance in England, and had provoked the revolution that Charles II had succeeded in avoiding.

Early successes made him overconfident. He introduced Catholics into the high command of both army and navy, and camped a standing army a few miles from London. He surrounded himself with Catholic advisers and attacked Anglican control of the universities. He claimed the power to suspend or dispense with acts of Parliament. In a vain attempt to win the support of Puritans as well as Catholics, he issued a Declaration of Indulgence along the lines of his brother's—thus further alienating the Anglican establishment. By revoking borough charters and browbeating sheriffs, he tried to ensure the election of a Parliament favorable to his policies. These measures, along with the example of Louis XIV's revocation of the Edict of Nantes in 1685, terrified England's Protestants.

The event that triggered James II's downfall was a happy one—the unexpected birth in June 1688 of a son to his Catholic queen. Until then, Protestants had consoled themselves with the thought that James II's two elder daughters by another marriage, Mary and Anne, were Protestants, and would succeed James. Now the existence of a Catholic male heir prolonged the Catholic absolutist threat indefinitely into the future. But unlike the events of 1641, the king had no "king's party." He had alienated Anglicans and

James II, who swiftly alienated even traditional supporters of the monarchy (engraved after a painting by Sir Godfrey Kneller, 1688).

dissenters, Tories and Whigs, aristocracy and commoners. The result was a bloodless "revolution," a rapid and fundamental political change that established the limited or parliamentary monarchy that has persisted to the present.

The agent of James II's downfall was William of Orange, *stadholder* and hero of the Dutch Republic, the man who had opened the dikes to halt the French invasion in 1672. In 1677, in pursuit of allies against France, he had married James II's eldest daughter, Mary, and had thus acquired a claim to the English throne. In June 1688 a group of prominent Englishmen, both Whigs and Tories, invited William to cross the English Channel and save the Protestant cause in England. That November William landed a Dutch army on the southern coast and marched slowly toward London. The countryside rose against James II, and William tactfully allowed the friendless king to flee to France. An improvised Parliament declared that James had abdicated the throne by flight and invited William and Mary to become joint sovereigns on condition that they accept a "Bill of Rights" that severely limited royal power.

This bloodless "Glorious Revolution" established at last the sovereignty of Parliament, which had made a king. William was strong-willed, but his priorities were continental and Dutch—the forging of an ever more powerful coalition against Louis XIV. He therefore grudgingly accepted Parliament's conditions. The "Jacobite" supporters of James II and his son invaded Ireland in 1690 and staged two bloody rebellions in the Scottish Highlands in 1715 and 1745, but all attempts at a second Restoration failed. Parliament had won. England had decisively rejected the French absolutist model of Louis XIV.

The Bill of Rights emphatically barred the king from suspending acts of Parliament or interfering with the courts. It furnished a base for the steady expansion of civil liberties in the generation after 1688. Parliament established religious toleration and freedom from arbitrary arrest. Censorship of the press quietly withered. The king had to summon Parliament annually, for he could neither pay nor control his

The speaker of the House of Lords offers William and Mary the English crown (from a contemporary engraving).

armed forces without parliamentary consent. Regular meetings of Parliament in turn strengthened the political parties and made the king dependent on their support. The monarch vetoed a parliamentary bill for the last time in 1707.

Hobbes Answered: John Locke and the Theory of Limited Government

The English Civil War and Glorious Revolution followed the Dutch revolt against Spain as the second of the Western revolutions that ended absolute monarchy and ultimately led to democratic representative government. Tradition demanded that English leaders in 1641–49 and 1688–89 deny that their acts were revolutionary. Parliament chopped off the head of one king and replaced another in the name of the *traditional* "liberties of England." But that half-fiction was unsatisfactory.

John Locke (1632–1704), a friend of the Earl of Shaftesbury who had founded the Whig party, provided a theoretical foundation for what Parliament had done and for the subsequent evolution of representative government. Locke probably wrote most of his *Of Civil Government: Two Treatises* while in political exile in Holland in 1683–89, but it emerged from the presses in 1690 as a belated rationale for the acts of Parliament during the Glorious Revolution. In it he at last answered Thomas Hobbes's justification of absolute sovereignty with a convincing theory of limited government.

Locke attacked the divine-right theory of monarchy and challenged Hobbes's claim that the only alternative to anarchy was absolute authority. Locke's first principle was that all individuals possess a natural right to "life, liberty, and property." That notion was revolutionary in an age of entrenched privilege. It remains revolutionary in our own, in which dictatorships or narrow oligarchies rule much of humanity. Locke derived the rest of his system from this premise of "natural rights," and from a more optimistic view of human nature than that of Hobbes. Like Hobbes and many predecessors and contemporaries, Locke argued that government was a contract in which humanity exchanged the anarchy of the "state of nature" for the security that government provided. But Locke's insistence that human rights were "natural" and prior to all government allowed him—unlike Hobbes—to limit the authority of government. The source of sovereignty, thanks to the natural rights of the governed, was the governed themselves: "The people alone can appoint the form of the commonwealth." It therefore followed, for Locke, that a government that acted without the consent of the governed dissolved the contract and gave the subjects a right to resistance or to revolution.

Locke also provided a principle for organizing government. Fearing concentration of power, he proposed a strict separation of powers that would allow the elected representatives of the people to check a tyrannical executive. Above all, he relentlessly emphasized property as the foundation of all freedom and the purpose of government itself: "The great and chief end. . . . of men's uniting into commonwealths and putting themselves under

John Locke (1632–1704), champion of "natural rights" and government by consent.

I I I I I I I I I I I I

Locke on Government by Consent   1690

Compare with "Bishop Bossuet on Absolutism," page XXX.

Men being, as has been said, by nature all free, equal, and independent, no one can be put out of this estate and subjected to the political power of another without his own consent, which is done by agreeing with other men, to join and unite into a community for their comfortable, safe, and peaceful living, one amongst another, in a secure enjoyment of their properties, and a greater security against any that are not of it. . . . When any number of men have so consented to make one community or government, they are thereby presently incorporated, and make one body politic, wherein the majority have the right to act and conclude the rest. . . . Absolute, arbitrary power, or governing without settled standing laws, can neither of them consist with the ends of society and government, which men would not quit the freedom of the state of Nature for, and tie themselves up under, were it not to preserve their lives, liberties, and fortunes, and by stated rules of right and property to secure their peace and quiet.

From John Locke, Of Civil Government: Two Treatises *(New York: Everyman's Library, 1924), pp. 164–65, 186.*

government is the preservation of their property." Some twentieth-century commentators have denigrated what they describe as Locke's doctrine of "possessive individualism," his equation of property and liberty—but have failed to offer examples of societies that enjoy liberty without property.

In the eighteenth century, Locke's ideas were a powerful rationale for a society based on wealth rather than on inherited privilege and for a new kind of government, limited in its powers. Inalienable natural rights, government by consent, the right of revolution, and the sanctity of property seemed increasingly "self-evident" to Englishmen after 1688, and ultimately to the American colonists in 1776.

The Emergence of the Cabinet System

At the level of practice rather than theory, factional struggles in Parliament replaced struggles between king and Parliament after 1688. The Glorious Revolution made gentry and merchants the real masters of both central and local government in England. Generally speaking, aristocratic landowners, bankers, merchants, and most dissenters were Whigs, while the smaller gentry, the Anglican parish clergy, and some great lords were Tories. But parties were still loosely organized, and small cliques often held the balance of power.

Given the fluidity of parliamentary alignments and the monarchy's residual powers, it took more than a century for a smoothly operating system of constitutional government to emerge through the slow accretion of precedent. The ultimate answer was the "cabinet system."

Under Charles II, a "cabinet council," or inner circle of important ministers had taken shape. Gradually the members of this "cabinet" discovered that settling major issues among themselves and then presenting a united front to the king was the most efficient way to conduct business. A leader—the "prime minister"—inevitably emerged within the cabinet.

During the reigns of William and Mary (1689–1702) and of Mary's sister, Queen

Anne (1702–14), monarchs still considered their ministers responsible to the crown rather than to Parliament. But to gain Parliament's support in war or peace both William and Anne found it advisable to choose their ministers from the majority party in Parliament. By Queen Anne's death in 1714, real power in England was slowly falling into the hands of a cabinet of ministers who controlled a parliamentary majority, often by bribery, and who felt themselves ultimately responsible to the political interests of the landed and moneyed classes represented in Parliament. By almost imperceptible stages, the world's first—and most influential—representative parliamentary government was evolving.

The Religious Settlement

The Glorious Revolution also produced an unprecedented measure of religious toleration. The fanaticism unleashed in the Civil War had given religious intolerance a bad name, and both Anglicans and Puritans were now more afraid of Catholic France than of one another. In addition, King William, thanks to the Dutch Republic's unique tradition of toleration, insisted on a religious truce. The result was the "Toleration Act" of 1689, which allowed dissenters to worship as they pleased and to educate their clergy and laity in schools of their own. Most of the existing anti-Catholic statutes, along with the acts excluding dissenters from civil and military offices remained in effect, but after 1689 their enforcement lacked vigor.

The Act of Settlement of 1701 provided that the sovereign should always be an Anglican Protestant. That finally quieted fear that a Catholic might succeed to the throne. The act also settled the succession, in case James II's two daughters should die without children, on the descendants of the daughter of James I who had married the ill-fated Frederick V of the Palatinate before the Thirty Years' War. That provision brought the Elector of Hanover to the throne in 1714, when Queen Anne died without direct heirs and ended the Stuart dynasty.

Medal of Queen Anne (1702–14).

Ireland and Scotland: Coercion and Union

Civil War and Glorious Revolution also indirectly furthered the unification of the British Isles. England, Ireland, and Scotland had all had the same king from the time of James I's succession in 1603, but union went no further than the common crown. The two smaller kingdoms, especially Ireland, suffered greatly during the seventeenth century from involvement in England's religious and political struggles.

The native Irish were Catholic; Protestant England therefore despised them and feared them as potential allies of Catholic Spain and France. To cope with that strategic threat, James I had settled Protestant colonists in the northeastern province of Ulster. But the Ulster Protestants were Presbyterians and soon became anti-Stuart, while the Catholic Irish were generally loyal to the Stuart dynasty. In 1641 the Catholics revolted. Cromwell crushed them with fire and terror in 1649, and massacred the Catholic garrisons at Drogheda and Wexford ("... being in the heat of action, I forbade them to spare any that were in arms in the town."). In 1690, James II landed in Ireland with French troops and Catholic support, but William of Orange routed him at the Battle of the Boyne. The much-celebrated anniversary of that Protestant victory remains to the present day an occasion for religious bloodshed in Ulster. After the Boyne, English and Irish Protestant landlords systematically persecuted the Catholic Irish and their religion, while reserving both economic and political power for themselves.

The Scots, who had given England a king in 1603, had somewhat better fortune. Scotland had only a sixth of England's population, but its Protestantism, its long tradition of parliamentarism, its military power, and its poverty—which made it unrewarding as prey—enabled it to make a satisfactory bargain. Scottish resistance to the imposition of Anglicanism had triggered the crisis that ultimately led to Civil War in 1642. Nevertheless, much of Scotland, especially the Highlands inhabited by the turbulent and ruthless Catholic clansmen, remained strongly attached to the native Stuart dynasty. From 1650 to 1745, the clans provided a base for risings in support of the Stuarts. The Scots parliament accepted the Revolution of 1688 but refused the Act of Settlement of 1701. It threatened to choose a king of its own—possibly the exiled pretender James II—if James II's last daughter, Anne, died without producing an heir.

That threat frightened England into serious negotiation. In 1707 the Whig government and the Scots agreed to an Act of Union that eliminated the risk that Scotland might choose a separate monarch and created the kingdom of "Great Britain." Scotland retained its own laws and its Presbyterian state religion but surrendered its separate parliament in return for representation in London and full participation in the dynamic English economy. The loss of political independence and the coming of a money economy even to the wild Highlands caused disgruntlement, especially among the clans. But the Act of Union was successful, unlike England's difficult relationships with Ireland or with the colonies in America. Scottish merchants and administrators helped build the British empire. Scottish philosophers, economists, and historians contributed mightily to the widening of human knowledge in the eighteenth century known as the Enlightenment (see pp. 543–48).

The Growth of British Power

A final consequence of the Glorious Revolution, after parliamentary government, religious toleration, and the settlement with Scotland, was to unite crown and Parliament on foreign policy and to turn the energies of the next generations from domestic conflict to foreign war. Given England's fear of Catholicism, William of Orange had no difficulty bringing his new kingdom into the Grand Alliance against Louis XIV, who had given refuge to James II. Parliamentary monarchy soon demonstrated that it was more deadly to its enemies than Stuart absolutism. The government of William and his successors was able to raise money, the sinew of war, in ways that only the Dutch could match.

Anti-Catholic woodcuts showing the "prodigious cruelties" of religious warfare in Ireland (1689).

In 1694 William's Whig ministers created a Bank of England to mobilize England's growing commercial and financial power against France. Within a few days of its founding, the Bank had raised over a million pounds of investors' money, and it promptly lent the money to the government at 8 percent interest. The resulting permanent national debt was a revolutionary instrument. It financed the defeat of Louis XIV and provided the foundation for the subsequent commercial and maritime supremacy of Britain. Throughout the next century British wealth, transmuted into ships of the line, gave the island kingdom a striking power out of all proportion to its size and population. The Peace of Utrecht of 1713 gave British sea power a position without serious rivals. Britain's victory heralded the elimination of France as a colonial competitor and Britain's domination of the world outside Europe.

CENTRAL AND EASTERN EUROPE, 1648–1721

An imaginary line running north from the Adriatic Sea to the Elbe River that flows into the North Sea divided the economy

The Economic and Social Division of Europe

of early modern Europe into two sharply defined halves. West of that line, the towns and their trade were increasingly dominant. The majority of the population still lived on the land, but most peasants were free workers and many of them small landowners. Most serfs had become agricultural wage laborers in and after the crisis of the Black Death. Most nobles had become landlords who hired labor for wages, or simply lived on rents from tenants. Though still a minority, the urban middle classes were growing in influence.

East of the line, in Hungary, Bohemia, Poland, Prussia, and Russia, lay a land of lord and peasant. Towns were small, poor, and weak. Noble estates were larger and the landed nobility far more powerful politically than in western Europe. And in the sixteenth and seventeenth centuries, noble power was still growing. Grain prices rose with the price revolution of the sixteenth century, and the growth of the trading networks centered on Antwerp and Amsterdam offered export markets. That situation provided an economic rationale for the imposition of a "second serfdom" in eastern Europe. The nobles sought to lower labor costs by binding their peasants to the land and imposing on them two to five days a week of compulsory labor. The profits they earned on exports in turn further increased the nobles' power. And in politics, the states of eastern Europe encouraged and promoted noble domination. Either the state *was* the nobility, as in Hungary or Poland, or it made a tacit bargain that delivered the peasants to the nobility in return for noble service to the state, as in Brandenburg-Prussia and Russia.

As in western Europe, states were machines for power. They had to be, for the flat plains of central and eastern Europe offered no "natural frontiers" to check the invader. A state could remain a state only if it had an army. But the gunpowder revolution of the fifteenth century had so raised the costs of armies that only strongly centralized states with relentless tax systems could afford them. Few such states existed in central and eastern Europe in the seventeenth century. Most eastern rulers faced the same obstacles to centralized government that western rulers had faced two centuries or more before—a powerful landed nobility, a church that owned large portions of the land, a middle class too small to bear the weight of heavy taxation, desperately poor agriculture, limited commerce, infant industries, and a peasantry tied to the land and thus incapable of meeting the need of new industries for labor.

The Holy Roman Empire

The one large political organization that bridged eastern and western Europe was the Holy Roman Empire. But the Thirty Years' War had left it a political fiction. A Habsburg remained emperor and a Diet or deliberative assembly met "perpetually" at Regensburg after 1663. But the Empire had no common army, administration, taxes, laws, calendar, or tariffs. It included perhaps 1,800 political units and petty rulers, including free cities, free imperial knights, Church principalities, and the kingdom of Bohemia. The Peace of Westphalia had recognized the full sovereignty of the 300 or so larger units within the Empire and had accorded France and Sweden the right to take part in the Diet's deliberations. This Empire, as Voltaire (see p. 545) remarked in the mid-eighteenth century, was "neither Holy, nor Roman, nor an Empire."

The ruling families of a few large states—Bavaria, Saxony, Hanover, Brandenburg, and Austria—sought to expand their territories and prestige by war or marriage. Augustus the Strong of Saxony, in addition to fathering, according to legend, more than 300 children, secured election in 1696 as king of Poland. In 1701 the Elector of Brandenberg obtained the emperor's consent to style himself "king in Prussia." And in 1714 the Elector of Hanover became king of Britain. But only two great powers emerged from the wreck of the Holy Roman Empire—Austria and Brandenburg-Prussia.

The Habsburgs: Europe and Austria Defended

The attempt of Emperor Ferdinand II (r. 1619–37) to revive and strengthen the Empire under Habsburg control collapsed in the Thirty Years' War. The Habsburgs of Vienna thereafter turned to a policy that Ferdinand had also fostered. They sought to consolidate and expand their hereditary lands in Austria and the Danube Valley into a centralized monarchy that could hold its own against the states of western Europe. The chief architect of that policy was Emperor Leopold I (r. 1658–1705), with the help and occasional prodding of capable civil servants and a remarkable general, Prince Eugene of Savoy.

Achieving the Habsburg objective required the reduction of Austria, Bohemia, and Hungary to obedience. In the Duchy of Austria and neighboring Tyrol, Leopold's lawyers established his ascendancy over the nobility. Bohemia was even less of an impediment. The Emperor Ferdinand II had smashed its native Czech nobility after the Battle of the White Mountain in 1620, and in 1627 had made the previously elective crown of Bohemia a hereditary possession of the Habsburg family. Hungary, on the fiercely contested border between the West and Islam, was different. Although the Habsburgs had usually been the elected monarchs there since early in the sixteenth century, the Ottoman Turks directly or indirectly ruled almost two-thirds of the kingdom. The Hungarian Protestants were numerous and inclined to fear the Turks less than they feared the Catholic Habsburgs.

But the Ottoman Empire was no longer the power that had taken Constantinople in 1453, smashed the Hungarians at Mohács in 1526, and sought Mediterranean mastery at Lepanto in 1571. The Ottomans failed to keep pace with the West in technology, above all in the technology of war. Their metal-working, their cannon and handguns, remained those of the sixteenth century. Ottoman logistics and tactics likewise failed to match the growing professionalization that overtook war in the West during and after the Thirty Years' War. But Ottoman troops nevertheless remained fearsome in the attack and tenacious in defense. And after 1656, the Ottoman central government briefly revived under a vigorous line of grand viziers (first ministers to the Sultan), the

The crown of the Holy Roman Empire of the German Nation, used from 961 to 1792.

Prince Eugene of Savoy, who ended the Ottoman Turk threat to central Europe.

Köprülü family. In the 1660s the Ottomans began a new thrust up the Danube Valley against their Habsburg antagonists.

But Austria prevailed in the end. From July to September 1683 a Turkish army of more than 100,000 besieged Vienna after laying waste to everything in its path. Volunteers rushed to Austria's aid from all across the Continent. The greatest pope of the century, Innocent XI, proclaimed Europe's last crusade against Islam. A coalition army under the leadership of King John Sobieski of Poland descended from the heights outside Vienna upon the Turks and routed them. For the next sixteen years, Austria and its allies fought their way laboriously back down the Danube Valley. In 1697, Prince Eugene of Savoy at last broke the Turkish army at the battle of Zenta, near the present Serbian-Hungarian border. Turkey ceased to be a threat, and soon became a victim.

The resulting Peace of Carlowitz in 1699 gave the Habsburgs all of Hungary. The Emperor crushed the Hungarian Protestants and executed many of them for treason. The Hungarian nobility retained its serfs and privileges in return for recognizing the ultimate sovereignty of Vienna. But the Habsburgs imprudently left local administration to the nobility and failed to create a uniform, centralized system of administration for all their possessions. Eugene's victories nevertheless established a strong state in the Danube Valley where none had existed before. The Treaties of Ryswick in 1697 and Carlowitz in 1699 thus marked the emergence of the two new great powers that had risen to check the overbearing ambition of Louis XIV—Britain and Austria. And two further contenders for great power status had also begun their ascent—Brandenburg-Prussia and Russia.

The Curious Rise of Brandenburg-Prussia, 1614–1701

Prussia, the power that emerged from the obscure Electorate of Brandenburg, was the most improbable of all seventeenth- and eighteenth-century claimants to great—power status. The Habsburgs

and even the primitive Grand Duchy of Muscovy had extensive territories. The Hohenzollern dynasty that created Prussia had been mere margraves—counts of a "mark," or frontier province—in Brandenburg since 1417. The one distinction of the small, sandy, barren principality around Berlin was that after about 1230 it was one of the seven "electorates" of the Holy Roman Empire, states whose rulers—at least in theory—voted to elect the emperor.

In the early seventeenth century, by the accidents of dynastic inheritance, the Hohenzollern family acquired two further territories of importance—the Duchy of Cleves and some neighboring lands on the Rhine in 1614, and the Duchy of Prussia on the Baltic coast to the northeast in 1618. The total population of all Hohenzollern possessions was perhaps 1.5 million. The provinces lacked defensible boundaries, standing military forces, and a central administration other than the household of the Elector. Each of the provincial estates jealously guarded its inherited privileges. Nothing suggested that these territories had the makings of a powerful state, especially after the Thirty Years' War had devastated Brandenburg. Berlin had lost more than half its population, and the Hohenzollern dominions as a whole had probably lost almost one-third of their people, a loss that took forty years to make up.

One man changed this situation. Frederick William of Hohenzollern, the Great Elector (r. 1640–88), was the first of the line of remarkable rulers that made Prussia. Born in 1620, he succeeded to power in 1640 after an education in Holland that had emphasized the latest in statecraft and technology. A devout Calvinist, he had learned toleration from the Dutch. In an age of fanaticism he respected the Lutheranism of his subjects. Above all, he learned from the helplessness of Brandenburg. "A ruler is treated with no consideration if he does not have troops and means of his own," he advised his son in 1667. "It is these, Thank God! which have made me considerable since the time that I began to have them."

Frederick William, the Great Elector, painted by his contemporary, Mathias Czwiczeic.

He inherited in 1640 a poorly equipped and mutinous army of 2,500 men. Before the end of the Thirty Years' War in 1648 his ceaseless efforts had increased it to 8,000 disciplined troops; by his death in 1688 he had a peacetime force of 30,000 that could expand to 40,000 in time of war. In the 48 years of his reign, the Great Elector built upon Brandenburg-Prussia's meager population the strongest military power in Germany, except for Austria.

That achievement rested on administrative centralization and the crushing of the provincial estates that largely controlled taxation. In Brandenburg he struck a bargain with the Estates in 1653 that provided a lump sum with which he raised further troops. The force in turn allowed him to collect taxes without further votes by the Estates, which—like Louis XIV—he never summoned again. In Prussia, far to the east, the townsmen were more stubborn than in Brandenburg, and the hard-bitten nobility, the *Junkers* (from *Jungherr,* "young lord"), proved unruly. The provincial opposition turned to Poland for support, but Frederick eventually crushed its resistance and executed its leaders. After campaigns against both Poland and Sweden, he also secured clear title to Prussia, which he had originally held as a fief from the king of Poland.

Despite some setbacks, Frederick nevertheless set up a tax system under civil servants of his own choosing that extended to all his territories. He deprived the nobility of the power it had exercised through the Estates and pressed it into state service as officers in the new standing army. In return, he confirmed and strengthened Junker control over the serfs. Power, not the betterment of the lowly, was the Great Elector's objective.

But against the background of the Thirty Years' War, the creation of the standing army and the order it brought was nevertheless a contribution to the welfare of the population. Devastation by foreign armies was even worse than Junker oppression. Moreover, Frederick William helped revive and improve agriculture after 1648 and encouraged industry and commerce. He made Brandenburg a haven for religious refugees—Lutherans, Calvinists, and large numbers of Huguenots after Louis XIV revoked the Edict of Nantes in 1685. These immigrants, together with Dutch, Swiss, and other newcomers, brought new skills in agriculture and industry, helped increase the population, and added considerably to the strength of the state. He welcomed even the more radical Protestant sects and the Jews but drew the line at the Jesuits, whom he considered too intolerant.

Frederick William's foreign policy was cautious. He sold his support to a succession of temporary allies in return for subsidies that helped pay for his army, while avoiding heavy fighting. The Swedes came close to Berlin in 1675, but he drove them off at the battle of Fehrbellin, a sign of Brandenburg-Prussia's rise and of Sweden's decline.

The recognition in 1701 of the Great Elector's son as Frederick I, "King in Prussia" (that is, in the province of Prussia, outside the boundary of the Empire), symbolized the appearance of a new power in Europe. In 1720, at the end of the Great Northern War that paralleled in eastern Europe the War of the Spanish Succession, the Hohenzollerns gained Pomerania and the vital port of Stettin from Sweden.

Prussia, as the Hohenzollern lands became known, had in eighty years transformed itself from a chance collection of feeble provinces into a state on the threshold of great power status. The weakness of its neighbors, rivals, or overlords—Sweden, Poland, Russia, and the Empire—gave it the opportunity. But this "Sparta of the North" rose primarily through its own efforts, through its army. All states in the fiercely competitive European system were machines for war, but Prussia devoted to its military relatively more of its population, resources, and energies than any other state. The army was the first institution common to all the Great Elector's lands, and its supporting bureaucracy was the model for Prussia's later organs of civil government. The nobility served the state in the army and bureaucracy and came to identify itself with state and army to an extent without parallel elsewhere.

That army, the army that conquered true great-power status for Prussia in the coming wars of the mid-eighteenth century, *was* the Prussian state.

Russia: Peter the Great's Revolution from Above

To the east of Prussia, Sweden, Poland, and the Ottoman Empire, no great power existed in the seventeenth century. The only contender was Muscovy, a state closer in constitution to the Ottoman Empire than to anything in Europe. As in the Ottoman Empire, India, and China, the Muscovite tsar "owned" his territory and his subjects, who enjoyed no rights against the state. That was no accident. Muscovy acquired its statecraft from Byzantium, and above all from the Mongols, its overlords from around 1240 until 1480 (see pp. 344–45).

The rulers of Muscovy were fully conscious of their uniqueness. They ridiculed the "limited" monarchs to the west as "men under contract" to their subjects and representative assemblies. In a letter addressed to Queen Elizabeth I of England in 1570, Tsar Ivan the Terrible had mocked her as no true sovereign but as one who had "men who rule beside you, and not only men, but trading boors." In Russia, even nobles lacked rights—even property rights—against the state; Ivan broke the hereditary nobility, or *boyars,* by torture, massacre, and wholesale confiscation of land in the 1560s and 1570s. He largely replaced them with a new "service nobility" that owed abject obedience to the autocrat. Scorn and hatred of foreigners characterized Muscovy's external relations. The alternation of despotism and anarchy marked its internal politics.

The unlamented death of Ivan the Terrible in 1584 indeed led to anarchy: a "Time of Troubles" that lasted until the coming in 1613 of the Romanov dynasty, which ruled Russia until 1917. Thereafter, religious strife compounded the weakness of the state. A reforming leader of the Orthodox Church, Patriarch Nikon, provoked a devastating schism in the 1660s by revising ritual and liturgy to bring them closer to the original Greek text of the Bible. That exasperated the traditionalist masses, to whom the Old Slavonic texts were sacrosanct. The Church split into a shallowly based state church and fiercely independent sects of "Old Believers" who braved execution and exile for their faith. As many as 20,000 may have burned themselves to death in the belief that the end of the world was at hand.

Abroad, Russia suffered defeats against Swedes, Poles, and Turks, and remained cut off from the Baltic and the Black Sea. English merchants made contact with Moscow in the 1550s by the icy route around Norway to the bleak port of Archangel on the White Sea. German merchants were also active in the capital. But Russia's chief import, then and later, was the West's technology, especially its military technology. Western culture—the Renaissance and Reformation—reached only as far as Catholic Poland.

In 1689, a new monarch, Peter I (r. 1682–1725), seized power at the age of seventeen in a palace coup. He was nearly seven feet tall, with inexhaustible energy and appetites, and a ferocious will. His insatiable curiosity led him to spend much time with the Dutch and Germans who lived in the "German Quarter" of Moscow. There he probably conceived the ambition of making Russia a great power by rapidly adopting Western technology, civil and military institutions, and customs. The partial realization of that ambition ultimately earned for him the title of Peter the Great.

Peter at first allowed others to rule for him. But in 1695 he ventured a first campaign against the Turkish fortress of Azov, where the Don River enters the Black Sea. The attack failed, but in 1696, with the help of Swiss, Dutch, and Habsburg experts, he built a fleet on the Don River, cut the fortress off from supplies and reinforcements, and stormed it. The lesson Peter I drew was that he needed additional Western experts to create a navy and to modernize his outmoded army.

In 1696–97, thinly disguised as a private citizen, Peter visited Holland, England, Germany, and Austria. There he learned how societies centuries ahead of

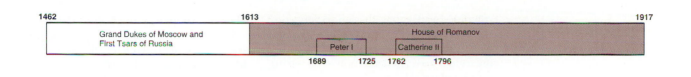

| 1462 | | 1613 | | | | 1917 |

Grand Dukes of Moscow and First Tsars of Russia — House of Romanov — Peter I — Catherine II

1689   1725   1762   1796

Russia built ships, made munitions, and conducted government and diplomacy. He worked in the shipyards, eagerly questioned everyone he met about Western naval and military technology, and drank steadily through the night with his Russian companions. When he returned to Russia, he brought with him more than a thousand Western experts—seamen, gunners, shipwrights, engineers, mathematicians, surgeons.

An outburst of xenophobia at home cut short his European tour. The *strel'tsy,* a barbarous and undisciplined palace guard that he had thwarted in his seizure of power in 1689, remained a threat. In 1696, in league with the "Old Believers" and distrustful of Peter's increasingly obvious intention of introducing Western innovations, the *strel'tsy* marched on the Kremlin. Peter hastened back to Moscow to find that trusted aides had suppressed the revolt. He then made an example of the rebels that long haunted even the memories of his countrymen, accustomed to indiscriminate bloodshed. He executed a thousand *strel'tsy* to the accompaniment of torture on a scale not seen since Ivan the Terrible.

Peter also determined to use his autocratic sovereign power to "westernize" his subjects externally, by force if need be. In 1699–1700 he forbade the traditional long robes and the beards that his subjects wore in the belief that God was bearded and that man was made in his image. The tsar himself took a hand in the shaving of his courtiers. He fought the resulting antiforeign and Orthodox reaction with brutal repression. He also ended the seclusion of women and instituted Western-style social gatherings of both sexes at which polite conversation and ballroom dancing rather than strong drink were the chief entertainments. In his will to transform Russia, he brooked no opposition; when his son and heir Alexis showed himself a slothful dev-

otee of tradition, Peter I had him arrested, tortured, and put to death in 1618.

But Peter I's priorities were above all military. He sought first to imitate Western power, not Western civilization. Beginning in 1699, he set up a new army using German and other foreign experts as officers. An overwhelming defeat by the Swedes at Narva in 1700 only spurred him on; Russia either had to modernize its army or perish. The tsar encouraged the vital iron industry of the Urals, set up cannon foundries, and created schools for gunnery, navigation, engineering, and officer training. By 1709, the year of his great victory over Charles XII of Sweden at Poltava, Russia had a modern army of more than 100,000 troops. By the end of Peter's reign in 1725, that army had swelled to 210,000 regulars and 100,000 auxiliaries that included the dreaded Cossack cavalry. The navy had grown from nothing to 24 ships of the line. Those were powerful forces indeed for a state with a population of only 8 million.

The army, the largest in eastern Europe, had the chance to achieve results, for Russia was at peace only one year in all of Peter's long reign. In the south, Peter failed to hold Azov and had to leave the Turks to his successors. But in the Great Northern War, the tsar seized from Sweden the vital coastline on the Gulf of Finland. That gave him the "window on the sea," the direct contact with western Europe through the ice-free southern Baltic that was his primary geopolitical goal.

Peter's subjects, who bore the weight of his gigantic social engineering project, paid dearly for these military successes. The effect of Peter's sometimes haphazard social and fiscal legislation was to divide a relatively complex society with a variety of subtle status gradations into two great classes—the "service nobility," and the more or less enserfed peasantry. A century after Peter I, a Russian intellectual could

Contemporary cartoon of Peter cutting the beard of a Russian noble. Those who kept their beards had to pay a tax and carry a license *(below).*

still quip bitterly that Russian society consisted of "slaves of the sovereign [the nobles], and slaves of the landlord [the serfs]; the former are called free only with regard to the latter."

Peter systematized the service nobility system he had inherited. All landowners owed service, and he decreed in 1714 the hated innovation of primogeniture, which forced noble younger sons off the land and into the army or navy. By instituting a fourteen-step "Table of Ranks" in 1722, Peter defined nobility in terms of one criterion alone, service. He made explicit what Louis XIV and the Great Elector could only practice—that service to the state, not birth, determined rank. In Russia, a lieutenant's commission now automatically brought noble status. That provided a career leading to ennoblement for the ambitious sons of commoners and helped divert them into state service and away from commerce and industry.

The peasantry, not the nobility, paid most heavily for Peter's innovations. In return for its service, the nobility gained a freer hand than ever before in dealing with serfs. A new tax census classified as a serf anyone whose position was doubtful. And the state demanded from the peasantry forced labor, military service, and taxes on an unprecedented scale. Supporting the new army required conscription, on the model of Sweden. After 1705 each twenty households had to furnish one recruit every year. The state provided the new military industries with serfs and convicts as labor, while a new head tax ("soul tax") tripled both state income and the tax burden. Forced labor and taxation, by one estimate, extorted from each household the equivalent of 125 to 187 days of labor each year. The ultimate result was depopulation, as peasants died of their privations or fled to the Don Cossacks to the southeast.

After 1709 Peter moved the seat of government from Moscow to a new city built on conquered territory on the Gulf of Finland: St. Petersburg, named for his patron saint. That change was the symbol of his aim to rival the West. The new city faced west, and its nearby naval base, Kronstadt ("royal city" *in German*),

claimed mastery of the Baltic. The methods that created the new capital, and its price, were also characteristic both of Peter's work and of that of later autocrats who sought to imitate him in Russia and in other backward states. St. Petersburg rose in an unhealthy marshland at the mouth of the Neva River and was a deliberate break with the Moscow-centered past. Peter compelled nobles and merchants to settle and build there. Construction proceeded rapidly through annual forced labor drafts of 20,000 peasants, many of whom perished from disease and exposure.

This new capital, founded on the bones of dead peasants, became the center of a new bureaucratic structure that Peter erected haphazardly over the primitive central administration he had inherited. The Western conception of "the state," as distinct from the private staff of the sovereign, now made its entry into Russian history. Peter set up provincial administrations, supervisory boards to coordinate the bureaucracy, and a "senate," or central administrative body to interpret his orders. He also created an organ, the *Preobrazhenskii Prikaz,* to ferret out "political crime," from tax evasion, to criticism of the tsar, to coup attempts. The deliberate vagueness of its charter, its sweeping authority, and its ruthless suppression of individuals for their political opinions rather than for their deeds made it the ancestor of the modern police state.

The new Russian state thus dominated its society in a way unknown even in Brandenburg-Prussia, much less in western Europe. The state mastered the Orthodox Church, already weakened by the great schism. After 1700 Peter neglected to appoint a patriarch and made the Church a mere department of his bureaucracy. The state defined the nobility by its service, and by demanding residence at St. Petersburg reinforced an already existing pattern of absentee landlordism that weakened the grip of the nobility on rural society. The state stunted the towns and ensured that the small and fearful middle classes that eventually emerged would be dependent on state employment and state contracts.

The bronze horseman: Peter the Great decrees the founding of St. Petersburg, Russia's window on the West.

The state then ordered its subjects to develop a consciousness, a public opinion. Peter was the first Russian sovereign to speak of "the common good." He founded Russia's first newspaper. He recognized that rivaling the West ultimately required voluntary collaboration from his subjects and the development of economic and intellectual initiative *from below*. But as his successors discovered, initiative from below was a deadly threat to the autocracy's own power. That tension, the result of grafting Western technology and military institutions onto non-Western social and political structures, was a pattern often seen later. Its consequence was a cycle of repression, "thaw," and further repression that has continued to the present.

But that ultimate consequence of Peter's work was far in the future when he died in 1725. What he left was a Russian great power, a military giant, irrevocably part of the European state system. And his example created a tradition of dynamic autocracy, of brutal revolutions from above carried through by pitiless force, that later Russian rulers sought to imitate or surpass.

The Losers: Sweden and Poland

While Prussia grew and Russia transformed itself, their Swedish and Polish neighbors declined. Sweden had burst on Europe as a military power of the first rank when Gustavus Adolphus swept into Germany in 1630–31. The Baltic virtually became a Swedish lake, with Swedish outposts that stretched from the Gulf of Finland to the North Sea. Copper, iron, and agriculture were Sweden's chief resources; superior cannon and muskets its chief military advantage. But Swedish power rested on shaky foundations. The country had a population of less than 2 million—not much larger than Brandenberg-Prussia or the Dutch Republic. The empire that Gustavus Adolphus had acquired was overextended; its enemies, from Russia and Poland to Prussia and Denmark, were hungry for revenge.

When young Charles XII (r. 1697–1718) came to the Swedish throne, a coali-

Peter the Great: The Bronze Horseman

The first and greatest modern Russian poet, Aleksandr Sergeyevich Pushkin (1799–1837), summed up Peter's place in Russian history in "The Bronze Horseman" (1833), named for the tsar's statue at St. Petersburg.

That square, the lions, and him—the one
Who, bronzen countenance upslanted
Into the dusk aloft, sat still,
The one by whose portentous will
The city by the sea was planted . . .
How awesome in the gloom he rides!
What thought upon his brow resides!
His charger with what fiery mettle,
His form with what dark strength endowed!
Where will you gallop, charger proud,
Where next your plunging hoofbeats settle?
Oh, Destiny's great potentate!
Was it not thus, a towering idol
Hard by the chasm, with iron bridle
You reared up Russia to her fate?

From Alexander Pushkin, Collected Narrative and Lyrical Poetry, *trans. by Walter Arndt (Ann Arbor: Ardis Publishers, 1984), p. 437.*

tion of Russia, Poland, and Denmark pounced on his Baltic territories. But Charles proved a greater commander even than Gustavus Adolphus. He crushed the coalition's forces in a series of lightning campaigns. Then success intoxicated him. In 1708–09 he launched Sweden into a foolhardy attempt to smash Russia and met devastating defeat at Poltava in the Ukraine. He subsequently escaped to Turkey, spent some years at the Ottoman court seeking allies, and died in the siege of an obscure Norwegian fortress in 1718. His meteoric career exhausted Sweden. In the peace settlements of 1719 to 1721 that ended this "Great Northern War," Hanover, Denmark, Prussia, and Russia divided up Sweden's Baltic empire. Sweden retired for good into the ranks of second-class powers.

Poland, an elective monarchy originally formed in 1386 through the union of the crowns of Poland and Lithuania (see p. 342), suffered a similar fate. Polish prosperity and culture had reached their peak

The Baltic: A Swedish Lake   1621–1721

in the sixteenth century. Roman Catholicism had linked Poland to western Europe and had conveyed the influence of the Renaissance, the Protestant revolt, and the Counter-Reformation. But by the beginning of the seventeenth century Poland's economic and political decline had begun.

In France, Prussia, and Russia the state tamed the nobility. In Poland the nobility gradually became the state, thanks to the elective character of the monarchy. Until the 1570s the Polish nobility had usually elected the legal heirs of their monarchs. But thereafter they chose candidates who appeared to favor their own interests. By 1700 the nobility had deprived the monarchy of most of its powers.

Noble power had consequences. It sank the peasants as deeply in serfdom as anywhere else in Europe. It checked the small, weak towns, prevented the rise of urban middle classes, and froze the Polish economy in rural backwardness. Above all, it concentrated political power in the Polish Diet, which now represented only the nobility, since representatives of the towns no longer dared attend.

The Diet's procedure, tailor-made to preserve noble domination, was notorious—one negative vote, the "*liberum veto*," could block any action. Moreover, the *liberum veto* allowed any member to "explode" a Diet session—to dissolve it and wipe out all legislation it had passed up to that moment. Of 57 Diets held in the century after 1652, all but nine "exploded." In one case a member cast a veto simply to see what would happen. And if by some accident legislation did emerge from the Diet, no machinery existed to enforce it against the provincial assemblies of lesser nobles or the private estate jurisdictions of the landed magnates. John Sobieski (1674–96), a native Pole of high integrity, was the last great king. He saved Vienna from the Turks but failed to save Poland from its nobility. After him, Poland declined into incoherence and eventual extinction at the hands of Austria, Russia, and Prussia between 1772 and 1795.

ABSOLUTISM, CONSTITUTIONALISM, AND THE BALANCE OF POWER

The half-century from 1660 to 1715 was thus a period of dramatic change. Internally, absolute divine-right monarchy reached its height in the France of Louis XIV. Powers from Madrid to St. Petersburg attempted to imitate the French model. Nevertheless, a few smaller peoples such as the Swiss had rejected monarchy in favor of republican government. The Dutch "Sea Beggars" had even shown that a republic could compete in the great-power arena. But it took England's Glorious Revolution and Marlborough's victories to demonstrate to Europe that even the greatest powers could choose alternatives to absolute monarchy.

Externally, relations between states and the workings of the balance of power almost completely superseded the religious-ideological conflicts that had rent Europe before 1648. France's bid for mastery after 1672 provoked the rise of England and Austria as great powers. Two great empires of the sixteenth century, Spain and the Ottoman Turks, continued their decline. Two peoples of limited resources and numbers, the Dutch and the Swedes, briefly claimed great-power status in the mid-seventeenth century but lacked staying power. Two new powers appeared in eastern Europe to join the balance—military Prussia and semi-barbaric Russia. The rivalries of these states—Britain against France, France against Austria, Austria against Prussia, Austria and Russia against the Ottoman Empire—were the forces that moved European war and diplomacy after 1715.

Medals celebrating an abortive "Treaty of Eternal Peace" between Russia and Poland (1686). (*Above*) King John Sobieski, Poland's last great king. (*Below*) Personification of Poland and Russia.

Suggestions for Further Reading

Western Europe

J. Stoye, *Europe Unfolding, 1648–88* (1969), and J. B. Wolf, *The Emergence of the Great Powers, 1685–1715* (1951), provide useful introductions, but see also W. Doyle, *The Old European Order, 1660–1800* (1978). C. J. Friedrich and C. Blitzer, *The Age of Power* (1957), covers the general theme of this chapter. R. Hatton, *Europe in the Age of Louis XIV* (1969), is excellent on social history. P. Goubert, *Louis XIV and Twenty Million Frenchmen* (1970), wittily relates the career of the king to the social history of France. See also J. B. Wolf, *Louis XIV* (1968), and W. H. Lewis, *The Splendid Century* (1954), an elegant account of the reign. On England, see especially C. Hill, *The Century of Revolution, 1603–1714* (1961). G. N. Clark, *The Later Stuarts, 1660–1714* (1934), is a fine synthesis. C. H. Wilson, *England's Apprenticeship, 1603–1763* (1965), covers England's emergence as a great power.

Eastern Europe

For the lands east of the Elbe, see especially S. H. Cross, *Slavic Civilization Through the Ages* (1948), and O. Halecki, *Borderlands of Western Civilization* (1952). On Germany, see H. Holborn, *A History of Modern Germany, 1648–1840* (1964). R. W. J. Evans, *The Making of the Habsburg Monarchy* (1979), and H. G. Koenigsberger, *The Habsburgs and Europe* (1971), are useful surveys. On Prussia, S. B. Fay and K. Epstein, *The Rise of Brandenburg-Prussia to 1786* (1937, 1964), is concise. See also F. Carsten, *The Origins of Prussia* (1954). B. H. Sumner, *Peter the Great and the Emergence of Russia* (1950), is a useful short account. For analysis, see especially R. Pipes, *Russia under the Old Regime* (1974), and J. Blum, *Lord and Peasant in Russia from the Ninth to the Nineteenth Century* (1961).

21

THE SCIENTIFIC REVOLUTION AND THE ENLIGHTENMENT

ntil the seventeenth century the growth of knowledge about nature had been slow, fumbling, and frequently interrupted. Scholars had observed events in nature, had in many cases recorded them, and had sometimes derived useful generalizations from them. But "experiments" in the modern sense had been largely absent, and scientific inquiry was scarcely distinguishable from theological speculation.

That changed. By the eighteenth century, during the age of rapidly broadening and deepening knowledge that became known as the Enlightenment, the West had accumulated a large body of principles verifiable by experiment. Those principles in turn allowed the prediction and manipulation of nature. That type of knowledge has continued to accumulate, with revolutionary effect. The ever-accelerating understanding of and mas-

tery over nature, for good or ill, was the achievement of the West, the first civilization in history to make a clear distinction between science on the one hand and religion or magic on the other.

THE SCIENTIFIC REVOLUTION

A new method of inquiry, later called the "scientific method," emerged from the universities of Western Europe in the late thirteenth and fourteenth centuries. After 1600 it achieved wide currency in western Europe. The new method was a combination of careful observation and controlled experiment with rational interpretation of the results, preferably using mathematics. That was the origin of modern science, an enterprise that a great twentieth-century mathematician-philosopher described as

(OPPOSITE) TWO OF GALILEO'S TELESCOPES.

the "vehement and passionate interest in the relation of general principles to irreducible and stubborn facts."

The Medieval Universe

Precisely *why* the West took the lead in scientific speculation over the other great civilizations, China, Islam, and India, remains unclear. Even in the West, deep-rooted traditional assumptions about the nature of the universe dominated thought for centuries. Medieval learning dictated that the universe was a finite sphere with the earth at the center. Between the center and the outermost limit, nine transparent spheres supposedly carried stars, planets, sun, and moon in their daily revolutions about a motionless earth. The earth was the realm of change, decay, and original sin. The heavens were the realm of perfection and changelessness. Sun, moon, and heavenly bodies were perfectly spherical and moved in spherical tracks to the accompaniment of an ethereal "music of the spheres." The assumed dichotomy between heavenly perfection and earthly corruption demanded a sharp separation

between the laws of heavenly and of earthly physics.

Even in the Middle Ages, not all scholars found this picture of the universe convincing. By the thirteenth and fourteenth centuries a small but increasing number had begun to question it, including Franciscan monks, perhaps inspired by their founder's sensitive feeling for nature. The study of the Greco-Arabic scientific texts that had reached the West stimulated a group of scholars at Oxford and Paris to apply mathematical reasoning to problems of physics and astronomy, such as motion and acceleration. Professors at the University of Padua continued these speculations in the fifteenth and sixteenth centuries. At Padua, a center of medical training for three centuries, scholars vigorously debated the proper method of studying nature in the course of arguments about Aristotle. The medieval universities kept interest in science alive and nurtured the first faint beginnings of the scientific revolution.

Most Europeans of 1500, however, did not question the Greek authorities, who had decreed that the normal state of everything in the universe was a state of rest. Aristotle had said that bodies moved only if a mover pushed or pulled them. Galen of Pergamum, in the second century A.D., had described the anatomy of the human body so convincingly that doctors still saw it through his eyes. In that same century, the Greco-Egyptian astronomer Ptolemy had compiled mathematical descriptions of the observed movements of the planets so ingenious that European authorities saw no need to discard them until after 1500. Ptolemy assumed that all motion in the heavens was circular and proceeded at a constant rate. But because the observed pattern of actual planetary motion in the heavens was not precisely circular, Ptolemy had invented the "epicycle," an additional small circle in which the planet moved while traveling around the circumference of its larger "sphere" around the earth. He and his successors needed eighty epicycles to force the observed motion of the planets to fit the theory, but in the end Ptolemy's system

The observatory of the Danish astronomer Tycho Brahe was the finest of the sixteenth century. Note the domes protecting the instruments.

explained what astronomers saw. Even more important, it permitted the prediction of lunar and planetary motion with some precision. At the close of the Middle Ages, few scholars saw much need to improve upon the observations and theories of the ancients.

The Background of Change

Nevertheless, forces in European society in the fourteenth, fifteenth, and sixteenth centuries prepared the way for a challenge to this orthodoxy. Artisans and craftsmen gradually adopted techniques more advanced than those of their medieval predecessors. Ever-smaller and more precise pocket watches took their place alongside the massive mechanical clocks of the medieval cathedrals. The development of the glass industry and the invention of the lens at some point before 1300, to take but one example, gave the promise of vastly extending humanity's ability to observe natural processes. Breakthroughs in shipbuilding and navigation (see p. 451) permitted the voyages of discovery, which in turn stimulated interest in nature generally.

The Renaissance, with its emphasis on literature and art and its veneration for the wisdom of the ancients, was in some respects hostile to the new science. But the Humanists were interested in Greek scientific texts as well as in Greek literature, and Renaissance patrons of artists were also patrons of inventors and technicians. Humanistic study revealed that ancient scientific authorities had differed among themselves on key issues, just at the moment when the authority of Galen and Ptolemy was becoming shaky for other reasons. Anatomical studies by the great Renaissance artists and the increasing practice of dissection suggested that Galen had made mistakes. Growing skill in mathematics exposed the clumsiness of Ptolemy's calculations. By the opening years of the sixteenth century, conditions were ripe for a dramatic shift in the West's underlying assumptions about the universe.

Vesalius and Copernicus: Observation and Calculation

In 1543 two notable scientific works heralded the end of medieval science. Andreas Vesalius, a Flemish anatomist at the University of Padua, published *On the Structure of the Human Body,* a marvelously careful description of human anatomy based on direct observation during dissection, and illustrated with accurate plates. Vesalius did not free himself completely from the authority of Galen, nor did his book offer much theoretical insight. But it was an influential example of the power of observation.

Even more powerful in its ultimate effect was the work of a Polish scholar, Mikolaj Kopérnik, better known as Copernicus. *On the Revolutions of the Heavenly Bodies* was a brilliant mathematical treatise that showed how to reduce Ptolemy's 80 epicycles to 34 by assuming that the earth turned on its axis once a day and moved around the sun once a year. Unlike Vesalius, Copernicus was not primarily an observer. During study at Padua in the early years of the century he had learned that some ancient authorities had held that the earth moved. That assumption made the motions of the moon and planets far simpler to explain mathematically than the medieval earth-centered theory. Copernicus, following the equally medieval notion that "nature always acts in the simplest ways," eventually discarded Ptolemy on grounds of logic, rather than from observation. His ideas gradually spread.

In 1600, the Inquisition tried a former monk named Giordano Bruno as a heretic and burned him at the stake in Rome. He had published works arguing that the universe was not a closed sphere but infinite in extent, that numberless suns and planets like our own filled it, and that God was equally present in every planet or atom in the cosmos. He also maintained that the existence of the infinite made it impossible to arrive at absolute truth, or find limits to the extent of knowledge. Copernicus had inspired him, although Copernicus himself believed in the finite

The Copernican revolution: the new sun-centered solar system.

sphere of the fixed stars and the uniqueness of the earth. Despite the fires of the Inquisition, Bruno's intuition of the infinity of the universe ultimately prevailed. It was the beginning of modern cosmology.

The Purposes and Method of Science: Bacon and Descartes

Two major prophets of the early Scientific Revolution, Francis Bacon (1561–1626) and René Descartes (1596–1650), followed Copernicus. Bacon, an English lawyer, statesman, and essayist, waged a vigorous scholarly battle against the deductive method of medieval scholasticism, which began with premises usually taken on authority and deduced from them their logical consequences. That might help to organize truths already known, argued Bacon, but it could never discover new truths. Only inductive reasoning, starting from direct observation of phenomena

and developing principles that explained them, could produce new truths.

Bacon set a practical goal for science, the "domination" of humanity over nature. He pictured an imaginary future society of scientists whose end was to benefit mankind by conducting hundreds of experiments that discovered useful facts. Bacon failed to appreciate the importance of mathematical models, and he found Copernicus unconvincing. Although he praised experimentation, he performed almost no experiments and collected his evidence in the traditional way, from books. His writings nevertheless dramatized the importance of empirical research. The founding in 1662 of the Royal Society of London, the first scientific society in England, owed much to Bacon's inspiration. He was the remote ancestor of the great laboratories and team-research projects of the twentieth century. His goal, the mastery of nature through rational analysis, has distinguished the West from the other historic civilizations.

Descartes, a French mathematician and philosopher, was an even more important figure than Bacon, but he lacked Bacon's intuitive understanding of the need for observation. To Descartes, the excitement of science lay in mathematical analysis and theory. In a famous autobiographical account, he told how the literature and philosophy that he had studied as a youth had left him unsatisfied because he reached no *certain* conclusions. By contrast, the precision and certainty of mathematics aroused his enthusiasm. He set out to discover a mathematical "method of rightly conducting the reason and discovering truth in the sciences."

In November 1619, in a moment of intuition, he saw the exact correspondence between geometry and algebra—the truth that equations and curves on graphs were interchangeable. That intoxicating vision suggested to him a new way of grasping ultimate truth. If humanity systematically doubted all notions based on authority or custom and started with clear and precise ideas known to be true, it might deduce systematically the entire universe from a few simple principles, just as he had derived curves from equations.

Descartes was one of the first to believe that science could save humanity. His enthusiasm was infectious and outran the knowledge available in the seventeenth century. He reduced the universe, including the human body, to a mathematically intelligible machine. Only the human intellect, he believed, resisted mathematical description. He therefore defined it as being outside the world of matter: The mind comprehended the world but did not exist in it. His generalizations in astronomy, physics, and anatomy were often premature, and his passion for system building went far beyond his capacity to confirm generalizations by experiment. He did important work in optics, but that in no way confirmed his far-ranging theories.

Nevertheless, Descartes' enthusiasm for scientific "method," his belief that mathematics could describe all phenomena, and his insistence on systematic doubt of all earlier theorizing left a profound mark on the scientific thinking of the three centuries that followed. Descartes made it easier for his successors to reject old ideas, and they gradually came to accept his belief that mathematics must be the language of science.

Experiment and Mathematics

Bacon and Descartes were too optimistic. Bacon thought that a generation of determined experimentation would establish a solid structure of knowledge about the universe. Descartes expected that a few basic mathematical axioms would soon lead, by deduction, to a universal science. He also believed in a universe far simpler than it now appears. One of Descartes' pupils even described the world as a gigantic piece of clockwork.

Meanwhile, experimentation and mathematics were developing steadily in the hands of a growing host of scientists. William Gilbert (1544–1603), court physician to Elizabeth I, coined the word "electricity" and deduced that the earth itself was a huge magnet. His *De magnete* (1600) remained the foremost work on magnetism until the early nineteenth century. William Harvey (1578–1627), who had studied at Padua, argued in a work published in 1628 that the blood must circulate from arteries to veins to heart, then on to the lungs, back to the heart and back once more to the arteries. He did this by estimating the amount of blood the heart pumped in a minute and arguing that it must go somewhere. Later in the century the new microscope revealed the tiny capillaries that actually connect arteries to veins.

Evangelista Torricelli (1608–47), Blaise Pascal, and others investigated the ancient proposition, long believed by most scholars, that "nature abhors a vacuum." They created vacuums in test tubes, invented the barometer, and discovered that the pressure of the atmosphere varies between sea level and mountain top. They proved inherited wisdom false, and their work showed a growing precision in observation and an increasing skill in

Scientific revolutionaries of the seventeenth century: Francis Bacon *(above)* and René Descartes *(below)*.

Harvey Discovers the Circulation of the Blood

Since calculations and visual demonstrations have confirmed all my suppositions, to wit, that the blood is passed through the lungs and the heart by the pulsation of the ventricles, is forcibly ejected to all parts of the body, therein steals into the veins . . . flows back everywhere . . . from small veins into larger ones, and thence comes at last into the vena cava and to the auricle of the heart; all this too in such amounts that it cannot be supplied from the ingesta [food] and is also in greater bulk than would suffice for nutrition.

I am obliged to conclude that in all animals the blood is driven around a circuit with an unceasing, circular sort of motion, that this is an activity of the heart which it carries out by virtue of its pulsation, and that in sum it constitutes the sole cause for the heart's pulsatile movement.

From C. C. Gillispie, The Edge of Objectivity *(Princeton, N.J.: Princeton University Press, 1960), p. 71.*

controlling experiments and in quantifying their results.

Mathematics likewise rapidly advanced. The invention of decimals and of logarithms early in the century made calculation easier. Pascal inaugurated the study of probability. At the end of the century Sir Isaac Newton and Baron Gottfried Wilhelm von Leibniz (1646–1716) crowned the work of many others by simultaneously but separately inventing the calculus, which provided the first mathematical method for describing accelerating or decelerating motion.

Kepler: The Foundations of Celestial Mechanics

Observational techniques and mathematical methods first united in astronomy and physics—producing results of a beauty and explanatory power that shattered for good all traditional notions of the place of science in human knowledge and of humanity in the universe.

The German astronomer Johannes Kepler (1571–1630) believed Copernicus's theory, but found discrepancies in it troubling. He worked from the observations of

his master, the Danish astronomer Tycho Brahe (1546–1601), which were far more accurate than those available to Copernicus. Brahe's data ultimately caused Kepler to discard reluctantly the universal belief, which Copernicus had not challenged, that heavenly bodies moved in circles.

Kepler concluded that the ellipse, whose properties scholars had studied since the time of the Greeks, fitted Brahe's observations of Mars, the planet whose motion most contradicted the Ptolemaic and Copernican systems. The orbits of the planets, Kepler suggested, were elliptical, with the sun at one of the two foci of the ellipse. Further, he demonstrated that a line from the sun to a planet swept out equal areas of the ellipse in equal times and that the cube of the distance of each planet from the sun was proportional to the square of the time of its revolution. That was astounding proof of the intuition of Descartes and others that nature was in some mysterious sense mathematical. A geometrical figure, studied for centuries as an abstract form, "fit" the facts of nature. By implication, nature was perhaps itself a machine, intelligible to the careful observer equipped with mathematics.

The New Universe: Galileo

Kepler's work describing many of his findings appeared in 1609. During that same year a professor at Padua and Pisa, Galileo Galilei (1564–1642), turned on the heavens a newly invented instrument, the telescope. He soon published an account of what he saw. The changeless perfection and perfect sphericity of the heavenly bodies had dissolved before his gaze. He saw that the moon had craters and mountains, that spots moved on the sun, that rings encircled Saturn, and that Jupiter had four moons of its own. A bright new star—a supernova—had already appeared in 1572, and Brahe had noted it. In 1577 a new comet had cut a path through what should have been unchanging crystalline spheres. Now Galileo's telescope shattered forever the unchanging, finite, spherical universe of the Middle Ages. Thoughtful scholars suspected that Bruno had been right. Humanity was looking out into infinite space, at a sparse population of stars like the sun that might themselves have solar systems.

The medieval distinction between earthly and celestial physics was apparently dissolving. The moon and sun were not perfect globes and the stars were not changeless. Nor was the earth any longer the motionless center of the universe. The earth, like Mars and Jupiter, was a planet circling the sun against a backdrop of silent, infinite space. Perhaps the same forces and laws operated both on earth and in the heavens.

Such views soon attracted the wrath of the Church of the Counter-Reformation, which had denounced the Copernican theory in 1616. The Roman Inquisition condemned Galileo himself in 1632, threatened him with torture, and forced him to retract his theories. The legend soon arose that after repudiating his "heretical" view that the earth moved around the sun, he nevertheless muttered stubbornly under his breath "*Eppur si muove*"—"It *does* move." Nor could the Inquisition suppress Galileo's brilliantly written dialogues, which contributed mightily to the overthrow not only of Ptolemy in favor of Copernicus, but also of Aristotle in favor of a new physics.

The speculations of the fourteenth-century Franciscan monks inspired Galileo's physics, but he was far more thorough and accurate than they in developing mathematical formulas to describe motion. He worked out by experiment the law of falling bodies—the distance fallen increases as the square of the time. He saw that projectiles followed parabolic paths that were the resultant of the two forces acting upon the projectile—the initial impetus that launched it and the downward pull of the earth. That insight was the beginning of modern ballistics, the scientific foundation of the new warfare.

Galileo also came close to formulating the key concept of modern mechanics, the law of inertia: that bodies tend to remain at rest or to continue in motion in straight lines unless outside forces act upon them. That deceptively simple proposition—fundamentally opposed to Aristotle's concept of motion as the result of

some mover's action—was the source of the law of gravitation. Galileo prepared the way, but it was a man born in the year Galileo died who made that decisive breakthrough.

The Synthesis of Celestial and Terrestrial Mechanics: Newton

Sir Isaac Newton (1642–1727), the greatest figure of the Scientific Revolution, was the man who married Kepler's astronomy to Galileo's mechanics, broke down all distinctions between celestial and terrestrial physics, and accomplished at least part of Descartes' dream of establishing a "universal science." A fundamental intuition came to Newton while he was still a student in his twenties at Cambridge University: the force that bends the moon into its orbit about the earth must be the same force that pulls an apple from its branch to the ground. A reciprocal force of attraction between every body in the universe must exist, and that force—although as yet unexplained—must be calculable.

Newton's earliest calculations came close enough to mathematical proof to persuade him that the same force indeed operated on the moon and on the apple, and that this force varied "directly as the product of the masses" involved and "inversely as the square of the distance" separating those masses. For some time after formulating this "law" of gravitation in 1664–66 he seems to have lost interest. But twenty years later a friend, the astronomer Edmund Halley (who calculated the orbit of the famous comet), persuaded Newton to publish. Newton developed the necessary mathematics—the calculus—to prove his theory to his own satisfaction. He published his conclusions in 1687 in his *Philosophiae naturalis principia mathematica,* the "mathematical principles of natural philosophy." It was one of the most influential books in the history of human thought.

Newton's law of gravitation provided a simple and elegant explanation of a growing mass of data in astronomy and physics and laid the foundations of future research in both sciences. Newton also

The greatest scientific revolutionary of all: Sir Isaac Newton, painted by Kneller.

improved on Bacon and Descartes by giving the scientific method its classic formulation in his fourth "Rule of Reasoning":

In experimental philosophy [science] we are to look upon propositions collected by general induction from phenomena as accurately or very nearly true, notwithstanding any contrary hypotheses [theories] that may be imagined, till such time as other phenomena occur, by which they may either be made more accurate or liable to exceptions.

Newton's support of the experimental or inductive approach was aimed against the premature generalizing, the theoretical "system[s] . . . little better than a Romance," of Descartes and his followers. But Newton, unlike Bacon, was fully convinced of the necessity of mathematical theory. Newton combined at last both celestial and terrestrial physics on the one hand, and empirical observation and mathematical interpretation on the other.

Newton's Universe

News of Newton's work spread rapidly among laymen, thanks to popular scientific works that soon began pouring from the presses of London and Amsterdam. The new universe that Newton disclosed was far different from the cozy finite universe of the Middle Ages. Bodies moved through infinite space in response to predictable, universally operating forces. Mass, force, and motion were the key concepts, and mathematics made them intelligible.

The question "Why?" had obsessed the scholars of the Middle Ages, who had felt they understood a natural phenomenon once they had discovered its purpose. Seventeenth-century scientists limited themselves to asking "How?" The discovery of regular patterns in natural processes satisfied most of them. The world of Kepler, Galileo, and Newton was a vast machine, working according to laws expressible in mathematics, laws understandable by anyone who followed the proper experimental and mathematical

methods. The telescope continued to reveal an ever-larger portion of an apparently infinite universe. The new astronomy, after displacing the earth as the center of the universe, displaced the sun as well. The microscope, after the 1660s, began to reveal the wonders of the infinitely small foundations of life—bacteria, spermatozoa, cells, capillaries.

The question "Why?" nevertheless remained unanswered. What was the place of God and of humanity in this universe? That question did not become acute until the eighteenth century. No prominent seventeenth-century scientist thought that he was reading God out of the universe. Descartes considered himself a good Catholic and apparently did not see the theological dangers inherent in his sharp separation of the world of matter from the world of mind. Newton spent many of his later years absorbed in theological speculation and alchemy. The border between science and religion or magic was still fluid, and possible contradictions between faith and science were not clearly evident to most seventeenth-century scientists, or to their audience.

The French philosopher-scientist Blaise Pascal (1623–62), inventor of probability theory and of the first calculating machine, and contributor to fields as diverse as the calculus and the dynamics of gases and fluids, indeed attempted a synthesis between faith and the new sciences. For Pascal, "the whole visible world [was] only an imperceptible atom in the ample bosom of nature," and the universe "an infinite sphere, the center of which is everywhere, the circumference nowhere." "The eternal silence of these infinite spaces frightens me," he confessed. Yet to examine a mite, "with its minute body and parts incomparably more minute, limbs with their joints, veins in the limbs, blood in the veins, humors in the blood, drops in the humors, vapors in the drops," was equally astonishing. "What is man in nature? A Nothing in comparison with the Infinite, an All in comparison with the Nothing, a mean between nothing and everything." Pascal related the new universe explicitly to Christianity, to Christ's sacrifice on the cross, which made human-

Newton invented and built this first reflecting telescope.

J.M. WILLIAMS

ity, despite its apparent insignificance, the greatest presence in the universe beside God. Others soon saw less need to invoke Christianity.

By the later seventeenth century the hold of religious orthodoxy on Europe's intellectual elite was beginning to weaken. Religious authorities could no longer simply forbid scientific speculation or experiment. The burning or torture of "heretics" like Giordano Bruno slowly went out of fashion, except in Spain. And scientists themselves began to demarcate their activities sharply from questions of faith. The charters of the many scientific societies and academies that sprang up throughout Europe during the century usually contained clauses forbidding purely theological or political discussion and establishing that the group would not investigate "ultimate" or "final" causes.

The earliest history of the Royal Society of London, published in 1667, suggests that scientific discussions offered a peculiar attraction to thoughtful individuals during and after a fanatically bitter religious and civil war such as the English Revolution. Science, which by definition dealt with the empirically verifiable, might thereby become politically and theologically neutral and benefit humanity in practical ways. Scientific truth gradually emerged as an alternative to theological truth. It was not entirely accidental that modern science arose as religious warfare went out of fashion, amid general revulsion at the devastation that fanaticism had wrought.

Nevertheless, Newton's new "world picture" did not explicitly contradict religious feeling. Some indeed found in the mechanistic universe a source of religious awe. Baruch or Benedict Spinoza (1632–77), an Amsterdam lens grinder and philosopher descended from the Jewish communities that Spain had expelled, concluded that the new universe of mass, force, and motion, operating in strict obedience to inexorable laws, *was* God. Spinoza saw no need to consider God as above, behind, or beyond nature, as a "free cause" apart from natural law. God was not "Creator" or "Redeemer," but a "God *or* Nature" that included all being

and incarnated natural law: "God never can decree, nor ever would have decreed, anything but what is; God did not exist before his decrees, and would not exist without them." Humanity, like all else, was part of the natural order and thus of God, and wisdom consisted of contemplating that order with serenity and delight.

Both Jewish and Christian contemporaries considered Spinoza a dangerous atheistic radical, although he was the mildest, kindliest, and most optimistic of men. Most of his works emerged in print only after his death. Contemporaries pointed out that to claim that humanity was part of God made it difficult to explain evil. Later critics discerned in "Whatever is, is in God" a dangerous fatalism. But Spinoza's notion of religion was destined to have great influence in the eighteenth century.

THE CULTURE OF THE BAROQUE

The age of the scientific revolution was also, especially in the Catholic areas of the Continent, the age of the "baroque" style in the visual arts. The baroque sprang up in the later sixteenth century, reached its climax about the middle of the seventeenth, and came to its end around the middle of the eighteenth. Eighteenth-century critics invented the term *baroque* (French for "odd" or "irregular"), after tastes had again changed, to stigmatize seventeenth-century art as a grotesque corruption of Renaissance styles. But by the late nineteenth century critics had come to consider the baroque a great achievement. More than most styles, it is difficult to define because it reflected the contrasts and contradictions of seventeenth-century culture as a whole—religious ecstasy and worldly sensuality, credulity and rationalism, violence and respect for order.

Baroque painters and sculptors portrayed voluptuous women in repose, heroes in battle, and saints in ecstasy with equal skill and zest. In general, the dominant notes of the baroque were tension, conflict, the grandiose, and the dramatic. Renaissance painters and writers had been interested in humanity itself. Baroque artists depicted the conflicts of humanity against the universe, of man against man, and of man within himself on a tragic and heroic scale.

Instructive parallels exist between the thought-worlds of the baroque artists and those of the seventeenth-century scientists. Galileo and Newton studied bodies or masses moving through space under the influence of conflicting forces such as gravitation and centrifugal force. To the great French dramatists of the age—Corneille, Racine, and Molière—the objects of study were typical human beings torn between conflicting forces such as love and duty. Space intrigued baroque painters. The Dutch master Jan Vermeer (1632–75) portrayed figures in a space bathed in and suffused with light. The greatest of Dutch painters, Rembrandt van Rijn (1606–69), spotlighted figures in the midst of darkened space, while others pictured them floating through apparently infinite voids. To baroque artists the supernatural was natural. The scientists' concern with mass, force, and motion paralleled the painters' and poets' concern with individuals caught in the tension between elemental forces. The typical hero of baroque literature, critics have suggested, is Satan in John Milton's *Paradise Lost* (1667), the

only great epic poem in English. Swayed by colossal passions, Satan moves through vast three-dimensional spaces and bends the forces of the universe to serve his implacable will to domination: "To reign is worth ambition though in hell:/Better to reign in hell than serve in heav'n." But God frustrates Satan's designs in the end.

The most typical, although not usually the most beautiful products of baroque architecture were the great palaces: Versailles and the remodeled Louvre in France, Schönbrunn in Austria, or Blenheim, the regal residence in England that Marlborough received for his victories. The style of these buildings was fundamentally Renaissance-classical, but grander, more ornate, and above all larger, often to the point of excess. As with the many descendants of Versailles, the neoclassical official buildings of later centuries, excess served a political purpose. Sheer mass emphasized the power of the state. In this, as in much else, Louis XIV led the way. Even some baroque religious architecture, such as the massive elliptical colonnades that the great Giovanni Lorenzo Bernini (1598–1680) erected to frame St. Peter's in Rome, conveyed the majesty of God rather than his mercy.

The most original creation of the baroque were the operas that originated in Italy early in the seventeenth century. Drama set to music had existed in the West since the twelfth century. But the music had been essentially choral and polyphonic until around 1600, when a group of Florentine composers devised a "*dramma per musica*" (drama through music) in which the characters sang their parts as simple melodies without choral accompaniment. Opera immediately became, and has remained, a vast popular success. The grandiose and palatial stage settings, the dramatic conflicts of the action, and the emotional power of the music exactly suited the taste of the period. Italian composers led the way until the end of the seventeenth century—Claudio Monteverdi (1567–1643), Girolamo Frescobaldi (1583–1643), Alessandro Scarlatti (1660–1725), and the greatest master of Italian Baroque music, Antonio Vivaldi (1675–1741). But it was an Englishman, Henry

The glories of the baroque: altarpiece in St. Peter's, Rome, by the Italian master Giovanni Lorenzo Bernini (1598–1680).

Purcell (*ca.* 1658–95), who wrote the most moving opera of the century, *Dido and Aeneas* (1687).

ORIGINS OF THE ENLIGHTENMENT: SEVENTEENTH-CENTURY THOUGHT ABOUT HUMANITY

While the vast majority of the population of western Europe remained medieval in outlook, the most adventurous minds of the seventeenth century fashioned notions about humanity that rested on Renaissance ideas but pressed far beyond them. The rediscovery of the ancient world, the great overseas voyages, and the scientific revolution led seventeenth-century thinkers into new territory. Their efforts ultimately inspired the greatest break in the history of European thought since the collapse of the Roman Empire, the eighteenth-century flowering of modern conceptions of humanity known as the Enlightenment. The new ideas of the seventeenth century fall conveniently into three categories: individualism, relativism, and a rationalism tempered with empiricism.

Individualism

Radical thinkers of the seventeenth century were increasingly inclined to celebrate the individual. The most intense Christian piety of the period—whether it was the Catholic devotion preached by St. François de Sales, the stern conscience of the Puritans and Jansenists, or the warm inner conviction of the German Pietists— was highly individualistic. That trend was equally evident in political theory. The fashion was to start with the individual and then seek explanations of and justifications for the existence of societies and states.

Supporters of the divine-right theory of kingship remained numerous, but by the middle of the seventeenth century the notion of an explicit or implicit "contract" between people and ruler was widespread. Hobbes and a few others, including Spinoza, argued that this contract, once made, was irrevocable and that it

Opera singers of the baroque: detail from an opera setting drawn by Ludovico Burnacinia, Vienna (1674).

bound the ruled but not the ruler. Others, like the Parliamentarians in the English Civil War and John Locke in political philosophy, argued for a right of rebellion against rulers who broke the terms of the contract by acting against the general welfare.

The idea of a "social contract" soon took its place alongside the notion of the "political contract." Society, according to social-contract theorists, was itself the result of a voluntary agreement among individuals who had been absolutely independent in their original "state of nature." The two ideas mixed, somewhat confusedly, in the works of Locke and of later political philosophers. In both contracts, the individual with his rights and his "natural" independence logically came first; then came society or the state. The more radical thinkers of the seventeenth century thus came to think of society as an artificial organization of independent individuals that rested on their consent. That was a radical break with the medieval conception of society as an organism or a "body" of which individuals were mere "members," each with an assigned place.

Relativism

The greatest thinkers of the Middle Ages were confident that the peoples of Christendom were chosen by God, and that divine revelation gave humanity all necessary truths. But that self-assurance weakened during the sixteenth and seventeenth centuries, thanks to Humanism, to the voyages of discovery, and to the development of science.

Humanism had begun to reveal Greco-Roman civilization in some detail. Ancient literature, art, and historical writing brought alive a long-dead society that offered numerous alternatives to the medieval Christian system of belief. The Renaissance had first created the modern disciplines of history, archaeology, and philology. Seventeenth-century scholars broadened and deepened them. Thoughtful Europeans thus learned that other societies had existed in other times with values, beliefs, and institutions quite different from their own. That recognition was the origin of the concept of historical relativism, of the notion that value systems—including those of Christian Europe—were historical phenomena subject to change.

The age of discovery added to historical relativism a geographical counterpart. The discovery in America and Asia of other societies shattered European provincialism. The tribal hunter-gatherers of America and Africa, the urban civilizations of Aztecs and Incas, and the great empires of Asia with their advanced arts and amenities inspired study and reflection. Perhaps the "noble savages" of the New World were happier than the more cultured but "corrupted" Christians of Europe. Perhaps Persian sages and Chinese philosophers had something to teach Christians. Each society had different standards—was any value system grounded on anything more solid than custom? Doubts on these points affected increasing numbers of European thinkers in the seventeenth and eighteenth centuries. And scientific discovery likewise widened their vision of humanity's place in nature. European Christianity was not alone in time and space, and humanity itself might not be alone in the universe.

The work of Pierre Bayle (1647–1706), the great scholarly skeptic of the later seventeenth century, exemplifies the results of historical study, geographical exploration, and scientific discovery. Bayle was born a Huguenot, briefly converted to Catholicism, and then renounced all orthodox belief when his brother died in a French dungeon during an attempt at forced conversion. Bayle took up residence in the relatively tolerant Dutch Netherlands and devoted the latter part of his life to a crusade against superstition, religious intolerance, and dogma of all kinds. In 1697 he published a huge rambling book, the *Historical and Critical Dictionary,* which had enormous influence on Enlightenment thought. Into the book he poured a relativism and skepticism acquired through extensive historical study, an amateur knowledge of science, and experience.

He defied convention by insisting that religion and political stability were not identical—atheists could be good citizens. He denounced religious conversions by force. He ridiculed astrology, a form of superstition even more current then than now. He derided tales of miracles. He distrusted all historical authorities, including the writers of the Old Testament, unless their account of events was inherently credible. An admirer of Descartes, his test of truth was "reason," and many scriptural accounts failed that test. Bayle was the most destructive critic of his generation. His war against traditional religion replaced, and in part derived from, the scarcely ended wars of religion.

Rationalism and Empiricism

The leading thinkers of the seventeenth century began a process that reached completion only in the eighteenth century: the replacement of the lost certainties of religious belief with a new object of worship—reason. It was the faculty that in theory distinguished humanity from the animal world. It was trustworthy; the triumphs of seventeenth-century science had proved that. An increasingly optimistic age concluded that reason gave humanity the *certain knowledge* of the world that religion no longer appeared to offer.

Reason also provided a law, "natural law," to replace the foundation that religious belief now failed to provide for human knowledge. The idea of a law of nature that served as a standard of behavior for all humans at all times was not new.

Greek philosophers such as Aristotle had enunciated a version of it, the Stoics had pressed it further, and Cicero had given the idea classic formulation:

> There is in fact a true law—namely, right reason—which is in accordance with nature, applies to all men, and is unchangeable and eternal. By its commands this law summons men to the performance of their duties; by its prohibitions it restrains them from doing wrong.

St. Augustine had then Christianized that law by identifying it with the law of God. The medieval scholastics had enthusiastically proclaimed that law to be the basis of earthly law and morality. During the Renaissance and the Reformation, the rediscovery of texts of the ancient Stoics and the work of Protestant scholars such as the father of modern international law, the Dutch jurist and diplomat Hugo Grotius (1583–1645), had secularized natural law once more, as a "law" inherent in the nature of humanity. Grotius, in *On the Law of War and Peace* (1625), attempted to find in natural law some basis for a "law of nations" that would transcend and moderate the religious fanaticisms of the Thirty Years' War. And the discovery of scientific "laws of nature," such as Kepler's laws of planetary motion, further reinforced the belief that natural laws of human behavior must also exist. Success in proving mathematical and scientific laws inspired faith that reason could discern "natural law" in human affairs.

The most influential example of that faith was John Locke's claim that every individual in the "state of nature," before the existence of organized societies, possessed certain "natural rights," most notably life, liberty, and property. From that premise it followed, as proof followed axiom, that humanity had formed societies and set up governments mainly to preserve those rights. Whereas Descartes had hoped to deduce the universe from a few central mathematical principles, Locke in his *Second Treatise of Government* (1690) assumed that he could deduce society and

government from a few simple axioms about humanity and natural law.

An undercurrent of empiricism, of respect for the evidence of the senses, nevertheless qualified that enthusiastic rationalism. Here too, Locke led the way in his *Essay Concerning Human Understanding* (1690), which many readers hailed as the counterpart in the study of humanity to Newton's work on the forces of nature. Locke argued that all human ideas came from the experience of the senses. The mind at birth was a *tabula rasa*, a clean slate, on which experience gained through the senses gradually imprinted conceptions. No "innate ideas" existed, and contrary to Descartes, no axioms were self-evident. Outside forces acting upon the mind explained all human ideas.

That was the purest empiricism. Locke hoped that it would provide a weapon for destroying the superstitions and prejudices of the past. It proved destructive of much else, including some of Locke's own doctrines. Locke's theory of the mind did away with original sin, for experience might mold the *tabula rasa* of the mind to do good rather than evil. It did away equally with the revelation on which Christianity rested and with mathematical axioms, for neither derived from the senses. Above all, it undermined Locke's own conception of "natural rights" that were innate and not based on experience.

The rationalism of Locke's natural-law theory of society clashed both with the empiricism of his theory of the mind and with the relativism in time and space that the Humanists and the great navigators had disclosed. The Enlightenment inherited this agonizing contradiction between rationalist faith in natural law and empiricist trust in sense-experience and in the evidence of comparative history.

THE EIGHTEENTH CENTURY: THE ENLIGHTENMENT

The task that the leading thinkers of the eighteenth century set themselves was to popularize the methods and principles of seventeenth-century natural science and to apply those methods and principles to God, humanity, and society. Scientific discovery continued, but the most brilliant writers of the age concentrated their effort on applying the new scientific method to long-festering human ills—economic, social, political, and ecclesiastical. Their concern was less to discover new truth about nature than to apply the methods of natural science to the transformation of society.

The eighteenth century's own name for this movement was "the Enlightenment"—*les lumières* in French. The term suggested the dawn of a new age of reason and knowledge after a long dark night of ignorance, superstition, intolerance, and despotism of kings and priests. That new light was the light of science, as the great English poet Alexander Pope (1688–1744) elegantly proclaimed:

> *Nature and nature's law lay hid in*
> *   night;*
> *God said, "Let Newton be," and all*
> *   was light.*

Correspondence, exchange of publications, and travel linked together a cultural movement that transcended state and religious boundaries. "Enlightened" writers and readers spanned Europe, from Russia to Spain, from Edinburgh to Naples, from the Philadelphia of Benjamin Franklin to the Virginia of Thomas Jefferson. But the center of the movement was indisputably Paris.

That was no accident. Most other countries were either too small or too backward to become major centers of Enlightenment thought and agitation. The major exception, England, had already fought its battles for religious toleration and political freedom. It had established after 1688 a freedom of thought and publication unprecedented elsewhere, even in the Dutch Netherlands. It had already had an Enlightenment, or "pre-Enlightenment," through Hobbes, Locke, and many others. By 1715, the England of gentry and merchants was too successful, both internally and externally, to provide much

nourishment for intellectual movements that fed on dissatisfaction with the existing order. Only the Scots, who delighted in stirring up their richer and duller neighbors to the south, were an exception. The philosopher and historian David Hume (1711–76) and the economist Adam Smith (1723–90) were major Enlightenment figures, and Edinburgh, the capital of Scotland, was one of the great centers of eighteenth-century European thought.

Three tendencies in French society united to make France the center of the Enlightenment. First, French government after the death of Louis XIV in 1715 became steadily more inept and ineffectual, both internally and in its wars and diplomacy (see pp. 563–64). Weakness at home and defeat abroad sapped the prestige of the existing order and of the Church that upheld it. Second, the aristocracy began to take its revenge on the monarchy that had reduced it to the role of courtly lapdog. In the realm of ideas, that revenge consisted of the articulation and eager propagation of potentially subversive ideas. Finally, the gradually increasing wealth that commerce and industry produced gave the growing urban middle classes an increasing consciousness of their own worth and importance. That consciousness led to rising social tension between the privileged and the less privileged. And that tension helped encourage an increasing body of literature that attacked the existing order at its weakest points: the obscurantism of the Church, the ineptitude of the noble-dominated royal administration, and the foolishness and arrogance of the nobility itself.

The weapons of the French Enlightenment writers were clarity, wit, and a deliberate ambiguity designed to ward off the wrath of officialdom. Government censors were often too slow-witted to catch hidden barbs aimed at Church or state, and after mid-century they often secretly agreed with the critics. Censorship stopped only the most blatantly subversive or obviously blasphemous attacks on the existing order. After the 1750s censorship was almost powerless against the flood of social criticism and satire that poured from the presses. The source of that flood was Paris, the center of the intellectual life of continental Europe. There the greatest intellectual figures of the age met and conversed in the *salons* or weekly gatherings that intellectual women of the aristocracy had begun to organize. The inhabitants of this world of ideas, whether commoner or noble, shared a common feeling that they were leading a revolution of ideas without precedent in European history, a crusade to end the absurdities and barbarities of the old order.

The "Philosophes": Voltaire, Montesquieu, Diderot

At first, London helped inspire Paris. The conventional date for the beginning of the Enlightenment as a movement was the visit to England in 1726–29 of a certain François Marie Arouet (1694–1778), better known by his pen-name, Voltaire. The French government had twice imprisoned Voltaire in the Bastille fortress in Paris for alleged or actual witticisms made at the expense of royal or noble personages. On the second occasion he had only achieved freedom by promising to leave for London. The man who came to personify the Enlightenment thus had good reason to hate the old regime.

In England, Voltaire read Newton and Locke, and relished the relative freedom of English society in comparison with his own. After returning to France he published *Philosophical Letters on the English* (1733), which passed on to his readers Newton's main principles and popularized Locke's theories of human nature and limited government. Voltaire skillfully contrasted the rationality of Newton's method and the tolerant reasonableness of the English way of life with the arbitrary and capricious realities of Church, state, and society in France.

Voltaire's English letters set the tone of Enlightenment propaganda in France for the next half-century. They were "philosophical" in the broad sense, because they reflected on the facts of human existence and attempted to discover their meaning, and because they searched for general principles useful to humanity as a whole. But the *philosophes*, as Voltaire

---

Voltaire on Superstition   1776

Almost everything that goes beyond the adoration of a Supreme Being and submission of the heart to his orders is superstition. One of the most dangerous is to believe that certain ceremonies entail the forgiveness of crimes. Do you believe that God will forget a murder you have committed if you bathe in a certain river, sacrifice a black sheep, or if someone says certain words over you? . . . Do better, miserable humans; have neither murders nor sacrifices of black sheep. . . .

Notice that the most superstitious ages have always been those of the most horrible crimes. . . . The superstitious man is ruled by fanatics, and he becomes one himself. On the whole, the less superstition, the less fanaticism, and the less fanaticism, the fewer miseries.

From Voltaire, Dictionnaire philosophique *(Paris: Editions de Cluny, n.d.; reproduction of the edition of 1776), Vol. III, pp. 218–25.*

---

and kindred spirits became known, had little use for metaphysical speculation. They were less philosophers than popularizers, crusaders for the application of the best intellectual tools of the century to social problems. Voltaire was the greatest of them—the most prolific, the wittiest, the most readable, and perhaps the angriest. His preferred targets were bigotry, superstition, and despotism.

"*Écrasez l' infâme*," cried Voltaire in his innumerable letters, pamphlets, stories, and satires: crush that "infamous thing," the Church. In the famous entry on "Religion" in his *Philosophical Dictionary* (1764), he described a vision he claimed to have had of a desert filled with piles of bones of "Christians with their throats slit by one another in theological disputes." He went on to report a philosophical conversation with the shades of Socrates and Jesus, who both deplored the spectacle he had just seen. And he attacked the religious intolerance of contemporary France as vigorously as the barbarism of the past. When he died in 1778, Voltaire was the most widely read author in Europe, the first writer to have made a fortune from the sale of his own writings. Paris buried him with a ceremony worthy of a king.

Voltaire, almost as skeptical as in life, by the master-sculptor Jean-Antoine Houdon (1781).

A second leading Enlightenment figure was the Baron Charles Louis de Secondat de Montesquieu (1689–1755), sometime president of the *Parlement* of Bordeaux. Montesquieu tried to create a "social science" by applying the methods of the natural sciences to the study of society. In his most famous work, *The Spirit of the Laws* (1748), he suggested that climate and other environmental factors helped determine forms of government, and he tried to discover what form of government best fitted a given set of environmental conditions. *The Spirit of the Laws* was not "scientific" by later standards, but it was the first serious attempt since the Greeks at tracing relationships between systems of government and the environment. In his popular *History of Civilization* (1756),

Voltaire took over and elaborated Montesquieu's concepts.

Montesquieu, like Voltaire, found Locke's theory of limited government persuasive. As a French noble he wished to limit the perceived excesses of royal absolutism. He followed Locke in concluding that the ideal political form called for the separation and balancing of powers within government. That conclusion later had great influence on the authors of the American Constitution (see p. 695).

A third major figure of the French Enlightenment was Denis Diderot (1713–84), co-editor of the famous *Encyclopédie,* an immense encyclopedia designed to sum up the totality of human knowledge. Despite Jesuit protests and cuts by timid printers, it appeared in 35 volumes between 1752 and 1780. Diderot was an enthusiast for science and saw the relationship between science and technology more clearly than most *philosophes.* The most remarkable feature of the *Encyclopédie* was the plates that show machinery and industrial processes. But Diderot was no mere compiler; he was a confident prophet of the Enlightenment's this-worldly religion of humanity. The entries and content of the *Encyclopédie* reflected the interests and enthusiasms of Diderot and his fellow *philosophes* and contained many of their most trenchant writings. The work was an immense success and became the bible of the "enlightened" everywhere. Through it ran faith in humanity's reason, pride in its accomplishments, and sublime confidence in its future.

The Enlightenment Faith

No intellectual movement is successful unless it has followers as well as leaders. The Enlightenment, like the Renaissance, produced its full quota of earnest hacks and disreputable scribblers. It also enjoyed a public, vast by previous standards, of silent supporters. Twentieth-century scholarship has shown that the *Encyclopédie* enjoyed astonishing sales in tiny provincial towns. Periodicals, libraries, book societies, and literary and scientific discussion groups spread knowledge,

Historical Relativism in Montesquieu: The Effects of Climate and Geography

In Asia they have always had great empires; in Europe these could never exist. Asia has larger plains; it is cut out into much larger divisions by mountains and seas . . . and the rivers being not so large form more contrasted boundaries. Power in Asia, then, should be always despotic; for if their subjugation be not severe they would soon make a division inconsistent with the nature of the country.

In Europe natural divisions form many nations of moderate extent, in which ruling by laws is not incompatible with the maintenance of the state: on the contrary, it is so favorable to it that without this the state would fall into decay. It is this that has formed a genius for liberty that renders each part extremely difficult to be subdued and subjected to a foreign power. . . . Africa is in a climate like that of the south of Asia and is in the same servitude. . . .

Monarchy is more frequently found in fertile countries and a republican government in those which are not so, and this is sometimes a sufficient compensation for the inconveniences they suffer by the sterility of the land. Thus the barrenness of the soil of Attica established a democracy there.

From Charles de Secondat de Montesquieu, The Spirit of the Laws *(Bohn Standard Library edition), Vol. I, Book XVII, Chs. 6, 7; Book XVIII, Ch. 1, pp. 289–91.*

social criticism, and scandalous gossip. The main ideas of the Enlightenment took root all over Europe, and a new generation absorbed from them entirely new conceptions of human nature, society, and religion. Five words, each of which bore a heavy freight of meaning in the eighteenth century, sum up these ruling ideas: *reason, nature, happiness, progress,* and *liberty.*

The eighteenth century believed as passionately in reason as the seventeenth, but with a difference. The "reason" of Voltaire relied more upon experience and less on mathematics than that of Descartes. It was a weapon of skeptical inquiry based on observed facts—or on what Voltaire thought were facts—rather than a method of deduction from axioms. To the thinkers of the Enlightenment, reason was the alternative to superstition and prejudice. It was the only sure guide to the principles that governed humanity and nature. Reason could discover the fundamental rationality of the universe, and it could also make human societies more rational. The *philosophes* were less interested in "pure" science than in applied science, less concerned with intellectual system-building than with specific reforms. They regarded reason as a down-to-earth tool, applicable equally to agriculture, government, social relations, astronomy, and physics.

Nature was a second favorite word of the Enlightenment. The precise meaning the *philosophes* attached to "nature" was not always clear, but to nearly all of them "nature" or "the natural" was the proper standard for measuring God and humanity. A thing "according to nature" was reasonable and therefore good. Voltaire and his contemporaries brought the idea of natural law to the peak of its prestige. One of them devised the following definition of natural law:

The regular and constant order of facts by which God rules the universe; the order which his wisdom presents to the sense and reason of men, to serve them as an equal and common rule of conduct, and to guide them, without distinction of race or sect, towards perfection and happiness.

Order and law, then, ruled throughout the universe of the *philosophes*—laws of economics, of politics, and of morality as well as of physics and astronomy. Reason permitted the discovery of those laws. Humans might ignore or defy them but did so at their peril. To the "enlightened," the road to happiness lay in conforming to nature and nature's laws. The enlightened elite of the eighteenth century looked on those who "broke" nature's laws in the same spirit as the clergy of the Middle Ages had looked on heretics who broke God's laws: they were rebels against the order of the universe.

Happiness in this world, not salvation and eternal rejoicing in the next, was the end the *philosophes* had in view. The Enlightenment, like the Scientific Revolution, was a secular movement. When Thomas Jefferson (see p. 579) cited "the pursuit of happiness" along with life and liberty as inalienable human rights, he was expressing a general sentiment of the age. Medieval Christianity's toleration of misery in this life in the expectation of rewards in the next angered the *philosophes*. They demanded the realization of Christian ideals here and now. They abominated cruelty, judicial torture, slavery, and the callous treatment of the insane. An enlightened Italian civil servant of the Habsburgs, Cesare Beccaria (1738–94), was the first to suggest that savage penalties do not necessarily prevent crime and to propose a theory of penology. The *philosophes* were also cosmopolitan and even pacifist in temper. Voltaire penned some of the bitterest passages ever written about the "insanity" of war and the absurdity of blind patriotism.

Progress was an even more central constituent of the Enlightenment faith than happiness. The *philosophes* took the Christian idea of the spiritual progression of humanity from the Creation through the Incarnation to the Last Judgment, and secularized it. The progress of civilization, they believed, was now out of God's hands and in those of humanity, thanks to the discovery and use of nature's laws in government, economics, and technology. The *philosophes* were in general confident that both humanity and society were perfectible through human effort.

This was a major revolution in Western thought. The Middle Ages could not have conceived of progress that was unrelated to God. Renaissance thinkers still felt themselves inferior to the heroic Greeks and Romans. But even before a symbolic literary battle between "ancients" and "moderns" that began in 1687, some thinkers had suggested that the "moderns" were as good as, and probably better than, the "ancients." By 1750 a French *philosophe*, economist, and civil servant, Anne-Robert-Jacques Turgot, could suggest that the essential element in history was humanity's slow struggle upward toward the discovery of the scientific method.

In 1794 the Marquis de Condorcet, a mathematician and aristocratic reformer under sentence of death during the French Revolution, wrote a *Sketch for a Historical Picture of the Progress of the Human Mind* that summed up all the optimism of his century. He saw "the strongest reasons for believing that nature has set no limit to the realization of our hopes" and foresaw "the abolition of inequality between nations, the progress of equality within nations, and the true perfection of humanity."

Progress, Condorcet concluded, was now "independent of any power that might wish to halt it" and "will never be reversed." The scientific method was irrevocably fixed in the human mind, and scientific knowledge of natural laws would continue to accumulate. Progress was thus accelerating, irreversible, and infinite. The coming "perfection of mankind" was an intoxicating vision, a vision the majority of the enlightened shared despite the abundance of historical evidence suggesting that civilizations declined as well as rose. How Condorcet reconciled his vision of progress with his own status as fugitive from the executioners of the Revolution of "Liberty, Equality, Fraternity" is unclear.

Liberty, indeed, was yet another favorite word of the *philosophes.* They were acutely aware of the prevalence in France of arbitrary arrest and restrictions on speech, religion, trade, and employment. Looking at England through lightly rose-tinted glasses, they envied Englishmen their economic, political, and religious liberties. Their concern for liberty was potentially the most explosive tenet of their faith, but few considered that violence was necessary to secure it. Liberty, for the *philosophes,* was inseparable from reason. Reason would soon reveal the true natural laws governing all things, from trade, to government, to religion. The artificiality and corruption of the present would become evident to all. A "benevolent despotism," an enlightened philosopher-king, would lead humanity into a new golden age—or so Voltaire and many other *Encyclopédie* authors hoped. But what if despotism was by its very nature not benevolent?

The Enlightenment and Religion

The new ideas inevitably had religious consequences. To the enlightened, religious fervor savored of the fanaticism of the wars of religion. The Enlightenment only prized enthusiasm for its new religion of reason, progress, and the "perfection of humanity." The fashionable form of belief common among the eighteenth century's educated elite came to be Deism, the belief in a God who is Creator but not Redeemer. The God of the Deists was a celestial watchmaker who had made the universe, wound it up, and then stepped aside to let it run according to natural law that he had laid down. God did not concern himself with humanity or act in or through human history.

The essence of religion, for the Deist, was thus awe and reverence before the rationality and perfection of the universe—a feeling reflected in the beautiful hymns of Isaac Watts still heard in many Protestant churches. To a Deist such as Voltaire, talk of revelation, miracles, or the special intervention of God in the natural order was false. Dogma and ritual were "superstition," for humanity needed only reason to see God. The heart of natural religion was a morality common to all mankind. "Light is uniform for the star

Sirius," Voltaire wrote, "and for us moral philosophy must be uniform."

Deism obviously tended to undermine orthodox Christianity and to substitute for it a rationalist belief in God as First Cause and in "natural law" as humanity's moral guide. A few *philosophes* such as Diderot went further and dared the censors by pushing beyond Deism to atheism. For Baron Paul Henri d'Holbach (1723–89), the universe contained nothing but matter, humanity itself was a conglomeration of atoms, and natural law determined all events. Holbach was the complete "materialist," an ancestor of much nineteenth-century thought.

Economics, Society, and Politics

The *philosophes* were interested in social and political issues, but they were reformers, not revolutionaries. Their formula for reform was simply to discover by reason and experience the natural laws that should operate in any given situation and to clear away all supposedly artificial obstacles to their operation. The result, "reason" indicated, would be "progress" toward happiness and freedom.

That outlook encouraged the beginnings of the modern discipline of economics. In 1758 François Quesnay published his *Economic Survey,* which proclaimed the existence of natural economic "laws" and urged an end to all restrictions, such as government control of grain supplies and prices, that prevented those laws from operating. But Quesnay and French economists of his school were too much the products of France's predominantly agricultural society. They saw agriculture as the source of all wealth and damned industry as "sterile" and commerce as parasitic. Adam Smith of Edinburgh saw more clearly. In *An Inquiry into the Nature and Causes of the Wealth of Nations* (1776), the first classic of modern economics, Smith extended the concept of "natural liberty" to commerce and industry.

He denounced all "mercantilist" practices, although he admitted that an age of warring states might make measures such as the Navigation Acts necessary for a time. In general, however, Smith maintained that state interference with the workings of the natural law of supply and demand decreased rather than increased national wealth. The "invisible hand" of natural law, Smith argued, was a self-regulating mechanism that automatically maximized the wealth and freedom of any society that respected it. To tamper with it was both dangerous and self-defeating.

In political theory, similar lines of reasoning led to three distinct schools of thought. The first rested on the notion of "enlightened absolutism." The *philosophes,* children of their age, were no democrats. Voltaire thought government should be for the people, but by kings: "The people, stupid and barbarous, needs a yoke, a cattle prod, and hay." Most *philosophes* hoped for a mellowing of divine-right monarchy into a benevolent "enlightened" philosopher-kingship that would govern—perhaps with well-rewarded *philosophe* advice—according to natural law rather than royal caprice. A second, smaller school believed that "reason" pointed in the direction of an English-style constitutional monarchy based on natural rights and on a contract that bound the sovereign to respect his subjects' liberties. And a very few advanced a third theory, still too radical to be of much immediate influence: the theory of democratic government. That school's foremost prophet was the eccentric Jean-Jacques Rousseau (1712–78), author of *The Social Contract* (1762).

Rousseau: Prophet of Democracy and Despotism

Rousseau, a native of Geneva, appeared in Paris in 1742 after a wandering youth. He came to know Diderot and other *philosophes* and for a time attempted to join them. But he was never easy in their company. He trusted reason but relied even more on emotion. He trusted nature, but to him nature was the unspoiled simplicity of the noble savage, of humanity before the coming of civilization. After a sudden vision experienced in 1749, he became convinced that humanity had lost more than it had gained by cultivating the arts and sciences. He lost all faith in progress.

An idealized view of Rousseau, misfit and social critic, from an eighteenth-century playing card.

The seeming artificiality of Paris society increasingly irritated him, and he broke with his former friends. Voltaire thought him insane, and in his miserable later years Rousseau indeed suffered from delusions of persecution.

Rousseau was the greatest social critic of the Enlightenment. By temperament he was a shy and sensitive misfit who desperately wanted to belong. He knew himself to be "good," on the model of the "noble savage." He therefore blamed his unhappiness, his failure to fit in, on the alleged artificiality of existing society. That society of kings, aristocrats, and priests—he felt—had "corrupted" and humiliated him. Consequently he imagined an alternative, not as a program for revolution—although many readers took it as one—but as a critique of existing societies.

Rousseau's utopia, described in *The Social Contract,* was a "direct democracy," a small and tightly knit community of free male citizens (like most men of the Enlightenment, Rousseau considered it part of "the order of nature that woman obeys man"). Government consisted of the citizens meeting face-to-face. From their de-liberations, Rousseau was confident, a "general will" would inevitably emerge. For humanity's essential goodness, in Rousseau's view, meant that a society that governed itself was immune from dissent and conflict. And by agreeing to form a community, Rousseau's citizens had in any case willingly sacrificed all individual rights to the group. Once the "general will" became known, all owed it absolute obedience.

Perhaps Rousseau had in mind an idealized image of Geneva as he wrote *The Social Contract.* In that city-state, citizens knew and trusted one another, and the minority normally accepted the majority's view with good grace, out of loyalty to the community. But it was Sparta, that least individualist and most austerely military of the Greek city-states, that recurred frequently in Rousseau's pages. It was his favorite model.

Perhaps Rousseau's knowledge of Sparta—of its relentless regimentation, its murderous *krypteia* or secret police, its ruthless enslavement of all surrounding cities—was imperfect. Perhaps, as some modern scholars assert, his proposals for a "progressive" education that would bring out the child's "natural" goodness and intellectual curiosity make Rousseau a prophet of individual freedom rather than Spartan uniformity. Perhaps his hostility to kings and aristocrats, indeed his aversion to all forms of authority, absolve him of responsibility for excesses committed after 1789 in the name of the "general will." But his theory of democracy was nevertheless a stunning illustration of the consequences—even the unintended consequences—of ideas.

Locke and Montesquieu had argued that the guarantee of political liberty was the separation of executive and legislative powers. Concentration of power threatened freedom. Their theory derived from an essential pessimism about human behavior, a long experience of human ambition and fallibility gained in the world of politics. Their theory of liberty was "negative"—liberty arose when institutional and legal checks limited the powers of government. That negative theory of liberty, of individual rights *against* government, was the foundation of modern representa-

Rousseau: The Despotism of the General Will

The problem is to find a form of association . . . in which each, while uniting himself with all, may still obey himself alone, and remain as free as before. This is the fundamental problem of which the Social Contract provides the solution: . . . the total alienation of each associate, together with all his rights, to the whole community. . . . Each man, in giving himself to all, gives himself to nobody. . . . Each of us puts his person and all his power in common under the supreme direction of the general will, and, in our corporate capacity, we receive each member as an indivisible part of the whole. . . . In order that the social compact may not be an empty formula, it tacitly includes the undertaking, which alone can give force to the rest, that whoever refuses to obey the general will shall be compelled to do so by the whole body. This means nothing less than that he will be forced to be free.

From Jean-Jacques Rousseau, The Social Contract *(New York and London: Everyman's Library, 1913), Book I, Chs. 6 and 7, pp. 14–18.*

tive democracies such as Britain and the United States.

Rousseau, an intellectual without worldly experience, took an entirely different view. For him humanity was "good" with the goodness of the noble savage. That goodness would express itself naturally in politics once the artificial restraints and corrupting influences of the old society fell away. Checks and balances, the separation of powers, the protection of specific rights would serve no purpose if "the people" governed itself. The "general will," by definition, could not will harm to itself! Rousseau's theory of liberty was "positive"—his liberty was the willing obedience to laws and decisions that the individual himself had helped to make. Rousseau's theory of liberty thus set no limit at all on what government could do if it expressed—*or claimed to express*—the general will. In a justly famous passage in *The Social Contract,* Rousseau even asserted that the community could force individuals to be free. That hard phrase was the precursor of an even harder reality after 1789.

Utopian visions like those of Rousseau, it later became clear, often originated among and appealed to intellectuals alienated from their societies. Utopianism flourished best under autocracies—like that of the successors of Louis XIV—that pursued policies sufficiently repressive to generate dissent, but not repressive enough to crush it. And the utopian search for a society without conflict, of which Rousseau was the greatest forerunner and prophet, could even lead to an attack on representative democracies whose "negative freedoms" appeared to foster doubt, unhappiness, and disunity. Rousseau died in 1778, but only chronology bound him to the Enlightenment. His true home was the post-1789 world of revolution, nationalism, and Romanticism that he helped to shape.

ARTS AND LETTERS IN THE EIGHTEENTH CENTURY

The art and literature of the later seventeenth and early eighteenth centuries reflected the belief of Enlightenment scientists and philosopers in the rationality, intelligibility, and order of the universe. Rationalism blended easily with classicism. The regularity and harmony of Newton's universe seemed to accord both with the balance, proportion, rationality, and restraint for which classical Greek architecture and Greek and Roman writers had striven. The dictators of literary and artistic taste at the close of the seventeenth century were classicists. When *philosophes* like Voltaire wrote dramas, they accepted classical standards as unquestioningly as had Corneille and Racine. The architects of the Georgian buildings of England and the beautifully proportioned Place de la Concorde in Paris accepted classical rules of balance and unity with equal zeal. Enthusiasm for classical antiquity reached its post-Renaissance climax after 1748, when Europe discovered the remains of the Roman city of Pompeii in startlingly well-preserved condition under the ashes and cinders from Mt. Vesuvius that had covered it in A.D. 79.

An Age of Prose

The "age of reason" was an age of prose. Essays, satirical tales, novels, letters, and histories were the characteristic literary forms of the eighteenth century. Authors bent their energies to description and narrative rather than to suggestion and imagination. The essays of Joseph Addison and Richard Steele, which began to appear in 1709, sketched a delightful picture of English rural society. Jonathan Swift's *Gulliver's Travels* (1726) and Voltaire's *Candide* (1759) offered biting social and philosophical commentary. As the century progressed, the novel emerged as the favorite form of literary expression; the most enjoyable example was perhaps Henry Fielding's *Tom Jones* (1749). Philosophy, economics, and history prospered alongside fiction. The eighteenth century's greatest monument of historical scholarship was Edward Gibbon's history of *The Decline and Fall of the Roman Empire* (1776–88), which in a luminous style that will forever delight its readers, sardonically described the "triumph of barbarism and religion" over the greatest empire of the ancient world.

Painting, especially fashionable portraits, well disclosed the elegant aristocratic flavor of eighteenth-century society. The delicate-featured and exquisitely groomed women who look coolly down on the observer, and the worldly, sometimes arrogant, faces of their husbands under their powdered wigs suggest the artificiality of aristocratic society, and sometimes the hardness of character of those who inhabited it. Opulent furniture and tableware, and the great town and country houses of nobles and wealthy merchants, reflect the same aristocratic elegance.

But not all books and art served the enjoyment of the aristocracy. The first newspapers written for a wide audience of educated readers emerged in the eighteenth century. William Hogarth (1697–1764) made engravings of his satirical sketches of English society and sold them by the thousands. Above all, novelists, dramatists, and musicians in London and Paris began to appeal to a middle-class audience. The Paris stage, with productions such as *The Barber of Seville* (1775) and *The Marriage of Figaro* (1784), by Pierre de Beaumarchais, turned a keen satirical edge against the aristocracy. The heroes and heroines of novels tended increasingly to imitate the middle-class origins of their audiences.

An Age of Music

But the greatest cultural achievement of the age was its music—above all, German music. Two great Germans dominated the musical world of the early eighteenth century: Johann Sebastian Bach (1685–1750) and George Frederick Handel (1685–1759). Handel in his oratorios for chorus and instruments and Bach in his richly varied works for keyboard instruments, chamber groups, orchestras, and choruses, realized all the dramatic and emotional possibilities of the baroque style. As the century drew on, the orchestra, which had originated in the seventeenth century, expanded and took in new instruments, the piano replaced the harpsichord, and music began to move from the aristocratic salon into the public hall.

Franz Joseph Haydn (1732–1809), who wrote both for chamber groups and for orchestras, developed the musical forms known as sonatas and symphonies. The other outstanding musical personality of the latter half of the century was Wolfgang Amadeus Mozart (1756–91), probably the most brilliant musician in history. Born at Salzburg in Austria, he began his career as a child prodigy, lived only 35 years, and died in poverty. But within that short span he produced over 600 compositions that included unequalled mas-

Eighteenth-century art for a popular audience: Hogarth, *The Village Fair*.

terpieces of invention and form—string quartets, sonatas, concertos, masses, symphonies, and operas such as *Le Nozze di Figaro* (The Marriage of Figaro, 1786), *Don Giovanni* (1787), and *Die Zauberflöte* (The Magic Flute, 1791).

THE LIMITS OF THE ENLIGHTENMENT: RELIGION, PHILOSOPHY, AND LITERATURE

The Enlightenment was the creation of a small elite, although many of its ideas circulated widely and penetrated far down the social scale. It was largely confined to western Europe and the English-speaking world. And countercurrents soon arose to challenge the supremacy of reason in philosophy and of rational structure and classical balance in art.

Contrary to the expectations of many Enlightenment figures, religion did not give way to Deism or wither away. Many Protestants found a compromise between Christian faith and the Enlightenment's rationalism, humanitarianism, and tolerance. The result was the nineteenth-century development of a liberal Protestantism. Others took the road of more intense piety. The cold rationality of Deism held no appeal for emotional natures, and only the educated could understand it. Hence the wide popularity of two warmly emotional Protestant movements, Pietism in Germany and Methodism in England and America. Both emphasized the importance of the inner religious experience of individual "conversion." Pietism was a second and milder Protestant Reformation that challenged not the pope, but the twin extremes of dogmatic orthodoxy and Deism that verged on unbelief. Individualist, tolerant, and indifferent to ceremonies, Pietism attracted followers among both Catholics and Protestants.

John Wesley (1703–91) was the leader of a somewhat parallel revival of a warm and personal Christian piety in England in the years following his conversion in 1738. When the Anglican clergy resisted his efforts, he took his message directly to the people. He addressed huge outdoor congregations and prayer meetings in remote chapels, taught his followers to sing their

Wolfgang Amadeus Mozart: the culmination of eighteenth-century music.

way to heaven with the hymns of his brother Charles, and deluged his congregations with streams of pamphlets from his printing presses. In the end, Anglican opposition forced Wesley to leave the established church and create a new denomination, Methodism, which took its name from the "methodical" piety of Wesley's followers that the orthodox had originally mocked. Methodism touched many thousands of Englishmen and women at home and in the colonies who found the dry intellectualism of much eighteenth-century Anglicanism repellent. Methodism's wide following, its emphasis on other-worldly concerns, and its conspicuous loyalty to existing political authority in this world made it a more effective buttress of the social order than Anglicanism.

Even philosophers saw reason's limits. David Hume, who along with Adam Smith was one of the greatest figures of the Scottish Enlightenment, started from a close study of the great French skeptic Bayle. Hume ended by denying the possibility of certainty. Only the experience of the senses, unverifiable by any independent means, kept the mind informed about external reality. And for Hume, sense-experience was a sequence of disjointed impressions, upon which the

John Wesley preaching.

mind—and the mind alone—imposed regularities, patterns, connections.

Hume's position, which has remained logically unassailable, cut at the root of the Enlightenment faith in the capacity of reason to discover laws in nature and human behavior. Hume did not doubt the validity of Newton's laws as a rule of thumb. What he denied was that anyone would ever be in a position to claim with certainty that Newton's laws applied to *all* times and in *all* places throughout the universe. Even observations that seemed to confirm those laws might not do so, for the evidence of the senses might be a snare. The sun *might* rise tomorrow; but then again it might not.

Hume was happy to concede that some kinds of knowledge were more certain than others. But he was the first philosopher to see the full depths of the predicament into which the collapse of the medieval religious certainties had plunged humanity. In the philosopher's study, if not in practical affairs, certainty was unattainable. That was "the whimsical condition of mankind." The observer's point of view helped determine what the observer saw. Knowledge, like the human value-systems that varied through historical time and geographic space, was relative.

Hume's skepticism did not yet shake an optimistic age that sought to replace God with Newton's clockwork universe. But a few farseeing figures nevertheless understood what he had done. The greatest philosopher of the century, Immanuel Kant (1724–1804), took up Hume's challenge, although Kant never traveled more than a few miles from his native city of Königsberg in East Prussia. In his *Critique of Pure Reason* (1781), the most demanding of all the great works of Western thought, Kant saved scientific reason, at least in his own judgment, by limiting its domain to appearances, to the data of sense-experience.

The mechanical world of physics, Kant argued, *was* knowable with certainty, although only knowable to an observer equipped with concepts built into the mind, such as space and time, What was not knowable with certainty, for Kant, were the *true* natures of the "things-in-themselves" that humans perceived through their senses. Nor could reason deal with the domain of metaphysics and religion, the realm of things that transcended experience. To many thinkers, Kant's refutation of Hume merely confirmed the Scot's skepticism. Others reacted by taking Kant, who himself argued for the necessity of belief in God as one foundation of morality, as a point of departure for a renewed leap into faith in religion.

In literature, the slowly gathering revolt against the Enlightenment took the form of a celebration of emotion that defied classical notions of rationality and balance. French and English novelists cultivated extremes of sentimentality. Heroines suffered heartrending misfortune and mistreatment, while the author sought at every turn to arouse the reader's anger, pity, love, or terror. The most influential example was Samuel Richardson's 2,000-page tear-jerker, *Clarissa* (1748), which influenced Rousseau's *Nouvelle Héloise* (1761). The bizarre, grotesque, and fantastic returned to fashion. In both architecture and literature, critics began to revive the Gothic style, despised since the Renaissance.

In Germany, which had never fallen totally under the sway of the French Enlightenment, a "Storm and Stress" (*Sturm und Drang*) movement in literature emphasized the great elemental emotions and denied the supremacy of reason. Johann Gottfried von Herder (1744–1803) conceived a philosophy of history that emphasized the uniqueness of each nation or race, the individuality of its genius, and the falsity of any view that denied that uniqueness in the name of universal reason. Johann Wolfgang von Goethe (1749–1832) published at the start of his long literary career *The Sorrows of Young Werther* (1774), a morbidly sentimental tale ending in suicide. The "Age of Reason" thus summoned up its opposite and successor—the age of Romanticism. The new age prized fierce emotion over harmony and equilibrium, and celebrated individual and national peculiarity over the Enlightenment's universal reason.

The Scientific Revolution and the Enlightenment were the most decisive break in the history of Western thought. The world picture of fifth-century Greece and of the Old and New Testaments, preserved through the Middle Ages and Renaissance, now gave way to a distinctively "modern" cast of mind. The world of Luther and Loyola, of Charles V and Philip II, was still organically related to the Middle Ages. The world of Newton and Locke, of Voltaire and Rousseau, was unmistakably our own.

Suggestions for Further Reading

The Scientific Revolution

M. Ashley, *The Golden Century* (1968), offers a fine survey of seventeenth-century social and cultural history. A. R. Hall, *The Scientific Revolution 1500–1800* (1966), is the best recent account. H. Butterfield, *The Origins of Modern Science 1300–1800* (1949), is highly readable, but C. Brinton, *The Shaping of the Modern Mind* (1953), covers a longer period. T. S. Kuhn, *The Copernican Revolution* (1957), describes the transformation of astronomical thought and offers an influential interpretation of how science advances. On the social background of scientific development, see D. Stimson, *Scientists and Amateurs: A History of the Royal Society* (1948). G. de Santillana, *The Crime of Galileo* (1955), elucidates the most famous case in the history of freedom of thought.

The Enlightenment

P. Hazard, *The European Mind: The Critical Years, 1680–1715* (1935, 1952), offers a still-useful study of the transition from Scientific Revolution to Enlightenment. The most searching interpretation of the Enlightenment as a whole is E. Cassirer, *The Philosophy of the Enlightenment* (1932, 1951). C. Becker, *The Heavenly City of the Eighteenth-Century Philosophers* (1932), attacks the *Philosophes* as doctrinaires, while P. Gay, *The Enlightenment: An Interpretation,* 2 vols. (1966–69), defends them. N. Hampson, *A Cultural History of the Enlightenment* (1969), is a useful introduction. C. R. Cragg, *Reason and Authority in the Eighteenth Century* (1964), and D. Mornet, *French Thought in the Eighteenth Century* (1929), deal with England and France respectively. R. S. Westfall, *Never at Rest: A Biography of Isaac Newton* (1981), discusses some of the leading intellectuals of the period, but see also T. Bestermann, *Voltaire* (1969), and J. N. Shklar, *Men and Citizens: A Study of Rousseau's Social Theory* (1969). L. Krieger, *Kings and Philosophers, 1689–1789* (1970), relates thought to politics. On specific topics, see M. F. Bukofzer, *Music in the Baroque Era* (1947); A. Boime, *A Social History of Modern Art,* vol. 1, *Art in an Age of Revolution, 1750–1800* (1987); B. Semmel, *The Methodist Revolution* (1973); G. R. Craig, *The Church in the Age of Reason* (1961); and E. Fox-Genovese, "Women and the Enlightenment," in R. Bridenthal et al., *Becoming Visible: Women in European History* (1987).

The Twilight of the Old Regime, 1715–1789

The 75 years between the death of Louis XIV in 1715 and the outbreak of the French Revolution in 1789 were a period of relative stability, without religious wars or great rebellions, except for a desperate serf uprising in distant Russia and the revolt of Britain's North American colonies in 1776. Monarchy remained the prevalent form of government, but divine-right monarchy evolved into "enlightened absolutism."

Yet monarchy, as in the seventeenth century, rested on a compromise with the aristocracy. Even the republican or constitutional governments of the eighteenth century were aristocratic in tone. Whig aristocrats and merchants dominated the English Parliament. After the death of Louis XIV, French nobles prevailed in the royal councils, and reestablished the powers of the *parlement* law courts. Junkers commanded the armies of Prussia. Polish nobles made the Polish Diet a farce. The "service nobility" of Russia gradually escaped from its duties to the state after the death of Peter the Great. And small oligarchies based on wealth ruled the Dutch Republic and the German "free cities" of the Holy Roman Empire.

Throughout Europe, the aristocracies of birth, office, and wealth reclaimed powers, rights, and privileges lost to the centralizing absolute monarchies of the seventeenth century. Only monarchs or chief ministers of unusual ability succeeded in bending the revival of aristocratic influence to the purposes of the state. The undeclared war between monarch and aristocrat normally led to an unspoken compromise, an uneasy balance between centralization and decentralization, between absolute monarchy and aristocratic privilege. That balance was perhaps lacking in clarity and logic. But all remembered how fanatical adherence to principle had given birth to the bloody religious and civil wars of the two preceding centuries. Those who had the luxury of choice were therefore usually glad to accept the structure of society and government as they found it after 1715.

Abject poverty, injustice, and brutality remained widespread, but to the elite, the brilliant "civilization"—a word that first appeared in the 1750s—of the Paris salons and the London coffeehouses appeared to outweigh the tribulations of the poor. To those who looked back on the devastation of the Thirty Years' War or the fanaticism of the "saints" of the English Revolution, social stability and political equilibrium were worth a high price in injustice. That eighteenth-century equilibrium later seemed a lost golden age to the generation of aristocrats that witnessed 1789. A French noble spoke for his caste when he remarked that those who had not lived before the Revolution lacked all conception of the sweetness of life.

THE STATE SYSTEM

Balance was likewise the rule in relations between states. The defeat of Louis XIV's bid for mastery had cost much blood and treasure. The great powers after 1715—France, Britain, Austria, Prussia, and Russia—agreed on few things. But all were determined to preserve the "balance of

Frederick the Great of Prussia inspects his troops (1778).

power," to ward off domination by a single state. That proved easier in the eighteenth century than either before or after. In the sixteenth and seventeenth centuries religious hatreds had devastated the Continent. In the age of revolution after 1789, national and ideological hatreds were again to tear it apart. But between 1715 and 1789 only issues of power divided the states of Europe, and those issues were often calculable and negotiable.

Preserving the balance meant ceaseless diplomatic haggling over "compensation"—the principle that if one state were fortunate or daring enough to acquire new territory, the other powers would receive compensating advantages to preserve the power balance. Compensation often meant that small states suffered mutilation or suppression at the hands of the great. But the practice of compensation helped preserve the balance and sometimes preserved the peace.

Wars remained frequent but were uniquely limited in both means and ends—although that happy situation was not always apparent to the relatively small numbers of professionals who fought, suffered, and died in them. Eighteenth-century war affected the civilian population far less than did war before 1715 and after 1789. Armies avoided pillaging, even on enemy territory. To allow the troops to forage gave them a chance to desert, and the devastation of territory that the victor might later annex was bad business. Conscription fell out of fashion except in Russia, where most troops were serfs, and to a limited extent in Prussia. The troops, in the words of a British commander of a slightly later period, tended to be "the scum of the earth, enlisted for drink," or foreign mercenaries. Only esprit de corps, constant drill that made obedience in battle automatic, and a discipline based on flogging and hanging welded these forces together. The aim, in the view of Prussia's greatest king, was to make the troops more terrified of their own officers than of the enemy.

Warfare itself consisted of elaborate maneuver. Commanders normally avoided pitched battles, for trained troops were a precious investment. The 43,000 casualties of Malplaquet (1709) had shown all too well the vast slaughter that ensued when armies equipped with muskets blasted one another at ranges of fifty paces or less. Armies also moved slowly, for the knee-deep mud of Europe's roads did not allow swift movement of the artillery or of the thousands of wagons needed to transport food. In winter, war usually ceased. Campaigns generally centered on a single province or fortified strongpoint and ended indecisively. The dominant system of naval tactics had similar results. Fleets sailing in rigid battle lines blasted at one another from a distance. Engagements were rarely decisive, for commanders feared losing control of their fleets and avoided the bloody, confused close-range ship-to-ship duels that alone ensured annihilation of the enemy.

Limited objectives corresponded to these limitations in methods. The enemy of today might be the ally of tomorrow. Defeating any power too thoroughly might disturb the power balance and summon up unforeseeable complications. In these "cabinet wars"—decided in and directed from the royal cabinet or secretariat—statesmen and generals normally sought concrete political and economic objectives, not unconditional surrender or total destruction. Once a power attained its objectives or became convinced that they were unattainable, it concluded a truce or a peace. In spite of relentless competition—over prestige, land, population, colonies, and trade—the monarchs, bureaucrats, and aristocrats of the eighteenth century felt themselves part of a common civilization. The secret of the eighteenth-century equilibrium was the absence of the twin forces that drive inter-state conflicts to extremes—religious or ideological strife, and bids for universal domination by a single power.

Eighteenth-century statesmen were not unaware of the similarities between their system and Newton's picture of the universe—a stable order of perfectly balanced gravitational attraction and centrifugal repulsion in which every mass moved along predictable lines of force. Ministers took pride in their mastery of "political algebra," the exact calculation of the

The French nobility lampooned: *The Baron* (1785).

forces acting on state policy. Soldiers created elaborate geometrical systems to describe the century's art of war. Only after mid-century did French theorists, such as Pierre de Bourcet and François de Guibert, begin to create a new strategy, operations, and tactics of movement, flexibility, surprise, and annihilation—the methods of the new revolutionary armies after 1792.

The eighteenth-century equilibrium remained precarious, a balance between dynamic forces. Powers still rose and fell, sometimes with alarming swiftness and decisiveness, as in the case of Poland. Wealth and trade increased steadily, for revolutions in both agriculture and industry were slowly beginning. Europe's economy and diplomacy were becoming global rather than continental; the struggle for empire reached toward the farthest corners of the earth. For the first time, battles fought in America, Africa, and Asia affected the balance of power in Europe. And in trying to maintain its position, each state accentuated its own particular strengths. Britain relied increasingly on naval power and commerce. Prussia depended on its army and bureaucracy. Russia further intensified its reliance on serfdom. Austria compensated for weakness in Germany by increasing its power in southeastern Europe. France, the one power that refused to specialize, condemned itself to naval weakness, while its intellectual and cultural leadership masked but did not remedy its failure to overtake its British rival in commerce and industry. Inept generalship and financial weakness even prevented France from profiting from its greatest strength before 1715 and after 1789—its land power.

Intellectual and political change intersected with the inter-state, social, and economic rivalries that culminated in the great upheavals after 1789. The years between 1715 and 1789, the twilight of the "old regime," fall conveniently into three periods of roughly a quarter-century each: (1) a generation of peace and relative prosperity from 1715 to 1740; (2) a period of worldwide warfare from 1740 to 1763; and (3) an interval of enlightened absolutism, aristocratic resurgence, and domestic unrest from 1763 to 1789.

PEACE AND PROSPERITY, 1715–40

Governments and peoples were thoroughly weary of war by the time the treaties of 1713–14 and 1719–21 restored peace to both western and eastern Europe. The age that followed was unheroic and happily corrupt, as postwar periods often are. But peace allowed the restoration of order and of law, and stimulated an enormous expansion of trade, particularly in western Europe.

Commerce and Industry

Seaborne commerce was the most conspicuous source of Europe's wealth during the eighteenth century. Thanks to the enterprise of their merchants and the technical skill of their mariners, the volume of foreign trade in Britain and France multiplied itself by five during the century. In the British case, colonial trade led the increase. Britain therefore needed and acquired a larger merchant marine than its rivals and the strongest navy in the world. For France, trade with other European states was the greatest source of increase. In both cases the accumulation of wealth in the hands of the upper classes was spectacular. For the first time, the total wealth of Europe began to eclipse that of Asia. The two preceding centuries of exploration, conquest, and establishment of overseas trading networks now paid off handsomely. Sugar from the West Indies, wine from Portugal, and tobacco from Virginia might grace the tables of Liverpool merchants. Their wives might wear printed calico from India in summer and furs from Canada in winter. Their daughters might marry the heirs of aristocrats whose large and elegant Georgian houses were the visible evidence of the combined profits of land and mercantile investment.

The labor of slaves or serfs produced many of the commodities on which Europe's thriving trade rested. The plantations of the West Indies serviced Europe's ever-increasing craving for sugar. That demand in turn created an almost insatiable demand for African slaves. Liverpool and

Europe in 1715

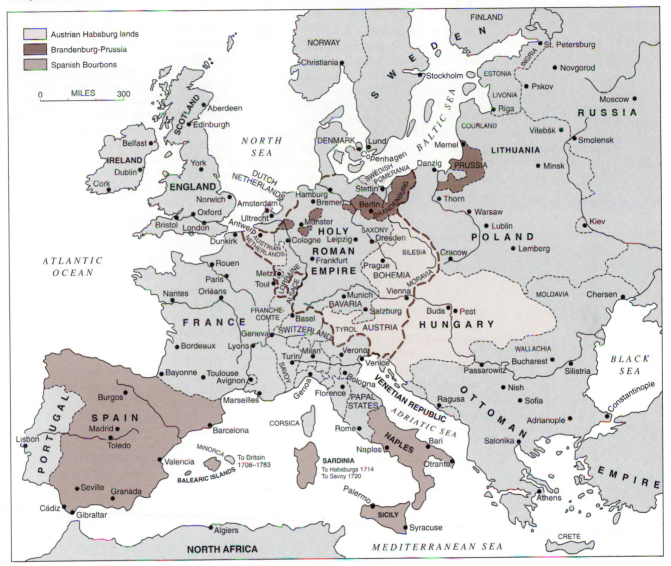

London slave traders met much of that demand. The serfs who toiled without recompense for their landlords in the grain-producing regions of eastern Europe played an economic role similar to that of the slaves of the West Indies. Some of the European economy still rested, as had the economy of the ancient world, on servile labor.

Despite the immense increase in overseas trade, the vast bulk of European commerce was within the European states themselves. And in all states except the Dutch Netherlands and perhaps Britain, most of the national product still came from agriculture. Even Britain's vast foreign trade in the last third of the century only amounted to perhaps 10 percent of the growing British economy. And it was in Britain that the coming of revolutionary changes in industry became visible after mid-century (see pp. 619–22).

Boom and Bust: The Mississippi and South Sea Bubbles

European commercial capitalism, which had created the first joint-stock companies, stock exchanges, and state banks, continued to expand. The coming of peace in 1713–14 encouraged both financial speculation and wildcat commercial ventures. Those ventures in turn led in 1719 and 1720 to the first large-scale example of a typically modern phenomenon, a stock crash—or, as contemporaries described it, a "bubble."

The wars of Louis XIV burdened both French and British governments with debt. In the French case only bankruptcy appeared to promise relief. That plight offered opportunities to plausible figures such as the Scottish promoter John Law, who appeared at the French court after the death of Louis XIV and offered to solve the monarchy's financial woes. After his commercial bank in Paris began to prosper, he received in 1717–20 control of French taxes, the right to issue paper money, a virtual monopoly on foreign trade, and the office of Controller General of Finances. His Mississippi Company, chartered to trade with France's colony in Louisiana, soon mutated into a "Company of the Indies" and assumed France's state debt, which it paid off by promoting a boom in its own stock. Law's "system"—his reforms of government finances, his paper money, and his expansion of the credit available to merchants—stimulated the French economy. But when the price of his company's stock reached 36 times its original value, investors began to cash in their paper profits. The market collapsed, and Law fled.

A parallel episode occurred in London. Promoters organized a South Sea Company to exploit the trade with the Spanish colonies provided for in the Peace of Utrecht. It likewise took over much of the government's debt, and it too deliberately promoted a boom in its own stock. In 1720, a few months after Law's failure had shown the precariousness of stock booms, the South Sea "bubble" burst.

These twin financial catastrophes slowed the development of joint-stock companies and ruined many individual investors. But despite their speculative excesses, the bold experimenters in London and Paris had shown new ways to mobilize capital for commerce and industry and to support the public debt from as yet untapped sources. After reorganization, both companies made money for their investors for many years. However, the French government, by partially repudiating its debt in the wake of the crash, lost the confidence of investors. The French acquired a fierce distrust of credit, an attitude that constricted their economic growth. London did not make that mistake. The British government never again permitted private interests to assume responsibility for the state debt. Britain thus assured itself the credit that meant the difference between victory and defeat in a world of warring states.

The England of Walpole

The generation of peace abroad after the death of Louis XIV allowed England to consolidate peace at home. Under the Act of Settlement of 1701, the Elector of Hanover succeeded Queen Anne as ruler of England in 1714. The first two Hanoverian monarchs, George I (r. 1714–27) and George II (r. 1727–60), were dull-witted and spoke little English. Their only claim to distinction was their patronage of the great composer Handel, whom they induced to settle permanently in England. In politics, their chief contribution was petty interference in minor details of government; the "inner cabinet" of ministers therefore became increasingly responsible for framing policy. Although the king in theory remained free to choose his own ministers, Parliament's control over finances meant that he had to select men who could influence elections and command a majority. By custom, ministers usually accepted the leadership of the ablest or most powerful minister, who presented their policy to the king. Those who disagreed with the group's majority lost their offices. These informal practices foreshadowed the nineteenth-century "prime minister" and "cabinet system" that

1660	1689	1714		1917	
Restored House of Stuart		Wm. & Mary, Anne	House of Hanover		(House of Windsor)

later became almost universal in the representative democracies of western Europe and of the English-speaking world.

Robert Walpole, a country squire with family connections to both the landed gentry and commercial interests, was the first prime minister, although he did not accept that title. For some twenty years, from 1721 to 1742, he managed the Whig party in Parliament and led the government. The first two Hanoverians necessarily chose their ministers from the Whigs who dominated the House of Commons, for affection for the Stuarts tainted the Tories after the abortive Scottish Jacobite rising in 1715.

Walpole was a consummate manipulator who held his parliamentary majority together by tact, persuasion, patronage, and bribery. He kept George I's favor by passing generous budgets for the king's household through Parliament, and by an occasional donation to the royal mistress. His enjoyment of drink and off-color stories—as well as his steely ambition—helped him to manage the Whig merchants and landed gentry who controlled Parliament and ran local government as justices of the peace. But his principal appeal was that he offered to England a political stability unknown since Elizabeth I.

"Let sleeping dogs lie" was Walpole's motto. He sought to defuse religious conflict. He maintained the Test Act to reassure the Anglicans but conciliated dissenters by annual parliamentary votes that in effect suspended the Test Act temporarily and allowed dissenters to hold public office. His policy of "salutary neglect" left the colonies to grow in population and wealth by their own efforts. Above all, he did his best to avoid war; he maintained until the 1730s the alliance with France that his predecessors had concluded in 1716–17 to safeguard Hanoverian possessions in Germany.

Under Walpole's ministry, Britain and its colonies prospered; the credit of the government remained high; the ruling aristocracy of landed and commercial wealth governed in its own interests, but far less repressively than did other European ruling classes. Voltaire, after his visit to England between 1726 and 1729, somewhat idealized English society and government. He neglected to mention to his French readers the ferocity of eighteenth-century English law toward crimes against property. In theory it imposed death by hanging for over 200 offenses, including on occasion the theft of items worth as little as five shillings. In practice, "transportation" to the colonies usually took the place of hanging, and English laws guaranteed equality and individual freedom to an extent unknown on the Continent except perhaps in the Dutch Netherlands and Switzerland.

But Walpole's golden age of the gentry did not last. In 1739 the London merchants and their spokesmen in Parliament forced him into a commercial war with Spain. Within three years his majority collapsed, and he left office.

France: Louis XV and Cardinal Fleury

The peace that brought strength to Britain brought weakness to France. Louis XIV's great-grandson, Louis XV (r. 1715–74), became king at the age of five. The Duke of Orléans, the nephew of Louis XIV who governed as regent during the new king's minority, secured his own power by concessions to the powerful elements in French society that the Sun King had kept leashed. Nobles reappeared as royal ministers. The *Parlement* of Paris boldly reasserted its ancient claim to register and enforce royal legislation—or not—as it saw fit. The French monarchy in theory

". . . to be hanged by the neck until dead": eighteenth-century English law, applied here to a debtor convicted of defrauding his creditors.

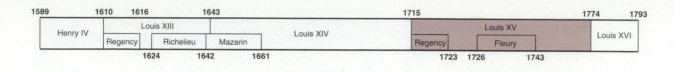

remained as absolute as ever, but after Louis XIV it lacked the ruthless will needed to translate theory into practice. The resulting reinforcement of the privileges of the aristocracy infuriated the middle classes and in the long run condemned the royal government to financial ruin.

Cardinal Fleury, the leading minister from 1726 to 1743, halted the decline for a time. But Fleury was no Richelieu. He came to power at the age of 73, and his policy, much like Walpole's, sought to avoid expensive wars and to conciliate rather than confront powerful domestic interests. Fleury dissociated himself from the courageous attempt of another minister to tax the nobility. He nevertheless stabilized the currency, encouraged trade, and had considerable success in damping down the continuing struggle between Jansenists and Jesuits. In foreign policy his overriding goal was to prevent the renewal of the coalitions against France that had blocked Louis XIV. Fleury therefore sought to cooperate with Walpole in making the Anglo-French alliance work.

When Fleury died in 1743 at the age of ninety, Louis XV took Louis XIV as his model. Henceforth he sought to govern personally, without a first minister. But although Louis XV had inherited many of his great-grandfather's tastes—women and the hunt above all—he lacked the Sun King's relentless capacity for sustained work. The court frivolity with which Louis XIV had sought to corrupt the aristocracy had also corrupted his own successor. Given the centralized administrative machine that the Sun King had left behind, the sloth of Louis XV meant a fatal lack of coordination of the various branches of the bureaucracy and frequent paralysis. Louis XV did not govern in person, and from 1743 until his death in 1774 he largely prevented others from governing for him.

The aristocracy and the royal mistresses, of whom the Marquise de Pompa-

dour (1745–51) and the Countess du Barry (1768–74) were the most notable, inevitably filled the resulting power vacuum. Louis XV was not unaware of the declining health of the state: "After me, the deluge" was his most famous—and justly remembered—remark. But France, thanks to its size, its population, and a growth rate in trade and industry as rapid as Britain's, remained potentially the most powerful nation in Europe.

Declining or Stagnant Powers

Elsewhere in Europe, with few exceptions, monarchical institutions likewise declined. In Spain a remarkable woman ruled: Elizabeth Farnese, the strong-willed Italian queen of Philip V of Bourbon (r. 1700–46), whom Louis XIV had put on the throne. With the help of her husband's chief ministers, Elizabeth Farnese beat back the claims of the nobility, encouraged trade and industry, and reestablished Spain's diplomatic status as a great power. But Spanish society and government failed to respond. Centralization that robbed subjects of all initiative, a taxation more crushing than anything west of Russia, absurd guild regulations, a pitilessly intolerant Church that was the single largest social institution, a sluggish nobility that amounted to 5 percent of the population, and a culturally rooted distaste for commerce and industry proved impossible to overcome. Spain's economy, colonies, army, and navy stagnated, while other powers pressed onward.

Austria remained an imperfectly united empire that linked the three kingdoms of Austria, Bohemia, and Hungary with two dependencies of entirely different cultures and traditions, northern Italy and the southern Netherlands. And the dynastic ties that bound together this bizarre assortment of territories were themselves open to challenge. The Habsburg Emperor Charles VI (r. 1711–40) had no son. He therefore spent almost thirty years persuading both his provinces and the powers to accept a "Pragmatic Sanction" that established his daughter Maria Theresa as heir to his scattered lands. By his death in 1740 he had secured the agreement on paper of all concerned. But in the absence of a strong Habsburg army and central bureaucracy, treaties were a fragile defense against the greed of neighboring monarchs and the restlessness of the Hungarian nobility.

Farther to the east, the Polish and Ottoman empires continued their decline. France and Spain fought a halfhearted and trivial war against Austria and Russia over the succession to the Polish crown between 1733 and 1738. The Russian candidate won. The losers received "compensation" in the form of scraps of territory elsewhere; Spain received Naples and Sicily from Austria. Simultaneously, Austria and Russia fought the Ottoman Turks, whose decline accelerated as Europe's technological lead continued to grow.

Russia after Peter I failed to make its full weight felt for a generation. His succession law, enacted after his mortal quarrel with his son Alexei, gave the autocrat power to choose his own successor. That in effect made Russia until after 1800 an elective monarchy—and the Guards regiments and court nobles did the electing, with bayonets. Between 1725 and 1741, palace coups gave the crown successively to women or children who reigned but did not rule. From 1741 to 1762 Elizabeth, a daughter of Peter I, ruled firmly after seizing power with the help of the Guards and eliminating her opponents in the customary fashion—by torture, execution, deportation, and confiscation of land.

German and particularly Prussian influence predominated at the Russian court. As in France, the nobility freed itself from many of the restrictions that a great monarch had placed upon it. The Russian nobility extended the power over the serfs that Peter I had given it, while gradually escaping its corresponding obligation to serve the state. In Russia, as in Hungary and Prussia during the eighteenth century, the peasants thus sank ever deeper into serfdom, while the government made re-

Habsburg domestic life, painted by Meytens: Empress Maria Theresa of Austria with her husband, Emperor Francis I, and their eleven children. The future emperor Joseph II stands at right center.

peated concessions to the nobility. Until the accession of Elizabeth, and especially of Catherine the Great in 1762, Russia lacked strong rulers. But the feebleness of Peter I's immediate successors showed the full extent of his greatness. Despite weakness at the center, Russia retained the great-power status that Peter had won for it.

Prussia: Sergeant King, Undisciplined Son

Prussia, as usual, was an exception to a general trend, for its monarchy became more rather than less absolute. King Frederick William I of Brandenburg-Prussia (r. 1713–40) was the most successful ruler of his generation. This strange, uncouth, and furious man, who smoked tobacco and drank beer in gargantuan quantities, was the second of the three great Hohenzollerns who made the poor and backward territories of Brandenburg-Prussia into a great power.

Frederick William followed in the footstep of the Great Elector, centralizing

Father and son: Frederick William I in a characteristic pose *(above)*, and the young Frederick II *(below)*.

as a pathetic figure, unmilitary in habits and possessed of decadent tastes such as reading Voltaire and playing the flute. The irate father burned books, smashed flutes, and had Frederick beaten. When the prince attempted to flee the country with a friend in 1730, the king had the friend beheaded before Frederick's eyes, threatened Frederick himself with death for "desertion," and set him to work in the provincial bureaucracy. The experience rendered Frederick cold, dissimulating, and supremely cynical. But he also acquired a passion for administration and war, and a burning ambition to acquire glory and "establish his sovereignty like a rock of bronze." His opportunity came in 1740, the year in which both his hated father and Charles VI of Habsburg died.

THE WORLD WARS OF MID-CENTURY, 1740–63

Two great wars, the War of the Austrian Succession (1740–48) and the Seven Years' War (1756–63) punctuated the middle of the century. The wars were linked, and derived from two irreconcilable rivalries—Hohenzollern against Habsburg in central Europe, and Britain against France in North America, the West Indies, Africa, and India. Twice these separate conflicts became entangled, although the powers exchanged partners between the two wars. In the end, Britain and Prussia defeated France and Austria.

The War of the Austrian Succession, 1740–48

In 1740 Maria Theresa (r. 1740–80), a beautiful, strong-willed, courageous, but inexperienced woman of 23, succeeded her father Charles VI in the Habsburg dominions, as provided for in the Pragmatic Sanction. That gave Frederick II of Prussia his opportunity. Although he had published an anonymous pamphlet against the supposed immorality of Machiavelli's political precepts, he had learned the great Florentine's lessons well. In December 1740 he seized Silesia, Austria's rich prov-

his administration, paring civil expenditures to the bone, and working his subordinates remorselessly. The purpose of this drill-sergeant king was to build the most formidable army in Europe. He echoed Richelieu in demanding absolute obedience to the state: "Salvation is from the Lord, but everything else is my business." After 1733, he militarized the peasantry by imposing a form of conscription, the "Canton System." Peasants in the ranks served Junker officers who were the brothers or cousins of their Junker landlords in civilian life. Frederick William doubled Prussia's peacetime standing army to 80,000, nearly equal to Austria's theoretical total of 100,000 men. But he was careful not to use his blue-coated and precisely drilled army, for he loved his "blue boys" too much to expend them in war.

His son Frederick II (r. 1740–86)—the third great Hohenzollern—thus inherited a treasury surplus, a ruthlessly efficient civil bureaucracy, and an army that was the fourth largest force on the continent and the most relentlessly trained. Frederick had initially impressed his father

ince to the northeast of Bohemia. Possession of Silesia, with its million inhabitants, its linen industry, and its iron ore, would finally make Brandenburg-Prussia a great power.

Frederick's thrust caught Maria Theresa off guard, and the success of his shameless aggression encouraged Bavaria, Spain, and finally France to join in the attack, in violation of their Pragmatic Sanction pledges. But Hungary, which resented Habsburg rule, ironically proved Maria Theresa's salvation. When she traveled to Budapest with her infant son and made an emotional appeal to the Hungarian Parliament, her bravery and tact inspired the Hungarian nobility to rise tumultuously to her support. An able minister, Count Haugwitz, centralized the Habsburg administration and reorganized the army during the wars that followed. Austria had been a helpless victim in 1740; now it became a formidable enemy. But Frederick's armies fought brilliantly, and at Hohenfriedberg in 1745 he achieved the first great Prussian victory due above all to his own generalship. The combined pressure of France, Bavaria, and Prussia— shaky though their alliance was—proved too much for Maria Theresa. In 1748, at Aix-la-Chapelle, she consented to a peace treaty that left Silesia in Frederick's hands.

The Anglo-French overseas rivalry intersected with the war on the Continent. Britain went to war with Spain in 1739 over Spanish maltreatment of English merchants smuggling goods to the Spanish empire. That "war of Jenkins' Ear" (named after an unfortunate English trader), and French intervention in Germany in support of a Bavarian claimant to the office of Holy Roman Emperor, made conflict between France and Britain almost inevitable. France and Spain, thanks to their Bourbon family ties, normally cooperated closely after 1700, and France had developed a large economic stake in the Spanish colonies, which it supplied with manufactured goods.

British and French interests also clashed in North America and India. The French military hold on Canada and Louisiana appeared to threaten the British colonies that stretched from Boston to Savannah. The fantastic rates of population growth of the British colonies on the eastern seaboard prompted a northward and westward expansion that seemed in turn to threaten the French. In the West Indies the British and French glowered at each other from their sugar-island strongholds. In India, where the Mughal empire had fallen into near-anarchy after the death in 1707 of the merciless Aurangzeb, its last strong ruler, the French and British East India companies sought to fill a power vacuum. From their respective bases at Pondicherry and Madras, each mobilized native rulers against the other. From Canada to the Carnatic Coast of India, France and Britain prepared for war, and British and French troops clashed in Germany as early as 1743.

In 1744 France declared war on Great Britain and merged the continental and overseas wars. In 1745 a force of American colonial militia with British naval support boldly seized the key to Canada, the great fortress of Louisbourg on Cape Breton Island in the St. Lawrence estuary. In 1746 the French seized Madras. But the overseas conflict was indecisive, because Britain failed to set clear objectives and establish priorities. In Parliament the "Patriot" partisans of overseas war denounced the British continental commitment as "Hanoverianism," a pandering to the interests of George II, who led a British army in Germany to defend his possessions as Elector of Hanover against France. The French defeated the British in a hard-fought battle at Fontenoy in the Austrian Netherlands in 1745, and in 1747 the British navy twice annihilated French fleets escorting West Indies convoys. George II's son, "Butcher" Cumberland, savaged the Highland clans after his victory over the last pro-Stuart rising, which had broken out with French encouragement in 1745.

Neither side pressed its successes far, except in Scotland. The War of the Austrian Succession was a typical "limited" war. The Anglo-French duel ended in stalemate. The French surrendered Madras, and the British government, much to the disgust of the American colonists, gave back Louisbourg. The French emerged from the war with increased prestige, an enlarged debt, and no concrete gains over either Britain or Austria. The British emerged with a clear sense of how to fight their next war with France.

The Overseas "War before the War," 1749–55

The peace of Aix-la-Chapelle did not end the overseas conflict between Britain and France. Joseph Dupleix, France's greatest colonial adventurer, sought after 1748 to make the French East India Company a political as well as a commercial power in India. By recruiting allies among the warring native states that contended within the hollow shell of the Mughal empire, he hoped to increase his company's revenue and ultimately drive the British from India. The English East India Company reinforced its outposts. Clashes ensued in which the British largely prevailed, thanks to their command of the sea and the brilliant leadership of the legendary Robert Clive. In 1754 the company directors, fearing that Dupleix had overreached himself, recalled him to France. The ensuing truce merely postponed the struggle for mastery in south Asia that Dupleix had begun.

In America, open warfare did not break out until 1752. The French in Canada used the interval of peace to build a chain of forts from the St. Lawrence down the Ohio to the Mississippi to block the westward thrust of Britain's American colonists. London countered, reinforcing the colonies with ships and troops. Britain held the advantage; 1.2 million British subjects, including slaves, faced about 60,000 French. The French sought to even the odds by an alliance with Indian tribes whose interest in preventing British westward penetration paralleled that of France. French raids in turn provoked in 1754 an unsuccessful attempt, under the leadership of Lieutenant Colonel George Washington of the Virginia militia, to capture the vital French base at Fort Duquesne, on the site of modern Pittsburgh. In 1755, near the same spot, General George Braddock and a force of British regulars discovered that rigid European tactics were poorly suited to war in the woods. The

French and Indian War, the final round of the Anglo-French struggle for North America, had begun.

The Climax of Old-Regime Statecraft: The "Diplomatic Revolution" of 1756

Overseas struggle was merely one prelude to a second round of war in Europe. The other prelude was a "diplomatic revolution" by which the chief enemies of the first general war of mid-century changed partners in preparation for the second. Britain had fought the War of the Austrian Succession in loose agreement with Austria, its traditional ally from the wars of 1689–97 and 1701–13. But London saw no British interest in fighting simply to restore Silesia to Maria Theresa. Bourbon France had fought against its traditional Habsburg enemy in a still looser alliance with Prussia; Frederick distrusted Paris and twice deserted it to make truces with Austria. By 1748, all four major powers were unhappy with their traditional allies.

The chief instigator of the ensuing revolution was Maria Theresa's chancellor, the wily Prince Wenzel Anton von Kaunitz. He began from the premise that the reconquest of Silesia—and the smashing of Prussia—was the prerequisite for Austria's resurgence as a great power. That aim prompted Kaunitz to think the unthinkable. He sought to replace the ancient antagonism between Bourbon and Habsburg with a Franco-Austrian alliance, possibly with Russian support, against Prussia. Even the battlefield genius of Frederick II, Kaunitz was confident, would be helpless against the three strongest land powers in Europe.

Kaunitz sought with success to win over the Marquise de Pompadour, the current mistress of Louis XV. But the king remained reluctant—until Britain and Prussia unintentionally convinced him. London had long feared that its Austrian ally lacked the will and ability to help Britain defend Hanover against France, and the outbreak of Anglo-French hostilities overseas increased British anxieties. In 1755 London therefore sought Russian help in the usual British way—subsidies

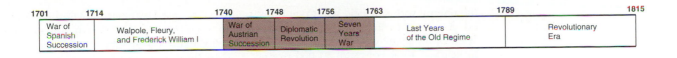

1701	1714		1740	1748	1756	1763		1789		1815
War of Spanish Succession	Walpole, Fleury, and Frederick William I		War of Austrian Succession	Diplomatic Revolution	Seven Years' War		Last Years of the Old Regime		Revolutionary Era	

that exchanged British gold for allied troops. That treaty alarmed Frederick II, for it raised the specter of a large Russian army encamped on his eastern border. He therefore approached London, and outbid Russia. By the treaty of Westminster of January 1756, Prussia itself agreed to defend Hanover, naturally in exchange for its own British subsidy.

The spectacle of Prussia, France's ally, contracting a quasi-alliance with Britain, a power already in conflict with France from the Ohio to the Carnatic, finally aroused the wrath of Louis XV. Bourbon France made a defensive alliance with Habsburg Austria. Kaunitz also enlisted Russia, and planned war for 1757. Frederick II judged that his only chance was to strike first. The Austrians had hoped for such a blow to weld Kaunitz's grand coalition together. Unfortunately for Kaunitz, Frederick II struck in August 1756, a year earlier than Vienna had anticipated. Unfortunately for Frederick, his aggression indeed did Kaunitz's work. It brought into play Austria's French alliance and created a grand coalition that almost destroyed Prussia.

The Seven Years' War, 1756–63

In the new war, the greatest worldwide conflict of the old regime, Britain thus fought for empire and Prussia for its life. After a feeble beginning, William Pitt became virtual prime minister of Britain. Pitt possessed a Roman nose, a talent for oratory, and a clear sense of Britain's global objectives. Convinced of his own indispensability ("I am sure I can save this country, and nobody else can") he pushed his way into the cabinet in spite of the disfavor of George II. From 1757 to 1760, he tirelessly directed Britain's war and drove his subordinates to their limits. In 1757, at Plassey near Calcutta, Robert Clive destroyed France's principal client, the Nawab of Bengal, and seized his rich province for Britain. That broke French power in India. Britain conquered France's chief slaving station at Gorée in Senegal and cut France's West Indian sugar islands off from their supplies of slaves and manufactured goods.

In 1759, the "year of miracles," Pitt conquered for Britain the domination of the outer seas that it held with only brief interruptions until 1941. A brilliant young general, James Wolfe, led an amphibious expedition up the St. Lawrence River. Outside the walls of Québec city he defeated France at the cost of his own life. That ended the French empire in North America. British fleets captured the rich West Indies sugar island of Guadeloupe and drove the French fleet onto the lee shore of Quiberon Bay in western France. Command of the sea was the key to Britain's triumphs.

On the Continent, Prussia survived only thanks to Frederick II and to his long-suffering troops, whom he drove toward

Britain's command of the sea in action: Wolfe takes Québec, 1759.

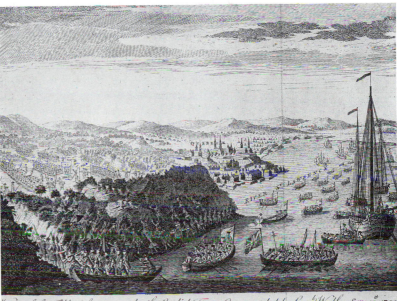

View of the Taking of QUEBECK by the English Forces Commanded by Gen.ˡ Wolfe Sep: 13. 1759.

the enemy with sarcastic wit: "You dogs, do you want to live for ever?" Prussia's "year of miracles" was 1757. At Rossbach in Saxony, Frederick with 21,000 troops decisively defeated a French army of 64,000 by attacking them in the flank. Having thus checked one of his three enemies, he hastened back to defend Silesia from Austrian invasion. A bare month after Rossbach, he smashed an Austrian army of 80,000 at Leuthen with a mere 36,000 Prussians.

But these great victories produced no decisive strategic result. Frederick was the supreme artist of eighteenth-century warfare, but his military instrument did not permit battles of annihilation. Pursuit, necessary to prevent a beaten enemy from re-forming to fight again, was impossible with troops that deserted once they were out of their officers' sight. And Prussia's desperate position, exposed to the French from the west, the Austrians from the south, and the Russians from the east, prevented the great king from finishing off any one of his adversaries. The war dragged on. Russia made its weight felt, and in 1759 an Austro-Russian army heavily defeated Frederick at Kunersdorf in Silesia.

Frederick thought despairingly of abdication. But dissension among his enemies saved him and Prussia. Kaunitz had not promised enough of the prospective spoils to France and Russia to inspire their all-out effort. Austria understandably feared that Russian troops, once invited into central Europe, would not leave. France's naval and overseas campaigns had exhausted its treasury, and the disgrace of Rossbach had shattered the monarchy's already low reputation at home. Pitt's lavish subsidies to the armies of German princelings, along with token British forces, pinned the French down in bloody fighting in western Germany.

In 1760 Frederick temporarily lost Berlin and by the end of 1761 he appeared close to total defeat, as 300,000 allied troops penned him into a fortified camp in Silesia. His British ally abandoned him. George III (r. 1760–1820), who had succeeded his grandfather, wished to prove himself thoroughly English, unlike the first

two Georges. He therefore withdrew from all involvement in German affairs and drove Pitt to resignation in October 1761. Lord Bute, George III's Scottish favorite, became chief minister and sought peace with France at almost any price, including the sacrifice of Prussia.

Then, on January 5, 1762, Elizabeth of Russia died. Her successor was the weak and eccentric Tsar Peter III, a German by birth and a fond admirer of Frederick the Great. He immediately withdrew Russia from the coalition. Only a crippled and sulking France now supported Vienna, and Maria Theresa and Kaunitz grudgingly abandoned their hopes of crushing the Prussian upstart. The long war was over.

Victory and Defeat: The Treaties of Hubertusburg and Paris, 1763

Two victors thus emerged from the treaties by which Prussia and Austria and Britain and France made peace in January–February 1763. At Hubertusburg, Austria conceded to Prussia the possession of Silesia and hard-won status as one of the five great powers of Europe. The Treaty of Paris almost eliminated France as Britain's overseas rival, although Britain did give back most of the economic outposts France had lost: trading stations in India, its slave-trade base at Gorée in west Africa, rich sugar islands in the West Indies, and two tiny islands off Newfoundland, St. Pierre and Miquelon.

But in the long run only the continents counted. Trading posts could flourish only if they controlled a large hinterland. Sugar islands produced great wealth in a few square miles but were incapable of defending themselves against a power, such as Britain, that controlled the sea. Failure at sea and the collapse of French land power in India and North America broke the first French colonial empire for good. France withdrew its troops from India and ceded to Britain all of Canada and of Louisiana east of the Mississippi, and Louisiana west of the Mississippi passed to Spain. Henceforth, the British had no serious rivals in North America except the colonists they had planted there.

ENLIGHTENED ABSOLUTISM, 1763–89

In the quarter century that followed the end of the Seven Years' War, the ancient institution of monarchy seemed briefly to take on new life. The major ideas of the Enlightenment—reason, natural law, happiness, progress, liberty—filtered through to the rulers. Some monarchs accepted the criticisms that *philosophes* had leveled at aristocratic and Church privileges, unequal taxation, and the degraded condition of the peasantry and the urban lower classes. In addition, the great wars of mid-century had strained the social fabric of most European states. The resurgence of the aristocracy forced monarchs to look to the middle classes for support. Only reforms could restore order, revive trade, refill the treasuries of Europe's monarchs, and check the pretensions of the nobility. The fusion of new ideas and practical needs produced the phenomenon that contemporaries described as "enlightened absolutism."

The concept of the enlightened absolutist inevitably fitted only a few rulers of the later eighteenth century. George III of England made no pretense to enlightenment, nor would his subjects have applauded if he had. English loyalty to the post-1688 status quo ran deep. In his last years, Louis XV of France showed unexpected resolution and zeal, but during most of his reign he was enlightened in few senses of the word. A few minor monarchs such as Gustavus III of Sweden (r. 1771–92) and Charles III of Spain (r. 1759–88) had some claims to the title. But the three rulers whom *philosophes* cited most often as enlightened absolutists were Catherine the Great of Russia, Frederick the Great of Prussia, and Joseph II of Austria.

The attack of the enlightened absolutists on irrational customs and vested interests, on aristocratic and Church power, and on town and provincial privileges was not new. It was in most respects a continuation of the centralizing drive of the seventeenth-century monarchies. What had changed was the climate of opinion in which monarchs acted. The ideas of the Enlightenment, the practical example of Britain, and the victorious struggle for self-government of the British colonies in North America after 1776 stripped of its persuasiveness the doctrine of the divine right of kings. Monarchs therefore had to appeal to their increasingly literate subjects with talk of following reason and of serving the public good. Frederick the Great described himself as "merely the first servant of the state." That monarchy now had to justify its existence was a sign of fatal weakness.

Russia: Catherine the Great

Catherine II (r. 1762–96), the most remarkable woman ruler of the century, was no Russian. Princess of the German line of Anhalt-Zerbst, she married the eccentric crown prince Peter in 1745. A woman of high intelligence, masterful cunning, implacable will, and a warm heart, she maintained a succession of lovers with lavish gifts of lands and serfs; as the poet Pushkin later remarked, "many were called, and many chosen." In her youth, Catherine survived the snake-pit of the St. Petersburg court by pretending to be frivolous, while

Catherine the Great looking the part.

finding allies and a lover among the officers of the crucial Guards regiments. Her husband Peter, after his coming to the throne as Peter III in 1762, alienated those same regiments by proposing to reform them along Prussian lines. He also appalled the pious by confiscating church lands. Within six months, Catherine seized power with the help of the Guards. Peter died under arrest, apparently at the hands of a relative of Grigori Orlov, Catherine's lover.

Catherine came to power with a genuine desire to improve the welfare of her subjects. She read the works of *philosophes* such as Montesquieu and advanced thinkers such as Beccaria. She corresponded with Voltaire, persuaded Diderot to visit her court, and proclaimed publicly her adherence to the Enlightenment. But as autocrat she could not afford too much enlightenment. Survival required independence from the faction that had brought her to power, and elimination of all potential rivals for the throne. She therefore sought to widen her political base by conciliating the nobility as a whole. She confirmed the most important act of her husband's brief reign, his release of the nobility from any obligation to serve the state. She made land ownership a monopoly of the nobility. She made promotion in the bureaucracy automatic, by seniority, a step that gravely weakened the power of her successors. In 1785 she granted the nobility a charter that conceded at last some rights against the state, some exemption from arbitrary arrest and from the barbaric punishments that Russian tradition demanded. But since the autocrat could still revoke noble status at any moment, the rights Catherine's charter granted were as much a matter of form as of substance.

In 1767–68 she even summoned a legislative commission to codify Russia's laws. Every social group except serfs sent representatives armed with statements of grievances. That was the autocracy's first open appeal to its subjects, its first attempt to give them a voice in Russia's central government. It was also the last before the twentieth century, when revolution forced the last tsar to concede a sham parliament.

Catherine dissolved the commission before it could suggest laws; its passing marked the waning of her "enlightened" phase.

She nevertheless drew from it a sense of what her subjects, especially the nobility, wanted. What they wanted and Catherine conceded was the strengthening of serfdom. As early as 1765 she gave landlords the power to condemn serfs to forced labor without legal formalities. In 1767 she banned serf complaints against landlords upon pain of hard labor for life and flogging with the dreaded Russian whip—the knout. The knout, now that the nobility was no longer obliged to do state service to justify their holding of serfs, was soon needed, for the freeing of the nobility in turn raised expectations among the serfs. When Catherine disappointed those expectations, the greatest of all Russian peasant revolts convulsed the Volga region from 1773 to 1775 under the leadership of the Cossack Emelyan Pugachev, who claimed to be Peter III. Catherine's army ultimately massacred the insurgents and brought Pugachev in an iron cage to Moscow. There, in time-honored fashion, Catherine had him broken on the wheel, beheaded, dismembered, and burned.

In the following years she sought to reorganize and strengthen local government to prevent further revolts, while extending the institution of serfdom to newly conquered provinces and to free categories of peasants. By the end of her reign, by one estimate, 34 million of the 36 million subjects of the Russian monarchy were serfs. By her encouragement of the nobility she furthered a process that never reached completion, the transformation of the service nobility into a Western-style aristocracy with rights against the state. In Russia, unlike western Europe, that process rested on the further enslavement of the peasantry. That left an explosive legacy.

Conquest, not reform, made Catherine II "the Great" in her own lifetime. Peter the Great had wrenched open a window to the West by driving the Swedes from the Baltic coast. Catherine pushed Russia's borders southward and westward against Poland and the Ottoman Empire.

Poland was her first victim, for its borders were a mere 200 miles from Moscow. In 1763 Catherine secured the election to the Polish throne of a former lover, Stanislaus Poniatowski. Thereafter, Catherine and Frederick II of Prussia worked to block constitutional reforms that might revive the fortunes of the Polish state. In 1772 the two monarchs joined to carry out a First Partition of Poland. Frederick took West Prussia, and thus secured a land bridge between Brandenburg and the province of Prussia. Catherine took a generous slice of northeastern Poland, with the pretext that Russian and Orthodox populations there were suffering under Polish rule. To preserve the balance of power, the two monarchs thought it wise to offer the province of Galicia, northeast of Hungary, to Maria Theresa. That gift distressed the pious empress, but reason of state triumphed over morality.

The First Partition shocked the Poles into a patriotic revival that swept up even Poniatowski, who forgot that he owed his throne to Catherine. In 1791, after the outbreak of the French Revolution, Poland enacted a remarkable reform constitution that abolished the *liberum veto* (see p. 528) and established a strong monarchy. Catherine gave a swift and ruthless answer. Early in 1792 she halted a promising war against the Turks, rushed an army to Poland, and restored the old anarchy. In 1793, in partnership with Prussia alone, she carried out a Second Partition that reduced Poland to a narrow strip wedged between Prussia, Russia, and Austria. The inhabitants of this rump-Poland, under the leadership of Thaddeus Kosciuszko, who had fought conspicuously in the American Revolution, rose in revolt against the partitioning powers. But Catherine's armies tracked down Kosciuszko and forced Poniatowski to abdicate. A Third Partition in 1795 wiped what was left of Poland off the map by dividing it between Russia, Prussia, and Austria. In the three partitions, Catherine secured almost two-thirds of Poland's original territory. A Polish state did not reemerge until the common ruin of the three partitioning powers in 1917–18.

Catherine's successes against the crumbling Ottoman Empire were almost

Russia's Drive to the West   1462–1796

as decisive. In wars in 1768–74 and 1787–92, Catherine secured most of the northern shore of the Black sea. By the Treaty of Kütchük Kainardji that ended the first war in 1774, Russia also received a vague right to protect Orthodox Christians in the Ottoman Empire, a right that later served as a perennial pretext for Russian intervention at Constantinople. Kütchük Kainardji marked the opening of the "Eastern Question"—the decay and partition of the Ottoman Empire—that bedeviled European diplomacy until its resolution by force in 1914–18. For the moment, the Ottoman Empire escaped the fate of Poland because of its size, its remoteness, and the mutual jealousies of its two European adversaries, Austria and Russia. But at Catherine's death in 1796, little seemed to stand between Russian power and Constantinople, the gate to the Mediterranean.

Maria Theresa on the First Partition of Poland

Frederick the Great, with his habitual cynicism, remarked that "Maria Theresa wept, but she kept on taking."

This unfortunate partition of Poland is costing me ten years of my life. . . . How many times have I refused to agree to it! But disaster after disaster heaped upon us by the Turks, misery, famine and pestilence at home, no hope of assistance from either France or England, and the prospect of being left isolated and threatened with war both by Prussia and Russia—it was all these considerations that finally forced me to accept that unhappy proposal which will remain a blot on my reign. God grant that I be not held responsible for it in the other world! I confess that I cannot keep from talking about this affair. I have taken it so to heart that it poisons and embitters all my days.

Excerpt from a letter to one of her diplomats, in Readings in Western Civilization, *ed. by Paul L. Hughes and Robert F. Fries (Paterson, N.J.: Littlefield, Adams, 1960), p. 134.*

Prussia: Frederick the Great

Frederick II of Prussia, who ruled until 1786, had better claims than Catherine to the title of "enlightened absolutist." The state he inherited, despite its narrow military traditions was unlike the "half-German, half-Tartar" autocracy that fell to Catherine II. Prussia's enserfed peasants suffered under the Junkers but had far more rights than the serfs of Russia. Prussia possessed a middle class and was a recognizably Western society capable of accepting gradual reform.

Frederick burnished his reputation for enlightenment by inviting Voltaire to Potsdam. They eventually quarreled over the merits of Frederick's rather awful poetry, but they agreed that the king's duty was to combat ignorance and superstition, to enhance the welfare of his subjects, and to promote religious toleration. The king welcomed all religious exiles, even Jesuits; only Jews remained hedged about with vexatious regulations. As a religious skeptic, Frederick found toleration easy.

In economic policy, Frederick was the most determined "mercantilist" since Louis XIV's minister Colbert. With his state-directed enterprises he sought to give Prussia self-sufficiency, above all in military supplies and equipment. He encouraged the new scientific agriculture that was slowly spreading from Holland. His policies induced 300,000 immigrants, including many skilled agricultural and industrial workers, to settle in Prussia. He also introduced Europe's first scheme for universal primary education, thus founding a tradition that in the nineteenth century became one of Prussia's greatest strengths. Finally, like other enlightened absolutists, Frederick rationalized laws and judicial procedures.

The Partitions of Poland

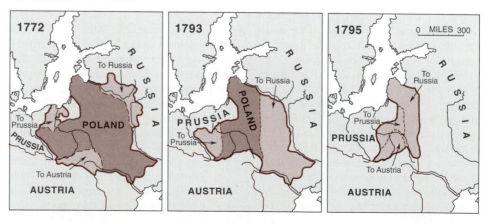

The Rise of Brandenburg-Prussia   1640–1795

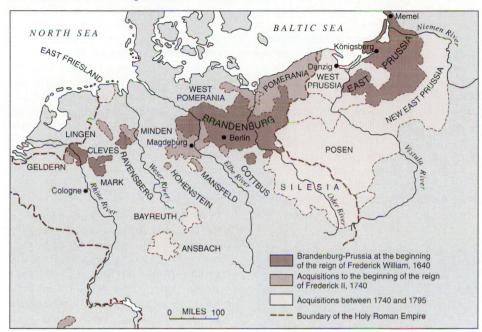

Brandenburg-Prussia at the beginning of the reign of Frederick William, 1640

Acquisitions to the beginning of the reign of Frederick II, 1740

Acquisitions between 1740 and 1795

Boundary of the Holy Roman Empire

0 MILES 100

Yet in many respects Frederick was less than enlightened. He believed firmly in birth and privilege. The Junkers served him well as officers in the most important organ of the state, the army. In return for that service he trusted the nobility far more than had his father or the Great Elector. Frederick improved the lot of serfs on his own estates but had little enthusiasm for emancipation. During his reign, noble estates expanded and the condition of the serfs worsened. His conception of society was static: nobles, townspeople, and peasants should remain at their respective posts. His preference for rigid caste lines over social mobility and for orders from above over economic initiative from below ultimately proved self-defeating.

Despite Frederick's enlightened pose, the discipline, efficiency, and ruthless centralization of the Prussian monarchy ultimately derived from a long Hohenzollern tradition entirely unrelated to the Enlightenment. The state that Frederick created in the wars between 1740 and 1763 and consolidated in peace from 1763 to 1786 was the most striking political achievement of his time. But without him, without

a genius at the helm, his economic and social policies doomed it to stagnation. Prussia's shattering military successes and Frederick's monopoly of diplomacy, strategy, and tactics put his officer corps to sleep. The coming storms of the revolutionary era almost destroyed Prussia. It survived only through the emergence of a "bureaucratic absolutism" in which the bureaucracy and army ran the state themselves, without much need for a monarch. That was Prussia's dangerous legacy to the German state that it ultimately created.

Austria: Joseph II

The monarch with the best claim to the title of enlightened absolutist was Joseph II of Austria (r. 1780–90). Although he professed contempt for the *philosophes,* he was more devoted to the main tenets of the Enlightenment and to the welfare of his peoples than any of his fellow monarchs.

Frederick II's conquest of Silesia in 1740 prompted a drastic reorganization of the Habsburg Empire that enabled it to survive until 1918. Maria Theresa, during her long reign (1740–80), developed an imperial bureaucracy that controlled from Vienna all provinces of the empire except Hungary. In 1775 that machine imposed a tariff union on the empire, except for Hungary. It compelled the nobles to assume some of the burden of taxation. It limited the amount of labor they could extort from the peasantry and curbed the power of private noble courts over the serfs, for whom Maria Theresa did more than any other ruler of her time.

Her son Joseph, who became emperor and co-regent after the death of her husband in 1765, took an increasingly energetic part in her efforts at reform. But

Joseph II, The Enlightened Despot   1783

The following extracts illustrate the paradox of enlightened absolutism; only autocratic methods made reform conceivable.

I have not confined myself simply to issuing orders; I have expounded and explained them. With enlightenment I have sought to weaken and with arguments I have sought to overcome the abuses which had arisen out of prejudice and deeply rooted customs. I have sought to imbue every official of the state with the love I myself feel for the wellbeing of the whole. . . .

The good of the state can be understood only in general terms, only in terms of the greatest number. Similarly, all the provinces of the monarchy constitute one whole and therefore can have only one aim. It is necessary therefore that there should be an end to all the prejudices and all the jealousies between provinces [and] all races which have caused so much fruitless bickering. [Circular letter of Joseph II, 1783.]

But given Austria's structure and traditions, only the monarch could dictate unity and the end of prejudices. The state needed a common language; Joseph II determined what it should be.

The German language is the universal tongue of my empire. I am the emperor of Germany. The states which I possess are provinces that form only one body—the state of which I am the head. If the kingdom of Hungary were the most important of my possessions, I would not hesitate to impose its language on the other countries. [Letter to a Hungarian noble, 1783.]

From T. C. W. Blanning, Joseph II and Enlightened Despotism *(London: Longman Group, 1970), pp. 131–32, and Louis Léger,* Histoire de l'Autriche Hongrie *(Paris, 1879), p. 373.*

Joseph sought to move farther and faster than his mother. Until her death in 1780 he chafed under Maria Theresa's compromises, particularly over religion. During the ten years that Joseph II ruled alone, thousands of decrees poured from the imperial chancellery in Vienna. He proclaimed religious toleration for all Christians and Jews. He dissolved monasteries that were devoted solely to religious contemplation and gave their revenues to the hospitals that in the next century made Vienna the medical center of Europe. He applied to everyone in the Habsburg dominions, regardless of rank or nationality, a system of equal taxation in proportion to income. He imposed one language for official business, German, on all parts of the empire, including Belgium, Italy, and Hungary. Above all, Joseph II abolished serfdom. Early in his reign he issued a number of decrees that gave all serfs in the Habsburg dominions personal freedom— freedom to leave the land, to marry as they pleased, to choose whatever job they liked. That act of Joseph II was permanent, even though his successors repealed other decrees by which he sought to make the peasants who remained on the land into property owners, free from forced labor obligations.

Through his policies of centralization and drastic reform, Joseph naturally made mortal enemies of the clergy, the landed nobility, non-German nationalities such as the Hungarians, and even peasants who failed to understand his intentions. In 1789, when revolution broke out in France, peasants in the Austrian Empire began to plunder and murder landlords to gain the rights Joseph had held out to them. By 1790 both Belgium and Hungary were in revolt against his rule, and the Church was bitterly hostile. Joseph lamented to his brother and successor Leopold: "I am the only one holding to the true course, and I am left to labor alone. . . . I am without any assistance whatsoever." Worn out, he died in 1790 after choosing a rueful epitaph: "Here lies Joseph II, who was unfortunate in everything that he undertook."

Joseph II, the "revolutionary Emperor," had built a structure stronger than he knew. It survived both the revolutionary era and the nineteenth century. The crippling limitations under which he labored stemmed above all from his position as a revolutionary without a party. His only supports were an unimaginative bureaucracy, a secret police that he had set up to combat opposition, and the Habsburg army. His brand of enlightened absolutism might have formed a bridge between divine-right monarchy and democratic politics. But his fate suggested that radical changes, at least on the Continent, demanded a broader base of popular support than he had been able to command.

Joseph II urging agricultural improvement on his peasants.

BRITAIN, FRANCE, AND THE AMERICAN REVOLUTION, 1763–89

In France and British North America, revolution from below took the place of reform from above. Louis XV made a belated but vigorous attempt to quell internal opposition between 1770 and 1774. Thereafter the French monarchy drifted until its collapse after 1789 in the greatest of modern European revolutions. Overseas, the American colonists claimed their independence in the name of reason and natural rights. When Britain resisted, the colonists broke away by force.

France: The Failure of Reform, 1770–74

The Seven Years' War severely strained British and French finances. Louis XV proposed to cope by making permanent a temporary war tax that fell on nobles and commoners alike, and by levying a new tax on those who had bought judicial and administrative offices from the monarchy. Such measures were necessary if the monarchy hoped to avoid bankruptcy. But they raised a storm of opposition from nobility and middle classes alike. The *parlements,* which were narrow oligarchies of officeholders who had bought their positions, rationalized their privileges by borrowing from Locke. Any attack on their own tax exemption, they arrogantly proclaimed, violated the "fun-damental laws" of the kingdom and the "natural rights" of Frenchmen.

In 1770–71 Louis XV finally acted. His forceful ministers, the lawyer René de Maupeou for political affairs and the Abbé Joseph Marie Terray for finances, closed the *parlements,* exiled their most fractious members to distant villages, and reassessed taxes. Public opinion—except, significantly, for Voltaire—rose in outrage. But the king held fast and won. A new system of royal law courts replaced the *parlements.* Maupeou prepared to rationalize at last France's administration and finances. Then, in 1774, Louis XV caught smallpox and died. His son, Louis XVI (r. 1774–92), well-meaning and lamentably weak, was the monarchy's downfall. He dismissed Maupeou, acquiesced in the restoration of the *parlements,* and presided first over bankruptcy, then over the beginnings of the French revolution, described in the next chapter.

The Revolt of Britain's American Colonies

France's revolution did not begin until 1788–89, but events overseas furnished a powerful example. Britain's "salutary neglect" of its North American colonies did not survive the Seven Years' War. As in France, the financial strain of that war prompted a search for new revenues. Parliament in London naturally looked to its colonists. The colonies had in the past paid no taxes to Britain. They had paid only customs duties that Parliament had imposed—but only loosely enforced—to channel colonial trade to Britain. The colonists' tax burden was thus a mere 4 percent of the average Englishman's. And while the colonists had done little fighting, London had paid dearly to defend them against the French, against France's Indian allies, and against the 1763 uprising of the Ottawa chief Pontiac. But unfortunately for the British government, its entirely reasonable efforts to raise revenue coincided with the elimination of French power in North America. That freed the colonists of their dependence on Britain. The result, thanks to the traditions of government that the colonies had acquired from England itself, was an explosion that shattered the British Empire.

Salutary neglect had permitted a political experiment possible in no other European colonial empire. The thirteen colonies from quasi-theocratic Massachusetts, to anarchic Rhode Island, to Catholic Maryland, to Anglican Virginia, were in effect self-governing. The ministry in London appointed royal governors, but under the charters granted to the colonies, the colonial legislatures, not Parliament, paid the governors' salaries and voted—or refused to vote—the revenues needed to carry on government. Elections to those legislatures were far more democratic than those for Parliament or for other European representative bodies. And the colonists took seriously John Locke's theory of limited government and the practice of England's Glorious Revolution of 1688. They regarded the British Empire as a quasi-federal structure that rested on consent.

Parliament took a differet view. Beginning in 1765 it sought to impose both direct taxes and new customs duties on the colonists. The colonists replied with boycotts of British imports, smuggling, and the demand "that no taxes be imposed on them but with their own consent." By 1773 a chasm had opened between Parliament's conception of sovereignty and the colonists' conception of freedom.

In December 1773 a radical Massachusetts minority not unconnected to the smuggling trade took direct action. A crowd thinly disguised as American Indians boarded three British merchant ships in Boston harbor and dumped into the murky water thousands of pounds' worth of tea—on which London had expected the colonists to pay import duty. The "Boston Tea Party" was at once an act of defiance against Parliament's claim to impose taxes and a blow against the smugglers' British competitors.

Parliament reacted with fury. In 1774 it closed the port of Boston, deprived the Massachusetts legislature of much of its power, and ordered the deportation of offenders for trial in England. That drove the other twelve colonies to rally behind Massachusetts out of fear that Parliament would likewise revoke or amend their charters.

Worse still, Parliament passed an otherwise statesmanlike measure, the Quebec Act of 1774, that appeared to be a further attack on the English-speaking colonies. The act guaranteed the preservation of the French language and the Catholic religion in Canada and defined Canada to include all territory north of the Ohio River and west of the Allegheny Mountains. It banned American settlement beyond the mountains. That—and the act's toleration for "Popery"—enraged both rich and poor, land speculators and pioneers, in the English-speaking colonies.

Between them, the Quebec Act and the so-called "Intolerable Acts" against Massachusetts marked the point of no return. To George III and to a large majority of his English subjects, the American colonists had proved themselves childish and irresponsible rebels. To a majority of the colonials, Parliament was seeking to impose an unbearable tyranny of the kind they now argued they had sought to escape by emigrating to the New World. The government of George III succeeded in driving toward rebellion even sober, propertied men who feared unrestrained democracy as "the madness of the multitude." The colonists began to arm themselves.

In April 1775, the British garrison at Boston sought to seize weapons and gunpowder that the colonists had assembled at Concord. The Massachusetts militia met the redcoats on Lexington green and fired the shots "heard 'round the world." Although the redcoats reached their objective at Concord, American fire from behind houses and stone walls harried them back to Boston. A Continental Congress assembled at Philadelphia and formally declared the colonies independent of king and Parliament on July 4, 1776. Its ringing words were Lockean to the very marrow:

We hold these truths to be self-evident, that all Men are created equal, that they are endowed by their Creator with certain unalienable Rights, that among these are Life, Liberty and the Pursuit of Happiness. That to secure these rights, Governments are insituted among Men, deriving their just Powers from the Consent of the Governed. That whenever any Form of Government becomes destructive of those ends, it is the Right of the People to alter or to abolish it, and to institute new Government. . . .

That was a call to revolution in the Old World as well as in the New.

The American War of Independence

The ensuing War of Independence was a civil war in both colonies and mother country. The colonists had sympathizers in both England and Ireland. A Whig faction that included the founder of modern conservatism, Edmund Burke, in vain urged George III and his inept prime minister, Lord North (1770–82) to conciliate the colonists. A group of "radicals," under the inspiration of a boisterous and debauched demagogue, John Wilkes, attacked the king's influence in Parliament, urged the publication of parliamentary debates, and agitated for a democratization

Third of the Hanoverians: the unfortunate George III.

of parliamentary elections. Wilkes eventually made his peace with the king, and the English radicals were too small a minority to carry much weight. But they nevertheless proclaimed the political faith of the Declaration of Independence, that government must rest on consent. Conversely, numerous "Tories" in the colonies, from Boston to the backwoods of North Carolina and Georgia, sympathized with or fought for the king. In the course of the war and its aftermath, some 80,000 fled or were driven out to Canada and their lands confiscated.

The war itself pitted the disorganized colonial militias and the small Continental Army under George Washington against a succession of seaborne British task forces. The Americans' strengths were Washington's unique combination of daring and caution, sluggish British generalship,

George Washington, victorious at the battle of Princeton (1777), by Charles Wilson Peale.

before France acted, but Vergennes, less idealistic than they, sought the humiliation of Britain. The French navy, improved since 1759, fought the British to a standstill in 1778 off Ushant, at the mouth of the English Channel. Across the Atlantic, it deprived Britain's forces of supplies and seaborne mobility until French defeat at the Battle of the Saintes (West Indies) in April 1782 restored Britain's naval supremacy.

That victory came too late for Britain in North America. At Yorktown in Virginia, a British force of 7,000, penned between the French navy and American and French troops, had surrendered on October 19, 1781. London, although it still occupied New York with 30,000 troops, recognized the futility of fighting on. In the Treaty of Versailles of 1783, Britain acknowledged the independence of the thirteen colonies and surrendered to them all of North America south of the Great Lakes, east of the Mississippi, and north of Florida. France gained revenge for the loss of Canada, some colonial outposts, and immense new debts that ultimately helped destroy its monarchy.

Yet independence did not settle the shape of the new American state. During the war most of the colonies had summoned conventions and drafted written constitutions with bills of rights. Between 1777 and 1781 the Continental Congress had united the former colonies in a loose federal union under the Articles of Confederation. In July 1787 Congress enacted the Northwest Ordinance, a momentous document that extended the principles for which the colonists had fought to the still unsettled western territories. When these territories became populated, they were to become not colonies or dependencies but "states," equal in status to the thirteen original members of the union.

Yet by 1787 it was clear that the Articles of Confederation failed to provide the necessary machinery for a common economic or foreign policy. The result was the summoning of a Constitutional Convention that hammered out a new federal constitution at secret meetings in Philadelphia. That document, which began with a characteristic flourish ("We, the People

smuggled muskets and powder that France supplied after 1776, and widespread popular support for the cause of independence. The British and their German mercenary troops rarely commanded more than the ground under their feet. Britain's assets were battlefield professionalism and command of the sea.

In October 1777, American forces cornered at Saratoga some 5,000 British troops that had descended from Canada. That victory, although it immediately followed Washington's loss of Philadelphia, ultimately decided the war. It induced Louis XVI and his ambitious foreign minister, the Comte de Vergennes, to intervene actively. French enthusiasts for American independence, including the Marquis de Lafayette, had joined Washington well

of the United States . . ."), has endured. The Constitution and the Revolution that created it founded the longest continuous tradition of democratic politics in history.

The American Revolution in History

The American Revolution had profound effects on Europe and eventually on the world. America was not the first "new nation"; the Dutch United provinces that had defeated Spain had that honor. But it was the only new nation of the Enlightenment. Its revolution was entirely secular and it claimed universal applicability for its principles. It had proclaimed and acted on Locke's theories of natural equality, unalienable natural rights, government by consent, and the right to revolution. Its state and federal constitutions demonstrated Montesquieu's theory of the separation of powers. Its constitutional conventions showed that a people could create a new government in an orderly fashion by formal contract, and that liberty need not mean anarchy. Its example showed that small political units could federate into a larger union. The American Revolution dramatized and propagated two of the West's principal political ideas—limited constitutional government and popular sovereignty, or democracy. The latter, but not the former, was destined to play a decisive role in the coming revolution in France.

By the last quarter of the eighteenth century, the tide of ideas and of politics was running strongly against the old regime. Aristocracy and enlightened absolutism were ceasing to command loyalty or even respect. The desire for equilibrium, whether social, international, or intellectual, no longer inspired educated Europeans. Balance and order in both art and politics were giving way to the thirst for emotion and change. The American Revolution accelerated that movement. After 1789, the greatest of European revolutions provided emotion, change, and violence enough for all.

Suggestions for Further Reading

General

For overviews, see especially G. Rudé, *Europe in the Eighteenth Century* (1972); L. Krieger, *Kings and Philosophers, 1689–1789* (1970); W. Doyle, *The Old European Order, 1660–1800* (1978); and I. Woloch, *Eighteenth-Century Europe* (1982). The relevant volumes of the *Rise of Modern Europe* series remain useful: P. Roberts, *The Quest for Security, 1715–1740* (1947); W. L. Dorn, *Competition for Empire, 1740–1763* (1940); and L. Gershoy, *From Despotism to Revolution, 1763–1789* (1944). O. H. Hufton, *The Poor of Eighteenth-Century France, 1750–1789* (1975), and L. Stone, *The Family, Sex and Marriage in England 1500–1800* (1977), are pioneering studies; A. Macfarlane, *Marriage and Love in England: Modes of Reproduction, 1300–1840* (1986), reaches conclusions radically different from those of Stone. J. H. Parry, *Trade and Dominion: The European Overseas Empires in the Eighteenth Century* (1971); C. G. Robertson, *Chatham and the British Empire* (1948); and L. B. Wright, *The Atlantic Frontier: Colonial American Civilization, 1607–1763* (1947), provide useful discussion of overseas expansion. On economic and social change, see above all F. Braudel, *Civilization and Capitalism, 15th–18th Centuries* (1982).

The Major States

For discussions of developments within the major states, see especially J. Lough, *Introduction to Eighteenth-Century France* (1960); G. Holmes, *The Making of a Great Power. Late Stuart and Early Georgian Britain* (1993); R. Vierhaus, *Germany in the Age of Absolutism* (1989); and H. Rosenberg, *Bureaucracy, Aristocracy, and Autocracy, the Prussian Experience, 1660–1815* (1958). For biographies of leading figures, see J. H. Plumb, *The First Four Georges* (1957); G. Ritter, *Frederick the Great* (trans. 1968); C. L. Morris, *Maria Theresa: The Last Conservative* (1937); and G. S. Thomson, *Catherine the Great and the Expansion of Russia* (1950). On the American Revolution, see especially E. S. Morgan, *The Birth of the Republic, 1763–1789* (1956); R. M. Calhoon, *Revolutionary America: An Interpretive Overview* (1976); and R. W. Tucker and D. C. Hendrickson, *The Fall of the First British Empire: Origins of the War of American Independence* (1982).

THE FRENCH REVOLUTION AND EUROPE, 1789–1815

The French Revolution, along with the industrial revolution in England (described in the next chapter), changed the face of Europe and ultimately of the world. It was both political and social. Politically, it destroyed the older order first in France and then in much of western Europe. The French monarchy, which traced its traditions to Charlemagne, collapsed. Its successor, the French Republic, created a belt of satellite republics from Holland to Italy. Socially, the Revolution swept away the rigidly defined ranks of the old order. A new hierarchy, based at least in theory on talent and wealth rather than on birth, replaced the Old Regime's three-part division by "orders," the nobles, clergy, and common people.

Above all, the Revolution changed the ways in which the peoples of western Europe viewed themselves. It created new words for new things. "Citizens," "revolu-tionary," "counter-revolutionary," "reac-tion," "guillotine," and the concept of the nation-state entered the West's political vocabulary. The Revolution gave birth to nationalism and mass politics. It opened the modern age of mass-based democracy and mass-based despotism in which we still live.

THE ORIGINS OF THE REVOLUTION

The collapse of the French monarchy in 1788–89 came suddenly. But like other great events, it had many causes. Underlying forces acting slowly over many years created a situation that made violent upheaval possible. Then the Revolution's immediate causes—the short-term forces and the events that detonated the explosion—came into play.

(OPPOSITE) THE TENNIS COURT OATH, BY JACQUES-LOUIS DAVID, OFFICIAL PAINTER TO THE CONSTITUENT ASSEMBLY AND LATER TO NAPOLEON. DAVID DID NOT COMPLETE THIS IMMENSE CANVAS, FOR MOST OF THOSE SHOWN IN IT FELL UNDER SUSPICION DURING THE TERROR.

The Forces That Made Revolution Possible

Three underlying forces in French society prepared the way for revolution: population growth, the expansion of the middle classes, and the rise of an informed public opinion permeated with Enlightenment ideas that were subversive of monarchy and aristocracy.

As world climate grew warmer, France's population swelled from 22 to 28 million between 1700 and 1789. That dramatic increase made *la grande nation,* as France called itself, Europe's most populous state. Rapid population growth meant youth. In 1789, 36 percent of France's population was under twenty years of age. And population growth was precarious. It rested on improvements in the transport and distribution of food, not on major advances in food production. Drought, storm, or grain blight produced serious food shortages in 1770, 1774, 1778, 1782, 1784, and 1786. After 1770, increasingly violent swings in agricultural output and prices coincided with a decline in daily wages that resulted from the rise in population.

An increase and spread of wealth at the top of the social scale paralleled this increase in numbers below. France's middle classes grew from around three-quarters of a million in 1700 to 2.3 million, or between 8 and 9 percent of the total population, by 1789. The nobility's share of the total population remained static throughout the century at between 0.5 and 1.5 percent. Ever-greater numbers of wealthy commoners might hope to rise into the nobility, but only slowly, over several generations. Although nobles increasingly took an interest in trade and industry, land ownership remained the chief source of wealth and the badge of social rank. The lines between noble and commoner were gradually blurring, but too slowly to suit many wealthy commoners.

With the downward spread of wealth came the growth of a phenomenon new to France, although it had been visible in England since the Civil War in the 1640s: a reading public. By 1789 perhaps 37 percent of France's people could read and write. In 1700, France had three semi-official newspapers; by 1789, it had several hundred weeklies and dailies. Libraries and reading rooms sprang up even in the provinces. Nobles and commoners alike collaborated in spreading the ideas of the Enlightenment. The condemnation of ignorance, prejudice, and superstition by Voltaire and Diderot and the egalitarian creed of Rousseau reached a widening audience. The example of the American Revolution, carried back to France after 1783 by the Marquis de Lafayette, hero of Yorktown, and by other French officers, suggested that the enlightened could remodel institutions and society at will.

The new ideas divided nobility and middle classes alike. Only a small minority of either gave up their loyalty to Church and monarchy in favor of Deism and a "republic of virtue." But the new ideas had consequences. In place of the old certainties—original sin, redemption, and obedience to priests, nobles, and a God-ordained king—they offered new myths: the perfectibility of man and society and the supremacy of the "general will."

The Immediate Causes: Government Crisis, Revolt by the Nobility, Crop Failure

The long-term forces would surely have brought change. That they triggered an explosion was the result of the coincidence of three short-term factors. First, the unusual incompetence of the royal government destroyed its authority. Then the nobility, sensing weakness, attacked. Finally, in the spring of 1789, France's peasants and urban crowds, unhinged by the last and worst of a series of poor harvests, brought the entire structure crashing down.

The crisis began in finance and administration. War, the sport of kings and nobles and the test of the greatness of the state, had always imposed crushing burdens. Prosperity after 1715 had freed France only gradually from the immense war debts of Louis XIV. The Seven Years' War of 1756–63 again brought heavy deficits. Then France's intervention in the American Revolution once more reduced the royal finances to near-collapse.

Louis XVI, unlike his two immediate predecessors, kept no mistresses and lived a modest life, for a monarch. But he had neither the brains nor the ruthlessness needed to master events. Under his loose supervision, his ministers struggled against approaching bankruptcy. Jacques Necker, a pompous and vain Swiss banker, coped during the American war by borrowing at ever-higher rates while assuring king and public that the budget balanced. His successors as Comptroller-General of Finances, especially Charles Alexandre de Calonne, followed Necker's example.

By 1786 Calonne could borrow no more. He concluded that the only solution to the financial crisis was fundamental reform of what he described as "a Kingdom made up of lands with estates, lands without, lands with provincial assemblies, lands of mixed administration, a Kingdom where provinces are foreign one to another, where multifarious internal barriers separate and divide the subjects of the same sovereign, where certain areas are totally freed from burdens of which the others bear the full weight, where the richest class contributes least, where it is impossible to have either a constant rule or a common will. . . ."

Calonne proposed to rationalize France's ramshackle administration and impose a single uniform land tax. The tax would strike the tax-exempt nobility and clergy who held between a quarter and a third of France's major source of wealth, its land. Since by custom the monarch needed some sort of approval for new taxes, Calonne in 1787 put his reform proposals to a hand-picked assembly of the two orders he proposed to tax.

This Assembly of Notables predictably put a price on approving Calonne's proposals. It demanded public scrutiny of the budget. Since that would inevitably expose the monarchy's financial incompetence, Louis dismissed Calonne and replaced him with one of his critics, Loménie de Brienne, archbishop of Toulouse. Brienne tried to cajole the notables into accepting the taxes that he himself had formerly denounced.

They again refused, and demanded that the king convene the Estates General of France, which had not met since 1614. Only that body, the notables now claimed, could approve new taxes. The nobility thus opened the attack on the monarchy in the name both of reform and of its own historic privileges. It was the first of many groups that fished in troubled waters and was swept away.

Louis XVI sent the notables home. He told the *Parlement* of Paris, the court whose task it was to register new laws, that the new taxes were legal "because I wish it." Louis' energetic minister of justice then closed the *parlements*. Despite a petition from the dukes and peers of France, and riots in the provinces under the leadership of nobles and *parlement* lawyers, Louis held firm. For a moment it looked as if the government had won.

Then drought, hailstorms, and crop failures struck all of France's major agricultural regions at once, for the first time since the famine year of 1709. The projected government deficit soared: starving peasants paid no taxes, and starving cities demanded expensive imported grain. The bankers, friends of the still-ambitious Necker, capped the disaster by refusing to lend the crown any more money. That blow brought the government to its knees. In August 1788 Louis XVI called the Estates General to meet in May 1789, and allowed Brienne to resign. The king reappointed Necker, who brought with him fresh loans but no policy. The government had confessed its incompetence and its bankruptcy, and had appealed to its subjects for help. The French Revolution had begun.

THE REVOLUTIONARY BREAKTHROUGH, 1788–89

What sort of revolution it would be was still unclear. The nobles and clergy who had defied their royal master expected to dominate the Estates General. But the nobles' protests in the spring and summer of 1788, and still more the approaching meeting of the Estates General, drew into politics groups that had until now played no role.

The "Third Estate" and the Masses

The first of these was the middle classes. The reinstated *Parlement* of Paris had decreed in September 1788 that the Estates General vote by order, with nobility, clergy, and commons balloting separately, as in 1614. That arrangement would make the commons, or Third Estate, a permanent minority—although they represented 98 percent of the population of France. Political clubs, many of them led by nobles with enlightened views, urged the "doubling" of the Third Estate, giving it twice its traditional number of representatives so that it would equal the other two orders combined. The Abbé Emmanuel Sieyès, chief theorist of this movement, published in January 1789 the most famous pamphlet of the Revolution: *What is the Third Estate?* It began with three questions: "What is the Third Estate?—*everything*. What has it been until now in the political order?—

nothing. What does it seek? *To be something*." Sieyès went on to demand the drafting of a constitution "which the nation alone has the right to do." That appeal to the *nation,* to popular sovereignty, meant the end of divine-right monarchy and ultimately of peace in Europe.

Initially Louis encouraged the commons as a counterweight to the nobility. He agreed at the end of December 1788 to double the Third Estate. His appeal to the privileged orders had begun the Revolution; his appeal to the Third Estaste led to the Revolution's breakthrough. But as the Estates General assembled at Versailles in May 1789, forces far more menacing to the established order than the lawyers, professional men, and bureaucrats of the Third Estate appeared on the scene—the peasantry and the urban lower classes. Their intervention converted a political struggle between elites, a conflict between the privileged and the merely rich or educated, into an upheaval that terrified nobles and Third Estate alike.

The motive force behind that upheaval was hunger, the result of the precarious balance between France's growing population and lagging agriculture. An extraordinarily hard winter followed the disastrous crop failures of 1788. The price of bread, the main food of the common people of Paris, rose by 60 percent between August 1788 and February 1789. Distress in the countryside depressed the demand for manufactured goods. Production of textiles, France's major industry, dropped perhaps 50 percent. Urban workers lost their jobs just as food prices soared.

The consequence was a rapid breakdown of public order in the spring and summer of 1789, before the new harvest arrived. The government had coped with past crises of this kind with price controls, emergency grain shipments, and police and army to enforce order. But now the royal administration itself was a wreck, the loyalty of the army's noble officer corps was shaky, and the revolt of the nobles and *parlements* had set a dangerous example.

Bread riots and disturbances broke out in the cities. In the countryside, the

Caricature of the French peasant supporting the clergy and nobility, while doves and rabbits, protected by the law for the sport of the nobility, eat the peasant's grain.

peasants stopped paying taxes. They also stopped paying the curious assortment of medieval obligations owed to landlords, local nobles, and the Church—money dues on land, tithes, and noble monopolies on flour mills, bakeries, wine presses, or law courts. These "seignorial dues," which a legal treatise of the day described as a "bizarre form of property," had long been the chief grievance of the peasants against what now, at one stroke, became the "Old Regime."

The peasants burned tax records and registers of dues. Where they could not find the registers, they burned the castles of the nobles to make sure. In late July 1789 rumors swept the countryside that "the brigands," the "English gang" (shades of the Hundred Years' War), or "the aristocrats" were approaching to slaughter and pillage. This "Great Fear," symptom of social breakdown, was both cause and consequence of peasant violence against the privileged orders.

From Estates General to Constituent Assembly, May–July 1789

When the Estates General met on May 23, 1789, the royal government, always indecisive, went back on the unspoken alliance with the Third Estate it had sought at the end of 1788. The king refused to allow the commoners to sit with the other two orders. He also rejected the demand of the Third Estate for voting "by head"— one delegate, one vote—which would have given the Third Estate a majority.

Under the leadership of Sieyès, the Third Estate reacted on June 17 by renaming itself the National Assembly—a new authority, independent of the monarchy and with an implicit claim to sovereignty. Liberal clergy and nobles joined the Third Estate. And when Louis ordered the Assembly's meeting-hall closed on June 20, it met at an indoor tennis court nearby. In the first of many scenes of drama and oratory that punctuated the Revolution, the representatives solemnly swore the "tennis court oath": not to disperse until they had given France a constitution.

Tom. I.   Pag. 417.

Emmanuel Joseph Sieyes

Theorist of the "Third Estate": the Abbé Sieyès.

Louis, suddenly resolute, replied on June 23 with a defense of "his" nobility and clergy and with veiled threats to dissolve the Estates General. After he had left the hall, the leaders of the Third Estate erupted: "The nation in assembly does not take orders." "We will not move from our seats unless forced by bayonets." The resistance of the privileged orders crumbled. More and more nobles and clergy joined the Assembly, which soon officially took the title of Constituent Assembly and named a committee to write a constitution for France.

Paris Speaks: The Fall of The Bastille, July 14, 1789

Louis XVI wavered, then swung again toward resistance. Royal troops, many of them Swiss and German regiments, concentrated around Paris. Louis dismissed Necker. Counter-revolution seemed imminent. Then the removal of Necker set off an explosion in Paris that put the Constituent Assembly firmly in power. This city of 600,000, which dwarfed even the largest French provincial towns, was hungry. Crowds of shop owners, artisans, and housewives, with the backing of a rapidly growing ward organization independent of the royal authorities, attacked jails and barracks, seeking weapons. The police, a mere 2,000 backed by 3,500 royal troops, were powerless.

On July 14, 1789—whether coincidentally or not the day on which Paris bread prices reached the highest level of the century—the crowd attacked the royal fortress at the center of Paris, the Bastille. Helped by mutinous troops, the crowd took the fortress and butchered its commander. With royal authority utterly destroyed and with Paris in the hands of the insurgents, Louis XVI temporarily re-

signed himself to being a constitutional monarch.

The Fourth of August and the "Rights of Man"

The Constituent Assembly soon faced an emergency more serious than any menace from royal bayonets, or even from the Paris crowd. By the end of July the revolt of the peasants threatened not only noble property but all property in the countryside. Some members of the Assembly called for the restoration of order by force. Other more radical elements had begun to meet in a political club that later become known as the Jacobins. On the night of August 4, 1789, they took the Assembly by surprise. They induced the liberal—and landless—Vicomte de Noailles to propose the voluntary renunciation of privileges by the nobles and the Church.

In a frenzied meeting that lasted until two the next morning, the delegates renounced tithes, dues, the privileges of their orders, and the traditional rights of their towns and provinces. On sober second thought, the Assembly decreed in the following days that some of the dues be paid off in installments. That hardly impressed the peasants, and seignorial dues were dead even before their final abolition without compensation in 1793. The old order, in law as well as in fact, was gone. But the Assembly had achieved its immediate aim: disorder in the countryside subsided for the moment.

At the end of August, in its second major act, the Constituent Assembly adopted a preamble for the new constitution—the "Declaration of the Rights of Man and the Citizen." That document owed something to the Declaration of Independence, Constitution, and Bill of Rights of the new American democracy. It proclaimed liberty, and equality of rights, in stark contrast to the legal and social distinctions between orders current across the Continent. It led in 1791 to the emancipation of the Jews from the legal disabilities imposed on them in the Middle Ages. Even women, whom most revolutionaries, like Rousseau, sought to confine to the role of wife and mother, began to

Rebellious troops and citizens bombard the Bastille, July 14, 1789 (from a contemporary print).

demand equality on the basis of its principles. Olympe de Gouges, a woman writer in Paris, published in the summer of 1791 a widely discussed "Declaration of the Rights of Women."

But the Declaration's fundamental ideas were not those of Locke nor of the English common law that had molded the American Revolution. The Americans sought above all to prevent the executive or the legislature, even if elected by a majority, from trampling on individuals or on local state governments. The French, however, rashly subscribed to Rousseau's notion that the people, once freed of "ignorance, forgetfulness, or contempt for the rights of man," would spontaneously express a General Will that would in turn produce laws. That Will and those laws would by definition be incapable of oppression, except the presumably justified oppression of those whose actions or opinions violated their "duties" as citizens.

To these potentially dangerous notions the Declarations of the Rights of Man added an even more explosive element— the concept of the sovereign *nation*. In the United States, and even in a Britain that included Welsh and Scots, popular sovereignty meant little more than rule by elected representatives under law. In continental Europe, following the French example, it soon came to mean rule by one's own linguistic or ethnic group. The political definition of the nation found in the 1789 Declaration superseded the vague cultural notions of nationhood that had spread in the course of the eighteenth century.

This invention of the revolutionaries of 1789 later became known as national self-determination or *nationalism*. It ultimately meant war of all against all, and war of unprecedented intensity. Monarchies might occasionally bow to custom, religion, or law. But the new *nation-state* recognized no law other than reason—its own reason. When that reason came into conflict with the reason of others, force was the final arbiter. And the concept of nation made possible, for the first time in Europe, near-total mobilization. What other cultures had achieved only through the labor of slaves the French revolution-

The Declaration of the Rights of Man and the Citizen   August 27, 1789

The representatives of the French people, constituted as a National Assembly, and considering that ignorance, forgetfulness, or contempt for the rights of man are the sole causes of public misfortunes and the degeneration of governments, have resolved to set forth in a solemn declaration the natural, inalienable, and sacred rights of man so that this declaration, constantly kept in mind by all members of society, may unceasingly recall to them their rights and duties. . . .

1. Men are born, and remain, free and equal in rights. Social distinctions can only be founded on usefulness to society.

2. The aim of every political bond is the preservation of the natural and inalienable rights of man. Those rights are liberty, property, security, and resistance to oppression.

3. The source of all sovereignty is in essence the nation. No body or individual can exercise authority that does not derive expressly from it. . . .

6. Law is the expression of the general will. All citizens have the right to contribute, personally or through their representatives, to its creation. It must be the same, whether it protects or punishes, for all. . . .

From Archives parlementaires de 1787 à 1860, *première série, (Paris: Librairie Administrative de Paul Dupont, 1877), Vol. 9, p. 236 (translation by M. Knox).*

aries and their successors across Europe accomplished through the enthusiasm of citizens.

The Monarchy Humiliated: The October Days

All this was still in the future in the late summer of 1789. The Constituent Assembly had partially pacified the peasantry, but it still faced revolutionary Paris. The grain harvest of 1789 was good, but it had not yet reached the market. Supplies from the disastrous harvest of 1788 had run out. By late September Paris rang with cries of "When shall we have bread?" (as a pamphlet title put it). In this atmosphere, the arrival of a fresh regiment of royal troops at Versailles, greeted conspicuously by

Revolutionary propaganda:
"Frenchwomen become free."

Louis XVI's unpopular queen, Marie Antoinette of Austria, set off a new explosion.

An armed crowd with 6,000 militant Paris housewives at its head marched on Versailles. They overwhelmed the royal guards and triumphantly brought king, queen, and crown prince ("the baker, the baker's wife, and the little baker's boy") back to Paris. Alongside the royal coach, the crowd carried on pikes the heads of guards who had been killed defending their king. That was an unpromising beginning for constitutional monarchy.

THE FAILURE OF CONSTITUTIONAL MONARCHY, 1789–91

With the royal family virtual prisoners in the Tuileries palace in Paris, and with the Constituent Assembly in control of government, the Revolution seemed to have won. What remained was to recast France's society and administration. A new social pyramid based on property replaced the Old Regime's society of orders. The Constituent Assembly wiped from the map the Old Regime's quaint provincial and regional boundaries, and substituted 87 "departments" of roughly uniform size. Elected assemblies took over local government, a brief reversal of the Old Regime's drive toward centralization. France's first constitution, adopted in September 1791, set up a single-chamber Legislative Assembly elected only by men wealthy enough to pay taxes equivalent to three days' wages. That group made up perhaps 15 percent of the population. A further, steeper property qualification restricted membership in the Legislative Assembly itself.

The new regime faced three problems for which it had no answer: the financial crisis that had felled the monarchy, the continuing agitation in Paris, and above all the king's refusal to play the part the Revolution had assigned him. The nimble Marquis Charles Maurice de Talleyrand, bishop of Autun, hit on an expedient that promised to rescue France's finances. The state—like Henry VIII of England two and a half centuries before—would dissolve all monasteries and nunneries, and would seize and sell off the Church lands. The

profits would reduce the national deficit and give the parish clergy and bishops guaranteed salaries as state employees. The confiscation of Church land went smoothly, but the July 1790 "Civil Constitution of the Clergy" aroused widespread resistance. Priests all over France refused to swear the required oath of loyalty to the state, and the papacy in Rome soon backed them. The Revolution had gained a new and formidable adversary and had opened a quarrel with the Church that divided France until the twentieth century.

Nor did the seizure of Church lands solve the financial crisis. The *assignats,* the new currency backed by the proceeds of the land sales, fueled an inflation that guaranteed further urban unrest even when harvests were good. The lands themselves, sold at scandalously low prices, enriched only their middle-class and peasant buyers. The main benefit to the state of this massive transfer of property was indirect: along with the sale after 1792 of the property of nobles who had fled abroad, it tied powerful middle-class and peasant groups to the Revolution.

The Constituent and Legislative Assemblies also failed to master Paris. The middle- and lower-middle classes of the great city had by 1790–91 reached a state of political excitement unthinkable under the Old Regime. The revolutionary ward organizations or *sections,* made up of fiercely radical butchers, bakers, innkeepers, and artisans, held frequent noisy meetings. The Paris municipal government, or *Commune,* was soon in the hands of extremists. Around these organizations and around the frequent "Jacobin Club" meetings at the former Jacobin monastery there arose a unique revolutionary subculture. The *sans-culottes,* literally those "without knee breeches," scrapped the aristocratic dress code of the Old Regime. Wearing trousers and red caps, carrying pikes and muskets, they addressed one another as "citizen" and demanded equality of wealth as well as equality of political rights. Professional agitators and extremist journalists—Jacques Hébert, Georges Danton, Jean-Paul Marat, and Camille Desmoulins—rubbed shoulders with foreign hangers-on of revolution like the Prussian ex-baron and "orator of the human race," Anacharsis Clootz. With such leaders to spur it, revolutionary Paris was soon ready to turn its pikes and cannon even on the Assembly, should it suspect it of betraying the Revolution.

Those representatives gave Paris its chance soon enough, for the conduct of the king rendered all forms of moderation suspect. Louis had maintained secret contacts with royalist elements in the Constituent Assembly, with his many relatives who had fled abroad, and with Austria. In June 1791 he made a dash for the nearest friendly border, that of Austrian Belgium. But town authorities blocked the royal family's escape at Varennes, just short of safety. Once more France's king, queen, and crown prince returned to the Tuileries in humiliating captivity.

Louis' failed escape made the constitution practically useless even before its formal adoption in September 1791. The Constituent Assembly found itself with a monarch who had publicly demonstrated his disloyalty to revolutionary France. Louis continued to appoint ministers and approve legislation, but neither his throne nor his head was safe. Nor did the new Legislative Assembly, which replaced the Constituent Assembly in October 1791, prove capable of giving France stable government. Thanks to a proposal of Maximilien Robespierre, the Jacobin provincial lawyer who claimed to be the most high-principled of the revolutionaries, the Constituent Assembly had voted to bar its own members from running for the new legislature. That act of self-denial did not encourage the republican virtue it symbolized. Its main effect was to eliminate the modest store of parliamentary experience and political common sense acquired since 1789.

WAR, TERROR, AND DICTATORSHIP, 1792–94

Rather than govern, the Legislative Assembly went to war with all Europe. The dominant force in the new chamber proved to be a Jacobin group loosely associated with the commercial center of western France, Bordeaux. Collectively known as the "Gironde" after the name of Bordeaux's estuary, their leaders—Vergniaud, Isnard, and Jacques Pierre Brissot—were above all brilliant orators. The Girondin recipe for leadership was simple—war.

Playing cards of the Revolution: "Equality" and "Freedom of Religion" have taken the place of kings and queens.

FIGURE 23.1   **France at War with Europe**   **1792–1815**

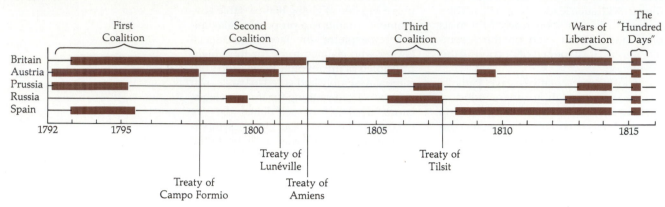

In August 1791, after the king's flight was blocked at Varennes, the emperor of Austria and the king of Prussia had proclaimed their intention to restore Louis XVI to his rightful place in full control of France. This "Declaration of Pillnitz" was a deliberately empty threat, for emperor and king had made Austro-Prussian action contingent on the improbable cooperation of the rest of Europe. Yet Austrian and Prussian hostility, and the assembling of vengeful French refugee nobles in the German states along the Rhine, gave the Paris war party its chance. War, in Isnard's fervent words to the Assembly, was "indispensable for completing the revolution." At home, it would consolidate Girondin power. Abroad, a "crusade for universal liberty," a war "of peoples against kings," would smash the old order in Europe as the Revolution had done in France.

Robespierre, almost alone, made a stand against war. The enemies of the Revolution, he insisted in debate with Brissot at the Jacobin Club, were inside France. King, court, and aristocrats wanted war and French defeat in order to reverse the Revolution. But Brissot's promises of easy victory over an immense conspiracy of "kings against peoples" carried the excitable members of the Legislative Assembly. In April 1792 France declared on Austria a war that soon expanded to embrace all Europe. Except for a brief interval in 1802–03, the war lasted until France's defeat in 1814–15 (see Figure 23-1).

The Fall of the Monarchy: August–September 1792

The Gironde did not survive that long. The first act of the war galvanized Paris, and Paris destroyed first the monarchy and then the Gironde. The 1792 campaign began badly. Revolutionary indiscipline, lack of supplies, and the emigration of many aristocratic officers crippled the army. Prussian

Robespierre, "the Incorruptible."

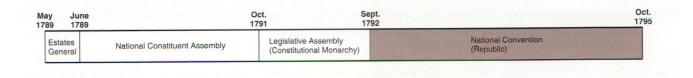

May 1789	June 1789		Oct. 1791	Sept. 1792		Oct. 1795
Estates General	National Constituent Assembly		Legislative Assembly (Constitutional Monarchy)	National Convention (Republic)		

and Austrian forces advanced clumsily into eastern France. On July 25 the Prussian commander, the Duke of Brunswick, publicly proclaimed his intention of "delivering the King, the Queen, and the royal family from their captivity." That well-intentioned announcement seemed to the revolutionary extremists the final proof that Louis XVI and his Austrian queen were conspiring with the enemy. The result was the "second revolution," the Paris insurrection of August 10, 1792.

That day far surpassed Bastille Day in violence. The king fled the Tuileries palace before the attacking crowd and revolutionary troops closed in. While his Swiss guards died at their posts, he placed himself and his family under the protection of the Legislative Assembly. That body, itself facing the pikes and cannon of the Paris wards, voted to "suspend" the king. A temporary executive council took charge until the election of a new legislature by universal male suffrage. The equality of "one man, one vote" thus came to France, and to Europe, for the first time. With it came equality of another kind. The guillotine (p. 596), set up in a Paris square for the first time on August 13, extended to all the nobility's former privilege of death by decapitation.

The fall of the monarchy moved the Marquis de Lafayette, now commander of the French army in Belgium, to defect to the Austrians; the Revolution had no more room for moderates. The Austro-Prussians seized the key border fortress of Verdun. In Paris, the fiery orator Danton urged the nation to rise: "Gentlemen, we need boldness [*de l'audace*], boldness, always boldness, and France is saved." On September 20, 1792, at the battle of Valmy, the revolutionary armies held, to the cry of "*Vive la Nation!*" The Old Regime's artillery, the best in Europe, persuaded the Prussians to withdraw.

Revolutionary Paris, without help from either Brissot or Robespierre, had again imposed its will on France on August 10. But it was not yet finished. Two hours after Danton's passionate plea for boldness, the Paris *Commune* summoned the crowds to arm themselves against Prussians and counter-revolutionaries. Deranged rumors of a plot—to release imprisoned aristocrats to slaughter the wives and children of patriots—inspired mobs to attack the Paris prisons. Brutal and sometimes drunken crowds massacred between 1,100 and 1,400 aristocrats of all ages and both sexes, along with priests and other prisoners. Robespierre immediately justified these "September Massacres": "Do you want a Revolution without revolution?" He and his Jacobin associates now sought to turn the fury of Paris against their Girondin rivals.

The Convention Executes the King

The new French Republic appeared to be the culmination of the Revolution. Within a year its partisans had remade even the calendar. September 22, 1793 became the first day of Year I, and Sundays disappeared. The red, white, and blue tricolor of France replaced the Bourbon family's white banner with lilies. The *Marseillaise,* rousing and bloodthirsty marching song of a battalion from Marseille called to Paris during the August 10 uprising, became the national anthem.

The new assembly, the National Convention, was the most revolutionary of France's many legislative bodies after 1789. For good reason. Public voting under the scrutiny of the revolutionaries, not secret ballot, had been the preferred method of election. Only 10 percent of France's eligible population was brave enough or friendly enough to the Revolution to vote. Brissot and his Girondin

Louis XVI in prison after the August 1792 insurrection, by Joseph Ducreux.

companions returned, reelected in the provinces and outnumbering Robespierre and his partisans.

But Robespierre took the initiative at home while the French armies, buoyed up by a fierce national pride, invaded Belgium and crossed the Rhine. In late November the revolutionaries discovered in the Tuileries palace a safe containing Louis XVI's secret correspondence with the refugee nobles. Robespierre and his terrifying young associate, Louis Antoine Saint-Just, demanded the Louis' execution without trial: he was guilty not merely of treason, but of being a king. The Convention nevertheless decided to try the case itself.

The trial desperately embarrassed the Gironde, which despite its hostility to the monarchy shrank from killing the king. Others were more resolute. Revolutionary conviction—and fear of Robespierre, the Jacobin extremists, and the Paris crowd—spurred the Convention to convict Louis XVI of treason and other crimes. He died under the guillotine on January 21, 1793. Now at last there was no going back. The Revolution had killed a king who had ruled by divine right. A week later, the French Republic declared war on Great Britain and its ally Holland.

The "Despotism of Liberty": The Committee of Public Safety

Internal crisis and external defeat again combined to drive the Revolution to extremes. Food riots in February and March 1793 kept the pressure on the Convention. In March, the military conscription decreed in revolutionary Paris provoked the Catholic peasants of the Vendée, in the backward far west of France, to revolt under royalist leaders. That guerrilla war dragged on for years and cost the young Republic dearly. The commander of the French army in the low countries, Charles Dumouriez, defected after losing decisively to the Austrians at the battle of Neerwinden. The supposedly oppressed peoples on France's borders fought against the French "crusade for universal liberty" rather than for it. The second city of France, Lyons, rose in May 1793. In June and July much of the south, including

Marseille, followed. Royalists handed over to a British fleet the great Mediterranean naval base of Toulon.

The Convention proved equal to these challenges. In March it established a revolutionary court and "surveillance committees" to crush dissent and counter-revolution. In April it gave France an executive, the Committee of Public Safety. To pacify Paris, it temporarily imposed price controls (the "maximum") on grain and flour, and sent rapacious foraging parties into the countryside. Danton and Robespierre attacked the Gironde for alleged complicity with the traitor Dumouriez. The Convention, surrounded by the crowds of the Paris wards armed with 150 cannon, decreed the arrest of the Gironde for treason in June 1793. In July, Robespierre and Saint-Just joined the Committee of Public Safety. France, for the first time since Louis XIV, had a government determined to rule.

The Committee included Lazare Carnot, the "organizer of victory," for the army, Lindet for food supplies, Barère for relations with the Convention, and the men of blood, Billaud-Varenne and Collot d'Herbois, for hunting down the Revolution's internal enemies. Ideological leadership rested with "the incorruptible," Robespierre, and with his associate Saint-Just. Although it was responsible in theory to the Convention, in practice the Committee of Public Safety ruled France alone for the next year. Its rule, which the revolutionary martyr Marat hailed as the "despotism of liberty," was more absolute than that of the Old Regime, and infinitely more effective.

Against the external enemy, the Committee ordered in August 1793 the mobilization of the entire population by the famed *levée en masse*. By 1794 850,000 men were under arms, far outnumbering the armies of the kings France faced. Against the peasant guerrillas of the Vendée, the Committee sent General Kellermann, victor over the Prussians at Valmy, with orders to deport noncombatants and seize crops and livestock. After the army reconquered Lyons, Collot d'Herbois and Joseph Fouché, emissaries of the Committee, killed thousands in reprisal for the revolt. The Convention changed the very name of Lyons to *Ville-Affranchie* ("Freed-City"). At Toulon an artillery major of Corsican birth, Napoleon Bonaparte, found the key to driving the British fleet from the harbor and retaking the city. His reward was promotion to brigadier general at the age of 23. By the end of 1793 the emergency in the south was over.

The Great Terror, 1793–94

The Committee and its lesser ally, the Committee of General Security, also moved to monopolize terror. That instrument was too important to leave to the Paris agitators and crowds to whom the Convention and the Committees owed their power. The Committee and the Convention damped down the Paris ward meetings, muzzled the press, and arrested some leading extremists in September 1793.

But the Committee of Public Safety's chief business was with those who were not extreme enough. "The gods," wrote the Robespierrist journalist Desmoulins, "are thirsty"—for blood. Marie Antoinette, tried for treason and on fraudulent charges of immorality, died bravely in October. The Gironde went to the guillotine in November. Aristocrats, monarchist politicians, failed generals ("to encourage the others") followed. In the provinces, the traveling representatives of the Committees dispensed death to priests, aristocrats, and moderates by portable guillotine, firing squad, grapeshot, and "vertical deportation" (drowning). Perhaps 20,000 men and women perished in the Great Terror of 1793–94. Although that was a small number by the standards set by twentieth-century revolutions, the Terror left memories in France that long endured.

Yet even after the elimination of the Girondins, Robespierre was unable to rest. The theories of the Enlightenment decreed that society, freed of the chains of the Old Regime, would spontaneously express a General Will. Yet Robespierre bitterly recognized that the Revolution had failed to produce "one will, *one.*" The fault therefore had to be that of the remaining evil men—plotters, traitors, Parisian ward extremists, lukewarm Jacobins, and counter-revolutionaries. It was not simply war and

---

The Modern State Mobilizes Its Citizens: The Levée en Masse

Barère to the Convention, August 23, 1793:

From this moment, until our enemies have been driven from the territory of the Republic, the entire French nation is permanently called to the colors. The young men will go into battle; married men will forge weapons and transport supplies; women will make tents and uniforms, and serve in the hospitals; children will make old cloth into bandages; old men will have themselves carried to the public squares to rouse the courage of the warriors and preach hatred of kings, and the unity of the Republic.

From Archives parlementaires de 1787 à 1860, *première série (Paris: Librairie Administrative de Paul Dupont, 1907), Vol. 72, p. 674 (translation by M. Knox).*

The Spirit of the Terror: Sayings of Saint-Just

This man [Louis XVI] must reign or die. . . . All kings are rebels and usurpers.

To the Convention, November 1792

The French people votes the liberty of the world.

Draft constitution, April 1793

The people and its enemies have nothing more in common except the sword. . . . *We must oppress tyrants.*

To the Convention, October 1793

Spare the aristocracy, and you will give yourselves fifty years of troubles. *Dare!* That one word summarizes the entire politics of our Revolution.

To the Convention, February 1794

There is something terrifying in the sacred love of one's country. It is so all-exclusive that it sacrifices everything, without pity, without fear, without regard for humanity, to the public interest. . . . You cannot make a republic with compromises, but only with ruthless severity, inflexible severity, toward those who have betrayed.

To the Convention, for the Committee of Public Safety, demanding the heads of Danton and others, March 1794

From Louis-Antoine de Saint-Just, Pages Choisies *(Paris: Éditions du Point du Jour, 1947), pp. 121, 123, 162, 199, 206, 223; and Denis Roche, ed.,* La liberté ou la mort *(Paris: Tchou, 1969), p. 49 (translation by M. Knox).*

Portrait de Marie Antoinette

Queen Marie Antoinette resolutely faces the guillotine (sketched from life by David).

internal threat that drove the revolutionaries to shed ever more blood. It was their faith in the perfectibility of humanity and their claim to embody the General Will.

The leaders of the Paris crowd, Hébert and the *Enragés,* or "wild men," were even more radical than the Committee of Public Safety. In March 1794 they tried to lead yet another Paris revolt. They failed and perished under the falling blade. Those more moderate than Robespierre—Danton, Desmoulins, and their allies in the center of the Convention—helped him against the Paris extremists. Then the moderate Jacobins began to plead for a relaxation of the Terror, for freedom of the press, and even for peace—for the spring of 1794 was a spring of French victories. Within a week of the decapitation of Hébert, the Committee arrested Danton and his allies. Saint-Just accused them of treason before the Convention. They too died.

With these blows against Hébertists and Dantonists, the Committee created a

wasteland around itself. The execution of the "wild men" destroyed its support in the Paris wards. That of the Dantonists weakened the Committee's hold on the center of the Convention, the moderates from the provinces who held the parliamentary balance. The Committee now ruled by terror alone. The pace of arrests and executions swiftly increased. More than 1,400 perished in Paris alone in June and July 1794.

The Revolution Ends: Thermidor, July–August 1794

Victory sealed the fate of Robespierre, as defeat had that of the Gironde. French troops, ever more experienced and more numerous, flooded once more across Belgium. The military emergency that had justified terror was over. The associates of Robespierre began to think of their own survival. Relative moderates such as Carnot joined with jealous members of the Committee of General Security. The bloodiest-handed of all, Collot d'Herbois and Billaud-Varenne, hoped the elimination of Robespierre would provide their own ticket to respectability. The center of the Convention secretly offered support.

An ominous speech in which Robespierre threatened unspecified enemies spurred the plotters to act before it was too late. On July 27, 1794—9 Thermidor by the revolutionary calendar—the plotters bodily prevented Robespierre from speaking to the Convention. Then they rushed through a decree for the arrest of the Robespierrists. The Paris wards, summoned to the rescue, responded poorly; they too had suffered under the Committee's dictatorship. The next day, 10 Thermidor, Robespierre, Saint-Just, and company went to the guillotine to which they had sent so many others. The Revolution had "iced over," Saint-Just wrote shortly before his arrest. The Robespierrists themselves, by their elimination of Hébert and the Paris ward agitators, had halted the seemingly unstoppable movement toward ever greater extremes. The Revolution was over, except for the endless war it had launched.

Here Lies All of France: cartoon of Robespierre executing the last Frenchman—the executioner.

FRANCE FROM THE CONVENTION TO THE DIRECTORY, 1794–99

The "reaction" of Thermidor, as it soon became known, produced a widespread sense of relief at the end of terror and of revolutionary attempts to remold human nature. French society, no longer cowed by terror and censorship, reasserted itself. The urban middle classes that had profited from the Revolution now sought to enjoy themselves in a frenetic round of banquets and dances. The *salons* reappeared, now led by educated women from the middle classes instead of the aristocracy. In their drawing rooms former terrorists drank champagne with former aristocrats and with the Revolution's new rich, the land speculators and army contractors. The "gilded youth" of the better-off quarters of Paris equipped themselves with clubs, and went to hunt Jacobins. In the provinces, a royalist "white terror" against republicans reenacted the horrors of the terror of the revolutionary Committees.

The relaxation of the price controls which the Robespierrists had imposed led to new Paris food riots in April and May 1795. But the Convention suppressed them, along with the last large-scale Paris revolt in October. In the last case, the young General Bonaparte mowed down the crowd with field artillery. Grapeshot, scientifically employed by loyal and experienced troops, had made 1789–style urban insurrection obsolete.

What Thermidor failed to provide was a stable government responsive to the new society, organized by wealth rather than rank, that was emerging from the Revolution. Ending the dictatorship of the revolutionary executive automatically meant increasing the danger of a restoration of the monarchy. The Convention nevertheless weakened the Committee of Public Safety by rotating its members and reducing its powers. In 1795, the Convention drafted and adopted yet another constitution, which remained in effect until the end of 1799. It replaced the Committee with a Directory of five members and supplanted the Convention itself with a new legislature, the Five Hundred. Wealth once more became a prerequisite for voting.

The five directors included Carnot, the Vicomte de Barras, and Jean-François Reubell, an Alsatian who believed that the Rhine was France's "natural frontier." Two-thirds of the Five Hundred were to come by law from the outgoing Convention—the so-called "perpetuals." The Convention intended this measure as a guarantee against royalist agitation in the provinces. It helped achieve that goal, but at the price of discrediting the new regime's claim that it represented the nation.

The remaining threat from Paris soon subsided. A poor harvest and an unprecedentedly severe winter in 1795–96 reduced the poor to near-starvation. Survival, not revolt, became the chief concern of the remaining *sans-culottes*. The last major attempt to mobilize Paris was the so-called "Conspiracy of the Equals" in the spring of 1796. The "Equals," especially Gracchus Babeuf and the Italian revolutionary Filippo Buonarroti, confusedly advocated extreme egalitarianism and a primitive agrarian communism. Their plot failed, but left an ideological legacy for the future.

It was the royalists who threatened the middle-class republic of 1795–99. But fortunately for the Directory, the young son of Louis XVI died in prison in June 1795. His uncle, in exile, took the title of Louis XVIII and announced his intention of restoring the Old Regime in its entirety. That program inevitably alienated both the constitutional monarchists and the powerful middle-class and peasant groups that had done well during the Revolution. A royalist uprising in the west of France poorly coordinated with a British and royalist landing at Quiberon ended in failure and massacre in 1795. Royalist deputies nevertheless did well enough in elections in 1797 and 1798 to force the Directors to undertake a series of coups d'état and purges to maintain control of the Five Hundred.

Stability and representative government had been impossible under the Convention because of the strength of the disloyal opposition and the exaggerated expectations of unity of ideologues such as Robespierre. They were likewise impossible under the Directory. By the end, by December 1799, the regime rested only on the army.

SON OF THE REVOLUTION: BONAPARTE, 1799–1815

That army had in the hard years since 1792 acquired matchless experience and prestige. The Old Regime had left it the most mobile and powerful artillery in Europe, and the innovative tactical and strategic theories of Guibert and Bourcet. The Revolution's war "of peoples against kings" had unleashed the energies and loyalties needed to use those theories to the fullest. The result was a new kind of warfare.

The man of destiny: the young Napoleon, by David.

Under the Old Regime, the eagerness of troops to desert and the inadequacy of the supply services had restricted the size and mobility of armies. No commander could easily control, feed, and move more than 70,000 men. But the new French armies, filled with nationalist fervor, deserted less often and showed a fierce initiative on the battlefield. Their leaders could trust them to fight as skirmishers, tormenting the rigid ranks of the Old Regime's armies as the American revolutionaries had tormented the British redcoats. The new armies could march dispersed, in self-contained "divisions" of 8,000 to 10,000 infantry equipped with their own artillery for support. This style of movement helped prevent bottlenecks and allowed the troops to feed themselves by looting the countryside as they passed. The division, and still more the next largest unit, the *army corps* of perhaps 30,000 men, had unparalleled offensive and defensive power. Corps could and did hold against an entire enemy army—until other French corps arrived with crushing effect on the flank or rear of the enemy. Concentration of forces on the move, on the field of battle itself, repalced the Old Regime's rigid and time-consuming deployments. The new system of warfare, the ruthlessness of the French revolutionary commanders, and the numbers, fervor, and readiness for sacrifice of the troops overwhelmed their traditionalist opponents.

The supreme master of the new techniques, and the ultimate beneficiary of the army's role as the Directory's sole support, was the young General Bonaparte. He had proved his usefulness to the Directory by crushing the Paris crowd in October 1795. After marriage to the fascinating Joséphine de Beauharnais, the former mistress of the Director Barras, Bonaparte received command of the Army of Italy in the spring of 1796. He was 27 years old.

The Directory's chief war aim was to secure the west bank of the Rhine; Italy was a sideshow. But Bonaparte made it the main theater. He began the fateful extension of French conquest far beyond the "natural frontiers" supposedly sought by Louis XIV. In the brilliant campaign of

1796–97, he smashed first the Piedmontese allies of the Austrians, then the Austrians themselves. Increasingly independent of the Directory, he ruled and looted north Italy as he pleased. In 1797 the Austrians sued for peace. By the Treaty of Campo Formio they relinquished their claims to Belgium and to the rich north Italian plain. In compensation they received from Bonaparte and the Directory a cynical gift, the once-proud republic of Venice.

By late 1797 France thus dominated Europe from Holland to north Italy. Prussia, busy seizing its share of the third and final partition of Poland, had made peace as early as 1795. Only Britain, surrounded by the seas and its fleet, fought on. The First Coalition against Revolutionary France had collapsed.

Bonaparte, the Revolution and Europe

For Bonaparte, the Revolution was "an idea that has found bayonets." France's ever-broadening rule indeed meant more than the rights of man. Intellectuals in lands as different as Britain, Germany, and Italy had initially greeted the Revolution with delight. "Bliss was it in that dawn to be alive / And to be young was very heaven," the English poet William Wordsworth wrote of 1789. Others were less optimistic. As early as 1790 the passionate Anglo-Irish parliamentarian and political philosopher Edmund Burke prophesied, in his *Reflections on the Revolution in France,* that the uprooting of historic institutions would lead to the rule of "some popular general."

The common people on France's borders soon found that occupation by the republic's armed hordes brought pillage and rape, the systematic exactions of French officialdom, and attacks on the Church. Even the "rights of man" offended deeply held popular prejudices such as those against the Jews. That liberty and equality came to much of Europe by French conquest was ominous: the counter-nationalisms that French ideas and French bayonets summoned up might eventually oppose democracy at home. For the moment, sporadic urban revolts and guerrilla struggles

CANONNIER.

did no more than annoy the victorious Republic.

"Great battles are won by artillery," wrote Napoleon of his favorite weapon.

A New French Empire in the Middle East?

Fearing inactivity, and wary of premature involvement in the intrigues around the Directory, Bonaparte sought the leadership of a French expedition to Egypt in 1798. That dependency of the Ottoman Empire, the Directory thought, had potential as a French colony that would help make up for the empire lost in 1763. It might also threaten Britain's road to India.

That French ambition did not survive the destruction of the French fleet at the battle of the Nile in August 1798. Horatio Nelson, Britain's greatest naval leader, cut Bonaparte's sea communications and marooned him and his 40,000 troops. After a year of difficult campaigning against

Egyptians, Turks, and British, Bonaparte slipped stealthily back to France. His abandoned army ultimately surrendered to the British.

Strategically, that outcome was no surprise. French domination, then and later, ended at the high-tide mark. But in cultural terms the Egyptian expedition gave an immense impulse to Western historical and linguistic studies. Bonaparte, a man of the Enlightenment, had taken with him to Egypt teams of experts to study the monuments and to loot the artifacts of one of the oldest civilizations in continuous existence. In the booty the French swept up and the British later captured was a stone slab found at Rosetta in the Nile delta (and now in the British Museum in London). On it are three inscriptions of the same text: one in ancient Greek, one in phonetic Egyptian script, and one in Egyptian hieroglyphics. The "Rosetta stone" provided the key with which a brilliant young scholar, Jean-François Champollion, deciphered the hieroglyphics in 1821–22. That achievement opened the road to the reconstruction of three millennia of Egyptian history. The Egyptian expedition symbolized more than European colonial greed. It also demonstrated the West's voracious curiosity, which in the coming century blossomed into a series of new disciplines aimed at understanding other cultures—comparative history, philology and linguistics, anthropology, and sociology.

From First Consul to Emperor, 1799–1804

Bonaparte timed his return to France in October 1799 perfectly. A Second Coalition against France had replaced the first. The Egyptian expedition had drawn Russia into the war, for Tsar Paul resented non-Russian attempts to bully the Turks. The Austrians also resumed fighting. A short but nasty Russian incursion into Switzerland and north Italy thoroughly alarmed French opinion. The Directory, its members at odds, was utterly discredited. Restoration of the monarchy threatened once more.

Sieyès, the propagandist of the Third Estate who had helped launch the Revolu-

tion, had survived the Terror by being discreet. In May 1799 he reemerged to join the Directory. He sought one last coup d'état to stabilize the rule of the beneficiaries of the Revolution, the Third Estate. For that he needed "a saber," a tame general. Sieyès approached Bonaparte, who accepted the role but with a difference: he would make this coup for himself.

And so, on November 9 and 10, 1799—18 Brumaire of the soon-to-be discarded revolutionary calendar—Bonaparte struck. With the help of his politician brother Lucien, Sieyès, and army bayonets, he cowed the legislature and assumed power as "First Consul." Sieyès found himself shunted off into gilded retirement. Much of French opinion had hoped for and expected a monarch. Instead, France got a dictator.

To consolidate his power, Bonaparte fell back on the technique of which he was the unparalleled master: battle. In the spring of 1800 he once more led a French army across the Alps, and attacked the Austrians in the rear. A close and bloody French victory at Marengo, and another on the German front, forced Austria to negotiate. The Second Coalition, as disunited as the first, collapsed. By the Treaty of Lunéville (February 1801), Austria conceded hegemony in Italy and the Rhine frontier to France. Russia, under the mad tsar Paul, had already withdrawn from the war. In March 1802, even Britain negotiated a grudging peace, the Treaty of Amiens. Britain's merchant elite was willing to try coexistence with the "Corsican tyrant," although continuing French control of Holland and Belgium was a far greater threat to British security than any conquest of Louis XIV.

Victory and peace enabled Napoleon, as he now began to style himself, to strengthen his grip on France. In 1802 he had himself proclaimed "First Consul for Life" and in 1804 "Emperor of the French." The pope, with whom Napoleon had signed in 1801 a treaty that partially bridged the gap between France and the Church, presided at the imperial coronation. But in an act contrary to custom that symbolized his will to power, Napoleon crowned himself.

Napoleon's rule brought France more than a new Bonaparte dynasty, complete with an improvised aristocracy of generals and Corsican relatives. For it was Napoleon, the former revolutionary, who at last brought enlightened absolutism to France by completing the Old Regime's drive toward centralization. In 1800 the Revolution's departments received permanent administrators sent from Paris. These "prefects," powerful successors to the Old Regime's *intendants* as the representatives of the central will in the provinces, long outlasted Napoleon. His model of the modern, centralized, bureaucratic state was one of the most powerful legacies of the Revolution. It swiftly found imitators throughout continental Europe and—much later—the non-Western world.

Along with centralization came legal uniformity. Napoleon's second major innovation in government was his law code, eventually known as the *Code Napoléon*. It replaced with a single national code the Old Regime's patchwork of customary and Roman law. It proclaimed equality before the law, reverence for property, and the supremacy of the male head of the family. The Code, like the prefects, was a much-imitated model. French bayonets imposed it in the ever-larger areas of Germany, Italy, and the Netherlands that Napoleon annexed. Its example moved French satellites and even enemies to institute legal reforms. Eventually only England, with its constitution formed through the slow accumulation of custom and precedent, remained untouched.

Napoleon's Conquest of Europe, 1803–07

Works of peace did not satisfy Napoleon's ambition for long. Starting in late 1802, he dispatched agents to the Middle East and prepared to stir up trouble for Britain in India. In Germany, after Lunéville, Napoleon oversaw a "princes' revolution" by which the larger states gobbled up lesser princes and Church rulers. That display of French power offended Austria, which still held token overlordship over the now crippled Holy Roman Empire.

The British, confident that a new coalition would soon form, resumed the war in May 1803. At first London stood alone, and Napoleon concentrated 400,000 men of his newly reorganized *Grande Armée* along the Channel coast. Southern England was virtually defenseless by land. "If we can be the masters of the narrows for six hours, we shall be masters of the world," Napoleon wrote to one of his admirals. But like Philip II of Spain and Louis XIV, Napoleon found the British fleet blocking his path to universal domination.

Thwarted at sea, Napoleon turned in 1805 to a land campaign in Germany. There he could bring his skill and France's power to bear. His coronation as emperor, with its overtones of a claim to the legacy of Charlemagne, had alarmed the Austrians. His crowning in May 1805 as "emperor" of the satellite kingdom of north Italy—where Charlemagne had also ruled—proved the final act that brought a new coalition into being. Austria and Russia now joined England. Irresolute Prussia, intent on absorbing the fat, English-ruled German state of Hanover, remained neutral.

Napoleon flung the *Grande Armée* from the Channel coast into south Germany before the Austrians and the Russians could join forces. One Austrian army, under the inept General Mack, found itself surrounded and forced to surrender at Ulm on October 20. But the next day, in the distant seas off Spain, the British navy reversed Napoleon's run of luck. At Cape Trafalgar Nelson captured or sank more than half the combined French-Spanish fleet. He paid with his life, but made sure that Napoleon could never repeat the invasion threat of 1803–04. Britain's victory at Trafalgar and the arrival of Russian armies in central Europe propelled Prussia slowly toward the coalition.

To free himself from this growing threat, Napoleon characteristically chose battle. He lured the combined Austro-Russian forces to attack him prematurely. On December 2, at Austerlitz north of Vienna, he faced 90,000 Austrians and Russians with 70,000 French, and broke the enemy line with an unexpected thrust. The Austro-Russians lost 27,000 dead and prisoners to Napoleon's 8,000 casualties, and Austria left the war. It was Napoleon's most brilliant victory.

Austria's collapse made Napoleon master of Germany, which he had already helped to remodel after Lunéville. Now Napoleon imposed a second round of revolution from above. The decrepit Holy Roman Empire died unlamented. Napoleon replaced it with a league of satellite states, the Confederation of the Rhine.

Napoleon's claim to universal domination: the emperor on his throne, by Ingres (1806).

Germany's remaining small states fell prey to their more powerful neighbors. In 1801 Germany had more than 1,800 separate political units. By the end of 1806 fewer than forty remained. Centralization was convenient for Napoleon's tax collectors, and for the Bonaparte relatives who received German states as gifts. But it also proved a mighty step toward the German nation-state that within a century came to dwarf and humiliate France.

Only Prussia, afraid that Napoleon would make peace with London and force it to give up Hanover, remained outside Napoleon's new German alliance. In October 1806, alone except for promises from distant St. Petersburg, Prussia went to war. Within a week Napoleon had launched the *Grande Armée* around the flank of the rigidly old-regime Prussian army. On October 14, 1806, converging French corps annihilated the Prussians at the twin battles of Jena and Auerstädt.

Within weeks Napoleon was in Potsdam with his generals, paying homage at the tomb of Frederick the Great: "Hats off, gentlemen; if *he* were still alive, we would not be here." But unlike Austria the year before, Prussia did not quit at once. Europe's resistance to Napoleon's increasingly open claim to universal domination was gradually stiffening. In cooperation with their Russian allies, the Prussians fought on in Poland. There, unlike the green lands of western Europe, the French found little to eat. The few roads were ice-covered bogs. The Russians appeared in force, and in the great slaughter at Eylau in February 1807 proved dogged though unimaginative foes. The coming of summer allowed the French to maneuver. At Friedland in June Napoleon finally crushed the Russians with a victory he proclaimed "as decisive as Austerlitz, Marengo, and Jena."

Tsar Alexander, the erratic grandson of the great Catherine and son of the madman Paul, whose murder in a palace coup in 1801 he had secretly welcomed, offered negotiations. Alexander met Napoleon at Tilsit on their common border, and totally reversed Russian policy. Not for the last time, Russia agreed to divide Europe into western and eastern spheres of influence.

Napoleon kept Germany, including Alexander's Prussian ally. To Russia fell Finland, Sweden, and Turkey. Alexander in return secertly promised to declare war on England and to help the French close the Continent to British trade.

That trade boycott, given the loss of much of the French navy at Trafalgar, was Napoleon's only weapon against Britain. In the Berlin Decree, issued in November 1806, he had declared a "blockade" against British exports to the Continent, confident that state bankruptcy and revolts by factory workers thrown suddenly out of work would force London to make peace. But this "Continental System" had leaks. Along the coastline that stretched from Spain to Russia, smugglers plied a roaring trade with the British, with corrupt French officials as accomplices. And Britain managed to keep its other markets open. Until 1812 it avoided war with its most powerful seagoing trading partner, the United States, despite bitter conflict over British searches and seizures of U.S. vessels. And in 1812–15, when the United States did go to war with Britain, Na-

poleon's break with Russia once again opened Scandinavia and Russia to British exports.

Europe Begins to Fight Back, 1808–12

The failure of the Continental System was only one sign that Napoleon's power had begun to wane after the agreement at Tilsit. More serious was rising resistance on the Continent. Revolutionary France had invented modern nationalism, and through it had tapped unprecedented military power. Now others, in Prussia and even in Austria, began to follow France's example. But Napoleon's first major setback on land came in a country scarcely touched by modern ideas—Spain.

There, in 1808, a savage guerrilla war broke out against the French troops Napoleon had sent to put his brother Joseph on the throne of the Spanish Bourbons. In scenes fixed forever in historical memory by the genius of the Spanish painter Francisco Goya, the French shot, hanged, and impaled the guerrillas, who in return

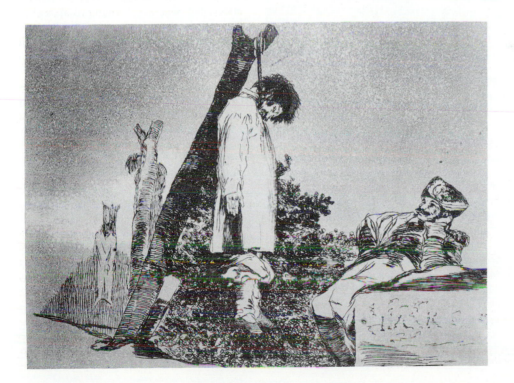

A Goya sketch of "The Disasters of War": A French dragoon contemplates Spaniards he has hanged.

hacked at the French with improvised weapons. Nobles, priests, and brigands led the masses, for the revolt was as much a reaction against the Enlightenment ideas the French brought as against the French themselves.

Unaided, the Spanish revolt might eventually have petered out, but Britain soon sent armies to Spain and Portugal. On the outskirts of Europe, sea communications were more efficient than the appalling Spanish roads that linked the French armies to Paris. The Duke of Wellington, a skillful commander already proven in India, found a secure base at Lisbon. The "Spanish ulcer" resisted treatment by Napoleon in person in late 1808. Thereafter he left Spain to less competent subordinates, and Wellington's army gradually wore the French down.

In Germany, the Tilsit settlement failed to stamp out the embers of a modern nationalism that eventually proved more terrifying than that of the French. Germany's sense of nationhood was at least as old as Luther's German Bible. The cultural revival of the late eighteenth century had given Germans a justified pride in their literature, which by the 1790s had begun to rival that of France. But it was French conquest that brought German nationalism into politics, while making it peculiarly militant. And the imposition of the "rights of man and the citizen" and of the *Code Napoléon* on Germany by an outside force helped make German nationalism potentially antidemocratic. In France, nationalism was subversive of the Old Regime. In Germany and farther east, nationalism might serve to reinforce it.

That was certainly the lesson that Prussian soldiers and bureaucrats drew from their defeat in 1806–07. King Frederick William III, with his territories halved after Tilsit, was even willing to appeal to his people in order to survive. He gave power to a cadre of unconventional civil servants and generals: Karl vom und zum Stein, Karl August von Hardenberg, August von Gneisenau, Gerhard von Scharnhorst. To defeat the French, Prussia needed what Hardenberg described as a "revolution in the good sense," an authoritarian "revolution from above." The reformers abolished serfdom, although dogged resistance from the nobility prevented full implementation. They gave towns and cities limited self-government in order to bring the population into politics in support of the Prussian state. They abolished most of Frederick the Great's restrictions on freedom of commerce and industry, and opened land ownership to non-nobles. Above all, they laid the basis for universal military service—decreed in 1814—and for the recruitment of non-noble officers. Their military-bureaucratic revolution from above sought to shore up enlightened absolutism with popular sup-

Prussia Responds: Revolution from Above

Baron von Hardenberg to King Frederick William III, "On the Reorganization of the Prussian State," September 12, 1807:

The French Revolution, of which the present wars are the continuation, has given the French amid bloodshed and upheaval entirely new energies. . . . Neighbors and conquered have been carried away by the flood. All barriers created to dam it up have proved feeble. . . .

The illusion that we could withstand the Revolution most effectively by holding fast to the old . . . has itself resulted in the promotion and ever greater extension of the Revolution. The power of its principles is so great, they are so generally recognized and widely spread, that the state that fails to take them up voluntarily will either suffer destruction or be compelled from outside to accept them. . . .

Therefore, our goal, our guiding principle, is a revolution in the good sense, leading straight to the great purpose of the ennoblement of humanity through the wisdom of those in authority, rather than through a violent upheaval from below or without. Democratic principles in a monarchical government: that seems to me the form appropriate to the current spirit of the age. . . .

In other, but similar circumstances, although under an entirely different spirit of the age, Elector Frederick William the Great revolutionized . . . his state and laid the foundations for its later greatness.

From Georg Winter, ed., Die Reorganisation des Preussischen Staates unter Stein und Hardenberg *(Leipzig: S. Hirzel, 1931), Vol. I, pp. 305–306 (translation by M. Knox).*

port. Its ultimate consequence was "bu-reaucratic absolutism," a power-state that bureaucrats and officers ruled under a thin veneer of royal authority.

For the moment, the Prussian reform-ers could only hope that Napoleon would somehow falter. Austria, in April 1809, took Napoleon's Spanish defeats as a sig-nal to renew the war. The Habsburgs in-cited the Tyrolean mountaineers, whom Napoleon had separated from Austria, to a desperate guerrilla revolt. Dynastic Vi-enna appealed publicly to "the German nation." The old regime was learning new tricks. The Habsburg Archduke Charles, one of the most talented of Napoleon's opponents, fought him to a standstill at Aspern, near Vienna. Then Napoleon tri-umphed in a grueling two-day struggle at Wagram on July 5–6, 1809. Victory was becoming more difficult. The rest of Eu-rope had begun to imitate the Revolution.

Austria nevertheless sued for peace after Wagram. Its new foreign minister, Clemens von Metternich, bought Napo-leon's good graces with the marriage offer of a Habsburg archduchess, Marie-Louise. Napoleon was happy to accept, and to discard Joséphine Beauharnais. A mar-riage alliance with the oldest major ruling house of Europe would give the upstart Bonaparte dynasty much-needed legit-imacy.

The End: From Moscow to Saint Helena, 1812–15

Yet Napoleon's power still rested on force, and with defeat in Russia in 1812, that force melted away. Until the end of 1811 Napoleon had expected to hold Tsar Alex-ander to the Tilsit bargain with threats. But Russian cooperation with the Continental System against Britain had always been

Napoleonic Europe   1812

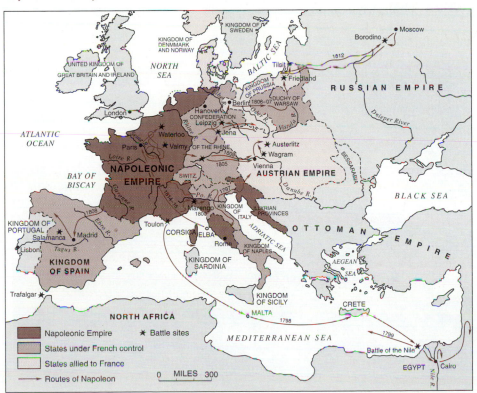

weak, and Alexander had secretly approached Prussia and Austria with proposals for a new coalition. In the spring of 1812 Napoleon broke relations with St. Petersburg and launched what he himself described as "the most difficult enterprise I have ever attempted," the invasion of Russia.

The vanguard of the largest army ever seen, more than a half-million men of whom 250,000 were French, crossed the Russian border in June 1812. The immense distances, the absence of roads, and shortage of food and fodder devoured Napoleon's *Grande Armée*. Russian resistance, compounded of equal parts courage, stubbornness, and vodka, stunned the French with its bitterness. As in Spain, guerrillas attacked French communications. Napoleon failed to force the ever-retreating Russian armies into a decisive battle. The immense slaughter at Borodino (almost 70,000 casualties) and the capture of Moscow in September 1812 were not victories. The Russian governor put the city to the torch. Tsar Alexander, perhaps fearful of being strangled like his father if he showed weakness, obstinately refused to negoti-

ate. After a fatal month of hesitation, Napoleon began an improvised withdrawal. The Russian winter and the pursuing Cossack cavalry did the rest. Perhaps 10,000 men out of the entire *Grande Armée* escaped from Russia in any condition to fight.

As Napoleon sprinted for Paris to raise a new army, Germany turned against the French. Princes, literati, and the middle classes united in an outpouring of national feeling. A mutinous Prussian general joined the advancing Russians with his army corps on New Year's Day, 1813. The Prussian state soon followed. Austria too joined the new coalition after Metternich vainly pressed Napoleon to settle for an empire confined to France and a return to the pre-1789 balance of power. Napoleon replied that any settlement short of victory would deprive him of the prestige he needed to rule France itself. It was that necessity, as well as his own immense ambition, that had spurred him toward universal empire.

Napoleon's dogged refusal to compromise thus created the coalition that finally brought France down. By August

The *Grande Armée's* flight across the icy Beresina River (late November 1812).

1813 the alliance was complete. Its forces caught and destroyed Napoleon's new and inexperienced army at Leipzig in October. The Allies had discovered how to defeat Napoleon—by coordinating their movements, giving battle only when united, and smashing Napoleon's less-talented subordinates separately before closing in on the Emperor himself.

With Germany gone and with Wellington advancing across the Pyrenees from Spain, Napoleon fought a last brilliant campaign to the north and east of Paris in the spring of 1814. He himself now suffered from a variety of ailments, his troops were green and badly outnumbered, his generals weary, and his subjects despairing from never-ending war. But he proved as dangerous as ever on the battlefield.

The coalition nevertheless held. Viscount Castlereagh, the British Foreign Secretary, welded together the unlikely allies—Britain, Austria, Russia, Prussia—with the Treaty of Chaumont (March 1814). That Quadruple Alliance pledged to fight to restore the balance of power and confine France to its traditional boundaries, and to remain united for twenty years after war's end. The Allies drove toward Paris and ignored Napoleon's last bold attempt to cut their communications. Military defeat, the plotting of his former foreign minister, Talleyrand, and the defection of key generals finally brought Napoleon down. In early April 1814 he abdicated and received from the Allies the Tuscan island of Elba for his retirement.

Louis XVIII, his relatives, and their court returned to France in the baggage trains of the victorious allied armies, and rapidly made themselves unloved. When Napoleon escaped from Elba and landed

The end, 1815: Napoleon and his staff, bound for exile on St. Helena.

in southern France in March 1815, the army rallied to him and joyous crowds carried him up the steps of the Tuileries palace.

The Allies were less delighted. Wellington and the Prussian commander, Blücher, rapidly concentrated their armies in Belgium. Napoleon, intent on one last throw of the dice, advanced to meet them. After drubbing the Prussians at Ligny he tried on June 18 to overwhelm Wellington at Waterloo before Blücher could join him. Wellington, as he freely if ungrammatically admitted, had been "never so near to being beat." Then Napoleon's Imperial Guard recoiled from the thin red line of British infantry and the Prussians attacked Napoleon's flank. Napoleon's last "Hundred Days" in power and France's career of conquest were over.

The Bourbons once more returned. Napoleon surrendered to the British, who shipped him off to the desolate South Atlantic island of St. Helena. There he occupied himself until his death in 1821 with the construction of the Napoleonic myth: that his empire built on force had been "a kind of republic" and that he himself had championed the principle of national self-determination for nations other than France.

The wars of the Republic and of the Empire had cost the *grande nation* perhaps 1.3 million lives—or one Frenchman in ten. The rapid population growth of the eighteenth century subsided as France's peasants concentrated on enjoying and conserving. France henceforth lacked the will for a serious bid to overturn the balance of power. But the Revolution and its wars had set loose in Europe ideas and forces that the victors could not still. It had unleashed, through the concept of the nation-state, new energies within and new conflicts without. It had demonstrated that a society could discard its rulers and freely adopt new myths and institutions. It had established the pattern of the modern bureaucratic state. And it had shown that popular sovereignty unlimited by law might produce a "despotism of liberty" instead of democracy. These were powerful lessons for the future.

Suggestions for Further Reading

The French Revolution

The best recent interpretive surveys are W. Doyle, *The Oxford History of the French Revolution* (1989), and D. M. G. Sutherland, *France 1789–1815: Revolution and Counter-Revolution* (1985). A. Cobban, *A History of Modern France,* Vol. I, *1715–1799* (1957), still offers a fine introductory summary. For the "classic" French Marxist view, see G. Lefebvre, *The French Revolution* (1962–64), and A. Soboul, *The French Revolution: 1787–1799* (1971). R. R. Palmer, *The World of the French Revolution* (1971), places the Revolution in its broader European context, as does E. J. Hobsbawm, *The Age of Revolution, 1789–1848* (1962), brilliantly, from a Marxist viewpoint. F. Furet and M. Ozouf, *A Critical Dictionary of the French Revolution* (1989), offers incisive discussions of key topics.

R.W. Greenlaw, ed., *The Social Origins of the French Revolution* (1975), and T. C. W. Blanning, *The French Revolution: Aristocrats versus Bourgeois?* (1988), offer useful introductions to the fierce debate over whether the Revolution was a class struggle. A. Cobban, *The Social Interpretation of the French Revolution* (1964), wittily attacks Lefebvre and Soboul. J. Tal-mon, *The Origins of Totalitarian Democracy* (1952), F. Furet, *Interpreting the French Revolution* (trans. 1981), and C. Blum, *Rousseau and the Republic of Virtue* (1986), stress ideology rather than class as the Revolution's driving force. F. Aftalion, *The French Revolution: An Economic Interpretation* (1990) explores the role of inflation. On the masses, see G. Rudé, *The Crowd in the French Revolution* (1959), and R. Cobb, *The Police and the People* (1970) and *The People's Armies* (1987). T. C. W. Blanning, *The Origins of the French Revolutionary Wars* (1986), is excellent on the Revolution's relations with Europe. The following also stand out: W. Doyle, *The Origin of the French Revolution* (1980); N. Hampson, *The Life and Opinions of Maximilien Robespierre* (1974); R. R. Palmer, *Twelve Who Ruled* (1941); A. Soboul, *The Parisian Sans-Culottes and the French Revolution* (1964); C. Tilly, *The Vendée* (1964); M. Lyons, *France under the Directory* (1975); A. Forrest, *The French Revolution and the Poor* (1981); L. A. Hunt, *Politics, Culture, and Class in the French Revolution* (1984).

Napoleon

G. Bruun, *Europe and the French Imperium, 1799–1814* (1938), and G. Bergeron, *France under Napoleon* (Princeton, 1981) offer useful surveys. G. Lefebvre's two-volume *Napoleon* (1969) is masterful and comprehensive. R. Holtman, *The Napoleonic Revolution* (1967), is useful on Napoleon's domestic policy; for the impact of Napoleonic France on Europe, see especially S. J. Woolf, *Napoleon's Integration of Europe* (1990). D. Chandler, *The Campaigns of Napoleon* (1966), offers a thorough treatment of Napoleon's wars, with good maps; for a shrewd contemporary's reflections on what those wars meant, see C. von Clausewitz, *On War* (1976), eds. M. Howard and P. Paret.

24

THE DEMOGRAPHIC AND INDUSTRIAL REVOLUTIONS 1750–1914

*H*istorical forces move at varying rates. The French Revolution transformed the politics of Europe in the two decades after 1789. But by then other even more powerful forces had begun to revolutionize the entire world: the leap from agriculture to industry and the continuing explosion of human knowledge ignited by the scientific revolution and the Enlightenment.

Those forces gathered strength only gradually in the course of the nineteenth century. And they are still at work. Understanding their origins, development, and consequences requires isolating them from other events and following their course through the long and relatively peaceful century from 1815 to 1914. That is the purpose of this chapter, which traces the coming of industrialization and the massive modern growth in population—

and of the next, which explores the movement of ideas. Both deal with the sweeping long-term forces that shaped both the nineteenth century and our own world.

The coming of the machine—the substitution of mechanical precision and power for human skill and human or animal strength—was the greatest single change in human existence since the agricultural revolution of the New Stone Age. In the late eighteenth century, the British economy began for the first time in history to generate an ever-increasing surplus of food and goods. Western Europe, the United States, and one non-European power, Japan, soon followed Britain's lead.

The coming of sustained and self-sustaining economic growth in Europe intersected with the "demographic revolution," the swift growth of population that began in the 1740s with the end of the

(*OPPOSITE*) THE FACE OF THE INDUSTRIAL REVOLUTION: "FRITZ," A GIGANTIC STEAM-HAMMER INSTALLED AT ESSEN IN THE RUHR BY THE FIRM OF KRUPP (1861).

"little ice age" (see p. 493). These two revolutions together laid the physical foundations of the societies of our own era, societies far larger, richer, and more powerful than any before. Machinery and population growth together also drove toward culmination the Europeanization or "Westernization" of the world that had begun in 1492.

THE STARTING POINT: THE BIOLOGICAL AND ECONOMIC "OLD REGIME"

Before the eighteenth century, the lives of all except kings, large landowners, upper clergy, and small merchant and professional classes tended to be "nasty, brutish, and short." In most of Western Europe farming was primitive and had changed relatively little from the eleventh century to the seventeenth. Nobility, clergy, and warring states devoured the small surpluses left after the people were fed. A precarious existence depended above all on two factors: favorable weather and the absence of disease. Drought or downpour, hail or frost—any whim of the climate might spell famine and death. Plant or animal diseases might cause disaster in small areas or across the continent. By one count, France suffered 13 general famines in the sixteenth century, 17 in the seventeenth, and 16 in the eighteenth.

Human epidemics were even less forgiving than those of the plant and animal world. The Black Death of the fourteenth century remained a serious threat, striking Amsterdam and Paris repeatedly and killing as much as a seventh of London's population in 1664–65. Columbus's discovery of America also contributed. It introduced smallpox to the Indians and syphilis to the Europeans. After 1493 syphilis spread with fierce virulence from Spain across the Continent. A new form of tuberculosis, more dangerous than its predecessors, arrived in Europe from India in the eighteenth century. As late as 1831–32 cholera from India produced a terrifying epidemic.

And along with the great diseases came the lesser endemic ones. Smallpox infected perhaps 95 percent of the inhabitants of early modern Europe—and roughly one in seven of those infected died. Malaria lessened life expectancy by perhaps a third. Before the eighteenth century it was endemic in marsh areas as far north as England. Typhus, typhoid fever, and many no longer identifiable but often fatal diseases were equally widespread.

Death was thus ever-present under the "biological old regime." The death rate exceeded the birth rate—population actually decreased—in times of famine and epidemic. Although a rapid rise in births followed each disaster, infant mortality was an even greater scourge than in today's Third World. In one prosperous French province in the seventeenth century infant deaths ran between 25 and 33 percent of all newborns in their first year. Only half of all newborns lived to the age of twenty.

Accompanying the familiar presence of death was an overwhelming dreariness of life. Since the industrial revolution it has been fashionable to lament, on well-filled stomachs and in the comfort of well-heated houses, the purity and authenticity of "the world we have lost." But the inhabitants of pre-industrial Europe did not live in picturesque rural bliss. They fought a grim and often losing struggle for survival amid squalid poverty without equivalent today except in the "Third World."

The vast majority of Europe's inhabitants lived through backbreaking toil in fields and cottage workshops. Children worked for their parents from the moment they were able. Those who did not work starved—as did many of those who did work. Agriculture followed the tyranny of the seasons: too little work in winter, and too much at ploughing and harvest time. Food had a desperate sameness. In the aftermath of the Black Death, population shortage and high wages had made meat a frequent food of the common people. But by the seventeenth century the population was again pressing against the limits of subsistence, and the vast majority of Europeans ate little but cereals. Wheat was the staple food, at least in western Europe. Rye, barley, or oats—"in England a food for horses, in Scotland for men"—prevailed in outlying areas of the east and north. Rice was an exotic eastern import until the creation of broad malarial ricefields in northern Italy after the fifteenth century. In the seventeenth and eighteenth centuries the New World crops, especially maize (corn) and potatoes, began to spread slowly but without changing the underlying pattern of the European diet. The population ate peasant bread baked a few times a year and stored like bricks. Ergot fungus, which causes hallucinations and convulsions, often contaminated rye. Too exclusive a diet of cornmeal mush (the Italian *polenta*) caused pellagra, a devastating vitamin deficiency disease. Only the rich, and the small populations in the mountains and wastelands given over to sheep and cattle, ate much meat.

As for shelter, the common people, until very late, lived in thatched hovels with dirt floors and one or two pieces of furniture. In many cases, the peasants shared the roof with their animals, as well as with bedbugs, fleas, and lice. Clothing was scarce, expensive, and rarely washed.

Isolation added to the monotony of work, food, and lodging. Few peasants journeyed beyond their native valleys. Peasant villages and even small towns were tight little societies torn by small hatreds and fiercely antagonistic toward outsiders. Only the rare visits to local market towns or fairs, or the brief village religious festivals with their ritualized overeating and drunkenness, punctuated a bleak existence. Small wonder that the peasants of the French Alps described the height of happiness in such macabre terms as "happy as a dead'un." Misery seemed tolerable because it was familiar; no alternative had ever existed except for the privileged few who lived above subsistence level.

The demographic and economic "old regime" began to give way to the new age in the course of the eighteenth century. The population of Europe had increased before, from 1100 to 1350; the Black Death had then reduced it by up to a third. Growth had resumed from 1450 to 1630, until the stagnation of the "little ice age."

Now, after 1750, Europe's population began to increase with unprecedented and apparently uncheckable speed.

The pattern was not unique. The populations of China and India, although statistics are sketchy, apparently grew at a similar rate and with a similar cause (see Figure 24-1). The most likely source of the general upturn after 1750 was a change in weather patterns. After the "little ice age" in the seventeenth and early eighteenth century, world climate appears to have warmed significantly. Agricultural production and nutrition improved. The death rate slowly declined and the birth rate rose. Population growth resumed at a rapid rate.

Two things that had little or no effect on the initial upturn of the population curve, despite the contrary impressions of contemporaries and historians, were modern medicine and sanitation, and industrialization itself. Medicine and sanitation, with the possible exception of vaccination for smallpox, introduced in 1796, played little role before the 1850s, and then primarily in England, the most advanced nation. The widespread draining of marshes, removal of rotting refuse from villages and towns, increased use of soap, baths, and cotton (and hence washable) underclothes probably cut the insect population of Europe. Malaria, transmitted by mosquitoes, and flea- and louse-borne plague and typhus did decrease. But the marshes were drained to reclaim land for farming, and the other changes served comfort, not medicine. Conscious efforts against disease had to await the discovery of its causes and carriers in the nineteenth century.

As for industrialization, it affected Britain first, and mainly after 1760. The 1780s was the decisive decade in which British economic growth turned sharply upward. Industry, in other words, did not itself cause the demographic revolution. Nor does industry's existence or absence fit neatly with population growth. Western Europe, which industralized, grew 280 percent between 1680 and 1900 (71.9 million to 201.4 million), whereas China, which did not industralize, grew at a roughly similar rate (150 million to 450

FIGURE 24.1   World Population   1000–2000

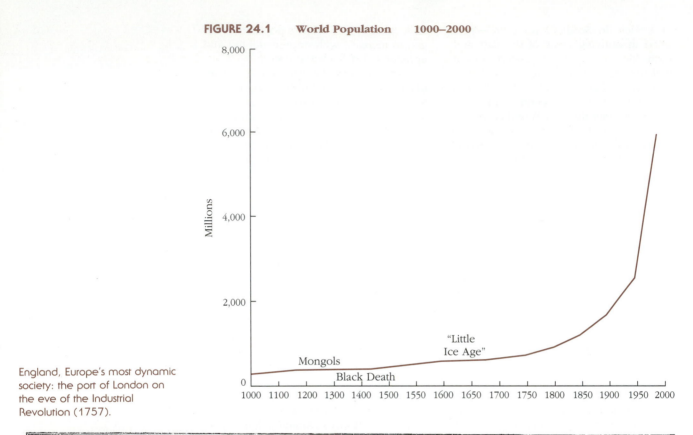

England, Europe's most dynamic society: the port of London on the eve of the Industrial Revolution (1757).

million). The peak growth rates of industrializing regions within Europe did outstrip most other areas. The presence of work encouraged both migration and earlier marriages that produced more children. England's population grew by a staggering 133 percent (from 4.93 million to 11.5 million) between 1680 and 1820, and 86 percent of that increase took place after 1760. But population also grew rapidly in nonindustrial areas. The population of England and Wales grew by 48 percent between 1751 and 1801; Ireland's grew by 75 percent.

Whatever its sources, the consequences of growth were startling. The total population of Europe west of the Ural Mountains grew from perhaps 140 million in 1750 to 390 million in 1900. England and Russia, at opposite ends of the Continent and of the scale of social and economic development, led the way (see Figure 24-2). In central Europe the populations of Germany and Austria-Hungary approximately doubled. Italy, thanks to massive emigration to the New World in the last quarter of the century, grew only 87 percent. France, whose career as *la grande nation* was ended demographi-

cally as well as militarily, increased only 65 percent.

Ireland, the classic European example of the consequences of unchecked population growth without industrialization, suffered catastrophe. Its population doubled in the seventeenth century, then more than doubled in the eighteenth century at the steepest rate in all Europe. That rise continued, from 5.25 million in 1800 to 8.5 million in 1845—of whom perhaps a quarter were unemployed. Then a potato blight and catastrophic famine in 1845–48 killed perhaps a million Irish, and flight to the New World cut population to around 4.5 million.

What prevented further demographic catastrophes of the kind that afflicted Ireland, or China in the 1850s and 1860s, when perhaps 20 million died in famines? As in Ireland and China, Europe's death rates gradually declined in the course of the century. Although birth rates also dropped, the spread between the death-rate and the birth-rate curves rapidly opened, and the population leapt upward. But unlike the outcome in Ireland and China, industrialization and medicine sustained Europe's increase. Only after the

FIGURE 24.2   **Population Increase by Country**   **1700–1900**

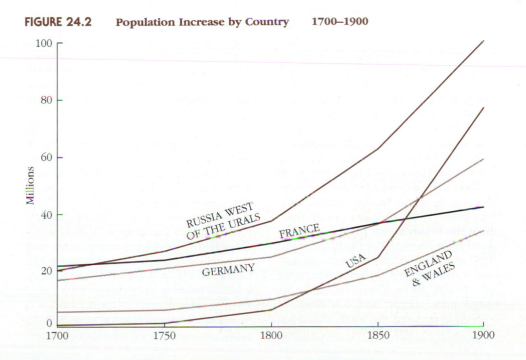

turn of the century did most of Europe pass through a "demographic transition" to a new pattern of lower birth rates. That transition was one symptom of the maturing of Europe's new industrial societies.

THE INDUSTRIAL REVOLUTION: CAUSES

The World Primacy of the West

Why did industrialization happen? Or, rather, why did it happen in the West? And why in Britain? Two other contenders, the Islamic world and China, might have led the way. They did not, although (as described earlier) in the early Middle Ages Islam had provided the then-backward West with lost Greek texts and vital concepts such as decimal numbers and algebra. And in 1078 China had briefly achieved a level of coal-smelted iron production (125,000 tons) that Britain did not match until 1796.

But the Islamic world and China shared common misfortunes. The savage waves of nomads from Central Asia hit them harder than they did Europe. Nomads conquered China's major iron-producing provinces. The Mongols sacked Baghdad and ruled China as the Yuan dynasty. The Ottoman Turks overran and held the core lands of Islamic civilization. In China a second "conquest dynasty," the Manchus, proved as disruptive as the Mongols.

Even more serious than invasion and foreign rule was a loss of impetus, an intellectual turning inward. In the Islamic world, that tendency may have had doctrinal roots. *Islam* means "submission"—to the will of God. From the beginning, Islam's thrust toward a life totally devoted to God meant potential hostility to nonreligious knowledge. In the tenth century, the "gates of independent judgment" about the Koran began to close. Further speculation about either theology or the physical world became increasingly suspect, and slowed dramatically (see pp. 217–18). As for China, the Ming dynasty's great trading and war fleets of 1405–33 dominated the South China Sea

and the Indian Ocean, and were technologically superior to those of the Portuguese who followed less than seventy years later. But China's confident ethnocentrism and the nomad threat to its northern border turned it inward for good.

Political disadvantages multiplied the disadvantages of circumstances and culture. The Islamic world and China shared a similar form of government—centralized despotism. Caliphs, Ottoman sultans, and emperors of China in theory *owned* their territory and its inhabitants. Human inefficiency, frequent struggles over the succession of the throne, and the need to rely on elites, such as China's scholar-gentry, that might in time become independent, often tempered that absolute power. But the claim to total power remained. All property in theory belonged to the ruler. He merely lent it to his subjects and could tax or reclaim it when he chose.

Europe—except for the Russian state (see pp. 343–47)—was different. After the assimilation or defeat of the Viking and Magyar raiders in the tenth century, Europe suffered relatively little from outside invasion. Mongols and Turks devastated only fringe areas such as Muscovy, Hungary, and the Balkans. And far from relapsing into self-satisfaction, Europeans developed that uniquely inquiring cast of mind already described in discussing the Renaissance and the scientific revolution. Theological speculation separated from inquiry about the physical world. Slowly and haltingly, the West crossed the divide between magic and science. And after 1100, Europe's science and technology slowly overtook and surpassed even those of China. The Western obsession with clocks, with the mechanical measurement of time, was symbolic of far more—the application of rationality, calculation, and step-by-step problem-solving to broader and broader areas of life.

Politics also helped. Despite the efforts of popes and emperors, Europe remained divided into warring states and principalities. Charlemagne, Gregory VII, Charles V, Philip II, Louis XIV, and Napoleon all failed to establish universal empires. Europe also lacked the identification of government and religion seen in both

Islam and China. The Investiture Conflict and the Protestant Reformation guaranteed that Caesar and God would remain distinct. That left space, however small at first, for freedom.

Finally, political fragmentation allowed subordinate groups and individuals to claim *rights*, even against their rulers—a concept almost unimaginable elsewhere. From the security of their fortified walls, medieval towns could defy their overlords. The barons extorted the *Magna Carta* from the English monarchy. The right of resistance to oppression became a stable principle of political thought in Europe, and nowhere else. Relative freedom under laws, however limited in practice, persisted and widened over the centuries.

And the close connection between political freedom and the free enjoyment of property allowed wide latitude and security for economic activity. In western Europe, and in western Europe alone, great bankers like the Medici and the Fuggers could deal almost as equals with emperors and kings. The straightjacket of the European mercantilist state was a small impediment to growth compared to the punitive taxation or confiscation that awaited Moslem or Chinese merchants whose economic success made them conspicuous. Relative freedom from devastation by nomads, the preeminence of curiosity and rationality, political pluralism and division between religious and secular power, and the concept of rights against the ruler propelled Europe past its rivals.

The Primacy of Britain in Europe

Within Europe, Britain led the way after the seventeenth century. Even more than the rest of Europe, it enjoyed freedom from external threat. The last successful invasion had been the Norman conquest in 1066. Internal turmoil, from the Wars of the Roses to the Civil War of the 1640s and the Highland clan risings of 1715 and 1745, was superficial and short-lived compared to the great wars that tore the Continent. An inquiring cast of mind had long distinguished the English, who contrib-

uted more than any other people to the scientific revolution. The Reformation and the breaking of the religious monopoly of the Anglican Church in the Civil War meant that religious restraints on speculation and on the free flow of knowledge were largely absent.

Finally, English politics and society helped establish England's primacy over rivals such as France, just as the nature of European politics and society gave Europe the lead it had acquired by 1700. The remnants of English feudal institutions and land tenure had disappeared by the sixteenth century. England had ceased to have serfs or even a hereditary peasantry. After the mid-sixteenth century even mining rights, except in gold and silver, belonged to the landowner and not to the king—a situation unique in Europe. When the Civil War of 1641–48 pitted the Crown against England's landowners organized in Parliament, the landowners had won, and had completed the process begun with the *Magna Carta*. Rights of property became absolute, dependent neither on service nor on the claims of overlords, tenants, or church. The purpose of government itself, as John Locke had spelled it out in 1690, was simple: "The great and chief end . . . of men's uniting into commonwealths and putting themselves under government is the preservation of their property." That concept of property was far more absolute than that prevailing even in old-regime France, much less in lands east and south of France.

By the eighteenth century, the inhabitants of England thus enjoyed guaranteed rights and a social mobility undreamed of on the continent. "All are accounted gentlemen in England who maintain themselves without manual labor," remarked an eighteenth-century traveler's handbook. In this relatively "open aristocracy," wealth bought status with a speed and directness not visible in France. That was an immense stimulus to the pursuit of wealth. Britain's upper classes were far less fastidious than their continental counterparts about how to acquire that wealth. The barriers against nobles engaging in trade and industry that were slowly breaking down in old-regime France scarcely existed in eighteenth-century Britain. And the guild restrictions that still hobbled industry on the continent had long vanished.

British family structure and inheritance customs also promoted mobility and growth. Unlike the practice in France, where all children of the nobility inherited their parents' status, the younger sons of the great English families received neither land nor title. On the Continent, caste-bound younger sons had to make do with careers in church or army. In Britain, younger sons went out into the world to earn money. These features made Britain into Europe's most dynamic society. It was the first to industrialize because it alone was ready.

Other factors help explain why Britain industrialized when it did. First among them was the gradual but impressive growth of English agriculture, which between 1700 and 1800 increased its output per acre by 44 percent. New timetables for ploughing, new methods of field rotation with crops such as clover or turnips that returned nitrogen to the soil and supplied fodder, larger numbers of sheep and cattle eating that fodder and manuring the fields, selective breeding of livestock—all contributed to growth. The absence of a hereditary peasantry allowed landowners, whether "gentlemen" or merely prosperous farmers, to consolidate the common lands of the medieval village into "enclosed" fields, either by agreement with the villagers or by act of Parliament. Consolidation of holdings was virtually complete by the first decades of the nineteenth century, and made England a land of economically efficient large and medium-sized farms, far different from the patchwork of open-field strips and small peasant holdings still found on the Continent.

This "agricultural revolution" had three major consequences for British industrialization. Contrary to widespread opinion, enclosure apparently did not contribute to industrialization by driving laborers off the land and into the new industrial labor force. The enclosed fields with their livestock and multiple crops required more, not less labor than the old system. It was the increase in the rural

population, not enclosure, that filled the new industrial cities. But agriculture did help to keep the new urban population fed, while enclosure freed land for industry or mining. And agricultural prosperity increased the market for industrial products.

But agriculture only provided a foundation for growth. On that foundation a rich commercial and industrial economy arose that as early as 1700 was supplying a third of England's national product. By comparison, at that date commerce and industry made up a fifth or less of the French economy. And England's commerce, unlike that of France, had by 1700 already created a national market that matched goods with buyers. A cash economy centered on London reached to the far corners of the island. Barter, still prevalent in backward areas of France, was relatively rare. The internal customs barriers that bedeviled French merchants and the inter-state ones that cut eighteenth-century Germany into incoherent dwarf economies did not exist in England.

Even geography favored the creation of a national market. No part of Britain is more than seventy miles from the sea. Navigable rivers—the Thames, Severn, Tyne, Humber—improved with dredging and locks, made possible the economical transport of bulk cargoes such as coal, of which London was already consuming 100,000 tons a year by the early seventeenth century. Especially after the 1760s, entrepreneurs promoted a massive expansion of canals that linked the major rivers into a national transport network. Similar private companies made British roads the best in Europe by the end of the eighteenth century (see Figure 24-3). Nor did the British market end with Britain itself. England's export trade, which grew sixfold during the eighteenth century, offered a further incentive for firms to expand production relentlessly.

Thus England was already rich, and its people, along with those of Holland and the United States, enjoyed the world's highest standard of living by the late eighteenth century. That wealth made it the only country in Europe that possessed the makings of a true mass market, a public

FIGURE 24.3   The Transport Revolution in Britain

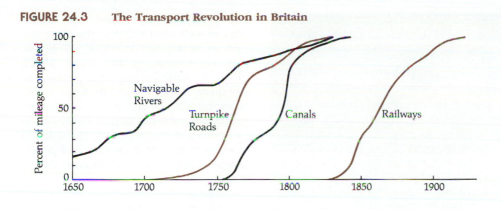

capable of buying large quantities of inexpensive goods. The pull of that market at last harnessed the West's love of gadgets and its willingness to search for practical results by trial and error to economic purposes. The pull of that market prompted the emergence of a cluster of technological innovations that propelled Britain into spectacular growth. For the first time in history, an economy expanded not primarily by increasing its labor input, but by replacing labor with machinery.

THE FIRST INDUSTRIAL REVOLUTION, 1750–1850

The innovations of this "first industrial revolution" affected above all three key industries: cotton, coal, and iron. Cotton, the miracle fiber from India, the Middle East, and the slave economies of the Caribbean and American South, led the way. Cotton was durable, lighter than linen, and easily washed, dyed, printed, and worked by machine. It was also in insatiable demand: As a London magazine put it in 1783, "every servant girl has her cotton gown and her cotton stockings."

In the 1730s the first of the major innovations, John Kay's flying shuttle, dramatically speeded up the weaving of cotton cloth. That increase created a bottleneck in spinning the raw fibers into thread. By the 1750s the flying shuttle was in general use, and tinkerers and entrepreneurs bent to the task of mechanizing spinning. James Hargreaves's "spinning jenny" of 1765, Richard Arkwright's larger and more pow-

erful "water frame," and Samuel Crompton's "mule," a hybrid with features from its two predecessors, filled the gap.

The new devices produced cotton thread in previously unimaginable quantities, and of a strength and fineness that hand spinners could not match. A twelvefold leap in cotton production and consumption between 1770 and 1800 in turn created further imbalances. The tiny chemical industry found itself pressed for vast quantities of soaps and bleaches for processing textiles. And the flying shuttle of the home weavers could no longer keep up with the output of thread. The answer was Arkwright's power-loom, invented in 1787. By 1833 one man with a twelve-year-old boy as helper could produce as much as twenty hand-weavers. Annual production of cotton cloth skyrocketed from perhaps a million pounds a year in 1730 to 100 million in 1815.

That expansion created an entirely new institution, the factory. The grouping together of workers in large workshops was not new. It had existed in the ancient world and in Europe before the Industrial Revolution. But in all except the heaviest metal industries, large workshops had little or no competitive advantage over cottage industry. In 1770, the date of Arkwright's first large factory, the vast bulk of production still took place at home under the "putting-out" system. The entrepreneur provided raw material to home workers (his subcontractors) and then collected and sold the finished product. The coming of power-driven machinery that was swifter, more efficient, and larger and

A replica of Arkwright's water frame, patented in 1769.

The factory: steam power and long rows of iron-framed machines. A cotton mill in the mid-1840s.

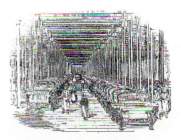

The Coming of Steam: A View from the Bottom   1818

When the spinning of cotton was in its infancy, and before those terrible machines for superseding the necessity of human labour, called steam engines came into use, there were a great number of what were then called *little masters;* men who with a small capital, could procure a few machines, and employ a few machines, and employ a few hands men and boys (say to twenty or thirty). . . . A few years however changed the face of things. Steam engines came into use, to purchase which, and to erect buildings sufficient to contain them and six or seven hundred hands, required a great capital. The engine power produced a more marketable (though not a better) article than the little masters could at the same price. The consequence was their ruin in a short time; and the overgrown capitalists triumphed in their fall.

Black Dwarf, *September 30, 1818, pp. 623–24, quoted in Theodore Hamerow,* The Birth of a New Europe *(Chapel Hill: University of North Carolina Press, 1983), p. 13.*

more expensive than anything possible in the home or in small workshops forced the concentration of industry into ever-larger units, into *factories* built around their machines and power sources. The "factory system" was an organizational and logistical leap comparable in importance to the technological advances that made it necessary and possible.

The take-off of the cotton industry, with its pattern of new machines perpetually challenging entrepreneurs to further mechanize the slower phases of the pro-

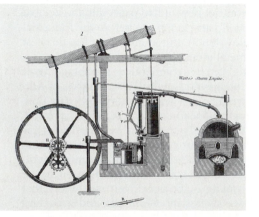

Watt's design drawing for his steam engine (1769).

duction cycle, encouraged other industries as well. Coal and iron, the other two sectors of this first industrial revolution, felt the stimulus. Water power, which drove the early factories, was proving inadequate by the 1790s. Its force varied with the seasons and it was found only on suitable streams, often far from markets or sources of raw materials. The solution was to tap an inanimate source of power whose supply seemed almost unlimited—coal.

The machine that turned the energy of coal into rotary motion to drive the new textile machines was the steam engine, the very symbol of the Industrial Revolution. Playthings such as the rotating kettle powered by a steam jet had existed since antiquity. But the first practical steam engine was Thomas Savery's "fire engine," or steam-powered pump, of 1698. Seven years later Thomas Newcomen, a blacksmith of Dartmouth in southern England, built the first true steam engine. It moved a crossbeam connected to a pump cylinder. Less than 1 percent of the energy released from its fuel did useful work. But that was enough. The machine was tireless and could be almost any size needed. It served at first to pump out and ventilate coal mines. It allowed the rapid expansion of coal production from ever-deeper seams, although its inefficiency prevented its use any distance from cheap coal.

Then, in the 1770s, James Watt invented an improved engine four times as efficient. That breakthrough created the "age of steam." The seemingly unlimited coal deposits of northern England could now power ever-larger spinning and weaving machines. Watt's partner was understandably immodest about their achievement: "I sell, Sir, what all the world desires to have—power."

Steam for pumping had permitted the expansion of coal production. Steam for industry in turn increased demand for coal. Steam power, coal, and the demands of war with France after 1793 between them revolutionized the iron industry. The English by 1740 already consumed ten or eleven pounds of iron per capita each year, far more than the French (although as late as the 1780s France's iron production was in absolute terms larger than Britain's). But English metallurgy soon came up against a seemingly unbreakable bottleneck: fuel. The supply of wood to make charcoal for smelting iron ore into pig iron was limited. Coal, in its charred form, coke, normally contaminated the iron with impurities that rendered the finished product unusable.

After long experiment, Abraham Darby successfully smelted iron ore with coke (as the Chinese had centuries before him) in 1709. But not until the 1750s did the technique become widespread. The triumph of coke smelting and further innovations, such as the steam-powered forced-blast furnace and the preheated air blast, drove British production of pig iron upward from 17,350 tons in 1740 to 2.7 million tons in 1852. That vast increase called forth further innovations elsewhere in the production cycle. The decisive breakthrough in the processing of pig iron (from 2.5 to 5 percent carbon) into wrought iron (less than .1 percent carbon) came in the 1780s with Henry Cort's "puddling" and steam-powered rolling process. Crude standardized shapes such as iron beams, bars, and rails became possible for the first time. Britain's iron industry left France's in the dust.

As iron became ever cheaper, new sources of demand appeared. Weapons had traditionally been the largest single use of iron, and remained so until after 1800. Royal Navy orders ensured the success of the Carron Company, Scotland's first major ironworks (1759). A new precision process for boring cannon from solid castings speeded production and made weapons more accurate. The steam engine's leaky cylinders also benefited from the new boring techniques. Iron beams began to appear in buildings and bridges in the 1770s, and the first practical iron-hulled ship emerged in 1815. Iron frames, rollers, gears, and pushrods replaced wood in the new generation of steam-powered textile machines, cutting vibration and permitting ever higher operating speeds.

The culmination of the age of steam was the application of coal power to transport—the railroad and the steamship, the

The new metallurgy: smelting iron with coke in Upper Silesia, 1841.

first self-moving vehicles in world history. The first practical steamships were the creation of a French marquis, Claude Jouffroy d'Abbans, in the late 1770s and early 1780s. Americans and British developed the innovation further, and the first partially steam-powered Atlantic crossing came in 1819. The railroad was a combination of the steam engine with the rail-wagons used since the late sixteenth century in mines and quarries. In the late 1750s iron rails had begun to replace wood. Then, after 1800, inventors sought to power a vehicle to run on those rails. In 1801–04 Richard Trevithick, developer

Iron ships: The huge *Great Eastern* (1858), built by Isambard Kingdom Brunel (1806–1859), one of Britain's greatest engineers.

The opening of the world's first freight and passenger rail line, the Stockton-Darlington Railway, on September 27, 1825. Photo courtesy of the Mansell collection.

of a high-pressure engine more efficient than Watt's, succeeded. After the mid-1820s the first railways began to spread across Britain and the United States.

Railroads and steamships drove forward the transport revolution begun with roads and canals. Rail immensely expanded the internal market, while the steamship widened the international one. Together they created a demand that stretched the iron industry, as the widening consumer market had stretched the cotton industry. Each mile of railway track required three hundred tons of iron. By 1851, the year of the Great Exhibition at London that measured Britain's achievements against those of its European rivals, Britain had more than 9,000 miles of track. Rails covered Britain like a web, linking mines, factories, ports, and huge new cities. The railroad was the last of the cluster of technologies of that first industrial revolution that made Britain the "workshop of the world."

THE SECOND INDUSTRIAL REVOLUTION: FROM THE NINETEENTH CENTURY TO THE TWENTIETH

By the time of the Great Exhibition, the Industrial Revolution was spreading rapidly. Societies on the Continent that were socially and economically ready to follow Britain's lead now began to close the gap. Britain's share of world industrial production dropped steadily as its rivals caught up (see Figure 24-4). And new rivals beyond the seas, in America and ultimately in Japan (see pp. 706–08), rose to challenge both Britain and Europe.

These "followers" suffered from one major disadvantage: their infant industries, especially in textiles, faced the competition of low-cost mass-produced British goods. But the followers also benefited from Britain's pioneering. After Britain, industralization would never again be unforeseen and unplanned: the followers

FIGURE 24.4   **Leader and Followers: Relative Shares of World Industrial Production**

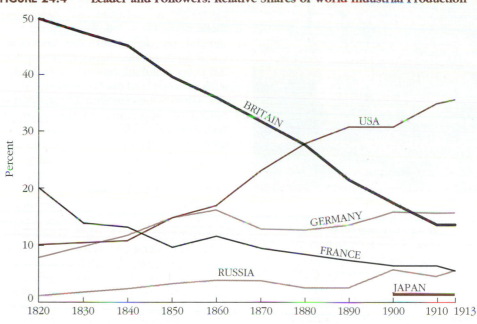

had a model. They could study and seek to avoid some of that model's shortcomings. They could adopt technology already pioneered in Britain, and save development costs. Finally, their industralization coincided roughly with a new wave of innovations, the "second industrial revolution," that appeared between 1850 and 1880. The followers could enter the new industries of this second wave without the burden of investment or labor force tied up in older industries. In the new industries the followers could in some cases compete on equal terms.

Four new technologies of the second industrial revolution propelled the world into the twentieth century: steel, chemicals, electricity, and the internal combustion engine. Steel was at first the most important. An alloy of iron known since antiquity, steel contains between .1 and 2 percent carbon. It combines strength, hardness, and elasticity in unique proportions. It holds under stresses that snap brittle pig or cast iron (2.5 to 5 percent carbon) and spread soft wrought iron (less than .1 percent carbon) like butter.

Until the 1850s no process existed for making steel cheaply and in quantity. The

oldest technique involved baking wrought iron bars at high temperature in a bed of carbon to diffuse the carbon into the iron. Then a blacksmith laboriously reheated, folded, and hammered the iron bars into themselves by hand to distribute the carbon throughout the iron evenly. In the

Rolling steel in a mill.

Steel for a new age: the
Bessemer process.

1740s, along with the other metallurgical discoveries of the early industrial revolution, came a process, long known in China and South Asia, for making steel in small melting pots, or crucibles. This crucible process was small-scale and expensive, but it produced the hardest and most uniform steel yet made in any quantity. And it made possible for the first time the casting of large steel objects such as drive shafts, railroad wheels or axles, and huge shell-firing cannon.

Then came two breakthroughs. In the 1850s Henry Bessemer, an armaments designer, discovered that blowing air through a crucible filled with molten pig iron rapidly burned off the excess carbon and in the process generated the heat needed to keep the iron molten. This "Bessemer converter" eliminated the laborious intermediate steps required in earlier processes. Amid spectacular showers of sparks, it accomplished in ten to twenty minutes what before had taken 24 hours and immense quantities of coal. The slightly later Siemens-Martin open-hearth furnace, which recirculated superhot combustion gases to create ever-higher temperatures, also produced steel that was as cheap as wrought iron. These breakthroughs made the age of steel, an age only now ending (see Figure 24-5).

In chemicals, another series of breakthroughs created entirely new industries. Until the mid-nineteenth century chemical production had mostly catered to the expanding textile industry's appetite for soaps and bleaches. Then, thanks to Brit-

ish and French laboratory work on organic chemicals derived from coal, came synthetic dyes. There followed mineral oils, mineral oil derivatives, the anesthetic chloroform, nitrated high explosives and fertilizers, celluloid, cellulose fiber textiles such as rayon, and the first primitive plastics. Alfred Nobel, Swedish inventor of stabilized nitroglycerine, the first practical high explosive, felt such remorse at the military uses of his product and the wealth he gained from it that he established the prizes—ironically including one for peace—that bear his name.

Electricity, the third key technology, came into its own by the 1880s. Its first practical use, the telegraph, dated from 1837–38. Undersea telegraph cable linked Britain and France by 1851 and spanned the Atlantic by 1866. The telegraph, Alexander Graham Bell's telephone (1876), and Guglielmo Marconi's radio (1897–1901) revolutionized communications. But electricity's most important use was as a source of power, after a series of inventions—generators, alternators, transformers—from the 1860s to the 1880s. Electricity lighted the new industrial cities, replacing the coal gas lighting pioneered in Britain around 1800. It also provided

FIGURE 24.5   The Age of Steel

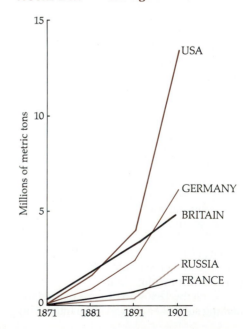

cheap, portable power in the factory, and ultimately replaced dangerous and unreliable webs of transmission belts with compact, powerful electric motors.

Last came the internal combustion engine. By the mid-nineteenth century the limitations of steam were apparent. Steam engines were heavy. Their usual fuel, coal, was equally so, and required legions of sweating stokers to feed the boilers. Consequently, steam was unsuitable for powering small vehicles. A German, Nicolaus Otto, provided the answer in 1876 with the first really practical internal combustion engine, which ran on coal gas. When converted to gasoline, it provided the motive power for the first automobiles in the 1890s, and for powered flight in 1903.

The technologies of the second industrial revolution in turn encouraged further changes in the methods and organization of production. Cheap steel and the machine tool industry it encouraged allowed the production for the first time of machines with interchangeable parts. That innovation, despite the claims of Samuel Colt for his early revolvers, remained more aspiration than reality until the 1870s. But after that, high-speed cutting steels, precision gauges, and a drive toward discipline and standardization in sizes and screw threads made possible the mass production of ever more intricate machines.

The new techniques of mass production with interchangeable parts found early application both in small arms and in the sewing machine. The American firm of Isaac Singer marketed this first domestic appliance on a worldwide scale after the 1850s. The same techniques, further rationalized, made possible in the twentieth century the production of automobiles on assembly lines. Mass production, in the proud words of the pioneer Henry Ford, was "the focusing upon a manufacturing system of the principle of power, accuracy, system, continuity, and speed."

The technology and organization of the second industrial revolution was different from that of the first. The new technologies required far greater amounts of capital than early textile innovators or even the eighteenth-century ironmasters had required. Until the coming of the railroads, entrepreneurs had tended to form closed partnerships that expanded by ploughing back profits into the enterprise. The scale of the new industries placed family firms and partnerships at a disadvantage, except for a few giants such as the firm of Friedrich and Alfred Krupp, the "cannon kings" of the Ruhr Valley. The solutions to this financial bottleneck, especially after mid-century, were the joint-stock company and large-scale bank loans to industry. Giant enterprises, bank financing, and close connections to the state became and remained conspicuous charcteristics of German industry, and of those of many other followers. Britain, by contrast, resisted concentration. It increasingly missed out on the economies of scale from which giant enterprises usually profit.

The second characteristic of the new technologies was their close connection to science. The inspired tinkerers that led the first industrial revolution shared the analytical, problem-solving, empirical cast of mind that had made the scientific revolution. But their discoveries had originated in workshop and forge, not in the laboratory. And their achievements were those of individual brilliance, not of teamwork. The new metallurgical, chemical, and electrical industries were different. From the beginning, the contribution of scientific theory to practice was great and ever-growing. Science-intensive industries in turn required ever-larger numbers of scientists and trained technicians. The sheer size of the new enterprises required a group effort of management, scientists, and technicians.

In France, state institutions such as the *École Polytechnique* and lesser provincial institutes supplied the necessary experts. But it was the reforming bureaucrats of Germany who triumphed in the new world of applied science and teamwork. Universal primary education and a widespread network of technical schools in many German states from the 1820s had no parallel on the Continent or anywhere else, except perhaps the United States after mid-century. Britain, where primary education did not become compulsory until 1880 and where the elite studied

Latin and Greek but not chemistry, suffered accordingly. By 1872 the University of Munich alone had more graduate research chemists than all English universities combined. And German and American management proved remarkably skillful at the large scale organization of research, development, and production.

The followers developed at different rates and achieved widely varying results. Belgium and France started first, in the 1820s. Belgium was probably the first society after Britain whose industry produced more by value than its agriculture. But it lacked the population and resources to be more than a minor industrial power. France was a potential rival to Britain, but it suffered from major constraints. Until the railway boom of the 1850s its communications were poor. Its large peasantry acted as a drag on the rest of the economy, lessening demand. Above all, old habits of mind died hard. The French entrepreneur, with some exceptions, bowed to the social pressures of a society that despite Revolution and Terror remained less competitive and more hierarchical than Britain's. The French and even the Germans tended until quite late to see business as a zero-sum game in which victory came only at the expense of others—who also had the right to a "fair" living. Robber-baron success seemed antisocial. The French economy grew steadily, but industry's share of the national product did not surpass that of agriculture until 1909.

Germany and the United States took up the British challenge most fully. By the end of the century, thanks to the coal and iron of the Ruhr Valley and to economic unity bloodily achieved in 1866–71 (see pp. 674–81), Germany had surpassed Britain. Pig-iron output increased twenty-fold between 1850 and 1870. Giants such as Krupps and the Borsig engineering works in Berlin dominated the production of locomotives, machinery, and engines of destruction. In chemicals, great firms such as AGFA, Höchst, and BASF had captured 90 percent of the world market for synthetic dyes by 1900. AEG and Siemens, the electrical giants, achieved positions in the world market that only their counterparts in the United States rivaled.

The economic development of the United States was if anything even more spectacular than Germany's. Growth rested on several factors. Land, once violently cleared of Indians, was "free." Vast mineral resources, from Appalachian coal to the Mesabi iron range to the gold of California, fueled development. The highest birth rate in the West and the immigration of 30 million people between 1845 and 1914 provided enough labor to meet needs, but not enough to depress wages or to discourage the introduction of labor-saving machinery. Relatively high wages in turn promoted consumer demand.

Mechanization began in textile production, as in Britain, in the 1770s in the water-powered mills of New England. Eli Whitney's cotton gin (1793), which separated fibers from seeds quickly and cheaply, helped create a boom in the slave South. Cotton shipments to the mills of Massachusetts and Lancashire leapt upwards. By 1840 the United States had already passed Britain in steam-engine horsepower. The Erie Canal, opened in 1825, cut across the Appalachians and connected the industry of the East with the grain of the Midwest. After 1830 railroads opened up sources of coal and iron and fed ever larger cities. Large farms and a relative shortage of labor encouraged the mechanization of agriculture on a scale undreamed of elsewhere. Cyrus McCormick's reaper (1831), the railroad, and the steamship allowed grain from the Great Plains to undersell European grain in European markets by the 1870s. Refrigeration, invented in the 1830s, made possible the mass distribution and export of meat by the 1880s. And in heavy industry, the United States created a zone of huge coal and steel firms, like those of Germany's Ruhr Valley, that stretched from Pittsburgh to Chicago and outclassed all rivals. By 1914 the industrial output of the United States was almost 80 percent of that of all Western Europe.

Last of the early followers came Italy, Russia, and Japan. Italy broke into rapid growth in the first decade of the twentieth century, but its depressed agriculture and lack of coal or oil held it back until after 1945. Russia and Japan were the first cases of a phenomenon increasingly familiar later in the new century—the industrialization of societies that were either partially (Russia) or wholly (Japan) non-Western in politics and culture. Economic growth in both cases was spectacular. But political and cultural traditions did not always encourage the sober use of the power that industrialization brought.

The second industrial revolution and the industrialization of the followers made a true world market. Before the wars of the French Revolution, Europe's mercantile world economy had shown some signs of the now familiar boom and bust pattern of the business cycle. The depression that followed the wars of the French Revolution had been unusually severe and widespread. By mid-century, transport and communications had begun to weld the world together. The California gold strike in 1848 and an outbreak of railway fever fueled an American, European, and world boom that broke in the first true world depression, the panic of 1857. Further growth culminated in a second collapse in 1873. That crash inaugurated a twenty-year period of falling prices known misleadingly as the nineteenth century "great depression." The term is a misnomer, because this was a period of unparalleled growth in output for the followers, especially Germany and the United States. Falling prices caused dislocation, especially in European agriculture. But they were a sign of health, a sign of the abundance that the mechanization of industry, agriculture, and transport made possible. And after 1896 a new boom lifted the world economy, with a brief interruption in 1907, until 1913.

THE INDUSTRIAL REVOLUTION: HUMAN AND SOCIAL CONSEQUENCES

The Industrial Revolution transformed every society it touched—in standard of living and life expectancy, the location and occupations of the population, the structure of the social hierarchy, and the character of the basic human unit, the family.

The Rise in Living Standards and Life Expectancy

England, along with Holland and the infant United States, already enjoyed the world's highest living standard in the eighteenth century, before industrialization. Britain preserved that lead throughout the nineteenth century except compared to the United States. Advance was nevertheless far from smooth; Britain, in particular, paid the price of pioneering. From the 1790s to the 1840s English real wages (wages adjusted for the cost of living) appear to have stagnated. The peak of Britain's birth rate coincided with the triumph of the factories over domestic handicrafts. Moreover, after the 1790s women and children made up an increasing proportion of the work force in factories and mines. Entrepreneurs could pay them less and dominate them more effectively than they could men. Factory work and the filth of the improvised industrial cities dragged urban life expectancy down below that of most rural areas.

The workers of the early industrial revolution also suffered less tangible losses. They exchanged the familiar if poverty-racked countryside or small-town workshop for filthy slum streets and "dark satanic mills" enveloped in clouds of coal soot. The "Black Country" around Birmingham came by its name honestly. The workers exchanged the tyranny of the seasons and of crop blights for the domination of the tireless machine. Breaking the new industrial labor force to the discipline of the clock was one of the major challenges facing the early entrepreneurs. Workers long resisted the habit of arriving for work on Mondays or arriving sober on Tuesdays. And the tyranny of the business cycle replaced that of nature. Overproduction or disruption of normal trade patterns could spell unemployment and massive distress for entire regions. The "cotton famine" that resulted from the U.S. Civil War (1861–65) caused near starvation in the mill-towns of Lancashire. In the new cities, overcrowding, poverty, and the sudden release from the traditional religious and social restraints of the tight rural community led to widespread illegitimacy, alcoholism, and prostitution.

But after 1840 conditions slowly improved. Between 1851 and 1878, British per capita real income increased by a startling 30 percent. Until 1900 it continued to rise at the unprecedented rate of between 17 and 25 percent per decade. And workers worked less; the average (estimated) workweek in British industry declined from almost 60 hours in the 1860s to around 53 hours in 1900. In Europe as a whole the estimated average workweek dropped from an appalling 84 hours in 1850 to 60 hours in 1910.

A dramatic increase in life expectancy reflected and paralleled the rise in real income. The crucial factor was a decline in infant mortality. The death rate of infants less than one year old dropped in England from 36 percent in 1751–60 to 11.7 percent in 1906–10. France's infant mortality after the turn of the twentieth century was slightly higher than Britain's, and Sweden's was somewhat lower. Russia's remained at 25 percent as late as 1900–09. Adults also lived longer. The decrease in infant mortality and greater longevity together raised life expectancy in western Europe from less than forty years in 1840 to the mid-50s by 1900. That rapid change was unparalleled in human history.

What did this mean for the bulk of the population? For the first time, appreciable numbers of people began living significantly above subsistence level and consuming an increasing variety of goods. Already in the 1780s English workers had come to expect tea, coffee, sugar, and inexpensive cottons. After 1850 workers paid a steadily decreasing proportion of their wages for food and lodging. They began to have money and time to spend on leisure and entertainment.

Industrialization naturally did not distribute its benefits equally. The elites had always lived better and longer than those at the bottom of the social pyramid. And industrialization opened further the gap between rich and poor: the rich grew richer faster than the poor. The concentration of wealth therefore increased. The immense fortunes of the entrepreneurs generated envy in the increasingly politically conscious workers and fear in the landowning elites which had until now dominated society.

Urbanization and Emigration

The new age also brought migrations unprecedented since the fall of the Roman Empire. Population growth dictated movement. The agricultural countryside simply could not support the increase in numbers after 1750. The growth of industry encouraged movement by providing jobs. After 1850 the revolution in transportation, the railroad and the steamship, made movement on an unprecedented scale possible. The result was urbanization and emigration.

Urbanization, the concentration of the population in cities, was most conspicuous in Britain, where the monster city, London, had long been the largest in Europe. In 1800 it contained about 12 percent of Britain's total population. By 1890 more than 60 percent of the British lived in cities of 10,000 or more. German and Belgian figures were in the 30 percent range, and France's only 25 percent (see Figure 24-6). Where sheep had grazed a generation or two before stood the largely unplanned cities of Manchester and Birmingham and the mine tailings and slag heaps of the Ruhr and of northeastern France. Not until after mid-century did the new cities gradually receive sewage systems, relatively clean water supplies, and housing that even remotely approximated the population's needs.

Emigration was the alternative to the cities. It tended to affect all countries with high rates of population increase, whether they led or followed industrially. Britain grew from 8.9 million in 1801 to 32.5 million in 1901, even while giving up millions of emigrants. Germany, between the "hungry forties" and the maturing of its industrial economy by 1900, gave up perhaps 5 million emigrants. France, with its stable peasant economy, low birth rate, and slow industrialization, showed a unique pattern of low emigration.

Predominantly agricultural countries also participated in this continent-wide

The new industrial city, crowded and sooty: London by Gustave Doré.

migration. Ireland, after the famine, gave up roughly 3 million emigrants before 1900. Scandinavian emigration peaked in the 1880s. Emigration from relatively backward areas such as Russia, Spain, and Italy continued to increase until World War I cut it short in 1914. Italy, with its overpopulated South and late industrialization, gave up an unprecedented 880,000 emigrants in 1913. The recipient of most of this great migration was the United States, which received 82 percent of all transatlantic emigration in 1866–70 and received still 61 percent in 1896–1900.

The combined effect of urbanization and emigration was to open up the old rural societies and to create new social relationships in the new cities and lands across the oceans. Returnees from the cities and even from the New World (10 million people *returned* to Europe between 1886 and 1915) brought new ideas into the narrow agricultural communities from

FIGURE 24.6   **The Urbanization of Europe**

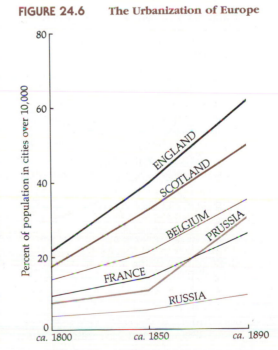

which they had escaped. Compulsory military service, which became almost universal after 1870, had similarly broadening effects. The knowledge that better or at least profoundly different patterns of life existed elsewhere helped dissolve what remained of the old order.

Social Structures

The industrial revolution weakened old social groups and created new ones. The rapid rise of a new business elite undermined the social power of the nobility far more than the events of 1789 had done. In Britain the aristocracy controlled perhaps 20 percent of the national product in 1820. By 1850 that proportion had sunk to 10 percent. A decline in the role of agriculture paralleled that of the nobility, the elite that defined itself by ownership of land. Britain's case was extreme: decline was so precipitous that by 1901 less than 5 percent of the population actually worked in agriculture or fishing. France, as usual, resisted the trend. Simultaneously, the industrial population and the proportion of the national wealth that industry produced swiftly increased

throughout western Europe (see Figure 24-7). Industry's proportion of the national product passed agriculture before 1820 in Britain, around 1890 in Germany, and in the first decade of the new century in France.

In the new cities, the middle classes expanded rapidly. By the end of the century they made up a far larger proportion of the total population than ever before— from perhaps 20 percent in northwestern Europe to 5 percent in the south and east. The middle classes consisted first of all of the entrepreneurs, the driving force and chief beneficiaries of the new age of cotton, coal, and steam. Then came the professional middle classes, the growing ranks of lawyers, doctors, higher bureaucrats, professors, and professional intellectuals. The nineteenth century was theirs as no other century has been, for the nobility had lost its monopoly of power and the masses were as yet hesitant in pressing their claims.

Below the entrepreneurial and professional middle classes, new groups proliferated. Increasing specialization of work paralleled and influenced the increasing number of subtle gradations in

FIGURE 24.7 **The Triumph of Industry over Agriculture: Germany and Britain**

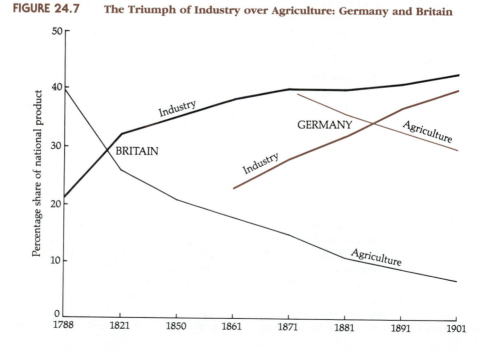

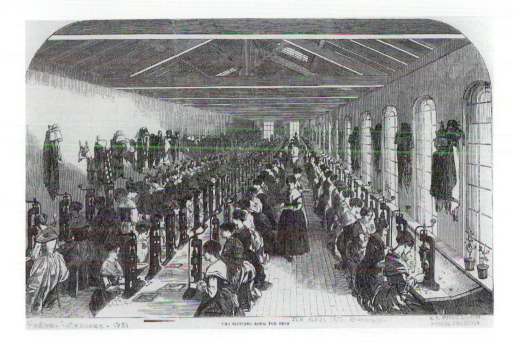

Women in the industrial work force: slitting pen nibs in a Birmingham factory (1851).

the social hierarchy. The artisans and home handicraft workers, victims of the machine, dwindled. Only the continued existence of trades difficult to mechanize fully, such as clothing manufacture, guaranteed their continued existence. Alongside this "old lower-middle class" of distressed artisans, there grew a "new lower-middle class" of white-collar workers in government or business bureaucracies. This group was as characteristic of the new industrial age as were the industrial workers below it.

The lower classes divided into numerous subcategories. Peasants and landless rural laborers stood at the bottom of the hierarchy in the countryside. A large class of domestic servants made possible the leisured existence of the new middle classes. The industrial workers themselves were anything but uniform. They ranged from the "labor aristocracy," skilled iron and steel workers, machinists, and foremen, to unskilled or semiskilled workers at starvation wages. Below the working classes was an underclass of pickpockets, prostitutes, and beggars, sometimes organized, but often anarchic and always violent.

The lines between groups remained far more fluid than under the old society

of orders on the Continent. Becoming an entrepreneur was relatively easy at first, at least in Britain, but class lines hardened as the century wore on. The amount of capital needed to enter industry increased dramatically with the coming of the steam engine and still more with the second industrial revolution. The new cities, unlike the old, were segregated by class. In the pre-industrial past, workers had lived in attics and cellars, above and below the rich. But in new industrial cities such as Manchester and Birmingham, the new rich instead retreated to villas in the countryside, leaving the pestilent city centers to the poor. And the growth of an independent working-class culture and ideologies in response to the Industrial Revolution (see pp. 652–53) acted as a barrier to mobility. Those who did rise socially risked ostracism for "betraying their class."

From Traditional to Nuclear Family

Finally, the processes of industrialization and urbanization affected the very structure of the family and the role of women. Even before industrialization, the early modern family, with its extended networks of kin and its family ties based on subordination and respect, had begun to give way to the nuclear family of parents and children. Nuclear families of parents and children, based at least in theory on love, may have existed in England since the late Middle Ages. They had in any case conquered the English middle classes by 1800. Family and workplace separated. The family became a private realm. The increasing fashion for romantic love as the chief reason for marriage undermined the old role of the father as a monarch in miniature. Once children chose their own mates, the authority of the father was under attack.

Similar developments, with a considerable lag, penetrated the urban areas of the Continent as well. First the upper middle classes adopted the new style, then the nobility. Finally it trickled down the social scale as the nineteenth century drew on. Increasing affluence, literacy, and longer lives encouraged the transition. Unlike the biological old regime, when plague or famine might at any moment strike down a spouse or child, affection was now a sounder emotional investment.

The new family structure hardly liberated women, but it did improve their status. The social conventions of romantic love ultimately sapped the Code Napoléon's attempts to bolster the power of the father and eroded the dominance of the

bewhiskered patriarchs of nineteenth-century Britain or Germany. A man could only with difficulty combine the roles of master, companion, and lover. And the separation of work from the home and the profusion of domestic servants meant that middle-class women had more leisure than before industrialization. A British male commentator noted in the 1850s that "the day is thrown idle on woman's hand. The thousand exciting events and undertakings that . . . stretch the faculties of man, are reckoned beyond her sphere." That leisure gave more and more educated women opportunity to reflect on their condition and eventually to revolt against it.

By 1914 most of western Europe had passed through the fires of industrialization. Britain, Germany, and France had become industrial great powers. The United States had outstripped all rivals. Russia and Japan were beginning to overtake Western Europe. Industrialization had transformed the ways of life of the peoples and classes it had touched. Some groups had lost; many more, despite the bitterness of the struggle, had won. And industrialization, along with that other revolution in France, had also helped transform the ideas and categories through which the West understood the world and sought to change it.

Suggestions for Further Reading

The Pre-industrial World

On the world before industrialization, see the analysis of C. Cipolla, *Before the Industrial Revolution* (1975); for England, P. Laslett offers a quasi-nostalgic view in *The World We Have Lost* (1971). For the adventurous, F. Braudel, *Civilization and* *Capitalism, 15th–18th Centuries* (1982), provides an unparalleled guided tour of the pre-industrial world economy. C. McEvedy and F. Jones, *Atlas of World Population History* (1978), is first-rate.

Why the West, and Why Britain?

On the West's primacy and its causes, see especially D. Landes, *The Unbound Prometheus* (1972); E. L. Jones, *The European Miracle* (1981); W. O'Neill, *The Pursuit of Power* (1982); and N. Rosenberg and L. Birdzell, *How the West Grew Rich* (1986). For England's peculiarities, see the contrasting accounts of A. Macfarlane, *Marriage and Love in England* (1986), and L. Stone, *The Family Sex, and Marriage in England 1500–1800* (1977), and the summary of recent demographic research in E. A. Wrigley, "The Growth of Population in Eighteenth-Century England," *Past and Present* (February, 1983), pp. 121–50. H. Perkin, *The Origins of Modern English Society 1780–1880* (1969), offers an excellent synthesis of the social causes of British industrialization.

The Industrial Revolution

On the interrelationship of technological change and economic growth, see above all D. Landes, *The Unbound Prometheus,* and J. Mokyr, *The Lever of Riches: Technological Creativity and Economic Progress* (1990). P. Deane, *The First Industrial Revolution* (1965), and E. Pawson, *The Early Industrial Revolution* (1979), are useful on Britain, as is T. S. Ashton, *The Industrial Revolution* (1970). On the industrialization of the followers, see T. Kemp, *Industrialization in Nineteenth-Century Europe* (1969), and C. Trebilcock, *The Industrialization of Continental Europe* (1981). B. Mitchell, *European Historical Statistics* (1981), is a useful source, and Paul Bairoch, "International Industrialization Levels from 1750 to 1980," *Journal of European Economic History 2,* no. 2, provides indispensable data on shifts in the economic balance of power. T. Hamerow, *The Birth of a New Europe* (1983), is a fine survey of the social and political consequences of industrialization.

25

THE NINETEENTH-CENTURY REVOLUTION OF IDEAS

The twin revolutions in France and in the mills and foundries of Britain generated new ideas and modified old ones. Yet the movement of ideas, like industrialization, was in part independent of other forces. Like industrialization, it was a continuous, expanding process operating throughout the relatively peaceful century that followed 1815. And like industrialization, it is best understood as a whole. This chapter therefore sketches the nineteenth century explosion of knowledge about nature and about humanity in its entirety. Then Chapters 26 and 27 introduce the political events of 1815–71 and European expansion into the wider world.

All across Europe, the old religious certainties, whether Catholic or Protestant, remained valid for the great mass of the population throughout the nineteenth century. But religion gradually became central to fewer lives. Science and scholarship appeared to undermine it. Urbaniza-tion and the decay of the traditional village community lessened its grip. In the realm of culture, a new movement, romanticism, fiercely attacked both the ideas and the style of the Enlightenment. In philosophy, two generations of Germans laid the foundations for much of nineteenth-century political thought. In politics, a "counter-Enlightenment" in some ways parallel to romanticism developed: conservatism, the ideology of opposition to revolutionary France and to all revolution. The adversary of conservatism was the ill-assorted conglomerate of economic and political doctrines known as liberalism. And beyond liberalism but related to it and locked in struggle with it came socialism, a political faith for the new industrial workers. Last of all, the French revolution's most powerful legacy, nationalism, spread eastward across Europe.

In the realm of practice, as opposed to that of ideas, new forces and tendencies modified European intellectual and social life. State bureaucracies hesitantly developed an interest in the education and welfare of their populations. Rising literacy and wealth led to the appearance of a new force that increasingly made rulers tremble: public opinion. Submerged social groups and categories, women and workers, began for the first time to make themselves heard.

THE FORCE OF IDEAS

Science and Scholarship

The nineteenth century opened new and unsuspected vistas. Mathematics, the discipline seemingly most remote from experience, equipped itself with the tools needed to inspire and describe the discoveries of twentieth-century physics. The creation of the first non-Euclidian geometry by a Russian, Nikolai Ivanovitch Lobachevsky (1793–1856), led to the invention of topology by Georg Friedrich Riemann (1826–66) of Göttingen. That, and the tensor calculus of Gregorio Ricci (1853–1925), in turn made possible the twentieth-century mathematics of space-time and gravity.

In physics, electricity and heat were the phenomena that nineteenth-century science explored most successfully. The discovery of electric current in 1786 led to Alessandro Volta's battery in 1799, to Hans Christian Oersted's discovery of a connection between magnetism and electricity in 1819, and to Michael Faraday's theory of electromagnetic induction in 1831. Ultimately James Clerk Maxwell, in *Electricity and Magnetism* (1873), provided a mathematical synthesis suggesting that light was also an electromagnetic phenomenon.

With electricity, advances in the laboratory created new industrial technologies. The reverse occurred with the steam engine. It inspired Sadi Carnot, son of the Carnot of the revolutionary Committee of Public Safety, to formulate in the 1820s the generalizations that later physicists codified as the first and second laws of thermodynamics.

The advance of chemistry was even more spectacular than that of physics. John Dalton's sketch of an atomic theory in the first decade of the century opened the way for the study of chemical compounds and structures. The synthesis in 1828 of urea, a compound found in nature, opened the study of organic chemistry, the chemistry of carbon. By the 1860s, chemists had begun to explore the molecular structure of simple carbon compounds such as benzene. In 1869 Dimitri Ivanovitch Mendeleev formulated a periodic law and table of elements that for the first time gave scientists a sketchy notion of some of the basic building blocks of the universe. The periodic table predicted the existence of elements as yet unknown; researchers using Mendeleev's theory isolated gallium (1871), scandium (1879), germanium (1886), and helium (1895).

But not until the end of the century did breakthroughs on the boundary of chemistry and physics revolutionize science's picture of the world and place the old Newtonian certainties in question. Wilhelm Roentgen's discovery of X rays (1895) soon led to the unearthing of radioactive elements that apparently emitted particles smaller than the atom. By the turn of the century, the theoreticians Max Planck and Albert Einstein had begun to lay the foundations for a non-Newtonian physics that unified the universe of subatomic particles with that of space-time and predicted the convertibility of matter into energy.

Biology, essentially a creation of the nineteenth century, developed practical uses after mid-century. The explorations of the world of bacteria by Louis Pasteur (1822–95) and Robert Koch (1843–1910) opened the door to an understanding of many diseases and aided Joseph Lister (1827–92) in the development of sterile surgical procedures.

But the greatest biological questions were theoretical. What caused the unparalleled diversity of life forms that eighteenth- and early nineteenth-century naturalists had classified? How had humanity originated? Studies in embryology in the 1820s implied that embryos, during their growth, might be recapitulating their species history, for bird embryos developed gill-slits. The study of fossils, still in its infancy, suggested change and development over immense periods of time. The discovery in 1856 of an apelike but large-brained skull at Neanderthal near the Ruhr (see p. 3) implied that humanity might have nonhuman ancestors.

Geology, an entirely new science, appeared to offer corroboration. Charles Lyell's *Principles of Geology* (1830–33) provided the first satisfactory explanation of the Earth's physical features and their origins. A variety of speculative thinkers suggested that life—including human life—might also be the result of evolutionary processes. But the mechanism by which that evolution occurred was still a mystery. Jean Baptiste Lamarck, who invented the term "biology," proposed in 1809 that creatures acquired characteristics in response to changes in their environment and subsequently passed those "acquired characteristics" to their offspring. That would account for diversity and change—if it were true.

It was Charles Darwin (1809–82) who most cogently suggested, after long investigations on the isolated Galápagos islands off Ecuador and elsewhere, that species evolved through a savage "struggle for life." Darwin announced that conclusion in 1858, after a fellow biologist, Alfred Russel Wallace (1823–1913), had sketched out a similar theory. The following year, Darwin published his path-breaking synthesis, *The Origin of Species by Means of Natural Selection, or the Preservation of Favored Races in the Struggle for Life.* Darwin argued, with a crushing weight of examples drawn from field research, that scarcity of food produced a fierce competition that killed off "unfit" variants of a given species before they could reproduce. "Sexual selection," or the triumph of the "fittest" males in competition for females further reinforced that mechanism. "Natural selection," working over immense spans of time, had produced the rich diversity visible in nature.

Darwin, although he recoiled from controversy with the religious establishment, ultimately extended his logic to humanity itself in *The Descent of Man* (1871): "Thus from the wars of nature, from famine and death, the most exalted object which we are capable of conceiving, namely the production of higher animals, directly follows." That claim, popularized in innumerable works by other "Darwinists," accomplished the most far-reaching revolution in the West's conception of itself since Copernicus had suggested that the Earth was not the motionless center of the universe. Darwin's explanation of humanity's place in the new world that science was uncovering made him the most widely influential scientific thinker of the century.

His theories also made him the father of modern biology. His single powerful generalization accounted for all the diversity of life. But Darwin's theory of evolution nevertheless had a major weakness: it accounted only for the change of *entire* species over time. Darwin could not find a convincing physical cause for the all-important variations between *individuals* that apparently drove those species changes. He fell back in part on Lamarck's untenable theory of the inheritance of acquired characteristics. Not until later did the long-neglected work of the Bohemian monk Gregor Mendel (1822–84), the father of genetics, provide the answer. In 1901 Hugo De Vries drew on Mendel's work to formulate a theory of genetic mutation by sudden random leaps. Later experiments using the fast-multiplying fruit fly laid the groundwork of modern genetics, which explained individual variation and provided Darwin's basic insights with powerful support.

In the social sciences, the nineteenth century likewise opened a new age. The eccentric Auguste Comte (1798–1857) invented the word sociology, if not the discipline it describes. A revolution in sources, methods, and subjects transformed history from a literary pastime into a scholarly profession. The German scholar Leopold von Ranke (1795–1886) laid down the doctrine that historians must first of all investigate and cross-check primary source materials, the evidence the histori-

Charles Darwin, father of modern biology and greatest scientific mind of the nineteenth century.

cal actors themselves had left. Ranke's notion that the historian's duty was to reconstruct events "as they actually happened" was not new. Thucydides the Athenian had suggested something of the sort in his fifth-century B.C. history of the Peloponnesian War (see pp. 56–57). But now, in the early nineteenth century, it was at last possible to attempt to translate that conception of history into systematic practice. In England, France, and Germany governments and private groups founded institutions such as London's Public Record Office for the collection and publication of historical source documents.

Vast multivolume national histories began to appear, monuments to the industry and learning of their authors, though, alas, not always readable. The Prussian professor of law, Karl von Savigny (1779–1861) founded a historical school dedicated to explaining the evolution of law. He proclaimed the superiority of Germanic law, which had grown by the slow accretion of precedent, over the artificial law codes of the French.

Historical scholarship even touched Scripture. David Friedrich Strauss's *Life of Jesus* (1835) examined the Gospels as historical documents and expressed skepticism about the divinity—and existence—of their subject. The French intellectual Ernest Renan provoked outrage in the 1860s by describing Christ as "an incomparable *man*." His biography of Christ was a popular success.

Finally, historians and philologists began investigating the diversity of human languages and deriving general laws. In 1835, a British scholar, Sir Henry Rawlinson, followed up Champollion's 1822 decipherment of hieroglyphics by reading the cuneiform inscriptions of the ancient Persians. German scholars studied the shifts of consonants in numerous languages over many centuries, and deduced laws governing the evolution of languages. They demonstrated that the Indian language Sanskrit and most European languages shared a common Indo-European origin. That discovery helped open up the study of the prehistory of Europe and of South and Central Asia (see pp. 8–10).

Religion

Religious skepticism had become commonplace among educated Europeans in the course of the eighteenth century. In the nineteenth century, that detachment from religion began to spread to the masses. That was partly a consequence of politics. The American and French revolutions, unlike the English Revolution of the 1640s, had been secular upheavals. Many French revolutionaries had been overtly anticlerical. Urbanization and its consequent social dislocation likewise undermined religion. In the jerry-built industrial city of Birmingham in 1851 the churches could hold less than a third of the population. And many of the new industrial workers resented the churches' defense of the social status quo. Finally, the retreat from religion was in part a consequence of the same process of scientific advance that had inspired the deists and skeptics of the Enlightenment.

But the science of the nineteenth century appeared far more powerful, and less compatible with traditional religion, than that of the eighteenth century. Lyell's geology and Darwin's evolution placed in question the biblical account of creation. That above all affected Protestants (and to a lesser extent Jews), given the central place of the biblical texts in their beliefs. Darwin's work provoked a veritable "warfare of science and theology." The Archbishop of Canterbury, in a furious debate in 1860, sarcastically asked "Darwin's Bulldog," the biologist Thomas H. Huxley, which side of his family descended from apes. A minority of "fundamentalist" Protestants, especially strong in the United States, continued to assert the literal truth of the biblical account of creation. The majority, thanks to Protestantism's emphasis on the individual's freedom and direct relationship with God, made a variety of compromises between faith and reason.

Strong forces nevertheless counteracted the decline of religion. Women of the lower classes, submerged by custom and illiteracy, tended to retain their traditional piety. The rural masses held to their faith whether they stayed at home or emigrated, as did so many Irish and Italians. Governments, whether of kings or liberals, continued to prize religion as a foundation for social order. Above all, religion itself showed continued vitality and expansive force.

In England and the United States the nineteenth century was a time of intense religious ferment. The impetus of German Pietism and of John Wesley's Methodism (see pp. 553–54) was far from spent. Other Protestant sects expanded with equal rapidity. Waves of religious enthusiasm swept over South Wales, for instance, in 1807–09, 1828–30, 1839–48, 1854, and 1859. In America after 1800 a "Great Revival" moved westward with the frontier.

The politics of Wesley, the Pietists, and their offshoots tended to bolster the social order. In the words of the *Statutes of the Wesleyan Body* (1792), "the oracles of God" commanded obedience to government. That attitude permeated English and American popular religion. Along with the early spread of democratic politics in those societies, it limited the appeal of the socialist panaceas for the ills of *this* world so popular in continental Europe, and described later in this chapter. And the spread of democracy helped the churches by providing a widely popular and defensible status quo.

European Catholicism was even more closely intertwined with the existing order than Protestantism, and after 1789 that order was under attack. Some advanced Catholic thinkers foresaw the need for the Church to distance itself from monarchy lest it perish in the monarchy's ruin. Félicité de Lamennais, a formerly ultraconservative French cleric, published *Words of a Believer* after the 1830 Paris revolution (see p. 662). He appealed for equality and democracy, and denounced "the passion to acquire and to possess." Rome damned Lamennais in two thundering encyclicals.

Pope Pius IX (r. 1846–78) appeared briefly as a champion of change. Then the revolutions of 1848 (described on pp. 666–69) dissuaded him. His encyclical

Quanta cura of 1864, with its appended *Syllabus errorum,* or "listing of errors," denounced the notion that "the Roman Pontiff can and ought to reconcile himself to and agree with progress, liberalism, and modern civilization." The reforming Pope Leo XIII (r. 1878–1903) reversed that uncompromising stance in a path-breaking encyclical of 1891 entitled *Rerum novarum* ("Of New Things"). The gradual dechristianization of the urban masses and the challenge of socialism had led to a rethinking. *Rerum novarum* was the charter of a new social and reforming Catholicism that condemned both capitalist greed and socialist denial of God. Leo XIII's successor, Pius X (r. 1903–14), reverted to rigid defense of received doctrine and purged the Church of "modernists" who sought to reconcile science with theology. But in the end it was Leo XIII's policy of adaptation to the new age that triumphed.

Romanticism

A new style, opposed to the rationalism and classicism of the Enlightenment (see pp. 543–48), emerged toward the end of the eighteenth century. The stormy young German writers of the *"Sturm und Drang"* movement of the 1780s, in particular, had defied convention and celebrated emotion. By 1800 German critics had coined the distinction between "classical" and "romantic," although "romantic" has no tidy definition.

Some romantics, such as the great English poet George Gordon, Lord Byron (1788–1824), thought of themselves as revolutionaries: "I have simplified my politics into a detestation of all existing governments." The French poet, dramatist, and novelist Victor Hugo (1802–85) could write that "romanticism is liberalism in literature." Byron's friend Percy Bysshe Shelley (1792–1822) proclaimed that "poets are the unacknowledged legislators of the world." Heinrich Heine (1797–1856), and last major German romantic poet and the greatest German lyric poet of the century, was a lifelong radical democrat. The French painter Eugène Delacroix (1798–1863) could paint, in *Liberty Leading the*

People (1834), the ultimate romantic vision of the triumph of revolution (see p. 656).

Other romantics, such as the English lyric poets William Blake (1757–1827) and William Wordsworth (1770–1850), outdid one another in their rejection of the "dark satanic mills" of the new industrial age. In politics, Wordsworth's original enthusiasm for the French Revolution gave way to bitter opposition even to modest Parliamentary reforms in England (see p. 660). Especially in Germany, romanticism turned increasingly into a celebration of the Middle Ages, which were supposedly more authentic than the Renaissance or the alleged artificiality and frenchified rationalism of the detested eighteenth century. The eerie landscapes of Caspar David Friedrich (1774–1840), painted from imagination rather than life, illustrated the romantic vision of the Middle Ages. In England, the medieval historical novels of Sir Walter Scott, the paintings of John Constable and Joseph Turner, and the revival of Gothic as an architectural style embodied similar tendencies.

But the romantics, however varied their politics and aesthetics, tended to share four things. First, they rejected the eighteenth century's "classical" limitations on form and structure in art. In music, romantics from the greatest master of the symphony, Ludwig van Beethoven (1770–1827) to the dogmatic theorist and practitioner of "total opera," Richard Wagner (1813–83), gleefully disregarded inherited conventions of form, and of orchestra size and make-up. Poets such as Wordsworth deliberately chose a vocabulary closer to spoken English than to the measured couplets of predecessors such as Alexander Pope. Continental dramatists discarded for good the restrictions on subject, time, and place that classical theories of drama had imposed.

Second, the romantics prized emotion, the stronger the better. That led even former fellow-travelers such as the great German poet Johann Wolfgang von Goethe (1749–1832) to conclude that "classic is that which is healthy, romantic that which is sick." The line between emo-

Cloister Graveyard in the Snow (1810) by Caspar David Friedrich.

tion and morbid self-preoccupation was a narrow one. But the romantic emphasis on the creative power of the individual imagination was a liberating force. If combined with craftsmanship and self-discipline it could produce masterpieces.

Third, the romantics tended to celebrate nature. Their nature was not the manicured eighteenth-century ornamental garden, but the craggy uplands of Wordsworth's imagination:

> *Once again*
> *Do I behold these steep and lofty cliffs*
> *That on a wild secluded scene impress*
> *Thoughts of more deep seclusion;*
>   *and connect*
> *The landscape with the quiet of the*
>   *sky.*

Rousseau, with his mystical *Reveries of a Solitary Wanderer* (1776–78) had shown the way. Nature, the "nature or God" of Spinoza (see p. 539) brought humanity—or at least skeptical intellectuals—closer to an otherwise unknowable God. The popularization of this "natural supernaturalism," as the English philosopher-historian Thomas Carlyle (1795–1881) called it, was one of the major legacies of romanticism.

Finally, the romantics both celebrated and embodied the cult of the solitary, youthful, misunderstood genius who defied convention and perhaps suffered persecution for political radicalism or, like Byron, for sexual peccadillos. Like Shelley, the genius might be dead by thirty; tuberculosis was as much the romantic disease as morbid introspection. The cult of the artist as misfit was in part an extension of the romantic emphasis on imagination, on the creative powers of the individual. The collapse of aristocratic art patronage after 1789 may also have contributed, for the middle classes were not yet rich enough to step in. Age, respectability, and middle-class patrons nevertheless tamed those romantics who survived. Although the movement did not outlast mid-century, it broke Enlightenment formalism for good. Art was henceforth what the artist, the individual as towering genius, decreed it to be.

The Revolution in German Philosophy: From Kant to Hegel

Parallel to romanticism and not unrelated to it came an explosion of creativity in German philosophy. Misty speculation, including opposition to Newton's mathematically precise account of matter and motion, had long been a German specialty. Immanuel Kant (see p. 554) had sought to rescue reason from the skepticism of Enlightenment philosophers such as David Hume, who refused to accept as certain the evidence of the senses. Kant saved reason by limiting its domain. He postulated that the human mind was capable of limited knowledge of the world around it, but only on the basis of categories such as space and time, categories already built into the structure of the mind itself. Humanity could not perceive "things in themselves," things as they really were, except through those categories.

Kant's second main contribution was related to his theory of knowledge. Moral judgment was similar to the mind's inborn mechanism of perception, Kant argued. Morality was the result of a universal law found within ourselves. And for Kant, freedom was obedience to that law. The poet Heine rightly remarked that as a revolutionary, Kant put Robespierre in the shade. Kant's notion of morality, in particular, opened the way for individuals to discover moral standards *for themselves*. Kant was a loyal supporter of the Prussian state, but his doctrine struck at the root of any claim to authority that individuals chose not to accept.

Kant's theory of knowledge provoked his successors, especially Johann Gottlieb Fichte (1762–1814) and Georg Wilhelm Friedrich Hegel (1770–1831), to a decisive step. Fichte saw the implausibility of saying that things-in-themselves existed but that the mind could not know them. If the mind knew about them, they must exist. Rather than falling back into Enlightenment rationalism, Fichte and Hegel took a leap of faith even greater than Kant's. Both things-in-themselves and the mind must be part of a larger whole, a universal consciousness, an all-encompassing "world spirit" that was a descendant of Spinoza's "nature or God."

Hegel, the most influential philosopher of the century, proclaimed that history was the process of the upward evolution or self-realization of that world spirit. History thus had a goal. It also had a mechanism, the "dialectic," a step-by-step progress through a series of reversals or negations. It had already passed through three stages: the oriental, in which the despot alone was free; the ancient world, in which a few men in Greece and Rome had been free; and the Christian-Germanic civilization of northern Europe, which had at last recognized that humanity itself was or could be free.

In this process, this ever-upward striving toward the self-realization of the world spirit, the role of the individual was clear. Kant's self-determining individual would inevitably will an ever-closer identification with Hegel's world spirit. And Hegel, as befitted a professor of philosophy at the University of Berlin, came to identify the world spirit with the Prussian power-state: "The State is the divine Idea as it exists on earth." Others took Kant's notion of self-determination, and Hegel's goal-oriented theory of history and put them to uses that their originators could hardly have foreseen.

Conservatism

Although Hegel's ideas helped to shore up the royal Prussian status quo, the doctrines later called conservatism had entirely different sources. First and most important was the Anglo-Irish Tory, Edmund Burke (1729–97). His inspired diatribe of 1790, *Reflections on the Revolution in France,* was uncannily prophetic (see p. 599). It still reads as if written in 1793–94, against the background of war and Terror. Burke denounced the doctrinaire logic of the French revolutionaries, whose "rage and frenzy will pull down more in half an hour than prudence, deliberation, and foresight can build in a hundred years." His model was the English constitution, that agglomeration of custom and precedent that over many centuries had created what freedom existed in Britain. Organic growth, not radical panaceas, was the only sound basis for a political system. Change was admissible, although "when I changed it should be to preserve." Even revolution, as in 1688 and 1776, might be acceptable if it reasserted a historic tradition. But plans for change should not assume human perfectibility. They should postulate, on the basis of long sad experience, the "ignorance and fallibility of mankind."

Burke's commitment to individual liberty, which had led him to sympathize with the complaints of the American colonists, did not survive translation into French and German. Burke the militant, the Burke who wrote in 1796 of the French Revolution that "it is with an *armed doctrine* that we are at war," was the Burke who inspired continental conservatives to create their own armed doctrines of counterrevolution. Joseph de Maistre (1754–1821), the most lively of the conservative theorists, acknowledged Burke's influence. But de Maistre's doctrine had little place for freedom: "All power, all discipline, are based on the executioner. He is at once the horror of human society and the tie that binds it together. . . ." In Germany, admirers of Burke invoked his name to support notions of a return to divine-right monarchy and medieval Christianity. That was not conservatism, but "reaction," an attempt to erase everything after 1789.

Liberalism

Conservatism, or reaction, was the ideology of what became, from its place in the seating arrangements of the post-1815 French assemblies, the "Right." Liberalism was the creed of the "Left." Like most "isms," the term is exceedingly vague. It has so broadened in the twentieth century that it now conveys a mood rather than a body of ideas.

Nineteenth-century liberalism was narrower. It meant, first of all, a body of economic thought that preached *laissez-faire,* the removal of all artificial restraints on the market. In politics, nineteenth-century liberalism stood, more or less squarely, for individual freedom and for equality of opportunity but not of outcome. Political liberalism—like Locke, its founding father—identified liberty with property; that identification was the link between political and economic liberalism. Liberalism was an optimistic creed that united capitalism and individualism under the banner of "progress," the faith of the Enlightenment. Liberalism was the creed of the middle classes, to whom the explosive growth of industry and trade gave increasing self-confidence.

The "classical economists," of whom the three most important were Adam Smith (1723–90), Thomas Robert Malthus (1766–1834), and David Ricardo (1772–1823), asked many of the questions that still occupy economists. Smith and Ricardo in particular argued that only the market could allocate resources efficiently. The "hidden hand" of supply and demand, by a self-operating law, would maximize the increase in wealth.

In his *Essay on the Principle of Population* (1798, revised 1803), Malthus explored the relationship between population and food. He concluded gloomily that "population, when unchecked, increases in a geometrical ratio. Subsistence only increases in an arithmetical ratio." Malthus' generalization that population—"when unchecked"—tends to outrun food made nineteenth-century economics the "dismal science." It also provided Darwin with his principle of the "struggle for survival" in the face of inevitable scarcity.

But Malthus qualified his theory in an important way that escaped many later critics. A "preventive check" on population increase existed: the tendency in Europe and especially in Britain for men and women to marry late, and hence have fewer children than their biological maximum. Malthus theorized that "moral restraint" or a growing taste for consumer luxuries might lead individuals to limit their families. Such tendencies could lead eventually to a shortage of labor, and "in the natural course of things" to a rise in wages. Malthus was a prophet of affluence as well as of doom.

His contemporary Ricardo had less foresight. In his *Principles of Political Economy and Taxation* (1817), the last great work of classical economics, Ricardo

proclaimed what soon became known as the "iron law of wages." Since population and hence labor supply supposedly increased geometrically, wages would always remain just above starvation level. Raising wages above that level would merely encourage overpopulation. That would in turn increase the supply of labor until wages once more dropped. Generosity toward the workers was thus futile, even pernicious. Ricardo's misunderstanding of Malthus was highly convenient to the early textile mill owners, hard men reared in a hard school. They enthusiastically embraced his doctrine. Economic science had shown conclusively, Ricardo's popularizers trumpeted, that poverty was inevitable and that efforts to avert it would produce ever more poverty.

Ricardo's other major contribution was to clarify a concept found in Adam Smith's work that had profound political implications. That was the "labor theory of value," the notion that the "value" of a manufactured article was proportional to the amount of labor required to make it. Ricardo used the theory to explain where profits came from. For him they were the difference between the cost of labor per article to the industrialist and the selling price of the article, after the deduction of the industrialist's overhead costs. Ricardo applauded profit; socialists later used his work to argue that profits were "surplus value" stolen from the workers.

The political ideas of nineteenth-century liberalism in part contradicted the "dismal science." The English philosopher and reformer Jeremy Bentham (1748–1832), the key figure in the transition from Enlightenment to nineteenth-century liberal thought, rejected the Lockean tradition of natural rights. Instead, as befitted an age of machinery, Bentham postulated that "utility" must guide humanity. Bentham's utility dictated the search for "the greatest happiness of the greatest number," and he defined happiness merely as "pleasurable feelings and . . . freedom from pain." For Bentham and the "Utilitarians," as his followers became known, the best government delivered the most pleasure and the least pain to the most people. Utility, in Bentham's view, replaced

Thomas Robert Malthus, pioneer of the study of population growth.

Locke's natural rights as the philosophical foundation of liberal democracy. But utility could also justify social engineering that trampled on those rights. For in Bentham's view, utility demanded the regimentation of the poor for their own supposed good.

Bentham's most influential successor, John Stuart Mill (1806–73), drove Benthamite liberalism to one possible logical conclusion, and inevitably made himself unpopular. Mill's *On Liberty* (1859) proclaimed utility as "the ultimate appeal in all ethical questions." Government was suspect: "That government is best that governs least." Mill asserted that "the only purpose for which power can rightfully be exercised over any member of a civilized community, against his will, is to prevent harm to others."

Mill, like Bentham, deduced that utility demanded democratic government. But what if that government, faced with the horrors of the early nineteenth-century factory system and with the plight of the poor, demanded limits on the economic freedom of the entrepreneur? Mill ultimately concluded that the state must intervene to protect children and improve living and working conditions. He also attacked the domination of men over women. After urging votes for women in Parliament in 1867, he published *The Subjection of Women* (1869). The work largely derived from ideas that his wife, Harriet Taylor Mill, had already put forward. It scandalized British middle-class opinion by insisting that women, too, should enjoy liberty. That demand followed from Mill's premises and from those of nineteenth-century liberalism generally. But few accepted that logic in the 1860s.

On the Continent, liberalism was more cautious than in Britain, thanks in part to the relative weakness of the middle classes there until industrialization was well under way. In politics, constitutionalism before liberty was the preference of Benjamin Constant (1767–1830), France's answer to Bentham. Constant proclaimed liberty as "the object of all human association" but resisted extension of France's limited franchise. German liberals (see p. 670) tended to confuse national self-assertion with liberty. And in economics, French and German thinkers resisted the full force of *laissez-faire,* with its tendency to dissolve all traditional social ties. Some German economists challenged liberal orthodoxy frontally. The influential Friedrich List (1789–1846) argued that industrialization in the face of British competition required a neo-mercantilist planned economy, protective tariffs, and state-supported railway construction.

Socialism

Despite its internal contradictions, economic and political liberalism was a thumping success as a secular religion of progress for the middle classes. But it inevitably summoned up a counter-ideology, "socialism." The term, almost as indefinable as liberalism, implies concern for the good of society as a whole, in opposition to liberalism's focus on individual liberty, property, and profit. Socialism and its overlapping but more extreme companion, "communism," had a pedigree going back at least to the abortive Paris rising of Gracchus Babeuf and the "Equals" in 1796 (see p. 597). But after 1815, as industrialization gathered force, it acquired new meaning.

Middle-class thinkers began to postulate an irrepressible conflict between workers and industrialists. Ricardo's economics, with its emphasis on inherent conflicts of interest between labor, capital, and landed wealth, provided tools for a radical attack on existing society. In England, a successful entrepreneur, Robert Owen (1771–1858), presented an alternative vision. Abolition of the profit motive and its replacement by "cooperation" would remake humanity, which Owen in Enlightenment fashion saw as a product of its environment. Across the Channel, Charles Fourier (1772–1837) pressed similar notions, which included the foundation of "phalanxes," or self-sufficient model agrarian communities. Owen demonstrated the fallacy of Ricardo's "iron law" by raising wages and providing housing for the workers in his model factories at New Lanark, Scotland, while at the same time increasing output and profits. His

John Stuart Mill, the conscience of nineteenth-century liberalism.

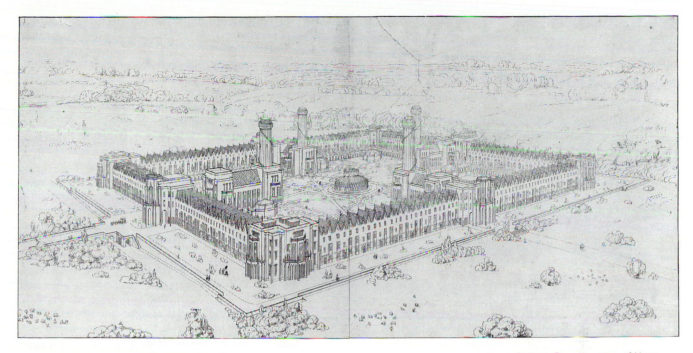

Robert Owen's vision of New Harmony, his utopian community in the Indiana wilderness.

later attempt to found a utopia at New Harmony, Indiana, was less successful.

A sterner prophet than Owen or Fourier was the French Count Henri de Saint-Simon (1760–1825). Although frequently classed with the "utopian" socialists Owen and Fourier, Saint-Simon was no enthusiast for model communities. He was the first to conceive of socialism as the outcome of an inexorable historical process that affected the whole of society. He prophesied that in the new society "rule over men" would give way to "the administration of things." His brave new world would be an earthly paradise in which *École Polytechnique* technocrats tamed nature for good with immense engineering projects. He was thus not only a father of socialism but also the inspiration of the heroic age of French engineering that produced the Suez Canal (1869) and the first railroad tunnels through the Alps.

The theory that came to dominate European socialism owed something to Saint-Simon but derived above all from a strange marriage between the misty realms of Hegelian philosophy and the apparent rigor of classical economics. Karl Marx (1818–83), a German Jew from the Prussian Rhineland, and Friedrich Engels, the scholarly son of a prosperous Rhineland industrialist, were its fathers. Marx became interested in philosophy while studying law at the University of Berlin. Following the example of Kant and Hegel, he set out to create a system.

By 1844–46, Marx had arrived with Engels' help at a preliminary synthesis. He kept Hegel's dialectical mechanism and goal-oriented stage-theory of history. But he replaced Hegel's mystical world spirit with humanity as a species. From the rigorous materialist Ludwig Feuerbach ("Man is what he eats"), Marx took the notion that the essence of the human species was work. Human nature was to be a "free producer."

Under capitalism, as Ricardo had seemingly demonstrated, humanity lost the product of its labor through the capitalist's confiscation of "surplus value." Under capitalism, Marx added, private property and specialization of work (the "division of labor") had "alienated" humanity from its true nature as "free producer." This was a sophisticated Hegelian

Karl Marx, the bourgeois patriarch (*right*), with his wife, two daughters, and Friedrich Engels in the 1860s.

Marx the Determinist Philosopher of History

In the social production of their existence, men enter into definite, predetermined relationships that are independent of their will. Those relations of production correspond to a given stage of the development of material productive forces. The totality of those relations of production forms the economic structure of the society, the real base, upon which a juridical and political superstructure rises, and to which given forms of social consciousness correspond. The mode of production of material life conditions the social, political, and intellectual life process itself. It is not the consciousness of men that determines their existence, but rather the reverse: their social existence determines their consciousness.

From Karl Marx, preface to A Contribution to the Critique of Political Economy *(1859; translation by M. Knox).*

version of the romantic and utopian socialist attack on early nineteenth-century industrial society.

But for Marx, unlike his "utopian" predecessors, history was destined to remedy the ills of past and present. He translated into economics Hegel's dialectical upward struggle of the world spirit toward self-realization. He joked that he had stood Hegel "right side up," and discovered the "rational kernel within the mystical shell." Work, not the Hegelian world spirit, powered history. Successive "modes of production," following one another dialectically, created new modes of consciousness, new stages in the upward progress of the human species. Instead of Hegel's oriental, ancient, and Germanic-Christian stages of history, Marx saw a progression of "modes of production," from ancient slave society, through "feudalism," to industrial capitalism, to a final stage: communism.

For the dialectic expressed itself politically as the struggle between economic classes: "The history of all existing society is the history of class struggle." That struggle now pitted the new industrial working class, the "proletariat" born of the Industrial Revolution, against the capitalist class or "bourgeoisie." That struggle, Marx con-

fidently predicted, would end with the victory of the proletariat, since capitalist industrialization would create ever-larger numbers of ever-poorer proletarians. And the proletariat's victory would bring the end of history—or rather the end of what Marx called "the pre-history of human society." For the proletariat, the class supposedly more alienated than any other in history from humanity's essence as "free producer," had a historic mission. Its revolution would be the last, and would turn philosophy into reality: "The government of persons is replaced by the administration of things, and by the conduct of the processes of production. The state is not 'abolished.' *It withers away.*"

Marx had worked out the main lines of his vision even before writing the famous *Communist Manifesto* with which he and Engels sought unsuccessfully to influence the 1848 revolutions described in Chapter 26. Marx spent the next thirty-five years as an exile in London, the center of world capitalism. There, drawing on the immense resources of the hospitable British Museum library, he fitted out his Hegelian framework with economic evidence that he believed proved its validity.

In *Capital,* the great unfinished work that began to appear in 1867 and set forth his system in its most elaborate form, Marx analyzed and damned the "capitalist mode of production." Its essence was greed: the capitalist was ". . . capital personified. His soul is the soul of capital." Capital was "dead labor, which, vampire-like, lives only by sucking living labor, and lives the more, the more labor it sucks." That demonic vision of capitalism appeared to derive from Marx's views on Judaism, as set forth in his notorious *On the Jewish Question* (1843). There, in pathological language, he had proclaimed that "money is the jealous God of Israel" and demanded an end to "the *empirical* essence of Judaism—huckstering."

Marx's system was at least three things: a philosophy of history, an economic theory and analysis of society, and a call to revolution. Logic and events have dealt harshly with the first two. His philosophy of history claimed scientific knowledge of the human future, and of the meaning of human history as a whole. But the whole past and the future are unknowable; statements about the meaning and destination of something largely unknowable are not science but a sort of religion.

And capitalism did not collapse. Capitalist industrialization did not polarize societies into ever-larger masses of increasingly degraded proletarians and ever-smaller groups of ever-richer capitalists. Revolution did not come to the most advanced capitalist countries, as Marx assumed it would. Instead, as described in Chapter 24, capitalist industrialization led to relative affluence and to an ever-broadening number of social groups. In the most advanced countries it was the industrial proletariat, not the state, that eventually withered away. And Marx's prediction of an ever-falling rate of profit under capitalism ignored the "dialectical" driving force of science and technology. New technologies create industries that are vastly profitable until they saturate their markets; then still newer technologies supersede them.

Marx's call to revolution proved to be the most powerful and durable part of his system. From the 1860s on, it made him the unchallenged intellectual leader of European and world socialism. But Marx's massive works concealed an underlying contradiction. His philosophy of history seemed to predict the almost automatic extinction of capitalism once economic conditions had ripened. That comforting thought might lead socialists to await the great day passively, a conclusion Marx and many later Marxists rejected. Marx left unresolved the tension in his writings between determinism and "voluntarism," between the temptation to await what was foreordained and the urge to force the pace of history through revolution.

Marx's endorsement of revolutionary terror and of the "dictatorship of the proletariat" also threatened his proclaimed goal of human freedom. Marx celebrated Jacobin-style violence as the midwife of history: under some circumstances there was "only one means to *curtail,* simplify and localize the bloody agony of the old society and the bloody birth-pangs of the new, only one means—the revolutionary ter-

ror." But he also recognized that humanity made its history not "as it please[d] . . . but under circumstances directly found, given, and transmitted from the past." Revolutionary terror would therefore constitute part of his new society's "past" and might influence its future in directions other than liberation.

And what if the "dictatorship of the proletariat" refused to wither away? Marx

Marx the Revolutionary Prophet

The history of all hitherto existing society is the history of class struggles.

Freeman and slave, patrician and plebeian, lord and serf, guildmaster and journeyman, in a word, oppressor and oppressed, stood in constant opposition to one another, carried on an uninterrupted, now hidden, now open fight, a fight that each time ended, either in a revolutionary reconstitution of society at large, or in the common ruin of the contending classes. . . .

The modern bourgeois society that has sprouted from the ruins of feudal society has not done away with class antagonisms. It has but established new classes, new conditions of oppression, new forms of struggle in place of the old ones.

Our epoch, the epoch of the bourgeoisie, possesses, however, this distinctive feature: it has simplified the class antagonisms: Society as a whole is more and more splitting up into two great hostile camps, into two great classes directly facing each other: Bourgeoisie and Proletariat. . . .

All previous historical movements were movements of minorities, or in the interests of minorities. The proletarian movement is the self-conscious, independent movement of the immense majority, in the interests of the immense majority. . . .

The advance of industry, whose involuntary promoter is the bourgeoisie, replaces the isolation of the laborers, due to competition, by their revolutionary combination, due to association. The development of Modern Industry, therefore, cuts from under its feet the very foundation on which the bourgeoisie produces and appropriates products. What the bourgeoisie, therefore, produces, above all, is its own grave-diggers. Its fall and the victory of the proletariat are equally inevitable.

From Karl Marx and Friedrich Engels, The Communist Manifesto *(1848).*

doggedly refused to take that question seriously, even when his rival in the international socialist movement, the eccentric Russian aristocrat Mikhail Bakunin (1814–76), attacked him publicly. Bakunin's anarchist answer to oppression was improbable: smashing the state would return humanity to a state of nature in which its essential goodness would at last prevail. But on the likely consequences of a transitional revolutionary dictatorship, Marx was the utopian and Bakunin the realist: "no dictatorship can have any other aim than to perpetuate itself."

Marx's vision conflicted in other ways with his goal of liberation. His claim to possess the meaning of history encouraged intolerance. If Marx, in Engels' famous words, was the Darwin of human society, if he had "discovered the fundamental law that determines the course and development of human history," then those who stood against him stood against history. Marx and his successors were not slow to point that out.

And as later critics have suggested, Marx's ideas contained implications for revolutionary regimes that went far beyond his advocacy of terror and temporary dictatorship. Since Marx claimed that all human conflict stemmed from the class struggle, conflict after the revolution could only be a result of resistance by the old ruling classes. Anyone who disagreed with the new regime thus became a legitimate target for further liberating violence. And if freedom meant social unity, as Marx—following thinkers as otherwise different as Rousseau and Hegel—assumed, then the more unity the more freedom. That belief could likewise point the way to the elimination of all who failed to fit in. And if, as Marx suggested, communism would enable humanity to control the conditions of its existence, then a regime that described itself as communist could do *anything it liked*. Nothing on earth, no law either economic or moral, need restrain it.

Marx's legacy was thus ambiguous. He made economics part of history. Economic forces, "modes of production," and social classes were henceforth objects of historical study alongside kings and battles. He offered a fierce critique of capitalism, although the credibility of that critique diminished as the brutal conditions of early British industrialization gave way to rising living standards. Above all, Marx created a messianic faith in revolution. That faith arrived on the scene too late in the nineteenth century to preside over a genuine revolution. The twentieth century offered new opportunities.

Bakunin the Anarchist Foresees a Dictatorship over the Proletariat

In 1874–75, Marx copied into his notebooks long passages from Statehood and Anarchy, *a work of his anarchist rival Mikhail Bakunin, and adorned them with furious comments (printed in brackets).*

(Bakunin) . . . the so-called people's state will be nothing other than the quite despotic administration of the masses of the people by a new and very non-numerous aristocracy of real and supposed learned ones. The people is not learned, so it will be entirely freed from the cares of governing, wholly incorporated into the governed herd. A fine liberation! The Marxists sense this [!] contradiction and, realizing that the regime of the learned [*quelle reverie!*], the hardest, most offensive, and most contemptuous in the world will in fact be a dictatorship in spite of all the democratic forms, console themselves with the thought that the dictatorship will be temporary and short-lived.

(Marx commentary) [*Non, mon cher!* The *class domination* of the workers over the resisting strata of the old world must last until the economic foundations of the existence of classes are destroyed.]

(Bakunin). . . . They say that such a state yoke, a dictatorship, is a necessary transitional means for attaining the most complete popular liberation. So, to liberate the masses of the people they first have to be enslaved. Our polemic rests and is founded on this contradiction. They maintain that only a dictatorship, their own naturally, can create the people's will; we answer: no dictatorship can have any other aim than to perpetuate itself. . . .

From Robert C. Tucker, ed., The Marx-Engels Reader, *2nd ed. (New York: W. W. Norton, 1978), pp. 546–47.*

Nationalism

From the beginning, socialism found itself competing with an even more powerful force: nationalism. The political idea of the nation-state, born in the French Revolution and spread by its wars, created deeper divisions than any between labor and capital. Two great forces, one political and one economic, acted throughout the nineteenth century to transmit nationalism eastward across Europe.

The first was the example of France's crushing military successes after 1792. Once French revolutionary nationalism had tapped the power of France's entire population, Europe's other peoples had to follow or go under. The second force was the Industrial Revolution. Once Britain showed the way to wealth and power, others had to follow. And survival, whether on the battlefield or in the cold marketplace world of profit and loss, demanded literate populations. Europe's states, as described in the next section of this chapter, responded by introducing compulsory schooling for their subjects. The new schools in turn had to teach a national language, for the days of medieval Latin as the universal language of western and central Europe were long past. National languages and state schools brought with them national cultures, complete with nationalist myths and historic grievances against neighbors.

This age of increasingly rapid change created emotional as well as political and economic needs. As money and goods and mass migrations dissolved Europe's traditional village communities, nationalism offered a new sense of belonging, a new anchor for popular loyalties. It offered that same sense of belonging—along with careers and power—to Europe's intellectuals. Yet the forces that spread nationalism did not determine and do not explain its ultimate effect, which was to tear Europe apart. Only the content of nationalist ideas can explain nationalism's consequences.

The nationalisms of nineteenth-century Europe were compounds of four major elements. First was the theory of the social contract and general will that the French Revolution had attempted to translate into reality. When the nation of king and nobles gave way to the nation of freely associating citizens, nothing except the "general will" limited the nation's ac-

tions. Second was Kant's doctrine of the moral autonomy of the individual. When extended to nations, that autonomy, that "self-determination," meant that nations needed to acknowledge no law they had not themselves chosen. Third was Hegel's notion of the state as the moral force in a history that was proceeding through struggle toward a goal. Hegel was no German nationalist; he had hailed Napoleon as a historic individual whose conquests advanced the self-realization of the world spirit. But his deification of the Prussian state had nationalist uses.

The fourth and most dangerous element of European nationalism was the ethnic concept of the nation. That too was above all a German contribution. Johann Gottfried von Herder (1744–1803), a prominent exponent of *Sturm und Drang,* had worked out in the 1770s and 1780s a philosophy of history that justified German resistance to the cultural domination of France. For Herder each nation, each *Volk,* was equally close to God. Each therefore had the duty to cultivate its own peculiarities: "Spew out the ugly slime of the Seine / Speak German, O you German!" Herder rejoiced in human diversity. Like Hegel, he was no nationalist. But once again, his ideas had nationalist uses.

German philosophers such as Fichte were soon proclaiming the *superiority* of the national language. The French, wrote Fichte after Napoleon's conquest of Germany in 1806, were a Germanic people who had foolishly abandoned their native tongue for a language derived from Latin. That had infected them with a "lack of seriousness." Herder's successors thus established a new test for nationhood: language. They made language the standard for drawing or redrawing boundaries. They made it what it had rarely been before: a matter of life and death.

In the decades after 1815, the French revolutionary conception of the general will, the notion of self-determination, the concept of the state as the moral force in history, and the ethnic-linguistic concept of the nation fused. The result was a uniquely European invention, *the secular religion of the nation-state.* For the nationalist, individual freedom and self-

Mikhail Bakunin, aristocrat and professional revolutionary.

The invention of national traditions: German peasant costume, as imagined by Ludwig Emil Grimm (1828).

Giuseppe Mazzini, prophet of the religion of the nation-state.

fulfillment lay only in service to such a state. That peculiar belief distinguishes nationalism from patriotism, the instinctive loyalty to homeland, and from xenophobia, the traditional and unthinking hatred and contempt for foreigners. Patriotism and xenophobia have existed throughout history; nationalism was an invention of the decades immediately after 1789.

It first spread in and through literature. Herder had provided a rationale for cultivating the language and culture of one's own *Volk*. The brothers Jakob and Wilhelm Grimm collected folk tales and Germanic mythology, and explored the roots of the German language. Poles, Czechs, Hungarians, and Balkan nationalities followed. Dictionaries and editions of medieval epic poems appeared, monuments to the peculiarities of each nation's history. Poets like Sándor Petöfi (1822–49) in Hungary and Giacomo Leopardi (1798–1837) in Italy wrote verse celebrating the national spirit and demanding national liberation.

Politics followed poetry. The defeat of revolutionary France did not remove nationalism from politics. Italy, which remained under Austrian domination after 1815, set the example. The conspiratorial sect of the *carbonari* ("charcoal-burners") had originated in south Italy as a protest against French rule. Although lacking a discernible program, it served as a magnet both for police spies and for youth hostile to the status quo. One such youth was Giuseppe Mazzini (1805–72), the greatest prophet of nineteenth-century nationalism.

Mazzini joined the *carbonari* in 1827 in his home town of Genoa and spent time in jail in 1830 for subversive activity. In exile in 1831 he founded a new type of conspiratorial organization: *Giovine Italia,* or "Young Italy." The movement had little practical success but its romantic emphasis on youthful enthusiasm set a powerful example. Mazzini proclaimed liberty, but his liberty was the liberty of the individual to serve the national idea. Nationalist politics was a *fede,* a faith, a political religion.

Mazzini proclaimed the liberty and equality of all nationalities and their inevitable brotherhood once Europe became a

"Europe of the Peoples." But he also insisted it was Italy's mission to provide "a new and more powerful Unity to all the nations of Europe." Italy had given Europe unity under the Roman Empire and the papacy. Now the "Third Rome," the "Rome of the Italian people," would fulfill that same universal mission. It would create a "third and still vaster Unity." That was no small claim, and it helped set a widely imitated pattern of nationalist megalomania. Nor did Mazzini address the decisive question: when the claims and "rights" of nationalities conflicted, who or what would decide?

Nationalist visionaries who followed Mazzini had less respect than he for liberty. As the century drew on, they increasingly emphasized the least tolerant strand of nationalism, its ethnic-linguistic element. Language and culture could nevertheless still be learned by outsiders. Nationalisms that retained them as the test for citizenship, as did France or Italy, remained relatively benign. But in Germany, where the ethnic-linguistic theory of the nation had originated, nationalism after the 1870s fused with a misunderstood Darwinism (see p. 729). By 1900 the German test for membership in the *Volk* was on its way to becoming implacably pseudo-biological. That leap from mother-tongue to "blood" and "race" was a crucial step toward the nationalist wars and genocides of the twentieth century.

IDEAS AND SOCIAL REALITY: THE STATE, WORKERS, AND WOMEN

Without a public capable of receiving them, ideas have little practical effect. In nineteenth-century Europe the gradual widening of literacy and of leisure created that public. States began to take responsibility for their subjects' welfare and education. And submerged groups such as workers and women reacted to new ideas and new conditions with broadening demands for social and political rights.

The Role of the State

States had traditionally been machines for power, not welfare. Yet in the seventeenth and eighteenth centuries, the states of western Europe began to recognize that the prosperity and education of their inhabitants might increase that power (see pp. 571–77). In the nineteenth century the industrial revolution further intensified the apparent need for states to supervise the education, health, and wealth of their citizens. Power, necessary for survival, remained the state's ultimate purpose, but alongside it there gradually emerged the modern bureaucratic "welfare state."

The states of the nineteenth century, as befitted the age of *laissez-faire,* removed economic restraints that appeared to impede the creation of wealth. By the 1860s, the centralizing bureaucracies of the German states had overcome the fearful rear-guard action of small-town Germany, with its xenophobic guilds and restrictions on free competition. In Britain, a militant middle-class movement institutionalized *laissez-faire.* In 1846 Parliament abolished the grain tariffs or "Corn Laws" that Britain's landed interests had imposed in the post-1815 slump. That step marked the political triumph of Britain's all-conquering industries over agriculture.

The state also intervened in the economy. Especially on the Continent, it took the lead in the creation of national markets and industrial economies. The obvious abuses of the factory system and the wretched sanitary conditions in the new industrial cities also provoked outcry and government action. In Britain, legislation as early as 1802 had attempted to regulate working hours for apprentices. In 1819 Parliament passed the first of a series of Factory Acts, forbidding the employment of children under nine and limiting the work day of children over nine to twelve hours. An act of 1831 forbade night work by those under 21; an act restricting the work day to ten and a half hours passed in 1850. The first Factory Acts applied only to cotton mills, but by the 1860s legislation covered most industries. Acts in 1841 and 1855 banned the employment of women and children in mining. Parliament also sought to regulate city sanitation and standards for wholesome food and drink, beginning with the Public Health Act of 1848. France and Prussia passed similar laws. Despite a long

record of poor enforcement and of collusion between factory inspectors and manufacturers, working and living conditions gradually improved.

In the face of British industrial competition, the continental states adopted protective tariffs. Prussia, in particular, made tariff policy an instrument of state power. Beginning in 1818, reforming Prussian bureaucrats aggressively pressed customs unions upon their smaller neighbors. In 1833, Prussia succeeded in creating a *Zollverein,* or customs union, that eventually covered all important German states except Austria. Prussia's bureaucracy and military also took the lead in the expansion of the railroad network. After mid-century, the army began gearing the railroads to its ever-faster mobilization system. Only the Russian state, in the period of its industrial "take-off" after 1880, surpassed the role of the Prussian state in economic development.

Prussia led in a second, absolutely decisive area: its school system pioneered mass literacy. That was a daring step. The value of widespread literacy in the eighteenth century was far from obvious, at least to the European upper classes. Catherine the Great neatly summarized their attitude in a letter reputedly sent to a subordinate: "We must not in any way provide instruction for the lower class of people. If they knew as much as you or I . . . they would no longer want to obey us. . . ." Even after 1800, members of the British Parliament railed against the democratization of knowledge; it might render the lower orders "insolent to their superiors."

The Prussian bureaucracy, ruling over what a French intellectual in the 1830s described as the "classic country of barracks and schools," had no such qualms. Prussia, after 1819, became the first state in history to enforce universal school attendance. A literate subject was a better soldier and a more productive subject. France followed in 1833 by requiring villages and towns to maintain schools. The Habsburg monarchy followed in the 1860s. Britain, in the spirit of *laissez-faire,* neglected its schools, and paid dearly. It made universal primary schooling compulsory only in 1880.

The coming of literacy worked yet another revolution. Throughout most of history, only very small elites had been able to read or write. At the beginning of the nineteenth century slightly more than half of all adult males in England and France and perhaps one in three or four women could write their own names. A century later, literacy in the developed countries of western Europe was well above 95 percent of both men and women (see Figure 25-1). The Industrial Revolution made mass literacy possible. But it was the state that turned that potential into reality.

Workers

Mass literacy, among its many side effects, made the claims of the outsiders increasingly difficult to ignore. In politics, both workers and women participated in the revolutionary ferment that culminated in

the Europe-wide uprisings of 1848, described in the next chapter. In the workplace, workers by that point had long since begun to organize against what they perceived as oppression. The introduction of machinery led to widespread artisan protest and machine-breaking both in England and on the Continent. From 1811 to 1816 English rioters rose repeatedly to smash knitting machines and power looms in the name of a mythical "King Ludd." Agricultural workers imitated the "Luddites" in 1830–32 by smashing threshing machines and burning barns.

But incoherent protest and anarchic violence had little chance even against the decentralized British state. Workers explored other paths, beginning in the 1820s. With the Combination Acts of 1799 and 1800 Parliament had ended early attempts by workers to organize rudimentary labor unions under the inspiration of the French Revolution. But in 1824–25 Parliament weakened the Acts in response to continued unrest and to the pleas of middle-class reformers for toleration of working-class "cooperation." Strikes remained illegal but unions could now organize. In 1829 Robert Owen presided over the founding of a Society for Promoting Co-operative Knowledge that in 1831 became the National Union of the Working Classes, the first true British trade union.

It turned out that regional and craft loyalties were stronger than working-class solidarity. Yet recurrent economic crises and the pressure of population growth kept unrest alive. In 1838 a leading workers' group, the London Working Men's Association, initiated a nationwide campaign to urge Parliament to adopt universal male suffrage and other reforms listed in a "People's Charter." Chartist agitation, under the leadership of the fiery journalist and speaker Feargus O'Connor, continued sporadically for the next ten years but failed to influence Parliament.

Chartism's internal rivalries and its political failure did not inhibit other working-class efforts. A national Association for the Protection of Labour emerged in 1845 and by 1859 was able to persuade Parliament to legalize peaceful picketing.

FIGURE 25.1   **The Decline of Illiteracy**

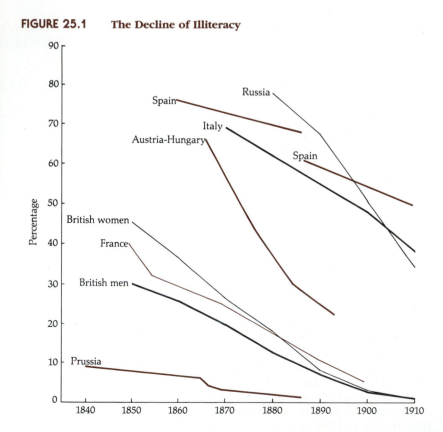

In 1868 a Trades Union Congress that represented more than 100,000 workers met at Manchester. By 1875 British trade unions had won the right to strike and picket.

On the Continent, working-class organization inevitably lagged, given the gap in development between Britain and its followers. Belgium prohibited labor unions until 1868. Revolutionary France had forbidden unions and strikes, and Napoleon's law code had confirmed that ban in 1803. Socialist underground secret societies, and uprisings such as those of the impoverished silk workers of Lyon in 1831 and 1834, merely provoked savage repression. Not until after 1871 did the French working classes organize effectively. In Germany, revolutionary sects such as the tailor Wilhelm Weitling's League of the Just emerged a generation before the creation of an organized German labor movement in the 1860s.

Despite rivalries between regions and crafts, home artisans and factory workers, highly skilled "labor aristocrats" and simple laborers, the European working classes were by the 1870s nevertheless well on their way to creating stable organizations to represent their interests. In England the ideological glue that held them together was frequently the piety of the Protestant sects. On the Continent, most of them adopted orthodox Marxism under the guidance or inspiration of the "First International," the "International Working Men's Organization" that Marx and Engels helped found in 1864. Workers' organizations soon made increasingly effective demands for change and gave birth to the first workers' political parties.

Women

The French and industrial revolutions made relative freedom for women possible, but did not produce it. As with workers, only struggle could do that. In revolutionary Paris, Olympe de Gouges had pointed out the inconsistency of proclaiming the Rights of Man while denying those same rights to women. In her pathbreaking *Vindication of the Rights of Women* (1792), the English writer Mary Wollstonecraft demanded equality, and freedom for women to employ their talents. The romantic poet Shelley, son-in-law of Mary Wollstonecraft, put the issue succinctly in 1817: "Can man be free if woman be a slave?"

That question passed through three overlapping phases in the course of the nineteenth century: literary self-assertion, theoretical elaboration, and political action. In the first phase, women intellectuals began to write with a frequency and eloquence that eventually won them grudging respect. Germaine de Staël, daughter of the banker Necker and France's leading woman writer until her death in 1817, took on Napoleon in print and had to take refuge in exile. Her novels *Corinne* (1804) and *Delphine* (1807) attacked conventional views of marriage and of women's education. She also played a decisive role in explaining German romanticism to the rest of Europe. Napoleon had the first edition of her *De l'Allemagne* (1811) burned as "un-French."

The French romantic novelist and social critic George Sand (Amantine-Lucile-Aurore, Baroness Dudevant, 1804–76) was an adherent of Fourierist utopianism who scandalized French polite society by wearing men's suits and smoking in public. Fleeing a provincial marriage of convenience, Sand went to Paris and wrote some eighty popular novels. She supported herself and her two children on the proceeds, an achievement almost without precedent. She also advocated and practiced "free love," by which she and other Fourierists and Saint-Simonians meant living together or marriage based on equality of the sexes and on sexual or emotional bonds rather than social convention. Sand, despite her deliberate unconventionality, was a prototype of the successful professional women who became common later in the century.

By midcentury, women authors were emerging whose achievements were unrivaled. Charlotte Brontë, in her novels *Jane Eyre* (1847) and *Shirley* (1849), presented strong women heroines in quest both of love and of independence. Her sister Emily, before her death of tuberculosis,

George Sand (1838).

produced the violent and terrifying *Wuthering Heights* (1847), one of the greatest of English nineteenth-century novels.

By that time both men and women had begun to explore the question of woman's role. Their views fall into three rough categories: those who reaffirmed woman's traditional subordination to man, those who argued that women were equal but different, and those who insisted on an absolute legal and political equality that would allow women to be like men if they chose.

Most males inevitably argued for woman's subordination. And many women still agreed. Woman's role was to obey, help, and comfort man the breadwinner, to bear and raise his children, and to preside over the home, a warm sanctuary in the cold and increasingly competitive new industrial world. That was the prescription of Sarah Stickney Ellis, an English writer of women's handbooks from the late 1830s on, and of numerous continental theorists from reactionaries such as De Maistre to liberals of all stripes.

The "equal but different" tradition was most prominent on the Continent. The title of a French tract of the 1830s sums up its message: *The Education of Mothers; or the Civilization of Mankind by Women.* Woman's first role was as mother. The mother's calling was to be the educator, the bearer of culture, the civilizer of the drunken, destructive, childlike male. As Jeanne Deroin (1805–94), the foremost French woman's advocate of midcentury, put it in the newspaper she published during the 1848 revolution, woman's "sublime humanitarian maternity" had the duty to "teach everyone how fraternity should be practiced." The world of politics and of relations between states should conform to the standards of the well-ordered home.

Nor should women seek to imitate men, insisted Louise Otto (1819–95), Deroin's foremost German counterpart. "True womanliness" was the goal. "Georgesandism" outraged Otto as much as it did any defender of the old order. Emancipation must not "[devalue] woman to become a caricature of a man." This tradition had appeal not only in Germany and France, but even in England and the United States. There it contributed not only to the assertion of women's rights but also to the temperance movement that gathered force as the nineteenth century drew on. And the notion of the mother as educator appealed to female theorists of eastern European nationalism. It gave woman a decisive role in the national struggle. Man's vocation was to fight; woman's was to transmit the *Volk* language and nationalize the minds of the young.

The third tradition that emerged in the course of the nineteenth century drew its ultimate inspiration from Locke. Men enjoyed autonomy and self-determination by natural right. To deny that same right to women was neither just nor civilized. Women must receive the same autonomy and education as men, even if that meant painful social readjustment. Wollstonecraft gave first expression to such views. John Stuart and Harriet Taylor Mill's *The Subjection of Women* (1869) provided the tradition's basic text. Its ideas were particularly influential in Britain and the United States, where they meshed with the Lockean political culture from which they derived.

Theorists of the "equal but different" tradition—and male supremacists—inevitably attacked the Mills for inciting women to what they described as antisocial self-indulgence. Ruthless individualism, the critics claimed, was no answer to the biological and social imperatives that governed women's conduct. Emancipation could not and must not mean emancipation from children, or from marriage, the building block of society. Women's biological role demanded special legal protection for the family, not the cold comfort of strict equality with men.

The issues at stake were so intractable and emotion-laden that the argument between the two schools has continued to the present. But regardless of theoretical differences, by the 1860s and 1870s a broadly based movement of women, primarily of the middle classes, had arisen both in Europe and in the United States. It increasingly turned to political action to secure women's rights (see pp. 727–29).

The new age of ideas after 1789 was both a continuation and a repudiation of the Enlightenment. Faith in "progress" and in the perfectibility of humanity swelled with the advance of science, the coming of steam-powered industry, and the spread of liberalism and socialism. Submerged groups found voices; states began to act as machines for welfare as well as for power. Yet strong countercurrents persisted. Conservatism or "reaction" inspired both nobles and intellectuals. Peasants and many in the middle classes still held to traditional community and dynastic loyalties. Romanticism damned the new industrial age but also undermined the remains of the old order through its stormy cult of the individual. And nationalism, which many conservatives mistook for liberalism, soon revealed itself as the overriding political faith of the nineteenth and twentieth centuries, the force that transmuted "geographical expressions" into nation-states.

Suggestions for Further Reading

Science, Religion, and Culture

For overviews that place nineteenth-century thought in its political and social setting, see E. J. Hobsbawm, *The Age of Revolution, 1789–1848* (1962), and *The Age of Capital, 1848–1875* (1975). F. L. Baumer, *Modern European Thought: Continuity and Change in Ideas, 1600–1950* (1977), offers a useful general survey of the movement of ideas. For the fate of religion, see O. Chadwick, *The Secularization of the European Mind in the Nineteenth Century* (1975). On the impact of Darwin and geology, see especially W. Irvine, *Angels, Apes, and Victorians* (1955); J. C. Greene, *The Death of Adam* (1959); and C. C. Gillispie, *Genesis and Geology* (1951). For romanticism, see especially J. Barzun, *Classic, Romantic, and Modern* (1961); J. B. Halstead, ed., *Romanticism* (1965); J. Clay, *Romanticism* (1981); and M. le Bris, *Romantics and Romanticism* (1981). On German philosophy, R. N. Stromberg, *European Intellectual History After 1789* (1981); R. Scruton, *From Descartes to Wittgenstein* (1981); K. Löwith, *From Hegel to Nietzsche* (1964); and G. D. O'Brien, *Hegel on Reason and History* (1975) are useful.

Social, Economic, and Political Thought

The best introduction to conservatism is still E. Burke, *Reflections on the Revolution in France;* K. Epstein, *The Genesis of German Conservatism* (1966), describes some of conservatism's continental ramifications. For liberalism, both economic and political, the classic texts are A. Smith, *The Wealth of Nations;* T. R. Malthus, *An Essay on Population;* and J. S. Mill, *Autobiography* and *On Liberty.* On Mill and his fellows, see especially J. Hamburger, *Intellectuals in Politics: John Stuart Mill and the Philosophic Radicals* (1965). G. Lichtheim, *The Origins of Socialism* (1969), and P. Singer, *Marx* (1980), offer concise introductions to socialism. R. Tucker, ed., *The Marx-Engels Reader* (1972), provides a selection of the essential texts. L. Kolakovski, *Main Currents of Marxism,* Vol. 1 (1978), lucidly analyzes the intellectual development of Marx and Engels, explains their debts to earlier thinkers, dissects the weaknesses of their system, and suggests some of the potential consequences of their ideas—but see also D. Conway, *A Farewell to Marx* (1987). E. Kedourie, *Nationalism* (1966), and Ernest Gellner, *Nations and Nationalism* (1983), offer complementary interpretations of a subject of overriding importance.

Consequences of the Industrial Revolution

For the intellectual and social impact of the industrial revolution, see especially the broadly conceived work of T. S. Hamerow, *The Birth of a New Europe* (1983). A. Briggs, *The Age of Improvement, 1783–1867* (1959), and E. P. Thompson, *The Making of the English Working Class* (1963), offer differing perspectives on English workers; L. Chevalier, *Working Classes and Dangerous Classes in Paris During the Nineteenth Century* (1971) and B. Moss, *The Origins of the French Labor Movement* (1976), cover France. R. Bridenthal et al., *Becoming Visible: Women in European History* (1987), offers a useful introduction to the changing status and aspirations of nineteenth-century women.

26

THE BREAKTHROUGH OF THE NATION-STATE, 1815–1871

hile population growth, industrialization, and the spread of literacy and new ideas were transforming Europe after 1815, the Continent enjoyed a century of relative peace. Four general wars and innumerable minor conflicts had punctuated the eighteenth century. Prussia and Russia had become great powers. Sweden had ceased to be one. Poland had ceased to be. But from 1815 to 1914 only three major conflicts—the Crimean War (1854–56) and the wars of Italian (1859–60) and German "unification" (1864, 1866, 1870–71)—affected even parts of Europe. And the nineteenth-century conflicts, unlike the great world wars of 1701–14, 1740–48, 1756–63, and 1792–1815, were short and involved only a few of the great powers.

Peace and stability were the result of both ideology and the structure of interna-tional politics. Conservative fear of "the Revolution" had welded together the final coalition that brought Napoleon down. That fear inspired a settlement in 1814–15 that bound the powers together in a network of treaties and mutual obliga-tions. Treaties, custom, and the consolida-tion of neutral buffer states separating the great powers made it harder than before for one power to challenge the rest. And fear of revolution, intensified by the three waves of unrest that convulsed the Conti-nent in 1820, 1830, and 1848, continued to hold the great powers back from foreign adventures until after mid-century.

Then the collapse of the revolutionary myth in 1848 ushered in a brief era of almost unrestrained rivalries between states, pursued under the banner of na-tionalism. The consequence was the breakthrough of the nation-state in central Europe: the creation of Italy in 1859–60

(Opposite) The romantic vision of the 1830 Revolution: *Liberty Leading the People,* by Eugène Delacroix.

and of Prussia-Germany in 1866–71. Those "revolutions from above," especially the German one, destroyed the small and intermediate buffer states that had been a key restraining element in the 1814–15 settlement. Nevertheless, thanks to the weakness of the new Italian state and the temporary self-restraint of the German one, the main lines of the 1814–15 settlement survived the wars of midcentury. Only after 1890 did a new challenge to the balance of power end the "long peace" and inaugurate a new century of world wars.

UNDER THE SHADOW OF REVOLUTION: THE CONGRESS OF VIENNA AND AFTER, 1814–48

The powers that had defeated Napoleon faced two intertwined tasks—the restoration of an international balance of power and of internal stability in the wide areas of Europe that France had conquered. As Britain's foreign secretary, Castlereagh, remarked, the victors needed to return Europe to "peaceful habits." The diplomats redrew the map in 1814–15 in ways that bore little relationship to the wishes of Europe's populations. Internally, the "re-

The Congress of Vienna: the official view, by Jean-Baptiste Isabey.

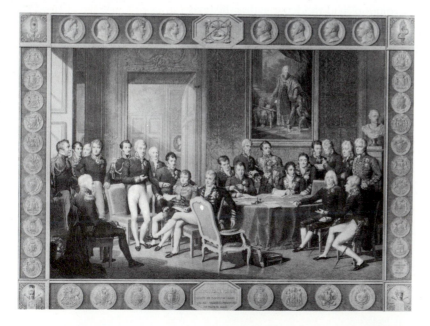

action" that followed the restoration of many of Europe's ruling houses was undeniably oppressive. But by the standards set in later peace settlements, the treaties of 1814–15 were both humane and durable.

Europe—or rather the five great powers—met at the Congress of Vienna in September 1814 to draw up the settlement. The four decisive figures in this first general European settlement since the Peace of Westphalia in 1648 were Tsar Alexander of Russia, Talleyrand for Bourbon France, Castlereagh for Britain, and the host, Chancellor Prince Metternich, for Austria. Frederick William III of Prussia and his ministers cut lesser figures. Around the principals danced the nobility of Europe and their innumerable hangers-on, while Metternich's secret police searched wastebaskets and boudoir drawers in search of diplomatic correspondence.

The two overriding issues were the settlement with France and the division of the booty in central and eastern Europe. The allies at first tried to exclude Talleyrand from their deliberations. But Russia's unpredictable ruler soon provoked a crisis that reversed the powers' roles. If France was the threat of yesterday, Alexander, with his insistence on entering Paris as a conqueror, might be the threat of tomorrow. His demand that the Congress confirm his control of most of Poland alarmed his allies, since a Russia that close to central Europe would be an over-mighty neighbor. Even Alexander's promise to equip his Polish territories with a constitution seemed a fig-leaf for the voracious expansionism of the Russian state. Metternich was in any case no lover of constitutions.

The tsar's Prussian ally also gave the impression that it might some day threaten the European balance. The Prussian military reformers, intoxicated with their victory over Napoleon, now demanded the annexation of Saxony, whose king had changed sides too late in 1813. (In revolutionary times, as that expert at well-timed shifts of allegiance, Talleyrand, remarked, treason was "a question of dates.") The upshot was deadlock. Russia and Prussia

Europe in 1815

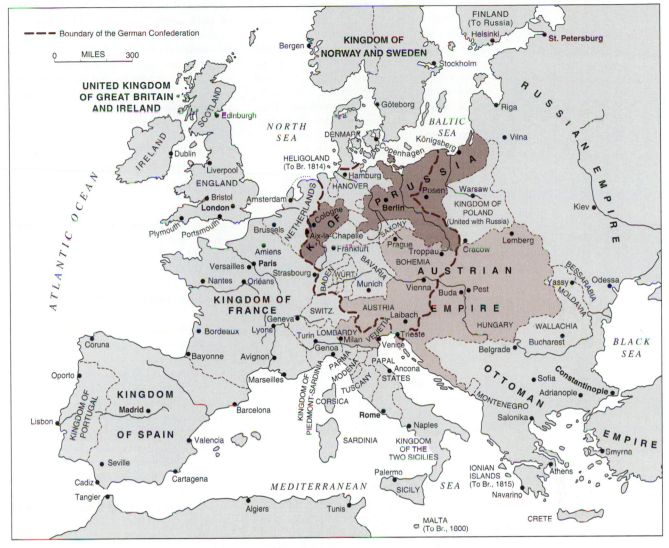

faced England and Austria, while the Prussian generals muttered threateningly. To defend the balance, Castlereagh and Metternich brought a willing Talleyrand into play. A brief triple alliance of the old enemies, France, Britain, and Austria, persuaded the Prussians and the tsar to back down.

France remained a great power, and preserved its pre-1789 borders almost unchanged. Russia gave up some Polish territory. Prussia kept some of Poland and secured only half of Saxony. In compensa-

tion, it gained the formerly Napoleonic territories in northwestern Germany. Castlereagh and Metternich placed a reluctant Prussia on the Rhine, in the front lines against a possible renewal of the French threat to the balance of power. England and Austria thus also unwittingly gave Prussia the immense coal and iron deposits of the Ruhr Valley, with economic and political consequences immeasurably important for the future of Prussia, Germany, and Europe. The separation of post-1815 Prussia into eastern and western halves generated additional pressure, if the Prussian power-state needed pressure, for further expansion—the annexation of the smaller states in between.

Other issues at Vienna generated less tension than the Poland-Saxony deadlock. In principle—as proclaimed by Talleyrand and Metternich—"legitimacy," or tradition, was to guide the settlement. That slogan was convenient for Bourbon France and Habsburg Austria. But it had less to do with the actual shape of the settlement than with the need for stability and balance that all felt deeply after almost 25 years of revolution and war.

The Bourbons returned to the thrones of France, Spain, and eventually Naples. The Pope reclaimed the Papal States, stretching across central Italy. Switzerland, released from its status as a satellite of revolutionary France, received a guarantee of perpetual independence and neutrality. But at British insistence, Holland received the former Austrian territory of Belgium to strengthen it as a barrier against France. Piedmont-Sardinia likewise and for the same reason received the former republic of Genoa. Austria kept Venetia and Lombardy.

In Germany expediency and the quest for stability triumphed. The surviving princes, whose territories had grown fat in the princes' revolution of 1801–03 and in Napoleon's redrawing of the map in 1806 and after, were poor examples indeed of "legitimacy." The deliberations of the German states at the Congress gave birth to a loose league, a German "united nations" of 39 states and mini-states, with an assembly sitting at Frankfurt. Austria held the presidency of this German Confederation with Prussia as its sometimes reluctant second. The Confederation's two-fold function was to give the awakening German nation a political home now that the Holy Roman Empire no longer existed, and to serve as a defensive barrier against a resurgent France or an aggressive Russia. The Confederation's principal weaknesses were the built-in split between Austria and Prussia and the egotism of its lesser princes. Both conspired against the greater unity that German nationalists were already demanding.

The inconsiderate and violent return of Napoleon during the "Hundred Days" of 1815 emphasized further the need for continuing great-power solidarity. The allies renewed the Quadruple Alliance for twenty years, and confirmed the principle established at Vienna that the great powers in concert would decide all major international questions.

But once the powers began to discuss the internal regimes of Europe's states, their ways parted. The symbol of the divergence between Britain on the one hand and Russia, Prussia, and Austria on the other was Tsar Alexander's treaty of the "Holy Alliance" of September 1815. This "piece of sublime mysticism and nonsense," in Castlereagh's scathing phrase, pledged the three eastern monarchies to conduct their policies in accordance with the principles of the Christian religion. Those principles, as interpreted by the eastern monarchies, apparently included the suppression of liberalism and revolution everywhere. Although the Holy Alliance itself had little practical effect, it gave its name to an era of obscurantism, arbitrary imprisonment, and muzzling of the press.

In Spain and Naples the restored Bourbons abolished the constitutions they had granted in 1812. Pope Pius VII reestablished his authority in the Papal States by again confining the Jews to ghettos, by reviving the Inquisition, and by abolishing the reforming law codes the French had brought. In Germany, Metternich attacked freedom of expression. In 1819 Prussia and the German Confederation adopted his repressive "Carlsbad Decrees" and suppressed liberal and nationalist agitation in Germany for a decade.

Even England passed through a brief repressive phase. The inevitable post-war economic slump in 1815, combined with population growth, brought widespread poverty and unemployment. Unlike their counterparts on the Continent, middle-class radicals called not for revolution but for reform of the corrupt parliamentary voting system. The Tory (Conservative) government nevertheless replied with ill-considered force in 1819. British troops routed a peaceful crowd of demonstra-

Cavalry disperses the crowd at the "Peterloo Massacre" (1819).

tors with considerable loss of life in the so-called Peterloo Massacre. Parliament passed the notorious "Six Acts" that made the expression of unorthodox political opinions a crime. But neither Britain nor the continental monarchies had the bureaucratic machinery or propaganda techniques needed to remold their subjects' thoughts; that was reserved for the despotisms of the twentieth century.

The "concert of Europe," for which the Quadruple Alliance had prescribed regular meetings, soon broke up. In 1820, the first of a series of disturbances in southern Europe posed the question of whether the great powers should intervene. A revolt to force parliamentary government on the Spanish Bourbons triggered disturbances in Naples, Piedmont, and Portugal. Castlereagh refused to attend the Congress of Troppau (1820) at which the three eastern monarchies declared their readiness to act. The ensuing Congress of Laibach (1821), over British protests, authorized Austrian military action to restore the Bourbons in Naples and Sicily. In October 1822, at Verona in north Italy, the last congress met to discuss intervention in Spain. Britain refused its con-

sent and withdrew: "Every nation for itself and God for us all," quipped George Canning, Castlereagh's successor.

Despite British disapproval, a royal French army crossed the Pyrenees to restore the Spanish Bourbons. Unlike 1808, no guerrilla resistance resulted. France was intervening for rather than against the Bourbons, the Church, and Spain's landowning nobles. The custom of consultation between great powers established at Vienna continued, though less formally than in the congress period.

If Britain's departure from Verona marked the effective end of the Quadruple Alliance, the Greek war of Independence (1821–29) soon crippled the Holy Alliance as well. The war was a major step in a process soon drearily familiar to European statesmen: the "Eastern Question," the breakup of the Ottoman Turk empire under the pressure of hostile great powers without and of nationalism within. Russia had humiliated the Turks in Catherine the Great's wars. The Serbs, under their chieftain "Black George," had set the example of national—or tribal—revolt against Constantinople in 1804. By 1817 the embryo of a Serb state had emerged, although it remained for the moment under Turkish overlordship. The Greeks followed in 1821 by massacring all Turks in the Peloponnese—a massacre the Turks repaid with interest.

The Greek cause attracted support among Western admirers of ancient Greece. Flamboyant figures such as the brilliant and dissolute English romantic poet Lord Byron flocked to Greece. Russia, always hostile to Turkey and now solicitous of its Slav "little brothers" under Turkish rule, broke with Metternich and lent aid to "the Revolution." A bizarre alignment of Britain and France with the Russia of Alexander's successor, the reactionary Tsar Nicholas I, annihilated the Turkish fleet at Navarino in 1827. In 1832 independent Greece received from Europe the quaint gift of a Bavarian prince as a ruler.

From 1830 Revolutions to 1840 Crisis

The second wave of revolutions, in 1830–32, was a more serious affair than the first. The breakdown of the Holy Alliance over

King Louis Philippe courts the public, in a contemporary cartoon.

the Greek war and the fading of the memory of revolutionary turmoil—but not of revolutionary achievements—contributed to its force. And, far more than in 1820–21, nationalism drove events. Finally, as in 1789, Paris set the example that had been missing in 1820. Louis XVIII, who had accepted a degree of constitutionalism after 1814, died in 1824. His successor, Charles X, considered himself king by divine right. He muzzled the press and defied the liberal majority in his Chamber of Deputies. His appointment of an ultra-monarchist ministry in 1829 brought deadlock in the middle of a series of poor harvests.

When Charles X attempted in July 1830 to dissolve the Chamber and reduce the already small electorate to a mere 25,000 wealthy men, Paris responded with the well-tried methods of July 1789. Charles, amazingly unprepared to crush the bloody revolt he had provoked, abdicated. Moderate liberals, with the help of that hardy perennial of Paris revolutions, the Marquis de Lafayette, took control. Their candidate, Louis Philippe of Orléans, son of a renegade cousin of Louis XVI who had helped unleash the revolution of 1789 and had taken the name "Philippe-Egalité," ascended the throne as first and last of the Orléans dynasty. This new "July Monarchy" promised France an end to experiments in absolutism.

News of the Paris revolution swept across Europe and ignited further outbreaks. But these, with the exception of stirrings in Britain and the overthrow of a number of unpopular German princelings, were of a different pattern than events in France. In Belgium, north-central Italy, and above all in Poland, the 1830 revolutions were nationalist revolts against foreign domination. The Catholic and French- or Flemish-speaking Belgians given to Holland in 1814–15 chafed increasingly under Protestant Dutch rule. Their revolution succeeded because Britain, France, and Prussia restrained the Dutch from attempting reconquest. In 1839, the five great powers gave Belgium the same guarantee of perpetual independence and neutrality that Switzerland had received in 1815. In Italy, revolutionaries seeking a unified Italian state, and cooperating more effectively than in 1820–21, took over Modena, Parma, and much of the Papal States. Then Metternich's armies marched south once more and restored the "legitimate" rulers.

The most tragic events of 1830 occurred in Poland. There intellectuals and patriots rose against the mild form of Russian rule experienced under Tsar Alexander's 1815 constitution. The Russian authorities initially showed the same unpreparedness and indecision as Charles X and the Dutch. But they soon corrected their mistake. The Russian reconquest, aided by dissension among the Poles, brought mass executions and imprisonment, military rule, and brutal attempts to Russify the population. A generation of Polish intellectuals died or emigrated.

In Germany, minor disturbances led to the granting of constitutions in some of the mid-sized states. In 1832, a nationalist mass movement staged a *Nationalfest* at Hambach near Frankfurt. A crowd of 30,000 heard speakers demand wider voting rights and a national state. Metternich replied with new Carlsbad-style decrees. Silence again descended in Germany.

Finally, the July Revolution of 1830 had repercussions even in Britain. The Conservative regime responsible for the Peterloo Massacre had slowly mellowed. In 1829 the Duke of Wellington's cabinet allowed Parliament to revoke Britain's longstanding discriminatory laws against Catholics. But the scandalous inequities of the electoral system persisted. The absence of any mechanism for redistricting meant that the new industrial cities such as Birmingham and Manchester had no representation in Parliament, while "pocket boroughs" and sleepy villages dominated by one or two great landowners did.

When the Conservatives balked at reform, elections in 1831 gave a majority to the opposition Whigs, or liberals. In 1832, after the House of Lords had tried and failed to block reform, the Reform Bill became law. It eliminated the worst abuses and extended the vote to one adult male in five, compared to one in twenty in Louis Philippe's France. Gradual reform, however grudgingly granted, helped Britain escape the Continent's cycle of bloody repression and bloodier revolution.

In international politics, the 1830 revolutions restored the solidarity between Russia, Prussia, and Austria that had collapsed during the Greek war. Each of the three occupied a part of Poland—and fear of their Polish subjects brought them together at Münchengrätz in Bohemia in 1833, where they concluded agreements against revolution in the spirit of the Holy Alliance that lasted until 1848 and after. Russia and Austria pledged to resist any threat to their Polish lands. They also agreed to oppose further changes in the status quo in Turkey and to act together if a change seemed unavoidable. This last agreement was a symptom of the continuing importance of the Eastern Question, which was to drive Austria and Russia apart repeatedly until the final crisis of 1914.

After the end of the Greek affair, Russia had moved to assume the position of "protector" to and eventual heir of the declining Ottoman Empire. A few months before Münchengrätz, Russia had landed troops at Constantinople to protect the Ottoman sultan from attack through Syria by his rebellious Egyptian vassal, the former Albanian bandit chieftain Mehemet Ali. This Russian protectorate of Turkey inevitably aroused Britain, whose strategic interest in maintaining a Mediterranean route to India required that Russia remain locked in the Black Sea.

But not until Mehemet Ali's second war with Turkey in 1839–40 did the British have an opportunity to act. The boisterous Lord Palmerston, a fit successor to Castlereagh and Canning as foreign secretary, made full use of British power, which thanks to industrialization was now reaching its zenith relative to its continental rivals. When Mehemet Ali's forces drove into Lebanon on their way to Constantinople, Palmerston persuaded Austria and Russia to support efforts to block him. The Royal Navy bombarded Beirut and a landing force cut the Egyptians to shreds. Mehemet Ali retreated; the Ottoman Empire for the moment survived.

THE REFORM BILL.

The Reform Bill of 1832, dramatized in a contemporary cartoon. Pocket boroughs go into the "Reform Mill" and a triumphant Britannia emerges.

The only opposition came from Louis Philippe's France. Nostalgic for the Egyptian colony that Napoleon had failed to bequeath, France broke with its "liberal" partner, Britain. In 1840 Paris briefly challenged all of Europe. Then British naval supremacy and a sudden blaze of hostility to France across the Rhine in Germany brought Louis Philippe's ministers to their senses. As the crisis subsided, Britain took Russia's place as chief "protector" of Turkey. The Turkish Straits, by an 1841 treaty between the great powers, were now closed to warships in time of peace. Russia was caged. If war came, Palmerston was confident Russia would remain caged, for Turkey and Britain would be allies and Russia's Black Sea coasts would lie open to bombardment by the Royal Navy.

In Europe itself, the chief importance of the 1839–40 crisis was as a warning for the future. Germany had reacted in kind to Frence hostility. Nationalist sentiment reached heights not touched at Hambach in 1832. Anti-French songs celebrating "the free German Rhine" enjoyed a fierce popularity. The marvelous Habsburg anthem of the great composer Haydn received new German-national words: "Germany, Germany, before everything, before everything in the world." The lack of moderation of *Deutschland über Alles* was symptomatic. Also symptomatic was Prussia's role in the crisis. As Germany's bulwark on the Rhine against France, the Prussian power-state gained a new prestige with German nationalists.

THE END OF REVOLUTION IN WESTERN EUROPE, 1848–50

Fear of revolution, the chief restraint on the great powers after 1815, still held German nationalism in check. Before the way was clear for attempts to redraw the borders established at Vienna, Europe had to pass in 1848–49 through a third and culminating round of the revolutions that had shaken it since 1815. These new upheavals combined features of 1789, 1820, and 1830.

The underlying conditions that made revolution possible in 1848 were similar to those of 1789 and 1830. Mainly agrarian societies with rapidly expanding populations and slowly increasing productivity faced a food crisis. The population of most European states had risen by 30 to 40 percent in the thirty years from 1815 to 1845. Urban workers spent between 60 and 70 percent of their wages on food. And in the previous fifty years, the working classes had come to depend disproportionately on one crop, an innovation from the Americas—the potato.

When a fungus rotted potato crops and grain blights struck most of Europe in 1845–47, the result was unrest from Ireland to Poland. Agricultural collapse, as in 1788–89, also generated a downturn in commerce and industry; food prices and unemployment rose together in the cities, with grim consequences. Grain prices peaked in early 1847 and then declined, but the business slump and unemployment continued (see Figure 26-1). And this temporary crisis sharpened the impact of a deeper structural change: by 1848 the introduction of machinery had begun to impoverish or drive from business many of the artisans who formed the majority of the population of Europe's cities. These conditions, in combination with the political myth of the Great Revolution of 1789, produced a chain reaction in the spring of 1848: western and central Europe's last 1789-style revolutions from below.

But 1848 was not 1789. Four essential differences made the Europe-wide movement of 1848–49 wider but far shallower than 1789. First, the example of the Terror of 1792–94 deterred the moderate liberals who led most of the revolutions from pushing too hard against the old order. A seasoned observer and participant in the events (Alexis de Tocqueville, whose *Democracy in America* is among the two or three greatest nineteenth-century works on politics) put it well: "We sought . . . to warm ourselves with the passions of our fathers, without quite managing it; we imitated their gestures and poses as we had seen them on the stage, since we could not imitate their enthusiasm or feel their rage."

Second, this absence of passionate leadership from above found a counterpart below, at least in the countryside. The

FIGURE 26.1   **France, 1848: Economic Forces and Revolution**

— Grain prices (average monthly prices per hectoliter)
— Industrial production (as a percentage of 1938 production)

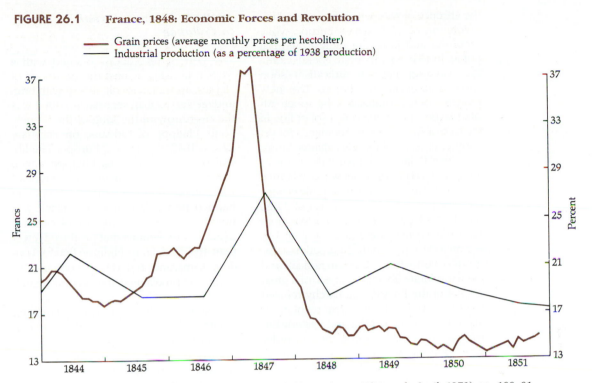

From Maurice Aqulhon, 1848 ou l'apprentissage de la République *(Paris: Editions du Seuil, 1973), pp. 100–01.*

peasants of central Europe sacked a few manor houses and attacked Jewish moneylenders. But the old order in the countryside did not collapse as it had in France in the Great Fear of 1789. The ingredient that had helped convert noble and urban revolt into the destruction of the old order was largely absent in 1848.

In France the peasants had profited from 1789 and were now indifferent or hostile to the revolutionaries in Paris. In Germany and Austria, both royal bureaucrats and liberals moved swiftly to bribe the peasants into passivity. Officials and parliamentarians rather than revolutionaries abolished most of the remaining peasant obligations to landowners. In Austrian Poland, in one of the earliest incidents in the wave of unrest that preceded 1848, the authorities even crushed a nationalist rising by inciting non-Polish peasants to massacre their Polish landlords.

The revolutions of 1848 were thus essentially urban, except where, as in Hun-

gary, the rural upper classes helped lead a national insurrection. And the revolutions came mainly from two groups: the intellectuals and the artisans. The intellectuals often hated the old regime for its failure, as they saw it, to recognize their talents. Hunger or fear of hunger moved the artisans. The intellectuals demanded political or national rights; the artisans economic ones. The intellectuals for the most part called for free competition, for industry, for "progress." The artisans aspired to return to the cozy world of guild restrictions, or, at a minimum, to a job guaranteed by the state. The intellectuals feared "the mob." The artisans in turn soon recognized how little the intellectuals offered them. This mutual hostility of the two main revolutionary forces (forces that had been briefly allied in 1793–94 under Robespierre) was the third major reason for the collapse of the 1848 revolutions.

The fourth and most important difference between 1848–49 and 1789–94 was the absence of war, which had spread the revolution of 1789 across Europe while requiring and justifying radicalization at home. In 1848 the moderate liberals riding the wave of Parisian radicalism soon showed unexpected caution. The new French foreign minister, the poet Alphonse de Lamartine, took a sober line in the face of Parisian radical demands for yet another crusade of peoples against kings: "We love Poland, we love Italy, we love all oppressed peoples, but we love France above all else. . . ." France's middle classes and peasantry, the beneficiaries of 1789, had lost all desire to export revolution. France once again became a republic, but continued to support the international status quo. Further east, German radicals and even moderate liberals yearned for a great war—but the Prussian monarchy refused to oblige. And without a great revolutionary war to throw central and eastern Europe into the melting pot, the old order was bound to recover.

The Vienna crowd mounts the barricades, March 1848.

1848–49: From Outbreak to Collapse

The year of revolutions opened with a Sicilian uprising against the Bourbons of Naples: an antitax revolt, mixed with brigandage and Sicilian separatism. But it was the overthrow of the king of the French, Louis Philippe of Orléans, on February 22–24, 1848, that roused Europe. The liberal opponents of Louis Philippe staged banquets featuring speeches in favor of wider voting rights. When the government banned further banquets, the result was the now-customary explosion of violence in Paris. After fighting that produced fewer than 400 dead, Louis Philippe fled for London. Lamartine and other moderate republicans proclaimed the second French republic.

News traveled rapidly. On March 13, crowd violence in Vienna led to panic at the Habsburg court, which proceeded to dismiss Metternich. The symbol of the reactionary Holy Alliance departed ignominiously for exile—in liberal London. Metternich's replacement by a cabinet of indecisive bureaucrats was the signal for further revolutionary outbreaks. The city of Milan, in the first mass example of Italian nationalism, revolted against Austria. In five days of bitter fighting in March, the Milanese, armed with a few muskets and with pikes from La Scala opera house, harried the Austrian garrison. Field Marshal Joseph Radetzky, veteran of the wars against Napoleon, withdrew in defeat. The Hungarians, the principal subject nation of the Habsburgs after the Germans, demanded and received the right to domestic self-government. To the north, news of Metternich's fall emboldened street demonstrators in Berlin and other German cities. In Berlin, after his troops fired on the crowd on March 18, the eccentric King Frederick William IV panicked and virtually surrendered. Military Prussia received a ministry of moderate liberals and a parliament.

The revolution seemed to have swept all before it. Only the two great powers at the opposite ends of Europe and of the scale of political, social, and economic development were exempt: Britain and

Russia. In Russia only the nobility was as yet politically conscious. In Britain the Chartist League's agitation for universal manhood suffrage never passed beyond the stage of peaceful mass meetings.

But even in Paris, Vienna, and Berlin appearances were deceptive, for the armies remained intact. France unexpectedly took the lead in reining in the revolution. In April 1848 the new republic held the first free elections under universal manhood suffrage of any major European power. The results were a stinging repudiation of revolutionary Paris. Peasants and provincial middle class voted for moderates and monarchists.

The new national assembly, faithfully representing the views of the majority of the electorate, soon began to dismantle the most striking gain the Paris crowd had achieved in the February revolution: the "national workshops" that gave work to the unemployed at government expense. The unemployed and the revolutionary artisans of Paris reacted. Without political leadership, without coordination, but with the tenacity of despair, they rose on June 22. The army and the paramilitary National Guard, under Eugène Cavaignac, a republican general who had learned his trade in colonial Algeria, fought back pitilessly. Perhaps 5,000 died in the Paris "June Days" of 1848; at least 3,000 were insurgents shot after resistance had ceased.

The republic, with its moderate republican and monarchist assembly, then faced the need to find a monarch. Bourbons and Orléans had in turn proved themselves unsuitable. As in 1799, a Bonaparte stepped in to fill the vacuum. In December 1848 the votes of moderate republicans and of France's conservative peasantry elected the eccentric Louis Napoleon Bonaparte—nephew of the great Napoleon and leader of failed conspiracies against the July Monarchy—to the presidency of the republic. Revolutionary universal suffrage had proved remarkably conservative in practice.

In central Europe as well, the revolutionary wave crested and began to recede in the summer of 1848. Prince Alfred Windischgrätz, commander of the Habsburg forces in the Czech lands, crushed a quasi-insurrection in Prague in mid-June and dispersed the Slav Congress that had met to call for Czech rights. A man "equally devoid of fear or pity," he hit upon the simple expedient of withdrawing his troops from the rebellious city and bombarding it into submission with artillery.

In Italy, the Habsburgs also recovered rapidly. Charles Albert of Piedmont-Sardinia followed up the victorious insurrection of the Milanese by declaring war on Austria. Italy, he proclaimed grandly, would "do it itself": Piedmont alone would defeat Austria and seize north Italy. But his poorly led army ran afoul of the canny Radetzky at the battle of Custoza in July. Charles Albert's attempt to reverse that verdict the next spring led to a second defeat at Novara and his own abdication. His principal legacy was the constitution he had grudgingly granted in March 1848. Further south, the visionary Mazzini and the greatest soldier of Italy's wars of independence, Giuseppe Garibaldi, led an epic defense of a Roman republic proclaimed by radical democrats in February 1849. French troops that Louis Napoleon sent—in a bid for French Catholic support—ultimately prevailed.

Victory at Prague and Custoza emboldened the Habsburg court. The addled young emperor Ferdinand ultimately abdicated in favor of his military-minded nephew Francis Joseph. Revolutionary Vienna received the Windischgrätz treatment, complete with executions of democrats. By late fall 1848 only Hungary, against which the Habsburgs had mobilized smaller nationalities such as the Croats, still asserted autonomy. In April 1849, after victories over invading Habsburg armies, Hungary's most radical leader, the fiery Lajos Kossuth, proclaimed Hungarian independence within "historic" borders that included large numbers of Slavs and Rumanians. Revolutionary greater Hungary proved more than a match for the Habsburgs and their Croat and Rumanian allies. But Russia, fearing that Austria's collapse would mean revolution throughout central Europe and confident by now that France would not launch a war over Poland, intervened massively. By August 1849 Russian troops

The adventurer: Napoleon III.

Nationalities of the Habsburg Empire

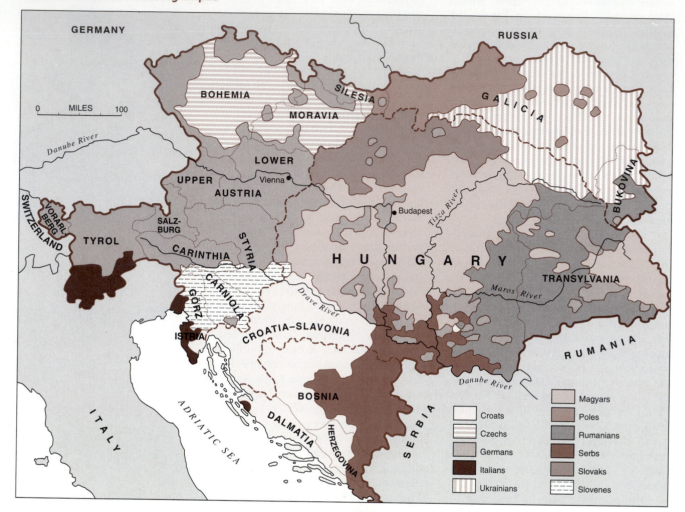

had bloodily restored Hungary to Habsburg control.

Far to the north, the German revolution also collapsed. In the spring of 1848 leading liberals such as Max von Gagern of Hesse-Darmstadt urged on Frederick William IV of Prussia a revolutionary German-nationalist war against Russia. Restoring Poland was to be the pretext, German unity and German domination of central Europe the real goal. But Frederick William, indecisive in many things, was firm about monarchical solidarity. He angrily rejected German liberalism's war: "By God, never, never shall I draw the sword against Russia."

The movement of German intellectuals that culminated in an all-German Parliament at Frankfurt in May 1848 therefore faced an insoluble dilemma. The war that nationalists yearned for to achieve unity required the cooperation of the very dynasties and princely armies that stood in the way of unity. The Frankfurt Parliament of lawyers and professors did succeed in launching a brief war against Denmark in April 1848, after the disputed but overwhelmingly German-speaking border duchies of Schleswig and Holstein had revolted against Denmark. But the Prussian troops who did most of the fighting stopped on Frederick William IV's orders when the king found he faced British, French, and above all Russian disapproval.

Inside Prussia itself the army and bureaucracy took heart after Windischgrätz's reduction of Vienna. Frederick William appointed a general as prime minister in November 1848. Then he closed parliament and imposed a conservative constitution to match his new government. In spring 1849 Prussian troops moved south to crush short-lived democratic republics in Saxony, the Bavarian Palatinate, and Baden. The democrats who had overthrown the grand duke of Baden fought with particular tenacity against a Prussian army under Frederick William IV's brother and eventual successor William. William in turn had a number of captured revolutionary leaders shot.

The end of revolution did not immediately restore stability to Germany. Frederick William had refused the crown of a united Germany that the discredited Frankfurt Parliament had offered him in April 1849. But his disdain for this "crown smelling of the gutter" did not prevent him from aspiring to a similar offer from his fellow princes. Embarrassment in Hungary might yet persuade Vienna to accept Prussian domination of Germany. By summer 1849 Frederick William had recruited most of the German princes for his "Prussian Union." Then Austria moved to reconstitute the German Confederation of 1815. Both powers appealed to Russia. In November 1850 a standoff nearly led to war when Austria and the Confederation challenged Prussia's control of the vital military roads across Hesse that linked the Prussian Rhineland to Berlin. Austrian and Prussian patrols traded shots for the first time since 1778. Prussia mobilized. Russia, seeking to restore the pre-1848 status quo and unenthusiastic about the emergence of a powerful united Germany, backed Austria. Some Prussian generals were confident of victory, but Frederick William was no more willing to fight Russia than he had been in 1848. By the treaty of Olmütz (November 1850), Prussia agreed to dismantle the Prussian Union and to demobilize. After long negotiation, Berlin also consented to restore the German Confederation of 1815. That agreement, which Prussian chauvinists denounced as the "humiliation of Olmütz," put off the struggle for mastery in central Europe for a generation.

From Revolution to Nationalism: The Consequences of 1848

The failure of revolution in 1848 meant the end of an era dominated by the example of 1789. The old pattern of repeated agricultural crises, urban and rural revolt, middle-class radical leadership, and government ineptitude had shown its limitation—at least in the absence of a continent-wide war. Railroads soon brought cheap food to urban markets and industrialization supplied work for impoverished and displaced former artisans. Middle-class intellectuals feared the masses they claimed to lead more than the old order they hoped to overthrow. And after the first shocks of March 1848, governments had swiftly recovered their nerve. The brilliant generalship of Radetzky and the successful brutality of Cavaignac, Windischgrätz, and Prince William of Prussia showed that the triumph of "the Revolution" was far from inevitable. Governments even began to imitate Britain in co-opting the lower orders.

The freedom from fear of revolution that Europe's statesmen now enjoyed liberated them from some pre-1848 restraints on the vigorous pursuit of power in the international arena. The year 1848 also changed the definition of those interests by revealing the full power of the revolution's child, nationalism. From the Turkish Balkans to Schleswig-Holstein, awakened nationalities clamored for self-determination. History and reason, their nationalist intellectuals claimed, gave them "historic rights."

Under the old dynastic order, ethnicity and language had only sometimes been a matter of life or death. Now they became the most powerful source of bloodshed in Europe. For each nationality defined "history" and "reason" according to its own convenience. And the ethnically mixed settlement pattern of central Europe ensured that right conflicted with right. The only remedy, as Kossuth had explained to the Serbs in 1849, was naked force: "The sword shall decide between us." That sword, the sword of nationalism, was to cleave first Europe and then the world.

In 1848—this too was a portent for the future—the most powerful of European nationalisms showed its cards. The Frankfurt Parliament was short on deeds and long on talk, but it had one great merit. Its discussions registered faithfully in cold print the aims of the German national movement. The Parliament debated the claims of the Poles in Posen, the activities of the Slav Congress in Prague, the rights of the Danes in Schleswig. Voices of moderation stood little chance in the face of calls for "healthy national egotism," of ex-

hortations to resist "the attempts of the puny little nationalities to set up housekeeping in our midst, and like parasites to destroy our own existence," and of proclamations that Germany's final mission was to wrest world mastery from Britain. The unanswered long-term question was whether Europe could tolerate such a Germany.

THE MAKING OF ITALY AND GERMANY, 1851–71

In the aftermath of the year of revolutions, the Holy Alliance alignment that had maintained stability since 1815 appeared restored. Russia had underwritten Austria's survival and had shepherded Frederick William IV back into the conservative fold. Appearances were deceptive: the stability of the Metternich era did not return.

The Concert of Europe Destroyed: The Crimean War

The chief agent of upheaval, for the last time in Europe's modern history, was France—or rather a Bonaparte. Louis Napoleon, political speculator and gangleader of the conspirators who had helped him to power, had none of the genius of his uncle and namesake, Napoleon I. What he did have was a mystical belief, derived from a naive reading of his uncle's cynical propaganda, in national self-determination. Even before taking power, he had conceived vague schemes for the reorganization of Europe. A coup d'état—in imitation of his uncle—made him First Consul in December 1851; a year later he proclaimed himself Napoleon III, Emperor of the French. Then he began his search for a way to tear up the 1814–15 settlement and redraw Europe's borders.

Russia's backing for Austria and for the status quo barred the way in central Europe and Italy. The Eastern Question therefore seemed to offer the best opening. A struggle over the Ottoman Empire might force Russia to abandon its role as protector of Austria, while giving Napoleon III the military prestige he needed to consolidate his rule at home. In 1851–52 he challenged Russian claims to a protec-

---

German Nationalism Speaks: Voices from the Frankfurt Parliament **1848**

To want to resurrect Poland merely because its downfall fills us with justified regret, I call moronic sentimentality. . . . Our right is none other than the right of the stronger, the right of conquest. . . . The German conquests in Poland were a necessity of nature. The law of history is not the same as that in the law books. History knows only the laws of nature, one of which tells us that a people does not gain the right to political independence through mere existence, but only through having the power to assert itself as a state among other states.

Wilhelm Jordan (Berlin), a member of the center-left, in the debate on Posen, July 25, 1848.

. . . but it is our aim to found a giant empire [*Reich*] of 70 million, and if possible of 80 or 100 million, and plant the standard of Arminius [a famous Germanic chieftain who had smashed three Roman legions in A.D. 9] in that *Reich,* to stand there armed against east and west, against the Slavic and Latin peoples, to wrest mastery of the seas from the English, and to become the most powerful nation [*Volk*] on this earth— *that* is Germany's future! With that prospect in view, petty debates over the drafting of our constitution, all petty debates, [must] retreat into the background. . . .

Count Friedrich Deym, a liberal Austrian noble, in the debate of October 27, 1848.

Stenographischer Bericht über die Verhandlungen der deutschen constituirenden Nationalversammlung zu Frankfurt am Main *(Leipzig: Teubner, 1848–49), Vol. 2, pp. 1144–46; Vol. 4, p. 2882 (translation by M. Knox).*

A CONSULTATION ABOUT THE STATE OF TURKEY.

A Consultation about the State of Turkey, a mid-nineteenth-century cartoon. The "Sick Man of Europe" (Turkey) is threatened by Death (Russia), while the physicians (France and England) hold their consultation.

Britain in the Crimea: bewhiskered officers of the 8th Hussars.

torate over the Christian holy sites in the Ottoman Empire, which included Palestine. That gambit triggered a diplomatic chain reaction—and a war that divided the great powers and left the road open, as Napoleon III had hoped, to further adventure.

Russia responded by putting pressure of its own on Turkey. That provoked France and Britain to send their fleets to Constantinople, and that in turn encouraged the Turks to declare war on Russia in October 1853. A crushing Russian victory over the Turkish navy—the so-called "Sinope massacre"—then brought into play a new factor in international politics: British public opinion. Liberal abhorrence of Russia—acute since its bloody intervention in Hungary in 1849—and the fiery Palmerston propelled Britain into a war to destroy for good Russia's power to threaten Turkey. Napoleon III also fought—to stir up trouble. Austria mobilized, but took only diplomatic steps against Russia. Austrian

The balance of power, by the French artist and caricaturist Honoré Daumier.

the right to have a Black Sea fleet, as Britain desired. But the war had other consequences London had neither bargained on nor greatly welcomed. Under Nicholas I's successor, Tsar Alexander II, Russia turned inward for a generation. Russian power no longer threatened Turkey. It also no longer upheld Austria. Indeed, Russia now sought revenge for the Austrian "ingratitude" that had repaid Russia's aid against Hungary in 1849 with a tilt toward the western powers in 1853–56.

France profited most from this breakdown of the conservative alignment. Napoleon III presided imperially over the 1856 Paris peace conference. Much to the disgust of the British, he was soon intriguing for a bargain with Russia that would help him to redraw the map of Europe. He was not alone.

The Making of Italy, 1858–60

In the last stages of the Crimean War, the "Italian Question" had reemerged from the limbo into which Radetzky's victories had thrust it in 1848–49. Charles Albert's successor, the fierce and erratic Victor Emmanuel II, had insisted on a war to restore the prestige tarnished by Piedmont's defeats at Custoza and Novara. His liberal prime minister, Count Camillo di Cavour, sent 15,000 troops to the Crimea as allies of Britain and France—and thus gained access to the Paris peace conference, at which he embarrassed the Austrians by criticizing their support of corrupt regimes in the Papal States and Bourbon Naples.

Dictatorial in temperament but an admirer of the British Parliament, Cavour was an unparalleled master of political improvisation, a "Piedmontese Machiavelli." His chief weakness was his tendency, striking even in the age of the deceitful and vacillating Napoleon III, to flagrant untruths that diminished his credibility: "If we did for ourselves what we are doing for Italy, we should be real scoundrels." His goal was to expand Piedmont, not to create an Italian nation-state. He also labored under severe constraints. National revolution, if encouraged too much, might yet turn into barbaric peasant revolt. And only north Italy appeared suitable for annexation to Piedmont. The South was a

fear of an all-out land war that it might lose, coupled with the neutrality of Prussia and the lesser German states, prevented a general European war.

Austrian and German passivity also meant that Britain and France could only strike Russia from the sea. In September 1854 the two allies therefore landed forces on the Crimean peninsula to attack Russia's principal Black Sea naval base, Sebastopol. Bitter Russian resistance and the immense effort of supplying large armies by sea made the expedition a predictable fiasco. Britain and France took Sebastopol only after a year of bloody fighting; industrial firepower was already beginning to make movement on the battlefield difficult. The Crimean War cost at least three quarters of a million dead, of whom 80 percent died of cholera, dysentery, or typhus.

The war's main consequence was disruption of the European state system, a disruption that ultimately permitted the wars that created Italian and German nation-states in 1859–60 and 1866–71. Russia indeed suffered a decisive check. It lost

world centuries behind Lombardy and Piedmont; great landowners and gangs—*Mafia, 'Ndrangheta,* and *Camorra*—dominated a downtrodden peasantry under the distant overlordship of pope and Bourbons. Above all, Cavour faced the unbroken power of Austria. The lesson of 1848–49 was that Italy could *not* do it itself.

Not all Italians agreed. Mazzini held to his vision of an Italy created through spontaneous uprising from below by the—nonexistent—nationalist masses. An Italian National Society came into being in 1857 with a more practical goal: support for a renewed Piedmontese bid for expansion. Garibaldi, revealed in 1848–49 as a great military talent, waited for his chance. The creation of an Italian state was ultimately the product both of a "royal war" of Cavour, king, and Napoleon III, and of pressure from below from Mazzini's ideas and Garibaldi's freebooters.

Initially everything depended on Napoleon III. In January 1858 the explosion of an Italian revolutionary's bomb outside the Paris Opera reminded Napoleon that he had yet to do "something for Italy." He soon approached Cavour. The two met in secret at Plombières near the Piedmontese border in July 1858 and agreed on a program. A French-Piedmontese war against Austria would seize Lombardy, Venetia, Parma, and Modena for Piedmont. In return for committing 200,000 troops, Napoleon would receive Savoy, an Italian satellite state, and the domestic prestige of a Napoleonic Italian campaign. The pope would lose territory but become head of an Italian confederation of states. Napoleon III gave to Cavour the task of provoking Austria into war without himself appearing the aggressor, and of providing 100,000 troops.

To present this French-Piedmontese war of conquest to international opinion as justified self-defense required all of Cavour's genius. At the end, in April 1859, Austrian recklessness saved him. Vienna's bullying ultimatum demanding that Piedmont demobilize destroyed what little was left of Austria's international backing. England, despite misgivings about Napoleon III, stood aside; the aftermath of the 1857 Indian mutiny (see pp. 689–90) had absorbed most of Britain's limited land

power. Russia watched Austria's humiliation with satisfaction. Only Prussia, Austria's other rival, offered aid. But its price was the reversal of Olmütz: Prussian supremacy in north Germany.

The war itself was swift, for Napoleon III and Cavour had isolated their opponent. The Piedmontese army scraped together only 50,000 men instead of the 100,000 Cavour had promised, but this time it faced no Radetzky. Piedmont fought a creditable holding action until the French arrived, partly by rail. In two bloody battles of June 1859 at Magenta and Solferino, the French drove the Austrians back with furious charges.

Then Napoleon III, appalled at a carnage for which he lacked his uncle's strong stomach, angry at the meagerness of his allies' contribution, disquieted by signs that Cavour coveted central as well as north Italy, and unnerved by a Prussian

The Making of Italy

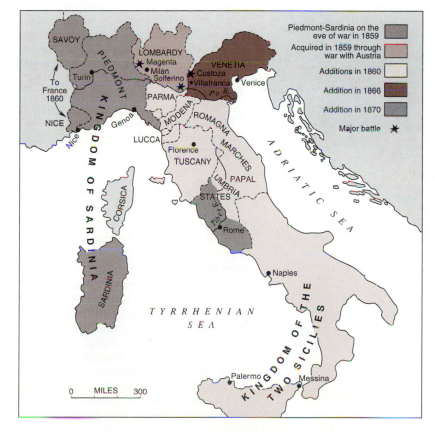

The makers of Italy: Count Camillo di Cavour (*top*) and Giuseppe Garibaldi (*bottom*).

threat on the Rhine, called a halt. By the July 1859 armistice of Villafranca with Emperor Francis Joseph, Napoleon III abandoned Cavour. Piedmont would receive only Lombardy. Cavour, when he heard that Victor Emmanuel II had agreed without consulting him, resigned in fury. He seemed to have lost.

But Cavour had proved his indispensability, and Victor Emmanuel II recalled him in January 1860. Cavour soon engineered the annexation of Tuscany, Romagna, Parma, and Modena to enlarged Piedmont. Rigged plebiscites, a favorite Napoleonic device, seemingly confirmed the unanimity of popular sentiment for Piedmontese annexation. Napoleon III, outwitted in his attempt to confine Piedmont to the north Italian plain, now demanded his price: Savoy, which was French-speaking, and the city of Nice, which was not. Cavour agreed, to the fury of Piedmontese public opinion. Garibaldi bitterly resented the loss of Nice, his home town, but he soon had his revenge. Despite Cavour's halfhearted attempts to stop them, Garibaldi and a volunteer "thousand" left Genoa for Sicily in early May 1860. Against Cavour's expectations and hopes, Garibaldi's ill-equipped troops routed the Bourbon army, roused the Sicilian peasantry to revolt, crossed to the mainland, and took Naples.

The epic campaign of Garibaldi's "Thousand" made Italy. To derail the social revolutionary elements of Garibaldi's program and to rescue the prestige of Piedmont, Cavour and Victor Emmanuel II had to act. The Piedmontese army invaded the Papal States and moved on Naples. Garibaldi, a monarchist at heart, unlike the fiercely republican Mazzini, yielded his conquests to the new Kingdom of Italy. He received little thanks from Cavour or from the Piedmontese army.

Italy was complete except for Venetia, which the new state received in 1866, Rome, which it took in 1870, and Trento and Trieste, which it did not conquer until 1918. As a colleague and rival of Cavour remarked, the process of "making Italians" remained. Cavour's representatives in the South soon made themselves more hated than the Bourbons. The brutal imposition of Piedmont's French-style prefects, mili-

tary conscription, and high taxes triggered a guerrilla war in the South that lasted more than five years and cost more dead than the wars of 1848–49 and 1859–60. Italy's *Risorgimento,* its "resurgence" and political unification, had come so swiftly and had joined areas so different in culture and traditions that "making Italians" took generations. Cavour, perhaps fortunately for his reputation, died of malaria and inept doctors in mid-1861. Time alone would tell if the foundations of the Italian nation-state that he and Garibaldi had created were sound.

The Struggle for Mastery in Germany: Prussia against Austria, 1862–66

Austria's international isolation had made a united Italy possible. That same isolation was the prerequisite for a far greater revolution in the state system than the birth of Italy, "least of the great powers." That revolution was the creation of a Prusso-German nation-state.

The Prussian military monarchy at first seemed an unlikely ally for the German nationalism it had rejected in 1848. But German unity, if it came at all, clearly had to come through one of the two German great powers, Prussia and Austria. And by the early 1860s Prussia possessed advantages Austria could not match. First, except for its Polish provinces, it was wholly German. Second, its Ruhr Valley coal and iron and its leadership since the 1830s of a German Customs Union, the *Zollverein,* had already made it the economic nucleus of any conceivable German nation-state. Third, its role as military bulwark against France and if need be Russia gave even its dynastic military establishment a certain national aura. Fourth, that military establishment soon proved that it had learned from Jena and Auerstädt. In its technique if not in its politics, the Prussian army was by 1860 the most innovative armed force in the world. Finally, after September 1862 Prussia had a leader as indispensable as Cavour—Otto von Bismarck.

Bismarck was a Pomeranian Junker by birth ("I am a Junker, and I mean to profit by it"). But his deep understanding of historical forces and political tactics far surpassed the blinkered outlook of his caste. He combined apparently genuine Pietist religious convictions with a total absence of political scruple. But like Cavour and unlike their successors in both countries, Bismarck recognized limits. Politics was "the art of the possible." Statesmen could exploit great historical forces but could not stand against them: "the stream carries you, but cannot be ruled" ran his favorite Latin motto. Bismarck's political technique—like that of the great Napoleon in warfare—was to aim at a range of alternative goals and to be prepared to achieve them by a variety of means, always leaving for himself a fallback position in the event of failure. When Bismarck gambled on war, it was only after exploring and ruling out less risky alternatives and after reducing incalculable dangers as far as possible. And once war had achieved his goals, he became as fierce a defender of the new status quo as he had been an opponent of the old.

Bismarck, like Cavour, did not set out to found a nation-state. His early career as fiery opponent of liberalism and nationalism in the Prussian Chamber in 1848 had branded him, in words that Frederick William IV had perhaps meant as a compliment, as a "red reactionary, smells of blood." But Bismarck's appointment as Prussian ambassador to the German Confederation in 1851 led to a slow change in his outlook. He came to recognize two things: that Austria's claim to leadership of the Confederation was incompatible with Prussia's dignity and security, and that Prussia's natural ally in the struggle for mastery in Germany was German nationalism. Monarchical solidarity abroad and unbending conservatism at home were contrary to Prussia's interests as a state: "Prussia's mission is to extend itself." Prussia must not tie its trim frigate to the "motheaten Austrian galleon." In 1859 he had urged Berlin to "let Austria get thoroughly bogged down in its war with France and then break out southwards with our entire army, taking our border posts in our knapsacks and planting them either on [the Swiss border] or wherever the Protestant religion ceases to predominate. . . ." Berlin ignored that shocking advice. What catapulted Bismarck into power as

prime minister and foreign minister in September 1862 was not his ruthless approach to foreign affairs. It was rather the deepening deadlock between the Prussian lower house and the new king, William I, who had succeeded his incapacitated brother Frederick William IV as regent in 1858 and as king in 1861. The military-minded new king sought to more than double the strength of the army's line units to half a million men and to reduce the role of the reserves, which had middle-class officers. This reorganization and the accompanying increase of compulsory military service from two years to three would drastically increase the weight of the army within Prussian society. It would also dramatically increase Prussia's external striking power. But the liberal majority in the Prussian Chamber repeatedly blocked funding of these plans. William, determined to have his way on grounds both of military efficiency and of monarchical authority, mournfully contemplated the English precedent, the struggle between Crown and Parliament in the 1640s. In this impasse the king turned to Bismarck as the one man steadfast enough to dominate the Chamber and see the king's will done.

Bismarck immediately sought to defuse the constitutional conflict by playing the card of German nationalism. In a speech that mixed insults with tempta-

"Mad Junker" and maker of Prussia-Germany: Otto von Bismarck.

Bismarck Takes Office: 1862
"Iron and Blood"

Germany looks not to Prussia's liberalism, but to its power; Bavaria, Württemberg, and Baden may indulge in liberalism, but Prussia's role is not for them. Prussia must concentrate its power and hold it concentrated for the favorable moment that we have already several times missed. Prussia's borders as drawn in the Vienna treaties do not favor a healthy state existence; the great questions of our time are not decided through speeches and majority votes—that was the great error of 1848 and 1849—but through iron and blood.

Bismarck, to the Prussian Chamber's budget committee, September 30, 1862.

From Bismarck: Die gesammelten Werke *(Berlin: Otto Stollberg Verlag, 1928), Vol. 10, p. 140 (translation by M. Knox).*

The new model Prussian army, 1861.

tions, he announced that "iron and blood" would settle the German question. The liberals professed to be shocked. Bismarck's first bid for liberal cooperation had failed, although some liberals had long called for "a great genius or mighty tyrant . . . capable of decisive action."

The "iron and blood" speech also appalled the king. But Bismarck put the issue to him in military terms: he could fight for his throne or tamely surrender. The fight involved muzzling the press, disciplining liberal sympathizers in the bureaucracy, and spending money that the Chamber had not appropriated on an army reorganization that it opposed. To the Chamber Bismarck impudently proclaimed his "loophole theory" of the constitution: when king and parliament disagreed, the king's latent powers entitled him to act for the general welfare. The conflict deepened. New elections returned the latest in a series of ever-larger liberal majorities. Thanks to the "three-class" Prussian election law, which weighted votes by wealth, those majorities represented only middle-class opinion. But Bismarck's fellow Junkers would not yet let him play the masses against the liberals.

Foreign policy ultimately offered a way around this stalemate, as Bismarck had hoped. A new Polish revolt, even more tragic than that of 1830, convulsed Russian Poland in 1863. Russian repression of the Poles alienated Napoleon III, whose alignment with Russia had underwritten the Italian war. Now *each* of the European great powers was isolated from the others—except Prussia, which maintained its "line to St. Petersburg." In this open situation, Bismarck soon found a cause that would allow him to undermine the status quo while claiming conservative intentions acceptable to Russia and Austria. In 1863 the Danish monarchy moved to incorporate Schleswig, with its minority of Danes and majority of Germans, into Denmark. That step was a flagrant breach of the 1852 Treaty of London that had ended the German-Danish fighting in 1848–49 and had confirmed the continued membership of the duchies of Schleswig and Holstein in the German Confederation. In January 1864 Bismarck therefore secured an alliance with Vienna to restore

the status quo, by force if need be. He secretly aimed at annexing the duchies to Prussia as the first step toward Prussia's long-sought domination of north Germany.

The Danish war of 1864 was swift and decisive, and British protests to Berlin and Vienna were halfhearted. Britain had tilted too close to the Confederacy in the U.S. Civil War (described in Chapter 27). By 1864, it found itself facing the eventual prospect of a million battle-hardened Union veterans on Canada's indefensible borders. It had no troops to spare to rescue Denmark. When the Danes foolishly rejected Bismarck's offer of a compromise, the Prussians stormed the key Danish position at Düppel in April 1864. In August a Prussian amphibious threat to Copenhagen forced the Danes to surrender both Schleswig and Holstein to Prussia and Austria.

That triumph demonstrated the power of the newly reorganized Prussian army and lessened pressure on Bismarck at home. Influential liberal publications soon came around to the view that Prussian state interest and German nationalism ran parallel: Prussia should annex the two duchies. Bismarck himself settled for a policy of gradual encroachment on his Austrian partner. He would "try all roads, the most dangerous road, last." If Austria would concede Schleswig and Holstein and the mastery of north Germany to Prussia, Prussia would perhaps underwrite Austria's survival. If Austria proved obstinate, force would decide.

The Austrians claimed to be shocked at Bismarck's suggestions of Prussian annexation of their joint property, the duchies. Vienna had joined Bismarck's Danish war in hopes of a conservative partnership to cement the status quo in central Europe. Too late it discovered that its partner had other ideas. But Bismarck was not ready for a new war in 1865, although the chief of the general staff, Helmuth von Moltke, was confident. Prussian and Austrian leaders met at Bad Gastein in August 1865 and "papered over the cracks." Prussia would administer Schleswig, Austria Holstein, and the partners would reject the claims to the Duchies of the German-national candidate, the Duke of Augustenburg.

The Gastein agreement lasted only a few months. Vienna was dimly aware that it could preserve its position in the German Confederation only with the support of the lesser states. It therefore broke the Gastein agreement and courted Augustenburg, the candidate of those states and of non-Prussian liberal opinion. Bismarck for his part sounded out Napoleon III in October 1865; the Emperor did not object to Prussian expansion. He presumably expected a long and indecisive Austro-Prussian war that would give France opportunities to intervene and demand its price. By February 1866 Bismarck was sure of his course. He put Austria's violations of the Gastein agreement to a Prussian crown council. William I, convinced of Austrian disloyalty, agreed that Prussia must prepare for war. The issue was simple: who was to be master in Germany.

Yet Bismarck still had to secure allies, and overcome William I's lingering scruples. Italy was happy to sign a three-month offensive alliance in April, thus performing the essential function of tying down large Austrian forces in Venetia. Bismarck, the conservative statesman, also conspired with Hungarian revolutionaries, justifying himself with a favorite quotation from Vergil: "If I cannot prevail on heaven, I shall mobilize hell." And he again appealed to German nationalism. Prussia promised after victory a German parliament elected under universal manhood suffrage.

Securing allies was easy compared to the frustrations of managing the king's conscience: "I have brought the horse to the ditch; he must jump!" Then, as in 1859, Austria rescued its enemies with an ill-timed gesture that appeared provocative. Vienna's slow and cumbersome mobilization system meant that it could not wait if war seemed inevitable. And Austrian mobilization, along with warnings from conservative aides against a "second Olmütz," finally induced William I to jump. On June 7, 1866, Prussian troops attacked the Austrians in Holstein and began to concentrate on the borders of Bohemia.

The "Seven Weeks' War" was a startling demonstration of Prussia's efficiency and might. Moltke used telegraph and railroad, proven in the U.S. Civil War (see pp. 699–702), effectively for the first time in a European conflict. Three Prussian armies detrained on the Bohemian border and converged with unexpected speed on the Austrian forces east of Prague. On July 3, 1866, two of the Prussian armies attacked the Austrian positions at Königgrätz (Sadowa). The firepower of Prussia's Dreyse breechloading rifle shocked the Austrians: it fired five rounds a minute to the Austrian muzzle-loader's one and a half. And unlike troops using muzzle-loaders, the Prussians could reload and fire while lying down. The Austrians held with counterattacks and heavy artillery fire. Then, in mid-afternoon, the third Prussian army, under Crown Prince Frederick, arrived on the Austrian flank and decided the fate of Germany. The Austrians lost 25,000 dead and wounded and 20,000 prisoners.

Bismarck stepped in to check the enthusiasm of king and generals for a push on Vienna. Further fighting would only provoke French intervention, without serving any useful purpose. Bismarck insisted that Protestant Prussia could not

Bismarck Demands War   February 1866

The Minister President spoke . . . [to the Prussian crown council] in the following terms: Prussia is the only workable political unit that has emerged from the ruins of the old German *Reich* [the Holy Roman Empire], and that is why Prussia had been called to lead Germany. Austria in its envy has always resisted the natural and entirely justified efforts of Prussia toward that goal; it has refused to concede to Prussia the leadership of Germany that it is incapable of exercising itself. . . . Austria has granted Prussia neither the influence due it in Germany, nor the secure position in the [Schleswig-Holstein] duchies necessary to both Prussia and Germany, nor the fruits of [Prussia's] victories. . . . It would be a humiliation, if Prussia now withdrew. Any such humiliation must be avoided at all costs. But in that case a break with Austria is probable. We must therefore discuss and decide the question of whether Prussia should pull back in fright from this obstacle—a break and possible war with Austria. . . . The whole historic development of German affairs and the hostile attitude of Austria drive us toward war. It would be an error to seek to avoid it now. . . .

From the Prussian crown council minutes, February 28, 1866, in Die auswärtige Politik Preussens 1858–1871 *(Berlin: G. Stalling, 1939), Vol. 6, pp. 611ff (translation by M. Knox).*

successfully absorb the Catholic German populations that the total destruction of the Habsburg Empire would give it. The king and Moltke grudgingly gave in. By the treaties of Nikolsburg and Prague (July–August 1866) Austria renounced any role in north Germany, accepted Prussia's absorption of Schleswig-Holstein, Hanover, Hesse-Cassel, and Frankfurt, and agreed to the dissolution of the German Confederation of 1815 and the creation in its place of a North German Confederation under Prussia. To avoid French intervention, Bismarck left nominal independence to defeated Baden, Württemberg, and Bavaria. But he fastened upon them military alliances that in wartime made their armies mere appendages of Prussia's.

Domestically, the war of 1866 ended the Prussian constitutional conflict. Elections, held on the day of Königgrätz, returned a conservative majority. Victory intoxicated the remaining liberal deputies; they gladly accepted Bismarck's promises that he would in future respect the Chamber's budget rights. With the liberals as allies, Bismarck now molded the North German Confederation, the pattern for the German nation-state. He personally supervised the drafting of the new constitution, which played off a universal male suffrage *Reichstag* or lower house against representatives of the princes in the upper house. Bismarck, as Prussian prime minister and foreign minister, and as chancellor of the new Confederation, held the balance. Prussia had conquered Germany, and Bismarck had conquered Prussia.

The Struggle for Mastery in Europe: Germany against France, 1867–71

Yet the North German Confederation was not the Germany that the German national movement dreamed of. Bismarck himself, while no nationalist, aimed from the beginning to draw the south German states into his greater Prussia. Unfortunately the economic attraction of the Prussian *Zollverein,* of a unified national market with uniform tariffs, weights, measures, and law codes, was not enough to overcome south German separatism. "Württemberg

wants to remain Württemberg as long as it has the power," said that state's chief minister—a sentiment heartily echoed in Bavaria and even Baden.

Bismarck therefore once more fell back on foreign policy to drive domestic affairs. Napoleon III offered the occasion. Disgruntled over his 1866 miscalculation, smarting over the 1867 defeat of his hare-brained scheme for an empire in Mexico (see p. 694), and under increasing pressure from a liberal public opinion he had helped create by loosening his control of press and politics in the early 1860s, Napoleon III too sought a foreign victory. An initial public clash with Bismarck in early 1867 over a French plan to buy Luxemburg from its ruler, the king of Holland, ended in humiliation for Napoleon. Both France and Prussia came to consider war inevitable as soon as frantic French military reforms were complete.

War came in 1870. The candidacy of a junior member of the Prussian royal house for the vacant throne of Spain offered the occasion. Bismarck had pressed the plan in secret, as one more small diplomatic blow against France, but he could not have known from the beginning that it would lead to war. When the candidacy prematurely became public, the French ambassador visited William I at the summer watering place of Ems and impertinently demanded that Prussia renounce the candidacy "forever." William I, miffed, cut the interview short. When Bismarck received the foreign office telegram describing the interview, he asked Moltke if the army was ready. The chief of the general staff replied that the sooner war came, the greater Prussia's relative strength would be. Bismarck then edited the "Ems telegram" for release to the press. The edited version implied that William I had curtly refused the French demand and had ruled out further negotiation, thus handing France a major diplomatic humiliation.

In Paris, Napoleon III's ministers and supporters reacted as Bismarck had expected. Hysterical at the visible loss since 1866 of France's leading role in Europe, they erupted: "To Berlin!" France declared war on July 19, 1870, without allies. Austria had no stomach for a rematch with Prussia. Italy wisely chose to remain neu-

The Making of Germany

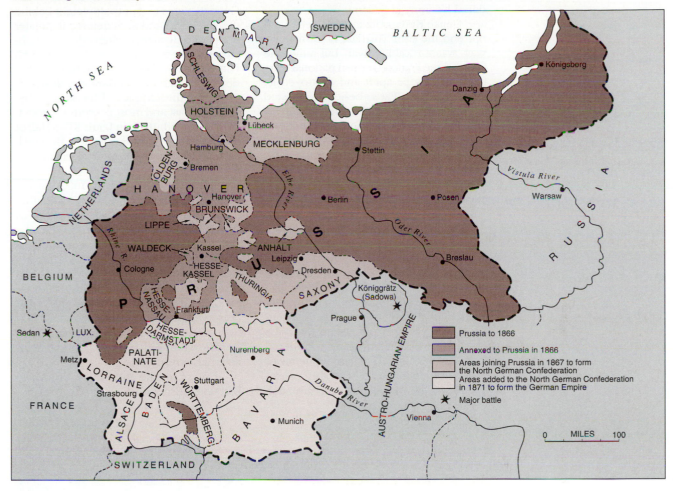

Legend:
- Prussia to 1866
- Annexed to Prussia in 1866
- Areas joining Prussia in 1867 to form the North German Confederation
- Areas added to the North German Confederation in 1871 to form the German Empire
- ★ Major battle

0   MILES   100

tral, despite the childlike enthusiasm of Victor Emmanuel II for war, any war. Russia's only thought was to free itself of the degrading Black Sea naval disarmament imposed after the Crimean War. Britain, without a mass army or a policy, watched impotently.

Moltke's mobilization timetables once again delivered three superlatively equipped Prussian and south German armies, now totalling 380,000 men, to their railheads. The French muddled about in tragic disorder. They now had a better breechloading rifle than the Germans, the Chassepot, and a secret weapon, the *mitrailleuse*, a primitive machine gun. But the cast-steel artillery of Krupp outclassed anything the French could field, and French logistics were chaotic.

The Germans drove across the border and pushed the French back in a series of punishing battles. At Gravelotte-St. Privat, on August 18, the elite Prussian Guard corps attacked uphill across open ground. French firepower killed or wounded 8,000 Prussians, most of them in the space of twenty minutes. Fortunately for the Germans, the ineptly led French then fell back on the fortified city of Metz. Leaving a force to screen the city, the German armies pressed on to squash Napoleon III's reserve army against the Belgian border. Desperate breakout attempts by French cavalry failed in a hail of Prussian rifle fire. The French charges were magnificent, but no longer a serious form of war. The armies of Europe were beginning to discover that industrial firepower killed. On

September 2, 1870, Napoleon III surrendered his army at Sedan.

Unlike Königgrätz in 1866, Sedan did not end the war. This last of Bismarck's wars was no "cabinet war" but rather the first of three Franco-German national wars that tore Europe apart and destroyed its world position. Paris, besieged, resisted under increasingly radical leadership. A French republic based on Tours and then on Bordeaux raised new armies in the style of 1793. Guerrillas, including the intrepid Garibaldi, harassed Prussian patrols and rail lines. The Prussians replied by executing civilians and burning farms and villages.

Finally, after much death, destruction, and bitterness, the French agreed to an armistice in January and signed a peace treaty at Frankfurt on May 10, 1871. The war had cost perhaps 190,000 lives. Bismarck exacted an indemnity equivalent to a billion dollars and annexed Alsace-Lorraine, whose inhabitants mostly spoke indeterminate dialects but considered themselves French. That least moderate of his peace settlements was the consequence of the nationalist furor Bismarck

had helped stir up—to force the south German states to put their weight behind the war effort and to acquiesce in greater unity. And Bismarck achieved that last objective even before the end of war with France. With bribes from the funds of the dispossessed house of Hanover, Bismarck overcame the scruples of the king of Bavaria, the last and most powerful holdout. On January 18, 1871, in Louis XIV's Hall of Mirrors in the Versailles palace, Bismarck had William I proclaimed German Emperor, or *Kaiser*.

Bismarck had said in 1866 that "If there is to be revolution, we would rather make it than suffer it." He had made it. His "revolution from above" had produced a German national state that dwarfed its neighbors militarily and was soon to do so economically. Internally, Bismarck had struck a compromise with middle-class national liberalism, a compromise that preserved Junker power far into the twentieth century. What he deliberately did not do was to fulfill all the aims of the German national movement.

Except for the annexation of Alsace-Lorraine, Bismarck had struck compro-

Europe in 1871

mises with the defeated. He had accepted limits. He had left the Catholic Austrian Germans outside his Protestant-dominated "lesser Germany." The unsatisfied aspiration of many German nationalists for a "greater Germany" spanning the Continent from Schleswig to Trieste and from Strasbourg to Riga might yet undo Bismarck's work.

Western and central Europe had traveled a long road since 1815. Revolution against the old order, the legacy of 1789, was played out. A final despairing outbreak, the "Paris Commune" of March–May 1871, gave in to the troops of the French republic soon after France's peace with Germany. The republic shot 20,000 insurgents and deported another 10,000 to a tropical death in French Guyana. The myths and realities of the new nation-state—flag-bedecked ceremonies, military conscription, compulsory schooling, elections, bureaucracies, and railroads—filled the place of revolution. The power of the nation-state held great potential for good, for the prosperity and freedom of its citizens, but also for evil.

Suggestions for Further Reading

General

A brilliant introduction to the period up to 1848 is E. J. Hobsbawm, *The Age of Revolution, 1789–1848* (1962). For more detail, see F. A. Artz, *Reaction and Revolution, 1814–1832* (1934); W. L. Langer, *Political and Social Upheaval, 1832–1852* (1969); and J. Droz, *Europe between Revolutions, 1815–1848* (1968). For the various powers, see especially A. Briggs, *The Making of Modern England* (1959); A. Cobban, *A History of Modern France*, Vol. II (1957); T. S. Hamerow, *Restoration, Revolution, Reaction: Economics and Politics in Germany, 1815–1871* (1958); A. J. P. Taylor, *The Habsburg Monarchy, 1809–1918* (1948); and the sardonic and brilliant R. Pipes, *Russia under the Old Regime* (1975).

Europe to 1848

On international politics before 1848, H. Nicolson, *The Congress of Vienna: A Study in Allied Unity, 1812–1822* (1946), and H. G. Schenk, *The Aftermath of the Napoleonic Wars* (1947), remain serviceable. The most successful overviews of 1848–49 are P. Robertson, *Revolutions of 1848: A Social History* (1952), and P. Stearns, *1848: The Revolutionary Tide in Europe* (1974). T. S. Hamerow, *Restoration, Revolution, Reaction* (1958), is outstanding on Germany. L. Namier, *1848: The Revolution of the Intellectuals* (1964), stresses the emergence of savagely competing nationalisms; see also, in general, E. Kedourie, *Nationalism* (1960).

Europe after 1848

The best survey of the post-1848 period is again E. J. Hobsbawm, *The Age of Capital, 1848–1875* (1975). A. J. P. Taylor's brilliant *The Struggle for Mastery in Europe, 1848–1918* (1954) is still the best synthesis of nineteenth-century international politics. M. S. Anderson, *The Eastern Question* (1966), expertly chronicles the decay of the Ottoman Empire and its consequences. On the Crimean War and after, see both W. E. Mosse, *The Rise and Fall of the Crimean System, 1855–1871* (1967), and P. W. Schroeder, *Austria, Great Britain and the Crimean War* (1979). For France after 1848, see J. M. Thompson, *Louis Napoleon and the Second Empire* (1955). D. Mack Smith, *Cavour and Garibaldi, 1860. A Study in Political Conflict* (1954); *Victor Emmanuel, Cavour, and the Risorgimento* (1971); and *Cavour* (1985), are excellent on the creation of the Italian state. On Bismarck's revolution from above, see especially O. Pflanze, *Bismarck and the Development of Germany: The Period of Unification 1815–1871* (1963), and L. Gall, *Bismarck* (1986); T. S. Hamerow, *The Social Foundations of German Unification, 1858–1871* (1969), supplies the domestic background. On the military events, D. E. Showalter, *Railroads and Rifles: Soldiers, Technology, and the Unification of Germany* (1975); G. Craig, *The Battle of Königgrätz* (1965); and M. Howard, *The Franco-Prussian War* (1961) are excellent. H. Strachan, *European Armies and the Conduct of War* (1983), provides a useful overview.

27

EUROPE AND THE WORLD IN THE NINETEENTH CENTURY

The forces that transformed the societies of Europe in the nineteenth century also propelled them outward, in a movement that flowed irresistibly and continuously throughout the century. In 1800 Europeans occupied or controlled a mere 35 percent of the world's land surface; by 1914 they controlled a staggering five-sixths of it.

Britain and its colonists led the way. British superiority at sea after Trafalgar (1805) ensured that the peace outside Europe would be a *pax Britannica*. Britain's growing industrial might and swiftly expanding population led to an expansion, virtually constant throughout the century, of the area under the British flag. By 1900 the British Empire ruled 23 percent of the world's land surface and 20 percent of its population. It was Britain that for the first time in history united most of humanity in a world market that pulsed with the erratic rhythms of the business cycle. The force of that market, more than anything else, drove to its culmination the Western conquest of the world begun in 1492.

But Britain's effortless superiority in the first decades after 1815 did not last. Its economic lead slackened as "followers" such as France and Germany industrialized, with political consequences in the wider world. By the 1840s and 1850s the power of Britain's offspring, the United States, was beginning to make its weight felt in North America and the Caribbean. As early as the 1850s America's naval reach touched Japan. Northern victory in the U.S. Civil War meant that Britain faced a unified industrial giant that it could not match in the long run. And by the 1880s European rivals were appearing in strength in Africa and East Asia: France in West Africa, Indochina, and China; Germany in Africa; and Russia in north China.

(OPPOSITE) THE IMPACT OF WESTERN POWER ON THE WIDER WORLD: A BRITISH WARSHIP ANNIHILATES A FLEET OF CHINESE WAR JUNKS DURING THE FIRST OPIUM WAR (1841).

By the end of the century a non-European power, Japan, had risen to dominate northeast Asia. That rise was a sign of the impermanence of the garish empires British and Europeans had patched together. For along with the world market, along with gunboats, rifles, rum, and Bibles, the Europeans brought nationalism to the wider world.

THE BRITISH WORLD EMPIRE

The 1815 Peace Settlement outside Europe

Britain had consolidated its first empire in the Seven Years' War in the mid-eighteenth century. The loss of the American Colonies and the inconclusive war of 1812, embarrassing to both parties, had given the British "official mind" a sharp lesson in the limitations of British power in North America. But elsewhere Britain was unchallenged. Wars in India after 1798 confirmed the verdict of the battle of Plassey (1757): Britain was paramount on the subcontinent.

That immense land empire in South Asia provided both the troops and the commercial and strategic motives for further British colonial annexations throughout the century. By 1819 the British had secured their route to India and their command of the Mediterranean, Atlantic, and Indian Oceans with a net of bases that stretched from Gibraltar and Cape Town to Singapore and Australia.

British naval supremacy had far-reaching effects. It largely ended piracy, from the Caribbean to the seas off Borneo. It also gradually cut off the African slave trade. Britain had controlled half of that trade by 1800 but had outlawed it by an act of Parliament in 1807, thanks to the pressure of crusading idealists such as William Wilberforce (1759–1833). The United States, despite fierce objections from its slave states, had followed suit the next year. In 1814–15, Castlereagh had extracted pledges from the powers at Vienna to work toward the end of the trans-Atlantic slave trade. In the following decades, Britain backed up that ban with Royal Navy patrols. That did not end the vast forced migration to the New World of perhaps 11.7 million Africans, of whom 1.9 million died on the crossing; only the closing of the slave markets in New Orleans, Havana, and Brazil could do that. But it was a start. And Britain was the first major power in history to abolish the institution of slavery itself, in 1833. For the moment, most other powers failed to imitate that example.

The Forces Driving British Expansion

Britain soon pressed on beyond the limits of 1815. The forces behind that expansion came not from the government in London but from the mills and foundries of the Midlands and North, the slums of Birmingham and Liverpool, and the crumbling peasant societies of Scotland and Ireland. Britain imported raw materials and food, especially after the repeal of the Corn Laws in 1846, from the far side of the globe. It exported both goods and people. First came the adventurers, in search of booty or high-profit trade, and the missionaries, intent on imposing Christianity and "progress" on "the heathen." Then came the trading companies with systematic plans for development. To states that were capable of aspiring to follow the West's lead—the Ottoman Empire, Egypt, and some societies in Latin America—bankers happily extended loans. Finally, in areas where "white" settlement appeared promising, increasing numbers of emigrants set up societies on the British and North American pattern.

The motive forces behind imperial expansion—economics and demography—remained virtually constant over the century except for a gradual decline in Britain's rate of population increase and economic growth. What changed, and what accounts for the changes in the forms that expansion took, was the available means. Western expansion had always faced constraints: distance and natural obstacles, disease, the resistance of native societies, and the unwillingness of European governments and peoples to make major sacrifices for empire. These limits

The British Empire in the Nineteenth Century

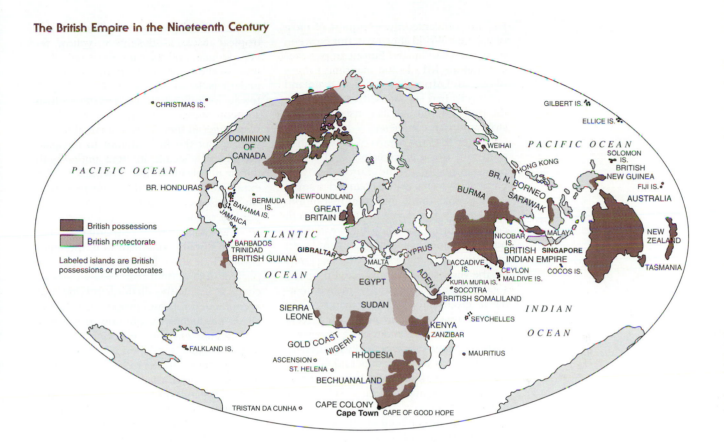

CHRISTMAS IS.

PACIFIC OCEAN

DOMINION OF CANADA

BR. HONDURAS

BERMUDA IS.

BAHAMA IS.

JAMAICA

NEWFOUNDLAND

GREAT BRITAIN

ATLANTIC

BARBADOS
TRINIDAD
BRITISH GUIANA

GIBRALTAR

OCEAN

CYPRUS

MALTA

EGYPT

SIERRA LEONE

SUDAN

GOLD COAST

NIGERIA

ASCENSION
ST. HELENA

RHODESIA

BECHUANALAND

TRISTAN DA CUNHA

CAPE COLONY
Cape Town   CAPE OF GOOD HOPE

FALKLAND IS.

ADEN

KURIA MURIA IS.
SOCOTRA
BRITISH SOMALILAND

SEYCHELLES

KENYA
ZANZIBAR

MAURITIUS

INDIAN

OCEAN

LACCADIVE IS.

CEYLON
MALDIVE IS.

NICOBAR IS.

BRITISH
INDIAN EMPIRE

MALAYA

BRITISH   SINGAPORE

COCOS IS.

BURMA

BR. N. BORNEO
SARAWAK

HONG KONG

WEIHAI

PACIFIC OCEAN

GILBERT IS.

ELLICE IS.

SOLOMON IS.
BRITISH
NEW GUINEA

FIJI IS.

AUSTRALIA

NEW ZEALAND

TASMANIA

British possessions

British protectorate

Labeled islands are British possessions or protectorates

Singapore, One of Britain's far-flung outposts, in 1830.

had not prevented the conquest of most of the New World after 1492. But between them they had limited European penetration before 1815 to the maritime fringes of Asia and Africa. On the Asian mainland only India had succumbed, after drawing the British in through its constant internal strife and rich commerce.

After 1815 the means of expansion— transport, tropical medicine, and weaponry—available to the Europeans and particularly to the British changed dramatically, thanks to the industrial revolution. First came steam. From the mid-sixteenth century, European sailing ships with their heavy cannon had outmaneuvered and outfought Arab dhows and Chinese junks on the high seas. But inshore, European square-riggers were clumsy and vulnerable to grounding or shifting winds. They could not move up narrow winding rivers against the current, and towing by rowers in ships' boats was pathetically inefficient. European naval power thus ended at the high-water mark except where the prize ashore was worth landing a substantial ground force.

Steamboats opened up the Asian and African coastal waters and at last allowed European trade and power to penetrate the interior with little effort. The British East India Company gave the first demonstration of the potential of a steam-powered "river war" in an 1824–26 conflict with India's eastern neighbor, the kingdom of Burma.

Iron-hulled steam vessels were the next step. They demonstrated their worth in the 1839–42 "First Opium War" between Britain and China. Chinese defenses and war-junks had been adequate against wooden-hulled sailing ships unable to maneuver on rivers. Against iron-hulled steamboats they were powerless. The war ended when the British steamed up the Yangtze River and cut the Grand Canal, which supplied Beijing (Peking) with rice. Steam played a decisive role in Commodore Matthew Perry's opening of Japan to American and European trade in 1853–54, and in the French conquest of Indochina in the 1870s and 1880s.

The second major innovation that made British and European expansion possible was quinine. Of all the major tropical diseases—dysentery, yellow fever, dengue, and the numerous nameless fevers—the African falciparum strain of malaria is the most consistently deadly. A few lucky individuals, such as the Scottish surgeon Mungo Park, who explored the river Niger in the 1790s, managed to survive it. But the first attempt to navigate the Niger by steam, in 1832, ended with the death of 40 of the 49 whites on the expedition. Between 1817 and 1836 British garrisons on the Gold Coast lost 66 percent of their strength each year.

The antimalarial properties of the bark of a South American tree, the chinchona, had long been known or suspected. But not until 1820 did two French chemists isolate the alkaloid, quinine, that accounted for those properties. By the 1830s production of quinine in quantity had begun; experience soon suggested that it worked best when taken regularly as a preventive. In 1854 a Niger expedition returned without casualties. The way lay open at last for trade far in the interior and ultimately for the extension of European power into all of sub-Saharan Africa.

The final factor that permitted the British and European conquest of the world was a revolution in weaponry. Until the 1840s, the chief advantages of the Europeans were their logistical organization, trained leadership, and cohesion under fire. The bayonet remained as important as fire from the one-round-per-minute musket, a weapon that some native societies could copy. Skilled enemies with muskets, such as the Algerians or Afghans who resisted the French and British in the 1830s and 1840s, could turn colonial conquest into an expensive, long-drawn-out, and exceedingly grim business—or block it altogether. The greatest European advantage in weaponry was artillery, which was hard to transport except by river and little help against guerrillas.

Then came the first effective muzzle-loading rifles, followed by breechloaders like the Sharps, Dreyse, and Chassepot. From the 1840s to the 1870s the range and rate of fire of European small arms increased at least fivefold—and no native blacksmith could copy the new industrially produced weapons or their ammunition. By the 1880s the box-magazine breechloading rifle and the first easily portable machine gun, the Maxim gun, enabled even small European forces to destroy native armies many times their size. In the climactic 1898 battle against the forces of the *Mahdi,* the Islamic prophet who had raised the Sudan against the unbeliever, the British lost 48 men. The *Mahdi's* armies lost 11,000. The Maxim gun made possible a brief age of military tourism.

The mid-nineteenth-century revolutions in transport, tropical medicine, and weaponry made colonial conquest far easier than before. They did not make it more orderly, however; Britain's steady expansion in particular was hardly a process planned or directed by London. The government from the beginning held to the utilitarian principle that the best government governed least. Until the 1860s those who made British policy were supremely confident that free trade would benefit the world as well as Britain. Palmerston had summed up that credo in a parliamentary speech in 1842, the year of the British victory that opened China. Commerce would lead "civilization with the one hand and peace with the other"; it would render mankind "happier, wiser, better." Free trade, one of its spokesmen announced in 1846, would make "foreign nations . . . valuable Colonies to us, without imposing on us the responsibility of governing them." The British formula, as two later historians have described it, was "informal empire"—"trade with informal control if possible; trade with rule when necessary."

As the century drew on, trade with rule seemed more and more necessary, despite the laments of a central bureaucracy bent on sparing the taxpayers. Trade might make humanity "better"—more like the British—but not in the short term. Trade, and the inevitable missionaries and settlers (where appropriate), invariably required the protection of the flag. Trade required enforceable contracts and security for money and goods. Trade frequently conflicted with the customs, laws, or policies of those it touched, from the tribal empires of Africa to the long-estab-

"Whatever happens we have got The Maxim Gun, and they have not," wrote the British satirist Hilaire Belloc (1870–1953) of this essential tool of empire.

lished states of China and Japan. Trade and loans in Latin America, the Ottoman Empire, and Egypt in many cases destroyed the authority of those who accepted them.

Trade, loans, missionaries, and settlers thus generated a variety of unstable mixtures of resistance and collaboration in the native societies they affected. The interaction between the outward thrust of Britain and its European imitators, and the resistance or lack of it in non-Western societies, was the mechanism that created the British Empire and extended Western domination throughout the world.

Resistance took many forms. Tribes from the Afghans northwest of India to the Kaffirs and Zulus of Africa raided British possessions on the innumerable turbulent frontiers of empire. Religious or proto-nationalist groups—the Mahdists of the Sudan, the Egyptian army, and the Boer farmers of South Africa—rose against the British or against rulers who collaborated with them. And states such as China and Japan refused to open their markets or provide security for the persons and property of British merchants. Resistance or defiance normally called forth a British response. Typically, London or its agents on the spot intervened militarily to protect what they perceived as existing British interests. The security of India's borders, of the China trade, of the Suez Canal or the Cape of Good Hope demanded increasingly strenuous action. That mechanism explains the patchwork character of expansion. Britain did not obey a grand design; it responded when action seemed unavoidable.

Collaboration by native societies also helped govern the timing, extent, and ultimate collapse of British and Western dominance. One corollary of London's belief in free trade and in a minimum of government intervention was the need for native auxiliaries. Princes and tribal rulers, native troops, and Western-educated natives might all serve as more or less willing collaborators with Britain's informal empire. The collaborators found themselves caught between two worlds: the British world market and their own societies. If the market pressed too rapidly and disruptively against the native economy, institutions, or religious and cultural traditions, collaborators might fumble and collapse in the face of antiforeign revolt. That presented Britain with a difficult choice: to get out, or to go in—at great and continuing expense—and rule directly. And to establish and maintain direct rule required the collaboration of the conquered. When that collaboration faltered or ceased, the European empires ultimately collapsed.

Britain's "White" Colonies: Canada, Australia, and New Zealand

The ideal collaborators were of course Britain's own colonists. The societies they created, with the exception of those of the French Canadians and Dutch-descended Boer farmers that London acquired in 1763 and 1814, were replicas of Britain. Britain's demographic expansion drove them onward. The satellite economies of Australia, New Zealand, and eventually Canada in turn contributed wool, grain, meat, and markets to British economic expansion. Along with the United States and Argentina, they also received most of Britain's immense overseas investments.

London, after its sad experience with the thirteen American colonies, did its best to defuse colonial discontent by conceding self-government as soon as possible. Canada, the most heavily populated and turbulent, came first. Conquest in the Seven Years' War and the subsequent arrival of large numbers of American loyalists after 1775–83 had disquieted the deeply rooted Catholic society of Norman peasants that France had planted in Québec. Britain's effort, in the Constitutional Act of 1791, to give each nationality its own province failed to quiet unrest.

In 1837 the suppression of a Québec rising and a revolt in the English-speaking province of Upper Canada (now Ontario) required British troops. In the aftermath, the Earl of Durham, one of the authors of Britain's 1832 Reform Bill, became governor-general. He recommended that Britain give Canada representative self-government as a unified province in which English-speakers would outnumber the French. London adopted his recommendations in the 1840s, but the French-English conflict inevitably persisted. By the time of the U.S. Civil War, the need for strong central government to promote internal cohesion, defense, and railway development was obvious. In 1867, after long negotiation between Canadian leaders, Parliament in London passed the British North America Act. Québec once again received its own administration within the "Dominion of Canada," a federation that included the maritime provinces. Britain happily gave the colonials management of their own affairs, including defense against rebellion and Indian raids.

Britain's invention of the self-governing "dominion" was decisive for Australia and New Zealand. The various territories of Australia, which had served from 1788 as a dumping ground for English convicts, received representative self-government in 1851–55. By then free immigrants far outnumbered the descendants of deported prisoners. In 1901 London conceded dominion status to the Commonwealth of Australia, a continent spanned by railroads and rich in wool, grain, and gold. The independence of New Zealand was a slower process, largely because of a series of unpleasant land wars with the native Maoris, a fierce and tenacious Polynesian warrior people. The land-hungry British settlers refused to dispense with London's protection until

British troops had broken Maori resistance. Self-government nevertheless came in 1876 and dominion status in 1907.

Britain's Indian Empire

In India the British, alone of the colonial powers, took steps in the nineteenth century to prepare the way for the ultimate independence of the non-European peoples they had conquered. The process was neither swift nor peaceful. To protect and extend its trade, the East India Company had succeeded the Mughal emperors as the paramount power on the subcontinent. In the Third Mahratta War of 1817–18 the Company broke for good the power of the Hindu warrior states. By that point the Company itself had ceased to be a private entity with a monopoly on India's trade. As early as 1773 the Crown had taken for itself the power to appoint a governor-general. In 1784 London had assumed control of the Company's political activities. In 1833 the Company lost its trading function entirely; henceforth its only mission was to govern India through the elite Indian Civil Service.

The end of the Company trade monopoly and the extension of British direct rule intensified pressure on the native societies of the subcontinent. The Company had usually been content to leave Indian social and religious custom undisturbed. But once it lost its monopoly, the way was open for the ever-intensifying penetration of independent British merchants and missionaries. Pressure in Parliament and in the British press for the reform of Indian society along British lines mounted.

By the 1830s the reformers had won. As true disciples of Jeremy Bentham (see p. 643), they felt passionately that India was theirs in trust, to Westernize and prepare for self-government at some point in the far distant future. The great British historian Thomas Babington Macaulay, one of the reformers, spelled out the goal: to create "a class of persons Indian in colour and blood, but English in tastes, opinions, and intellects." And Karl Marx celebrated in newspaper articles the creation in India of "a fresh class . . . endowed with the requirements for government and imbued with European science." Britain's mission, he triumphantly announced, was "the annihilation of the old Asiatic society, and the laying of the material foundations of Western society in Asia." Old East India Company hands had misgivings about this revolution from above and the blind self-confidence that drove it. "Englishmen are as great fanatics in politics as Mohommedans in religion. They suppose that no country can be saved without English institutions," fumed a former governor of Madras.

The reform effort culminated with the 1848–56 administration of governor-general Lord Dalhousie, the very personification of utilitarian enterprise and "progress." Dalhousie introduced the telegraph, built the famous Grand Trunk Road across northern India, and planned the railways that by 1905 were the longest and best in Asia. His irrigation canals made vast areas of northern India fertile.

In politics, a less tidy field than engineering, Dalhousie's messianic faith in the benefits of Western civilization made him an annexationist. He completed the conquest of the Sikhs of the Punjab, seized Sind in the west and lower Burma in the east, and gradually annexed Indian states whose thrones fell vacant. British rule now brought ever-increasing missionary activity, equality before the law that disrupted these societies of rigidly demarcated castes, and interference with Hindu religious customs such as *sati*, the ritual burning of widows on their husbands' funeral pyres.

By 1857, the strain on native society had grown intolerable. Over wide areas of northern India the population, from lord to peasant, had grown convinced that Britain's ultimate purpose was to abolish Indian society and religion, whether Hindu or Moslem. The occasion but not the cause of the ensuing explosion was the foolish introduction into the Company's Indian army of new rifles that took paper cartridges waterproofed with tallow Loading required biting the cartridge open. And when rumors, later confirmed, flew that the manufacturers had used tallow made from a blend of pig and cow

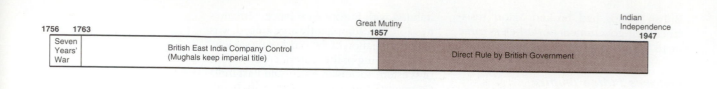

| | 1756 | 1763 | | Great Mutiny 1857 | | Indian Independence 1947 |

| Seven Years' War | British East India Company Control (Mughals keep imperial title) | Direct Rule by British Government |

fat, the *sepoys*—the Company's native sol-diers—faced an appalling dilemma. The cow was sacred to Hinduism, the pig for-bidden to Moslems. The troops could bite the cartridge and suffer loss of caste if Hindu or defilement if Moslem. Or they could betray their deeply felt oath to the army.

Many chose mutiny and rose against the British with the support of much of the population of the dusty plains around Delhi. Native leaders harked back to the proud days of Mahrattas and Mughals, and sought to drive the British from India. The *sepoys* committed numerous atrocities against British prisoners, women, and children. The British, isolated and fearful amid an immense and largely hostile pop-ulation, fought a pitiless race war. They celebrated the reconquest of Delhi by lashing *sepoy* prisoners across gun barrels and blasting them to shreds. London dis-solved the East India Company, drastically reorganized its Indian army, made India a possession of the Crown, and publicly disclaimed any intention of tampering with its subjects' religions.

The Great Mutiny of 1857–58 was a shock not only to the British rulers of India but to British imperial self-confidence. It drove home the obvious: non-Western so-cieties did not automatically take to West-ern values. It revealed that the reformers' "fresh class" of English-educated collabo-rators lacked roots in the Indian popula-tion. The English henceforth proceeded with greater caution and far lower expec-tations. Stability, not social revolution be-came their goal. Creeping annexation ceased. The Indian subject princes, who for the most part had remained loyal, pre-served their territories into the twentieth century. Britain now confined its activities primarily to administration, engineering, and the defense of India's borders.

Nevertheless, the reformers suc-ceeded in the long term. The Great Mutiny was the last sizable traditionalist Indian revolt. English-educated Indians took an increasing role in the junior ranks of the administration, in the new English-speak-ing law courts, and in the creation of tex-tile, coal, and steel industries. By the 1880s a modern Indian public opinion, both Hindu and Moslem, had come into being. The founding, with help from British liber-als, of the Indian Congress party in 1885 marked the birth of the force that ulti-mately succeeded the British. The Indians whom Britain had educated in turn in-vented Indian nationalism.

Britain in Africa to the 1880s

Except for the Cape Colony and a few fever-ridden trading stations on the west coast, Britain in 1815 had little use for Africa. That changed. The penetration of British palm-oil traders, missionaries, and antislavery reformers, especially after mid-century, brought increasing clashes with

A scene from the Great Mutiny, 1857: British firepower and discipline halt a sepoy attack during the siege of Delhi.

The Scramble for Africa   1884/1914

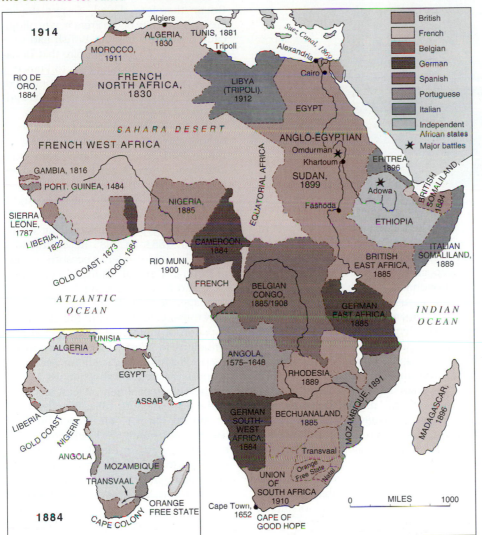

Map legend:
- British
- French
- Belgian
- German
- Spanish
- Portuguese
- Italian
- Independent African states
- ★ Major battles

1914

Algiers
ALGERIA, 1830
TUNIS, 1881
Tripoli
MOROCCO, 1911
Suez Canal, 1869
Alexandria
Cairo
RIO DE ORO, 1884
FRENCH NORTH AFRICA, 1830
LIBYA (TRIPOLI), 1912
EGYPT
SAHARA DESERT
FRENCH WEST AFRICA
ANGLO-EGYPTIAN
Omdurman
Khartoum
SUDAN, 1899
ERITREA, 1896
BRITISH SOMALILAND, 1884
GAMBIA, 1816
PORT. GUINEA, 1484
NIGERIA, 1885
Adowa
Fashoda
ETHIOPIA
SIERRA LEONE, 1787
LIBERIA, 1822
GOLD COAST, 1873
TOGO, 1884
CAMEROON, 1884
RIO MUNI, 1900
EQUATORIAL AFRICA
ITALIAN SOMALILAND, 1889
FRENCH
BELGIAN CONGO, 1885/1908
BRITISH EAST AFRICA, 1885
ATLANTIC OCEAN
GERMAN EAST AFRICA, 1885
INDIAN OCEAN
ANGOLA, 1575–1648
RHODESIA, 1889
MOZAMBIQUE, 1891
MADAGASCAR, 1896
GERMAN SOUTH-WEST AFRICA, 1884
BECHUANALAND, 1885
Transvaal
Orange Free State
Natal
UNION OF SOUTH AFRICA, 1910
Cape Town, 1652
CAPE OF GOOD HOPE
0 MILES 1000

1884

TUNISIA
ALGERIA
EGYPT
ASSAB
LIBERIA
GOLD COAST
NIGERIA
ANGOLA
MOZAMBIQUE
TRANSVAAL
ORANGE FREE STATE
CAPE COLONY

native forces. In West Africa, the warlike Ashanti kingdom in the hinterland of the Gold Coast was the main barrier. A British punitive expedition in 1874 checked its power, but Britain did not finally annex the kingdom until 1896. In East Africa, British attempts to put down the slave trade destroyed the authority of Britain's client, the Sultan of Zanzibar. That drew London ever deeper into the affairs of East Africa.

But the extension of British rule to much of Africa followed from two great crises in the 1880s and 1890s, both connected with the security of the routes to India. In North Africa the stake was the great canal across the Suez isthmus that the Saint-Simonian engineer and promoter, Ferdinand de Lesseps, had completed in 1869. In 1876 the Egyptian Khedivate, the regime of the successors of Mehemet Ali (see p. 663), collapsed in

The strategic Suez Canal, in the 1890s.

bankruptcy; it had attempted to modernize Egypt on European credit. The French and British governments took command of Egyptian finances and taxation to see their bondholders paid.

That intrusion was the latest of a long series of defeats at the hands of unbelievers since Bonaparte. It generated a radical response; unlike the Indian Mutiny, that response was recognizably modern. In 1882 a movement in the partially Westernized Egyptian army overthrew its own government and defied the West. The movement's ideological basis was a modernizing current of Islam; its program, Egypt for the Egyptians; its leader, the charismatic Colonel Ahmed Arabi Pasha.

That situation, now all too familiar, took Britain and France aback. A naval show of force of the traditional sort merely provoked a massacre of foreigners at Alexandria. The British responded with cannon fire. That was the point of no return: British prestige was committed, the prestige required to hold India. The pacific Liberal cabinet of William Ewart Gladstone (see p. 712) unhappily landed an army to restore a cooperative Egyptian government. The French had no need of a route to India, and refused to follow.

The British convincingly crushed Arabi's army, and found themselves ruling Egypt. To Gladstone's dismay, the old techniques of informal empire no longer served. British interests appeared too great, Egyptian resistance too fanatical. If Britain withdrew, its discredited clients would again collapse, leaving Canal and debt at the mercy of anti-Western forces. Britain therefore stayed, despite the increasing hostility of the French, who illogically concluded that the British had slyly usurpted the Egyptian empire that Bonaparte had failed to bequeath to France.

Worse, Egypt was not self-contained: the mighty river Nile upon which its agriculture depended rose in the Sudan, far to the south. That province was in theory Egypt's, held through isolated garrisons. But in 1881 an Islamic figure even more charismatic than Arabi had arisen there and had begun to weld the region's Dervish religious orders into an army and a state. The *Mahdi,* Mohammed Ahmad, swept the Egyptian garrisons out of the Sudan in 1883. In 1885 he destroyed a British-led force under an eccentric soldier of fortune, General "Chinese" Gordon.

Gladstone, lamenting his "Egyptian bondage," left the *Mahdi* for later British governments to deal with. But British occupation of Egypt had unleashed French ambitions in West Africa. Other powers also took a hand. The resulting "scramble" for protectorates and annexations divided up the African continent, at least on paper, in the 25 years after 1882. In West Africa Britain left much to the French but kept Nigeria and a number of smaller river colonies. In East Africa the British were less generous to their rivals. Proximity to India impelled them to keep most of the coast, except for areas conceded, graciously or not, to Italians and Germans.

And a second great crisis far to the south drove Britain to extend its control still further. Britain's principal stake at the Cape of Good Hope was also originally strategic. The Cape was an indispensable base, "the true centre of the Empire . . . clear of the Suez complications, almost equally distant from Australia, China, India, Gibraltar, the West Indies, and the Falklands," as a Colonial Office official pointed out in the 1870s. Unfortunately, the Cape had a land frontier. It also had non-British white inhabitants: the settlers whom the Dutch East India Company had planted in 1652 to provide supplies for its shipping.

British relations with the Cape Dutch after annexation were friendly; the colony received representative self-government in 1872. Dealings with the Boer ("peasant") farmers of the inland frontier were less satisfactory; British humanitarians frowned on the Boer habit of enslaving the Africans. Between 1835 and 1844, hungry for land and determined to preserve a white supremacy they felt God had ordained, the Boers streamed north across the Vaal River and out of British control. The climax of that "Great Trek" came at the battle of Blood River in 1838. A Boer wagon train defeated the onslaught of the Zulu king Dingaan, heir of the great Shaka, who had created the mightiest army south of the Sahara. To the *"Trekboers,"* reared in the stern Old Testament faith of the Dutch Reformed Church, victory at Blood River proved that God had chosen them.

The Trekboers founded twin republics, the Orange Free State and the Transvaal—states that in their very origins represented an almost tribal reaction against Britain. When London sought in the 1870s to force them into a Cape federation that would eventually become a dominion, Transvaal Boer rifles replied. A British defeat in 1881 persuaded Gladstone to recognize Boer independence, subject only to a vague right of veto over Boer relations with foreign powers. Unlike the situation in Egypt, the stakes were not high enough to warrant a major British commitment, and Boer nationalism was clearly too tough to take on lightly.

Gladstone's retreat postponed the struggle for mastery in South Africa. That development, like the climax of the British-French struggle for the Nile and the crises in East Asia around the turn of the century, is best left for discussion in its international context (see pp. 750–53). But even before the second round against the Boers, and despite doubts and hesitations in London, Britain had annexed most of a new empire in Africa. Egyptian revolt, the fanaticism of the *Mahdi*, and Boer proto-nationalism had marked the limits of informal influence. Africa's resistance drove Britain to defend by ever-broader annexations what Britain already held. And the growing rivalry from the other European powers increasingly confirmed the British on the path they had chosen.

BRITAIN'S RIVALS: FRANCE, GERMANY, ITALY, RUSSIA

The other European powers inevitably sought to imitate Britain. But each power did so in its own way. And they ultimately did so at Britain's pleasure, for neither separately nor together could they challenge British naval supremacy.

France

French imperialism, which created the second largest nineteenth-century European empire, was primarily military in inspiration. It began in 1830 with an attack on the pirate kingdom of Algiers. The dying Bourbon dynasty sought the prestige of conquest; Louis Philippe inherited some coastal outposts and a hinterland that resisted fiercely. The French army, in almost twenty years of bloody campaigns and hair-raising atrocities, prevailed by 1847 against the canny resistance leader Abd-el-Kader.

The Algerian outpost provided security for French Mediterranean shipping. Its conquest produced and gave a home to that quintessential French colonial force, the Foreign Legion. It offered a training ground for generations of colonial officers. And thanks to French and European immigration and agricultural settlement, Algeria almost began to pay for itself after the suppression of a further Moslem uprising in 1870.

But Algeria was no product of trade and industry, the forces behind British expansion. And even if the French had aspired to an informal commercial empire in North Africa, Moslem resistance would have thwarted them. The French empire did have economic functions. But its reason for existence lay above all in the belief of successive French governments before 1870 that France's claim to European primacy required colonial possessions. And the loss of that primacy in 1870 made colonial self-assertion a necessary compensation for European humiliation.

Under Napoleon III, General Louis Faidherbe made Senegal, France's most important West African outpost, a major source of native troops. In 1858–59 Napoleon seized Saigon and Da Nang in Vietnam as a reprisal for native killings of French missionaries. In the 1860s France annexed the southern areas of Vietnam. Napoleon III exploited the U.S. Civil War to impose the Austrian Archduke Maximilian as Emperor of Mexico, with the support of Foreign Legion bayonets. Union victory and Mexican resistance brought French withdrawal and the Archduke's death by firing squad in 1867.

The Franco-Prussian war inevitably imposed a pause. But by the early 1880s France had again begun to expand. It forced a protectorate on Tunis, Algeria's difficult neighbor, in 1881. After humiliation in the Egyptian crisis of 1882, French consuls and officers on the West African rivers began feverishly staking claims that Paris until then had been unwilling to back. Collision with a series of unbending Moslem theocracies in the West African interior compelled the French to make good their paper claims with Maxim guns. The colonial army and France's formidable naval infantry happily bent to that task. By 1902 the French empire extended from Algeria to the Gulf of Guinea, and France had annexed Madagascar on the Indian Ocean side of the Cape of Good Hope.

Germany and Italy

The German and Italian empires had even less economic function than the French; as latecomers, Germany and Italy could only seize territories so worthless that Britain and France had passed them by. Bismarck had utter contempt for the German colonial enthusiasts who had emerged after 1871. He nevertheless set them loose in 1884–85 to claim Togo, Cameroons, South-West Africa, and German East Africa to create artificial friction with London. At the 1884–85 Berlin colonial conference he also helped give the brutal King Leopold II of Belgium control of the Congo basin; British-French rivalry benefited other powers besides Berlin.

Bismarck's purposes in picking a colonial quarrel with Britain were diplomatic and domestic, not colonial: rapprochement with France, a thumping German

nationalist vote in the 1884 elections, and reinsurance against dismissal by the mildly liberal and pro-British Crown Prince Frederick when William I ultimately died. Those passing needs saddled Germany with expensive and useless African territories and an assortment of Pacific islands. Bismarck's successors acquired a Chinese port. That unsatisfactory empire did not disillusion German opinion; it whetted its appetite for larger things.

Italy, as the least of the great powers, found even slimmer pickings than Germany. It acquired the Red Sea port of Assab in 1882 and asserted a protectorate over the Coptic Christian kingdom of Ethiopia in 1889. The Amhara rulers of Ethiopia appeared to accept, but then resisted further Italian encroachment. Menelik, the emperor, acquired European rifles and French military experts. On March 1, 1896, at Adowa he dealt the Italians the worst defeat inflicted upon a would-be European colonizer in the nineteenth century. In the face of an enemy that outnumbered them by five to one, the Italians had divided their forces and had struck out on divergent routes across unmapped mountains. They lost 6,000 dead and 4,000 wounded or captured; political chaos at home prevented a renewal of the war. Italy made do for a generation with the coastal enclaves of Eritrea and Somalia.

Russia in Asia

Finally, Russia rounded out an empire in central and east Asia in the course of the nineteenth century. That process was like French expansion in that it was military, and like that of the United States in that it pursued geopolitical "manifest destiny." The Crimean War checked Russia in Europe but sharpened its appetites elsewhere. In 1853–54 it annexed large areas around the Aral Sea. In the next twenty years it methodically crushed the central Asian nomad peoples and the surviving Tartar khanates of Bukhara, Khiva, and Kokand. By 1884 Russia had reached the Afghan border. Farther east, it pressed into Mongolia. And in 1858 and 1860, by the army's bayonets and the treaties of Aigun and Beijing (Peking), Russia seized from

Colonial troops: An Algerian officer in the French army of the 1880s.

the Chinese the Amur and maritime provinces opposite Japan. At the southern tip of the maritime province it founded a naval base with a name that was a program: Vladivostok, "Ruler of the East." And from 1891 Russia began pushing a railroad across Siberia toward the Pacific at Vladivostok, to make that program reality.

BRITAIN'S LEGACY IN NORTH AMERICA: THE EXPANSION OF THE UNITED STATES

The Young Republic

By the 1890s an entirely different sort of state had reached the Pacific shores of the New World. The United States that emerged from the Revolutionary War of 1775–83 and the Constitutional Convention of 1787 was a unique experiment. It was a new state, not founded through the slow processes of dynastic and military-bureaucratic consolidation that had made the states of Europe. Its sovereign people—"We the people of the United States"—did not claim to be a "nation," a political unit preordained by language, culture, and historic boundaries. America's language and culture were initially British, and its territorial boundaries were lost in the endless forests of the Appalachians and the swamps of southern Georgia. The foundation of the new state was its principles: "We hold these truths to be self-evident, that all Men are created equal, that they are endowed by their Creator with certain unalienable rights, that among these are Life, Liberty, and the Pursuit of Happiness. . . ." The securing of those natural rights was the purpose of American government, the unity of the thirteen colonies was the means.

Hard experience in town and county meetings, state assemblies, and the Revolutionary War had given the framers of the Constitution a realism—or a pessimism—about human nature that contrasted sharply with the Rousseauite optimism of later European revolutionaries. As James Madison of Virginia, one of the Constitution's principal architects, observed: "If men were angels, no government would

Tocqueville Foresees the World Domination of Russia and America   1835

There are at the present time two great nations in the world, which started from different points, but seem to tend towards the same end. I allude to the Russians and the Americans. . . . All other nations seem to have nearly reached their natural limits, and they have only to maintain their power; but these are still in the act of growth. . . . These alone are proceeding with ease and celerity along a path to which no limit can be perceived. The American struggles against the obstacles that nature opposes to him; the adversaries of the Russian are men. The former combats the wilderness and savage life; the latter, civilization with all its arms. The conquests of the American are therefore gained by the plowshare; those of the Russian by the sword. The Anglo-American relies upon personal interest to accomplish his ends and gives free scope to the unguided strength and common sense of the people; the Russian centers all the authority of society in a single arm. The principle instrument of the former is freedom; of the latter, servitude. Their starting-point is different and their courses are not the same; yet each of them seems marked by the will of Heaven to sway the destinies of half the globe.

From Alexis de Tocqueville, Democracy in America *(New York: Vintage Books, 1953), Vol. I, p. 434.*

be necessary." Majority will unchecked by law meant tyranny over both individuals and states. Madison and others therefore built into the Constitution what a great American historian has described as a "harmonious system of mutual frustration": the separation of powers.

Legislature, executive, and judiciary checked and balanced one another, as did the new federal government and the thirteen states. Within Congress, the indirectly elected Senate moderated the impetuous House of Representatives. Neither majority whim in Congress, nor the authority of that elected monarch, the president, nor any caprice of the Supreme Court's judges could prevail for long without the cooperation of the other branches. That system, so cumbersome in theory, in practice usually forced the deliberate creation of the compromise and consensus without which democratic polities fall into chaos or despotism. The Constitution did not guarantee the success of the American experiment. That depended above all on the common sense, civic spirit, and political experience of the citizenry. But it did provide a framework that used those qualities to advantage.

The Constitution was above all a democratic document, although its framers were men of property and social distinction and although it made allowances for the South's "peculiar institution," slavery. To secure the agreement of the southern states, the framers counted each slave, for purposes of apportioning representatives, as three-fifths of a white citizen. Despite that concession to inequality, the Constitution swiftly developed in the direction of still greater democracy. To overcome opposition to its adoption, Madison and others put forward a further series of guarantees that the new federal government would not imitate the "tyranny" of George III. The first ten amendments, or Bill of Rights, adopted in 1789–91, placed the rights of the individual against the state at the center of the new political system. Those rights gradually grew as the country expanded and the political weight of the socially stratified east coast states decreased. Most states that had restricted voting through religious tests or property qualifications had enacted universal male suffrage by the 1820s.

The founders gradually passed from the scene, leaving a vacuum that political parties ultimately filled. The first grouping of importance was the Federalists, whose advocacy of a strong central government helped push the Constitution through. Their leading light was Alexander Hamilton, first Secretary of the Treasury and prophet of the economic development of the United States. Their program implied the supremacy of industry and commerce over agriculture and of the cultivated elite over the masses. Thomas Jefferson and Madison of Virginia formed a Democratic-Republican party that opposed Hamilton with a vision of an egalitarian farmers' republic. Great cities, Jefferson wrote, were "pestilential to the morals, the health, and the liberties of man."

"Old Hickory": Andrew Jackson (1767–1845)

That conflict of ideologies and interests persisted throughout the century and beyond. It soon became at least in part a regional division. The egalitarian frontier triumphed in the 1828 election, the first fought by recognizable national parties. Andrew Jackson, "the People's Choice" against the eastern elites, was ironically a Kentucky landowner. But his overwhelming popular-vote victory at the head of the Democratic party was a mighty step toward the emergence of the system of two national parties, powerful engines of consensus, that still exists.

By 1828 the United States was well on its way to territorial consolidation. Jefferson, as president in 1803, had bought from Napoleon the Louisiana territory that commanded the mouth of the Mississippi and stretched west to the Rocky Mountains and north to the still unmarked Canadian border. In the aftermath of the War of 1812, Britain and the United States agreed to demilitarize the Great Lakes and establish the 49th parallel as their mutual border as far as the Rockies. In 1819 Spain sold Florida to the United States. By 1837 the original thirteen states had doubled in number. Jackson encouraged and speeded the "removal" by force of most of the remaining Indian tribes east of the Mississippi. Only Mexico to the south was now a potential rival.

The United States even began to interest itself in Latin American affairs. Napoleon, by deposing the Bourbons in 1808, had cut adrift the Spanish Empire in Latin America. The revolts against Spain that followed had produced by the early 1820s a collection of weak and internally divided states. After France's 1823 invasion of Spain to restore the Bourbons, French backing for Spanish efforts at reconquest appeared to threaten what Britain considered a promising market. George Canning, Castlereagh's successor as British Foreign Secretary, suggested a joint British-United States declaration to ward off European intervention.

But President James Monroe preferred to act unilaterally. With a characteristically American statement of republican principles, the Monroe Doctrine, he announced to Congress in December 1823 that the United States would regard attempts to establish or reestablish European control in the western hemisphere as signs of "an unfriendly disposition towards the United States." Canning could boast to Parliament that he had "called the New World into existence to redress the balance of the Old." But it was the Royal Navy, not the still minuscule seapower of the United States, that initially backed the Doctrine with force. Until the very end of the century the Royal Navy, in Britain's own interest, served as ultimate guarantor of the maritime security of the United States.

The mechanization of the slave economy: Eli Whitney's cotton gin.

Expansion and Disunion: The Origins of the Civil War

Economic and territorial expansion soon strained both the principles and the political fabric of the Republic. The trading Northeast, which acquired a merchant marine second only to Britain's, industrialized rapidly (see p. 626). The Erie Canal and the railroad opened the Midwest to settlers, and gave those settlers new markets in the East for their grain.

The South, despite the misgivings of figures such as Jefferson ("Indeed I tremble for my country, when I reflect that God is just"), further refined the slave economy established in the seventeenth century. Tobacco was less and less profitable, but after 1793 the cotton gin, a machine invented by the Yankee Eli Whitney, made the short-fiber cotton that grew in the South into a fabulously profitable plantation crop. The slave economy spread rapidly westward, creating a "Cotton Kingdom" from Savannah to Mobile and New Orleans. By the 1820s the South was shipping 60 million pounds of raw cotton annually to the mills of Europe.

Old divisions between states blurred. Divisions between Puritan trading New England, the religiously and socially varied central Atlantic states, and the Anglican slave South had been less important than the gulf between the settled and hierarchical societies of the coastal plains and the egalitarian frontiersmen of the Appala-

chians and beyond. Now canal, railroad, and river steamer riveted North and South firmly to their respective hinterlands. Free labor spread across the northern backcountry, slave labor across the South.

Economic and territorial expansion brought to a head the fundamental conflict of principles: could a system founded on individual freedom ultimately tolerate slavery? By the 1830s stern New England voices had begun to attack the Cotton Kingdom at its most vulnerable point—its principles. Agitators such as William Lloyd Garrison and Wendell Phillips ceaselessly pounded at the irreconcilability of black slavery and white freedom. Garrison denounced the Constitution itself as "a covenant with death and an agreement with hell," for it permitted slavery. The Southern response was increasingly implausible and hysterical. John C. Calhoun, the South's greatest national political figure, told the Senate in 1837 that slavery was no evil, "but a good, sir, a positive good." The Abolitionists were and remained a tiny though noisy minority, but they inspired a persecution mania in the South that in the end drove it to revolt and ruin.

Economic issues also helped strain relations between the two regions. The South, as befitted a satellite economy of Britain, demanded free trade; the industrializing North with its Midwestern markets sought protective tariffs. In 1832 that conflict led to a great crisis. The "sovereign state" of South Carolina, under Calhoun's leadership, "nullified" a protective tariff that Congress had passed. President Jackson prepared to use force: "The laws of the United States must be executed." Since the issue was not slavery itself, the other Southern states were not prepared to back South Carolina. A compromise deferred until later the issue of "states' rights." The rebellious state withdrew nullification and Congress agreed to reduce tariffs. Nor did economics always pull the sections apart. Northern industry's dependence on Southern cotton led the South to bet heavily though in vain upon the existence of an implicit alliance between plantation chattel slavery and factory "wage slavery," between the "lords of the lash and the lords of the loom."

The relentless territorial expansion of the United States, by constantly raising the stakes in the competition between two irreconcilable systems, ultimately brought war. Admitting new states created a series of ever-greater crises. Missouri's admission as a slave state was possible only as part of an 1820 compromise that established latitude 36° 30′, Missouri's southern border, as the future boundary between slave and free territories.

Then, in the 1820s and 1830s, settlers, including planters and their slaves, flocked into the Mexican territories west of Louisiana, ironically at the invitation of the Mexican government. Attempts to reassert Mexican control led to revolt by the settlers in 1835–36 and the proclamation of a "Republic of Texas." Eight years later the Democratic party under James K. Polk carried the presidential election by promising to annex Texas, which had asked to join the Union. Mexico's warnings that it would fight what it regarded as aggression, and clashes with Mexican patrols on the Rio Grande, brought war in 1846–48. The minuscule U.S. Army outclassed its adversary. It captured Mexico City and seized by force the entire Southwest from Texas westward to California.

This extension of U.S. power, and Polk's compromise with the British to extend the 49th parallel border with Canada westward to the Pacific across the Oregon territory, created a far greater North-South crisis than had Missouri. Polk had promised the northern states an Oregon-Canada border ("Fifty-four forty or fight!") far to the north of the one he ultimately secured. Northern leaders retaliated by demanding that Congress exclude slavery from the territories seized from Mexico. The South, which had contributed disproportionately to victory, replied with threats of secession from the Union.

The Compromise of 1850 failed to paper over the cracks. It admitted California as a free state but left the status of the lands between California and Texas to the choice of their eventual inhabitants. It also pledged the North to return fugitive slaves, thus forcing northern authorities to choose between conscience and federal law. And Harriet Beecher Stowe's popular novel, *Uncle Tom's Cabin* (1852), dramatized the nature and consequences of slavery for the Northern public. The conflict deepened.

Congress and the Southern-dominated Supreme Court tore up the Missouri Compromise in the Kansas-Nebraska Act of 1854 and the Dred Scott decision of 1857. All territories, even those previously covered by the Missouri Compromise, could now choose to be free or slave. The consequence was a savage guerrilla struggle punctuated by mob violence in "bleeding Kansas," west of Missouri but north of the Missouri Compromise line.

Quasi-war over Kansas opened the door to the men of blood on both sides. There an Abolitionist extremist, John Brown, made a name for himself with a series of unsavory killings. In October 1859, impelled by visions of arming the slaves and provoking an immense revolt, he and a band of followers seized the federal arsenal at Harpers Ferry, Virginia. Colonel Robert E. Lee, U.S. Army, swiftly turned him out. Virginia as swiftly hanged him. Brown provided Abolition with a martyr and convinced the increasingly deluded South that it stood alone, for "states' rights" and slavery, against the rest of the Union.

The election of 1860 showed that North-South polarization was complete. Abraham Lincoln of Illinois ran for the new Republican party ("free soil, free men") that represented the North and Northwest. He carried seventeen of the

Slave States and Free States   1861

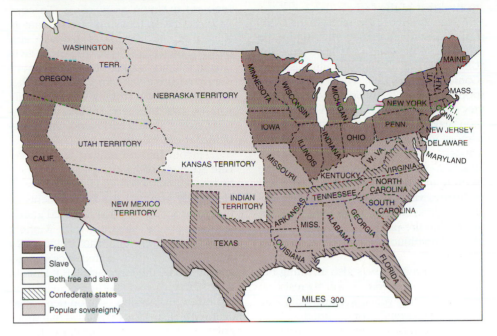

eighteen free states. The fifteen slave states overwhelmingly opposed him. Lincoln sought to preserve the Union with conciliatory gestures. He abhorred slavery but was a practical politician, not a zealot. The fire-eaters of the South, trusting in the economic power of "King Cotton" over both New England and Lancashire, and in their military spirit and talent as a planter aristocracy, decided for secession. On April 12–14, 1861, South Carolina bombarded and took Fort Sumter, the federal outpost in Charleston harbor. The "irrepressible conflict" had begun.

The Second American Revolution, 1861–65

The slave South's appeal to arms unleashed the world's first industrialized war, the longest, bloodiest, and most consequential struggle in the Western world between 1815 and 1914. The Crimean War had come too early and Bismarck's wars were too short to show what happened when industrialized powers collided. The U.S. Civil War was different. It was the first conflict between Western powers un-

limited in aims since the Wars of Religion. To the South's limited war to assert the "right" of states to preserve slavery, the North replied with *unconditional surrender*—a war aim the French revolutionaries had hinted at but which even Napoleon had hesitated to pursue. Reestablishment of the Union ultimately demanded the total destruction of the South's military power, the elimination of slavery, and the remaking of Southern society through a second American Revolution.

Neither side possessed at the outset a serious military establishment by European standards. The 16,367 officers and men of the peacetime U.S. Army split. A quarter of the 1,066 regular officers went South, including Colonel Lee, who stood with Virginia when it seceded to join the Confederate States of America. The Confederacy used these defectors wisely, to train and lead the state militias that became its army. The Union inherited the regular army, and kept its officers with regular army units. The Northern militias, sketchily trained and led by political appointees and elected officers, paid in blood for that mistake. Not until 1863–64 did Union battlefield effectiveness begin to rival that of the "rebels."

The Confederacy faced a daunting task. It produced 26,000 tons of pig iron annually to the Union's 160,000 tons. The Union had 22,000 miles of railroads to the Confederacy's 9,000. The Union had a population of 22 million; the Confederacy's whites were 6 million, with 3.5 million slaves. Weight of numbers and an almost infinitely expandable productive capacity were thus the Union's greatest assets. Yet the Confederacy coped in the short term. It improvised military-run war industries virtually overnight in Birmingham, Selma, Atlanta, Richmond. And the new rifled fire-power provided by the industrial revolution favored the tactical defensive.

Union morale was also anything but firm; the Confederacy's will to resist, at least in the early years, was unconditional. "Peace Democrats"— or "Copperheads" to the supporters of the Union cause— sought with considerable success to undermine Lincoln. In the border states partisans of the Confederacy intrigued, plotted, and spied. The 1863 introduction of a draft in the North caused an insurrection in New York City; mobs burned government offices and killed blacks as scapegoats for

the war. Putting these "draft riots" down required a Union army corps. To cope with Confederate sympathizers Lincoln took the drastic step of partially suspending the Bill of Rights and trying civilians in military courts. The Confederacy's purely negative war aim gave it a further advantage. A few striking victories might win the war. Northern opinion might desert Lincoln; Britain and France might recognize the Confederacy.

Lincoln had no military experience. Like so many of his troops and generals, he learned on the job and he learned well. He swiftly adopted the key elements of the "Anaconda plan" that the aged generalissimo of the Mexican war, Winfield Scott, had proposed. The Union navy would blockade the Confederacy's coasts and dominate the Mississippi. But Lincoln could not afford to wait for strangulation to do its work; Union opinion demanded action. He also soon concluded that strangulation alone could not produce unconditional surrender. Union armies had to penetrate the heart of the Confederacy and destroy it.

The Confederate armies in northern Virginia dominated the first phase of the war, which lasted until mid-1863. They repeatedly threw back inept Union

Industrial fire-power: "The Dictator," a Union 13-inch mortar.

attempts to seize Richmond. But Lee failed to exploit the inexperience of the Union armies to deliver the crushing counteroffensive blow needed to unseat Lincoln.

The Confederacy's two major attempts to invade the North ended in disaster. The first, in September 1862, led to the appalling bloody draw at Antietam Creek in Maryland. The Union won a strategic victory, for Lee had to retreat. That gave Lincoln the platform to launch the political offensive that secured his place in history. On September 23, 1862, he announced that after January 1863 all slaves in states still in rebellion would be free. And on New Year's Day he issued the Emancipation Proclamation, which made the war a crusade to end slavery. It captured for the Union the support of European liberal opinion. It threatened the cohesion of the Confederacy's home front. It gave the Union armies, by the end of the war, almost 180,000 black soldiers, an eighth of their strength.

Lee's second invasion of the North, in June–July 1863, ended at Gettysburg, the largest battle fought in North America to this day. Lee's instinct for the Napoleonic tactical offense betrayed him. The artillery and rifle fire of the new industrial age shredded the ten brigades he launched at the Union center. His army, reduced by more than 20,000 dead, wounded, or missing, retreated through rain and mud to defend Virginia.

The Union had not merely halted Lee's last offensive. In the neglected western theater Lincoln had found a winning strategy and two generals equal to any who fought for the Confederacy. Ulysses S. Grant, a whisky-sodden failure in peace, had shown himself in 1861–62 to be a brilliant strategist and dogged tactician. On July 4, 1863, the day after Gettysburg, the Confederate citadel at Vicksburg in Mississippi fell to Grant and his subordinate William Tecumseh Sherman after a long amphibious campaign. The greatest river of the continent belonged to the Union from Ohio to New Orleans; the Confederacy was cut in two. After Grant and Sherman took Chattanooga at the end of 1863, the way was open for a Union

The South in ruins: Richmond, 1865.

drive through the Appalachians to cut the South in three and tear out its heart.

That task fell to Sherman, who practiced to the fullest his insight that "War is hell." He marched on Atlanta, the hinge of the rail system that linked the arsenals of Alabama with the Richmond front. He took and burned Atlanta and its factories. Then he discarded his rail supply links and marched to meet the Union navy at Savannah, cutting a fifty-mile-wide swath of scorched earth across Georgia's richest plantations. Sherman's victories gave Lincoln the decisive edge against Democrats and Copperheads in the hotly contested 1864 election.

To the north, Grant had become commander-in-chief under Lincoln. He methodically ground Lee's forces down in a year of staggeringly bloody battles of attrition around Richmond. Lincoln had at last found the method appropriate to the Union's unlimited war aim. As a Union general remarked to the Prussians while observing their 1870–71 campaign, the aim was to leave enemy civilians with "nothing but their eyes to weep with over the war."

The end came in March–April 1865. While Sherman savaged the Carolinas on his way north toward Lee's rear, the Confederate armies began to melt. Sherman's destruction of the South's farms and livestock created an irresistible urge to desert. And the pressure of Grant's will and of the Union's immense manpower on the

The strain of war: Abraham Lincoln, April 1865.

Confederate trenches at Petersburg near Richmond ultimately forced Lee out. Cornered in the open at Appomattox Court House, he surrendered to Grant on April 9, 1865. Five days later, a Confederate sympathizer assassinated Lincoln.

Reconstruction, the process of reintegrating the South into the Union, would have to go forward without the political genius of this greatest of presidents. The North faced a choice: it could simply return the South to the rule of the unrepentant planters in return for promises not to repeat the experiment of secession. Or it could attempt to reconstruct the South on a Northern pattern, ensuring that the newly freed slaves would receive the equality that blacks and many Northern whites had fought to achieve.

Lincoln's successor Andrew Jackson took the first path. It led to his impeachment at the hands of the Republican majority in Congress, which imposed the second alternative, "radical reconstruction." But martial law and federal aid for the ex-slaves were not enough to break the united resistance of planters and poor whites. The South's commitment to victory was as fierce after 1865 as before, and the North's staying power was limited.

Within twelve years, Ku Klux Klan terrorism and the more subtle opposition of the South's ruling class had won. To win the disputed election of 1876 the Republicans in Congress agreed to end Reconstruction. Henceforth the white South, in return for being left alone, gave the Democratic party a bloc of safe congressional seats. Blacks in effect lost the guarantees of life, liberty, property, and the vote given them in the thirteenth through fifteenth amendments of 1865–70. Compulsory labor, sharecropping, and debt bondage to the landlord replaced the old slave order and guaranteed a future of poverty. Sharecroppers and their masters do not innovate, nor do they give industry the markets needed to support growth. And in the course of the war Egyptian and Indian cotton had conquered the South's export markets. Low cotton prices further slowed recovery from the devastation of war.

Despite its immense cost—roughly 359,000 Union and 258,000 Confederate

dead and a legacy of resentment and economic stagnation in the South—the Civil War had decided issues as vital as those decided in the Revolutionary War. The United States would remain united, rather than splitting into rival assortments of squabbling states; Napoleon III had to end his Mexican escapade or face war. Slavery was dead; the United States would be a predominantly industrial society of free men and women. And Reconstruction was a battle better fought and lost than not fought at all.

Toward an Industrial Society

In the North and West, the years after the war were a time of unprecedented expansion and change. William H. Seward, secretary of state to Lincoln and Johnson, bought Alaska from Russia in 1867 for $7.2 million. He also annexed the island of Midway, halfway across the Pacific. The completion of the first transcontinental railroad in 1869 welded California to the East. The Great Plains went under the new steel plows or suffered division by barbed wire. By 1890 the frontier was passing.

The new age brought to the North and West the usual social conflicts of industrialization. The towns and cities, in which more than one-third of the North's population already lived in 1860, asserted their power over the countryside. Railroads and banks dominated the farmers of the plains, setting freight rates and conceding credit on whatever terms they pleased. "Trusts," vertically integrated monopolies such as John D. Rockefeller's Standard Oil, and giant corporations, such as Andrew Carnegie's U.S. Steel, replaced old-style family firms. Wall Street buccaneers such as Jay Gould and Jim Fisk left behind them trails of looted companies.

Industry demanded and received the highest protective tariffs in the world from the most uproariously corrupt Congresses in U.S. history. But a reaction against monopolies eventually set in. The Interstate Commerce Act of 1887 sought to regulate the railroads in the interests of the farmers. The Sherman Antitrust Act of 1890 made a gesture toward controlling the trusts. And in national politics, farmers organized. From the National Grange of 1867 through the Farmers' Alliance of the 1880s to the People's party, or Populists, of 1891, they sought to defend the Jeffersonian vision of a farmers' republic. They stood against banks, cities, and the ever-growing masses of immigrants. The "prolific womb of governmental injustice," the Populists thundered, was breeding "two great classes—tramps and millionaires."

In the 1896 election the Populists coalesced with the Democratic party under the leadership of William Jennings Bryan, later famous as an opponent of the teaching of Darwinism. His florid oratory failed to carry the Northeast and Midwest against the Republican and industrial candidate, William McKinley. Industry, which had already surpassed agriculture's share of the national product in the 1860s, had defeated agriculture for good.

In the cities that the Populists so abhorred, new forms of organization were emerging. The Knights of Labor, formed in 1869, had more than 700,000 members at its height. An 1886 episode of European-style anarchist bomb violence at the Haymarket in Chicago helped discredit the Knights, although they were not involved. The American Federation of Labor (AFL), an organization of skilled craft unions under the reformist Samuel Gompers, replaced them. The first major union actions inevitably brought defeat. Andrew Carnegie and his partner Henry C. Frick called in troops to crush AFL opponents in the great 1892 Homestead steel strike in Pittsburg. Eugene Debs' American Railway Union likewise failed in its bitter confrontation with the Pullman Company in 1894. But the unions survived.

In politics, the industrial cities of the Northeast and Midwest were the scene of a vast social experiment—the creation of Americans out of speakers of languages other than English. This was relatively new, for until the 1870s the only non-English-speakers to arrive in large numbers had been Germans. The waves from eastern and southern Europe after 1870 learned swiftly. Their children grew up as Americans, thanks to compulsory elementary schooling. Their political participation, with the hearty encouragement of the big city machines ("Vote early and often"), gave new meaning to the liberties proclaimed in the Constitution. A country as empty and short of labor as America, a country founded on principles rather than on notions of ethnic identity, was open to anyone willing to subscribe to those principles—except for the Chinese and Japanese, excluded by racist public opinion in 1882 and 1907 respectively. Industry and immigrants together transformed the United States from farmers' republic into cosmopolitan industrial empire, another Europe in size, ethnic variety, and power.

THE NON-WESTERN WORLD: RESISTANCE AND EMULATION, FAILURE AND SUCCESS

Others were less fortunate. The major non-European states of the nineteenth century responded to the Western challenge in a variety of ways. Some vegetated. Some collapsed. Some attempted to adapt Western technology while rejecting the ideas that had created it. And one, the empire of Japan, carried out a revolution from above that in forty years, from the 1850s to the 1890s, transformed it from victim into conqueror.

Latin America: Anarchy and Dictatorship

The states that emerged from the collapse of Spain's New World empire between 1808 and 1824 suffered serious disabilities. Spain had created societies stratified by blood. First came the Spanish administrators, then the Creoles—native-born of Spanish blood—then the *mestizos*—those of mixed Indian and Spanish descent. At the bottom were the Indians and the African slaves or ex-slaves of the Caribbean and Brazil. These societies had no tradition of self-rule; the jealous centralization of Spain, which distrusted the Creoles, had seen to that. And racial stratification meant weak states in which the masters had more in common with their counterparts in neighboring states than with their own peasants.

Repeated Creole revolts against Spain produced an unstable collection of fifteen

Hero of the independence struggle against Spain: Simón Bolívar, el Libertador.

Sultan Abd al-Hamid II, known for his cunning and cruelty.

states. Only Brazil, which achieved independence under the heir to the Portuguese throne, escaped a major upheaval. The new states oscillated between anarchy and the rule of narrow landowner oligarchies or despotic *caudillos*. Simón Bolívar (1783–1830), liberator of half the continent, despaired: ". . . America is ungovernable." By 1826 he already foresaw the future: "Many tyrants will rise upon my tomb."

The inland state of Paraguay provided the most spectacular example of those tyrants. Three men ruled it mercilessly between 1811 and 1870: José Gaspar Rodríguez de Francia (1811–40), Carlos Antonio López (1840–62), and his son, Francisco Solano López (1862–70). Francia created a police state cut off from the outside world and an army that under his successors became the most powerful in Latin America. In 1864 López junior took that army to war against all three of Paraguay's neighbors: Brazil, Argentina, and Uruguay. By the end, in 1870, the population of Paraguay had fallen from more than half a million to less than a quarter; almost all adult males were dead.

A few states, especially after midcentury, began to develop economically, as part of the British informal empire—Argentina, Brazil, Chile. Increased European immigration, especially to Argentina, speeded the pace of change. Elsewhere, savage struggles between peasants, rancher oligarchs, and the immensely powerful landowning Church produced repeated civil wars. Mexico changed chief executives 46 times in its first thirty years. It suffered a massive civil war and French intervention in mid-century, and the quasi-dictatorship of Porfirio Díaz from 1877 to 1911. Much of Latin America ended the century further behind the West in economic and social terms than it had been in 1800.

Egypt and the Ottoman Empire: Collapse and Survival

Closer to Europe, the Islamic world faced the full force of Western power. Algeria, Tunisia, and Morocco (in 1911) succumbed to French military colonialism.

Persia and the weak states of the Persian Gulf fell under the protectorate of Britain's Indian Empire. Only Egypt and Turkey were strong enough to have a chance at survival.

Egypt failed. The cotton boom of the 1860s encouraged the successors of Mehemet Ali to launch ambitious public works such as the reconstruction of Cairo in the image of Napoleon III's Paris. By the 1870s the Khedive Ismail was spending twice Egypt's revenue annually and plugging his deficit with European loans. Bankruptcy and the fierce reaction of Egypt's partially Westernized elites to the Khedive's subservience to Britain and France produced the explosion that led an unhappy Gladstone to occupy Egypt. The country's vital strategic importance to Britain, its easily controlled terrain, and its still largely peasant society doomed it.

The Ottoman Empire was both more fortunate and less digestible than its sometime vassal Egypt. It faced stirrings of nationalism, reinforced by religion, among its Balkan peoples. Russia, despite defeat in the Crimea, remained a major threat. Bankruptcy and foreign financial controls, as in Egypt, followed upon rash borrowing and frivolous expenditure in the 1870s. But the empire's international situation and military tradition saved it from dismemberment in the nineteenth century. Britain propped it up to keep Russia away from the Middle East. Austria supported it lest the demise of the Ottoman multinational empire free Balkan nationalities to turn against the multinational Habsburg empire. Germany supported it to stabilize Austria and as a field for German "informal empire." France supported it because France held much of the Ottoman debt. The powers would not tolerate one of their numbers monopolizing the Ottoman Empire, nor could they agree on how to divide it. Its poor but warlike peoples and its mountainous terrain made it an unpromising conquest.

Under the stubborn and wily Abd al-Hamid II ("the damned"), who ruled from 1876 to 1908–09, the Empire survived war with Russia in 1877–78 (see p. 745). It received military equipment and training from Prussia-Germany. In 1908–09 a

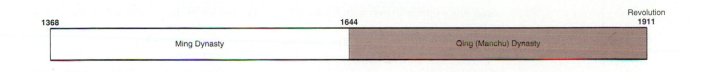

1368	1644	Revolution 1911
Ming Dynasty	Qing (Manchu) Dynasty	

group of Westernized "Young Turk" officers on the pattern of Arabi made the sultan a figurehead. In the following years they proved that the Ottoman warrior tradition could inspire a twentieth-century fighting force. That force ultimately upheld Turkish independence.

China: Resistance and Decline

The China that faced the Europeans in the middle decades of the nineteenth century was the most populous state on earth, with a historical tradition that stretched back three millennia. To the Manchu aristocrats of the Qing (Ch'ing) dynasty (1644–1911) and to the Confucian scholar-gentry who ruled China, the "Middle Kingdom" was the center of the universe. The overseas "barbarians" who had first appeared along China's coasts in the sixteenth century seemed no different than the nomads of central Asia or the tributary kingdoms of Vietnam, Korea, and Tibet. Barbarians

China in the Nineteenth Century

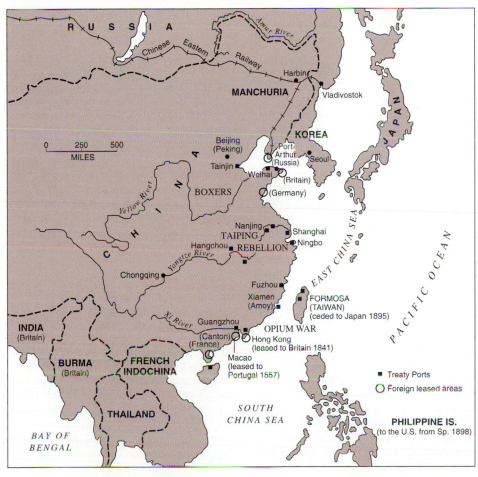

could enter into relations with China only by bringing tribute and prostrating themselves before the emperor. The dynasty kept them in their proper place in the eighteenth century by restricting them to the single trading port of Canton.

But China proved less and less capable of imposing Chinese norms on the seaborne barbarians or on the Russian land power to the north. The barbarian technological lead lengthened decisively with the coming of steamships and shell-firing cannon. And the Qing dynasty appeared to be following the law of cyclical rise, crisis, and decay that had long shaped Chinese thought about history and politics. By 1800 the dynasty had passed its peak and was descending, amid secret-society agitation, peasant rebellions, massive overpopulation, and immense natural catastrophes that took millions of lives. The sheer size of the empire, along with administrative inefficiency, corruption, and the inherent conflict between Manchu and Chinese, crippled efforts at reform.

The end of the East India Company's monopoly of the China trade in 1833 stimulated a rush to Canton by private British merchants, and led to the opening of China by force. British traders developed a profitable black market in China for the Indian-grown opium that paid for the West's imports of tea, silk, and the gleaming ceramics that had inspired envy and imitation in eighteenth-century Europe. When the Peking government made a desperate attempt to close down the opium trade for both fiscal and health reasons, the British replied with gunboats. The first and second Opium Wars of 1839–42 and 1856–60 flattened the dynasty's armed forces, opened numerous ports to European trade, delivered Hong Kong to Britain and vast northern territories to Russia, and gave foreigners immunity from Chinese law, with its custom of judicial torture. Traders, missionaries, and diplomats flocked in, rousing xenophobia. Killings of foreigners and frequent gunboat reprisals were the predictable result.

Internally, defeat in the First Opium War and the strains of dynastic decline unleashed an immense civil war. Hong Xiuquan (Hung Hsiu-ch'üan), the princi-

The Empress Dowager Ci Xi (Tz'u Hsi), r. 1861–1908, whose fierce resistance to change helped doom the Qing dynasty.

pal leader of the "Taiping Rebellion" that conquered south-central China in the 1850s, believed that he was the younger brother of Jesus and that his mission was to exterminate the Manchus. Hong's unstable blend of Western religious ideas and Chinese peasant millenarianism attracted a wide and fanatical following. But its foreign elements made it suspect to the Confucian provincial gentry. Eventually the dynasty rallied, thanks to armies that the gentry raised and led. With help from foreign military experts such as "Chinese" Gordon, they crushed the Taiping rebels by 1864. The European powers, in the end, preferred the Qing to chaos. Twenty million peasants perished in the war and its accompanying famines.

Qing survival now required drastic measures—not merely the adoption of Western techniques, but of the ideas on which they rested. The dynasty made a start in the late 1860s under the leadership of the Manchu Prince Gong (Kung). But Gong lost a series of palace struggles to the pitiless Empress Dowager Ci Xi (Tz'u Hsi), who henceforth dominated court and central administration until her death in 1908. Her hostility to anything she did not control paralyzed the regime. And to a true Confucian, the West's material and military success was irrelevant; tradition and virtue were their own reward. China's "self-strengthening" program grudgingly acquired armament plants, railways, and a military academy, but it lacked conviction. Neither dynasty nor scholar-gentry created the leadership and institutions required to save China from further dismemberment by the Europeans and Japanese.

Japan: From Victim to Great Power

Japan, until the arrival of Commodore Matthew Perry of the U.S. Navy in 1853–54, was even more closed than China. The great lord Tokugawa Ieyasu (1542–1616) had unified it in a series of wars that lasted until 1600. He and his successors imposed peace, exterminated or forced underground the Christian communities that the Jesuits had founded, and recognized only

A Japanese view: Commodore Matthew C. Perry, charged by President Millard Fillmore with opening Japan to Western trade, parades through the streets of Yokohama (1854).

the Dutch—limited to one port and one ship a year—as trading partners. The Tokugawa discouraged and occasionally persecuted Japanese who pursued "Dutch learning," the new European knowledge.

The Japanese system after 1600 was nevertheless quite different from anything in China. Both Western scholars and their twentieth-century Japanese counterparts have frequently described it as "feudal," for its basis was some 250 domains, or *han*, whose lords were dependents or vassals of the Tokugawa family. But a key element in European feudal institutions, the rights of the vassal against the lord, was lacking. And the system was infinitely more centralized than anything in medieval Europe. Most of Japan's hereditary warrior caste, the samurai, did not even own land, but received allowances in rice from their *han*. Their ethos stressed above all service to their lord.

Japanese politics were thus far different from those of China. The Tokugawa ruled, at least in theory, as deputies (*Shōgun*) of the imperial house, which had reigned, although rarely ruled, from time immemorial. The emperor was both a figurehead for the Tokugawa and the most powerful symbol of Japanese unity. He might become a figurehead for others, legitimizing revolution. And the division of Japan into domains offered regional bases for movements to overthrow the Tokugawa.

Culturally, Japan had a tradition of borrowing. It acquired Confucianism and Buddhism from China and sixteenth-century guns from the Portuguese. The early curiosity of Japanese scholars about the outside world had few parallels in China. And the practical warrior ethos of the samurai took precedence over Confucianism. On the battlefield virtue was irrelevant; the issue was victory or defeat. A leader in "Dutch learning," Sakuma Shōzan (1811–64), compiler of foreign-language dictionaries and cannon-foundry master, commented caustically: China had lost the First Opium War "because foreign learning is rational and Chinese learning is not."

Structurally, Japan was small and ethnically homogeneous, with a fierce sense

1598		1868		1912
	Tokugawa Shogunate		Meiji Era	

of distinctness. During the long Tokugawa peace, it had developed a flourishing agricultural economy and a large and growing merchant class. The Tokugawa, although still in control in 1854, were losing their grip on an increasingly rich and diverse society. Like eighteenth-century Britain, Japan had the cultural and social potential for a vast leap in productivity.

Finally, Japan's economy, although dynamic, was—unlike China's—not conspicuously rich enough to attract Western greed immediately. The opening of Japan was an afterthought. That was why Perry got there before the British. And the Japanese, in framing their response to Perry's peremptory demands for trading ports, had the advantage of knowing what had happened to China. Collaboration, not resistance, was clearly wisest until Japan was stronger.

Perry's arrival created a revolutionary situation. The Tokugawa shogunate grudgingly opened Japanese ports and accepted "unequal treaties." Xenophobic "men of spirit" among the lower samurai replied by assassinating foreigners and the Tokugawa officials who collaborated with them. In 1863 Britain bombarded the city of Kagoshima in reprisal. The shogunate's impotent collaboration with the West, like that of the khedivate in Egypt, deprived it of the legitimacy needed to rule.

But Japan took a different path than Egypt or China. The shogunate avoided open war with the West. And in the outer *han* of Satsuma, Chōshu, Tosa, and Hizen, middle and lower samurai with some understanding of the outer world offered an alternative to supine acquiescence or self-destructive fanaticism. In 1868 they persuaded their lords to revolt in the name both of tradition and modernity. The Tokugawa shogunate fell after a brief but bloody civil war.

The insurgents "restored" the emperor, who took the reign-title of Meiji. The new leaders were ruthless and clearsighted. Backed by imperial authority and

the newly invented tradition of the Shinto state religion, they swiftly swept away all perceived obstacles to a "rich country, strong army." Loyalty previously given to "feudal" superiors proved readily transferable to emperor and nation.

The Meiji oligarchs pensioned off the domain lords in 1871. In 1873 they began the creation of a Prussian-style conscript army, breaking the "feudal" samurai monopoly of arms. The oligarchs abolished their own caste, the samurai, to mobilize all energies in a race against time to preserve Japan's independence. In 1877 their new army pitilessly crushed a last great rising of dissident samurai under a former comrade. The oligarchs created state enterprises with Western machinery, and sold them off to a merchant class that rose eagerly to the challenge of creating an industrial economy. The oligarchs imposed Western-style code law and compulsory education to reinforce Japan's existing traditions of learning, hard work, and respect for authority. They secured French, Prussian, and British advisers for army and navy. They created a military-bureaucratic absolutism with a Bismarckian constitution (1889) as fig-leaf. And in foreign affairs, they succeeded in appearing meek until Japan was strong enough to face the West on equal terms. The oligarchs of the Meiji Restoration created a mighty modern state, a powerful engine of change and conquest, the first modern non-Western great power. Its chief defect, it later emerged, was a lack of brakes.

Early in Britain's century, its seapower and its industrial lead had allowed it to dominate the wider world without apparent effort. Non-European peoples and states, from Latin America, to Egypt, to Burma, to China failed to rise to the challenge and suffered colonial occupation or "informal" domination through gunboats and treaties. When Africa went under the knife, divided by diplomacy and the

Maxim gun in less than twenty years, Britain took the lion's share. But ultimately both Britain's European "followers" and the two new non-European great powers proved dangerous rivals. The United States, thanks to swift demographic and economic growth and Northern victory in the Civil War, was by the 1890s poised to dominate the Americas. And Japan was about to create an empire that foreshad-owed the collapse of European domination in Asia. As the century ended, the world hegemony of Britain and of Europe rested precariously on narrow demographic foundations, on the grudging collaboration of the non-European peoples, on the toleration of the new non-European great powers, and on the long but increasingly fragile peace in Europe itself.

Suggestions for Further Reading

British and European Expansion

For much of the conceptual framework of this chapter, see the essays of J. Gallagher and R. Robinson in W. R. Louis, ed., *Imperialism* (1976), and D. Headrick, *Tools of Empire: Technology and European Imperialism in the Nineteenth Century* (1981). B. Porter, *The Lion's Share: A Short History of British Imperialism, 1850–1983* (1984), is useful on Britain. D. K. Fieldhouse, *The Colonial Empires* (1966), and *Colonialism, 1870–1945* (1981), offers a comparative perspective, as do S. K. Betts, *Europe Overseas* (1968); the sardonic V. Kiernan, *From Conquest to Collapse: European Empires from 1815 to 1960* (1982); and W. Baumgart, *Imperialism: The Idea and Reality of British and French Colonial Expansion, 1880–1914* (1982). For Britain's "white" colonies, see D. G. Creighton, *Canada's First Century* (1970); E. McInnis, *Canada: A Political and Social History* (1947); and C. H. Grattan, *The Southwest Pacific to 1900* (1963). On India, see J. M. Brown, *Modern India: The Origins of an Asian Democracy* (1985), and S. Wolpert, *A New History of India* (1982). R. Robinson, J. Gallagher, and A. Denny, *Africa and the Victorians: The Climax of Imperialism* (1968), is delightfully provocative on the "scramble for Africa."

The United States

The literature on the United States is distressingly vast; J. M. Blum et al., *The National Experience: A History of the United States,* 8th ed. (1993), is an excellent introductory survey with detailed bibliographies. On the pre-Jacksonian period, see G. Dangerfield, *The Awakening of American Nationalism* (1965); J. C. Curtis, *Andrew Jackson and the Search for Vindication* (1976), covers the "Age of Jackson." For the road west, see R. A. Billington, *Westward Expansion* (1967). On slavery, see especially E. D. Genovese, *Roll, Jordan, Roll: The World the Slaves Made* (1974). J. M. McPherson, *Battle Cry of Freedom: The Civil War Era* (1988), describes the greatest crisis in America's history; C. Royster, *The Destructive War* (1991), analyzes its peculiarly violent character; C. V. Woodward, *Origins of the New South, 1877–1913* (1951), covers its long-term impact.

Latin America, the Islamic World, and East Asia

For general surveys of Latin America, see J. F. Rippy, *Latin America: A Modern History* (1958, 1968), and T. H. Skidmore and P. H. Smith, *Modern Latin America* (1984); J. Lynch, *The Latin American Revolutions, 1810–1826* (1973), describes the initial upheaval that brought independence. For the fates of Ottoman Turkey and Egypt, see respectively B. Lewis, *The Emergence of Modern Turkey* (1968), and J. C. B. Richmond, *Egypt, 1798–1952* (1977). On China and Japan see C. Schirokauer, *A Brief History of Chinese and Japanese Civilizations,* 2nd ed. (1989); J. K. Fairbank, *The Great Chinese Revolution, 1800–1985* (1986), *The Cambridge History of China,* Vols. 10 and 11 (1978, 1980); and W. G. Beasley, *The Modern History of Japan* (1981), and *The Meiji Restoration* (1972).

28

EUROPE IN THE LONG PEACE 1871–1914

The years between 1871 and 1914 were the longest period of uninterrupted peace in Europe since the "five good emperors" of the first and second centuries A.D. Only minor Balkan conflicts disturbed the peace. The workings of the balance of power and especially the self-restraint of the new Germany prevented war between the great powers. Only after 1890 did a German bid for European domination and world-power status (see pp. 757–67) lead to a new age of world wars.

Monarchy and its attendant aristocracy remained the preeminent form of government. Landed wealth still dominated state administrations, diplomatic services, and standing armies. Revolution was no longer practical politics in western Europe, although faith in it persisted and even broadened. The demands of the working classes had little political weight until after 1900. The welfare state, with its bureaucracies, regulations, and taxes

was still in its infancy. These conditions, along with the immense strides of industry and commerce, made these decades the golden age of the middle classes. Money was now the foremost badge of social status, although those with money still sought to climb socially by marrying into the aristocracy. The middle-class citizens of Europe, thanks to steam, electricity, and the absence of government restrictions on movement, could travel as never before or after. Letters of credit and British bank-notes took the place of passports.

This golden age was short. Both liberal principles and the preservation of domestic peace after the coming of mass education and the second industrial revolution seemed to demand an ever-wider expansion of the vote. Universal male suffrage in turn created the first workers' parties and encouraged women to demand the vote for themselves. In the realm of ideology and culture, a confident middle-class materialism compounded of

(*Opposite*) THE GOLDEN AGE OF THE MIDDLE CLASSES: *A SUMMER SUNDAY AFTERNOON ON THE ISLAND OF LA GRANDE JATTE*, BY THE INNOVATIVE PARISIAN PAINTER GEORGES SEURAT (1884–86).

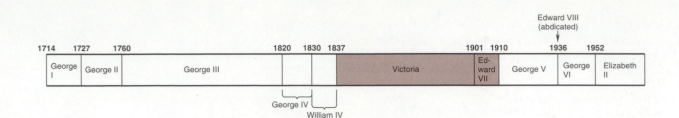

Darwin, steel, and electricity provoked a response: outright hostility to the gospel of science and "progress." The very rapidity of change created immense tensions, psychological as much as political and intellectual. Those tensions ultimately discharged in spontaneous rejoicing among the urban masses at the coming of war in August 1914.

EUROPEAN POLITICS AND SOCIETY

England: The Limits of Gradualism

By the 1860s Britain's spurt of dramatic economic growth was ending. From the 1870s its rivals began pressing ever more insistently at its heels. Yet as late as 1914 London remained the center of the world economy. Britain's money market was the largest, although upstart New York increasingly rivaled it. Britain dominated insurance and financial services, and controlled the world's largest merchant marine. Britain's overseas investments more than doubled between 1870 and 1900; in 1914 they still dwarfed those of other powers and underwrote economic growth on every continent. Britain's export of know-how and import of interest and insurance premiums increasingly rivaled its trade in goods. But financial dominance proved a poor substitute for the mastery of world manufacturing that was passing to others (see Figure 24–4, p. 623).

Politically, the Britain of Queen Victoria (r. 1837–1901) was a time of gradual adjustment. The temperamental Palmerston had dominated shifting factional alignments in Parliament until his death in 1865. Parties remained incoherent collections of notables, without central machinery or discipline. The Queen was thus able to assert considerable power as constitutional monarch. But under Palmerston's two great successors, Benjamin Disraeli and William Ewart Gladstone, Liberals and Tories (Conservatives) took on their modern shape, following a pattern also visible in the United States. The monarchy's influence receded as the mass electorate and mass parties advanced.

The parties alternated in power, spurring each other to enlarge the franchise and appeal to the new electorate. Gladstone, "the People's William," took the initiative on the franchise in 1866. But it was Disraeli, son of a converted Jew, author of novels about the social question, and radical Tory, who shot ahead of his rival

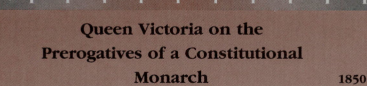

Queen Victoria on the Prerogatives of a Constitutional Monarch   1850

She requires: 1. That he [Lord Palmerston, the Foreign Secretary] will distinctly state what he proposes in a given case, in order that the Queen may know distinctly to *what* she has given her Royal sanction. 2. Having *once given* her sanction to a measure, that it be not arbitrarily altered or modified by the Minister: such an act she must consider as failing in sincerity towards the Crown, and justly to be visited by the exercise of her Constitutional right of dismissing that Minister. She expects to be kept informed of what passes between him and the Foreign ministers before important decisions are taken . . . ; to receive the Foreign Dispatches in good time, and to have the drafts for her approval sent to her in sufficient time to make herself acquainted with their contents before they must be sent off.

From Queen Victoria to Lord John Russell (the Prime Minister), August 12, 1850, The Letters of Queen Victoria, ed. by A. C. Benson and Viscount Esher (London: John Murray, 1907), Vol. II, p. 315.

with a Second Reform Bill of 1867 that almost doubled the electorate. Gladstone, during his governments of 1868–74 and 1880–85, then introduced the secret ballot in 1872 and a Third Reform Bill in 1884 that gave most adult males the vote.

The consequences of the coming of democracy to Britain were at least three. First, it created the modern machinery of mass parties. In the 1874 election Disraeli pioneered the use of grass-roots committees coordinated from the center. Gladstone replied in 1880, attacking Disraeli's foreign policy in Britain's first populist stump speeches by a major political leader. Gladstone's tactics had once prompted Disraeli to describe his rival as an "unprincipled maniac, and with one commanding characteristic—whether preaching, praying, speechifying or scribbling—never a gentlemen." The day of the gentleman in politics was indeed passing. The Liberal party machine, under "Radical Joe" Chamberlain, self-made businessman and reforming mayor of Birmingham, improved on Disraeli's 1874 example and converted Gladstone's "speechifying" into victory. Appeals to and organization of the new mass electorate replaced social standing as the key to political success.

The second major consequence of democracy was to raise the problem of Ireland, Britain's earliest colony. Elizabeth I, James I, and Cromwell had imposed Protestant landlords on Ireland's Catholic peasants. An Irish nationalist revolt in the 1790s had failed. The famine of the 1840s had cut the population by a third, but peasant resistance to the landlords remained strong. A "Fenian Brotherhood" founded in 1858 in New York pressed the Irish cause with intermittent terrorism. And the Second Reform Bill and the secret ballot between them brought more than fifty Irish nationalist members to Parliament. There they obstructed proceedings with long speeches demanding rights for the peasantry and autonomy within the British empire—home rule—for Ireland.

Gladstone's first administration (1868–74) made an inadequate start on the peasant question; his second (1880–85) settled it with the Land Act of 1881. But he was already too late. Exorbitant rents, arbitrary evictions, peasant boycotts, violence against landlords, and Irish nationalist assassinations of high British officials had unleashed the extremists on both sides. Gladstone's conversion to Irish home rule and his attempts to implement it in 1886 and during his tragic last government in 1892–94 were in vain. Home rule meant placing Protestant landlords and the Presbyterian Scottish settlers of Ulster under the "Rome rule" of the Catholic majority.

To the delight of the Tories, who as a result gained uninterrupted power from 1895 to 1905, home rule split Gladstone's party. "Radical Joe" Chamberlain and the imperialist wing of the Liberals joined the Tories. The Irish question, which had now become a religious-national conflict between Protestant Ulster and the Catholic south and west, festered. On the eve of World War I, the Liberals made a final attempt to impose home rule. The Protestants of Ulster, armed to the teeth, defied London. The army officer corps, as closely connected to Ulster as its Prusso-German counterpart was to Prussia's Polish borderlands, resisted government policy in a fashion not seen since Cromwell. Then war in Europe postponed civil war in Ireland.

Queen Victoria, symbol of an era (r. 1837–1901).

The great antagonists: Disraeli (*above*) and Gladstone (*below*).

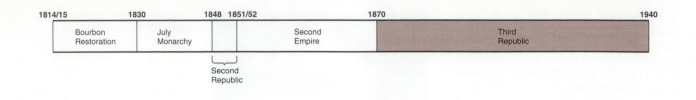

1814/15		1830		1848	1851/52		1870		1940
Bourbon Restoration		July Monarchy				Second Empire		Third Republic	

Second Republic

The expansion of the vote had brought the Irish question, which seemingly had no peaceful solution, to a head. Ballot and Irish question together introduced the third major consequence of democracy in Britain: the rise of a workers' party. Until the 1890s the working-class movement had confined itself to trade unionism. Craft unions had organized the Trades Union Congress in 1868; unskilled workers won their first major victory in the great London dock strike of 1889. But Gladstone and Liberals to his left on social issues, such as Chamberlain, held the working man's vote—until the party split over home rule.

Chamberlain's defection to the Tories created the political space for a working-class party. Keir Hardie, Scottish leader of the miners, organized the Independent Labor Party (ILP) in 1893. In 1900 the ILP, the gradualist middle-class "Fabian Socialists" of Sidney and Beatrice Webb, and a variety of other groups coalesced to form what became the Labour Party. In the 1906 election it won 29 seats. Although the Liberals won the election of 1906, they now had to reckon with an increasingly formidable force to their left. That strengthened the Liberal commitment to expensive social reforms such as old-age pensions (1908) and unemployment and health insurance (1911) under the leadership of the "Welsh magician," David Lloyd George.

When the unrepresentative Tory majority in the House of Lords balked at Lloyd George's "People's Budget," the Liberals rammed through a Parliament Act in 1911 that stripped the Lords of their veto over money bills. But the Liberals did not recapture Labour. Indeed, a wave of strikes after 1911 culminated in the ominous 1914 "Triple Alliance" of railwaymen, transport workers, and miners. Here also the coming of war rescued the Liberals from

crisis—but that rescue proved only temporary.

France: The Third Republic under Siege

France entered the long peace with a difficult legacy. Since 1789 three constitutional monarchies (1789–92, 1815–30, 1830–48), two republics (1792–99, 1848–51), and two Bonaparte dictatorships (1799–1815, 1851–70) had tried to rule it. All had collapsed within twenty years. Savage disputes divided Bourbon Legitimists, Orleanists, and Bonapartists, moderate "opportunists" and radical republicans, clericals and anticlericals. War, defeat, and the crushing of the Paris Commune in 1871 (see p. 681) had created lasting bitterness. Yet by 1879 France had established a regime that weathered one world war and collapsed only after crushing defeat in a second.

The Third Republic would have gladdened the heart of Edmund Burke. It represented the triumph of the provinces over radical Paris. Thanks to its middle-class leadership and its peasant voters, it proved remarkably conservative.

Its origin was Bismarck's demand for a French regime with a popular mandate to make peace. The universal male suffrage elections of February 1871 produced a chamber of monarchists, because the republicans had discredited themselves by preaching war to the bitter end. But the monarchists did not restore the monarchy. The Legitimist claimant, the childless Count of Chambord, refused to abandon the white flag with lilies of his royal forefathers. The country would not give up the Revolutionary and Napoleonic tricolor. Nor while Chambord lived would the Legitimists support the more flexible Orleanist claimant, the Count of Paris.

David Lloyd George (1863–1945), last of the great Liberal Party reformers and war prime minister, 1916–22.

The monarchy's moment soon passed. The monarchists had brought peace, but the peasantry feared that if they stayed in office they would restore the pre-1789 old regime. Elections gradually tipped the parliamentary balance toward the republicans. In 1877 they captured a majority in a hotly contested election called by the monarchists' figurehead president, Marshal MacMahon. In 1879 MacMahon resigned and Jules Grévy became the Third Republic's first republican president.

The president, however, was not to be the Third Republic's executive. A strong presidency might fall to another Louis Napoleon or MacMahon. Prime minister and cabinet, ever-changing according to the Chamber's whims, ruled France. The Third Republic spread power so widely that paralysis sometimes resulted.

Yet it could act decisively. Under the stern leadership of Jules Ferry, minister of education from 1879 to 1881 and prime minister in 1880–81 and 1883–85, the Republic created a national educational system independent of the implacably hostile Church. The mission of France's new schoolteachers was to nationalize and republicanize the rural masses, and to make France competitive with Prussia-Germany. In the villages, the "schoolmaster's party" now faced the "priest's party." Railways, another priority of Ferry and of his colleague Charles de Freycinet, likewise opened up the countryside to new ideas. The Republic finished the rail network that Napoleon III had begun, and at last consolidated France as a national market.

Its successes did not save the Republic from two major internal crises before the turn of the century. Despite the collapse of the royalists and the extinction of Bonapartist hopes with the death of Napoleon III's son in 1879, the Right remained hostile. The agricultural downturn of the 1880s, the phylloxera vine blight that almost destroyed France's historic wine industry, and a slowdown in industrial growth sapped the regime's popularity. After 1885 the moderate "opportunist" republicans who had presided over the establishment of the Republic no longer

had a majority. Three groupings of roughly equal size, the Right, the Opportunists, and the radical republicans, faced one another.

In this tense situation the chief figure among the Radicals, Georges Clemenceau, imposed his protégé, General Georges Boulanger, on the cabinet as minister of war. Boulanger, an impressive figure on horseback, cultivated popularity with the troops and made hostile remarks about Germany, remarks Bismarck gleefully exploited. When the government fell in 1887, Boulanger intrigued with both Catholic Right and extreme Left. In his support the ferocious anti-Semite Edouard Drumont joined the demagogue Paul Déroulède, one of the first of those nationalist extremists, common in the twentieth century, whose politics failed to fit the classic nineteenth-century categories of Left and Right. Boulanger began posing as a potential Bonaparte—until a resolute Opportunist government frightened him into exile in 1889. There he committed suicide on the grave of his mistress.

The Republic survived, despite continuing depression and a series of scandals that included revelations that de Lesseps' Panama Canal company, which had failed to repeat his triumph at Suez, had paid off numerous deputies. The Republic's second major crisis came from a different direction. In 1894 army intelligence recovered from a wastebasket at the German embassy a document suggesting that a member of the French general staff was selling war plans to Germany. The army immediately fixed upon a culprit, Captain Alfred Dreyfus, the only Jew on the staff. It court-martialed him without a shred of evidence, stripped him of his rank, and condemned him to imprisonment on Devil's Island off French Guyana. His family protested but failed to gain a hearing until evidence emerged that the leaks to Germany were continuing.

In 1898 the flamboyant novelist Émile Zola wrote an open letter to the president of the Republic entitled "*J'accuse!*" He accused the army of unjustly condemning an innocent man and of covering the real traitor. He challenged the authorities to sue him for libel. The "*Affaire Dreyfus,*"

Statesman of the Third Republic: Jules Grévy, president, 1879–87.

The young Georges Clemenceau, "Tiger" of the Radicals and war prime minister, 1917–20.

The French army, determined to brand Dreyfus as a traitor, provides him with a "guard of dishonor" whose backs are turned (1899).

or simply "the Affair," split France into warring camps. The clericals, who had in 1892 refused a pressing invitation from the reforming Pope Leo XIII to "rally" to the Republic, stood with officer corps, monarchists, anti-Semites, and the radical Right of the streets. For them, Dreyfus was guilty; he must be guilty—for his innocence meant the guilt of army, aristocracy, and Church. The Left stood in general for Dreyfus, although nationalism led many Opportunists and Radicals to support the army.

The government, which had foolishly claimed in 1897 that "there is no *Affaire Dreyfus*," collapsed. The suicide of the officer who had forged the cover-up evidence and the flight of the real traitor, a Lieutenant Esterhazy, led to a succession of new trials and Dreyfus's eventual rehabilitation. A Déroulède coup attempt in 1899 failed. Anticlerical Radical governments dissolved religious orders that had attacked the Republic, took the Church off the state payroll, and purged the army. The Republic won its confrontation with the Right and carried to completion the process of secularization begun with the Civil Constitution of the Clergy of 1790 (see p. 590).

Finally, the Republic even deflected or absorbed the workers' movement. The elections of 1893 brought almost fifty socialists into the Chamber. The economic upturn after 1896 eased France's domestic distress and encouraged socialist and trade-union struggles. The General Confederation of Labor (CGT) and the socialist groups that coalesced in 1905 to form a united Socialist Party gave France a workers' movement second only to that of Germany. Marxism, which the austere Jules Guesde had introduced into the French labor movement in the late 1870s, prospered. Yet the greatest of all French Socialists was a Marxist only by courtesy. Jean Jaurès, the man who unified the movement's quarreling sects, had concluded that capitalism did not necessarily lead to revolution. By temperament he preferred conciliation to violence. And in the advocacy of violence the Marxists had a powerful rival—the anarchist myth of the revolutionary general strike, creation of the eccentric Georges Sorel, author of *Reflexions on Violence* (1908). Militants influenced by Sorel captured the CGT amid violent strikes in 1905–06. Clemenceau and Aristide Briand, prime ministers in 1906–10, ruthlessly suppressed them. But the Republic demonstrated that it could absorb as well as repress hostile forces. To the left of the now-respectable Radicals an exotic new hybrid, the "Radical-Socialists," sprang up. A genuine though non-Marxist Socialist joined a French government for the first time in 1899. Others eventually followed.

The Republic, to the surprise of all, far outlasted its predecessors. It proved strong enough to face war squarely in 1914. As international tension mounted after 1911 the Chamber swallowed its qualms about leadership. It appointed as president Georges Poincaré, a dour, forceful, and uncompromising Alsatian. It increased compulsory military service from two years to three to compensate partially for Germany's population advantage. When war came, even the Socialists marched.

Germany: Bismarck and After

The new German Reich of 1871 was a hybrid—partly centralized and partly federal, part military dictatorship and part constitutional monarchy. The King of Prussia and German Emperor (Kaiser), as

"Supreme War-Lord," personally controlled the German army. The Emperor appointed and dismissed the Reich chancellor without reference to the Reich's legislature. Prussia, which made up more than three-fifths of the Reich, dominated the upper house of that legislature, which consisted of representatives of the German princes. The lower house, or *Reichstag*, elected under universal male suffrage, had the indispensable right to approve or disapprove the budget; that much the Prussian Liberals had won in the constitutional conflict of 1862–66. Nor could the Reich government levy direct taxes. The states retained that right, and made occasional contributions to Reich finances at their pleasure. Finally, the constitutions of the states, especially the inequitable "three-class" franchise law of Prussia, which weighted votes by wealth, balanced the universal suffrage of the *Reichstag*.

This was a system of checks that only Bismarck could balance. Its complexity was in part a result of his desire to make himself indispensable, and in part a reflection of the strength of the various mutually hostile forces with which he had to deal. The "National" Liberals, who had chosen to cooperate with Bismarck after 1866, at first controlled the *Reichstag*. The Conservatives, thanks to the weighting of votes by income in the Prussian elections, held Prussia. The states retained the power to paralyze Reich finances.

All three forces were losers in the long term. The National Liberals failed to make the leap from mid-nineteenth century party of notables to mass party that British Liberals and Tories had made between 1868 and 1880. That failure doomed the German liberals to long-term decline. The Conservatives, despite an increasingly populist style from the 1890s on, survived because of the three-class franchise in Prussia and the votes of the landless peasants of the great estates of eastern Germany. Conservatism lost whatever Pietist ethical content it may have once had, and became the party of Junker "agribusiness." And the states lost vitality as national integration proceeded. That left a vacuum into which other forces gradually moved.

First of those forces were the German Catholics, who made up more than 30 percent of the Reich's population. They responded to Bismarck's Protestant "Greater Prussia" with a national Catholic political party, the Center. When Bismarck and the National Liberals attacked them in the

The Dreyfus Affair: Zola Accuses   January 1898

I accuse Lieutenant Colonel Du Paty de Clam [the investigating officer] of having been the diabolical author of the [original] judicial error— unknowingly, I may hope—and of thereafter defending his evil work, for the last three years, by the most bizarre and reprehensible machinations.

I accuse General Mercier [the former Minister of War] of having become the accomplice, at best through weakness of intellect, of one of the greatest iniquities of the century.

I accuse General Billot [the present Minister of War] of having had in his hands the indisputable proofs of the innocence of Dreyfus, and of having suppressed them. . . .

I accuse General de Boisdeffre and General Gonse [chief and deputy chief of staff of the army] of having become accomplices in that same crime. . . .

I accuse the first court martial [of Dreyfus] of having violated the law by condemning the accused on secret evidence, and I accuse the second court martial of having covered up that illegality, on orders from above. . . .

In making these accusations, I am not unaware that I am placing myself in jeopardy under articles 30 and 31 of the press law of July 29, 1889, which punishes the crime of defamation of character. I do so voluntarily. . . .

I have only one passion, that of enlightenment, in the name of humanity, which has suffered much and has a right to happiness. . . . Therefore let them dare to take me to court, and may the investigation take place in the light of day!

I am waiting.

From Émile Zola, Oeuvres Complètes *(Paris: Cercle du Livre Précieux, 1969), Vol. 14, pp. 930–31 (translation by M. Knox).*

early 1870s as "enemies of the Reich" who took their orders from Rome, Catholics rallied to the Church and the Center party. This *Kulturkampf* or "cultural struggle" between the Prusso-German state and the Catholic Church consolidated German political Catholicism as a party holding as much as a quarter of the popular vote. The Center's electorate, precisely because its bond was religion, came from all classes, although it was concentrated regionally in the Catholic south and west of Germany.

The second German mass party was that of the workers. Various workers' parties had emerged in the course of the 1860s, and in 1875 they coalesced to form the Social Democratic Party of Germany (SPD). Like the Center, the SPD suffered a preemptive attack by Bismarck. In 1878–79, in the course of a major policy change that involved alliance with Vienna, heavy protective tariffs, and the deliberate splitting of his National Liberal allies, Bismarck persuaded the *Reichstag* to outlaw SPD propaganda and mass meetings. He and his successors attempted to wean the workers away from the SPD with factory legislation and with the world's first state sickness and accident insurance (1883–84) and old-age and disability pensions (1889). Neither stick nor carrot checked the SPD's growth. The masses flooding into the new industrial cities voted, and voted Socialist.

By 1891, affiliated with highly disciplined trade unions and equipped with a Marxist program, the SPD was poised for expansion. By the Reich's last election in 1912, it had conquered 29 percent of the vote, the largest of any single party—and the largest vote for any workers' party in the world. This massive bureaucratic organization, with its women's and youth affiliates, its social clubs and workers' libraries, its newspapers and periodicals, was the mainstay of the international working-class movement, the "Second International" that emerged in 1889 after the collapse of Marx's "First International."

Despite its verbal commitment to revolution, its "proletarian internationalism," and its hostility to "militarism," the SPD was a working-class copy of the organiza-tion, sobriety, and discipline of the Prussian army. But it was not monolithic. The "revisionists" of its center and right, under the leadership of Edouard Bernstein, proposed to "revise" Marx. Like Jaurès in France, Bernstein believed that revolution was neither inevitable nor necessary, for the standard of living of the workers was rising. Social reform should come through ballot box and trade union. The SPD left, whose leading theoretician was the formidable Rosa Luxemburg, replied with insults. Reform was a "bourgeois swindle" and the revolutionary general strike was the just and necessary weapon of the "proletariat." That split increasingly threatened to crack the party open.

Failure to strangle the SPD at birth was the greatest of Bismarck's domestic defeats, but not the only one. His turn to protective tariffs in 1878–79 missed its two main goals. It did not provide the Reich with adequate revenues independent of the states. Nor did it give the government a stable *Reichstag* majority. The often stormy alliance between right National Liberals and Conservatives, industry and agriculture, "iron and rye" that Bismarck created around protective tariffs gained an absolute majority only once, in the 1887 elections. Without a Boulanger, without an emergency real or imagined with which to rouse the electorate with cries of "the Fatherland in danger," neither Bismarck nor his successors were able to dominate the universal-suffrage *Reichstag* he had created.

Ultimately Bismarck was unable to dominate the Kaiser either. The dependable William I died in 1888 at age 91. His successor, the reputedly liberal Frederick III, died of throat cancer shortly after ascending the throne. Instead, William I's brilliant but unstable grandson became Kaiser William II. His mother, Queen Victoria's daughter, voiced private forebodings: "My son will be the ruin of Germany."

William II did not merely lead the new German industrial military monarchy forward, as he put it, "toward glorious times." He personified its blend of manic self-confidence and inward self-doubt, of fear and aggression. He soon quarreled with Bismarck—who, to render himself indis-

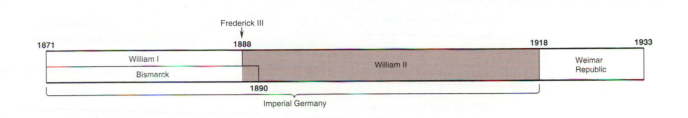

Frederick III

1871 1888 1918 1933

| William I | | William II | Weimar Republic |
| Bismarck | | | |

1890

Imperial Germany

pensable, wrecked the *Reichstag* coalition of 1887 and proposed to suppress the SPD with Maxim guns. In March 1890, after an exchange of insults, the Kaiser sent Bismarck into vengeful retirement.

William II then tried to rule in person. But he failed to fill Bismarck's heroic role, and he and his subjects increasingly lacked Bismarck's sense of limits. The Kaiser's frequent "oratorical derailments" created chaos in both foreign and domestic affairs. By 1897 he did acquire a team capable of translating his enthusiasms into coherent policy: the 78-year-old Prince Chlodwig von Hohenlohe-Schillingsfürst as figurehead chancellor, the slippery Bernhard von Bülow as foreign secretary, and the supremely devious Admiral Alfred von Tirpitz as chief of the navy that was to make the new Germany a world power (see pp. 757–59). But William's short attention span and failure to resist the influences of the fire-eating young Guards officers who surrounded him guaranteed further crises.

In 1908, after a series of scandals at court had undermined the monarchy's reputation, William gave an interview to the British *Daily Telegraph* in which he offended both British and German public opinion at once. The ensuing outcry gave him a nervous breakdown. After 1908, his interventions in Reich policy were less frequent, although his fear of being thought weak played a fateful role in 1914.

German nationalism increasingly took the monarchy's place and filled the political vacuum left by the failure of the National Liberals. The Liberals themselves promoted a growing Bismarck cult to combat regionalism. On the far right a variety of groups emerged with more extreme visions. The Farmers' League, a rabble-rousing spin-off of the Conservatives, began in the 1890s to mobilize the rural masses with anti-Semitism. Jews, money, machinery, cities, the SPD, modernity—all were allegedly ruining the world of authentic German values and destroying the *Volk* community.

This sort of racist "cultural pessimism" was not unique to Germany. French racist fanatics such as Count Arthur de Gobineau (*On the Inequality of Human Races,* 1859) and Drumont had thought up or spread many of the notions that became current in Germany in the 1880s and 1890s. But France was industrializing less rapidly than Germany and was thus under less intense social strain. Above all, its political tradition since 1789 had stressed equality and rights. In Germany, once religious anti-Semitism met Darwin's ambiguous legacy in the 1880s, restraints collapsed. The Conservatives made anti-Semitism socially respectable, part of the ideological armory of the new nationalism.

Other groups, such as the Navy League to which Tirpitz played sorcerer's

William II, king of Prussia and emperor of Germany, 1888–1918, in a favorite uniform—that of the Death's Head Hussars.

apprentice and the Pan-German League founded in 1890, put forward megalomaniacal foreign policy programs with domestic implications. Their more extreme members created a grass-roots right-wing politics of a new kind, independent of the parties and the government. This loose movement was increasingly divorced from the monarchy and from the nobility, whom the new nationalists saw as castebound and inadequate. Erich Ludendorff, non-noble general staff officer and anti-Semite, personified the new outlook. While his seniors still looked to the Kaiser, Ludendorff pledged his loyalty to the "Fatherland." All that such people lacked was a vehicle and an occasion for mobilizing the masses. The coming great war gave them that and much else.

Russia: Despotism and Revolution

"Russian government is an absolute monarchy tempered by assassination," wrote a French observer in the 1830s. Despite Catherine the Great's concessions to the nobility, the tsar, thanks to the Tartar autocratic tradition of the Russian state, remained a ruler more absolute than any eighteenth-century Western monarch. Preserving autocracy as the nineteenth century drew on required ever-sterner measures.

Nicholas I succeeded the neurotic Alexander I in December 1825. Confusion over the succession led dissident noble officers under the influence of half-understood French liberalism to attempt a palace coup. After its failure, Nicholas had personally interrogated the surviving "Decembrist" leaders. He also vowed to prevent a recurrence. His remedy was an ever more extensive and powerful secret police and laws against what the next century came to call "thoughtcrime." The tsarist criminal code of 1845 was unique in Europe. It devoted 54 pages to "crimes against the state" and decreed savage penalties for merely raising "doubts" about the authority of the tsar.

Like his predecessors since Peter the Great, and like many non-Western regimes in both the nineteenth and twentieth centuries, the Russian autocrat faced an impossible choice. His power rested on external success. Yet the bayonets of conscripted serfs were no longer enough; defeat in the Crimea in 1854–56 had proved that. Success, and thus autocracy, in the machine age required a society capable of economic growth. But growth in turn created demands for political participation that threatened autocracy.

The successor of Nicholas, Tsar Alexander II (r. 1855–81), chose economic growth, but with what he hoped were safeguards. In 1861, following the example of Peter the Great, he imposed on Russia a revolution from above: the freeing of the serfs. The end of serfdom would permit universal military service, raise agricultural productivity, free labor for industrialization, and galvanize society into a prosperity that would restore Russia's threatened power position. Alexander's great Emancipation Edict of 1861 freed from the rule of their landlords the 22.5 million serfs who made up almost 38 percent of the Russian empire's population. What it did not do was free them from the land. To aid tax collection and to retain control of the peasantry, the autocracy kept the peasants bound to their village community, the *mir*. The landowners retained two thirds of the land and the former serfs received only a third, for which they had to pay by installments over the following 49 years.

Land redemption debt, the stifling effects of the *mir* on peasant enterprise, and massive population growth ensured that emancipation merely turned a serf problem into a peasant problem. The rural population leapt upward from 50 million in the early 1860s to 82 million in 1897. Competition from newly created industries in the cities lessened peasant income from traditional village handicrafts. Peasants who stayed on rather than migrating to mines and cities waited expectantly for a final redivision of the land that would wipe the landlords out.

More immediately damaging to the autocracy than the growing possibility of rural revolt was a loss of control over educated society. Russia had few cities and no middle class of any size in 1800. It developed them hesitantly, with the support of the autocracy's effort at industrialization. What it developed above all was an *intelligentsia*, a minority defined first by its education and then by its opposition to the autocracy. That minority produced some of the nineteenth century's greatest literature, from the poetry of Pushkin to the novels of Turgenev, Tolstoy, and Dostoyevsky. But thanks to the autocracy that prevented it from acquiring political experience, the intelligentsia also developed, like the thinkers of Enlightenment France, a variety of dangerous utopias.

The generation that followed the Decembrist plotters of 1825 took their inspiration from Hegel rather than from liberalism. They asked how Russia might contribute to the self-realization of the world spirit. In the 1840s and 1850s their dominant school, the "Slavophiles," argued that Russia's very differences from the West were Russia's strength. The Westernizing experiment of Peter the Great, they insisted, had been a disastrous mistake. But thanks to Orthodox Church and *mir*, Russia had not succumbed to rationalism, individualism, alienation. Russia's mission, they proclaimed, was therefore to give humanity back its soul. A variety of critics, often called "Westerners," pointed out that the *mir* was primarily an invention of the autocracy's tax collectors, and suggested that talk of Russia's soul was utopian glorification of backwardness. But Slavophilism persisted, and furnished much of the substance of Muscovite "Great Russian" nationalism.

The generation that followed the emancipation of the serfs argued more about politics than about Russia's soul. By the 1860s non-nobles had reached the universities in numbers. The learned professions were beginning to multiply, providing political radicalism with a social base. A Left emerged that mocked the reforms of the 1860s as insufficient and dedicated itself to overthrowing the autocracy. In 1874 several thousand students went "to the people" to create a peasant revolutionary movement. Peasants reacted to these "populists" with suspicion, and revealed a deep interest in private property that shocked students brought up on Slavophile visions of peasant communism.

Defeat in the countryside and mass arrests impelled some radicals toward terrorism. A tiny conspiratorial group, with the boldness characteristic of those who believe they possess the absolute truth, named itself "The People's Will" (*Narodnaya Volya*). It hunted down the tsar himself and killed him in March 1881. The new tsar, Alexander III (r. 1881–94), crushed *Narodnaya Volya* and created the dreaded *Okhrana*, a secret police even more powerful than its predecessors. Repression froze what little political life Russia possessed. An anti-Semitic radical Right grew, with government support, to oppose the revolutionary intelligentsia. Slavophilism mutated into Russian nationalism and Pan-Slavism, the claim that the Russian state was the patron of Slavs everywhere. Right-wing opinion, as in Imperial Germany, began to place limits on the autocracy's flexibility in foreign affairs.

At home, after the defeat of *Narodnaya Volya*, the radicals turned increasingly to the "scientific" certainties of Marxism. But Marxism was a theory of revolution for advanced countries. It hardly fitted Russia, which still awaited both a "bourgeoisie" and a "bourgeois revolution." Vladimir Ilyitch Ulyanov, brother of a hanged member of *Narodnaya Volya* and son of an imperial bureaucrat, found the answer. Under the alias of V. I. Lenin, he embraced the voluntarism, the faith in the primacy of the human will, that was one part of Marx's legacy. It was the task of Russian Social Democracy, Lenin announced, to force the pace of history. It must take command of Russia's small but growing industrial working class and overthrow the autocracy.

For that task, Lenin created a new kind of organization, the embryo of the twentieth-century one-party state. The history of Europe after 1848, Lenin saw, demonstrated that Marx had been wrong. The proletariat under capitalism was not revolutionary. "The working class, exclusively by its own effort, is able to develop only trade-union consciousness," he wrote with contempt. Logically enough, Lenin recognized that the vehicle of socialist revolution was not the working class

The professional revolutionary: Vladimir Ilyitch Lenin (*center*) with associates (1895).

but the "bourgeois intelligentsia: contemporary socialism was born in the heads of individual members of that class." Only the mobilization of that "class" could bring revolution. In 1902 he spelled out what was needed in a famous tract, *What Is to Be Done?* An organized minority of "professional revolutionaries" must serve as vanguard to the childlike masses. "Give us an organization of revolutionaries," wrote Lenin, "and we will overturn Russia!" Lenin's splitting of the Russian Social Democratic party at its conference in London in 1903 created that organization. His faction claimed for themselves the title of "men of the majority," or *Bolsheviki,* and imposed on their irresolute opponents the demeaning title of *Mensheviki,* or "men of the minority." Lenin's narrow sect ("better fewer, but better") slowly grew.

Imperial Russia's first revolution owed nothing to the Bolsheviks. The autocracy sought reinforcement by "a victorious little war" against Japan in 1904 (see p. 756). Defeat instead led to urban and rural revolt. Russia after 1890 had begun to industrialize at a startling rate under the impulse of French loans and of bureau-

crats such as Sergei Witte, creator of the Trans-Siberian Railway. The opening up of the coal and iron of the Donetz Basin and the oil of the Caucasus made Russia an industrial world power. In the cities of northern Russia, textile and mechanical industries grew feverishly. And an industrial work force torn from its villages and as yet largely unprotected by factory legislation proved far more radical than Lenin had expected.

The shooting in front of the Winter Palace of an unarmed crowd petitioning the tsar on January 22, 1905, "Bloody Sunday," touched off widespread anarchic revolt in the cities. But that spontaneous popular insurrection failed to find leaders. The Mensheviks lacked the will; they expected that in the fullness of time a "bourgeois revolution" would pave the way for their own socialist one. The Socialist Revolutionaries, heirs to the Populists, expected peasant uprisings and were unprepared to lead the workers. The Bolsheviks were too few and naturally distrusted this spontaneous expression of the popular will. The last tsar, the fatuous Nicholas II (r. 1894–1917), was thus able to end the Revolution of 1905. He gave his subjects a legislature, or *Duma,* while loyal troops, bureaucrats, and police gradually suppressed the revolutionary workers' councils, or *Soviets,* that had given the revolution what little organization it possessed. The far Right, organized with official approval in the "League of the Russian People," or Black Hundreds, massacred Jews and opponents of the autocracy.

Constitutional experiments soon ended. Two successive *Dumas* defied the government, demanding civil rights and reforms. Nicholas refused to surrender his autocratic power. Restriction of the franchise produced a Third *Duma* (1907–12) of "masters, priests, and lackeys" that proved more obedient. Under its last strong minister, Peter Stolypin, the autocracy attempted belatedly to finish the emancipation of the peasants from the *mir,* while suppressing all opposition. Stolypin died by assassination in 1911. More despotism bred further extremism and pushed Russia's few Liberals to believe naively that the far Left was preferable to the autocracy. As a new war approached in 1914, waves of massive strikes con-

---

Lenin Invents the Dictatorship of the Vanguard Party   1902

I assert:

1. that no revolutionary movement can endure without a stable organization of leaders maintaining continuity;

2. that the broader the popular mass drawn spontaneously into the struggle, which forms the basis of the movement and participates in it, the more urgent the need for such an organization, and the more solid this organization must be (for it is much easier for all sorts of demagogues to side-track the more backward sections of the masses);

3. that such an organization must consist chiefly of people professionally engaged in revolutionary activity;

4. that in an autocratic state, the more we *confine* the membership of such an organization to people who are professionally trained in the art of combating the political police, the more difficult it will be to unearth the organization.

From Vladimir Ilyitch Lenin, What Is to Be Done? Burning Questions of Our Movement *(New York: International Publishers, 1969), p. 121.*

Bloody Sunday, January 22, 1905. Tsarist troops fire on a procession of workers, killing 70 and wounding 240.

vulsed urban Russia. Tsarism desperately needed victory, but victory might not be enough to save it.

Austria-Hungary: Dynastic Empire in an Age of National States

For Austria, 1866 was not merely a military defeat, but an omen. The breakthrough of the national state in central Europe threatened the breakup of the Habsburg empire itself. Austria survived because Bismarck needed it. "If you ask me what we have promised Austria in return for her friendship, I should answer 'life,'" remarked Prussia's ambassador in Vienna to his Russian colleague in the fall of 1870. Austrian collapse would saddle Protestant Prussia with the Catholic Austrian Germans and with Austria's Balkan quarrels with Russia.

But German goodwill alone could not ensure Austria's long-term survival. That required an ideology, an "Austrian Idea," to counter the nationalism of the empire's subject peoples. The economic integration of the Danube Basin, the ties of agrarian Hungary to industrial Vienna and Bohemia, was not sufficiently inspiring. Good government from the most efficient bureaucracy of east central Europe was likewise no answer to the growing clamor of the nationalities for rule—or misrule— by their own. And Austria's substitute for colonial expansion, its "civilizing mission" in the Balkans, encouraged the same sort of nationalist reaction that bedeviled the European powers in Asia and Africa.

Emperor Francis Joseph (r. 1848–1916) and his ministers faced a paradox. Preserving Habsburg freedom of action, as always, required playing off the empire's provinces and nationalities against one another. But in the age of nationalism, that strategy could only encourage the nationalities to greater and greater mutual intolerance, and tear the monarchy apart. And if, by some miracle, the monarchy should successfully promote compromise between the nationalities, they would then be free to combine against the monarchy itself.

The dynasty therefore played for time. In 1866–67 Francis Joseph grudgingly struck a bargain with Hungary to prepare the way for a war of revenge against Prussia. That "*Ausgleich,*" or compromise of 1867, gave the Hungarians what their moderates had sought in 1848: full control of affairs within the far-flung borders of a "greater Hungary" that included millions of Rumanians, Serbs, and Croats. The only institutions of importance that Hungary shared with the rest of the monarchy after 1867 were the emperor and the ministries of foreign affairs and war. And Hungary received, in effect, a veto over Habsburg foreign and military policy.

When Austrian revenge on Prussia seemed possible in alliance with France in the war of 1870, the Hungarians exercised that veto. Prussia had made the *Ausgleich* possible; a Habsburg reversal of the verdict of 1866 would automatically place Hungary's hard-won autonomy in question. The revolutionary alliance with Hungary against Vienna that Bismarck had toyed with in 1866 thereby became a tacit German-Magyar agreement to preserve the new status quo. Thus the provisional became permanent. The *Ausgleich* made Austria the "Dual Monarchy" of Austria-Hungary until 1918. In Hungary, the gentry ruthlessly Magyarized the subject nationalities and dominated the voteless and voiceless Hungarian peasantry. In the rest of the empire, the German "ruling *Volk*" fought a losing battle against the rise of the Czechs.

After a series of unsatisfactory German liberal ministries, Francis Joseph turned in 1879 to an aristocrat of Irish extraction, Count Eduard Taafe. Taafe's formula was simple and for a time effective. In the *Reichsrat,* the legislature of the non-Hungarian parts of the empire, he created a government bloc of loyal Poles, clericals, and Czechs, the so-called "iron ring." With that support, and with the aim of keeping "all the nationalities of the empire in a balanced state of mild dissatisfaction," he kept the peace until his fall in 1893.

The German-Czech conflict over rich and rapidly industrializing Bohemia destroyed Taafe's framework. Since 1848 the Czechs had developed a high culture, complete with composers such as Bedřich Smetana and Antonín Dvořák, that put to shame German claims of cultural superiority. The Czechs had nationalized their masses with schooling in Czech and with a university at Prague. They were developing an industrial middle class. And their most advanced politicians, the "young Czechs" (shades of Mazzini) refused to subscribe to Taafe's proposed arrangement for sharing power with the Germans in Bohemia.

The Germans were equally obstinate. In Vienna, that cosmopolitan city of art and vice, a variety of anti-Slav and anti-Semitic demagogues arose. The fanatical Georg von Schönerer preached that "religion is irrelevant, *race* is the source of the swinishness" that he ascribed to the Jews. The mayor of Vienna, Karl Lueger, organized a "Christian Social" party that mixed populist clericalism with an anti-Semitism less crude than that of Schönerer; its descendants still give Austrian politics their peculiar tone. Even Austrian social democracy divided into German and Czech national socialisms. Language and culture proved, there and elsewhere, more powerful than class.

In 1897 the dynasty tilted decisively toward the Czechs. It pushed through a decree requiring that state officials in Bohemia be bilingual in Czech and German. Since no German would stoop to learn Czech, the decree in effect excluded the Germans from state employment and from power. The Germans rioted. Schönerer thundered at the dynasty's betrayal of Germandom. He and other lesser fanatics looked to Prussia-Germany against a Habsburg state that they accused of submerging the Austrian Germans in Slavs and Jews.

In the short term the Germans won. The monarchy dismissed Count Casimir Badeni, responsible for the language decree, and retracted the decree itself in 1899. Naturally the Czechs rioted in response. Slovenes and Italians fought in Trieste. Some Croats began to feel the pull of the notion of a "South Slav" (Yugoslav) state of Croats, Slovenes, and Serbs across the border. The "South Slav" idea had little basis in history, culture, or religion, for Slovenes and Croats were Catholic and Western in orientation, and Serbs were

Orthodox and Balkan. But it gradually spread; fear that independent Serbia might prove the "Piedmont of the South Slavs" provoked hysteria in Vienna.

In 1906–07 the dynasty at last fell back on universal suffrage, hoping to submerge the competing nationalisms in a flood of loyal peasant votes. But universal schooling had made the peasants into Germans, Czechs, Croats, and Slovenes. After 1909, Francis Joseph and his ministers ignored the *Reichsrat* and ruled by decree. Reformers floated a variety of federal or "trialist" plans to give Slavs equality with Germans and Magyars. But Germans and Magyars preferred to wreck the monarchy rather than suffer diminution of their "historic rights." In the face of ever-intensifying internal conflict, Austria-Hungary's "idea" remained Church, dynasty, bureaucracy, and army. By 1914 those institutions were strong but wasting assets.

Italy: Least of the Great Powers

The weight of Italy's historic greatness almost crushed the new Italian national state. Nationalists from the radical Mazzini rightward insisted that the new Italy must be and act as a great power. The legacy of the Roman Empire and of Italy's economic and cultural primacy in the Renaissance demanded no less.

Italian reality was ill-equipped to live up to such expectations. The South, where the landlords' horses lived better than the peasants, was two centuries or more behind the North. At unification in 1861, illiteracy ranged from 54 percent of the population over six years of age in the North to 89 percent in the South and the islands. Even the relatively prosperous North lacked an industrial base, for Italy had little iron and almost no coal.

The new state also had a narrow political base. In part, this was deliberate. Cavour and his heirs feared the masses with their potential for anarchic radicalism or Bourbon-clerical revolt. Until 1882 the electoral law gave 2 percent or less of the population the vote; after that date 7 to 9.4 percent could vote. In part, narrowness was unavoidable. The illiterate, until the coming of conscription, had little idea that they even belonged to a national state. And after 1870, furious at his loss of Rome, Pope Pius IX had locked himself in the Vatican and ordered a Catholic boycott of Italian politics. That was no small loss for a state with a population that was nominally 99 percent Catholic.

Finally, the later stages of unification were demoralizing. War in 1866 brought Venetia into the state, but only because Prussia won at Königgrätz; Italy itself suffered humiliating defeats by land and sea. The taking of Rome from the Pope in 1870 was inglorious. The petty spectacle of parliamentary politics provoked the scorn of the aged Mazzini and of nationalists such as the poet Giosuè Carducci: "Oh for the days of sun, of liberty and glory in 1860. . . . Oh for the struggles of titans between Cavour and Garibaldi in 1861!" "What have we become?" asked Carducci despairingly.

What Italy had become was a moderately successful parliamentary regime under a series of centrist coalitions resembling those of France's Third Republic. Defeat in 1866 at least prevented any revival of royal absolutism. Victor Emmanuel II and his army lacked the prestige for Bismarckian solutions. Under Cavour's heirs, the moderate liberal *Destra,* or Right, Italy paid the immense debts of the wars of unification and balanced the budget. The money came mostly from the hard-pressed peasantry, but at least Italy did not follow Egypt and Turkey into debt bondage. The *Destra* reformed the army, although that institution still lacked the prestige needed to attract first-rate officer material. Finally, the *Destra* gave Italy some small voice in the councils of the great powers.

In 1876 a motley coalition of northern left-liberals and southern landowners henceforth known as the *Sinistra,* or Left, ousted the *Destra*. The *Sinistra* extended the franchise and made elementary education free and compulsory in law if not yet in fact. It also created a parliamentary tradition that outlasted the century, for the southern landlords, in return for patronage jobs and public works, gave the government of the day their votes. That

bargain, rather like the tacit agreement that ended Reconstruction in the United States, helped stabilize parliament at the price of social and political stagnation in Italy's south.

By the 1890s new forces pressed against the system. The steamship brought in cheap grain and ruined southern agriculture, then bore away the resulting emigrants. Peasant unrest in Sicily unnerved the governments of the early 1890s. A socialist movement, anarchist in the 1870s and Marxist by the 1890s, gained ground. And unlike their counterparts elsewhere, the Italian socialists successfully organized parts of the countryside. By the first decade of the new century, the unions of the landless agricultural laborers of the rich Po Valley in north Italy were strong enough to stage bitter province-wide strikes.

Even Catholicism began to stir politically. Leo XIII (r. 1878–1903) weakened his predecessor's prohibitions on Catholic political participation in Italy, just as he had urged Catholics to rally to the Third Republic in France. Then his successor Pius X (r. 1903–14) revived some of Pius IX's denunciations of modernity. The entry of organized Catholicism into Italian politics was thus slow. But by the 1913 election, it was an accomplished fact.

The *Sinistra* had its last incarnation under the charismatic Sicilian and former Mazzinian, Francesco Crispi (prime minister, 1887–91, 1893–96). It fell resoundingly after catastrophe at Adowa ended Crispi's bid for a vast East African empire. Riots against the African war and hard times at home inaugurated a period of bayonets in the streets and right-wing governments. The king, Victor Emmanuel II's son Umberto I, imposed a general as prime minister before his own assassination by an anarchist in 1900. Parliament fought back and won decisively.

With the new century came economic takeoff and political stability under the greatest of Cavour's successors, Giovanni Giolitti (prime minister 1903–05, 1906–09, 1911–14). Giolitti despised rhetoric; that won him respect but no fanatical followers. He knew well that Italy's uneven economic and social development had produced bizarre political effects—including his own need to pay southern deputies for their support. If you cut a suit for a hunchback, he once remarked, you get a hunchbacked suit.

What he attempted was gradual reforms that would integrate the new mass forces, the Socialists and Catholics, into the Liberal parliamentary system without destroying it. He refused to persecute the Socialists. To the horror of Italy's industrialists, he did his best to keep the state neutral in labor disputes. His greatest monument was the enactment in 1912 of virtual universal male suffrage, which expanded the electorate from 3.3 million to 8.6 million. It was also his downfall.

The Catholics proved difficult and demanding allies. On the Left, extremists that included a certain Benito Mussolini (see pp. 834–38) captured the socialist party-leadership and closed off any chance of cooperation with Giolitti. The prime minister's own supporters in parliament resented concessions he had made to the Catholics and overthrew him in March 1914. "Red Week," an immense wave of riots led by Anarchists and Left-Socialists that swept north Italy in June 1914, soon made Giolitti's sober common sense and conciliation look outdated and naive.

Intellectuals of all stripes had long railed against his lack of charisma. The young literary firebrands of the Italian Nationalist Association lamented that Italy "had been too much made with diplomatic intrigues and foreign arms." They and others forcefully revived a myth widespread since the anticlimax of the *Risorgimento* in the 1860s. "Making Italians," the completion of national integration, required a great war. Giolitti's right-Liberal successor Antonio Salandra was soon to find that war, and with it destroy Liberal Italy.

BATTLES FOR WOMEN'S RIGHTS

The coming of mass politics for men inevitably raised the question of the rights of women. It opened an arena in which large numbers of women could for the first time

Facts, not rhetoric: Giovanni Giolitti (1842–1928), five times prime minister of Italy.

press their case not merely for the vote but for equality between the sexes. That was a question that went far beyond politics.

Male domination of women has taken many forms. Its foremost mid-nineteenth-century version was middle-class woman's role as pedestal-mounted "angel in the house." That notion was in part a consequence of the separation of life into work and home, male and female domains, that came with industrialization. But it also had pseudoscientific underpinnings. Learned doctors discoursed on women's presumed lack of sexual passion and on the alleged "gigantic power and influence of the ovaries" over a women's whole being. For such pundits, women's position was biologically determined. "What was decided among the prehistoric Protozoa, cannot be annulled by Act of Parliament." Even liberals could claim that the scientific wisdom of the day freed them from having to give women the same natural rights as men.

Religion contributed as well to the myth of women's domestic nature. In the 1820s the churches took to insisting that women, who were proving more resistant than men to the temptations of religious skepticism, were also "purer" than men.

Preservation of that purity required their continued confinement to the home.

By the 1860s, especially in Britain, these notions were under attack. Women had penetrated previously male citadels such as hospitals and schools. Florence Nightingale made nursing a profession for women by her crusade against the British army's grotesque mismanagement of medical services in the Crimea. Soon a broad women's movement pressed for higher education and careers for single middle-class women. In the 1870s Girton and Newnham Colleges at Cambridge began granting degrees to women. Pioneers opened up medicine and the law. Agitation led to reforms in the 1870s and 1880s of Britain's crude laws governing marriage, divorce, and the age of consent. Women's bodies and property ceased to belong to their husbands in a literal, legal sense.

The British "feminists"—the French word became current in the 1890s—also attacked the legal double standard in a more spectacular way. They crusaded successfully against the Contagious Diseases Act (repealed 1886) that required veneral disease examinations and quarantine for prostitutes—but not soldiers—in garrison towns. The acts, they insisted, were government endorsement of the creation of "a *slave* class of women to minister to lust."

Crusader for hospital reform: Florence Nightingale (1820–1910).

The crusaders sought to do more than raise the status of women. They proposed to reform men and revolutionize the relationship between the sexes.

When the Liberals came to power in the 1906 election, the women's movement tried to hold them to liberal principles. But the evasive Herbert Asquith (prime minister, 1908–16) and the even more slippery Lloyd George torpedoed women's suffrage legislation in 1910. The Women's Social and Political Union (WSPU), under the leadership of Emmeline Pankhurst and her daughter Christabel ("Votes for Women, and Chastity for Men"), then declared war on government, Parliament, and men. "Suffragette" activists attempted to break police cordons in Parliament Square; the police and male bystanders replied with violence and sexual abuse. Christabel Pankhurst orchestrated a campaign of window-smashing, burning of country houses, attacks on art galleries, and bombs in Westminster Abbey. To trial and imprisonment, the WSPU replied with hunger strikes. The government countered with forced feeding. Opinion, including opinion among women, was overwhelmingly against WSPU defiance of the law. But WSPU tactics provoked the government to acts that weakened its position.

Finally, in June 1914, Asquith agreed to receive a delegation of working women under the leadership of Sylvia Pankhurst, Christabel's sister and a labor activist. The specter of a potential mobilization of working-class women into a genuine mass movement apparently made Asquith quail. He lost all stomach for further warfare between the sexes and undertook to support a women's suffrage bill. The war delayed it until 1918 but eased its passage. The contribution of women to the war effort made it impossible to deny them the vote.

Continental feminists faced societies far less tolerant than Britain (or than the United States, where suffrage agitation was intertwined with evangelical religion and the temperance movement). And like continental liberalism, continental feminism tended to be far less radical than its British counterpart. In France and Germany, middle-class feminists inclined toward the "equal but different" school. Woman's role as mother and her right to control reproduction was the focus of the work of widely influential figures such as Ellen Key (1849–1926) of Sweden and Nelly Roussel (1878–1922) of France. The most radical continental women tended to gravitate to the women's affiliates of the socialist parties, which took more interest in woman's presumed oppression by capitalism than her domination by man. Nevertheless, the socialist parties of the Second International were the first continental political parties to endorse women's suffrage. By the end of the great war that began in 1914, much of western Europe was ready to follow them.

RISE AND FALL OF THE CULT OF SCIENCE

A policeman carries Emmeline Pankhurst bodily off to jail during a 1911 suffrage demonstration.

The waning of traditional forms of religious belief helped open space for a variety of other faiths. Nationalism and socialism gave their adherents many of the consolations that earlier generations had gained from religion. After mid-century a misunderstood science provided a third secular religion: the "cult of science."

The furious attacks of religious figures on Darwin and Lyell were misplaced; the rise of science did not challenge religion in any direct, logical sense. God is not subject to empirical proof or disproof. But the new science did provide a semblance of empirical underpinning for statements of faith—in science. The source of the cult was the Enlightenment vision of a machine-like universe in which everything was in principle knowable. The cult's nineteenth-century founder, Auguste Comte (1798–1857), attempted from the 1820s to the 1850s to systematize all of human knowledge. He postulated—like Hegel and Marx—a series of stages. For Comte, humanity's road led from theology to metaphysics and from metaphysics to science, which was the domain of what Comte called "positive" or empirically verifiable knowledge. The "Positivism" of Comte and successors enshrined science as the new diety. Comte was confident

that even the messy affairs of humanity would eventually yield scientific general laws in the form of a discipline of "sociology."

That discipline has still to yield general laws. That did not stop Comte's most conspicuous successor, the indefatigable Herbert Spencer (1820–1903) from following in his footsteps. Spencer's *Synthetic Philosophy* (1862–96) attempted in ten volumes what Comte had attempted in six, the compression of all of human knowledge into a positivist framework. Darwin was the centerpiece of Spencer's work, but a Darwin misapplied to social phenomena. Darwin himself was in part responsible for this misunderstanding. In *The Descent of Man* he incautiously speculated that "the wonderful progress of the United States, as well of that character of its people, are the results of natural selection; the more energetic, courageous, and restless men from all parts of Europe having emigrated during the last ten or twelve generations to that great country. . . ."

Alongside Spencer a wide variety of "social Darwinists" proliferated. Most argued (in the words of Walter Bagehot, high priest of the English constitution) that "the majority of the groups which win and conquer are better than that majority which fail and perish." That was a wonderfully convenient rationalization for "might makes right" among nations, social groups, and individuals. The oil king John D. Rockefeller trumpeted that business was "merely the survival of the fittest . . . the working out of a law of nature and a law of God."

In Germany the task of propagating and popularizing Darwinian biology fell to Ernst Haeckel (1834–1919). He followed in the footsteps of Feuerbach (whose materialism had influenced Marx) and of the best-selling crank Ludwig Büchner (1824–99). Büchner's *Force and Matter* (1852) confidently asserted that since matter and energy were eternal, it was "impossible that the world can have been created. How could anything have been created that cannot be annihilated?"

Haeckel, simultaneously Darwinist and social Darwinist, defied 25 centuries of Western thought by abolishing any distinction between humanity and nature; he called the cult he founded and led "Monism." In his international best-seller of 1899, *The Riddle of the Universe,* he mocked theological and metaphysical speculation. Questions without empirical answers were not questions. And "Monism" meant that upon pain of degeneration humanity must live in harmony with "the laws of nature." Chief of those laws was natural selection. When Haeckel's notion of nature as legislator for man met the ideas of racist cranks such as Gobi-

neau, the results were intellectual high explosive. Marx had abolished all theoretical restraints on revolutionary dictatorship and on the elimination of the "class enemy." Haeckel, Gobineau, and Kaiser William II's friend, the racist–social Darwinist Houston Stuart Chamberlain (*The Foundations of the Nineteenth Century,* 1899) similarly abolished intellectual and moral restrictions on the liquidation of the "racial enemy."

The Revolt against Positivism

The domination of the positivist cult of science was shortlived, although its influence persists to our own day. In philosophy, a commanding figure soon emerged who denounced almost every aspect of the present, science and its worshipers included. Friedrich Nietzsche (1844–1900), son of a Protestant pastor, was the last great German philosopher of the nineteenth century. He was the antithesis of system-building predecessors such as Hegel, whose work he ridiculed. From 1872 until his final collapse into syphilitic madness in 1889 he bombarded his growing public with at least one work each year. One of the greatest masters of the German language, he leapt from one striking aphorism to the next. He frequently contradicted himself, and always contradicted others. He damned the smugness of the age.

Nietzsche's message was at bottom consistent. Contradiction was life. Philosophy was not systemic, but perpetual question and experiment. Morality—for Nietzsche in his eccentric way was the last great moralist—took precedence over knowledge. Scientific truth was valuable only insofar as it contributed to "life." And to Nietzsche the law of the modern world was not the survival of the fittest, but the inevitable triumph of mediocrity. Darwin had it backwards. In reality "happy accidents are eliminated, the more highly evolved types lead nowhere, it is the average and below average types which ineluctably ascend to power." Women's emancipation was "one of the worst developments of the general *uglification* of Europe." Nationalism was unbearably crass:

The Thinker: Friedrich Nietzsche, the last great German philosopher.

the new Reich of 1871, bristling "hedge-hog-fashion" with arms, was "the most stupid, the most depraved, the most mendacious form of 'the German spirit' that ever was." Nietzsche likewise denounced anti-Semitism and the Germanic tribal cult of the composer Richard Wagner, whom he had originally admired.

Christianity, for Nietzsche, was worst of all. It stifled "life" and dragged down the exceptional individual with its "slave morality" of meekness and compassion. Nietzsche consoled himself by contemplating what he described as "the greatest event of recent times—that 'God is dead,' that the belief in the Christian God is no longer tenable." Nietzsche's morality was that of the isolated exception, the aristocratic *Übermensch,* or "superman," living "beyond good and evil" and outside society and politics. "Life," the *"will to power,"* was supreme over all else.

That proved a dangerous legacy. In the short term, Nietzsche appealed to socialists, anarchists, and outsiders. His denunciations of German nationalism infuriated the pan-Germans. But the spread of Nietzsche's ideas, which ironically accelerated immediately after his descent into madness, ultimately made "the will to power" and the "superman" into myths of the new populist Right. "Everything is permitted" became a credo for political "supermen" riding the coming wave of war and revolution.

Other late nineteenth- and early twentieth-century philosophers, especially the Frenchman Henri Bergson (1859–1941), shared Nietzsche's horror of rationalist system-building. But it was the world of medicine and scholarship that offered the most decisive rejection of positivism. In the mid-1890s a Vienna medical figure, Sigmund Freud (1856–1939), launched the first serious medical—rather than philosophical—attempt to understand the human mind. Freud, like Nietzsche, saw that secretive, cunning, savage forces dominated the mind. But where Nietzsche saw *power* as the central human lust, Freud merely saw sex—a more comforting conclusion, although still shocking to a prudish age. In treating his patients, Freud tapped the uncon-

Nietzsche Speaks

Truths are illusions that one has forgotten *are* illusions.

Nothing is true, everything is permitted.

Why morality, when life, nature, and history are "unmoral"?

The common man alone has the prospect of carrying on, of propagating himself—he is the man of the future, the only survivor; "Be like him! Become mediocre!" is now the only morality that still has a meaning or an audience. But it is hard to preach, this morality of mediocrity.

Objection, evasion, gleeful mistrust and irony are signs of health. Everything absolute belongs to pathology.

In individuals, insanity is rare, but in groups, parties, nations and epochs, it is the rule.

The thought of suicide is a powerful consolation; with it one can get through many a bad night.

Man must be trained for war and woman for the recreation of the warrior: anything else is silliness.

I have only rarely the courage of what I know.

Dear Professor, in the end I would have much preferred being a Basel professor to being God. But I did not dare carry my private egotism so far as to omit—for its sake—the creation of the world. . . . [Nietzsche's last letter, to the Basel historian Jacob Burckhart, January 1889]

From Friedrich Nietzsche, Werke in Drei Bänden, *ed. by Karl Schlechta (Munich: Karl Hanser Verlag, 1954–56), 3:314, 2:889, 2:645, 2:737, 2:637, 2:328, 3:1272, 3:1351 (translation by M. Knox).*

scious mind with novel techniques: hypnosis, dream interpretation, and free association. What Marx did for economics as a historical force, Freud did for the unconscious.

Unfortunately for the further development of his new discipline of psychoanalysis, it soon emerged that Freud's elaborate theoretical structure was metaphor rather than a verifiable scientific

Sigmund Freud, explorer of the
unconscious mind.

theory. Freud warred with prominent disciples such as Carl Gustav Jung (1875–
1961) and Alfred Adler (1870–1937) over
key points of interpretation. Even more
than Marxism, Freudianism and the larger
psychoanalytic movement that it created
relished the hunt for error and deviation.
That placed in question its claim to be
science; for good or ill science is about
empirical proof. And Freud's attitude toward women, whom his odd theory of
"penis envy" consigned yet again to biological inferiority, has not gone unchallenged. But Freud was in some ways a
good prophet of the twentieth century,
thanks to his experience of Austria-
Hungary's vicious ethnic quarrels and to
his membership in Vienna's most conspicuously persecuted minority, the Jews. Humanity, Freud asserted, was incurably
predatory.

A final challenge to positivism
emerged in the social sciences. The man
who actually founded the "sociology" that
Comte had named was Max Weber (1864–
1920), Prussian reserve lieutenant and
professor. Weber, the "bourgeois Marx,"
was a realist: "All ideas aimed at abolishing

the dominance of men over men are 'Utopian.' " He began by asking a question that
Marx had neglected: how did capitalism
originate? Weber hit upon religion as the
key variable that distinguished societies
that had industrialized from those that
lagged. And within Western society he
found a close historical association between the "Protestant ethic," especially
that of Calvinism (see p. 439), and the
joyless drive to accumulate ever-greater
masses of capital. This "Weber thesis" has
proved a fruitful source of argument from
his day to the present, although critics
have pointed out that the earliest European capitalism—in the Italian city-
states—was Catholic.

Weber's other major contribution was
his attempt, in a massive unfinished work
entitled *Economy and Society,* to make
sense of the relationships between economics and social and political institutions. But unlike many later sociologists,
Weber rejected the Comtean notion that
the social sciences, like the natural sciences, must formulate general laws. In the
human sciences, Weber pointed out, veri-
fication through controlled experiment
was unfeasible. The researcher's own
value system inevitably intruded on the
results. Truth was only possible within
narrow limits. Weber's work on method
demolished the positivist approach to society and history. Humanity would have
to make do with lawlike hypotheses like
the "Protestant ethic."

Finally, Weber was in his way a
prophet, although a self-limiting and modest one. Like Marx but without Marx's dogmatism, he saw goal-oriented movement
in history: the "disenchantment of the
world," the decay of traditional religious
and social certainties in the face of ever-
increasing rationalization and bureau-
cratization. Weber feared that in the new
century that process would end with humanity bound in a static "iron cage of serfdom" under immense self-perpetuating
state and capitalist institutions. His prophecy ignored both the growing freedoms of
the West's democratic societies—of which
Weber the Prussian lieutenant had little
understanding—and the dynamism of

technological change. But Weber's "iron cage" metaphor proved less off-center than the prophecies of Marx.

ART IN AN AGE OF SCIENCE

In the realm of culture, the last half of the nineteenth century was a period of crisis. Romanticism had broken all restraints on form and content. Everything was permitted. A bewildering variety of styles and radical disagreement about the purposes of "art" were the result. The notion that art should imitate reality or nature, the central idea of Western art since Plato and Aristotle (see pp. 57–58) was passing.

Architecture and design were the principal exceptions to this growing confusion of styles. The fragmentation of architecture had begun well before that of literature and the visual arts. In the late eighteenth century, a profusion of "revivals" had followed the dying Baroque. As the nineteenth century drew on, Greek temples mutated into churches, museums, and banks; Gothic cathedrals provided models for hideous town halls in grimy industrial cities; Romanesque arches adorned the massive temples of science at the universities. Furniture became steadily heavier, more overstuffed, and more hideously carved. But by the end of the century a reaction had set in.

In design, the opening of Japan in 1854 was as important to the nineteenth century as the influence of Chinese art had been to the eighteenth. The geometric shapes and absence of ornament of Japanese interiors were a revelation to European designers and architects. Simultaneously, the machine age stimulated new thought. Some, such as England's William Morris (1834–96), revolted against mass production. Morris's politics were a romantic socialism, his taste an attempt to relive a lost golden age of craftsmanship now submerged in shoddy machine-made furniture. His "Arts and Crafts Movement" created a spare geometric style that was the beginning of modern home furnishing. German designers in the *Werkbund,* or Craft League, that flourished from 1907 to 1914 pioneered a style that in some ways resembled Morris's—but they did not share his hostility to the machine.

Architecture developed in a like manner. Steel and glass were its materials. The Crystal Palace of the 1851 Great Exhibition, the immense canopy of St. Pancras station in London (1863–65), and the Eiffel Tower (1889) pioneered their use. But it was America, thanks to sheer technological exuberance and to the high property costs in its new city centers, that invented the steel-framed skyscraper in the 1880s. The Americans Louis Sullivan (1856–1924) and his pupil Frank Lloyd Wright (1869–1959) gave the new architecture its slogan: "form follows function." Sullivan did not disdain ornament, although he aspired to buildings that would be "comely in the nude." After 1890, his buildings took on a geometric grid-like pattern. German architects associated with the *Werkbund,* especially Walter Gropius (1883–1969) and Bruno Taut (1880–1938), had also begun before 1914 to design functional steel and glass buildings. The "international style" of the twentieth century, the first unified style in Western architecture since the Baroque, had arrived.

The fate of literature and the visual arts was entirely different. Old conventions of form and substance collapsed, but fragmentation instead of unity was the consequence. The novel, the nineteenth century's foremost art form, passed from the psychological "realism" of Gustave Flaubert (1821–80) to the pseudopositivist "naturalism" of Émile Zola (1840–1902). Flaubert, in his great *Madame Bovary* (1856), dissected the consciousness of a small-town doctor's wife whose dreamy reading of romantic novels leads her to adultery and destruction. Both subject and technique scandalized contemporaries. The far less talented but more prolific Zola churned out a sequence of twenty novels between 1871 and 1893 that traced "the social and natural history of a family" during the Second Empire. Zola kept careful track of his "facts" and propounded laws of human nature. But his sometimes lurid style suggested the opposite of scientific detachment. His Naturalism was above all social criticism; his intervention in the Dreyfus case and brief exile to escape prison were the high point of his career.

The work of the great Russians, Count Leo Tolstoy (1828–1910) and Feodor Mikhailovitch Dostoyevsky (1821–81), showed a similar tension between psychological observation and social and political commitment. Tolstoy eventually repudiated his greatest works, *War and Peace* (1869) and *Anna Karenina* (1871), and turned his back on Russian society in favor of a mystical New Testament faith and pacifist "nonresistance to evil." Dostoyevsky migrated from advanced revolutionary beliefs to a mystic Slavophilism. In *The Possessed* (1871–72) he drew on his youthful experiences and his deep psychological insight to suggest the demonic nature of revolutionary messianism—just as much of the Russian *intelligentsia* embraced that messianism.

One conspicuous exception to this pattern of ideological commitment was the American expatriate, Henry James (1843–1916). His many novels, novellas, and short stories combined Flaubert-like psychological observation with penetrating commentary on the contrast between European and American manners and morals. James's European-style novels earned him an international reputation; his most conspicuous American contemporaries, Herman Melville (1819–91) and Mark Twain (1835–1910), remained curiosities to Europeans. Melville's symbolic epic of whaling and the struggle between evil and good, *Moby Dick* (1851), derived from the Protestant biblical tradition, not the European novel. Twain achieved the impossible. In *The Adventures of Huckleberry Finn* (1884) he rendered backwoods dialect—or rather a carefully contrived illusion of dialect—into art, in a comic yet often grim tale of life on the Mississippi against the ominous background of the slave South. Twain was deliberately and aggressively provincial; he frequently spoofed European social and linguistic snobbishness.

While Flaubert, James, and the Russians between them seemingly exhausted most of the novel's possibilities, the Norwegian Henrik Ibsen (1828–1906), the Swede Johan August Strindberg (1849–1912), and the Russian Anton Pavlovitch Chekhov (1860–1904) did the same for drama. Ibsen mercilessly attacked social pretension and the oppression of women. He depicted the quest of the modern individual for self-understanding. The truth, he suggested, could destroy as well as free. But humanity was not irredeemable; love was still conceivable. Not so for Strindberg, who created increasingly dreamlike plays in which unlovely characters, "bound together by guilt and crime," inexorably destroyed one another. Chekhov, who depicted symbolically the dissolution of Russian aristocratic society, pioneered a drama that turned its back on conventional notions of plot. He gave artistic form to the anarchy of life. Chekhov's characters speak in seemingly disconnected remarks, dramatic development occurs within the characters themselves, and action is inconclusive.

It was in poetry, music, and painting that the breakthrough to the artistic fragmentation of the twentieth century was most dramatic. In poetry, late Romantic lyricism dissolved into Symbolism. Intended for a few initiates rather than for a mass audience, Symbolism was in part a reaction to the dreary Naturalist notion that art should serve social and political betterment. Symbolism's predecessor was the dissipated "accursed poet," Charles Baudelaire (1821–67), and its banner "art for art's sake." The Symbolists, above all the schoolboy prodigy Arthur Rimbaud (1854–91), Stéphane Mallarmé (1842–98), and Paul Verlaine (1844–96), wrote a poetry of deliberate obscurity and musical effects. Their style influenced the two greatest German poets of the new century, Rainer Maria Rilke (1875–1926) and Stefan George (1868–1933). It furnished the basis for much twentieth-century poetry.

In music, Richard Wagner's "total work of art," his four-evening-long *Ring of the Nibelungen* opera cycle (1853–74), was the end of romantic music as well as one starting point of the new German Reich's political mythology. Gustav Mahler (1860–1911) and others continued

Wagner's tradition of orchestral excess and startling effects, but with less conviction. In France, Claude Debussy (1862–1918) and Maurice Ravel (1875–1937) pioneered a new style that deliberately paralleled Symbolist poetry. The irregular rhythms and harsh dissonances of Igor Fëdorovitch Stravinsky's *Rite of Spring* caused a riot at its Paris premiere in 1913. Arnold Schönberg (1874–1951) and his pupils created a new "atonal" music that defied traditional notions of melody.

In painting, an entire epoch in Western art ended with the school known as the Impressionists. Claude Monet (1840–1926) and Auguste Renoir (1841–1919) were its originators and masters. They discarded the age-old attempt to render reality on canvas literally. Photography, invented in the 1820s, had by the 1860s rendered realism seemingly superfluous. Instead, the Impressionists sought to use the play of light, represented with dabs of color, to show scenes as they appeared to the mind's eye. Their paintings shocked contemporaries accustomed to increasingly sterile imitations of ancient or Renaissance models. But the Impressionists were not revolutionaries; they were the brilliant end of a long tradition.

After them came Paul Cézanne (1839–1906), proclaiming both in words and on canvas that "all of nature is formed by the cylinder, the sphere, and the cone." Vincent van Gogh (1853–90) reproduced a tortured life in violent colors and swirling shapes. Georges Seurat (1859–91) composed stiff, flat figures out of thousands of tiny colored dots. And after 1900 Pablo Picasso (1881–1973), Wassily Kandinsky (1866–1944), the "Cubists," and Italy's fiercely irreverent "Futurists" began to cut painting's links with visual reality. The art of the twentieth century was to be an art of increasing abstraction and of proliferating schools and slogans.

It was also increasingly an art for the few rather than the many. Until the nineteenth century Western art had always spoken to a unified audience, a cultivated and largely aristocratic elite. Mass literacy and mass market ended that. Wood-pulp paper and the machine-driven rotary press

Thickly applied paint and new ways of representing light: *van Gogh's Chair* (1888).

made possible the first truly cheap newspapers, the first modern "mass media" based on advertising. Great press barons arose, profiteers of ignorance with a secret

The "Yellow Press": A Novelist's View

In New Grub Street *(1891), the English novelist George Gissing presented through the mouth of his fictional editor, Whelpdale, a view of the mass media's conception of its audience that is still surprisingly up-to-date.*

No article in the paper is to measure more than two inches in length, and every inch must be broken into at least two paragraphs. . . . Let me explain my principle. I would have the paper address itself to the quarter-educated; . . . the young men and women who can just read, but are incapable of sustained attention. People of this kind want something to occupy them in trains, and on buses and trams. . . . What they want is the lightest and frothiest of chit-chatty information—bits of stories, bits of description, bits of scandal, bits of jokes, bits of statistics, bits of foolery. Am I not right? Everything must be very short, two inches at the utmost; their attention can't sustain itself beyond two inches.

From George Gissing, New Grub Street *(London: Eveleigh Nash & Grayson, 1927), p. 419.*

contempt for their public. Alfred Harmsworth (later Lord Northcliffe) of the London *Daily Mail* first achieved a daily circulation of more than a million, with a paper that combined gossip and crude xenophobia in equal proportions. Publishers churned out vapid "best-sellers" by the hundreds of thousands. The mass press was not responsible for its readers' lack of sophistication, but it worked hard to perpetuate it. That narrowed the market for genuine art and gave it a snobbish exclusiveness that further deepened the gap between high and low culture characteristic of the twentieth century.

Like the aristocrats who after 1789 lamented a lost golden age, the middle classes of Europe were soon to mourn the long peace. The years from 1871 to 1914 were the peak of Europe's power and wealth relative to the other continents. The cultural brilliance of Europe's capitals, above all Paris and Vienna, made the last decades of peace a "*belle époque,*" a delectable era. But powerful forces were working against equilibrium and tolerance. Those forces, above all the force of nationalism and the growing economic power of the new Germany, slowly undermined the stability of the European state system. That shift, invisible to peoples absorbed in their everyday lives, in the end proved a matter of life and death for millions of Europeans.

Suggestions for Further Reading

General

E. J. Hobsbawn, *The Age of Capital, 1848–1875* (1975), and *The Age of Empire, 1875–1914* (1987), are outstanding works of synthesis. Readable surveys include N. Rich, *The Age of Nationalism and Reform, 1850–1890* (1977), C. J. H. Hayes, *A Generation of Materialism, 1871–1900* (1941), and O. J. Hale, *The Great Illusion, 1900–1914* (1971).

Domestic Affairs

On Britain, see above all A. Wood, *Nineteenth Century Britain* (1960); G. Dangerfield, *The Strange Death of Liberal England, 1910–1914* (1935); and F. Bédarida, *A Social History of England, 1851–1975* (1979). The most accessible discussions of France are A. Cobban, *A History of Modern France,* Vol. 2 (1957), and R. D. Anderson, *France, 1870–1914: Politics and Society* (1977); E. Weber, *Peasants into Frenchmen: The Modernization of Rural France* (1976), is full of wonderful material. For Germany, H. U. Wehler, *The German Empire, 1871–1918* (1985), is short and provocative, but the relevant portions of G. Craig, *Germany, 1866–1945* (1978), are a better guide to what actually happened. For Russia, see R. Pipes, *Russia under the Old Regime* (1974); H. Seton-Watson, *The Russian Empire, 1807–1917* (1967); A. Ulam, *Lenin and the Bolsheviks* (1966); and the intelligent popular account of E. Crankshaw, *The Shadow of the Winter Palace; Russia's Drift to Revolution, 1825–1917* (1976). On Austria-Hungary, C. A. Macartney, *The Habsburg Empire* (1969), is lucid and balanced; A. J. P. Taylor, *The Habsburg Monarchy, 1809–1918* (1948), is one-sided and entertaining. On Italy, the best treatment is C. Seton-Watson, *Italy from Liberalism to Fascism, 1870–1925* (1967), but see also the pertinent portions of D. Mack Smith, *Italy, a Modern History* (1959–   ), and M. Clark, *Modern Italy, 1870–1982* (1984). J. A. Thayer, *Italy and the Great War: Politics and Culture, 1890–1914* (1964), describes the fatal fascination that a last great war to achieve national integration exercised over Italy's elites.

Society and Culture

On the rise of feminism, see especially R. Bridenthal et al., *Becoming Visible: Women in European History* (1987), and S. K. Kent, *Women and Suffrage in Britain, 1860–1914* (1987). The best introductions to Nietzsche are J. P. Stern, *Nietzsche* (1978); W. Kaufmann, *Nietzsche: Philosopher, Psychologist, Antichrist* (1956); and R. Heyman, *Nietzsche: A Critical Life* (1980). On Freud and his legacy, see especially R. Wollheim, *Sigmund Freud* (1971); the critical treatment of H. J. Eysenck, *The Decline and Fall of the Freudian Empire* (1984); and Ernest Gellner, *The Psychoanalytic Movement* (1985). On Freud's environment, see above all C. Schorske, *Fin-de-Siècle Vienna: Politics and Culture* (1980). W. J. Mommsen, *The Age of Bureaucracy* (1974), offers an excellent short introduction of Max Weber and his ideas. E. Wilson, *Axel's Castle: A Study of the Imaginative Litera-* *ture of 1870–1930* (1931), is still the best introduction to literature from the Symbolists onward. R. Raynal, *The Nineteenth Century: New Sources of Emotion from Goya to Gauguin* (1951), with fine illustrations, and F. Mathey, *The World of the Impressionists* (1961), remain excellent introductions to the new painting.

29

EUROPE FROM BALANCE TO BREAKDOWN, 1871–1914

In international politics, the long peace between Bismarck's wars and the First World War was the classic age of the European balance of power. Fear of revolution and the solidarity of the great powers, which had damped down rivalries after 1815, were gone. The princes and their standing armies had defeated revolution in 1848–49, and the Crimean War had destroyed the European concert. Europe, Bismarck scoffed, was a mere "geographic expression": "I only hear a statesman use the word 'Europe' when he wants something for himself." The long peace after 1871 rested almost exclusively on the balance of power, a mechanism seemingly as self-operating as the free market. Threats by one power automatically led the others to combine and force it to retreat.

But by the 1890s the European system was no longer self-contained. The rise of two great powers outside Europe, the United States and Japan, made it for the first time a world balance. That undermined the balance on the European continent itself—just as industrialization tilted that balance toward a single mighty state. That state was Germany, whose industry surpassed Britain's between 1900 and 1913. And Germany, already the greatest land power, also challenged Britain after 1897 for world mastery at sea. New technologies of war and transport improved the position of the great continental powers and increasingly threatened Britain's ability to bring its seapower to bear. The shift of the balance in Germany's favor, and Germany's ill-advised attempts to exploit that shift, eventually drove Britain to ally itself with France and Russia, Ger-

(OPPOSITE) SARAJEVO, JUNE 28, 1914: ARCHDUKE FRANCIS FERDINAND AND HIS WIFE WALKING TO THE AUTOMOBILE IN WHICH THEY WERE TO DIE.

many's neighbors. Germany answered with war.

THE FORCES BEHIND DIPLOMACY

The industrialization and democratization of Europe also meant the industrialization and democratization of war and foreign policy. Generals, admirals, and diplomats resisted but could not reverse those forces. The war of 1866 was the last "cabinet war." After that, victory required and nationalism inspired the participation of the masses. The expansion of literacy and the extension of the vote also meant that the masses began to influence foreign policy as well.

Toward Mass Armies and Industrial War

Until 1871 only Prussia had a genuine mass army based on universal military service. The other powers followed the lead of post-1815 France in preferring long-service professional armies. Then the Prussian army, created in 1814 and doubled in size by William I's military reforms in the 1860s, crushed the Austrians in 1866 and the French in 1870. That forced the others to imitate Prussia—and conscript much of their male population—if they hoped to remain or become great powers. Austria-Hungary introduced universal ser-

The French 75mm field gun.

vice in 1868; France, Italy, Russia, and Japan had followed by the 1880s. Only Britain and the United States, which faced no land threats, could afford the luxury of volunteer armies.

Military power thus rested more than ever on demographic strength. That weakened the position of France even more than had defeat in 1870, for France's population almost ceased to grow after 1840, while Germany's increase continued (see p. 615). Of the great powers, only Russia and the distant United States surpassed Germany in total population. And Russia's economic weakness and political fragility meant that numbers were its only great asset.

An accelerating revolution in destructiveness of weapons paralleled the revolution in the size of armies. Alfred Nobel's nitrated explosives, ever-tougher steels, precision manufacturing, and advances in optics vastly increased the range and power of small arms and artillery. Between the 1860s and 1914 the battlefield of the twentieth century—empty because all visible movement draws fire—took shape. A hail of shell splinters and machine-gun bullets reversed the advantage that the attack had enjoyed in the days of the great Napoleon. Only crushing superiority of fire and manpower could now break a determined defense, and success might extend only so far as the next belt of enemy positions.

By 1900 the railroad had also worked a revolution, by vastly increasing the strategic mobility of land powers. In the Napoleonic wars, Wellington's sea communications proved better than the road links of the French. The railroad changed that; land powers could now meet amphibious threats rapidly and with overwhelming force. And the new mass armies could mobilize with unheard-of rapidity. Mobilization and concentration for battle became a single continuous operation. Speed, as the Prussians had demonstrated in 1866 and 1870, was all-important. The state that mobilized first and fastest, the general staffs of Europe concluded, would win.

What the staffs failed to see was that industrialization and industrial firepower

FIGURE 29-1 The Balance Shifts: Total Industrial Potential of the Great Powers

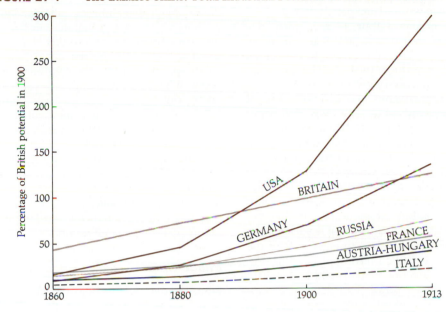

made a swift decision increasingly un-likely. Prussia's victory in 1870 had been a fluke, a consequence of France's disor-ganized mobilization and ineptitude in the first battles. War between industrial pow-ers, as the U.S. Civil War had shown, could easily become an immense struggle of at-trition. The outcome of a protracted war between industrial powers depended less on rifle strength in the first battles than on industrial might and financial stamina.

And in total industrial potential, by 1913, one power had surpassed all others ex-cept the United States: the Germany of Kaiser William II (see Figure 29-1). That was a fateful shift in the balance of power.

Technology also revolutionized war at sea—and likewise threatened Britain's position. France and the contenders in the U.S. Civil War had pioneered steam-powered armored warships. By the 1880s steel cannon, turrets, and armor had out-

The first duel between armored warships: the *Monitor* against the *Merrimac* (renamed *Virginia*) at Hampton Roads, March 1862.

classed and replaced the wooden ships that had won at Trafalgar. By 1900 a battleship mounted four 12-inch guns, displaced 14,000 tons, and was capable of 18 knots. Then the British, to outrace all rivals, introduced the first all-big-gun ship, H.M.S. *Dreadnought,* in 1904–05. With its ten 12-inch guns and 21-knot speed, it could stand off at long range and batter older battleships into flaming scrap.

Fleet size was as vital—and as much a matter of international competition—as warship design. Growing threats moved the British in 1889 to launch a crash rearmament program, the Naval Defense Act. London adopted the "Two-Power Standard" as a yardstick of naval strength: British strength had to equal that of the two next-ranked naval powers. But Britain's rivals continued to build, and by 1912 every great power had fleets of Dreadnoughts. And other weapons challenged the supremacy of the battleship. Torpedoes, mines, submarines, and eventually aircraft evened the contest between Britain and its rivals, between the greatest sea power and the land powers.

Technology inevitably raised the cost of warfare and of preparation for war. Britain's defense expenditure more than doubled between 1890 and 1914. Germany's almost quadrupled. But since their economies were also expanding, the burden of military expenditure as a percentage of gross national product did not increase as sharply as did the absolute amounts spent. What many contemporaries saw as an uncontrolled upward-spiraling "arms race"—a metaphor that gained currency in the decade before 1914—was in reality a slow climb. Nevertheless, the weaker or slower-growing powers—Italy, Austria-Hungary, Russia, and France—found it harder to become or remain great powers than did the economic giants. In a long war, those that had difficulty keeping up before 1914 might well go under.

Public Opinion and Foreign Policy

Educated opinion first began to affect foreign policy in Britain and the United States. Public opinion made the Crimean War, and destroyed the British Cabinet that bungled it. Public opinion was decisive in making and—under Lincoln's inspired leadership—in deciding the U.S. Civil War. Gladstone mobilized public opinion against Disraeli's foreign policy in the 1880 election; his own command

The ten 12-inch guns of the H.M.S. *Dreadnought* (launched 1906), outclassed all previous warships.

of Parliament crumbled after the public discovered that his muddling had sent Gordon to his death at Khartoum in 1885.

As public opinion broadened to include an ever-larger segment of the population, it began to affect policy in four principal ways. First, its often confusing message increasingly aggravated—or excused—the indecision of policy-makers. As Gladstone's Conservative successor Lord Salisbury lamented in 1895, "When the great oracle speaks, we are never quite certain what the great oracle said." Public opinion, it often seemed, wanted no foreign policy at all.

Second, public opinion made it increasingly difficult to maintain consistency and continuity in policy. Democracy, as Tocqueville pointed out in the 1830s, "can only with great difficulty regulate the details of an important undertaking, persevere in a fixed design, and work out its execution in spite of serious obstacles. It cannot combine its measures with secrecy or await their consequences with patience." The British foreign office made the fickleness of Parliament and public into a virtue, a ready excuse when other powers pressed for inconvenient British commitments. The French Chamber destroyed its government for attempting to cooperate with Britain in Egypt in 1882, then held a grudge against the British for going ahead alone. In 1885 the Chamber suddenly overthrew Ferry after a minor defeat in Indochina. Italian governments fell for "losing" Tunisia to France in 1881 and for losing to the Ethiopians at Adowa in 1896. The coming of democracy confronted the makers of foreign policy with entirely new pressures and limits.

Third, Liberal opinion in Britain and Socialist opinion on the Continent tended to confuse morality with policy, to the dismay of self-proclaimed realists such as Disraeli or Bismarck. The interest of the state often appeared to require actions (such as the threat of war) or allies (such as the Turks), that were distasteful to an electorate influenced by Gladstone-style moralizing. Extreme moralists rejected the rules of the international game altogether. Richard Cobden and John Bright, middle-class crusaders against Britain's Corn Laws, denounced the Crimean War and lost their seats in Parliament. They shared a faith that free trade would act "on the moral world as the principle of gravitation in the universe—drawing men together, thrusting aside the antagonism of race, and creed, and language, and uniting us in the bonds of eternal peace." Free trade triumphed, but eternal peace did not appear. Cobden and Bright blamed that "foul idol," the balance of power, and the aristocracy, a historical fossil for which the British diplomatic service allegedly served as a gigantic welfare system.

Socialist opinion saw a different villain. Capitalism, the root of all evil, must also be the cause of war, not its cure (as Cobden and Bright had claimed). Rosa Luxemburg and Lenin clashed over whether party leadership or spontaneous risings by the masses were the key to revolutionary struggle, but they fervently agreed that imperialism and war were the inevitable result of capitalism. They and others in the revolutionary wing of the Second International insisted that capitalist-imperialist war would and must lead to socialist revolution. Thinkers less committed to Marxism merely deplored armaments spending. Countess Bertha von Suttner, an Austrian writer, gained wide success with her pacifist novel, *Lay Down Your Arms!* (1889). She helped inspire the guilt-ridden Alfred Nobel to establish the peace prizes that bear his name, and in 1905 she was the first woman to receive one.

Some states even courted pacifist opinion. Nicholas II of Russia, fearing that his ramshackle finances would not support re-equipping his army with new artillery, proposed a ten-year "holiday" on armaments in 1898. But the disarmament conference held the following year at the Hague in Holland failed. So did a second in 1907; its only results were agreements on the treatment in war of neutrals, prisoners, wounded, and noncombatants, the stipulation that small-arms bullets must have full metal jackets rather than the far more lethal expanding lead tip, and a World Court incapable of resolving major disputes. Most rulers and military figures were secretly grateful to William II for sab-

Bertha von Suttner (1843–1914), recipient of the 1905 Nobel Peace Prize.

otaging the conferences. The Kaiser scoffed rudely in private and proclaimed his reliance "on God and on my sharp sword." Sir John ("Jacky") Fisher, the reforming admiral responsible for the *Dreadnought,* was equally forthright: "The essence of war is violence. Moderation in war is imbecility." What counted was winning, and winning required the swift application of overwhelming force.

William II and Fisher need not have worried. In an age of nationalism, the more democracy, the more nationalism. That was the fourth major consequence of the growing power of public opinion. Pacifism remained the faith of small minorities. The principal pre-1914 leader of the German Social Democrats, August Bebel, admitted in 1892 that even his own party was "a sort of preparatory school for militarism." In Britain and France, "jingoism" and Boulangism (see pp. 745 and 715) showed that universal male suffrage did not necessarily bring peace.

Even authoritarian regimes had to consider the views of their publics and their officer corps. Nationalist opinion had driven Napoleon III, against his better judgment, to war and his doom in 1870. Nationalist opinion, originally unleashed with government support, helped drive Imperial Germany after 1905 to make a violent bid for the mastery of Europe. By the 1870s, Slavophilism had mutated into Russian nationalism and "pan-Slavism." Russia was the patron and protector of its Slav "little brothers" everywhere—a sacred duty that extended the Russian state's potential claims far into central Europe and the Balkans. Journalists like Nikolai Katkov of the *Moscow Gazette* preached that duty and those claims in a manner that the tsars, given Russia's tradition of assassination, found hard to ignore. Even in Japan, the Meiji oligarchs and their successors were responsive to opinion, especially military opinion. Assassination sometimes struck down Japanese statesmen who appeared insufficiently resolute in defending Japan's security and rights.

BISMARCK THE CONSERVATIVE, 1871–90

Disraeli had greeted with dismay Germany's victory over France in 1870: "The balance of power has been entirely destroyed. . . ." That prophecy came thirty years too soon. In the 1860s Bismarck had harnessed German nationalism to the purposes of the Prussian state; after 1871 he kept it harnessed. The new Germany, he repeatedly declared, was a "satiated" power. Bismarck merely sought to preserve the dominant position in Europe that he and Moltke had won.

That meant keeping the peace. In a future great war the powers whose mutual hostility had neutralized them in 1866 and 1870 might yet combine against Germany. France, which had refused to accept the loss of Alsace-Lorraine in 1870–71, was the chief threat. If France found allies, Germany would face a dangerous coalition. And if Russia's traditional friction in the Balkans with Austria-Hungary led to open conflict, Germany might have to support Vienna. Russia would then bid for French support. Bismarck's annexation of Alsace-Lorraine meant that any open conflict between Austria and Russia would almost

Bismarck the conservative.

certainly become a general European war in which Germany would have to fight on two fronts.

Bismarck therefore encouraged the mutual tensions of the powers to keep them dependent on Berlin. He exploited any colonial rivalry that might divert the attention of his neighbors from Alsace-Lorraine. Bismarck's policy, as much as Germany's strength, made Berlin the center of European diplomacy for a generation. To freeze the status quo, Bismarck also attempted to restore the unity between Vienna, St. Petersburg, and Berlin that had guaranteed stability before the Crimean War. The aim of his German-Russian-Austrian "Three Emperors' Leagues" of 1872–73 and 1881 was to prevent Austria-Hungary and Russia from clashing in the Balkans. Bismarck was less successful than Metternich; the three eastern monarchies were now incapable of marching in step for long.

Bismarck himself unintentionally fractured the first Three Emperors' League in early 1875, when he tried to bully a fast-reviving France with newspaper warnings ("Is War in Sight?") and private threats of war. Those threats led Russia, for the first time since Prussia's thrusts against Denmark in 1848–49, to join Britain. When the Tsar and Disraeli jointly warned Berlin that they would not permit Germany to crush France again, Bismarck retreated. The balance of power, the mechanism that thirty years later was to bring Britain, Russia, and France together against Germany once more, had shown Bismarck his limits. Germany was the single most powerful continental state, but it was not the master of Europe—yet.

The First Great Eastern Crisis and the Congress of Berlin, 1875–78

The "war-in-sight crisis" of 1875 passed quickly, despite its menacing undertone for Germany. It was the Balkans that ultimately wrecked Bismarck's attempts to keep Germany, Russia, and Austria-Hungary together.

The two great Balkan crises of 1875–78 and 1885–87 were entirely different from their predecessor, the Crimean War.

Balkan nationalism had come of age; the Balkan nationalities, not the great powers, were now the main threat to the Ottoman Empire. The Christian Slavs of Bosnia triggered the first and greatest of the two crises by rising in revolt in July 1875. When the revolt spread to the province of Bulgaria, the Turkish overlords replied with massacres. Tsar Alexander II, under pressure from pan-Slav opinion, prepared to rescue Russia's Balkan "little brothers" from the Turks—and seize Constantinople.

But this time, unlike 1854–56, France did not move. Britain was paralyzed: Gladstone used the Turkish massacres to undermine the government of his rival Disraeli and to attack Britain's traditional policy of supporting Turkey to bar Russia from the Mediterranean. Austria-Hungary also stood aside, fearing that any victory by the Balkan peoples over Turkey would make Austria-Hungary itself the next "sick man" of Europe. The Russians offered Ottoman territory to Vienna as compensation for eventual Russian and Slav gains, and promised not to create a "large compact Slav state" that would threaten the Habsburg monarchy.

To everyone's surprise, the Turks fought well when Russia went to war in April 1877. At the entrenched camp of Plevna on the main road to Constantinople, their British rifles stalled the ill-equipped Russians until December 1877. That victory gave the Ottoman Empire another forty years of life. Britain's fickle public opinion swung decisively: the Turks were no longer the Moslem butchers of Christian Slavs, but the plucky defenders of Plevna. That freed Disraeli to send the British fleet to face Russia at the Turkish Straits. And it gave the world a new word for populist aggressiveness, "jingosim":

> We don't want to fight,
> But by Jingo, if we do,
> We've got the ships,
> We've got the men,
> We've got the money, too.

Russia, exhausted by Turkish resistance, was soon in no condition to fight

The Treaty of San Stefano   1878

The Congress of Berlin   1878

Britain. But the Tsar's peace treaty of San Stefano with Turkey (March 1878) nevertheless went too far. It created a great Bulgaria covering the entire eastern Balkans. That "large compact Slav state," and Russia's failure to offer the compensation it

had promised, led Austria-Hungary to join Britain. Then Bismarck stepped in as "honest broker" and convened an international "Congress of Berlin" in June–July 1878. The location of the meeting symbolized the new Germany's decisive role in Europe.

Russia backed down, and grudgingly divided the great Bulgaria of San Stefano into three: Bulgaria, an "Eastern Rumelia" technically under Turkish overlordship, and a "Macedonia" that reverted to Turkey. In compensation, Austria-Hungary received the Serb-inhabited provinces of Bosnia and Hercegovina to administer as a sort of trust. Serbia officially became independent of Turkey, although in 1881 Austria-Hungary made it a client state for a generation. Disraeli returned from Berlin triumphant, with Turkish Cyprus as a sort of payment for saving Constantinople from the Russians. The Congress of Berlin had patched up a map of the Balkans that lasted with only minor modifications until 1912. Russia turned to expansion in central Asia.

Bismarck's Alliance System, 1879–83

In the aftermath of the first great eastern crisis, Bismarck took the very step for which he had reproached the Prussian governments of the 1850s: he tied the "trim Prussian frigate" to the "moth-eaten Austrian galleon." In September 1879 he signed at Vienna a defensive military alliance against Russia that lasted until both Austria-Hungary and Germany collapsed in 1918.

With this Dual Alliance—the first peacetime alliance between great powers since the eighteenth century—Bismarck pursued three fundamental goals. It would reassure Austria-Hungary about its security. It would restrain Austro-Hungarian aggressiveness in the Balkans and against Russia—for Bismarck could at any time point out that the alliance was defensive, and threaten to leave Vienna to its fate if it provoked a war. Finally, the Dual Alliance would give German nationalism a surrogate for the "greater Germany" from the Baltic to the Adriatic that Bismarck had blocked by creating his greater Prussia in 1866–71.

Bismarck's new policy held great dangers. Berlin's promise of support in fact increased rather than decreased Vienna's aggressiveness. And the German public's vocal support for the Germans of Austria-Hungary made it less and less possible for Bismarck to threaten to leave Vienna in the lurch. His successors felt themselves bound to Vienna by German nationalist "*Nibelung* loyalty"—a doom-laden Wagnerian tune repeatedly sounded as both empires went down in 1914–18. Finally, the Dual Alliance tied Alsace-Lorraine and the Eastern Question together even more tightly than before. Germany, bound to Austria-Hungary by alliance and divided from France by an insoluble quarrel, was the link between East and West. No matter how a great-power war started, Germany and Austria-Hungary would now face both France and Russia.

To put off that day, Bismarck followed the Dual Alliance with a second Three Emperors' League in 1881. Russia agreed for the moment not to join France in a war against Germany, and the three powers agreed to take no action in the Balkans except by mutual agreement. The second League rested on even weaker foundations than the first. Alexander III, now in power thanks to his father's assassination in 1881 (see p. 721), was a narrow autocrat of nationalist instincts. The solidarity between monarchs of the age of Metternich meant little to him, and still less to Vienna, which Bismarck had to pressure into signing the three emperors' agreement.

To compensate Vienna for this forced cohabitation with Russia, Bismarck made yet another treaty. In 1882 he roped the Italians into a Berlin-Vienna-Rome triangle, the Triple Alliance. Rome, humiliated over France's seizure of Tunisia in 1881, was delighted at this recognition of Italy's importance, however insincere. Vienna received an unconvincing Italian promise not to seek Trento and Trieste, the Dual Monarchy's remaining Italian-speaking areas, if Russia attacked Austria-Hungary. Bismarck paid the bill by promising to support Italy against French attack, an event he thought unlikely.

In 1883 Bismarck added Rumania to this increasingly bizarre treaty structure. That action ran directly counter to assurances he had given Russia that he had underwritten Austria-Hungary's survival but not its Balkan interests. Secret pledges that Berlin and Vienna would defend Rumania against attack in effect blocked Russia's land route to Constantinople. The Balkans, as Bismarck had told the *Reichstag* in 1876, contained no German interests worth the "bones of a Pomeranian musketeer." Yet Bismarck had now committed Germany to defend the eastern Balkans against Russia.

The Second Eastern Crisis and the Reinsurance Treaty, 1885–87

Bismarck's diplomacy more and more resembled an elaborate juggling performance. The second of the great Balkan crises, which arose in 1885, tested his genius to the fullest. The issues this time were fortunately less explosive than in 1877–78. Russia's principal goal was now security against British naval attack in the Black Sea and free passage through the Turkish Straits for its growing grain exports from the Ukraine.

Russia nevertheless quarreled with Britain in 1885–87, first by encroaching on Afghanistan, India's vital buffer, then over Bulgaria, the gateway to the Turkish Straits. Ultimately, both issues led to stand-offs; Russian ambitions turned toward East Asia. But the crisis also drove Britain, under Gladstone's Conservative successor, Lord Salisbury, toward the Triple Alliance. In two "Mediterranean Agreements" of 1887, Salisbury joined Italy and Austria-Hungary in guaranteeing—against Russia and France—the territorial status quo in the Mediterranean and Black Sea. Britain, France, and Italy thus blocked Russia at Constantinople, with Bismarck's blessing.

Bismarck added the final touch to this eccentric combination by negotiating a secret agreement with the Russians to replace the collapsed Three Emperors' League. The three-year "Reinsurance Treaty" of June 1887 seemed to pledge

German support for Russian action against Constantinople if the Turks allied themselves with the Western powers. Germany and Russia also promised each other neutrality should war come, except if Germany attacked France or Russia attacked Austria-Hungary.

That secret pledge contradicted the spirit if not the letter of the Dual Alliance that linked Berlin and Vienna, and the German alliance with Rumania as well. And by promising Russia support at the Turkish Straits, the Reinsurance Treaty also ran counter to the second Mediterranean Agreement that linked Bismarck's Italian and Austro-Hungarian allies with Britain against Russia. Bismarck had created a system of mutually contradictory commitments that froze the Austro-Russian quarrel while keeping Germany's "line to St. Petersburg" open. But if treaties alone could not keep the Balkans quiet, he would have to choose sides. Germany could only choose Austria-Hungary, and a clash with Russia.

The Collapse of Bismarck's System, 1887–90

This astounding performance taxed even Bismarck. It also had unforeseen effects. France, weary of diplomatic isolation, reluctantly drew closer to Russia. The tsar, annoyed at Bismarck's closing of the Berlin loan market during the Bulgarian crisis and his continued backing of Austria-Hungary, swallowed his royal doubts about accepting the French Republic's money. The Russians gained their first sizable French loan in October 1888. In January 1889 they ordered large quantities of French rifles after promising not to use them against France.

Bismarck was no longer sufficiently in control in Berlin to counter this threat. The new Kaiser, William II, had fallen under the influence of Moltke's successor, Count von Waldersee, who insistently urged "preventive" war against Russia before Russia became too strong. In fall 1889, without Bismarck's approval, William II assured Vienna that whatever the source of the quarrel, Germany would mobilize its forces alongside Austria-Hungary. Ger-

many was abandoning its Russian connection.

Then, in March 1890, Bismarck and the young Kaiser quarreled over domestic policy. When the Russians anxiously suggested a renewal of the Reinsurance Treaty, Bismarck was gone. His successor was a conscientious but limited general, Count Leo von Caprivi, who found Bismarck's foreign policy too complex and self-contradictory. He feared that St. Petersburg might leak word of Germany's promise to support Russia at the Turkish Straits. That would destroy Germany's ties to Russia's enemy, Britain. Nor would German opinion or the Vienna government take kindly to Germany's sins against the nationalist loyalty-unto-death supposedly enshrined in the Dual Alliance.

Germany therefore turned down the Russian offer and drew temporarily closer to Britain with an 1890 agreement over colonial issues. The end of the Reinsurance Treaty and Germany's wooing of Britain accelerated a process already under way: Russia's move toward France. In July 1891 a surly Tsar Alexander III stood at attention for the playing of the *Marseillaise,* hymn of revolution, during a visit by the French fleet. Bismarck had deliberately isolated France; William II and Caprivi had left Russia isolated. In August 1891 France and Russia agreed to coordinate their foreign policies. Both sought the independence from Berlin that Bismarck had denied them.

By 1892 French and Russian negotiators had hammered out a military pact that pledged France to attack Germany if Germany attacked Russia, and Russia to attack Germany if Germany attacked France. If Austria-Hungary alone mobilized, France pledged to mobilize too. That promise broke with France's previous reluctance to enter Balkan quarrels. But Paris agreed because it desperately wanted security against Germany and did not expect Austria-Hungary would ever act alone. The Franco-Russian alliance was intended to last as long as the Triple Alliance of its adversaries.

The ratification of the alliance in December–January 1893–94 did not, as is often claimed, make a general war proba-

Tsar Alexander III, the French Republic's grudging alliance partner.

Alliances and Alignments before 1914

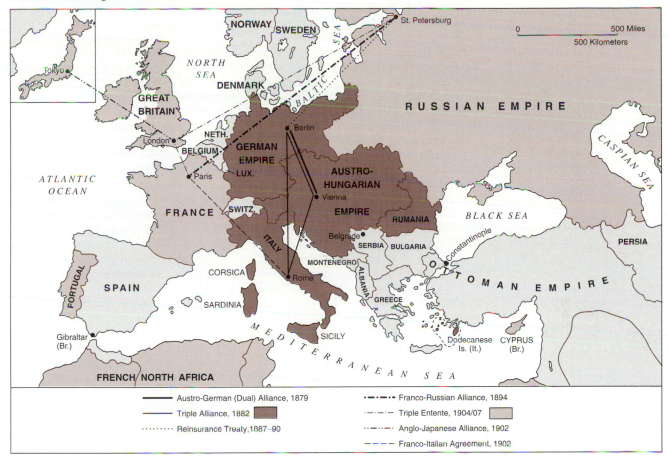

——— Austro-German (Dual) Alliance, 1879	—·—·— Franco-Russian Alliance, 1894
——— Triple Alliance, 1882	—··—··— Triple Entente, 1904/07
·········· Reinsurance Treaty, 1887–90	—···—···— Anglo-Japanese Alliance, 1902
	– – – – Franco-Italian Agreement, 1902

ble. The annexation of Alsace-Lorraine and Bismarck's Dual Alliance had already done that. What the Franco-Russian alliance did was to reassert the European balance of power and end the German political domination of Europe that Bismarck had established. As late as 1892 the young Kaiser could confide to associates his vision of establishing "a sort of Napoleonic supremacy" in Europe "in the peaceful sense." But after the Franco-Russian alliance, a German "Napoleonic supremacy" could come only through war.

THE BREAKTHROUGH TO WORLD POLITICS, 1890–1904

Europe nevertheless enjoyed peace for another twenty years. The Franco-Russian alliance gave France and Russia security

in Europe. Russia and Austria-Hungary remained calm when a new Near Eastern crisis erupted in 1895 over Turkish massacres of Armenians, and in 1897 they agreed to put the Balkans "on ice." For a generation Europe turned its attention to Africa and East Asia. And for the first time non-European great powers, Japan and the United States, made their presence felt. That made the European balance a world balance of power, dwarfing powers like France that were merely European in scale.

Theories of World Politics

Theorists such as Sir John Seeley (1834–95) had long noticed that even the British Empire lacked the vast territorial and demographic base of continent-spanning powers like the United States and Russia.

Britain could compete, argued Seeley in the 1880s, only if it welded its white colonies and home islands into a world-spanning trans-national federation, a "Greater Britain." That remedy appeared less and less plausible: the white colonies, like the thirteen colonies before them, were developing away from Britain, not toward it. Particularly after 1900, informed British opinion feared the disintegration of the empire.

In Germany, nationalist professors provided a conceptual framework suitable for a "rising" power. From the summit of the German historical profession, the liberal Johann Gustav Droysen and the far less liberal Heinrich von Treitschke declared that unity under Prussia was the culmination of all previous German history. Droysen's fourteen-volume *History of Prussian Policy* (1853–86) and Treitschke's five-volume *History of Germany in the Nineteenth Century* (1879–94) portrayed the past, in good Hegelian fashion, as the upward struggle of a Prussian state embodying the world spirit. They also looked forward to higher things: Germany's mission in the world paralleled Prussia's mission in Germany. An entire generation absorbed their outlook.

The sociologist Max Weber suggested in a famous 1895 speech that the achievement of German unity had been a waste of time unless it was to serve as prelude to a "German world-power policy." The founder of the odd quasi-discipline of geopolitics, Friedrich Ratzel, suggested in his *Political Geography* (1897) and other publications that national borders were fluid and ever-changing. Organization and numbers were the key elements in an eternal struggle for "living space." Political pressure groups like the Pan-German League, founded in 1891, agitated fervently for more "space" for Germany. Britain's decline, the Germans argued, was Germany's opportunity to break through into the charmed circle of true world powers alongside Russia and the United States.

In Russia, figures like Katkov temporarily set aside pan-Slav fantasies for a Russian nationalist "manifest destiny" in East Asia. Russia in Asia, Katkov argued, was

"as much at home as in Moscow." As the trans-Siberian railroad crept eastward, the Tsar and his subordinates began to look to control of northeast Asia as the foundation of Russia's world power status.

In the United States, pundits urged a search for new frontiers beyond the seas to replace the land frontier that was passing. "Manifest destiny," a phrase coined by a Southern journalist in 1850, appeared to extend beyond the Pacific shores to "universal empire." But America's most influential prophet of empire was more modest. When Captain Alfred Thayer Mahan of the U.S. Naval War College published *The Influence of Seapower Upon History, 1660–1783* in 1889, it enjoyed instant success.

Mahan derived two simple laws from the great age of British naval power. One he merely implied: power, from the Roman empire to the British empire, meant *sea* power. The second he stated baldly: sea power meant a battle fleet. These notions made Mahan's book the bible of the U.S. Navy and of its great-power rivals, for he offered a recipe for success in the new age of world politics: build battle fleets and seize overseas bases and colonies to protect and foster an ever-expanding commerce. Ironically, Mahan achieved prominence just as technology—railroad, torpedo, mine, and submarine—was evening the contest between land power and sea power, and just as non-European nationalism was making colonies an increasingly doubtful investment.

The Struggle for Mastery in Africa, 1895–1902

The rivalries of the new age of world politics unfolded in two main theaters of action. In Africa, Britain and France confronted each other at the climax of the "scramble" for territory that had begun with the British occupation of Egypt in 1882. In East Asia, China's failure to keep pace with Japan or with the European powers led to a decade of bitter conflict.

France's refusal to accept British control of Egypt led it into dangerous paths in Africa. In 1897 Paris sent a small expedition under a Captain Marchand to stake a claim on the Upper Nile, the key to Egypt's water supply. But London, after Salisbury and the Conservatives returned to power in 1895, had decided to avenge the Mahdi's defeat of Gordon at Khartoum (see p. 692). Britain's security in Egypt demanded command of the Sudan.

A British army under Sir Herbert Kitchener ascended the Nile by steamer to face the army of the Mahdi. That made the issue between Britain and France one of power alone. At Omdurman, in September 1898, Kitchener crushed the Mahdists. Three weeks later, Kitchener found Marchand and his small force at Fashoda on the Upper Nile. To make good its territorial claims, France would now have to go to war. Salisbury refused to negotiate: "We claim the Sudan by right of conquest. . . ." The Dreyfus affair had crippled Paris politically, and France suddenly remembered that Britain still held the naval control of the Mediterranean that Nelson had won in 1798 at the Battle of the Nile. Marchand withdrew.

The Fashoda crisis was not the end of Britain's African woes. The great conflict with the Boers that Gladstone had postponed by retreating in 1881 finally erupted in the 1890s. The discovery of gold on Boer territory in 1886 made the Transvaal republic the greatest power in southern Africa. British entrepreneurs rushed in to exploit the Transvaal mines—but every ounce of gold they extracted increased the wealth and power of the Boers. After 1894 a railroad through Portuguese East Africa gave the Transvaal an independent link to the outside world. German political and economic influence flowed in, to the alarm of the British.

Most alarmed was Cecil Rhodes, the great robber baron of the Transvaal diamond mines and gold fields, and Britain's governor of the Cape Colony. In 1895 Rhodes decided to destroy Boer independence before Britain lost control of the Cape—and before his own mining interests suffered. With the secret help of the former Liberal Joseph Chamberlain, now Salisbury's secretary for colonies, Rhodes planned a raid against the Transvaal in support of a promised uprising of British

settlers and miners inside the Boer Republic itself. But these "Uitlanders," as the Boers called them, failed to move when Rhodes's raiders, under the leadership of a Dr. Jameson, struck in January 1896. The mounted infantry of the Boers neatly trapped the attackers, humiliating both Rhodes and Britain.

The main consequence of this "Jameson raid" was to provoke the unpredictable German Kaiser, William II, to send a foolish telegram of congratulation to the president of the Transvaal, the bearded patriarch Oom Paul Kruger. That gesture, which seemed to foreshadow further German meddling in southern Africa, made British action more urgent. Chamberlain, convinced that Britain must fight for its position at the Cape before it was too late, began preparing British public opinion for war. Salisbury, the prime minister, was unhappy: "I see before us the necessity for considerable military effort, and all for people whom we despise and for territory which will bring no power and profit for England." Yet Chamberlain and his deputy at the Cape, Sir Alfred Milner, had their way. In October 1899 Milner at last provoked the Boers into declaring war.

Contrary to expectation, the Boer War was no walkover. Britain controlled the sea; despite European disapproval and violent pro-Boer agitation in Germany, Britain's European rivals were helpless. But the Boers were not. Unlike Mahdists or Zulus they did not obligingly charge into British machine guns. Instead, they allowed the British to attack, and sent them reeling with German-supplied rifles and

Architects of empire, and of the Boer War: Joseph Chamberlain (*above*) and Cecil Rhodes (relaxing in the bush during the Matabele war, 1896).

Three generations of defiant Boers, with their Mauser rifles.

field guns. Boer knowledge of the country made their swift-moving mounted infantry hard to find as well as hard to defeat. Not until June 1900 did a huge and clumsy British army conquer the Boer capital, Pretoria. To defeat a few thousand backwoods farmers, Britain ultimately had to commit 450,000 men.

The conquest of Pretoria did not give Britain control of southern Africa. The Boers fought on in a bitter guerrilla struggle. The British replied with savage reprisals and "concentration camps": barbed-wire open-air prisons for the Boer civilians and their African dependents, to keep them from supplying the guerrillas. Roughly 20,000 Boers and 12,000 Africans died in the camps from disease and British

Asia in 1880

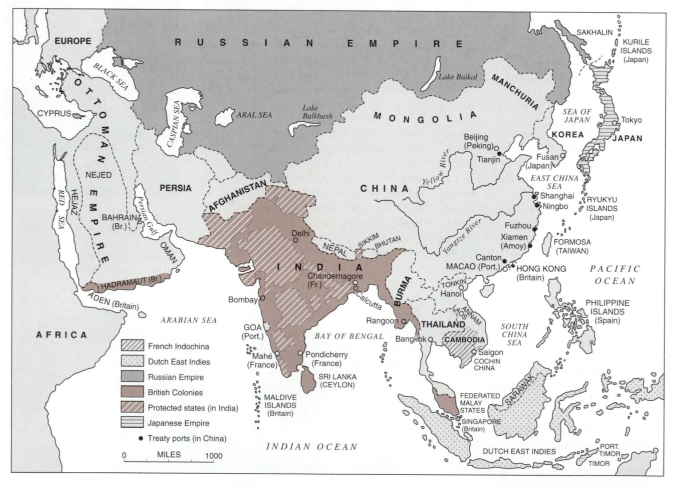

mismanagement. The Liberal opposition in London attacked the Conservative government for defending civilization with the "methods of barbarism." Soon all except the most determined "jingoes" were heartily tired of the brutality and sacrifices that empire required.

Attrition and Britain's increasing use of Boer turncoats and African volunteers finally persuaded the Boers to give up in May 1902. The greatest colonial war of the nineteenth century was over. But the fierceness of Boer resistance forced concessions from London as well. In 1910, Britain gave dominion status to a Boer-dominated Union of South Africa. The Boers had won in all but name.

The Struggle for Mastery in East Asia, 1894–98

African struggles were still part of the old framework of European and colonial rivalries. East Asia was different. There a new power, Japan, burst upon the scene by attacking China in September 1894. In the 1870s the Meiji oligarchs had restrained Japanese extremists who had urged a war with China's dependent kingdom, Korea. Now Japan was ready, and friction over Korea provided the occasion. Japan's new European-style army drove the Chinese from Korea and invaded Manchuria. Japan's new navy battered the poorly trained Chinese fleet off the mouth of the

Asia in 1914

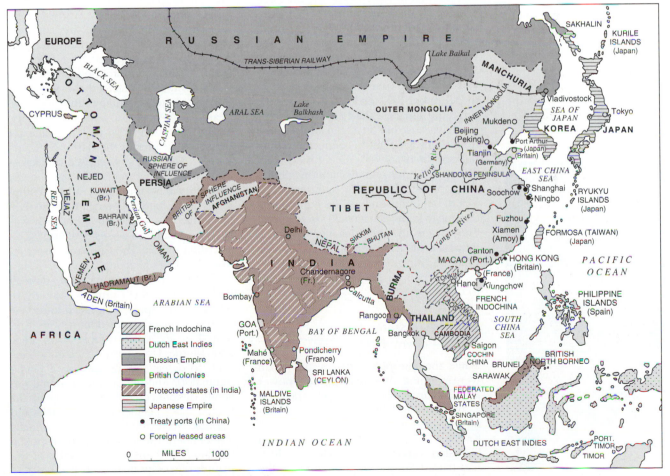

Yalu River. Japan seized the vital base of Port Arthur on the Liaodong peninsula. By the Treaty of Shimonoseki of April 1895, Japan forced China to give up Port Arthur to Japan and to recognize Korean independence—but independence from China, not from Japan.

Then disaster struck. Russia and its French ally intervened diplomatically, posing as China's protectors. Their adversary in Europe, Germany, joined them in the hope of regaining favor with the Russia it had estranged in 1890. The three powers "advised" Japan against keeping Port Arthur and the Liaodong peninsula. The resentful Japanese agreed to give them up. Japan's main prizes were Taiwan, which it took as a colony, and an unstable joint overlordship with Russia over Korea.

Japan's victory over China opened a new scramble for concessions and ports that seemed to foreshadow the final collapse of the decrepit Chinese empire. Russia now made its bid for control of north China. It plied China with loans and gained the right to build a spur of the trans-Siberian railway directly across Manchuria to Vladivostok (see the map on p. 753). In December 1897 the Russians seized the prize the Japanese had sought, the ice-free naval base of Port Arthur, and secured from China the right to connect it to their railroad. In 1897–98 Germany and Britain also seized ports on the Shandong peninsula, opposite Port Arthur. Italy demanded a port, but China understood Europe well enough to know that it could safely refuse. The powers divided China into spheres of influence: Manchuria to Russia, southwest China to France, the great Yangtse Valley in the center to Britain, and Shandong to Germany.

The United States as a World Power: 1898

While the European powers and Japan were stripping China to the bone, a power greater than any of them began to develop a foreign policy of its own. That was a novelty, and not always a welcome one, for the United States. Thanks to its ocean boundaries and to the British fleet—which had barred European interference in the

New World in Britain's own interests—the United States had largely ignored the European balance throughout the nineteenth century. But a new assertiveness emerged in the 1890s, as industrial America reached maturity. In 1895 President Grover Cleveland's secretary of state intervened in a boundary dispute between Britain and Venezuela with the brash claim that "the United States is practically sovereign on this continent, and its fiat is law. . . ."

In 1898 the second of two Cuban revolts against Spain tempted the United States to make good that assertion. The battleship *Maine,* sent to Havana as a symbol of U.S. support for the revolt, exploded and sank in harbor, probably by accident. But the jingoist press of William Randolph Hearst claimed a Spanish plot: "Remember the *Maine*!" That agitation and the coming election moved President William McKinley to strike.

The shining new U.S. Navy, built up since the early 1890s on Mahan's theories, swept Spain's antiquated fleet from the seas. A hastily improvised landing on Cuba eventually defeated the Spaniards despite sketchy training and logistical chaos. Theodore Roosevelt, soon to be McKinley's successor, made a name for himself as leader of the dashing "Rough Riders." The navy too reached out across the Pacific: Commodore George Dewey crushed the Spanish fleet in the Philippines at the battle of Manila Bay. He then challenged a German squadron that was loitering nearby in hopes of snapping up a coaling station. The Germans wisely refused Dewey's challenge.

The Filipinos proved more difficult than Spain or the Germans. Already in revolt against Spain, they failed to see the charm of United States domination. It required up to 70,000 troops, three years, and all the U.S. Army's Indian-fighting skills to defeat the insurgency of Emilio Aguinaldo. Anti-imperialists at home fervently denounced the war. Ultimately the United States pacified the Philippines and stabilized its relationship with a nominally independent Cuba through an unspoken bargain. In return for the loyalty of the planter oligarchy that Spain had created,

Theodore ("Teddy") Roosevelt, Rough Rider and future president, 1898.

the United States promised to maintain order. That guaranteed short-term stability, but offered no long-term release from the fierce conflicts within these sharply stratified colonial societies.

The United States rounded out its new overseas empire by annexing Guam, Puerto Rico, and Hawaii. It also intervened diplomatically—mixing moralism and American interests in the style of the Monroe Doctrine—in faraway China. In 1899 McKinley's secretary of state, John Hay, urged the powers to preserve an "Open Door" to trade and to respect China's territorial integrity, rather than dividing China into exclusive spheres. The powers humored the newcomer and agreed. Paper promises were cheap, and easy to disavow.

Closer to home, the United States also made good the claim to the exclusive Latin American sphere of influence, free of European interference, first implied in the Monroe Doctrine in 1823. Britain in effect conceded United States domination of the Caribbean in the Hay-Pauncefote treaty of 1901. Under Theodore Roosevelt and his successors William Howard Taft (1909–13) and Woodrow Wilson (1913–21), the United States engineered the secession from Colombia of a new state—"Panama"—and between 1904 and 1914 carried through the Panama Canal project that had defeated de Lesseps. U.S. Marines brought imperial order to Central America and the Caribbean while diplomats sought, in Wilson's words, to teach the inhabitants "to elect good men." A navy of Dreadnoughts, with bases stretching from Manila Bay to Norfolk, Virginia, assured the security of the new empire and of America's growing trade. And America's immense and still-growing share of the world's industrial production reinforced its claims as a power.

The Struggle for Mastery in East Asia and the European Balance, 1899–1905

Meanwhile Western intrusion into China after 1897 triggered the largest spontaneous anti-Western rising since the Indian Mutiny of 1857–58. The "Righteous and Harmonious Fists," or "Boxers," had originated as an anti-dynastic secret society. They claimed that Taoist magic powers protected them from Western bullets. In 1898–99 the society spread across north China as a mass movement to "expel the foreign bandits and kill the Christian converts." The Dowager Empress and her conservative advisers in Beijing (Peking) quietly encouraged the Boxers, who obligingly ceased opposing the Qing dynasty itself.

International intervention to protect missionaries triggered a Boxer-led rising that besieged the Westerners in Beijing. Boxers assassinated the German minister. The Qing declared war on the European powers. As an Italian nationalist cynically remarked a year or two later, only an invasion from Mars could unite humanity. China briefly had the same effect; Europe, Japan, and the United States momentarily forgot their quarrels. William II dispatched Field Marshal Waldersee to lead the conquest of north China, sending the troops off with an impromptu speech that urged them to take no prisoners and to rival the fearsome reputation of Attila and his Huns. That was a phrase that Germany's enemies later remembered.

Even before Waldersee's arrival, Maxim guns had defeated Taoist magic. The powers imposed a stiff settlement but preserved the dynasty with the fiction that the Boxers had been an anti-Qing rebellion. The dynasty staggered on; the death of the Empress Dowager in 1908 and a revolution of provincial armies and Westernized intellectuals in 1911 ultimately destroyed it.

In the present, Russia's occupation of Manchuria and of Beijing itself worried Britain. London now felt little need for allies in Europe, for by the mid-1890s Salisbury at last felt strong enough to quietly abandon Britain's commitment to defend the Turkish Straits. The revival of British naval power and Britain's possession of Egypt had made "splendid isolation" practical. But to resist Russia in China, Britain needed a land power as an ally. That led Chamberlain to seek an agreement with Germany between 1899 and 1901. The Germans proved slippery, for good

The Western Powers line up for their slices of China (from a German cartoon, 1900).

reason. British goodwill and Germany's small stake in China were not sufficient cause for Germany to alienate Russia further. Germany shared European borders with Russia and with Russia's French ally; Britain did not.

In January 1902 Britain therefore found a different partner, that other "island empire," Japan. Tokyo and London pledged to go to war if either of them faced *two* great powers in East Asia. That meant that Britain and Japan would fight side by side only if France intervened alongside its Russian ally. Britain's role was to keep the French neutral while Japan, if necessary, stood up to Russia.

Russian recklessness soon made that necessary. In March 1903 the first train across the trans-Siberian railway reached Port Arthur. With their supply line apparently secure, the expansionists in St. Petersburg could look forward to ousting their Japanese partners and seizing Korea—and the domination of northeast Asia—for themselves. But Korea, as a Prussian general staff adviser had taught his Japanese pupils, was "a dagger pointed at the heart of Japan," a position of supreme geopolitical importance. Yamagata Aritomo, founder of Japan's modern army and the most Prussian of the surviving Meiji oligarchs, demanded war to stop Russia before it was ready to move.

When Russia refused to accept Japanese predominance in Korea in return for Japanese recognition of Russian control of Manchuria, Japan chose war. On January 8, 1904, the Japanese navy surprised and crippled the Russian fleet at Port Arthur. Command of the sea enabled Japan to lay seige to Port Arthur and to invade Man-

churia. Russian machine gun and artillery fire exacted a terrible price from the attackers, but Port Arthur ultimately fell in January 1905. By March the Japanese had worn the Russians down in great battles of attrition in Manchuria. The trans-Siberian railway was still single-tracked, and Russian supplies and reinforcements were precarious. The Russians retreated northward.

At the end of May 1905 the Russian Baltic fleet, sent halfway around the world to rescue Port Arthur, met the Japanese off the island of Tsushima, south of Korea. The Japanese "crossed the T" of the advancing Russian fleet, sweeping the leading Russian ships with the long-range broadsides of their entire force. The annihilation of that last Russian fleet and the revolution that had broken out in European Russia in January 1905 (see pp. 722–23) forced Russia to cease fighting. "Teddy" Roosevelt, trying out America's new status as a Pacific great power, stepped in to mediate and to preserve a balance that would keep China alive. His Treaty of Portsmouth (New Hampshire) of September 1905 recognized Japan's "paramount interests" in Korea, forced Russia to return Manchuria to China, and gave Port Arthur, its railway, and the southern half of Sakhalin island to Japan (see the map on p. 753). Within five years Japan had annexed Korea. A non-European power had for the first time defeated a European great power. That set a powerful example for all non-Western peoples.

The Russo-Japanese war also decisively altered the European scene. The approach of war in Asia had caused the French deep anxiety: would Russia's war with Japan, a British ally, drag France into war with Britain? Théophile Delcassé, France's crafty foreign minister, therefore turned toward Britain. The British, equally intent on avoiding a clash, turned toward France. Queen Victoria's successor, the high-living Edward VII, wooed French opinion with a state visit in 1903 and with less official gastronomic and amorous cross-Channel excursions. By April 1904 the British and French had settled the colonial disputes that had divided them since the occupation of Egypt in 1882. France traded its useless claims in Egypt for a British promise to support the eventual French annexation of Algeria's western neighbor, the decrepit Sultanate of Morocco. This Anglo-French *Entente Cordiale* was thus East Asian in origin and colonial in nature. But it soon became an alliance in all but name, facing the greatest European power, Germany.

That fateful development was a consequence of a second major effect of Russia's defeat by Japan: the disruption of the European naval and military balance. Until Russia recovered, Germany was supreme on the Continent. Its naval buildup, of which more below, soon outpaced the fleets of the Franco-Russian alliance and threatened to outpace that of Britain. Its land forces, freed temporarily from the two-front threat, held France hostage. And its efforts to reduce France to vassalage moved Britain, for the first time since Waterloo, to think of committing British forces to a land war in western Europe.

GERMANY ON THE LOOSE, 1905–14

Perhaps Germany's ever-greater industrial power should have inspired its leaders to *buy* Europe rather than conquer it. But German nationalist prophets, from the Liberals of the Frankfurt Parliament in 1848 to the Pan-Germans of the 1890s (see pp. 670 and 720), dreamt of "wrest[ing] mastery of the seas from the English, and . . . become[ing] the most powerful *Volk* on this earth." That was a goal only force could achieve.

Germany Challenges Britain, 1897–1905

Once the Franco-Russian alliance had barred the road to "Napoleonic supremacy" on land, the Kaiser looked seaward. Personal rivalry with his English royal cousins, an amateur interest in naval technology, and identification with the world-spanning goals of German middle-class nationalism made him from the early 1890s the chief advocate of enlarging Ger-

many's coastal defense navy into something far more impressive. In 1894 the Kaiser read the *Influence of Seapower Upon History* and became a convert to Mahan's gospel of the battle fleet. But not until 1897 did he find the team capable of translating his wishes into budgets and battleships: Bernhard von Bülow at the foreign office and Admiral Alfred Tirpitz at the Reich naval office.

Bülow provided the foreign policy cover for the fleet program. Germany was to avoid entanglement with either England or Russia while it created a fleet that would alter the world balance of power. It was the task of Tirpitz, with a formidable bifurcated beard and the wiliest political mind in Germany, to provide that fleet. To convince the *Reichstag* of the need for a battleship navy, he mounted Germany's first modern advertising campaign; the admiral's enemies did not call him "the Father of the Lie" for nothing. Charts showing Germany's comparative naval strength appeared in dentists' waiting rooms all over Germany. Schoolchildren chipped in pennies to pay for the fleet. Professors and industrialists spoke and wrote fervently of Germany's "sea interests" and world mission. In 1898 the *Reichstag* passed a first naval law providing for 19 battleships, and in 1900 accepted a second that doubled the fleet to 38 battleships and stepped up the building tempo to 3 ships each year.

To justify the enormous expense and *Reichstag* advance appropriations stretching over decades, Tirpitz claimed that Germany's increasing foreign trade and colonial empire required a fleet for its security. Only a fleet capable of placing "the greatest naval power" at serious risk would provide that security. Tirpitz's so-called "risk theory" appeared on the surface to be defensive, a strategy of deterrence. But no power threatened Germany's commerce or its largely useless colonial empire. Nor was deterrence Tirpitz's aim. In private memoranda for the Kaiser and others, he preached decisive battle "between Helgoland [an island off the German coast] and the Thames." For the "greatest naval power," the opponent Tirpitz had chosen, was Britain.

Admiral von Tirpitz, who built the fleet against Britain.

Germany's World Mission in the Words of Its Leaders

Even before 1900, the Kaiser's frequent "oratorical derailments"—as an aide privately described them—and the more cautious remarks of his chief foreign policy assistant, Bernhard von Bülow, had suggested the magnitude of Germany's ambitions:

Germany is gradually growing out of its children's shoes, and entering its youth. . . . We are bound for great things, and I shall yet lead you into glorious times.

The Kaiser, February 24, 1892 [speech in Berlin]

The German Empire has grown into a world empire. . . . German goods, German know-how, [and] German enterprise span the oceans.

The Kaiser, January 18, 1896 [speech in Berlin]

We do not seek to put anyone in the shade, but we demand our place in the sun! (Bravo!)

Bernhard von Bülow, December 6, 1897 [to the Reichstag]

If we look around us, we can see how the face of the world has changed in the last few years. Old world empires are passing away and new ones are coming into being.

The Kaiser, October 18, 1899 [speech in Hamburg]

Some have said . . . that in each century a conflict, a massive settlement of accounts redistributes influence, power, and possessions around the globe. In the sixteenth century the Spaniards and Portuguese divided the New World. In the seventeenth century the Dutch, French, and English entered the race while *we* were beating in each other's heads [in the Thirty Years' War] (merriment). In the eighteenth century the Dutch and French lost most of what they had gained to the English. In our own nineteenth century England has ceaselessly extended its colonial empire, the mightiest the world has seen since the days of the Romans, while the French have planted themselves firmly in North and East Africa and have created a new empire in Indochina, and Russia has begun a mighty procession of victories in Asia that has carried it to the high plateau of the Pamirs and the shores of the Pacific. . . . Are we once again facing a new division of the world, as the poets fancied a century ago? I think not, or rather I do not think it yet. But in any case we cannot permit any foreign power, any foreign Jupiter, to say to us: "Hard luck. The world had already been given away." We do not seek to injure other powers, but we also seek to keep other powers from kicking us around (Bravo!). . . . In the coming century the German people will either be a hammer or an anvil.

Bernhard von Bülow, December 11, 1899 [to the Reichstag]

From Michael Behnen, ed., Quellen zur deutschen Aussenpolitik im Zeitalter des Imperialismus 1890–1911 (Darmstadt: Wissenschaftliche Buchgesellschaft, 1977), pp. 63, 146, 166, 225, 230–31 (translation by M. Knox).

Victory over Britain, Tirpitz calculated, depended on four assumptions. Rivalry with France and Russia would tie up the British navy in China and the Mediterranean, leaving Britain weak in the North Sea. The feeble British would neither pay for nor be able to man the additional ships needed to keep pace with the German buildup. Technology, Tirpitz assumed, would remain static; German battleships built in 1900 would be roughly equivalent to British and German ships commissioned later. Finally, in the event of war the British fleet would charge into Germany's mine- and submarine-infested waters to mount its traditional close blockade of enemy ports, as in the days of Nelson. That would give the Germans their opportunity to fight close to their bases on advantageous terms.

The Kaiser was enthusiastic. The fleet would assure him his place in Prusso-German history. Just as his grandfather William I—thanks to Bismarck—had used the Prussian army to give the new Germany a dominant position on the Continent, so he himself would use the navy to break through into the circle of authentic world powers. And just as William I and Bismarck had defeated Prussian Liberalism by victory abroad in 1866–71, so he and his "second Bismarck," Bülow, would defeat Social Democracy. And the Kaiser's fleet, thanks to provisions in the naval laws that automatically replaced over-age ships without the need for further *Reichstag* votes, would ultimately become independent of the hated legislature.

The British were not amused. Britain by 1900 was closer than Germany to being an industrial society; more than half of Britain's food was imported, and those imports came by sea. Naval supremacy in home waters was no luxury for Britain, but a matter of survival. The British navy scrapped its Chinese river gunboats and its Caribbean squadron to free manpower for the North Sea. After 1903 it created new naval bases facing Germany at Rosyth in Scotland and at Scapa Flow in the Orkneys (see map, p. 770). Admiral "Jacky" Fisher, as Admiralty chief after 1904, supervised Britain's technological leap to the all-big-gun ship, the Dreadnought. He also urged destruction of the German fleet in harbor before it was strong enough to challenge Britain. Finally, Britain sought allies against Germany: France and eventually Russia. By 1905, the principal assumptions of Tirpitz's plan were all proving false. Germany had challenged Britain to a naval race that the British dared not lose, and had isolated itself diplomatically except for its alliance with an increasingly ramshackle Austria-Hungary.

The First Morocco Crisis and the Anglo-Russian Entente, 1905–07

Germany might have sought to loosen by good behavior the "encirclement"—as Germans now began to call it—that Germany had created around itself. Britain, France, and Russia were an odd assortment: two parliamentary regimes, one brutal autocracy. Britain and Russia might still clash anywhere from China to Persia, if Germany lay low. But Bülow and the chief brain at the German foreign office, the secretive Friedrich von Holstein, chose to break "encirclement" with threats. Japan's defeat of Russia in 1904–05 had temporarily paralyzed France's continental ally. Bülow and Holstein, seeking to exploit that weakness, picked a quarrel with France in the expectation that Britain would abandon France to German domination.

As a pretext the Germans chose French encroachment on the decaying Sultanate of Morocco. But this "First Morocco Crisis" was in reality not a colonial quarrel. It was rather a crisis of the European balance of power. In March 1905, with Russia in revolutionary chaos, Bülow and Holstein diverted to Tangier the Kaiser's habitual Mediterranean cruise. There William II blusteringly asserted Germany's nonexistent "great and growing interests in Morrocco" against France. Tension mounted as summer, the season for war, drew near. In June the French cabinet's nerve cracked, and Paris accepted the humiliating German demand that Delcassé resign as foreign minister.

Germany seemed to have won; William II made Bülow a prince. And in July William II succeeded in persuading his cousin "Nicky"—Tsar Nicholas II—to sign an alliance with Germany at a meeting of their yachts off the Finnish island of Björkö. Nicholas agreed, hoping that German backing would help him get better peace terms from Japan. Germany had apparently broken the Franco-Russian alliance and had achieved supremacy on the Continent.

But Russia in defeat and revolution needed French money more than ever before. And France would only supply that money if Russia abandoned the Björkö agreement—which the Russians in any case no longer needed once they had made peace with Japan in September 1905. The Germans also made a fatal error. Instead of working out a private bargain with France over Morocco, they called for an international conference.

The representatives of the powers met at Algeciras, opposite Gibraltar, in January 1906. Germany found itself isolated except for Austria-Hungary. Even its Triple Alliance partner Italy stood alongside France. In 1900 Italy had secured secret French agreement to its eventual annexation of Libya in return for its support of France in Morocco. In 1902 Rome had even sinned secretly against the Triple Alliance by promising France that Italy would remain neutral if Germany "provoked" France to declare war. The Algeciras conference therefore handed Germany a major diplomatic defeat. And Britain had already taken secret steps to bolster the French. In December 1905, as the Liberals took office, talks had begun between the British and French army staffs over the commitment of a British army on the left wing of the French if Germany attacked.

The crisis Germany had provoked had mightily reinforced the ring forming around Germany. By their actions, Bülow and Holstein had converted the Anglo-French colonial agreement of 1904 into a quasi-alliance against Germany to preserve the European balance of power. And on August 31, 1907, Russia and Britain, the two most persistent great-power enemies of the nineteenth century, signed an agreement settling their long-standing disputes in China, Tibet, and Persia. The

"Triple Entente" of Britain, France, and Russia now faced the Triple Alliance of Germany, Austria-Hungary, and Italy.

Naval Race and Bosnian Crisis, 1907–09

The Germans learned little from this First Morocco crisis. The noisy diplomacy of Bülow and Holstein had contradicted Tirpitz's need for quiet in which to build a fleet against Britain; now the building of Tirpitz's fleet thwarted Germany's far greater need to lie low. By 1908 Tirpitz could see that he might fail. The Liberals in Britain, despite their loathing of "great armaments" and their desire to increase social-welfare spending, refused to give up Britain's lead over the German fleet. Tirpitz, amid noisy anti-British propaganda from the German Navy League, therefore pushed a third naval law through the *Reichstag* that raised the German building tempo to four Dreadnoughts per year.

Britain replied by proposing a one-year halt in building, a "naval holiday." Berlin refused. Except for the pacifist Cobdenite wing of the Liberals, British public opinion was now unanimous. Britain must keep its naval lead whatever the cost. "We want eight [Dreadnoughts] and we won't wait!" thundered the popular press. In 1909–10 Britain began construction of ten battleships and battle cruisers. When the time came to pay the bill, the Liberals raised the income tax, slapped on inheritance taxes, and overrode aristocratic protests in the House of Lords; the knowledge that naval superiority was a matter of life or death strengthened British resolve. In Germany, Bülow's attempt to raise taxes to cover the vast increases in fleet costs led to the defection of the *Junker* Conservatives, the collapse of the government's *Reichstag* majority, and ultimately to Bülow's own dismissal.

As Anglo-German tension mounted, Germany's ally Austria-Hungary made its own contribution to the growing European crisis. For a decade it had held to its 1897 agreement with Russia to keep the Balkans quiet. But in 1903 a group of fanatical Serb officers slaughtered Vienna's clients, King Alexander and Queen Draga

Obrenovitch of Serbia. As Austria-Hungary's relations with Serbia deteriorated, France offered Serbia economic support. By 1908 the Austro-Hungarian foreign minister, Count Aehrenthal, had concluded that Vienna's prestige was at stake.

In October 1908, as a blow against Serbia, he announced Austria-Hungary's formal annexation of Bosnia and Hercegovina, the largely Serb-inhabited provinces bordering Serbia that the Congress of Berlin had allowed Austria-Hungary to occupy in 1878. Aehrenthal's Russian counterpart, Count Isvolsky, had secretly agreed—but only if Austria-Hungary helped toward a long-standing Russian goal, the opening of the Turkish Straits to Russian warships. Aehrenthal's announcement thus caught the Russians before they had secured their reward. Austria-Hungary kept Bosnia and Hercegovina, while Russia grumbled and threatened and Serb crowds demanded war against Austria. Eventually William II appeared, as he himself put it, "in shining armor" at Austria-Hungary's side. Berlin demanded that Russia and Serbia accept the annexation, or else. The Russians gave in; they had not yet recovered from war with Japan. But what seemed to Berlin a triumphant reassertion of German and Austro-Hungarian prestige struck the other powers as dramatic evidence of German aggressiveness. Bülow later claimed that he had warned the Kaiser—when William dismissed him in summer 1909 after a personal clash—not to "repeat the Bosnian affair." It was sound advice.

The Second Morocco Crisis, 1911

Bülow's successors, Chancellor Theobald von Bethmann Hollweg and foreign secretary Alfred von Kiderlen-Wächter, did not act on it. Instead, Kiderlen tried once again to use Morocco as a pretext for bullying France, in the hope of breaking the Triple Entente and riding German nationalist enthusiasm to a government victory in the 1912 *Reichstag* elections. In May 1911 the French occupied Fez, the capital of Morocco, after rebellion and anti-foreign riots like those in Egypt in 1882. Kiderlen reacted by dispatching a gunboat, the *Pan-*

ther, to the Moroccan Atlantic port of Agadir on the pretext of protecting German lives—which were not threatened. The German press was ecstatic: "Finally, a Deed!"

Kiderlen also secretly threatened Paris with war, while offering to settle for the entire French Congo in compensation for France's seizure of Morocco and as a symbol of France's vassalage to Germany. But the French and Russian armies were now stronger than they had been in 1905. Lloyd George, whom the Germans had taken for a pacifist Liberal, stiffened the French with jingo oratory promising British support.

Bethmann Hollweg shared what his private secretary described as "the authentic and fitting German idealist conviction that the *Volk* needs a war." But the Kaiser was less enthusiastic. Germany ultimately settled for several strips of swamp in the French Congo. France retained its independence. The Pan-Germans, whose backing Kiderlen had courted throughout the crisis, vented their fury on the Reich government for this "new Olmütz" (see p. 669). And Britain made further secret commitments to France. London reaffirmed its decision to send a British Expeditionary Force (B.E.F.) to France in the event of German attack. Sir Edward Grey, the foreign secretary, authorized further military discussions with the French while keeping the cabinet's pacifist Liberals in the dark. And Sir Winston Churchill, civilian chief of the navy after 1911—and a distant descendent of the great Duke of Marlborough who had halted the France of Louis XIV—called the Mediterranean fleet home to the North Sea to face the Germany of William II. The French took over Britain's Mediterranean responsibilities in return for a secret British pledge to protect the coasts of northern France against the German fleet. That was Britain's most far-reaching commitment against Germany to date.

Germany Prepares for War, 1912–13

The German response to defeat in the Second Morocco Crisis was retrenchment—of a sort. Tirpitz lost the unchallenged right to funding that his navy had enjoyed since 1897; in 1913 and 1914 the German building tempo fell to two battleships a year, Berlin at last recognized that it must secure its continental position before taking on Britain. The Kaiser and Bethmann Hollweg now gave the army priority. Radical nationalists on the general staff such as Erich Ludendorff broke *Junker* resistance to expanding the army and thus bringing more and more non-nobles into the officer corps. In 1912 and 1913 two army bills increased the army's size by a quarter, and the *Reichstag* paid the bill by passing an inheritance tax over Conservative objections. Tirpitz's only consolation was the Kaiser's rejection of another British proposal for a "naval holiday."

The increase in the size of the army was necessary, if Germany was to implement its chosen strategy in war. Waldersee's successor as Chief of the Great General Staff, Count Alfred von Schlieffen (1891–1905), faced the same nightmare of a two-front war as his predecessors. But his answer was different. Instead of attacking Russia and defending in fortified Alsace-Lorraine, as both Moltke and Waldersee had proposed, Schlieffen planned to strike France first. France, he reasoned, was vulnerable to a swift decisive blow, whereas the Russians could always retreat into their limitless spaces as they had in 1812.

Schlieffen had studied military history, classifying battles as an entomologist does insects. Decisive battles, he concluded, were all envelopments. The most perfect was Hannibal's crushing double envelopment of the Romans in 216 B.C., at Cannae in south Italy (see p. 78). But mountains, French fortifications, and the absence of space for Germany's million-man army would not permit the attack across the Franco-German border needed for a double envelopment. Instead, Schlieffen planned a holding action there to distract the French. Meanwhile an immense right wing, three-quarters of the entire German army, would swing down through neutral Belgium and attack the unfortified and undefended French rear.

Timing was everything: if Germany did not mobilize in time, or if it failed to knock France out immediately, the

Schlieffen's Plan

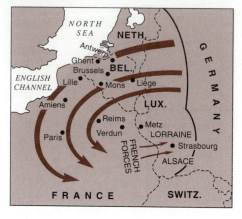

"Russian Steamroller" would crush Germany's skeleton forces in East Prussia and drive on Berlin. And Schlieffen, in his admiration of Hannibal, had forgotten one vital fact. In the end, Rome had defeated Hannibal and destroyed Carthage through attrition and through its command of the sea.

Schlieffen's plan had at least two fatal strategic flaws. It required that any German war, even one stemming from a Bal-

kan quarrel, must begin with an attack on France that staked Germany's future on a single card. And the violation of Belgium, whose neutrality Prussia and the other great powers had guaranteed in 1839, virtually ensured that Britain would join Germany's enemies. To Schlieffen that seemed unimportant. Britain had no mass army, and the war would be over—*must* be over—before it had time to raise one. Those were dangerous illusions.

Schlieffen retired in 1905 and died in 1913, leaving his plan to Helmuth von Moltke the younger, the high-strung and indecisive nephew of the great Moltke. The new chief of staff had doubts about Schlieffen's "infallible recipe for victory," but kept them to himself. And at the end of 1912 the German leaders apparently decided to act. A British warning that Britain would stand by France in the event of war enraged the Kaiser. On December 8, 1912, he presided over a conference of his military advisers at Berlin. Moltke urged war "the sooner the better," to crush Germany's adversaries before they grew too strong. New Russian railways in Poland and rearmament of the Russian army with modern weapons would make the Schlieffen plan impractical by 1917. Tirpitz advised restraint for the moment; the navy was not ready. The conference, without consulting Bethmann Hollweg, decided to mobilize the press to prepare the public for war. With government encouragement, newspaper stories increasingly hostile to Russia began to appear.

At the general staff, Moltke and his assistant Ludendorff made two fateful decisions in 1913. First, they discarded Germany's one remaining alternate plan, which had provided for an offensive against Russia and defense against France. Second, Ludendorff added to the Schlieffen plan an immediate thrust through neutral Luxembourg and Belgium, starting the moment the German army mobilized, to seize the key rail junction of Liège. If danger threatened, Germany—unlike the other powers—could not mobilize and wait to see what happened. It planned to violate Belgium in the process of mobilizing its army, and to attack France regardless of what triggered the crisis.

"War the sooner the better": Helmuth von Moltke the younger, Prussia-Germany's chief of staff, 1906–14.

The Balkan Wars, 1912–13

While the Germans prepared, the great powers lost control of the Balkans. France's seizure of Morocco had set off a chain reaction. Giovanni Giolitti of Italy feared that the French—now that they had secured Morocco with Italian approval—would forget their earlier promise to support Italy's claim to Libya. In September 1911, Giolitti therefore declared war on Turkey, Libya's nominal overlord, and sent a fleet to Tripoli. A hastily improvised landing failed to subdue the warlike Arabs of Libya or their Turkish advisers. Italy then seized Turkish islands in the Aegean and attacked the Turkish Straits. Not until October 1912 did the Turks give up a still unpacified Libya to Italy.

The Italian example encouraged the Balkan states. Serbia and Bulgaria, with Russia as godfather, signed an alliance in March 1912. Greece and Montenegro joined them. The Russians thought of the new alliance as defensive; the Balkan states had other ideas. In September 1912 this Balkan League attacked and swiftly divided up the remaining Ottoman territories in the Balkans. Then the victors quarreled over the booty. Bulgaria attacked Serbia in the hope of seizing Macedonia, claiming that the powers had defrauded it of that province in 1878. Serbia, Greece, Montenegro, Rumania, and Turkey repelled the Bulgarians.

In the aftermath of the two Balkan Wars, the great powers worked together under the leadership of Sir Edward Grey of Britain to calm the triumphant Serbs and stabilize the new Balkan order; an independent Albania that barred Serbia from the Adriatic was one result. But the Balkan Wars were clearly not the last Balkan crisis. The collapse of the multinational Turkish empire in Europe made Austria-Hungary, the new "Sick Man" of Europe, increasingly desperate to reassert its shrinking prestige against the growing

The Dissolution of the Ottoman Empire to 1914

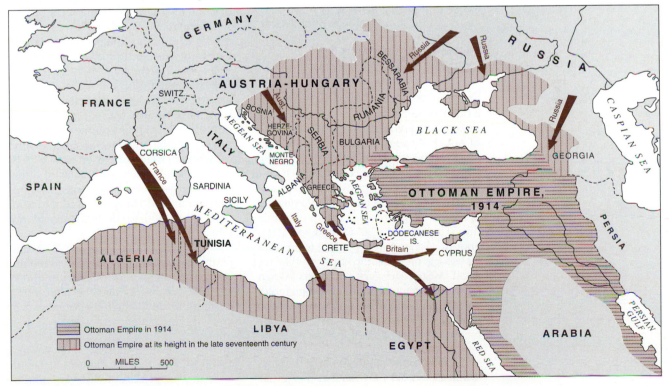

The Balkan Wars: Turkish infantry moves up.

power of Serbia, the self-proclaimed "Piedmont of the South Slavs."

FROM BALKAN CRISIS TO GERMAN WAR: JULY 1914

On June 28, 1914, at Sarajevo in Bosnia, a Bosnian Serb terrorist assassinated Archduke Franz Ferdinand, heir to the throne of Austria-Hungary. The terrorists, following a pattern common later in the century, were associated with a secret society—the "Black Hand"—sponsored by Serbian military intelligence. Although Vienna did not know that, it reacted with predictable fury. The chief of staff, Conrad von Hötzendorff, longed for a war to restore Habsburg prestige and crush Serbia for good. Austria-Hungary's frivolous foreign minister, Count Leopold von Berchtold, concurred. Only the Hungarians, whose privileged position within the monarchy might suffer if Vienna annexed yet more Slavs, urged caution.

Berlin broke the deadlock in Vienna. When Berchtold's envoy met the Kaiser on July 5, 1914, the Kaiser urged an immediate attack on Serbia, regardless of Russia's reaction. He repeatedly assured a friend, Krupp von Bohlen, that "this time I will not chicken out [*Diesmal falle ich nicht um*]." Bethmann Hollweg told his closest confidant on July 8 that Germany would probably win a general war. If Russia shrank from a war, Germany would nevertheless split the Entente and achieve a decisive diplomatic and strategic victory. In Vienna, Berchtold used Berlin's so-called "blank check"—in reality a virtual order to act—to break the Hungarians' opposition to war. Hungary owed its autonomy after 1866 to Berlin; it could not refuse Berlin's command.

But partly from Viennese sloth and partly from calculation, Berchtold did not deliver his ultimatum to Serbia until July 23. That long delay and the ultimatum's contents made Berchtold's actions seem coldly premeditated, and weakened Austria-Hungary's position. One senior German diplomat could not believe that Vienna had drafted the ultimatum; its brutal tone was "Prussian to the very bones."

Berchtold made the deliberately humiliating demand that Austro-Hungarian police be permitted to enter Serbia and join the hunt for the terrorists and their accomplices. He also announced that Vienna would treat refusal of any single condition in the ultimatum as a total rejection. The Serbs returned a conciliatory answer. But they refused to accept Austro-Hungarian intervention inside Serbia itself.

For Vienna, that was pretext enough for war. And for Berlin, where the leadership, in the words of a participant, "worried only that the Serbs might swallow the [Austro-Hungarian conditions]." Bethmann Hollweg sabotaged efforts by Britain to arrange a conference of the kind that had prevented the Balkan Wars from growing into a great-power conflict. On July 28, with strong German encouragement, Austria-Hungary declared war on Serbia. Vienna's mobilization was too slow to permit an invasion for several weeks, but Vienna and Berlin were determined to present the other great powers with a violent *fait accompli*. Austria-Hungary therefore shelled Belgrade, the Serb capital.

Now Russia had to respond or suffer a humiliation far worse than the Bosnian crisis. On July 28, Nicholas II and his foreign minister, Sergei Dimitrievich Sazonov, tried to deter Vienna by ordering mobilization of the four Russian military districts opposite Austria-Hungary. But then the Russian generals reported that their cumbersome mobilization system permitted only a general mobilization. On July 31 Russia published the order for general mobilization. That was the point of no return, although the Russian purpose was still deterrence, not war.

In Berlin, the news of Russian mobilization was welcome indeed. The Kaiser had begun to waver, and Moltke was pressing Bethmann Hollweg with increasing fierceness to mobilize before Russia could. Bethmann Hollweg himself feared the domestic consequences of being first to mobilize; his task was to keep the German Social Democrats loyal to the coming war effort. Consequently, Russia's mobilization appeared heaven-sent. "The mood is brilliant," wrote the Kaiser's chief naval

Sarajevo, June 28, 1914: The arrest of the assassin, Gavrilo Princip.

aide in his diary on August 1. "The government has succeeded very well in making us appear as the attacked." Germany dispatched an ultimatum to Russia summoning it to demobilize. Russia refused.

On August 1 Germany declared war on Russia and ordered mobilization. France honored its alliance obligations to Russia by mobilizing also, in defiance of a German ultimatum to Paris demanding French neutrality in a Russo-German war. The ultimatum was for show only; German strategy dictated an attack on France. If France dared to upset the Schlieffen plan by abandoning its Russian ally and

Conrad von Hötzendorff, Austria-Hungary's chief of staff, contemplates war on three fronts (1914).

come by emotion: "Even if we end in ruin, it was beautiful." That was a fitting epitaph for Imperial Germany and for the long peace.

"War Guilt," War Causes

After 1918, it became fashionable to dispute Germany's preeminent responsibility for the war of 1914–18. German scholars rallied around their foreign office and accused Russia or Britain. Anglo-Saxon "revisionists" charged Vienna, St. Petersburg, Paris, and even London with "war guilt." Guilt is a notion best left to psychoanalysts—but causes and responsibilities are the historian's business.

The long-term causes of the war were two: Austria-Hungary's decline and—above all—Germany's rise. Balkan nationalism threatened an Austria-Hungary entangled in a perennial struggle with Russia. After 1890, German nationalism proved not at all "satiated"—and the transition to a world balance-of-power system excited it still further. Bismarck, with his alliance with Austria-Hungary in 1879, had tied together these two principal sources of European conflict. After 1905 they interacted explosively. Balkan nationalism undermined Austria-Hungary just as the growing German threat drove Britain, France, and Russia to coalesce against Germany.

In the final crisis, responsibility was unevenly divided. Britain intervened only when the Germans invaded Belgium. France merely accepted a war that Germany forced on it. The Serb government did not seek war, although its army had nurtured the terrorists. Russia had backed Serbian expansion in the Balkan Wars, and in July 1914 it may have encouraged the Serbs to refuse the most humiliating of Austria-Hungary's demands. Russia had also been the first to mobilize, although it aimed not at war, but at getting Vienna's attention.

The responsibilities of Austria-Hungary were more serious. It sought war with Serbia, made sure that its ultimatum would lead to war, and shelled Belgrade. But Berlin took the key decision: without German pressure, Austria-Hungary would

---

The Kaiser Spurs Vienna On   July 5, 1914

The Kaiser's message, as reported by Austria-Hungary's ambassador, Count Ladislaus Szögyény, was no simple "blank check" or assurance of support. It was an incitement to war.

After lunch, when I once again underscored with the greatest emphasis the seriousness of the situation, His Majesty [Kaiser William II] authorized me to report to our most gracious Majesty [Emperor Francis Joseph] that in this case as in others we could count on Germany's full support. . . . He (Kaiser William) was of the opinion that this action must not be delayed. Russia's attitude will in any event be hostile, but he had been prepared for that for years, and should it come to a war between Austria-Hungary and Russia, we could be assured that Germany would stand by our side with its usual faithfulness to its alliances. . . . He understands full well that His royal and imperial Apostolic Majesty [Emperor Francis Joseph] would be reluctant, given his well-known love of peace, to march into Serbia. But if we had really become convinced of the necessity of military action against Serbia, he (Kaiser William) would regret it if we allowed the present highly favorable moment to pass unused.

From Imanuel Geiss, ed., Julikrise und Kriegsausbruch 1914 *(Hannover: Verlag für Literatur und Zeitgeschehen GmbH, 1963), pp. 83–84 (translation by M. Knox).*

---

remaining neutral, the German ambassador in Paris was to ask provocatively for the surrender of French border fortifications. That would force France to fight. In the event, France did not accept Berlin's ultimatum. On August 2 Germany invaded Luxembourg and demanded that Belgium give free passage to German troops. Belgium refused. On August 3 Germany declared war on France. On the morning of August 4 German troops entered Belgium—and pushed the indecisive British cabinet into war. The violation of Belgium allowed the Liberals to feel moral about a war to defend British security and the balance of power; the Cobdenite pacifist Liberals resigned, and Britain dispatched an ultimatum demanding that Germany withdraw from Belgium. At midnight on August 4, that ultimatum expired, and all the European great powers were at war. As the Kaiser addressed the *Reichstag* amid stormy applause, the Prussian war minister, Erich von Falkenhayn, was over-

never have acted, and the crisis would have fizzled out. Since late 1912 Germany's leaders had looked forward to a general war, given a suitable occasion. Moltke actively sought war "the sooner the better." His purpose was to strike down Germany's *potential* enemies before they became too strong—a goal little different from outright aggression. Bethmann Hollweg, obsessed with the ever-growing—though hollow—Russian colossus, and optimistic about German chances of victory if general war came soon, was willing to risk it. All trusted in a "fresh and joyous war" (in the phrase of the Kaiser's boister-

ous son, Crown Prince William), victorious in the style of 1870.

Germany's minimum goal was a small Balkan war to shore up a flagging Austria-Hungary and split the Triple Entente. Its maximum goal was to destroy the balance of power and make Germany supreme in Europe. And the Schlieffen plan—after 1913 Germany's *only* war plan—guaranteed that any German war against Russia would begin with an attack on Belgium and France. That assured British intervention. Germany unleashed a Balkan war, then turned it into a general war that destroyed Europe's world position.

Suggestions for Further Reading

The European Balance

The relevant chapters of A. J. P. Taylor's indispensable *The Struggle for Mastery in Europe* (1954) give a detailed and brilliant general account, but see also N. Rich, *Great Power Diplomacy, 1814–1914* (1992), and P. Kennedy, *The Rise and Fall of the Great Powers* (1987). W. L. Langer, *European Alliances and Alignments, 1871–1890* (1950), is still useful on Bismarck's conservative phase. M. Hurst, ed., *Key Treaties for the Great*

Powers, Vol. 2, (1871–1914) (1972), gives English texts of key agreements such as the Triple Alliance. Among the many accounts of the policies of the various powers, see especially G. Bourne, *The Foreign Policy of Victorian England* (1970); B. Porter, *The Lion's Share* (1984); and D. Geyer, *Russian Imperialism* (1987). On military affairs, see the relevant chapter in H. Strachan, *European Armies and the Conduct of War* (1983).

World Politics

The chapter on international affairs in G. Barraclough, *An Introduction to Contemporary History* (1964), remains the best short introduction to the rise of "world politics." W. L. Langer, *The Diplomacy of Imperialism* (1950), covers the 1890–1902 period in informative detail. H. W. Morgan, *America's Road to Empire* (1965), conveniently summarizes America's entry into world politics; see also C. S. Campbell, *The Transformation of Ameri-*

can Foreign Relations, 1865–1900 (1976), and H. K. Beale, *Theodore Roosevelt and the Rise of America to World Power* (1956). R. Van Alstyne, *The Rising American Empire* (1960), offers a jaundiced view of U.S. motives. T. Pakenham, *The Boer War* (1978), and I. Nish, *The Anglo-Japanese Alliance* (1966), are excellent.

The Road to the First World War

The best single work on the origins of the First World War remains L. Albertini, *The Origins of the War of 1914* (1952). P. Kennedy, *The Origins of the Anglo-German Antagonism, 1860–1914* (1980), is a model of analysis. V. Berghahn, *Germany and the Approach of War in 1914* (1973), and Z. Steiner, *Britain and the Origins of the First World War* (1977), offer parallel accounts that emphasize German responsibility. On France, Russia, Austria-Hungary, and Italy, see J. Keiger, *France and the Origins of the First World War* (1983); D. Lieven, *Russia and the Origins of the First World War* (1983); F. R. Bridge, *From Sadowa to Sarajevo: The Foreign Policy of Austria-Hungary, 1866–1914* (1972); and R. Bosworth, *Italy and the*

Approach of the First World War (1983). V. Dedijer, *The Road to Sarajevo* (1967), throws some light on Serb machinations. G. Ritter, *The Schlieffen Plan* (1958), and P. M. Kennedy, ed., *The War Plans of the Great Powers, 1880–1914* (1979), are useful on military planning. For the final crisis, I. Geiss, ed., *July 1914* (1967), is indispensable. F. Fischer, *Germany's Aims in the First World War* (1967) and War of Illusions (1975), make a strong case for a premeditated German war of aggression. G. Schöllgen, ed., *Escape into War? The Foreign Policy of Imperial Germany* (1990), summarizes the resulting "Fischer debate."

WAR AND REVOLUTION
1914–1929

The war that began in August 1914 smashed nineteenth-century Europe beyond repair. Contrary to almost universal expectation, the first battles did not decide the war. Instead, as in the U.S. Civil War, industrialized states summoned up their full reserves of human and machine power and battered each another into collapse. In the process, Europe lost its world economic leadership, already threatened by the growth of the United States. The nationalism of the colonial peoples received powerful reinforcement. The four great empires of Europe and the Middle East perished. One of them, Russia, suffered a revolution utopian in its aims and unparalleled in its ferocity, the first Marxist revolution. The European balance of power collapsed, and only the intervention of an outside power, the United States, brought Germany's defeat. Then the swift withdrawal of the United States after 1919 left the exhausted victors, Britain and France, face to face with a vengeful Germany that refused to accept the outcome. The Great War of 1914–18 was merely the *First World War*.

THE WAR OF MOVEMENT, 1914

The German Gamble Fails

On August 4, Schlieffen's great right wing—a million men in four German armies deployed in northwestern Germany—began to swing across Belgium. The French obligingly attacked the fortifications of the German left wing in Lorraine, and plunged deeper into the trap. The Lorraine offensive cost France 300,000 dead, wounded, and missing.

But Schlieffen and Moltke the younger had made no allowance for enemy reaction. Nor had they given enough thought

(*OPPOSITE*) TOTAL WAR: WOMEN, STEEL, AND HIGH EXPLOSIVES AT A BRITISH MUNITIONS PLANT, 1917.

The First World War   1914–18

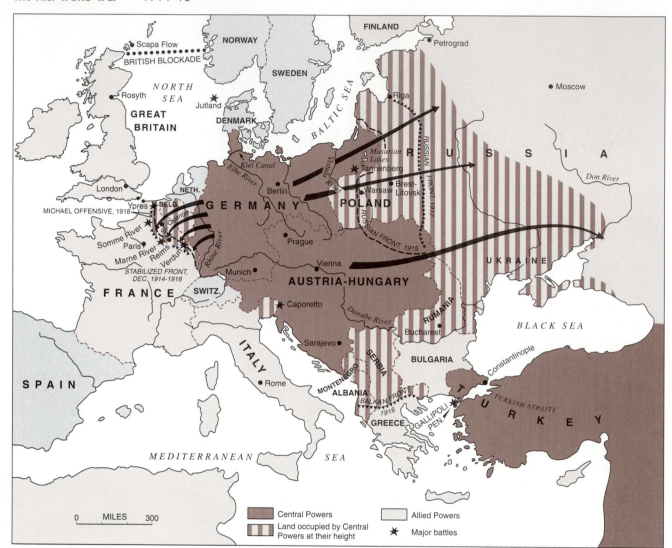

Central Powers
Land occupied by Central Powers at their height
Allied Powers
★ Major battles

to "friction," the forces of accident, error, and confusion that make even the simplest plans in war heartbreakingly difficult to carry out. Belgian civilians sniped at German troops, despite German massacres in reprisal. The Belgians wrecked their railroads to keep supplies from reaching the German armies. And the long marches exhausted the German reservists. By September, wrote an officer on the far right wing, "the men stagger forward, their faces coated with dust, their uniforms in rags, looking like living scarecrows. They march with their eyes closed, singing in chorus so as not to fall asleep. . . . It is only the delirium of victory that sustains our men."

Delirium soon receded. As the Germans neared the Franco-Belgian border, they met both the French and the 120,000 professionals of the British Expeditionary Force. The Kaiser spurred his commanders to "exterminate the treacherous English" and to walk over their "contemptible little army." The B.E.F. replied with shockingly accurate and rapid rifle fire. German numerical superiority finally forced the British and French to withdraw southward, but the price of German victory was high. That price rose further as the French commander in chief, the un-flappable "Papa" Joseph Joffre, gave up his offensive in Lorraine and switched forces by rail to face the main German attack as it swept down from Belgium. Schlieffen had simply assumed that the French would be too paralyzed to strike back; the French decided otherwise.

The Germans, footsore in the August heat, found by the end of the month that they lacked enough troops to swing west and north of Paris, as Schlieffen had origi-nally planned. And as the outermost Ger-man army swung south and east of Paris, it exposed its flank and rear to French forces in the city. Joseph Galliéni, con-queror of Tonkin and Madagascar, threw his troops against the German weak point, and marshaled the taxis of Paris to bring up reserves. The German commander on the spot frantically turned back to the northwest to counter Galliéni, and opened a fatal gap between his army and its neigh-bor. On September 8–9, spurred on by fierce demands from Joffre ("the honor of England is at stake"), the battered B.E.F. staggered northward across the Marne River into the gap between the two Ger-man armies. That break in the German line threatened disaster; Moltke's liaison officer and commanders on the spot pan-icked. On September 9 the exhausted Germans withdrew northward. Moltke suffered a nervous breakdown. France's defensive victory on the Marne meant that Europe faced a long war.

Moltke's replacement, the moody Er-ich von Falkenhayn, dissipated German reserves in a series of piecemeal attacks north of Paris. The B.E.F. and the French held with difficulty, but they held. This "race to the sea" ended in October–November 1914 with a huge slaughter in Flanders. At Langemarck, near Ypres, Fal-kenhayn committed scarcely trained vol-unteers, fresh from school or university, against the remnants of the B.E.F. It was a "massacre of the innocents." Little re-mained of the volunteers, of whom Ger-many had much need later, or of the B.E.F., the only source of experienced leaders for Britain's coming mass armies.

In mid-November Falkenhayn admitted to Bethmann Hollweg that the Imperial German Army was "a broken instrument," incapable of forcing a decision. By year's end Germany had lost almost a million dead and wounded, and France at least 900,000. Trenches and barbed wire stretched from the Channel to Switzerland. Until early 1918 the lines on the western front scarcely moved, despite unparal-leled carnage.

In the East the Germans had better luck. The "Russian Steamroller" rolled into East Prussia, and then broke down. When the outnumbered German defenders wa-vered, Moltke dragged a senior general, Paul von Hindenburg, out of retirement and gave him Ludendorff as chief of staff. Ludendorff, with the help of intercepted Russian radio communications, concen-trated his forces against one of the two Russian armies and crushed it at Tannen-berg by August 29. Russia lost 92,000 men and 400 guns. Then Ludendorff turned on the other Russian army and drove it back in disorder. Hindenburg and Ludendorff emerged as much-needed symbols of Ger-man invincibility.

Germany's ally fared less well. Aus-tria-Hungary's first invasion of Serbia was a fiasco, and the main Russian attack in Galicia drove Conrad von Hötzendorff's

Victors on the eastern front: Hindenburg (*left*) and Ludendorff.

armies back in confusion. But by the end of the year German troops had retrieved the situation. In the vast spaces of eastern Europe, movement was still possible, although here too siege warfare around key fortresses and rail junctions was frequent.

The War Spreads beyond Europe

To the south, one member of the Triple Alliance did not go to war in August 1914: Italy. Its grounds were entirely reasonable, for the alliance did not require it to share a war of aggression about which Berlin and Vienna had failed to consult it in advance. But Italian neutrality did not prevent the spread of the war beyond Europe. A German Mediterranean force, the battle cruiser *Goeben* and the cruiser *Breslau,* evaded an inept British pursuit and sought refuge at Constantinople in August 1914. The Turkish government then gambled on the victory of Germany, its longtime patron, over Russia, its perpetual enemy. When *Goeben* and *Breslau* bombarded Odessa in October, Russia declared war and attacked Turkey by land in the distant Caucasus. The entry of Turkey extended the war to the Middle East, from the Caucasus to Suez to the Persian Gulf.

Farther afield, British sea power was supreme. Britain swept the seas clear of German surface raiders by the end of 1914. And Britain's Grand Fleet did not charge into the mines and the submarine ambushes off the German fleet base of Wilhelmshaven, as Tirpitz had expected. Instead, it established blockade lines at the Channel and from Scotland to Norway, a "distant blockade" outside the reach of the fleet that Tirpitz had built. Britain, thanks to its geographic position, could cut Germany off from the outer world without fighting the fleet action on German terms for which Tirpitz had planned.

Thanks to sea power, the Dominions were free to join Britain, and the German colonies were easy prey. Even the Boer leaders cooperated with London. French and British forces seized Togo, Cameroons, and South-West Africa. Only in and around German East Africa (now Tanzania) did the Germans hold out. There,

until 1918, Paul von Lettow-Vorbeck and his native *askaris* repeatedly made fools of their British, Indian, British-African, and Boer pursuers. The "war of the white tribes" of Europe and the sight of Lettow-Vorbeck's *askaris* defeating whites proved a major stimulus to African nationalism.

In Asia the war gave Japan its opportunity to reverse the verdict of 1895, when the powers had forced it to give up its gains in China. Tokyo enthusiastically offered Britain its support in August 1914. It gobbled up the German outpost in Shandong, and the German island possessions in the Pacific that Australia did not. In January–May 1915 it imposed on China the "twenty-one demands," which included recognition of Japan's possession of Shandong and of its claims to southern Manchuria, Inner Mongolia, and an industrial region in central China. Britain persuaded Japan to "postpone" its most extreme demands, such as a right to impose advisers on China's central government. But diplomacy was an increasingly flimsy barrier against Japan's growing threat to China—and to Europe's domination of Asia and the Pacific.

THE INDUSTRIAL AND GEOGRAPHIC BALANCE

The reasons for the stalemate after September 1914 are clearer now than they were then. Railroads allowed the mobilization and movement to battle of immense armies. The size of those armies allowed the occupation of ever-wider defensive frontages. Finding an enemy flank against which to launch a decisive attack, as the 1914 "race to the sea" demonstrated, was almost impossible. And on the battlefield itself, the storm of steel and lead, the ever-thicker coils of barbed wire, and the absence of transport for troops, ammunition, and food immobilized the mass armies. Cars, trucks, and motorcycles were neither bulletproof nor available in adequate numbers. The defenders' reserves, thanks to railroad, telephone, and radio, could always reach a threatened point faster than the attackers could break through on foot. And air reconnaissance and air photography enabled defenders to detect offensive preparations. Strategic mobility checkmated tactical decision, firepower crushed movement, communications and air reconnaissance removed surprise.

Two other factors made the war of 1914–18 an unprecedented struggle of attrition. First, although the general staffs of Europe had largely ignored it, the U.S. Civil War had demonstrated that wars between industrial powers could last for years even when one contender was far stronger industrially than the other. In the absence of striking military ineptitude of the sort the French had displayed in 1870, only attrition could decide the outcome. And the coalition nature of the 1914–18 war likewise prolonged the struggle. As in the world wars of the eighteenth century but unlike 1859, 1866, and 1870–71, the belligerents of 1914–18 had great-power allies. When the weak faltered, their allies usually sustained them. And although Russia collapsed in 1917, the United States simultaneously intervened to shore up a flagging France and Britain with money, food, munitions, and troops.

The keys to victory in this world struggle were industrial might, geographic position, and access to raw materials. The three Allied powers, Britain, France, and Russia, had in 1913 a total industrial potential a third greater than that of the Central Powers, Germany and Austria-Hungary. But the Central Powers were superior to France and Russia alone and after 1914 probably also to Britain and France combined. The Schlieffen Plan had at least deprived France of a fifth of its wheat, half of its coal, and two-thirds of its iron production. Only U.S. intervention in 1917 gave the Allies the better than two-to-one margin in total industrial power that brought victory.

In geographic position, the Central Powers enjoyed one major advantage and one serious but not insuperable drawback. The advantage was the result of Germany's two-front predicament; German possession of "interior lines" allowed swift transfer of forces from west to east to meet successive threats. Given the stalemate at the tactical level, that was no small advantage. The Allies, conversely, were unable to link Russia, their major source of manpower, with the weapons and ammunition produced in the West.

But "encirclement" was also a major disadvantage for the Central Powers: it cut them off from the world market. Shortages of vital materials such as nitrates, rubber, and copper set in immediately. The Germans at first coped. Holland and Scandinavia served as channels for German imports and exports. A German Jewish research chemist, Fritz Haber, broke the nitrate bottleneck with his nitrogen-fixation process, perfected in 1913: the inexhausible nitrogen available in the atmosphere gave Germany the explosives it needed to continue the war.

In the long run, Germany suffered. Command of the sea enabled Britain and France to draw on munitions made in the United States and on loans to pay for them. The United States, at least at first, would have gladly done business with the Germans as well. But German shipping remained locked in the Baltic and North Sea. The loss of overseas food and fertilizer imports, the forced slaughter of livestock to save fodder, and farm labor shortages crippled German agriculture. First potatoes and then turnips became the staple of the German diet. The British blockade failed to paralyze German industrial production, but it did slowly sap civilian morale.

On balance, the Germans had the advantage until 1918. German possession of northern France forced the Allies to take the offensive. Given the devastating effects of defensive firepower and the dogged ineptitude of most Allied generals, that meant immense slaughter for no gain. Geography isolated Russia and political and industrial weakness made it increasingly vulnerable. Finally, the quality of German leadership at the tactical and operational levels compensated for the Central Powers' two-to-three disadvantage in total potential against the Triple Entente. Germany, by 1917, had virtually won the war it had started. It went under only because it started another war—with another continent, the United States.

POLITICS, SOCIETY, AND THE "HOME FRONT"

All the powers, except perhaps Italy and Rumania, entered the war with the certainty—in some cases bogus—that they were victims of unprovoked aggression. That conviction—and the sense of sudden release from the cares, frustrations, and social tensions of Europe's rapidly changing yet narrowly class-bound societies—brought widespread rejoicing. Especially in the cities, reservists marched to the stations through crowds waving flags and pelting them with flowers. As the trains rolled, the troops chalked "To Paris!" or "To Berlin!" on the boxcars. They expected to be home before the autumn leaves fell.

Those who lived through the August days never forgot the spontaneous outpouring of a national enthusiasm that momentarily abolished social distinctions. An assistant to Bethmann Hollweg noted with wonder on August 14: "War, war, the *Volk* has risen! . . . All deeply joyful, to live, for once, caught up in a great cause." And a recent immigrant to Munich from Austria-Hungary named Adolf Hitler later wrote in his memoirs that "overpowered by stormy enthusiasm, I fell down on my knees and thanked Heaven from an overflowing heart for granting me the good fortune of being permitted to live at this time." Then as later, he expressed a widely felt emotion.

That emotion guaranteed national cohesion across class and party lines. The socialist Second International collapsed amid mutual recriminations by its members. In Germany, the government declared a political truce, the *Burgfrieden* ("peace inside the fortress"). Even revolutionary Social Democrats, at the request of the SPD leadership, voted for the first war appropriations. Good Marxists could not refuse a seemingly defensive war against tsarist Russia, the European state Marx had hated above all others. But Germany's unity was short-lived.

For the Reich, despite its public claims, fought to create an immense central European empire as the basis for German world domination. In September, as the German armies began their retreat from the Marne, Bethmann Hollweg drafted a confidential memorandum setting forth Germany's aims: annexations in France and Belgium that would reduce those nations to vassalage, the absorption of Luxembourg, and the creation of a central European customs union that would guarantee Germany's economic as well as military supremacy on the Continent. German war aims in eastern Europe were even more voracious. And the leaders of the Reich looked beyond Europe to vast African annexations and to a victory that would give Britain's world position to Germany. The war, as the chancellor's assistant noted in his diary in mid-1916, was in part a "struggle with England for world mastery."

Public discussion of Germany's aims, despite the attempts of Bethmann Hollweg to still it, increasingly broke into the open. By 1915 politicians, business figures, and pan-Germans were vying with one another to claim ever-larger areas of Europe and ever-tighter control over the small states, Germany's vassals-to-be. Racist pan-Germans urged the removal of inconvenient Poles from the annexed lands. Much of the Left soon concluded that the war was a war of conquest. The Right coupled demands for total victory and immense annexations with refusal to reform the inequitable Prussian franchise, which weighed votes according to wealth. Germany's lack of cohesion at home was its weak point. But only military defeat could transform weakness into collapse.

In France, all political forces joined a *Union Sacrée* against the German invader. In Britain, German aggression against Belgium utterly discredited the Cobdenite pacifist Liberals. Volunteers swamped the British army. In Austria-Hungary, quarreling nationalities loyally answered the call to the Habsburg colors. Even the Russian autocracy gained a brief reprieve: the prewar wave of strikes subsided and the peasant reservists marched. Only Italy, which chose intervention in 1915 without disguising it as national defense, faced from the beginning an internal struggle against those who failed to see the necessity of war.

Parliamentary regimes showed greater staying power than their autocratic counterparts. Warfare in the age of the masses required popular support and only political participation guaranteed that support. That was one secret of France's survival, despite the death or wounding of 60 percent of all Frenchmen who reported for duty between 1914 and 1918. Britain, with amazing unanimity, abolished cherished traditions of *laissez-faire*. When volunteers began to fall short in 1916, the British cabinet took the radical step of conscription. Conversely, once the war turned sour in 1915–16, internal social and national tensions placed Austria-Hungary, Russia, Italy, and even Germany at risk.

Parliamentary regimes also proved surprisingly successful at directing their war efforts. At first the soldiers dominated in Britain, France, and Italy, thanks to their alleged professional wisdom. But much of that wisdom proved wrong. When the generals failed to force a decision, the civilians took a hand. In December 1916 the feeble—or too humane—Asquith gave way to a Liberal-Conservative-Labour coalition under Lloyd George, a man known to have "fire in his belly." Lloyd George asserted, not always successfully, London's control over Britain's obstinate commander on the western front, Sir Douglas Haig. The French Chamber made Joffre a figurehead in December 1916. The national emergency of 1917 made the cynical and iron-willed Clemenceau, "the Tiger" of the Radicals, prime minister and virtual dictator by consent of the Chamber and the nation. Vittorio Emanuele Orlando, a less compelling figure, assumed some of the same powers in Italy's dark winter of 1917–18.

The autocracies took two paths. In Russia and Austria-Hungary, the monarchies held jealously to power, while inefficiency and defeat sapped their store of prestige and public trust. The essential question on the eastern front until 1917 was which of the two great empires would win the race to military collapse and political disintegration. Germany traveled another road. The Kaiser's bloodcurdling speeches and blustering orders of the day imperfectly concealed his weak nerves.

By 1916 he had become a figurehead for Hindenburg and Ludendorff.

Socially, the war marked the real beginning of the "century of the common man." Until 1914 aristocrats and landowners had dominated the bureaucracies, diplomatic services, and officer corps of Europe. The war did not end that domination everywhere, but it made a mighty start. The military aristocracies paid in blood for their privileges. Pomeranian Junkers, Ulster landowners, Russian nobles, Hungarian gentry, and the impoverished aristocracy of France led their peasant soldiers from in front, and suffered accordingly. Noble families without daughters died out, their sons fallen on the Marne, in Galicia, or in the great 1915–16 battles of attrition in the West. By 1916 most of the professional officers of 1914 were dead or disabled. Those who survived graduated gratefully to staff jobs and high commands.

The middle classes took their place as company and battalion officers. The lower middle classes, which in peacetime had rarely aspired to ranks higher than sergeant, suddenly became lieutenants. These "temporary gentlemen" suffered the sneers of the officers' mess at their accents and bearing. The Germans created a special indeterminate rank of "officer substitute" to avoid giving deserving sergeants

Britain recruits a mass army, 1915: the appeal (*above*), and the result (*below*).

commissions. But the new men proved themselves in battle. The Great War, along with death and bereavement, brought social promotion to an entire class. That sudden increase in social mobility, along with the classless society of shared danger at the front, was the origin of powerful myths. Finally, the war integrated the peasantry into the nations of the middle and upper classes far more effectively than universal schooling or even peacetime military service had done. Enforced travel, mixing with men from different regions and backgrounds, and above all the experience of fighting together for the national cause made Pomeranian, Swabian, or Bavarian peasants into Germans and made Bretons, Normans, or Gascons into Frenchmen.

At home, industrial mass warfare dictated a new sort of labor force. With men at the front, women and unskilled adolescents joined the work force in numbers not seen since the early industrial revolution in Britain. Almost a quarter of the workers in France's war industries were women, as were 60 percent of the workers in Britain's munitions plants. British craft unions fought jealously against this "dilution" of the work force, but lost. War work expanded women's horizons and gave them a new sense of confidence and competence.

Industrial mass warfare also dictated an unprecedented intensity and extent of state action. The autocracies already had strong traditions of "state capitalism." The democracies mobilized their economies with similar and often more drastic methods: a bewildering variety of war-production and raw-materials allocation boards and bureaucracies, and close coordination between the state, the labor unions, and the military. The wartime industrial state seemed to confirm Weber's depressing vision of the "iron cage" of bureaucracy and furnished the model for the welfare state of the later twentieth century.

Finally, mass warfare dictated the mobilization of mass opinion. German propaganda damned the barbaric British "hunger blockade" and stressed the German world cultural mission that over-rode the rights of "parasitic" small nations such as Belgium. British, French, and (after 1917) U.S. propaganda dwelt on examples of "Hun" barbarism that included poison gas and Zeppelin or submarine warfare against noncombatants and neutrals. Opinion was as powerful as high explosive, and both sides sought to exploit it to the full.

ATTRITION, 1915–16

Deadlock, 1915

Throughout 1915 the powers made confused attempts to break the unexpected stalemate. The Germans were most successful. In the West, Falkenhayn stood on the defensive. He remained so until 1916, except for a brief experiment of Fritz Haber's with chlorine gas near Ypres in April 1915. The German command failed to mass reserves to exploit the unexpected gap the gas opened in the Franco-British lines. Introduction of this new and apparently barbaric weapon profited the Germans nothing and mightily helped the Allies in the battle for neutral opinion.

For most of the year, Britain and France attacked. Their strategic goal was to drive Germany out of France and win the war; that dictated the offensive. But their generals had no better method for restoring movement to the battlefield than steadily increasing weights of high-explosive shell to blast the German wire flat and silence the machine guns. At Neuve Chappelle, and Loos, and in the repeated French "pushes" in Artois and Champagne, and Allies suffered repeated bloody reverses and gained virtually no ground. The Germans became ever cannier at sheltering their troops in dugouts and in positioning reserves and artillery in depth. In 1915 the French lost 1,500,000 dead and wounded, Britain 300,000, and the German defenders perhaps 875,000.

In eastern Europe, Generals August von Mackensen and Hans von Seeckt broke through the Russian front in Galicia. By September 1915 they had sent the tsar's armies reeling back 300 miles with a loss of 1.7 million dead, wounded, and captured. Yet Falkenhayn still did not believe that the eastern front offered a chance of decisive victory. He halted his advance, although the immense defeat of 1915 had opened wide the fractures between Russia's rulers and their subjects that the German declaration of war had temporarily closed in 1914. The Germans, totally discarding what little remained of European traditions of monarchical and noble solidarity, attempted to widen those fractures by covert action. SPD leaders with ties to their Russian counterparts funneled large sums into Russia to create unrest among the Russian Empire's workers and border nationalities. And in the Middle East, German agents based in Turkey sought with some success to raise Islam against the Allies.

Far to the southeast, new fronts opened. Britain, thanks to the genius for war of the impulsive young Winston Churchill at the Admiralty, attempted to seize Constantinople and open a year-round warm-water supply route to Russia. But the muddled British high command was unequal to the task of coordinating a simultaneous land and sea assault. The British navy, using expendable pre-Dreadnought battleships, failed to force its way past the shore batteries and mines defending the Dardanelles in February–March 1915. The Turks ran out of ammunition just as the British navy pulled back. Then it was the turn of the army. British and Australian landings on the Gallipoli Peninsula in April soon bogged down; the Turks proved unexpectedly stubborn and skillful. The only British success was the brilliantly planned and coordinated evacuation of the failed beachheads by January 1916; France and Britain retained a toe-hold at Salonika in Greece.

The Gallipoli landings, before British bungling became apparent, moved the least of the great powers to take a hand. In October 1914, Salandra, Italy's prime minister, had incautiously announced that henceforth "holy national egoism"—*sacro egoismo*—would guide Italy's course. In winter–spring 1914–15 he proved as good as his word. Salandra and his foreign minister, Sidney Sonnino, secretly auctioned Italy to the two groups of powers. The Allied bid was the higher: Trento,

Trieste, and Dalmatia (where Italian-speakers were a tiny minority) from Austria-Hungary, a piece of Turkey, and unspecified colonial gains. On May 24, 1915, Salandra, Sonnino and King Victor Emmanuel III took Italy to war against the will of its parliament. Italy's armies crossed the Austro-Hungarian border and ran headlong into long-prepared defenses on the Isonzo River. There the Italians stalled, despite repeated bloody offensives.

And in fall and winter 1915 the Germans confirmed the verdict of Gallipoli. Bulgaria joined the Central Powers after an auction similar to that in Rome. German, Austro-Hungarian, and Bulgarian armies attacked Serbia from three sides. By luring Bulgaria into the war and by smashing Serbia, Germany had secured its communications through the Balkans to Turkey. Russia would receive no Allied aid through the Straits. Only the icy sea route to Murmansk and Archangel and the single track of the Trans-Siberian Railway linked Russia to the West.

Yet by December 1915 Falkenhayn was not satisfied. Germany's immense losses had brought it no closer to its goal: a strategic decision over one of its three adversaries. In his 1915 "Christmas Memorandum," Falkenhayn concluded that Britain was the keystone of the enemy

Between the Turks and the sea: Gallipoli, 1915.

Pétain of Verdun.

alliance. To strike it required the intensification of submarine warfare against British and neutral merchant shipping, which the Germans had introduced in February 1915, and of terror attacks on British civilian targets with Zeppelin airships.

Falkenhayn identified French morale as Germany's second, and most promising, target. The collapse of France would "strike England's best sword from her hand." The method he chose was attrition, and he sought an objective "for the retention of which the French leadership will commit their last man. If they do this, France's strength will be bled white, since once committed to such a course there is no alternative for them, whether we reach the objective itself or not." Limited German infantry attacks would pin the French defenders under a giant mincing machine: the German artillery. Falkenhayn baptized

his brainchild Operation GERICHT— "execution place."

1916: Verdun and the Somme

On February 21, 1916, the army of the German Crown Prince attacked the fortified city of Verdun at the hinge of the French line. More than 2,000 German guns tore the French to pieces with the heaviest artillery fire so far seen. As the French gave way, Joffre appointed Henri Pétain, a master of the defensive, to command Verdun. "Courage! We'll get them!" was his watchword. In the course of the next eight months, over three-quarters of the French army passed down the muddy truck route to Verdun and emerged shattered.

Yet France held. By May 1916, despite German innovations such as flamethrowers, phosgene gas shells, and masses of fighter aircraft, Falkenhayn himself was caught fast in the snare he had rigged for the French. The Germans had themselves invested so much prestige, morale, and blood at Verdun that they had to take the city. The French fought them to a standstill by July, then counterattacked in October, November, and December to regain the lost ground. Verdun cost the French 377,000 dead, wounded, and missing and the Germans at least 337,000. Neither army, but especially that of France, was ever the same again.

The agony of France had repercussions. As in 1914, Russia sought to help its ally. Russia's most brilliant general, Alexei Brusilov, launched a surprise offensive in the Ukraine in June. Austria-Hungary's eastern armies collapsed; the Russians took 200,000 prisoners. Conrad von Hötzendorff had to break off a promising "punitive expedition" against his favorite victim, Italy. Falkenhayn loosened his grip at Verdun and sent divisions eastward to prop up Austria-Hungary.

Then, on July 1, 1916, Sir Douglas Haig attacked the German defenses north and south of the Somme River. On a day of "intense blue summer beauty," after a seven-day bombardment of unprecedented weight, the infantrymen of Britain's volunteer "New Armies" climbed

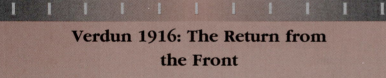

Verdun 1916: The Return from the Front

I have never seen anything more heart-rending than the passage of the two regiments of the brigade that flowed past me on that road [from Verdun] the whole day long. . . .

First came skeletons of companies, sometimes with a surviving officer in front, propping himself up with a cane; all walked or rather moved with short steps, bent knees forward, folded into themselves, staggering as if gripped by drink. Then came groups that were perhaps squads, or even platoons; there was no telling. They advanced, head down, staring blankly, crushed under their rucksacks, holding by the slings rifles red with mud. The color of their faces scarcely differed from that of their over-coats. Mud had covered everything and dried, then more mud had covered them once more. . . . Cars thundered past in close-packed columns, scattering this pitiable flotsam, survivors of the great slaughter. But [the troops] said nothing, made no sound. They had lost even the strength to complain. . . .

Some reservists, from the roadside, looked on somberly. . . . I heard one saying: "It's not an army; it's corpses!". . . . Two of the reservists cried silently, like women.

From Georges Gaudy, Les trous d'obus de Verdun (février-août 1916) *(Paris: Plon, 1922), pp. 233–34 (translation by M. Knox).*

from their trenches. Loaded with a minimum of 66 pounds of gear per man, aligned in rigid formations, they walked toward the German wire, which in most areas the British artillery had failed to cut. As the British bombardment lifted, German machine-gunners scrambled unhurt from their deep concrete-lined dugouts and massacred the British infantry. German artillery observers had never before seen such tempting targets. The French, further south, advanced in small groups, taking cover wherever possible. They did rather better.

Haig's army lost 57,470 dead and wounded—nearly half the men engaged—on the first day. But Haig, "brilliant to the top of his army boots" (as Lloyd George later put it) remained convinced that German losses were so severe that the enemy was bound to crack. Using the same unimaginative tactics, he persevered until the battlefield became a sea of icy mud in November. The maximum British penetration was less than six miles. British losses were 419,000, those of the French, over 200,000. The German defenders lost more than half a million.

As Brusilov's push petered out and the British pressed on the Somme, a sudden emergency led to Falkenhayn's downfall. Rumania, like Italy, had been associated with the Triple Alliance; it had likewise chosen neutrality in 1914. Now, in August 1916, Brusilov's success moved the Rumanians to join the Allies. Their timing was remarkably poor. The Kaiser dismissed Falkenhayn as chief of staff but gave him Rumania as a consolation prize. Falkenhayn, Mackensen, and Seeckt rolled up the inept Rumanians within four months.

At German supreme army headquarters, a new team took control—Hindenburg and Ludendorff. Hindenburg, the "wooden Titan," was content to be a symbol of national resistance. Ludendorff, the dominant partner, brought a new ethos to the supreme command, the ethos of the pan-German "right opposition." He despised the Kaiser as a weakling. His devious aide, Colonel Max Bauer, cultivated pan-Germans and right radicals. The Kaiser feared his nominal subordinates;

Hindenburg and Ludendorff alone commanded the confidence of the masses. Once he had appointed them, the Kaiser could remove them only at the risk of his throne.

The new team had two recipes for victory. First, total war demanded total mobilization. Under the "Hindenburg Program," Germany planned to double its production of munitions and treble that of artillery and machine guns. The army, with the assistance of the SPD unions and of the industrialists, applied compulsory service to the work force. Substitute—*ersatz*—materials would make up for shortages. Germany, by a supreme effort of will, would submerge its opponents in fire and steel. The new team's second innovation was to stake Germany's future on one card, in the manner of Schlieffen. That card was the submarine.

THE WAR IN THE BALANCE, 1917

Germany Challenges America

The U-boat question had been long in ripening. Tirpitz had realized by late 1914 that the British distant blockade had neutralized his battle fleet. He therefore pressed for the use of submarines, which he had neglected before 1914, against British merchant shipping. But submarines were effective only if used from ambush. Attempts to board and search merchant ships before sinking them, as international law required, might expose the surfaced submarine to deadly fire from camouflaged guns on the merchant ship. The Germans therefore adopted in February 1915 a policy of "sink on sight" around the British isles. On May 7, 1915, Germany's U-20 sank the British liner *Lusitania* off the southern tip of Ireland and killed 1,198 people, of whom 128 were U.S. civilians. The Germans struck a medal to commemorate their feat.

President Woodrow Wilson, a grim former academic of messianic bent, had no intention of leading the United States into war. Unlike his rival, "Teddy" Roosevelt of the Rough Riders, Wilson was proud of being "too proud to fight." He

OCEAN STEAMSHIPS.

CUNARD

EUROPE VIA LIVERPOOL
LUSITANIA

Fastest and Largest Steamer
now in Atlantic Service Sails
SATURDAY, MAY 1, 10 A. M.

Transylvania, Fri., May 7, 5 P.M.
Orduna, - - Tues.,May 18, 10 A.M.
Tuscania, - - Fri., May 21, 5 P.M.
LUSITANIA, Sat., May 29, 10 A.M.
Transylvania, Fri., June 4, 5 P.M.

Gibraltar—Genoa—Naples—Piraeus
S.S. Carpathia, Thur., May 13, Noon

ROUND THE WORLD TOURS
Through bookings to all principal Ports
of the World.
Company's Office, 21-24 State St., N. Y.

NOTICE!

TRAVELLERS intending to
embark on the Atlantic voyage
are reminded that a state of
war exists between Germany
and her allies and Great Britain
and her allies; that the zone of
war includes the waters adjacent to the British Isles; that,
in accordance with formal notice given by the Imperial German Government, vessels flying
the flag of Great Britain, or of
any of her allies, are liable to
destruction in those waters and
that travellers sailing in the
war zone on ships of Great
Britain or her allies do so at
their own risk.

IMPERIAL GERMAN EMBASSY

WASHINGTON, D. C., APRIL 22, 1915

U-boat warfare: Germany warns
neutral travelers that it will sink
the *Lusitania* if it can (*above*).
U-boats at sea in the
Mediterranean (*below*).

was soon to run for reelection in 1916 on the slogan "He kept us out of the war." But the *Lusitania* outrage prompted even Wilson to bombard Berlin with stern summonses to obey international law.

The United States had long been suspicious of Imperial Germany. Germany's treatment of Belgium and use of poison gas had appalled American opinion. The *Lusitania* sinking swung America heavily against the Central Powers. Bethmann Hollweg persuaded the Kaiser and the navy to retreat and postpone confrontation. Then Falkenhayn, in his "Christmas Memorandum," urged the renewal of unrestricted U-boat warfare. In February 1916, the Germans synchronized "intensified" submarine warfare around Britain with their attack at Verdun. A further sinking involving U.S. citizens followed inevitably in March, and Wilson's typewriter clattered threateningly once more. The Germans again retreated. Bethmann Hollweg, at least, was now aware that further sinkings might goad Wilson into "a sort of crusade against Germany."

The German navy tried to make do with surface action. On May 31, 1916, Admiral Reinhard Scheer took the German High Seas Fleet out. But the British had intercepted Scheer's radio messages, and Admiral John Jellicoe's Grand Fleet was waiting off Jutland. The German Dreadnoughts and their British rivals faced one another for less than thirty minutes, until

the outnumbered Scheer frantically turned away into clouds and smoke and ran for Wilhelmshaven. The Germans lost fewer ships, and claimed victory. But the British were the strategic victors, for they still controlled the exits from the North Sea. And the Germans concluded from their narrow escape that surface action could not break the blockade.

Thus when Hindenburg and Ludendorff arrived on the scene in August 1916, they found the navy once more pressing for a decision to unleash the submarines. Tirpitz had resigned over the issue in March and had raised a fanatical public outcry for U-boat war. To buy time and to preempt a mediation attempt by Wilson, Bethmann Hollweg launched a Central Powers "peace offer" in mid-December 1916. The offer failed to mention the freeing of Belgium, and was thus unacceptable to the Allies. Its inevitable rejection, Bethmann Hollweg apparently hoped, might turn Wilson's wrath on Paris and London. That would give Germany a convincing pretext for launching unrestricted submarine warfare.

At the Castle of Pless in Silesia, on January 9, 1917, the Germans took the decision that doomed them. The navy sang its usual tune: U-boats would bring Britain "to its knees" in a few months. Hindenburg and Ludendorff argued fiercely for action, regardless of consequences. They made the same error with the United States that Moltke had made with Britain in 1914. Because their new enemy had no mass army, they assumed that it was safe to defy it. Germany's U-boats received orders to sink all shipping around Britain after midnight on January 31, 1917. Wilson broke relations with Germany but still hoped to keep the United States neutral in order to mediate a "peace without victory."

But by 1917 the powers had invested too much blood and money to settle for any peace short of victory or defeat. Nor, thanks to the Germans, could Wilson remain neutral for long. The Reich foreign secretary, Arthur Zimmermann, proved that the stresses of total war had caused Berlin to take leave of its senses. Using the telegraph channel that Wilson had thoughtfully provided the Germans for possible peace negotiations, he secretly cabled the German ambassador in Mexico City. The message offered the Mexicans a military alliance and the recovery of Texas and the Southwest. The British intercepted it, deciphered it, and delivered it to Wilson along with proofs of its authenticity. It arrived in Washington at the end of February, along with news that a U-boat had sunk the British liner *Laconia* with the death of three Americans, two of them women.

Wilson gave the Zimmermann telegram to the press on March 1. Zimmermann compounded his amazing blunder by admitting that the telegram was genuine. Even voices of the isolationist Midwest, such as the Chicago *Tribune* and the Cleveland *Plain Dealer,* accepted war. A Germany that encouraged Mexico to attack the United States was intolerable. On April 2, Wilson, to repeated applause, addressed Congress: "The world must be made safe for democracy." The United States declared war on Imperial Germany. The New World was coming belatedly to restore the balance of the old.

The Russian Revolutions: February and October

While Wilson debated his course, events in eastern Europe disclosed the full magnitude of Germany's blunder in provoking the United States. Russia now ceased to count as a belligerent, and Germany faced only a weakening France and Britain. In 1916 munitions strikes paralyzed industry in Moscow and Petrograd (the new non-German name given to St. Petersburg in 1914). Russia's railroads broke down. Refugees and wounded soldiers swamped Russia's ramshackle administrative machinery. Food ran short in the cities; conscription and government purchases of food at artifically low fixed prices alienated the peasantry. The failure of the Brusilov offensive to decide the war and the antics of the tsarina's favorite, the faith-healing charlatan Grigorii Rasputin, lost the autocracy what little public support it still possessed. Strikes and food riots by workers and housewives in Petrograd

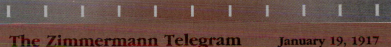

The Zimmermann Telegram   January 19, 1917

[To German Ambassador, Mexico City]
Top Secret—Decipher Personally

We intend on 1 February to begin unrestricted U-boat warfare. We shall nevertheless attempt to keep America neutral. Should that not succeed, we propose to Mexico an alliance on the following basis. Joint conduct of the war. Joint peace settlement. Lavish financial support and agreement on our part that Mexico should reconquer its lost territories in Texas, New Mexico, and Arizona. We leave settlement of the details to your Excellency.

Your Excellency should disclose the above offer in the greatest secrecy to the President [of Mexico, Don Venustiano Carranza] as soon as outbreak of war with the United States seems certain, and add the suggestion that he should on his own initiative invite Japan to join the alliance, and [that he should] simultaneously mediate between Japan and ourselves.

Please call to the President's attention the fact that merciless use of our U-boats now offers the prospect of forcing England to make peace within a few months.

Acknowledge receipt.

Zimmermann

From Herbert Michaelis, Ernst Schraepler, eds., Ursachen und Folgen vom deutschen Zusammenbruch 1918 und 1945 *(Berlin: Dokumenten-Verlag Dr. Herbert Wendler, 1958), Vol. 1, pp. 151–52 (translation by M. Knox).*

challenged the autocracy in early March 1917 (February by the "old style" Julian calendar that symbolized Russia's isolation from Europe). The peasant soldiers deserted the autocracy on March 12; it fell without a struggle.

A provisional government of liberals, of Lenin's Menshevik rivals, and of Socialist Revolutionaries attempted to fill the vacuum this "February Revolution" had left. But in Petrograd the Soviets, or councils of workers, soldiers, and sailors, now controlled the streets. On March 14, 1917, the central Petrograd Soviet addressed to the war-weary world a proclamation that blamed "monarchs, landholders, and bankers" for the war and demanded an immediate end to the "horrible slaughter."

"The Russian Ruling House":
a contemporary cartoon of
Rasputin manipulating Tsar
Nicholas II and Tsarina
Alexandra.

The new master: Lenin in
Moscow, 1917.

Similar appeals in 1915 and 1916 from the wrangling representatives of the parties of the socialist Second International had lacked resonance. The call of the Petrograd Soviet was different: it came from a body with power. And its claim to world ideological leadership conflicted with the call for "war to end war" that Wilson was soon to issue from Washington.

Soon after the Petrograd Soviet's peace message, the Germans made a further contribution to the disruption of Russia. They shipped Lenin and a few chosen Bolsheviks home to Russia from their place of exile in neutral Switzerland in a sealed boxcar ("like a plague bacillus," as Winston Churchill later observed). Lenin arrived at Petrograd's Finland Station on April 16, 1917, and dictated to his party a few simple policies: support of the Soviets, implacable hostility to the provisional government, and an immediate end to the war.

In June 1917, Lenin launched a slogan of vast appeal to the peasantry, which made up 80 percent of Russia's population, and to the overwhelming majority of Russia's 7 million troops: "Bread, Peace, Land." His aim was as simple as his slogan. He proposed to seize power and hurl backward Russia directly into socialism. Revolutionary breakthrough in Russia would then trigger the revolutions in western Europe and the world without which a socialist Russia, isolated, would inevitably perish.

The provisional government was divided and inexperienced, thanks to the stifling effect the autocracy had had on Russian political life. It shared power uneasily with the Petrograd Soviet while seeking to continue the war against Germany. The government's most conspicuous personality, the Socialist Revolutionary Alexander Kerensky, identified himself with a final bungled offensive in July 1917. Bolshevik appeals spread through the army and undermined what little discipline remained. Peasant soldiers, weary of war and obsessed with the notion that revolution meant the long-awaited final redivision of the *mir* land (see p. 720), "voted with their feet." Many

went home; those that stayed demanded an end to the fighting.

A Petrograd insurrection against the provisional government in July showed that the Bolsheviks were gaining ground. Their unyielding utopian radicalism was better attuned to the mood in the cities than their more responsible or faint-hearted opponents. Kerensky arrested some Bolsheviks but lacked the ruthlessness or perhaps the power to suppress them outright. Then, in August, General Lavr Kornilov, Kerensky's army commander in chief, marched on Petrograd to restore order. Workers and mutinuous troops from the capital persuaded Kornilov's forces to defect.

Kornilov's failed coup from the Right further weakened Kerensky and his allies. Mensheviks and Socialist Revolutionaries, by their association with the provisional government and the continuing war, lost much of the popular support they had enjoyed in Petrograd in the spring. The Bolsheviks painted the disintegrating provisional government and its parties as Kornilov's accomplices; Bolshevik numbers swelled.

On November 6–7 (October 24–25 by the Russian calendar), Lenin and his dashing ex-Menshevik associate, Leon Trotsky, launched their own coup from the Left. The Military Revolutionary Committee of the Petrograd Soviet, of which Trotsky had gained control, seized key points with picked troops. On the evening of November 7 (October 25), the provisional government's last stronghold, the tsar's Winter Palace, fell. Kerensky fled. The Bolsheviks had acted in the name of the Soviets against the provisional government. The Bolsheviks soon infiltrated or cowed the Soviets while taking for themselves the mantle of legitimacy that the Soviets provided. And in January 1918 Bolshevik bayonets dispersed Russia's first and only democratically elected parliament, the Constituent Assembly.

The Bolsheviks had won less than 25 percent of the seats in the Constituent Assembly. But they had guns and organization, and they briefly commanded a popular majority in Petrograd and Moscow. Above all, they moved swiftly to institutionalize terror. In December 1917 Lenin's security officer, the fanatical Pole Feliks Dzerzhinsky, became chief of a new organization, the "All-Russian Extraordinary Commission for the Struggle Against Counterrevolution and Sabotage," known by its acronym of CHEKA. Its task was to exterminate the enemies of the revolution; their place, in Lenin's words, was "against the wall."

In January 1918 the Socialist Revolutionaries, whose peasant loyalists had given them more votes than any other party, fought back against the dissolution of the Constituent Assembly. They rose against Bolshevik dictatorship—and Lenin and Dzerzhinsky massacred them. In July 1918 the Bolsheviks likewise shot—with Lenin's approval—the ex-Tsar Nicholas II and his entire family. By that point Lenin and his CHEKA had discarded the concept of individual responsibility for actions, the basis of Western and even tsarist law. The CHEKA defined its enemies by class, and killed them not as individuals but as members of a category. The bourgeoisie was "objectively"—by its very existence—guilty of counterrevolution. That was a logic not seen in action in the West since the September massacres of 1792 and the Jacobin Terror of 1793–94. It was the logic of genocide.

Terror worked well internally. Externally, Lenin faced an immediate crisis. The German masses did not overthrow their rulers in response to the "Decree on Peace" that Lenin and Trotsky published immediately after the October Revolution. Instead, Russia's peasant armies continued to melt, while the Germans advanced toward Petrograd. Lenin therefore sought a breathing space for the Revolution, to give time for the western European and world revolution he unrealistically expected; he had predicted in September 1917, before taking power, that "to secure an armistice means *to conquer the world.*"

Lenin secured that armistice from the Germans in December and began negotiations at Brest-Litovsk in Poland for a Russo-German peace. But the Bolshevik negotiators soon found that self-determi-

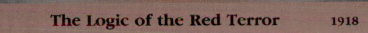

The Logic of the Red Terror   1918

M. Y. Latsis, the terrifying Latvian who was Dzerzhinsky's chief subordinate at the CHEKA, spelled out in a 1918 newspaper article the logic under which his organization acted.

We are not carrying out war against individuals. We are exterminating the bourgeoisie as a class. We aren't looking for evidence or witnesses to reveal deeds or words against the Soviet power. The first question which we ask is—to what class does he belong, what are his origins, upbringing, education, or profession? These questions define the fate of the accused. This is the essence of Red Terror.

Quoted in Harrison Salisbury, Black Night, White Snow: Russia's Revolutions, 1905–1917 *(Garden City: Doubleday, 1978), p. 565.*

nation, as the Germans interpreted it, meant stripping away the conquests of all tsars since the seventeenth century. The border peoples, from Finland through the Ukraine to the Caucasus, were to become independent under German "protection." When the Bolsheviks refused, the Germans resumed their effortless advance on Petrograd. Lenin then dragooned his wavering comrades into signing; the Revolution had to swallow the German terms if it hoped to survive. On March 3, 1918, the Bolsheviks signed the treaty of Brest-Litovsk, which deprived Russia of a quarter of its European territory, a third of its population, more than half of its coal and iron, and a third of its industry. But it left the Bolsheviks in power.

The Crisis of the Allies, 1917

The collapse of Russia came close to wrecking the Allies. The October Revolution, which took Russia out of the war for good, followed a series of catastrophes. Germany's submarines almost throttled Britain's Atlantic supply line between March and August 1917. British food stocks, despite rationing, fell to a mere two months' supply. But the German navy soon found that it was unable to sink ships faster than the United States could build them. Lloyd George stormed into the Admiralty and compelled it to set up convoys, which it had originally despised as a "defensive" and therefore inferior form of war. Mine barriers partially closed the exits from the North Sea even to U-boats. The U.S. Navy, with its eight Dreadnoughts and its indispensable escort craft, reinforced the British.

As the U-boats battered Britain, France faltered. Joffre's replacement, Robert Nivelle, was convinced that he had found the secret of victory: surprise. The discovery was not original, and both sides could use it. In Operation ALBERICH, named after the malevolent dwarf in Wagner's *Ring of the Nibelungen,* Ludendorff secretly withdrew to a new line 12 to 25 miles behind the original front. The Germans had a further surprise for the French: flexible defensive tactics far superior to the thin and brittle trench lines of 1914–16. The German "defense in depth"—deep belts of strongpoints interlocked by fire, coordinated artillery barrages, and swift and terrifying counterattacks—broke Nivelle's offensive of April 1917, and inflicted 200,000 casualties. The French army had believed in Nivelle; now its morale cracked. From the end of April until June 1917, units mutinied. Some waved red flags; the example of the Petrograd Soviet, with its call for immediate and unconditional peace, was contagious.

Fortunately, German intelligence was characteristically poor. Had Ludendorff known of the mutinies, he might have driven France from the war. Instead, Pétain, who had saved France at Verdun, now had time to save it once more. He suppressed the mutinies with a judicious combination of firing squad and conciliation. He listened to the troops and gave them what they wanted: home leave, better food, and no more offensives. The French army would do its part in defense, but others would have to break Germany.

The mutinies gave Haig what he thought was his opportunity. In the third battle of Ypres, from July to December 1917, he threw his troops again and again at the German lines as heavy artillery and rain churned the soil of Flanders into "a porridge of mud." As in 1916, Haig suffered from the delusion that the Germans were about to crack. The maximum British and Canadian penetration was about five miles around the village of Passchendaele; the cost, perhaps 400,000 dead and wounded. By the end of the year British morale was scarcely higher than that of the French.

Finally, far to the south, the Germans showed that they were developing a tactical answer to the riddle of the trenches. On October 24, 1917, after a brief surprise bombardment, an Austro-German army crashed through the Italian defenses on the Isonzo River around the village of Caporetto. The Germans moved in small, stealthy groups equipped with light machine guns. Instead of advancing on a broad front and slowing to tidy their flanks, they pushed rapidly through weak points and on into the Italian rear, sowing alarm and despondency. Positions too difficult to take they simply bypassed.

The Italian army crumbled and withdrew almost to Venice. Then, to the surprise of Germans and Austrians, it held on the Piave River even before British and French troops arrived to prop Italy up. Caporetto and the resulting loss of most of Italy east of Venice had at last made the unpopular war of 1915 a war of national defense.

On the home front, 1917 was equally disastrous for the Allies. Commodity shortages and the indiscriminate printing of money to finance the immense war expenditures drove prices steadily upward. Inflation and scarcity generated popular discontent (although troops on leave found civilian complaints about rationing tiresome—the civilians were safe from shellfire). The extreme left of the European socialist parties took up with enthusiasm the slogans of the Petrograd Soviet and of the Bolsheviks. Shortly before Caporetto, a workers' revolt convulsed one of Italy's principal industrial centers, Turin. Civilian disturbances and demonstrations accompanied the French army mutinies. Even Britain experienced unrest.

Nevertheless, the outlook was not totally bleak either on the western front, in the Middle East, or in central Europe. In

November 1917, at Cambrai, Haig for the first time committed en masse that bizarre British invention, the tank. The British high command had failed to find a tactical answer to the trench deadlock, but a few innovators, among them Winston Churchill, had found a technological one. The combination of the internal combustion engine, caterpillar track, armor, and machine guns or cannon might yet restore mobility to the battlefield. Unfortunately, Haig had squandered surprise by using a few isolated tanks on the Somme in 1916. At Cambrai, the 400 tanks that Haig committed overwhelmed the terrified Germans. But the usual British failure to coordinate infantry, artillery, and reserves left the tanks exposed to a German counterattack that regained most of the ground lost.

In the Middle East, Turkey was beginning to crumble, despite its victory at Gallipoli and an appalling series of British blunders in Mesopotamia in 1914–16. Sir Edmund Allenby, perhaps the most imaginative British commander of the war, took Jerusalem in November 1917 after a push northward from Egypt into Ottoman Palestine. Simultaneously, Britain issued the Balfour Declaration, which appeared to promise "the establishment in Palestine of a national home for the Jewish people." London sought to mobilize Zionist—Jewish nationalist—support in Europe and to create a buffer between the Suez Canal and the postwar sphere allotted to the French in Syria. With the aid of Arab irregulars led by the eccentric T. E. Lawrence (later "Lawrence of Arabia"), Allenby pressed on for Damascus and Constantinople.

Finally, Austria-Hungary too was beginning to crumble. Allied statesmen had reluctantly dabbled in the subversion of Austria-Hungary as early as 1916. The "old Kaiser," Francis Joseph, who had reigned since 1848 and had become the symbol of the Dual Monarchy, died that November. His death deprived Austria-Hungary of its essential symbol of unity. In 1917 the Petrograd Soviet and the Bolsheviks, among their many slogans, launched that of "self-determination." Wilson took it up to prevent the Bolsheviks from monopo-

LETTING DOWN A LADDER

The Kaiser and Wilson's Fourteen Points (an American view).

lizing it. In his statement of American war aims of January 1918, the famous "Fourteen Points," he demanded "autonomous development" for the peoples of Austria-Hungary and the resurrection of the Polish state destroyed in 1795. Self-determination was a powerful political weapon in the hands of the Allies. But it was a weapon of desperation that might well destroy any prospect of postwar order in central and eastern Europe.

As the year 1917 closed, the Allied leaders contemplated their position with alarm. Russia had dissolved. Britain, France, and Italy had each in turn come close to collapse. Germany was victorious in eastern Europe and in Italy. It seemed poised to attack in the West. The home front was wavering. The "Yanks," Allied propaganda insisted, were coming. Would they come in time?

GERMANY'S LAST THROW, 1918

"Michael"

Ludendorff might have played for time and trusted to his army's defensive skill to blunt Allied offensives in 1918. But time appeared to be working against Germany. Since the "turnip winter" of 1916 the British blockade had bitten deeper and deeper into German civilian morale and health. Austria-Hungary, Bulgaria, and Turkey were on the verge of collapse. Time would allow the Americans to mobilize a mass army and would fortify the Allies with U.S. food and munitions. Ludendorff also rejected a political solution that the war-weary Allies might have had to accept in the dark winter of 1917–18: German withdrawal from Belgium and northern France in return for a peace that left to Germany its immense gains in eastern Europe—and thus the mastery of the Continent.

With defense and negotiation ruled out, the remaining solution was attack. Russia's collapse freed enough German forces to give them rough equality in France by March 1918—although Ludendorff's megalomania nevertheless kept a million Germans in eastern Europe to bring in the grain of the Ukraine and to seize the oil of the Caucasus. Ludendorff planned to use the reinforcements and the methods proven in Russia and at Caporetto to "hack a hole" in the western front. The rest, Ludendorff insisted, would "take care of itself." The great German offensive, in the words of a member of his staff, "would not be a battering ram, pounding head-on against a wall, but rather like a flood of water, flowing around obstacles, isolating them, and following the path of least resistance deep into the enemy's territory." Throughout the winter the German staffs pulled divisions out of the line, formed assault battalions (*Stosstruppen*), trained them in the new "infiltration" tactics, and rested them for a last supreme effort. Ludendorff knew the risks. When a politician asked him what would happen if he failed, he was frank: "Then Germany is finished."

The German objective of dominating Europe, the German style of all-or-nothing gambles, and the immense expectations that victory over Russia had aroused in the German public all dictated action. No political check on Ludendorff existed. In January 1917 Bethmann Hollweg had given up his small remaining authority by agreeing to unrestricted submarine warfare. In July 1917 Hindenburg and Ludendorff forced Bethmann Hollweg's resignation by threatening their own. The intimidated Kaiser appointed an unknown bureaucrat as chancellor. Tirpitz organized the political underpinnings of the Hindenburg-Ludendorff regime. On Sedan Day, September 2, 1917, a "Fatherland Party" (*Vaterlandspartei*) emerged, proclaiming pitiless war until final victory over both Allies and SPD, and massive annexations in east and west to secure that victory for all time. Germany's mission, Tirpitz announced, was to lead Europe against the "all-devouring tyranny of Anglo-Americanism." The *Vaterlandspartei* soon had more members than the SPD. It was the first—but not the last—fanatical mass party of German nationalism. Its spirit momentarily galvanized the home front in the expectation of final victory.

On March 21, 1918, the first of Ludendorff's offensives, baptized MICHAEL, struck the British line between St. Quentin and La Fère. The British defenders massed in their forward trenches, where German high explosive and gas shells massacred them. Haig had failed to learn from the German defense-in-depth that had cost the Allies so dear in 1917. Then the new German offensive tactics—attack in depth—tore a hole through the British lines thirty miles deep. It was the greatest gain on the western front by either side since 1914. The French prepared to withdraw to defend Paris.

But the British ultimately held. Ludendorff broke his own rule of always bypassing resistance, and shattered his reserves against the stubborn British defense of Arras. In April a second German offensive in Flanders took back the gains Britain had achieved at heartbreaking cost in the 1917 Passchendaele offensive. A third attack, in May–June 1918, drove the French back to the Marne and came within forty miles of Paris. Each time, Ludendorff achieved operational freedom but failed to translate it into a strategic victory that would force the Allies to make peace before the Americans appeared in force.

The Yanks Arrive

And on the Marne, U.S. Army and Marine Corps units at last joined the French in counterattacks at Belleau Wood and Château-Thierry. The Americans lacked experience. But they were willing to die in a manner not seen since 1914–16, the manner of Langemarck and the Somme. That spirit, and American numbers and weight of artillery terrified the Germans even as they shot the Americans down in droves.

Ludendorff's fourth and fifth offensives failed miserably, at great cost. Ludendorff had bled the German army to death. In March his forces in the West had numbered 3,800,000. By July they had suffered almost a million casualties. German troops shipped in from Russia as replacements began to vote with their feet, jumping from the slow-moving troop trains before they reached the western front. Yet in the face of hunger, desertion, demoralization, and defeat, Ludendorff still refused to allow negotiations with the Allies.

In July, August, and September, the Allies began to counterattack in a series of carefully limited operations. An inter-Allied high command under the hard-driving Marshal Ferdinand Foch of France at last began to coordinate Allied actions effectively. Allied infantry, often with tank support, would break into the German lines until German reserves arrived and resistance stiffened. Then the Allies would shift to another sector.

These attacks slowly nibbled away the German gains of the spring and further demoralized the Germans. On August 8, the "black day of the German army," whole German units surrendered for the first time to British tanks and infantry. In September, Haig broke through the strongest German defenses in the West, the "Hindenburg Line." By now the U.S. Army in France was 1,500,000 strong and under its own commander, John "Black Jack" Pershing. It pinched out the St. Mihiel salient east of Verdun and prepared for a massive drive into Lorraine to roll up the German front and meet the British in central Belgium.

March 21, 1918: Germany Attacks

Ernst Jünger, winner of Germany's highest decoration, the Pour le Mérite, *and of its foremost literary award, the Goethe Prize, led a* Stosstrupp *in the 1918 offensives. His vision of war, set forth in postwar memoirs such as* Storm of Steel, *was widely popular in 1920s Germany, and very different from the laments over war's futility and waste frequently found in British and French war writing.*

Here Jünger describes Ludendorff's stunning opening bombardment and the initial German assault.

The minute hand moved closer and closer; we counted off the last minutes. Finally it stood at 0505. The hurricane broke loose.

A fiery curtain rose high in the air, supported by sudden, unceasing upwellings. A raging thunder, into which even the heaviest shell-bursts merged, shook the earth. The gigantic eruption of annihilation from the innumerable [German] cannon [firing overhead from] behind us was so frightful, that the greatest of the battles we had passed through before this seemed like children's games. . . . The enemy artillery remained dumb; it was flattened as if by a single blow from a giant's club. . . .

It had become day. Behind us the immense din still grew. Before us rose an unpierceable wall of smoke, dust and gas. Men ran through the trench and yelled joyfully in one another's ears. Infantry and artillery, combat engineers and field telephone linemen, Prussians and Bavarians, officers and men, all were overmastered and gripped with enthusiasm by this elemental outpouring of our power, and were burning for the assault at 0940. . . .

The great moment had come. The barrage rolled across our first line. We attacked. . . . The overpowering desire to kill gave my feet wings. Rage squeezed bitter tears from my eyes. The immense desire to destroy and annihilate that hovered over the battlefield thickened our minds and dipped them as if in a red haze. We called to each other stumbling and stammering disjointed phrases, and an outside observer might perhaps have believed that we were overcome by an excess of joy.

From Ernst Jünger, In Stahlgewittern *(Berlin: E. S. Mittler, 1941 [1st ed., 1920]), pp. 253–57 (translation by M. Knox).*

At the end of September, Ludendorff's fears about Germany's allies at last proved correct. The Franco-British army at Salonika broke the Bulgarians and drove north through the Balkans, threatening

The Yanks arrive: General John J. ("Black Jack") Pershing (*right*) meets Haig.

Austria-Hungary and Germany's southern border. Ludendorff panicked and demanded the appointment of a German civilian government to take the blame for the approaching defeat. He insisted that Germany seek an armistice from Wilson before total collapse ensued. The Fourteen Points, Ludendorff slyly assumed, would allow Germany to keep at least some of its gains. Pershing foresaw that the Germans would deny they had lost unless the Allies dictated peace in Berlin. Wilson, less far-sighted, entered negotiations in October.

Then events took command. Italy attacked on October 24 and reached Trieste by November 3. Austria-Hungary collapsed into a chaotic mass of seething nationalities, each attempting to carve out its own state. The German naval command, knowing the war was lost and hoping to create a suitably Wagnerian legend for the future, attempted to send the High Seas Fleet on a death ride down the English Channel. The sailors understandably mutinied and seized Kiel naval base. Revolution spread to Munich and Berlin. The SPD leaders in Berlin proclaimed a German Republic on November 9; the Kaiser abdicated and fled to Holland. And the Allies, under pressure from Wilson and from their own war-weary public opinion, permitted

the Germans an armistice while Germany still occupied most of Belgium and some French territory.

On the "eleventh hour of the eleventh day of the eleventh month" of 1918, silence at last descended on the western front. As the armistice terms commanded, the Germans withdrew to the Rhine, demobilized, and sailed their fleet to the British fleet base at Scapa Flow. The war had cost at least 20 million lives. Germany suffered approximately 2 million military dead, Russia 1.7 million, France 1.3 million, Austria-Hungary 1.1 million, Britain and its empire 750,000 and 250,000 respectively, Italy about 500,000, Turkey somewhat less, and the United States 114,000. Civilian casualties included 100,000 killed by U-boats and air raids, 30,000 Belgians killed by German forced labor, reprisals, or artillery fire, and at least 1.5 million Armenians whom the Turks had massacred in 1915. A further 20 million died in the great influenza pandemic that struck the world in 1918.

TREATIES WITHOUT PEACE, 1919–22

The first general European peace conference since Vienna in 1814–15 met at Paris in January 1919. It faced a more difficult task than Metternich and Castlereagh (see pp. 000–00). They had merely attempted to return the world "to peaceful habits" and reestablish a balance of power that France had upset. The peacemakers at Paris in 1919 faced similar requirements, and far more.

Scores of outraged nationalities, mercifully silent at Vienna, now clamored for self-determination and "rights"—including the right to oppress minorities or neighboring nationalities. Public opinion, mobilized to hate for four long years and politically potent thanks to universal suffrage, made moderation difficult. Bolshevism, a revolutionary threat without parallel in 1814–15, appeared to menace central Europe. War and the new national boundaries had disrupted complex industrial economies; the permanence of peace might depend in part on

The Peace Settlements in Europe   1919–20

Legend:
- Boundaries of German, Russian, and Austro-Hungarian empires in 1914
- Areas lost by Austro-Hungarian Empire
- Areas lost by Russian Empire
- Areas lost by German Empire
- Areas lost by Bulgaria
- Demilitarized Zone
- Boundaries of 1926

FINLAND

Helsinki

NORWAY

Leningrad
(St. Petersburg)

Stockholm

SWEDEN

Tallinn

ESTONIA

BALTIC SEA

Riga

LATVIA

DENMARK

Memel

LITHUANIA

NORTH
SEA

Danzig

EAST
PRUSSIA

NETHERLANDS

Amsterdam

GERMANY

Berlin

POLISH CORRIDOR

Warsaw

Vistula River

POLAND

Kiev

RUHR

Brussels

Cologne

BELGIUM

LUXEMBOURG

Frankfurt

Weimar

Rhine River

Elbe River

Prague

CZECHOSLOVAKIA

GALICIA

Paris

Versailles

LORRAINE

ALSACE

Strasbourg

Vienna

Dniester River

BESSARABIA

FRANCE

Berne

SWITZERLAND

Locarno

Geneva

S.
TYROL

AUSTRIA

HUNGARY

Budapest

RUMANIA

Milan

Trieste

Zagreb

Genoa

Rapallo

Venice

CROATIA

Belgrade

Bucharest

BLACK SEA

ITALY

YUGOSLAVIA

SERBIA

BULGARIA

Sofia

Rome

MONTENEGRO
(To Yugoslavia, 1921)

Istanbul (Constantinople)

Naples

ALBANIA

GREECE

TURKEY

Athens

MEDITERRANEAN SEA

0   300 MILES

0   300 KILOMETERS

the economic solutions the peacemakers found. And Wilson, who insisted on attending the conference in person, rejected a French proposal for drafting a clear agenda and order of business. The "Big Four," Wilson, Lloyd George, Clemenceau, and Orlando, leapt from issue to issue. From confusion they created chaos.

The Big Four at Paris, 1919: Orlando makes a point to Lloyd George, while Clemenceau (*center*) and Wilson (*far right*) look on.

Germany and the Versailles "Diktat"

Germany's fate was the chief issue facing the conference, and its chief failure. In the abstract, two courses were available that might have prevented Germany from attempting again the experiment of 1914. The Allies and the United States could conciliate the new German republic by offering a lenient peace. Or they could fasten on Germany a genuinely Carthaginian peace that would undo Bismarck's work and divide Germany into two or three: Prussia, Catholic south Germany, and an independent Rhineland. Clemenceau, who had seen two German invasions of France in his lifetime, naturally preferred the second alternative. But neither Lloyd George nor Wilson was a neighbor of Germany. Britain already controlled the German fleet; it could afford to scoff at Clemenceau's fears and reject the open-ended military commitment needed to enforce his drastic solution. And Germany was an economic unit essential to European and British prosperity, as well as the only remaining counterweight to Bolshevik Russia in eastern Europe.

The Big Four therefore compromised. Bismarck's Reich remained in existence, and Britain and the United States calmed France with the offer of an Anglo-American security guarantee, a military al-

liance against German resurgence. But having decided to preserve Germany, the Allies failed to adopt the corollary of that decision, a peace as lenient as that offered to Bourbon France in 1814–15. Allied public opinion, even in Britain, shouted "Hang the Kaiser!" The disorderly procedure of the Paris conference meant that demands on Germany accumulated piecemeal and found their way into the peace treaty without any weighing of their cumulative effect. And their own disunity prevented the Big Four from inviting the Germans to help draft the treaty, as the French had in 1814.

The treaty that the German delegation grudgingly signed in the Hall of Mirrors at Versailles on the fifth anniversary of Sarajevo (June 28, 1919) was relatively lenient—compared to Brest-Litovsk. Germany lost only 13.5 percent of its 1914 territory, mostly areas inhabited by Poles, Danes, and French. The Allies piled on (1) financial "reparations"; (2) disarmament to an army of 100,000 men without heavy equipment, aircraft, or general staff, and a navy of 15,000 manning obsolete battleships; (3) temporary Allied occupation and permanent demilitarization of the Rhineland; (4) loss of the Silesian coalfields and most of Posen and West Prussia to Poland, with the German-inhabited port of Danzig in West Prussia becoming a self-governing "Free City"; (5) loss of Memel in East Prussia to Lithuania; (6) temporary cession to France of the Saar; (7) loss of Germany's useless overseas colonies; and (8) a prohibition on union with the Germans of Austria. The core of Bismarck's Germany nevertheless remained intact.

Yet compared to German expectations, the "*Diktat*" or dictated peace that the Germans received at Versailles was a nightmare. For four years German propaganda had told the German people that a savage ring of aggressors had attacked Germany out of Cossack bloodlust, French thirst for revenge, and British "trade envy." Germany's leaders had assured their public that victorious occupation of Belgium, northern France, and vast stretches of Russia guaranteed Germany a victorious peace. And the Germans had also, quite without justification, expected a Wilsonian "peace without annexations or indemnities" as their reward for proclaiming a republic. They had evidently not read Point thirteen of Wilson's Fourteen Points, which specified the creation of a Poland with access to the sea, inevitably across German territory.

The abrupt transition in 1918 from the expectation of victory to the reality of defeat, territorial loss, and national humiliation lessened the German public's already tenuous grip on reality. Germany, its political leaders at its head, denied the obvious. Germany, they claimed, had not provoked the war—although numerous German documents soon emerged indicating that it had, and few could deny that Germany had attacked Belgium without provocation. The Germans damned as a "war-guilt lie" the Allied attempt, in Article 231 of the Versailles Treaty, to establish the financial responsibility of Germany and its allies for "loss and damage" resulting from the war imposed on the Allied Powers "by the aggression of Germany and its allies." The Germans, from the beginning, furiously denied the Treaty's moral validity.

Nor had Germany suffered military defeat, according to most German leaders, including the new SPD president of the republic, Fritz Ebert. Through the mouth of Hindenburg, the German Right added the crucial corollary. If the Allies had not defeated Germany, the culprits could only be the "November Criminals" of the SPD, whose Revolution had allegedly stabbed the heroic troops "in the back." The twin legends of Allied victory through trickery and German defeat through a "stab-in-the-back" ensured that Germany would have the will to reverse the verdict of 1914–18.

And the Versailles Treaty's relative lenience ensured that Germany would have the means. For east-central Europe was now a power vacuum. The collapse of Austria-Hungary brought into being five miniature Austria-Hungaries: rump Austria, a diminished Hungary, Czechoslovakia, Poland, and a Serb-dominated kingdom of Serbs, Croats, and Slovenes that later took the name of Yugoslavia. Rumania, which now absorbed both the Hungarians of Transylvania and the Rumanian-inhabited ex-Russian territory of

Bessarabia, formed a sixth weak state between Germany and Russia. Italy, by seizing Trento and Trieste, became the seventh "successor state" of the defunct Habsburg empire.

With Russia in eclipse and German economic and demographic power virtually intact, only the United States could balance Germany once it began to revive.

National Minorities in Central Europe   1919

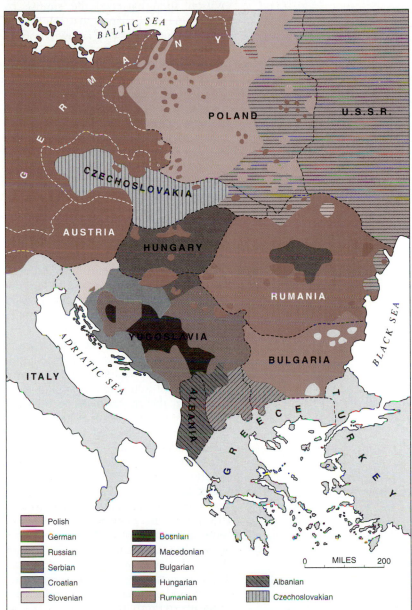

Polish
German
Russian
Serbian
Croatian
Slovenian
Bosnian
Macedonian
Bulgarian
Hungarian
Rumanian
Albanian
Czechoslovakian

0   MILES   200

The war, despite Germany's defeat, had paradoxically made Germany potentially stronger *relative to the rest of Europe* than in 1914. The states of eastern Europe, the Germans correctly judged, were *Saison-staaten,* "states for a season" destined to wilt under the hot sun of renewed German greatness.

Wilson, the League, and the U.S. Commitment to Europe

Wilson soon hastened the sunrise by destroying any chance that the United States would underwrite a new European balance. In the course of 1917–18 the notion of a "League of Nations," brainchild of British pacifist Liberals, had captivated the President. He saw in the League an alternative to the alleged evils of the balance of power and of secret treaties that Cobdenite mythology blamed for the war.

In the Paris negotiations Wilson therefore devoted an increasing portion of his energy to writing the League's "Covenant" into the Versailles Treaty, thus confusing further the process of settlement with Germany. The League, Wilson came to hope, would remedy imperfections in the Treaty, bind the potentially isolationist United States to Europe, and ensure the perpetual peace that he had promised would come out of this war to "make the world safe for democracy."

In pursuing the mirage of the League, Wilson destroyed any chance that the United States would underwrite European stability by a permanent commitment of its power, the power that had defeated Germany. The Republicans took control of the Senate in the fall 1918 elections. They balked at the open-ended global commitments that League "collective security" entailed. Their leader, Henry Cabot Lodge, was no isolationist; he favored a continued commitment of American power to prevent Germany from renewing its "war of world conquest." But Wilson rejected Lodge's offer to ratify the Treaty with reservations. Wilson—dogmatic about presidential prerogatives, always rigid of character, and now increasingly ill—defied an essential feature of the Constitution: the requirement that the President lead rather than command the Congress.

Wilson's reward, after he had suffered nervous collapse and an incapacitating stroke while taking his case to the people, was Senate rejection of the Treaty in March 1920. The British economist John Maynard Keynes influenced the Senate with his merciless pamphlet against Wilson and the Treaty, *The Economic Consequences of the Peace.* Wilson himself ensured rejection by ordering his loyalists to vote against the amended version the Republicans proposed. And the wreck of Wilson's policy and presidency destroyed any prospect of any Anglo-American security guarantee for France. The Republican presidential candidate, Warren G. Harding, summed up the rising national yearning for a return to the womb with a word of his own invention: America needed "normalcy." Harding carried the 1920 election. The United States retreated into resentful isolation, except for its petulant demands for repayment of Allied war debts.

Peace in the Pacific? The Washington Conference, 1921–22

The Pacific proved the one area in which the United States continued to play a great-power role. Wilson had sought unsuccessfully at Paris to lever the Japanese out of Shandong and compel them to retract the "twenty-one demands" they had forced on China in 1915. U.S. opinion also looked unkindly on the Anglo-Japanese alliance, and U.S. admirals saw it as a two-ocean threat that demanded a fleet larger than the navy "second to none" projected in 1916, after the first submarine outrages. The United States, with the help of Canada, forced Britain to choose between its alliance with Japan and its friendship with the United States. Britain, in no condition to engage in a naval "race" with the United States, acquiesced. Britain had abandoned the "Two-Power Standard" (see p. 742) to face the German challenge; now it abandoned its alliance with Japan and accepted formal parity with the greatest naval power, the United States.

At the Washington Conference on arms limitation and Pacific affairs in 1921–22, the powers laid down a new naval and East Asian order. The Washington Naval Treaty of February 1922 apparently froze the world ranking of naval power. It decreed a ten-year "holiday" in battleship construction and limited total tonnage of capital ships to 525,000 each for Britain and the United States, 315,000 for Japan, and 175,000 each for France and Italy. The powers relieved China of most Japanese encroachments and reaffirmed the "Open Door." The Anglo-Japanese Alliance dissolved into a meaningless Four-Power Treaty in which Britain, France, Japan, and the United States pledged to preserve the Pacific status quo. Japan agreed to the Washington settlement in return for British and American pledges not to build fortified bases north of Singapore and east of Hawaii. Tokyo retained naval supremacy in northeast Asia, along with Hong Kong and the Philippines as hostages to ensure British and American good behavior. The Washington treaties seemed to promise an era of peace. Their real results were a perilous complacency in the democracies and the cutting loose of Japan from the restraining influence of its alliance with Britain.

debris of the Imperial German Army, authorized the recruitment of right-wing freebooters, the *Freikorps*. These units appealed to Germans of the Ernst Jünger type, who had enjoyed the Great War and were reluctant to give it up, and to nationalist students too young to have fought in 1914–18. In January 1919, after an abortive Communist ("Spartacist") coup in Berlin, the *Freikorps* shot Rosa Luxemburg and other leaders of the far Left "while attempting to escape." That was a euphemism much used later. A *Putsch,* or military coup, by *Freikorps* elements and a Communist uprising in the Ruhr almost destroyed the German republic in 1920.

In Italy, the Liberals lost control of the mass political forces that Giolitti had unleashed with universal male suffrage in 1912–13. The delusion that Italy was Russia gripped the Italian socialists. Their verbal threats of revolution and occasional violence against landowners and veterans soon provoked a virtual civil war, which the socialists inevitably lost (see p. 834).

Further east, Bolshevik Russia fought for survival. The 1918 Armistice had forced Germany to give up the gains of Brest-Litovsk. But the Bolsheviks continued to

Postwar wars: street fighting in Berlin, 1919.

WARS AFTER THE WAR, 1919–23

Meanwhile, U.S. withdrawal left Europe on its own. Peaceful habits did not return. Social and national struggles convulsed Europe until 1923. The League of Nations generated immense masses of paper and gave small nations a forum for interminable talk. But it was impotent whenever it faced a great power. Even Italy defied the League in 1923 over an incident with Greece.

Civil Wars in Germany, Italy, and Russia

In Germany and Hungary, short-lived Left-extremist uprisings or regimes perished when faced with ruthless force from the Right. The SPD government of the German republic, unable to impose order with the

proclaim the goal of world revolution, without which they expected a Communist Russia to succumb to "capitalist encirclement." Lenin and his associates split the European socialist parties by founding their own Third ("Communist") International in March 1919. They also appealed to the colonial peoples, furthering the disruption of the European empires that the war had begun.

Trotsky raised Bolshevik armies and fought with increasing success against "White Russian" forces under former tsarist generals who sought to restore the old regime. The Allies landed troops in 1918 at Vladivostok and Murmansk to secure the supplies they had sent to the tsar and to support the Whites. Except for the eager Japanese, who remained at Vladivostok until 1922, the Allies soon withdrew. By 1920 the Red Army had defeated the Whites, but the Poles made the error of attempting to seize the Ukraine. In July 1920 the Red Army drove into Poland with hopes of continuing westward. Then the Poles under Marshal Josef Pilsudski held at Warsaw. Russia's borders stabilized. Finland, Estonia, Latvia, and Lithuania kept their newly acquired independence; Rumania kept Bessarabia. In other respects Bolshevik Russia preserved the territories of the tsarist empire.

Eastern Europe and the Balkans

In the vacuum between Germany and Russia, the successor states quarreled. The diplomats at Paris did their best to draw new borders for Germany's former allies by the treaties of St. Germain (September 1919) for Austria, for Neuilly (November 1919) for Bulgaria, and of Trianon (June 1920) for Hungary. These frontiers, although much criticized as a source of conflict, in most cases merely ratified what the nationalities of eastern Europe had already done in pulling Austria-Hungary down. The great powers thereafter failed to moderate the squabbles of the small. Poland and Czechoslovakia disputed the border town of Teschen. Lithuania quarreled over its borders with Poland and Germany. Hungary claimed territory from all three of its neighbors—Rumania,

Czechoslovakia, and Yugoslavia. Those powers sought security through alliances with one another, a combination the Hungarians mocked as the "Little Entente." France, seeking an eastern ally to replace Russia, contracted alliances with Poland and Czechoslovakia, and entered into consultative pacts with Rumania and Yugoslavia.

Germany and Bolshevik Russia, the pariahs of the international scene, sought comfort together. In 1922, at Rapallo, they publicly canceled their mutual debt and reparations claims. Secretly, Red Army and German *Reichswehr* contracted a profitable bargain. Germany gave the Bolsheviks modern military technology and in return received an opportunity to secretly experiment in Russia with weapons such as gas and aircraft which were forbidden under the Versailles Treaty.

Far to the south, the Turks reacted to the collapse of their empire by creating a national state, under the leadership of the victor of Gallipoli, Mustafa Kemal Pasha. A foolhardy Greek advance into Turkey in pursuit of the "Great Idea" (*Megali Idea*) of a Greek empire from the Adriatic to the Black Sea led to disaster in 1922. The Turks then massacred or expelled the 1.35 million Greeks in Asia Minor whose ancestors had lived there for three millennia. The Greeks in turn drove almost half a million Turks from Greek Thrace. This "exchange of populations," as League bureaucrats euphemistically described it, still appeared barbaric in the 1920s. Unfortunately it did not appear so for long.

After a confrontation with British troops at Chanak near Constantinople that brought down Lloyd George's government in October 1922, the Turks permitted the Allies to leave them alone. The 1923 Treaty of Lausanne recognized the independent Turkish state. Kemal, who later took the name Atatürk ("father of the Turks"), abolished the Ottoman sultanate and ruled ruthlessly until his death in 1938. The Eastern Question was closed. Its worthy successors were the merciless struggles throughout the Middle East between the Ottoman Empire's former subjects.

The Final Battle of World War I: The Ruhr

Meanwhile, France and Germany fought a deadly although largely bloodless struggle. The issue was simple: would Germany accept its apparent demotion to second-rate power? The Germans refused to accept as final the loss of Posen, West Prussia, and Upper Silesia to Poland. Above all, Germany refused to pay promptly and fully the reparations that the Allies had fixed in 1921 at a theoretical total of $32 billion dollars (although they seem to have expected the Germans to actually pay only $12.5 billion).

The French faced immense expenses to repair the devastation wrought by the war and by the Germans, who had systematically wrecked French territory as they retreated in 1917 and 1918. France also hoped that heavy reparations would make it harder for Germany to rearm, and was confident that $12.5 billion was well within the German capacity to pay. It therefore did its best to hold Germany to the Allied payment schedule.

When the Germans defaulted massively in late 1922, France and its ally Belgium acted. Poincaré sent French troops into the Ruhr Valley to seize Germany's mines and factories. Mining coal with bayonets was expensive, but the French made a modest profit. The German government of Wilhelm Cuno ordered passive resistance. Cuno began printing marks feverishly, fuelling the inflation already under way as a result of Germany's immense internal war debt. Cuno wrecked Germany's currency to prove that Germany could not pay. What he proved was that Germany would not pay.

In August–September 1923 Cuno and passive resistance collapsed as the mark rose from 4 million to 160 million to the dollar. Gustav Stresemann, a crafty former National Liberal with an extreme annexationist past, took power as chancellor. He mastered internal disorder, which included a radical nationalist uprising in Bavaria under the leadership of a fanatical ex-corporal and winner of the Iron Cross, Adolf Hitler (see pp. 838–39).

France occupies the Ruhr Valley, 1923.

Stresemann sought a compromise with France that would give Germany a breathing space. Britain and the United States, concerned over the economic repercussions of chaos in Germany, helped. They threatened economic reprisals if Poincaré did not withdraw from the Ruhr. By spring 1924 Stresemann had stabilized the currency by introducing a new mark. Poincaré gave way to a left-wing coalition in the May 1924 French elections. His successor, Aristide Briand, was a weaker and more conciliatory man. An emissary of the United States, Charles G. Dawes, patched together a temporary reparations settlement, the Dawes Plan. It lowered payments to a level Germany consented to pay and underwrote Germany's solvency with a U.S. loan, the first of many. U.S. credit to Germany after 1924 indirectly furnished the sums Germany paid as reparations. The last French troops left the Ruhr in August 1925. France had lost a great trial of strength.

THE ILLUSIONS OF LOCARNO, 1925–29

From the French viewpoint, worse followed. Austen Chamberlain, Britain's

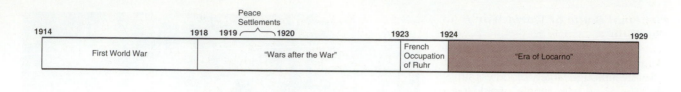

1914		1918	1919	Peace Settlements	1920	1923	1924	1929
	First World War			"Wars after the War"		French Occupation of Ruhr	"Era of Locarno"	

foreign secretary, hoped to prevent a repetition of the Ruhr occupation by giving France security against Germany in an Anglo-French pact that would replace the failed 1919 Treaty of Guarantee. Stresemann got wind of the project and slyly preempted it with an offer of a general western security pact that Germany would also sign.

Instead of a revival of the Anglo-French Entente Cordiale, the French received the multilateral Treaty of Locarno (October 16, 1925). France, Germany, and Belgium pledged to respect their mutual borders, as drawn in the Versailles Treaty, and to preserve the demilitarization of the Rhineland. Britain and Italy acted as outside guarantors against "unprovoked attack," a vague and elastic phrase. And France could now respond militarily only to "flagrant" violations of the demilitarization of the Rhineland. Locarno thus significantly weakened a key provision of Versailles.

Despite Stresemann's claims of conversion to being a "good European," Locarno was an immense German victory. It prevented a repetition of the Ruhr: if France sought to use force to uphold the Versailles Treaty, Britain might be treaty-bound to fight France! Locarno also ruled out Anglo-French staff talks on the pre-1914 model, much to the relief of the British army and government. And Locarno covered only the West. Germany retained freedom to redraw, by force if necessary, its eastern borders.

A brief Indian summer of illusion, the "era of Locarno," followed the treaty. France and Britain repeatedly ignored massive German violations of the Versailles Treaty's disarmament provisions, and soon gave up their right of on-site inspection. Germany entered the League of Nations. In 1929, in a second reparations settlement (the "Young Plan") negotiated under U.S. auspices, Germany

agreed to make modest payments until 1988. France in turn undertook to evacuate its Rhineland occupation zone by summer 1930, five years ahead of the Versailles Treaty schedule.

Western public opinion demanded forgetfulness and illusion from its political leaders, and it received them. The Great War, much of the public concluded, had been an exercise in criminal futility that must never be repeated. Alliances and armaments—not German aggression—had caused the war. Therefore alliances and armaments (except semiclandestine German armaments) were evil. Enlightened international public opinion, working through the League of Nations, would prevent war.

Illusion reached its height with the famous pact "outlawing war" that Aristide Briand and Frank B. Kellogg, the U.S. secretary of state, drafted in 1928. Briand hoped the pact would bind the United States, however sketchily, to Europe. But the Kellogg-Briand Pact, which 62 nations happily signed, contained no enforcement provisions whatsoever. It also included an escape clause wide enough to accommodate entire tank armies: signatories could still fight in self-defense. The pact had all the force of a pious declaration against sin.

Fifteen years of war and revolution broke for good the "peaceful habits" acquired in the nineteenth century. For four years millions of men had killed one another in mud holes while Europe had transformed its vast accumulated wealth into steel and high explosives. Those who returned from the front carried the language and habit of violence into politics. In the East, a pitiless utopian sect had taken control of a great power of immense economic and military potential. In central Europe, the greatest European power of all had emerged from the war unreconciled to defeat. The victors had checked

The god of war scoffs at the Kellogg-Briand Pact (a Dutch view).

A DUTCH JAB
Mars: "If your disarmament talkers don't stop, I'll die laughing."

at heartbreaking cost the German bid for European and world mastery but had left Germany capable of repeating that bid. Soon—with the onset of the Great Depression in 1929—the world economy collapsed. That collapse enfeebled the democracies and unleashed voracious "have-not" powers first in Asia and then in Europe. As the Great War receded into memory, another even greater war took its place.

Suggestions for Further Reading

General Works

No up-to-date one-volume history of the war exists. M. Ferro, *The Great War, 1914–1918* (1973), A. J. P. Taylor, *The First World War* (1972); and C. R. M. F. Cruttwell, *A History of the Great War, 1914–1918* (1934/1991), offer intelligent surveys. M. Eksteins, *Rites of Spring: The Great War and the Birth of the Modern Age* (1989), probes its cultural significance with exceptional insight. Z. Zeman, *The Gentlemen Negotiators* (1971), and D. Stevenson, *The First World War and International Politics* (1988), cover diplomacy and strategy with style. P. Kennedy, "The First World War and the International Power System," *International Security,* 9 (1984), analyzes the relative strength of the powers. A. Offer, *The First World War: An Agrarian Interpretation* (1989), offers a new look at economics, strategy, and the nature of the contending societies. For life and death on the western front, see particularly the chapter on the Somme in J. Keegan, *The Face of Battle* (1976).

War and Revolution

For Germany's war, see F. Fischer, *War of Illusions* (1975), and *Germany's Aims in the First World War* (1967); H. W. Gatzke, *Germany's Drive to the West* (1950); T. Lupfer, *The Dynamics of Doctrine: The Changes in German Tactical Doctrine During the First World War* (1981); and J. Kocka, *Facing Total War: German Society, 1914–1918* (1984). On Britain, E. L. Woodward, *Great Britain and the War of 1914–1918* (1967), is unsurpassed, but see also A. Marwick, *The Deluge. British Society and the First World War* (1965). For France, see especially P. Bernard and H. Dubief, *The Decline of the Third Republic, 1914–1938* (1985), and A. Horne, *The Price of Glory; Verdun, 1916* (1962). S. Fitzpatrick, *The Russian Revolution, 1917–1932* (1982), gives a useful overview; A. Ulam, *Lenin and the Bolsheviks* (1965), and R. Pipes, *The Russian Revolution* (1990), are more detailed; L. Trotsky, *History of the Russian Revolution* (1936), is an unparalleled history-memoir by a key participant. On United States intervention, see especially B. Tuchman, *The Zimmermann Telegram* (1958); E. May, *The World War and American Isolation, 1914–1917* (1959); and D. Smith, *The Great Departure: The United States and World War I* (1965).

Settlement and Aftermath

On the power consequences of the war, see Kennedy, "The First World War" (above); G. Weinberg, "The Defeat of Germany in 1918 and the European Balance of Power," *Central European History,* 2 (1969); and H. Holborn, *The Political Collapse of Europe* (1954). P. Birdsall, *Versailles Twenty Years After* (1941), remains the best treatment of the peace conference, but see also K. Schawbe, *Woodrow Wilson, Revolutionary Germany, and Peacemaking, 1918–1919: Missionary Diplomacy and the Realities of Power* (1985). On the aftermath, S. Marks, *The Illusion of Peace. International Relations in Europe, 1918–1933* (1976), is unsurpassed. C. A. Macartney and A. W. Palmer, *Independent Eastern Europe* (1962), is excellent. S. Marks, "The Myths of Reparation," *Central European History,* 11 (1978), demystifies a widely misunderstood issue.

31

THE WORLD BETWEEN THE WARS, 1919–1939

The virtual withdrawal of the United States and Russia from world politics created a fleeting illusion: that Britain and France, the victors in 1914–18, dominated Europe and the wider world as in the early nineteenth century. But France's failure to coerce even a disarmed Germany and Britain's economic and imperial troubles soon revealed the hollowness of appearances. Germany enjoyed a brief prosperity after 1924, thanks to U.S. credit. But political stability eluded it. Few of the new states of central and eastern Europe found either stability or prosperity. The United States enjoyed an unprecedented economic boom—in isolation.

Then, in 1929–30, came the Great Depression. It extinguished the few surviving parliamentary regimes between Germany and Russia. It almost destroyed world lending and trade. It mortally wounded the great democracies, confirmed the United States in its isolationism, and freed "have not" powers to attack the West both in Europe and Asia. Fascist Italy under Benito Mussolini, a racist Germany under Adolf Hitler, and a militarized Japan destroyed the order established in the Versailles and Washington treaties, while Lenin's implacable successor, Joseph Stalin, sought to profit from the resulting chaos. Britain, France, and the United States met these global challenges demoralized and disunited. France went under; Britain nearly perished; the United States paid dearly for its irresponsibility after 1919.

THE TWENTIES: A GOLDEN AGE?

Britain: Stability and Stagnation

War and its aftermath broke the Liberals. In 1916 Asquith gave way to Lloyd

George, and then, in May 1918, attacked him in the House of Commons and split the Liberal party. In the "khaki election" of December 1918 Lloyd George led his wartime Liberal-Conservative coalition to a crushing victory over both Asquith and Labour. That victory condemned the divided Liberal party to permanent opposition and decline.

But the Conservatives soon found Lloyd George's leadership irritating. His brinkmanship in the Chanak crisis with Turkey in October 1922 gave the stolid foot soldiers of the Conservative party their opportunity. The comfortable, avuncular, pipe-smoking Stanley Baldwin rose up and denounced Lloyd George as "a great dynamic force"—"a very terrible thing." By 1923 Baldwin, whose enemies mocked him as "a man of the utmost insignificance," was prime minister.

He remained until 1929, except for a brief Labour minority government in 1924. Baldwin was the tweedy personification of a largely extinct rural England. A master of conciliation, of fudging issues, he defused social conflict with the soothing syrup of his "fireside chats" on that new medium, the radio. He found foreign policy boring. The Locarno treaty seemed to make foreign policy unnecessary; Baldwin did his best to have none.

The British mass army that had broken the Hindenburg Line in 1918 shrank to an insignificant imperial police force. The new Royal Air Force remained a hollow shell. The navy vegetated. In 1928 Britain adopted as permanent a 1919 budgetary invention of Lloyd George— the "ten-year rule." All defense expenditure and planning was to rest on the assumption that Britain would not fight a great power for at least ten years. That assumption was in effect a rationalization for Britain's unilateral disarmament.

In 1926, Baldwin's government weathered the general strike feared since the miners, dockers, and railwaymen had formed a "triple alliance" in 1914. The Polish and German mining industries had recovered from war and disruption and had forced coal prices down. Britain's miners struck to protest the resulting pay cuts. Transport and other workers joined the miners in sympathy. But the government did not need the armored cars that

The General Strike, 1926: London police protect delivery workers from possible reprisals by strikers.

Churchill, by then a defector to the Baldwin cabinet from the dying Liberals, gleefully displayed in Hyde Park to intimidate the strikers. Baldwin supervised a conciliatory settlement for the transport workers; the miners eventually surrendered.

The General Strike of 1926 left a legacy of bitterness, especially among the miners. But Baldwin's tranquilizing manner nevertheless preserved Britain's traditions of gradualism and social peace, despite the rise of Labour and the strain of unemployment in declining areas and industries that idled more than 10 percent of Britain's labor force in every year except 1927. But Baldwin was certainly no "dynamic force." Neither he nor his Labour successor of 1929–31, Ramsay MacDonald, was the man to counter the decay of Britain's heavy industry or arrest Britain's military decline.

France: Instability and Resilience

France, at least superficially, contrasted sharply with Britain's orderly alternation between Conservatives and Labour. France went through seventeen governments between 1920 and 1929. Once the war emergency was past, the Chamber reasserted its dislike of leaders. It did away with Clemenceau in 1920. The Ruhr crisis with Germany over reparations brought Poincaré to the fore in 1922–24. Then *"Poincaruhr"* departed when the May 1924 victory of the moderate left *Cartel des Gauches* displaced the nationalist chamber elected in the enthusiasm of 1919. The Cartel, in turn, was politically incoherent. Radical-Socialists and Socialists squabbled. The Communists, who had captured from the Socialists most of the members of the largest union, the General Confederation of Labor (CGT), gleefully attacked the Cartel from the left. Moscow demanded then and later that all Communist parties concentrate their fire not on the Right but on their Socialist rivals. A "cascade" of short-lived Cartel ministries proved incapable of governing in 1925–26, as the franc declined catastrophically after the Ruhr crisis. Poincaré returned in July 1926; his authority saved the franc.

Remarkably, he remained—and retired voluntarily in 1929.

The appearance of chaos, except under Poincaré, was deceptive. The Third Republic rebuilt the war-devastated areas by the end of the 1920s. The coal and iron of Lorraine, now liberated from Germany, fueled a sharp rise in steel production. André Citroën pioneered the mass production of automobiles in Europe, an innovation the British were slow to follow. Hydroelectric power and bauxite deposits in southern France made it a major producer of that new light metal, aluminum. While unemployment was laying waste to Britain's mining and shipbuilding areas, France was suffering a labor shortage. Prosperity and the immense wartime losses created job openings that 1.5 million immigrants from eastern Europe and the colonies filled.

But France's position was precarious; it rested above all on German disarmament. For as in 1914, France's industrial economy was about half the size of Germany's, and three Germans of military age still faced every two Frenchmen. After the Ruhr fiasco and the Locarno treaty, which barred France from invading western Germany, the French sought security in defense and implicitly abandoned their allies in eastern Europe. In 1929, the government initiated a gigantic engineering project to seal France's eastern borders and protect its vital industries from a repetition of 1914. The Maginot Line, named for the minister of war of the moment, André Maginot, was an immensely strong crust of obstacles and fortresses linked with tunnels and underground railways. It had one weakness: it did not cover the Belgian border. Belgium was a French ally and had its own fortifications facing Germany. If Belgium ceased to be an ally, both the Maginot Line and France might fall.

Germany: Republic without Republicans

Germany's new democracy showed neither British stability nor French resilience. The SPD, Center, and German Democratic (left-Liberal) parties received 75 percent of the vote in the January 1919 elections,

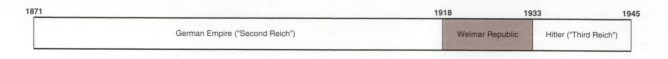

thanks to Germany's need to appear democratic for the Paris peace conference. The new legislature convened under their leadership in the provincial town of Weimar, safe from the Spartacist radicals in Berlin, and drafted the most democratic constitution conceivable. It gave the vote to both sexes at age twenty and employed an extreme form of proportional representation that measured, like a delicate seismograph, every quirk and blip of public opinion. Any party that could collect 60,000 votes in all of Germany could have a *Reichstag* seat. That was an invitation to political fragmentation; by 1928 Germany had at least 45 parties.

The Weimar constitution had a further weakness that in the end proved fatal. Max Weber, who helped draft the constitution, believed that a strong American-style presidency would ward off what he took to be democracy's tendency toward incoherence. Thanks to Weber and to Germany's monarchical tradition, the Republic received *both* a chancellor responsible to the legislature *and* a popularly elected Reich president. And the Reich president had something his American counterpart did not have, although Lincoln at war had in practice claimed it: emergency powers to make law by decree.

Underground in the Maginot Line.

The Weimar constitution failed to work because its drafters superimposed it upon a state and an electorate that were anything but democratic. The officer corps, core of the old Reich, saved itself in 1918–19 by cooperation with the SPD. Thereafter, under General von Seeckt, it supported the Republic grudgingly so long as the Republic tolerated the army's semi-independent status as a "state within the state." As for the electorate, it voted its convictions in the 1920 election and placed the founding parties of the Republic in a permanent minority. Democracy had failed as a means of ensuring a lenient peace. Middle-class Germans had no natural love of democracy for its own sake, and therefore deserted the German Democratic party for the Right. Even the SPD and Center parties were scarcely democratic by vocation. The SPD had to retain its Marxist rhetoric to prevent further defections to the increasingly vocal Communists to its left; the Center had a built-in authoritarian bent.

That the Republic survived as long as it did, and that it provided the backing for Stresemann's moderate foreign policy from 1923 to 1929, was almost miraculous. This was a political system unable to reach agreement on the colors of the national flag; a cabinet fell over that issue in 1926. Coalitions, to command a *Reichstag* majority, had to extend so far left or right that they were prone to break down at any moment.

Nevertheless, three factors preserved the Republic. No alternative existed. The monarchy was politically dead; Communist risings failed in 1919, 1920, and 1923; *Putsches* from the Right collapsed in 1920 and 1923 because Seeckt and his army were neutral or hostile. Second, the Republic acquired an unexpected respectability in 1925. Tirpitz, in his last contribution to German politics, persuaded Field Marshal von Hindenburg to run for Reich president. Hindenburg's triumphant election compelled the old Right to moderate its hatred for the Republic. Finally, Germany after 1924 began to recover its pre-1914 prosperity, thanks primarily to U.S. short-term loans. But if a political alternative arose, if Hindenburg disappeared, if the army turned against the Republic, or if prosperity ended, Weimar might end as well.

The Habsburg Successor States: Democracies and Dictatorships

German democracy, however precarious, was an earthly paradise compared to conditions further east. The states of eastern Europe greeted 1919 clothed in Wilsonian democratic garb. Within a decade, the absence of native parliamentary traditions and the pressures of nationalism and peasant-landlord conflict had turned most of them into dictatorships.

As Austria-Hungary collapsed, its peoples had erected national states. Inevitably, given central and eastern Europe's mixed pattern of settlement, the new borders included large national minorities. Rumania forcibly incorporated the 1.5 million Hungarians of Transylvania, and returned with interest harsh Hungarian treatment of the minorities of pre-1914 greater Hungary. The Poles sometimes dealt arrogantly with their German minority, despite the danger of provoking the German state. In Yugoslavia, Orthodox Serbs lorded it over Catholic Croats and Slovenes, former subjects of Austria-Hungary. Virtually all states and peoples mistreated the Jews. League of Nations safeguards for ethnic minorities proved mere scraps of paper.

Social oppression was almost as pervasive as national oppression. Except in industrial Czechoslovakia and in post-1918 Austria (which consisted of Vienna and an assortment of Alps), the chief class was the peasantry. It ranged in size from 80 percent of the population in Bulgaria to 55 percent in Hungary. Controlling it was the chief preoccupation of eastern Europe's landholding ruling classes. In the Baltic states of Estonia, Latvia, and Lithuania, the landlords were predominantly Russians, Germans, or Poles; the new nationalist governments happily took their

Seeckt, planner of German victories over the Russians and Romanians in 1915–16, made Germany's postwar 100,000-man force an elite "army of leaders," cadres for a future mass army.

land. Elsewhere, peasant land hunger and landlord resistance contributed mightily to political instability.

By 1930, Hungary, Poland, Lithuania, Yugoslavia, Bulgaria, and Rumania were all essentially dictatorships. Hungary went first. From March to November 1919 it suffered the Bolshevik dictatorship of Béla Kun, Rumanian invasion, and finally a bloody reconquest by the Right under the

The dreariness of Weimar, depicted by Georg Grosz, an artist of the Left who bitterly attacked the Republic.

"Strong men" of eastern Europe:
Horthy of Hungary (*above*) and
Pilsudski of Poland (*below*).

leadership of Austria-Hungary's greatest naval leader, Admiral Nicholas Horthy. The result was a gentry-controlled sham parliament under a narrow oligarchy with Horthy at its head. A nationalist dictatorship of the peasant Right emerged in Lithuania in 1926. Poland's parliamentary interlude yielded to a 1926 coup by an ex-socialist "man on horseback," Marshal Joseph Pilsudski. In Yugoslavia, the assassination in parliament of the chief Croat leader in 1928 rendered the country ungovernable. King Alexander imposed a royal dictatorship supported by Serb bayonets. Some Croats replied with terrorism. And in Bulgaria, a military coup in 1923 displaced the ruthless peasant leader, Alexander Stambolisky, who had ruled since 1919. Stambolisky and some 10,000 of his followers perished in ensuing uprisings and massacres. In 1925 a Communist bomb dropped the roof of Sofia cathedral on the representatives of the Right. Enough survived to massacre the Left and impose a royal and military dictatorship with parliamentary trimmings. In 1930 the dissolute King Carol of Rumania returned from exile and adopted a similar solution.

There were two exceptions to this pattern. Austria, despite the economic ruin of separation from Hungary and Bohemia and a built-in cleavage between "Red Vienna" and the *Freikorps*-like hearties of its Alpine valleys, managed to last out the decade as a parliamentary regime. Czechoslovakia, although a veritable patchwork of nationalities, was an island of relative freedom and prosperity under the enlightened leadership of its Czech founders, Thomas Masaryck and Eduard Beneš. But no eastern European state was equipped to face the coming storm.

The United States: The "Roaring Twenties"

Unprecedented domestic prosperity appeared to reward the international irresponsibility of the United States. The economy grew steadily after the brief worldwide slump of 1920–21. By 1929 the real per capita income of the average American had improved by more than a third compared to 1921. The automobile

came into its own as the engine of growth and symbol of the "American way of life." By 1926, Henry Ford had sold 16 million Model T's, the first true mass-production automobile. By 1929, the United States had one car for every five people; European automobile production was a mere 13 percent of the U.S. level. The U.S. electrical industry followed suit: radios, refrigerators, and vacuum cleaners deluged a public that displayed an apparently insatiable appetite for consumer goods.

Politically, the 1920s were a placidly Republican decade. President Harding died suddenly in 1923 during the revelation of financial scandals involving his associates. His Vice President, Calvin ("Silent Cal") Coolidge, then presided in masterful inactivity until 1928. A man of few words but pithy ones, he made no secret of his conviction that "the business of America is business."

The 1920s were also a decade of stern intolerance. As President Wilson lay paralyzed, his attorney general, A. Mitchell Palmer, mercilessly hunted foreign-born "Reds." In laws of 1921 and 1924, under the guise of immigration quotas, Congress extended to southern and eastern Europeans the policy of exclusion adopted earlier against Chinese and Japanese. The Ku Klux Klan revived, and lynched blacks and Jews. And after 1917, temperance crusaders dragooned the state legislatures into ratifying an Eighteenth Amendment that prohibited "the manufacture, sale, and transportation of alcoholic beverages."

Prohibition—not repealed until 1933—was in part revenge of rural and Protestant America upon the great cities and their immigrants. But Prohibition also took revenge on its supporters. The Eighteenth Amendment and the Volstead Act of 1919 that enforced it created an immense illegal beer and liquor industry under the control of the very immigrants whom the temperance movement had sought to discipline.

License accompanied intolerance. War, Prohibition, and prosperity broke down inherited standards. Prohibition, an unenforceable law, led to contempt for all laws; it also increased the appeal of alcohol. Relief from the strain of war, the growing emancipation of women not

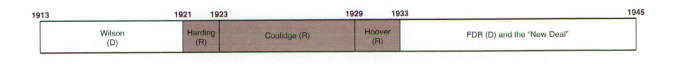

1913		1921	1923		1929	1933		1945
	Wilson (D)	Harding (R)		Coolidge (R)		Hoover (R)	FDR (D) and the "New Deal"	

merely politically but sexually, and the freedom that affluence and automobiles conferred created a hectic and exhilarating "Jazz Age." But all things end. The 1920s ended in an economic catastrophe that appeared to put capitalism itself in question.

THE GREAT DEPRESSION

The collapse of the New York stock market in October 1929 helped trigger a depression that lasted until the next great war, for which it was partially responsible. The Great Depression's ultimate causes, a subject of much dispute, were essentially three.

First, the war distorted the fabric of world trade, and politics prevented readjustment after 1918. Britain and Germany had hurled the products of their industries at each other for four years. When they resumed peacetime production the result was worldwide overcapacity, thanks to a vast economic expansion in the United States and Japan that had filled the wartime gap in the world market. The same process operated in agriculture: the United States, Canada, Argentina, Australia, and New Zealand had multiplied their agricultural production after 1914. After 1919, governments dared not permit the free market to slash the resulting surpluses. Industrialists and bankers made their money talk; workers and farmers voted. Instead of allowing production to fall, most states chose price subsidies and tariffs—a choice that simply prolonged overproduction. Despite the best efforts of the bureaucrats, agricultural prices soon dropped, and kept on dropping. Cotton peaked in 1923, and grain in 1924–25; by 1927 the slide in prices was general.

Second, the war burned up the capital needed to propel Europe's growth. France lost more than half its 1914 foreign investments—a quarter had been in Russia. Britain took on a debt of $1 billion in paying for U.S. supplies. Britain's allies owed it $1.7 billion. The resumption of economic growth depended on renewed U.S. lending.

And the policies of the United States—the third major cause of the Great Depression—were irresponsible and self-contradictory. During the war, America had replaced Britain as the world's greatest creditor. U.S. foreign investments rose from $2 billion in 1913 to $15 billion in 1930. But the isolationist United States of the 1920s refused to play the role that its wealth thrust upon it, the role of leader and ultimate guarantor of the stability of the world market. It rejected any thought of canceling the crushing burden of war debts, incurred in a common cause, under which its allies labored. Coolidge well expressed the implacable American view of those debts in a famous remark in his Vermont twang: "They hired the money, didn't they? Let them pay it!"

The age of jazz: King Oliver's Jazz Band in Chicago (1922), with the young Louis Armstrong (*center*).

Worse, the United States barricaded itself behind the Fordney-McCumber tariff in 1922. High tariffs were traditional in the United States, but now they deprived Europe of a market desperately needed to earn profits with which to pay its war debts. As the president of the Chase National Bank remarked: "The debts of the outside world to us are ropes about their necks, by means of which we pull them towards us. Our trade restrictions are pitchforks pressed against their bodies, by which we hold them off."

The United States nevertheless had a foreign economic policy of sorts. Well-meaning emissaries such as Dawes and Young attempted to stabilize Europe economically. But in the absence of tariff reduction and debt cancellation they merely produced a financial merry-go-round. U.S. short-term loans fueled the German economic expansion that underwrote reparations to France, which in turn paid war debts to Britain. Both Britain and France then paid war debts to the United States. But what if Europe's economy turned downward, or U.S. lending ceased?

Both began to happen 1927–28. Germany's agricultural prices crumbled and its industrial growth stopped. In the United States the Federal Reserve System, an innovation of Wilson's first administration designed to stabilize the banking system, made economic instability worse. Since 1921 the "Fed" had happily pumped in credit, creating hectic growth. In mid-1927, sensing a possible downturn, it pumped harder than before. Easy credit helped stimulate an already foolhardy stock market to the greatest speculative boom in history. The Dow Jones index doubled in value, from 191 to 381, between early 1928 and September 1929. The Wall Street boom put pressure on Europe by siphoning off money from foreign lending. It squeezed U.S. banks and industry by sucking funds out of bank savings, industrial investment, and consumer spending.

In spring and summer 1929, U.S. economic activity turned downward. Production outran demand as speculative mania drained cash from the pockets of businesses and consumers. The market contin-

ued giddily upward. Then the bubble burst. Wall Street slipped on October 3, 1929. By the end of the month, after "Black Thursday" (October 24) and "Black Tuesday" (October 29), the Dow index was falling free. Investors who had bought stocks on credit trampled each other to sell, or leapt from high windows onto Wall Street. Business activity, commodity prices, foreign trade, and the vital lending to Europe all collapsed.

Congress reacted predictably. In March–June 1930, it passed the notorious Smoot-Hawley Tariff, the highest in U.S. history. Coolidge's successor, the unlucky and unloved Herbert Hoover, signed that tariff into law despite a monster petition from a thousand U.S. economists begging him to veto it. The tariff and the cut-off of American short-term credit on which Europe depended were the principal forces that transformed the Wall Street crash into the Great Depression.

All nations sought to keep their own industries and farmers afloat by barring imports. In spring and summer of 1931, the year of wrath, the banking system of central Europe collapsed. A subversive German scheme for economic union with Austria—a disguised annexation—provoked French financial retaliation. An already frail Austrian bank, the Credit Anstalt, failed. The resulting sudden flight of U.S. short-term loans from Germany almost destroyed a banking system enfeebled by agricultural depression and industrial malaise. The German economy, the motor of central Europe, stalled; 17,000 industrial enterprises shut down.

Britain also came under pressure. In September 1931 London suspended payments in gold, which it had discontinued during the war and had painfully reestablished in 1925 only with U.S. help. The pound sterling became just another paper currency, rather than the unchanging world standard it had been throughout the nineteenth century. That was the end of Britain's already shattered claim to world economic leadership. Hoover belatedly and half-heartedly tried to fill Britain's role by proposing a one-year moratorium on reparations and war-debt payments in June 1931. Cancellation would have been more appropriate, but U.S. opinion would not permit it. Regardless of U.S. wishes, war-debt and reparations payments effectively ceased, although negotiations lingered until 1932–33.

Governments sought to promote economic recovery by drastic expenditure cuts to balance their budgets. That further depressed their economies by lessening demand. Tariff and currency-devaluation wars escalated, further deepening and widening the Depression. Britain, formerly the world bastion of free trade, adopted tariffs in 1932. The United States left the gold standard and devalued the dollar in 1933. In Germany and the United States, the worst-hit powers, roughly one worker in four was unemployed by the time the Depression reached bottom in 1932. The Great Depression cut world industrial production by almost a third and world trade by two-thirds. The world market almost ceased to exist (see Figure 31-1). Then the precarious peace of 1919 collapsed.

THE WEST AND THE WIDER WORLD, 1919–39

The war discredited the concept of empire, as well as destroying empires. The victors received German colonies, chunks of the Ottoman Empire, and Pacific islands not as outright possessions, but as "mandates" from the League of Nations. In theory, the purpose of colonialism was now to prepare the subject peoples for independence. That colonialism now needed political fig-leaves was a sign of its coming collapse.

Especially in Asia and the Middle East, war and Bolshevism encouraged the ultimate agent of that collapse—nationalism. Japan's economic expansion encouraged it to press its claim to domination in East Asia. China's reaction and the Great Depression soon moved Japan to make good that claim by force. Japanese defiance of the West undermined the essential foundation of colonialism everywhere, the prestige won in the nineteenth century through the West's effortless domination of the wider world.

FIGURE 31-1   Down the Drain: The Contracting Spiral of World Trade 1929–33

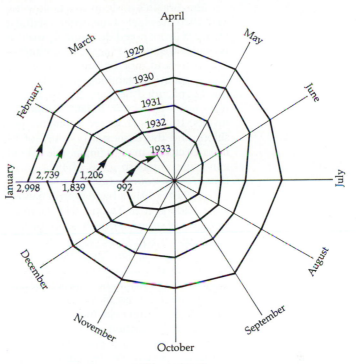

Millions of Dollars

From *Charles P. Kindleberger*, The World in Depression, 1929–1939 *(Berkeley: University of California Press, 1973), p. 172.*

Culmination and Twilight of the Colonial Empires: Britain and France

In 1919, Britain appeared more supreme outside Europe than at any time since the 1870s. Along with its South African and Australian dominions, Britain had taken the lion's share of the war's colonial booty. It had at last secured the east coast of Africa from the Cape to Cairo. It had triumphantly completed the partition of the Ottoman Empire that the Balkan nationalities had begun in 1878. Its major rivals were out of the running. Germany was defeated, Russia was in chaos, and the United States had no desire for further colonial acquisitions; in 1933–34 it pledged to give the Philippines independence by 1945 and unilaterally gave up its treaty right to intervene in Cuba. Britain's only remaining competitors were its allies, France and Japan.

But Britain's position was hollow. By May 1920 the chief of the general staff, Sir Henry Wilson, noted despairingly that "in no single theater are we strong enough—not in Ireland, nor England, not on the Rhine, not in Constantinople, nor Batoum, nor Egypt, nor Palestine, nor Mesopotamia, nor Persia, nor India." Nationalist revolts, Britain's shattered economic position, and the domestic priorities of its mass electorate made it impossible to hold either the immense gains of 1914–18 or Britain's first colony, Ireland.

At Easter 1916 a band of Irish nationalists had risen in Dublin with German promises of support. British troops put the rebels down and tactlessly executed the movement's leaders. That "blood sacrifice" destroyed the position of the Irish moderates and made the radical nationalist Sinn Fein a mass movement. In 1919 an offshoot of Sinn Fein, the "Irish Republican Army," launched a campaign of assassination and urban guerrilla war. The British responded. The feared "Black and Tans," former western-front desperadoes, reinforced the Royal Irish Constabulary. Anonymous gangs caused suspected I.R.A. members and sympathizers to disappear. Even partition in 1921–22 between an Irish Free State in the south and Protestant Ulster in the north did not end "the troubles." I.R.A. diehards refused to accept partition, continued to assassinate

British officials, and forced on the Free State itself a civil war more savage than the one the British had waged. A semblance of peace did not return until 1923, and in Ulster sporadic violence has continued to the present.

In Egypt, nationalist riots and assassinations in March 1919 likewise showed the limits of British power. Britain gave Egypt nominal independence in 1922 while retaining control of foreign policy, defense, and the all-important Suez Canal. In Iraq the British conceded sham-independence, inexpensively enforced by punitive raids with the fighter-bombers of the infant Royal Air Force.

Palestine was more difficult. The Balfour declaration of 1917 and the world war itself speeded Jewish emigration from Europe to Palestine. The ideal of a Jewish state was the creation of Theodor Herzl, who in 1897 had founded a Zionist Organization to promote it. Jewish immigration and aspirations to statehood inevitably cut across the claims of Palestine's Arab inhabitants, many of whom, paradoxically, had moved to Palestine to benefit from the economic upsurge the Jews had brought. In 1929 Arab-Jewish conflict erupted in the "Wailing Wall" riots in Jerusalem. After 1933, thanks to Adolf Hitler, Jewish immigration to Palestine doubled the Jewish population in three years. After 1936–37, a guerrilla struggle between Arabs and Jews tied down two British divisions sorely needed elsewhere. A British

The Easter Rising, 1916: ruins in central Dublin after British artillery bombardment.

ban on Jewish immigration in 1939 failed to placate the Arabs and aroused the fierce hostility of the Zionists.

Worse still for Britain, India repeatedly erupted in violence. Among the many ambiguous British promises of the dark year of 1917—when a mere 15,000 troops upheld British rule on the subcontinent—was a pledge of "responsible government" as reward for India's notable contribution to the war effort. Postwar British conduct appeared to betray that pledge. In April 1919, after a series of attacks on British civilians at Amritsar in the Punjab, General Reginald Dyer ordered his troops to disperse a crowd with rifle fire. In this "Amritsar Massacre" at least 379 died and more than 1,200 suffered wounds. The massacre, and the ensuing celebration of Dyer in British Conservative circles as the man who had prevented a second Indian Mutiny, opened an unbridgeable gulf between Britain and educated Indian opinion.

Amritsar impelled Mohandas K. Gandhi, a Hindu lawyer who had made his name as a leader of the Indian community in South Africa, to launch the Congress party on a campaign of nonviolent civil disobedience. That agitation collapsed in 1922, but British concessions did not follow. Gandhi revived his movement in 1930. The imprisonment of 60,000 demonstrators and Gandhi's rejection of British compromise offers again led to the movement's collapse; Gandhi had outrun Indian opinion. Then Britain gave in. The Government of India Act of 1935 gave India a constitution and a firm promise of independence, despite fierce opposition in London from Conservative diehards such as Winston Churchill. The Congress party swept the 1937 elections. But by that point, despite Gandhi's charismatic appeal, Indian nationalism had divided along the Hindu-Moslem line, A Westernized Moslem lawyer-politician, Mohammed Ali Jinnah, created a Moslem League that by 1940 was demanding partition of the subcontinent into Hindu and Moslem states.

India's movement toward independence was only one sign of the British Empire's decline; not even the white Do-

The Balfour Declaration

Foreign Office
November 2nd, 1917

Dear Lord Rothschild,

I have much pleasure in conveying to you, on behalf of His Majesty's Government, the following declaration of sympathy with Jewish Zionist aspirations which has been submitted to, and approved by, the Cabinet.

"His Majesty's Government view with favour the establishment in Palestine of a National Home for the Jewish people, and will use their best endeavors to facilitate the achievement of this object, it being clearly understood that nothing shall be done which may prejudice the civil and religious rights of existing non-Jewish communities in Palestine, or the rights and political status enjoyed by Jews in any other country."

I should be grateful if you would bring this declaration to the knowledge of the Zionist Federation.

Yours sincerely,
(Signed) Arthur James Balfour

Quoted in L. Stein, Zionism *(London: Ernest Benn, 1925) p. 377.*

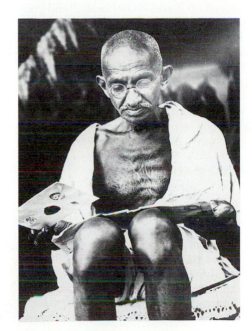

Gandhi (1931) in his everyday garb as a Hindu holy man.

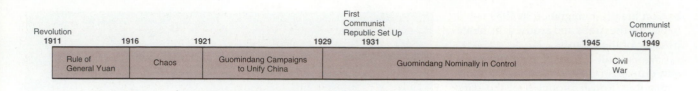

minions showed the unquestioning loyalty for which British imperialists had hoped. Their share in Britain's 1914–18 sacrifices and victory gave the Dominions claims on Britain. With Canada and South Africa in the lead, they sought full sovereignty at the Imperial Conference of 1926. By the Statute of Westminster of 1931 they received it. The British Empire adopted the ambiguous title of "British Commonwealth of Nations." And in 1932, Eamon De Valera, sole survivor of the rebel leaders of Easter 1916, became prime minister of the Irish Free State. In 1937 he took the Free State out of the Commonwealth in everything but name and set a powerful example.

France preferred the Foreign Legion bayonet to the subtleties of negotiation. It was little more successful than Britain. Its 1919 booty, Syria and Lebanon, proved hostile and unrewarding; the French battered Damascus with artillery as late as 1925. The Berbers of Morocco destroyed a Spanish army in 1921 and attacked the French. It took Pétain, tanks, and four years of fighting to reestablish colonial order. Algeria and Tunisia were intermittently restless.

In Indochina, beneath a placid surface, nationalist and Communist clandestine organizations spread, with encouragement from China. The Depression brought starvation to the Vietnamese peasantry and the first serious insurrections since French conquest in the nineteenth century. At Yen Bay, north of Hanoi, nationalists rose in 1930; Communists organized strikes and risings. Ho Chi Minh ("the bringer of enlightenment"), agent of the Communist International for Southeast Asia, founded a Communist Party of Indochina. French reprisals were brutal even by French standards. Ho escaped to China and Moscow, and dryly observed that had the nonviolent Gandhi been born in a French colony he "would

long since have entered heaven." France's control appeared unshaken. But soon white power everywhere in East Asia was at risk.

The Struggle for Mastery in East Asia Renewed: China and Japan

The Depression unleashed a struggle for supremacy in Asia that pitted Japanese imperial claims against both Chinese nationalism and the remnants of European domination.

In 1911–12 military revolt in southern and central China had at last overthrown the decrepit Qing dynasty. The leading proponent of a Western-style Chinese nationalism, Sun Yat-sen, supported that outcome—which destroyed what little prospect remained for a Japanese-style revolution from above that would harness dynastic loyalty to the task of transformation. Sun instead helped found a political party, the Guomindang, and strove to give China constitutional government.

But power in the new China—as in most other societies whose traditional order collapsed under the impact of the West—now came from the barrel of a gun. The end of the Qing dynasty and the crumbling of Confucianism in the face of Western ideas left no other form of legitimacy. Yuan Shikai, most successful leader of the Western-armed provincial armies, had the most guns. He attempted to make himself emperor. Regional warlords resisted; Yuan fell ill and died in 1916. After that, warlord armies fought obscure struggles the length and breadth of China. Those around Beijing (Peking) contended for the honor of manipulating a sham parliament. Chinese nationalism, outraged at continuing European and Japanese encroachments, sought in vain for a political vehicle.

Two contenders arose. Sun discarded parliamentary government for Leninism

Sun Yat-sen, theorist of Chinese nationalism (1923).

without Marxism. The Soviet Union, seeking a sphere of influence in China, delightedly offered advisers and arms. With the help of Michael Borodin, the Communist International's man in China, Sun drafted a new statute for the Guomindang that made it a centralized "vanguard party"—but one without a coherent ideology. Sun's military assistant, Chiang Kai-shek, created a party army in southern China with Soviet rifles and advisers, and inherited the Guomindang after Sun's death in 1925. But the Soviet Union had a second string to its bow: the Chinese Communist Party (CCP), founded in 1920–21 with Soviet advice by groups of Beijing and Shanghai intellectuals. Those groups included the sturdy and pugnacious son of a rich peasant, Mao Zedong (Mao Tse-tung).

In 1927, as Chiang extended Guomindang control to central China, collaboration between the Communists and the Guomindang broke down. Chiang crushed the Communists in Shanghai and elsewhere with much slaughter. Soon the CCP had lost its original base, the small working classes of the industrializing coastal cities. Mao escaped to the hills on the Jiangxi-Hunan border, created a Party army of peasants and bandits, and ultimately purged his remaining rivals in the Party leadership. Lenin had adapted Marxism to a largely peasant country but had kept Marx's notion of the industrial proletariat as chosen people. Mao discarded even that; his Marxism for Chinese conditions was to be an ideology of peasant revolt *against* the cities.

After temporarily suppressing the Communists, Chiang Kai-shek defeated the northern warlords and seized Beijing in 1928. That nominally unified China. But Chiang's rule was precarious; the Guomindang absorbed a variety of quarrelsome warlords as it expanded. The Communists in the hills remained a threat, despite five Guomindang "bandit-extermination campaigns." In 1934–35 Mao's forces escaped from south-central China and in an epic "Long March" of 6,000 miles sought refuge at Yenan in the remote north-west.

By then, Chiang had another enemy to occupy him. Japan had given up most of its claims on China in the Washington treaties of 1922. The Western-style political parties permitted under Japan's Bismarckian constitution of 1889 were at the height of their influence in the early and middle 1920s, despite occasional assassinations of politicians by ultra-nationalist sects. But internal and external pressures made Japan's era of liberalism at home and peace abroad a brief one. At Paris the powers had humiliated Japan by refusing its request to incorporate into the Versailles Treaty a declaration on racial equality. The corollary of that refusal was the banning of Japanese immigration to the United States and to Australia. Simultaneously, U.S. tariffs squeezed Japanese exports, and U.S. pressure dictated in 1921–22 the end of the alliance with Britain that had tied Japan to the international status quo.

Inside Japan itself, by the late 1920s, explosive economic growth, population increase, and radical ideologies pressed against that status quo. Economic growth between 1900 and 1929, at 4.2 percent a year, was faster than that of any other power. Population grew from 43.8 million in 1900 to 71.1 million in 1940. American tariffs and immigration restrictions pushed Japan toward dependence on mainland raw materials and emigration outlets, especially in coal- and iron-rich Manchuria.

Ultra-nationalist sects, a feature of the Japanese scene since the "men of spirit" of the 1850s, proliferated. Ideologues such as Kita Ikki (1883–1939) proposed vague syntheses of Marxism and Japanese nationalism, and looked forward to a world-dominating Japan with vast colonial possessions and a population of 250 million. Such ideas prospered in the military, especially among middle-level and junior officers with rural backgrounds. Ishiwara Kanji, most formidable of the middle-level officers, foresaw world conquest by stages. Japan would seize Manchuria, and would then fight Russia, Britain, and the United States in turn. Each victory would bring Japan the resources needed for the next step: "war can maintain war." Ishiwara was no isolated dreamer; he had the ear of the army's chiefs. And the army, like its German counterpart during the Hindenburg-Ludendorff dictatorship,

Rivals for the mastery of China: Chiang Kai-shek (*above*) and Mao Zedong (*below*).

Mao Proposes a Peasant Revolution   1927

Mao's "Report on an Investigation of the Agrarian Movement in Hunan" of March 1927 was his earliest attempt to persuade his Party that it must either lead China's peasantry or succumb to it.

The force of the peasantry is like that of the raging winds and driving rain. It is rapidly increasing in violence. No force can stand in its way. The peasantry will tear apart all nets which bind it, and hasten along the road to liberation. They will bury beneath them all forces of imperialism, militarism, corrupt officialdom, village bosses and evil gentry. Every revolutionary party, every revolutionary comrade will be subjected to their scrutiny and be accepted or rejected by them. Shall we stand in the vanguard and lead them or stand behind them and oppose them? Every Chinese is free to pick his answer. However, destiny will force us to pick an answer soon. . . .

From Benjamin I. Schwartz, Chinese Communism and the Rise of Mao *(Cambridge: Harvard University Press, 1964), pp. 74–75.*

soon became the decisive force in the state, responsible only to a figurehead emperor.

Chiang's conquest of northern China almost coincided with the Depression. Together they triggered this explosive mixture. Chinese nationalist boycotts of Japanese goods, Chinese aspirations to regain full control of Manchuria, and the collapse of Japan's already stagnant peasant economy in the Depression drove the Japanese army officer corps to strike, to

secure Japan's vital Manchurian hinterland before it was too late. In September 1931, Ishiwara and a group of like-minded officers planted explosives on Japan's railway in Manchuria and blamed the Chinese. The army swiftly cleared Manchuria of Chinese forces and created the puppet state of Manchukuo. The navy attacked the Chinese at Shanghai and ruthlessly bombarded the Chinese quarters of the city—in front of Western newsreel cameras. The cabinet in Tokyo, divided and terrified of assassination, backed the army. When the League of Nations mildly criticized Japan in February 1933, the Japanese delegation stalked out, never to return.

The West failed to do anything effective, despite its outrage over Shanghai. Britain now faced the same unpleasant situation that Russian occupation of northern China had created in 1900. London could not realistically fight a great war to preserve distant China; no vital British interest was at stake. In 1901–02 London had therefore taken on Japan as junior partner. But now Japan itself was the threat, and its strength was far greater than in 1902. This time Britain's only potential allies were the Soviet Union and the United States. But the Soviets were as great a threat as Japan to British interests in China. And while Washington sternly refused to recognize Japan's conquest of Manchuria, it refused with equal sternness to back its moralistic talk with economic reprisals, much less with force. Britain therefore soothed the Japanese and attempted to limit the damage.

Japan made that difficult. Its navy began a massive new building program; in 1934 Japan withdrew from the Washington naval treaty. The elaborate structure of interwar naval disarmament came crashing down. Japanese politicians increasingly submitted to the demands of the military. Those slow to submit risked the fate suffered by prime minister Inukai Tsuyoshi in 1932: assassination. In 1936 junior officers, with the collaboration of Kita Ikki, launched a coup in Tokyo and slaughtered several ministers. The high command reasserted itself with loyal troops and executions.

The rising sun, 1931: Japanese infantry in Manchuria await the order to attack the Chinese.

That ended the day of junior officers and freelance ideologues. Senior generals such as Tōjō Hideki increasingly directed Japanese policy in rivalry with the admirals. And in July 1937 a brush with Guomindang forces near Beijing swiftly escalated into an open-ended China war. A militarized Japan, fighting under the unintentionally ironic slogan of "Asia for the Asians," sought to make China a Japanese colony. The first of the wars that ultimately converged to make the Second World War had begun.

THE THIRTIES: THE DEMOCRACIES FALTER

The Japanese threat caught the democracies just as the Depression and their own demoralization touched bottom. Japan's success soon emboldened others. Fascist Italy, the Germany of Adolf Hitler, and ultimately even the Soviet Union broke the peace (see pp. 833–54). They met little opposition until very late.

Britain: Highmindedness and Decline, 1931–37

The Depression destroyed Ramsay MacDonald's second Labour government, which had taken office in 1929. Labour, trembling at the displeasure of the financial markets and lacking imagination, met the Depression by imposing balanced budgets. That required cuts in unemployment payments and provoked a cabinet and labor-union revolt in the catastrophic month of August 1931. MacDonald stayed on at the head of a "National Coalition" with Liberal and Conservative backing; Labour went into opposition.

As in Lloyd George's coalition, the Conservatives were the dominant partner. Baldwin flattered Parliament and the public; Neville Chamberlain provided the efficiency and drive. He was Austen Chamberlain's unlovable and iron-willed younger brother, in Lloyd George's unkind words "a good mayor of Birmingham in an off-year." In 1935 an enfeebled MacDonald retired, and Baldwin led the Conservatives to victory over Labour by

pretending to block Italy's conquest of Ethiopia (see p. 837). Then Baldwin left his iron-clad House of Commons majority to Chamberlain in 1937.

By that point Britain's world position was precarious. Japan's thrust into Manchuria had moved London to scrap the "ten year rule" and create a committee to look into defense needs—but nothing more concrete. MacDonald, a quasi-pacifist during the First World War, delayed while the World Disarmament Conference met in 1932–34, just as the revolt of the discontented powers took shape. Not until March 1934, after the Conference's inevitable collapse, did the British cabinet begin to debate rearmament. And only Winston Churchill, ceaselessly harassing the cabinet from outside, viewed the German threat with any urgency. Conservative opinion considered Churchill "unsound" since his association with the Dardanelles fiasco in 1915 (which others had mismanaged). His fierce opposition to the government over independence for India had not enhanced his reputation.

Churchill Warns MacDonald and Baldwin   1932

On November 23, 1932, in the House of Commons, Churchill denounced MacDonald's continued pursuit of Western disarmament in the face of the growing German threat:

Do not delude yourselves. Do not let His Majesty's Government believe—I am sure they do not believe—that all Germany is asking for is equal status. . . . That is not what Germany is seeking. All these bands of sturdy Teutonic youths, marching through the streets and roads of Germany, with the light of desire in their eyes to suffer for their Fatherland, are not looking for status. They are looking for weapons, and, when they have the weapons, believe me they will then ask for the return of lost territories and lost colonies, and when that demand is made it cannot fail to shake and possibly shatter to their foundations every one of the countries I have mentioned [France, Belgium, Poland, Rumania, Czechoslovakia, Yugoslavia], and some other countries I have not mentioned. . . .

From Martin Gilbert, Winston S. Churchill, *Vol. V, 1922–1939. The Prophet* of Truth *(Boston: Houghton Mifflin, 1977), p. 451.*

Baldwin's sloth and Chamberlain's niggling defense of financial orthodoxy triumphed. Large-scale British rearmament did not begin until 1936–37. It was too little and too late.

France: Cynicism and Decline, 1932–37

Highminded professions of faith in the League and disarmament accompanied the decline of Britain. The French were more cynical. The only disarmament that interested them was that of Germany, which collapsed in 1932–33. Yet France did not react. The Depression struck France later than Britain or Germany, mainly because France was less industrialized. But it hit hard and kept hitting. Industrial production stagnated at between 80 and 90 percent of its 1928 level from 1931 to mid-1939 (see Figure 31-2). Economic stagnation worsened the central vice of French politics, ideological polarization. The Third Republic, always disorganized, began to totter.

The Communists polled a million votes in 1928 and had gained another half million by 1936. A further sharpening of Moscow's anti-Socialist line in 1928 produced open war between French Communists and Socialists. That conflict stopped the Socialists from collaborating for long with the Radical-Socialists to their right, for fear of losing yet more voters and union members to the Communists. Nor were the deputies of the center numerous enough to command the Chamber. And alongside the old Right of the Dreyfus era and the "two hundred families" that supposedly controlled French industry, a new populist right emerged. The "Leagues," bands of trench-coated anti-Semitic thugs with lead pipes and revolvers, supported ideologies ranging from monarchism to extreme nationalist authoritarianism.

In January 1934, after two years of weak governments of the Left that rivaled the merry-go-round of 1925–26, one of the Republic's characteristic scandals erupted. A shady financier of eastern European extraction, Alexander Stavisky, committed suicide or was murdered after the exposure of frauds apparently committed with the backing of prominent politicians. The Republic seemed even less reputable than usual. On February 6, 1934, the Leagues attacked parliament while Communists rioted in the industrial suburbs of Paris. Police firepower saved the Republic amid

FIGURE 31-2   **Depression and Recovery: Failure and Success**

(Industrial Production as a Percentage of 1928 Production)

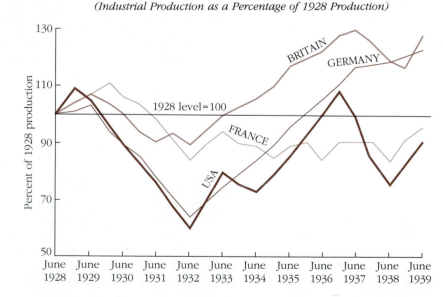

tension not seen in Paris since Boulanger and Dreyfus. The *"six février"* served notice that the Republic lived on borrowed time.

A change of line in Moscow gave the Left a second wind. In 1935 the Communist International, faced with the rise of Hitler's Germany, reversed its previous attempt to stamp out its Socialist rivals. In France the result was a "Popular Front" coalition of Radical-Socialists, Socialists, and Communists. Léon Blum, a vacillating Socialist intellectual, led the government that emerged from the Popular Front's election triumph of April–May 1936. Blum suppressed the Leagues. To the accompaniment of sit-in strikes and industrial turmoil he decreed paid vacations, the forty-hour week, and other concessions that French workers considered long overdue. Those restrictions on industry slowed rearmament and caused French investors to move their capital into harder currencies than the franc. Capital flight in turn brought Blum down in June 1937. The Left could win elections but could not govern.

Nor did Blum, torn between his own horror of war and the pressing need for rearmament to face Germany, find a coherent foreign policy. Not that the Right would have necessarily performed better; much of it mouthed the slogan "Better Hitler than Blum." Blum's foremost successor, Edouard Daladier, was a Radical of Napoleonic appearance but less than Napoleonic strength. His minister of finance, Paul Reynaud, saved the franc in the manner of Poincaré. But that success proved irrelevant. Under Daladier and Reynaud, France first abandoned its eastern allies, then itself collapsed.

The United States: Political Success and Economic Failure of the New Deal, 1933–38

Hoover appeared helpless as the economic fabric of the United States disintegrated. Stock prices continued to slide, wiping out much of the savings of a generation. By 1932, U.S. industrial production had dropped to half of its 1929 level. Only unemployment rose: from 5 million in December 1930 to 13 million in December 1932. The unemployed and their families sought refuge in shantytowns, named with bitter irony "Hoovervilles."

Hoover lost the 1932 election. His threadbare claims that prosperity was "just around the corner" were unconvincing. His spending on public works, although far greater than that of any previous administration, was not enough to spark the economy. His Democratic opponent, the New York grandee Franklin Delano Roosevelt, accepted the nomination with a pledge of a "new deal for the American people." But before Roosevelt could take office the overstrained banking system followed the rest of the economy, as panicked depositors stormed the tellers' windows. On inauguration day, March 4, 1933, Roosevelt shut the remaining banks before they collapsed. Capitalism itself seemed in ruins.

Roosevelt brought a short-term remedy that had eluded Hoover: force of conviction. "So first of all let me assert my firm belief that the only thing we have to fear is fear itself—nameless, unreasoning, unjustified terror . . . ," rang his presidential address. In a mere five days he pushed through Congress a Hoover plan to shore up the banks. In the first of a series of radio "fireside chats" that gave the nation back some of its lost self-confidence, he announced that the banks would reopen. By June 1933 he had averted the threat of total economic collapse. Industrial production briefly equaled the level of 1929.

Roosevelt and his "brain trust" of young intellectuals directed at Congress a torrent of legislation that established public works programs far more vast than those of Hoover and recruited the unemployed into a quasi-military Civilian Conservation Corps. The first New Deal administration created 6 million jobs. To raise agricultural prices, the government paid farmers not to plant crops. Government extended to farmers and householders some protection from the mortgage foreclosures that meant economic ruin and gave unemployment benefits to workers. Government ultimately guaranteed the right to organize unions and created the compulsory pension plan known as Social Security. And thanks to the free-

The impact of the Depression.

trade convictions of Roosevelt's otherwise ineffectual Secretary of State, Cordell Hull, U.S. trade barriers dropped after 1934. That was too late to save the fragmented world market—but better late than not at all.

The New Deal's European-style welfare-state measures seemed revolutionary—and aroused the bitter enmity of business interests. Soon the Republican establishment was denouncing Roosevelt as a "dictator" and traitor to his class. Labor, blacks, and most middle-class Americans took a different view. Roosevelt won his second term in 1936 by an unprecedented margin of 11 million votes; his Republican opponent carried only Maine and Vermont.

But stability and prosperity failed to return. Production briefly surpassed 1928 levels in 1936–37, then dropped again catastrophically (see Figure 31-2 on p. 814). By December 1937, the largest steel industry in the world was operating at 26 percent of capacity. Roosevelt had vastly increased the role of government in the economy—but until 1938 he held to the Hoover line of balanced budgets. Unfortunately, unbalanced budgets were precisely what the economy required to stimulate demand. Not until his 1938 recovery plan did Roosevelt halfheartedly endorse deficits. Necessity, not New Deal economic policies, led to recovery after 1939. Armament production for global war dragged the United States out of the Depression, just as the revolt of the discontented powers in Europe and Asia dragged it unwillingly back into world affairs.

THE AGE OF UNCERTAINTY: SCIENCE, SOCIETY, AND CULTURE BETWEEN TWO WARS

The twenty-year truce was not merely a time of demoralization for the democracies or of triumph for savage dictatorships—a theme taken up in the following chapter. It was also an era of disorienting intellectual, social, and cultural change. Science continued its rapid expansion of knowledge of the cosmos and of the building blocks of matter itself. Technology transformed everyday life. The state took on vast new duties. The war had accelerated the rise of workers' parties and the political, economic, and sexual emancipation of women. It had speeded the breakdown, among much else, of previous notions of what constituted art. A new writing, art, and architecture, reflecting disenchantment with the certainties of the pre-1914 era and rejection of the war, flourished. The mass culture born before the war reached maturity, especially in the United States, to the horror of many traditionalist intellectuals. And the war acted as catalyst for new and terrifying ideologies.

Science: The End of Certainty

By 1900, and still more by 1919, phenomena had emerged that were puzzling or inexplicable to physicists. Neither electromagnetism nor light precisely fitted the traditional Newtonian framework. Worse, the theorists soon had to cope with X rays (1895), radioactivity (1896), and Ernest Rutherford's 1911 discovery that atoms were not solid, as had been assumed since the first atomic theories had emerged in ancient Greece. Atoms apparently contained electrons, nuclei, and much empty space. A chemist discovered radioactive decay in 1913; uranium and thorium, it appeared, turned into lead. Atomic nuclei might contain additional particles.

Further experiment showed that the elements were not the unchangeable basic building blocks in which scientists had believed since the birth of modern chemistry in the eighteenth century. In 1919 Rutherford bombarded nitrogen with helium nuclei and produced oxygen. Researchers discovered neutrons and positrons in 1932 and 1933. The "cyclotron" or racetrack-like particle accelerator first proposed in 1932 allowed laboratory creation of the "transuranic" heavy elements. The first were neptunium and plutonium in 1940.

The theorists soon attempted to explain some of what the researchers were finding. Max Planck of Berlin suggested in 1900 that energy from warm bodies did not radiate at uniform levels across the spectrum but jumped in steps or *quanta;* the amount of energy released varied with its wavelength. Albert Einstein, at that point an obscure patent examiner in Switzerland, suggested in 1905 that light too was "quantized." Niels Bohr of Denmark applied the quantum concept in 1913 to Rutherford's new atom and explained both atomic structure and the differing spectra that various elements emitted. In 1927 Werner Heisenberg of Leipzig, in the course of researches on quantum theory, suggested that the very act of measuring the position, velocity, or mass of a particle interacted with the particle, introducing uncertainty into the measurement. Prediction of the action of subatomic particles fell back on mere statistics—a most un-Newtonian and disquieting state of affairs.

By that point Einstein had established the theory of relativity, the foundation, along with quantum theory, of modern physics. In 1905, in a paper that outlined his "Special Theory of Relativity," Einstein asserted that time and space were not absolute entities, as Newtonian physics required; rather, they varied relative to the observer's velocity and location. The only absolute in Einstein's new universe was the speed of light—186,300 miles per sec-

ond—which was the absolute limit of velocity. Mass increased with velocity, and mass, multiplied by a constant squared, was equivalent to energy: $E = mc^2$. That fateful notion as yet lacked empirical confirmation.

By 1916 Einstein had incorporated gravitation into his theory, which now became the "General Theory of Relativity." And in 1919 an eclipse permitted the first confirmation of the General Theory. Starlight passing through the sun's gravitational field bent by the amount Einstein's theory predicted. Newton's tidy universe gave way to a four-dimensional and curved "space-time continuum." Attempts to unify the General Theory of Relativity with quantum theory, and to explain everything from gravitation to the birth and death of the cosmos and the ever-expanding world of subatomic particles, soon followed.

It also emerged that Einstein's insights had dramatic practical application. In January 1939, building on work by Niels Bohr, Enrico Fermi, and others, Otto Hahn and Fritz Strassmann of Berlin announced that they had split the nuclei of uranium atoms by bombarding them with neutrons. The process transmuted the uranium into barium and a small amount of the uranium's original mass into an astounding amount of energy, as Einstein's formula suggested. The race to create a self-sustaining atomic chain reaction—and weapons of unprecedented destructive power—began.

Biology and medicine experienced the same accelerated pace of advance that was visible in physics. Even before the First World War, the first crude antibiotics—organic poisons that killed disease organisms but not their human hosts—had appeared. Salvarsan, an arsenic compound that revolutionized the treatment of syphilis, became available as early as 1909. The sulfonamides, effective against pneumonia and gangrene, followed in 1935–38. Penicillin emerged in the laboratory in 1929; its first medical use in 1940 proved it startlingly effective against a wide range of diseases and infections.

Advances in immunization had in 1914–18 at least spared western Europe

Giant of the new physics: Albert Einstein in Berlin, 1920.

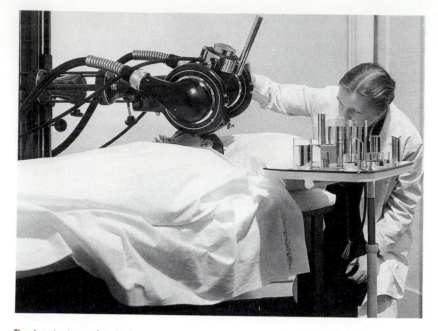

The beginnings of radiation therapy: X-ray treatment for skin cancer, 1930.

the typhoid epidemics that had accompanied previous great wars. In the interwar period inoculations for diphtheria, yellow fever, typhus, and bubonic plague became available. The discovery of hormones, such as insulin (1922) and cortisone (1936), permitted the development of therapies for previously untreatable conditions such as diabetes. The identification and isolation of vitamins helped eradicate deficiency diseases such as pellagra. Thanks to improvements in blood typing, transfusions became normal procedure after 1940. And insecticides, especially DDT (1939), showed promise of eliminating insect carriers of disease. For the Germans, who first developed them, the new insecticides also showed promise of another sort. In 1936 the great German chemical trust, I. G. Farben, began a crash program to develop, from a family of insecticides that killed by disrupting nerve impulses, a weapon for use against humans: the first nerve gas.

Technology: Steel, Oil, and Electricity

The war and the interwar period accelerated dramatic changes in materials and energy sources that were already under

way. Steel remained king, thanks to a bewildering variety of new stainless or extremely hard alloys with metals such as chromium, vanadium, tungsten, nickel, and molybdenum. Concrete, reinforced with steel rods, came into its own as a structural material that permitted the most astounding architectural shapes. Aluminum, refined with electric power, found its way into everything from aircraft to cooking pots. Plastics developed rapidly; by 1939 they provided transparent canopies and windows for aircraft and flexible insulation for electrical cables. Synthetic rubber, another German innovation, became vitally important both to Germany and to the United States after 1939. Artificial fibers such as rayon made possible garments even less expensive than cotton. But artificial yarns made from wood or cellulose fibers were only the first step. In the 1930s the first truly synthetic fiber, derived from oil, became available—nylon. Its great strength made it ideal for everything from stockings to parachutes.

In the realm of energy sources, oil and electricity now triumphed. The First World War had made demands for transport that only the internal combustion engine could meet, and had immensely accelerated motorization. Trucks, tanks, and tractors supplemented and in many cases replaced the horse. Oil-fired high-compression steam turbines or diesel engines replaced clumsy coal, which required stokers and prevented refueling at sea. By the mid-1920s aircraft had ceased to be underpowered kite-like objects of wood, cloth, and wire. By the early 1930s the first multi-engine all-metal airliners were carrying passengers rich and daring enough to try them. Even humanity's oldest form of combustion-propelled projectile revived. In 1926 the visionary Robert Goddard developed the first practical liquid-fueled rocket. His work attracted little attention in his native United States, but observers in Russia and Germany found it intriguing.

Electricity revolutionized communications and created new mass media: motion pictures, sound recordings, radio, and television. Motion-picture technology originated in the 1890s in the United States and France; by 1914 "movie houses" were common. Record players and radios, thanks to Lee DeForest's triode amplifier tube (1906–07), were widespread by 1928, the year of the first "talkie." Television—images electronically scanned, transmitted by radio, and displayed on a cathode ray tube—emerged in U.S. and British laboratories in the mid-1920s, although it did not reach the public for another two decades.

Electronics had more deadly uses: the detection of submarines by sound ranging (sonar) and especially of aircraft and surface ships by radio ranging (radar). After 1935 Britain and Germany raced one another for mastery over those vital auxiliaries to air and sea warfare. As the interwar truce ended, science was developing a potential it had not possessed in 1914: the potential to decide the outcome of war between great powers.

The State in Crisis

The First World War ended for good the state that governed best by governing least. The state now took responsibility for guaranteeing the survival and welfare of the individual. Prewar programs such as old-age pensions and industrial-accident insurance expanded. Unemployment benefits became law. In Germany, workers briefly gained a state-sanctioned voice in management decisions. The United States of Coolidge and Hoover resisted such allegedly socialist measures; then Roosevelt adopted many of them.

The war had also introduced management of currency and foreign exchange, and vast bureaucracies to plan investment and allocate raw materials. Peace had dismantled that planning machinery, but the example of the Hindenburg Program lived on in the Soviet Union (see pp. 830–32). The Depression, a crisis in some ways more severe than the war, gave the state back its wartime role—in "peacetime." The state grudgingly took responsibility for the fate of the economy.

Most democracies adopted some kind of economic planning. But as Roosevelt's confused experiments suggest, they lacked a theory. In 1936, John Maynard

Keynes at last provided a theory for an era in which *laissez-faire* appeared to lead ever deeper into depression. In his *General Theory of Employment, Interest, and Money,* Keynes argued that government deficit financing—the creation of money by decree—was the obvious antidote to deflation and unemployment. Government spending put people to work; their spending, through the "multiplier effect," put others to work. Ideas require time to penetrate, and Keynes's arrived too late. The old orthodoxy dominated as late as 1937, when a tax increase and a tightening of the money supply produced a renewed economic nosedive in the United States. To recover, Roosevelt adopted by trial and error a mild version of deficit financing. Within a decade, Keynes's theories had become conventional wisdom, the charter for continuous state management of market economies.

Workers: Expectations Disappointed

At the outbreak of war in 1914, Britain's Liberal foreign secretary, Sir Edward Grey, dolefully foretold its political and social consequences: "There will be Labour governments everywhere after this." Britain, France, and Weimar Germany indeed received governments led or dominated by workers' parties. But those governments, and the labor unions that supported them, operated under severe limitations.

First, the workers were themselves divided. Regional and craft quarrels fractured the unions of Britain and the United States; racial and ethnic lines also divided U.S. workers. On the Continent, Communists sought to destroy Socialists in the unions as well as in the political arena. In Germany, as described in Chapter 32, the Communist offensive after 1928 helped kill the Weimar Republic; both Socialist and Communist parties perished in the common ruin.

Second, the Depression dramatically lowered worker morale. Especially in Europe, it weakened the main weapon of industrial workers, the strike. Few can strike when one worker in four has no job. Finally, industrial workers, contrary to the predictions of Marx, found themselves in the minority in advanced capitalist societies. Except in egalitarian Scandinavia, political parties claiming to represent workers consistently failed to achieve more than a third of the vote. Insuperable social and ideological barriers prevented further growth—a profoundly demoralizing situation.

If workers accepted democratic rules, socialism was clearly impossible, for the "bourgeoisie" would hardly vote its own demise. But if the workers chose the path of revolution, the other two-thirds of society, with the help of the state apparatus, would inevitably crush them. That threat and the moderate instincts of western Europe's social democrats forced unions and workers' parties in the interwar period to fight a "war of position"—a trench struggle for gradual reform of the economic system rather than for its overthrow. Given their minority status, workers' parties that did achieve power rarely governed long. In the Depression many even failed to prevent their political opponents from reducing unemployment benefits and state employee salaries.

Women: New Predicaments for Old

Women in Britain, Germany, Scandinavia, and the United States likewise discovered that the vote and the workings of the political system changed their lives only slowly. Giving women the vote prevented a repetition of the prewar confrontations in Britain. It channeled women's political activities into the existing parties. It helped women's groups to lobby for full equality before the law and for legislation protecting mothers and children. But the onset of the Depression and the coming of a new war soon diverted politically active women from "women's issues" to more general ones.

Many countries, among them France, Italy, Belgium, and Switzerland, did not even give women the vote, thanks to the weight of male opinion and of the Church. And women's economic position between the wars was even more precarious than that of men. Demobilization of the mass armies and conversion to peacetime pro-

duction led to mass dismissals of women from industry. Structural changes—the continuing decline of peasant agriculture and of "mom and pop" retailing—likewise narrowed women's employment possibilities.

But women were unwilling to give up their new-found economic independence. Many had no choice: their husbands were dead. The interwar growth of business bureaucracies and of that temple of consumer goods, the department store, offered a substitute for industrial employment. Women entered the professions at a greater rate than before, especially in the United States, Britain, and Scandinavia. They maintained their positions in fields such as nursing, primary-school teaching, and librarianship. They nevertheless usually received less money than men—for the same work.

In one vital area the interwar period was the scene of truly dramatic change—control of reproduction. During and immediately after the war, pioneers such as the American Margaret Sanger (1883–1966) and Englishwoman Marie Stopes (1880–1958) made contraceptive information available to a mass audience for the first time in human history. A Dutch invention, the diaphragm, joined the condom, an eighteenth-century device popularized—like cigarettes—in the First World War.

Women thus for the first time acquired effective means to determine when and by whom they had children. Improved childbirth techniques and nutrition ensured that fewer of those children died. Fewer children in turn meant that the average woman now spent four years or less—instead of fifteen or more—pregnant or nursing. That historic achievement allowed some women, for the first time, to aspire to have both a career and a family.

Most men still objected. And the new science of the mind offered small improvement over nineteenth-century medical notions of female inferiority. In Freud's view, woman's unconscious yearning for a penis allegedly led her to seek a penis-substitute: babies. Above all, the course of interwar politics menaced emancipated women; Fascists and Nazis sought to crush all challenges to male su-

Margaret Sanger, pioneer of birth control for the masses, about to appear in court (1917).

premacy. The mission of the allegedly "inferior sex of the master race" was to breed large broods of heroes. But even those regimes failed to reverse the decline of the birth rate brought by industrialization and accelerated by contraception.

The High Culture of Disenchantment

The war broke down inhibitions in literature and art as well as in life. William II had insisted that "an art that transgresses the laws and barriers recognized by me ceases to be an art." Now he was gone; censorship, both formal and informal, diminished in intensity throughout northern Europe. Avant-garde literary and artistic trends that had originated before 1914 now became dominant, at least in high culture.

The prevailing mood was one of disenchantment. The war was the formative experience of an entire generation. Its apparent futility marked their writing, especially in highminded Britain, where the sordid brutality of war had come as a greater shock than elsewhere. British "war poets," including Wilfred Owen and Siegfried Sassoon, wrote eloquent verse that damned the war and the western front. The peculiar conditions of the war, the stark contrast between apparently futile slaughter at the front and almost complete safety beyond artillery range, engendered a fierce hatred of all symbols of authority. Sassoon, a highly decorated officer, railed with particular bitterness at generals, staffs, politicians, and civilians. French war writing, especially *Under Fire* (1917) by Henri Barbusse, who later became a Communist, reflected France's immense losses. Even German war literature occasionally sounded a despondent note, as in Erich Maria Remarque's *All Quiet on the Western Front* (1929).

But Germany was different from the West. There, heroic nihilists of the Ernst Jünger stamp dominated. Works such as *Battle as an Inner Experience* (1922) and *Fire and Blood* (1925) convinced the German young that they had missed something. Jünger spoke or claimed to speak for his generation: "War, the father of all

things, is also our father; it has hammered, hewn, and tempered us into what we are. And so long as the spinning wheel of life turns within us, this war will be the axis about which it whirls."

In England, the aesthetes of the "Bloomsbury Group" devoted themselves to the destruction of what little remained of Victorian morality in their own private lives. Freud appeared to suggest that conventional morality was an elaborate hypocritical cloak over unconfessable desires. He appeared to legitimate not merely confessing those desires, but advertising and gratifying them as well. And his doctrines were an inexhaustible source of small talk. Freud's works now became a popular success.

Bloomsbury also attacked the symbols of Victorianism. Lytton Strachey's *Eminent Victorians* (1918), with its inaccurate but compelling demolitions of Florence Nightingale, "Chinese" Gordon, and other British national totems, was an instant success. John Maynard Keynes, a Bloomsburyite by adoption, atoned for his guilt—in Bloomsbury's eyes—at having worked for the government during the war by savaging his former chief, Lloyd George, in *The Economic Consequences of the Peace* (1919).

In poetry, two transplanted Americans and an Irishman—T. S. Eliot (1888–1965), Ezra Pound (1885–1972), and William Butler Yeats (1865–1939)—gave English poetry a modern shape that ultimately derived from the French Symbolists: loose in structure and playing on layer upon layer of symbolism and allusion to mythology and literature. Eliot's greatest work, a manifesto for the new English poetry, was *The Waste Land* (1922). Its bleak vision of London and modern life as Dante's *Inferno* fitted precisely the postwar mood among intellectuals:

> *Unreal City,*
> *Under the brown fog of a winter*
> *   dawn,*
> *A crowd flowed over London Bridge, so*
> *   many,*
> *I had not thought death had undone*
> *   so many.*

Pound, more difficult and allusive even than Eliot, eventually succumbed to an obsessive anti-Semitism and took Fascist Italy as his adopted country. Yeats, like the others, wove symbols and bizarre occult or cosmological references into his poems. But he also wrote some of the most lucid and musical English verses of the twentieth century, such as the famous lines of "The Second Coming" (1921) that prophesied the triumph of political barbarism:

> Things fall apart; the centre cannot
>   hold;
> Mere anarchy is loosed upon the
>   world,
> The blood-dimmed tide is loosed, and
>   everywhere
> The ceremony of innocence is
>   drowned;
> The best lack all conviction, while the
>   worst
> Are full of passionate intensity.

In the novel, a new technique, the "stream of consciousness," prevailed briefly. Marcel Proust pioneered it in his monumental *Remembrance of Things Past* (1913–27), in which he abandoned narrative in favor of an apparent reconstruction of the thoughts and memories of the novel's protagonist. Virginia Woolf, the one great literary talent of Bloomsbury, experimented with it. But its greatest master was the Irish expatriate, James

Joyce. His *Ulysses* (1921) was a minute reconstruction of a day in the life of a Dublin salesman, Leopold Bloom, organized around themes from Homer's *Odyssey*. Its occasional passages about sex at first prevented it from appearing in England or the United States, much less in Ireland. Banning, and its spread through copies smuggled from Paris, only enhanced its reputation. It was the most influential English novel of the century. In its sequel, *Finnegan's Wake* (1939), Joyce pushed his language beyond comprehensibility and left his audience behind.

On the Continent, Thomas Mann confirmed his position, acquired before the war, as Germany's greatest living man of letters. His monumental symbolic novel, *The Magic Mountain* (1924), was an ambiguous saga of good and evil that conveyed despair in the power of reason in human affairs. Despair in reason was a step forward for Mann. During the war, he had actively urged the rejection of reason, democratic politics, and the West in a massive tract entitled *Reflections of an Unpolitical Man* (1918).

German writers of the "Expressionist" school experimented with a drama of unbridled emotion, Freudian symbolism, and Left politics. Expressionist sons messily murdered their fathers and the other figures of authority discredited by the lost war. The greatest talents of the school were Bertolt Brecht (1898–1956), and the novelist and short-story writer Franz Kafka (1883–1926). Brecht soon exchanged Expressionism for Leninism. Kafka constructed a symbolic world in which fear, guilt, and merciless, incomprehensible forces torture the isolated individual. Kafka's novella, *The Metamorphosis* (1915), sums up Kafka's view of humanity's fate in the modern world. His hero, Gregor Samsa, wakes up one morning and discovers that he has inexplicably become a giant cockroach.

In the visual arts and architecture, new schools multiplied. The Great War slaked Italian Futurism's thirst for violence and change; Futurism emerged enfeebled. "Dada," a Parisian fashion of the teens and twenties, poked fun at art itself and celebrated the absurd and the unpredict-

The Bauhaus school of architecture and design, Dessau, Germany (1926).

able. Its progeny, "Surrealism," sought to represent inner reality in paintings strewn with half-melted pocket watches and Freudian symbols. The center of excitement in the visual arts moved briefly from Paris to Berlin and Munich, thanks to Expressionist masters such as Paul Klee (1879–1940). And in architecture, Walter Gropius, Mies van der Rohe, Bruno Taut, and others secured the first large-scale commissions for the new functional architecture, the "international style." The architects at least were optimists; they sought to remake humanity by remaking its environment. That was too ambitious a project—but they did revolutionize architecture and design.

Mass Culture and Its Critics

One source, beside the shock of the great war, of the despondency that afflicted many intellectuals in the 1920s was the appalling discovery that this was indeed the "age of the masses." A variety of German thinkers stigmatized democracy as the "rule of the inferior." Ortega y Gasset, a Spanish philosopher and literary critic, won immediate fame with his denunciation of *The Revolt of the Masses* (1929). Ortega complained that the unwashed legions, half-educated through universal primary schooling and given power through the vote, were besieging the citadel of Western civilization. The liberal elites born in the nineteenth century had ceased to lead; chaos had resulted.

The reason for that failure of leadership was obscure to Ortega. But it was plain enough. Liberals deplored as an affront to their own cultural standards or to human dignity the methods seemingly needed to exert leadership. Others were less squeamish. Georges Sorel, the pre-1914 French seer of revolution, had developed the concept of "political myths" that mobilized the masses. The French psychologist Gustave Le Bon (1841–1931) had argued that "the crowd" was "feminine" and had claimed that it demanded the domination of a charismatic male. In the Anglo-Saxon countries, vast engines of publicity sold everything from soap to vacuum cleaners to wartime hatred of "the

Hun." The foremost characteristic of the operators of that machinery was their contempt for the public they manipulated.

The "age of the masses" was thus to be an age of emotion, not reason. Advertising used the same techniques to sell a charismatic leader or a Lucky Strike. New media such as film, radio, and illustrated magazines proved especially effective at conveying and appealing to emotion. Politics in Fascist Italy and in Germany after 1933 took on quasi-religious overtones as vast regimented throngs hailed their leaders.

What most critics of interwar mass culture forgot was that, historically speaking, the alternative to semiliteracy had been no literacy at all. Until the nineteenth century only narrow elites had fully enjoyed the written word. Its extension to the majority of the population inevitably involved a lowering of standards, by the standards of the elite. But that was not the end of the world. One answer to semiliteracy was better mass education. Nor was the thrust of the mass market toward the lowest common denominator an all-encompassing and uniform thrust.

The continuing rise in living standards, except during the Depression, did not only foster mediocrity and uniformity. It also permitted excellence and diversity. Bauhaus architecture and design was a genuine popular success. In film, German directors before 1933 created popular successes that were also works of art. Even Hollywood, which established an absolute dominance over the world film industry in the 1930s, occasionally made movies that were not totally frivolous. And in politics, as Roosevelt's radio talks demonstrated, genuine democrats could mobilize a mass public as effectively as the new barbarians.

The Revolt against Reason

War and Depression unleashed those barbarians. In Germany above all, defeat and revolution made anti-Semitic conspiracy theories seem plausible to a wide audience. The wartime propaganda of Tirpitz's *Vaterlandspartei* against the West, the Left, and the Jews found its logical continuation in scores of radical nationalist prophets and sects.

An eccentric Munich schoolmaster, Oswald Spengler (1880–1936), provided a pseudo-historical justification for the new barbarism of the racists and of the visionaries of "soldierly nationalism" such as Jünger. In the summer of 1918, Spengler published the first volume of a turgid 900-page work entitled *The Collapse of the West*. For Spengler, history was a vast cyclical process in which civilizations, the products of creative minorities of Nietzschean supermen, rose, decayed, and collapsed. The West was nearing the end of its cycle. Amid chaos and the brutal self-assertion of new creative minorities, a new civilization might soon be born.

As history, Spengler's grandiose vision was oddly compelling although sometimes laughably distorted. As prophecy it proved almost self-fulfilling. The book's coincidence with Germany's defeat ensured its success. To many Germans, war and an unwanted revolution indeed seemed like the collapse of civilization. And in ensuing years, in works such as *Prussianism and Socialism* (1920) and "The Political Duties of German Youth" (1924), Spengler spelled out in detail the ruthless commitment he thought the new age demanded.

German philosophy added its authority to the chorus of unreason. Nietzsche had denounced Judeo-Christian values as a "slave morality" and had subordinated all morality to "life." His most prominent successor, Martin Heidegger (1889–1976), altogether denied that moral values had a rational basis. In Heidegger's *Being and Time* (1927), the individual was utterly alone, imprisoned in time. The only certainties were *Angst* (usually translated, too strongly, as "dread") and death. Only by living in full awareness of *Angst* and death could a select few define themselves and live "authentically"—a claim that ironically smacked of moral judgment.

This quest for authenticity—in a world where values apparently have no foundation or validity outside the individual—had curious consequences. It often led to self-affirmation through radical poli-

tics: the more radical, the more self-affirming. Heidegger himself made his choice in 1933. Academic freedom, he announced in his inaugural speech as rector of Freiburg University, was "inauthentic." Like Spengler, he enthusiastically urged German youth to serve German radical nationalism and a great leader. Unlike Spengler, Heidegger had a specific leader in mind—Adolf Hitler.

Others chose different leaders. Bertolt Brecht and the literary critic György Lukács (1885–1971) picked Stalin, to whom Lukács made embarrassing obeisance. Lukács's commitment to an irrational political faith did not make him self-conscious; he later wrote an entire volume lovingly demolishing German "irrationalism" from the romantics to Heidegger and Hitler. Brecht, in one of his Depression plays, used his unmatched command of German to celebrate the omniscience and ruthlessness of the Leninist "vanguard of the masses" in verses that the German Communist Party found excessively enthusiastic and frank.

Even in strongholds of middle-class values such as Britain and the United States, the war, the Depression, and the crises of the 1930s prompted intellectuals to irrational enthusiasms. Freud, although he claimed to be a rationalist, undermined reason through his faith in the overwhelming power of the savage forces he saw in the unconscious mind. Those who nevertheless retained a faith in "progress" and reason tended to lean leftward. Lincoln Steffens, a crusading American journalist, returned in 1919 from Russia with a jubilant announcement: "I have been over into the future, and it works!" He was the first of many. Widespread loss of faith in the future of Western society engendered an irrational desire to believe in progress *somewhere*. Visiting Western liberals noisily embraced the Soviet Union and resolutely ignored all evidence that contradicted the facade behind which their jolly Soviet hosts hid the reality of mass executions and starvation. In the mid-1930s American Communism successfully wooed some disenchanted liberals; it claimed to be "twentieth-century Americanism."

War and Depression together created a disorienting and demoralizing world. Empires fell. Political and social landmarks crumbled. Religious, moral, political, and even scientific certainties undermined in the nineteenth century now collapsed. An exaggerated faith in the power of reason gave way to the fanatical celebration and cynical manipulation of emotion. The "best," the defenders of Western civilization and of democracy, lacked the conviction to squarely face the "passionate intensity" of their enemies, the nationalist-racist and Marxist-Leninist dictatorships. The 1920s were no golden age, even in western Europe. The 1930s opened with war in East Asia. They closed with the greatest war in history.

Suggestions for Further Reading

Interwar Politics

For a good introduction to interwar Europe, see especially R. J. Sontag, *A Broken World, 1919–1939* (1971). S. Marks, *The Illusion of Peace, International Relations in Europe, 1918–1933* (1976), is excellent on the peace settlement and its aftermath; for eastern Europe see C. A. Macartney and A. W. Palmer, *Independent Eastern Europe* (1962). On Britain, A. J. P. Taylor, *English History, 1914–1945* (1965), is highly readable, but see also M. Muggeridge, *The Thirties* (1940) and G. Orwell, *The Road to Wigan Pier* and *Down and Out in Paris and London*. On France, see especially P. Bernard and H. Dubief, *The Decline of the Third Republic, 1914–1938* (1985), and A. Adamthwaite, *France and the Coming of the Second World War* (1977). On the United States, W. E. Leuchtenburg, *The Perils of Prosperity, 1914–1932* (1958), is still rewarding, but see also E. W. Hawley, *The Great War and the Search for a Modern Order* (1979); for the 1930s, R. S. McElwaine, *The Great Depression: America, 1929–1941* (1984), is excellent. A. J. Nicholls, *Weimar and the Rise of Hitler* (1968), and E. Kolb, *The Weimar Republic* (1988), offer useful summaries of Germany's brief democratic experiment.

The Great Depression

For the causes and course of the Great Depression, J. K. Galbraith, *The Great Crash, 1929* (1955), and C. Kindleberger, *The World in Depression, 1929–1939* (1973), are useful; D. Landes, *The Unbound Prometheus* (1972), places the event in long-term perspective. For events in the colonial empires, see especially E. Monroe, *Britain's Moment in the Middle East, 1914–1956* (1963); A. Williams, *Britain and France in the Middle East and North Africa, 1914–1967* (1968); B. N. Pandey, *The Break-up of British India* (1969); and J. M. Brown, *Modern India: the Origins of an Asian Democracy* (1985). On China, see J. K. Fairbank, *The Great Chinese Revolution, 1800–1985* (1986) and *The Cambridge History of China*, vol. 12, part I (1983), and J. E. Sheridan, *China in Disintegration* (1975). For Japan, see especially W. G. Beasley, *Japanese Imperialism, 1894–1945* (1987), and J. B. Crowley, *Japan's Quest for Autonomy* (1966).

Culture between Two World Wars

On the intellectual impact of the war, see the wonderful M. Eksteins, *Rites of Spring: The Great War and the Birth of the Modern Age* (1989); also R. Wohl, *The Generation of 1914* (1979). For the sharp contrast between Germany and the West, compare the German outlook depicted in E. Jünger, *The Storm of Steel* (1920; tr. 1929), with that of the writers discussed in P. Fussell, *The Great War and Modern Memory* (1975). For Germany's decisive contributions to interwar high culture, see especially P. Gay, *Weimar Culture* (1968); J. Willett, *Art and Politics in the Weimar Period: The New Sobriety, 1917–1933* (1979); and B. M. Lane, *Architecture and Politics in Germany, 1918–1945* (1968). For the many interwar intellectuals who despaired of their own societies and sought consolation in Moscow, see P. Hollander, *Political Pilgrims: the Travels of Western Intellectuals to the Soviet Union, China, and Cuba, 1928–1978* (1981).

32

THE TOTALITARIAN STATES

By 1933 the demoralized democracies faced not only a militant Japan but three great dictatorships: the Soviet Union of Joseph Stalin, the Fascist Italy of Benito Mussolini, and the National Socialist Germany of Adolf Hitler. Dictatorship was not new. Lenin, an expert, defined it as "a power that is not limited by any laws, not bound by any rules, and based directly on force." Despots from the god-emperors of the ancient world to the tsars of Russia had ruled without laws or rules that limited the sovereign. But custom, the merciful inefficiency of their bureaucracies, and the inadequacies of the technologies at their command had limited their power.

Robespierre and the Committee of Public Safety had briefly wielded, in the name of the General Will, power more total than that of any preceding European state. Now, in the twentieth century, war

and revolution made possible the perfection of the dictatorship of the General Will sketched out in 1793–94. It soon acquired a name. Giovanni Amendola, an Italian liberal later murdered by the thugs of the Italian dictatorship, coined in 1923–24 the adjective *"totalitario"* to describe Fascist election methods. Mussolini happily plagiarized it in 1925; he relished its brutal sound.

"Totalitarianism" thus became a generic term for the dictatorship of the age of mass politics, a dictatorship that set itself a limitless goal: *total power over the individual.* That goal distinguished it from traditional despotisms, and from "authoritarian" regimes such as the dictatorships of interwar eastern Europe or Latin America, which sought mainly to preserve their power. The totalitarian states sought instead to create a "new man," to remodel humanity. And their external goals were

(OPPOSITE) TOTALITARIAN RITUAL: ADOLF HITLER (FRONT RANK, CENTER) PAYS HOMAGE TO HIS PARTY'S DEAD ON THE FIFTEENTH ANNIVERSARY OF THE 1923 "BEER HALL PUTSCH."

almost equally limitless, for the example of freedom anywhere was a mortal threat for all such regimes.

Yet the three regimes were far from identical, despite their habit of imitating one another and their ultimate cooperation in launching the Second World War. Russia, the only Marxist-Leninist state of the three, was also the most economically and socially backward. Russia's middle class was small and its Orthodox Church relatively weak even before the Bolsheviks decided to exterminate the one and virtually abolish the other. Bolshevik power came from victory in a merciless civil war; from the beginning it rested "directly on force." Lenin and his successor Stalin faced none of the constitutional or social obstacles to total power present in the more developed societies of the West.

Mussolini and Hitler, by contrast, came to power with apparent legality in societies that had parliamentary regimes. They faced mighty entrenched interests and institutions—armies, industrialists, and churches—whose assistance was necessary for the consolidation and expansion of their power. In Russia the regime was free from birth to begin the total transformation of Russian society accomplished by the late 1930s. All it lacked was an implacable will. Stalin supplied that. In Italy and Germany the dictators had to buy their freedom. The method they chose was war.

RUSSIA: FROM REVOLUTION TO GENOCIDE

From Tsarist to Communist Autocracy

Within five years of the collapse of tsarism in 1917, Russia was once again an autocracy. After October 1917, Lenin systematically crushed all opposition—the short-lived Constitutional Assembly, the other left-wing parties, and the counterrevolutionary "Whites." The grass-roots workers' Soviets withered; the secret police (CHEKA) swelled to 30,000 and the Red Army to 5.3 million. Soon all that remained of the workers' Soviets was the name, which the Party took over for its new state: the Union of Soviet Socialist Republics.

The Bolsheviks defeated the Whites by 1921, only to face economic crisis and internal revolt. War, revolution, and civil war had cost Russia more than 10 percent of its 1913 population of 159 million. At least 2 million had died in the First World War, a million had emigrated, up to 10 million had died in the civil war and accompanying famines, and as many as 5 million had perished in drought and famine in 1921–22. Between 1917 and 1920, food shortages, Bolshevik brutality and mismanagement, and civil-war chaos had cut Russia's "proletariat" in half, from 3 million to 1.5 million. The industrial work force, recently recruited from the peasantry, simply returned to its villages. The peasantry itself fiercely resented the ruthless Bolshevik confiscation of crops to feed the cities. Externally, defeat in Poland in 1920 and the failure of world revolution to materialize meant isolation and apparent danger.

In February 1921 strikes against the self-proclaimed "workers' state" swept Petrograd. In March, sailors at Kronstadt, the nearby naval base that had once furnished fanatical recruits to Bolshevism, rose against Bolshevism on behalf of the half-starved remnant of Russia's workers. Millions of peasants in central Russia were already in armed revolt against the exactions of "war communism," the forced requisition of food. The regime appeared close to collapse.

Lenin and the Party acted. Mass arrests clamped Petrograd down. Trotsky besieged Kronstadt and annihilated the sailors at the cost of 10,000 Red Army casualties. Lenin outlawed "factionalism" in the Party and attacked those comrades who still took seriously the Party's claim to represent the *existing* Russian proletariat. In the Party's eyes, those workers and Kronstadt sailors who demanded free elections to the Soviets had ceased to be proletarians.

To placate the peasantry, the only great social group the Party was not yet strong enough to crush by force alone, Lenin and his associates retreated from "war communism." The "new economic policy" or NEP of 1921–28 restored some free enterprise to the countryside and even to industry. It was a recognition of reality—external isolation and internal weakness—that ended for the moment Lenin's attempt to force the pace of history and leap directly from tsarism to Communism.

The NEP was an economic success. Agricultural production passed 1913 levels in 1924. Enterprising peasants prospered. By 1926–27 even the cities had begun to revive. But the NEP proved a brief respite. In May 1922, Lenin suffered the first of a series of deadly strokes. In January 1924 he died. By that point the struggle for the succession had already begun: Trotsky was the leading candidate. But his Menshevik past, Red Army ties, and lack of modesty alienated a fiercely clannish Party that feared "Bonapartism"—the rule of a successful general. Trotsky's rival was a self-effacing bureaucrat from Georgia in the Caucasus, Joseph Stalin, a former seminary pupil and revolutionary bank robber. Lenin had placed Stalin in charge of the central Party machine, and thus of recruitment. Stalin soon allied himself with Trotsky's rivals on the Party "Left," Grigorii Zinoviev and Lev Kamenev.

Stalin craftily cloaked his ambition in mock humility and easily deflected Lenin's dying demand that the Party demote the uncouth Georgian, who was "too rude," a fault "insupportable in a general secretary." Stalin's foolish allies from the "Left" found him less threatening than Trotsky. And the new Party rank and file with whom Stalin was rapidly swamping the "Old Bolsheviks" owed their careers to him alone.

Stalin was careful to speak in the name of the Party, while consolidating his own power. Since Lenin had forbidden "factionalism," opponents of Stalin automatically became opponents of the Party. They forfeited both legitimacy and self-confidence; Stalin used the Party's cult of unity against them to force humiliating recantations and "self-criticisms." The CHEKA, renamed GPU, then OGPU, and finally NKVD, became Stalin's ally and in-

Trotsky, victorious Commissar for War, reviews his troops (1920).

strument; it soon overshadowed the Party. And Stalin had Lenin embalmed and placed on exhibit as a holy relic of the new state religion: "Leninism." Petrograd became Leningrad; all across the Soviet Union statues of the prophet arose. The cult of Lenin legitimated Bolshevik power and created the role that Stalin himself was soon to fill.

In 1925 Zinoviev and Kamenev led the attack on Trotsky, and expelled him from his Party and army offices. In 1926 Stalin turned on his allies and in turn demoted them with the help of the Party "Right" formed around the theorist Nikolai Bukharin. Trotsky had urged continued conflict: "permanent revolution" abroad and, at home, increased pressure on the peasants to squeeze from them capital for a crash industrialization program to achieve the Communist utopia. Stalin and Bukharin triumphed within the Party by asserting a seemingly more moderate course: "socialism in one country" and continuance of the NEP.

But once Trotsky, Zinoviev, and Kamenev were disposed of, Stalin took over their domestic policy. The naive Bukharin suddenly discovered that Stalin was "an unprincipled intriguer who . . . changes his theories depending on whom he wants to get rid of at any particular moment." Terrified, Bukharin sought alliance with Kamenev and Zinoviev: Stalin was "a new Ghenghis Khan; he will strangle us all."

Stalin's ambitions extended far beyond the death of his Party rivals. The world, he told the Party in 1926, had "two centers of gravity," the Soviet Union for socialism and "Anglo-America" for capitalism. "To win conclusively," the Soviet Union must replace its present "capitalist encirclement" with a "socialist encirclement" by a ring of satellites. And Stalin also foresaw a new world war; the Soviet Union, he predicted, would enter last of all, "in order to throw a decisive weight onto the scales."

To survive the coming war and to expand Soviet power, Stalin needed arma-

ments before anything else. A war scare that he invented in 1927–28 helped make the case for a Five-Year Plan of crash industrialization. The NEP was already failing to provide enough grain for the towns, as the peasantry resisted Party attempts to keep agricultural prices artificially low. Stalin could therefore argue that the NEP, if it continued, would make it impossible to extract from the peasants the surplus needed to finance industrialization and feed a larger factory work force. Party and OGPU pressure on the most prosperous peasants—the so-called *kulaks* ("fists")—increased.

By early 1929, Stalin had forced Trotsky into exile (and had him murdered in 1940, after erasing his name from the history of the Bolshevik Revolution). Stalin then demoted Bukharin and the "Right" by exposing their attempts to ally themselves with the discredited "Left." And he put an end to the NEP.

Lenin's party had erected a new autocracy over Russia. Stalin, whom the Soviet press increasingly hailed as the "Great Leader," was now close to erecting an autocracy over the Party. In the absence of laws and rules, Bolshevik dictatorship over the proletariat was swiftly becoming the dictatorship of an individual. And that individual, because he controlled the instrument of terror and claimed to embody the will of the proletariat and the supposed laws of history, could do anything he pleased.

The Great Famine, 1929–34

On December 27, 1929, as the first Five-Year Plan went into effect, Stalin informed Russia of its fate: "either we go backward to capitalism or forward to socialism. What does this mean? It means that after a policy that consisted in limiting the exploitative tendencies of the *kulaks,* we have switched to a policy of liquidating the *kulaks* as a class."

In Stalin's view, crash military-industrialization and the consolidation of Soviet power required making the landowning peasantry into a rural proletariat—serfs of the Soviet state—to work the land with state-owned machinery. The goal of

Stalin Demands Crash Industrialization

Stalin shrewdly blended Marxism-Leninism and Russian nationalism in his rationale for crash industrialization. He advanced his thesis most forcefully in a speech of early 1931.

To reduce the tempo [of industrialization] would mean to fall behind. And those who fall behind get beaten. But we do not want to be beaten. No, we refuse to be beaten! One feature of the history of old Russia was the continual beating she suffered because of her backwardness. She was beaten by the Mongol Khans. She was beaten by the Turkish beys. She was beaten by the Swedish feudal lords. She was beaten by the Polish and Lithuanian gentry. She was beaten by the British and French capitalists. She was beaten by the Japanese barons. All beat her—because of her backwardness, military backwardness, cultural backwardness, industrial backwardness, and agricultural backwardness. They beat her because to do so was profitable and could be done with impunity. . . . It is the jungle law of capitalism. You are backward, you are weak—therefore you are wrong; hence, you can be beaten and enslaved. You are mighty—therefore you are right. . . . We are fifty or a hundred years behind the advanced countries. We must make good this distance in ten years. Either we do it, or we shall be crushed.

From Basil Dmytryshyn, USSR: A Concise History *(New York: Charles Scribner's Sons, 1978), p. 158.*

"complete collectivization" that Stalin announced in December 1929 would end forever the mortal internal threat that Lenin had feared: "Capitalism begins in the village marketplace." It would also provide external might, to defend and advance the Revolution. With collectivization, Stalin made good his claim to be Lenin's true heir—despite the doubts Lenin had expressed about Stalin's manners. Stalin proposed to force the pace of history and complete the revolution that Lenin had launched in 1917.

Nor was Stalin's choice of the word *liquidate* an accident. The Party activists, army, and OGPU troops who forced the peasants into state-controlled collective farms received orders to select fixed quotas of *kulaks* and "*kulak* henchmen" for removal. Between 5 and 20 percent of the rural population, depending on the area, were deported to Siberia and central Asia. Most of them died, either on the march or under the care of the OGPU's newly established "Main Administration of Corrective Labor Camps," best known by its sinister acronym, GULAG. The peasants who remained resisted. They slaughtered and ate their livestock rather than deliver it to the collective farms. They refused to plant more than a bare minimum of crops. Villages and entire regions defied the regime. Red Army sweeps and mass executions gradually subdued them.

Stalin's war on the Soviet Union's 120 million peasants culminated in a devastating famine in the Ukraine and elsewhere in 1932–33. Stalin barred food relief shipments, to bring home to the peasantry the cost of defying him; Soviet food *exports* during the famine exceeded those during the prosperous years of the NEP. With macabre relish Stalin publicly commanded merriment: "Life has become more joyous, comrades; life has become gayer." Privately he remarked much later, to Winston Churchill, that 10 million had suffered death or deportation. Soviet demographers later admitted a population loss of 7.5 million; the true figure may have been as high as 15 million.

Stalin's war on the peasantry so devastated Soviet agriculture that in per capita terms it produced scarcely more in 1953

The "Mutability of the Past"

In his novel 1984, *published in 1949, the British essayist and novelist George Orwell (1903–50) depicted a nightmare totalitarian future that drew on Stalin's attempts to control the past.*

The mutability of the past is the central tenet of Ingsoc [Orwell's fictional state ideology]. Past events, it is argued, have no objective existence, but survive only in written records and in human memories. The past is whatever the records and the memories agree upon. And since the Party is in full control of all records, and in equally full control of the minds of its members, it follows that the past is whatever the Party chooses to make it. It also follows that though the past is alterable, it never has been altered in any specific instance. For when it has been recreated in whatever shape is needed at the moment, then this new version *is* the past, and no different past can ever have existed. . . . At all times the Party is in possession of the absolute truth, and clearly the absolute can never have been different from what it is now. . . .

From George Orwell, 1984 *(New York: Signet, 1961), p. 176.*

than it had in 1913. The catastrophic losses to agriculture probably exceeded the gains of the rapidly expanding industrial sector. But the terror-famine achieved its political purpose. The Party broke the one great social force in Russia. By 1932 the state had seized 88 percent of Russia's farmland; by 1937 collectivization was almost total.

And Stalin did extract the labor and some of the needed capital for the Five-Year Plan. According to some estimates, "de-kulakized" slave laborers furnished more than 5 percent of the Soviet labor force by 1933. Peasants fled the land for the industrial cities and mines of the Don Basin and the Urals. Food extracted from the peasantry at gunpoint helped the regime to more than triple Russia's industrial work force. Terror and propaganda whipped the exhausted workers onward, amid immense waste and confusion. Vast hydroelectric dams, steel mills, and armaments factories rose, based on technology bought from the West with exported grain and with gold that GULAG inmates dug from the arctic tundra. The first Five-Year

Joseph Stalin (1937): "To choose one's victims, to prepare one's plans minutely, to slake an implacable vengeance, and then to go to bed . . . there is nothing sweeter in the world."

1917		1924	1928		1953

Lenin | Stalin against Trotsky | Stalin

Plan multiplied Soviet capital-goods production by two and a half. At the "Party Congress of Victors" in January 1934 Stalin savored a success bought through the crippling and stunting of his society: "The line of the Party has triumphed."

The Great Terror, 1934–39

As the crisis of collectivization passed, Stalin nevertheless found himself under attack. In 1932 opponents circulated a long document full of devastating criticism of his wasteful and erratic economic leadership, and of the Party's alienation of the working class it claimed to incarnate. Stalin responded with orders to scrutinize the Party membership and purge those suspected of opposition. But he failed to persuade his colleagues on the Party's ruling committee, the Politburo, to redefine dissent within the Party as "counterrevolutionary activity," which carried the death penalty.

That impasse ended on December 1, 1934. A dissident Party member, with the apparent complicity of the NKVD, assassinated Sergei Kirov, boss of Leningrad and rising young star of the Party. Much later, after Stalin's death, Soviet leaders hinted broadly that Stalin was behind the murder. It gave him a pretext to clamp down once more. Having enserfed the peasantry, he now set as his goal the destruction of all doubters and *potential* sources of opposition. Hitler had set the example in June 1934 with a massacre of associates who had become politically inconvenient (see p. 842).

In the aftermath of Kirov's assassination, the NKVD under Stalin's personal direction received the power to shoot summarily anyone it pleased. It soon discovered a mythical "terrorist center" in Leningrad. In early 1935 it dredged up Zinoviev and Kamenev for the first of a series of show trials, an art form already perfected in trials of Socialist Revolution-

aries, Mensheviks, and foreign engineers falsely accused of sabotage. Calls went out to the Party to unmask "Trotskyites" and "Zinovievites." Soviet law soon provided swift death not only for alleged spies and "parasites," but also for those who had knowledge of their activities and failed to denounce them—including children of twelve years or older. The families and children of those arrested became hostages, liable to punishment—a further extension of the genocidal notion of "class justice" that Dzerzhinsky and Latsis of the CHEKA had pioneered. *Pravda,* the Party newspaper, began to carry stories praising children who had reported their parents to the NKVD.

In August 1936, amid mounting anxiety, Stalin announced a new Soviet constitution that contained lavish guarantees of individual freedoms. But woe to those who failed to exercise those freedoms "in accordance with the interests of the workers and for the purpose of strengthening the socialist system." That same month Zinoviev and Kamenev obligingly admitted to having planned Stalin's assassination; the court had them shot. Terror became all-pervasive.

But Stalin was not content. He accused the NKVD leaders of footdragging and replaced them with a new man, the "bloodthirsty dwarf," Nikolai Yezhov. In January 1937 Yezhov mounted yet another Moscow show trial, of the fancifully named "terrorist counterrevolutionary Trotskyite-Zinovievite bloc." Mass arrests and lesser trials occupied the rest of the year. The NKVD and its informers feverishly invented conspiracies, beat prisoners into confessions that implicated ever more suspects, and shot in the prison cellars those who were no longer of use.

Stalin also turned on the Red Army, which he apparently feared might threaten his power in the event of an ever more probable European war. The generals were tougher than the Party; they refused to confess to being in league with Germany and Japan. Stalin had his own high command shot in secret in June and July 1937 and announced the executions after the event.

The last great trial, in March 1938, was that of the so-called "bloc of anti-Soviet rightists and Trotskyites." It included a wide range of victims, from Bukharin to Genrikh Yagoda, the former head of the NKVD whom Stalin had replaced in 1936 for insufficient zeal. Old Bolsheviks confessed to sabotaging butter production with ground glass and to conspiring with Trotsky, Germany, Japan, Britain, and Poland. Western observers, including Roosevelt's ambassador and the correspondent of the *New York Times,* swallowed these absurd tales whole. Bukharin was puzzling, however. He confessed to almost everything, then hinted he was not guilty. Above all, he refused to admit to having plotted Lenin's murder, as Stalin's vindictive prosecutor, Andrei Vishinsky, claimed. The court had Bukharin shot with the rest, but he had marred the illusion of guilt that Stalin sought to create.

The great terror, like the terror-famine that preceded it, accomplished its objective. It remade the Party. Seventy percent of the Central Committee of 1934 perished; Stalin wiped out the leading Old Bolsheviks and any alternative within the Party to his own domination. Terror remade the armed forces. Half of the officer corps, 35,000 men, fell victim. And only 10 percent of those destroyed in the great terror were members of the Party or army. The rest were victims of chance associations, of neighbors' denunciations, of family relationships to suspects, of the envy of subordinates at work, of membership in national minorities. The victims of Stalin's genocide died not because of anything they had done but because of what they were. They perished *by categories,* from *kulaks* and "*kulak* henchmen," to Ukrainians, to Old Bolsheviks, to suspects of "Trotskyism," to relatives of suspects, to individuals whose only "crime" was that they belonged to a generation that remembered Russia before 1917.

The replacements of those "purged" were younger, with fewer memories than their predecessors. They were unlikely to question Stalin's leadership. Above all they were bound to Stalin: they owed their rapid promotions to the vacancies he and his NKVD had created. In many cases they had helped, with a word to the NKVD about their superiors—for Stalin was not the sole author of the terror. He had millions of helpers, bound forever to their master by fear, gratitude, and complicity. Stalin had created a new ruling class in his own image.

The cost was high. The secret 1937 census, according to some accounts, showed that the Soviet Union had 21.5 million people fewer than the second Five-Year Plan had forecast. Stalin, furious, had the demographers shot or sent to GULAG for having allegedly "exerted themselves to diminish the numbers of the population of the Soviet Union." Stalin reserved that privilege to himself. By 1939, the GULAG concentration camps held an estimated 10.4 million people—10 percent of the Soviet labor force. The death rate in the camps was as high as 10 percent a year. By 1940, Stalin's genocide had through famine, terror, and slave labor killed between 12.7 and 22.1 million people—on top of the immense losses between 1914 and 1922. Stalin had also signed a pact with Hitler.

ITALY: FROM DICTATORSHIP TO EXPANSION, 1922–40

To achieve total power in a developed Western society was a challenge more difficult than that facing Stalin. But the First World War created conditions that made it thinkable. For war—a war the rulers had imposed on a resentful parliament and a divided public—caught Italy at a particularly dangerous moment, as the coming of universal male suffrage in 1912–13 launched it into the age of mass politics.

The Crisis of Liberal Italy, 1919–22

War and the example of the Russian revolution mobilized the Italian masses; the 1919 election destroyed the dominance of the Liberals. Two great mass parties, the Catholic People's Party (*Popolari*) and the Socialists, now commanded between them a majority in parliament. But unlike Weimar Germany, the mass parties refused to cooperate and rule. Socialists embraced the half-understood example of Lenin. The *Popolari,* under Vatican influence, had entered politics partly to counter the Socialists. Parliamentary deadlock and a series of weak Liberal cabinets resulted. And for the Right, the Liberal regime had lost its small stock of prestige when the Allies at Paris had "mutilated" Italy's victory by refusing to concede its far-reaching Balkan and colonial claims.

Outside parliament, the Socialists took the offensive in the "two red years" of 1919–20. Their agricultural unions and political machines organized the landless laborers and were soon ruling Italy's richest farming region, the Po Valley. Landowners who refused to hire labor at the rates and in the numbers that the Socialists decreed suffered boycotts, arson, mutilation of livestock, and worse. Factory and transport workers struck repeatedly. But the Socialists' incessant talk of revolution, their violence against landowners, and their abuse of veterans as warmongers and capitalist dupes inevitably backfired.

In October 1914 Benito Mussolini, whom Lenin had seen as the future revolutionary leader of Italian Socialism, had quarreled with the party over its refusal to support war. Mussolini, the brutal and charismatic son of a village blacksmith, had agitated for war and had served in the infantry until he was wounded. In March 1919, he founded a movement to carry the war into politics: the *Fasci di Combattimento* ("combat leagues"). Its first recruits were a curious mixture of former assault troops, wartime junior officers, nationalist students, and socialists who had chosen war in 1914–15. "Fascist" ideology was and remained amorphous, but its principal components were a fierce hostility to the Left and a resentful and expansionist nationalism.

The Socialist offensive in the Po Valley flatlands and agitation by the Slovenes of newly annexed Trieste made the summer of 1920 "the hour of Fascism." Fascist *squadre,* gangs in black shirts or wartime field-gray, attacked Socialists and Slovenes with clubs, knives, pistols, and hand grenades. Landowners and a few industrialists happily contributed funds. Army units secretly provided trucks and weapons. The numerous landowning peasants, whom the Socialists had alienated with talk of collectivization of the land, joined the Fascist *squadre.* Some Liberals in Rome deplored Fascist violence but lacked the resolve to restore order. Other Liberals, among them Giovanni Giolitti, saw the Fascists as a healthy patriotic reaction against the excesses of the Socialists and the encroachments of the *Popolari* on the Liberal state.

By the summer of 1921 the Fascists had smashed the Socialists in the Po Valley and Tuscany, and had set themselves the task of conquering Italy. In Rome, Fascist deputies took the battle into parliament after Giolitti offered an electoral alliance. In the countryside, motorized "punitive expeditions" by the "blackshirts" grew ever larger and more ferociously effective. But hostility between the Socialists and the *Popolari* prevented them from joining hands against the Fascist threat.

By October 1922 Liberal Italy was finished. Right Liberals such as Salandra sought to co-opt Mussolini, to tame him by bringing him into the government. In a two-track maneuver that combined an insurrectionary "March on Rome" with negotiations with Salandra and others, Mussolini demanded to be named prime minister. The last Liberal cabinet feebly urged the King to bring in the army to restore order. Victor Emmanuel III consulted his generals, who answered that the army would do its duty, but that it would be better not to put it to the test. King, army, and Right Liberals chose Mussolini over a civil war they feared would strengthen the Left. They made Mussolini prime minister of Italy on October 31, 1922.

The Fascist State, 1922–29

As Mussolini admitted privately in 1924, the "March on Rome" was no revolution: "The revolution comes later." He had no

majority in parliament and therefore had to take fellow-traveling Liberals and *Popolari* into his first cabinet. He depended on Italy's industrialists and on foreign bankers to shore up the economy. And to the end his authority ultimately derived from the king who had appointed him. The Fascist regime remained a "dyarchy," with dictator and king sharing power. The regime was thus the least "totalitarian" of the three great dictatorships: Mussolini's "NEP" lasted until 1935–36.

But Mussolini nevertheless aspired to total power, and moved to achieve it by stages. From the beginning he chipped away both at opponents and at conservative "flankers" who sought to use him merely to tame the Left. Fascist violence continued in the provinces; a new electoral law guaranteed a Fascist majority in the 1924 elections.

That victory led Mussolini to overreach. Fascism's most conspicuous opponent, Giacomo Matteotti of the Socialists, claimed in parliament that the new regime rested on force and fraud. Then he vanished. It soon emerged that the "CHEKA," as Mussolini only half-jokingly called his bodyguard of thugs, had taken Matteotti for a fatal ride in the country.

Mussolini himself preserved what a later age was to call "plausible deniability." Pressure for his resignation nevertheless mounted among Liberals in the cabinet and in parliament. Mussolini privately railed at the Italian people's "absurd fuss" over the death of one man. Then and later he secretly envied the Bolsheviks, who faced no such limits.

Socialists, *Popolari,* and Left Liberals, united at last, seceded from parliament in protest. That was suicidal; it split the opposition between those who seceded and those who stayed. Mussolini bought off with concessions some of the Liberals who remained. He faced down waverers in the cabinet by threatening to fight the opposition in the streets rather than yield power. As in 1922, he offered the Italian establishment a simple choice: him or civil war.

On January 3, 1925, with the King's silent support, Mussolini announced that he would remain in power indefinitely. The police shut down the opposition press. A succession of botched attempts to assassinate Mussolini soon gave him welcome pretexts to rule by decree and outlaw all opposition parties. Within the Fascist party, Mussolini abolished the few shreds of internal democracy that had survived from 1919–21: "The Revolution has one Leader." By 1928 he had grafted the party onto the state and had given the party's highest organ, the Grand Council of Fascism, power to regulate the succession to the throne. He created a Fascist youth movement to permeate the coming generations with a brutish nationalism and a pagan "sense of virility, of power, of conquest."

Mussolini, surrounded by the commanders of the "March on Rome," strikes a pose before assuming power in 1922.

Mussolini also secured a prize that had eluded his Liberal predecessors: a settlement of Italy's festering quarrel with the Church. The Lateran Pact of February 1929 created a Vatican City mini-state and gave the Vatican a large sum in Italian state bonds as compensation for the territory seized in 1870; a Concordat between Church and state made Catholicism the state religion. In return, Pope Pius XI hailed Mussolini as "the man whom Providence has placed in Our path." That blessing and the rural clergy's enthusiastic support for the regime made Mussolini's position unassailable. A plebiscite and a one-party election in March 1929 gave Mussolini an overwhelming and mostly genuine majority, and a black-shirted parliament. The dictatorship rested on monarchy, army, and police, but also on the acclamation of the masses and the blessings of the Church.

Mussolini Breaks Through to Empire: Ethiopia and after, 1935–40

Yet control of government and the growing cult of the *Duce* was not enough. In 1925 Mussolini had expressed many of his ultimate goals in a speech to the party. Fascism's "fierce totalitarian will" would " 'fascistize' the nation, so that tomorrow Italian and Fascist, more or less like Italian and Catholic, will be the same thing." He also had a method for achieving that goal. Like the Girondin orator Isnard (see p. 592), who in 1792 had foreseen a war "indispensable for completing the revolution," Mussolini saw a connection between war and revolution. In 1914–15 he had demanded a "revolutionary war." That war had destroyed Liberal Italy and placed him in power. Only more war could make that power total.

And from the extremists of Italy's Nationalist party and from his navy, Mussolini acquired a vision of Italy's goals in that war. "A nation," he informed a group of high officers in 1926–27, "that has no free access to the sea cannot be considered a free nation; a nation that has no free access to the oceans cannot be considered a great power. Italy must become a great power." Britain and France, and Italy's ties to the world market, stood in the way of Mediterranean domination and of what Mussolini later described as Italy's "march to the ocean." By 1923–24, if not before, Mussolini had already foreseen that a vengeful nationalist Germany would be Italy's most promising ally in that march.

Waiting for Germany was tedious. Between 1922 and 1931 Mussolini crushed with massacres and concentration camps the Arabs of Libya, whom the Liberal state had been unable to subdue. He dabbled with plans for attacking Turkey and sponsored Croat and Macedonian terrorist attacks on neighboring Yugoslavia. But British disapproval, Italy's economic and financial weakness, and the Depression forced Mussolini to pretend he had a deep love for peace—although the Depression also ended the foreign trade and loans that bound Fascist Italy to the international status quo.

In early 1933, as Hitler came to power, Mussolini briefly thought he had blackmailed the French into abandoning their support of their Yugoslav ally, a Mussolini target since the 1920s. Then the king and

---

Mussolini: War, Revolution, and Empire   1925

At times I look with favor on the idea of [creating] generations in the laboratory, of creating, in other words, the class of the warriors, who are always ready to die, the class of the inventors, who pursue the secrets of the mysteries [of nature]; the class of judges; the class of the great captains of industry; of the great governors. It is through this sort of methodical selection that one creates the great elites that in turn establish empires. . . . War and revolution are two terms that are almost always linked. Either war produces revolution or it is revolution that leads to war. Even the strategy of the two movements is alike: as in war, in revolution you do not always attack. Sometimes you must make more or less strategic retreats. Sometimes you must rest for long periods on positions you have conquered. But the goal is there: empire.

Speech to the Fascist party congress, June 22, 1925, from Opera Omnia di Benito Mussolini *(Florence: La Fenice, 1956), Vol. 21, pp. 362–63 (translation by M. Knox).*

the generals vetoed a Balkan war that would risk French retaliation and "a lesson that would last us for a century." France, terrified at the rise of Hitler, nevertheless soon gave Mussolini the opening he sought. In July 1931 France's prime minister, the unscrupulous and gullible Pierre Laval, had suggested to an Italian emissary that Italy might quench its thirst for expansion in Ethiopia. France would stand aside in return for Italy's help in maintaining the status quo in Europe against Germany.

Mussolini had at first rejected this offer as a French trick to bog Italy down in Africa just as Germany was opening up possibilities in Europe. Then, in early 1934, he reversed himself. He had quarreled with his would-be ally, Hitler, over Austria. If war in Europe was impossible, war in Africa might yet serve his purpose. The king, the military, and the Italian establishment were lukewarm rather than actively hostile, as they had been over Yugoslavia. They were willing to "avenge Adowa" if Mussolini insisted and if no great power objected.

In January 1935, Mussolini and Laval signed the Rome Agreements, which conceded Italy a "free hand" in East Africa in return for the abandonment of longstanding Italian colonial claims on France and for Italian backing for France in Europe. The last part of the bargain Mussolini regarded skeptically; to Berlin he confided through intermediaries that "he would exploit the French, if they offered him anything, without becoming dependent upon them."

Large Italian forces, the first of almost half a million troops and laborers, began shipping out for East Africa in March 1935. Britain feebly objected. War in Africa would make cooperation with Italy against the German threat impossible, and in an election year Baldwin could not abandon the League of Nations, of which Ethiopia was a member. When Mussolini rejected British efforts at compromise, London reluctantly sent more battleships to the Mediterranean to deter him. The League, impotent in the Manchurian crisis because no great power had been willing to fight Japan, now rallied behind Britain—and the overwhelming power of the

British fleet. But Baldwin's foreign secretary secretly assured Mussolini that Britain did not intend war. That pledge, together with intercepted British radio messages suggesting the fleet was short of ammunition, enabled Mussolini to overrule his hesitant military and the King. On October 3, 1935, Italy attacked Ethiopia.

Britain reacted with economic sanctions against Italy organized through the League of Nations. Sanctions proved easy to evade, and thanks to a British failure of nerve they did not cover the imported oil that fueled Italy's armed forces. Their main consequence was to cut Italian dependence on British coal—in favor of the coal of the Ruhr.

On the battlefield, the armies of emperor Haile Selassie of Ethiopia almost routed the Italians in December–January 1936; then Italy's lavish use of tanks, artillery, aircraft, and mustard gas crushed them. At the beginning of May 1936, Italian forces entered the Ethiopian capital, Addis Ababa. From his balcony, Mussolini hailed before a delirious crowd the "reappearance of empire, after fifteen centuries, on the fateful hills of Rome." War and the brutal Italian occupation of 1936–41 cost the lives of a million Ethiopians.

War also made Mussolini "founder of the Empire," with a prestige matching that of his conservative allies, the generals, and the king. Mussolini listened less and his advisers dared offer less and less advice. Sanctions inflamed Italian opinion against the West and made it easier for Mussolini to bully the industrialists and militarize the Italian economy under the banner of "autarky," the illusory pursuit of self-sufficiency in raw materials. And Italy's quarrel with the League and subsequent intervention in the Spanish Civil War in July–August 1936 gave him the opportunity to move closer to Berlin. In October 1936, he and Hitler inaugurated the "Rome-Berlin Axis." And in 1938 he imitated Hitler's anti-Semitic legislation.

On June 10, 1940, after a long struggle with the generals, king, and moderate opinion, Mussolini led Italy into the Second World War. Only war, he told a cheering crowd, would "resolve . . . the problem of our maritime frontiers" and "break the military and territorial chains that suffocate us in our sea, for a people of forty-five million souls is not truly free unless it has free access to the ocean." Victory would give him the prestige needed to smash the monarchy and to break the Church's grip on Italian society. Defeat instead hurled the Fascist regime and Italy itself into the abyss.

GERMANY: FROM WAR TO WAR

Adolf Hitler

The man who opened the road for Mussolini and invited Stalin into central Europe began as modestly as his fellow dictators. Son of an Austro-Hungarian customs official, Adolf Hitler absorbed pan-Germanism and anti-Semitism from his surroundings. After failing admission to the Vienna Art Academy in 1907–08, he drifted to Munich in 1913 rather than serve in the armies of the Habsburg dynasty he despised for its compromises with Slavs and Jews. War in 1914 he regarded as a deliverance (see p. 774). Always a loner, he found in the German army a home and in battle a vocation. From October 1914 to October 1918 he served at the front in the most dangerous job the infantry offered: battalion messenger. He earned two Iron Crosses, decorations rarely given to lance-corporals.

Word of the 1918 revolution and Germany's defeat reached him as he lay in hospital, temporarily blinded by British gas; the news roused him to fury. As the army demobilized, he remained in service at Munich for lack of anything better. The army's propaganda branch took him in. There he made a discovery that changed Europe and the world: "I could 'speak.' " In September 1919 his superiors sent him to observe a meeting of a radical rightist sect of Munich railway workers, the German Workers' Party (DAP).

Hitler immediately attracted attention and an invitation to join the Party. News of his talent as a speaker spread rapidly in Munich's right-radical circles. By July 1921 he had taken the DAP away from its founders, had changed its name to National Socialist German Workers' Party (NSDAP), and had made himself its dictatorial leader. By late 1923 his party had 55,000 members and a paramilitary mass army, the brown-shirted SA (*Sturmabteilungen,* "storm troop sections"), under the leadership of Ernst Röhm, a fiercely politicized former army officer.

The *Führer,* as Hitler now became, spoke powerfully to a nation that had become convinced, however perversely, that it had suffered foreign aggression in 1914–18 and unmerited demotion to second-class power in 1919. Hitler's ideological delusions and those of his ever-larger audiences coincided, thanks to Germany's defeat. His starting point was the extremist form of social Darwinism that had long been popular in Germany. Following pseudo-biological prophets such as Ernst Haeckel (see p. 730), Hitler assumed that nature's laws—the "survival of the fittest" or the "free play of forces"—offered the only "healthy" rule for human conduct. Humanity was one with nature, not apart from it or above it; biology was supreme in all spheres of human activity.

That insight, Hitler insisted, was science. Like his rivals the Marxist-Leninists, Hitler and his followers combined pseudo-scientific materialism with bizarre ideological claims. For Communists, economics was the secret essence of human history, which was the history of class struggle. For Hitler, biology held the key: race—not class—was "the driving force of world history." And like the Marxist-Leninists, who saw "the capitalist" as demon, Hitler too saw a historic villain.

For Hitler, the Jewish people were a "race-tuberculosis of nations" who had supposedly lived "parasitically" throughout history from the labors of peoples that had given them shelter—especially the "Aryan" or "Nordic" peoples of Europe for whom Hitler claimed biological superiority. Throughout history, the Jews had allegedly sought the "eternal Jewish goal—world domination." They were responsible for Germany's internal weakness and thus for its defeat through the purported stab-in-the-back of 1918.

The Jewish threat, Hitler ranted to enthusiastic audiences, now placed before

"Vote National Socialist, or the sacrifices [of 1914–18] were in vain": the entire appeal of Hitler's party, born of war and bound for revenge, distilled into a single electoral slogan.

the world a stark alternative: "either victory of the Aryan side or its annihilation and victory of the Jews." Only Germany could ensure "Aryan" victory; its "historic mission" was to found "an Aryan world order." And death awaited Germany's adversaries: as early as 1920 Hitler proclaimed his determination to "strike the [Jewish] evil at its root and exterminate it root and branch." His ultimate goal was racist world revolution.

Meanwhile, recovery from the lost war required a new state: "We need a dictator who is a genius, if we want to rise again." But in the age of mass politics, even dictatorship required pseudo-democratic phrases and mass enthusiasm or mass terror to make it work. Hitler therefore proclaimed that nationalist dictatorship was "Germanic democracy." His mass following, and many of Munich's social elite, seemed to agree.

The Ruhr crisis of 1923 shook Weimar's authority and led Hitler to bid for power before inaction drained away the enthusiasm of his increasingly fanatical following. On the night of November 8–9, 1923, Hitler and the SA seized key points in Munich and sought to launch a "March on Berlin" modeled on Mussolini's October 1922 exploit. But unlike Mussolini, Hitler failed to secure the support of army and police, who soon crushed this "Beer Hall *Putsch*." Hitler's oratory at his subsequent treason trial nevertheless turned defeat into victory. His allies, who included Ludendorff, sheepishly denied their responsibility. Hitler affirmed his own and appealed to a higher court: Weimar judges might condemn the rebels, but history would acquit them. He emerged from the trial as uncontested leader of German radical nationalism.

His short term in prison was a welcome rest, a chance to "confirm his ideas by the study of natural history." There he began a memoir and political tract entitled "A Four and One-Half Year Struggle against Lies, Stupidity, and Cowardice." A merciful editor later shortened the title to the catchier *Mein Kampf*—"My Struggle." Its 600 turgid pages included much wisdom about propaganda technique, expressed with a cynical frankness that

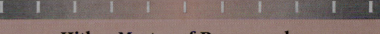

Hitler, Master of Propaganda   1925

Hitler set forth four mutually reinforcing principles for effective propaganda: it addressed "the most limited intelligence" in its audience, it appealed to emotion rather than intellect, it was relentlessly repetitive, and it displayed and fostered a fanatical one-sidedness.

All propaganda must be popular and its intellectual level must be adjusted to the most limited intelligence among those it is addressed to. . . . The more modest its intellectual ballast, the more exclusively it takes into consideration the emotions of the masses, the more effective it will be. . . . The art of propaganda lies in understanding the emotional ideas of the great masses and finding . . . the way to the attention and thence to the heart of the broad masses. . . .

The receptivity of the great masses is very limited, their intelligence is small, but their power of forgetting is enormous. In consequence . . . all effective propaganda must be limited to a very few points and must harp on these in slogans until the very last member of the public understands what you want him to understand. . . .

What . . . would we say about a poster that was supposed to advertise a new soap and that described other soaps as "good"? We would only shake our heads. Exactly the same applies to political advertising. The function of propaganda is . . . not to make an objective study of the truth . . . ; its task is to serve our own right, always and unflinchingly. . . . It does not have multiple shadings; it has a positive and a negative: love or hate, right or wrong, truth or lie, never half this way and half that way. . . .

From Adolf Hitler, Mein Kampf, *trans. by Ralph Manheim (Boston: Houghton Mifflin, 1943), pp. 180–83.*

distinguished Hitler from the theorists of commercial advertising. It also suggested that Hitler saw himself as that rare phenomenon, a combination of prophet and political leader.

Last but not least, *Mein Kampf* offered a foreign-policy program. In late 1922, Hitler had formulated in private how he proposed to go about fulfilling Germany's world mission: "We should attempt the carving up of Russia with English help." In *Mein Kampf* Hitler laid that program out in detail, beginning with a critique of William II's too ambitious foreign policy, which had alienated Britain, France, and Russia all at once. Germany should instead proceed to world domination by stages, smashing one adversary at a time: first the internal enemies, then France, and finally Russia, where Germany would seize the *Lebensraum* ("living space") it required, the vast blockade-proof empire Ludendorff had briefly grasped in 1918. Britain and Italy, both hostile to France during the Ruhr crisis, appeared available as allies; Hitler had inevitably conceived an admiration for Mussolini, who furnished a welcome prototype for nationalist dictatorship. In an unpublished "second book" of 1928 Hitler also discovered Germany's final adversary in the quest for world domination: the United States.

For the moment, these vistas were beside the point. Prosperity and the success of Stresemann's foreign policy lessened the appeal of radical nationalism. The NSDAP, which Hitler had reorganized as a tightly centralized "Führer-party" after his release from prison, received a mere twelve *Reichstag* seats in the 1928 election. But two things suggested that it was ready for further growth: its relentless emphasis on organization and propaganda, and its growing success with the hard-hit peasantry of north Germany as the agricultural depression deepened after 1927.

Hitler's Road to Power, 1929–33

Hitler's breakthrough into national politics came in 1929–30, even before the Depression hit Germany in full force. The press and film magnate Alfred Hugenberg, an extreme pan-German, had taken over the party of the traditional Junker Right, the German National People's Party (DNVP). Hugenberg, unlike the DNVP's earlier leaders, was fanatically committed to destroying the Weimar Republic. The Young Plan reparations settlement of 1929 offered him an occasion for a massive propaganda campaign against the Republic for allegedly consenting to the "enslavement of the German people" through reparations.

Hugenberg enlisted the help of Hitler and the NSDAP—and firmly established Hitler on the national political scene. Then the last Weimar coalition government collapsed because the SPD, like Labour in

Britain in 1931, rejected balancing the budget by cutting unemployment benefits. The government, under the authoritarian Center Party leader, Heinrich Brüning, lacked a firm *Reichstag* majority. Brüning therefore committed an act of folly. He called an election for September 1930.

The French had evacuated their last Rhineland occupation zone that June; the Germans were now free to vote their nationalist views without fear of consequences. Brüning's cost-cutting measures against the deepening Depression made him unloved. Hugenberg's campaign against the Young Plan had enabled Hitler to create an agitation and propaganda machine that utterly outclassed that of the other parties. The 1930 vote was an electoral earthquake: 107 Nazi *Reichstag* seats, and almost a fifth of the popular vote.

The NSDAP was now Germany's second largest party after the SPD. It tailored its appeals to every conceivable interest group, but its program was above all a name: Adolf Hitler. Hitler offered to fill the role that Bismarck had created and that William II had failed to fill, the role of national *Führer*. He symbolized a radical alternative to Weimar's economic misery, dreary indecisiveness, class and religious division, and national humiliation. The NSDAP, ranted one of Hitler's lieutenants, was "the opposite of everything that now exists." Increasing numbers of Germans found that deliberately vague appeal compelling.

The principal question in German politics after September 1930 was when, and under what conditions, Hitler would come to power. In the next two years, as the Depression shrank Brüning's authority, the Junker kitchen cabinet around Reich President Hindenburg became increasingly desperate. They applauded the NSDAP's nationalist fanaticism and sought to use it to buttress their own power, while resisting Hitler's increasingly pressing demands for the chancellorship. But like the similar efforts of Salandra and Giolitti in 1921–24, repeated conservative attempts to domesticate Hitler failed.

In spring 1932, Brüning sponsored Hindenburg's reelection for a second seven-year term, and Hitler unchivalrously ran against the "Old Gentleman." Hindenburg won, but only with the support of the SPD, which preferred even a Prussian field marshal to Hitler. After the election, Hindenburg dismissed Brüning, who had outlived his usefulness and had provoked Hitler by attempting to abolish the SA. The army, which played an increasingly political role, resisted curbs on what it naively perceived as the SA's violent young "idealists."

A *Reichstag* election in July 1932 gave the NSDAP an unprecedented 230 seats, amid SA violence that left hundreds dead. With the help of the 89 Communists, who opposed democracy as bitterly as the NSDAP, Hitler now had a *Reichstag* majority that was hostile not merely to any democratic or conservative cabinet or chancellor, but to Weimar democracy itself. NSDAP obstruction and Hitler's demand for the chancellorship produced parliamentary paralysis. Hindenburg still refused to hand over Germany "like a laboratory rabbit" to the bold experimenters of the NSDAP. But Brüning's two successors as chancellor failed to master the Depression, the *Reichstag,* the continuing Nazi street violence, and backbiting in the conservative camp. On January 30, 1933, Hindenburg gave in and made Adolf Hitler chancellor of the German Reich in a coalition cabinet with Hugenberg and numerous other conservatives.

The Nazi Revolution, 1933–37

Hitler soon showed his conservative allies that he was no puppet "hired" for the occasion, as they foolishly assumed. He established a direct alliance with the military high command on February 3 by promising to "exterminate Marxism root and branch," reawaken the German people's "will to arms," and create a new armed forces (*Wehrmacht*) once more based on universal military service. He extracted from Hindenburg permission to hold a new election, and emergency presidential powers that restricted press and other freedoms. The SA and its elite offshoot, the SS (*Schutzstaffel* or "security echelon"), terrorized political opponents and Ger-

man Jews with the approval of the Prussian police, which was now under the management of Hitler's close associate Hermann Göring.

On February 27, 1933, the *Reichstag* building in Berlin mysteriously burned; Hitler and his propaganda chief, the malevolent Joseph Goebbels, seized on this as evidence of a "Communist plot" that justified the suppression by presidential decree of all remaining constitutional freedoms. The election on March 5, 1933, gave the conservative-NSDAP coalition a majority. Hitler then bullied the new *Reichstag* into voting an "Enabling Act" that gave him as chancellor the power to make law by decree. That made him independent of both *Reichstag* and Hindenburg. By July 1933, Hitler had abolished all parties other than the NSDAP, including the DNVP of his conservative allies. He had purged the civil service of political opponents and Jews—a measure that began an intensifying effort to define who was a Jew and to isolate those so defined from the rest of the population.

Hindenburg and the army yielded. They approved heartily of Hitler's crushing of Communists and SPD, and swallowed whatever modest qualms they may have had over the anti-Jewish measures, which roused a storm of protest abroad. Hitler also received the blessings of the Vatican, which abandoned the Catholic Center party as it had the Italian Catholic *Popolari* and signed in July 1933 a Concordat with Hitler similar to its 1929 arrangement with Mussolini. In November 1933 a plebiscite and a *Reichstag* election gave Hitler a brown-shirted parliament and an 87.8 percent majority. Hitler had achieved in nine months what Mussolini, with far less mass support in 1922 than Hitler had in 1933, had needed seven years to accomplish.

But while the aged Hindenburg lived, Hitler still faced an authority higher than his own. In preparation for the "Old Gentleman's" death, Hitler consolidated his alliance with the army. That "state within the state" was equally indispensable to his domestic power and to his plans for war. When the SA under its chief Ernst Röhm challenged the army for leadership of the

On Hitler's order, the party organized a boycott of Jewish shops and offices in April 1933. The placard reads: "Germans! Defend yourselves! Don't buy from Jews!"

rearmament effort, Hitler chose the army. On June 30, 1934, with trucks and weapons the army provided, Hitler's SS forces rounded up and shot Röhm and more than 200 SA leaders. That "night of the long knives" sealed with blood Hitler's alliance with the military leadership. On August 2, after Hindenburg finally died, the *Wehrmacht* took an oath to Hitler personally. As "*Führer* and Reich Chancellor," a position that united his own powers with those of the Reich President, Hitler now enjoyed powers that far surpassed Mussolini's.

Hitler soon consolidated and extended that power. The NSDAP did its best to mobilize the population, including the industrial workers, who received membership in a Nazi "German Labor Front" in place of the smashed SPD trade unions. German youth, by 1936, was subject to compulsory membership in the "Hitler Youth" and "League of German Maidens." And the SS proved a far more formidable rival to the army than had Röhm's SA. Its fanatically loyal and fastidiously precise leader, Heinrich Himmler, had by 1934

Heinrich Himmler (*left*) and Ernst Röhm a few months before Himmler had Röhm shot at Hitler's order.

seized control of the Reich police forces, established a network of concentration camps outside the control of the normal judiciary, and set up a small but growing private army that included an SS bodyguard regiment for the *Führer*. By 1936, Himmler was officially "Reich leader of the SS and Chief of the German Police," a unique party-state hybrid.

And the regime struck once more at Germany's half-million Jews. In September 1935, at the annual Nuremberg party rally, Hitler proclaimed a "Reich citizenship law" that made the German Jews less than full citizens and forbade the intermarriage of "Germans" and "Jews." The definition and increasing segregation of the "racial enemy" proved a mighty step toward extermination.

By 1936–37, within the shell of the Weimar constitution, Hitler had created a system that German jurists described as a "*Führer*-state." Party organizations proliferated alongside the state bureaucracy and with Hitler's approval gradually usurped its powers. The SS, with Hitler's backing, encroached on both army and judiciary. "Political free enterprise," as one scholar has well described it, was the ruling principle of Hitler's Reich. From his villa in the Bavarian Alps, far above the struggle, Hitler encouraged the rivalries of his subordinates. Those rivalries strengthened his own power and served as a form of "natural selection" in molding the new National Socialist governing elite. The regime's dynamism was in part a consequence of Hitler's method of leadership, which contrasted with the more rigid top-down style of Stalin and even Mussolini. Hitler defined the goal of competition— to fulfill the *Führer's* will—and left it to his subordinates to guess that will and to strive frenetically to implement it. That was his most original contribution to the technique of total power.

Germany Rearms: "Everything for the Wehrmacht!"

Nazi Germany's road to total power led through massive rearmament and conquest. On February 3, 1933, five days after taking office, Hitler addressed a private meeting of his generals and admirals. As well as promising them the elimination of the Left and rearmament, he announced that the power of the new *Wehrmacht* would serve for "the conquest of new *Lebensraum* in the East and its ruthless Germanization." The generals did not take that statement seriously until much later. But they were delighted to rearm.

In the following year the army, Germany's dominant service, accelerated the clandestine rearmament plan that it had already begun under Weimar. When the Disarmament Conference of the League of Nations threatened to get in the way of that plan, Hitler left both the Conference and the League in October 1933, with the unanimous support of his generals, former conservatives, and diplomats. His establishment "flankers" enabled him to rearm and to launch the war that culminated in their own ruin.

Externally, rearmament inevitably led Germany into a "danger zone" in which it ran the risk of preventive war. Hitler warned his generals in February 1933 that they would soon find out "if France has statesmen; if so, it will not give us time but will attack us (presumably with [its] eastern hangers-on)." France had no statesmen, and Hitler neutralized Poland with a surprise non-aggression pact in January 1934. Each time Western outrage at Germany's anti-Jewish measures or its rearmament reached dangerous heights, Hitler soothed foreign opinion with a "peace speech" that played on the democracies' credulity and yearning for peace.

That tactic served even to cover Germany's March 1935 declaration that it had unilaterally torn up the disarmament provisions of Versailles. Germany, Hitler triumphantly announced, had an air force—the *Luftwaffe*—and would soon have a vast mass army based on universal service. London and Paris made feeble protests; then Britain legalized Germany's violations of the Versailles treaty by allowing Hitler a fleet a third the size of Britain's in the Anglo-German Naval Agreement of June 1935.

Internally, Hitler broke the opposition to breakneck rearmament that emerged in 1935–36, as the economy

Germany's first and last "Minister for Public Enlightenment and Propaganda," Joseph Goebbels.

achieved virtual full employment. Germany's steel barons, whose excess capacity had almost ruined them in the Depression, balked at investing in new plants. Big business leaders warned that the armament boom was overheating the economy; labor and raw material shortages would soon lead to massive inflation and financial ruin. Hitler treated the doubters with contempt. He was secretly confident that the loot that the *Wehrmacht* would seize in war would keep the economy going. He also had the support of the army leaders, who wanted armaments and did not share the industrialists' doubts. Hitler gave Hermann Göring, now chief of the *Luftwaffe* and second man in the Nazi state, full powers over the economy in mid-1936, and simple orders: "Within four years the German *Wehrmacht* must be ready to fight; within four years the German economy must be ready for war."

Rearmament itself proceeded rapidly, gobbling up an ever-greater portion of Germany's gross national product (see Figure 32-1). By 1939, despite the belated beginnings of rearmament in the democracies, Germany was out-spending all its Western rivals combined by a factor of almost two to one. Hitler's effort produced results: the most powerful air force and army in the world. All that remained was to use them. As Hitler remarked retrospectively in November 1939, "I did not create the *Wehrmacht* in order not to strike."

THE ROAD TO WAR, 1936–39

Germany's massive rearmament soon became the decisive driving force in world politics. But what did the *Wehrmacht* mean? The powers sought to guess Hitler's intentions but shrank from the obvious answer, that German rearmament served the purpose announced in *Mein Kampf,* the conquest of *Lebensraum*. To recognize Hitler's warlike intentions meant giving up a cherished myth: that World War I had been so terrible that another great war was unthinkable. It also meant war—

to stop Hitler before he grew too strong. The Western democracies shrank from that conclusion. Their reward was war— once Hitler was too strong to stop.

Diplomatic Revolution in Europe, 1936

By 1936, Germany's growing might and the Ethiopian quarrel between Italy and the League of Nations offered Hitler a unique opportunity. In February 1936 he sounded out the Italian attitude toward Locarno; Mussolini made clear that he would not object if Germany broke that treaty, of which Italy was a guarantor. On March 7, 1936, Hitler's forces occupied the demilitarized Rhineland without warning. Germany had broken not only the "dictated peace" of Versailles, but also Locarno, a treaty Germany had freely signed.

Hitler's action was by far the greatest risk he had so far taken. The German army was in the initial phases of massive expansion and was correspondingly disorganized. The French could have used overwhelming force. Victory would not have been bloodless; Hitler had given orders to fight, and to hold the line of the

FIGURE 32-1   **Hitler Rearms, the Democracies Falter: Military Expenditure 1932–39**

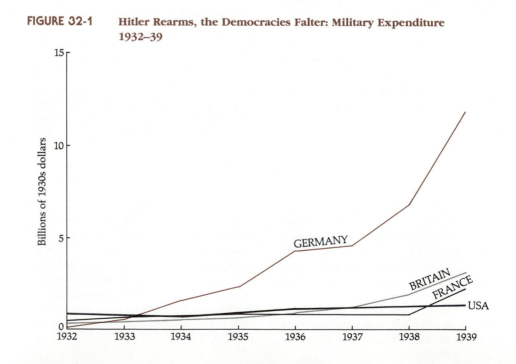

Europe before the Second World War   1930–39

Germany in 1930

German acquisitions, 1930-39

German allies in 1939

0   MILES   200

Rhine. But Germany was not yet ready to fight for long.

In the event, it did not need to fight at all. Britain, with much of its navy tied up facing Italy, urged Paris not to take rash action. As *The Times* of London indulgently commented, Hitler's coup was no more than the occupation of "territory indisputably under German sovereignty." The French military made clear to its politicians that it likewise preferred inaction. The French politicians in turn happily seized on Britain's pusillanimity as an excuse for their own. Hitler, who launched the crisis despite doubts among his generals, saw the outcome as confirmation of his own superior judgment. He had now taken the measure both of the West and of his own timid high command.

The remilitarization of the Rhineland was a strategic and diplomatic revolution. Now Hitler could fortify Germany's western border and prevent France from defending its Polish and Czechoslovak allies by threatening to attack Germany. The smaller powers rushed to seek favor with the new master. Belgium, convinced of the futility of its French alliance, retreated into neutrality in November 1936. That move uncovered France's northeastern border, which the Maginot line did not protect. Austria, which Mussolini had quietly abandoned to Hitler in January 1936, signed a pact with Hitler in July that gave Germany the right to interfere in its foreign and domestic affairs. The Balkan states expanded their already close economic ties with Germany. Stalin, apparently after reading *Mein Kampf,* had in 1934 become a belated convert to the League of Nations and "collective security"—but he now intensified his efforts to tempt Hitler into a mutually profitable arrangement. Hitler saw no need to answer. He had the initiative.

Spain and China, 1936–39

Hitler found the quarrels of others tactically useful. Mussolini's Ethiopian adventure had distracted attention from German rearmament and had offered the opportunity to seize the Rhineland. New conflicts in Spain and China offered similar opportunities.

In July 1936, a group of traditionalist Spanish generals rose against the republic that had taken the place of Spain's enfeebled monarchy in 1931. Resistance by the population blocked the coup in most of Spain. Generals Francisco Franco and Emilio Mola then appealed for help to Fascist Italy and Nazi Germany. Help came. Mussolini had visions of dominating the western Mediterranean and saw Spain, like Ethiopia, as an opportunity to strengthen his power at home through what he described as the "permanent revolution" of warfare. He sent aircraft and a ground force that ultimately amounted to 50,000 men.

Hitler simply wanted a conflict in Spain that would divert the West from his doings in central Europe. He sent arms and *Luftwaffe* units. Even Stalin, who apparently saw the Spanish Civil War as a vehicle for keeping the "capitalist" powers at one another's throats, intervened on the side of the Republic with arms, advisers, and Communist-organized "International Brigades." Only Britain and France abstained. London viewed both sides with distaste and feared that the Spanish Civil War might lead to general war. Léon Blum's France offered hesitant unofficial assistance to the Spanish Republic but shrank from greater risks.

In the next three years, more than half a million Spaniards died in massacres of prisoners and civilians, in battles around Madrid in 1936–37, in bloody winter fighting in 1937–38, and in the final campaigns in southeastern Spain that ended with the collapse of the Republic in March–April 1939. The war became a symbol. For Germany and Italy, the battle against the Republic was a struggle against "Bolshevism"—a convenient propaganda theme to cloak the Italian and German threat to the status quo. For the Left of western Europe and the United States, the war was a struggle against "fascism"—a generic concept that the Communist International had invented to distinguish "capitalist" dictatorships from the dictatorship of Lenin and Stalin. Few recognized that this was above all a *Spanish* civil war, last of a long series of struggles between military-clerical Right and liberal or socialist Left that had convulsed Spain since Napoleon's invasion in 1808. It ended with the victory of the military dictatorship of Francisco Franco, who cannily outlasted his Nazi and Fascist patrons and died in power, and in bed, in 1975.

Full-scale war in East Asia soon overshadowed the events in Spain. In July 1937, a shooting incident between Japanese and Guomindang troops at the Marco Polo Bridge near Beijing (Peking) led both sides to escalate. Chiang Kai-shek had grudgingly agreed in 1936 to a temporary alliance with the Chinese Communists against the Japanese, and he now felt compelled to fight. The Japanese army welcomed the chance to reduce all China to colonial subjection. The Tokyo government, under a prime minister who had made his name as an expansionist ideologue, Prince Konoe Fumimaro, backed the army.

A Japanese landing force took Shanghai with much slaughter. In a series of swift campaigns, the Japanese forced Chiang southward. In December 1937, they seized Chiang's capital at Nanjing and massacred between 100,000 and 300,000 Chinese amid scenes of mass rape and displays of swordsmanship against unarmed prisoners. Almost simultaneously, Japanese aircraft sank the U.S. gunboat *Panay* on the Yangtze River. That seemed a warning to the West that China was Japan's preserve: "Asia for the Asians."

The West showed little resolve. Baldwin's successor, Neville Chamberlain, hoped to avoid provoking Japan until he had conciliated Hitler and Mussolini. American opinion, after abandoning Europe in the 1920s, had justified itself by creating the myth that bankers and armaments barons—rather than Ludendorff and Zimmermann—had forced the United States into war in 1917. Between 1935 and 1937 an isolationist Congress passed three "Neutrality Acts" to prevent U.S. sales of arms and ammunition to belligerents. Isolation would supposedly avoid another war.

When Roosevelt vaguely urged the democracies to "quarantine" the aggressors in an October 1937 speech, a fierce isolationist chorus attacked him. His modest rearmament plan of January 1938 provoked a furor in Congress but eventually passed. Roosevelt did join the British in January 1938 in secret naval talks directed against Japan. He contemplated imposing economic sanctions on Tokyo and eventually entering hostilities undeclared and by stages, bypassing the isolationists in Congress. Both notions came into their own in 1941. But Roosevelt was a master of ambiguity, of avoiding commitment until it was inescapable. Chamberlain found no reason to reverse his judgment of late 1937 that it was "always best and safest to count on *nothing* from the Americans except words."

Japan's war in China therefore went forward without Western interference. By 1939 the Guomindang had retreated to Chongqing (Chungking) in Sichuan province in the far southwest. Japan had won the war but could not end it. The "New Order in Asia" that Konoe proclaimed in November 1938 was upheld only by Japanese bayonets. Japan had neither subdued China nor secured the resources that its own economy lacked.

Alliances against the West, 1936–37

By late 1937, Hitler had reached a number of conclusions and decisions. He recognized that Britain was willing to accept the peaceful achievement of German aspirations in Austria, Czechoslovakia, and the Polish Corridor. But it was unlikely to tolerate the far wider program put forward in *Mein Kampf*, and become junior partner in a German quest for *Lebensraum* and world domination. Hitler therefore decided to seek alliances against Britain, to deter it or to distract it militarily.

In the fall of 1936, Mussolini's parallel search for allies against the West and Italo-German cooperation in Spain brought Hitler and Mussolini together in a "Rome-Berlin Axis." Footdragging by Mussolini's conservative flankers and fear of becoming a satellite of the Reich kept him from seeking a formal military alliance until early 1939. But he gave Hitler evidence of his good faith by ostentatiously adopting German-style laws against Italy's 50,000 Jews in the summer–fall of 1938, over opposition that included powerful elements within the Fascist party. Japan signed on with Hitler in November 1936, in an agreement publicly directed against the Communist International. That "Anti-Comintern Pact" in reality involved a secret military commitment against the Soviet Union and an unspoken hostility to Britain. Italy joined the Anti-Comintern Pact in November 1937 when it followed the German and Japanese example by leaving the dying League of Nations.

None of these "Hitler coalition" pacts as yet offered firm guarantees that Germany would have allies in war. But they scared London, which intensified—in the hope of binding Hitler to the status quo—its efforts to "appease" what it regarded as his legitimate claims in central Europe. Hitler inevitably viewed such efforts as signs of British weakness and as an invitation to further German coups. On November 5, 1937, he told his high command and his conservative foreign minister that Germany might have the opportunity to seize Austria or Czechoslovakia or both in the near future. War with Britain and France must in any event come before 1943–45. Germany was ready to move from rearmament to war.

His listeners, except for Göring of the *Luftwaffe* and Admiral Erich Raeder of the navy, found Hitler's resolve to launch a war of aggression imprudent. The generals grumbled that Germany's strategic situation was still unfavorable. Hitler took note. And in January–February of 1938 he exploited questions about the moral character of his minister of war and army commander in chief to dismiss them both, along with his conservative foreign minister. He himself became minister of war and chose new military subordinates pathetically eager to please their *Führer*. Joachim von Ribbentrop, the former champagne salesman and NSDAP foreign-policy pundit who had negotiated the

Anglo-German Naval Treaty and the Anti-Comintern Pact, became the new foreign minister. Hitler had cleared the way for further expansion by consolidating his control over the German army and the foreign office, the last preserves of the conservatives who had brought him to power.

Bloodless Conquests: Vienna, Munich, Prague, 1938–39

An opportunity for further expansion immediately arose. In February 1938 the prime minister of Austria, Kurt von Schuschnigg, visited Hitler, hoping to placate him. Hitler bullied Schuschnigg unmercifully and extorted his agreement to take two Austrian NSDAP leaders into his cabinet as minister of war and minister of the interior. Once back in Vienna, Schuschnigg thought better of his promise to hand Austria over to Hitler. But British and French support was not forthcoming, and Italy had given up its claim to be Austria's protector in 1936. On March 11–12, 1938 the *Wehrmacht* rolled bloodlessly across the Austrian border.

The Austrians received the *Wehrmacht* and its *Führer* with flowers and delirious applause. Hitler responded by proclaiming the immediate *Anschluss* ("merging") of Austria into Germany. Savage SS persecution of Vienna's Jews began immediately; the Austrian army received new uniforms and Prussian drill instructors. And "Greater Germany" now surrounded Czechoslovakia on three sides.

Unlike Austria, Czechoslovakia had a military alliance with France, 35 well-equipped divisions, and fortifications that in some areas rivaled the Maginot line. But like Austria, it lacked Western support. The France of Daladier shamefacedly sought a way of avoiding its alliance obligations. A prominent Englishman privately advised a German acquaintance not to shoot Czechoslovakia, but to strangle it.

Strangulation, or what his diplomats jokingly described as an ethnic "chemical solution," was indeed Hitler's first thought. The German minority of 3.25 million in Czechoslovakia's northern border area— the Sudetenland—was his chosen instru-

Anschluss, March 1938: The German army takes possession of Vienna.

ment. In April he instructed the political leadership of the Sudeten Germans to press Prague with a series of ever-escalating demands that would lead ultimately to the dissolution of the Czech state. "Autonomy" for the Sudetenland would render Czechoslovakia indefensible by depriving it of its border fortifications and industries.

When the Czechs mobilized their army in May 1938 in response to bogus rumors of an impending German attack, Hitler changed his policy. Force would replace subversion: "It is my unalterable intention to smash Czechoslovakia by military action in the near future." He set a target date of October 1, 1938, and intensified work on Germany's fortified *Westwall* to keep the French at bay while he crushed Czechoslovakia.

By early September, as Goebbels' propaganda about fictitious Czech atrocities against the Sudeten Germans reached a crescendo, a covert mobilization had readied the *Wehrmacht.* Sudeten Ger-

mans rioted on orders from Berlin, and Hitler demanded their "self-determination" at the close of the last annual Nuremberg party rally on September 12. Mussolini mocked the Czechs and pledged his support to Hitler. The Czechs, despite intense pressure from London and Paris, got ready to fight for their existence.

This crisis moved Neville Chamberlain to act, to carry to its logical conclusion the policy of active, preemptive "appeasement" he had followed since becoming prime minister in 1937. He flew to Germany twice and urged the dictator to accept the Sudetenland by slices rather than all at once. Hitler naturally responded to Chamberlain's attempts at conciliation with further demands: the entire Sudetenland by October 1. But Chamberlain failed to persuade his cabinet colleagues to accept that humiliating ultimatum. Hitler, in a speech at the Berlin Sports Palace on September 26, then raved at the Czechs and offered them a stark choice: "Peace or war!" Chamberlain's reply was a mournful

The Munich Conference,
September 29–30, 1938.
Chamberlain, Daladier, Hitler,
Mussolini, and Ciano decide
Czechoslovakia's fate.

"Peace for our time?"
Chamberlain returns from
Munich, 1938.

radio address in which he confessed his dismay over this "quarrel in a far away country between people of whom we know nothing." Chamberlain's colleagues displayed greater resolve; they ordered the Royal Navy mobilized and a blockade prepared. The French unhappily followed. Hitler's insistence on unilateral violent solutions appeared at last to have created a coalition capable of blocking Germany before it achieved European hegemony.

Then Hitler had second thoughts. German crowds greeted the approach of war with a sullen silence far different from the delirious enthusiasm of August 1914. Germany could crush the Czechs. But Czech fortifications would exact a stiff price and the army was still far from ready for general war; it was not scheduled to reach full strength until 1940–41. Finally, Germany in 1938 lacked the oil and raw materials required for a long war against Britain and France.

When Chamberlain proposed a further compromise through Mussolini, Hitler resentfully acquiesced to a four-power

conference at Munich on September 29–30, 1938. There Chamberlain and Daladier pressed on him a phased occupation of the Sudetenland by October 10. Roosevelt, from the background, urged London and Paris to avoid war. To save the West's face, the dictator agreed to an unenforceable four-power guarantee of the mutilated and militarily defenseless remnant of Czechoslovakia.

The Munich agreement was an immense moral, political, and strategic defeat for the West, a defeat that made possible Hitler's destruction of the European and world order in 1940–41. The West abandoned its one industrialized eastern European ally, and Germany's annexations in the Sudetenland included a rich booty: more than 70 percent of Czechoslovakia's major industries.

Chamberlain nevertheless returned from Munich with what he claimed was "peace with honor," "peace for our time." Churchill and a small band of dissident Conservatives thought otherwise. So did Hitler, who immediately and publicly rejected British attempts to hold him to the

Munich agreement: "We will suffer the tutelage of governesses no longer!" He was privately furious that his "entry into Prague had been spoiled." In a secret speech to his press representatives on November 10, he regretted that his peace speeches had misled the German people: "Force of circumstances was the reason I spoke for years only of peace." Now the task was to turn the *Volk* around: it must stand like "formed-up troops" behind his leadership. Doubters in the "intellectual strata" unfortunately still possessed necessary skills: "otherwise one could exterminate them, or whatever." As Hitler spoke, party activists devastated synagogues and Jewish shops all over Germany at his command, in the regime's last public attempt to mobilize the German people against the Jews.

By early 1939, Hitler had begun to see the realization of his program within his grasp. He inaugurated a new naval building plan: by the mid-1940s Germany would have an 800-ship fleet far superior to Britain's and capable of taking on the United States. He accelerated an immense construction plan to remake Germany's city centers within ten years. Huge domes and halls, designed so that their ruins would be impressive thousands of years hence, were to fit Berlin for its new status as capital of the world. To his officer corps, he insisted that Munich was not an end but a beginning; Germany was bound for world domination. It must move forward as it had since 1933, "without letup, exploiting every opportunity, however small, to move immediately toward a new success." And he publicly warned that "international Jewry" was the source of foreign accusations that he was seeking war. He promised retribution.

Convinced of the feebleness of Western resistance, Hitler saw no reason not to absorb the remainder of Czechoslovakia. On March 14–15, 1939, he bullied its helpless government into placing itself under German "protection." Hitler and the *Wehrmacht* entered Prague. Germany's overheated war economy received a new infusion of booty. But Hitler had at last gone too far. His conquest of territories inhabited almost entirely by Czechs disproved his claims that he sought only self-

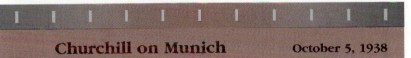

Churchill on Munich   October 5, 1938

To the accompaniment of heckling from Chamberlain loyalists, Churchill sought unsuccessfully to convince the House of Commons that "peace for our time" was defeat without war.

CHURCHILL: . . . I will . . . begin by saying the most unpopular and most unwelcome thing. I will begin by saying what everybody would like to ignore or forget but which must nevertheless be stated, namely, that we have sustained a total and unmitigated defeat, and that France has suffered even more than we have.

VISCOUNTESS ASTOR: Nonsense.

CHURCHILL: When the Noble Lady cries "nonsense," she could not have heard the Chancellor of the Exchequer [Sir John Simon, speaking for the Chamberlain government] admit in his illuminating and comprehensive speech just now that Herr Hitler had gained in this particular leap forward in substance all he set out to gain. The utmost my right hon[orable] Friend the Prime Minister [Chamberlain] has been able to secure by all his immense exertions . . . the utmost he has been able to gain—[*Hon Members:* "Is peace."]. . . . The utmost he has been able to gain . . . has been that the German dictator, instead of snatching his victuals from the table, has been content to have them served to him course by course. . . .

From Martin Gilbert, Winston S. Churchill, *Vol. V, 1922–1939:* The Prophet of Truth *(Boston: Houghton Mifflin, 1977), p. 997.*

determination for Germans. His breach of the Munich agreement and of his September 1938 promise that the Sudetenland was his "last territorial demand in Europe" showed that he was utterly untrustworthy. The Prague coup crystallized opinion in Britain, which had turned increasingly against Germany after Munich and the November 1938 attack on Germany's Jews.

The Totalitarians United, and the Coming of Hitler's War

A storm of public protest enveloped Chamberlain, who had initially sought to avoid responding to the Prague coup. His answer, when it came on March 31, 1939, was ill-considered. Britain and France guaranteed Poland, which appeared to be

Hitler's likely next victim, against threats to its independence. The Western Allies soon extended similar guarantees to Rumania and to Greece, which Mussolini appeared to menace by his annexation of helpless Albania on April 7. Chamberlain, with Paris in tow, belatedly attempted to create a structure of diplomatic deterrence that would halt Hitler.

But Hitler played by war-fighting rules. Paper guarantees of states that the Western powers could not defend in war did not impress him. The Western pledge to Poland simply convinced him that the Poles, who had already resisted secret German demands for the German-inhabited city of Danzig and for West Prussian territory lost to Poland in 1918–19, should definitely be his next target. On April 3 he set September 1, 1939, as the planning date for an attack on Poland.

The Western guarantee to Poland also made Stalin the man of the hour: the "capitalist" powers were now pledged to fight among themselves. All Stalin had to do was to await bids for his support. Soviet participation in war might not even be necessary; the Soviet Union and Nazi Germany might exercise joint domination of

the Eurasian land mass. Stalin's daughter, who later defected to the West, testified to her father's conviction that "together with the Germans, we would have been invincible!"

In May 1939, Stalin dismissed his foreign minister, Maxim Litvinov, lest Litvinov's Jewish antecedents complicate negotiations with Berlin. Stalin's creature Vyacheslav Molotov took Litvinov's place and renewed Moscow's longstanding secret proposals for a German-Soviet political agreement. The British and French also explored cooperation with Russia, but they sent their negotiators to Leningrad by slow boat. Chamberlain had no enthusiasm for a Bolshevik alliance, and London, in view of Stalin's liquidation of half the Soviet officer corps, doubted the military usefulness of that alliance.

Hitler also moved to ensure that Italy would serve to distract Britain and France in the Mediterranean while he attacked Poland. The Axis powers concluded a war alliance, the so-called "Pact of Steel," on May 22, 1939. It was to operate automatically if either power "became . . . involved in warlike actions," regardless of who had provoked the conflict. Mussolini tried to limit his commitment by pointing out that Italy needed another three years to strengthen its armaments; Hitler was silent.

The day after the signing of the Pact of Steel, Hitler addressed his generals. The German-Polish border dispute over Danzig and West Prussia was merely the pretext for war. The real issue was "the enlargement of *Lebensraum* in the East." That must come soon; Germany faced a choice between continuing rise, and decline. And this action would be different from Czechoslovakia: "There will be fighting." If Britain and France objected, he would fight them as well.

By mid-August, as the Goebbels propaganda machine blasted the Poles, the *Wehrmacht* had again covertly mobilized. Talks with Moscow progressed well: Hitler and Stalin spoke the same language. On August 20 Hitler wrote urging Stalin to receive Ribbentrop to put the finishing touches on a Russo-German "non-aggression" pact. Stalin agreed. The British

The morning after *Kristallnacht* ("plate glass night"), the Nazi party attack on synagogues, Jewish businesses, and Jews that Goebbels organized on November 9–10, 1938.

and French negotiators were in essence offering Stalin war with Germany, and no gains. Hitler was offering him no war, and a division of eastern Europe into Nazi and Soviet spheres. Stalin thus achieved objectives sought since the beginning of the Soviet state. The foundation of the non-aggression pact, Stalin later informed the British ambassador with amazing openness, was the common Russo-German aim of destroying the "old balance" of power that had existed in Europe.

On the night of August 23–24, in the Kremlin, Ribbentrop and Molotov signed the Nazi-Soviet Non-Aggression Pact in Stalin's presence. Its name was misleading: it promised benevolent neutrality in the event that either power became involved in war, even a war of aggression. And its secret protocol drew a line through eastern Europe and Poland that divided the two parties' respective booty. At the close of the negotiations, Ribbentrop ventured a joke: Berlin humorists were saying that Stalin was about to join the Anti-Comintern Pact. Stalin too offered a witticism: "The Germans wanted peace. . . ." And Stalin then toasted both Hitler and Heinrich Himmler, that "guarantor of order in Germany."

Even before Ribbentrop had closed his deal with the Russians, Hitler again spoke to his generals: "We must act." Now was the point of Germany's greatest relative strength. His own leadership was irreplaceable, and he could "at any time be removed by an idiot or criminal." In a few years British and French armaments would begin to catch up, while Germany's war economy would run down for lack of raw materials. Hitler's sole fear, according to one account of his remarks, was "that Chamberlain or some other swine [*Saukerl*] might arrive at the last moment" with peace proposals. He ordered the attack on Poland for August 26.

Hitler wavered briefly on August 25, when Britain signed a military alliance with Poland and Mussolini shamefacedly confessed that Italy was too weak to fight. Then, surrounded by SS advisers, he confirmed his decision for war. Germany's long-term situation was "very difficult, perhaps hopeless." But as he had written

Hitler "Foresees" the Holocaust 1939

In his Reichstag *anniversary speech of January 30, 1939, Hitler made clear publicly that he reserved a special fate for Europe's Jews.*

I have in my life very often been a prophet, and was generally laughed at. In the period of my struggle for power it was the Jewish people who first of all received my prophecies exclusively with laughter, [when I said] that I would one day take over the leadership of the state and thus of the entire German people, and that I would among many other things also bring to solution the Jewish problem. I believe that the laughter of German Jewry that then resounded has since died in their throats.

I will today once more be a prophet: if international finance Jewry inside and outside Europe succeeds in plunging the nations into a new world war, the outcome will not be the Bolshevization of the earth and thus the victory of Jewry, but the extermination [*Vernichtung*] of the Jewish race in Europe.

From Hitler: Reden und Proklamationen 1932–1945, *ed. Max Domarus (Munich, 1965), Vol. 2:1, p. 1058 (translation by M. Knox).*

Stalin and Ribbentrop enjoy a joke at the signing of the Nazi-Soviet Pact, August 23–24, 1939.

in *Mein Kampf,* Germany would "either be a world power, or would cease to be."

At 4:45 A.M., German summer time on September 1, 1939, the *Webrmacht* attacked Poland from north, west, and south. In the next two days a sorrowing Chamberlain and the fearful French sought to promote, with Italian help, yet another conference. But the House of Commons refused. The Labour opposition and dissident Conservatives combined to "speak for England" and demand that Chamberlain honor Britain's pledge to Poland.

The March guarantee had perhaps been a tactical diplomatic error, but it had one great virtue at the end. Hitler, by challenging it, forced Chamberlain to declare war or suffer the collapse of his government. Britain's ultimatum to Germany expired at 11:00 A.M. on September 3. The Second World War had begun.

The causes of the war of 1939 have generated less dispute than those of World War I, of which it was a continuation. Britain, France, and the United States made a second war possible by failing either to dismember or conciliate Germany in 1919. Subsequently, their supine inaction and preemptive concessions permitted Hitler to rearm and strike. The Prusso-German conservatives helped Hitler to power and collaborated enthusiastically with him in creating the *Webrmacht* that destroyed the European and world balance. Stalin sought alliance with Hitler for the overthrow of the European balance and the extension of Soviet power. Stalin gave Hitler the chance to strike when he did. But in the end, it was Hitler's drive toward total power and his vision of racist world revolution that made this greatest of wars: "The decision to strike was always in me."

Suggestions for Further Reading

Totalitarianism

H. Arendt, *Totalitarianism* (1951), remains the classic description of the phenomenon, but is often eccentric. W. Laqueur, *The Fate of the Revolution,* rev. ed. (1987), conveniently summarizes debate about the concept of totalitarianism and about the Soviet regime. G. Orwell, *1984* (1949) and *Animal Farm* (1946), offers biting analysis in fictional form of totalitarianism in general and of Stalin in particular.

Stalin

On the Soviet Union, M. Heller and A. Nekritch, *Utopia in Power* (1982), is a lively introduction; B. Dmytryshyn, *USSR: A Concise History* (1978), provides a brief narrative and key documents. H. Carrère d'Encausse, *Lenin: Revolution and Power* (1981) and *Stalin: Order Through Terror* (1981), offer clearsighted analysis. On Stalin, see especially A. Ulam, *Stalin* (1973), and R. Conquest, *Stalin, Breaker of Nations* (1991). On Stalin's consequences, see R. Conquest, *The Harvest of Sorrow* (1986), *The Great Terror* (1968), *Kolyma: the Arctic Death Camps* (1978), and A. I. Solzhenitsyn, *The GULAG Archipelago* (1973). The numbers Stalin killed remain a subject of hot debate; for useful estimates, see S. Rosefielde, "An Assessment of the Sources and Uses of GULAG Forced Labour, 1929–56," "Excess Mortality in the Soviet Union," and "Incriminating Evidence: Excess Deaths and Forced Labour Under Stalin," *Soviet Studies,* 1:1981, 3:1983, 2:1987. On Stalin's foreign policy, see above all A. Ulam, *Expansion and Coexistence* (1968).

Mussolini

The Italian dictatorship is insufficiently studied. C. Seton-Watson, *Italy from Liberalism to Fascism* (1967), offers an excellent introduction to the circumstances that made it possible. A. Lyttelton, *The Seizure of Power* (1973), ably describes its first decade. M. Knox, *Mussolini Unleashed, 1939–1941* (1982) and "Conquest, Foreign and Domestic, in Fascist Italy and Nazi Germany," *Journal of Modern History,* 56:1 (1984), explores where it was going.

Hitler and War

The best introduction to Nazi Germany remains K. D. Bracher, *The German Dictatorship* (1970). K. Hildebrand, *The Third Reich* (1984), and P. Ayçoberry, *The Nazi Question* (1981), are excellent on the interpretive issues. On Hitler himself, see first of all his own words: A. Hitler, *Mein Kampf* (Ralph Manheim translation, 1943), and *Hitler's Second Book* (1961). J. Fest, *Hitler* (1975), is by far the best biography. On the inner workings of the regime, M. Broszat, *The Hitler State* (1981), is outstanding. W. Deist, *The Wehrmacht and German Rearmament* (1981), is the best introduction to Hitler's war preparations. K. Hildebrand, *The Foreign Policy of the Third Reich* (1973), and G. Weinberg, *The Foreign Policy of Hitler's Germany* (1970, 1980), are excellent on foreign policy. W. Murray, *The Change in the European Balance of Power, 1938–39* (1984), provides outstanding analysis of the strategic consequences of Munich and dissects the West's failure to stop Hitler before he became too strong. On Hitler's responsibility for and movement toward genocide, see especially G. Fleming, *Hitler and the Final Solution* (1982), and R. Hilberg's classic, *The Destruction of the European Jews* (1961; revised and expanded, 1985).

Finally, A. J. P. Taylor's *The Origins of the Second World War* (1961), raised a storm by arguing that Hitler had no long-term vision and that war in 1939 was simply a result of opportunism and miscalculation. That view has found few supporters; Hitler's words, both public and private, demonstrate otherwise. P. M. H. Bell, *The Origins of the Second World War in Europe* (1986), provides a useful summary of recent research; G. Martel, ed., *The Origins of the Second World War Reconsidered* (1986), offers mostly hostile retrospective comment on Taylor.

33

FROM SECOND WORLD WAR TO COLD WAR 1939–1949

In the next two and a half years, the war that began on September 1, 1939, grew into a global conflict. Hitler destroyed Poland, invaded Scandinavia, and crushed France. Those victories opened Mussolini's road to a Mediterranean and Balkan war. They encouraged Japan to move south on a collision course with Britain and the United States. And they gave Hitler the strategic and economic base he needed to begin "his" war for *Lebensraum* in the East and for racist world revolution.

On June 22, 1941, Germany attacked Soviet Russia. That at last brought into existence an "anti-Hitler coalition"—Britain, Russia, and a still reluctant United States—powerful enough to bring the Reich down. On December 7, 1941, Japan completed that coalition by forcing the United States into war. Hitler and Japan made the European war of 1939–41 into a global struggle that destroyed Europe's independence.

Only Hitler united his enemies. As the Reich faltered in its desperate struggle against the three allied world powers, the allies began to break up. Stalin sought an empire stretching far beyond the eastern European sphere gained from Hitler in 1939. Britain and America hesitantly sought Stalin's cooperation in a postwar system of world order, a successor to the defunct League of Nations. Given the underlying incompatibility between the Soviet Union and the Western Allies, "cold war" predictably followed world war once Hitler was dead. By 1947–48, the peoples of eastern Europe, already ruined by Hitler, had suffered a second—Soviet style—revolution from above. But this time the United States did not withdraw as it had in 1919. It reluctantly committed forces to hold in "peacetime" against Stalin the positions it had stormed in war against Hitler. Global war gave way to global confrontation between the American and

(*OPPOSITE*) THE FACE OF A NEW WORLD WAR: GERMAN MECHANIZED INFANTRY DESTROYS A RUSSIAN VILLAGE, 1941.

Russian superpowers, under the shadow of weapons of unimaginable power, atomic and then thermonuclear bombs.

THE NEW WARFARE

Technology and Science at War

The internal combustion engine restored the battlefield mobility that industrial firepower had taken away in 1914–18. The second German war was a war of movement; its pace sometimes rivaled or exceeded that of Napoleon's campaigns. Only in fortified areas or when evenly matched forces met head-on did the fighting congeal for months at a time into something that resembled Verdun.

The tank came into its own. In the 1920s British theorists had suggested that the future of war on land resembled war at sea: vast armored formations sweeping across the battlefield like great fleets. But the conservatism of Britain's cavalrymen, Chamberlain's budget stringency, and his government's resolve never to fight again on the Continent killed innovation in Britain. In Germany the tank caught on during

the *Wehrmacht*'s rapid expansion after 1933; in 1935 the German army set up its first *Panzerdivisionen*—armored divisions. By September 1939 it had six of them.

Contrary to myth, Germany's armored forces were not a response to a demand by Hitler for weapons with which to implement a "*Blitzkrieg*" or "lightning war" strategy of short decisive campaigns. Until 1938, Hitler let the German army do its own planning. He was fortunate—and the world unfortunate—that his generals successfully combined motors, armor, radios, and the German deep-penetration tactics of 1917–18 into an instrument that could smash the European balance of power.

At sea, oil-fired turbines and diesel engines gave the fleets far greater range than the coal-fired navies of the First World War. A new capital ship, the aircraft carrier, rivaled and soon replaced the Dreadnought as the backbone of sea power. By 1941 the aircraft of the fast fleet carriers of the Imperial Japanese and U.S. navies could reach out hundreds of miles beyond the horizon to rain armor-piercing bombs on the enemy. Refueling at sea

Fleet carrier: the USS *Lexington* in 1939.

gave the fleets ranges of thousands of miles. And the amphibious techniques pioneered by the U.S. Marine Corps—partly to defend its budget between the wars—enabled Americans and British to fight their way back after the early Allied disasters.

In the air, the scene had also changed. Airpower was no longer in its infancy. Aircraft were now capable of tasks ranging from "strategic" bombing of the enemy's homeland to transport of troops and supplies, dropping of parachute or glider infantry, close support of ground troops, deep photo-reconnaissance, attack on surface fleets, antisubmarine patrol, and air defense. Air superiority was the key to rapid movement by land or sea. Only the Germans, in the last phases of the war, were tough and expert enough to fight successfully for long without air cover.

The greatest novelty of all was the contribution of science. Fritz Haber's nitrate process had given Germany the explosives that enabled it to fight on until 1918. But in World War I science had in other respects been a mere auxiliary to warfare. By 1939 that was no longer true. The development and production of decisive or potentially decisive weapons such as radar, computers to decipher enemy signals, liquid-fuel ballistic missiles, jet aircraft, and the atomic bomb required a high level of scientific skill, technological expertise, and economic power.

The bomb—the first nuclear weapon— was the result of an unprecedented commitment of scientific talent and resources, a commitment only the United States could make. The spur for this first example of "command science"—a vast government-directed research project aiming at a goal—was fear that Hitler would get the bomb first. Fortunately, German physicists advanced slowly and hesitantly, and Hitler gave priority to projects that promised quick results. The U.S. "Manhattan Project" spent a staggering $2 billion and drained the hydroelectric power of the Tennessee Valley and Pacific Northwest. But by July 1945 it had produced the uranium and plutonium bombs used against Japan. Science made possible—and war appeared to demand—

weapons of mass destruction that were potentially capable, for the first time, of annihilating all humanity.

The Industrial and Geographic Balance

Even more than 1914–18, the Second World War was a struggle between war economies as well as between armed forces. Germany began at a slight disadvantage in total industrial potential compared to Britain and France. But its unassailable geographic position, control of Rumania's oil, and economic aid from Stalin more than made up for that shortcoming. Much of Germany's rubber supply flowed in through Vladivostok. Soviet oil fueled Hitler's U-boats, aircraft, and tanks. Turkey's chrome and Finland's nickel hardened the armor of the *Panzer* divisions. In 1940 Sweden provided almost half of Hitler's iron ore through the Baltic and the coastal waters of Norway. This time, the British blockade was ineffectual.

The collapse of France brought Germany much military and economic booty, and France's industries, which now worked for the Reich rather than against it. But Italy's simultaneous entry into the war extended Germany's military and economic risks without compensation; Britain now had an enemy it could defeat in Africa and the Mediterranean. And by the fall and winter of 1940, the economic power of the United States had begun to swing against Germany.

That threat helped decide Hitler for war against the Soviet Union, which he expected to crumble swiftly. But the Soviets held, although barely. Germany thereafter faced a coalition of world powers with at least three times Germany's industrial potential. The addition of Japan to the Axis powers in December 1941 was only a small gain; Britain, the United States, and the Soviet Union still had more than two and a half times the industrial potential of the "Hitler-coalition" of Germany, Italy, and Japan (see Figure 33-1). Soviet Russia's refusal to collapse and Hitler's rejection of Stalin's secret bids for an armistice led to the destruction of the

FIGURE 33-1   The Axis Defeated: War Production   1940–43

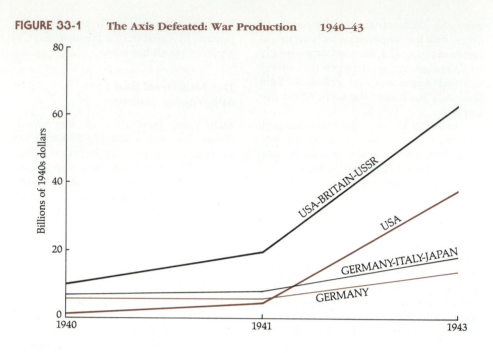

Reich under a rain of fire and steel from the east, the west, and the skies.

FROM EUROPEAN TO GLOBAL WAR, 1939–41

Poland: Defeat and Occupation

Poland fought bravely, but not for long. By September 15 the most serious fighting was over; German armor and airpower had sliced the Polish forces into helpless fragments. Stalin attacked the Poles from the rear on September 17 and claimed the Polish territories promised him under the secret protocol to the Nazi-Soviet pact.

In their occupation of Poland, Soviets and Nazis showed remarkable similarities in their methods. As Stalin remarked much later to a Yugoslav Communist, "This war is not as in the past; whoever occupies a territory also imposes on it his own social system. . . . It cannot be otherwise." Beginning in September 1939, Stalin deported to the GULAG more than a million Polish civilians and prisoners of war. To decapitate any future Polish national resistance, Stalin and the Politburo ordered the NKVD to shoot more than 20,000 Polish officers, members of the upper classes,

and clergy in March–April 1940; many of their bodies turned up in 1943 in a mass grave in Katyn forest in western Russia. The Baltic states suffered similar treatment when the Soviet Union swallowed them in June–July 1940. And Stalin, who so loved foreign Communists that he had liquidated many of them in the Great Terror, also handed over to Himmler hundreds of German and Austrian Communists who had sought refuge in the Soviet Union. Stalin was not joking when he publicly hailed "Russo-German friendship, cemented by blood."

Himmler and his sinister subordinate Reinhard Heydrich lacked Stalin's long experience in truly large-scale killing. They found Poland a splendid training ground. With the advancing German army came *Einsatzkommandos* ("task forces") of SS and Police whose mission was to kill Jews and educated Poles, especially priests. Thousands perished in experimental massacres; German army protests led to a brief halt. Then the army sheepishly handed over control of occupied Poland to the Party and the SS.

Hitler himself, on October 18, made clear to his subordinates what he expected from Poland: "cheap slaves." Himmler herded the Jews of Poland into newly created ghettos as a "first prerequisite" for an as yet unspecified "final goal." He also shipped in ethnic Germans from the Baltic and carpetbaggers from the "Old Reich" to settle the areas cleared of Poles and Jews. And war freed Hitler even inside Germany. In October 1939 he ordered—in secret—the killing of mental patients and the handicapped to rid the "race" of "worthless life." The totalitarian reshaping of Europe had begun.

"Greater Germany" Triumphant, 1940

The West made no attempt to help the Poles, despite repeated French pledges to attack Germany from the west. The French instead peered fearfully from their Maginot Line bunkers and sent out a few inept patrols. By the end of September 1939 the Germans were happily redeploying their forces from Poland to the French and Belgian borders.

Hitler immediately demanded that his generals attack in the West. Time was against Germany. The British were at last creating a mass army; Allied war production was rising; America "was still not dangerous to us because of her neutrality laws," but that might change. The generals grumbled that they needed more time. Some hesitantly plotted against the regime.

Unfortunately for the West, bad weather repeatedly forced Hitler to postpone the attack. The breathing space gave the German army time to add more vehicles, draw lessons from the fighting in Poland, and train relentlessly. It also gave Hitler and a brilliant junior general, Erich von Manstein, time to replace the army staff's uninspired copy of the Schlieffen Plan (see p. 762) with a surprise armored thrust through the hills around Luxembourg.

Distractions in Scandinavia also dogged Germany throughout the winter. Stalin had misjudged the Finns: unlike the defenseless Baltic states, they did not tamely give in to Soviet demands for military bases and territory. On November 30 Stalin therefore attacked Finland and set up a puppet Finnish Communist government in a captured border town. The League of Nations, in its last memorable act, expelled the Soviet Union as an aggressor. But the Finns and the great powers, not world opinion, determined the outcome. Soviet numerical superiority finally wore the Finns down in February–March 1940, but by that time Stalin's amateurishly led troops had suffered several hundred thousand dead and wounded. Fearing that Soviet occupation of all of Finland would lead to continued fighting and Allied intervention in Scandinavia, Stalin settled for the small annexations he had demanded at the outset.

War in Scandinavia indeed attracted Allied and German hopes and fears. Paris hoped to divert the war away from the plains of northern France. Winston Churchill, whom Chamberlain had unwillingly taken into the cabinet as chief of the Royal Navy, urged attacks on Germany's vulnerable iron ore supply line from neutral Sweden. The Germans also prepared; they longed for a window on the Atlantic in Norway for their submarines and commerce raiders.

The Germans moved first. On April 9, using the *Luftwaffe* to compensate for their naval inferiority, they seized key points in Norway with brilliantly executed amphibious and airborne attacks. German ground troops swiftly seized Denmark. Britain and France belatedly landed forces in central and northern Norway. But German speed, skill, and air superiority drove them out by early June.

Defeat in Scandinavia destroyed the mournful Chamberlain as a war leader. On May 10, 1940, Winston Churchill came to power as prime minister at the head of an all-party coalition. Labour, which had damned Churchill in earlier years for his uncompromising hostility to striking miners, Gandhi, and Hitler, now staunchly agreed to share with Churchill the responsibility for leading Britain's war effort. Churchill had been right about Hitler.

But Churchill arrived almost too late. The day of his appointment was the day on which the Germans launched their long-awaited offensive against France and the Low Countries. They had prepared well. The *Luftwaffe,* despite heavy losses, swept the skies of French aircraft and savagely bombed Rotterdam to terrorize the Dutch. German infantry swiftly crushed the small and inexperienced armies of Holland and Belgium. Seven *Panzerdivisionenen* and three motorized infantry divisions struck through Luxembourg and the Ardennes hills, and reached the Channel on May 20, cutting off in the Low Countries forty of the best-equipped Allied divisions. Of that huge force, 1.2 million fell prisoner; only 226,000 British and 112,000 French escaped to Britain from the beaches of Dunkirk.

On June 17, after the Germans had seized Paris, a new French government under the aged Marshal Pétain sued for armistice. By June 24 France was out of the war; only small "Free French" forces

The victor: Hitler tours Paris, 1940.

under the command of a charismatic junior general, Charles de Gaulle, fought on with British help. Hitler occupied the north and west of France, leaving Pétain only an enclave in the south with its capital at Vichy. Greater Germany—*Grossdeutschland*—now controlled Europe from the North Cape of Norway to the Spanish border. Hitler had succeeded where William II and Ludendorff had failed. In the intoxication of victory and looted champagne, the German generals and Hitler's conservative allies forgot their earlier doubts. War, as Hitler had hoped, had made him *Führer* indeed.

Britain, America, Russia and the German Strategic Impasse, 1940–41

But the war did not end in France; victory there proved a strategic dead end. Hitler expected Britain to "see reason" and join the Reich as a junior partner, but Churchill refused to give in: "Nations that went down fighting rose again but those which surrendered tamely were finished." Chamberlain and Halifax sought negotiations from weakness in the name of "realism," but Churchill beat them down in cabinet debate. He was confident that Britain's rising production of fighter aircraft would prevent the Germans from achieving air superiority and invading Britain.

Churchill also bid ruthlessly for the American support Britain needed to fight on; better Roosevelt as senior partner than Hitler. On May 20 Churchill secretly warned Roosevelt that failure to support Britain might lead to a new British government committed to surrender. That government might swing the British fleet to the Axis side and mortally threaten the United States in the North Atlantic. And to show Roosevelt and the world that Britain would fight so long as he was in command, Churchill's navy on July 3 sank or captured in harbor much of the fleet of Britain's former ally, France. The Axis could no longer gain naval superiority by seizing French battleships from the Pétain government.

The fall of France at last galvanized American opinion and freed Roosevelt to respond to Churchill's polite blackmail and to his display of resolve. The U.S. Congress ordered America's first peace-time military draft in August 1940; America's dwarf army of 280,000 could now once more become a serious force—in a few years. Roosevelt also defied the spirit of a congressional ban on weapons sales. In September 1940 he traded fifty obsolete U.S. destroyers for the right to use British bases in Newfoundland, Bermuda, and the Caribbean, and for a pledge that Britain would never turn its fleet over to the Germans. In November 1940 he trounced his Republican opponent, Wendell Willkie, and won an unprecedented third term as president.

Hitler saw the coming American threat—and a possible remedy—as early as July 31: "England's hope is Russia and America. If hope in Russia falls away, America too falls away, for after elimination of Russia an immense increase in Japan's power in east Asia follows." If Germany destroyed Soviet Russia, Hitler assumed, Japan would be free of threat on its northern flank and could keep the Americans busy in the Pacific. Hitler therefore sought an immediate attack on the Soviet Union. War in the East was not only "his" war, the war he had looked for since 1922 to secure for Germany a vast blockade-proof eastern empire, a "German India." It was also the answer to the growing support of the United States for Britain. A German "world *Blitzkrieg*" in Russia would make Germany unassailable by conquering Eurasia before Roosevelt could bring to bear the immense economic and military potential of the United States.

But Hitler's planners soon told him that Russia's harsh climate would prevent an eastern campaign that fall. He therefore fell back on stopgaps. Germany launched a sea and air war against Britain's Atlantic supply lines, but a strategy of attrition offered no promise of immediate results, and threatened to speed up Roosevelt's drift toward war. A second possibility was operation SEA LION, an invasion of Britain for which the Germans began to prepare in July. But in the vast "Battle of Britain" that reached its climax over southern Eng-

Churchill inspects the ruins of the House of Commons after a German attack.

land on September 15, the Spitfires and Hurricanes of the Royal Air Force (RAF) denied the *Luftwaffe* air superiority. The Germans then switched to night bombing in the "Blitz" of winter 1940–41. Their raids flattened large areas of London and killed civilians by the thousands, but failed to break British morale.

The German navy and Ribbentrop offered other options. The navy pressed for a Mediterranean campaign: seizing Britain's outpost at Gibraltar with the help of Franco's Spain and galvanizing the Italians to take Suez. Ribbentrop tried to fashion a world coalition from Madrid to Tokyo

Spitfire!

against Britain and the United States. On September 27, 1940, he succeeded in enlisting the Japanese and Mussolini in a "Tripartite Pact" in which all three pledged to come to each other's aid in the event of war with the United States.

St. Paul's Cathedral, London, under *Luftwaffe* bombardment, January 23, 1941.

Franco and Mussolini between them wrecked both the German navy plan and the European part of Ribbentrop's coalition. The price Franco set for Spain's intervention was higher, in supplies and territory, than Hitler was willing to pay; Gibraltar remained British. And Mussolini threw the Mediterranean theater into chaos by attacking Greece at the end of October 1940. The Greeks hurled the ill-trained Italians back into Albania. British torpedo bombers then sank three Italian battleships at anchor, and British armored forces from Egypt crushed the large but poorly led Italian army in Libya between December 1940 and February 1941.

Italy's disasters forced Hitler to intervene in the Mediterranean not to achieve final victory over Britain, but merely to rescue his ally. U-boats, a *Luftwaffe* air corps, and armored units under the brilliant but erratic Erwin Rommel arrived in time to prevent the collapse of Italy's position in Africa, and of Mussolini's regime. In spring 1941 Hitler ended Mussolini's Balkan war by striking south into Greece through Rumania and Bulgaria, and by bloodily dismantling a potentially hostile Yugoslavia.

But these new victories offered Hitler no way to end the war. German triumphs in the Mediterranean or Middle East could not force Britain to negotiate so long as it controlled the North Atlantic and had the support of the United States. And Roosevelt, despite a continuing isolationist opposition which trumpeted that "the British, the Jew[s], and the Roosevelt administration" were seeking to force America into war, was at last achieving results. In February–March 1941, Anglo-American staff talks secretly laid down the strategy governing the future U.S. war effort: *Germany first*. If and when the United States entered the war, it would concentrate its power against the West's most dangerous enemy. In March 1941 Congress passed a "Lend-Lease Act" which offered to a financially exhausted Britain, and thereafter to other U.S. allies, an almost unlimited supply of arms on long-term credit. Credits later turned into outright gifts, and ultimately amounted to $43 billion.

Racist War of Annihilation: BARBAROSSA

Even before Lend-Lease made clear that the United States was moving toward Britain, Hitler had decided on his response: "his" war, the war in the East. Ribbentrop had invited the Soviets to explore the possibility of Soviet participation in the Tripartite Pact. But the uncouth Molotov's visit to Berlin on November 12 and 13, 1940, wrecked that project. To Ribbentrop's fantasies about a Soviet Russian outlet to ice-free oceans through Iran and British India, Molotov replied with a long shopping list in Europe—*Germany's* chosen sphere. Stalin wanted Soviet bases at the Turkish Straits, the addition of Bulgaria to the Soviet "security zone," the removal of German protection over Finland, and joint Soviet-Danish—but not Soviet-German—control over the exits from the Baltic. Molotov also stressed the Soviet Union's "interest" in Rumania, Hungary, Yugoslavia, Greece, and even the portion of Poland currently assigned to Germany under the Nazi-Soviet Pact. The tactlessness and extravagance of Molotov's demands suggested that Stalin expected the Anglo-Saxon powers to defeat Germany, and was claiming his booty in advance.

Hitler was relieved. Stalin had "let the cat out of the bag." The Soviet-German "marriage of convenience" was over. On December 18, Hitler issued a directive for the greatest land war in history, Operation BARBAROSSA: "The German *Wehrmacht* must be prepared to *overthrow Soviet Russia in a swift campaign,* even before the end of the war with England." BARBAROSSA would annihilate all Soviet forces in European Russia and seize all Soviet territory up to a line that stretched from Archangel on the Arctic Ocean to Astrakhan on the Caspian Sea. That stroke, Hitler and his generals assumed, would crush the Soviet regime and give Germany world mastery.

The German military planners shared Hitler's racist contempt for the Red Army, and regarded the destruction of the Soviet Union as an "intriguing" operational problem. But for Hitler it was more than that.

"The coming campaign," he told his subordinates on March 3, "is more than a mere armed conflict; it also entails a struggle between two ideologies." And since, by Hitler's racist logic, Bolshevism was an outgrowth of Judaism, the ideological struggle required "racial" measures: "the Jewish-Bolshevik intelligentsia . . . must be removed."

What that meant soon became clear. Hitler's military assistants issued orders empowering Himmler of the SS to carry out "special tasks" in the coming area of operations. *Einsatzgruppen* ("task groups") of the SS and Police, with army help, were to take "executive measures with respect to the civilian population" of Russia. The army itself, under the "Commissar Order" of May–June 1941, became for the first time a direct extension of Hitler's racial goals. That order required shooting upon capture all Red Army political officers and Communist party members. The *Wehrmacht* estimated that it would take 3.5 million prisoners of war but allocated rations for only 790,000; the rest would presumably starve. And the experts of Göring's economic planning staff decided that the conquered territories would have to feed the *Wehrmacht*—leaving no food for the cities of European Russia. "X millions of people will die out," noted the bureaucrats dispassionately. BARBAROSSA was to be a racial and ideological war of extermination that trampled underfoot all limits on interstate violence established in Europe since the Thirty Years' War. Colonial war had come home to Europe.

On June 22, 1941, the *Wehrmacht*'s three million men attacked the Soviet Union on a front that stretched from the Baltic to the Black Sea. Stalin had received numerous warnings, but had spurned them as "capitalist provocations" designed to trick him into an unwanted and unnecessary war with Hitler. He had preferred to believe rumors planted by the Germans that the *Wehrmacht* deployment was a gigantic attempt to extort more raw materials from the Soviet Union. German deception worked; until the last, Stalin apparently expected a German ultimatum.

What he got instead was war. "What shall we do?" he reportedly asked the Politburo before suffering a nervous collapse. Not until July 3 did he belatedly take to the radio and urge his Soviet "brothers and sisters" in a broken voice to resist to the end. Stalin evidently had difficulty believing that those he had terrorized would fight for him. They fought above all for biological survival and for Great Russian nationalism. Wholesale massacres by the Germans of Soviet prisoners of war and Jews stiffened Soviet resistance. And the Soviet regime now appealed not to "proletarian internationalism" but to something far deeper. It invoked the Russian traditions that Stalin had promoted through the historical rehabilitation, in the 1930s, of past rulers whose methods resembled his own: Ivan the Terrible and Peter the Great.

The Germans advanced swiftly, thanks to strategic surprise and to their overwhelming advantages in military doctrine, experience, and *Luftwaffe* airpower. By early August they had taken Smolensk, halfway to Moscow, and had killed or captured more than a million Soviets. Hitler looked to the future; he believed he had won. He ordered German armament efforts shifted to air and sea warfare against the British. Subordinates drafted a directive for German thrusts through the Caucasus to the Middle East oilfields in the coming "period after BARBAROSSA." Germany, Hitler privately declared, would raze Moscow and Leningrad to the ground, exterminate much of the population of European Russia, and replace it with German settlers. The term "Greater German World Empire," which Goebbels had banned from his press in 1940 as premature, no longer seemed inappropriate.

July–December 1941: The Culmination of the War

Others saw the future differently. Churchill and Roosevelt immediately offered aid to a surprised Stalin, who accepted it in the spirit in which it was offered; as he once remarked, "In war I would deal with the Devil and his mother." But the Western powers nevertheless assumed that the Germans would destroy Soviet Russia. Roosevelt and Churchill met on shipboard near Newfoundland in mid-August 1941, and produced an "Atlantic Charter," a declaration of war aims in the style of Woodrow Wilson.

The Charter implied that the United States would eventually enter the war. It proclaimed that Britain and the United States sought "no aggrandizement, territorial or other" and desired "no territorial changes that [did] not accord with the freely expressed wishes of the people concerned." It announced that both powers would seek free markets, freedom of the seas, and "freedom from fear and want" for all humanity. But it made no reference to the third member of the new "Grand Alliance," or to that power's entirely different principles and methods. Roosevelt and Churchill evidently expected that they alone would dictate the outcome of the war. The United States began to ready an army that would surpass the *Wehrmacht:* a projected 215 divisions of which 61 would be armored.

The Newfoundland meeting was the outward expression of a halting change in Roosevelt's policy. In the conviction that the aid "short of war" promised with Lend-Lease was not enough to defeat Hitler, he began to move toward war itself. Without the formal approval of Congress, Roosevelt began between July and September 1941 an undeclared naval war in the North Atlantic. U.S. forces took over Iceland, an outpost Hitler coveted, from the British. Roosevelt agreed to convoy British shipping from Canada to Iceland. In September, after the inevitable clash between a U-boat and a U.S. destroyer, he gave the U.S. Navy orders to "shoot on sight" at Hitler's navy.

Before sailing to meet Churchill, Roosevelt had also moved against Japan. Hitler's May–June 1940 victory in Europe had encouraged Tokyo to turn southward toward the vital oil of the Dutch East Indies. Then a Soviet-Japanese nonaggression pact signed in April 1941, coupled with Hitler's attack on the Soviet Union in June, had ended Tokyo's fear of a Soviet threat on its northern flank in Manchuria.

In July 1941 Japan occupied bases in the southern part of French Indochina in preparation for a further jump southward. Roosevelt reacted by freezing all Japanese assets in the United States and by restricting the U.S. oil exports on which Japan depended. The Dutch took similar measures. In the space of a week, Japan had lost 90 percent of its oil supply. Roosevelt himself seems to have intended only to cut back U.S. oil exports as a warning, but zealous subordinates announced a total cutoff.

Tokyo then offered to moderate its activities in China and Indochina. But Roosevelt and his advisers judged Japan's offer insincere; the Japanese army in any event privately refused to give up its Chinese colony. In September 1941, Tokyo decided to go to war with the United States while its navy still had oil reserves and before the United States completed its naval rearmament—unless a breakthrough occurred in negotiations. None did. In mid-October the military rulers of Japan dropped their facade; Prince Konoye's civilian cabinet gave way to the government of General Tōjō Hideki. On November 26, as Roosevelt again insisted on Japanese withdrawal from China, Japan's fast carrier forces secretly sailed.

In Russia, the Germans at last closed on Moscow. In July and August Hitler had diverted armored forces south to the Ukraine, where they took another 650,000 prisoners in a great encirclement at Kiev. The Ukraine operation, troop exhaustion, and supply difficulties delayed the final drive on Moscow until early October. But once launched, operation TYPHOON made dramatic progress. The Germans demolished yet another Soviet army group and seized a further 600,000 prisoners in great battles at Vyazma and Bryansk.

In Moscow, the NKVD disappeared from the street corners. Bonfires in the ministry courtyards consumed mountains of files. Bureaucrats fled for Kuibyshev on the Volga River, which had been designated as the alternative capital. An announcement that Stalin remained in the Kremlin and a few NKVD shootings stabilized the situation briefly—but the Soviet regime appeared close to collapse. Then

Pearl Harbor, December 7, 1941.

the fall rains bogged the *Panzerdivisionen* and their supply echelons in Russian mud. The freeze that followed briefly speeded the advance once more, but Soviet resistance stiffened. German reconnaissance units reached the outskirts of Moscow; they could see the flashes of the antiaircraft guns on the Kremlin roof. But the Germans were desperate. By early December, only a quarter of their original tank force could move; 23 of every 100 German soldiers who had invaded the Soviet Union were dead, wounded, or missing. On December 5–6, fresh Soviet troops launched a counteroffensive that threw the Germans into confusion. Hitler had failed to destroy the Soviet Union.

The following day, December 7, 1941, the Japanese naval air arm struck at Hawaii, and crippled the battleship force of the U.S. Pacific Fleet at Pearl Harbor. The military logic of the Japanese attack was as impeccable as its execution was flawless—except that it missed the fleet carriers, which were at sea. Because the U.S. fleet was the main obstacle to Japan's southward advance to the oil of the Dutch

East Indies, a preemptive strike to eliminate that fleet had seemed essential. But the Japanese in their desperation had ignored the political and strategic consequences of attacking Pearl Harbor. Japan's "date which will live in infamy"—as Roosevelt described December 7—freed him of the delicate task of persuading Congress to declare war in defense of the British and Dutch colonial empires. And Pearl Harbor produced instant unanimity in the United States. Isolationists, many of whom saw themselves as defenders of American ethnic purity against contamination from the outside world, took up with a fierce racism the cause of crushing Japan. Nor had Tokyo—given its own racist disdain for outsiders and consequent underestimation of American resolve—thought how to end the war it had begun against an enemy with at least ten times its military-industrial power.

Hitler closed the circle on December 11, 1941, by declaring war on the United States. He apparently hoped that a two-ocean war would prevent America from concentrating its power decisively in either theater. His decision, like that of the Japanese, handed the United States an immense political-strategic victory. Roosevelt now had no need to persuade Congress to declare the war on Germany needed to implement his long-decided strategy of "Germany first." Hitler's declaration forced America to fight in Europe and guaranteed that it would fight hard. Hitler and Tokyo between them made certain the defeat of the Axis and the end of Europe's independence.

THE "FINAL SOLUTION"

The realization that Germany might lose spurred Hitler to greater military efforts. It also led him to make sure of one thing: the accomplishment of the "historic mission" he had long ago defined for Germany, the elimination of the alleged threat of "Jewish world domination."

The "executive measures" of the SS against the civilian population of Russia that Hitler ordered in March–April 1941 took effect during the headlong *Wehrmacht* advance from June to December. SS and Police *Einsatzkommandos* rounded up and shot as many of European Russia's 4.7 million Jews as they could catch. The *Wehrmacht* protested far less now than it had over the 1939 killings in Poland. Hitler's victories had immeasurably reinforced his authority and the prestige of his ideology, and the army itself had inherited from the *Freikorps* of 1918–21 (see p. 793) the tradition of shooting Bolsheviks "while attempting to escape." Until the war turned in December 1941, high German commanders had no qualms about ordering their units to massacre Soviet prisoners and Jews: "The [German] soldier must be fully convinced of the necessity of harsh, but just expiation by the Jewish-Bolshevik subhumans."

But the Jews of Russia were only part of Hitler's target. At the height of his victories in July 1941, Hitler remarked that "if any [European] state . . . permits a Jewish family to remain, that [family] will become the bacteria-breeding-ground for a new

---

Hitler Gloats Openly over the Extermination of the Jews   1942

Few Germans later admitted to having known about it, but Hitler publicly boasted in scarcely veiled language about the "Final Solution" on four occasions in 1942 (January 30, February 24, September 30, and November 8):

I told the *Reichstag* session [January 30, 1939; see p. 853] two things: First, that once they had forced the war upon us, neither armed force nor passage of time would bring us down, and second, that if Jewry were to unleash an international world war for the purpose of exterminating the Aryan peoples of Europe, then it would not be the Aryan peoples that would be exterminated, but Jewry. . . . The Jews in Germany once upon a time laughed at my prophesying. I do not know if they still laugh, or whether their laughter has already ceased. I can however now assure you that they will never laugh again [*es wird ihnen das Lachen überall vergehen*]. And *that* prophecy of mine will also be confirmed.

Hitler speech at Berlin, September 30, 1942, in Hitler: Reden und Proklamationen 1932–1945, *ed. Max Domarus (Munich, 1965), Vol. II:2, p. 1920 (translation by M. Knox).*

infection." On July 31, 1941, Himmler's subordinate Reinhard Heydrich received orders to organize, "with the participation of all necessary German central bureaucracies, all preparations for a general solution of the Jewish Question in Europe."

Hitler himself was apparently careful not to sign a document authorizing what soon became known in the SS and the German ministries as the "Final Solution of the Jewish Question." But both his public remarks and his private actions leave little doubt that he was the driving force behind it. He repeatedly demanded reports of the progress of the killings, and in November 1941 he promised the Grand Mufti of Jerusalem, leader of the Palestinian Arabs, that when Germany conquered the Middle East he would "annihilate" the Jews there as well.

In September–October 1941 the SS began deporting to Poland and occupied Russia the German and Austrian Jews. The SS shot many of them in mass executions. But that method soon proved cumbersome. In the fall, winter, and spring of 1941–42, Himmler and his subordinates therefore set up camps in occupied Poland designed as factories of death, with gas chambers and crematoria: Auschwitz-Birkenau, Treblinka, Lublin, Sobibor, Belzec, Chelmno. In January 1942, at a conference in the flossy Berlin suburb of Wannsee, Heydrich tasked the major Reich ministries to assist him in deporting the Jews—men, women, and children—to these death camps: "Europe will be combed through from west to east."

The "Final Solution" did not end until November 1944, when Himmler, on his own initiative, suspended it as the Reich neared collapse. Its consequence was the murder of more than 6 million Jews, including a quarter of a million from Germany, more than 1 million from Russia, 3 million from Poland, 200,000 from western Europe, and at least 750,000 from eastern Europe.

The Jews were the victims with the highest priority. But the Gypsies of Europe also suffered deportation to the death camps on "racial" grounds; hundreds of thousands perished. German experts tested killing-factory techniques on Soviet

The "Final Solution": Jewish deportees arrive at Auschwitz.

prisoners and on German mental patients and handicapped as well as on Jews. Between 1941 and 1945 the SS and the German army between them killed the staggering total of 3.3 million Red Army prisoners by shooting or maltreatment. More than 2 million Poles died during German conquest and occupation. And Hitler's intention, in the event of victory, was to exterminate most of the population of eastern Europe and European Russia. Hitler's genocide was more than a Holocaust of the Jewish people. It was the first step in a pseudo-biological attempt to remodel humanity—a racist world revolution.

It also went almost unchallenged, except on distant battlefields and in a doomed 1943 Jewish uprising in the Warsaw ghetto. French police and Dutch SS helped round up Jews for deportation. Slovaks, Greeks, and Hungarians cooperated with greater or lesser enthusiasm. Rumania and Germany's Croat puppet-state vigorously organized their own massacres of Jews; Latvians, Lithuanians, and Ukrainians provided the SS with valuable helpers. The major exceptions were Denmark, Norway, Bulgaria, and even Fascist Italy, which baffled the Germans with bureau-

The "Final Solution"

The first train arrived . . . 45 freight cars with 6,700 people, of whom 1,450 were already dead on arrival. . . . A large loudspeaker blares instructions: undress completely, take off artificial limbs, glasses, etc. Hand in all valuables. Shoes to be tied together (for the clothing collection). . . . Women and girls to the barber, who cuts off their hair in two or three strokes and stuffs it into potato sacks.

Then the line starts moving. . . . At the corner a strapping SS-man announces in a pastoral voice: Nothing will happen to you! Just breathe deeply inside the chambers, that stretches the lungs; this inhalation is necessary against the illnesses and epidemics. When asked what would happen to them, he replies: Well, of course the men will have to work, build houses and roads, but the women won't have to work. If they want to they can help in the household or the kitchen. For a few of these unfortunates a small glimmer of hope which suffices to have them take the few steps to the chambers without resistance—the majority knows what is ahead, the stench tells their fate. . . .

The wooden doors are opened. . . . Inside the chambers, the dead are closely pressed together, like pillars of stone. . . . Even in death one recognizes the families. They still hold hands, so they have to be torn apart to get the chambers ready for the next occupants. The corpses are thrown out—wet with sweat and urine, covered with excrement, menstrual blood. Children's bodies fly through the air. . . . Two dozen workers use hooks to pry open mouths and look for gold. . . . Others search genitals and anuses for gold, diamonds, and valuables. Wirth [an SS guard] motions to me: Just lift this can of gold teeth, this is only from today and the day before! . . .

From an eyewitness account of mass gassings, in Vierteljahrshefte für Zeit-geschichte *(1953), Vol. I, pp. 190–91.*

American bureaucrats harbored a poorly concealed distaste for Jewish refugees.

At first the Allies discounted the reports of the killings; deliberate, mechanized mass murder seemed too monstrous an act even for Hitler. Britain did issue a declaration describing the deportations in December 1942, and Churchill pressed for air attacks on the rail lines leading to Auschwitz. But the great distances to the target, the military demands of the air war and of the Normandy invasion, and bureaucratic sabotage by his subordinates prevented action.

This time Churchill did not use the public threats with which he had answered rumors in early 1942 that Hitler planned to use poison gas against Britain's Soviet ally. Then Churchill had promised reprisals: a deluge of mustard gas from the air upon Germany. That entirely credible threat had deterred Hitler, although he had secretly stockpiled large quantities of nerve gas, a weapon far more deadly than anything in the Allied chemical arsenal. But unlike the Soviet Union, the Jews of Europe were not a state—or an ally of Britain and the United States. They had last call on Allied resources. The victims of Hitler's genocide, like those of Stalin's, perished without even token assistance from that elusive force, world public opinion.

THE HOME FRONT: BUREAUCRACY, PROPAGANDA, TERROR, DEATH

On the home fronts, the war followed some of the precedents laid down in the First World War and the Great Depression. All the major belligerents mobilized immense masses of men for war and industry. Women again joined the work force in vast numbers, even in Germany, where the regime's ideology supposedly dictated that they remain at home. The Reich also mobilized up to 12 million Soviet prisoners of war, slave laborers, and foreign workers.

The totalitarian states had acted even in "peacetime" as if they were at war. Their

cratic roadblocks and passive resistance, and saved many of their Jews.

The churches and the Allies did little. Most Protestants, except in Scandinavia, were silent. Pope Pius XII, despite excellent information about the death camps, offered only general condemnations of the killing of civilians. Even the October 1943 deportation of Roman Jews to Auschwitz—"from under his windows," as the German ambassador put it—did not move Pius XII to public protest, although the Church secretly helped to hide Jews. Stalin was himself a longstanding and virulent anti-Semite, and many high British and

economies, even when "capitalist" in formal terms, were largely state-directed even before 1939. War provided justification in Germany for still greater state and Nazi Party intervention in the economy and in daily life, and the occasion for evermore intense barrages of lies from Goebbels' "Ministry of Public Enlightenment and Propaganda."

As the ring around Germany drew tighter, terror itself became a key ingredient in the war effort; Hitler was fanatically determined to prevent a repetition of Germany's 1918 political collapse. Civilians who expressed doubts about "final victory" disappeared into Himmler's camps. Military personnel guilty of "subverting the will to fight" perished by the thousands on portable *Wehrmacht* gallows. Conversely, Stalin in 1941 and 1942 gave survival priority even over domestic terror. NKVD pressure on the population and the army briefly relaxed. But once the Soviet Union gained the upper hand after 1943, arrests increased once more.

The democracies, as in 1914–18, improvised vast wartime bureaucracies to guide public opinion and to ration food, raw materials, and labor. Press, radio, and film became an arm of the war effort. Censorship, often voluntary, prevented the publication of news deemed harmful to morale. Photographs of American battle dead rarely appeared. And as in 1914–18, public discussion of war aims aroused extravagant expectations. At home, especially in Britain, those expectations spurred the planning of a postwar "welfare state" that would banish the misery of the Great Depression. In international politics, similar hopes accompanied the "United Nations"—a new and better League that would replace that supposed evil, the balance of power, and secure peace through universal goodwill without effort by the democracies. British and American war propaganda also encouraged illusions about the lovable nature and supposed agreement with the principles of the Atlantic Charter of jovial, pipe-smoking "Uncle Joe" Stalin.

Traditional democratic freedoms also suffered partial eclipse, especially for groups that appeared somehow linked with the enemy. Churchill's government rounded up 30,000 German and Italian "enemy aliens" during the great invasion emergency of 1940 and imprisoned them not for offenses committed but for *suspected* disloyalty. Although the United States faced an external threat far less immediate than Germans across the Channel, Pearl Harbor nevertheless triggered a hysterical racist clamor against the Japanese-American minority on the West Coast. Roosevelt ordered 112,000 of them deported to the interior; many lost farms and businesses. Deportees of military age shamed those responsible for this shabby treatment by volunteering to fight. Many served as linguists in the Pacific. Their unit in Europe, the 442nd Regimental Combat Team, terrified the Germans and earned more decorations for valor than any other American force of its size and time in combat.

Except for fortunate North America and distant Australia and New Zealand, all major belligerents suffered either foreign military occupation or devastation from the air. Many suffered both. That was the most striking difference between the two world wars. In the first, those behind the front had been almost immune from violent death. In the second, scorched earth and famine, guerrilla warfare and assassinations, reprisals and massacres, and the rain of high explosive, magnesium, white phosphorus, and napalm from the skies bound "front" and "rear" in shared danger. This was a "total war" far more total than its predecessor.

GLOBAL WAR, 1941–45

The global war of December 1941 turned swiftly against the Axis. By summer–fall 1942, Germany and Japan were stalled everywhere, from the Russian steppes to the South Pacific. Then Allied counterattacks drove the Axis back while air bombardment and submarine blockade wrecked the economies that sustained the Axis forces. And as the Allies advanced, discord between them became increasingly visible.

The Last Successes of the Axis, 1942

While the Germans sought to rebuild the forces shattered in the 1941–42 winter fighting in Russia, Japan seized a perimeter from India's western border to Wake Island, west of Hawaii (see the map on p. 873). Hong Kong, the Philippines, Singapore, and the Dutch East Indies swiftly fell to air and amphibious attack. Douglas MacArthur, photogenic commander of U.S. forces in the Philippines, left for Australia in March at Roosevelt's order. His troops fought on until the Japanese overwhelmed them in May. The inglorious surrender on February 15 of more than 80,000 British and Empire troops at Singapore—to a smaller Japanese force—was the deathblow to "white" imperial prestige in Asia. By summer 1942, Japan appeared poised to attack India from Burma, while Gandhi (see p. 809) inspired a new wave of demonstrations and riots against British rule.

But after a thrust southward toward New Guinea that led to a first indecisive action between carrier fleets, Japan struck at Midway Island, west of Hawaii. U.S. decipherment of Japanese signals enabled Chester Nimitz, the U.S. theater commander, to lay an ambush. On June 3–6, 1942, the two fleets traded air attacks near Midway—and the outnumbered U.S. Navy almost miraculously destroyed four Japanese fleet carriers and their highly trained pilots. The Battle of Midway tore the heart from the Japanese naval air force and made Japan's far-flung perimeter untenable.

By June 1942, Hitler was himself ready for a last major thrust, toward the oil of the Caucasus region. The *Panzerdivisionen* once again ripped immense gaps in the Soviet front. But as in 1941 Hitler failed to choose one objective and stick to it. As the Soviets crumbled, he ordered a second major thrust at Stalingrad, the key Soviet communications point on the Volga. There the Germans soon found themselves locked in street fighting in the rubble, where German armor and skill were of little use. The Red Army's bitter resistance made Stalin's city the Verdun of the Second World War.

Hitler had lost the strategic initiative in December 1941. He now lost even the operational initiative; Germany had no more troops or equipment for wide-ranging offensives. Even in Africa, where Rommel had improvised a modest *Blitzkrieg* at the end of a long and precarious supply line, Germany halted in July 1942 at El Alamein, 75 miles short of Alexandria.

The Allies Strike Back, 1942–43

Allied counterblows soon came. In the Pacific, a U.S. Marine Corps landing on Guadalcanal, at the southern tip of the Solomon Islands, countered the Japanese threat to the U.S. supply line to Australia. In a savage land, sea, and air battle of attrition that lasted from August 1942 to February 1943, the Marines and the U.S. Army forced the Japanese out. U.S. submarines began a ruthless campaign against Japanese merchant shipping that cut Japan's seaborne empire into isolated fragments.

Rivalry between MacArthur and the Navy prevented the concentration of U.S. effort on a single thrust back across the Pacific. Instead, MacArthur laboriously ascended the Solomons and New Guinea toward the Philippines, to which he had theatrically promised to return. Further north, the Navy—using Marine and U.S. Army landing forces backed by battleship gunfire and carrier aircraft—seized a succession of bloodstained central Pacific islands: Tarawa, Kwajalein, Eniwetok, Saipan, Guam, Ulithi, Palau. In fall 1944 MacArthur and the Navy joined to invade the Philippines. From Saipan, Tinian, and Guam, the shining new B-29s, the largest and farthest-ranging bombers in existence, could now batter the Japanese homeland.

British and U.S. troops soon drove the Germans from North Africa. In October–November 1942 the British desert commander, Bernard Montgomery, at last attacked Rommel at El Alamein. Montgomery deliberately fought a methodical 1918–style battle. Weight of fire, not skill, crushed his nimbler opponent. Rommel escaped, but then faced an unexpected attack from the rear after an American-British task force landed in French North

The Road to Tokyo Bay   1942–45

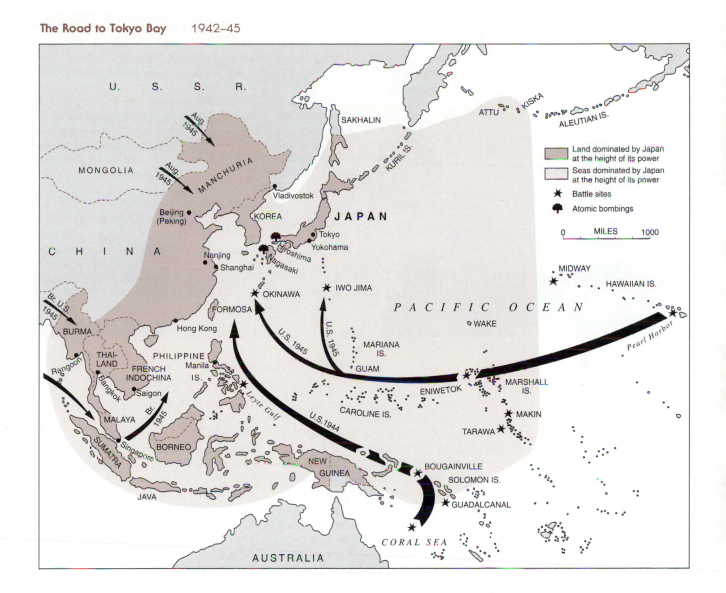

Land dominated by Japan
at the height of its power

Seas dominated by Japan
at the height of its power

★ Battle sites

Atomic bombings

0   MILES   1000

Africa on November 9, 1942. The slow-footed Allies failed to take Tunis before the Germans, but then they laid siege to Rommel and his Italian allies by land, sea, and air. In May 1943, the Axis bridgehead around Tunis collapsed; Hitler and Mussolini had lost North Africa and almost a quarter of a million irreplaceable veterans. In July, the Allies leapt to Sicily. As Mussolini's regime crumbled and Italy fled the war, Americans and British seized positions south of Rome in September–October.

On the eastern front, the Soviets launched the greatest counteroffensive of all. On November 19, 1942, the Red Army struck from the north and southeast of Stalingrad and encircled 300,000 Germans and German allies in and around the city. Hitler, as was his habit, ordered implacable resistance: no withdrawal, no breakout, no surrender. At the end, in February 1943, only 93,000 Germans remained alive to surrender as food and ammunition ran out. In July 1943 Hitler ventured a last local offensive at Kursk, south of Moscow.

Counterattack! Soviet infantry in
the ruins of Stalingrad, 1943.

Surprise was lacking, and Soviet antitank guns smashed the Germans in the greatest armored battle of the war. Germany had lost even the tactical initiative in the East.

In the Atlantic, the U-boats that had savaged British and U.S. shipping in 1941–42 soon found themselves under siege. British microwave radar, British decipherment of German navy communications, and the addition of U.S. escorts and airpower to those of Britain won the "Battle of the Atlantic" by May 1943. In that month the Germans sank 50 merchant ships at too steep a price: 41 U-boats and crews. The defeat of the U-boats made possible the American build-up in Britain for the coming assault on Hitler's "Fortress Europe."

That fortress, as Churchill had pointed out in a speech, had no roof. Stalin's increasingly bitter demands for an Allied "second front" in Europe had led Britain to pour vast resources into heavy bomber forces; only in the air could Britain strike directly at Germany. Since German fighters made daylight bombing suicidal, RAF Bomber Command concentrated on night raids. And at night, it was clear by summer

1941, British bombers could hit no target smaller than a German city. The bomber offensive, for lack of alternatives, therefore sought to dislocate the German economy indirectly through what the chief of RAF Bomber Command described with relish as "de-housing" the Germans.

The Reich now paid dearly for having trampled on all the conventions of "civilized" European warfare, including inhibitions against bombing cities; the *Luftwaffe* had done its best to flatten Warsaw, Rotterdam, London, Coventry, and Belgrade. From March 1942 on RAF massed bomber raids devastated the cities of western and central Germany: Lübeck, Rostock, Cologne, Essen, Bremen, Düsseldorf. In July–August 1943, the RAF burned most of Hamburg, killing 50,000 civilians and de-housing 800,000 others. The *Luftwaffe,* overcommitted on all fronts, took the bombers on in a bitter struggle of attrition. But fresh Allied aircraft and crews joined the battle faster than the Germans could shoot them down.

Hitler and Goebbels used the fall of Stalingrad and the coming of the bombers to demand total mobilization for "total war" from the German people. SS terror, loyalty to a still revered *Führer,* and fear of retribution for Germany's war of extermination in the East thereafter kept the German people in the war to the bitter end. War production, thanks to fanatical German efforts and to the mobilization of millions of foreign workers, slave laborers, and prisoners of war, rose until 1944. New "reprisal" weapons, such as the V-1 "buzz-bomb" and the V-2 ballistic missile, poured from slave-built underground factories. Jet-propelled fighters, by late 1944, briefly challenged Allied control of the skies. But the Reich failed to overcome the combined forces of the coalition it had created.

The "Grand Alliance": Stalin and the West, 1941–43

That coalition, by fall 1943, had begun to define its war aims. By December 1941, when Churchill's foreign secretary, Sir Anthony Eden, visited Moscow, Stalin had recovered from his panic of the previous summer. The Soviet Union was going to survive. Eden discovered, as Hitler and Ribbentrop had before him, that Stalin had ambitions. He insisted, for example, on keeping the Baltic states he had acquired in his 1939 bargain with Hitler. That was a violation of the Atlantic Charter's promise of self-determination, which the Soviet Union had accepted, although with reservations, in September 1941. But Stalin jovially sought to reassure Eden: he was different from Hitler, whose "fatal defect" was that "he does not know where to stop. . . . I can assure you that I will always know where to stop."

Stalin shrewdly capitalized on the Soviet Union's immense casualties and on the prestige gained as the only ally fighting large German land forces. He ceaselessly demanded that Roosevelt and Churchill establish a "second front" in Europe—the front that had existed in 1939–40 and had collapsed thanks in part to Stalin's support for Hitler. Stalin also played masterfully on Anglo-American fears that Germany and the Soviet Union would conclude a separate peace that would leave the Western Allies facing Hitler alone. He repeatedly approached Hitler in secret with offers of an armistice that would restore the borders of 1939 and the Russo-German quasi-alliance against the Western powers.

Roosevelt and Churchill failed to counter Stalin effectively. Almost apologetically—and unsuccessfully—they asked him to declare war on Japan, with whom the Soviet Union had signed a non-aggression pact in April 1941. Roosevelt, too anxious to please, promised a second front in Europe in 1942, a logistical and military impossibility. Partly to placate Stalin, Roosevelt also proclaimed at a January 1943 conference with Churchill at Casablanca that the Allies would accept nothing less than "unconditional surrender" from Germany, Italy, and Japan. A further purpose of that policy, which Roosevelt derived from the implacable Union war aim in the U.S. Civil War, was to prevent a repetition of 1918–19. This time the Western Allies planned to smash Germany for good, stamping out "stab-in-the-back" legends and any desire for yet another rematch. Stalin responded with an inexpensive gesture: in May 1943 he announced the dissolution of the Communist International, which had become redundant now that he had placed his own men firmly at the head of the International's "fraternal parties."

As with Chamberlain's 1939 guarantee to Poland, Roosevelt's assurances that the "capitalists" would fight Hitler to the bitter end only encouraged Stalin to continue his secret courtship of Hitler. What the Anglo-Americans apparently did not know was that Hitler flatly refused to compromise; Germany's *Lebensraum* was at stake. Hitler would have willingly struck a deal with the Anglo-Americans—but *they* demanded Germany's total defeat. Stalin offered Hitler a chance for survival—but Hitler refused to bargain in the East. That deadlock ensured that the war would continue until Germany either won or ceased to exist.

By November–December 1943, when the ill-assorted Allies met for the first "Big Three" conference at Teheran in occupied Iran, Stalin held the advantage. The British and Americans were stalled in bloody

D-Day: Normandy, June 6, 1944.

fighting against a handful of German divisions south of Rome, while the Red Army was driving back some 2.5 million Germans. Lend-Lease aid, which gave the Red Army the 700,000 U.S. and British trucks it needed for the far-ranging offensive thrusts of 1944–45, was no substitute for a second front in the West. The United States drastically weakened its diplomatic position by scaling down its projected army from the 215 divisions planned in 1941 to a mere 89 by early 1944. Roosevelt sought to avoid war-weariness and his own defeat in the 1944 election. But that decision meant that the Western Allies now *needed* the Soviet Union to defeat Germany, and perhaps even Japan.

Churchill therefore offered preemptive concessions. To give Stalin back the western border he had secured in the Nazi-Soviet Pact of 1939, Churchill proposed that Poland "move westward" into Germany. Stalin, for his part, agreed to enter the Pacific war after the defeat of Germany. That was a prize the Anglo-Americans need not have paid for, since

the Soviet Union was certain in any event to seek booty in Manchuria and Korea after Germany's defeat.

The Reconquest of Europe, 1944–45

Throughout 1943 Germany had been strong enough to throw into the sea any green American or British troops landed on the mined and fortified shores of "Fortress Europe." By spring 1944, that had changed. The campaigns in North Africa and Italy had taught the U.S. Army about the Germans and about amphibious landings, the most difficult operation in war. The long-range P-51 Mustang fighters of the U.S. Army Air Corps had secured daylight air superiority over France and the western parts of Germany. British decipherment of German signals (code-named ULTRA) gave the Allies advance warning of German moves. A massive Allied deception operation persuaded Hitler and his generals that the main Allied landing on the Continent would come near Calais—or as far north as Norway.

On June 6, 1944, British, Canadian, and U.S. forces under the supreme command of an American, Dwight D. Eisenhower, landed on the Normandy beaches. Three airborne divisions descended on the German rear. Overwhelming air superiority, Allied logistical mastery, and messy ground fighting resembling that of 1918 expanded the Allied beachhead. Then, in late July, the U.S. First Army broke through at St. Lô and launched the Third Army of George S. Patton around the German western flank. Patton, unlike his cautious superior Eisenhower, understood mobile warfare as well as his German adversaries. By August he had overrun Paris and was reaching toward the German border. Charles de Gaulle, now head of a sizable Free French army, returned to claim the presidency of a new French republic. Even Montgomery, commanding the British and Canadians, showed unexpected speed in pursuit of a thoroughly beaten enemy. For a brief moment Hitler's subordinates despaired of halting the Allies short of the Rhine. In the East, the *Wehrmacht*'s Army Group Center folded up, crushed by a massive Soviet summer offensive that advanced more than 400 miles, from Smolensk to the outskirts of Warsaw, and cost the Germans half a million troops.

But Hitler held on, despite an assassination attempt on July 20 by a conspiracy of anti-Nazi staff officers. Himmler received the welcome task of purging the army and the bureaucracy. The Prussian conservatives who had invited Hitler into power—and then regretted it—now perished in the concentration camps they had made possible. Goebbels and the Nazi Party spurred the German population to fanatical resistance.

Eisenhower reined Patton in and gave Montgomery most of the shrinking stream of supplies reaching the Allied armies from their beachheads and improvised ports in Normandy. In mid-September Montgomery launched three U.S. and British airborne divisions in a straight line across Holland toward the Ruhr Valley and sent his armored divisions forward to link up. But the purpose of the attack was obvious, and Montgomery's armor was slow. An SS *Panzer* division resting near the northernmost drop zone at Arnhem crushed the British paratroops and de-

railed the Allied thrust. Bitter positional fighting amid the minefields and camouflaged bunkers of Hitler's *Westwall* ran on into winter.

Hitler still hoped that a last stunning blow at the Western Allies would break the unnatural Grand Alliance and leave him to fight Stalin alone. In mid-December 1944, at the scene of his May 1940 victory in the Ardennes, he flung a last offensive at the Americans, whom he considered soft. His luck was no better than Ludendorff's in 1918, despite a penetration of fifty miles and a massacre of U.S. prisoners by SS troops. The U.S. 101st Airborne division, outnumbered and ringed by German armor, defiantly held the key road junction at Bastogne. Patton spun the U.S. Third Army around by ninety degrees on icy roads and within a week struck northward at the vulnerable German flank. As the skies cleared, Allied fighter-bombers hunted the roads clear of German tanks and trucks. This "Battle of the Bulge" consumed most of Germany's reserves of armor, ammunition, and gasoline, just as U.S. precision bombing of Germany's synthetic petroleum plants eliminated its sole source of fuel.

Allied airpower in the Bulge: a supply drop to the 101st Airborne Division at Bastogne, December 1944.

The Road to Berlin   1942–45

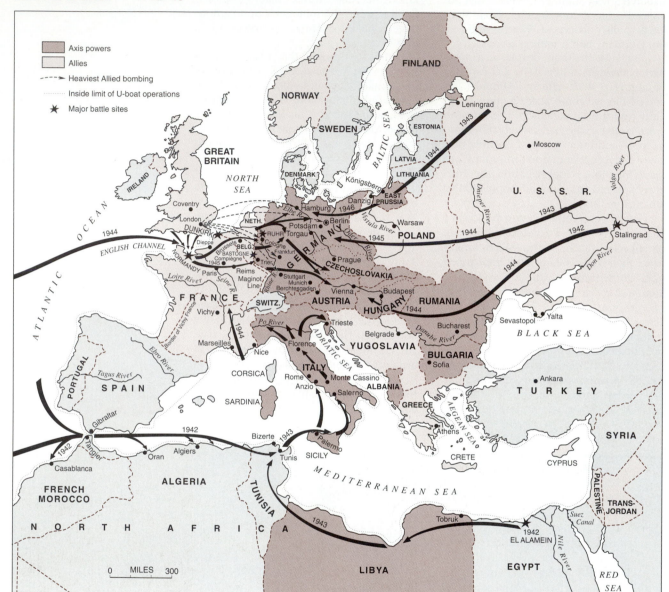

In the East, Stalin had by that point gone far toward the objectives staked out in 1939–40. By late July, the great Soviet drive that crushed Hitler's Army Group Center had seized the Polish city of Lublin. There Stalin established a Communist puppet regime (the "Lublin Committee") like the one he had tried to force on Finland in the 1939 Winter War. On August 1, 1944, as the Red Army approached Warsaw for the second time in a quarter-century, the Polish resistance movement rose against the Germans inside the city in a desperate effort to liberate the capital before the Red Army and the NKVD arrived.

Stalin halted his army across the Vistula River and gave Himmler's pitiless counterinsurgency forces time to crush the Poles in a two-month struggle. The SS eliminated on Stalin's behalf much of the remaining national leadership of Poland. Stalin met Churchill's protests by denouncing the Polish resistance fighters as "criminals." He denied to British and American aircraft the use of his airfields to drop supplies to the Poles. Despite pleas from Churchill, Roosevelt refused to use the considerable leverage over Stalin that the great Allied victories in France now gave. And while it marked time in Poland, the Red Army drove Rumania and Finland from the war, overran Bulgaria, and slowly conquered Hungary. Soviet troops seized Belgrade, but the Yugoslav Communist guerrilla army of Josip Broz Tito largely cleared the rest of Yugoslavia of Germans by its own efforts—a fact of much political importance later.

As Stalin carved out a Soviet empire, Churchill made a last attempt to secure a modest measure of independence for eastern Europe. He faced Stalin in the Kremlin in October 1944 and reached an agreement—to which Roosevelt never subscribed—that divided Europe into spheres of influence. By this informal "percentage deal" Stalin conceded Britain a 90 percent preponderance in Greece, where Communist partisans were soon to attack the British and the Greek government that had returned from exile in London. Stalin received a similar predominance in Rumania and slightly less in Bulgaria. Yugoslavia was to be split "50-50." On Poland, Churchill failed to shake Stalin from his support of the Lublin Poles.

When the "Big Three" met for the second time, at Yalta in the Crimea in February 1945, Stalin's position was even stronger than it had been the preceding fall. Roosevelt was mortally ill, and even in good health lacked Stalin's relentless mastery of detail. Churchill was now totally dependent on the United States; Britain was financially and militarily exhausted.

Above all, the Red Army now held practically all of Poland. It was advancing into East Prussia amid the rape and slaughter of civilians, while the Anglo-Americans were still grinding their way painfully through Hitler's *Westwall* fortifications. Roosevelt's advisers assumed that the United States still needed Stalin's assistance against Japan and that they must pay for that assistance with concessions both in Europe and Asia. Finally, Roosevelt himself, although no zealot for world government, assumed that only a new and better League, the United Nations, could prevent a second American retreat into isolationism. The success of the United Nations clearly required Soviet postwar cooperation.

Yalta was thus the masterpiece of Soviet wartime diplomacy. Stalin had already brushed aside Western objections and had recognized his Lublin Committee as Poland's government. At Yalta he agreed that a few Poles from the London government-in-exile could enter the Lublin government as individuals—and as hostages to the Red Army and the NKVD. And he secured a firm commitment to the division of Germany into occupation zones, one for each major ally. He also presumably noted with interest Roosevelt's unguarded remark that United States troops would probably remain in Europe less than two years after the war.

The "Big Three" at Yalta, February 1945.

In Asia, Roosevelt capitulated to Stalin's demands for Russia's pre-1904 privileges and more: railroad rights in Manchuria, the vital warm-water base of Port Arthur, and the annexation of southern Sakhalin and the Kurile islands north of Japan. Roosevelt even accepted the delicate task of securing the agreement of Chiang Kai-shek to this renewal of tsarist colonialism. In return, Stalin generously promised to enter the war against Japan three months after Germany's defeat. He pledged Soviet cooperation in founding the United Nations, which eventually came into being at a conference at San Francisco between April and June 1945. Finally, Stalin agreed at Yalta to a vaguely worded "Declaration on Liberated Europe" promising free elections in all countries the Allies occupied. Within a month of that promise, Stalin's tanks forced on Rumania a Communist-led government, while NKVD roundups and deportations in Poland intensified.

In early March 1945 Americans and British at last fought their way across the Rhine at several points; it was the Soviet turn to mark time while the Red Army cleared up the Baltic coast. British in the north and Americans to the south swiftly encircled 325,000 German troops in the Ruhr Valley. Patton drove across central Germany toward Czechoslovakia. The U.S. Ninth Army reached the Elbe River, sixty miles from Berlin, two weeks before the Soviets surrounded the city. Two battle-tried U.S. airborne divisions stood ready to descend on the rubble of Hitler's capital.

But Eisenhower and his superiors in Washington, in the disarray of Roosevelt's final illness and death on April 12, failed to seize Berlin. George Marshall, the U.S. chief of staff, opposed the sacrifice of American lives for "purely political purposes"—an oddly innocent remark, given that war *is* politics. Marshall and Eisenhower abandoned to the Red Army the symbol of victory over Germany, along with vital German territory. The United States ignored Churchill's desperate urging that it counter Stalin's all too obvious appetites by pushing as far east as possible.

The Red Army took Berlin against fanatical SS and *Wehrmacht* resistance, while Hitler committed suicide on April 30 in his bunker under the Reich chancellory. Mussolini had preceded him on April 28; the Italian Communist partisans who captured the *Duce* shot him "in the name of the Italian people." On May 7 and 9, the *Wehrmacht* surrendered unconditionally to the United States, Britain, and the Soviet Union. Germany, as Hitler had half-promised, had for the moment ceased to exist.

Japan in Ashes, 1945

As the members of the "anti-Hitler coalition" faced one another across the rubble of central Europe, the United States readied itself for the final assault on Japan. Hundreds of B-29 bombers were now in action. On the night of March 9–10 they turned central Tokyo into a sea of fire, and killed between 80,000 and 120,000 civilians. By July 1945 the United States had burned out half of the surface area of Japan's cities.

In February–March and April–June, two huge and bloody amphibious landings seized first Iwo Jima and then Okinawa, within fighter range of the Japanese home islands. Japanese pilots, following a tactic tested in the Philippines the previous fall, crashed explosive-laden *kamikaze* ("divine wind") suicide aircraft into U.S. carriers, transports, and escorts. They sank 21 U.S. ships and damaged more than 60 others. On land, the Japanese were equally merciless—toward themselves and toward the prisoners they rarely took. The Marines replied in kind; only 212 of the 22,000 Japanese troops on Iwo Jima ended as prisoners of war. The coming landings on the Japanese home islands, in the view of U.S. military planners, might cost as many as a million U.S. casualties, and many millions of Japanese. The war might last until mid-1946.

The Japanese cabinet saw defeat coming. But Japan's army, the decisive force now as before, refused to accept defeat. It still held southeast Asia, much of China, and Manchuria, Korea, and Japan. Japanese peace feelers through Moscow, deciphered by U.S. intelligence, suggested that Tokyo's diplomats now sought peace. But feverish military preparation for a last-ditch defense of the home islands sent a different signal. And Allied insistence on "unconditional surrender," which suggested the removal of the Emperor, gave the military diehards an apparently unanswerable argument for a fight to the death.

This difficult situation fell to Harry S. Truman, Roosevelt's vice president and successor. Truman, a man of personal and political courage ("The buck stops here."), underestimated by his contemporaries, entered the presidency with no experience of foreign affairs. He gradually turned against Stalin, but too slowly to affect the outcome in Europe. After July 1, 1945, the U.S. Army, despite continuing pleas from Churchill, withdrew from the wide areas it had conquered east of the planned Western zones of occupation.

On July 17, at Potsdam in the center of conquered Prussia-Germany, Truman met Stalin and Churchill at the last major wartime conference. Stalin confirmed his promise to enter the war in Asia. He secured half of a scheduled $20 billion in German reparations for the Soviet Union but pledged in return to deliver food from agricultural eastern Germany to the industrial Western zones. He also demanded a voice in the Ruhr occupation; the Western Allies refused. And he voiced a series of disquieting desires: naval bases in Greece, a United Nations mandate over the Italian colony of Libya, an interest in French Syria and Lebanon, and a role in the international administration of Tangier in Morocco. When Churchill congratulated Stalin on his military successes, Stalin grumpily remarked that at least one predecessor in the Kremlin had done better: in 1814 "Tsar Alexander got to Paris." That was an aspiration far beyond anything the Soviets had disclosed to Hitler in the Berlin talks of November 1940.

During the Potsdam conference an ungrateful British electorate replaced Churchill with the leader of the Labour party, Clement Attlee. That redoubled the burden on Truman. But Truman had discovered that the United States possessed a weapon that Roosevelt had concealed

Stalin, radiating self-confidence, with Churchill and Truman at Potsdam, July 1945.

from him—the still highly secret atomic bomb. Hitler had died before it was ready for use, but it might speed Japan's collapse. Stalin, informed of it officially for the first time at Potsdam, pretended indifference and expressed the hope that it would be used on the Japanese. His own atomic bomb project had begun secretly in 1942–43, after Soviet intelligence had alerted him to the British, American, and German nuclear efforts.

Truman shared the impatience of most citizens of the democracies. The war must end soon, so that "our boys" could return and happily demobilize. Neither Truman nor his planners explored the possibility of persuading Japan to surrender by siege, without an invasion; that would require too much time. Nor, despite advice from some State Department experts, was Truman willing to abandon publicly the demand for unconditional surrender. That formula had long outlived its supposed usefulness in soothing Stalin—but the public overwhelmingly supported it as a fitting revenge for Pearl Harbor.

The ruins of Hiroshima, August 1945.

Truman and Churchill did attempt to warn Tokyo with a declaration that promised "prompt and utter destruction" unless Japan surrendered, but hinted at Allied flexibility about Japan's postwar form of government. Japan ignored the hint. Truman therefore ordered that the first two operational bombs be dropped on Japanese industrial cities containing military installations. He could not "disinvent" the weapon on which the United States had spent $2 billion. U.S. opinion, from extreme Left to far Right, was in 1945 virtually unanimous in approving the use of the bomb to end the war. Most thankful of all were the infantry awaiting orders to storm the mined and barbed-wired beaches of Japan.

On August 6 and 9, B-29s from Tinian island dropped two atomic weapons on Hiroshima and Nagasaki, in southwestern Japan. Roughly 120,000 Japanese perished outright and many died later from long-term radiation injuries. The Hiroshima bomb failed to persuade, but the shock of the Nagasaki bomb and the simultaneous Soviet declaration of war and *Blitzkrieg* in Manchuria produced crisis in Tokyo. The

prime minister, Suzuki Kantarō, urged acceptance of the Potsdam declaration before worse followed. The war minister, General Anami Korechika, demanded continued resistance; most of the high command agreed. To break the deadlock, Suzuki made an unprecedented appeal to Emperor Hirohito, who by ancient but disused custom could in exceptional circumstances decide vital issues.

The Emperor, speaking softly, reproached his military for a wartime performance that had fallen far short of its promises. He insisted that Japan had no choice; it must "bear the unbearable." On August 15, after the suppression of a diehard military revolt, Japan's god-emperor broadcast to a people who had never before heard his voice and revealed that Japan would end the war. On September 2, 1945, Japan surrendered unconditionally to MacArthur and Nimitz on the deck of the battleship *Missouri*, at anchor in Tokyo Bay.

After six years and a day, the Second World War was over. It had cost the Soviet Union roughly 17 million military and civilian dead. Germany had lost 6.2 million; Poland, 6 million including its Jews; China, perhaps 4 million, not counting victims of famine and disease; Japan, 2 million; Yugoslavia 1.7 million; France somewhat more than and Italy somewhat less than half a million. Britain lost 325,000; the United States escaped with combat losses of only 292,000. More than 50 million people had perished in the most destructive conflict in history. Germany and Japan lay in ruins; tens of millions of destitute refugees, prisoners of war, slave laborers, and concentration camp survivors thronged central Europe. Economic chaos and political vacuum followed the defeat of the Axis in both Europe and Asia.

THE COLD WAR

As in 1918, victory did not bring peace. In bringing order out of chaos, the United States and the Soviet Union collided. The "Cold War" that followed divided Europe and the world for the next four decades. Its origins, chronological boundaries, and nature later provoked bitter debate, at least in the West. But its origins were no mystery. Conflict between great powers of differing aims, interests, and ideologies was neither new nor startling. What was surprising about the Cold War was the slowness of its coming. It took two years of ever more brutal Soviet measures in eastern Europe, of Soviet demands and encroachments in divided Germany, and of Soviet pressure on Europe's flanks to provoke the United States to a coherent response.

Before the Cold War: 1945–46

As in 1939–41, Stalin imposed the Soviet system on his new territories. And as in his destruction of his domestic rivals in the 1920s, he proceeded by stages, keeping his goals deliberately ambiguous. These "salami tactics," as Stalin's man in Hungary, Matyás Rákosi, described them, also owed a debt to Mussolini and Hitler, who had pioneered the technique of "legal" revolution through the power of the state apparatus. Stalin's relative caution, as Rákosi explained to a secret party meeting in May 1945, resulted above all from the need to divide Britain and the United States. If he did not provoke the United States, Stalin apparently thought, it might follow Roosevelt's prediction at Yalta and soon withdraw its troops from Germany. That would leave the Soviet Union dominant in Europe.

The Sovietization of eastern Europe therefore proceeded cautiously, in three phases. First came Red Army and NKVD control in 1944–45, then in 1945–47 a slow slicing away of the non-Communist parties. Finally, after the United States showed that it was prepared to stay in Europe and resist, came the creation of one-party Communist dictatorships in 1947–49.

In Rumania and Bulgaria, Stalin's lieutenants rapidly imposed Communist-dominated coalition governments. Churchill had in effect left both countries to Stalin in the "percentage deal" of fall 1944, and Stalin rightly assumed that action there would not unduly provoke the United States. Stalin was almost equally dictatorial in Poland, his vital land bridge

to the Soviet occupation zone in Germany; leaders of the Polish resistance who surfaced in March 1945 disappeared into NKVD custody. But Stalin was nevertheless careful to maintain a façade. Until 1947 he permitted the leader of the London Poles, Stanislaw Mikolajczyk, to remain as "second deputy prime minister" in the puppet government of Stalin's Lublin Committee.

Territorial Adjustments after the Second World War   1945

The boundaries shown on this map date from the beginning of World War II.

Axis states after World War II

Lands that changed hands after World War II

The Soviet flag rises over the *Reichstag,* April 1945.

Reichstag, a small group of German Communist émigrés under the leadership of the ice-cold and ruthless Walter Ulbricht landed in Berlin from Moscow. The Western Allies at first shut down German political activity in their zones and gave priority to the large-scale hunt for war criminals that culminated in the trials of the surviving Nazi leaders at Nuremberg in 1945–46. The Soviets shot a few prominent Nazis but gave priority in their zone to the creation of a regime around Ulbricht.

In early 1946, Ulbricht's resurrected German Communist Party cajoled and coerced the much larger SPD organizations in the Soviet zone into a merger that produced a "Socialist Unity Party," the SED. That tactic, which Stalin attempted to apply unsuccessfully through other Communist parties in western as well as eastern Europe, ultimately aimed at a united Communist Germany—a goal Stalin and his associates disclosed to Yugoslav and Bulgarian Communist leaders in early 1946.

Stalin's gradual destruction of non-Communist forces both in the Soviet zone of Germany and elsewhere in east-central Europe was not the only Soviet policy that aroused alarm in the West. Stalin insisted on receiving reparations from the western zones of Germany without in turn delivering the food from eastern Germany that he had pledged at Potsdam. He continued to demand a Soviet share in the occupation of the Ruhr while blocking with unacceptable conditions the fitful inter-allied negotiations over a German peace treaty. That provoked the United States, in September 1946, to announce that its occupation force would remain in Germany indefinitely.

On the Soviet Union's other borders, Stalin sought gains far beyond those the Red Army had already secured. He pressed the Norwegians for bases on their island outpost of Spitzbergen and repeatedly demanded Dardanelles bases and parts of the Caucasus from Turkey. In Greece, the Communist guerrilla movement, defeated in December 1944 after it had attacked the British in Athens, renewed the struggle in May 1946. Tito, the

Hungary and Czechoslovakia enjoyed relatively free elections in 1945–46. Especially in Czechoslovakia, Stalin did not at first need to use force. The Czech government-in-exile of President Beneš chose to collaborate from the beginning; unlike the Poles, the Czechs had no prior experience of Russian occupation. The Czech Communist Party of Kliment Gottwald achieved a plurality of 38 percent in the 1946 election.

In his zone of Germany, which he rightly regarded, even in ruins, as Europe's greatest power, Stalin applied similar methods. The day after the Red Army hoisted its flag on the remains of the

leader of newly Communist Yugoslavia, provided weapons and supplies. Stalin remained in the background but at first made no objection. Communist victory in Greece would isolate Turkey and assure the Soviet Union the foothold in the eastern Mediterranean that Stalin had demanded in vain from Britain and the United States.

In three areas Stalin made tactical retreats. He held back from Sovietizing his occupation zone in Austria, probably for fear of provoking an *Anschluss* of the western zones of Austria with the western zones of Germany. In Finland, he contented himself with imposing a military alliance that left Finland's parliamentary institutions intact. That compromise, which rested on Finland's proven determination to resist Soviet invasion, Finland's political caution, and Sweden's continuing neutrality, lasted until the Cold War's end. Finally, in March 1946 Stalin suddenly agreed to honor his Teheran promise to evacuate the northern parts of Iran that he had occupied in 1941.

That swift—and unique—postwar withdrawal was symptomatic of Stalin's policy. Churchill, out of office but still forceful, had just spoken eloquently under Truman's sponsorship of an "Iron Curtain" that had descended across Europe. U.S. protests over the Soviet creation of satellite "republics" in Iran, together with Churchill's call for a new Anglo-American alliance to block further Soviet expansion apparently made a temporary retreat seem advisable to Stalin. It was his last.

"Containment" against Soviet Expansion, 1946–47

Within Washington's disorganized policy machinery, those who distrusted Soviet intentions gradually gained the upper hand after 1945. Truman, who had remarked in June 1941 that he hoped that Nazis and Soviets would kill each other off, was from the beginning inclined to resist Soviet demands. But in the absence of Soviet acts of direct hostility toward the United States, domestic opinion prevented the translation of sentiment into policy. U.S. wartime propaganda stressing Stalin's amiability

---

Churchill: "The Iron Curtain"   March 1946

In a speech given at Fulton, Missouri, with Truman in the audience, Churchill sought to educate the American public.

From Stettin in the Baltic to Trieste in the Adriatic, an iron curtain has descended across the Continent. Behind that line lie all the capitals of the ancient states of Central and Eastern Europe. Warsaw, Berlin, Prague, Vienna, Budapest, Belgrade, Bucharest and Sofia, all these famous cities and the populations around them lie in what I must call the Soviet sphere, and all are subject in one form or another, not only to Soviet influence but to a very high and, in many cases, increasing measure of control from Moscow. . . .

The Russian-dominated Polish government has been encouraged to make enormous and wrongful inroads upon Germany, and mass expulsions of millions of Germans on a scale grievous and undreamed-of are now taking place. The Communist parties, which were very small in all these Eastern States of Europe, have been raised to pre-eminence and power far beyond their numbers and are seeking everywhere to obtain totalitarian control. Police governments are prevailing in nearly every case. . . . These are sombre facts for anyone to have to recite on the morrow of a victory gained by so much splendid comradeship in arms and in the cause of freedom and democracy; but we should be most unwise not to face them squarely while time remains. . . . I do not believe that Soviet Russia desires war. What they desire is the fruits of war and the indefinite expansion of their power and doctrines.

From Lewis Broad, Winston Churchill 1874–1951 *(London: Hutchinson & Co., 1951), pp. 574–75.*

---

and promising world peace through the United Nations had succeeded too well. That "Uncle Joe" was as merciless though more cautious than Hitler and that no disunited "United Nations" could repeal the balance of power came as a rude shock.

While the political education of the American public proceeded with help from both Churchill and Stalin, the military power of the United States shrank dramatically. The 12.1 million men under arms in August 1945 demanded release. By June 1946 those vast and battle-hardened forces had dwindled to 3 million, and a year later stood at a mere 1.4 million, most of them without combat experience. Possession of the bomb led to complacency.

And Stalin's demobilization was far less rapid than that of the United States. By 1948–49 the Soviet armed forces were the largest in the world, with roughly 4 million men. An estimated thirty or more Soviet divisions under unified command in eastern Europe faced a scratch assortment of two U.S. and nine British, French, and Belgian divisions in western Europe. The West lacked a high command, and Soviet tank forces held a crushing edge in numbers and quality.

In the United States, the Republicans achieved majorities in both houses of Congress in November 1946, paralyzing Truman. But to the surprise of the doomsayers, the U.S. economy, which now briefly accounted for half of world industrial production, did not relapse into depression. Global war had forced the United States to take up at last the world economic leadership it had spurned in 1919. At the Bretton Woods Conference of July 1944, the Western powers agreed under U.S. sponsorship to a new international economic order, complete with a World Bank and International Monetary Fund. The Bretton Woods system offered a framework for world trade and the expansion of U.S. exports that had not existed between the wars. But a prerequisite for that expansion was the recovery of Europe. By the bitter winter of 1946–47 that recovery was disturbingly overdue.

Stalin's appetites and Europe's distress, which might strengthen the large Communist parties in France and Italy and choke off world trade once again, finally moved Truman to act. Britain, besieged as in 1919 with nationalist revolts from Egypt to India, furnished the occasion. In February 1947 Britain confessed that it could no longer back Turkey against Soviet pressure or support the Greek government against the Communist partisans. The collapse of the British position in the eastern Mediterranean left a power vacuum. If Truman did not fill it, Stalin clearly would.

On March 12, 1947, after gaining promises of Republican support in Congress, Truman announced the "doctrine" that bears his name. The United States would help Greece, Turkey, and all "free peoples" against "armed minorities or . . . outside pressures." The Republicans, under the leadership of Senator Arthur Vandenberg, enlisted with enthusiasm. But Vandenberg and U.S. public opinion exacted a price. As Vandenberg explained to Truman, Congress would spend money only if Truman "scared hell out of the American people." Truman therefore transformed an essentially pragmatic decision to support two strategic countries into something entirely different: a worldwide ideological struggle between light and darkness. And Truman's choice of words inadvertently placed an intolerable burden on many of America's allies-to-be. To qualify for U.S. aid, they now had to seem virtuous and "free," rather than merely strategically important.

In the short term, the Truman Doctrine succeeded brilliantly; aid to Greece and Turkey passed Congress. In June 1947 Truman's new secretary of state, the wartime chief of staff George Marshall, announced a second major initiative. The United States offered to both western and eastern Europe, including the Soviet Union, a massive infusion of economic aid to set the postwar recovery in motion at last. Although Congress would never have approved aid to the Soviets, the authors of the Marshall Plan left to Stalin the burden of refusal.

A senior State Department official, George Kennan, meanwhile supplied a much-needed statement of the Truman Doctrine's rationale. Writing as "Mr. X" in the July 1947 issue of *Foreign Affairs,* Kennan urged a "policy of firm containment, designed to confront the Russians with unalterable counterforce at every point where they show signs of encroaching upon a peaceful and stable world." Containment, Kennan argued, would ultimately lead "either [to] the break-up or the gradual mellowing of Soviet power." He later explained with embarrassment that by "counterforce" he had not necessarily meant the use of force, and that not "*every* point" at which the Soviet Union might seek expansion was equally vital to the United States. But his article, and other semiofficial and official pronouncements from Washington, in theory made U.S. commitments almost unlimited.

To uphold those commitments, the United States reorganized its armed forces in July 1947, creating a nuclear-armed air force independent of army and navy, and a Department of Defense. It also acquired new institutions that until now, alone of the great powers, it had disdained. Permanent peacetime secret services, the Central Intelligence Agency (CIA) for foreign intelligence and "covert action" (1947) and the National Security Agency (NSA) for codebreaking (1952), arose from the debris of the wartime intelligence effort.

Europe Divided, 1947–49

Stalin did not disappoint the framers of the Marshall Plan. Molotov attended the conference held in Paris to launch the Plan but soon uttered his characteristic stone-faced "*Nyet*." Stalin commanded his satellites to refuse Marshall aid and ordered the Communist parties of western Europe to oppose the Plan with strikes and riots.

In fall and winter 1947–48 Stalin swiftly completed his "revolution by conquest" in the Soviet Union's new central and eastern European empire. In Hungary, Rákosi had already arrested key opposition leaders in May 1947. In October, Mikolajczyk fled Poland in fear of his life. In December King Michael of Rumania abdicated. In Czechoslovakia, Kliment Gottwald and his Communist Party seized control in February 1948 from inside the popularly elected government. Jan Masarcyk, the protégé of Beneš at the foreign ministry, fell, jumped—or was pushed—from a window to his death. Beneš, as in 1938, declined to fight; Gottwald shunted him aside. The new Communist regimes took the remarkable name of "people's democracies"—Stalin too was a master of packaging dictatorship for the age of mass politics.

The United States, Britain, and France now went ahead rapidly to restore economic and political life in their sectors of Germany. When they attempted to include the Western part of Berlin in the

The Berlin airlift, June 1948–May 1949.

creation of a new currency that foreshadowed a West German state, Stalin reacted angrily. In June 1948, in violation of the wartime inter-allied agreements providing for free access to Berlin, he blockaded the western sectors with Soviet tanks.

Truman and his advisers thought of sending their own—desperately few—tanks down the *Autobahn*. But in the face of the Soviet Union's crushing ground superiority (roughly twenty Soviet against two U.S. divisions in Germany), they chose in characteristically American fashion an engineering remedy for a political or military problem. To keep alive the same West Berliners they had bombed three years before, the Allies organized an endless chain of transport aircraft that delivered millions of tons of food, coal, and gasoline. In November 1948, Truman won reelection against heavy odds. In May 1949 Stalin abandoned the Berlin blockade.

Its effects, however, were lasting. The blockade led to the founding in April 1949 of the North Atlantic Treaty Organization

(NATO), the military alliance of the United States and the western European democracies that Wilson had failed to create in 1919. The blockade also pushed the United States and its Allies into speeding the transformation of the western zones into a "Federal Republic of Germany." That new German state adopted a constitution in May 1949 and held its first election that August. In the Soviet zone Ulbricht received Stalin's permission to proclaim a "German Democratic Republic" (DDR). The two superpowers now confronted each other with unbending hostility from northern Norway to the Turkish Caucasus.

As well as provoking—in the form of NATO—the "unalterable counterforce" Kennan had prescribed, Stalin also failed to Sovietize one key nation in east-central Europe. In 1947–48 he attempted to reduce Yugoslavia to the same subservience as his other eastern European satellites. When Tito fought back by purging Soviet agents from his party, Stalin expelled Yugoslavia from the international Communist movement for "nationalist tendencies." Then he sought to orchestrate a pro-Soviet coup: "I shall shake my little finger and there will be no Tito." But Tito remained. That first split in the international Communist movement scuttled the Greek Communist insurgency. Stalin had already told the Yugoslavs that the Greek civil war should be "rolled up" as unprofitable now that Truman was backing the Greek government. After the break with Moscow, Tito abandoned the Greek guerrillas; he needed Western economic support to survive.

Increased tension with the United States and the quarrel with Yugoslavia gave Stalin a chance to tighten further his control at home. Alleged external threat and genuine internal terror went together, as after 1927, to force the population to accept the privation caused by Stalin's military-economic priorities. In war and its aftermath, Stalin deported to Siberia and central Asia millions from nationalities— Crimean Tartars, Volga Germans, and the Baltic and Caucasus peoples—that he accused of collaboration with the German invaders. He vengefully transferred to his own concentration camps all returned Soviet prisoners of war ("In Hitler's camps there are no Russian prisoners of war, only Russian traitors, and we shall do away with them when the war is over.") He demoted prominent military leaders now that he no longer needed them, and arrested many whose sole crime was having seen with their own eyes the wealth of the world west of the Soviet borders. The GULAG had suffered a labor shortage after 1941; by 1950 it once more held an estimated 8 to 10 million prisoners.

After war's end, Stalin's lieutenant Andrei Zhdanov began a purge of Soviet writers and scientists that continued even after Zhdanov died a sudden and perhaps unnatural death in 1948. Zhdanov's rival Georgi Malenkov and Yezhov's sinister successor at the NKVD, Lavrenty Beria, subsequently had Zhdanov's former associates in the Leningrad party apparatus eliminated. The gradually intensifying purge, which Stalin extended to the new eastern European satellites, soon took on an overtly anti-Semitic character. "Rootless cosmopolitanism" and "Zionism" were the chief charges under which prominent satellite leaders, many of them of Jewish descent, went to gallows or execution cellars after show trials in 1951–52. Stalin thus applied to the satellites the remedy imposed at home after Kirov's murder in 1934: the removal of all who were not his creatures and the creation of a new ruling class of grateful accomplices.

As Tocqueville had foreseen in the 1830s, America and Russia had each come to "sway the destinies of half the globe." Their confrontation in 1947–49 resulted from and ended a century of ever more destructive European national struggles. Hitler, the most extreme of all nationalist prophets, had invited the superpowers onto the scene. Then he had created chaos and destruction so vast that at the end only superpowers could master it.

That they proceeded to do—with methods that were mutually exclusive. Here too Tocqueville had seen clearly: "The principal instrument of [America] is freedom; of [Russia], servitude." The democracies of western Europe, despite occasional grumbling, conceded hegemony to Washington. They repeated, against Stalin, the choice Churchill had made in 1940: better to serve as the junior partner to another democracy, the United States, than to suffer the domination of a continent-wide slave state. In east-central Europe, Stalin's new multinational empire replaced the Habsburg order that had collapsed in 1918. Supranational American-Soviet confrontation dwarfed and repressed Europe's nationalisms and froze the borders of 1945. But outside Europe both geography and the alignment of forces were far different. There Stalin failed to discern "where to stop," and nationalism, Europe's most successful export, opened new worlds of violent conflict.

Suggestions for Further Reading

The Second World War

As with the First World War, there is no comprehensive, up-to-date, and readable one-volume history of the war of 1939–45. G. Wright, *The Ordeal of Total War, 1939–1945* (1968), is a useful survey. J. Lukacs, *The Last European War, September 1939/December 1941* (1976), offers a brilliant synthesis of everything from grand strategy to the intellectual impact of the first two years of war. K. Hildebrand, *The Foreign Policy of the Third Reich* (1973), and A. Hillgruber, *Germany and the Two World Wars* (1981), lay out German strategy and objectives, but see also H. R. Trevor-Roper, ed., *Hitler's Secret Conversations, 1941–1944* (1953), and N. Rich, *Hitler's War Aims* (1973–74). G. Fleming, *Hitler and the Final Solution* (1982), and R. Hilberg, *The Destruction of the European Jews* (1961; revised and expanded, 1985), cover the "Final Solution" and Hitler's responsibility for it in chilling detail. On Germany's "barbarization of warfare" in the East and the army's role in genocide, see especially the brilliant book of O. Bartov, *Hitler's Army: Soldiers, Nazis, and War in the Third Reich* (1991); Bartov and M. van Creveld, *Fighting Power* (1982), also suggest why the Germans were so hard to defeat. Among the many excellent books on aspects of the war, W. Murray, *Luftwaffe* (1984), and M. Hastings, *Overlord: D-Day and the Battle for Normandy* (1984), stand out.

Of Hitler's principal enemies only Churchill left memoirs: his wonderfully readable *The Second World War,* 6 vols. (1948–1953), remains the best history of the war as seen from London. On Roosevelt and American policy, see R. Sherwood, *Roosevelt and Hopkins* (1950); R. A. Divine, *The Reluctant Belligerent: American Entry into World War II* (1965); and G. Smith, *American Diplomacy in the Second World War, 1941–1945* (revised, 1985). On the Pacific war, see especially A. Iriye, *The Origins of the Second World War in Asia and the Pacific* (1987) and *Power and Culture: The Japanese-American War, 1941–1945* (1981); H. P. Willmott, *Empires in the Balance: Japanese and Allied Pacific Strategies to April 1942* (1982); R. H. Spector, *Eagle Against the Sun: The American War Against Japan* (1985); C. Thorne, *Allies of a Kind: The United States, Britain, and the War Against Japan, 1941–1945* (1978); and H. Feis, *The Atomic Bomb and the End of World War II* (1966).

The Cold War

On wartime diplomacy and the origins of the Cold War, H. Feis, *Churchill, Roosevelt, Stalin* (1957), still provides useful narrative; D. S. Gaddis, *The United States and the Origins of the Cold War, 1941–1947* (1972), and V. Mastny, *Russia's Road to the Cold War* (1979), use a wider selection of sources. H. Seton-Watson, *The East European Revolution* (1951, 1956), still offers a useful overview of the Communist seizure of power in eastern Europe; A. Ulam, *The Rivals: America and Russia Since World War II* (1971), is a succinct and witty narrative; P. Seabury, *The Rise and Decline of the Cold War* (1967), introduces some of the interpretive issues.

34

THE AGE OF CONTAINMENT
1949–1975

*T*he Prague coup and the Berlin Blockade marked the beginning of the "classic" Cold War, the fiercest phase of the superpower confrontation around which international politics pivoted for the next forty years. In Europe, the war remained cold. In Asia, by Stalin's choice, cold war became a shooting war in Korea in June 1950. Then military stalemate and Stalin's death in March 1953 ended the most acute period of hostility between the United States and the Soviet Union.

But truces in Korea and elsewhere in Asia did not end the superpower conflict. Anti-Soviet revolts in the east European satellites and recurrent Soviet threats over Germany repeatedly interrupted the post-Stalin "thaw." Tension between the superpowers culminated in 1962 with the attempt of Stalin's successor, Nikita Sergeyevich Khrushchev, to tilt the strate-gic balance by placing nuclear missiles in Cuba. Khrushchev's shamefaced withdrawal and U.S. distraction in Vietnam then inaugurated a period of gradual superpower "détente" or relaxation of tension, despite wars between U.S. and Soviet allies or clients in the Middle East. The Soviet Union looked on in masterful inactivity as the United States, convulsed at home, ultimately abandoned "containment" in Vietnam in 1972–75.

Unheard-of prosperity in the United States, western Europe, and a resurgent Japan accompanied superpower conflict. American-style material culture—appliances and automobiles, Hollywood films, television serials, and rock and roll—enveloped the world. A new generation arose in the West that remembered neither Depression nor war, and fiercely attacked its elders. A transnational women's movement that originated in France and the

(Opposite) America in Vietnam: Men of the 173rd Airborne Brigade scramble from their vulnerable helicopters during an air assault operation near Saigon (1966).

United States at last pushed women's rights beyond the vote. For the democracies, the age of containment was an era of unprecedented technological advance and of wealth and well-being that spread far down the social scale. But as in earlier ages, the price of change and economic growth was unease and discontent.

CONFRONTATION IN EUROPE AND ASIA, 1949–53

Stalin's Temptation in Asia

Japan left the Western Allies a difficult legacy. Its slogan of "Asia for the Asians" had masked its own colonialism. But that slogan, together with the inglorious defeat of the British at Singapore in February 1942, mightily encouraged Asian nationalism. Thanks to the "Germany first" strategy of the United States, southeast Asia had enjoyed the lowest priority of all the Allied theaters of war. In August 1945, when Imperial Japan collapsed, the British had only half reconquered Burma. The Guomindang was still hiding in a remote enclave in southeast China. Indochina—Vietnam, Laos, and Cambodia—and the Dutch East Indies were still under Japanese control. Japan handed that control over not to the former colonial masters, but to armed native movements.

Cold War Europe

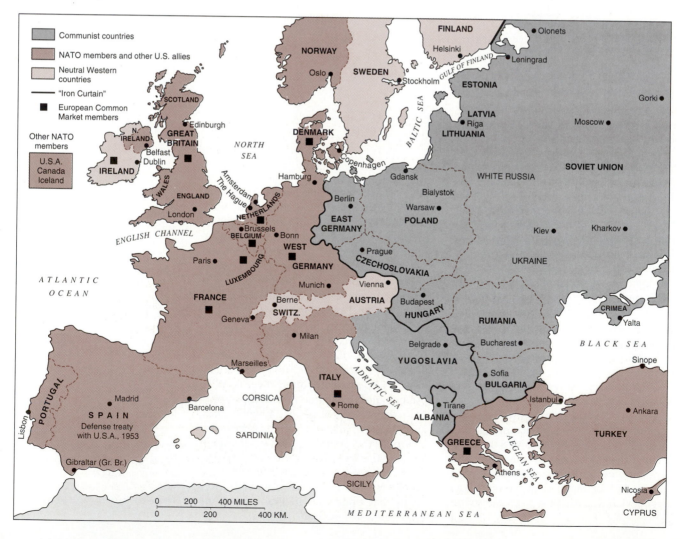

The Dutch gave up in 1949 under U.S. pressure, and granted the East Indies—renamed Indonesia—its independence. In Vietnam, Ho Chi Minh's Communist Party of Indochina destroyed its non-Communist nationalist rivals and in September 1945 declared Vietnam's independence from France. France's effort at reconquest led to fierce guerrilla conflict after November 1946.

To the north, the Soviets took Manchuria in their twelve-day war of August 1945 and remained there until 1946. They took only half of the former Japanese colony of Korea; the United States, warned by Stalin's drive for total control of occupied eastern Europe, insisted on dividing the strategically vital Korean peninsula into Soviet and U.S. zones at the 38th parallel. By 1947–48, two Korean states, one Communist and one with American "advisers," were locked in bitter hostility and intermittent border conflict. Japan itself fell to the United States alone. Douglas MacArthur, installed in Tokyo as a sort of American Shōgun, contemptuously dismissed Soviet bids to share in the occupation. In the Pacific, Moscow had contributed little to victory.

In China, the Guomindang of Chiang Kai-shek and the Chinese Communist Party (CCP) of Mao Zedong (Mao Tse-tung) ended the war against Japan as nominal allies. Their marriage of convenience inevitably turned to renewed civil war in July 1946. China could not have *two* dictatorships. Truman and his advisers wavered between trying to revive the Guomindang-CCP coalition, backing the Guomindang, and abstaining. Washington tried all three policies in succession. Stalin at first sought to maintain a balance between the CCP and the Guomindang favorable to the Soviet Union, as in the 1920s. But once CCP victory seemed certain, Stalin bet on Mao.

In January 1949, Mao's "People's Liberation Army" entered Beijing (Peking), and in October Mao proclaimed the People's Republic of China (PRC). Chiang and the remnants of the Guomindang took refuge on the offshore island of Taiwan. Mao traveled to Moscow and after difficult negotiations signed a "treaty of friendship" with Stalin in February 1950; it promised the return to China of the Manchurian railway and Port Arthur, and allied China and the Soviet Union against Japan. After almost forty years of war, turmoil, and famine, something resembling a new dynasty had at last replaced the Qing.

The "loss" of China and the concurrent explosion of the first Soviet atomic bomb in August 1949 created turmoil in the United States. Truman now paid for having "scared hell out of the American people" and for having funded resistance to Soviet expansion in Europe by a pledge of aid to opponents of "armed minorities" everywhere. The Republican Right, in the unsavory person of Senator Joseph McCarthy of Wisconsin, attacked the president by claiming that he was not anti-Communist enough.

McCarthy and his many supporters were convinced of American omnipotence. For them neither Chinese Communists nor Soviets were serious enemies. Only treason at home by U.S. officials could have delivered China to Mao and the secret of the atomic bomb to Moscow. They saw and relentlessly pursued a largely imaginary internal menace—"Caaamunism" (as McCarthy and his supporters pronounced it) at the State Department and in the academic world. The public's sudden realization that it faced a

The Cold War comes home: McCarthy at work, October 1951.

Soviet nuclear threat added to the hysteria. The pattern of ideological witch-hunts and populist-isolationist demagogy visible in the 1920s and 1930s reasserted itself. Not until 1954 did McCarthy's wild charges discredit him; in the long term he gave resistance to Communism a bad name.

In response to the threatening new situation of 1949–50, Truman decided to build a thermonuclear, or hydrogen, bomb. Stalin, unknown to the Americans, had initiated his own H-bomb research in 1948. The new weapons were hundreds or even thousands of times more destructive than the Hiroshima bomb, which had been equivalent to a mere 20,000 tons of high explosive. Truman also ordered a review of U.S. defense preparations and strategy; his advisers embodied their conclusions in National Security Council paper NSC-68 of April 1950. It urged a major U.S. conventional as well as nuclear build-up to maintain a balance of power threatened by the Soviet Union's bomb, its ever-growing military, and its alliance with China. But the recommendations of NSC-68 were politically impractical. The Republicans in Congress continued to demand budget cuts—while at the same time attacking the administration for being "soft on Caaamunism."

Then Stalin, by yet another ill-timed display of appetite, gave Truman the domestic support he needed to counter the Soviet build-up. Defeat in the Berlin Blockade turned Stalin toward Asia; in mid-1949 he secured Mao's help for an accelerated military build-up of the Soviet-sponsored North Korean state. At the end of 1949 (as Stalin's successor Nikita Khrushchev disclosed in his memoirs), Stalin received Kim Il-Sung, the former Red Army major who led the North, and authorized him to attack South Korea. Mao apparently agreed. On June 25, 1950, Kim's T-34 tanks—the weapon that had opened Stalin's road to Berlin—crossed the 38th parallel and rolled over the South Korean army.

The Korean War: Armed Containment in Asia, Rearmament in Europe

Truman scarcely hesitated. On June 30, 1950, he ordered American ground troops from Japan into combat. U.S. control of Japan and the credibility of the U.S. defense of Europe appeared to be at stake. Like Roosevelt in the Atlantic in 1941, Truman acted without a congressional declaration of war—and without congressional opposition. At the United Nations, a Soviet walkout ordered by Stalin allowed the Security Council, for the first time in its history, to vote with the necessary unanimity to fight in defense of a member. The United States provided supplies and a force that eventually grew to 350,000, alongside 400,000 South Koreans and 44,000 troops from fourteen other nations fighting under the U.N. flag.

The North Koreans, well-trained by their Soviet and Chinese advisers, stormed south and almost swallowed the peninsula in one gulp. But by early August, with much air and naval support, an Army, Marine, and South Korean force ground them to a halt around the vital port of Pusan, in the far southeastern corner of Korea. Then MacArthur landed the Marines and

One of Kim Il-Sung's T-34s meets the U.S. Marine Corps (1950).

the U.S. Army at Inchon, halfway up the Korean peninsula, cut the North Koreans to shreds, and reached the old border along the 38th parallel. Truman and the United Nations imprudently gave MacArthur permission to conquer North Korea, unless Chinese or Soviet intervention appeared likely. Containment briefly became "rollback." To MacArthur, who knew neither doubts nor humility, permission to cross the parallel was a blank check. As winter deepened, he drove headlong for the Yalu River that divides Korea and China, and strung his forces out on North Korea's icy mountain roads.

China made clear that it would fight to drive MacArthur back from its borders. In mid-October MacArthur disregarded a sudden appearance of Chinese "volunteers." In mid-November a massive Chinese counteroffensive took him completely by surprise and flung the U.N. forces back below the 38th parallel. Only the Marines, who walked out grimly from Chosin reservoir near the Yalu—through snow and seven Chinese divisions—emerged with credit from the disaster.

MacArthur, to redeem his reputation, demanded the bombing and blockade of China itself. In a letter to a Republican congressman, he criticized his commander in chief by insisting that "in war there is no substitute for victory." Truman dismissed him in April 1951 for insubordination; the president and his advisers saw no profit in a wider war against China that would pin down an ever-increasing proportion of U.S. forces and might lead to a direct U.S.-Soviet clash. That would be "the wrong war, at the wrong place, at the wrong time, and with the wrong enemy," and might damage Washington's ultimate Cold War goal of keeping the Soviets out of western Europe and Japan, the largest non-Communist concentrations of economic power and talent in the world beside the United States.

After MacArthur's defeat, Truman therefore fought a "limited war" in Korea, using U.S. reinforcements and firepower to push the Chinese back above the parallel. By July 1951, U.S. and allied forces had inflicted immense casualties on the Chinese and had stabilized the front. Bitter

Korea   1950–53

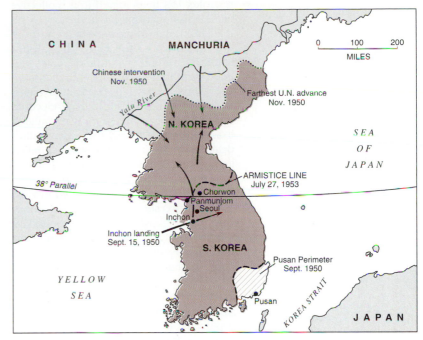

truce talks began, while trench raids and local offensives continued on Korea's bare and jagged hills. Chinese and North Koreans sought to wear down the resolve of an impatient and peacefully inclined democracy by talking and fighting at the same time. Stalin willed the continuation of the war. In January 1951, immediately after MacArthur's disaster, Stalin had told a secret meeting of his satellite leaders that the United States was so feeble militarily that a Soviet attack on western Europe would become feasible in the next three to four years. Wearing U.S. forces down in Asia would help guarantee success.

But Stalin was not immortal. He apparently began in 1952 to orchestrate one last purge, based on false charges that the Kremlin doctors—most of whom were of Jewish descent—had plotted to murder the Soviet leadership. The doctors' coming trial, like that of Zinoviev and Kamenev in 1936, promised to unleash a flood of denunciations, arrests, and liquidations. Stalin's associates trembled for their heads. "The Boss" was apparently about to inaugurate yet another round of social mobility, Soviet style.

But on March 5, 1953, Stalin died of a stroke. His heirs joined in a "collective leadership" that sought hesitantly to retreat from Stalin's terror within and from confrontation without. In the United States, impatience with the Korean stalemate ("die for a tie") carried the Republican candidate, Dwight D. Eisenhower, to victory in the 1952 presidential election. Eisenhower promised to apply his military experience to ending the war. Stalin's death gave the Communist side flexibility, and Eisenhower's expressed willingness to use nuclear weapons in Korea helped concentrate minds in Beijing. On July 27, 1953, the two sides finally signed an armistice that established a de facto boundary separating North and South Korea. After three years and the death of a million Chinese, perhaps 2 million Koreans, and 52,246 Americans, the war was over. Only a little more than a third of the 10,000 Americans whom the Communists had captured returned alive.

Containment in northeast Asia had succeeded, but at a price. Part of that price was that Washington began to perceive all Communist actions, even unrelated ones, as part of a grand design framed in Moscow. Truman sent the U.S. Navy to shield Taiwan from Mao's forces on the mainland, although Washington had earlier shunned Chiang Kai-shek. The United States looked on approvingly as Britain tamed a Communist insurgency among the overseas Chinese of Malaya. Mao's victory in China had already led Truman in May 1950 to order aid to France in Indochina, a cause of which Washington had earlier disapproved. The North Korean attack the following month led Washington to flood Indochina with weapons and funds that amounted to $1 billion a year by 1954.

But Ho Chi Minh skillfully identified Vietnamese Communism with national resistance to colonial rule. The Vietnamese Communist regular army that Mao's forces trained and equipped in southern China after 1949 showed unparalleled fighting power. U.S. prodding drove Paris to create non-Communist nationalist forces in Vietnam, Laos, and Cambodia, and to promise eventual independence; more Vietnamese indeed fought on the French side than on

Ho Chi Minh's. But few of them fought as hard. In late 1953 the French staked everything on luring Ho's forces to attack an isolated French outpost on the Laotian border at Dien Bien Phu. There the excellent artillery that the United States had given Chiang, who had lost it to Mao, who had given it to Ho, trapped the French instead. Dien Bien Phu fell in May 1954. France agreed to withdraw from Indochina, subject to a satisfactory truce. The United States, Soviet Union, China, France, and Britain met at Geneva in the first major East-West conference since 1947 and agreed to a cease-fire and the division of Vietnam at the 17th parallel. Laos and Cambodia were to be independent and neutral. The First Indochina War was over.

Contrary to later claims, the powers at Geneva did not formally agree on free elections and the reunification of all Vietnam by 1956. The United States rejected elections without United Nations supervision to ensure a fair vote. Neither Ho's newly minted "Democratic Republic of Vietnam" (DRV) north of the 17th parallel nor its southern counterpart supported the conference's unsigned face-saving declaration calling for elections. Ho and his associates were the least satisfied of the parties at Geneva; they felt that Beijing and Moscow had sold them out by failing to deliver all of Indochina. An unquiet truce nevertheless descended in Asia.

The attack by Stalin's North Korean clients on South Korea thus had worldwide consequences. It helped entangle the United States in southeast as well as in northeast Asia. And it at last roused the United States to remedy the military imbalance created by its hasty demobilization in 1945–46. Truman persuaded Congress to commit additional U.S. divisions and substantial military aid to Europe. The United States acquired its first large-scale peacetime draft, and built a standing military establishment twice the size of that of 1949, with a network of bases ringing the Soviet Union. Thanks to Stalin, Washington was able to implement many of the recommendations of NSC-68.

And Stalin also spurred the United States to look for allies among its former enemies. In 1952 Washington restored

Ho Chi Minh ("the Bringer of Enlightenment"), architect of Vietnamese Communism (1954).

sovereignty to a partially democratized Japan, linked to the United States by military bases and a security treaty. West Germany received back its sovereignty in a peace treaty with the Western powers in 1954, and began to rearm in 1955. By the late 1950s, NATO at last had enough forces, both American and German, to stop a Soviet armored thrust short of the Rhine. The Soviet Union answered with more armored divisions, intermediate-range nuclear missiles, and an alliance against NATO founded in 1955, the Warsaw Pact.

THE ADVENTURES OF NIKITA SERGEYEVICH KHRUSHCHEV, 1953–64

In Moscow, Stalin's death apparently prevented the last great purge, a new stage in his remodeling of Soviet society. Instead, the Soviet Union fell back into a drab bureaucratic "failed totalitarianism." The messianic claim to remake humanity remained, but the will to do so by terror was now gone. And without terror, the system was doomed to economic stagnation and collapse.

"Thaw" at Home and Abroad

Stalin's heirs fought to take credit for the "thaw" that set in after March 1953. Lavrenty Beria, master of the secret police, moved first. But his rivals united, called on the Red Army for support, and had him shot. The new "collective leadership," under Georgi Malenkov for the state bureaucracy and Nikita S. Khrushchev for the Communist Party, then announced implausibly that Beria had been a British intelligence agent since 1919. Some of Stalin's habits survived him.

Beria's liquidation was nevertheless the last. When Khrushchev displaced Malenkov in 1955, he merely demoted him. When Malenkov, Molotov, and Stalin's most bloodstained surviving associate, Lazar Kaganovich, allied themselves against Khrushchev in 1957, he merely dismissed them from their posts in the Party and government. Thanks to Khrushchev, the new Soviet ruling class that Stalin had created at last achieved job security. Amnes-

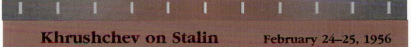

Khrushchev on Stalin   February 24–25, 1956

Khrushchev sought above all to differentiate between Lenin and Stalin, to present Stalin's terror and "cult of personality" as an accident rather than as a logical consequence of Lenin's party autocracy.

Lenin used severe methods only in the most necessary cases, when the exploiting classes were still in existence and were vigorously opposing the revolution, when the struggle for survival was decidedly assuming the sharpest forms, even including a civil war.

Stalin, on the other hand, used extreme methods and mass repressions at a time when the revolution was already victorious, when the Soviet state was strengthened, when the exploiting classes were already liquidated. . . . It is clear that here Stalin showed in a whole series of cases his intolerance, his brutality and his abuse of power. Instead of proving his political correctness and mobilizing the masses, he often chose the path of repression and physical annihilation, not only against actual enemies, but also against individuals who had not committed any crimes against the party and the Soviet Government.

From Basil Dmytryshyn, USSR: A Concise History *(New York: Charles Scribner's Sons, 1978), p. 501.*

ties gradually thinned the population of the GULAG after a series of bloody prisoner revolts.

And Khrushchev, whose deliberately uncouth peasant exterior concealed both shrewdness and a moral courage he had been careful to repress while Stalin had lived, soon set about destroying the legacy of his former "Boss." As the Twentieth Party Congress of February 1956 approached, all mention of the former "great leader" and "guide of progressive humanity" dropped from the Soviet press. At the Congress, Khrushchev attacked Stalin in a secret speech that shook the foundations of the Soviet system.

Khrushchev was careful to brand Stalin's "cult of personality" and his "extreme methods and mass repressions" as an exception, a historical accident that owed nothing to Lenin, much less to Marx. But Marx had justified dictatorship and terror, and Lenin had authorized terror against the "class enemy," and had erected the dictatorship of a Party that he insisted must be monolithic. Stalin had merely followed that logic to its conclusion and had attempted to make the Party monolithic through terror.

Khrushchev's secret speech nevertheless contained a wealth of information about the purges, from the technique of extorting false confessions to the startling numbers of victims in the higher ranks of the Party. Its text soon leaked to the outside world and devastated Communist parties and their sympathizers everywhere. Some left the Party, disillusioned with Communism. Others attacked Khrushchev for betraying the faith. In the Soviet Union, as Khrushchev had apparently intended, the speech made a return to Stalin's methods difficult. Dissidents now risked years in labor camps or torture in psychiatric hospitals, but executions were increasingly rare. Khrushchev replaced mass terror with subtle and calculated repression by the post-Beria secret police and intelligence service, the Committee for State Security (KGB).

Externally, "de-Stalinization" made Soviet policy less rigid. Khrushchev announced that "war was not fatalistically inevitable" between the "socialist camp" and the Western "capitalist" powers. In a belated attempt to woo German and European public opinion, he agreed to withdraw Soviet forces from Austria in 1955. He visited Tito that same year and apologized for Stalin's vindictiveness against Yugoslavia; the Soviet Union thus recognized that the "Soviet path" was not the sole road to Communism.

But de-Stalinization had limits abroad as well as at home. In the Soviet Union, the "great patriotic war" of 1941–45 and Stalin's rehabilitation of the tsarist past had partially merged Great Russian nationalism with Communism. But in the satellites, Communism was a Red Army import and nationalism was from the beginning its mortal enemy. The "people's democracies" consequently suffered repeated waves of unrest throughout the Cold War era. In East Berlin, Stalin's death and Ulbricht's imposition of wage cuts in June 1953 had triggered a new Kronstadt 1921—a desperate workers' revolt, soon crushed by Ulbricht's "People's Police" and Soviet armor.

Khrushchev's secret speech led to further ferment. In Poland, workers at Poznán demonstrated against wage cuts in June 1956. Street fighting between workers and troops then triggered a struggle within the Polish Communist Party between Stalinists and "moderates." But instead of sending tanks, Khrushchev grudgingly accepted assurances from the chief of the "moderates," Wladyslaw Gomulka, that Poland would remain within the Soviet empire. Gomulka then persuaded the population to subside in the name of national survival.

In Hungary, similar events led to tragedy. Rákosi, Stalin's man in Budapest, clung to power until Khrushchev ordered him to resign in July 1956. But his successor was another lesser Stalinist. When Hungary's equivalent to Gomulka, Imre Nagy, finally came to power in late October, the Hungarian Communist regime was disintegrating in the face of spontaneous national revolt. Demonstrators toppled the immense statue of Stalin in Budapest. Communist leaders hid or ran for the Soviet border. A small force of Soviet tanks withdrew from Budapest in the

Soviet tanks dominate the streets of Berlin after crushing the East German workers' revolt (June 1953).

face of popular fury. Nagy tried to persuade Moscow to hold back, while he calmed popular demands for multiparty democracy and for withdrawal from the Warsaw Pact.

Nagy failed. Like the Habsburgs whose role he now filled, Khrushchev could not permit the defection of one nationality, for fear the others might follow. Simultaneous Western disarray over the Suez crisis (see p. 927) made the decision to act easier. On November 4, 1956, Moscow flooded Budapest with tanks and crushed the revolt. During the fighting and aftermath, the Soviets and their collaborators killed thousands of Hungarians; 190,000 refugees fled west. Khrushchev had saved Stalin's empire with Stalin's methods.

The Sino-Soviet Split

To the east, where the Soviet Union faced a new phenomenon, a second Communist great power, those methods were less effective. Stalin had preserved an uneasy dominance over Mao even after 1949. Khrushchev and his colleagues could not. Mao was his own Lenin and Stalin; he regarded Stalin's puny successors with poorly concealed contempt. The Chinese also resented having to carry the military burden of Stalin's misjudgment in Korea, and grumbled about the poor quality and small quantity of Soviet economic aid. They nevertheless tolerated Khrushchev, despite de-Stalinization, which Mao read as unspoken criticism of his own thriving "cult of personality."

The parting of the ways, the greatest single defeat to Soviet policy since 1941, soon came. In October 1957, in a final bid to keep Beijing as a loyal vassal, Khrushchev signed a secret treaty providing China with assistance in developing the atomic bomb. But the following year, Mao staked a claim to world ideological leadership of the Communist movement. He launched an economic "Great Leap Forward" complete with collectivization and crash industrialization. The "attainment of Communism in China is no longer a remote future event," Mao's Central Committee trumpeted. That statement was a

Stalin dethroned: Budapest, November 2, 1956.

direct challenge to Moscow, which had never dared to promise the rapid attainment of Communism—the blissful end of history amid untold abundance—to its long-suffering subjects. And to add to the horror of the Soviets, Mao also challenged the United States by seeking war—unsuccessfully—in the Taiwan straits in the fall of 1958.

In June 1959, Soviet aid to China's nuclear program abruptly ended. Khrushchev decided not to give the bomb to his over-mighty and reckless vassal, and recalled his military and industrial experts from China. By 1960 the Sino-Soviet split was almost public. By the summer of 1963 the two "fraternal parties" were trading mortal insults and staging mass displays of ritual hatred. Moscow damned Beijing for its fanatical rigidity ("dogmatism"). Beijing denounced Moscow for betraying the Marxist-Leninist gospel ("modern revisionism"). The international Communist movement had irrevocably split.

From Berlin to Cuba

On the Soviet Union's western front, Khrushchev took the offensive. His objective was probably to settle the German question through a peace treaty that recognized as an international border the 1945 boundary between the western and Soviet occupation zones, and ended the West's nonrecognition of Ulbricht's shaky puppet regime. That would consolidate Soviet control of East Germany and east-central Europe.

But Khrushchev lacked subtlety. He had already, in the Suez crisis of 1956,

Kennedy's inaugural address contained some of the most stirring phrases ever spoken by an American president. It also unwisely proclaimed a willingness to "pay any price."

Let the word go forth from this time and place, to friend and foe alike, that the torch has been passed to a new generation of Americans, born in this century, tempered by war, disciplined by a hard and bitter peace, proud of our ancient heritage, and unwilling to witness or permit the slow undoing of those human rights to which this nation has always been committed, and to which we are committed today at home and around the world.

Let every nation know, whether it wishes us well or ill, that we shall pay any price, bear any burden, meet any hardship, support any friend, oppose any foe to assure the survival and the success of liberty. . . .

In the long history of the world, only a few generations have been granted the role of defending freedom in its hour of maximum danger. I do not shrink from this responsibility; I welcome it. I do not believe that any of us would exchange places with any other people or any other generation. The energy, the faith, the devotion which we bring to this endeavor will light our country and all who serve it, and the glow from that fire can truly light the world.

And so, my fellow Americans, ask not what your country can do for you; ask what you can do for your country.

From Theodore C. Sorensen, Kennedy *(New York: Harper & Row, 1965), pp. 245–48.*

gleefully brandished the Soviet Union's small but growing arsenal of nuclear missiles. In October 1957 the Soviet Union's triumphant launching of the first artificial satellite, *Sputnik,* suggested that Soviet military technology was surpassing that of the United States. In November Khrushchev delivered an ultimatum to the West demanding a German peace treaty within six months.

The ultimatum became a rolling one, always extended. The exuberant Khrushchev accompanied it with a drumfire of nuclear threats that punctuated four years of steadily increasing superpower tension. His declared commitment to "peaceful coexistence" did not inhibit him from occa-

sionally predicting in ominous tones the ultimate triumph of Communism: "We will bury you." In September 1959 Khrushchev nevertheless became the first Soviet ruler to visit the United States, for an inconclusive summit with Eisenhower. After a Soviet antiaircraft missile knocked down one of the CIA's U-2 high-altitude reconnaissance aircraft over central Russia, Khrushchev canceled the return visit in May 1960 by staging a propaganda circus complete with personal slurs against Eisenhower.

The 1960 U.S. presidential election brought in a new Democratic administration under the debonair young Boston-Irish grandee, John Fitzgerald Kennedy. That offered Khrushchev new opportunities. Kennedy inherited from Eisenhower a Caribbean problem: Cuba. There a revolutionary adventurer, Fidel Castro, had come to power when the military regime of the incompetent Fulgencio Batista had collapsed in January 1959. Castro, who later claimed—not implausibly—to have been a lifelong Marxist-Leninist, immediately began to court Moscow. Khrushchev happily responded during a visit to the United Nations at which he distinguished himself by pounding his shoe on his desk during a General Assembly speech by Britain's prime minister.

Along with the Cuban problem, Kennedy inherited from Eisenhower a solution: an amateurish CIA-organized invasion of Cuba by anti-Communist Cuban exiles seeking to trigger an uprising against Castro. The invasion force landed at the Bay of Pigs on Cuba's south coast on April 17, 1961. But Kennedy refused to authorize the naval air support that would have given the lightly armed attackers a chance of survival; Castro swiftly crushed them with his Soviet tanks.

In the aftermath of that delicious humiliation of the "*Yanquis,*" Castro consolidated his dictatorship. He took over for his own purposes the Cuban Communist Party, won increased military, police, and economic aid from the Soviet Union, and hastened the departure of the best-educated and most articulate 15 percent of Cuba's population to southern Florida. The Soviet Union acquired a Caribbean satellite, complete with Leninist vanguard party, secret police, and GULAG; the United States received in the course of the decade up to a million enterprising new citizens.

Kennedy, sheepish over failure, met Khrushchev at a summit at Vienna in June 1961. There Khrushchev bullied him unmercifully and apparently concluded that Kennedy was soft. On August 13, Khrushchev proceeded to solve his German difficulties on his own. East German forces backed by Soviet armor sealed East Berlin off from the Western sectors with a massive wall of prefabricated concrete and electrified barbed wire. This "Berlin Wall" closed the last avenue of escape from Ulbricht's "German Democratic Republic" (DDR), which had lost 3 million citizens to the West in the preceding decade.

Kennedy and other Western leaders failed to respond to that unexpected Soviet stroke, although Kennedy called up U.S. reserve forces as a warning to Khrushchev not to press his luck. Worse followed. Khrushchev ordered nuclear tests that violated assurances he had given to Kennedy as well as a moratorium on atmospheric testing to which he had subscribed in 1958. In October 1961 the Soviet Union triumphantly detonated a bomb twice as large as any U.S. weapon, with a force equivalent to 58 million tons of high explosive.

In mid-1962, with Ulbricht's DDR at last on its way to consolidation behind barbed wire, the irrepressible Khrushchev launched a spectacular Caribbean gamble. In July he persuaded the Cubans to accept a Soviet garrison of 43,000 ground troops and technicians, armed with 48 medium-range and 32 intermediate-range ballistic missiles capable of striking most of the United States. The missiles would triple Soviet capacity to deliver thermonuclear warheads to United States targets. A *fait accompli* might also make possible the deployment of additional missiles that would give the Soviet Union parity or superiority. And success would shift the psychological superpower balance in favor of the Soviet Union. Khrushchev had evidently failed to learn one lesson from Korea—that the United States, if and when aroused, acted unpredictably.

The "New Frontier": Kennedy takes office (1961).

By early September 1962, the Cuban missile sites were under construction and were clearly visible from the air. Khrushchev and his diplomats lied repeatedly to Kennedy: the Soviet Union was merely installing antiaircraft rockets, not offensive missiles. But on October 14, 1962, photographs from a high-flying U-2 showed patterns already familiar from intermediate-range missile sites in the Soviet Union. Khrushchev's gamble that he could install the weapons before the United States noticed had failed.

Kennedy and his advisers consulted feverishly. The more militant urged an immediate air strike and an airborne and amphibious invasion of Cuba. Others pleaded for a predictably futile appeal to

Berlin divided by concrete and barbed wire: the Berlin Wall.

Khrushchev makes a point (1962).

tinued feverishly; the first missiles were apparently approaching operational readiness, and up to 45 nuclear warheads (it later became known) had reached the island.

On October 27, Kennedy sent his brother Bobby, the administration's enforcer, to tell the Soviet ambassador sternly that "the point of escalation was at hand." If Moscow did not agree to withdraw the missiles, the United States would remove them itself. That threat, backed with a strategic nuclear superiority of 10 to 1 or better and by overwhelming air, sea, and ground power in the Caribbean, at last persuaded Khrushchev to back down. The Soviet Union withdrew its missiles. But it left behind advisers, intelligence listening posts, and a mechanized brigade based near Havana. The United States pointedly avoided making a formal promise not to invade.

Like Stalin's death, the Cuban Missile Crisis marked the end of a major phase in the Cold War. It was the closest that Soviet and U.S. forces had come to fighting since the Berlin blockade—but on that occasion the United States had possessed a nuclear monopoly. In the aftermath of the far more dangerous Cuban crisis, both powers sought to curb their mutual hostility. A 1963 treaty banning nuclear tests in the atmosphere and in space was the first and most durable result of that effort.

But in other respects the two rivals drew entirely different lessons from the confrontation. The United States, reassured about the superpower balance, overcommitted itself in Asia. It also sought to limit nuclear weapons, and by 1969 had by deliberate inaction discarded the superiority that had helped checkmate Khrushchev in Cuba. Nuclear "parity," U.S. leaders theorized, would lead the Soviets to embrace arms control and eventual reductions. Thermonuclear weapons, U.S. academics suggested, were so destructive that their only use was to deter their use by others.

The Soviets took a different view. "You Americans will never be able to do this to us again." a Soviet negotiator grimly informed his American counterpart in the aftermath of the crisis. Khrushchev's col-

the United Nations. Kennedy chose a naval blockade that would give Khrushchev time to retreat without too great a humiliation. But Kennedy also prepared for air strikes and an invasion, should they be necessary to prevent the missiles from becoming operational. His televised announcement on October 22 of a U.S. Navy "quarantine" of Cuba initiated a week of crisis that many feared was the prelude to "nuclear holocaust." But only Castro seems to have sought war; at the height of the crisis, he reportedly urged Khrushchev to launch a nuclear strike against the United States and proclaimed that "the Cuban people [were] prepared to sacrifice themselves for the cause of the destruction of imperialism and the victory of world revolution."

When the blockade took effect on October 24, Soviet ships loaded with additional missiles halted on their way to Cuba. Khrushchev belatedly admitted having placed offensive nuclear forces in Cuba but retreated behind the improbable claim that he had acted only to prevent a United States invasion—a threat the Bay of Pigs fiasco had dissipated, and which the Soviet missiles themselves had revived. He offered to withdraw them in return for a U.S. pledge not to invade Cuba. Work on the missile sites in Cuba meanwhile con-

The Soviet ballistic missile site at San Cristóbal, Cuba (October 1962).

leagues forcibly retired him in October 1964, in part because he had begun to threaten the privileges of the Party elite, but also for mishandling the missile crisis. Under the stone-faced new leadership of Leonid Brezhnev and Alexei Kosygin, the Soviet regime tightened KGB controls at home and increased its defense budget from an already heavy 10 percent of gross national product in 1965 to 25 percent or more by 1980.

The Soviet goal was nuclear superiority (see Figure 34-1). Unlike Western academics, Soviet leaders saw nuclear weapons as militarily decisive and politically useful. The United States and its allies relied on the U.S. nuclear "umbrella" to hold back superior Soviet ground forces. If the Soviet Union could threaten the United States itself with nuclear destruction, U.S. threats to use nuclear weapons against the Soviet Union if the Soviet armies attacked U.S. allies would lose credibility. Nuclear superiority would also give the Soviet Union a global reach and greater freedom to support "wars of national liberation" that indirectly undermined the West's position. Finally, the growth of Soviet power would presumably intimidate the Europeans and the Japanese, and divide them from the United States.

PEACE AND WAR IN THE SHADOW OF THE COLD WAR

While the superpowers struggled, Japan and the once-great powers of Europe enjoyed unprecedented economic growth. Not so the Middle East, where after 1945 the West no longer filled the vacuum created by Ottoman collapse. The foundation of a Jewish state and the conflicting ambitions of the Arabs led to two generations of bitter wars.

The Mid-Sized Powers in Eclipse

The revival of world trade was essential for the recovery of Europe and Japan. In the previous long peace, from 1871 to 1914, world trade had grown at an average annual rate of 3.4 percent; then the German bid for world mastery had pushed growth down to an average of 1 percent per year from 1913 to 1938. But after 1948,

Figure 34-1   After Cuba: Missile Power   1962–72

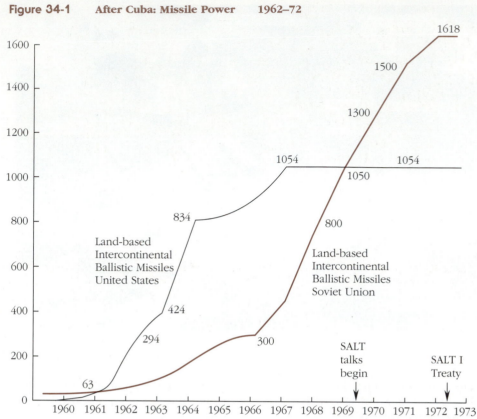

Adapted from Le Monde, *November 22, 1972, p. 2.*

more than $20 billion in Marshall Plan and other U.S. aid, together with a boom caused by the Korean War, galvanized the world economy. The Bretton Woods system installed in 1944–47 brought the stability and predictability that had been lacking in the 1920s and 1930s.

The result was astonishing growth. From 1950 to 1960, the volume of world trade grew by 6.4 percent each year. Europe and Japan rebuilt their economies under the military protection and economic leadership of the United States. The West German "economic miracle" was the most dramatic in Europe, with a growth rate of 7.7 percent per year. France followed, then Italy, which started as a far poorer country. Britain's longstanding failure to channel its best brains into industry and commerce helped condemn it to last place, with a growth rate of 2.6 percent per year.

But despite the aspirations of Europe's technocratic visionaries, no "United States of Europe" emerged. The European Community (EC) or European common market, founded at Rome in 1957, slowly developed a transnational political superstructure and a European parliament. But its powers remained small. The nation-state remained the principal focus of loyalty. And France crippled the EC for a decade by checkmating a halfhearted British attempt to enter it in 1963.

In Britain after 1945, Labour and Conservatives alternated in government with their customary decorum. Labour under Clement Attlee nationalized major industries, thereby protecting them from much-needed rationalization and modernization. Government health care and social insurance extended "cradle to grave" security to the entire population. When the aging Churchill returned to

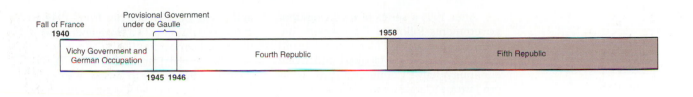

Fall of France 1940	Provisional Government under de Gaulle		1958
Vichy Government and German Occupation		Fourth Republic	Fifth Republic
	1945 1946		

power in 1951, he left the welfare state intact but sold off some of Britain's nationalized industries. His foreign secretary and successor, Anthony Eden, resigned in disarray after the Suez crisis of 1956 (see p.927), but the reassuring leadership of Harold Macmillan kept the Conservatives in office until 1963–64. Labour then returned under the bland Harold Wilson, Labour's answer to Stanley Baldwin. Both parties pursued roughly similar policies: the welfare state at home, a "special relationship" with the United States abroad, and the retention of as much empire as Britain could hold without excessive effort.

France, as usual, was livelier. The Fourth Republic was similar in political habits and alignments to the Third Republic that had died in 1940. The founders of the new republic pushed de Gaulle, the savior of France, into premature retirement in early 1946. He repaid the compliment by damning the vagaries of the Chamber of Deputies as "the convolutions of this absurd ballet." His successors half-heartedly waged the Indochina war into which de Gaulle's emissaries had blundered in 1945–46. The Fourth Republic's one hour of glory was the 1954–55 premiership of Pierre Mendès-France, who set a deadline for French withdrawal from Indochina and made it stick.

But the Mendès-France government soon collapsed over the Algerian insurrection against France (see pp. 929–31) that erupted less than six months after the Indochina settlement. That second great colonial war wrecked the Fourth Republic. The French Right supported NATO but claimed that Algeria was part of France, although nine-tenths of Algeria's inhabitants were Moslems. Left-wing opinion and a strong Communist Party opposed NATO but—after some hesitation—favored Algerian independence. Parliamentary

deadlock followed. The army in Algeria was already restless; those who had served in Indochina grimly reproached the politicians for France's long record of defeat. A sense of betrayal impelled the army to swing its support behind de Gaulle's tumultuous return in a quasi-coup in May 1958.

De Gaulle demanded and received from parliament the right to draft a new constitution. His Fifth Republic was more durable than its predecessor; de Gaulle as president assumed stronger powers than any French executive since Napoleon III. And he used those powers wisely. He led France out of the Algerian war in 1962 without splitting the highly politicized army or provoking the bloody civil war between Right and Left that had seemed imminent in 1958. He gave France unprecedented economic growth. The France of landowning peasants consolidated in the Revolution of 1789 at last became a land of urban workers.

Italy surprised everyone. It achieved stability and unprecedented prosperity. Because of its collaboration with Mussolini, the monarchy failed to win a majority in a 1946 referendum. Italy became a republic, under the leadership of the political parties that reemerged after the collapse of Fascism. The Catholic *Popolari,* renamed Christian Democrats, were the largest; they faced small middle-class parties and a Socialist-Communist alliance. By 1947–48, as the lines of the Cold War hardened, Italy's new political system had also set. Alcide De Gasperi, a Catholic politician whom Mussolini had once persecuted and imprisoned, led the Christian Democrats and the government. The Communist-Socialist alliance lost heavily in the decisive election of April 1948, which De Gasperi fought with massive U.S. and Vatican support and with a remarkable platform: "For or Against Christ."

DeGaulle in Algiers (1958).

After 1953 a series of revolving-door governments followed De Gasperi. But even more than in France, the "absurd ballet" in parliament cloaked underlying continuity. Italy's Communist Party, western Europe's largest, formed a permanent "disloyal opposition" capable of overthrowing the system--if permitted to enter the government. By parliamentary arithmetic, only a coalition of the political center around the Christian Democrats could govern. With adjustments such as the addition of the Socialists to the coalition in 1963 after they broke with the Communists, that formula gave Italy forty years of remarkably stable although increasingly corrupt government. And the economy of Italy's industrial north grew with breakneck speed from the mid-1950s to the late 1960s, thanks to the skill of its entrepreneurs. That economic "miracle" enabled Italy, by the 1970s, to challenge Britain and France for economic primacy. That was an astounding achievement for a society that in 1913 had possessed less than a quarter of Britain's industrial power.

West Germany was western Europe's most dramatic success. Bonn—the Federal Republic's provisional capital, chosen in the expectation of an eventual move to Berlin—was not Weimar. The West German constitution of 1949 barred from parliament any party that received less than 5 percent of the vote. That "five-percent hurdle" restrained the political fragmentation that had helped destroy the first German republic. The new presidency, unlike the presidency of Weimar that had made Hitler chancellor, was a purely ceremonial position. And Hitler, through war, terror, and defeat, had destroyed—along with much else—the conservative elites that had so despised Weimar democracy that they had helped bring the Nazis to power.

The new Republic's first chancellor was an aged but vigorous former mayor of Cologne and pre-1933 opponent of Hitler, Konrad Adenauer. His party, the Christian Democratic Union/Christian Social Union (CDU/CSU), was a successor to the Catholic Center party that also appealed to Protestants. It became the mass party of the German urban and rural middle classes,

and ruled uninterruptedly from 1949 to 1966 in coalition with a small liberal party, the Free Democrats (FDP).

The Social Democratic Party (SPD), the only major party to survive from Weimar, opposed the CDU/CSU. After publicly discarding Marxism in 1959, the SPD at last broke the class barrier that had stunted its growth before 1933. Like the CDU/CSU, it appealed to an ever-larger and more prosperous middle and working class; it offered "good government" and the welfare state. Under Willy Brandt, a dynamic mayor of Berlin who had passed the Hitler years in political exile, the SPD achieved by 1966 a share of power in coalition with Adenauer's successors in the CDU/CSU. In 1969, in alliance with the FDP, Brandt and the SPD replaced the CDU/CSU in power. West Germany had achieved an orderly alternation between two large coherent parties. Antidemocratic fringe groups survived on the far Right and Left, but their clamor was infinitely greater than their influence. And the West German economy had grown into the largest in western Europe and the fourth largest in the world.

Finally, Japan amazed its American occupiers. MacArthur's democratic revolution from above, the greatest internal upheaval since the Meiji Restoration of 1868, was a qualified success. Drawing on the precedents of the parliamentary 1920s, Japanese politicians created a powerful machine of electoral consensus, the Liberal Democratic party. Its ruling oligarchy achieved and maintained a parliamentary majority based on the votes of Japan's peasantry and urban middle classes. That majority permanently excluded from power a fragmented opposition that included Communists, Socialists, and a Buddhist political cult. This "half democracy," as Japanese critics described it, provided a political stability that fostered spectacular economic growth.

The United States provided other ingredients as well: the technology offered by U.S. corporations to their Japanese subsidiaries, and markets and raw materials to replace Japan's lost empire in China and southeast Asia. Direct U.S. aid to Japan after 1954 totaled about $2 billion,

"In the beginning, there was Adenauer": Konrad Adenauer (chancellor, 1949–63), founder of West German democracy.

but the expenditure by 1970 of more than $10 billion in orders by the U.S. military for the wars in Korea and Vietnam was more significant. The goods the U.S. armed forces ordered were mostly civilian; their production fostered the manufacturing techniques that Japan used to storm the world's export markets after the mid-1960s. In Japan, the United States provided the catalyst for the "economic miracle" of the 1950s and 1960s even more than it had in Europe. But it was the relentless hard work of the highly skilled and well-educated Japanese labor force that by the 1970s had made Japan the third largest economy in the world, after the United States and the Soviet Union.

The New Eastern Question, 1947–73

Hitler failed to kill all the Jews of Europe. Instead, paradoxically and unintentionally, he made possible the first Jewish state since the Roman reconquest of Jerusalem in A.D. 70. His genocide inspired a disgust for Europe among many of the Jews who survived, and led to a flood of emigration to Palestine. His genocide taught the lesson that only a Jewish state, weapons in hand, could ensure Jewish survival. His genocide temporarily discredited anti-Semitism in western Europe and the United States, and inspired guilt in those who had failed to aid the Jews of Europe in time. That unspoken guilt dissipated with time, but it was a powerful source of international support for the creation of a Jewish state.

In the aftermath of Hitler's war, Britain tried to uphold its 1939 ban on further Jewish immigration to Palestine (see p. 809). British interests in the Arab world—the world of oil—seemed to demand that Britain block the Zionist aspiration to found a Jewish state. But by 1945 the 600,000 Jews of Palestine constituted a third of the population, and many of them had fought for Britain against Hitler. They now resisted Britain as they had resisted the Arabs in the guerrilla conflict after 1936. By 1946 Zionist guerrilla groups, the Irgun and the "Stern Gang," were at war with both Arabs and British.

Chaim Weizmann, the Zionist leader who had secured Balfour's promise in 1917, tirelessly lobbied the powers for his cause.

By 1946, Britain's position was untenable. As in Ireland after 1919, the British army could not control a spreading guerrilla war without using methods that no democracy could defend. Truman backed the creation of a Jewish state. Even Stalin, who despite his anti-Semitism saw the Jews of Palestine as possible allies against Britain, did not oppose it. In 1947 Attlee's Labour government thankfully handed the poisoned gift of Palestine over to the United Nations, which proposed partition along ethnic-religious lines. The Jewish organizations accepted, but the Palestinian Arabs and their supports in the Arab states refused. An Arab "Liberation Army" attacked Jewish communities. In May 1948, as in Greece and India (see pp. 886 and 926), the exhausted British departed.

That left Palestine to anyone who could conquer it. On May 14, 1948, David Ben-Gurion, charismatic veteran of the Jewish settler communities, proclaimed a Jewish state—the state of Israel. The armies of Egypt, Jordan, Syria, Lebanon, and Iraq invaded Palestine with the announced intention of driving the Jews into the sea. Israel, outnumbered and outgunned, fought that "Arab League" to a standstill and drew Israel's precarious borders by force. Many Palestinian Arabs obeyed calls from their leaders to leave the Jewish-controlled areas, expecting a swift return with the Arab armies. In some cases Jewish forces drove Arab civilians out. Defeat left some 600,000 embittered Palestinian refugees in Jordan and Egypt, and made the Arab states more determined than ever to destroy the Jews.

The core of the new "Eastern Question"—the struggle between the successor states of the Ottoman Empire—was the irreconcilable conflict between the Palestinian Arabs, the Arab states, and Israel. But the antagonism also drew nourishment from a broader and more ancient conflict. The Arabs regarded Israel as yet another intrusion by the West, a successor to the Crusader kingdoms of the twelfth and thirteenth centuries and to the European imperialism of the nineteenth. Israel was a galling symbol of the Islamic world's humiliating weakness, first exposed by Napoleon's 1798–99 campaign in Egypt. Only Israel's destruction, many Arabs increasingly felt, could restore their self-respect.

Arab hostility was self-defeating. The fierce external threat welded Israel's disparate inhabitants together and consolidated its parliamentary system under Ben-Gurion's Labor party. A modern economy took shape, the result of native ingenuity and money from Jewish organizations abroad. In 1951 the gross national product of Egypt, the most prosperous of the Arab states, was three to four times that of Israel; by 1966–67 the ratio had declined to 1.6 to 1.

War had given birth to Israel, a Jewish state, the only democracy in the Middle East. Only war could preserve it, for the Arab powers refused to recognize the "Zionist entity" as a state and made no secret of their continuing desire to destroy it and its inhabitants. Egypt took the lead. Abdel Gamal Nasser, a visionary who dreamed of uniting the Arabs from the Atlantic to the Persian Gulf, emerged as dictator of Egypt after an army coup in 1952. From 1955 on, he secured lavish supplies of arms from the Soviet Union.

Twice, in 1956 and 1967, Nasser provoked Israel with Palestinian guerrilla raids from Gaza and closure of the straits of Tiran that commanded access to Israel's Red Sea port of Eilat. Twice Israel struck first and routed the Egyptians in short but devastating wars in the Sinai Peninsula. Indefensible borders and immense numerical odds left Israel no alternative to preemptive war. Nasser's proclaimed desire for a "war of annihilation" suggested that the price of failure would be a new "Final Solution."

In 1956, thanks to the sheepish withdrawal of its British and French allies, Israel had to leave the conquered Sinai to a United Nations "peacekeeping" force that later failed to keep the peace. In 1967, Israel therefore refused to withdraw after victory—and not only from the Sinai and Gaza. Syria and Jordan had joined Egypt in that "Six Days' War" and had lost the west bank of the Jordan River and the strategic Golan heights from which Syrian artillery had shelled the farming settlements of northern Israel. The conquests of 1967 brought a measure of security, but with it a dangerous gift: the million new Arabs of the "occupied territories" of the West Bank and Gaza.

The Palestinian guerrilla organizations drew a lesson from the 1967 war: they could not look to the Arab states for victory. In 1968 the "Palestine Liberation Organization" (PLO) and its offshoots therefore launched a campaign of terror against soft targets such as Israeli airliners. Israel replied with air strikes against Palestinian refugee camps and open season on PLO leaders. Israeli reprisals against Jordan for Palestinian raids prompted Jordan's King Hussein to discipline the armed Palestinians who constituted a state within his state. In "Black September" 1970, Hussein's highly professional army crushed them. Lebanon, a state too weak to defend itself, became the last stronghold of the PLO.

An embarrassed Soviet Union soon replenished Nasser's arms and manned his radars, antiaircraft missiles, and fighters. In 1969–70 Nasser and the Soviets waged a "war of attrition" against Israel's forward defenses along the Suez Canal. Negotiations sponsored by the United Nations and United States proved predictably futile. Nasser died of a heart attack in September 1970. By that time Egypt had suffered 30,000 casualties, and Washington and Moscow—embarrassed still—had together imposed a cease-fire along the Canal. Nasser's successor, Colonel Anwar Sadat, prepared for yet another round against Israel. The increasing economic power of the Arab oil states had begun to isolate Israel from the timid and oil-dependent western Europeans. But this time, instead of a "war of annihilation," Sadat planned a limited attack to take back the east bank of the Canal and bloody the Israelis.

The Soviet Union supplied advanced antiaircraft and antitank missiles by the shipload. But Sadat was careful to distance himself from his Soviet patrons, who for their part perhaps feared that too close association with a new Arab war might damage the developing "détente" with the United States (see below). In July 1972 Sadat asked for the withdrawal of most of his Soviet "advisers." In 1973, with Egypt's army mobilized and deployed and with Syrian armor drawn up opposite the Golan heights, Sadat attacked. The date he chose was Yom Kippur, the Jewish Day of Atonement, October 6, 1973.

As Sadat had hoped, Israel's political isolation deterred it from repeating its preemptive strikes of 1956 and 1967. Sadat's carefully planned crossing of the Canal broke through Israel's thinly held fortifications, and his Soviet antitank missiles shattered the first hasty Israeli armored counterattacks. But then the Egyptians strayed inland from the Canal and into a battle of movement which the Israelis dominated with their usual skill and drive. In the north, outnumbered Israeli forces in the Golan routed more than 1,000 Syrian and Iraqi tanks and advanced to within artillery range of Damascus. In the south, Israel at last crossed the Canal into Egypt and encircled one of Sadat's two armies. The road to Cairo lay open. Then the superpowers imposed a cease-fire, although not before an unprecedented Soviet threat to commit paratroops in support of Egypt had provoked the United States to alert its nuclear forces.

Militarily the Yom Kippur War was yet another crushing defeat for the Arab cause. But unlike 1967, it was not a total humiliation. Sadat's initial success along the Canal allowed him to claim a moral victory. That made Egypt—although not the Palestinians or the other Arab states—more willing to negotiate. Israel's near disaster also compelled rethinking in Jerusalem. The ultimate result of 1973 was a first break in the wall of Arab hostility surrounding Israel and the transition from war to grudging peace between Israel and Egypt (see p. 964).

And yet the international implications of the Yom Kippur War were ominous. It encouraged the oil-producing states of OPEC (Organization of Petroleum Exporting Countries) to more than double the real (inflation-adjusted) price of oil from October 1973 to 1975—while placing a total embargo on the United States in revenge for its support of Israel. The Europeans cowered. They cut off trade with Israel and, except for Portugal, refused to allow the United States to use NATO bases in support of the massive airlift of ammunition that the beleaguered Jewish state needed to survive. Only Holland failed to comply swiftly enough with Arab demands; it suffered both Arab oil embargo and ostracism by its EC partners. That display of NATO and European disunity inevitably encouraged adversaries of the West to whom events in southeast Asia had already given heart.

THE AGONY OF CONTAINMENT: AMERICA IN VIETNAM

The United States emerged from the Cuban Missile Crisis convinced that nothing was impossible. Then Kennedy's brilliant rhetoric, the self-confidence of the academic elite he had drawn into government, and the pressures of domestic politics combined to commit the United States to a second war of containment in Vietnam.

The Illusion of Omnipotence, 1962–68

Containment by war had proved an effective though costly answer to Stalin's adventure in Korea. Against indirect methods, against insurgency, it was less successful. That familiar technique was the ultimate choice of Ho Chi Minh and his associates, who ruled the "Democratic Republic of Vietnam" (DRV) north of the 17th parallel from their capital at Hanoi. They had consolidated their control in the north in 1955–56 by killing as many as 50,000 peasants who resisted collectivization. They had also maintained their network of party cadres south of the 17th parallel, in South Vietnam.

There Ngo Dinh Diem, a Catholic anti-Communist from the precolonial Mandarin ruling class, established a "Republic of Vietnam" at Saigon, the capital of the South. Diem's regime rested on the traditional landowning elite and on the Vietnamese army France had organized to fight the Communists. The regime had little support among the South's peasants, whose loyalty Ho's party had secured during the war against the French by driving out landlords and redistributing land.

Eisenhower, after much hesitation, committed the United States to support Diem. If South Vietnam fell to Hanoi and to its apparent backers in Beijing, Eisenhower theorized, other southeast Asian "dominoes"—Laos, Cambodia, Thailand, Malaya, and Indonesia—would also fall. The United States had first tolerated France's Indochina war, and then, after 1950, had funded it. After 1954 the United States gradually took France's place. But Washington failed to foresee the sacrifices that policy might entail, or to understand

that Vietnam was unlike Korea in three essential ways. South Vietnam lacked a government or leader with even the frayed legitimacy of a Syngman Rhee. Vietnam was not a peninsula surrounded on three sides by a sea dominated by the U.S. Navy. And Vietnam was only distantly related to the fundamental American Cold War goal of maintaining its major allies in Europe and Japan.

In January 1959 Ho Chi Minh and his Party's inner circle decided to resume "armed struggle" in South Vietnam with the aim of annexing it to the DRV. A party-dominated army, called "Viet Cong" (Vietnamese Communists) by its enemies, took shape in the South. Between 1961 and 1963 it assassinated more than 3,000 Diem

War in Southeast Asia   1954–88

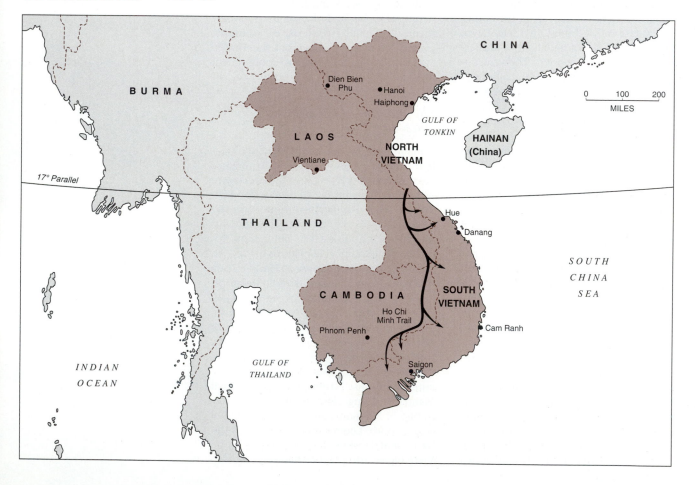

administrators or civilians connected with the government. Hanoi announced in December 1960 the creation of a political cover for that army, the "National Liberation Front" (NLF), a "popular front" that included many non-Communists but secretly took its orders from Hanoi. It was important that NLF and Viet Cong activities appear to Western public opinion as a Southern revolt against what Hanoi described as the "U.S.-Diem dictatorship."

Diem's shaky regime crumbled by 1962–63. His Catholicism, his autocratic manner, and his sinister brother and minister of police, Ngo Dinh Nhu, alienated the influential Buddhist clergy, some of whom burned themselves to death in acts of protest well-publicized on U.S. television. Diem's association with the Americans offended South Vietnam's urban, educated elites. His closeness to the landowners estranged the peasants. The NLF offered the city-dwellers a romantic nationalism and false assurances that its victory would mean autonomy for the South. To the peasants the NLF offered land, but made no mention of the fate of the collectivized peasants of the north. Viet Cong units and political cadres established control over ever-wider areas.

Kennedy, an enthusiast for spy novels and unconventional warfare, increased the number of U.S. military advisers in Vietnam from the 900 he had inherited from Eisenhower to more than 15,000, including helicopter and fighter-bomber units. They were not enough to stave off approaching defeat, and Kennedy apparently concluded that winning the war required Diem's removal. When Diem's confrontation with the Buddhists provoked unrest among his generals, Washington quietly encouraged them to plan a coup. Kennedy made it known in Saigon that if Diem did not dismiss Nhu "we must face the possibility that Diem himself cannot be preserved." That was a green light to the Vietnamese military plotters, who overthrew Diem on November 1, 1963. Contrary to Kennedy's intentions, but all too predictably, the coup forces shot Diem and Nhu.

The United States, confident that it could control events in a society of which

Lyndon Baines Johnson takes the oath of office after Kennedy's assassination, November 22, 1963.

it was deeply ignorant, in this way took total responsibility for the fate of South Vietnam. Kennedy himself died three weeks after Diem, on November 22, 1963, assassinated in Dallas in circumstances that later generated endless conspiracy theories. His vice president and successor, Lyndon Baines Johnson of Texas, proved wily and resourceful in his domestic policy. He accomplished what Kennedy had begun, the belated abolition of the "Jim Crow" segregation laws of the southern United States and the launching of a federal "war on poverty." But his confused attempts to cope with the disaster that he had inherited in Vietnam wrecked his presidency.

The coming 1964 presidential election and the legacy of the Chinese-American war in Korea made disengagement from Vietnam almost unthinkable. "Who lost Vietnam?" was a question Johnson dreaded as much as Eisenhower and Kennedy before him. Looming behind Hanoi was Beijing, where Mao and associates were proclaiming a worldwide peasant revolutionary war against the urban capitalism of the West. And China seemed all the more menacing after it exploded its first atomic bomb in October 1964. Withdrawal from Vietnam, the Washington elite and press assumed, would weaken the credibility of U.S. guarantees to its other allies and unleash a wave of Communist expansion that would engulf "dominoes" from the rice fields of Thailand to the oilfields of Indonesia.

Johnson therefore sought to dissuade Hanoi from pursuing its ambitions. The academic strategists whom Kennedy had brought from Harvard to Washington offered a method: carefully calibrated air and sea pinpricks by U.S. and South Vietnamese forces that would convince Hanoi to give up its attempt to annex the South. The DRV was not convinced; it sent ever-larger forces southward through Laos. By early 1965 South Vietnam seemed on the verge of collapse.

With congressional authorization to "prevent further aggression" in southeast Asia in his pocket, and with victory in the 1964 presidential election safely behind him, Johnson launched a major air campaign against the North in March 1965. But fear of provoking Chinese intervention—as in Korea—and the illusion that bombing by increments would "send a message" kept U.S. bombing safely below the level needed to cripple Hanoi's economy, society, and Soviet-supplied air-defense network.

The air war might eventually have worn the North down, but it could not save South Vietnam in the critical early months of 1965. Between March and May 1965 Johnson therefore committed U.S. Marines and paratroopers to the South. They were the first units of an expeditionary force that grew to 543,000 men and women by spring 1969. That force—or rather the roughly 75,000 infantrymen and 50,000 artillerymen and helicopter crewmen who actually did the fighting—had almost everything: apparently limitless firepower on call, helicopter medical evacuation, lavish supplies, and rotation back to the United States if they survived their 365 allotted days in Vietnam.

What they lacked was a strategy. Washington sought only to force Hanoi to negotiate; that was even less inspiring to the troops than "dying for a tie" in Korea. The U.S. Army command in the South sought to defeat the Viet Cong and the North Vietnamese through attrition. The U.S. Navy and Air Force competed to see which service could drop more bombs on strategically irrelevant targets in and around the North. Both air and ground wars maximized *American* attrition, without bringing a decision closer.

The U.S. ground war did buy time, however. Saigon's battlefield performance and political stability slowly improved. In January–February 1968 the victor of Dien Bien Phu, General Vo Nguyen Giap, launched Viet Cong and North Vietnamese forces at the cities of the South. Timed for Tết, the Vietnamese lunar new year, Giap's "General Uprising" was a stinging operational and tactical reverse for Hanoi. U.S. troops held and counterattacked. Saigon's troops, their backs to the wall, stood and fought. Contrary to Giap's expectation, the population of the cities did not join his troops; at Hue on the central coast, retreating North Vietnamese took revenge by massacring 2,800 civilians. Yet out of tactical defeat Hanoi gained strategic victory. The confusion and bloodshed of Tết shocked the American press and television reporters in Saigon, who interpreted fighting in the cities as a massive U.S. defeat.

Under a rough and profane exterior, Johnson concealed a fatal desire to be loved. Increasing fire from the press and the growth in 1967–68 of raucous student demonstrations against the war effort ("Hey, hey, LBJ, how many kids did ya kill today?") deeply wounded him. The Tết fighting and the strong showing of an "antiwar" candidate in the New Hampshire presidential primary broke what little nerve he had left. He had failed to define a war aim and to lead; now he concurred with his critics.

On March 31, 1968, Johnson appeared on television and announced three things: that the United States would cease bombing the North except for the area immediately north of the 17th parallel, that it would seek a negotiated withdrawal from the war, and that he himself would not run for reelection in the fall. Assassination had brought Johnson to power; he departed by committing political suicide.

His public confession that he thought the war unwinnable changed the terms of debate. After March 1968, Americans battled over how to leave Vietnam, not over how to win or whether to fight.

Defeat, 1968–75

Johnson's ill-fated vice president, Hubert Humphrey, lost the 1968 presidential election. On the Right, a racist third-party revolt against Johnson's domestic policies deprived the Democrats of their usually solid Southern vote. From the Left, violent student demonstrations against Humphrey outside the Democratic Convention in Chicago and the abstention of many "dovish" voters—in protest against Johnson's Vietnam policy—likewise cut into the Democratic vote. To the horror of most "doves," the victor was the Republican candidate, Richard M. Nixon, a former associate of Senator McCarthy.

Nixon had claimed during the campaign that he had a "secret peace plan." It remained secret. In spring 1969 he announced the "Vietnamization" of the war and the gradual withdrawal of American troops; by late 1972 fewer than 25,000 remained. To buy time, Nixon launched in May–June 1970 a last brief offensive thrust, an attack on the elaborate bases the North Vietnamese had established in Cambodia.

Nixon and his devious National Security Adviser, Henry Kissinger of Harvard, may had deluded themselves as well as others that "Vietnamization" would achieve a Korea-style stalemate. More probably, they aimed from the beginning at a gradual retreat from Vietnam in the style of de Gaulle's withdrawal from Algeria. But Hanoi refused to negotiate. Its delegates to the Paris talks that began in May 1968 demanded instantaneous and total withdrawal by the United States and the dismantling of its ally in Saigon. Hanoi also refused to promise the release of U.S. prisoners, mostly Navy and Air Force aircrews, from its concentration camps. The death of Ho Chi Minh in September 1969 made no difference. The Leninist party he had created lived on.

Tết, 1968: Marines advance warily through the ruins of Hue.

But by now the international situation surrounding the U.S. plunge into Vietnam had entirely changed. A Communist coup attempt in Indonesia had failed in 1965; the Indonesian military and Islamic militants retaliated with the massacre of hundreds of thousands of Indonesian Communists and sympathizers. *That* vital domino and its oil was not going to fall.

As for China, it had ironically ceased to need containment. Mao had reduced it to chaos with his "Great Proletarian Cultural Revolution" of 1966–69 (see p. 934), and the Sino-Soviet split had ripened into full-scale military confrontation between the two Communist giants along their 7,000-mile border.

In the spring and summer of 1969 Soviet and Chinese troops fought bitterly on the Ussuri River, north of Vladivostok. A Soviet journalist with close ties to the KGB reported ominously in the British press that "Marxist theoreticians" were discussing the possibility of a full-scale Sino-Soviet war. Soviet spokesmen secretly approached the United States, suggesting that a Soviet strike against China's infant nuclear weapons program would serve the interests of both superpowers. But Nixon sternly warned Moscow off. Kissinger secretly visited Beijing in July 1971 for talks with the shrewd Zhou Enlai, the second man in China. Nixon sought to exploit the mutual fears and hatreds of the Communist great powers to put pressure on Hanoi, to promote arms control, and to secure a Berlin settlement.

In February 1972, Nixon visited Beijing in person and ended the Chinese-American enmity that had endured since war in 1950. Ideology took a back seat to power relationships. As a Middle Eastern saying put it, the enemy of my enemy is my friend. The U.S. "opening to China" so worried Brezhnev that he agreed to a Nixon visit and retreated both in negotiations over Berlin and over strategic arms limitation.

Immediately before the Moscow summit of May 1972, Nixon blocked the vital North Vietnamese port of Haiphong with air-dropped mines, in reprisal for a failed North Vietnamese offensive aimed at Saigon. The mines and the fact that Brezhnev—like Mao—greeted Nixon warmly, apparently provoked second thoughts in Hanoi. But even Nixon's landslide reelection in November failed to persuade Hanoi to settle for less than Saigon's swift collapse. In December 1972 Nixon therefore ordered attacks on vital targets in and around Hanoi with the full firepower of the B-52 heavy bombers of the U.S. Air Force. Following that "Christmas bombing," Hanoi at last consented to release the United States from the war on terms short of utter humiliation.

On January 27, 1973, the DRV representatives signed a peace agreement in Paris providing for the return of U.S. prisoners, the withdrawal of U.S. advisers still in South Vietnam, and a precarious truce. Publicly, Nixon and Kissinger claimed they had achieved "peace with honor," a phrase rich in historical irony. Privately they apparently hoped for a "decent interval" between U.S. withdrawal and South Vietnamese collapse.

The interval was indecently short. Nixon, like Johnson, wanted to be loved. Unceasing personal attacks by his domestic opponents and frequent leakages to the press from within his administration warped his sometimes eccentric judgment. During the 1972 election campaign he ordered the "plumbers," a secret White House unit formed to combat the leaks, to plant electronic listening devices in the national Democratic Party headquarters at Washington's Watergate Hotel. In June 1972, an alert security guard caught the inept "plumbers" as they attempted to break in, and in spring–summer 1973

The opening to China: Nixon and Mao (1972).

Nixon's frantic attempts to cover up his own role in this "Watergate Affair" collapsed. Televised hearings before Congress left his administration in a shambles. On August 9, 1974, he left the presidency by a unique route—resignation to escape impeachment, criminal prosecution, and probable imprisonment.

Internally, the outcome of Watergate was a triumph for the rule of law. Externally, it enabled Congress to seize control of foreign policy and cut off aid to South Vietnam and to anti-Communist forces in Laos and Cambodia. Fierce congressional opposition paralyzed Nixon's vice president and successor, Gerald R. Ford. In January 1975 the North Vietnamese Politburo took the measure of Congress and of Ford: "Having withdrawn from Vietnam, the United States could hardly return." Hanoi, newly reequipped with Soviet tanks and heavy weapons, prepared a North Korean-style offensive across South Vietnam's northern and western borders.

In April 1975, DRV armor overran the exhausted and demoralized South Vietnamese army. The United States watched impotently and then organized one last operation: the evacuation from Saigon of all remaining Americans and some of the many South Vietnamese who had worked for the United States. The North annexed the South and renamed Saigon "Ho Chi Minh City." The Second Indochina War was over. It had cost the lives of roughly 725,000 North Vietnamese, 525,000 South Vietnamese, and 58,000 Americans. Its end brought not peace, but massacres in Vietnam and Cambodia, millions of refugees, and a Third Indochina War between the Communist victors (see pp. 957–58).

A "Generation of Peace"? Détente and Arms Control, 1968–75

As they disengaged from Vietnam, Kissinger and Nixon proclaimed that a new international order was being born. The opening to China would not only release the United States from southeast Asia. It would also open the road to a lasting "détente," or relaxation of tensions, between Moscow and Washington.

Talk of détente was not new. The atmospheric test ban treaty of 1963 was its first monument. In 1968 Johnson had signed with Moscow a nuclear nonproliferation treaty—which China and France rejected in favor of exploding their own hydrogen bombs. Strategic arms talks and a 1968 summit with Brezhnev proved abortive. But in Europe, the West Germans abandoned Adenauer's rigid policy of nonrecognition of Ulbricht's East German regime. Willy Brandt of the SPD, upon his entrance into Bonn's governing coalition in 1966, inaugurated a new "eastern policy." Brandt's *Ostpolitik* sought to lessen tensions both with the DDR and with the nations of eastern Europe on which Germany had trampled in 1938–45. Extreme versions of *Ostpolitik* looked forward to an end to NATO and the Warsaw Pact, and the reunification of Germany.

As a French intellectual once remarked, Germany's neighbors loved Germany so much that they were delighted to have two of them. *Ostpolitik* was nevertheless a modest success. It suffered a setback in August 1968, when the Soviet Union and its Warsaw Pact allies invaded Czechoslovakia to crush the "Prague Spring," a liberalization movement in the Czech Communist party. But embarrassment at Soviet brutality did not long deter Brandt, Johnson, or Nixon from seeking further negotiations.

Brandt became Chancellor of West Germany in 1969 and concluded nonaggression treaties with the Soviet Union, Poland, Czechoslovakia, and the DDR in 1970–73. Kissinger's opening to China helped move the Soviet Union in 1971 to sign a treaty with the United States, Britain, and France that formally guaranteed Western access to Berlin. In theory that prevented a renewal of Stalin's blockade or of Khrushchev's threats to West Berlin.

Kissinger judged that Brezhnev badly needed reinsurance against Beijing and an infusion of Western technology and money to bolster Soviet economic growth, which had peaked in the 1950s and declined thereafter. He assumed, in essence, that the West could bribe the Soviets. Economic ties and arms control would in good

Cobdenite fashion (see p. 743) enmesh Moscow in a structure of "interdependence." As Kennan had hoped in 1947, the Soviet Union would at last "mellow" and become a status quo power. The need for containment would end, and the world, in Nixon's self-inflating phrase, would enjoy a "generation of peace."

The Soviet view was quite different. Despite Moscow's sensitivity about Kissinger's flirtation with Beijing, the Soviets did not consider China a near-term threat. The vast bulk of Soviet divisions continued to menace western Europe. Brezhnev sought détente as a tool for achieving Soviet objectives, not as an occasion to abandon them. Western money, technology, and grain would shore up a flagging economy and upgrade Soviet weapons technology. Détente need not hold the Soviet Union back outside Europe, as the Soviet Union immediately demonstrated by backing Sadat's October 1973 war. Nor did détente mean the end of ideological struggle.

Soviet reservations thus undermined the two greatest monuments of détente, the strategic arms limitation treaty of May 1972 (SALT I) and the Helsinki security treaty of 1975. SALT I and its accompanying "ABM Treaty" limiting antimissile defenses wrote into international law the quantitative advantage that the Soviet buildup had gained since 1962. The Soviets retained 1,618 land-based and 950 submarine-launched intercontinental ballistic missiles to the 1,054 and 710 of the United States. But SALT I limited numbers of missiles only; it placed no restrictions on the "multiple independently targeted" warheads (MIRVs) that soon equipped those missiles. The treaty appeared to make the superpower arms competition more predictable than before but did little to end it. And its duration was only five years.

The Helsinki treaty of 1975, the final cap on the eastern treaties of 1970–73, was equally ambiguous. The West, in a Europe-wide conference at Helsinki that included neutral powers, at last bestowed legitimacy on Stalin's conquests of 1944–45. In return, Moscow offered cultural exchanges, and promises, immediately violated, of respect for human rights and of free movement of people and ideas across the borders of the Soviet empire.

MASS CULTURE AND "COUNTERCULTURE"

Socially and politically, the 1950s were placid times in the West. Sociologists prematurely hailed the "end of ideology," the demise of messianic political faiths in the wake of Khrushchev's 1956 revelations. Then worldwide communications, anti-American discontents, a student generation of unprecedented size and wealth, and the twin catalysts of the Vietnam War and the independence struggles in the "Third World" (see pp. 926–32) created a wave of disturbances unprecedented since 1848.

The Americanization of the World

The growth of the world market amid undreamed-of prosperity also meant the rapid worldwide spread of the mass culture of the leading state. Two things speeded up that process: the dying British Empire's legacy of English as the universal language of commerce, and a new revolution in transportation and communications that paralleled the coming of steam and the telegraph in the nineteenth century. In 1950, almost all intercontinental travel was by ship. By 1960 four-engined jet aircraft had cut the trip from Paris to New York to eight hours; no spot on the globe was more than 24 hours away. By the 1970s, satellite television relays provided instantaneous transmission of pictures and sound from anywhere on Earth.

American film and television conveyed sparkling images of affluence and made few intellectual demands on their audiences. When dubbed into local languages, they acquired a wide following wherever governments allowed their citizens to view them. They also aroused appetites for wealth and growth that most societies found difficult to satisfy. Even the relatively rich Europeans did not duplicate the credit-card prosperity of the American middle classes until the 1970s.

Along with Hollywood movies and television serials came the gray legions of corporate America, from General Electric to ITT to Coca Cola. They established or widened beachheads for American commerce in Europe, Japan, and the "Third World." That massive expansion of America's cultural and economic visibility aroused a variety of reactions. European business at first gratefully embraced the Marshall Plan and private American investment in Europe. Welcome turned to distrust by the 1960s. U.S. capital export was so massive that Europeans feared losing control of their economies to America's allegedly sinister "multinational corporations." Then the burden of Vietnam undermined U.S. economic performance. Europeans created multinationals of their own and invested in the United States.

Culturally, reaction was likewise mixed. The defeated nations of Germany, Italy, and Japan embraced some elements of American democracy or industrial organization. But especially in Britain, France, and the Islamic world, native traditions resisted fiercely. Britons like the philosopher and unilateral-disarmament crusader Bertrand Russell looked down their noses at what they took to be American provincialism and irresponsibility. Conservative critics, from traditionalist Catholics to stern Gaullists to Shiite Moslems, decried "Coca-colonization" and the moral laxity that American wealth allegedly brought. The academic Left, from Mexico City and Tokyo to the cafés of the Left Bank in Paris, turned withering Marxist scorn on America, the leading capitalist state.

Student Revolt and Middle-Class Terrorism

After 1945 the United States sought to create the first society in history in which a majority of citizens had some higher education. In the 1960s much of western Europe began to follow. The rapid expansion of colleges and universities created a shortage of faculty that consigned students to boredom in immense factory-like classrooms. Affluence apparently removed any pressing need to work. Leisure and the outrageous example of "beat generation" rebels of the 1950s fostered the

The Americanization of the world: the supermarket comes to France.

rise in the early 1960s of a youth "counterculture." Its adherents were passionately contemptuous of inherited standards of behavior and dedicated to the joys that contraceptive pills, mind-distorting drugs, and the electric guitar had recently made available.

The rebellion of the youthful rich began appropriately enough in the richest country, the United States. In 1964, the University of California at Berkeley exploded in violent confrontation between a rigid central administration and a radical "Free Speech Movement" determined to shock and provoke. Vietnam loomed on the horizon as early as 1963, but it was Johnson's plunge into full-scale war in 1965 that gave the rebels their cause and mass base. College students received draft deferments, but those who graduated or flunked out faced army service unless they discovered a convenient medical condition.

In these circumstances a "New Left" arose that mocked predictions of the "end of ideology." From 1964–65 on, it savaged the American political and academic establishment from the Left with a zeal that recalled the 1950s attacks of Senator McCarthy from the Right. It proclaimed a "second American revolution" against "imperialism" in Vietnam and against middle-class society at home. Student insurrections paralyzed Columbia, Harvard, and other campuses in 1967–68. Nixon's 1970 thrust into Cambodia inspired an immense wave of protest.

By then the most determined student radicals had formed a terrorist group that called itself the "Weathermen." The name came from a line of the folk-rock cult figure Bob Dylan: ". . . you don't need a weatherman to know which way the wind blows." The Weathermen sought to "bring the war home," to imitate the "armed struggle" of the Viet Cong and of urban guerrillas like the Tupamaros in Uruguay (see p. 941). Their most striking achievement was the accidental demolition in 1970 of a Greenwich Village townhouse and bomb factory belonging to the parent of a member. And the broader "Movement" deflated swiftly after 1970, thanks

to the end of the draft and to the inherent contradiction between Leninist commitment and countercultural hedonism. Not "armed struggle" but drugs, sex, rock and roll, and imported Buddhist or Hindu mysticism were the most widespread forms of protest against middle-class America.

The American example helped inspire disturbances in Europe far more serious than mere campus revolts. The European rebels had inherited a tradition of romantic student radicalism stretching back into the nineteenth century. They also drew on the discipline and doctrine of their countries' Communist parties, although they condemned those parties as stodgy. Even more than their American counterparts they found inspiration in "Third World" revolutionary movements.

The Paris "days" of May 1968 turned back the clock to the Paris Commune of 1871; urban insurrection once more seemed to be practical politics. A student uprising with support from the industrial workers briefly controlled the Left Bank of Paris. Hundreds of thousands marched demanding de Gaulle's overthrow. The General flew off in disgust ("reforms yes; bed-messing no") to visit his army and to secure the support of the officer corps. He then returned to Paris and rallied the "forces of order" with a television speech that brought millions into the streets singing the "Marseillaise"—a revolutionary anthem transmuted into a call to arms against revolution. The student movement deflated. The Left lost votes in the election that followed. De Gaulle resigned in 1969 when a referendum went against him, but he resigned in favor of a hand-picked successor. The modern state had again shown its ability to tame upheavals from below.

In Germany, student revolt was in deadly earnest—as it had been under Weimar, when the Nazis had captured the student movement long before they seized the state. Some German "New Left" radicals, Freudian-Marxist in ideology and Stalinist in practice, turned to "armed struggle" in the late 1960s. Their most prominent group, the "Red Army Faction" or "Baader-Meinhof gang," attacked U.S. bases in West Germany and assassinated industrialists, judges, and politicians with ruthless precision. But computerized tracking of suspects eventually demolished the guerrillas. In 1976–77 Andreas Baader, Ulrike Meinhof, and other "Red Army Faction" leaders committed suicide in prison to embarrass "the system." Bombings, assassinations, and revolution by suicide failed to inspire the placid West German "masses" to revolt. After 1979, the German student Left largely abandoned "armed struggle" for ecological and antinuclear protest (see p. 961).

Italy's student radicals mounted the most determined challenge to the democratic state. Students and industrial workers combined in 1969 to make a deadly serious "hot autumn" of riots, strikes, and factory or university occupations. Throughout the 1970s terrorist groups of former students from both leftist and Catholic backgrounds sought to provoke the Italian parliamentary regime into revealing its allegedly "Fascist" nature. Some had received training in KGB-sponsored schools in Czechoslovakia, others with the PLO in Lebanon. Their instrument was the "knee-capping" or assassination of judges, factory managers, journalists, and politicians. In 1978 the terrorist "Red Brigades" kidnaped and killed a former prime minister, the Christian Democrat Aldo Moro. That stroke united Italian opinion against the terrorists and galvanized police and prosecutors. The "Red Brigades" and their offshoots ended in prison. Throughout the West youthful rebellion gave way to middle-class careers.

The Feminist Revolution

Among the movements that flourished in the 1960s alongside student and "countercultural" protest was a renewed and militant feminism. The vote, the Depression, and two world wars had damped feminist agitation from the 1920s to the 1950s. But in the intoxicating atmosphere of the 1960s, the continuing growth of women's share in the work force—often in poorly paid part-time or temporary jobs—helped ignite protest. The contradiction between women's claims to rights and the facts of

The power of the state: French police beat Paris students, May 1968.

male power in the family, at work, and in politics inspired radical theorists, especially in the United States and France. Precursors such as Simone de Beauvoir, France's leading female intellectual and author of *The Second Sex* (1949), soon appeared insufficiently militant. Beauvoir's elegant and learned analysis of "the slavery of half of humanity" appeared to lack a political program.

Numerous theorists and groups sought to supply one. In the United States, where women entered the labor force earlier and in greater numbers than in Europe, a broad front of women's organizations had arisen by the mid-1960s. It sought to open hitherto male professions to women and to secure "reproductive freedom": the removal of restrictions on contraception and abortion. This "first wave" of feminists ranged from mild liberalism to New Left radicalism. But in practice it flowed from the Lockean natural rights tradition, as Harriet and John Stuart Mill (see p. 644) had applied it in the nineteenth century— women should enjoy by right the same autonomy as men. To at last assert that autonomy, women now had to learn to compete successfully with men in all fields of human activity. The most radical "first wave" theorists concluded that women's autonomy demanded the destruction of the "patriarchal" family and the liberation of women from childbirth and child-rearing.

As the euphoria of the 1960s subsided, a "second wave" of American feminist theorists began to celebrate—rather than seeking to eliminate—women's differences from men. The new "woman-centered" school had counterparts in western Europe and was related to the "equal but different" tradition of the nineteenth century (see p. 654). It asserted the superiority of women's nature, which was allegedly more intuitive, warm, compassionate, "nurturing," peace-loving, and practical than that of the purportedly cold, calculating, competitive, violent, power-mad male. It dismissed masterful women leaders from Margaret Thatcher of Britain to Indira Gandhi of India (see pp. 937 and 960) as victims who had in effect become men. It proclaimed that women were a "sex class" whose shared nature and experience overrode all ideological, social, national, and racial divisions. "Universal sisterhood" would inaugurate a new and purely female culture that would ultimately save humanity. Ironically, that vi-

sion caught on just as ideological, social, ethnic, and racial divisions fractured the women's movement—and as a counteroffensive by fiercely antifeminist "pro-family" women sought to roll it back.

But despite internal struggles and external opposition, the feminist revolt had decisive consequences. In the United States and western Europe, it spurred reforms that gave women a greater measure of formal equality than ever before in history. It inspired the creation of institutions such as day-care centers that helped to free women to join the work force in ever-greater numbers. Above all, it provided middle-class women with encouragement to pursue careers equivalent to those of men, encouragement that their mothers had lacked. Demographically, the consequence was later marriages and fewer children. Emotionally, the attempt to "have it all," to pursue a career and raise a family, sometimes provoked intolerable strain. Men inevitably proved slow to adjust to the equality in practical matters that the new "two-career family" demanded. But change was nevertheless perceptible. The feminist revolution brought closer to reality than ever before the nineteenth-century ideal of equality between the sexes.

Protests within the West were merely one sign of the passing of the "age of containment." The Middle East explosion of 1973 revealed the full extent of Western disunity. The swift escalation of oil prices that followed struck a stinging blow to the world economy. U.S. foreign policy succumbed temporarily to paralysis as Congress sought to demolish the "imperial presidency" that it blamed for Vietnam. Geography and political circumstances had favored containment in Korea, at a price. The agony of containment in Vietnam hastened the end of America's strategic dominance over the Soviet Union and of its economic edge over Japan. By the mid-1970s, commentators saw a new age of another kind emerging. Détente, they proclaimed, had ended the Cold War. In place of superpower conflict they saw a growing international class struggle between rich and poor states.

Career woman of the 1970s: the strain of family and work.

Suggestions for Further Reading

The Superpower Conflict

Few intelligent syntheses cover the post-1945 period. Recent events arouse too much retrospective passion and carry too heavy a weight of current hopes and fears. Sources are simultaneously too wide and too shallow. Much remains buried in the archives, especially the former Soviet archives. A. Ulam, *The Rivals: America and Russia Since World War II* (1971), is nevertheless excellent on the central U.S.-Soviet conflict. P. Seabury, *The Rise and Decline of the Cold War* (1967), is acute on that conflict's nature and dimensions. R. Aron, *The Imperial Republic: The United States and the World, 1945–1973* (1974), is both brilliant and detached. On the Soviet Union, see first the inside views of M. Djilas, *Conversations with Stalin* (1962), and (with caution) N. Khrushchev, *Khrushchev Remembers* (1974). A. Ulam, *The Communists* (1992), traces the entire post-1945 trajectory of the Communist powers, but see also his *Expansion and Coexistence* (1968) and *Dangerous Relations: the Soviet Union in World Politics, 1970–1982* (1983). For the Cuban Missile Crisis, G. Allison, *Essence of Decision* (1971), is still rewarding, despite much new evidence from the Soviet and Cuban side.

The Mid-Sized Powers

W. Laqueur, *Europe in Our Time: A History, 1945–1992* (1992), is a masterful synthesis. M. Schaller, *The American Occupation of Japan* (1985), traces the process that put Japan back on the road to supremacy in East Asia; K. van Wolferen, *The Enigma of Japanese Power* (1989), offers a compelling (and depressing) analysis of Japanese politics and society; H. C. Hinton, *Three and a Half Powers: The New Balance in Asia* (1975), places Japan in its international context.

The Middle East

The Middle East arouses even more passion than the Cold War; no reliable narrative history of the area since 1945 exists. L. C. Brown, *International Politics and the Middle East* (1984), is a fine introduction to how it got the way it is. P. Mansfield, *The Middle East: A Political and Economic Survey* (1980), is a useful handbook. Y. Harkabi, *Arab Strategies and Israel's Response* (1977), offers one Israeli view; for Arab difficulties with Israel and the modern world, see especially F. Ajami, *The Arab Predicament: Arab Political Thought and Practice Since 1967* (1992). W. Laqueur, *Confrontation: The Middle East War and World Politics* (1974), remains the best book on the Yom Kippur War.

From Korea to Vietnam

Few dispassionate accounts of America's wars of containment exist, but see D. Rees, *Korea: the Limited War* (1964), and G. Lewy, *America in Vietnam* (1978). G. Race, *War Comes to Long An* (1972), and E. M. Bergerud, *The Dynamics of Defeat* (1991), explain the perplexities—and the enemy—encountered in America's longest war. *Dispatches* (1978) conveys the atmosphere of Vietnam with unparalleled skill. P. Braestrup, *Big Story* (1977), describes with candor and irony the role of the U.S. press. H. Summers, *On Strategy* (1982), is a not always successful attempt to figure out what went wrong. For détente and the opening to China, see (with caution) H. Kissinger, *White House Years* (1979) and *Years of Decision* (1982).

Students and Feminists

The transnational student revolt still awaits its historian. D. Caute, *The Year of the Barricades. A Journey Through 1968* (1988); R. V. Daniels, *The Year of the Heroic Guerrilla. World Revolution and Counterrevolution in 1968* (1989); and R. Johnson, *The French Communist Party Versus the Students* (1972), are nevertheless useful. On the women's movement, see especially J. Mitchell and A. Oakley, *What Is Feminism?* (1986); C. Duchen, *Feminism in France* (1986); and H. Eisenstein, *Contemporary Feminist Thought* (1983).

35

THE NON-WESTERN WORLD FROM THE FORTIES TO THE NINETIES

Under the shadow of superpower conflict, an entire world of "new nations" arose in the years after 1945. The collapse of the European empires under the pressure of that most successful of European exports, nationalism, ultimately created more than 120 new states. Most of them were poor compared to the developed West. But that was almost the only characteristic they had in common. For despite claims that all non-Western societies shared a common "Third World" or southern-hemisphere heritage, the new states were dramatically different in history, culture, politics, economic structure, and wealth. By the 1990s it was clear that the notion of a unified "Third World" with interests that were implacably opposed to those of the West—or "North"—was misleading. For increasing numbers of non-Western states were making the leap from poverty to wealth that the West had made in the nineteenth century. One prerequisite for that leap—but no guarantee of success—was independence, achieved in the era of "decolonization" that gave birth to the vast majority of non-Western states.

DECOLONIZATION: IDEOLOGICAL WINDS OF CHANGE

The force of ideas was the most powerful of the "winds of change" that swept over the Western colonial empires in the two decades after Britain's defeat at Singapore in 1942. Nationalism, the political religion of the nation-state, arose spontaneously in the non-Western world whenever native ruling classes sought to resist Western power by acquiring Western ideas.

(*OPPOSITE*) WARS OF DECOLONIZATION: SUSPECTED GUERRILLAS UNDER GUARD DURING THE MAU MAU UPRISING IN KENYA (1952).

From China to Ghana, nationalism offered an ideology to replace the old communities and beliefs that Western power had shattered in the nineteenth century. The creation of nation-states, independent and sovereign externally and the focus of *all* loyalties internally, would wipe out the humiliation that Western domination had brought, provide a sense of belonging—and help nationalist intellectuals to power and wealth.

Some parts of the world took to the new ideas more readily than others. The societies of east Asia were cultural units of long standing. That eased their conversion into nation-states on the European pattern. In the Islamic world, loyalties were simultaneously too wide and too narrow to fit the new pattern easily. "Arab unity," "Islamic solidarity," or "Islamic Revolu-

tion" coexisted uneasily with centuries-old tribal, religious, and linguistic-ethnic rivalries. In Latin America, the world's oldest group of "new nations" except for Holland and the United States, the persistence of stratification by blood—Creole, *mestizo*, Indian, African—meant that the elites were often closer to their counterparts in neighboring states than to their own peasants. And in black Africa, state borders bore little relationship to the ethnographic map.

As an ideology of revolt against the West, nationalism inevitably had competitors—of which Marxism-Leninism was the most successful. Although in theory an ideology of class war, in practice it often merged—outside Europe—with nationalism. As Sun Yat-sen of China had recognized (see p. 810), nationalism and

South and East Asia since the Second World War

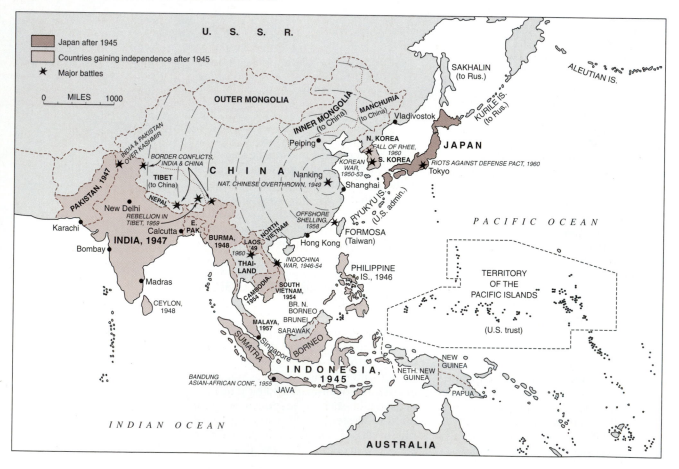

Leninist organizational techniques were a powerful combination. In the "Third World" as in the Soviet Union, Marxism-Leninism provided legitimation for "cults of personality" and for the almost unlimited power of Party elites. The resulting regimes were the most regimented and fiercely nationalist in history: China, North Vietnam, North Korea, Cuba, and Ethiopia from the 1970s to the 1980s. But those strange offspring of the European traditions of nationalism and Marxism were nationalist with a difference. Paradoxically, they also belonged to the "socialist camp"—a multinational Soviet empire based on the denial of nationalism. Only China, Yugoslavia, and Albania developed Marxist-Leninist nationalisms *opposed to* Moscow.

An assortment of "pan-movements" also competed with nationalism. The Islamic world gave birth to two mutually contradictory ones—Arab nationalism and pan-Islamism. Arab nationalism, whose chief manifestation was the Arab League of states with its periodic meetings and communiqués, proved weak indeed. Even when wielded by charismatic figures such as Gamal Abdel Nasser, it failed to unify the Arab world politically. Its religious counterpart, pan-Islamism, suffered from even greater weaknesses. Of Islam's close to a billion adherents, roughly a quarter were Arabs. The rest, from Senegal through Iran, Pakistan, and India to Indonesia and the Philippines, included such a wide variety of linguistic and ethnic groups that common action even in the United Nations rarely proved possible. Islam itself, like Christianity, also had internal divisions, especially the hostility between the minority Shiites—10 percent of all Moslems—and the majority Sunni (see p. 201). South of Islam, "pan-Africanism" found expression in 1963 in an "Organization of African Unity"; the organization endured but unity remained absent.

A final contender was—for lack of a better term—"Third Worldism": the ideology that proclaimed the division of humanity into a rich, oppressive, capitalist "North" and an innocent, victimized, agrarian "South." In 1955, at Bandung in Indonesia, 29 African and Asian states met and inaugurated a series of "Third World" meetings that promoted the notion of "nonalignment" in the Cold War and made increasingly insistent demands that the West atone for its "imperialist" past.

Third Worldism, as it developed in the 1960s and 1970s, was a powerful mixture. First of its ingredients was the notion that the reduction of the "Third World" to poverty had been the result of Western development and wealth. Second was a romantic faith in revolution and its supposed modernizing effects; that faith rested in part on a misreading of Soviet history. The final component was the claim that the "Third World" was a cohesive unit, that its solidarity against "imperialism" overrode all its many linguistic, ethnic, religious, and cultural divisions. Those were powerful myths, but they proved less powerful than nationalism, the cult of the nation-state.

DECOLONIZATION: BIRTH OF THE NEW NATIONS

The empires that survived the Second World War were doomed by demography, once the colonized peoples revolted. Britain, with roughly 41 million inhabitants in 1939, dominated an empire of more than 500 million. The colonial empires of France, Holland, Belgium, and Portugal were less disproportionate in size to the European powers that held them. But even there colonial rule rested on the continuing willingness of the colonized to submit and collaborate.

Overwhelming European power, the power of the Maxim gun, had produced submission and collaboration in the past. But now the balance of forces had changed. The rise and widening reach of the Soviet Union and of Mao's China gave colonial nationalists powerful allies. The dependable Soviet AK-47 assault rifle, copied from a German weapon of 1943–44, became the Maxim gun of *decolonization*. Economic growth and Western schooling produced native intellectuals who sought both peaceful and violent ways to force the colonizers to go. These intellectuals created nationalist mass movements far better at reconquering independence than the pre-colonial native rulers had been at keeping it. In Europe, the vast bloodletting of the two world wars and the economic uselessness of many of the colonies persuaded most European democracies to abandon their empires once native nationalists mounted a serious challenge.

Britain: The Long Retreat

British decolonization began first and lasted longest, given the British Empire's size and bizarre variety. It was also the least traumatic, thanks to London's pragmatic willingness to concede, graciously or not, what it no longer had the power to withhold. Ireland went first in 1921–37 (see p. 808). Its leader, the former rebel Eamonn De Valera, was the first of many nationalist leaders whose road to power led through British jails.

In the aftermath of the Second World War, the British empire found itself under even more determined siege than in 1919–21. Mohandas Gandhi—fortunately for India—had failed to drag down British rule in 1942 when the Japanese were at the gate. But after 1945 the Labour government of Clement Attlee had no choice but to quit India; Britain lacked the troops and money to hold by force a subcontinent of more than 400 million inhabitants.

Two mass movements had arisen that fought both Britain and each other: Gandhi's Congress Party and Mohammed Ali Jinnah's Moslem League. The Congress Party claimed all India by right of Hindu nationalism; the Moslem League claimed a Moslem state—Pakistan—around Karachi and in Bengal, east and west of the Hindu majority. By March 1947, in the words of a subordinate of Britain's last viceroy, the Indian empire was "a ship on fire in mid-ocean with ammunition in the hold." In August 1947 the British simply left. Then the excellent British-trained armies of the two successor states, India and Pakistan, went to war over the province of Kashmir. Hindu and Moslem populations on the

The partition of British India, 1947: Moslem refugees on a road near New Delhi strewn with Moslem dead.

wrong side of the partition lines fled for their lives. Independence brought 15 million refugees and 500,000 to 750,000 dead in religious-ethnic massacres.

Keeping India secure had moved Britain to conquer Ceylon, Burma, Malaya, and the north coast of Borneo. The end of empire in India led London to give independence to Burma and Ceylon (later Sri Lanka) in early 1948. Britain stayed on until 1957 in Malaya and Singapore to quell a Communist insurgency that sprang from Malaya's overseas Chinese minority. In 1963 Britain gave independence to its possessions in Borneo. It kept only Hong Kong, which it pledged in 1984 to transfer to China in 1997.

In the Middle East, around the oilfields essential to Britain and western Europe, London tried to hang on. It left Egypt in 1945 and gave up its thankless task in Palestine in 1948. But until the mid-1950s it managed to hold the irreducible minimum: the vital base of Cyprus, the oil states of the Persian Gulf, and a zone around the Suez Canal through which the oil passed to Europe. But soon the sad tale of 1882 repeated itself—with a different outcome. Like the Khedive before him, Britain's Egyptian client King Farouk was unseated in 1952 by a nationalist officers' revolt. After Farouk's overthrow, a charismatic figure on the model of Arabi Pasha took command: Colonel Abdel Gamal Nasser.

Nasser proposed to unify "the Arabs" from Morocco to Iraq. As a first step, he sought to evict Britain from the Suez Canal and lead the Arabs against Israel. In June 1956, weary of terrorist attacks on British sentries, Britain withdrew its last troops from the Canal Zone—and Nasser almost immediately confiscated the Canal from its European owners. He also challenged Israel by organizing guerrilla raids from the Gaza Strip, and provoked the United States by purchasing arms from the Soviet Union. Anthony Eden, Churchill's wartime foreign secretary and successor, took up the challenge: Nasser was another Hitler. Had Nasser not written a booklet, *Philosophy of the Revolution* (1953)? Was the Suez Canal in 1956 not the Rhineland of 1936? (But in 1936 Eden had merely thought

Hitler's action "deplorable.") The French, bogged down in war against the Algerian rebels and convinced that Nasser the pan-Arab zealot was behind it, were happy to help.

British and French airborne and amphibious forces, in secret coordination with Israel's conquest of the Sinai, seized the Mediterranean end of the canal on November 5–6, 1956. But Eden failed to understand that Washington sought to woo "Arab nationalism" and would not tolerate a British and French reconquest of Egypt. Eisenhower and his Secretary of State, John Foster Dulles, panicked Eden by suspending U.S. support for the stability of Britain's currency. That forced British withdrawal. The French, fuming over British timidity, resentfully followed.

Nasser claimed victory, although his army had suffered a worse rout than in 1948–49 and Cairo was defenseless against the British, French, and Israelis. Suez, a British military victory, ended Britain's prestige in the Middle East as defeat at Singapore had done in Asia. A coup against the British-backed Arab monarchy in Iraq, unrest in Jordan, and the beginnings of a civil war between Moslems and Maronite Christians in Lebanon followed in 1958. Iraq bloodily left the British orbit; British paratroops and U.S. Marines briefly landed in Jordan and Lebanon to maintain "stability." In Cyprus, a campaign launched by Greek guerrillas in 1955 led to Britain's departure in 1959–60. A low-intensity war within Cyprus between the Greek majority and the Turkish minority followed; it ended only in 1974, with a Greek coup that provoked a Turkish invasion and the forcible partition of the island.

If the 1940s were Britain's decade of decolonization in south Asia, and the 1950s the decade of Middle East, the 1960s were the decade of sub-Saharan Africa and the Caribbean. Harold Macmillan, Eden's successor, spoke grandly in January 1960 of the "wind of change" sweeping the African continent. In the next five years, in a "scramble for Africa" like that of the 1880s and 1890s but in reverse, Britain and France gave their African empires away. In 1956–57 Britain had already

The Collapse of the British Empire

1946	Jordan
1947	India
1948	Ceylon [later Sri Lanka], Burma, Palestine
1956	Sudan
1957	Ghana, Gold Coast, Malaya
1960	Cyprus, Nigeria, British Somaliland [joined ex-Italian Somalia]
1961	Sierra Leone, Cameroons, Tanganyika, Kuwait
1962	Jamaica, Trinidad and Tobago, Uganda
1963	Kenya, Zanzibar [joined Tanganyika to form Tanzania, 1964], Singapore, North Borneo, Sarawak [joined Malaya to form Malaysia; Singapore broke away in 1965].
1964	Malawi, Malta, Zambia
1965	Gambia
1966	Guyana, Botswana, Lesotho, Barbados
1967	Aden, Leeward Islands, Windward Islands
1968	Mauritius, Nauru, Swaziland
1970	Fiji
1971	United Arab Emirates, Bahrein, Qatar

given independence to the Sudan and to Ghana and the Gold Coast in west Africa. Independence for Nigeria, Africa's richest and most populous "new nation," came in 1960. In south-central Africa, Britain delayed for a while out of concern for its white settler population in Rhodesia. But in 1965 the whites unilaterally declared their independence from Britain, defied Harold Wilson's Labour government and the United Nations, and fought to maintain control over the black majority. The settlers were too few, and too isolated internationally to win; negotiations transformed Rhodesia into black-ruled Zimbabwe in 1978–79.

South of Rhodesia, the Union of South Africa under Boer leadership had achieved virtual independence after the First World War, but its politics remained balanced precariously between English-speakers, pro-British Boers, and vengeful backwoods *Trekboers*. In 1948 the *Trekboers* came to power, and imposed through laws a rigid system of racial oppression called *Apartheid* ("apartness") that already existed in fact. The Boers crushed black demonstrations, like the one at Sharpeville in 1960, with gunfire. In 1961 South Africa withdrew from the British Commonwealth rather than tolerate further criticism of its peculiar institutions.

Britain took the final steps in its abandonment of empire in the late 1960s and early 1970s. Its vital naval base at Aden, at the entrance to the Red Sea, went in 1967 after a bloody guerrilla war with Arab tribal "Marxists." Soviet warships in its harbor replaced those of the Royal Navy. Aden mutated into a "People's Democratic Republic of Yemen," complete with AK-47 massacres at Politburo meetings. And in 1971 Britain in effect handed over to the mercy of the Shah of Iran (see pp. 965–67) its oil-rich clients in the Gulf, from

The Sharpeville massacre, 1960: Blacks flee the guns of the South African police.

Kuwait in the north to the United Arab Emirates in the south.

All that remained of the British Empire were a few small Caribbean, Atlantic, and Pacific islands along with outposts whose populations feared that independence would lead to annexation by grasping neighbors: Hong Kong, Gibraltar, and the Falkland Islands off Argentina. The Commonwealth, in which many of Britain's former colonies remained, became a debating society.

France: The Suitcase or the Coffin

France did not give up as easily as Britain. Its second colonial empire, acquired after defeat by Germany in 1870–71, was a symbol of national vitality. French schoolteachers had zealously propagated the political myth of France's "civilizing mission" in Africa and Indochina. French politicians, Right, Center, and Left, refused to give up their empire. De Gaulle began in 1945 the failed attempt to reconquer Indochina. Socialists such as prime minister Guy Mollet, who later dispatched France's task force to Suez, sought at least to hold Algeria. The French army, miserably defeated by the *Wehrmacht* in 1940, committed its soul to victory in Indochina. But it failed at Dien Bien Phu (see p. 896), and the survivors returned in 1954 convinced that the Fourth Republic's politicians had stabbed the army in the back: "*On nous a fait le coup*" ("They shafted us").

In November 1954, Algerian rebels who took the name of the National Liberation Front (FLN) attacked French settlers and police stations. The war that followed was both colonial and civil; it destroyed the Fourth Republic and created an Algerian nation. For Algeria was not simply a colony. Its population included, in addition to 140,000 Jews and a swiftly growing Moslem population of 9 million, slightly more than 1 million European settlers, the *pieds-noirs* ("black-feet"): privileged immigrants from France, Spain, Italy, Malta. Administratively, Algeria was part of France.

France reacted to the Algerian revolt by reinforcing its army there, bombing

Apartheid defied (South Africa, 1970).

Moslem villages, and cutting its commitments elsewhere. It gave Tunisia and Morocco their independence in 1956. The FLN, with some arms from outside but more captured from the French, soon found a winning strategy. At Philippeville in August 1955, FLN guerrillas and Arab crowds killed some 70 *pieds-noirs*; the French obligingly killed more than 1,200 Moslems in reprisals. FLN assassination teams sought out and eliminated all Moslems who maintained contacts with the French. FLN enforcers amputated the noses of Moslems who smoked tobacco, a French monopoly. The FLN divided the European and Moslem communities with a river of blood; that polarization gave the FLN domination of the Algerian "camp."

By 1955–56, the two communities were at war. *Pieds-noirs* launched vengeful "rat-hunts" against any and all Moslems, even those who had nothing to do with the insurgents. FLN time bombs shredded young Europeans in the cafés of the once-pleasant city of Algiers. To end the bloodshed, the Fourth Republic abdicated to the army. In January 1957 it called in the *paras*, the pride of the army, and made them secret policemen. In the ensuing "Battle of Algiers" the paratroops took over the Arab quarters, swept up suspects at random, tortured them with electric shock and water, and gradually tracked down the FLN bomb networks. Many thousands of Algerian suspects simply "disappeared."

Torture won the Battle of Algiers but helped lose the war. In France, intellectuals of the Left but also of the Center and the Right denounced the army. Officers resigned in disgust. FLN spokesmen abroad and states sympathetic to the FLN—including the United States—denounced French methods. And the civilian ministers who had ordered the army to win by any and all means were already

seeking negotiations with the FLN. The army had vowed that *this* time it would win; if winning required the removal of the politicians before they "betrayed" the army, so be it. In May 1958, as *pied-noir* and military plots simmered, the theater commander in Algeria, General Raoul Salan, demanded that Charles de Gaulle be recalled to power.

De Gaulle came once more, as he had in 1940–45, to save France. But to the fury of the army and of the *pieds-noirs*, he soon gave signs of a hidden agenda. In 1958–59 the army decimated what remained of the FLN in the countryside and sought to win Moslem loyalty with promises

Africa and Southeast Asia in 1988

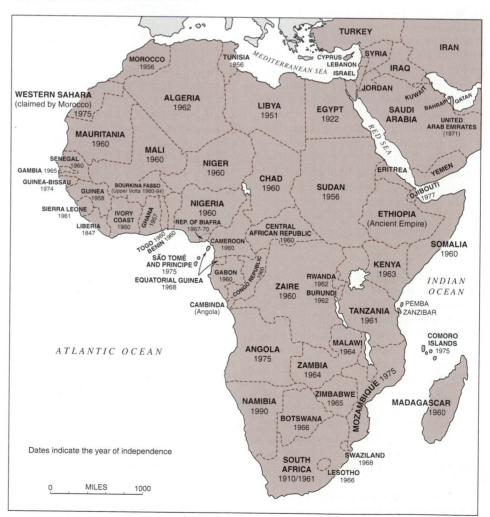

Dates indicate the year of independence

0   MILES   1000

of "integration." More Moslems, indeed, fought for France than against it. But the FLN maintained its political organization and its claim to represent the Moslem majority. At last it began to dawn on the French that winning through "integration" would mean a large and ever-growing Moslem presence in the French parliament; the Moslem birthrate was ten times that of the *pieds-noirs*. De Gaulle, with perfect timing, said the magic word in a speech of September 1959: "self-determination."

Pieds-noirs and army reacted. In 1961 the high command in Algiers, the *paras*, and the Foreign Legion revolted against de Gaulle as they had revolted against the Fourth Republic. But de Gaulle held fast. He appealed by radio to the half million draftees in Algeria and convinced the generals that they were isolated. The Algiers *Putsch* collapsed. In 1962, despite a *pied-noir* terrorist campaign and an uprising in the European quarter of Algiers, de Gaulle achieved a negotiated settlement. In effect, he conceded Algerian independence unconditionally, and left the *pieds-noirs* to choose "the suitcase or the coffin." Most chose the suitcase.

The Algerian war was traumatic for France, and still more so for the Algerians, who suffered the vast majority of the war's million or so casualties. It demonstrated the lengths to which communities driven by nationalism would go to defend or assert control of territory. It also stripped France of its African empire. During the course of the war, de Gaulle gave independence to almost all of France's colonies in sub-Saharan Africa: Guinea in 1958, and Cameroon, Chad, the Central African Republic, Congo-Brazzaville, Dahomey, Gabon, Ivory Coast, Mali, Niger, Senegal, and Togo in 1960.

Holland, Belgium, Portugal

The lesser empires of Holland and Belgium passed more quietly than did that of France. The Dutch found a "Republic of Indonesia" barring their return to the East Indies in 1945. Its leader was Achmet Sukarno, a charismatic nationalist who had collaborated with the Japanese to gain In-

Chaos in the Congo, 1963: Government paratroopers chase a mutinous policeman.

donesian independence. Four years of intermittent negotiations and "police actions" by the Dutch armed forces ultimately led—under U.S. pressure—to an agreement in November 1949 that granted independence. The Dutch kept only West Irian (the Dutch half of New Guinea) until Sukarno seized it in 1962–63.

The Belgians gave the most spectacular example of irresponsible decolonization. Their Congo empire, which the Berlin Conference of 1884–85 had assigned to King Leopold, had long been a byword for relentless brutality. Its rubber plantations, worked by native forced labor, were the subject of international protest even before the First World War. And the Belgian state, which took the colony over from Leopold's private Congo Company, did far less than other colonizers to create a Western-educated elite. When the approaching independence of the neighboring French Congo (Congo Republic) inspired nationalist riots, the Belgians panicked, packed up, and left in mid-1960. The Congolese army mutinied. A multi-cornered civil war and massacres of both tribal enemies and whites followed. Belgian mining companies hired mercenaries to hold the copper-rich province of Katanga. It took four years and 20,000 United Nations troops to restore even a semblance of order. The ultimate victor was the head of the Congolese army, Joseph Mobuto, who established a corrupt but durable dictatorship in 1966 and changed the country's name to Zaire.

Portugal's colonies were the first European seaborne empire; they were also the last. The Portuguese military-clerical dictatorship of Antonio Salazar (1932–68) lost its Indian enclave of Goa to an unprovoked Indian attack in 1961. In Africa—in Angola, Mozambique, and the west African mini-colony of Guinea-Bissau—Portugal chose to fight. But the commitment of 150,000 troops from the early 1960s until 1974 bled Portugal's already backward economy. In the end, Salazar gave way to a less-effective successor. The Portuguese army, politicized by its long struggle in Africa, overthrew the government in Lisbon in 1974 and dismantled Portugal's empire.

A bloody scramble followed. Indonesia invaded the Portuguese island of East Timor and killed as much as a third of its almost 700,000 people. In Angola, Portugal's withdrawal led to the flight of most of the remaining white settlers, economic collapse, civil war between rival groups, and intervention by the Soviet Union, Cuba, and South Africa (see p. 950). In Mozambique, the Marxist-Leninist *Frelimo* ("Front for the Liberation of Mozambique") of Samora Machel took power. In Guinea-Bissau, the Lisbon-educated Amilcar Cabral, the most skillful of Portugal's opponents, built a movement that achieved independence in 1973–74. But by then Cabral himself had perished by assassination, a victim of rivalries within his own movement. As he had foreseen, the real test of that movement—and of the rulers of all "new nations"—came after independence.

Losers and Winners, 1965–90

The two halves of the table illustrate the striking differences in rates of economic growth within the non-Western world. Some states stagnated or regressed. Others grew with startling rapidity.

	1990 population (millions)	Per capita GNP (1990 dollars)	Average annual growth rate in per capita GNP, 1965–90 (percent)	Life expectancy at birth, 1990	Adult illiteracy, 1990 (percent)
Tanzania	24.5	110	−0.2	48	54
Ethiopia	51.2	120	−0.2	48	na
Somalia	7.8	120	−0.1	48	76
Zaire	37.3	220	−2.2	52	28
Uganda	16.3	220	−2.4	47	52
Madagascar	11.7	230	−1.9	51	20
Niger	7.7	310	−2.4	45	72
Bolivia	7.2	630	−0.7	60	23
Jamaica	2.4	1,500	−1.3	73	2
Libya	4.5	1,760	−3.0	62	36
Argentina	32.3	2,370	−0.3	71	5
Venezuela	19.7	2,560	−1.0	70	12
China (PRC)	1,133.7	370	5.8	70	27
Indonesia	178.2	570	4.5	62	23
Cameroon	11.7	960	3.0	57	46
Thailand	55.8	1,420	4.4	66	7
South Korea	42.8	5,400	7.1	71	4
Singapore	3.0	11,160	6.5	74	na
Hong Kong	5.8	11,490	6.2	78	na

From World Bank, World Development Report 1992 *(New York: Oxford University Press, 1992), pp. 218–19.*

AFTER INDEPENDENCE: THE "THIRD WORLD" DIVIDED

In the 1960s, the poorest of the newly independent states had annual per capita levels of gross national product (GNP)—the best indicator of a society's overall wealth or poverty—of 100 or fewer 1965 dollars. Yet some very poor states grew swiftly, and some richer ones stagnated or regressed. Breaking the non-Western world into its major component parts—the Chinese cultural area, south Asia and its island offshoots, the Islamic Middle East, Latin America, and Africa south of the Sahara—makes that wide variety of outcomes easier to understand.

Confucian East Asia

Culturally, China had influenced its neighbors—Vietnam to the south and Korea and Japan to the northeast—from the beginning of recorded history. The Confucian pattern that China exemplified placed a high value on literacy, hierarchy, and the subordination of the individual to the group. Those qualities made east Asia's densely populated rice-growing economies work. But that pattern may initially have retarded economic growth in China by its very success and durability. Japan, which rose to the nineteenth-century Western challenge most readily, was always less Confucian than China, thanks to its hereditary warrior ruling caste. China and its neighbors, highly developed cultures with an ethos of literacy, duty, and relentless hard work, were nevertheless the best equipped for economic growth of all the non-Western world.

But politics and geography imposed differing outcomes. Japan's small size helped its consolidation as a modern state. And a fortunate combination of centralization (the Tokugawa shogunate and the traditions of the Imperial house) and decentralization (the "feudal" domains) gave innovators both a political and military vehicle for change and an opportunity to seize power. In China, the empire's unwieldiness, the rigidity of its Manchu rulers, and its choice of armed resistance rather than accommodation to the "barbarians" all led to a collapse that seemed to follow the cyclical pattern of dynastic decline hallowed by Chinese tradition. The immense Taiping rebellion of the 1850s and 1860s foreshadowed the far greater upheaval of the twentieth century: four decades (1911–53) of devastating civil war, invasion by Japan, and war in Korea against the United States.

Mao Zedong and his Communist Party mobilized the peasantry by appealing to their land hunger and roused the urban intellectuals by offering a vehicle for nationalism. That was a winning combination. But Mao, intoxicated with revolutionary messianism, soon sought to pioneer in economic development as he had in adapting Marxism-Leninism to a peasant society. In two disastrous experiments, the "Great Leap Forward" (1958–59) and the "Great Proletarian Cultural Revolution" (1966–69), he almost destroyed both the Chinese economy and his own Party. "Politics in command!" was Mao's guiding principle; the death by famine of as many as 25 million in the "three lean years" of 1959–61 was the result. The forcing of China's peasantry into "communes" and a crash industrialization

Why Maoism?

Lu Xun (Lu Hsün, 1881–1936), China's greatest twentieth century short-story writer and social critic, wrote bitter pages in the 1920s that suggest some of the ingredients of Mao's success.

It has never been granted to the Chinese people that they are human beings; at best, they have been raised to the level of slaves, and this is still the case today. In the past, they were often lower than slaves. The Chinese masses are neutral; in time of war they do not know what faction they belong to, and in fact they belong to any faction. Come the rebels: considering the people as being the government's, they loot and murder. Comes the regular army: instead of recognizing its own, it loots and murders too, as if the people belonged to the rebels. At this point, the only wish of the population is to find a Master, a Master who would deign to accept them as his people—no, not even that—who would deign to accept them as his cattle. The people would be ready to eat grass if necessary; all they ask is that the Master point out in what direction they must trot. . . .

As a rule, after each period of anarchy, when chaos reaches its climax, some personality appears—more powerful, more clever, more cunning (sometimes a foreigner)—to unify the empire and grant it some measure of order. . . .

In the end, the simplest and most adequate way of describing the history of China would be to distinguish between two types of periods: (1) the periods when the people wish in vain to enjoy a stable slave condition; and (2) the periods when the people manage to enjoy a stable slave condition. The alternation of these two states is what our old scholars called "the cycle of chaos and order."

From Simon Leys (Pierre Ryckmans), Chinese Shadows *(New York: Penguin Books, 1978), pp. 200–201.*

based on amateur backyard blast furnaces reduced the economy to a shambles. Mao's comrades then removed him from direct control of Party and state while retaining him as a living symbol of the Revolution and of the Party's legitimacy.

But Mao was not ready to be embalmed and placed on display like the dead Lenin. With the help of Jiang Qing, the former Shanghai film actress who had become his second wife, and of the Red Army political leader Lin Biao, Mao took power back in 1966 through a coup in Beijing. Then he mobilized China's youth for a unique all-out struggle against his *own* Party and government bureaucracy. Only rebellion could ensure the "continued development of the Revolution towards communism."

Mao's "Great Proletarian Cultural Revolution" of 1966–69 delighted revolutionary enthusiasts in the West; to China, it brought chaos. The force behind it was the sudden release from totalitarian control that Mao offered his millions of youthful and fanatical "Red Guards": "To rebel is justified!" He urged them to take charge of China's destiny, and of their own. They took him at his word, and beat and murdered foreigners, high Party figures, government bureaucrats, and one another. The economy again threatened to disintegrate. Perhaps half a million Chinese perished in Red Guard purges and widespread fighting. The army ultimately restored order by force; Mao himself lost his grip on power with increasing age and died in 1976.

The final defeat of the radicals followed swiftly. Deng Xiaoping, the most cunning of the Party leaders who had attempted to cage Mao in the early 1960s, outmaneuvered Mao's designated successor, Hua Guofeng. With the apparent toleration of Deng and his faction, urban intellectuals posted slogans and essays on a "Democracy Wall" in Beijing in 1979. Deng then exploited the unrest to oust Hua in 1980–81.

In the saddle at last at the age of 76, Deng impartially destroyed both the democratic dissidents and the radical "Gang of Four," Jiang Qing and her three principal allies. He also hastened the "de-Maoization" of the economy. China's survival as a great power and the Party's own legitimacy demanded the adoption of the capitalist methods pioneered by China's small neighbors, Hong Kong, Singapore, South Korea, and the hated "Guomindang remnants" on Taiwan (see p. 936). China's peasants now received the right to sell their surpluses in free markets. The state leased back the farmland it had swallowed up during Mao's collectivization drives. Factory managers gained some measure of freedom from central planning. Around Hong Kong and other coastal cities, huge "free enterprise zones" arose to attact foreign investors. China's GNP growth in the 1980s and early 1990s surged to between 8 and 12 percent per year, recovering much of the ground that Mao had lost and giving China, by some estimates, the world's third largest economy.

Yet the Party retained control of heavy industry, and relaxed its grip on the rest of the economy only with great reluctance. It also soon found itself—like autocrats elsewhere—caught between the contradictory requirements of economic growth and those of political self-preservation. Deng's first choice as successor, Hu Yaobang, raised the hopes of China's intellectuals. In 1985 he denounced Mao for having plunged China into chaos through "radical leftist nonsense." In December 1986 the students of China took the new leadership at its word and demonstrated massively for Western-style democratic freedoms. The police contained the demonstrations.

Deng removed Hu Yaobang and party zealots campaigned against the pestilence of "bourgeois liberalism" spreading into China from the West. But Deng nevertheless held to his economic policies, despite inflation, corruption, a growing regional split between the booming coastal cities and the poor inland countryside, and the dangerously close contact between ordinary Chinese and Westerners that swift economic growth required.

A further explosion inevitably followed in April–June 1989. Beijing crowds of as many as a million people repeatedly

The cult of Mao: National Day celebrations, 1966.

demanded reforms. Students occupied Tienanmen Square ("The Square of Heavenly Peace") at the center of the capital and refused to leave until the government granted democracy. Deng knew that unless he crushed this open defiance, his authority would collapse. He brought in army units manned by grim-faced peasants from remote provinces and smashed the students with machine-gun fire and tanks on June 4, 1989. Demonstrators who survived joined the 15 million inmates of China's GULAG. A brief international outcry followed, but the pace of foreign investment scarcely slackened.

The Party had covertly abandoned Marxism, but not Leninism. Deng was clearly a believer in Lenin's axiom that "a regime that is prepared to use limitless terror cannot be overthrown." Yet in the long run, the course that Deng had set for China offered no relief from the contradiction between Leninist autocracy and capitalist economic revolution. At best, his successors might hope to preside over China's evolution into an unstable capitalist authoritarian regime like that of South Korea or Taiwan. But more and greater bloodshed—internal and possibly external—seemed equally likely.

North Korea and Vietnam, although they began under foreign rule rather than under informal Western domination, followed the Stalinist-Maoist pattern. The North Korean Communist "monarchy" of the aged Kim Il-Sung, who in 1984 appointed as his successor his son Kim Jong-Il, remained into the 1990s one of the world's most closed and Stalinist states. Its army remained poised to attack South Korea, its clandestine atomic bomb program threatened all of northeast Asia, and its only noteworthy export was weaponry—including primitive V-2 style ballistic missiles—and advice on war and terrorism to states as far afield as Iran, Iraq, Libya, Syria, Zimbabwe, Grenada, and Nicaragua. Vietnam imposed on South Vietnam after April 1975 the same Stalinist system that had already proven an economic failure in the North. The result was a decade of economic stagnation and hunger; politics and economics together led

---

Democracy Wall: A Chinese Dissident Speaks   1978

Wei Jingsheng was the most daring of those who wrote on the wall in Beijing; he then disappeared into prison. His 1978 essay, "Democracy, the Fifth Modernization," shows the bitterness of the generation that suffered the full force of Mao's "Great Proletarian Cultural Revolution."

Today, it is perfectly irrelevant to try to determine the balance account of Mao Zedong's achievements and mistakes. . . . The question which the people should now be asking is this: without Mao Zedong's personal despotism, could China ever have fallen as low as we see her today? Or are we to believe that Chinese people are stupid, or lazy, or devoid of any desire to improve their lot? We know very well that this is not the case. Then what happened? The answer is obvious: the Chinese have taken a path they should never have entered; if they followed it, it is because a despot, who knew how shrewdly to peddle his trash, simply took them for a ride. . . .

German fascism, of stinking memory, was actually called "national socialism." It too was led by a tyrant; it too told the people to tighten their belts; it too deceived the people, assuring them: "You are a great nation!" Above all, it too suppressed basic democracy, because it clearly saw that democracy was for it the greatest danger, the most frightful enemy. Stalin and Hitler could shake hands and sign the famous German-Soviet pact, and on this basis the German and Russian peoples were condemned to suffer slavery and misery. Do we, too, need to continue suffering such slavery and misery? If we wish to break away from it, there is only one way: democracy.

From Simon Leys, The Chairman's New Clothes: Mao and the Cultural Revolution *(London: Allison and Busby Limited, 1981), pp. 260–61.*

---

to a flood of refugees, the million or million and a half "boat people" who risked death from drowning or from Thai pirates rather than remain in Vietnam. A younger generation of leaders came to power in 1986 and announced a sort of NEP (see p. 829): a grudging latitude for private enterprise "within the socialist system." Yet as late as 1988 much of the North suffered famine. Despite a modest economic upturn and foreign capitalist investment in the early 1990s, no loosening of Leninist party control seemed in sight.

The individual against the party-state: A lone Chinese democrat pleads with a platoon of tanks on the day after the Tienanmen massacre, June 1989.

By contrast, the non-Communist states of the Chinese cultural area of east Asia and southeast Asia prospered mightily. Malaysia, politically Malay but with an economy under the control of its large overseas Chinese minority, grew at a per capita rate of more than 4 percent. Thailand, the one south or southeast Asian state that had avoided colonial occupation, grew at a comparable rate, thanks to its Chinese minority and relatively literate population. It benefited both from an infusion of dollars during the Vietnam War and a subsequent boom in Pacific trade.

In South Korea, Japanese colonialism (1905–45) and United States patronage helped provide an industrial infrastructure and a Western-educated and technologically expert elite capable of swiftly following Japan's example. Politically, South Korea enjoyed enforced stability. The harsh domination after 1948 of a Harvard-educated politician, Syngman Rhee, gave way in 1960–61 to almost thirty years of military dictatorship. In 1986–87 the new

middle class that Korea's industrialization had created began to demand political rights; the authoritarian solutions of the past no longer worked. The military loosened its grip and permitted an election. The military candidate won, but offered an increasing measure of democratization; the presidency passed to a civilian in 1991–93.

A similar absence of democracy, but likewise mellowed by a gradual loosening of single-party or British colonial control, accompanied the spectacular per capita growth rates of culturally Chinese and economically capitalist Taiwan, Singapore, and Hong Kong. Their economic growth outstripped all other contenders including Japan, and suggested in miniature the world-shaking potential of China itself.

South Asia and the Islands

Four of the lands of south Asia—India, Pakistan, Bangladesh (East Pakistan until

1971), and Sri Lanka (Ceylon until 1972)—were closely linked by geography and history. They were the ultimate successors, after the British interlude, to the Mughal empire. To the east lay Burma, a borderland between south Asian and Chinese culture. Indonesia, dominated by Islam, and the Philippines, a compound of Malay, Islamic, Spanish, and U.S. influences, were unique, but their village-based societies were similar in many ways to the pattern of south Asia. They were Asian but not Confucian.

India and Pakistan remained locked in struggle after 1947–48. Pakistan, split between the dominant Punjab to the west and East Bengal to the east, failed to consolidate itself. When Gandhi's violent successor, Jawaharlal Nehru, quarreled with China over border areas in Tibet in 1961–62, the Chinese army gave India a sharp and persuasive defeat. Fighting between India and Pakistan erupted once more in 1965–66, and the Soviet Union, seeking favor with India as a counterweight to Mao's increasingly hostile China, brokered a compromise. In 1970–71, when the East Bengalis sought autonomy from Pakistan, the generals who ruled West Pakistan answered with massacres. Under Nehru's combative daughter, Indira Gandhi (unrelated to Mohandas Gandhi either by blood or political philosophy), India went to war and swiftly dismembered Pakistan. East Bengal became independent Bangladesh. India was now supreme on the subcontinent and confirmed that status by exploding in 1974 what it whimsically described as a "peaceful nuclear device." Secret Pakistani acquisition of Western nuclear fuel technology and China's apparent gift in the early 1980s of a tested bomb design apparently evened the contest. Endless friction over Kashmir offered ready occasions for renewed war.

Yet despite the Indian-Pakistani wars and periodic ethnic-religious riots and massacres, economic growth in south Asia was steady, although post-colonial "socialist" red tape slowed growth in India until the 1990s. In per capita terms, India grew between 1965 and 1990 at a rate of 1.9 percent per year, Pakistan at 2.5 percent; Bangladesh, one of the world's poorest states, stagnated at .7 percent. In the north Indian plain, new strains of rice and wheat and the entrepreneurship of India's Sikh minority brought an agricultural "Green Revolution" that promised to give India self-sufficiency in food. A powerful industrial economy arose around Bombay and other cities. By the early 1990s a growing proportion of India's 850 million people had achieved a standard of living approaching that of southern Europe.

Pakistan, except for brief periods in the 1950s and 1970s, remained a military dictatorship with parliamentary trimmings. But India persisted for a time in the democratic traditions it had inherited from Britain. An attempt at dictatorship in 1975–77 by Indira Gandhi collapsed amid universal condemnation, although she returned with a parliamentary majority in 1980 after promising not to repeat the experiment. Her eventual downfall was the Sikh minority, whose extremists sought an independent Sikh state, "Khalistan," carved from the Punjab, India's agricultural heart. When heavily armed Sikh militants seized the Sikh Golden Temple at Amritsar in 1984, Indira Gandhi evicted them using the Indian army. Sikhs assassinated her in retaliation; Hindus then killed many thousands of Sikhs living in Hindu areas. Indira Gandhi's son Rajiv Gandhi, third and last of the Congress Party dynasty that Nehru founded, ruled as her successor until defeat in a 1989 election. Then he too died by assassination, blown up by Tamil guerrillas in revenge for Indian intervention in Sri Lanka (see the following paragraphs). And by the early 1990s, a Hindu radical nationalist movement had emerged as a contender for power. It offered India's 100 million Moslems a stark choice: "The cemetery or Pakistan." And it sought to force that choice on the Moslems by riot and massacre. Nationalism and religion seemed poised to destroy India's parliamentary experiment and tear the subcontinent apart.

To the south, Sri Lanka showed great promise. Its peoples were 60 percent literate at independence; its agricultural export economy grew rapidly until the 1960s. Then nationalism caught up with

Indira Gandhi (prime minister, 1966–77, 1980–84), daughter of Nehru and architect of India's hegemony over South Asia.

it. Alongside the majority Sinhalese, who were Buddhist in religion and made up 70 percent of the population, lived a Hindu Tamil minority that had originally immigrated from southern India. Under British rule, the two communities had lived together in relative peace. But the creation of an independent sovereign state in 1948 brought with it a struggle for mastery over that state. By the mid-1950s, Sinhalese politicians had imposed Sinhalese as the official language, and ideologues were proclaiming Sinhalese superiority as the descendants of conquerors from the north in the sixth century B.C.

The Tamils, and enterprising group that dominated commerce and the professions, responded first with riots and then, after 1983, with guerrilla war and demands for a separate Tamil state around the city of Jaffna in northern Sri Lanka. A cycle of terror and reprisal similar to that in Algeria after 1954 locked Sinhalese and Tamil nationalisms into seemingly irreconcilable conflict for land and power. Indian army intervention in 1987 to broker a peace in turn goaded the "Tamil Tiger" guerrillas to savage attacks on the Indians and to further massacres of Sinhalese civilians. Despite the war, Sri Lanka maintained a growth rate from 1980 to 1990 of 4 percent, but continued growth remained hostage to the possibility of further bloodshed.

To the east, Burma retreated into resentful isolation after independence; in 1974 its most durable leader, General Ne Win, proclaimed a non-aligned "Burmese Road to Socialism" that led to poverty for all except bureaucrats and black marketeers. In 1988 the military government, which had in the interim changed the country's name to "Myanmar," killed as many as 2,000 pro-democracy protesters. It then lost an election in 1990, but predictably failed to hand power over to the democrats. Despite a gradual opening of the economy to Japanese investment, Burma's cycle of poverty and government violence seemed likely to continue.

Indonesia, further south, enjoyed the massive advantage of oil. Sukarno ruled until the late 1960s and squandered that wealth on palaces, monuments, and mistresses. His successor, General Suharto, took power in the aftermath of the failed Communist coup of 1965 and the wholesale massacre of Communists that followed. His regime began to realize Indonesia's economic potential, thanks to close economic ties with Japan, but showed few signs of movement toward parliamentary government.

The Philippines suppressed a Communist insurgency after receiving independence in 1947, and then succumbed to military dictatorship under General Ferdinand Marcos (1965–86). A second and exceedingly bloody Communist insurgency followed. Marcos' power disintegrated after 1983, when his associates arranged the assassination of a key opponent, Benigno Aquino. When Marcos sought to steal the 1986 election, the dead man's widow, Corazon Aquino, took power in 1986 in a largely bloodless "people power" uprising backed by key army figures, the Catholic Church, U.S. public opinion, and the overwhelming majority of politically active Filipinos. Aquino's presidency was a qualified success, despite a series of military coup attempts and continued attacks by the Communist guerrillas of the New People's Army. But economic growth remained agonizingly slow.

The Islamic Middle East

Deep fissures divided the newly independent states of the Middle East from one another. The most important were two: the ideological and political antagonisms between different types of regime, and the envies and hatreds between states that lacked oil and those that had it. Hostility between tribes and between branches of Islam created further tensions both between and within the Middle Eastern states.

The region contained three main types of regime. First came the traditional monarchies and sheikdoms, usually based on Bedouin or other tribal loyalties: Saudi Arabia, Morocco, Jordan, the Gulf states from Kuwait to Oman, and the Iranian monarchy of the Pahlavi dynasty (1921–79). Egypt, Iraq, and Libya had also originally been monarchies—until military coups in 1952, 1958, and 1969 respectively. The second category was the "secular" states—Egypt, Syria, Iraq, Tunisia, Algeria, Libya. The Turkey of Kemal Atatürk provided the model: a military-dominated state dedicated to introducing Western technology and ideas. Like Turkey, most of the secular states tried to use the state bureaucracy as the chief motor of economic development. And most of them claimed to embody an "Arab socialism" that in practice meant deadening bureaucratic controls that fathered corruption and black markets. Finally, a third model, a revolutionary "Islamic Republic" based on Shiite Islam, arose in Iran after 1979 (see pp. 965–67).

Throughout the Cold War era, the Middle Eastern states tended to tilt in their foreign relations toward one of the two superpowers. Conservative states such as the traditional monarchies normally favored the United States. Roosevelt took over Britain's patronage of Saudi Arabia and of its oil in 1943–45—a relationship that endured. Morocco, under its durable monarch King Hassan II (1961–), also maintained close ties with Washington, as did moderate secular states such as Tunisia under Habib Bourguiba (1956–87) and Egypt after Anwar Sadat broke with Moscow in 1976. Algeria, "non-aligned" in rhetoric but less so in practice, also tended to tilt toward western Europe and the United States, valued customers for its natural gas and oil. Iran, until its 1978–79 revolution, posed as a bulwark of Western influence in the Gulf to mask its monarch's megalomaniacal ambitions.

The Soviets tended to recruit the most expansionist Middle Eastern states—Nasser's Egypt, Libya after the revolution of Colonel Muammar al-Qaddafi in 1969, Syria under the merciless Hafez al-Assad (1970–), the Iraq of Assad's equally remorseless counterpart Saddam Hussein (1979–), and the Marxist-Leninist "People's Democratic Republic of Yemen." Lavish shipments of arms, the Soviet Union's only major industrial export, along with numerous military and "police" advisers, cemented these ties. Yet Soviet influence was sometimes brief. Moscow never regained the position in the region

that it had held before the loss of Egypt in 1972–76 (see p. 964).

The possession or lack of oil also divided the Middle Eastern states into two groups. Saudi Arabia, Libya, Algeria, Iran, Iraq, Kuwait, the Gulf sheikdoms, and even Egypt after its recovery of Sinai in 1982 all enjoyed the bounty of oil in varying degrees. After 1973, when the Arab and other oil-producing states of the OPEC cartel more than doubled the real price of oil within a year, that bounty increased markedly. But the newly rich were slow to convert their oil wealth into modern economies. The small populations of Saudi Arabia and the sheikdoms were still in part wedded to their desert traditions. Some of the secular states, such as Egypt and Algeria, had some oil but not enough. Others smothered initiative beneath layers of bureaucracy or tried to ban enterprise entirely, as did Qaddafi's Libya.

Religious and ethnic fractures likewise divided the Islamic Middle East. Iran, after its 1978–79 revolution, emerged as the world's only Shiite state; religion and Iranian nationalism combined to set it at odds with its Sunni Arab neighbors. Iraq, although Arab in population, was mostly Shiite in religion; the cleavage between Shiite and Sunni was a major source of internal weakness. Turkey, Iraq, Iran, and even Syria had sizable armed minorities of Kurds, a mountain warrior people who had fought all their neighbors for more than 2,000 years. Syria contained large Christian communities, and its officer corps and rulers were Alawites, a small Shiite sect that ruthlessly dominated the Sunni majority.

In Lebanon, five major communities struggled for mastery. The last census (1932) showed that 29 percent of the population was Maronite Christian, 22 percent Sunni Moslem, 20 percent Shiite Moslem, and 7 percent Druze, a heretical and combative Moslem sect. The French, on their departure in 1946, left a parliamentary regime that gave the presidency to the Maronites, the prime ministership to the Sunni, and the office of army chief of staff to the Druzes. But demography soon shifted the religious-ethnic balance, and a fifth group, the Palestinian refugees, entered the arena

after 1970. By 1984, the Shiites made up an estimated 31 percent of the population, the Maronites 25 percent, the Sunni 20 percent, and the Druzes only 6 percent. By 1975 the PLO's creation of a state within a state, at war with Israel, ignited a religious-ethnic civil war throughout Lebanon that continued, despite Israeli and Syrian intervention, until 1991.

Finally, nationalism divided rather than united the Middle Eastern states, even though all except Iran and Turkey were Arab. Efforts at union between Arab states, such as Nasser's attempt to absorb Syria into a "United Arab Republic" (1958–61) or Qaddafi's federations with Egypt (1972–73), Tunisia (1974), and Morocco (1984–86), all collapsed. The rulers of Syria, for instance, had no desire to become a mere province of Egypt; they possessed their own national consciousness and sense of mission, the creation of a "Greater Syria" that included Lebanon and Palestine. Nasser also failed to subjugate the Arabs of North Yemen between 1962 and 1968 despite massive use of Soviet tanks and mustard gas.

The multiple divisions between sects, tribes, and states tended to stunt the states of the region both politically and econom-

ically. And the state machines and armies of the secular states also provided a classic arena for assassinations and coups. In the absence of settled political traditions and long-established legitimacy, as elsewhere in the "Third World," power grew out of the barrel of a gun. Those with the guns and the smattering of Western technical knowledge needed to use them saw no reason why they should not rule the state and direct the economy. The resulting one-party regimes ranged from the merely inefficient (Egypt, Tunisia, Algeria) to the terrifying (Libya, Syria, Iraq). Hafez al-Assad of Syria and his Soviet advisers dealt with Sunni unrest in 1982 by shelling flat much of the city of Hama and killing as many as 30,000. The monarchies tended to be less aggressive, somewhat less oppressive, and better economic performers than the secular states—but economic development undermined the traditions on which their stability rested. No lasting order to replace the Ottoman Empire or the Anglo-French domination that had followed it seemed in sight, and the rise of Islamic militance generated new and savage conflicts.

The Three Latin Americas

The "new nations" of Latin America had received their independence between 1811 and 1839, long before the post-1945 waves of decolonization. Yet the colonial conquest that had created them had marked them forever. Spain had ruled through a centralized bureaucracy that had prevented the Creoles, native-born of Spanish descent, from gaining experience in self-government—in sharp contrast to the pattern of the British settlement colonies from North America to Australia. After independence, narrow landed oligarchies and a disproportionately powerful land-owning Church had taken Spain's place as the rulers. And Spain had imposed on its colonial economies a pattern similar to that in politics—centralized controls and ruinous taxation that stunted enterprise. Anarchy and despotism, economic stagnation or regression had in most cases followed independence (see pp. 703–4).

Traditional monarchs and secular rulers: King Faisal of Saudi Arabia (1964–75, *above*) and (*below, left to right*) a 1970 encounter between Gaafar Mohammed Nimeiri of the Sudan (1969–85), Muammar al-Qaddafi of Libya (1969–), and Nasser of Egypt (1954–70).

But not all of the new states suffered the same misfortunes; Latin America was almost as divided as the Islamic Middle East or the Third World itself. With the exception of miscellaneous small states such as Guyana and Suriname, the former British and Dutch colonies between Venezuela and Brazil, the states of the region fell into three principal categories. First were those with a Creole or European majority: Costa Rica, Uruguay, and Argentina. They began as classic settler economies: Europe transported to the New World. They thrived throughout the nineteenth and early twentieth centuries on commodity exports such as coffee, beef, hides, wool, and grain. But—as elsewhere—politics intervened to decide their fate in the post-1945 world market.

Costa Rica's parliamentary regime rested on a base of prosperous small landowners, and maintained an enviable degree of stability and prosperity after the late 1940s. In Uruguay, however, a drop in world commodity prices and an economy crippled by bureaucratic bloat brought stagnation and massive inflation by the 1960s. Soon a Marxist-Leninist urban guerrilla movement, the "Tupamaro National Liberation Front," arose among the disaffected young of the upper classes. It sought to destroy parliamentary democracy by provoking the state to violent reprisals that would "unmask" its "true nature" as an organ of repression in the service of domestic "capitalism" and foreign "neocolonialism." The Tupamaros duly brought down the parliamentary regime in 1973–74. The military dictatorship that followed erased the guerrillas with torture and "disappearances." Parliamentary democracy had perished, but implacable Rightist dictatorship—not the Marxist millennium—had replaced it. Civilian government returned hesitantly in 1985.

Argentina traveled a road similar to Uruguay's, but even more savage. Its settler population had been overwhelmingly Spanish and Italian, with large German, British, French, and Jewish communities; in 1900 the country had appeared poised to become another Australia. But the Great Depression ended what little political stability it had enjoyed. Oligarchic military regimes gave way in 1944–46 to the populist dictatorship of Colonel Juan Perón, admirer of Mussolini and husband of the charismatic Eva (Evita) Duarte, patron saint of Argentina's "shirtless" dispossessed. An army coup destroyed Perón's regime in 1955, but his Peronist party lived on as Argentina's most powerful political force. Although it was too weak and disunited to overthrow the military, it was strong enough to make Argentina ungovernable until the army wearily permitted Perón to return to power in 1973. Then Perón died in 1974. His third wife, Isabel Martínez Perón, a former cabaret dancer, sought to rule with advice from the Peronist party and her astrologer. Inflation and Tupamaro-style Leftist guerrillas reduced Argentina to a shambles.

In 1976 the military again seized power and destroyed the guerrillas with torture and mass murder, dumping planeloads of drugged prisoners into the South Atlantic. Between 5,000 and 20,000 suspects "disappeared." The military killed with such abandon that fear of retribution then locked it into power. Finally the inglorious defeat of its 1982 attempt to seize the Falkland Islands from Britain (see p. 960) led to its fall, and to elections that returned Raul Alfonsín, a genuine democrat, as president. Alfonsín ruled until hyperinflation brought on by economic mismanagement chased him from office in 1989. His successor, the moderate Peronist Carlos Menem, sold off many inefficient state industries, balanced the budget, and by 1992 had tamed inflation. Argentina, for the first time in decades, seemed ready for economic growth. It was time; between 1965 to 1990 Argentina's GNP per capita had declined at an average annual rate of −0.3 percent.

The second category of Latin American states were the former colonies of Spain with a majority of Indians or *mestizos*—those of mixed blood. Of these states, Chile had the largest Creole population, at around 25 percent. There and in most other states from Bolivia through Central America to Mexico, large *mestizo* or Indian groups remained permanently excluded from a share in power. In Peru

Central and South America in 1993

and Bolivia, between 30 and 55 percent of the population consisted of Indians speaking Quechua or Aymara rather than Spanish; literacy in many of these states was relatively low.

They nevertheless traveled diverse paths. Mexico and Ecuador, thanks in part to their oilfields, enjoyed relatively high rates of growth from the 1950s to the 1980s, although Mexico's ruling "Institutional Revolutionary Party" (PRI) slowed the economy through corruption, state ownership of industry, and unpredictable banking policies. Growth accelerated after the disputed 1988 presidential election of a Harvard-trained economist, Carlos Salinas de Gortari. Salinas sold off wasteful state-owned firms, loosened controls on foreign investment, and in 1992 defied Mexican nationalist sentiment by joining the United States and Canada in the North American Free Trade Agreement (NAFTA). Mexico seemed close at last to sustained economic growth.

Colombia also prospered relative to many other Latin American states, despite a long-running "*violencia*" or permanent civil war between political parties, Leftist guerrillas, and cocaine lords. But oil did not save Venezuela, nor did copper save Chile. Generals ruled Venezuela for much of the twentieth century; the most conspicuous and brutal were Juan Vincente Gomez (1908–35) and Marcos Peréz Jiménez (1952–58). Then a succession of weak parliamentary regimes nationalized more and more of the economy. A drop in world oil prices after 1982 cut Venezuela's per capita GNP by a quarter, and triggered repeated riots and military coup attempts.

The government of Chile, the oldest stable parliamentary regime on the continent, collapsed in 1973. For many years its politics had been deadlocked between a Marxist Left, a Catholic Christian Democratic center, and a conservative Right. In 1969 the candidate of the Left, Salvador Allende, took power as president on the strength of a plurality of 36.3 percent, less than two points ahead of his closest rival. Despite promises to the contrary—made to opposition parties that represented a majority of Chileans—Allende attempted to transform the economy in a "socialist" direction. He also invited Fidel Castro for a long and lavish state visit. Both the Nixon administration and the Chilean middle classes objected.

Allende's policies produced massive inflation and economic paralysis—in an economy already vulnerable because it rested on one commodity, copper, and on inefficient protected industry. Politically, Allende remained intent on a Marxist revolution for which he had no mandate; enthusiasts from the Latin American and European Left flocked to Chile. In September 1973, with the support of the Right and even of some Christian Democrats, the armed forces rocketed and stormed the presidential palace, and rounded up the Left. Allende apparently killed himself with a treasured machine pistol, a gift of Castro. Allende's supporters accused Nixon, Henry Kissinger, and the CIA of complicity in the coup. Washington had indeed subsidized Allende's political opponents and had tried in 1970 to provoke the Chilean army to remove him. But no firm evidence of U.S. involvement in the 1973 coup surfaced, despite lengthy congressional investigations. In any event, the generals and admirals who overthrew Allende had a domestic mandate.

Their leader, General Augusto Pinochet, soon converted that mandate into one of Latin America's most ruthless dictatorships. In the months after the coup, the military shot between 3,000 and 10,000 Leftists. Too late, the Christian Democrats and moderate Rightists realized that Pinochet, like Allende, was a man with a mission. But his mission was to eradicate Chilean Marxism rather than bring it to power. Pinochet privatized the state-owned firms, put down protests with unyielding brutality, and left the presidency on his own terms in 1988, while remaining commander of the armed forces. His Christian Democratic successor, Patricio Aylwin, reaped the benefits of Pinochet's economic reforms.

To the north, in Peru and Bolivia, military regimes predominated until the early 1980s. The Peruvian military, which ruled from 1968 to 1980, adopted Third Worldist notions of economic development, and nationalized banks and foreign firms. The result was prolonged stagnation. The civilian governments that followed presided over hyperinflation and an implacable insurgency of Quechua-speaking Indians led by university-educated Maoists, the *Sendero Luminoso* or "Shining Path" to revolution. *Sendero* grew swiftly, thanks

The face of military dictatorship: Augusto Pinochet (1986).

to Peru's economic failure and the socio-economic chasm between the Indian population and Peruvians of Spanish descent. In 1992 President Alberto Fujimori imposed a dictatorship that he described as a temporary measure against the guerrillas. The capture of *Sendero*'s leader, Abimael Guzmán Reynoso, a former philosophy professor also known as "the Fourth Sword of Marxism," gave the government a momentary advantage. But Peru's situation remained precarious.

Bolivia too acquired a civilian government in the 1980s, but showed little sign of stability or economic growth. The Central American states of Guatemala, El Salvador, and Nicaragua, already among the poorest in Latin America, suffered in the 1980s from civil wars between landowners and peasants, Creoles and Indians, Left and Right—and extremely low or negative per capita growth rates.

Finally, the largest of all Latin American states, Brazil, was in a category by itself. Its ethnic mixture, a unique compound of Portuguese, Africans, Italians, Germans, Slavs, East Indians, Japanese, Chinese, and native Indians, defies categorization; blacks remained at the bottom of the social scale, although color lines were less sharp than in Spanish America. Above all, Portugal had left its colonial subjects far more freedom for local and individual initiative than had Spain. The result was a society capable of growth—despite the extremes of wealth and poverty common elsewhere in Latin America, foreign debts of $122 billion (1990), a bloated state bureaucracy, repeated bouts of hyperinflation, and political turmoil that led to military rule between 1964 and 1985 and the dismissal of a president for corruption in 1992. By the 1980s, Brazil had become the world's tenth-largest economy. Its per capita growth rate from 1965 to 1990 was 3.3 percent, and its industries had achieved dramatic export successes. But political and economic mismanagement could yet slow or halt development.

The Sorrows of Africa

No wretchedness in Latin America compared with the misery found between the fringes of the Sahara and the Cape of Good Hope. Of the 23 states in the world with populations of more than 1 million and negative per capita growth between 1965 and 1990, 15 were in sub-Saharan Africa. The region's 450 million people produce roughly as much annually as Belgium's 10 million.

Africa's states were poorest of all the "new nations" at independence. All suffered from a variety of disabilities. Literacy in some of them was below 30 percent, and those who learned to read in government or missionary schools lost touch with their still non-literate societies. Traditional animist cults, based on magic, did little to prepare their followers to function in the cold "disenchanted" world of cause and effect, profit and loss. Islam, Africa's fastest-growing religion, carried a hostility to the "Christian" West that often extended to Western economic ideas. And the Christian missionaries who remained after independence to teach often had priorities other than economic development.

Independence came within boundaries drawn by figures such as Bismarck, Lord Salisbury, and Leopold of Belgium, which cut across tribal zones and traditional economic units. Pre-colonial political structures, a rich jumble of city-states and small kingdoms, interspersed with larger tribal confederations and empires that tended to expand rapidly for several generations and then crumble from lack of cohesion, offered little precedent for the creation of European-style nation-states. Independence led to bloody inter-tribal competition for control of the guns and money of the new post-colonial state machines. One-party (or one-tribe) dictatorships and short-lived parliamentary regimes fractured by ethnically based parties were the norm.

Economies tended toward subsistence agriculture or export-oriented one-crop systems. Only Nigeria with its massive oil reserves and large population, Botswana with its diamonds, and Rhodesia and South Africa with their European economies based on the labor of the black majority appeared to have solid economic prospects in the 1960s. Most black African states worsened their economic plight by ill-conceived "socialist" measures, such as requiring that peasants sell their produce to the state at fixed prices that were often below the cost of production. That destroyed incentives to farm; much of the African continent had been self-sufficient in food at independence, but soon imported it. And food-price subsidies swelled government debts and encouraged migration to the continent's growing shantytowns.

Some states appeared poor prospects from the beginning. Uganda and the Central African Republic succumbed to terrifying dictatorships by former army sergeants, Idi Amin Dada and Jean-Bedel Bokassa. Amin killed as many as 300,000 Ugandans between 1971 and 1979, and left behind a civil war from which the country recovered only slowly. In Liberia, a West African state founded in the early nineteenth century by freed slaves from the United States, a bloody coup led by a Sergeant Samuel Doe of the Krahn tribe overthrew the descendants of the founders in 1980. Doe's tribal adversaries rebelled, and in 1990 seized the capital and killed Doe. Anarchy—the collapse of the Liberian state amid bloodshed and mass suffering—followed, despite intervention by forces from neighboring African states. Inland from Liberia, the cruelty of nature replaced or reinforced the effects of war. The Saharan fringe—Mali, Burkina Faso, Niger, Chad, and the Sudan—suffered repeated disasters from drought and from population pressure on their fragile semi-desert environment.

Ethiopia, east and south of the Sudan, suffered both from drought and from the backward-looking monarchy of Haile Selassie—until its overthrow in 1974. His successors, the Marxist-Leninist zealots of the *Derg* ("Provisional Military Administrative Council"), proved far more terrifying than the aged "Lion of Judah." In 1977–78, amid purges and massacres, a Lieutenant Colonel Mengistu Haile Mariam took command of state and army. With Soviet aid, he sought to subjugate the Eritreans, the people of the former Italian colony whom the United Nations had forced into federation with Ethiopia in 1952. Mengistu pursued a Stalinist program of collectivization ("villagization") that ruthlessly dispossessed and displaced millions of peasants, and in 1987 he proclaimed Ethiopia a

Communist "People's Democratic Republic." Between 1977 and the collapse of Mengistu's regime in 1991, war, purges, collectivization, and famine between them killed more Ethiopians and Eritreans than had Mussolini. Neighboring Somalia, under the dictatorship of Siad Barre (1969–91), passed from Soviet to U.S. clientage in the late 1970s; Barre's overthrow in 1991 led—as in Liberia—to the collapse of the state. A bloody civil war between rival clans and gangs followed, while hundreds of thousands of Somalis starved. Belated United States and United Nations military intervention helped guarantee the delivery of food, but could not force the Somalis to form a stable government.

Other sub-Saharan states adopted forms of "African socialism" less extreme than that of Ethiopia, but with little better results. The Marxist regimes of Angola and Mozambique pressed nationalization and collectivization schemes with similar economic consequences, although less drastic human ones. Ghana achieved independence under Kwame Nkrumah, who styled himself "the Redeemer," established a dictatorship, invited in East German and Chinese advisers, and cut a bold figure at "nonaligned" meetings until Ghana's army removed him in 1966. Ghana's economy fell steadily further behind that of its similar but more "capitalist" neighbor, the Ivory Coast, until the dictatorship of an air force lieutenant, Jerry Rawlings, imposed free-market reforms in

Famine and the state: A Sudanese policeman drives back a hungry crowd (1985).

Mobuto in 1965, shortly after taking power.

the late 1980s. Tanzania's experiment with village collective farming supposedly based on traditional African practices proved an economic disaster. Its "capitalist" northern neighbor, Kenya, enjoyed relative success. Zambia's nationalization of industries and land in the 1970s, along with drought, produced negative per capita growth. Guinea-Bissau's one-party "socialist" dictatorship and self-inflicted economic failures exasperated even the Swedes, those most patient donors of development aid.

Sub-Saharan Africa's largest and most populous states, Nigeria and Zaire, also failed to live up to post-independence expectations. Nigeria's British-style parliamentary regime fell victim to tribal strains and religious conflict between the Moslem north and the Christian and animist south (a conflict also found in the Sudan). An attempt by the Ibo people of southeast Nigeria to create an independent "Biafra" in 1967–70 met with defeat in a pitiless civil war; more than a million died. The army then ruled Nigeria until a brief parliamentary interlude in 1979–83, which ended in yet another coup. Nigeria's oil wealth prompted it to build prestige projects such as a useless $4 billion steel mill, and to found a new capital—a common symbol of state power and national integration, from St. Petersburg and Washington to Brasilia and Islamabad (Pakistan).

But heavy bureaucratic controls and the resulting corruption slowed economic growth.

Zaire profited from its huge mineral wealth even less than Nigeria did from its oil. Belgian and French military intervention helped the dictatorship of Mobutu survive numerous challenges from the provinces. The regime proved skillful at borrowing from Western banks and spending the money on prestige projects and its own pleasures. Opposition groups forced Mobutu to give up some of his powers after disturbances in 1991, but eventual chaos seemed as likely as orderly reform.

Finally, Rhodesia-Zimbabwe and South Africa, the European economies in Africa, survived. Defeat in 1978 did not mean "the suitcase or the coffin" for Zimbabwe's whites. The Marxist victor, Robert Mugabe, pursued a unique course: he convinced the white minority to remain provisionally and run the economy. In South Africa, despite increasing political isolation and worldwide economic sanctions, the Boer "white tribe" maintained its racial domination throughout the 1970s and 1980s. But the sanctions drastically slowed economic growth. In 1989–90, after a change of leadership in the ruling National Party, the Boer government moved with surprising speed to conciliate the black majority and regain international respectability. President Frederik W. De Klerk abolished most *Apartheid* restrictions, released Nelson Mandela of the opposition African National Congress (ANC) from prison, and began negotiations with the ANC over a new constitution that would bring the black majority to power. Talks continued despite widespread fighting—covertly encouraged for a time by the government's security forces—between the Zulus and the Xhosa, the tribe most closely associated with the ANC. But it remained unclear how to reconcile white demands for guarantees of life and property with the ANC's insistence on majority rule.

Nelson Mandela addresses his followers after his release from almost three decades of imprisonment by the Boer regime (1990).

From the 1940s to the 1970s the forces that had once driven Europe's expansion into the wider world operated in reverse.

Europe's demographic outward thrust had ended, thanks to industrialization and the carnage of the World Wars. The colonized peoples had learned to resist with Europe's own weapons and military-political techniques. And the rise of native nationalisms made empire unprofitable or untenable. Yet despite their common origins as formal or informal dependencies of Europe, the new nations traveled widely divergent paths through the Cold War era. The capitalist states of east Asia set an example that forced China to discard Marxist-Leninist economics, even while it sought to keep Marxist-Leninist politics.

South Asia, amid religious wars and stifling bureaucratic controls, gradually advanced. The warring states of the Middle East failed to find a new balance to replace the Ottoman and colonial orders. Many of the older new nations of Latin America missed the path to sustained economic growth. And in Africa south of the Sahara a few states prospered, many regressed, and some lapsed into chaos or civil war. Politics, culture, and responsiveness to the capitalist world market seemed to determine—for good or ill—which states were capable of making the perilous leap from poverty to power and wealth.

Suggestions for Further Reading

General Works

No adequate survey of the post-1945 "Third World" exists; few reliable or readable works cover even parts of it. G. Chaliand, *Revolution in the Third World* (1978, revised 1988), offers a lively guided tour that is now in some respects dated. It nevertheless provides an excellent analysis of the wide cultural differences within the "Third World." See also C. Rangel, *Third World*

Ideology and Western Reality (1986). The World Bank's annual *World Development Report* offers comprehensive statistical data with which to test generalizations about the "Third World." E. Luttwak, *Coup d'Etat: A Practical Handbook* (1969, 1979), analyzes its dominant method of political change.

Decolonization

Nor is there any adequate comparative history of decolonization. E. Monroe, *Britain's Moment in the Middle East, 1914–1956* (1963); A. Williams, *Britain and France in the Middle East and North Africa, 1914–1967* (1968); W. R. Louis, *The British Empire in the Middle East, 1945–1951* (1984); and

A. Horne, *A Savage War of Peace: Algeria 1954–1962* (1977), are useful on the Middle East and North Africa. B. N. Pandey, *The Break-up of British India* (1969) and *South and Southeast Asia, 1945–1979* (1980), ably cover south and southeast Asia.

The Diversity of the Non-Western World

For the varied cultures of the "Third World" and for post-1945 events, see—for East Asia—H. C. Hinton, *Three and a Half Powers: the New Balance in Asia* (1975); S. Leys, *Chinese Shadows* (1978) and *The Chairman's New Clothes: Mao and the Cultural Revolution* (1981); and R. MacFarquhar and J. K. Fairbank, eds., *The Cambridge History of China*, vols. 14 and 15 (1987, 1991). On South Asia, see Pandey (listed earlier) and J. M. Brown, *Modern India: The Origins of an Asian Democracy* (1985). V. S. Naipaul, *India: A Wounded Civilization* (1977), offers pessimistic cultural criticism; N. Maxwell, *India's China War* (1970), is an eye-opening case study in Indian foreign policy. On the Middle East, D. Pipes, *In the Path of God: Islam and Political Power* (1983), is useful on the force of ideas; P. Slugett and M. Farouk-Slugett, eds., *Tuttle Guide to the Middle*

East (1992), imparts basic facts. On Latin America, see especially L. E. Harrison, *Underdevelopment Is a State of Mind: The Latin American Case* (1985); P. Sigmund, *The Overthrow of Allende and the Politics of Chile, 1964–1976* (1977); M. Falcoff, *Modern Chile, 1970–1989* (1989); C. Rangel, *The Latin Americans: Their Love-Hate Relationship with the United States* (1986); and V. S. Naipaul, *The Return of Eva Perón* (1980). On Africa, see D. K. Fieldhouse, *Black Africa 1945–1980. Economic Decolonization and Arrested Development* (1986), and the informed popular account of S. J. Unger, *Africa: People and Politics of an Emerging Continent* (1986); C. Young and T. Turner, *The Rise and Decline of the Zairian State* (1985), provide a depressing case study.

36

THE END OF
THE COLD WAR ERA

The 1975 Helsinki security treaty and other symbols of détente did not change the underlying realities of the Cold War. The international order born in 1941–47 in the struggle between the two superpowers remained the pivot of international politics. But within the framework of the Cold War order, other powers went about their business. Japan's industries stormed the world's markets. Western Europe suffered stagnation, unemployment, and disorientation in the late 1970s and early 1980s, and then acquired new purpose in attempts to construct a European superpower. In the Middle East, an "Islamic Revolution" swept Iran in 1978–79, generating potent new strains of terrorism and triggering the most destructive war between non-Western states in the Cold War era. The victor in that struggle, the Arab national socialist dictatorship of Iraq,

then pressed on toward collision with the United States and much of the rest of the world in 1990–91. That collision coincided with a seemingly unthinkable event: the end of the Cold War through Soviet collapse. But as in 1918, the fall of empires unleashed not peace but savage ethnic-religious conflict.

In the realm of knowledge, the last half of the century was a period of staggering advance and growing bewilderment about the foundations and purposes of science and scholarship. The geometric expansion of human knowledge brought fragmentation. No single mind could fully grasp more than a small range of subjects. The gap between high culture and popular culture inherited from the late nineteenth century grew wider, just as the popular culture of the West swept the non-Western world with tides of unprecedented intensity. In this disoriented condi-

(*OPPOSITE*) THE FALL OF EMPIRES, 1989–91: IN A SCENE REPEATED THROUGHOUT THE FORMER SOVIET BLOC, THE IMMENSE STATUE OF LENIN IN RIGA, LATVIA, LIES IN THE DUST.

tion, as the momentum of population growth drove humanity's numbers relentlessly upward, the world prepared to meet the third millennium of the Western era.

THE SOVIET EMPIRE FROM EXPANSION TO COLLAPSE, 1975–91

The Soviet Union seemed well launched on an upward trajectory by 1970, the year it surpassed the United States in numbers of intercontinental nuclear missiles. American indecision in the wake of Vietnam and the continued growth of Soviet military power then tempted Brezhnev to seek a second Soviet empire far beyond the "Yalta line" of 1945. That expansion in the end met determined resistance. Soviet economic growth, which had turned downward after Stalin's death, slowed and stopped. Then the Soviet empire and the Soviet Union itself crumbled under Western counterpressure, external defeat, eastern European unrest, economic and ecological catastrophe, and the demoralization of the Soviet rulers themselves.

The Culmination of Soviet Power, 1975–79

Détente was brief. The 1973 Yom Kippur war and the Arab oil embargo revealed western Europe's lack of resolve. In Washington, the Nixon administration self-destructed. Congress turned against America's "imperial presidency" and sought to bring the executive branch to heel. North Vietnam's victory in April 1975 suggested that the United States was paralyzed. Simultaneously, new openings tempted the Soviet Union in Europe, Africa, Asia, and the Caribbean.

In Portugal, a power vacuum opened up after the 1974 military revolution that put an end to its colonial empire. The Portuguese Communist Party, with Soviet money and advice, sought power through the "salami tactics" that Stalin had applied in eastern Europe in the late 1940s. But without Red Army backing, those tactics failed. Portugal was a member of NATO, which was unwilling to see it pass into the Soviet orbit. Aid from western Europe and the United States helped Portugal's Socialist party to defeat its Communist rival, and to found a parliamentary democracy.

In Africa, the Soviets skillfully drew Portugal's former colonies, Mozambique and Angola, into their orbit. In Angola they helped to victory their chosen ally among the three guerrilla armies contending for power in the wake of Portuguese withdrawal. But putting the Marxist-Leninist MPLA ("Popular Movement for the Liberation of Angola") in power and keeping it there against rivals backed by the United States, Zaire, China, and South Africa required an ocean-spanning airlift, as many as 50,000 Cuban troops, and fifteen costly years of war (1976–91).

Further north, the Soviets established two other bridgeheads, at Aden and in Somalia, commanding the entrance to the Red Sea. They also wooed Somalia's rival, Mengistu Haile Mariam of Ethiopia. In 1977–78, Mengistu received over $1 billion in Soviet arms, Soviet and Cuban advisers, and a Cuban armored brigade under Soviet command. That help won a war in the Ogaden desert against Somalia—which then drifted toward the United States. But even with Soviet arms, Mengistu was unable to crush resistance in Eritrea. Ceaseless purges, general famine, and ever-growing ethnic revolt all around Ethiopia's periphery ultimately made Mengistu a Soviet burden rather than an asset.

In Asia, Soviet patronage of North Vietnam continued after Hanoi's conquest of the South in March–April 1975. In return the Soviets secured the huge U.S. base at Cam Ranh Bay for air and sea forces capable of threatening both southern China and Japan's sea lanes to the oil of the Middle East. But that patronage cost Brezhnev several billion dollars a year after 1979, when Vietnam opened a Third Indochina War (see p. 957) by seizing Cambodia.

In the Caribbean, two events in 1979 offered further openings. On the tiny island of Grenada, a shaky post-colonial regime fell victim to a coup by Marxist-Leninist enthusiasts, the "New Jewel Party." Their attempts to politicize the Grenadan "masses" and their appetite for weapons soon led them into close ties with the Soviet Union, East Germany, Cuba, Nicaragua, Bulgaria, North Korea, and the PLO.

On the Central American mainland, in Nicaragua, the withdrawal of U.S. support for the dictatorship of Anastasio Somoza Debayle led to his regime's collapse and the seizure of power in July 1979 by a Cuban-educated insurgent movement, the "Sandinista National Liberation Front" (FSLN). Within a month the new FSLN regime had clinched relations with the Soviet Union, Bulgaria, and Libya. It soon acquired ties to the PLO and North Korea. Cuban and Soviet bloc advisers poured in, and the FSLN proclaimed the United States "the enemy of all humanity." Shipments of Soviet-bloc arms soon arrived not only for the "Sandinista Armed Forces" (as the new party-army called itself) but also for insurgencies kindled or rekindled in El Salvador and Guatemala.

Swift expansion of the Soviet Navy, which gained a global reach from bases that stretched from Cuba to Cam Ranh Bay, accompanied the Soviet Union's disturbing military activism in the non-Western world. But most alarming of all was the swift buildup of Soviet conventional and nuclear forces aimed at western Europe. Brezhnev's decision to ratchet military spending upward toward a quarter of Soviet GNP—a figure similar to that of Nazi Germany in 1939—paid off. The Soviet Union had already achieved a numerical advantage of 2 to 1 or better over NATO in deployed divisions, tanks, and artillery; now it seemed to be catching up to the West in the sophistication of its armored vehicles, aircraft, and electronics.

And despite the cap on most strategic forces established by an unratified U. S.–Soviet SALT II treaty signed in 1979, the Soviets pressed their build-up of intermediate, or theater, nuclear forces. From 1978 onward they deployed an entirely new class of intermediate-range ballistic missiles, the three-warhead SS-20. These truck-mounted behemoths were easily hidden, reasonably accurate, and could reach Iceland, Portugal, Japan, and China from deep within the USSR. They also could fire with a minimum of preparation, in keeping with the Soviet emphasis on

preemptive surprise attack. By 1979 the Soviet Union had deployed 120 SS-20s, and no limit appeared in sight. NATO had nothing remotely similar.

But then Brezhnev succumbed to a further—fatal—temptation. On December 27, 1979, KGB commandos and Soviet paratroops descended on Kabul, the capital of Afghanistan, and approximately 100,000 Soviet troops rumbled across the Afghan borders. This latest and most violent expansion of Soviet power, like its predecessors, was an outgrowth of events not entirely of Moscow's making. In 1978 a Marxist-Leninist Afghan party, the "Democratic Party of the People of Afghanistan" (DPPA), had overthrown the five-year-old Afghan republic and had provoked the fiercely independent and devoutly Islamic Afghan tribes with talk of secularism and land "reform." By spring 1979, despite the commitment of additional Soviet arms and advisers, a powerful insurgency was under way that drew on Afghanistan's proud nineteenth-century tradition of ferocious resistance to both Britain and Russia. A factional struggle within the DPPA replaced its original leader with Hafizullah Amin, a bloodthirsty figure whom Moscow regarded as untrustworthy.

Amin's seizure of power and the spreading revolt apparently led to the drastic Soviet measures of December 1979: Amin's assassination by the KGB and Red Army occupation of Afghanistan. But unlike Angola and Ethiopia, where the Cubans had done most of the Soviet Union's fighting, this was no proxy war. The Red Army's DPPA auxiliaries numbered only 30,000 and were so unreliable that they normally fought with Soviet tanks watching them from the rear. The Soviet Union had begun a war that it could neither win, nor end without giving up its claim to represent humanity's future. The Soviet empire had reached its point of culmination, and was about to enter a swift and final descent.

The Fall of Empires, 1979–91

As in Korea in June 1950, the unpredictable American reaction stunned the Soviets. Gerald Ford's Democratic successor as president, James E. ("Jimmy") Carter,

Afghanistan and the Persian Gulf

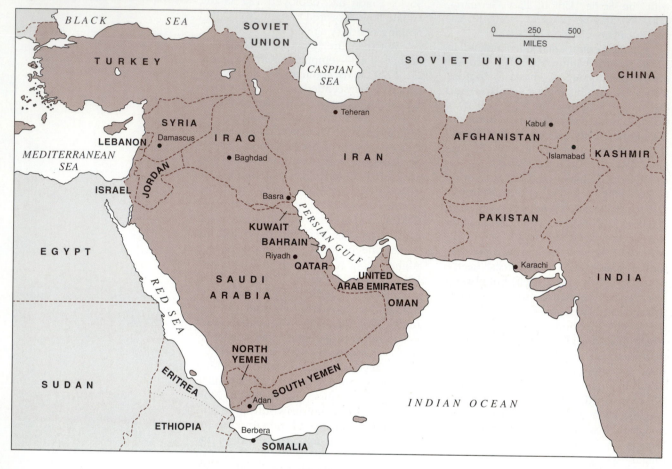

had in 1977 condemned the foreign policy of his predecessors for its "inordinate fear of Communism." The Soviet invasion of Afghanistan, he now confessed, proved that they had been right. He slapped an embargo on U.S. grain sales to the Soviet Union. He sought to humiliate the Soviets with a boycott of the 1980 Moscow Summer Olympics. He spurred U.S. defense spending. And he announced a "Carter Doctrine" to bar further Soviet expansion southward from Afghanistan: the United States would use military force to block attempts "by any outside force to gain control of the Persian Gulf region." Détente was dead.

Carter's successor, Ronald Reagan, proved an even more dangerous and unpredictable adversary. He announced—

and seemed to believe—that the Soviet Union was an "Evil Empire." He doubled the U.S. national debt from $1 trillion in 1981 to $2.1 trillion in 1986 to rebuild the U.S. armed forces at a pace and in a style the Soviets could not match. He promoted an antiballistic missile shield project, the Strategic Defense Initiative (SDI), based on computer and optical technologies that the Soviet Union did not possess and could not develop. News of SDI, together with the demonstration—in 1982 air fighting between Israelis and Syrians in Lebanon—of the effortless superiority of the latest generation of U.S. fighters over their Soviet counterparts, provoked near-panic in Moscow. And Reagan followed through on a pledge by Carter to the NATO allies to deploy a force of U.S.

medium-range nuclear missiles in Europe to counter Brezhnev's SS-20s.

But that was not all. For the first time since MacArthur's drive to the Yalu in 1950, the United States replaced containment with "rollback." Reagan proclaimed a policy soon known as the "Reagan Doctrine": the United States would support *anti-Communist* insurgencies around the world. The CIA received orders to furnish the Afghan rebels with arms, including advanced antiaircraft missiles. That paralyzed the Soviets' main asset in Afghanistan, command of the air. From 1981–82 on, the CIA also organized and supported a growing insurgency, the *contras,* or "counter-revolutionaries," against the Sandinista regime in Nicaragua. And when the leaders of Grenada's New Jewel Party split into warring factions in October 1983, and the widening bloodshed seemed to threaten American citizens on the island, Reagan swiftly sent U.S. Marines and paratroops. Small parties of Cuban troops offered fierce but short-lived resistance; most Grenadans seemed happy to see the Americans. For the first time since 1917, a Western democracy had deposed a Marxist-Leninist regime.

Even the inner empire in eastern Europe that Stalin had conquered in 1945 was now far from secure. Of all the satellites, Poland had plunged most deeply into debt to Western bankers during détente. Misconceived industrial investments and rising inflation struck at the living standards of Poland's downtrodden workers, whose riots had toppled Gomulka in 1970 as they had toppled his predecessor in 1956. In summer 1980 Polish workers at Gdansk—once known as Danzig—went on strike: a class struggle against a Marxist-Leninist state. Poland's intellectuals and the Catholic Church, the historic vehicle of Polish nationalism, backed the strike. Against all precedent, the workers won the right to replace their Party-run sham unions with an independent national trade union, *Solidarnosc* ("Solidarity"). The demoralized Polish Communist Party lost control even of the press, and began to disintegrate. Poland, the largest and most strategically vital of all the satellites, appeared about to crumble—with dangerous repercussions in the DDR, Czechoslovakia, and Hungary.

Brezhnev and his associates found the answer: a Polish general. Moscow

A Solidarity demonstration defies martial law (1982).

placed the Polish Communist Party in the hands of Wojciech Jaruzelski, a prim and ruthless military figure with a long record of absolute obedience to the Soviet Union. In December 1981 Jaruzelski crushed Solidarity with riot police and the army; Soviet tank forces in East Germany, Poland, and western Russia stood ready to back him up. Jaruzelski placed before the Polish people a grim choice: either his dictatorship, or a Soviet intervention that would endanger the survival of the nation. Solidarity survived underground and Polish workers began a permanent although unspoken slowdown strike.

The Soviet domestic scene was by now at least as threatening as the foreign and imperial one. Soviet military procurement at last ceased to grow in the early 1980s; the economy was floundering. The annual rate of GNP increase had fallen inexorably from roughly 5 percent in the 1950s to negative growth by the early 1980s. Without terror—which Stalin's successors lacked the ideological conviction to wield—growth was apparently no longer possible. The diversion of up to a third of Soviet industrial and research resources to the military, the inefficiency of central planning, the rewarding of political loyalty over brains, and a demoralized work force ("they pretend to pay us, we pretend to work") meant that even massive investment produced only stagnation.

Rudimentary medical services, a rising industrial accident rate, intense chemical pollution, radiation from more than a hundred underground nuclear blasts in mines and oilfields, astounding levels of vodka consumption, and widespread hopelessness made the Soviet Union the only industrialized society in history to experience a long-term decline in the life expectancy of its population. Male life expectancy dropped from age 65 in 1965 to an estimated 61 or worse in 1981; the life expectancy of Soviet women from 73 in the early 1970s to 69 in 1985.

Nor did the Soviet Union—one of Europe's last two multinational empires—escape the demographic trends that had sapped its former imperial rivals. By 1970 only 51 percent of the Soviet population were Great Russians, the ruling nationality. The subject peoples, especially the Moslems of Central Asia, were growing at rates of up to three times that of the peoples of European Russia. Great Russians probably ceased to be a majority in the early 1980s, although they remained the largest single nationality within the Soviet Union. Nationalist unrest in Soviet Central Asia and the Caucasus accompanied the shift in numbers; demonstrations erupted whenever KGB pressure relaxed.

These trends clearly threatened the Soviet Union with the loss of superpower status by Brezhnev's death in 1982. Two

Soviet industrial pollution: a paper pulp plant near Archangel, 1990.

transitional figures, Yuri Andropov of the KGB and the colorless Konstantin Chernenko, followed Brezhnev to the grave after brief spells in power. Then in March 1985 the Politburo chose a far younger man, Mikhail Gorbachev. Andrei Gromyko, Molotov's pupil and heir at the foreign ministry, reportedly put Gorbachev over the top by remarking that he had a very nice smile and very hard teeth.

Gromyko was wrong. Gorbachev immediately revealed a genius for disastrous half-measures. His goal was to preserve and consolidate his own power, that of the Party, and that of a revived "socialism." But from the beginning he faced the same contradiction that had snared earlier autocrats from Peter the Great onward. Success in inter-state competition—the preservation of the Soviet Union's superpower status—was only possible in the long run through the development of a society and economy on the Western model. But that society would demand an end to autocracy. And failure in interstate competition likewise led, as Nicholas the Last had discovered in 1917, to autocracy's collapse.

Gorbachev's economic reform, *perestroika* (restructuring) soon developed into "catastroika." Gorbachev's reforms broke Stalin's central planning mechanism without creating functioning markets to replace it. Gorbachev failed to follow the Chinese example of reversing Stalinism in agriculture first, buying off the peasantry with profits and swamping urban discontent with food. Worse still—given his aim of preserving his own power and that of the Party—he also failed to follow the Chinese in keeping an iron grip on politics. To checkmate the opponents of *perestroika*, the remaining Stalinists in the Party, the military, and military-industry, he loosened Party and KGB control over the press, over broadcasting, and over access to the Western media. He naively intended this new policy of *Glasnost* (openness) as the decisive blow for *perestroika*. Instead, *Glasnost* destroyed Gorbachev, the Party, and the Soviet Union.

Glasnost, together with the 1986 meltdown and fire in a Soviet nuclear reactor at Chernobyl in the Ukraine, demolished the Party's claim that it held the key to history.

The accident contaminated livestock, milk, and crops from Lapland to Portugal, killed 31 outright and thousands more in the following years from radiation-induced illnesses. Large areas of the Ukraine and Byelorussia remained contaminated. And *Glasnost* mercilessly exposed the regime's incompetence in everything from reactor design to medical countermeasures to post-accident cleanup. Over the next three years the Soviet press and an increasingly vocal public opinion stripped away the legitimacy of the Soviet state.

Gorbachev had already begun the destruction of that legitimacy by blaming economic stagnation on Brezhnev. Then Stalin came under attack, as massive new evidence of his genocide leaked from the archives into the Soviet press. The term "totalitarianism," long banned as Western Cold War rhetoric, became the preferred description of the Soviet past. Finally, the public and the new free press turned on Lenin—the regime's embalmed saint—and damned him as the author of a historic wrong turning that had led Russia and its subject peoples to misery and ruin. By May 1990, demonstrators were appearing in Red Square carrying placards that certified the regime's death: "Socialism? No Thanks!" "Seventy-Two Years on the Road to Nowhere." "Down with the Red Fascist Empire."

By that point, the Soviet external empire was gone. Gorbachev sought throughout 1986–89 to trade his steady retreat for Western concessions. But his rising dependence on Western—and especially German—loans to finance *perestroika* stripped him of his bargaining power. Between 1987 and 1990 he agreed to scrap his SS-20s and other theater nuclear weapons, and to limit the Soviet Union's nuclear and conventional forces on terms virtually dictated by the United States. Between 1988 and 1991 he wound up Brezhnev's second Soviet empire—withdrawing the Red Army from Afghanistan, pledging to withdraw it from Cuba, helping to ease the Cubans out of Angola and the Vietnamese out of Cambodia and abandoning Ethiopia.

But once defeat in Afghanistan had destroyed the Red Army's aura of invincibility, and once the Soviet regime had confessed its failures and its dependence on the West, Stalin's inner eastern European empire began to crumble as well. Poland and Hungary led the way toward independence; Solidarity and the Hungarian opposition won the right to exist legally in early 1989. That fall, after Hungary tore down the stretch of fortified Iron Curtain along its border with Austria, East Germans flooded westward through Budapest to seek asylum in West Germany. Massive demonstrations against the East German regime in the East German city of Leipzig then threw the DDR leaders into panic. Erich Honecker, their chief, called Gorbachev to ask permission to shoot the demonstrators. But Gorbachev, although faced with the collapse of the DDR and the loss of the symbol of Soviet victory in the Second World War, advised Honecker to avoid bloodshed. This time, unlike 1953, 1956, and 1968, Soviet tanks did not roll.

Gorbachev's gesture, whatever its motives, earned him a Nobel Peace Prize. It also ended the eastern European empire that Stalin had created and that his successors had maintained by force. The collapsing DDR opened the Berlin Wall on November 9, 1989, and happy crowds surged through the Brandenburg Gate. Of the satellite leaders, only Nicolae Ceausescu of Rumania chose to fight it out when Party and army rivals hijacked popular disturbances and launched a coup in December 1989. But the Rumanian army's tanks prevailed over Ceausescu's secret police. The new rulers named themselves the "Council of National Salvation," shot their former boss, and set up an ex-Communist dictatorship. Elsewhere the collapse of the satellite regimes was largely peaceful and led to freely elected non-Communist governments and the withdrawal of the Red Army. The "former DDR," after free elections, chose reunification with West Germany on October 3, 1990.

By that point the Soviet Union itself was in crisis. The inner ring of subject peoples, conquered by the tsars and reconquered by Stalin, began a slow-motion revolt: demonstrations, declarations of independence, appeals to the West. Soviet troops crushed demonstrators in Lithuania and elsewhere, but by spring 1991 United States warnings set limits on Gorbachev's use of force. Party and KGB diehards whom he had placed in key positions then sought to remove Gorbachev himself in a bungled coup d'état in August 1991. The protests of Reagan's successor George Bush, the incompetence of the plotters, and the resistance of Boris Yeltsin, recently elected president of the Russian Republic, led to the collapse of the coup and the banning of the Communist Party.

The failed coup and the death of the Party made the Soviet Union ungovernable. Between August and December 1991 the multinational empire of Lenin and the tsars dissolved into its national component parts. Fourteen new states split off in an arc around Russia: Estonia, Latvia, and Lithuania on the Baltic, Byelorussia (Belarus), Ukraine, Moldavia (Moldova) in the west; Georgia, Armenia, and Azerbaijan in the Caucasus; and the five predominantly Moslem republics of what had been Soviet Central Asia. At the initiative of Yeltsin and the Ukraine, a ramshackle "Confederation of Independent States" (CIS) emerged as heir-apparent to the Soviet Union's military establishment, nuclear arsenal, and defense policy. At the end of December

Boris Yeltsin of Russia (1991): from Communist bureaucrat to democratic reformer?

1991 Gorbachev resigned as president of a state that no longer existed. The white, blue, and red Russian tricolor replaced the red flag of Communism over the Kremlin's towers. The Cold War had ended with the dissolution of the Soviet superpower.

WAR AND PEACE IN ASIA

The final phase of the Cold War was a time of sharp contrasts in Asia. U.S. withdrawal in 1973–75 removed war in southeast Asia from American television screens. But it did not end war there. Japan and the smaller states within Japan's economic orbit prospered mightily. The island empire became an economic superpower, the world's second largest economy. But it showed few signs of taking up the responsibilities that accompanied that power.

Cambodian Genocide and Third Indochina War

North Vietnam's conquest of the South in March–April 1975 led to direct annexation. Hanoi abolished what was left of the southern "National Liberation Front" in 1976. Hundreds of thousands of former Saigon officials and soldiers disappeared into "re-education camps." Many thousands died.

In Cambodia, Hanoi had long sponsored a Communist guerrilla movement, the Khmer Rouge, that soon showed itself even more terrifying than its patrons. The Khmer Rouge leaders, Pol Pot (born Saloth Sar), Ieng Sary, and Khieu Samphan had acquired their Maoism at Left Bank cafés while studying in Paris in the 1940s and 1950s. There they conceived a utopian goal of a kind common among uprooted intellectuals: the forging of a unique "Cambodian Road to Socialism" through the elimination of the old society and the breaking of all ties between Cambodia and the outside world.

Pol Pot and his associates followed that road with pitiless consistency when they seized power in Cambodia in the wake of Hanoi's conquest of South Vietnam. In a few days in April 1975 they

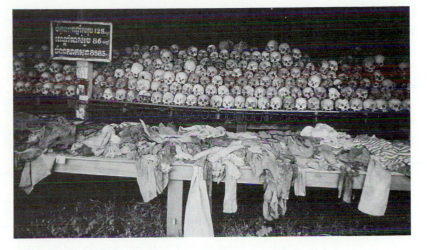

Bones of victims of the Khmer Rouge, Tonle Bati, Takeo Province, Cambodia.

forcibly emptied Phnom Penh, a capital city containing perhaps 3 million inhabitants and refugees; many starved. The teenage peasant zealots of the Khmer Rouge hunted and killed all Cambodians with an education and anyone whose support for the collectivized and "ruralized" new order seemed less than total. In 1970, Cambodia's population had stood at an estimated 8 million. By 1980 the population of "Democractic Kampuchea" had fallen to between 5.5 and 6.5 million. Perhaps 750,000 of the 1.5 to 2.5 million missing people had fled across the minefields to Thailand. The rest had died.

World opinion showed its usual paralysis. Many in the West at first dismissed the accounts of torture, massacre, and starvation conveyed by refugees. Nor did Khmer Rouge genocide (or "autogenocide") play any part in Pol Pot's downfall; that followed instead from his fierce nationalist resentment of his former patrons in Hanoi. In 1977–78 Khmer Rouge forces clashed savagely with the Vietnamese along the Cambodia-Vietnam border. In December 1978 more than 100,000 Vietnamese troops launched a classic mechanized *Blitzkrieg* that dispersed the Khmer Rouge armies and seized Phnom Penh.

That "Third Indochina War" did not remain entirely isolated. China had long objected to Hanoi's close ties with Moscow. Hanoi likewise had no love for Beijing. In 1978 Vietnam began to expel its 900,000 to 1.2 million overseas Chinese. That brutal measure, together with the invasion of Cambodia, prompted a brief Chinese attack on North Vietnam in February–March 1979. China's inexperienced army did poorly, however, and Brezhnev apparently cautioned Beijing against pressing the attack. Vietnam proceeded to impose a semicolonial regime on Cambodia, complete with hundreds of thousands of Vietnamese settlers. Nearly 200,000 troops stayed on until 1988–89 to fight both Khmer Rouge and anti-Communist guerrillas. Not until Soviet backing faltered did Hanoi agree to withdraw, and a precarious truce, brokered and supervised by the United Nations, descended in 1991. The Third Indochina War had cost tens of thousands of dead beyond those who had perished by Khmer Rouge genocide, and the Khmer Rouge still held much of Cambodia.

Japan: The Fragility of Success

While the United States was floundering in Indochina, Japan was emerging as the "workshop of Asia." Its gross national product swelled from roughly 13 percent of U.S. GNP in 1965 to 54 percent in 1990. Its economy rested overwhelmingly on industry rather than agriculture or mining, for Japan's narrow, poor and mountainous islands had almost no oil and few minerals. As in the United States, the production of automobiles and electrical devices led the way. Unlike the United States, Japan's industries immediately targeted export markets from the United States to southeast Asia to Europe; to import food and oil, Japan had to export. By the mid-1970s Japan had conquered the U.S. market for television sets and seized a bridgehead in the automobile market. By the 1980s even the manufacturers of the United States' most innovative product, the computer chip, were complaining of "unfair" Japanese competition. Europe reacted with even greater hostility. Japan even took over the U.S. role as the world's greatest creditor—a position Washington had held since 1914–18.

Japanese success flowed in part from thirty years of relentless hard work and attention to detail by Japanese management and by Japan's highly educated and dedicated work force. It also derived in part from a social and political system in

The face of Japanese industry: Robots weld automobile bodies at a factory near Tokyo.

which big business, the government bureaucracies, and the ruling Liberal Democratic Party acted in unison to promote limitless economic growth.

But with growth came perplexities that the Japanese system was ill-prepared to master. Defeat in 1945 had not changed the fundamental nature of the Meiji state. Army and navy had ceased to count in decision-making, but the vacuum at the center, the lack of steering and of brakes that had led Japan to ruin in 1931–45, persisted. Internal debate on Japan's course, on the possible reactions abroad to Japan's seemingly ever-widening share of its trading partners' domestic markets, was strangely absent. Japanese government spokesmen routinely pledged to consume and import more, and to export less. Yet throughout the 1970s and 1980s, Japan's trade surpluses with Europe and the United States continued to swell.

Japan was nevertheless extremely vulnerable. The pacifist constitution that MacArthur had imposed in 1947 kept the island empire partially disarmed, unable to defend its shipping lanes to the oil of the Persian Gulf or to the vast "co-prosperity sphere" stretching southward to Thailand, Malaysia, and Indonesia which it had at last acquired under United States protection. Nor did its neighbors want it rearmed. Beijing repeatedly reminded Tokyo of the immense massacres committed during Japan's attempt to conquer China in 1937–45.

And so great was Japan's dependence on foreign trade that a severe downturn could easily unhinge both society and government. For Japan's defeat in 1945 had largely failed to produce the rethinking and repentance found in West Germany. The nationalist myths of racial and cultural superiority that had propelled Japan toward the conquest of Asia had survived the Pacific War. Many Japanese continued to view Pearl Harbor as a justified response to American economic aggression. And unlike West Germany and the other Western democracies, Japan's social and political order did not derive its strength from religious or legal-ethical principles—such as Locke's notions of inherent rights for individuals—that were

independent of government or society. The foundation of "Japan, Inc." was simply the collective will of the ruling elites, a will legitimized by success alone. Yet Japan's pace of economic growth had gradually slowed since the 1960s. And in the early 1990s Japan's inflated land and stock prices collapsed dramatically, the economy tipped into recession, and the resistance of Japan's trading partners intensified. Recurring corruption scandals crippled the Liberal Democratic Party; it splintered in mid-1993 and lost its long-standing parliamentary majority. Political paralysis seemed possible, just as the economic success required for social and political stability was less assured than in the past.

WESTERN EUROPE IN SEARCH OF ITSELF

The sharp rise in the world price of oil in 1973–75, a further oil-price shock in 1979–80, and the simultaneous collapse of superpower détente shook western Europe. Yet its states remained stable, relatively prosperous, and increasingly bent on achieving greater economic and political unity within the European Community (EC). Then came the end of the Cold War, and rising uncertainty.

Britain, France, and Italy from the Seventies to the Nineties

Britain in the 1970s was still recognizably the class-ridden society of the past. Workers voted Labour; the middle and upper-middle classes supported Conservatives or Liberals. Ineffectual governments alternated, while Britain's slow relative economic decline continued. The bland Edward Heath of the Conservatives (1970–74) followed Labour's even blander Harold Wilson (1964–70); Labour returned with Wilson in 1974–76; Wilson's tougher successor James Callaghan hung on until 1979.

Then came an electoral and ultimately a social earthquake. Margaret Thatcher, the daughter of a provincial grocer, led the Conservatives to a landslide victory on a radical platform: the dismantling of inefficient state-owned industry and the freeing of Britain's markets from bureaucratic controls and high taxes. Thatcher's ready wit in debate, immense capacity for work, bloody-minded persistence, and political courage made her Britain's longest-ruling prime minister (1979–90) since the early nineteenth century. She temporarily crushed the upper-class "old-school-tie" elements within her own party, and forced competition and efficiency on Britain's obstinate labor unions and unimaginative businessmen. She crushed Argentina as well in a brief war when its military rulers foolishly seized the Falkland Islands from Britain in 1982.

She also largely accomplished her self-proclaimed mission of changing welfare-state Britain from a "dependent to a self-reliant society—from a give-it-to-me to a do-it-yourself nation." The state's share of GNP dropped. Britain's industrial productivity leapt upward. Strikes declined dramatically. Stockholders, by 1989, outnumbered union members for the first time in Britain's history. Families bought their state-owned apartments. Profits became socially respectable. Class ceased to be the decisive barrier to achievement; Thatcher at last brought to Britain the revolutionary "career open to talent." Yet her grip on power proved fragile amid the economic storms of the late 1980s. In late 1990, as Britain slid into a deep recession, her own party ungraciously dumped her. The background of Thatcher's successor nevertheless showed the depth of her mark on British politics. John Major, who went on to defeat Labour narrowly in 1991, came from a working-class family.

In France, voter boredom and the worldwide economic slowdown of the late 1970s brought a turning point similar to that in Britain, but from the Left rather than the Right. De Gaulle's first two successors as president of France, Georges Pompidou (1969–74) and Valéry Giscard d'Estaing (1974–81), were men of the moderate Right. But in 1981 the elder statesman of the Socialist party, François Mitterand, took power in coalition with a Communist Party that still held almost a sixth of the vote.

Yet by mid-decade, France's politics had set in a new mold. Mitterand and his party tried "socialist" economics with dismal results, then rapidly reversed course away from nationalized industry and state planning. They surrendered to local government many of the powers that Paris had wielded—since Napoleon I—through its representatives in the provinces, the prefects (see p. 601). Prosperity, its last-ditch defense of Stalinist dogma, and its stout support of the Soviet invasion of Afghanistan shrank the Communist Party toward electoral insignificance. A new anti-immigrant party, the National Front, rose on the far Right. And the longstanding gap between the parties of the political center—the moderate Right and the Socialists—narrowed dramatically. In 1986–88 Mitterand as president successfully "cohabited" with a prime minister and parliamentary majority drawn from his Center-Right opponents. The ideological gulf between great blocs on the Left and Right that had poisoned French politics since 1789–94 had finally closed—leaving the Socialists without a distinctive political message and dooming them to defeat in the 1993 elections. The Revolution, French historians and political commentators gratefully concluded, was over. France seemed at last to have become a stable industrial society.

Italy's road from the 1970s to the 1990s was less smooth than that of Britain or France. Northern Italy's dynamic private firms gave Italy more overall growth in the 1980s than France or West Germany, and made it by 1990 the world's seventh-largest economy, ahead of Britain and level with France. In the early 1980s the Italian state defeated the terrorists of the Left, the "Red Brigades" and their offshoots. But it also failed in other vital respects. The state's deadening hand controlled a larger share of industry and commerce than in any other major capitalist economy. Italy's politics revolved around the division of patronage in the government bureaucracies and state-controlled firms, the buying off of interest groups with pensions and bribes, and the financing of the governing parties through massive kickbacks by industry. In 1990, total national debt surpassed annual GNP.

And the state had less luck against a far greater threat than the Red Brigades: the criminal empires of the Mafia (Sicily), Camorra (Naples), and 'Ndrangheta (Calabria) that dominated the economics and politics of the South, diverting economic development aid and making their wishes known through terror-bombings and the assassination of government prosecutors, police officials, and politicians. By the early 1990s, the apparent complicity of the Christian Democratic ruling party with organized crime in the South and the exposure of widespread political corruption in the North utterly discredited the parliamentary regime that had ruled Italy since 1948. Italy's party system crumbled, as crusading prosecutors investigated or jailed national leaders of the Christian Democrats and Socialists. Soviet collapse also split the Communists, the traditional alternative to the ruling system, into would-be social democrats and diehard Leninists. And an anti-Southern backlash made the North-South divide, unbridged since Garibaldi and Cavour had annexed the South in 1860–61, into a political as well as a social and economic divide. A new regional party, the "Northern League," denounced Rome's bloated government bureaucracies, state subsidies for the South, southern migrants, non-European immigrants, and the very notion of Italy's unity. Electoral reforms demanded by an irate public seemed likely to split Italy into a North dominated by the Northern League, a Center under the ex-Communists, and a Christian Democratic South and islands. As so often in the past, Italy's survival seemed in doubt.

Germany Reunited

The end of détente in 1979 hit West Germany harder than it hit its European partners. Willy Brandt's successor as chancellor, Helmut Schmidt (1974–82), practically led NATO during the Carter era. The socialist "Iron Chancellor" was the main force behind the alliance's 1979 decision to counter—with the deployment in western Europe of U.S. Pershing and cruise

missiles—the Soviet Union's ever-increasing SS-20 missile force. But Schmidt's own party, the SPD, proved less cooperative than NATO. It abandoned him and turned against the Western alliance; in vain Schmidt urged his critics to "stop behaving as if the Americans were your enemies and the Soviets your friends!" A new ecological and antinuclear party, the Greens, appealed to German nationalism—from the Left—against the United States. Hundreds of thousands of West Germans demonstrated repeatedly against U.S. nuclear weapons, but not against Soviet ones. The SS-20s seemed to be driving a wedge into the heart of NATO.

But West Germany's political center held. The small liberal party, the FDP, after concluding that the SPD was abandoning the Western alliance, abandoned its Socialist coalition partners and joined the Christian Democrats (CDU/CSU) in 1982. That move brought Schmidt's government down. Under the leadership of Helmut Kohl, a bear-like provincial figure whose enemies unfailingly underestimated him, the CDU/CSU-FDP coalition won the 1983 "missile election" decisively. In 1983–84 the first American missiles deployed—and the world did not end, as the protesters had insisted it would. Instead, NATO's apparent resolve to defend itself further demoralized the Soviet leadership.

Despite a talent for spectacular verbal gaffes that rivaled that of Ronald Reagan, Kohl dominated German politics into the 1990s. His durable FDP foreign minister, Hans-Dietrich Genscher, detected Soviet weakness earlier than most Western leaders. Genscher went to work with determination and tact, offering ever-increasing loans that tied Gorbachev to West German goodwill while flattering him shamelessly. By 1989–90, as the Soviet empire crumbled, Genscher and Kohl moved swiftly to secure the primary goal of West German foreign policy ever since 1949, the annexation of East Germany. George Bush offered firm support. By summer 1990, after a majority of East Germans had voted to join the West, Gorbachev was in no position to refuse.

But once East Germany had merged with West Germany on October 3, 1990,

The end of the East German economy.

The power of symbols: the new German Right (1992).

and immigrants that flooded Germany at the Cold War's end, heightened the appeal of the far Right. Shaved heads, black leather, combat boots, racist slogans, and the murder of refugees, Jews, Gypsies, and Turkish immigrants became the order of the day in 1991–92 among disaffected working-class youth in both East and West Germany. Kohl belatedly mobilized against these new barbarians the police apparatus that had demolished leftist terrorism in the 1970s and early 1980s. The great majority of Germans rejected *Fremdenhass*—hatred of foreigners. West Germany's constitutional order had successfully resisted neo-Nazi revivals in the past. But the financial and social strains of reunification seemed likely to put that order to a lengthy test.

The European Community—An Emerging European Superpower?

Germany's trials were also the trials of its neighbors, thanks to the growing importance of the European Community. In 1986 France's bureaucrats at the EC's headquarters in Brussels launched a far-reaching initiative toward greater economic and ultimately political unity among the Community's twelve states. Their target was the creation by January 1, 1993, of a unified European market embracing 325 million people. The unspoken purpose of the initiative was to tame Germany for the future by embedding it in a unitary European economic and political structure.

Despite the large income gap between the EC's rich states (West Germany, France, and northern Italy) and poor states (Greece, Portugal, Ireland, and even Britain), and the slowness of some states to bend their legal and commercial systems to fit EC standards, the "single market" initiative enjoyed general approval. Other EC projects were less immediately successful. Germany's refugee crisis led it to freeze implementation of a 1990 agreement with France and seven other EC states to abolish passport checks along their mutual borders. EC attempts to peg Europe's currencies to the German mark led to a spectacular crisis in 1992 when

the bill came due. Four-fifths of the DDR's industry was uncompetitive, fit only for the scrap heap. Pools of toxic waste dotted a bleak landscape beneath clouds of soft-coal smog. The work force, after 45 years of socialism, had lost the habits of initiative and efficiency that West Germans took for granted. It soon emerged that a wide cultural gap had opened between the two German societies of the Cold War era. To the "Wessis," their "Ossi" counterparts seemed caught in a time warp, a people at once incompetent, dim-witted, and lazy. To the "Ossis," their rich West German cousins seemed overworked, self-important know-it-alls.

Worse still, the economic recovery of the East seemed likely to take a generation, rather than the few years that Kohl had counted on in pushing for unification. The former DDR sucked in hundreds of billions of marks in West German aid but remained economically stagnant. Yet funding that aid forced on Bonn increasing budget deficits, higher taxes, high interest rates, and inflation. The German economy slowed amid fierce protests from Germany's suffering EC partners.

And East German unemployment, along with the million or more refugees

Germany's high interest rates, a consequence of the need to raise vast sums to save the former DDR, drove Germany's partners into a deepening recession.

Above all, the road seemed far from clear for implementing the EC's most far-reaching initiative, the Maastricht treaty of 1991. That agreement foresaw a single European currency, a central European bank and monetary policy, a common European citizenship, and a common defense and foreign policy before the year 2000. But the voters had other ideas; public hostility to bureaucratic centralization, growing dissatisfaction with western Europe's governing parties, and economic recession threatened to wreck Maastricht. Denmark's citizens at first voted against the treaty; France's approved it by a narrow majority; Britain's seemed hostile. Germans did not fancy exchanging the sacred German mark for European "Esperanto money." Nationalist intellectuals bemoaned the likely loss of national traditions and peculiarities. And Maastricht raised a further perplexity. Prospective new EC members, from Norway, Sweden, Finland and Austria to Turkey, Poland, and Hungary, pressed to join. Yet widening the EC by admitting further members might damage the Maastricht attempt to deepen unity among the original twelve members.

Finally, the external crises that accompanied the end of the Cold War showed how little the EC had changed Europe politically; it still remained a continent of national states. In the Second Gulf War (see the next section) the EC split; Britain, France, and Italy, although with wide differences in enthusiasm, sent forces to fight Iraq under United States command in 1990–91. Germany, whose industrialists had aided Saddam's nerve gas and missile programs, offered only cash. Belgium refused even to sell ammunition to its NATO ally, Britain. Saddam's threat to one of the EC's most vital interests, its supply of oil, failed to produce a common European policy.

In the savage conflicts between the peoples of Yugoslavia that broke out in summer 1991, the EC likewise split along lines ordained by history: France for the

Serbs, Germany for the Slovenes and Croats. Britain vetoed military action: experience in Northern Ireland showed that it was easy to send troops in, but hard to get them out. Germany's postwar constitution restricted the EC's most powerful army to self-defense, and Germany's 1941–45 sponsorship of Croat genocide and its brutal occupation of Serbia ruled out any German military role in the Balkans. Serbs and Croats therefore simply ignored EC-brokered ceasefires; "EC threatens Serbia with lengthy debate," ran an ironic German headline. Soon the EC gratefully handed the Balkan wars over to the United Nations and the United States. Europe had the makings of a superpower, but whether its peoples were ready to sacrifice their historic traditions and national independence for the sake of unity was uncertain.

WAR AND PEACE IN THE MIDDLE EAST, 1975–93

The final phase of the Cold War era was a time of ever-fiercer conflict in the Middle East. The Arab world seemed incapable of creating stable regimes except by force. Even the traditional monarchies, from Saudi Arabia and Jordan to Morocco, relied on all-pervasive internal security machines. In the secular states, families, clans, tribes, and sects fought one another for survival—the control of the army and the police. The failure of states without oil to generate enough economic growth to outpace their swelling populations undermined what little legitimacy those regimes possessed. From Algeria to Egypt and Jordan, Islamic zealots attacked their governments at the grass-roots. Israeli-Arab conflict continued. But a second strand of the new "Eastern Question," a series of conflicts between Arabs and Iranians, Arabs and Arabs, and Arabs and the West over the immense oil riches of the Persian Gulf generated violence that far surpassed the struggle for Palestine.

Israel and its Neighbors, 1975–93

A brief relaxation followed the Yom Kippur War of October 1973. Anwar Sadat of Egypt cut his last Soviet ties and aligned

European unity at risk: frenzied London currency traders during the crisis of the European exchange rate mechanism, 1992.

himself with the United States in 1976. In 1977 he broke all precedent and flew to Jerusalem in search of peace with Israel; Egypt was war-weary and economically desperate. At a 1978 summit meeting at Camp David near Washington, Carter pushed Menachem Begin of Israel into a peace agreement underwritten with lavish United States aid for both Egypt and Israel. In March 1979 Egypt and Israel signed a treaty that ended thirty years of war. Despite Sadat's assassination by Islamic militants in October 1981, Israel returned the last slice of Sinai to Egypt in 1982. At least one of the Middle East's many borders was momentarily at peace.

Peace did not descend on Israel's northern border. The PLO and its offshoots in their "state-within-a-state" in southern Lebanon repeatedly bombarded and raided northern Israel. Israel replied with air strikes and armored thrusts. In 1982 it intervened in the multi-cornered civil war that had simmered since 1975–76 between Lebanon's principal communities, the Maronite Christians, Sunni Moslems, Shiite Moslems, Druzes, and Palestinians. Israeli forces brushed the Syrians aside and drove for Beirut, seeking to stamp out the PLO for good.

Snipers and terrorists soon convinced Israel that it could not hold Lebanon; it withdrew in 1983. An ill-considered U.S. and European attempt to prop up the Maronite Christian-dominated Lebanese central government followed, but came to grief when suicide truck-bombers penetrated

the U.S. and French perimeters and killed 241 U.S. Marines and 58 French paratroopers. The Marines and the European forces withdrew sheepishly in February–March 1984, while Lebanese Shiites took Western hostages and attacked targets in Europe. Western retreat left the mastery of Lebanon to Syria, if it could conquer it. Syria sought first to destroy all armed Palestinians not loyal to itself. Yasser Arafat, the chief political leader of the Palestinian movement, fled for his life. Many of his followers perished. Syria then moved into Beirut and by late 1990 had ended Lebanon's civil war.

PLO defeat in Lebanon did not mean the end of Palestinian militance. Israel had been from the beginning a demographic time bomb. Several hundred thousand Palestinians had remained within Israel's borders in 1948–49; by the 1980s they were twice as prolific as Israel's Jewish population. Israel acquired a further one million Arabs on the west bank of the Jordan and in the Gaza Strip through its great victories in the Six Days' War of 1967. By the mid–1980s, 3.6 million Jews faced 2.1 million Arabs within the post–1967 borders of "greater Israel." Demographic trends, if continued, would have given the Arabs close to a majority by 2005. And rapid population growth inevitably increased the numerical weight of the young, the most easily aroused and least tolerant segment of any population.

The Palestinians had no intention of waiting until the next century; they wanted all of Palestine now. In December 1987, the young of the occupied Gaza Strip took on Israel's police and army with rocks and firebombs in an uprising or "*Intifada*" that attracted global television coverage and sympathy. But then Palestinian support for Iraq and Iraqi defeat in the Second Gulf War (see pp. 968–70) undermined the *Intifada*'s reputation and morale, and the rise of Islamic extremist groups split the movement. By 1991–92 fighting among the PLO, the Islamic movement Hamas, and other Arab groups was killing more Palestinians than the Israeli army. Fear of Hamas ultimately drove Yasser Arafat, most of the PLO, and Israel together in a dramatic September 1993

Sadat, Carter, and Begin clasp hands at the signing of the Israeli-Egyptian peace treaty, March 26, 1979.

agreement to establish self-governing Palestinian enclaves in Gaza and the West Bank. Peace and a Palestinian state seemed conceivable at last, although violent rejection of the accord by Hamas and PLO splinter groups foreshadowed further bloodshed.

The Iranian Revolution and the First Gulf War, 1978–88

Anwar Sadat had died by assassination in 1981, a victim of the widespread upsurge of religious militance of which he had once remarked, "This is not Islam, this is madness." The source of that "madness" was the Islamic world's impotence in the face of nineteenth- and twentieth-century Western power, and the failure of the secular states of the Middle East to catch up with the West—or even to defeat the Jewish state, the West's Middle Eastern outpost. The main trigger of that "madness" was the 1978–79 revolution that convulsed Iran.

Shah Mohammed Reza Pahlavi, "King of Kings" and ruler of Iran from 1941 to 1979, was a man of large ambitions. He sought to use Iran's oil wealth to force his subjects into the twentieth century. Land reform, Western education, and the partial emancipation of women outraged the powerful landowning Shiite clergy. In 1963 one of the clergy's most influential figures, the Ayatollah Ruhollah Khomeini of the holy city of Qum, attacked the Shah and all his works. Khomeini went first to jail and then into exile. There he ceaselessly reviled the Shah as an "unclean" tool of the "satanic" West.

The Shah for his part relied increasingly on his secret police, the dreaded SAVAK. He faced the same desperate choice as other "modernizing" autocrats. The introduction of Western ideas and economic practices soon created an intelligentsia that rejected the autocracy—just as those same ideas and practices alienated or shrank the traditional sectors of society on which the autocracy rested. The Shah nevertheless pressed on. With Kissinger's encouragement, he took over from Britain the role of lord of the Persian Gulf after 1971. In 1973–74 he led OPEC's

Israel in 1993

assault on the world economy, and used Iran's fabulous oil profits to buy the latest in tanks, ships, and aircraft from the United States and Europe.

But the Shah failed to spread the profits from the oil boom widely enough to defuse the resentments of his urban lower classes. His apparent sponsorship of the invasion of Iran by European and United States goods and customs, from alcohol to tailored blue jeans for women, outraged the devout. The intelligentsia deplored his refusal to offer them parliamentary government. In January 1978 the Shiite clergy led riots at Qum against the regime. Disorder spread across Iran. The Shah, ill with cancer and irresolute, failed to crush the unrest while his conscript soldiers were still loyal. In the Teheran riots of September 1978, the army began

The *Intifada.*

Militant Islam: Religious
extremists assassinate President
Sadat, October 1981.

to crack. Khomeini's unarmed zealots taunted the troops to make them martyrs; the troops deserted or shot their sergeants and officers. The Shah's nerve shattered along with a cherished illusion: that his people loved him. In January 1979, he fled.

Khomeini arrived from Paris—a stern medieval figure alighting from a jumbo jet—to sweep a feeble provisional government from office. He then established a form of government never before seen, a theocratic "Islamic Republic" under the rule of Shiite clergy. Student militants, revolutionary committees, "Revolutionary Guards," and the shaven-headed zealots of Hezbollah (the "Party of God") enforced political conformity. They also ruthlessly reimposed Islamic dress on Iran's women. Teheran crowds enthusiastically chanting "Death to America" filled the West's television screens. When Carter allowed the dying Shah to visit New York in October 1979 for cancer treatment, Khomeini's "Islamic students" violated diplomatic tradition and seized the United States embassy in Teheran with its staff of over fifty.

Khomeini may not have originated the embassy coup, but he swiftly exploited it. What better way to mobilize domestic support, dramatize the Islamic Revolution abroad, and humiliate the "Great Satan" America than to hold its diplomats hostage? The Iranians had learned from North Vietnam, which had tied American negotiators in knots over the release of U.S. prisoners. The American television networks rose to the occasion. Soon each evening news broadcast began with an announcement of the number of days the hostages had been imprisoned.

The crisis placed intolerable pressure on Carter; 1980 was an election year. Iran's position between the Soviet Union and the Gulf deterred him from taking military action, lest Moscow use United States intervention as a pretext to expand its Afghan bridgehead southward. In April 1980 Carter nevertheless launched an ineptly planned hostage rescue mission that broke down in the Iranian desert; fierce interservice rivalry and Carter's eccentric insistence on the *minimum* use of force

had made failure likely. The hostage crisis decided the 1980 election against Carter; Iran packed the hostages onto an Air France jet as Ronald Reagan took the oath of office in January 1981.

By then Khomeini had a greater and more immediate worry than the "Great Satan." Like other revolutionary leaders before him, he aspired to world revolution—and he repeatedly called for Islamic upheavals throughout the Middle East. Among his preferred targets was Saddam Hussein, ruthless and fanatical Sunni ruler of the Shiite majority of neighboring Iraq. The Iraqi dictator, apparently thinking that revolutionary chaos had undermined Iranian military power, in return launched an armored thrust into Iran's oilfields in September 1980. Iran's 3 to 1 advantage in population soon began to tell. This was no war of maneuver between sophisticated opponents, but a tropical Somme 1916, a demolition derby of military ineptitude.

In early 1982 Iraq lost the oilfields it had seized. By 1985–86 it was close to losing Basra, its second city after Baghdad. Iranian "Revolutionary Guards," many of them adolescents carrying toylike plastic "keys to Paradise" furnished by the clergy, pressed the attack at immense cost. "Fountains of blood" foamed with red dye at Teheran cemeteries in macabre commemoration of the fallen. Religious war, an "Islamic" successor to SAVAK, and mass executions silenced opponents and doubters.

Iraq responded to defeat by appealing to other Arab regimes for aid against the Iranian Shiite menace. If Iraq went under, Kuwait and Saudi Arabia might follow. Iran secured clandestine assistance from Israel, which considered Saddam Hussein a worse threat than Khomeini. Israel also struck a blow against Iraq's nuclear ambitions by sending its F-16 fighter-bombers to destroy Iraq's French-built reactor in June 1981.

As Iran advanced, Iraq in desperation expanded the war by air and sea. It drenched Iranian troops and Kurdish villages with mustard gas, nerve gas, and hydrogen cyanide. Its air force attacked Iranian cities and the oil exports that fi-

The return of the Ayatollah: Khomeini in Teheran, February 1979.

nanced Iran's war. Iran in reply struck at international shipping bound for the oil ports of Iraq's Persian Gulf allies and launched missiles at Baghdad in the manner of Hitler's V-2 bombardment of London in 1944. Iraqi missiles in turn flattened entire blocks in Teheran and Qum.

In 1987, Washington responded to an appeal from Kuwait to escort its tankers through the Gulf. Britain, France, and Italy likewise committed ships to the Gulf. In spring 1988 the Iranians imprudently challenged the U.S. fleet and lost much of their navy in a flurry of U.S. cruise missiles. The Western navies hemmed Iran in, while Iraqi offensives forced a bitter Khomeini to accept a ceasefire in July–August 1988. The First Gulf War had cost up to a million dead and had lasted longer than any other twentieth century war between major states.

The Second Gulf War: Iraq against the World, 1990–91

Victory over the hated Iranians inspired Saddam Hussein to further conquests. By profession a political assassin and secret policeman, he had held undisputed power since 1979 by killing all potential rivals in the army and the ruling Ba'th ("Arab Renaissance") Party. His regime, like those of his models, Hitler and Stalin, rested on terror with an admixture of propaganda. It had to, for its ethnic-religious base, the Sunni Arabs in Iraq's center, was a mere fifth of Iraq's population. Dissident Kurds made up another fifth and Shiite Arabs the other three-fifths. Saddam's ultimate aim was to unite all Arabs from Morocco to Iran into a superpower based on control of oil, armed with nuclear weapons, and capable of destroying Israel and defying the "imperialist" West. Iraq, the self-proclaimed "Prussia of the Arabs," was for Saddam the foreordained core of that coming superpower.

Saddam had played skillfully on Western and Arab hopes and fears during his eight-year war with Iran. He posed as the protector of Saudi Arabia, Sunni Islam, and the oil of the Gulf against the Iranian Shiite threat. The Gulf Arabs responded with long-term loans; the West sold him arms and military technology that included equipment for his secret nerve gas, ballistic missile, and nuclear bomb projects. France, West Germany, Switzerland, Holland, Britain, and the United States were conspicuous suppliers. Saddam's longstanding friends in Moscow also provided arms and military advice. Within a decade or less, Iraq would be ready.

But Saddam lacked the necessary patience. In spring 1990 he boasted publicly of his chemical weapons and declared that he could "make the fire eat up half of Israel." He also convinced himself that no power stood between him and mastery of the Gulf. His army was the world's fourth largest, and decadent America would never accept "10,000 dead in one battle" to stop him. On August 2, 1990, on the pretext of settling a financial and territorial dispute, his armored divisions invaded and brutally occupied his small neighbor, Kuwait.

Like Kim Il-Sung before him, Saddam had gone too far. Iraq already owned a tenth of the world's oil reserves. After conquering Kuwait, it controlled almost a fifth. Had Saddam's tanks continued southward and seized the Saudi oilfields—as they seemed poised to do—he would control 45 percent of the world's oil and more than two-thirds of the Gulf's. He could then dictate the world price of oil and extort limitless deliveries of arms and technology from the West. The resulting economic chaos might plunge the world into depression and destroy the domestic political stability of the industrial democracies.

The Americans once again proved unpredictable. George Bush, with backstage prodding from Margaret Thatcher, answered the threat from Saddam that United States and European policies had helped create. Despite widespread press criticism of his daring commitment, Bush pledged almost immediately that "this [aggression] will not stand." He convinced Saudi Arabia to accept the deployment on its territory of a quarter of a million U.S. and allied troops. With Soviet support guaranteed by Gorbachev's desperate need for Western aid, Bush led the U.N. to declare Saddam's annexation of Kuwait "null and void." Through the U.N. he imposed on Iraq economic sanctions and a blockade enforced by the U.S. and allied navies. His Gulf coalition ultimately included 37 states, with troop contingents or ships and aircraft from much of NATO, Hungary, Poland, the Gulf Arabs, Egypt, Morocco, Pakistan, Bangladesh, and even the Syria of Hafez al-Assad. Only Jordan, Yemen, Cuba, and the Palestinians stood with Saddam.

When Saddam failed to withdraw from Kuwait, Bush ordered a further 250,000 American troops—including armored divisions no longer needed for a Third World War in central Europe—to the Gulf. Britain sent 43,000 soldiers, sailors, and airmen, and France 16,000. On November 29, 1990, the United States pushed through the U.N. Security Council a resolution authorizing the use of "all means necessary" to liberate Kuwait if Saddam did not withdraw by January 15, 1991. That resolution, and Saddam's continued defiance, checkmated opponents of war in the United States. Economic sanctions might evict Saddam from Kuwait at some distant future date, or they might not. U.S. air power and armor clearly would, although some feared the possible human cost. Bush pledged that the United States would use its full power from the outset rather than the "graduated pressure" that had failed in Vietnam. The U.S. Senate endorsed the U.N. resolution by a small majority, the House of Representatives by a far larger one. Saddam, perhaps deceived by memories of Vietnam and by the images of antiwar protest outside the White House conveyed by global television, answered with defiance.

On January 16–17, 1991, the first moonless night of the new year, the U.S. Air Force and Navy struck at Baghdad and at targets throughout Iraq. Effortless technological and tactical superiority stripped away Iraq's many-layered air defenses, wrecked chemical and nuclear plants, broke Saddam's communications with his ill-trained and poorly led army, and starved that army of food, water, and ammunition before bombing much of it to shreds. Saddam replied with a missile bombardment of Israel aimed at turning

America in the Gulf: one of the 35,000 U.S. women who served in the war against Saddam Hussein.

the war into an Arab-Israeli struggle and splitting the Western-Arab coalition. But Israel's leaders refused to rise to the bait; they did not retaliate against Iraq. Not even ecological terrorism—the burning of Kuwait's oil wells and the dumping of crude oil into the Gulf at Saddam's orders—halted the allied air campaign. On February 23 the coalition launched a long-prepared ground attack that swept by surprise around the Iraqi army's unprotected

"First we're going to cut it off, and then we're going to kill it." General Colin L. Powell, chairman of the Joint Chiefs of Staff, predicts that the United States will destroy Saddam's invasion force in Kuwait (January 23, 1991).

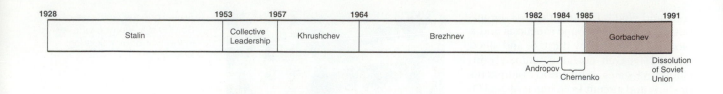

1928		1953	1957	1964		1982	1984	1985		1991
Stalin		Collective Leadership	Khrushchev	Brezhnev				Gorbachev		

Andropov   Chernenko

Dissolution of Soviet Union

desert flank, drove it from Kuwait, and pinned its battered remnants against Basra. U.S. casualties, at 148 killed in action, were wildly disproportionate to the many thousands of Iraqi dead.

Yet at the very end, Bush held back. He apparently feared that demolishing Iraq entirely would make Iran the master of the Gulf. Saudi and Turkish fears that Iraq's disintegration would create troublesome Kurdish and Shiite ministates on their borders also influenced U.S. policy. Bush spared Saddam—after the U.S. Air Force had destroyed several bunkers where the Iraqi leader was thought to be hiding. The ground war ended after 100 hours, leaving Saddam enough tanks and helicopters to put down bloodily the risings by Kurds and Shiites that immediately followed the coalition's victory. A belated U.S. and NATO humanitarian mission in northern Iraq helped save hundreds of thousands of Kurdish refugees. An even more belated "no-fly zone" shielded the Shiites in the south from Saddam's air force. U.N. inspectors picked over the remains of Iraq's chemical, missile, and nuclear projects, and economic sanctions remained in effect. Yet Saddam remained defiantly in power, while his Iranian neighbor rearmed with an eye to future opportunities. The United States and its allies had restored order to the Gulf for a few years.

NEW WORLD DISORDER

The "New World Order" that Bush proclaimed would follow the Cold War proved long on novelty but short on order. From 1947–48 until 1989–90 the superpowers had generally maintained discipline among their respective clients. They had also avoided—with the exception of Khrushchev's adventure in Cuba—direct

challenges to each other's vital interests. Before Soviet collapse, Saddam would probably have lacked the freedom to challenge the West for control of oil. The United States would undoubtedly also have hesitated before attacking a Soviet client so close to the USSR's borders. The end of the Cold War ended all such restraints. And as relations between Moscow and Washington thawed, so too did ancient European quarrels. States and peoples reveled in their newly recovered freedom. Some used it to seek conquest or revenge. And new mechanisms for restraining those violent impulses seemed absent.

Nationalism, the Final Stage of Communism

History had divided Europe into three bands or zones. In west and west-central Europe, great wars and the building of nation-states had settled—one way or another—all major religious-ethnic quarrels. In east-central Europe and the Balkans, the second zone, the two world wars and Hitler's genocide had only partially disentangled historic patterns of mixed settlement. Finally, the rubble of the Soviet multinational empire made up a third zone in which colonial Great Russian outposts planted by the tsars or by Stalin overlaid an already complex ethnic-religious pattern ordained by history.

The quarrels and potential quarrels of east-central Europe intensified from north to south. Soviet collapse stranded between independent Lithuania and Poland a Russian military enclave around Kaliningrad (formerly Königsberg) in what until 1945 had been East Prussia. Poland had seized and held Lithuania's capital, Vilnius, throughout the interwar period, and a sizable Polish minority remained in Lithuania. Poles and Germans coexisted un-

Saddam Hussein, in a favorite pose, celebrates the election defeat of George Bush, November 1992.

easily along the Oder-Neisse line that Stalin had laid down in 1945. Czechoslovakia split into separate Czech and Slovak states in 1992–93, leaving Slovakia with a disgruntled Hungarian minority of more than half a million. Hungary looked to its minorities not only in Slovakia, but also in Serbia and above all in Rumania, where the 2.1 million Hungarians of Transylvania lamented Romanian maltreatment that stretched back to 1918–20.

The quarrels that divided the peoples of Yugoslavia generated the greatest immediate violence. There the old border between the eastern and western Roman empires had become the border between Catholicism and Orthodoxy, between Croats and Slovenes on the one hand and Serbs on the other. Ottoman conquest had imposed an overlay of Islam. The many nationalities and groups each regarded their neighbors as mortal enemies; usually they were correct. In the interwar era, Serb royal dictatorship had welded them together in a miniature multinational empire. In the Cold War era, Tito's Communist autocracy and fear of Soviet invasion had done likewise. But like Stalin, Tito was mortal. He died in 1980, and the collapse of Communism and of the Soviet threat in 1989–91 freed Yugoslavia's peoples—for civil war. Ex-Communist leaders, Franjo Tudjman of Croatia and Slobodan Milosevic of Serbia, played the nationalist card. Tudjman denied that Hitler's Croat puppet-state had massacred more than half a million Serbs in 1941–45. Milosevic announced that "borders . . . are always dictated by the strong."

The Serbs were indeed strong. Their population, at roughly 9 million, was larger and more widely scattered than that of the other peoples within Yugoslavia's borders. They also controlled most of the Yugoslav army's artillery and tanks. Fear of a repetition of the massacres of 1941–45 and ambition for a "Greater Serbia" led them to take the offensive against Slovenia and Croatia when fighting broke out in June 1991 between Croat police and Serb militiamen. Slovenia defeated the Serbs and asserted its independence, thanks to geography and smuggled antitank rockets. Croatia fought doggedly but lost the

third of its territory that was partially inhabited by Serbs. Milosevic's army and Serb freebooters massacred, raped, and drove Croats from their homes in the conquered areas. Croats massacred Serbs when they could catch them.

In April 1992 Yugoslavia's breakup forced independence upon Bosnia-Hercegovina, a region split among Moslem Slavs, Serbs, and Croats. Serb offensives and massacres then "cleansed" two-thirds of Bosnia of Moslems and Croats. The Serbs scornfully ignored repeated but purely verbal protests from the

The Ethnic Groups of East-Central Europe

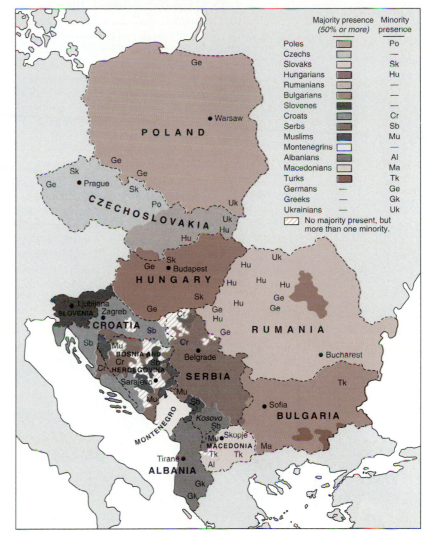

	Majority presence (50% or more)	Minority presence
Poles		Po
Czechs		—
Slovaks		Sk
Hungarians		Hu
Rumanians		—
Bulgarians		—
Slovenes		—
Croats		Cr
Serbs		Sb
Muslims		Mu
Montenegrins		—
Albanians		Al
Macedonians		Ma
Turks		Tk
Germans	—	Ge
Greeks	—	Gk
Ukrainians	—	Uk

No majority present, but more than one minority.

Europeans, the U.N., and Bush's Democratic successor, President Bill Clinton; they remained confident that no outside power would go to war to stop them. More than 150,000 died and 3 million fled their homes in the first two years of this Third Balkan War—by far the most massive violence in Europe since 1945. And the precarious Serb position in the southern province of Kosovo, historic "cradle of Serb civilization" but inhabited overwhelmingly by Albanian Moslems, threatened further war with Albania and with other Balkan states.

Europe's easternmost zone of ethnic-religious conflict was almost equally active. Soviet collapse stranded almost 26 million Great Russian colonists outside Russia and more than 27 million non-Russians inside it. Great Russian outposts, from Estonia and Latvia to Moldova to the Crimea to Kazakhstan, coexisted uneasily with newly independent peoples divided from them by language and religion. Fighting tore Moldova. Festering disputes between Russia and Ukraine over ownership of the ex-Soviet Black Sea Fleet and of the Crimea threatened for the future. In the Caucasus, Georgians fought their national minorities and each other. Armenia and Azerbaijan battered each other over enclaves within their territories inhabited by minorities from the other. The shadowy "Confederation of Independent States" had neither the will nor the force to reimpose order.

Only Great Russian nationalism could do that. Communism's collapse left it the only idea—the only imperial ideology— that might claim to unite the vast spaces stretching from Poland to the Pacific. And as in the past the fall of empires generated

The Soviet Successor States

towering resentments. Great Russian nationalist prophets spun vengeful anti-Semitic and anti-Western conspiracy theories to explain the empire's collapse. Radical newspapers quoted Hitler with approval, and demanded a ruler with Stalin's iron hand. Ex-Communist ideologues demanded alliance with China—and support for the Orthodox Serbs—against the West. Uncertainty, inflation, unemployment, the suffering of Great Russians stranded outside Russia, and the separatist agitation of the non-Russian nationalities locked within it unsettled a politically naive population. Powerful interests and structures inherited from the Soviet "old regime," from the nuclear-armed armed forces and the KGB to military-industry, repeatedly embarrassed Gorbachev's successor in the Kremlin, Boris Yeltsin of the Russian Republic. If the Russian democratic experiment collapsed, Great Russian nationalism might yet seek to re-establish the empire of the tsars and of Stalin.

New Worlds Emerging

Prospects for controlling the bloodshed and disorder of the post–Cold War world seemed to rest in part with a revived United Nations. From Angola to Cambodia to Bosnia, U.N. observers and U.N.-flagged peacekeeping forces sought earnestly—and often vainly—to bridge mortal enmities. Other post-Communist struggles, such as the collapse of Liberia and of Ethiopia, the tribal wars that engulfed Afghanistan in the wake of Soviet withdrawal, and the endless civil war and famine in the Sudan, seemed so intractable that the United Nations largely ignored them.

The United Nations was and remained a bureaucracy, not a power. Only the military forces of the great powers could repel attempts by "the strong" to dictate their borders, or force peace on ethnic groups bent on mutual slaughter. The U.N.'s contribution to world order appeared to depend in part on how much its richer member states were willing to pay—in money and in blood—to enforce that order. National sovereignty

"Borders . . . are always dictated by the strong": A Serb patrol searches for Bosnian Moslems, 1993.

also remained a barrier to action. All states, but especially non-Western states, looked on interference in their "internal affairs" with continued suspicion. The United Nations still functioned mainly as a forum for agreement—when its member states did agree—on issues such as the protection of the environment and famine relief.

And the United Nations was powerless against a further side-effect of Soviet collapse, the accelerated spread of deadly technologies that promised to multiply many-fold the dangers of ethnic-religious conflict. At the very moment that Western governments and industrialists began to realize the risks they had run in arming Saddam, the defense establishment and black market of the defunct Soviet Union opened an immense bankruptcy sale. Amid the ruins of the Soviet empire, hard currency could buy virtually anything, from scientific and technical brainpower to tactical nuclear warheads, radioactive materials, submarines, missiles, advanced aircraft, and tanks. The Soviet Union, China, and North Korea had long sold ballistic missiles to powers such as Iran, Iraq, Syria, Libya, and Egypt. Algeria, Libya, Iran and North Korea concealed nuclear ambitions of varying intensities. India and Pakistan had both nuclear weapons and missiles to carry them; Pakistan allegedly owed its bomb design to China. Brazil and Argentina, which had also helped arm Saddam, waited in the wings. China loomed on the horizon as the Asian superpower of the twenty-first century—or as an unparalleled source of chaos. All had presumably learned from Saddam's lack of patience and stealth.

The world that faced this explosive mixture of new technologies and old hatreds was by the early 1990s so closely knit that a shock to any of its key economies might drag the others down as well. Computers and instantaneous communications had welded the world's stock, currency, and commodity exchanges into a seamless 24-hour world market. The electronic transfer of financial information and funds sent trillions of dollars, marks, yen, and lesser currencies sloshing from market to market. Automatic stock and futures trading driven by computer programs turned market hiccups into jagged ascents or hair-raising plunges.

Since 1944–45 the United States had acted as stabilizer for the entire system. But by the 1980s the rise of Japan and Europe, the fiscal hangover from Reagan's debt binge, and the failure of U.S. primary and secondary education to keep pace with competing societies had shrunk America's margin of superiority. The passage of world economic leadership from Britain to America in 1914–44 had been stormy. World depression or the division of the world into hostile economic blocks—Japan and Asia, German-Europe, and the Americas—might also accompany the relative loss of U.S. economic power. Yet for a moment, Soviet collapse left the United States in a stronger relative position than at any time since the 1920s. For good or ill, it still surpassed or even dwarfed possible rivals in all three dimensions of

power: overall economic strength, political leadership, and military might.

TOWARD THE TWENTY-FIRST CENTURY

Broad and swift scientific and technological advance paralleled the expansion of the world economy under the umbrella of U.S. power after 1945. Simultaneously, the proliferation of knowledge in innumerable highly specialized scientific and scholarly subdisciplines posed a threat already visible in the nineteenth century—that educated people, each locked in the jargon of a specialty, would cease to speak a common language. Especially in the social sciences and humanities, skepticism about the possibility of establishing truth corroded all established standards. And as the Americanization of the world through television proceeded, high culture retreated into a cloistered existence in the universities.

The Thrust of Science and Technology

"Command science," the systematic mobilization by governments of scientific knowledge for a specific purpose, came into its own after 1945. The Manhattan Project had shown the way. Its successors were the postwar programs of the great powers that created thermonuclear bombs, and atomic reactors to generate electricity and to power submarines and surface ships.

Yet by the 1980s reactor accidents had lessened enthusiasm for nuclear power. A power reactor at Three Mile Island in Pennsylvania partially melted in 1979; its containment vessel held, and only small amounts of radioactivity reached the atmosphere. The far worse Soviet nuclear accident at Chernobyl in 1986 seemed a portent of the limits of technology. The many similarly constructed reactors still functioning in the former Soviet territories struck many Western experts as potential time bombs. Yet increasing fear of ecological catastrophe through nuclear power intersected with claims that burning coal and oil would lead to a dangerous rise in global temperatures through the "greenhouse effect."

Command science was also the instrument of the conquest of space—a dream entertained since the seventeenth century, but now suddenly practical. The Soviet effort that launched *Sputnik* in 1957 put Yuri Gagarin into Earth orbit in 1961. Kennedy responded with a pledge to put an American on the moon by the end of the decade. The National Aeronautics and Space Administration (NASA), which Eisenhower had established after *Sputnik,* assembled the largest community of scientific talent ever mobilized for a single purpose, and spent up to $40 billion. On July 20, 1969, Neil Armstrong of the United States became the first human to walk on the Moon. The Soviet Union stuck closer to Earth; its space program was military in inspiration and priorities. After its moon voyage triumph, NASA bet virtually its entire shrinking budget on one program, the reusable "space shuttle." The explosion after launch of the shuttle *Challenger* in January 1986 temporarily paralyzed both civilian and military space programs. NASA ultimately pressed on in hopes of building a permanent orbital space station and sending missions to Mars in the twenty-first century.

Command science, despite its magnitude and its many spin-offs, was only a small part of the continuing scientific and technological revolution. During and after the Second World War, new materials came into their own. Plastics and glass fiber increasingly replaced steel and other metals. Composites of plastic and boron or carbon fiber, lighter and stronger than steel, became available in the 1970s. Titanium, almost 50 percent lighter than steel and with a higher melting point than aluminum, found innumerable uses in supersonic jet aircraft, nuclear reactors, and submarines.

But the most spectacular advances— a wave of innovation as potentially powerful as the "second industrial revolution" of steel, chemicals and electricity—came in electronics and biology. Semiconductors, materials such as germanium and silicon that conducted current only hesitatingly at room temperature, had been a subject of curiosity since the primitive germanium diodes of the early radio receivers. In 1947 William Shockley, John Bardeen, and Walter H. Brattain of Bell Laboratories invented the transistor, the first semiconductor amplifying device. By the early 1960s the transistor had evolved into the integrated circuit, or "chip," consisting of innumerable microscopic transistors linked in complex patterns and imprinted on a silicon wafer.

The arrival of the transistor coincided with the birth, speeded by wartime cryptographic needs, of the new discipline of computing. Its theoretical roots reached back into the nineteenth century; its two leading theoreticians were Alan Turing (1912–54) of Cambridge, who played a leading role in Britain's decipherment of the *Wehrmacht*'s supposedly uncrackable codes, and the Hungarian refugee physicist-mathematician John von Neumann (1903–57) of Princeton. By the 1960s their successors had created theories, computer languages, and machines capable of the unimaginably complex and rapid calculations needed to model thermonuclear explosions, solve engineering problems through simulation, predict the paths of space vehicles, guide missiles and robots, and store and manipulate evergreater masses of information.

From 1959 to the 1990s, chips and therefore computers doubled in computing power each year. The cost per transistor decreased over twenty years by a factor of more than *1 million*. That pace of advance showed no signs of slowing. As chip fabricators approached the apparent limits that silicon places on computer speed, those limits receded, and other faster materials such as gallium arsenide emerged. The invention in the 1960s of lasers, devices that generated focused light of a single frequency, added to the potential of semiconductors. Lasers offered innumerable applications from surgery to weaponry, and allowed long-distance transmission of information through glass fibers at densities far exceeding the limits of electrical or microwave circuits.

Potentially even more powerful than semiconductors and lasers were

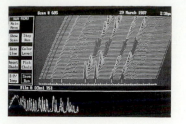

The structure of life: the computer display of an automatic DNA-sequencing machine.

the new techniques of molecular biology. In 1951–53 James D. Watson of the United States and Francis H. C. Crick of Britain jointly deciphered the "double helix," the complex molecular structure of deoxyribonucleic acid, or DNA, the material in which cells encode their genetic information. That research led eventually to the beginnings of an understanding of evolution at the molecular level and to the manipulation of plant and animal genes to make bizarre hybrids that crossed species lines. The mapping of the entire human genetic code—all 100,000 genes, each consisting of 1,500 subunits—appeared a realistic prospect by the end of the century.

Molecular biology opened immense possibilities for good, for the eradication of most diseases and the understanding and possible slowing of aging. It provided the most powerful weapons for fighting the great viral pandemic of the 1980s and 1990s, AIDS (Acquired Immune Deficiency Syndrome). The virus, against which conventional medical techniques were almost as powerless as those of the Middle Ages against the Black Death, spread mainly through sexual intercourse and the sharing of unsterilized drug hypodermics by addicts. By the early 1990s it threatened tens of millions of victims around the world.

But together with hope and life, the new biology also appeared to offer death, through biological weapons of unprecedented subtlety and power—and transfiguration, through "human perfectibility" in a quite literal sense: the genetic re-engineering of the human species. Nuclear weapons had given humanity a chance to annihilate itself, but also the long European peace after 1945. Molecular biology held out the prospect both of healing and of a new kind of annihilation, the transformation of humanity into something less or more than human.

The Disintegration of Scholarship and High Culture

In the realm of ideas, specialization and the triumph of the relativism that had flourished since the Enlightenment fur-

thered the fragmentation already visible as the twentieth century began. Especially in the Anglo-Saxon countries, most philosophers abandoned speculation. The new "analytical" philosophers scorned metaphysics—the exploration through imagination of the nature of existence. They sought instead what Bertrand Russell (1872–1970), an early leader of the analytical school, described as the "unattainable ideal of impeccable knowledge." Their method was the close examination of language and meaning through logic and mathematics. Their quest led them to narrow increasingly the domain of truth to establish certainty.

Ultimately they so narrowed the domain of truth that it vanished. The reclusive Ludwig Wittgenstein (1889–1951), perhaps the greatest of twentieth-century philosophers, abandoned all attempts to describe the world and retreated acerbically into the analysis of language. His taunt that "the belief in the causal nexus is superstition" denigrated all forms of knowledge about nature and human affairs. But as Wittgenstein's eighteenth-century percursor David Hume had pointed out, the philosopher's study was the place for skepticism. Survival in the hard outside world that Wittgenstein shunned still required such "superstitions" as cause and effect.

On the Continent, after Heidegger, traditional forms of philosophy still prospered. The Left Bank sage Jean-Paul Sartre (1905–80) was Heidegger's principal heir. After 1945, Sartre's "existentialism" became a cult phenomenon from Paris to San Francisco that endured until the 1960s. Its basis was Heidegger's call for "authenticity" and his denial of a rational foundation for values. For Sartre, individuals were utterly free to choose their values. Any denial that such freedom existed was inauthentic, was an evasion of responsibility, was "bad faith." But Sartre offered no advice on what values to choose, for advice would constrict freedom and constitute "bad faith." He merely commanded choice, for only heroic choice was "authentic." Heidegger had chosen Nazism. Sartre, whose only gestures against Nazism had been literary, chose Marxism, which he described as the "unsurpassable philosophy of our time."

French intellectual fashions change as rapidly and wield as powerful an influence throughout the West as the hemlines of Paris designers. After the collapse of the May 1968 student revolt that Sartre's doctrines of heroic commitment had helped inspire, new preoccupations emerged. The most important was an intellectual tendency known as "structuralism." It had originated in linguistics between the world wars and thence had spread to anthropology, literary criticism, history, sociology, psychoanalysis, and philosophy. Its lowest common denominator was the claim that the *structure* of a language, myth, or literary or historical "text" was a more fundamental characteristic than other attributes such as its origin, history, purpose, or content.

In linguistics, its point of origin, structuralism was largely the product of the insights of the Swiss scholar Ferdinand de Saussure (1857–1913), who suggested that meaning was a product of oppositions or differences between the "signs" that made up language. Meaning was thus entirely relative. "Signs" had meaning only by virtue of their structural relationship to other "signs." An influential American scholar, Noam Chomsky (1928–), added a fruitful conjecture of his own—that *all* languages shared a common "deep structure" that grew out of the structure of the human mind itself. Chomsky's apparent biological determinism clashed with his politics; a combative Left-utopian, he rejected the "capitalist" West and implicitly demanded faith in the perfectibility of humanity, a perfectibility doubtful indeed if the human mind was as "hard-wired" as Chomsky the linguist assumed.

In anthropology, Claude Lévi-Strauss (1908–), investigated the myths of Brazilian and American Indians as clues to the structures of the "primitive mind." Structure was primary, content far less important; meaning existed only as part of a structure. Critics like Roland Barthes (1915–80) carried similar notions into literary criticism. The literary "text" became a subject for a decipherment or "deconstruction" that deliberately ignored the "text's" author, historical context, literary excellence or lack of it, and commonsense meaning. For the structuralist critic, the interpreter not the author gave meaning. That doctrine allowed the interpreter to give a "text" any meaning at all. And the implication that all "texts" were of equal value frequently produced bizarre results. Structuralist critics examined with deep seriousness works that few non-structuralists even considered to be literature.

Historians, beginning in France, took a Lévi-Straussian interest in the "collective mentalities" of past social groups. Analysis of social or intellectual "structures" began to supersede narrative. The study of long-term change—climatic, economic, and demographic—triumphed for a time over short-term "event history" and the history of ideas. Devotees of economics subjected small portions of the past to "cliometric" statistical examination. Historians increasingly though not always wisely borrowed methods from sociology and psychology. Marxism revived, until the ruin of Soviet "real socialism" left many of its adherents disoriented. For the first time in history, historians wrote works incomprehensible to the educated public.

Structuralism and the disciplines it influenced mirrored the disorientation of the age. If *all* truths were relative, tolerance even of bizarre claims was the highest virtue. In the humanities and social sciences few dared affirm that some "truths" were less relative than others and that the test of all generalizations was confrontation with empirical evidence. The natural sciences proved more resistant to bewilderment; experiment remained the test of truth or falsehood, and mathematics offered an empirically effective means of describing nature.

In the arts, disintegration was almost total as the century drew toward its end. In the visual arts the last undisputed master was Pablo Picasso (1881–1973). In the 1940s, with Europe at war, abstract expressionist painters such as Jackson Pollock and Willem de Kooning seized artistic leadership for New York. Yet some American experiments, such as the "pop art" of the 1960s that took its images from advertising, appeared almost self-consciously sterile. In architecture, the "international style" persisted, although architects increasingly adorned their buildings with "post-modernist" classical flourishes. In music, few composers after Igor Stravinsky (1882–1971) and Sergei Prokofieff (1891–1953) commanded mass audiences. Dissonance and disjointed rhythms bored or repelled all except specialists. Symphony orchestras and opera companies made do with the time-honored works of Mozart, Beethoven, Wagner, and other eighteenth- and nineteenth-century giants. In literature, especially in the United States, poetry and the serious novel fled to the universities to be embalmed in "creative writing" courses. Even Paris began to flag as a fountainhead of novelty. Soviet-bloc dissident and emigré writers, along with those of Latin America, showed more life than their European or American counterparts. Western high culture increasingly lacked the vitality and self-confidence of earlier ages.

One world? Japanese youth, Western mass culture (1989).

THE WIDENING AND NARROWING OF THE WEST

As the century drew to a close, Western ideas dominated the globe as never before. In the nineteenth century, the zenith of the West's relative power, its culture had only touched the surface of non-European societies. By the late twentieth century, instant communications relentlessly drove forward the economic and cultural integration of the world. That drive generated fierce reactions, above all from Islam. The Western conception of government resting on and limited by the right of the governed—*democratic government*—found few successful imitators. But the extension of the West's scientific and industrial revolution to all humanity appeared likely to continue. As James Watt's partner had boasted of the new steam-engines, "I sell, Sir, what all the world desires to have—power." The West offered power over nature and over the conditions of human existence to those willing to learn. That temptation has so far proved almost irresistible.

Yet the West has also narrowed in relative terms. By the 1980s the birth rate of Europe from France to the Urals had fallen to roughly equal the death rate. The United States continued to grow, but at a rate lower than ever before. Not so the other continents. As China passed the 1.1 billion mark in the 1980s, its growth slowed only slightly despite ruthless post-Mao laws against unlicensed births. South Asia's relentless rise hardly slowed. Africa's population expanded at a pace faster than that of any other continent, although the AIDS pandemic seemed to be slowing it—tragically—by the 1990s. World population was 4 billion in 1975 and will probably surpass 6.1 billion by the year 2000. Thereafter either economic development will reduce birth rates or natural catastrophes, overcrowding, environmental degradation, epidemics, and wars will increase death rates. Projections suggest that world population may finally level off at around 12.5 billion in the middle of the twenty-second century. East and South Asia would have more than 6 billion, sub-Saharan Africa 2.5 billion, North Africa and the Middle East 1 billion, Latin America and the Caribbean 1 billion, and North America and Europe together less than 1 billion. The West's share of the human species is contracting as the West's influence as the "mainstream of civilization" expands to embrace all humanity.

Suggestions for Further Reading

The Superpowers

As the present approaches, perspective vanishes and perceptive works become ever more sparse. *The New York Times* and *The Economist* (London) offer a better guide to how the world works than jargon-ridden books by policy gurus. J. Keegan and A. Wheatcroft, *Zones of Conflict: An Atlas of Future Wars* (1986), offer a military and political geography of the antagonisms of the 1980s. A. Ulam, *Dangerous Relations: The Soviet Union in World Politics, 1970–1982* (1983), dissects superpower relations in the Brezhnev period. Ronald Reagan's foreign policy still awaits a balanced assessment; some of the essays in J. L. Gaddis, *The United States and the End of the Cold War* (1992),

offer a start. H. Carrère d'Encausse, *Confiscated Power: How Soviet Russia Really Works* (1982) and *The End of the Soviet Empire* (1993), are excellent on the dynamics of Soviet collapse. M. Feschbach, *Ecocide in the Soviet Union* (1992), provides chilling data on the system's effects on its peoples. A. Ulam, *The Communists* (1992), covers its entire post-1948 trajectory. J. F. Brown, *Surge to Freedom* (1992), describes the fall of Stalin's east-European empire. On the ethnic struggles let loose by the end of the Cold War, see especially M. Glenny, *The Fall of Yugoslavia: The Third Balkan War* (1992).

East Asia and Europe

Nguyen Van Canh, *Vietnam Under Communism, 1975–1982* (1983), describes the fate of South Vietnam after the departure of the United States. The Khmer Rouge are still poorly understood, but see F. Ponchaud, *Cambodia Year Zero* (1978); W. Shawcross, *The Quality of Mercy: Cambodia, Holocaust, and Modern Conscience* (1984); and K. D. Jackson, ed., *Cambodia, 1975–1978: Rendezvous with Death* (1992). K. van

Wolferen, *The Enigma of Japanese Power* (1989), offers deep and sometimes disturbing insights. For Europe, see W. Laqueur, *A Continent Astray: Europe, 1970–1978* (1979) and *Europe in Our Time: A History, 1945–1992*. J. Herf, *War by Other Means: Soviet Power, West German Resistance, and the Battle of the Euromissiles* (1991), explains the NATO crisis of the early 1980s.

The Middle East from Peace to War

On the Middle East and Islamic militance, see especially D. Pipes, *In the Path of God: Islam and Political Power* (1983); F. Ajami, *The Arab Predicament: Arab Political Thought and Practice Since 1967* (1992); S. Bakhash, *The Reign of the Ayatollahs* (1984); G. Sick, *All Fall Down: America's Tragic Confrontation with Iran* (1985); and I. Rabinovich, *The War for Lebanon, 1970–1983* (1984). S. al-Khalil (Kanan Makiya), *Republic of Fear* (1989), analyzes Saddam's Iraq with unparalleled penetration and foresight; his *Cruelty and Silence* (1933) offers further

evidence on Saddam's domestic terror, and explores the complicity of Arab intellectuals with the Ba'athist regime. D. Hiro, *The Longest War* (1991) and *Desert Shield to Desert Storm: The Second Gulf War* (1992), cover Saddam's two wars; R. Hallion, *Storm Over Iraq: Air Power and the Gulf War* (1992), helps explain why the Second Gulf War was not Vietnam. P. Slugett and M. Farouk-Slugett, eds., *Tuttle Guide to the Middle East* (1992), offer an up-to-date area handbook.

Technology and Culture

W. A. McDougall, *The Heavens and the Earth: A Political History of the Space Age* (1985), offers analysis of one great monument of "command science." For intellectual developments since the Second World War, see especially J. A. Passmore, *A Hundred Years of Philosophy* (1968) and *Recent Philosophers* (1985); N. Cantor, *Twentieth-Century Culture: Modernism to Decon-*

struction (1988); R. N. Stromberg, *After Everything: Western Intellectual History Since 1945* (1975); and the merciless G. Himmelfarb, *The New History and the Old* (1987). D. Ravitch, *What Do Our 17-Year-Olds Know?* (1987), documents America's educational collapse.

ILLUSTRATION CREDITS

INDEX